PHILIP'S

STREET ATLAS
Surrey

Contents

4 *Key to maps*

6 *Administrative boundaries*

7 *Street maps*

161 *Index of street names*

229 *Index of towns and villages*

232 *Approaches to Heathrow*

Considerable effort has been made by checking on the ground and by innumerable consultations with various authorities to make the information contained in the maps as up-to-date as possible (although in some congested areas it has not been possible to show certain very small roads and names). However, because of the highly detailed and changing nature of the area, it is difficult to be precisely correct in every respect and the publishers would welcome any comments which readers may care to make and which will help towards maintaining accuracy in future editions. Please address correspondence to the CARTOGRAPHIC DIVISION, George Philip Limited, 1 Marlin House, Marlins Meadow, Croxley Business Park, Watford WD1 8YA.

We should like to thank the Engineers, Surveyors and Planners of the Authorities throughout the county who have helped so readily and also the many firms and individuals who have contributed with their local knowledge and expert advice.

Published by Philip's
an imprint of Reed Consumer Books Limited
Michelin House, 81 Fulham Road, London SW3 6RB
and Auckland, Melbourne, Singapore and Toronto

First edition 1966
Sixteenth edition 1994

Cartography by Philip's
Copyright © 1994 Reed International Books Limited

ISBN 0 540 05984 6 (Softback)
ISBN 0 540 05983 8 (Hardback)

Printed and bound in Great Britain by
Butler and Tanner Limited, Frome and London

────▬────	**Railway and station**
⊖	**London Transport station**
✛	**Place of worship**

Important buildings
Hosp.: Hospital   P.H.: Public house
P.O.: Post office   Sch.: School
T.H.: Town hall   Mus.: Museum

P Ⓟ	**Car park**
𝑖	**Tourist information centre**
Ⱳ	**Country park**
❷	**Motorway junction**
══M4══	**Motorway**
──A3──	**A road**
──B376──	**B road**
──────	**Connecting road**
─ ─═══	**Other road**
─ ─ᴮ─ ─	**Bridleway**
──────	**Footpath**
─·─·─·	**County boundary**
· · · · · ·	**Borough and district boundary**

'Connecting roads' and 'other roads' may sometimes be private, narrow or unfit for road vehicles.

The representation in this atlas of a road, street or footpath is no evidence of the existence of a right of way.

0	440yds.	880yds.	1320yds.	1mile
0	500m	1000m		1500 metres

Scale: 3 inches to 1 mile

1 kilometre = 0.6214 miles
1 mile = 1.6093 kilometres

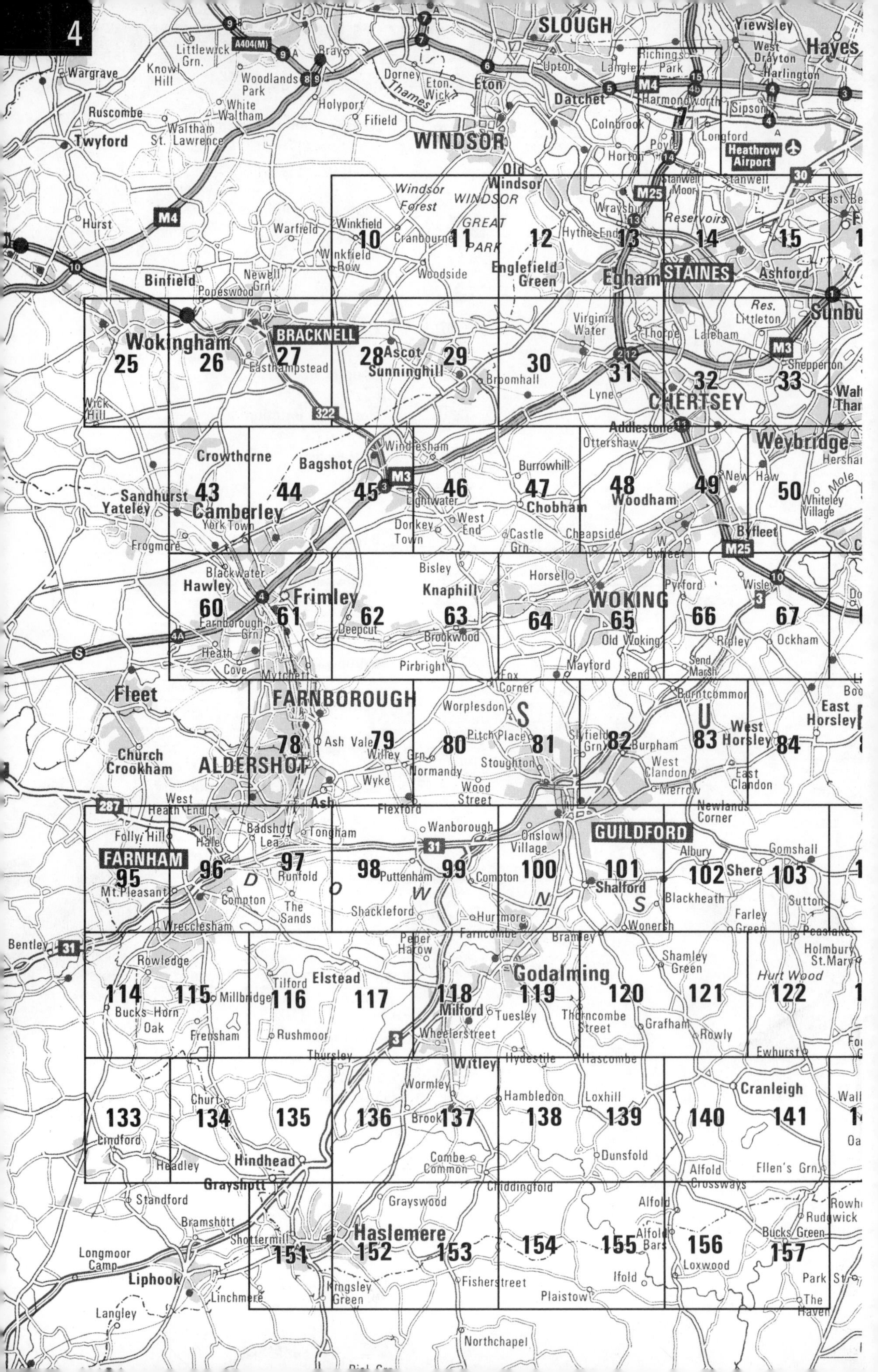

SLOUGH
Yiewsley
West Drayton
Hayes
Harlington
Littlewick Grn.
A404(M)
Bray
Wargrave
Knowl Hill
Woodlands Park
Dorney
Eton Wick
Eton
Upton
Langley
Richings Park
Harmondsworth
Sipson
Datchet
M4
Ruscombe
White Waltham
Waltham St. Lawrence
Holyport
Fifield
Thames
Twyford
WINDSOR
Colnbrook
Longford
Poyle
Horton
Heathrow Airport
Old Windsor
Stanwell Moor
Stanwell
Windsor Forest
WINDSOR GREAT PARK
M25
Wraysbury
Reservoirs
East Bedfont
Hurst
M4
Warfield
Winkfield
Cranbourne
Hythe End
10
11
12
13
14
15
Winkfield Row
Woodside
Englefield Green
Egham
STAINES
Ashford
Binfield
Newell Grn.
Popeswood
Res.
Littleton
Sunbury
Virginia Water
Thorpe
Laleham
M3
Shepperton
Wokingham
BRACKNELL
Ascot
Sunninghill
25
26
27
28
29
30
31
32
33
Easthampstead
Broomhall
Lyne
CHERTSEY
Walton-on-Thames
Wick Hill
322
Addlestone
Weybridge
Hersham
Crowthorne
Bagshot
Windlesham
Ottershaw
Burrowhill
M3
New Haw
Mole
Sandhurst
Yateley
43
44
45
46
47
48
49
50
Camberley
York Town
Lightwater
Chobham
Woodham
Whiteley Village
Frogmore
Donkey Town
West End
Castle Grn.
Cheapside
W Byfleet
Byfleet
M25
Blackwater
Hawley
Bisley
Knaphill
Horsell
Pyrford
Wisley
Frimley
WOKING
60
61
62
63
64
65
66
67
Farnborough Grn.
Deepcut
Brookwood
Old Woking
Ripley
Ockham
4A
Heath
Cove
Mytchett
Pirbright
Fox Corner
Mayford
Send
Send Marsh
Fleet
FARNBOROUGH
Burntcommon
Worplesdon
East Horsley
Pitch Place
Slyfield Grn
Burpham
West Horsley
Church Crookham
ALDERSHOT
Ash Vale
Willey Grn.
78
79
80
81
82
83
84
Stoughton
West Clandon
East Clandon
Wyke
Normandy
Wood Street
Merrow
West End
Heath End
Ash
Flexford
Newlands Corner
287
Folly Hill
Upr. Hale
Badshot Lea
Tongham
Wanborough
Onslow Village
GUILDFORD
Albury
Gomshall
FARNHAM
31
95
96
97
98
99
100
101
102
103
Runfold
Puttenham
Compton
Shalford
Shere
Mt.Pleasant
Compton
The Sands
Shackleford
Hurtmore
Blackheath
Sutton
Wonersh
Farley Green
Wrecclesham
Farncombe
Bramley
Peaslake
Bentley
31
Peper Harow
Shamley Green
Holmbury St.Mary
Rowledge
Godalming
Tilford
Elstead
Hurt Wood
114
115
116
117
118
119
120
121
122
Millbridge
Milford
Tuesley
Thorncombe Street
Bucks Horn Oak
Frensham
Rushmoor
Wheelerstreet
Grafham
Rowly
Thursley
Hydestile
Hascombe
Ewhurst
Witley
Wormley
Churt
Hambledon
Loxhill
Cranleigh
133
134
135
136
137
138
139
140
141
Brook
Lindford
Headley
Hindhead
Combe Common
Dunsfold
Alfold Crossways
Ellen's Grn.
Grayshott
Chiddingfold
Standford
Grayswood
Alfold
Rudgwick
Bramshott
Bucks Green
Shottermill
Haslemere
Alfold Bars
Longmoor Camp
151
152
153
154
155
156
157
Liphook
Fisherstreet
Ifold
Loxwood
Park Street
Kingsley Green
Linchmere
Plaistow
The Haven
Langley
Northchapel

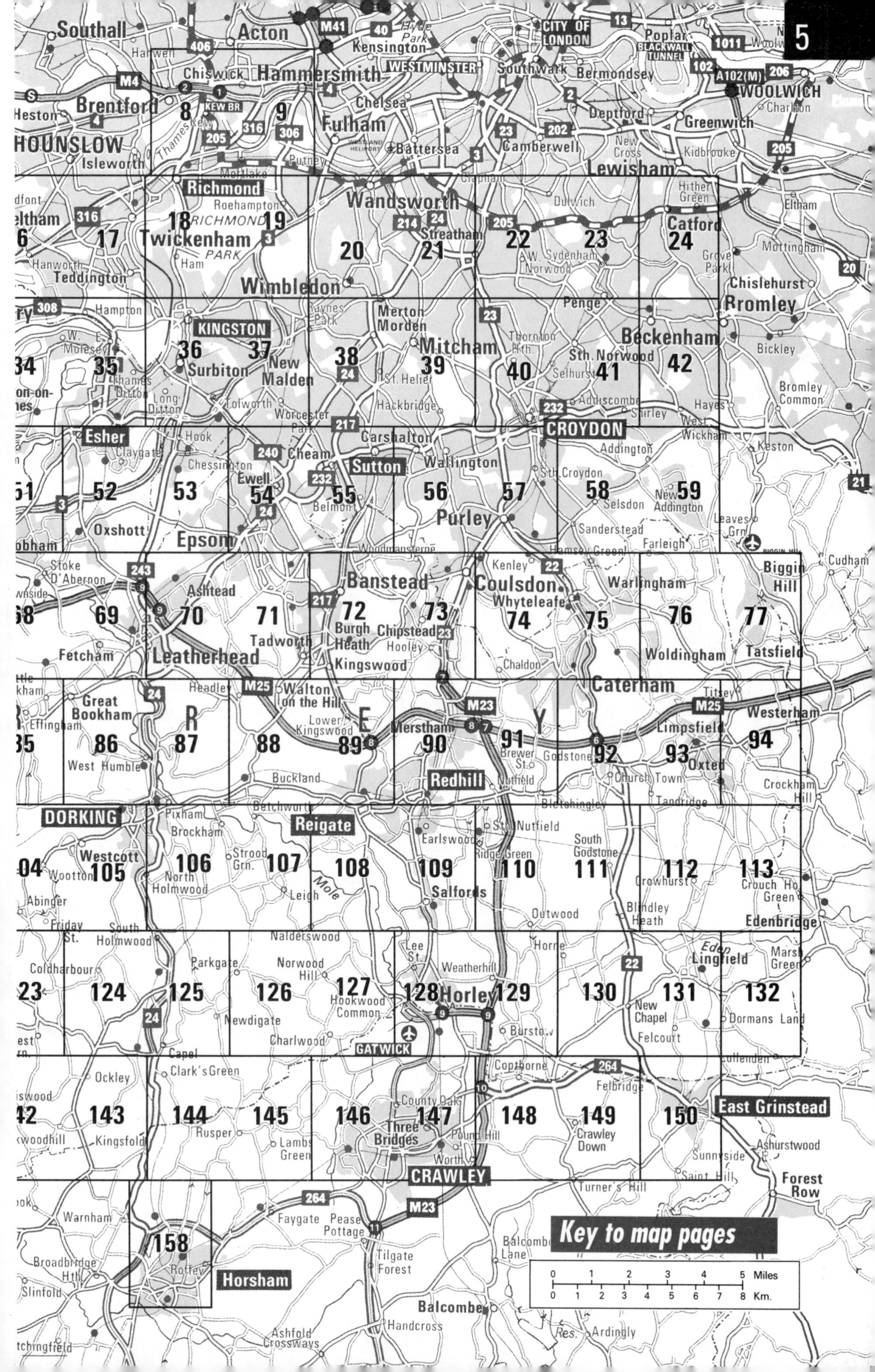
Key to map pages
Southall
Acton
Kensington
Hyde Park
CITY OF LONDON
Poplar
BLACKWALL TUNNEL
Woolwich
Chiswick
Hammersmith
WESTMINSTER
Southwark
Bermondsey
WOOLWICH
Charlton
Brentford
KEW BR.
Chelsea
Deptford
Greenwich
Heston
Fulham
HOUNSLOW
Isleworth
Battersea
Camberwell
New Cross
Kidbrooke
Lewisham
Mortlake
Putney
Clapham
Richmond
Roehampton
Wandsworth
Dulwich
Hither Green
Eltham
RICHMOND PARK
Twickenham
Streatham
Catford
Mottingham
Ham
W. Sydenham
Norwood
Grove Park
Hanworth
Teddington
Wimbledon
Chislehurst
Hampton
Raynes Park
Merton
Morden
Penge
Bromley
KINGSTON
Mitcham
Thornton Hth.
Beckenham
W. Molesey
E. Molesey
New Malden
Sth. Norwood
Bickley
Thames Ditton
Surbiton
St. Helier
Selhurst
Long Ditton
Tolworth
Worcester Park
Hackbridge
Addiscombe
Shirley
Hayes
Bromley Common
CROYDON
West Wickham
Esher
Hook
Carshalton
Addington
Keston
Claygate
Chessington
Cheam
Sutton
Wallington
Ewell
Sth. Croydon
Belmont
Selsdon
New Addington
Oxshott
Purley
Sanderstead
Leaves Grn.
Epsom
Woodmansterne
Hamsey Green
Farleigh
Cudham
Stoke D'Abernon
Kenley
Biggin Hill
Ashtead
Banstead
Coulsdon
Warlingham
Whyteleafe
Burgh Heath
Chipstead
Tadworth
Hooley
Fetcham
Kingswood
Woldingham
Tatsfield
Leatherhead
Chaldon
Headley
Walton on the Hill
Caterham
Great Bookham
Titsey
Effingham
Lower Kingswood
Merstham
Westerham
Limpsfield
Brewer St.
Godstone
Oxted
West Humble
Buckland
Redhill
Nutfield
Church Town
Crockham Hill
Bletchingley
Tandridge
DORKING
Pixham
Betchworth
Reigate
Sth. Nutfield
Brockham
Earlswood
South Godstone
Westcott
Strood Grn.
Ridge Green
Wootton
North Holmwood
Leigh
Mole
Salfords
Crowhurst
Crouch Ho. Green
Abinger
Blindley Heath
Friday St.
South Holmwood
Outwood
Edenbridge
Nalderswood
Lee St.
Horne
Eden
Lingfield
Coldharbour
Parkgate
Norwood Hill
Weatherhill
Marsh Green
Hookwood Common
Horley
New Chapel
Newdigate
Dormans Land
Charlwood
Burstow
Felcourt
Capel
GATWICK
Copthorne
Clark's Green
Ockley
Felbridge
County Oak
Three Bridges
Crawley Down
East Grinstead
Rusper
Lambs Green
Pound Hill
Kingsfold
Ashurstwood
Worth
Sunnyside
CRAWLEY
Saint Hill
Forest Row
Turner's Hill
Warnham
Faygate
Pease Pottage
Balcombe Lane
Broadbridge Hth.
Roffey
Tilgate Forest
Horsham
Slinfold
Balcombe
Handcross
Res.
Ardingly
Ashfold Crossways
0 1 2 3 4 5 Miles
0 1 2 3 4 5 6 7 8 Km.
M4
M41
M23
M25
A102(M)
8 9 17 18 19 20 21 22 23 24 34 35 36 37 38 39 40 41 42
52 53 54 55 56 57 58 59 69 70 71 72 73 74 75 76 77
86 87 88 89 90 91 92 93 94 105 106 107 108 109 110 111 112 113
124 125 126 127 128 129 130 131 132 143 144 145 146 147 148 149 150 158

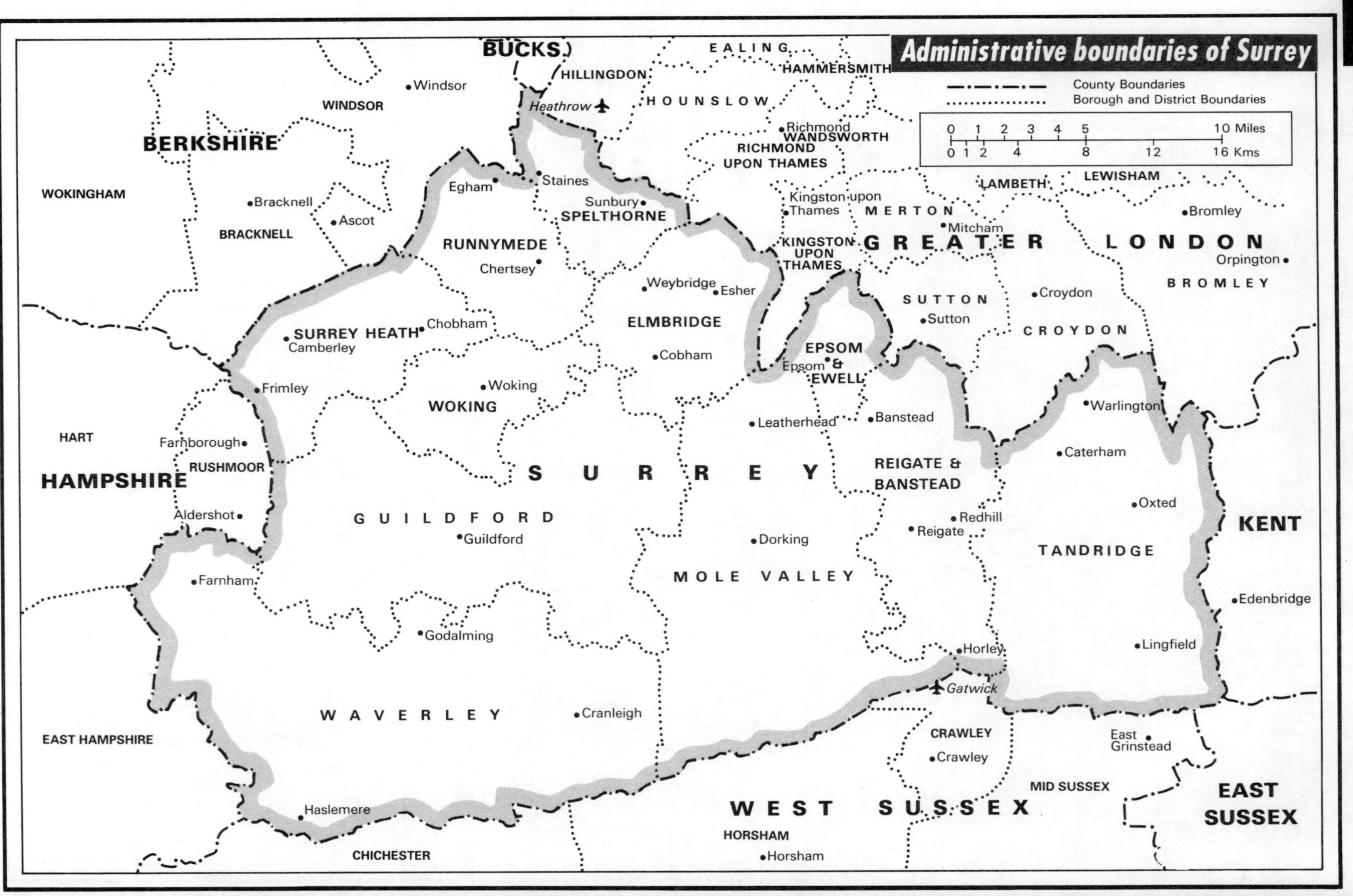

Administrative boundaries of Surrey
County Boundaries
Borough and District Boundaries
0 1 2 3 4 5 10 Miles
0 1 2 4 8 12 16 Kms
BUCKS.
EALING
HILLINGDON
HAMMERSMITH
HOUNSLOW
Heathrow
Windsor
WINDSOR
BERKSHIRE
WOKINGHAM
Bracknell
BRACKNELL
Ascot
Egham
Staines
Sunbury
SPELTHORNE
Richmond
WANDSWORTH
RICHMOND UPON THAMES
Kingston upon Thames
MERTON
Mitcham
LAMBETH
LEWISHAM
Bromley
GREATER LONDON
Orpington
BROMLEY
KINGSTON UPON THAMES
RUNNYMEDE
Chertsey
Weybridge
Esher
ELMBRIDGE
Cobham
SUTTON
Sutton
Croydon
CROYDON
SURREY HEATH
Camberley
Chobham
EPSOM & EWELL
Epsom
Frimley
Woking
WOKING
Leatherhead
Banstead
Warlington
Caterham
HART
Farnborough
RUSHMOOR
HAMPSHIRE
Aldershot
SURREY
REIGATE & BANSTEAD
GUILDFORD
Guildford
Redhill
Reigate
Oxted
Dorking
TANDRIDGE
KENT
Farnham
MOLE VALLEY
Edenbridge
Godalming
Horley
Lingfield
Gatwick
WAVERLEY
Cranleigh
EAST HAMPSHIRE
CRAWLEY
Crawley
East Grinstead
MID SUSSEX
EAST SUSSEX
Haslemere
WEST SUSSEX
HORSHAM
Horsham
CHICHESTER

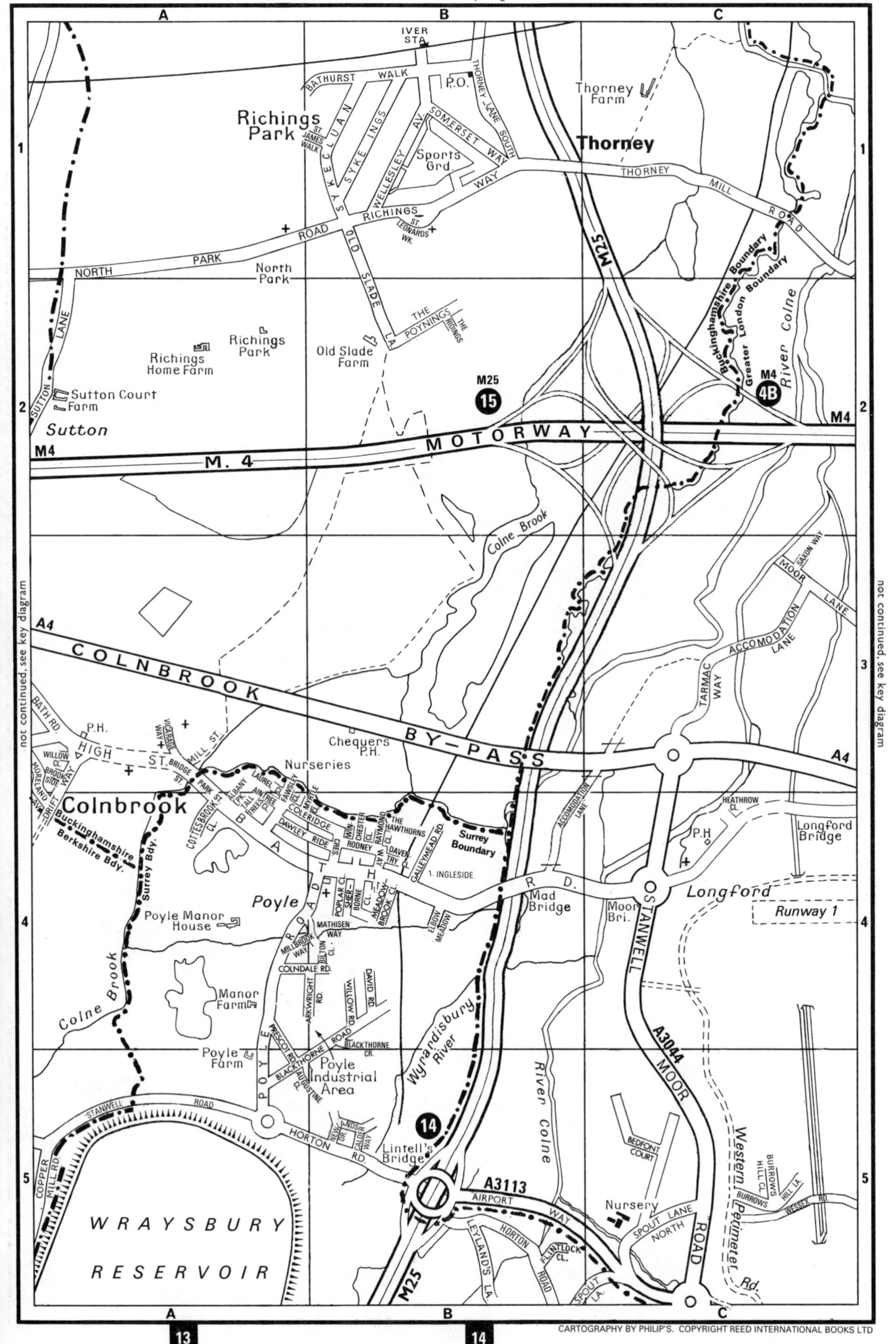

IVER STA.

Richings Park

Thorney Farm

Thorney

BATHURST WALK

P.O.

THORNEY LANE SOUTH

THORNEY MILL ROAD

SYKE CLUAN
ST.
ST JAMES WALK
SYKE INGS
WELLESLEY AV.
SOMERSET WAY
RICHINGS WAY

Sports Grd.

RICHINGS ST.
ST. LEONARDS WK.

ROAD

NORTH PARK

North Park

M25

OLD SLADE LA.
THE POYNINGS
THE RICHINGS

River Colne

Buckinghamshire Boundary
Greater London Boundary

M4
4B

Richings Park

Richings Home Farm

Old Slade Farm

M25
15

SUTTON LANE

Sutton Court Farm

Sutton

M4

M. 4 **M O T O R W A Y**

M4

Colne Brook

not continued, see key diagram

A4

C O L N B R O O K **B Y - P A S S**

MOOR LANE
SAXON WAY

ACCOMMODATION LANE

TARMAC WAY

A4

BATH RD.
P.H.
WILLOW WAY
VICARAGE WAY
MILL ST.

HIGH ST.
BRIDGE ST.

MORELAND DRIFT
BROOKSIDE

Chequers P.H.

Nurseries

Colnbrook

Buckinghamshire Berkshire Bdy.

Surrey Bdy.

COTTESBROOK CL.
PARK AV.
ELBANY
LAUREL CL.
AINTREE CL.
FIRS CL.
FAMLEY
COLERIDGE
DAWLEY RIDE

KIMBER
SOHO
RODNEY
CHESTER CL.

THE HAWTHORNS

GALLEYMEAD RD.

Surrey Boundary

HEATHROW CL.

P.H.

Longford Bridge

Colne Brook

Poyle

A ROAD
T

POPLAR CL.
SHREE
BOURNE CL.
MEADOW CL.

BAYMOND
DAVENTRY

1. INGLESIDE

MEADOW BROOK
ELBOW MEADOW

ACCOMODATION LANE

R D.

Mad Bridge

Moor Bri.

Longford

OSTANWELL

Runway 1

Poyle Manor House

Manor Farm

MILLBROOK WAY
BILTON CL.
COLNDALE RD.
ARKWRIGHT RD.
WOTLUM RD.
DAVID RD.

Wyrardisbury River

River Colne

A3044

MOOR ROAD

Western Perimeter Rd.

Poyle Farm

POYLE ROAD
PRESCOT RD.
BLACKTHORNE RD.
FIRESTINE
Blackthorne Cr.

Poyle Industrial Area

BEDFONT COURT

Nursery

BURROWS HILL CL.
BURROWS HILL LA.
WESSEX RD.

STANWELL ROAD
COPPER MILL RD.

HORTON RD.

NEW HAW CL.
WEIR CL.
VALLEY CL.

14

Lintell's Bridge

A3113

AIRPORT WAY

SPOUT LANE NORTH

M25

LEYLANDS LA.
HORTON ROAD
FLINTLOCK CL.
SPOUT LA.

W R A Y S B U R Y
R E S E R V O I R

CARTOGRAPHY BY PHILIP'S. COPYRIGHT REED INTERNATIONAL BOOKS LTD

not continued, see key diagram

A   B   C

Acton Hosp.

Sports Grd.

Lammas Park

St. George's Ave.

Gunnersbury Park

King Edward Hosp. (Clayponds Wing)

Gunnersbury

Cem.

1. Packington Rd.
2. Greenock Rd. Acton Works   Level Crossings

(L.T.E.)

Chiswick Works

Gunnersbury Sta.

Chiswick

Wellesley

2

1

M4 MOTORWAY   over   GREAT   WEST   ROAD

M4 MOTORWAY

Kew Bridge Sta.

Leisure Centre

BRENTFORD
Living Steam Museum
Musical Museum

Brentford Cent. Sta.

The Boathouse

Kew Green

The "City Barge" (P.H.)

Kew

Jodrell Lab.

1. Willow Cottages
2. Cambridge Cottages

Pal.

Brentford Dock

Syon Park

Syon House

Royal Botanic Gardens

Queen's Cottage

Temperate House

Pagoda

Public Records Office

North Sheen

Crematorium Cem.

Golf Course

Kew Observatory

Club Ho.

Old Deer Park

Rec. Grd.

Sports Grd.

Athletic Grd.

Lr. Mortlake

North Sheen Sta.
Level Crossing

Lower

Richmond

Derby Arms P.O.

Twickenham

Richmond Sta.

Richmond Green

A316   A305 SHEEN RD.

Upper

A   B322   B353   C

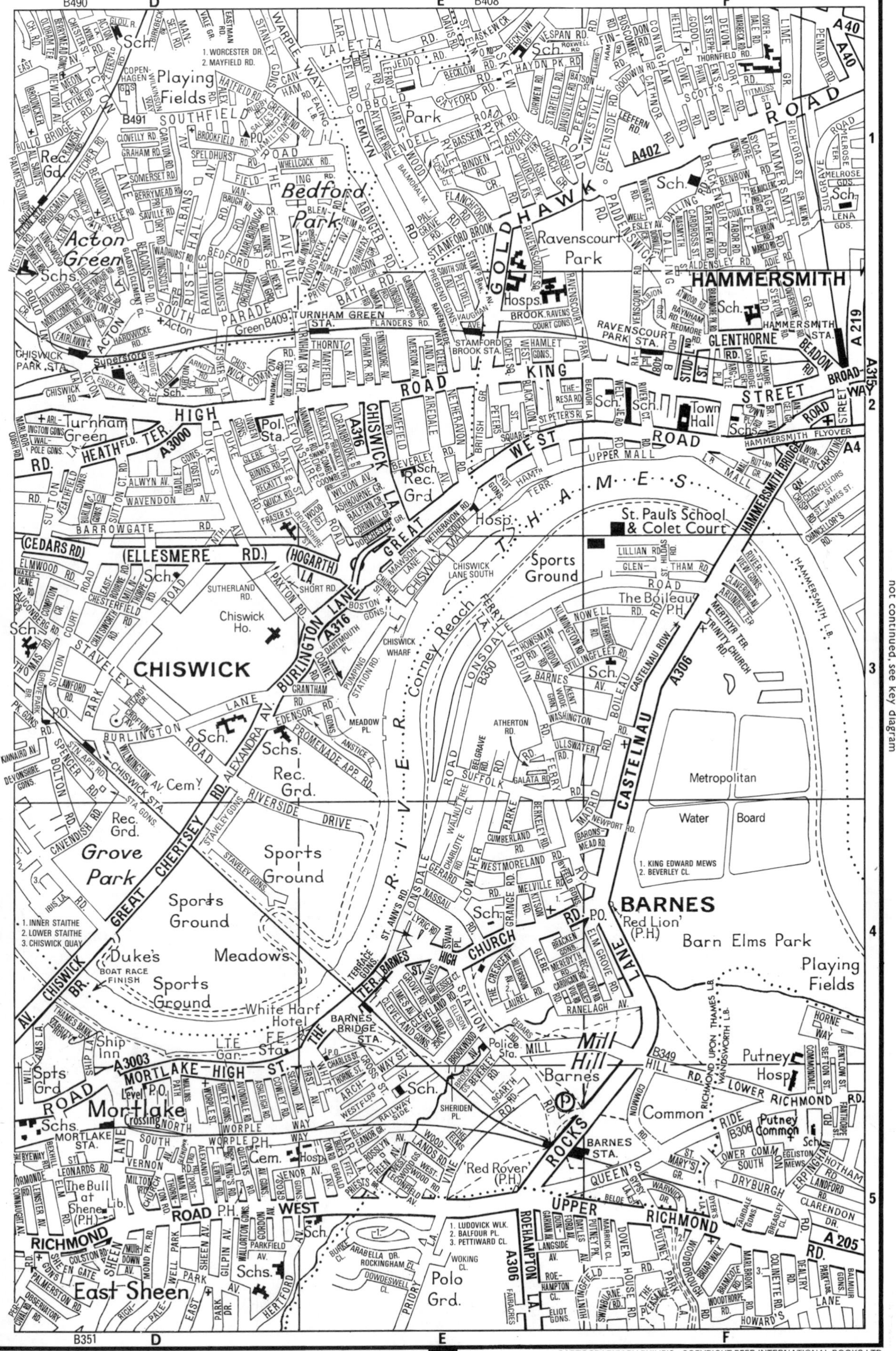

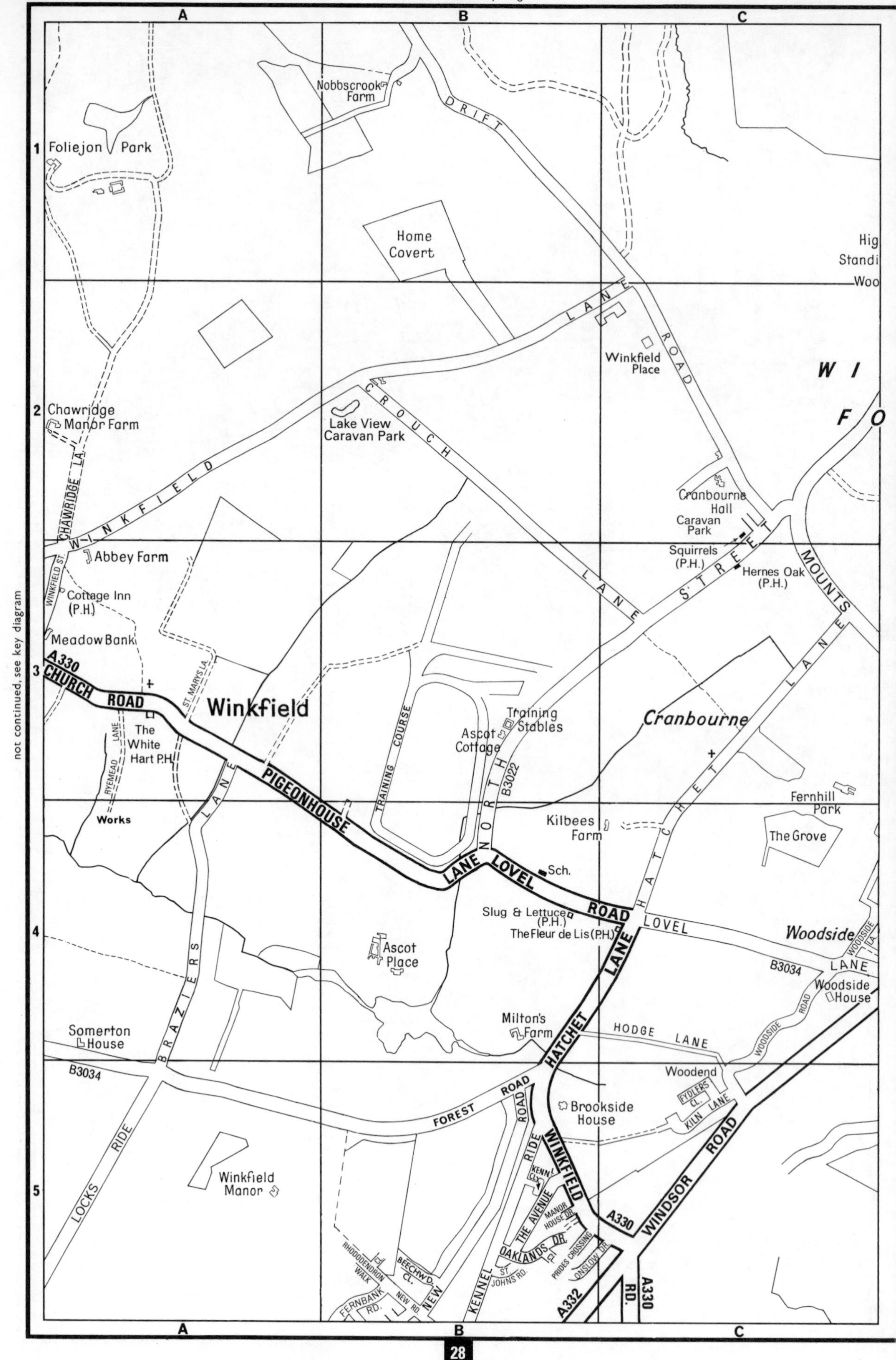

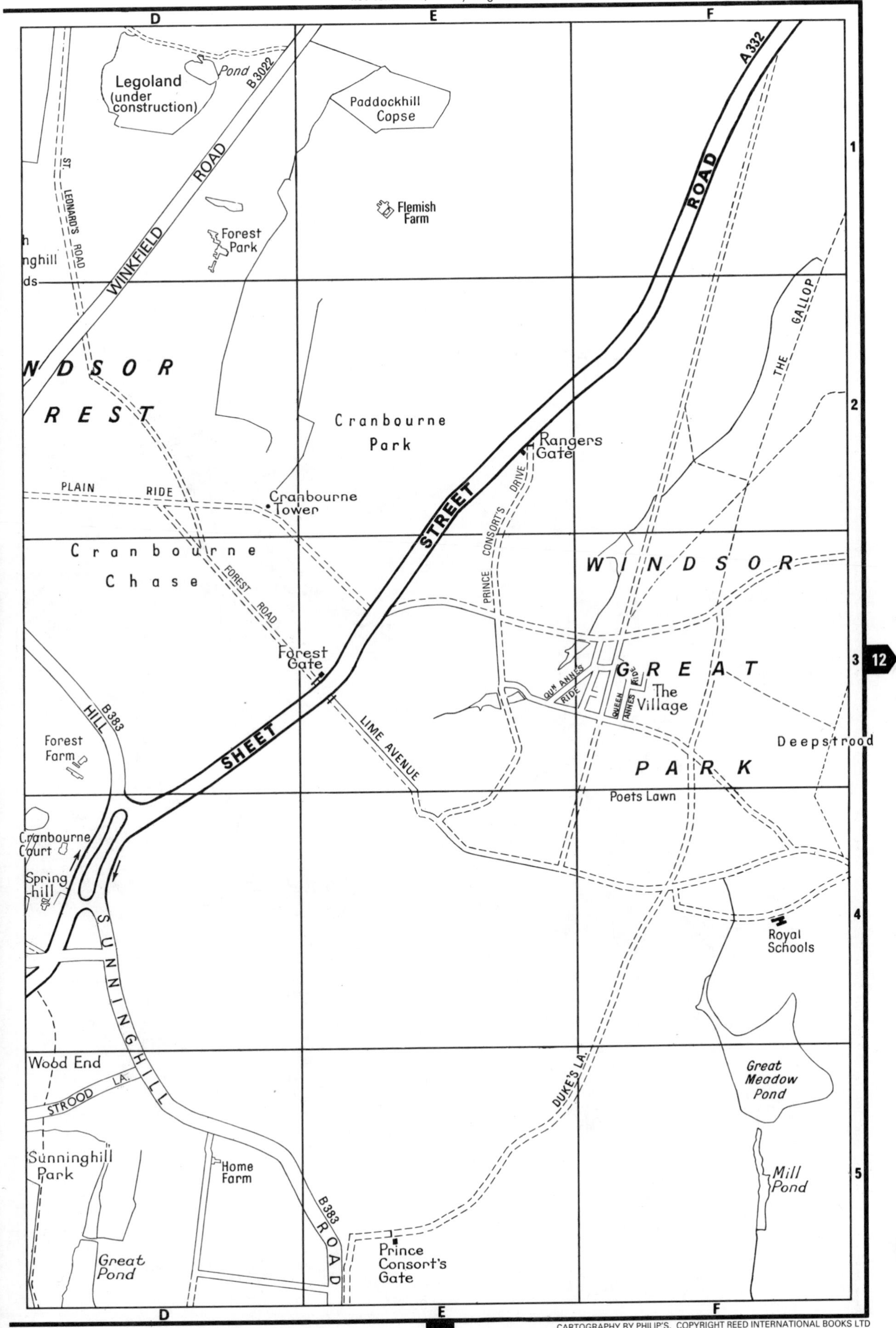

Legoland
(under construction)

Pond
B 3022

Paddockhill
Copse

ST. LEONARD'S ROAD

WINKFIELD ROAD

Flemish Farm

Forest Park

D

E

F

A 332

1

h nghill ds

WNDSOR REST

THE GALLOP

2

Cranbourne Park

PLAIN RIDE

Cranbourne Tower

STREET

PRINCE CONSORT'S DRIVE

Rangers Gate

WINDSOR

C r a n b o u r n e   C h a s e

FOREST ROAD

Forest Gate

QU. ANNES RIDE

GREAT

The Village

QUEEN ANNES RIDE

3

12

HILL B 383

SHEET

Forest Farm

LIME AVENUE

Deepstrood

Forest Gate

PARK

Poets Lawn

Cranbourne Court

Spring hill

SUNNINGHILL

Royal Schools

4

Wood End

STROOD LA.

Home Farm

DUKE'S LA.

Great Meadow Pond

Sunninghill Park

B 383 ROAD

Mill Pond

5

Great Pond

Prince Consort's Gate

D

E

F

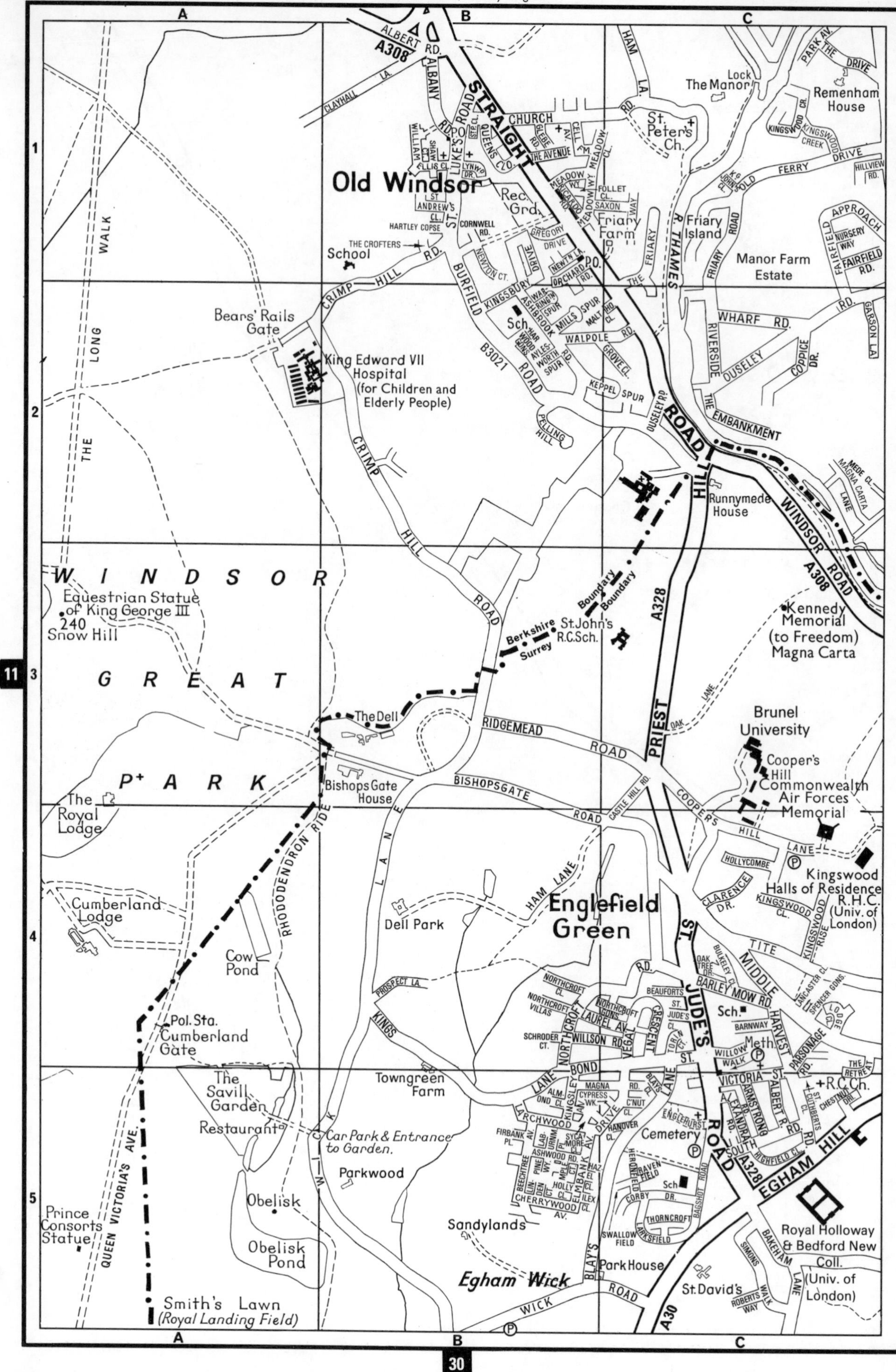

A308
ALBERT RD.
ALBANY
CLAYHALL LA.
CHURCH
STRAIGHT

Old Windsor

St. Peter's Ch.
The Manor
Lock
Remenham House
KINGSW.
KINGSWOOD
CREEK
PARK AV.
THE DRIVE
HILLVIEW RD.
FERRY DRIVE
THE
KINGSWOOD

ST. LUKE'S ROAD
RD.
WILLIAM ST.
LYNW. DR.
SHAW FLD.
ELLIS CL.
QUEENS CLO.
MEADOWY.
GLEBE
MEADOW RD.
THE AVENUE
FOLLET CL.
HAM LA.

ST. ANDREW'S CL.
HARTLEY COPSE
THE CROFTERS
School
CORNWELL RD.
HILL RD.
CRIMP HILL RD.
BURFIELD
KINGSBURY
NEWTON CT.
ORCHARD
GREGORY DRIVE
P.O.
SAXON WAY
Friary Farm
THE
Friary Island
FAIRFIELD
APPROACH
NURSERY WAY
FAIRFIELD RD.

Bears' Rails Gate
King Edward VII Hospital (for Children and Elderly People)
Sch.
AYLWARD SPUR
ALLENBROOK
MILLS SPUR
MALT SPUR
WALPOLE RD.
GROVE CL.
KEPPEL SPUR
Manor Farm Estate
WHARF RD.
RIVERSIDE
OUSELEY RD.
COPPICE DR.
GARSON LA.

B3021
ROAD
AYLES WORTH SPUR
PELLING HILL
OUSELEY ROAD
THE EMBANKMENT
MEDE
MAGNA CARTA LANE

CRIMP HILL

Runnymede House

WINDSOR
Equestrian Statue of King George III
240 Snow Hill

Boundary
Boundary

GREAT

HILL ROAD
Berkshire
Surrey
St. John's R.C.Sch.
A328
PRIEST HILL
WINDSOR ROAD
A308
Kennedy Memorial (to Freedom) Magna Carta

PARK
The Dell
RIDGEMEAD ROAD
Brunel University
Cooper's Hill
Commonwealth Air Forces Memorial
OAK LANE
COOPERS HILL

The Royal Lodge
RHODODENDRON RIDE
Bishops Gate House
BISHOPSGATE ROAD
CASTLE HILL RD.
HOLLYCOMBE
Kingswood Halls of Residence R.H.C. (Univ. of London)
CLARENCE DR.
KINGSWOOD CL.
KINGSWOOD RISE
TITE

Cumberland Lodge
Dell Park
HAM LANE
LANE
Englefield Green
OAK TREE DR.
BARLEY MOW RD.
MIDDLE
HARVEST
BLUNLEY CL.
LANCASTER CL.
SPENCER GDNS.
THE LODGE

Cow Pond
PROSPECT LA.
NORTHCROFT VILLAS
NORTHCROFT GDNS.
Sch.
BARNWAY
WILLOW WALK
Meth.
PARSONAGE
THE RETREAT

Pol. Sta.
Cumberland Gate
KINGS
NORTHCROFT
SCHRODER CT.
LAUDEL AV.
ST. JUDE'S
WILLSON RD.
VEGA
ST. JUDE'S ROAD
VICTORIA ST.
ARMSTRONG
ALEXANDRA RD.
ALBERT RD.
THE CHESTNUTS
ST. COLUMBA'S DR.
R.C. Ch.

The Savill Garden Restaurant
QUEEN VICTORIA'S AVE.
Towngreen Farm
LANE
BOND
ALM. HO.
MAGNA RD.
CYPRESS WK.
LARCHWOOD
KINGSLEY
C'NUT
TORR.
ENGLEHURST
Cemetery
VICTORIA ST.
SOUTH AV.
ENGLEHURST
HIGHFIELD CL.
HIGHFIELD RD.
EGHAM HILL
A328

Car Park & Entrance to Garden.
Parkwood
WICK
FIRBANK PL.
SYCA. MORE AV.
ASHWOOD RD.
BEECHTREE
LIN. DEN AV.
PINE AV.
HOLLY CL.
HANOVER
ALMOND AV.
HAZ. EL
HEL
BRAVEN FIELD
HEREFIELD CL.
Sch.
CORBY
THORNCROFT
SWALLOW FIELD
PARKSFIELD
BAGSHOT RD.

Obelisk
CHERRYWOOD AV.
Sandylands
Park House
BLAY'S LANE

Prince Consorts Statue
Obelisk Pond
Egham Wick
ST. DAVID'S
A30
SIMONS WALK WAY
BAKEHAM LANE
Royal Holloway & Bedford New Coll. (Univ. of London)

Smith's Lawn (Royal Landing Field)
WICK ROAD

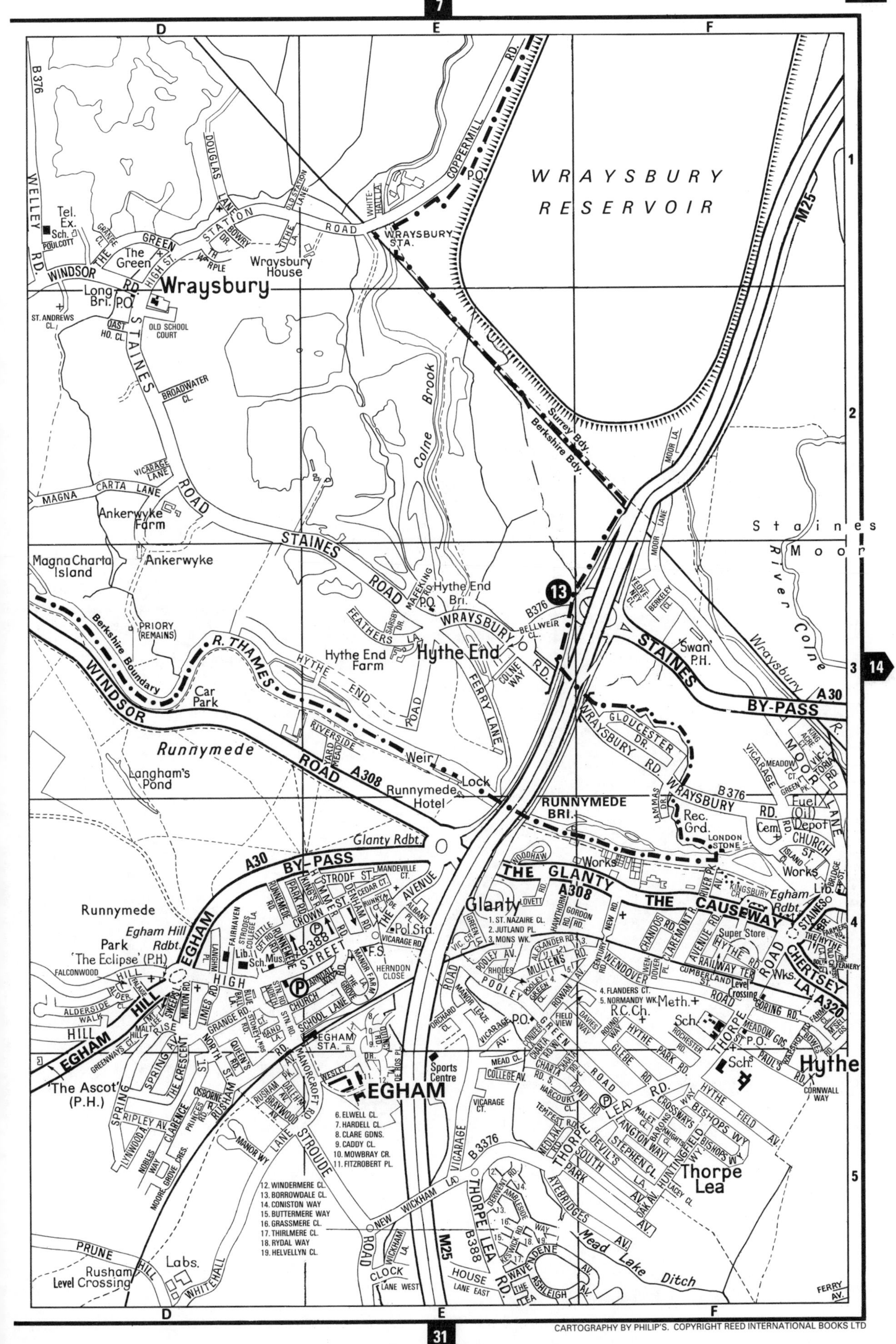

CARTOGRAPHY BY PHILIP'S. COPYRIGHT REED INTERNATIONAL BOOKS LTD

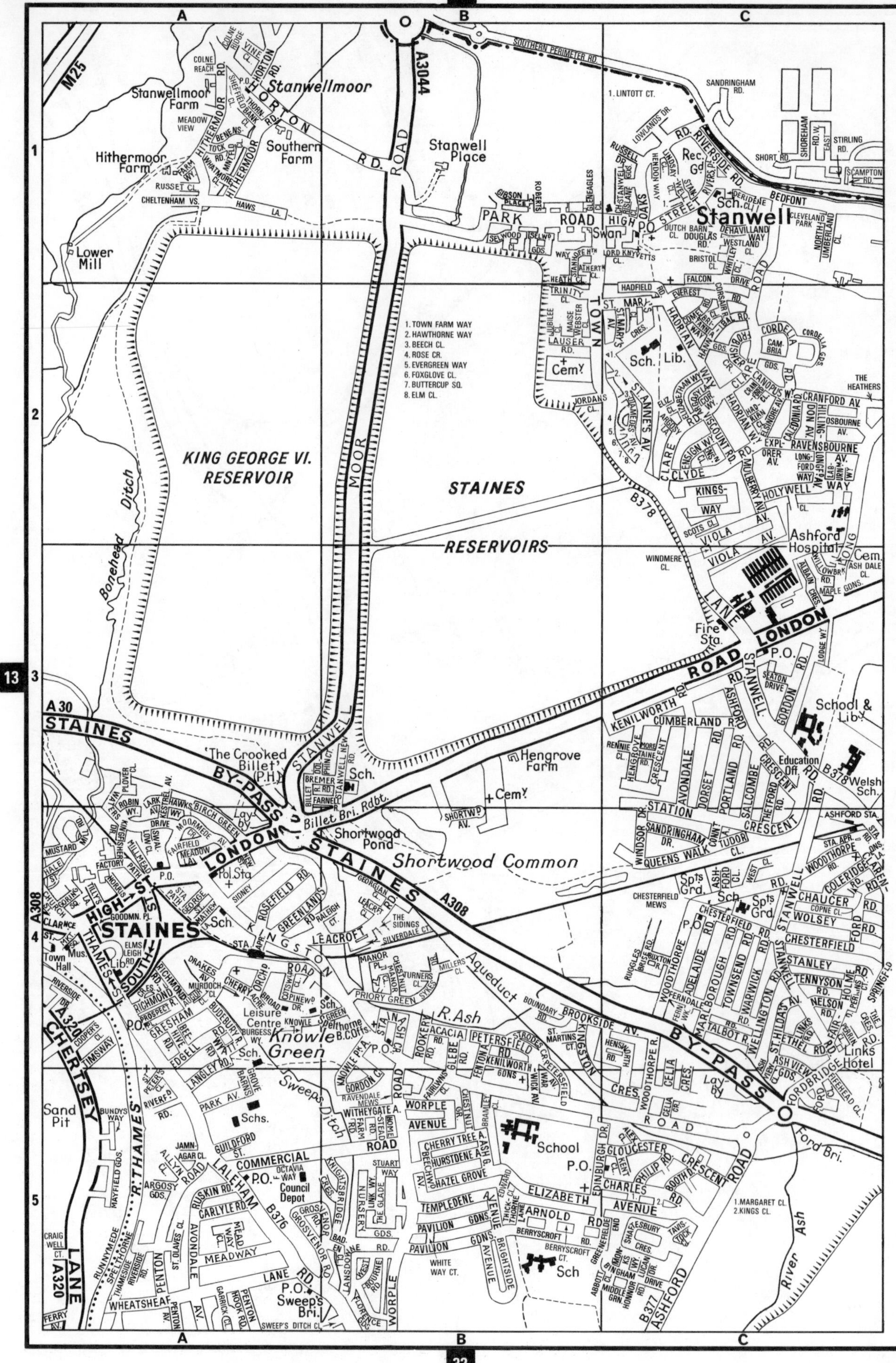

7
13
32
A
B
C
1
2
3
4
5
M25
A3044
Stanwellmoor
Stanwellmoor Farm
Hithermoor Farm
Southern Farm
Stanwell Place
Lower Mill
HORTON RD.
HITHERMOOR RD.
HAWS LA.
CHELTENHAM VS.
SOUTHERN PERIMETER RD.
MOOR ROAD
1. LINTOTT CT.
SANDRINGHAM RD.
Stanwell
PARK ROAD
HIGH STREET
Swan
BEDFONT RD.
RIVERSIDE RD.
FALCON DRIVE
TOWN LANE
KING GEORGE VI. RESERVOIR
STAINES
RESERVOIRS
1. TOWN FARM WAY
2. HAWTHORNE WAY
3. BEECH CL.
4. ROSE CR.
5. EVERGREEN WAY
6. FOXGLOVE CL.
7. BUTTERCUP SQ.
8. ELM CL.
Bonehead Ditch
B378
Ashford Hospital
Cem.
Fire Sta.
LONDON ROAD
STANWELL RD.
KENILWORTH RD.
School & Lib.
Education Off.
Welsh Sch.
A30
STAINES BY-PASS
'The Crooked Billet' (P.H.)
Hengrove Farm
Billet Bri. Rdbt.
Shortwood Pond
Shortwood Common
STATION CRESCENT
ASHFORD STA.
STAINES
A308
HIGH ST.
Town Hall
Mus.
Lib.
KINGSTON ROAD
Leisure Centre
Knowle Green
R. Ash
Aqueduct
BROOKSIDE AV.
Links Hotel
Sweeps Ditch
Sand Pit
CHERTSEY LANE
A320
R. THAMES
COMMERCIAL ROAD
Council Depot
LALEHAM RD.
B376
School
GLOUCESTER CRESCENT
ELIZABETH AVENUE
B377
ASHFORD ROAD
Ford Bri.
River Ash
1. MARGARET CL.
2. KINGS CL.
Sweep's Bri.
WHEATSHEAF LA.

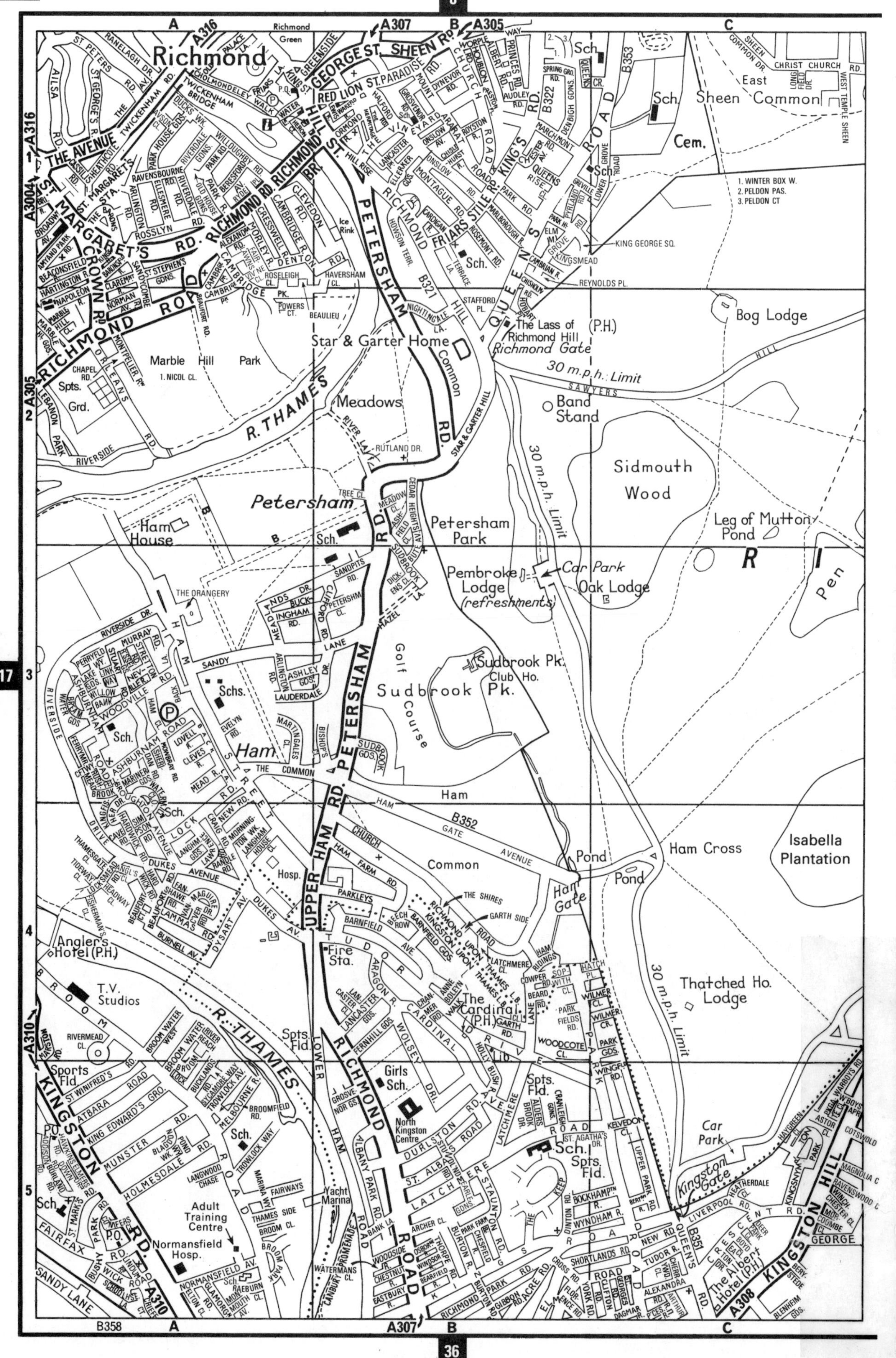
8
A
B
C
A316
A307
A305
Richmond Green
Richmond
RANELAGH DR.
ST. PETERS RD.
ST. GEORGE'S RD.
AILSA
THE AVENUE
TWICKENHAM BRIDGE
CHOLMONDELEY WALK
GEORGE ST.
SHEEN RD.
RED LION ST.
PARADISE RD.
KING ST.
GREENSIDE
WORPLE WAY
ALBERT RD.
PRINCES RD.
AUDLEY RD.
SPRING GRO. RD.
DENBIGH GDNS.
MARCHMONT RD.
QUEENS CR.
B353
B322
Sch.
Sheen Common
East Sheen Common
CHRIST CHURCH RD.
SHEEN COMMON DR.
LONGFIELD DR.
WEST TEMPLE SHEEN
Cem.
1. WINTER BOX W.
2. PELDON PAS.
3. PELDON CT
A3004
ST. MARGARET'S RD.
ST. MARGARETS STA.
CROWN RD.
RICHMOND RD.
RICHMOND BR.
HILL ST.
HILL RISE
PETERSHAM RD.
B321
THE VINEYARD
ONSLOW AV.
MONTAGUE RD.
FRIARS STILE RD.
KING'S RD.
QUEENS RISE
QUEEN'S RD.
ROSEMONT RD.
ELLERKER GDNS.
HOWSON TERR.
RICHMOND HILL
Ice Rink
ARLINGTON RD.
ROSSLYN RD.
CAMBRIDGE RD.
CLEVEDON RD.
DENTON RD.
HAVERSHAM CL.
ROSELEIGH CL.
POWERS CT.
BEAULIEU
KING GEORGE SQ.
KINGSMEAD
REYNOLDS PL.
STAFFORD PL.
NIGHTINGALE LA.
Bog Lodge
The Lass of Richmond Hill (P.H.)
Richmond Gate
Star & Garter Home
Common
Marble Hill Park
1. NICOL CL.
CHAPEL RD.
ORLEANS RD.
MONTPELIER RD.
Spts. Grd.
LEBANON PARK
RIVERSIDE
R. THAMES
Meadows
RIVER LA.
RUTLAND DR.
STAR & GARTER HILL
SAWYERS HILL
30 m.p.h. Limit
Band Stand
Sidmouth Wood
Petersham
Ham House
Sch.
TREE CL.
MEADOW CL.
CEDAR HEIGHTS
SUDBROOK LA.
Petersham Park
Leg of Mutton Pond
R
Pen
Pembroke Lodge (refreshments)
Car Park
Oak Lodge
THE ORANGERY
SANDPITS RD.
PETERSHAM CL.
MEADLANDS DR.
BUCKINGHAM RD.
CLIFFORD RD.
DICKENS CL.
RIVERSIDE DR.
MURRAY
SANDY LANE
ARLINGTON RD.
ASHLEY GDNS.
LAUDERDALE DR.
Golf Course
Sudbrook Pk. Club Ho.
Sudbrook Pk.
17
Schs.
Sch.
Ham
THE COMMON
MARTINGALES CL.
BISHOP'S CL.
SUDBROOK GDNS.
PETERSHAM RD.
ASHBURNHAM RD.
WOODVILLE RD.
EVELYN RD.
LOVELL RD.
CLEVES RD.
MEAD RD.
NEW RD.
BACK LA.
HAM STREET
KINGFISHER DR.
LOCK RD.
DUKES AVENUE
THAMESGATE CL.
TIDEWAY CL.
HEADWAY CL.
BEAUFORT RD.
BURNELL AV.
DYSART AV.
UPPER HAM RD.
HAM GATE AVENUE
B352
Ham Common
CHURCH RD.
HAM FARM RD.
PARKLEYS
BARNFIELD AVE.
BEECH ROW
RICHMOND RD.
KINGSTON UPON THAMES L.B.
THE SHIRES
GARTH SIDE
Pond
Ham Gate
Ham Cross
Isabella Plantation
Angler's Hotel (P.H.)
T.V. Studios
BROOM ROAD
A310
RIVERMEAD CL.
Fire Sta.
TUDOR DR.
ARAGON R.
LANCASTER GDNS.
CARDINAL AV.
ANNE BOLEYN WALK
The Cardinal (P.H.)
HAM RIDINGS
FLATCHMERE CL.
COWPER RD.
WILMER CL.
PARK FIELDS RD.
WOODCOTE CL.
PARK GDNS.
Thatched Ho. Lodge
Sports Fld
Spts. Fld.
KINGSTON RD.
ST WINIFRED'S RD.
ATBARA ROAD
KING EDWARD'S GRO.
MUNSTER RD.
HOLMESDALE RD.
BROOM WATER
BROOMFIELD RD.
Sch.
TROWLOCK WAY
MELBOURNE R.
LOWER HAM RD.
FERNHILL GDS.
WOLSEY DRI.
Girls Sch.
North Kingston Centre
DURLSTON RD.
ST. ALBANS ROAD
LATCHMERE RD.
STAUNTON RD.
LATCHMERE LA.
Spts. Fld.
ALDERS GRO.
CRANLEIGH GDNS.
WINGFIELD RD.
KELVEDON CL.
UPPER PARK RD.
ST. AGATHA'S DR.
Sch.
Spts. Fld.
Car Park
Kingston Gate
HAYGREEN CL.
HEATHERDALE
CRESCENT RD.
KINGSTON HILL
COTSWOLD
MAGNOLIA C
RAVENSWOOD C
GEORGE
Adult Training Centre
Normansfield Hosp.
Yacht Marina
FAIRWAYS
THAMES SIDE
BROOM CL.
BROOM PARK
LANGWOOD CHASE
ALBANY PARK RD.
BANK LA.
WOODSIDE
CHESTNUT R.
EASTBURY R.
RICHMOND ROAD
WATERMANS CL.
CANBURY PROMENADE
ARCHER CL.
BURTON RD.
PARK FARM
CHESFIELD
WYNDHAM R.
BOCKHAMPTON
DINTON RD.
NEW RD.
SHORTLANDS RD.
TUDOR R.
ALEXANDRA
QUEEN'S RD.
B351
The Albert Hotel (P.H.)
A308
KINGSTON HILL
BLENHEIM GDS.
P.O.
Sch.
ST. MARKS RD.
FAIRFAX RD.
SANDY LANE
BUSHY PARK RD.
WICK ROAD
NORMANSFIELD AV.
ELTON CL.
GLAMORGAN CL.
MONMOUTH CL.
RAEBURN CL.
RICHMOND PARK RD.
GIBBON RD.
ACRE RD.
ELM RD.
YORK RD.
CLIFTON RD.
DAGMAR
B358
A307
36

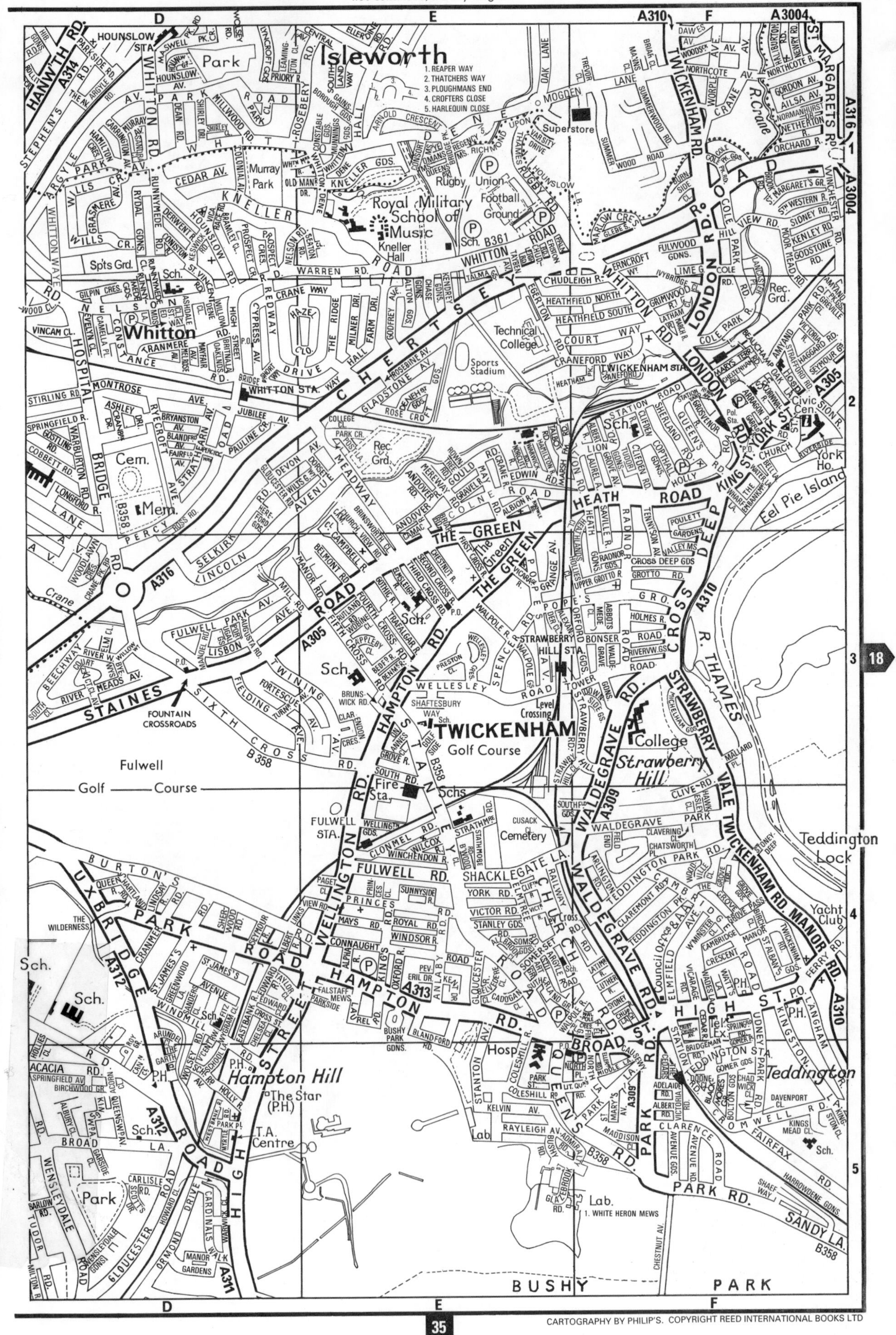

Isleworth

1. REAPER WAY
2. THATCHERS WAY
3. PLOUGHMANS END
4. CROFTERS CLOSE
5. HARLEQUIN CLOSE

Park

Murray Park

Royal Military School of Music
Kneller Hall

Whitton

Technical College

Sports Stadium

Civic Cen.

York Ho.

Eel Pie Island

THE GREEN

Strawberry Hill

TWICKENHAM
Golf Course

Strawberry Hill

College

Teddington Lock

Yacht Club

FOUNTAIN CROSSROADS

STAINES

Fulwell
Golf — Course

THE WILDERNESS

Fulwell STA.

Sch.

Hampton Hill
The Star (P.H.)
T.A. Centre

ACACIA

Park

Teddington

Hosp.

Lab.

1. WHITE HERON MEWS

BUSHY PARK

CARTOGRAPHY BY PHILIP'S. COPYRIGHT REED INTERNATIONAL BOOKS LTD

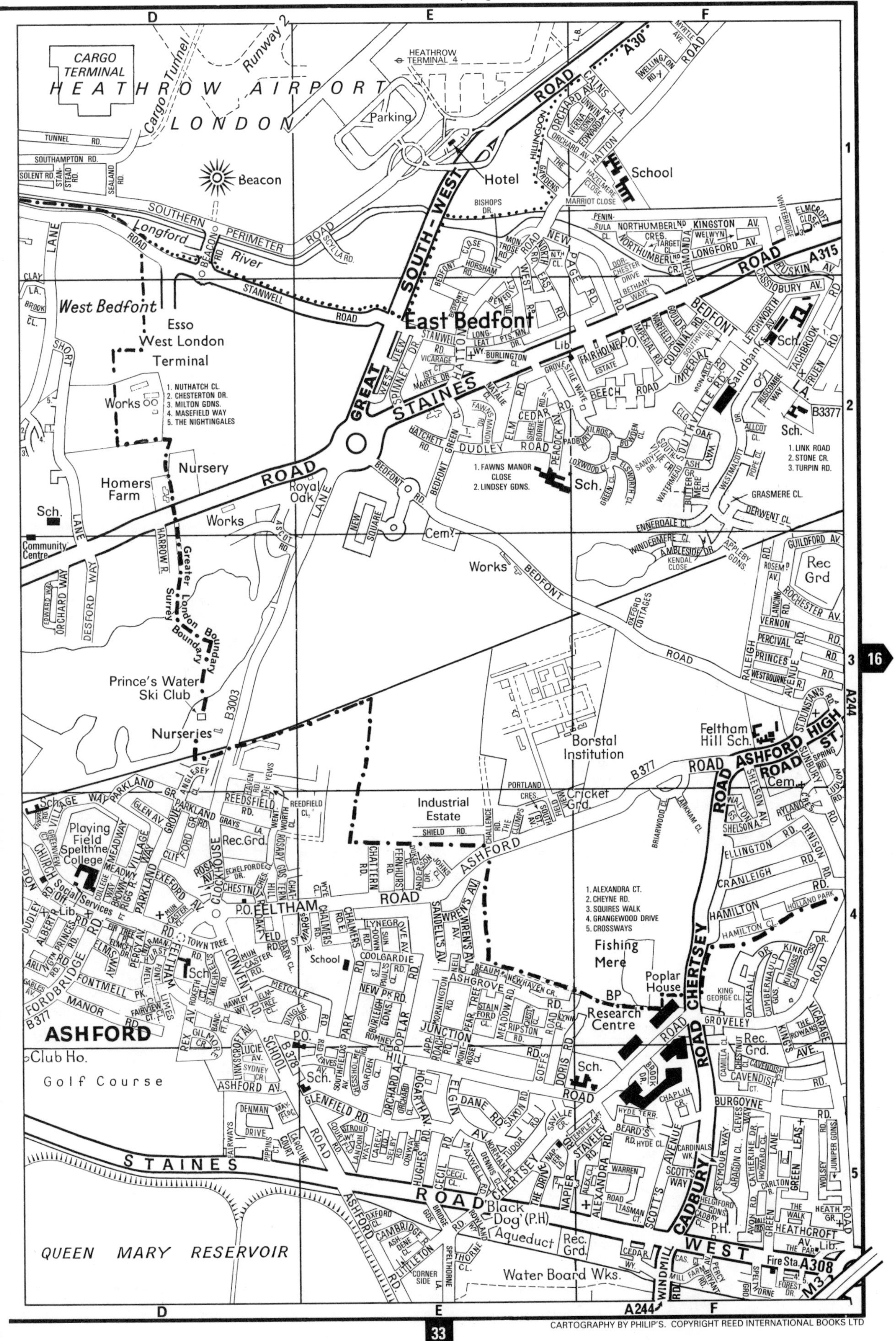

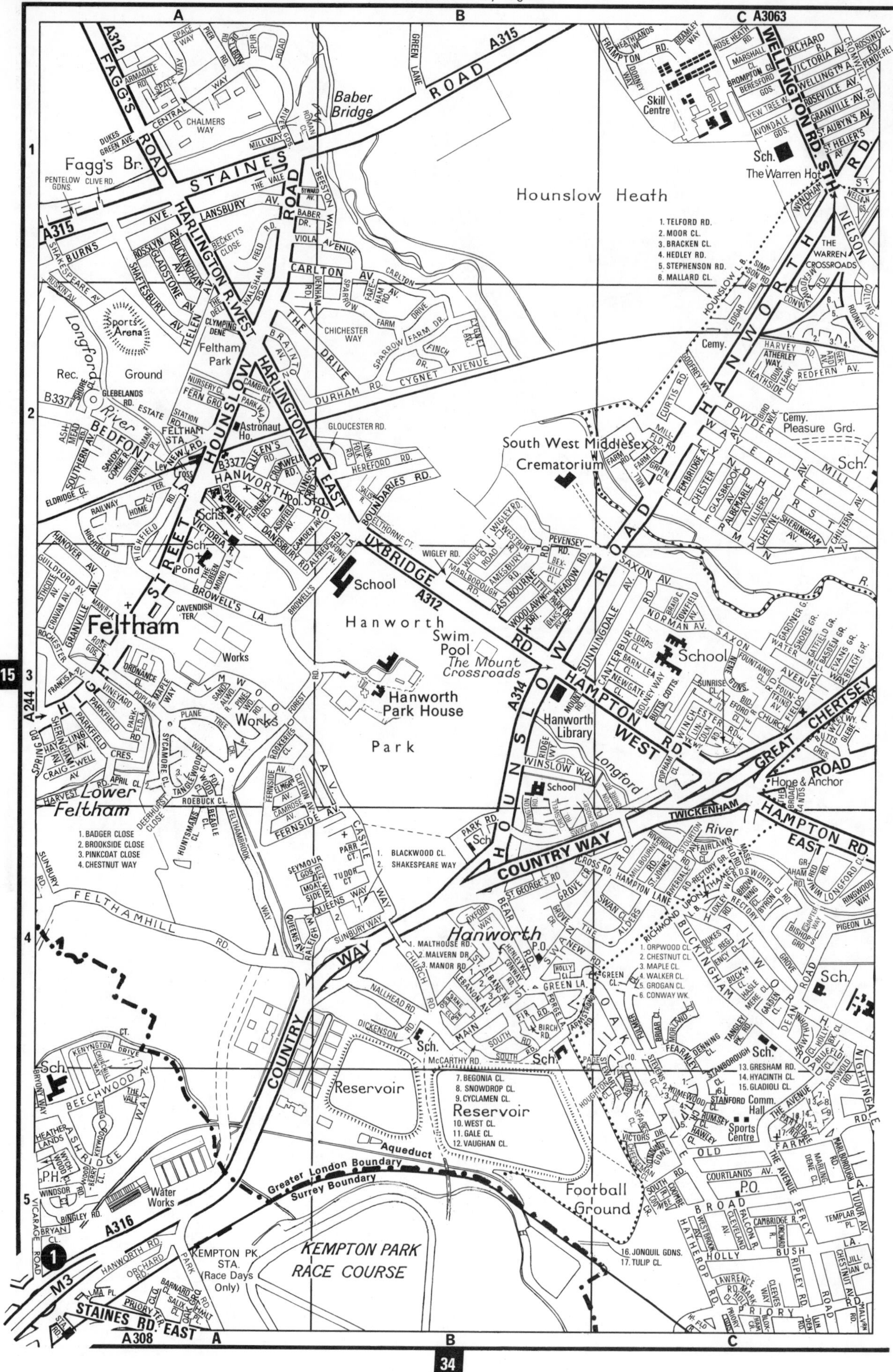

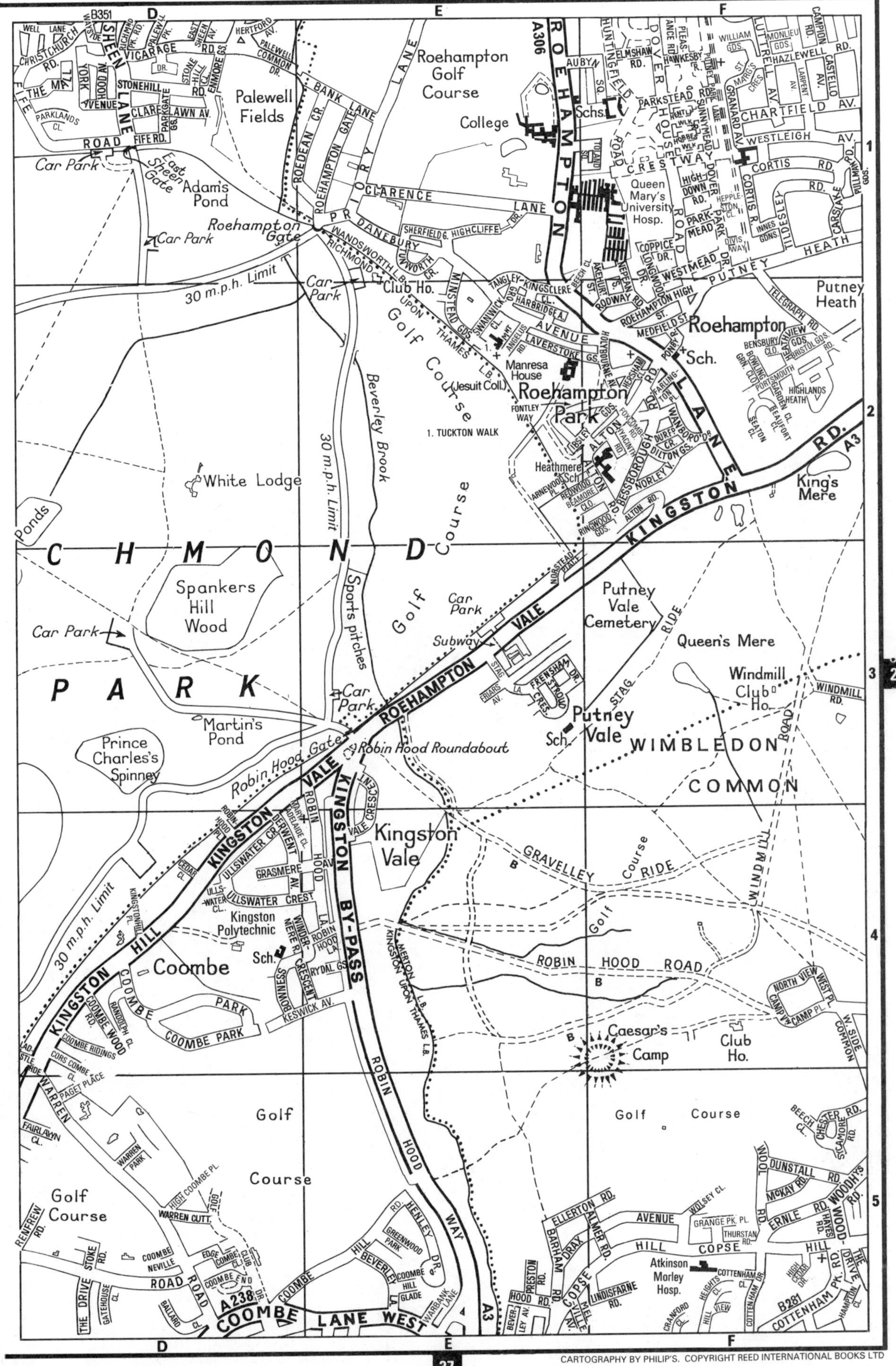
9
D
E
F
B351
A306
ROEHAMPTON LANE
SHEEN LANE
VICARAGE RD.
CHRISTCHURCH RD.
THE MALL
FIFE ROAD
PARKLANDS CL.
STONEHILL RD.
CLARE LAWN AV.
FIFE RD.
HERTFORD AV.
PALEWELL COMMON DR.
Palewell Fields
BANK LANE
ROEDEAN CR.
ROEHAMPTON GATE
PRIORY LANE
CLARENCE LANE
Roehampton Golf Course
College
Schs.
AUBYN SQ.
ELMSHAW RD.
PARKSTEAD RD.
DOVER HOUSE ROAD
CRESTWAY
Queen Mary's University Hosp.
CHARTFIELD AV.
WESTLEIGH AV.
CORTIS RD.
HAZLEWELL RD.
LUTTRELL AV.
CASTELLO AV.
CARSLAKE RD.
TILDESLEY RD.
PUTNEY HEATH
WESTMEAD
Car Park
East Sheen Gate
Adam's Pond
Roehampton Gate
Car Park
DANEBURY AV.
SHERFIELD G.
HIGHCLIFFE DR.
TUNWORTH CR.
WANDSWORTH L.B.
RICHMOND UPON THAMES L.B.
Club Ho.
30 m.p.h. Limit
Car Park
MINSTEAD GDS.
AVENUE
LAVERSTOKE GS.
ROEHAMPTON HIGH ST.
MEDFIELD ST.
Roehampton
Sch.
Putney Heath
TELEGRAPH RD.
HEATHVIEW GDS.
BENSBURY CLO.
BRISTOL GDS.
PORTSMOUTH RD.
HIGHLANDS HEATH
SEATON CL.
Golf Course
Manresa House
(Jesuit Coll.)
Roehampton Park
FONTLEY WAY
1. TUCKTON WALK
ALTON RD.
BESSBOROUGH RD.
Heathmere Sch.
KINGSTON RD.
A3
King's Mere
Beverley Brook
30 m.p.h. Limit
White Lodge
Ponds
RICHMOND PARK
Spankers Hill Wood
Car Park
Sports pitches
Golf Course
Car Park
NORSTEAD PL.
Putney Vale Cemetery
STAG RIDE
Queen's Mere
Windmill Club Ho.
WINDMILL RD.
Subway
ROEHAMPTON VALE
FRIARS AV.
FRENSHAM DR.
Putney Vale
Sch.
WIMBLEDON COMMON
Car Park
Martin's Pond
Prince Charles's Spinney
Robin Hood Gate
Robin Hood Roundabout
ROBIN HOOD WAY
KINGSTON VALE
KINGSTON BY-PASS
Kingston Vale
VALE CRESCENT
ULLSWATER CR.
GRASMERE AV.
ULLSWATER CREST
Kingston Polytechnic
Sch.
WINDERMERE RD.
BOWNESS CRESCENT
RYDAL GS.
KESWICK AV.
KINGSTON HILL
30 m.p.h. Limit
Coombe
COOMBE PARK
COOMBE RIDINGS
COOMBE WOOD RD.
GRAVELLEY RIDE
Golf Course
ROBIN HOOD ROAD
WINDMILL
MERTON L.B.
KINGSTON UPON THAMES L.B.
Caesar's Camp
Club Ho.
NORTH VIEW
CAMP RD.
WEST PL.
W. SIDE COMMON
PAGET PLACE
WARREN RD.
FAIRLAWN CL.
WARREN PARK
Golf Course
Golf Course
HIGH COOMBE PL.
WARREN CUTT.
RENFREW RD.
STOKE RD.
COOMBE NEVILLE
COOMBE END
THE DRIVE
GATEHOUSE CL.
BALLARD CL.
A238
COOMBE LANE WEST
COOMBE HILL RD.
BEVERLEY LA.
HENLEY DR.
WARBANK LANE
A3
Golf Course
BEECH CL.
CHESTER RD.
SYCAMORE RD.
DUNSTALL RD.
McKAY RD.
ERNLE RD.
WOODHAYES RD.
ELLERTON RD.
AVENUE
WOLSEY CL.
GRANGE PK. PL.
THURSTAN RD.
HILL COPSE
BARHAM RD.
DRAX AV.
ALMER RD.
COPSE HILL
Atkinson Morley Hosp.
COTTENHAM DR.
COTTENHAM PK. RD.
B281
PRESTON RD.
HOOD RD.
LINDISFARNE RD.
1
2
3
4
5
20
37

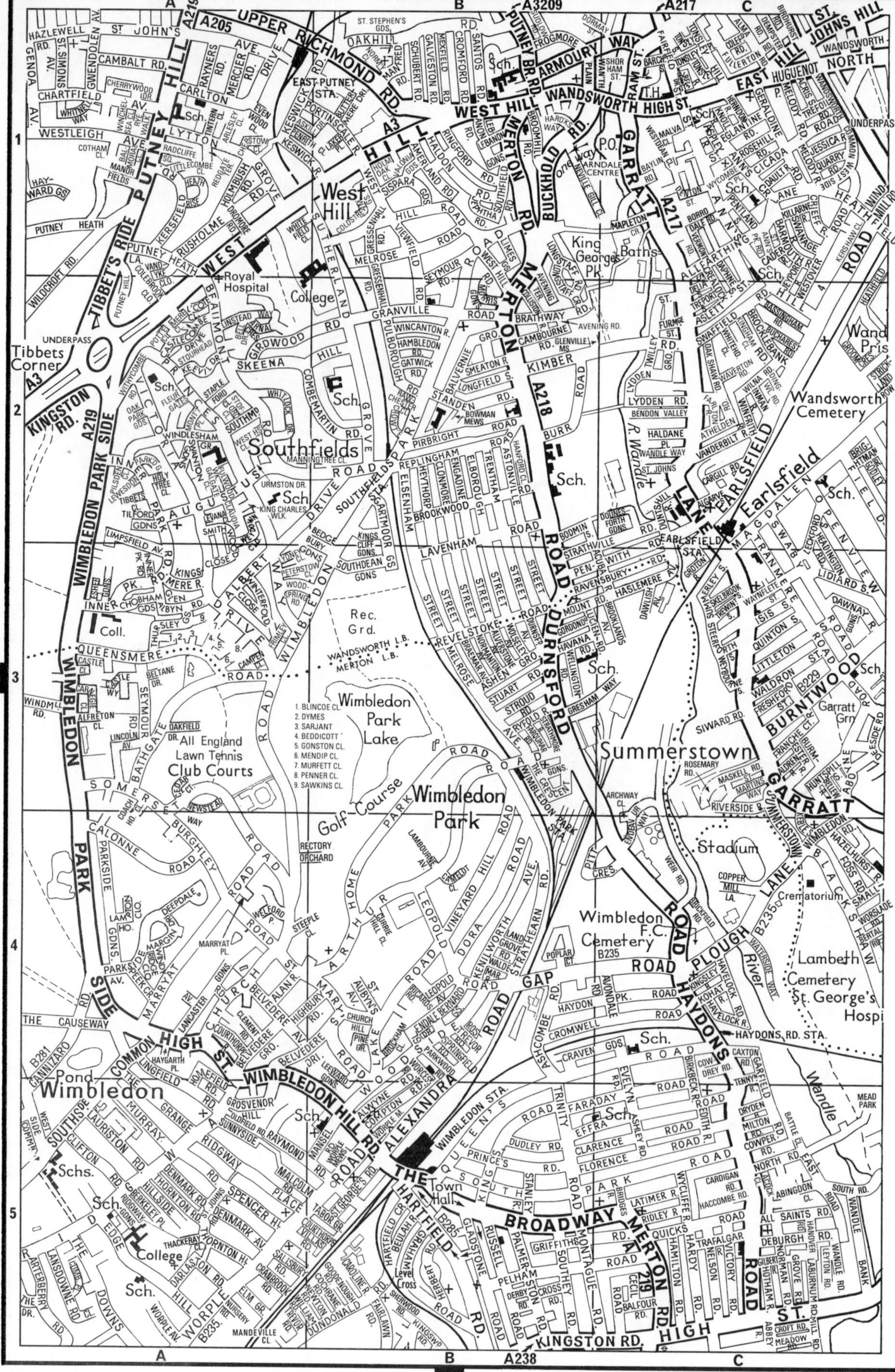

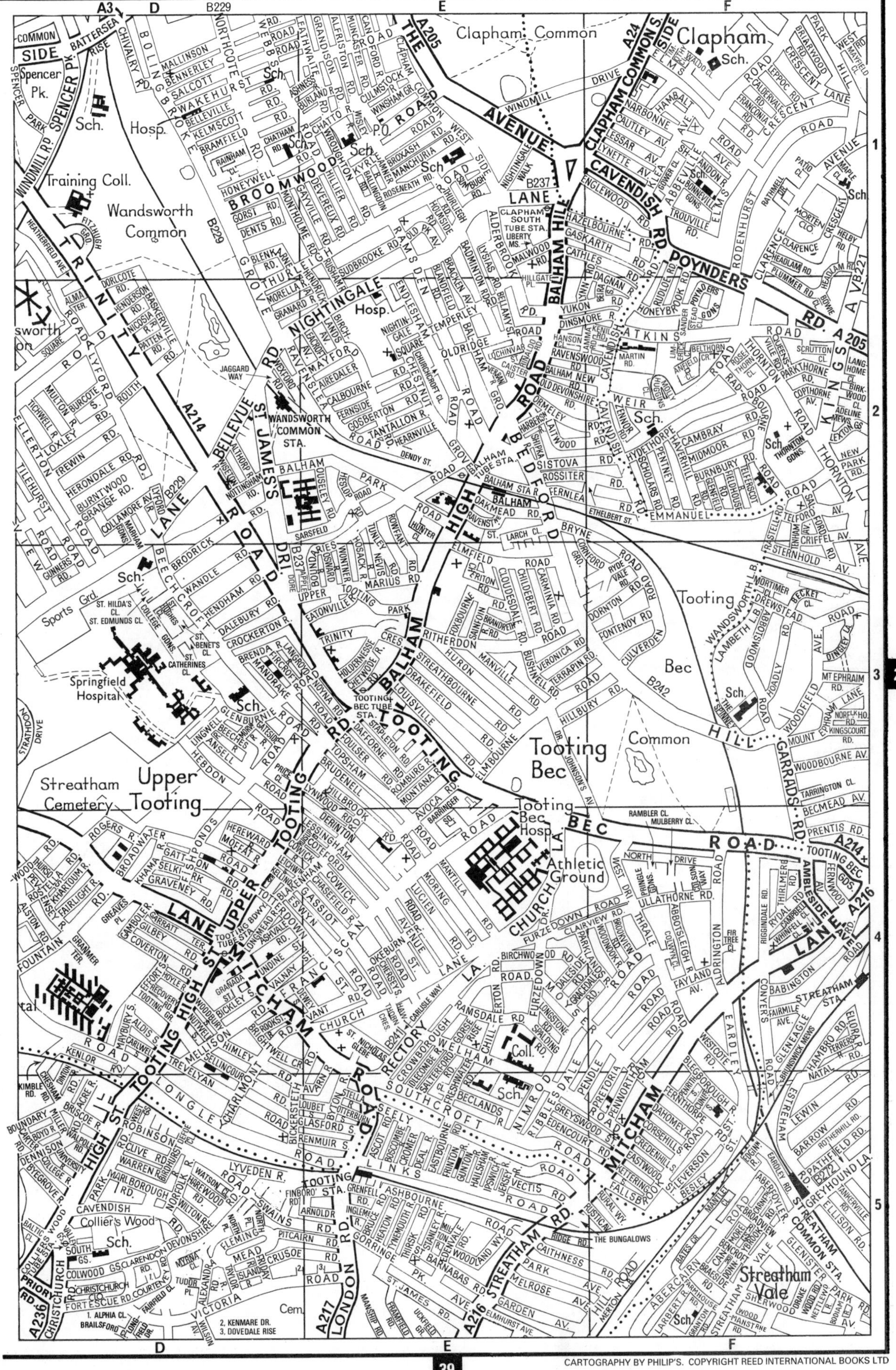

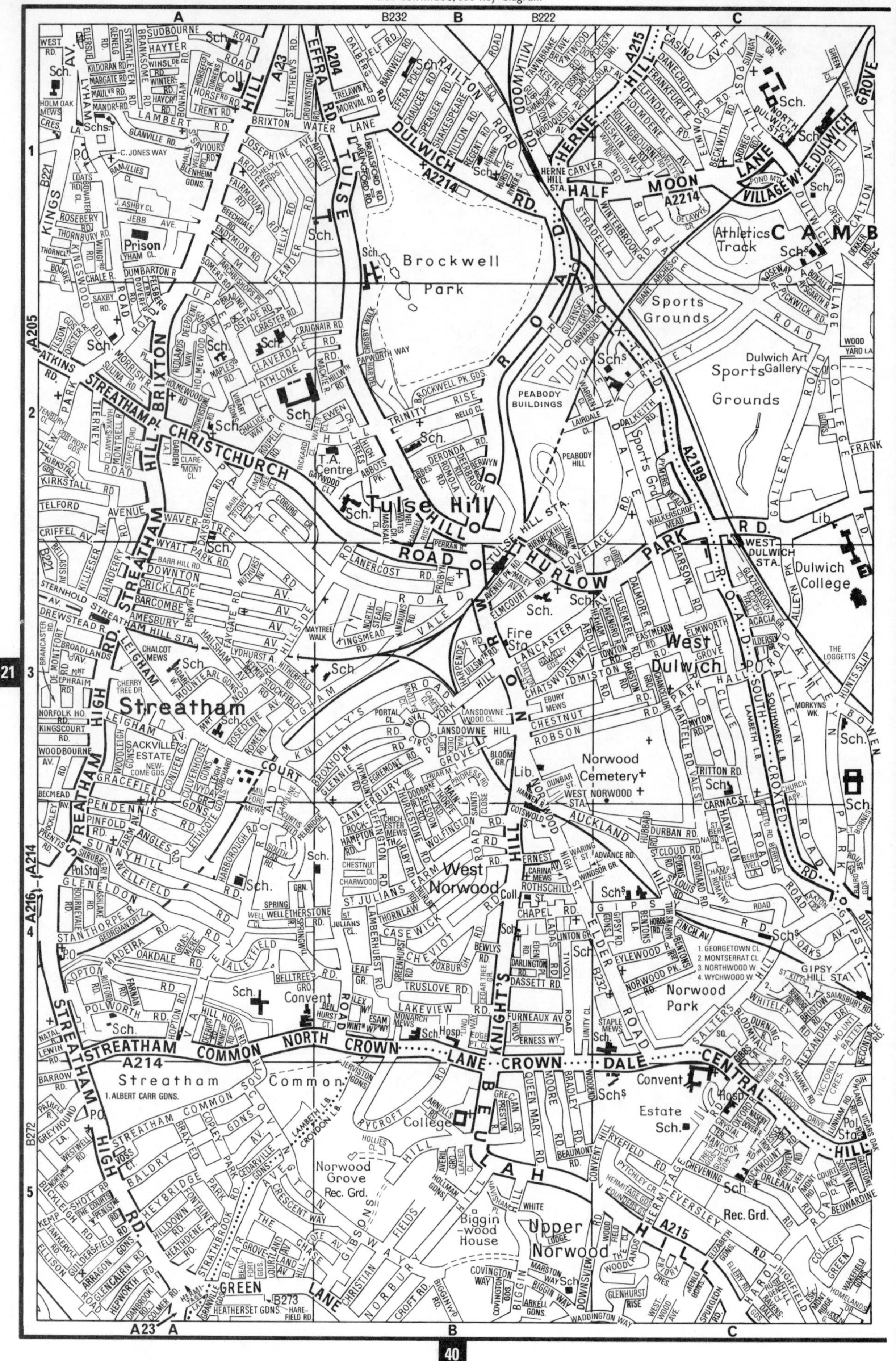

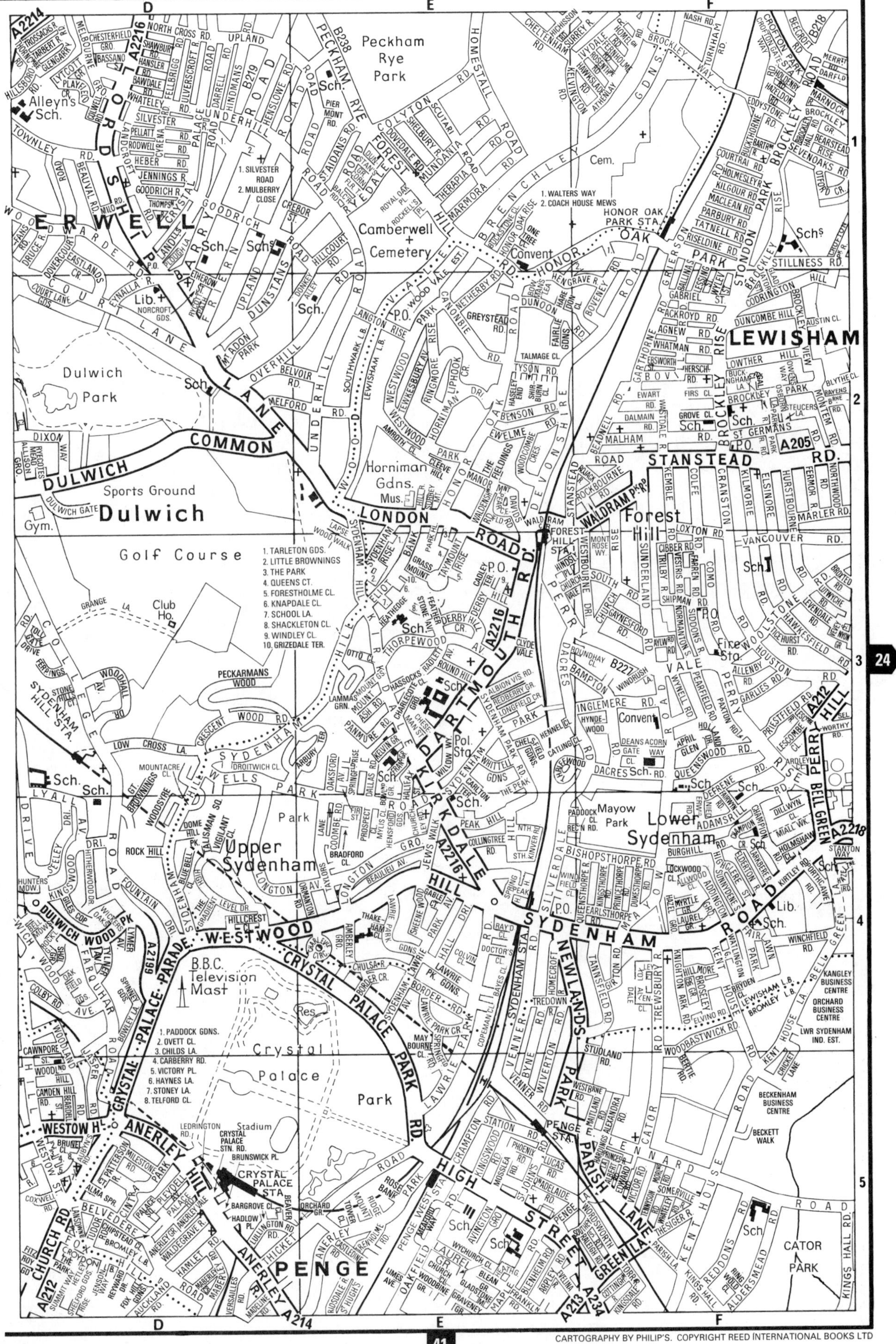

CARTOGRAPHY BY PHILIP'S. COPYRIGHT REED INTERNATIONAL BOOKS LTD

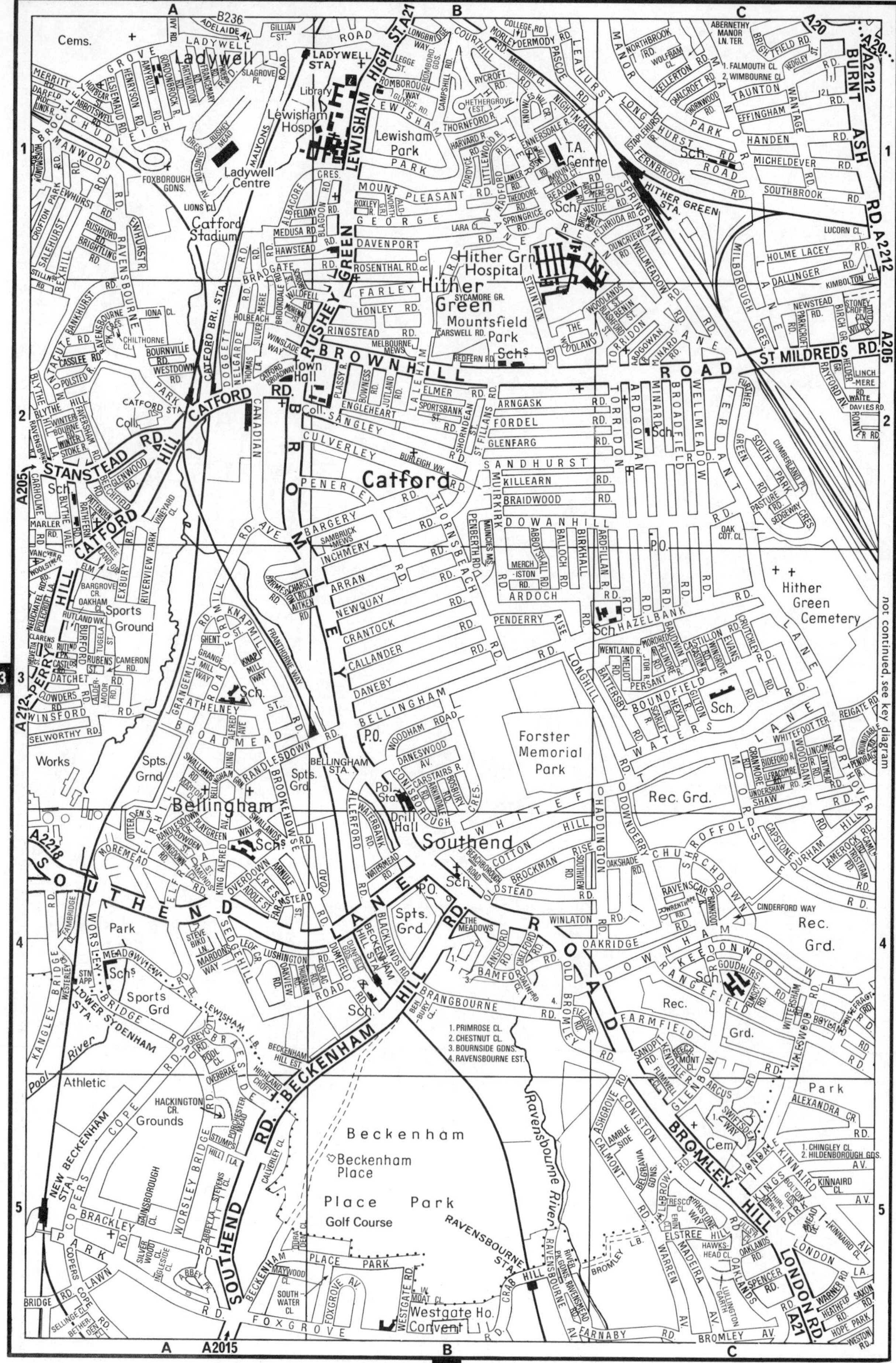

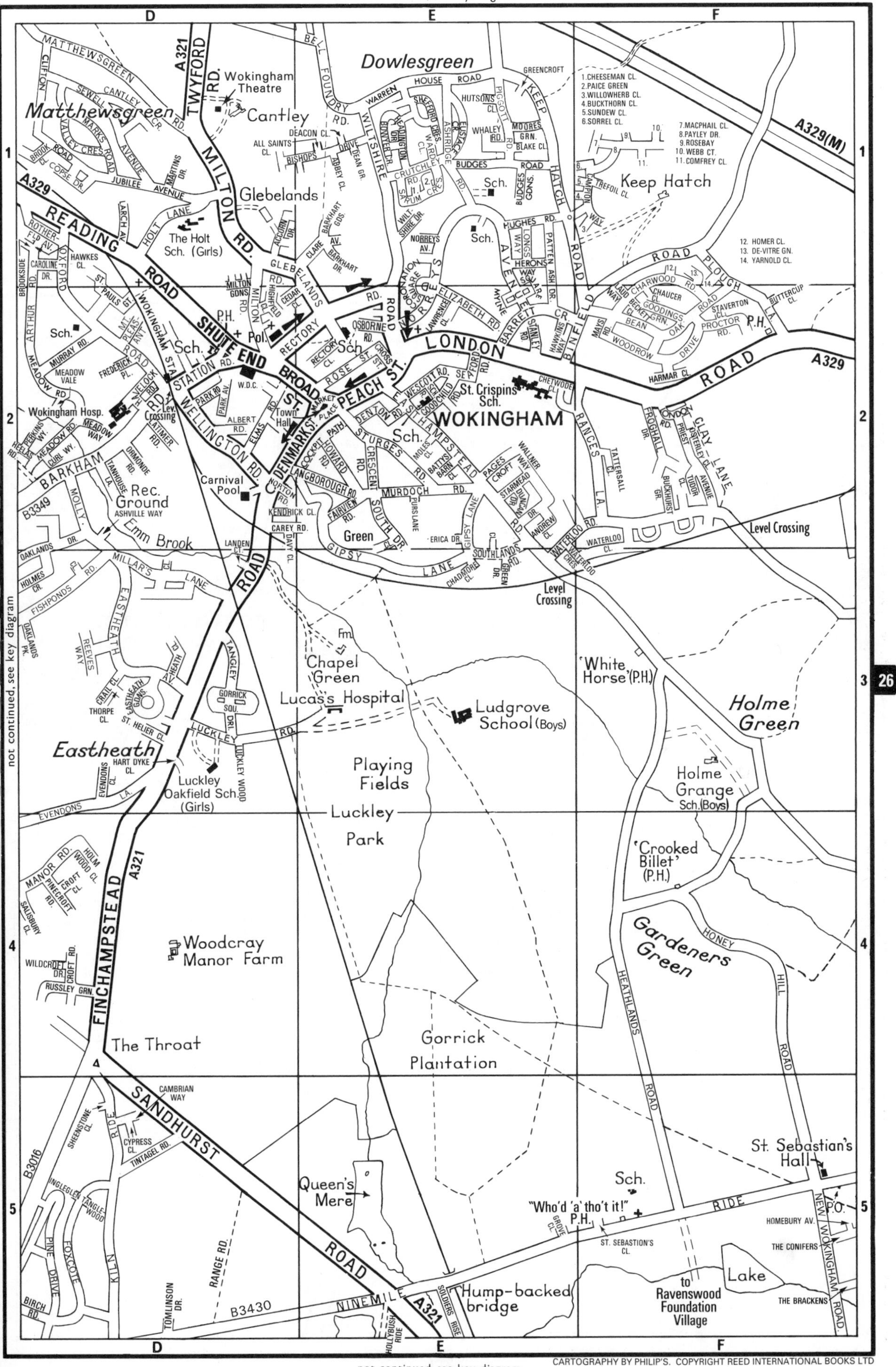

A   B   C

Pockets Copse

Murrellhill Farm

Blackman's Copse

Masts

A329(M)

A329

The Shoulder of Mutton (P.H.)

Springfield Rd.

LONDON ROAD

B3408

Farley Hall

P.O.

Sch.

Beehive La.

Buckhouse Farm

Hotel
Sport Complex

Rose Farm

Riggs Copse

St. Ann's Manor Hotel

Big Wood

BERKSHIRE WAY

1. Radcliffe Way
2. Simmonds Close
3. Statham Court

WOKINGHAM

B3408

WESTERN ROAD

The Bridge (P.H.)

Priestwood

Admiral Cunningham (P.H.)

Windmill Rd.

DOWNMILL

Arlington Sq.

SKIMPEDHILL LA.

DOWNSHIRE LA.

MILL LANE

A3095

A329

Peacock Lane

Lovelace Rd.

Doncastle Rd.

Elles Field

Oldbury

Willoughby

Green Man P.H.

Jun. Sch.

Mill Pond

Lodge
(PRIVATE ROAD)

Lack's House

Waterloo Road

Jennett's Hill

Ringmead

Welbeck
Wheatley
Winscombe
Wordsworth
Wroxham

Prim. Sch.

Easthampstead

Church Hill House Hospital

REEDS

Great Hollands

Easthampstead Park Educational Centre

Gate

4. Wickham Vale
5. Eddington Road
6. Ramsbury Close
7. Penwood Gdns.
8. Hatchgate Copse
9. Flexford Green
10. Compton Close

Vandyke
Cunworth Cl.
Beedon
Drive

Six Oaks

Easthampstead Rd.

Sutton Court Farm

Downshire Golf Course

Golf Club House

WEST ROAD

Easthampstead Park Crematorium & Cemetery

Easthampstead Park Water Pollution Control Centre

Beaufort Park (Met. Office)

Ullswater

Holland Pines

CROWTHORNE ROAD

MILL LANE

South Hill

RIDE

Pinewood Leisure Centre

NINEMILE RIDE

B3430

NINEMILE

OLD WOKINGHAM ROAD

Road Research Laboratory

Earthworks

Caesar's Camp

UPPER STAR POST RIDE

Honeysuckle Cl.

HATCH

Play. Fld.

Sch.

Oaklands

A3095

B3348 BRACKNELL RD.

25

43

not continued, see key diagram

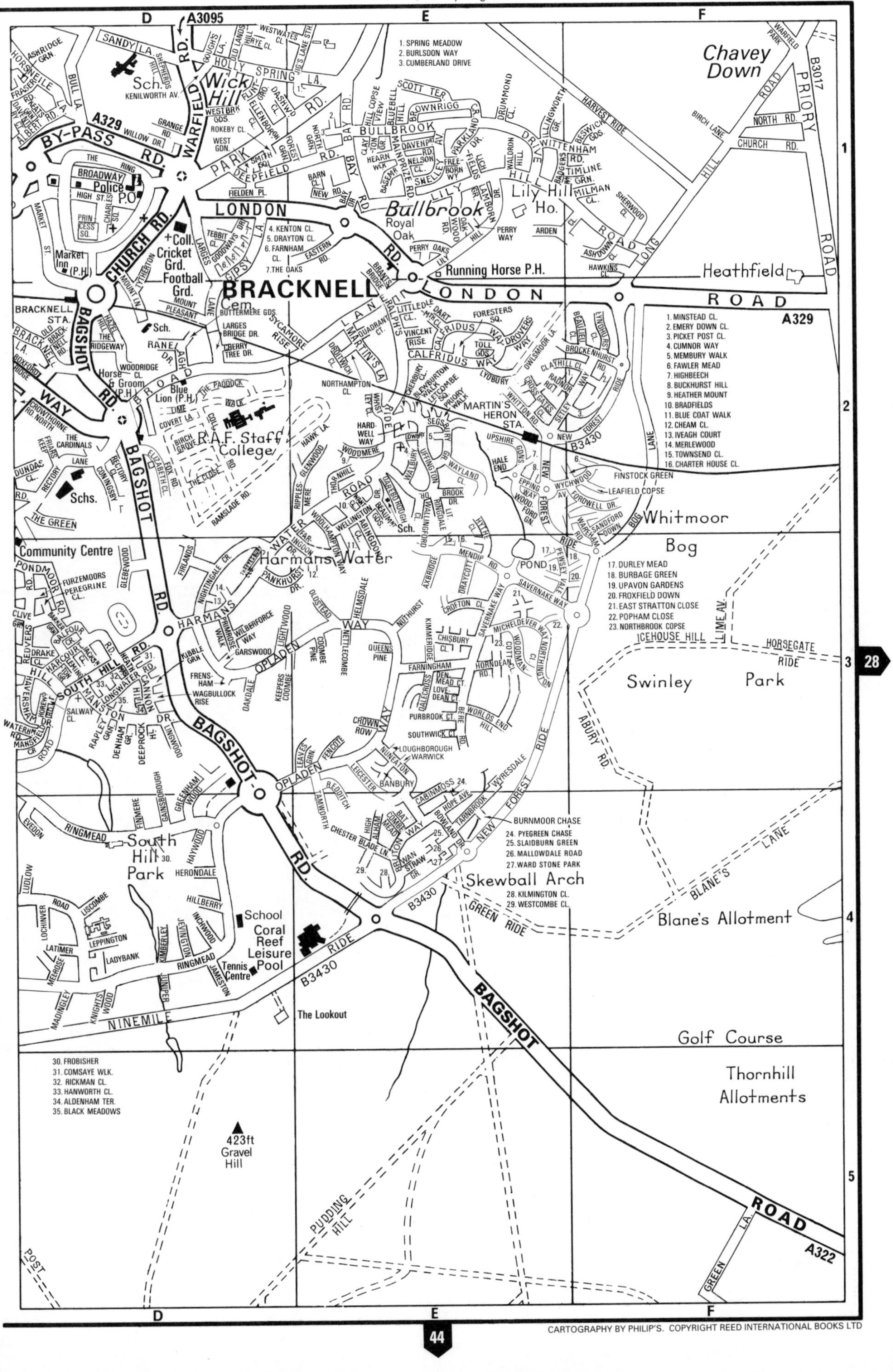

Chavey
Down

BRACKNELL

Bullbrook

Wick Hill

LONDON ROAD

Heathfield

Running Horse P.H.

Royal Oak

Martin's Heron Sta.

Whitmoor Bog

Harmans Water

Community Centre

R.A.F. Staff College

Swinley Park

Horsegate Ride

Icehouse Hill

Blane's Lane

Blane's Allotment

Skewball Arch

South Hill Park

School Coral Reef Leisure Pool

Tennis Centre

The Lookout

Golf Course

Thornhill Allotments

▲ 423ft Gravel Hill

Pudding Hill

Ninemile

1. SPRING MEADOW
2. BURLSDON WAY
3. CUMBERLAND DRIVE
4. KENTON CL.
5. DRAYTON CL.
6. FARNHAM CL.
7. THE OAKS

1. MINSTEAD CL.
2. EMERY DOWN CL.
3. PICKET POST CL.
4. CUMNOR WAY
5. MEMBURY WALK
6. FAWLER MEAD
7. HIGHBEECH
8. BUCKHURST HILL
9. HEATHER MOUNT
10. BRADFIELDS
11. BLUE COAT WALK
12. CHEAM CL.
13. IVEAGH COURT
14. MERLEWOOD
15. TOWNSEND CL.
16. CHARTER HOUSE CL.

17. DURLEY MEAD
18. BURBAGE GREEN
19. UPAVON GARDENS
20. FROXFIELD DOWN
21. EAST STRATTON CLOSE
22. POPHAM CLOSE
23. NORTHBROOK COPSE

24. PYEGREEN CHASE
25. SLAIDBURN GREEN
26. MALLOWDALE ROAD
27. WARD STONE PARK
28. KILMINGTON CL.
29. WESTCOMBE CL.

30. FROBISHER
31. COMSAYE WLK.
32. RICKMAN CL.
33. HANWORTH CL.
34. ALDENHAM TER.
35. BLACK MEADOWS

BURNMOOR CHASE

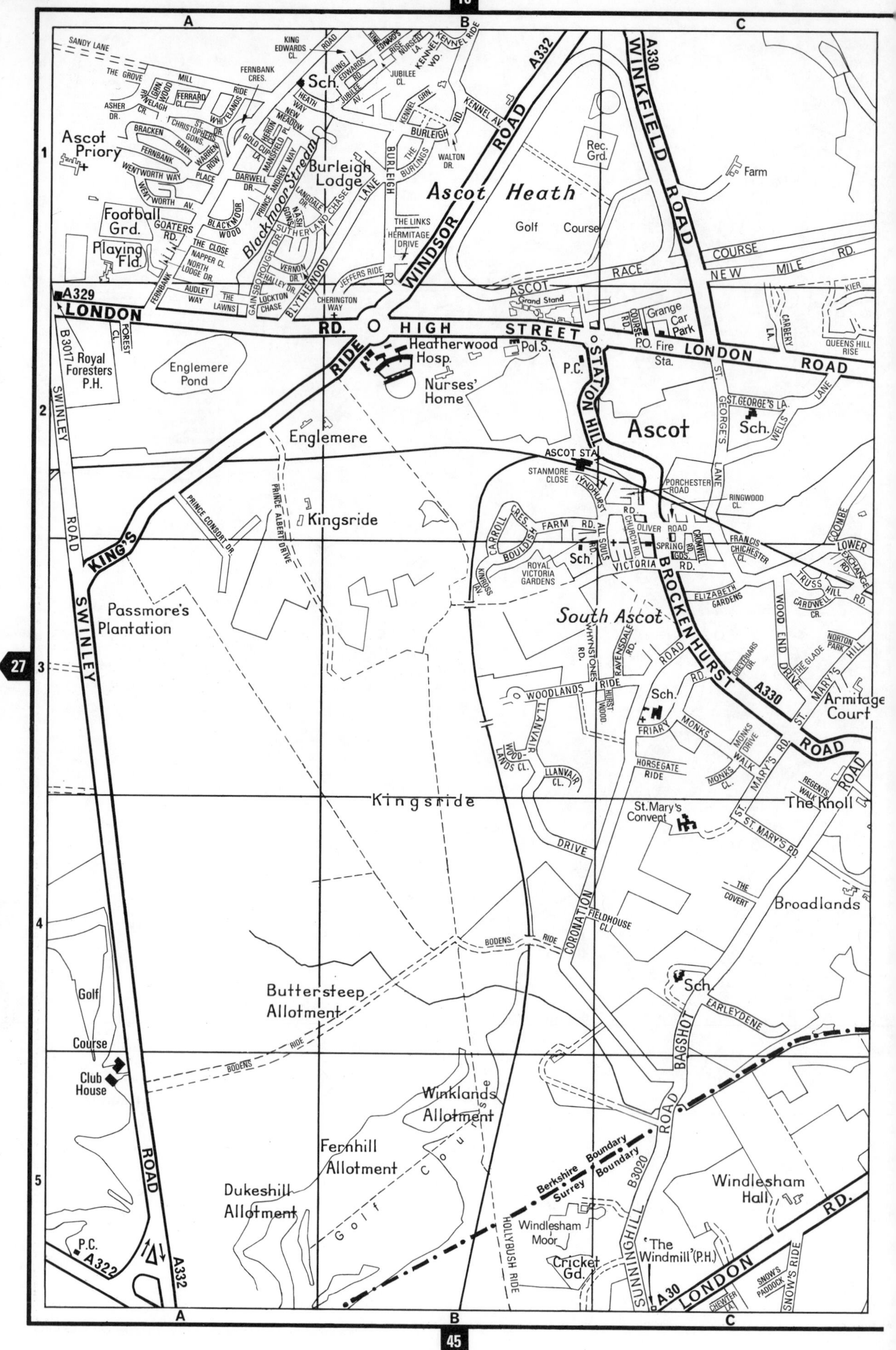

10
27
45
Ascot Heath
Ascot
South Ascot
Ascot Priory
Burleigh Lodge
Englemere
Englemere Pond
Kingsride
Passmore's Plantation
Buttersteep Allotment
Winklands Allotment
Fernhill Allotment
Dukeshill Allotment
Windlesham Moor
Windlesham Hall
Broadlands
Armitage Court
The Knoll
St. Mary's Convent
Heatherwood Hosp.
Nurses' Home
Royal Foresters P.H.
'The Windmill' (P.H.)
Berkshire Boundary
Surrey Boundary
Golf Course
Football Grd.
Playing Fld.
Rec. Grd.
Club House
Cricket Gd.
LONDON RD.
HIGH STREET
WINDSOR ROAD
WINKFIELD ROAD
KING'S RIDE
SWINLEY ROAD
BROCKENHURST ROAD
BAGSHOT ROAD
SUNNINGHILL ROAD
STATION HILL
COURSE RD.
NEW MILE RD.
RACE
CORONATION DRIVE
BODENS RIDE
HOLLYBUSH RIDE
ST. GEORGE'S LANE

D E F

Johnson's Pond

Lower Farm

Buckhurst Park

WATERSPLASH

PUMP LA.
SUNNINGHILL
B383

GREEN
LANE
Sch.
+
Pemberton Lodge

HILLTOP CL.

Cheapside

BUCKHURST
MILL

ROSY BOTTOM

New Golden Gates

SILWOOD CL.

PARK

Brook Lodge

Harewood Lodge

LANE

Blacknest Gate

Car Pk.

VIRGINIA WATER

Frostfarm Plantation

CHEAPSIDE LANE

Tetworth

The Cedars

CHURCH PATH

Silwood Park

B383 BUCKHURST

Titness Park

ROAD

LANE

BLACKNEST

A329 RD.

Swan Lake

1

2

Ashurst Lodge

SHENSTONE PARK

BEECH CROFT CL.
SWANNELL'S WAY
CHURCH LA.
KINGSWICK CL.

The Oaks

Silwood Park

B383

LONDON

ROAD

Tittenhurst

Coworth Park

Belvedere Fort

A329

Sch. Council Offices

ORIENTAL RD.
SUNNINGHILL
ROAD
KINGSWICK
Sch.

QUINCE RD.
VILLAGE RD.

SANDHIDE
AVENUE
SILWOOD RD.
B383
SILWOOD
ROAD

KILN LANE

1. LOWER NURSERY
2. LEACROFT
3. UPPER NURSERY

LANE

The Red Lion (P.H.)

A30

Sunninghill

UPP. VILLAGE
NIVEN RD.
BOWDEN RD.
HIGH ST.
KING'S
QUEEN'S SQ.
P.O.
HIGH
CLERE

1. Pembroke Lodge
2. Pembroke Cl.
3. Tenby Dr.
4. Pinehurst

THE SPINNEY

HEATHFIELD AV.
RD.
LARCH

Sunningdale Park

DALE
LODGE RD.
SANDY
COWORTH RD.
1. 2. 3.
LA.
PARKSIDE RD.
SIDBURY RD.
TRY CL.
WHITMORE

CHURCH

LANE

Sunningdale

LONDON ROAD

TRUSS HILL RD.
FOX COVERT LANE
BRIDGE RD.
CHARTERS COTTS.
LAVENDISH MEADS
Works

BAGSHOT
B3017
HANCOCK'S MT.

Charters

HIGHFIELD
PARK DR.
PARK CRES.
LYNDWOOD CR.
RISE
OAKDENE
CHARINWOOD
BROOMHALL
STATION RD.
B383

BEDFORD

LANE

MANOR RD.

SHRUBBS HILL LANE

LAWSON WAY
REDWOOD DRIVE

BROOMFIELD FIELD RD.

SHEDLEY END
A.G. GREEN'S DR.

30

3

Sch.

P.O.

Broomhall Farm

Berkshire
Surrey
B.
Bay Bay.

DEVENISH

Sch.

King's Beeches

BROADLANDS
DRIVE
FIREBALL HILL

CHARTERS

Sch.

BEECH HILL RD.
DRYARCH
WOODBY DR.
RD.

CEDAR RD.

Sunningdale STA.

LONDON ROAD
CHOBHAM

BROOMFIELD
PARK

1. NORTH END LANE
2. GUARDS COURT

RUNNYMEDE
SURREY HEATH

SUNNING

CHARTERS
AVENUE
Sch.
BALLENCRIEF RD.
PINEDITE DR.
HAMILTON DR.
CHANCTONBURY
GRANTS AV.

LADY MARGARET RD.
CHARTERS WAY

Level Crossing
P.H.
P.O.
CLAREFIELD

ONSLOW RD.
FEATHER DR.

Broomhall

4

Old Windsor Bog

Thankerton House

DEVENISH LA.
GREENWAYS DR.
KNOLE WOOD
ELM PK.

ROAD

HILLSIDE
CROSS

Ridge Mount

RIDGE RD.
WINKFIELD COURT
WINKFIELD RD.

Sunningdale Golf Club Ho.

MOUNT
CUNISTON
PRIORY RD.
ABBEY WOOD
BRIDGE VIEW
RICHMOND WOOD

FISHERS WOOD

Hills End

TITLARKS HILL RD.

Monument

RD.

Little Arm

+

LONDON
WESTWOOD
WOODHALL
ROAD
LA.

Sunning Ho.

Wood Hall

Sunningdale Golf Course

B

CHOBHAM COMMON

B

B383

5

Windlesham Court

WINDLESHAM COURT DRIVE

Long Down

Nurseries

Nurseries

D E F

CARTOGRAPHY BY PHILIP'S. COPYRIGHT REED INTERNATIONAL BOOKS LTD

A   B   C

Berkshire Boundary
Surrey Boundary

1

Totem Pole

Wood Lee

The Dell

Valley Gardens

VIRGINIA   WATER

HILL CALLOW

HOLLOW   B   LANE

Virginia Beeches

Merlewood

Car Park

Frostfarm Plantation

Wheatsheaf Hotel

BLACKNEST   RD.
A329

Waterfall

B389
CHRISTCHURCH

WOODSIDE WAY

Christ Ch.+

WAVERLEY
WAVERLEY CL.
Sch.

SPRING WOODS

WOODLANDS ROW
WOODLANDS RD.

GORSE HILL RD.
PIPERS END

2

ROAD

WENTWORTH
ROAD

GLENDALE
CHESTNUT AV.

Wentworth Farm

PINEWOOD
STAYNE END

QUENTIN WAY

LAKE RD.
LAKE

WELLINGTON AV.

DRIVE
ABBOTTS DR.
ABBOTTS

BROCKWAY

VIRGINIA

OAKWOOD

MONKS   ROAD

HEATH RISE
HEATH CL.
MORELLA CL.
GORSE HILL RD.

STA. PARADE
WALK

ABBEY RD.

LONDON
A30

MEADOW RD.

DRIVE
PORTNALL
PORTNALL
RD.

Wentworth Club

WENTWORTH   DRIVE

Wellington Bridge

HARPESFORD AV.

BADGERS HILL
VIRGINIA
NUNS
KEEPERS WLK

THIS RD.

Virginia Water
+Bourne

SHERBOURNE DR.
Golf Course

FIRWOOD RD.
NORTH
NORTH DR.

(West)

WOODLEE
DRIVE
HEATHERSIDE DR.

WELLINGTON

HILLSIDE
SUNDON CR.

ROAD

CABRERA AV.
CAB. CL.
MERESIDE RD.
TRUMPSGREEN AV.
BOURNE RD.

29

3

Course

THE FAIRWAYS

CROWN

Knowlehill
Stag & Hounds (P.H.)

CROWN LA.
THE MEADOWS
RD.
THE MOUNT
OAK TREE CL.

RISE
DRIVE
BOURNESIDE

DRIVE   EAST

Wentworth Golf
Course (East)

AVENUE
KNOWLE GROVE CL.
KNOWLE GROVE

WEST
DRIVE

Wentworth

Three Gables

Great   Wood

MERESIDE PL.
BEECHWOOD RD.

TRUMPSGREEN
KNOWLE HILL

CORRIE GDNS.

4

SOUTH   LANE

PITSMEAD

Longcross Bridge

Little Arm

LONGCROSS STA.

RUNNYMEDE
SURREY HEATH

Barrowhills

Ship Hill

Long Arm

BURMA RD.

M3

LANE
P.O.

B386
ROAD

5

CHOBHAM
COMMON

CHOBHAM

ALBURY
TANGLEWOOD CL.
HILL

Old School Cafe

B386

LONGCROSS

Longcross House

Flutters Hill

A   B   C

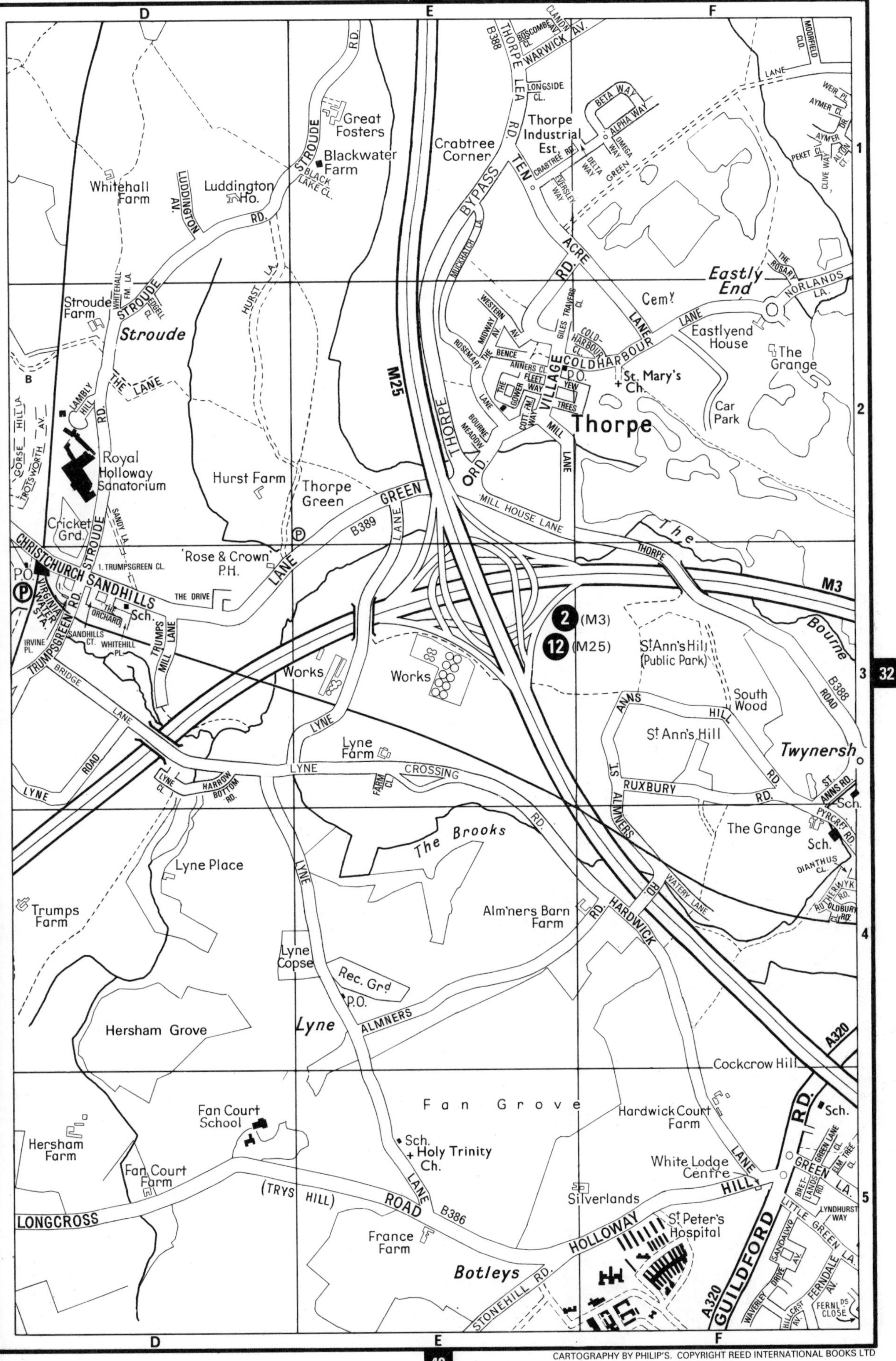

CARTOGRAPHY BY PHILIP'S. COPYRIGHT REED INTERNATIONAL BOOKS LTD

14

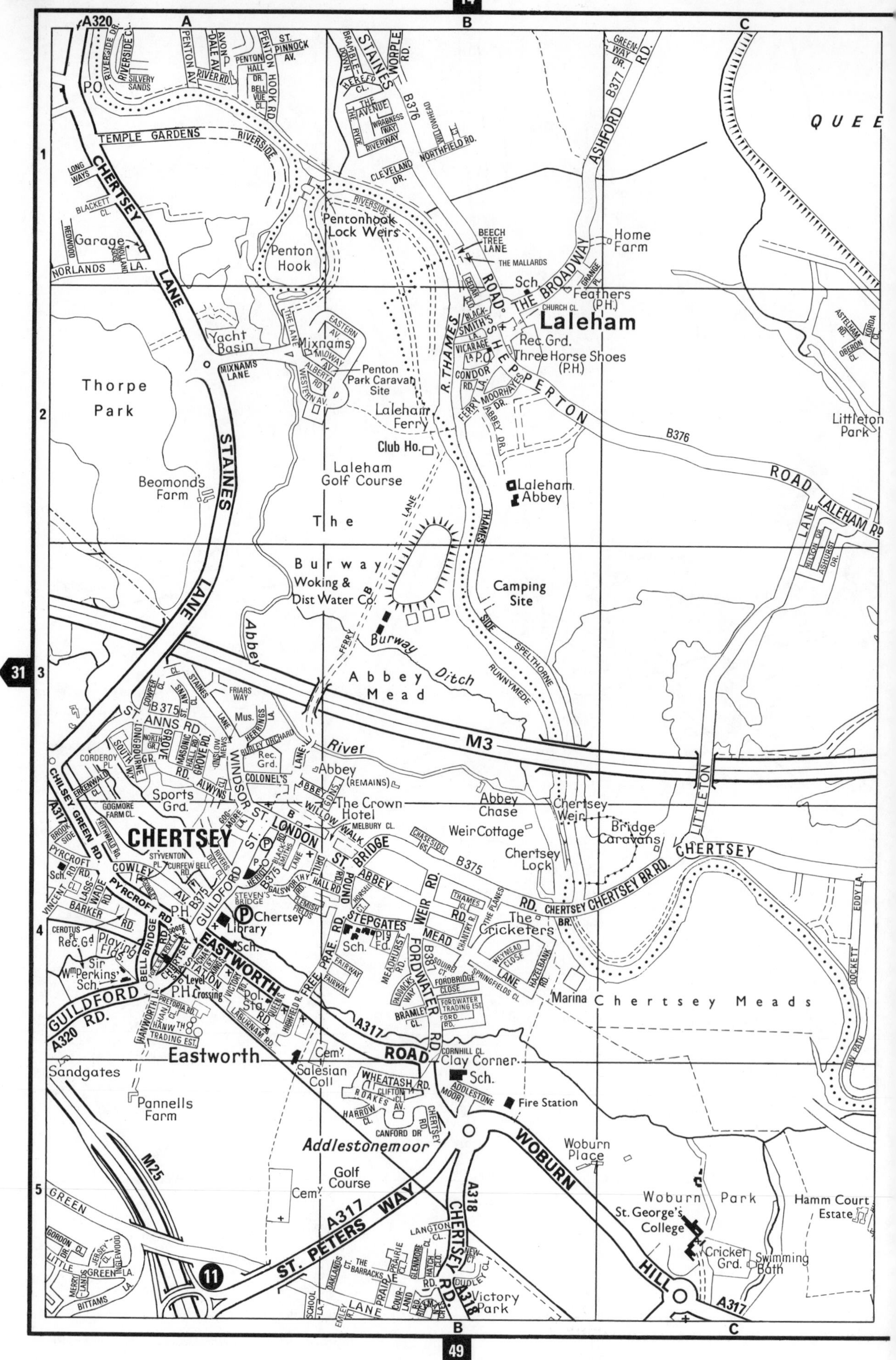

A
B
C
1
2
3
4
5
A320
RIVERSIDE DR.
RIVERSIDE CL.
SILVERY SANDS
PENTON AV.
DALE AV.
AVON CL.
RIVER RD.
PENTON HALL DR.
BELL VUE CL.
PENTON HOOK RD.
ST. PINNOCK AV.
P.O.
TEMPLE GARDENS
RIVERSIDE
LONG WAYS
CHERTSEY
BLACKETT CL.
REDWOOD
Garage
NORLANDS LA.
LANE
BRAMBLE DOWN
STAINES
WORPLE RD.
HEREFORD CL.
THE AVENUE
THE RYDE
WRABNESS WAY
RIVERWAY
B376
NORTHFIELD RD.
CLEVELAND DR.
GREEN WAY DR.
RD.
B377
ASHFORD
QUEE
Pentonhook Lock Weirs
Penton Hook
BEECH TREE LANE
THE MALLARDS
Home Farm
THE BROADWAY
Sch.
GRANGE PL.
Feathers (P.H.)
CHURCH CL.
Laleham
ROAD
SHEPPERTON
R. THAMES
CEDAR RD.
BLACKSMITH'S LA.
VICARAGE
P.O.
Rec. Grd.
Three Horse Shoes (P.H.)
CONDOR RD.
FERRY LA.
MOORHAYES DR.
ABBEY DR.
Yacht Basin
MIXNAMS LANE
THE LANE
EASTERN AV.
Mixnams
MIDWAY AV.
ALBERTA RD.
WESTERN AV.
Penton Park Caravan Site
Laleham Ferry
Thorpe Park
STAINES
Beomond's Farm
Club Ho.
Laleham Golf Course
The
Laleham Abbey
B376
ROAD
LALEHAM RD.
Littleton Park
ASTLEHAM RD.
KORDA CL.
OBERON CL.
MILTON DR.
ASHURST DR.
LANE
THAMES
Burway
Woking & Dist Water Co.
Camping Site
Abbey
FERRY LANE
Burway Ditch
Abbey Mead
SIDE
SPELTHORNE
RUNNYMEDE
M3
River
LITTLETON
COWPER CL.
STAINES LANE CL.
FRIARS WAY
ST. ANNS RD.
B 375
GROVE
MASONIC HALL RD.
GROVE RD.
Mus.
HERRINGS LA.
NORTH GR.
LONGBOURNE GR.
SOUTH WAY
CORDEROY PL.
WINDSOR
BURLEY ORCHARD
Rec. Grd.
COLONEL'S LANE
ALWYNS LA.
Abbey (REMAINS)
ABBEY GDNS.
WILLOW WALK
The Crown Hotel
MELBURY CL.
Abbey Chase
Chertsey Weir
Bridge Caravans
Weir Cottage
Chertsey Lock
CHERTSEY
CHERTSEY BR. RD.
CHILSEY GREEN RD.
A317
BROOK SIDE
Sports Grd.
GOGMORE FARM CL.
GOGMORE LA.
CHERTSEY
ST.
LONDON
ST.
BRIDGE
CHASESIDE GDNS.
B375
PYRCROFT
Sch.
COWLEY
STYVENTON PL.
CURFEW BELL RD.
GUILDFORD
HERIOT RD.
BLACKSMITHS
LANE
DRILL HALL RD.
POUND RD.
ABBEY
WEIR RD.
THAMES CL.
RD.
THE PLANES
CHERTSEY
BR.
The Cricketers
EDDY LA.
AV.
B375
P.H.
STEVEN'S BRIDGE
Chertsey
Library
Sch.
STEPGATES
Sch.
Plg. Fd.
MEAD
CHANTRY RD.
WEYMEAD CLOSE
HAZELBANK RD.
PYRCROFT RD.
VINCENT
BARKER
RD.
CEROTUS PL.
Rec. Gd.
Playing Flds.
Sir Wm. Perkins' Sch.
BELL BRIDGE RD.
EASTWORTH
STATION RD.
P.H.
Level Crossing
Pol. Sta.
FREE PRAE. RD.
FAIRWAY
MEADHURST RD.
FORDWATER
B388
SQUIRE CT.
FORDBRIDGE CLOSE
FORDWATER TRADING EST.
FORD RD.
SPRINGFIELDS CL.
LANE
Marina
Chertsey Meads
DOCKETT
GUILDFORD
A320 RD.
HANWORTH LA.
PRETORIA RD.
HANWORTH TRADING EST.
LABURNAM RD.
HIGHFIELD RD.
A317
ROAD
BRAMLEY CL.
RD.
CORNHILL CL.
Clay Corner
Sch.
Eastworth
Cemy.
Salesian Coll
WHEATASH RD.
CLIFTON CL.
ROAKES AV.
HARROW CL.
CANFORD DR.
CHERTSEY RD.
MOOR
ADDLESTONE
Fire Station
TOW PATH
Sandgates
Pannells Farm
Addlestonemoor
WOBURN
Woburn Place
M25
Golf Course
Cemy.
A318
GREEN
A317
ST. PETERS WAY
CHERTSEY
Woburn Park
St. George's College
Hamm Court Estate
GORDON CL.
JERSEY CL.
INGLEWOOD
LITTLE GREEN LA.
MERRYLANDS
BITTAMS LA.
11
LANGTON CL.
PRAIRIE CL.
GLENMORE CL.
HATCH CL.
NEW CT.
DUDLEY CL.
THE BARRACKS
OAKLANDS CT.
COURLAND RD.
PRAIRIE RD.
RD.
A318
Victory Park
HILL
Cricket Grd.
Swimming Bath
A317
SCHOOL LA.
EMLEY
LANE

31

49

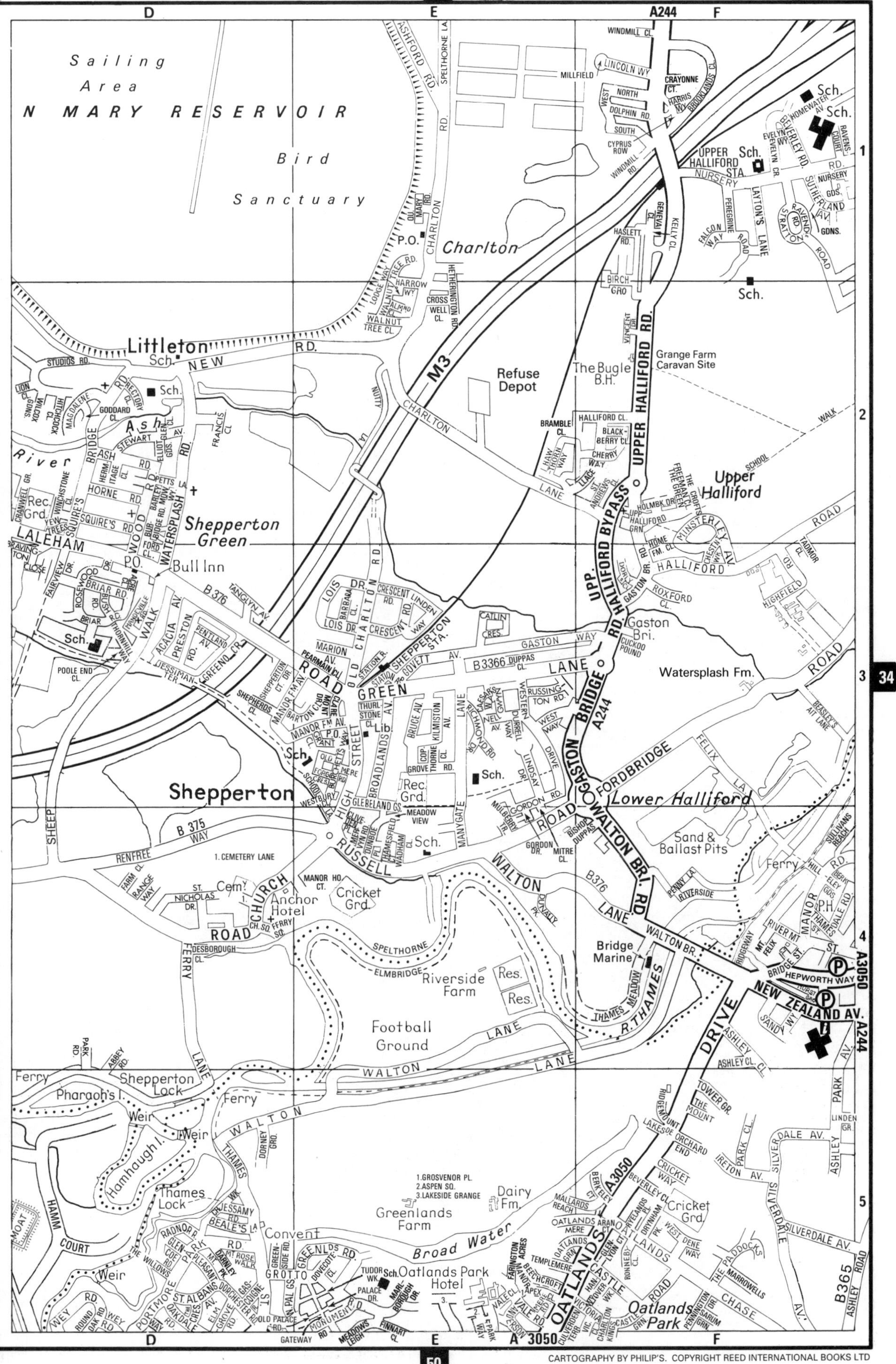

CARTOGRAPHY BY PHILIP'S. COPYRIGHT REED INTERNATIONAL BOOKS LTD

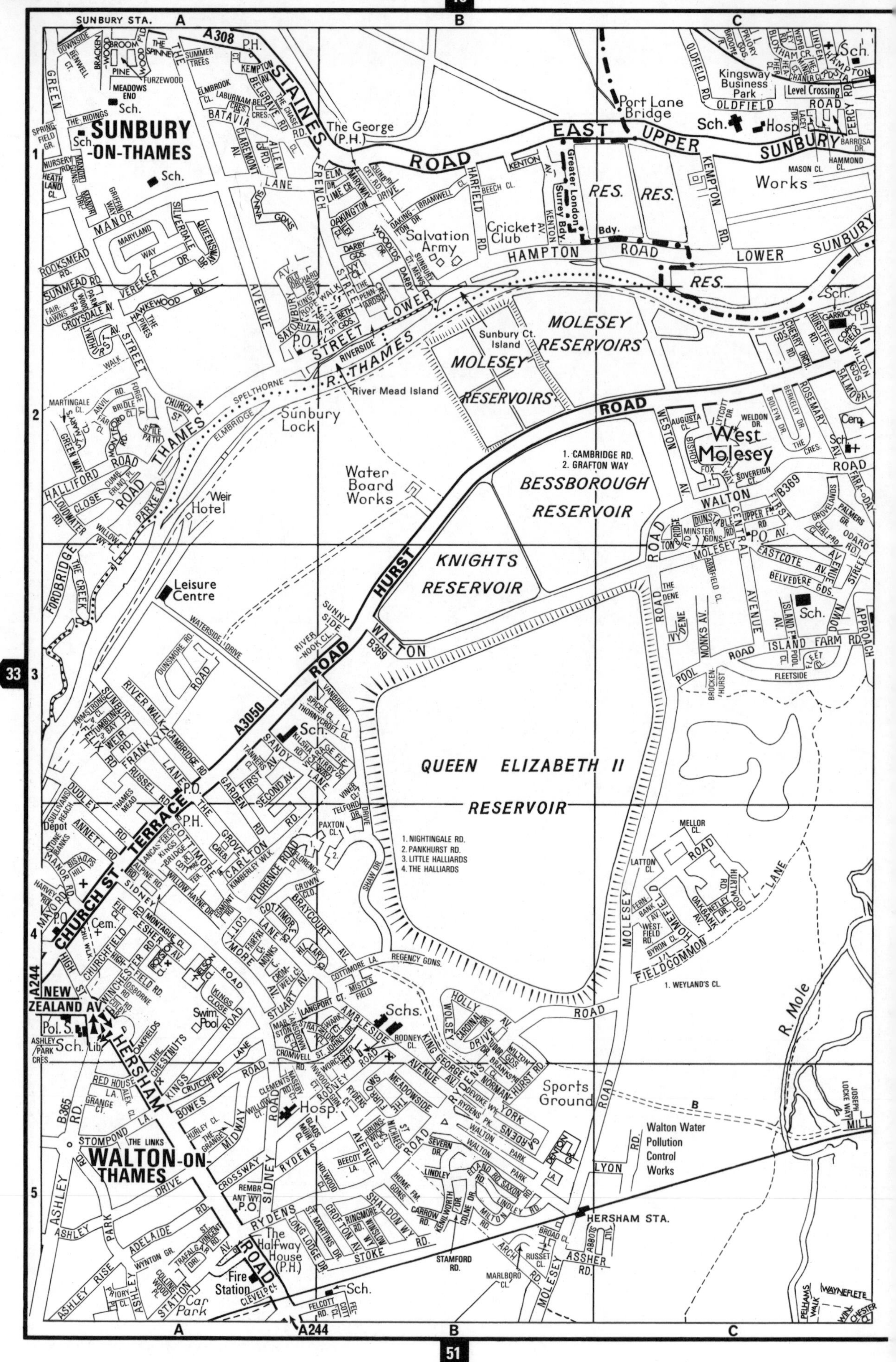
16
33
51
A
B
C
1
2
3
4
5
SUNBURY STA.
SUNBURY
-ON-THAMES
Sch.
MEADOWS END
A308
P.H.
STAINES
ROAD
The George
(P.H.)
EAST
UPPER
SUNBURY
Port Lane Bridge
Kingsway Business Park
Level Crossing
OLDFIELD
ROAD
Hosp.
Works
RES.
Greater London Surrey Bdy.
Bdy.
Cricket Club
Salvation Army
HAMPTON
ROAD
LOWER
SUNBURY
KEMPTON
FRENCH
MANOR
MARYLAND WAY
SILVERDALE DR.
ROOKSMEAD RD.
SUNMEAD RD.
VEREKER DR.
HAWKEWOOD RD.
CROYSDALE AV.
AVENUE
P.O.
STREET
LOWER
THAMES
R. THAMES
RIVERSIDE
Sunbury Ct. Island
MOLESEY RESERVOIRS
River Mead Island
Sunbury Lock
SPELTHORNE
ELMBRIDGE
CHURCH ST.
THAMES
ROAD
HALLIFORD
CLOSE
PARKE RD.
Weir Hotel
Water Board Works
1. CAMBRIDGE RD.
2. GRAFTON WAY
BESSBOROUGH RESERVOIR
West Molesey
WALTON
ROAD
B369
MOLESEY
KNIGHTS RESERVOIR
HURST
ROAD
A3050
Leisure Centre
WATERSIDE DRIVE
SUNNY SIDE
RIVER-NOOK CL.
WALTON
B369
Sch.
ISLAND FARM RD.
POOL
ROAD
FLEETSIDE
QUEEN ELIZABETH II
RESERVOIR
1. NIGHTINGALE RD.
2. PANKHURST RD.
3. LITTLE HALLIARDS
4. THE HALLIARDS
FIELDCOMMON
1. WEYLAND'S CL.
R. Mole
CHURCH ST.
TERRACE
P.H.
P.O.
Depot
Cem.
HIGH ST.
NEW ZEALAND AV.
A244
Pol. S.
Sch.
Lib.
HERSHAM
ROAD
Swim. Pool
Schs.
Hosp.
Sports Ground
Walton Water Pollution Control Works
HERSHAM STA.
WALTON-ON-THAMES
B365
ASHLEY
DRIVE
ASHLEY PARK
The Halfway House (P.H.)
Fire Station
Car Park
STATION
LYON
MOLESEY
ROAD

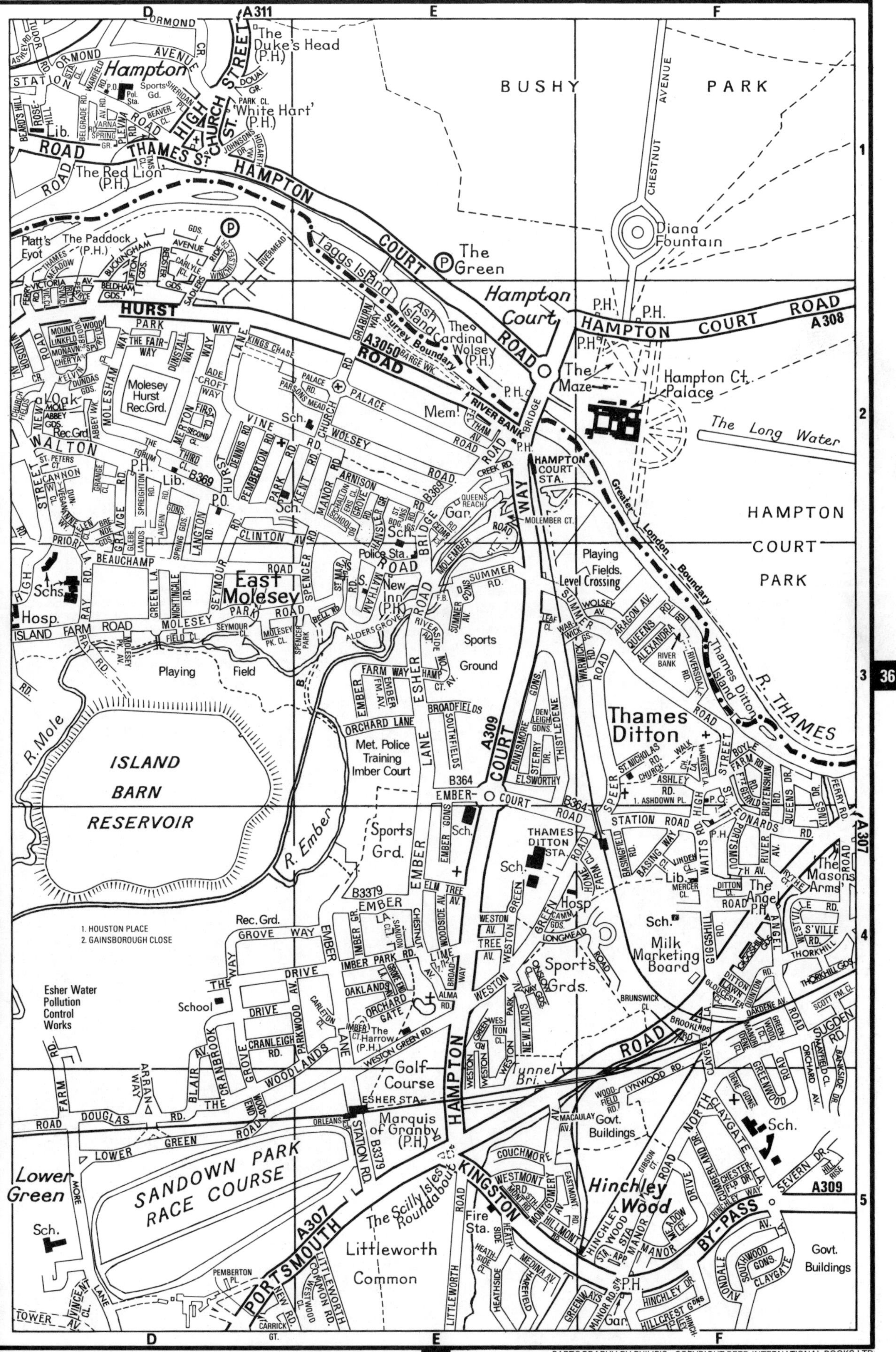

CARTOGRAPHY BY PHILIP'S. COPYRIGHT REED INTERNATIONAL BOOKS LTD

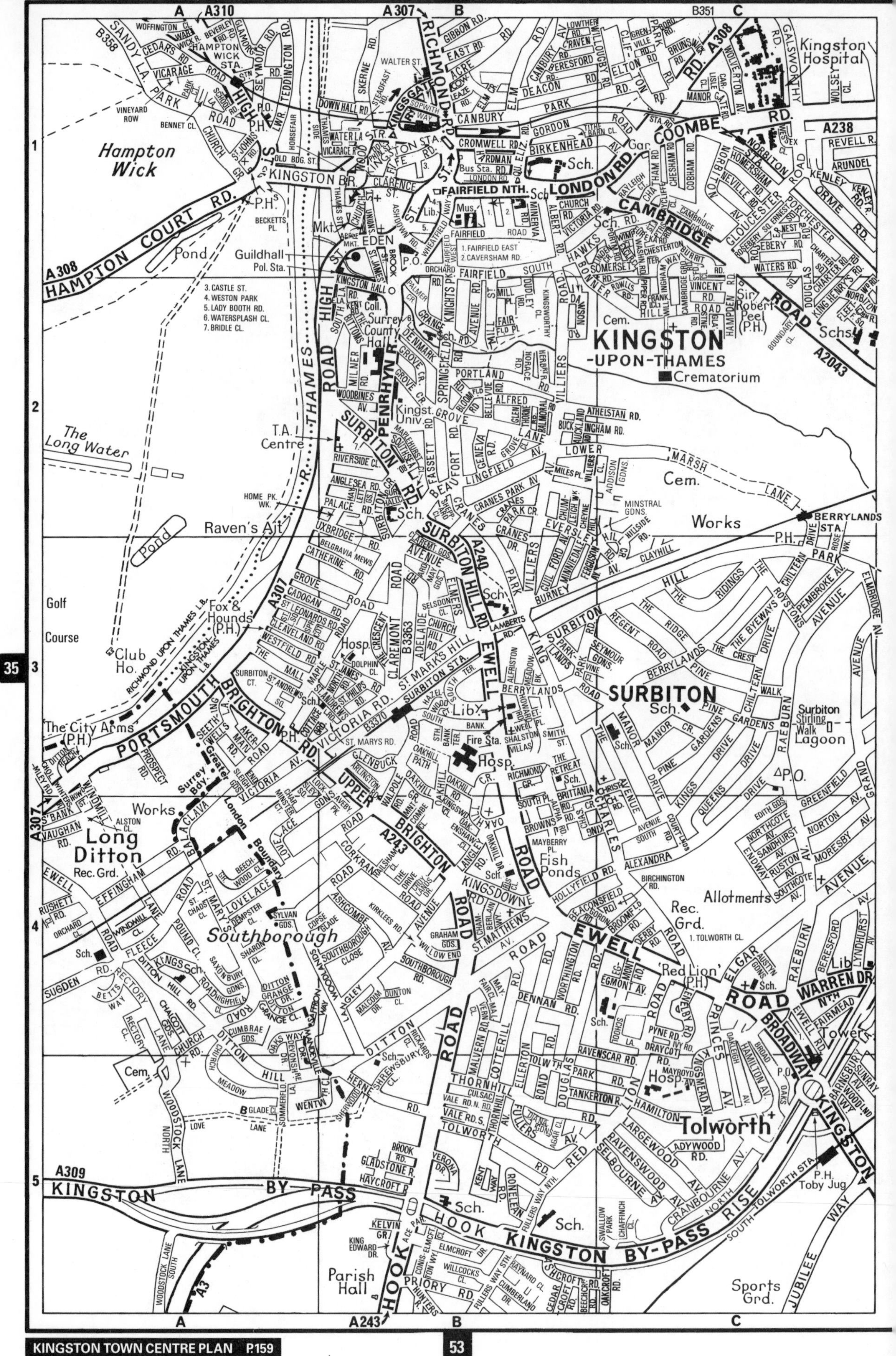

KINGSTON TOWN CENTRE PLAN   P.159

18
B
2
3
4
A310
A307
B351
A308
A238
A2043
A240
A243
B3363
B3370
A309
A3
B358
Hampton Wick
Kingston Hospital
KINGSTON -UPON-THAMES
Crematorium
SURBITON
Long Ditton
Southborough
Tolworth
The Long Water
Raven's Ait
Golf Course
Club Ho.
Pond
Guildhall
Pol. Sta.
Mkt.
Surrey County Hall
Kingst. Univ.
T.A. Centre
Cem.
Works
BERRYLANDS STA.
Surbiton Stirling Walk Lagoon
The City Arms (P.H.)
Fox & Hounds (P.H.)
Fire Sta.
Hosp.
Fish Ponds
Allotments
Rec. Grd.
'Red Lion' (P.H.)
Sir Robert Peel (P.H.)
Parish Hall
Sports Grd.
P.H. Toby Jug
HAMPTON COURT RD.
PORTSMOUTH RD.
BRIGHTON RD.
HIGH ST.
RICHMOND RD.
LONDON RD.
CAMBRIDGE RD.
COOMBE RD.
KINGSTON BR.
KINGSTON BY-PASS
HOOK RD.
EWELL RD.
SURBITON HILL RD.
PENRHYN RD.
UPPER BRIGHTON RD.
KING CHARLES RD.
VICTORIA RD.
ALEXANDRA DRIVE
ELGAR AV.
WARREN DR. NTH
BROADWAY
1. FAIRFIELD EAST
2. CAVERSHAM RD.
3. CASTLE ST.
4. WESTON PARK
5. LADY BOOTH RD.
6. WATERSPLASH CL.
7. BRIDLE CL.
1. TOLWORTH CL.
RICHMOND UPON THAMES L.B.
KINGSTON UPON THAMES L.B.
Surrey Bdy.
Greater London Boundary
35
53

19

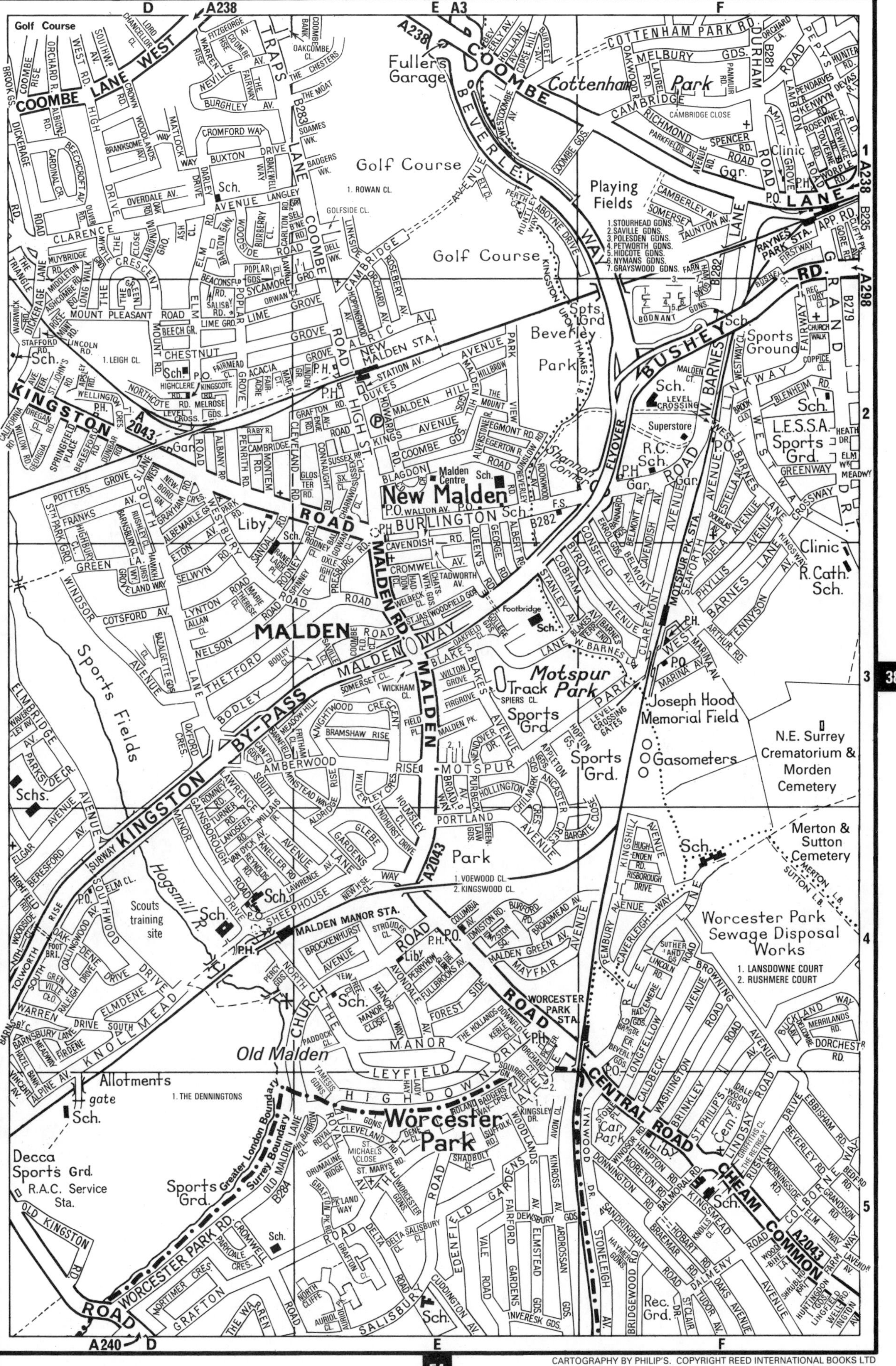
Golf Course
COOMBE LANE WEST
Fuller's Garage
COOMBE
Cottenham Park
Playing Fields
Golf Course
Golf Course
BEVERLEY WAY
KINGSTON UPON THAMES L.B.
Spts. Grd
Beverley Park
New Malden
NEW MALDEN STA.
KINGSTON ROAD
Shannon Corner
BUSHEY RD.
Sports Ground
L.E.S.S.A. Sports Grd.
Superstore
R.C. Sch.
MALDEN
MALDEN RD.
MALDEN WAY
Motspur Park
Track
Sports Grd.
MOTSPUR PK. STA.
Joseph Hood Memorial Field
Gasometers
N.E. Surrey Crematorium & Morden Cemetery
Clinic
R. Cath. Sch.
Sports Fields
KINGSTON BY-PASS
Hogsmill R.
Scouts training site
MALDEN MANOR STA.
Park
Merton & Sutton Cemetery
MERTON L.B.
SUTTON L.B.
Worcester Park Sewage Disposal Works
1. LANSDOWNE COURT
2. RUSHMERE COURT
WORCESTER PARK STA.
Old Malden
Allotments
gate
Worcester Park
CENTRAL ROAD
CHEAM COMMON
Greater London Boundary
Surrey Boundary
Decca Sports Grd.
R.A.C. Service Sta.
Sports Grd.
WORCESTER PARK RD.
Rec. Grd.
Car Park
A238
A3
A298
A2043
A240
B235
B279
B281
B282
B283
B284

38

54

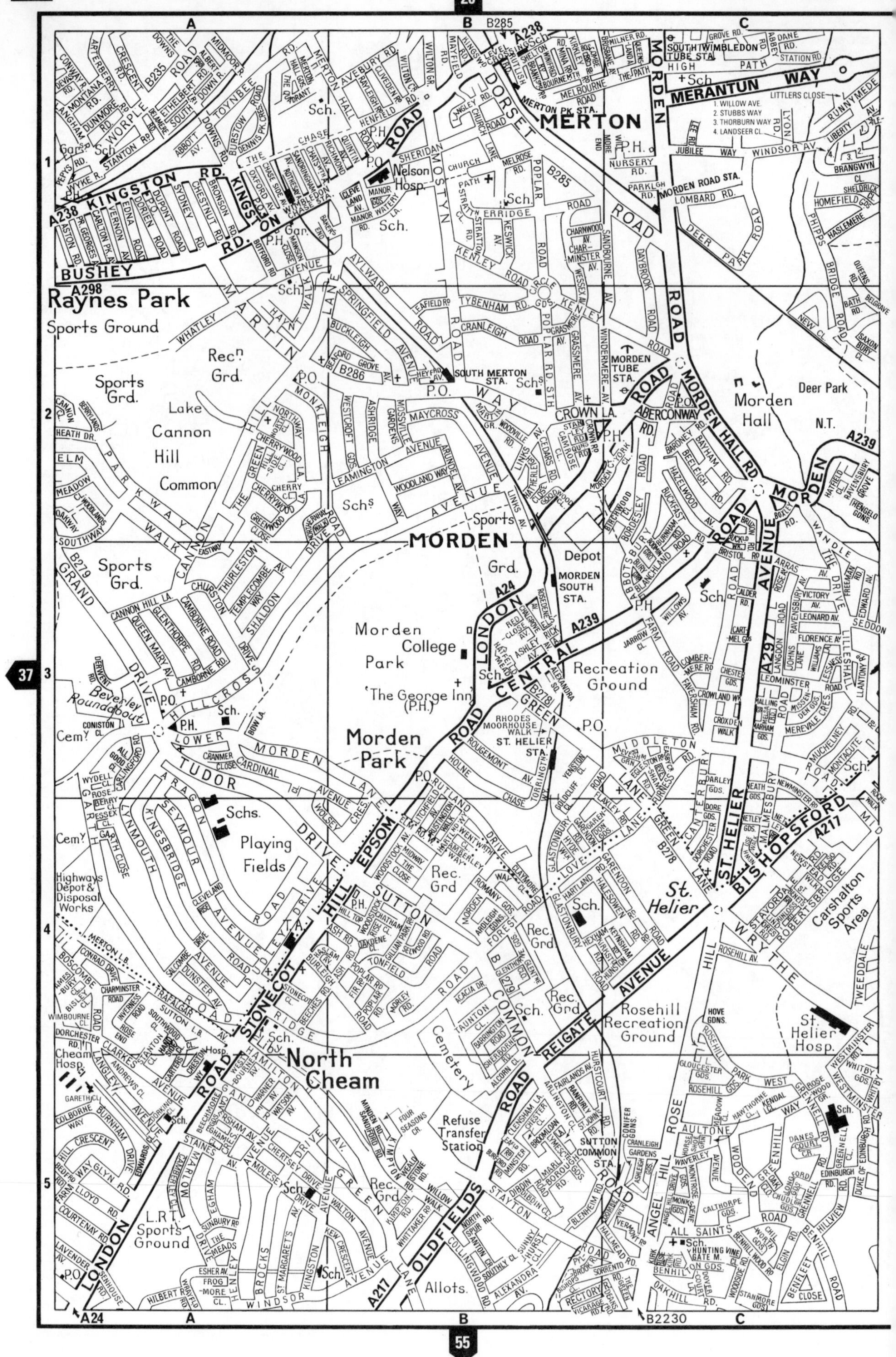
20
37
55
A
B
C
1
2
3
4
5
B285
A238
MERTON
Raynes Park
Sports Ground
A298
BUSHEY
KINGSTON RD.
MORDEN
North Cheam
St. Helier
Morden Park
Morden Hall
Deer Park
N.T.
Lake
Cannon Hill Common
Sports Grd.
Recn Grd.
Morden College Park
'The George Inn' (P.H.)
Recreation Ground
Rosehill Recreation Ground
Carshalton Sports Area
St. Helier Hosp.
Nelson Hosp.
Cheam Hosp.
Beverley Roundabout
Playing Fields
Cemetery
Refuse Transfer Station
Allots.
L.R.T. Sports Ground
Highways Depot & Disposal Works
SOUTH WIMBLEDON TUBE STA.
MERTON PK. STA.
MORDEN ROAD STA.
SOUTH MERTON STA.
MORDEN TUBE STA.
MORDEN SOUTH STA.
ST. HELIER STA.
SUTTON COMMON STA.
MERANTUN WAY
1. WILLOW AVE.
2. STUBBS WAY
3. THORBURN WAY
4. LANDSEER CL.
LITTLERS CLOSE
MORDEN HALL RD.
LONDON ROAD
CENTRAL ROAD
EPSOM ROAD
STONECOT HILL
SUTTON COMMON ROAD
REIGATE AVENUE
BISHOPSFORD ROAD
ST. HELIER AVENUE
OLDFIELDS ROAD
A24
A239
A217
A297
B278
B279
B286
B2230

MITCHAM

WESTERN ROAD

Schools

Cemetery

1. MOORE CL.
2. POTTER CL.
3. PAINS CL.
4. THRUPP CL.

1. JUNIPER GDNS. CL.
2. EBENEZER WK.

Sports Grd

Sch.

Level Crossing

Town Hall

Hosp.

1. KINGSLEIGH PL.
2. CHATSWORTH PL.

CRICKET GRN

MADEIRA RD

CRANMER RD

Mitcham Pond

Mitcham Golf Course (Public)

Mitcham GDN. VILL.

MITCHAM JUNC STA.

Club House

Common

The Watermeads

Sports Grd.

Park

Rec. Grd.

R. Wandle

Industrial Estate

Schools

Peterborough

Level Crossing
BEDDINGTON LANE STA.

Beddington Corner

MERTON L.B.
SUTTON L.B.

1. POPPY CL.
2. VIOLET CL.
3. FOXGLOVE WAY
4. PRIMROSE CL.
5. BLUEBELL CL.

Beddington Farm

Beddington Sewage Farm

Sports Grd.

Schools

1. SEVERN ACRES
2. MARFLEET CL.

Hackbridge STA.

Hackbridge

1. ENDALE CL.
2. ROSSIGNOL GDNS.

Sports Field

Beddington Park

PR. CHARLES WAY

Beddington Corner

The Grange

Carew Manor Sch.

PRINCE OF WALES RD.

The Wrythe

A 232 CROYDON RD. A 232

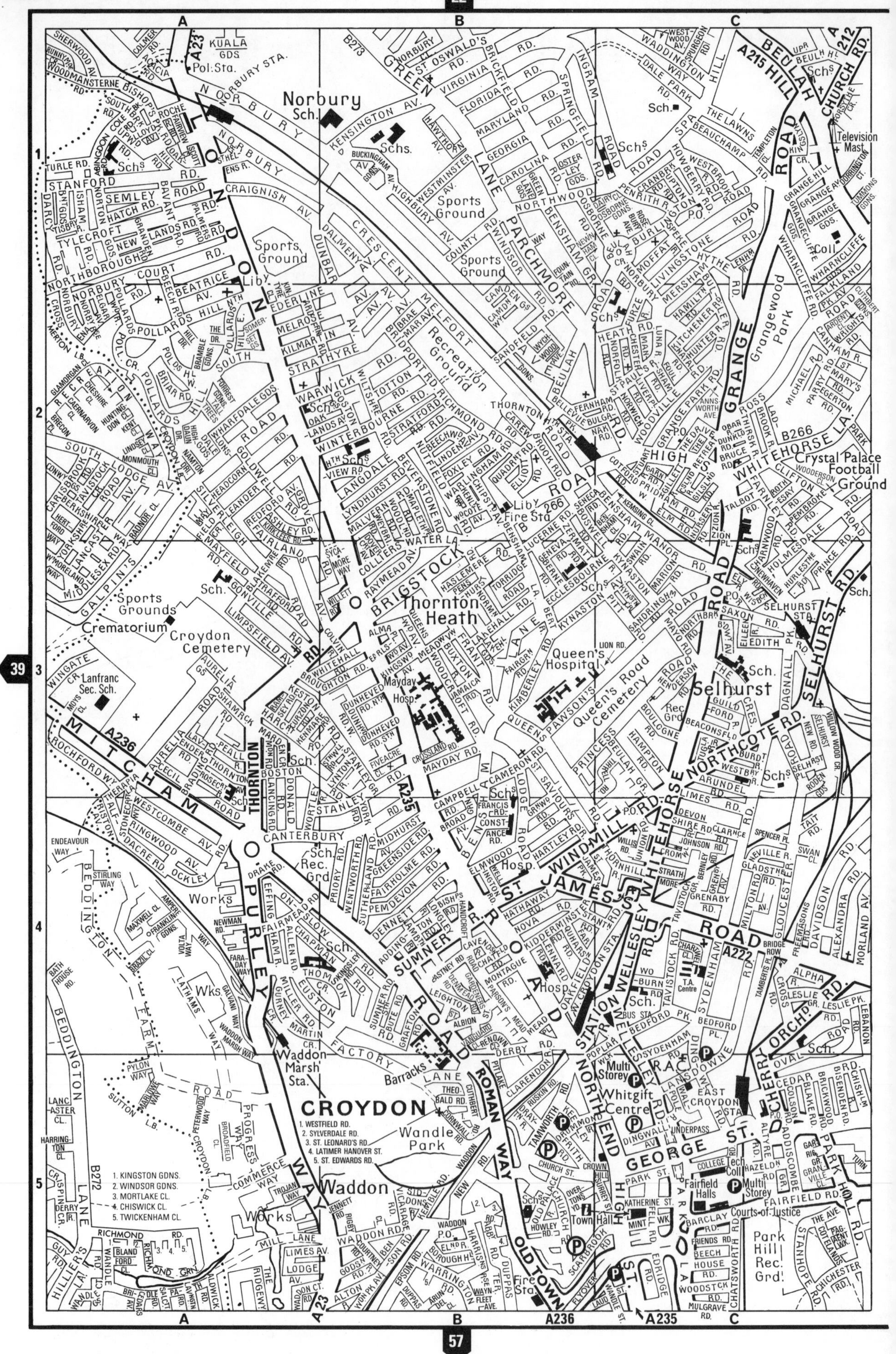
22
A
B
C
1
2
3
4
5
39
57
A236
A235
Norbury Sch.
NORBURY STA.
Pol. Sta.
KUALA GDS.
SHERWOOD AV.
WOODMANSTERNE RD.
BISHOP'S PK. RD.
NORBURY
LONDON ROAD
CRAIGNISH AV.
STANFORD
SEMLEY
HATCH RD.
TYLECROFT
NEW LANDS RD.
NORTHBOROUGH RD.
NORBURY COURT RD.
BEATRICE AV.
Liby.
POLLARDS HILL
Sports Ground
DUNBAR AV.
DALMENY AV.
CRESCENT
MELFORT
KENSINGTON AV.
Schs.
BUCKINGHAM AV.
HIGHBURY AV.
WESTMINSTER AV.
Sports Ground
ST. OSWALD'S RD.
VIRGINIA RD.
FLORIDA RD.
MARYLAND RD.
GEORGIA RD.
CAROLINA RD.
GREEN LANE
PARCHMORE
NORTHWOOD RD.
COUNTY RD.
WINDSOR RD.
BENSHAM GR.
INGRAM RD.
SPRINGFIELD RD.
WADDINGTON WAY
DALE PARK
SPA HILL
BEAUCHAMP
THE LAWNS
BEULAH HILL
A215
CHURCH RD.
A212
Television Mast
GRANGE HILL
Coll.
WHARNCLIFFE
Grangewood Park
GRANGE ROAD
LIVINGSTONE ROAD
MERSHAM
HYTHE RD.
MOFFAT
BURLINGTON
BEULAH CR.
Recreation Ground
SANDFIELD
BEULAH RD.
THORNTON HEATH STA.
ROAD
HIGH ST.
WHITEHORSE LA.
B266
Crystal Palace Football Ground
CLIFTON
Sch.
SELHURST RD.
SELHURST STA.
Selhurst
BRIGSTOCK RD.
Thornton Heath
WARWICK RD.
WINTERBOURNE RD.
LANGDALE
Liby.
Fire Sta.
266
BENSHAM MANOR
ECCLESBOURNE
KYNASTON AV.
Queen's Hospital
Queen's Road Cemetery
LION RD.
Mayday Hosp.
MAYDAY RD.
QUEENS
PRINCESS
HAMPTON
NORTHCOTE RD.
WHITEHORSE
GALPIN'S
MAYFIELD
Sports Grounds
Crematorium
Croydon Cemetery
Lanfranc Sec. Sch.
WINGATE
MITCHAM
A236
ROCHFORD WY.
AURELIA RD.
THORNTON
BOSTON
CANTERBURY
WESTCOMBE AV.
RINGWOOD AV.
DACRE RD.
OCKLEY
PURLEY
Works
Wks.
BEDDINGTON
FARM ROAD
WINDMILL RD.
ST. JAMES'S
WELLESLEY RD.
ROAD
A222
T.A. Centre
SYDENHAM
CHERRY ORCHD. RD.
OVAL ROAD
Sch.
Hosp.
STATION RD.
W. CROYDON STA.
NORTHEND
Multi Storey
Whitgift Centre
EAST CROYDON STA.
GEORGE ST.
Tech. Coll.
Fairfield Halls
Multi Storey
Courts of Justice
Park Hill Rec. Grd.
Waddon Marsh Sta.
Barracks
CROYDON
1. WESTFIELD RD.
2. SYLVERDALE RD.
3. ST. LEONARD'S RD.
4. LATIMER HANOVER ST.
5. ST. EDWARDS RD.
Wandle Park
ROMAN WAY
Waddon
Works
PURLEY WAY
FACTORY LANE
SUMNER RD.
OLD TOWN
Town Hall
KATHERINE ST.
Fire Sta.
FLYOVER
CHURCH ST.
CROWN HILL
HIGH ST.
DINGWALL AV.
LANSDOWNE
PARK LANE
FAIRFIELD RD.
BARCLAY
PARK HILL RD.
CHICHESTER RD.
CHATSWORTH RD.
MULGRAVE RD.
1. KINGSTON GDNS.
2. WINDSOR GDNS.
3. MORTLAKE CL.
4. CHISWICK CL.
5. TWICKENHAM CL.
B272
BEDDINGTON LANE
RICHMOND RD.
MILL LANE
WADDON RD.
SUTTON
PROGRESS WAY
COMMERCE WAY
DUPPAS
WARRINGTON RD.

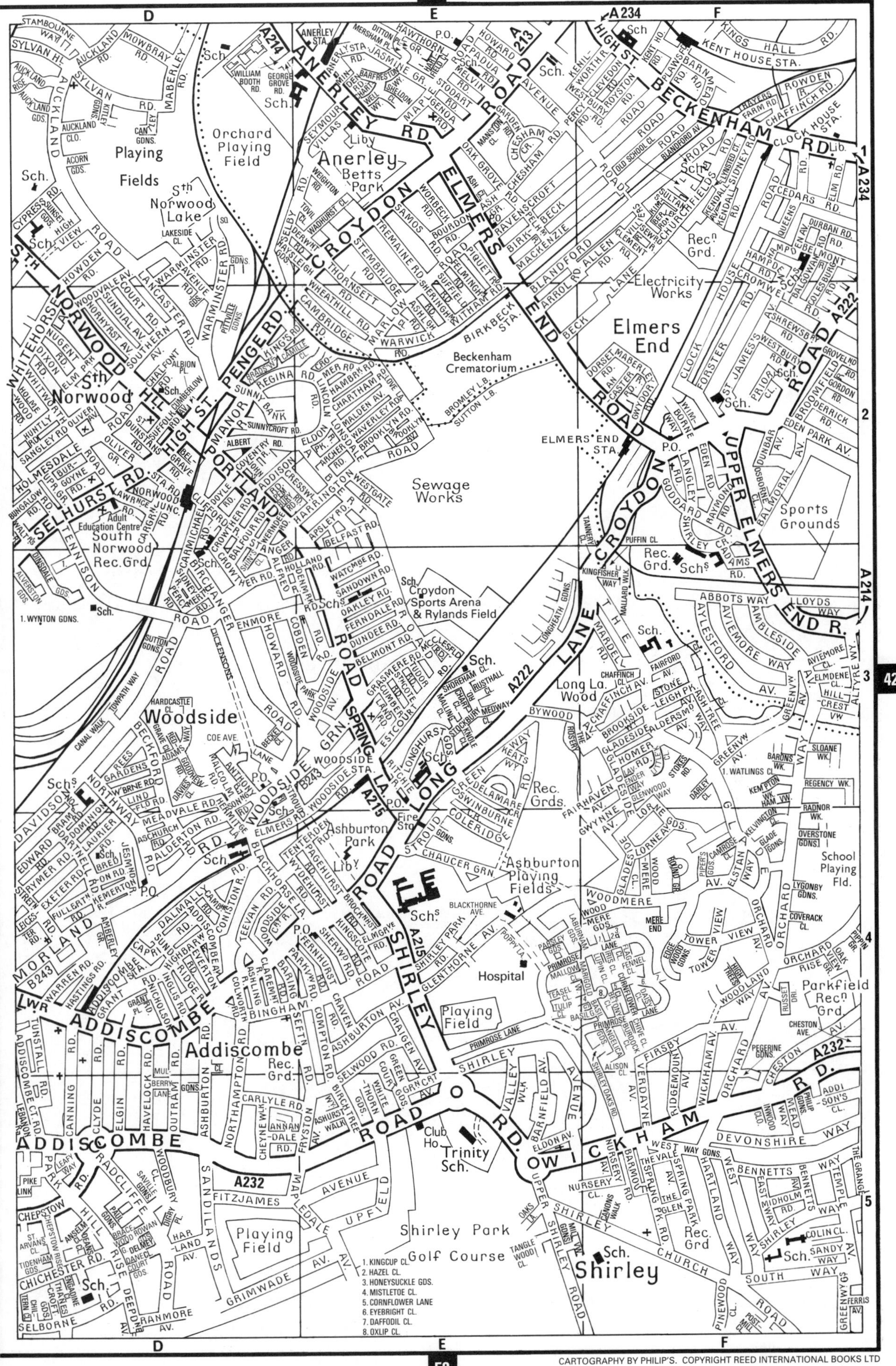

CARTOGRAPHY BY PHILIP'S. COPYRIGHT REED INTERNATIONAL BOOKS LTD

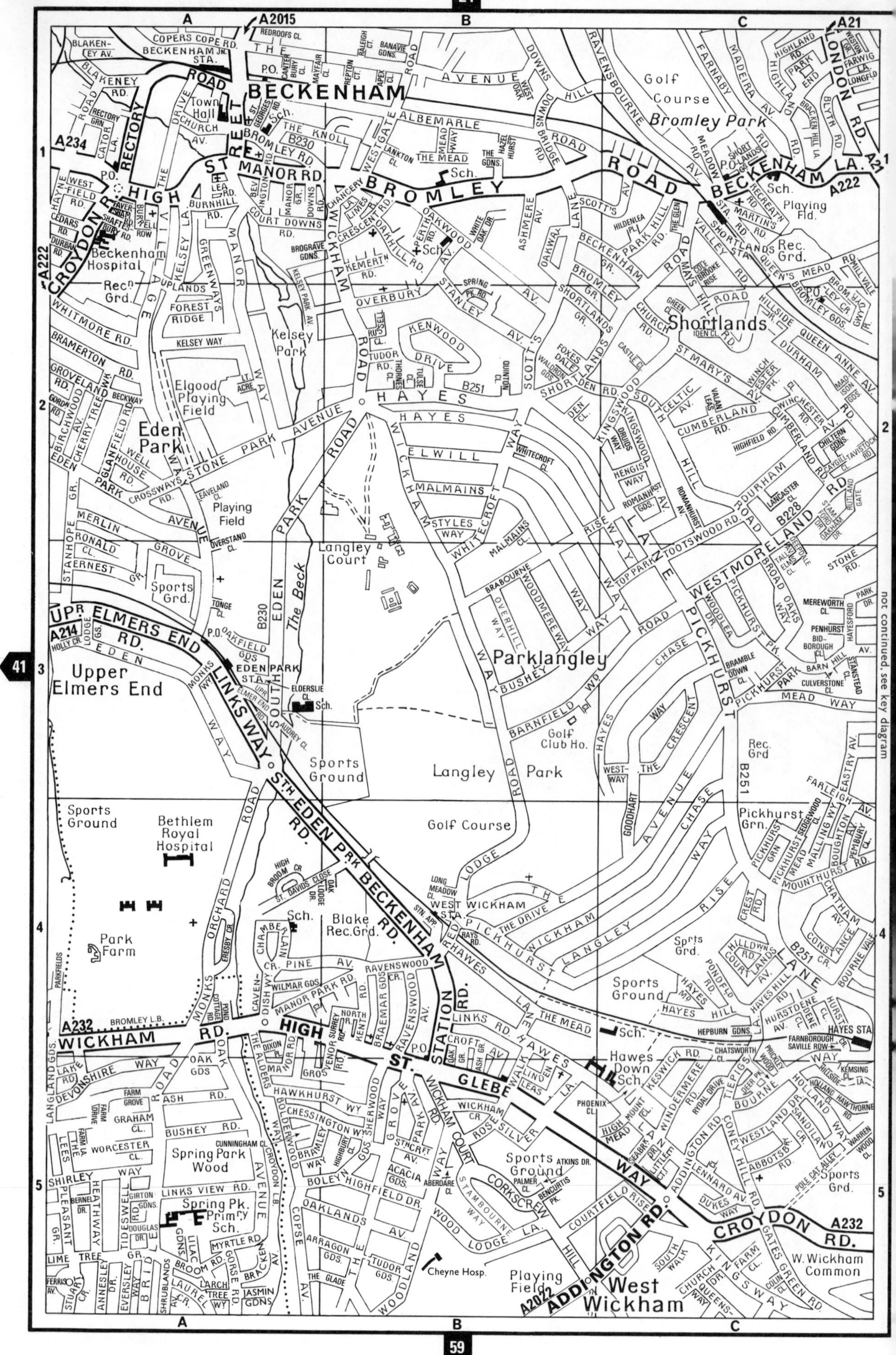
24
41
59
A
B
C
1
2
3
4
5
A2015
A21
A234
A222
A214
A232
A2022
B230
B251
B228
BECKENHAM
Beckenham Jn. Sta.
Town Hall
Beckenham Hospital
Recn Grd.
Bromley Park
Golf Course
Shortlands
Playing Fld.
Rec. Grd.
Kelsey Park
Elgood Playing Field
Eden Park
Playing Field
Sports Grd.
Langley Court
Parklangley
Upper Elmers End
Eden Park Sta.
Golf Club Ho.
Langley Park
Sports Ground
Golf Course
Bethlem Royal Hospital
Park Farm
Blake Rec.Grd.
West Wickham Sta.
Pickhurst Grn.
Rec. Grd
Hayes Sta
Hawes Down Sch.
Sports Grd.
Sports Ground
Spring Park Wood
Spring Pk. Primry Sch.
Cheyne Hosp.
Playing Field
West Wickham
W. Wickham Common
CROYDON RD.
HIGH STREET
BROMLEY ROAD
BECKENHAM LA.
HAYES
WICKHAM RD.
HIGH ST.
ADDINGTON RD.
LINKS WAY
UPR. ELMERS END RD.
STH. EDEN PRK. RD.
BECKENHAM RD.
WESTMORELAND RD.
PICKHURST LANE
HAYES LANE
WEST WICKHAM
LONDON RD.
not continued, see key diagram

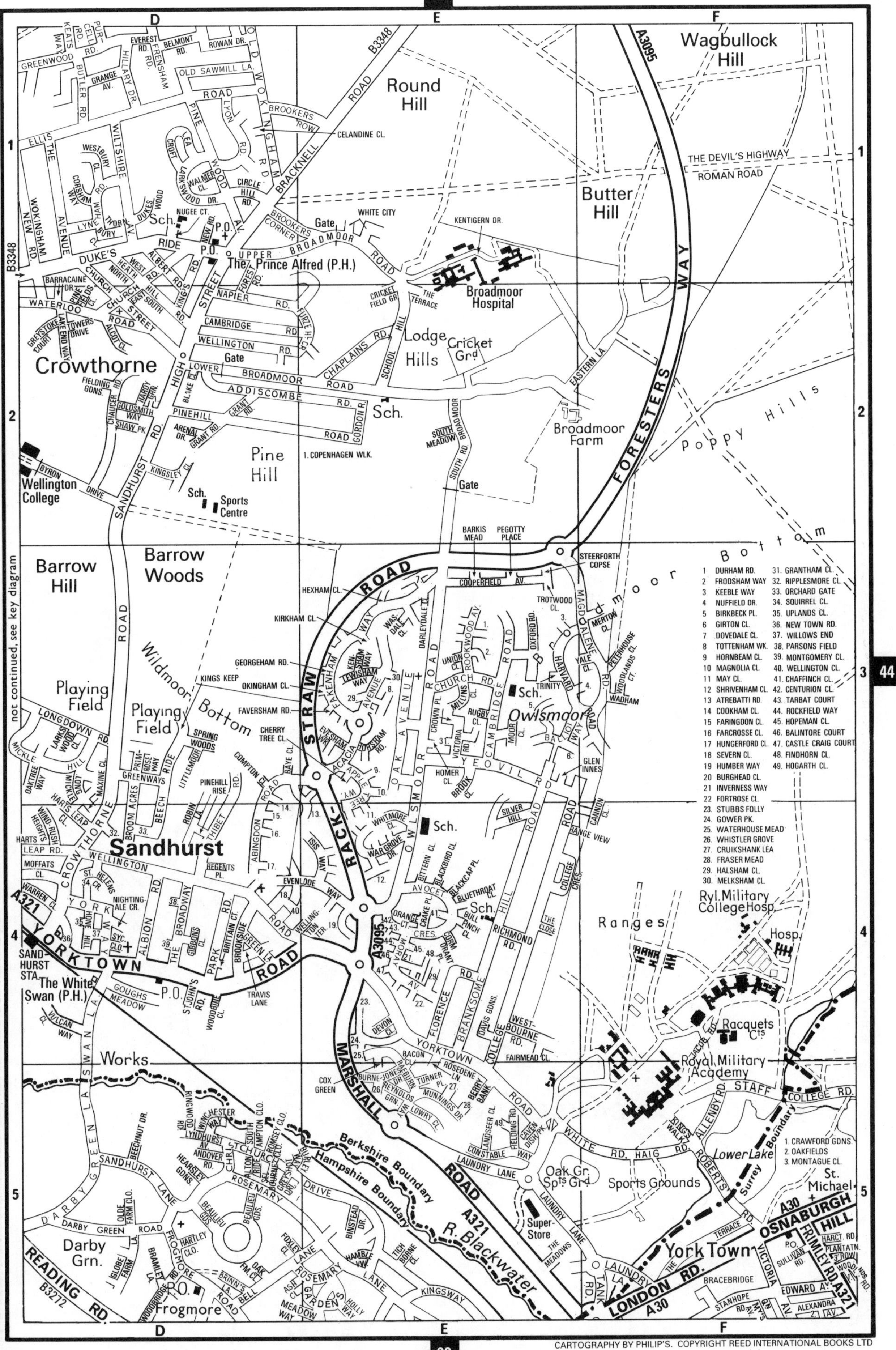

1 DURHAM RD.
2 FRODSHAM WAY
3 KEEBLE WAY
4 NUFFIELD DR.
5 BIRKBECK PL.
6 GIRTON CL.
7 DOVEDALE CL.
8 TOTTENHAM WK.
9 HORNBEAM CL.
10 MAGNOLIA CL.
11 MAY CL.
12 SHRIVENHAM CL.
13 ATREBATTI RD.
14 COOKHAM CL.
15 FARINGDON CL.
16 FARCROSSE CL.
17 HUNGERFORD CL.
18 SEVERN CL.
19 HUMBER WAY
20 BURGHEAD CL.
21 INVERNESS WAY
22 FORTROSE CL.
23 STUBBS FOLLY
24 GOWER PK.
25 WATERHOUSE MEAD
26 WHISTLER GROVE
27 CRUIKSHANK LEA
28 FRASER MEAD
29 HALSHAM CL.
30 MELKSHAM CL.
31 GRANTHAM CL.
32 RIPPLESMORE CL.
33 ORCHARD GATE
34 SQUIRREL CL.
35 UPLANDS CL.
36 NEW TOWN RD.
37 WILLOWS END
38 PARSONS FIELD
39 MONTGOMERY CL.
40 WELLINGTON CL.
41 CHAFFINCH CL.
42 CENTURION CL.
43 TARBAT COURT
44 ROCKFIELD WAY
45 HOPEMAN CL.
46 BALINTORE COURT
47 CASTLE CRAIG COURT
48 FINDHORN CL.
49 HOGARTH CL.

1. CRAWFORD GDNS.
2. OAKFIELDS
3. MONTAGUE CL.

A B C

1

Roman Stud or
Upper Star Post

THE DEVIL'S HIGHWAY
ROMAN ROAD
Rapley Lake

Surrey
Hill
427 ft.

Lower Star
Post

VICARAGE LANE

BRACKNELL ROAD

2

Deer Rock
Hill

Pascha Wood

COLLEGE RIDE

43 3

Saddleback
Hill

Olddean Common

Pennyhill
Park
Hotel

Sch.

Wish Stream
Wishmoor Bottom

Berkshire Boundary
Surrey Boundary

Barossa
Common

1. DORSET CT.

HIGHVIEW CR.
WIMBLEDON
CL.
WIMBLEDON RD.
BRACKNELL CL.
MITCHAM
WALLINGTON RD.
CASHALTON RD.
SUTTON RD.
ESHER RD.
WYCHWOOD PL.

Cricket
Grd.
Sch.
Sch.

Jolly
Farmer
Inn

4

EPSOM CL.
MATTHEWS RD.
KINGS RD.
DAWNAY RD.
MATTHEWS RD.
QUEEN ELIZABETH RD.
CORNWALL AV.
EVEREST RD.

BIRCH CL.
ACADEMY CL.
WHITE HILL
COLLEGE RIDE
ROSEWOOD CL.
OLD DEAN RD.
DIAMOND RD.
UPLAND RD.
COLLEGE CL.
DIAMOND RIDGE

HORSESHOE CR.
ROMAN RD.
STAR POST RD.
WISHMOOR
UPPER COLLEGE RIDE
Sch.
HIGHLAND RD.
WIGHAM RD.
POPPYHILLS RD.
DEER ROCK RD.

HAMPSHIRE RD.
HORSE SHOE RD.
BALLARD
RAPLEY
CORDWALLES RD.
LORRAINE RD.
P.O.
Fire Sta.
CAESAR'S RD.
CAESAR'S RD.
NAPIER RD.
COBB RD.
PASCHAL
TURTHILL RD.

Play.Fld
Sch.
PADDOCKS

Sch.

PORTSMOUTH ROAD

LT.
MWAY
COLLINGWOOD CRES.
GRANDE CL.
FOXHILL
CRES.

THE
GIBBET
LANE

Officer's
Quarters

Cricket Grds.
OLD GREEN LA.
OLD GREEN PLA.
KINGS RIDE
COLLEGE RIDE
BAROSSA RD.
CROMWELL RD.
YORK RD.
HARTFORD RISE
GEORGINA CL.
CLAREWOOD RD.
PORTESBERY HILL DR.
DIAMOND HILL

AMBERWOOD DR.
KNIGHTSBRIDGE RD.
GAINSBOROUGH RD.
KNIGHTS RD.
LINDEN CL.
CROSBY WALL CL.
DEVONSHIRE RD.
NORTH GATE
ELSENWOOD CRES.
BUCHAN
HIGHBURY CRES.
LARCHWOOD
GLADE
HILLCREST
MAYWOOD
Beaufront
BEAUFRONT RD.
CHATSWORTH
SILVER WOOD DR.
HIGHCLERE
ELSENWOOD DR.
Hill Crest

COLLINGWOOD RISE
LODDON
COOL-ARNE RISE
MILROY DRI.
AZALEA
CLEWBOROUGH DR.

5

STAFF COLLEGE ROAD
Upper Lake
Drill Hall
A30
Cen. Hall
St. Michaels
HEATHERLY CL.
THE AVENUE
HEATHERLY RD.
SEATON RD.
CAMBRIDGE CL.
FIRWOOD
FRANCE HILL DR.
GORDON RD.
PARK STREET
SOUTHWELL PK. RD.
LONDON ROAD
HIGH ST.
CARLISLE
GRAND AV.
APPLEY RD.
PRINCESS WY.
PEMBROKE B'WY.
UPPER GORDON RD.
MIDDLE GORDON RD.
ST. MARY'S R.
HEATHCOTE RD.
PARK LA.
COURT RD.
CHAUCER GR.
TEKELS AV.
DENISTOUN CL.
GARFIELD RD.
BRACKENDALE

CAMBERLEY
Council
Offices & Mus.
Lib.
Civic Hall
Police Sta.
R.C.Sch.
LANGLEY DR.
CHURCH HILL

Staff
College

1. WILLINGTON CL.
2. DEREK HORN CT.
3. TWYNHAM RD.

UPPER PARK RD.
PARK RD.
HA-I.CL.
ASHNELL RD.
MARLBOROUGH RISE
BRANKSOME PK. RD.
SANDY LA.
GRANGE RD.
BELTON RD.
YEO-MANS WAY
DEEPWELL DR.
BELLEVER HILL
GROVE RD.
WAVERLEY RD.
REDCREST GDNS.
WOOD RISE
RAVENS CL.
STOCK WOOD RISE
CRAWLEY WD.
CRAWLEY DR.
CONNAUGHT RD.
ALISON DR.
CRAWLEY HILL
SOUTH-COTE DR.
AMBROSDEN AV.

Frimley
Hall
Hotel
FRIMLEY HALL DR.
LIME AV.
CONIFER DR.
COPSE END
COPSE RD.
PADDOCK CL.
IBERIAN WY.
CHESTNUT
FAIRWAY
HEIGHTS
BURGOYNE RD.
YOULDEN DR.
YOULDEN CL.
SPRINGFIELD RD.
SAVILLE GDNS.
CHESTERS RD.
RAWDON RISE
PRIOR END
PRIOR RD.
DANDRIDGE CL.
Sch.

Camberley
Golf

HOLLYFIELDS CLO.

A B M3 A325 C

A322 BRACKNELL ROAD

Berkshire Boundary
Surrey Boundary

B3020

A30

Erlwood House
Glenhurst

The Cricketers Inn

Bagshot Park

The Pantiles Restaurant

Pol. Sta.

BAGSHOT STA.

HALF MOON ST.

'Three Mariners' (P.H.)

'Hero of Inkerman' (P.H.)

Bagshot

The White Hart (P.H.)

Foot bridge

Hallgrove Sch.

Freemantle Cottage

1. Faulkner Pl.
2. Hewlett Pl.
3. Kepple Pl.
4. Duval Pl.
5. Bell Pl.
6. Gloucester Gds.
7. Chewter Cl.
8. Wardle Cl.

Windle Brook

Swift Lane

M3

Nurseries
South Fm.

Beeches La.

LIGHTWATER BYPASS A322

Guildford Road

Hammond Way

Vicarage

'Bird in Hand' (P.H.)

'Foresters Arms' (P.H.)

JENKINS HILL

Lupin Cafe

1. Surridge Ct.
2. Laird Ct.
3. Victoria Ct.
4. Princes Way

Hammond's Pond

Lightwater Country Park

Lightwater

Bagshot Test Course

Sch.

Bagshot Heath

Curley Hill 400 ft.

HIGHVIEW RD.

AMBLESIDE

Turf Hill
B311

1. Lowfield Cl.
2. Shrublands Dr.
3. Myrtle Cl.
4. The Orchard
5. Bluebell Rise

Pol. Sta.

Woodcote House School

ROAD KENNEL LA.

Windlesham House

The Half Moon (P.H.)

The Bee (P.H.)

Heath Course

White Hill

Redroad Hill

B311 RED ROAD

Brackenwood

B3015 MAULTWAY

46

CARTOGRAPHY BY PHILIP'S. COPYRIGHT REED INTERNATIONAL BOOKS LTD

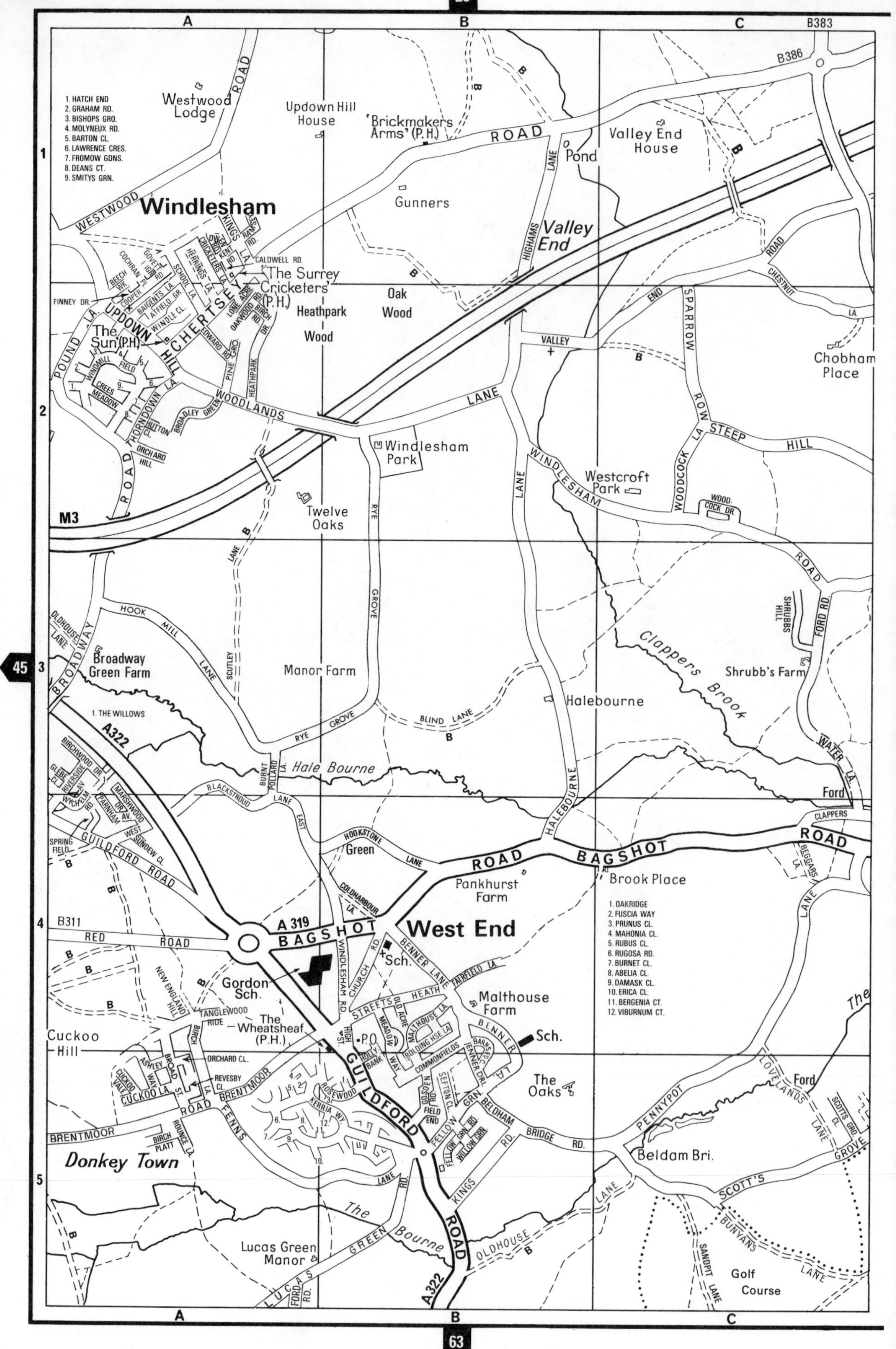
29
45
63
A
B
C
1
2
3
4
5
B383
B386
1. HATCH END
2. GRAHAM RD.
3. BISHOPS GRO.
4. MOLYNEUX RD.
5. BARTON CL.
6. LAWRENCE CRES.
7. FROMOW GDNS.
8. DEANS CT.
9. SMITYS GRN.
Westwood Lodge
Updown Hill House
'Brickmakers Arms' (P.H.)
ROAD
Valley End House
Pond
Gunners
Windlesham
WESTWOOD
Valley End
HIGHAMS LANE
CALDWELL RD.
The Surrey Cricketers' (P.H.)
Oak Wood
Heathpark Wood
CHERTSEY
UPDOWN HILL
The Sun (P.H.)
FINNEY DR.
POUND LA.
CHESTNUT LA.
SPARROW ROW
Chobham Place
VALLEY END
WOODLANDS LANE
STEEP HILL
Windlesham Park
WINDLESHAM
Westcroft Park
WOODCOCK LA.
WOODCOCK DR.
Twelve Oaks
M3
HOOK MILL LANE
RYE GROVE
BROADWAY
OLDHOUSE LANE
Broadway Green Farm
SCUTLEY
Manor Farm
Clappers Brook
SHRUBBS HILL
FORD RD.
Shrubb's Farm
Halebourne
1. THE WILLOWS
A322
BLIND LANE
WATER LA.
BURNT POLLARD LA.
Hale Bourne
HALEBOURNE LANE
Ford
CLAPPERS
BLACKSTROUD LANE EAST
HOOKSTONE LANE
Green
BAGSHOT ROAD
BEGGARS LA.
Brook Place
Pankhurst Farm
GUILDFORD ROAD
COLDHARBOUR LA.
1. OAKRIDGE
2. FUSCIA WAY
3. PRUNUS CL.
4. MAHONIA CL.
5. RUBUS CL.
6. RUGOSA RD.
7. BURNET CL.
8. ABELIA CL.
9. DAMASK CL.
10. ERICA CL.
11. BERGENIA CT.
12. VIBURNUM CT.
B311
RED ROAD
A 319
BAGSHOT
West End
Sch.
BENNER LANE
FAIRFIELD LA.
WINDLESHAM RD.
CHURCH RD.
Gordon Sch.
NEW ENGLAND HILL
TANGLEWOOD RIDE
The Wheatsheaf (P.H.)
HEATH
STREETS
Malthouse Farm
Sch.
The
Cuckoo Hill
ORCHARD CL.
REVESBY CL.
P.O.
COMMONFIELDS
GUILDFORD
The Oaks
LOVELANDS LANE
Ford
CUCKOO LA.
BRENTMOOR ROAD
FENNS
FIELD END
FELLOW GRN.
BELDHAM BRIDGE RD.
KINGS RD.
PENNYPOT
Beldam Bri.
SCOTT'S GROVE
BRENTMOOR
BIRCH PLATT
ROUNCE LA.
Donkey Town
LANE RD.
The Bourne
Lucas Green Manor
LUCAS GREEN
ROAD
OLDHOUSE
LANE
SANDPIT LANE
BUNYANS LANE
Golf Course
A322
FORD RD.

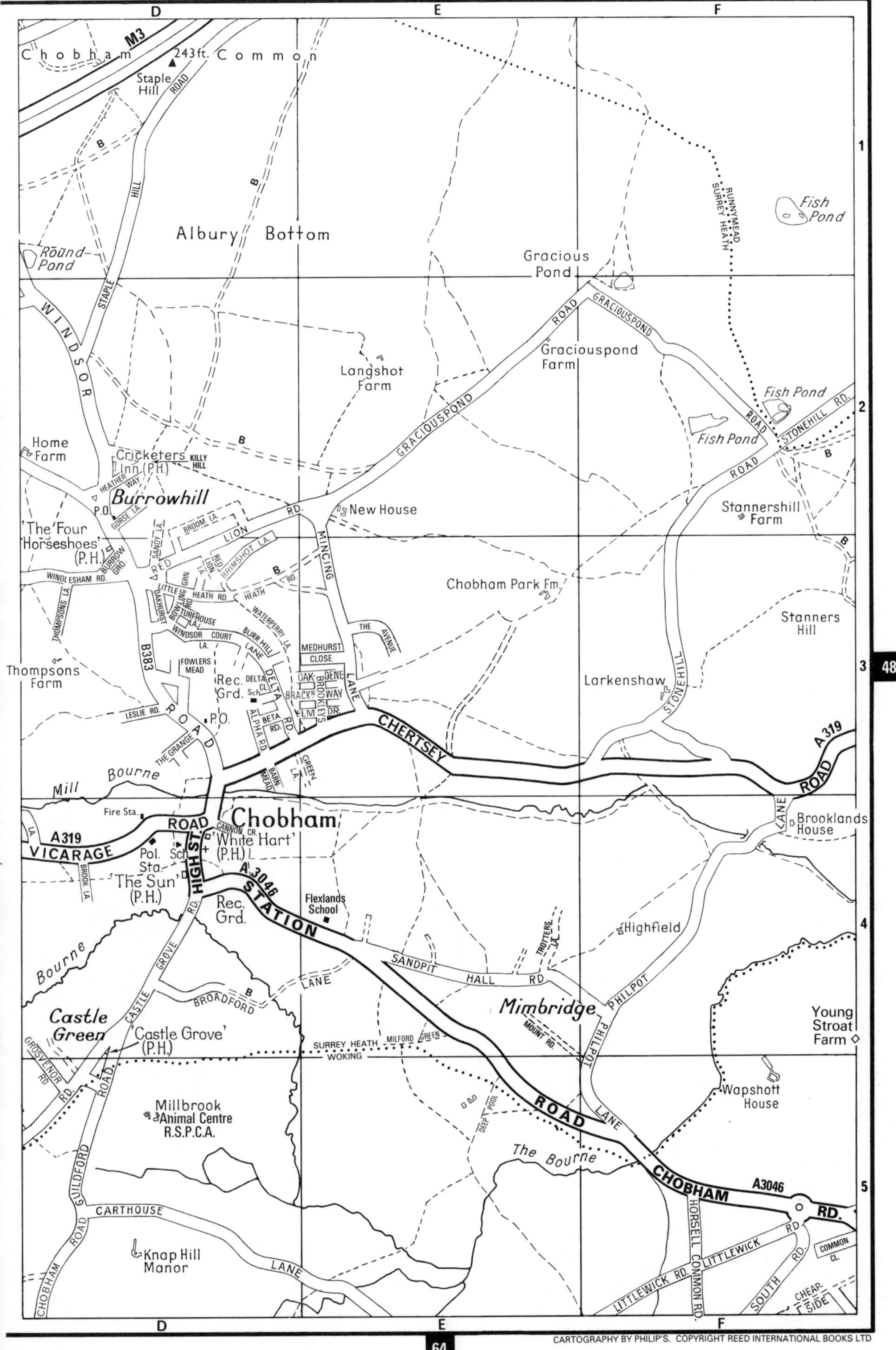

CARTOGRAPHY BY PHILIP'S. COPYRIGHT REED INTERNATIONAL BOOKS LTD

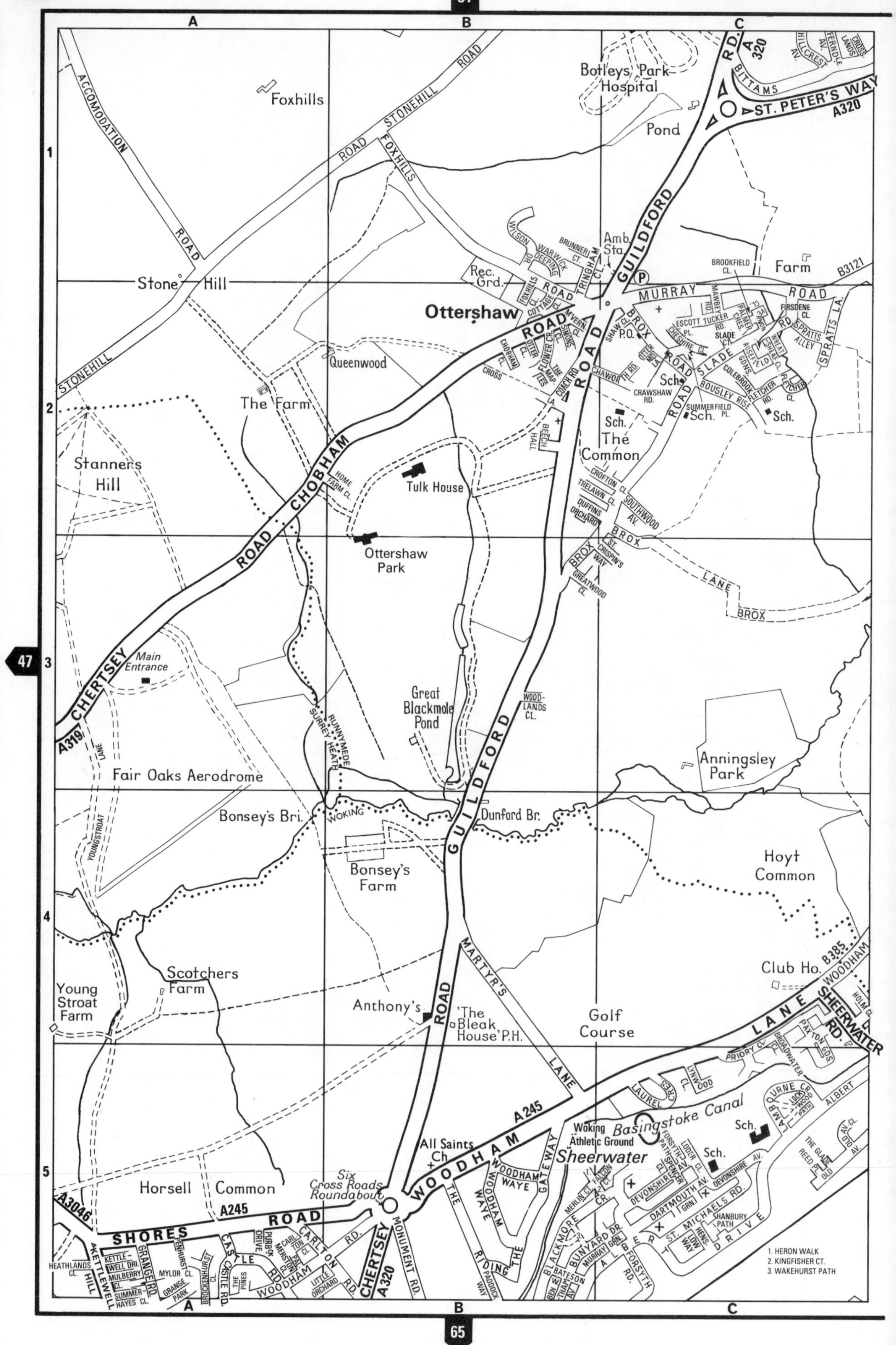
31
47
65
Foxhills
Botleys Park Hospital
Pond
Stone Hill
Ottershaw
Queenwood
The Farm
Stanners Hill
Tulk House
Ottershaw Park
The Common
Main Entrance
Great Blackmole Pond
Fair Oaks Aerodrome
Anningsley Park
Bonsey's Bri.
Dunford Br.
Bonsey's Farm
Hoyt Common
Scotchers Farm
Young Stroat Farm
Anthony's
'The Bleak House' P.H.
Golf Course
Club Ho.
Basingstoke Canal
Woking Athletic Ground
Sheerwater
All Saints Ch.
Six Cross Roads Roundabout
Horsell Common
CHOBHAM ROAD
CHERTSEY ROAD
GUILDFORD ROAD
WOODHAM LANE
WOODHAM ROAD
SHORES ROAD
MURRAY ROAD
ST. PETER'S WAY
STONEHILL ROAD
ACCOMODATION ROAD
FOXHILLS ROAD
BROX ROAD
BROX LANE
SLADE ROAD
MARTYR'S LANE
MONUMENT RD.
ALBERT DRIVE
SHEERWATER RD.
1. HERON WALK
2. KINGFISHER CT.
3. WAKEHURST PATH

WEYBRIDGE RD.

LA.
D
11

WESTON AV.
SIMPLEMARSH ROAD
MARSH LA.
CHAPEL AV.
SCHOOL ROAD
MEADOW RD.
ECTON RD.
HIGH ST.
B.C. HOUSES
GEORGE V. CT.
VICTORY PL.
ALBERT RD.
VICTORIA ROAD
ADDLESTONE
Trading Estate
ADDLESTONE
The Pelican Ham (P.H.) Moor

SUMNER CL.
St. Pauls Sch.
ST. PAULS CL.
PEARTREE CL.
LIBRARY
STATION RD.
BRIGHTON RD.
Civic Cen.
Pol. Sta.
Runnymede
B.C. Offs.
Inn
PARK
BOURNESIDE
HAM
Trading Estate
Level Crossing

1

B3121
HILL
SPINNEY
HILLSIDE GDNS.
LEDGER DR.
COPPER
ONGAR CL.
DICKENS DR.
MARLEY CL.
COOMBELANDS LA.
CHURCH HILL
ONGAR RD.
LIBERTY LANE
ORCHARD LANE
Sch.
CROCKFORD
Crockford Bridge
Addlestone
1. CROCKFORD CL.
2. FRENCHAYE
3. HAZEL DENE
4. MARNHAM PL.
Mill Pond
Coxes Lock

HARE LA.
Rowhill
FIVE OAKS
ROWHILL
OAKHILL RD.
BEARWOOD CLOSE
CAXTON AV.
FRANKLANDS DR.
CHAUCER WAY
HART LA.
Works
Coombelands
M25
NEW HAW ROAD
1. WILLIAMS CLOSE
2. STEEPLE GDNS.
3. COMPTON GDNS.
4. RANGER WALK
5. GRAY CLOSE
TEMPLEFIELD CL.
BROOKHURST RD.
WESTERHAM CL.
Black Horse (P.H.)
River Wey Navigation
BURCOTT GDNS.
BATES
2

P.H.
ROWTOWN RD.
Row Town
Rodwell Fm.
LANE
Rose Park
Holme Farm
Hall's Farm
WOODHAM PARK RD.
The Bourne
Min. of Agriculture Central Veterinary Laboratory
Moated Farm
HALLEY'S WALK
MEADWAY DR.
White Hart' (P.H.)
P.O.
New Haw
B385
COMMON LANE
BYFLEET RD.
MANOR ROAD
Wey Manor Farm
3 **50**

WOODHAM
FULLMEAD WAY
WENDLEY DR.
MANOR DR.
GRANGE RD.
SELBOURNE CL.
SELBOURNE AVENUE
THE PADDOCKS
PINEWOOD AV.
MAYFIELD AV.
WESTFIELD PARADE
Byfleet & New Haw Sta.
MINTSELLS RD.
VICKERS DR. NORTH
AVRO WAY
BROOK-LANDS
DE HAVILLAND DR.
SOPWITH DR.

Woodham
WOODHAM LODGE
ACACIA DR.
QUEEN MARY'S DR.
KING GEORGE'S AV.
HOLLY LANE
KINGSTON RD.
PINEWOOD GROVE
PARK
B385
Library
P.O.
LINDSAY RD.
KINGS RD.
SCOTLAND BRIDGE RD.
BROOM-FIELD RD.
Heathervale Mun. Caravan Park
Rec. Grd.
RUNNYMEDE
WOKING
MAXWELL DR.
WILDACRES
SALISBURY PL.
BERRY'S LA.
CHERTSEY RD.
Sch.
KINGS HEAD
DAWSON RD.
Barnes Wallis Dr.
1. VISCOUNT GDNS.
2. BARNATO CL.
4

OAK END WAY
SHEERWATER AV.
FARIS AV.
ORCHARD AV.
FULBROOK AV.
SELSDON RD.
BRIAR WK.
BIRCHWOOD RD.
Sch.
DARTNELL AV.
SCOTLAND BRIDGE
BRAESIDE RD.
DARTNELL
PARK ROAD
DARTNELL CLOSE
SQUIRREL WOOD
BLACKWOOD
PARVIS ROAD
QUEENS AV.
YORK RD.
PETERSHAM AV.
Parvis
A318
A245 RD.
FOXLAKE RD.

SILVER BIRCH AV.
WEST BYFLEET STA.
CLAREMONT ROAD
STATION RD.
CAMPHILL ROAD
P.O.
Lib.
CAMPHILL COURT
Sch.
PARVIS ROAD
2. WAKEFIELD CL.
3. CHUTERS CL.
4. THE MALTINGS
Pol. Sta.
HIGH RD.
MOWBRAY AV.
Byfleet
P.O.
EDEN GROVE RD.
BREWERY RD.

SHEERWATER BRI.
WOODLANDS AV.
THISTLE DENE
HOLLIES AV.
PYRFORD RD.
HIGHFIELD RD.
HOBBS CL.
HIGHFIELD
6. MADEIRA CL.
7. LONGRIDGE GROVE
8. TIMBER CL.
9. WILDWOOD CL.
RECTORY
HART RD.
WINERN GLEBE
CHURCH ROAD
West Hall
Sch.
A245
SHEERWATER RD.
Club Ho.
West Byfleet Golf Course
FAIRFORD CL.
Sch.
MAITLAND CL.
MELBURY CL.
West Byfleet
BROADOAKS CR.
BUCKS CL.
WEY LA.
GREEN-WAY CL.
5. BLACK PRINCE CL.
MAGDALEN DR.
SANWAY RD.
Sch.

WOKING
B367
OLD WOKING RD.
CALDHARBOUR RD.
OAKCROFT
Sch.
THORLEY GDNS.
DODD'S LANE
Murray's Bridge
Dodd's Bridge
WOKING GUILDFORD

33

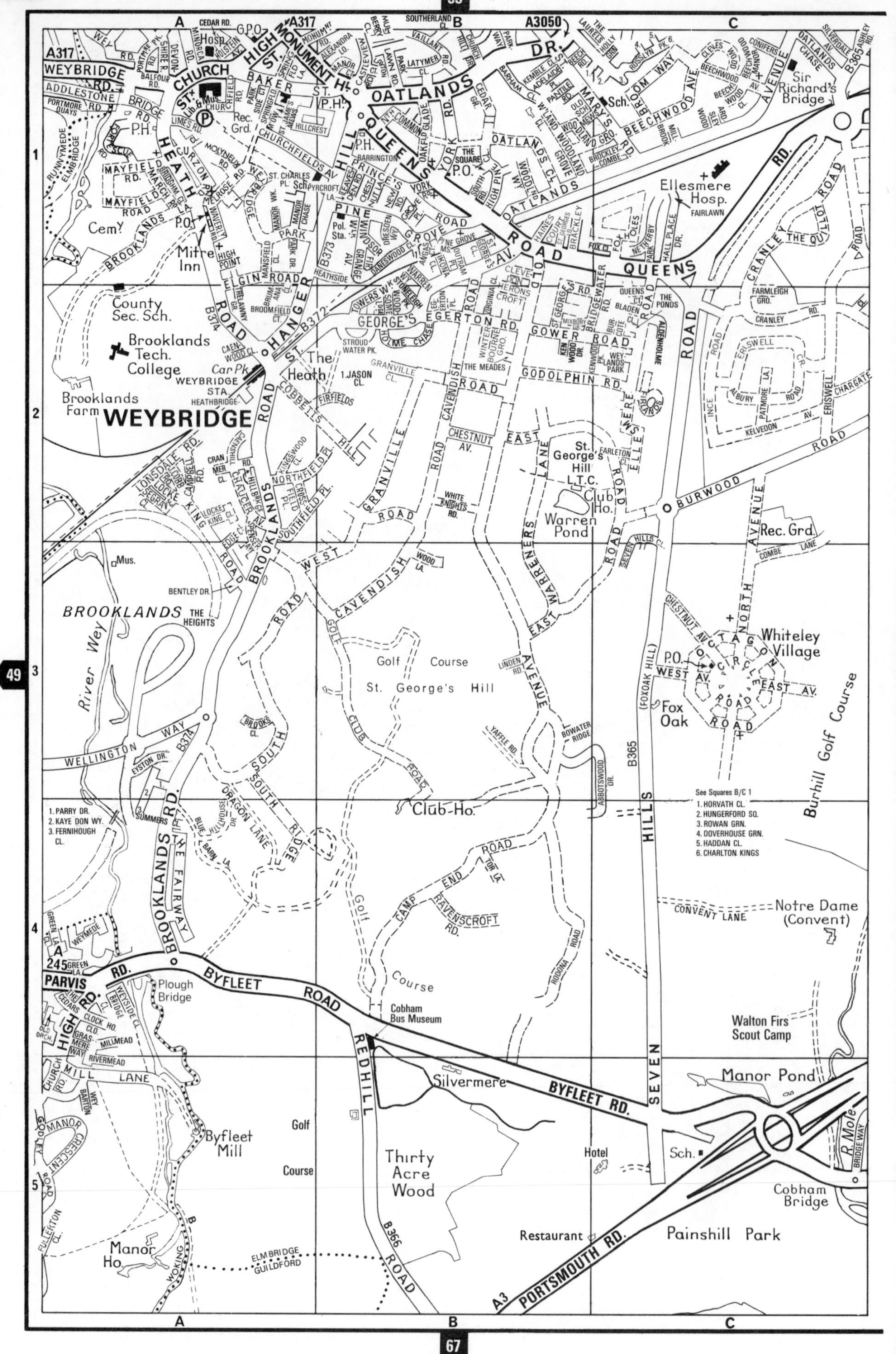
A
B
C
1
2
3
4
5
A317
A3050
WEYBRIDGE RD.
ADDLESTONE
BRIDGE RD.
CHURCH ST.
HIGH ST.
MONUMENT HILL
BAKER ST.
OATLANDS DR.
OATLANDS
QUEENS RD.
QUEENS ROAD
Sch.
Sir Richard's Bridge
Ellesmere Hosp.
FAIRLAWN
Lib. & Mus.
Rec. Grd.
P.H.
P.O.
Pol. Sta.
THE SQUARE
HEATH RD.
MAYFIELD RD.
BROOKLANDS RD.
Cemy.
Mitre Inn
HIGH POINT
ELGIN ROAD
HANGER HILL
County Sec. Sch.
Brooklands Tech. College
Car Pk.
WEYBRIDGE STA.
HEATHBRIDGE
The Heath
Brooklands Farm
WEYBRIDGE
ST. GEORGE'S AV.
EGERTON RD.
GOWER ROAD
GODOLPHIN RD.
CAVENDISH ROAD
GRANVILLE ROAD
CHESTNUT AV.
EAST ROAD
St. George's Hill L.T.C.
Club Ho.
Warren Pond
BURWOOD ROAD
CRANLEY RD.
Rec. Grd.
COMBE LANE
NORTH AVENUE
Whiteley Village
OCTAGON ROAD
CIRCLE ROAD
WEST AV.
EAST AV.
Fox Oak
(FOXOAK HILL)
B365
SEVEN HILLS ROAD
Burhill Golf Course
Mus.
BROOKLANDS
THE HEIGHTS
BENTLEY DR.
River Wey
WELLINGTON WAY
B374
WEST ROAD
Golf Course
St. George's Hill
CLUB ROAD
WARRENERS LANE
AVENUE
SOUTH ROAD
SOUTH RIDGE
DRAGON LANE
THE FAIRWAY
Club-Ho.
CAMP END ROAD
RAVENSCROFT RD.
RODONA ROAD
See Squares B/C 1
1. HORVATH CL.
2. HUNGERFORD SQ.
3. ROWAN GRN.
4. DOVERHOUSE GRN.
5. HADDAN CL.
6. CHARLTON KINGS
1. PARRY DR.
2. KAYE DON WY.
3. FERNIHOUGH CL.
CONVENT LANE
Notre Dame (Convent)
A245
PARVIS RD.
BYFLEET ROAD
Plough Bridge
Cobham Bus Museum
Walton Firs Scout Camp
HIGH RD.
MILL LANE
Silvermere
BYFLEET RD.
Manor Pond
REDHILL ROAD
B366
Golf Course
Byfleet Mill
Thirty Acre Wood
Hotel
Sch.
R. Mole
Cobham Bridge
Restaurant
Painshill Park
PORTSMOUTH RD.
A3
Manor Ho.
ELMBRIDGE
GUILDFORD
WOKING RD.
MANOR CRESCENT
GODLEY RD.

49

67

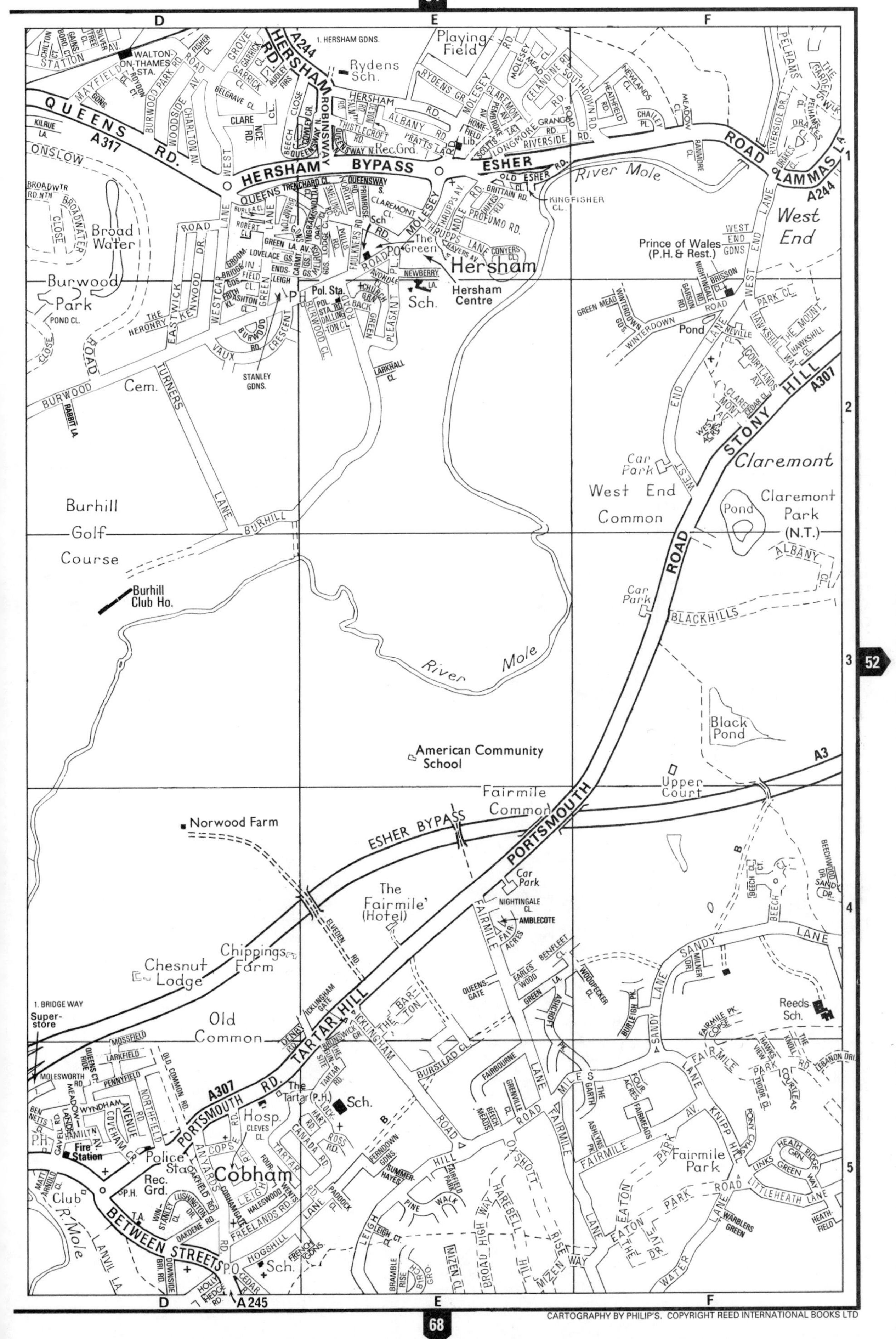

CARTOGRAPHY BY PHILIP'S. COPYRIGHT REED INTERNATIONAL BOOKS LTD

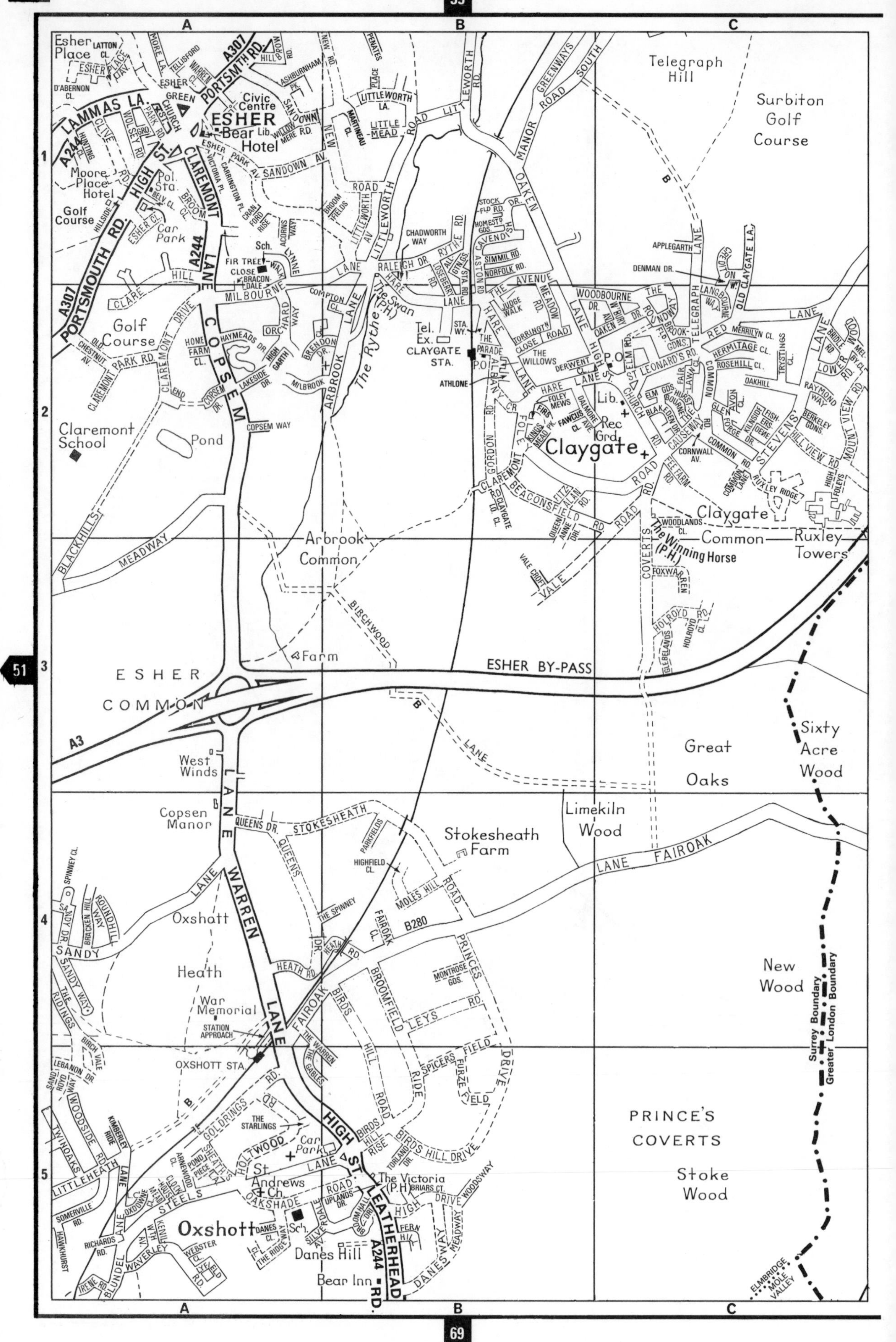
35
51
69
A
B
C
1
2
3
4
5
Esher Place
ESHER
Civic Centre
Bear Hotel
Lib.
Moore Place Hotel
Golf Course
Pol. Sta.
Car Park
Sch.
LAMMAS LA.
A244
A307
PORTSMOUTH RD.
HIGH ST.
CLAREMONT LANE
COPSEM LANE
MILBOURNE LANE
SANDOWN AV.
LITTLEWORTH RD.
LITTLEWORTH LANE
MANOR ROAD SOUTH
OAKEN LANE
Telegraph Hill
Surbiton Golf Course
CLAREMONT PARK RD.
CLAREMONT DRIVE
Claremont School
Pond
COPSEM WAY
ARBROOK LANE
The Rythe
The Swan (P.H.)
Tel. Ex.
CLAYGATE STA.
P.O.
ATHLONE
THE AVENUE
WOODBOURNE
TELEGRAPH LANE
OLD CLAYGATE LA.
HARE LANE
HIGH ST.
Lib.
Rec Grd.
Claygate
ST LEONARD'S RD.
COMMON RD.
STEVENS' LANE
FOLEY RD.
CLAREMONT RD.
BEACONSFIELD RD.
Claygate Common
The Winning Horse (P.H.)
Ruxley Towers
MEADWAY
BLACKHILLS
Arbrook Common
BIRCHWOOD
Farm
ESHER BY-PASS
ESHER COMMON
A3
West Winds
B
Great Oaks
Sixty Acre Wood
Copsen Manor
QUEENS DR.
STOKESHEATH
Limekiln Wood
Stokesheath Farm
FAIROAK LANE
WARREN LANE
Oxshott Heath
SANDY LANE
B280
PRINCES DRIVE
BROOMFIELD
New Wood
War Memorial
STATION APPROACH
OXSHOTT STA.
BIRDS HILL ROAD
Surrey Boundary
Greater London Boundary
PRINCE'S COVERTS
Stoke Wood
Car Park
St. Andrews Ch.
The Victoria (P.H.)
Oxshott
Sch.
Danes Hill
Bear Inn
LEATHERHEAD RD.
A244
STEELS LANE
LITTLEHEATH LANE
ELMBRIDGE
MOLE VALLEY

Hook

Club House

A3

CLAYTON

Lower Wood

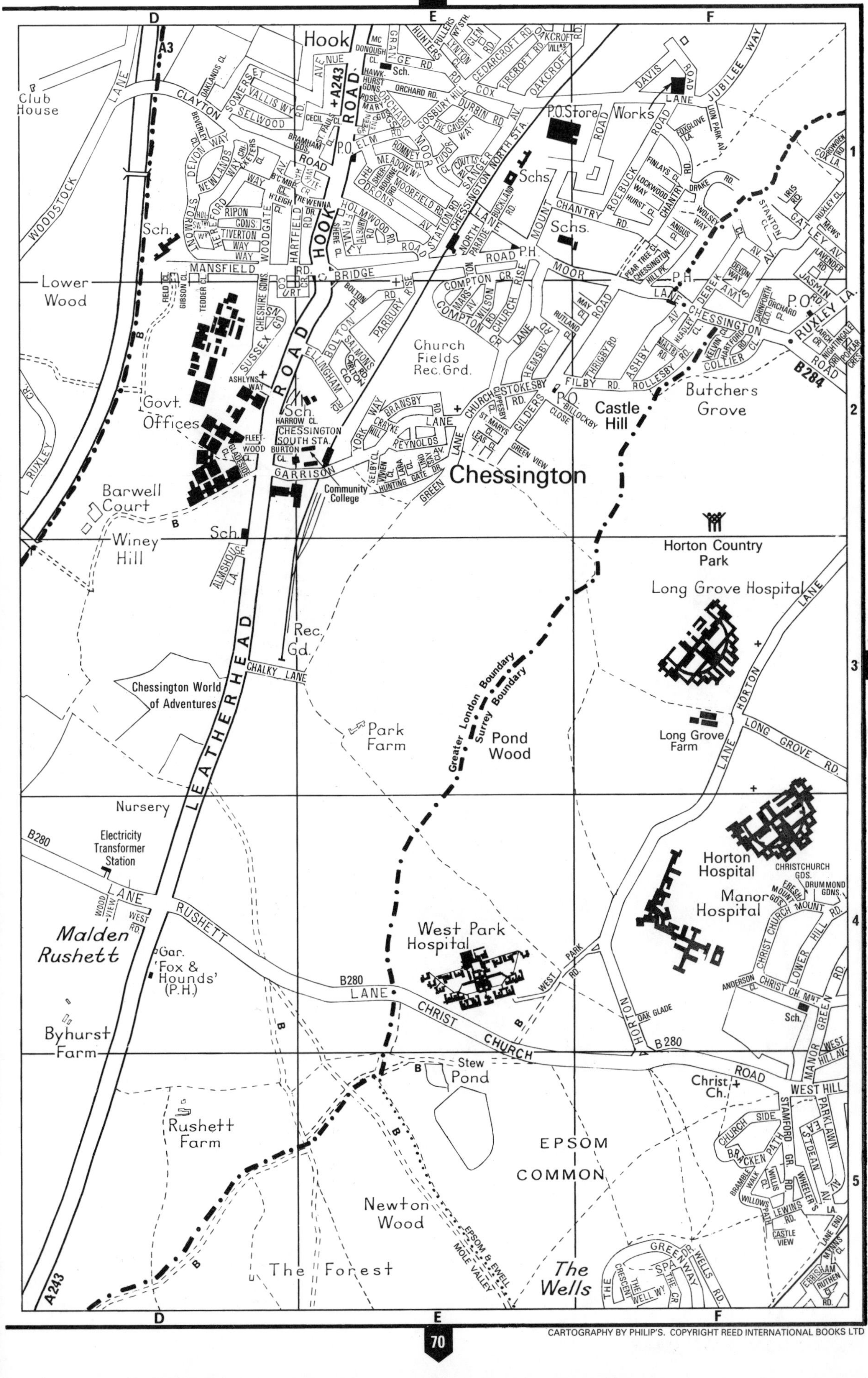

Sch.

Govt. Offices

Barwell Court

Winey Hill

Sch.

HOOK ROAD A243

MANSFIELD RD.

Sussex Cheshire Gdns.

Ashlyns Way

CHESSINGTON SOUTH STA.

GARRISON

Chessington World of Adventures

LEATHERHEAD ROAD

CHALKY LANE

Rec. Gd.

Park Farm

Nursery

B280

Electricity Transformer Station

RUSHETT LANE

Malden Rushett

Gar. 'Fox & Hounds' (P.H.)

Byhurst Farm

Rushett Farm

Newton Wood

The Forest

A243

Church Fields Rec. Grd.

COMPTON CR.

Chessington

P.O.

Castle Hill

Butchers Grove

P.O. Store Works

Schs.

Schs.

CHANTRY

MOOR LANE

RUXLEY LA.

B284

JUBILEE WAY

Community College

Greater London Boundary
Surrey Boundary

Pond Wood

West Park Hospital

B280 LANE

CHRIST CHURCH LANE

Stew Pond

B280

EPSOM COMMON

The Wells

Horton Country Park

Long Grove Hospital

Long Grove Farm

HORTON LANE

LONG GROVE RD.

Horton Hospital

Manor Hospital

CHRISTCHURCH GDS.

DRUMMOND GDNS.

WEST PARK RD.

Sch.

Christ Ch.

WEST HILL

MANOR GREEN ROAD

The Greenway

CARTOGRAPHY BY PHILIP'S. COPYRIGHT REED INTERNATIONAL BOOKS LTD

54

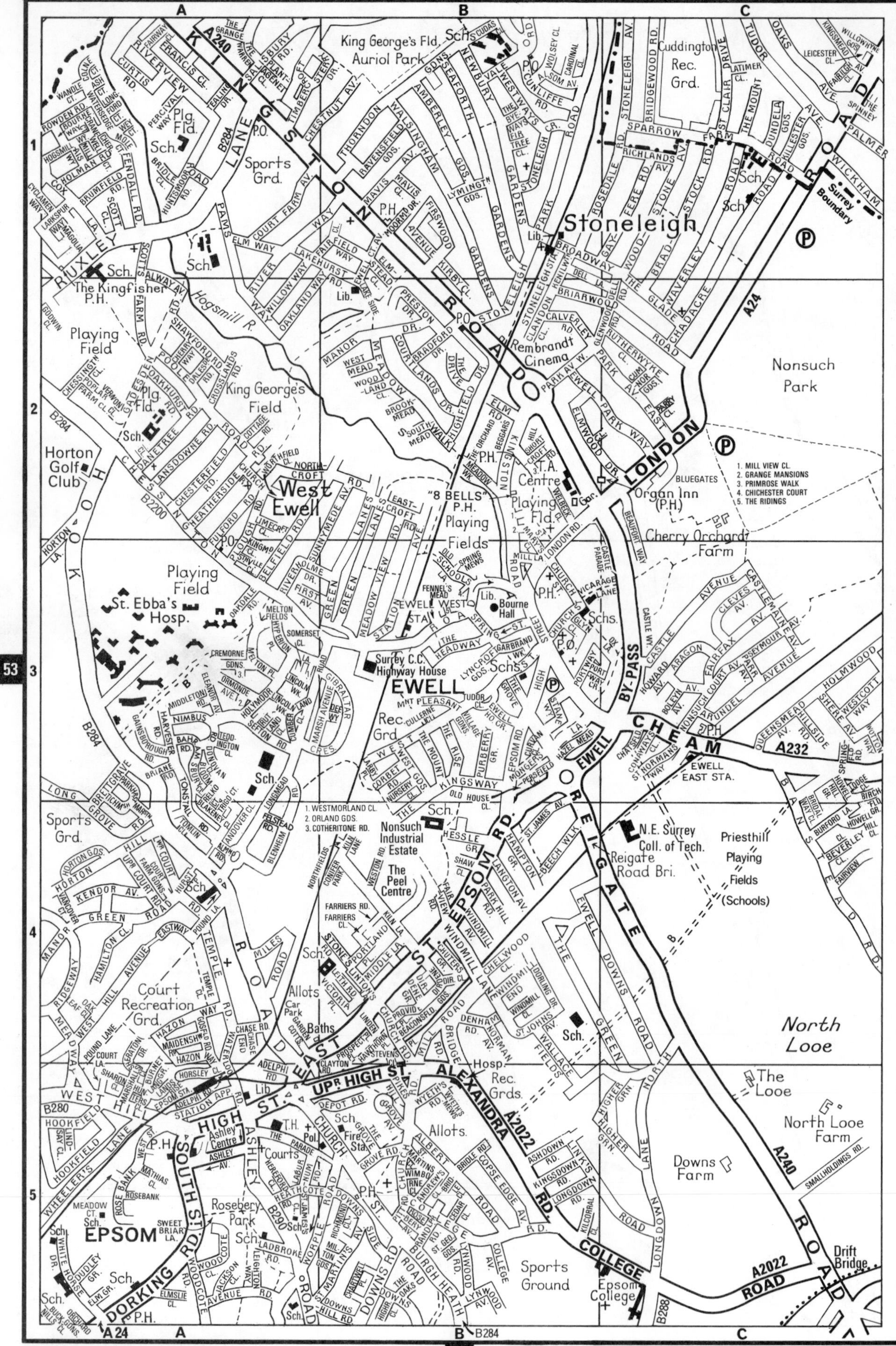

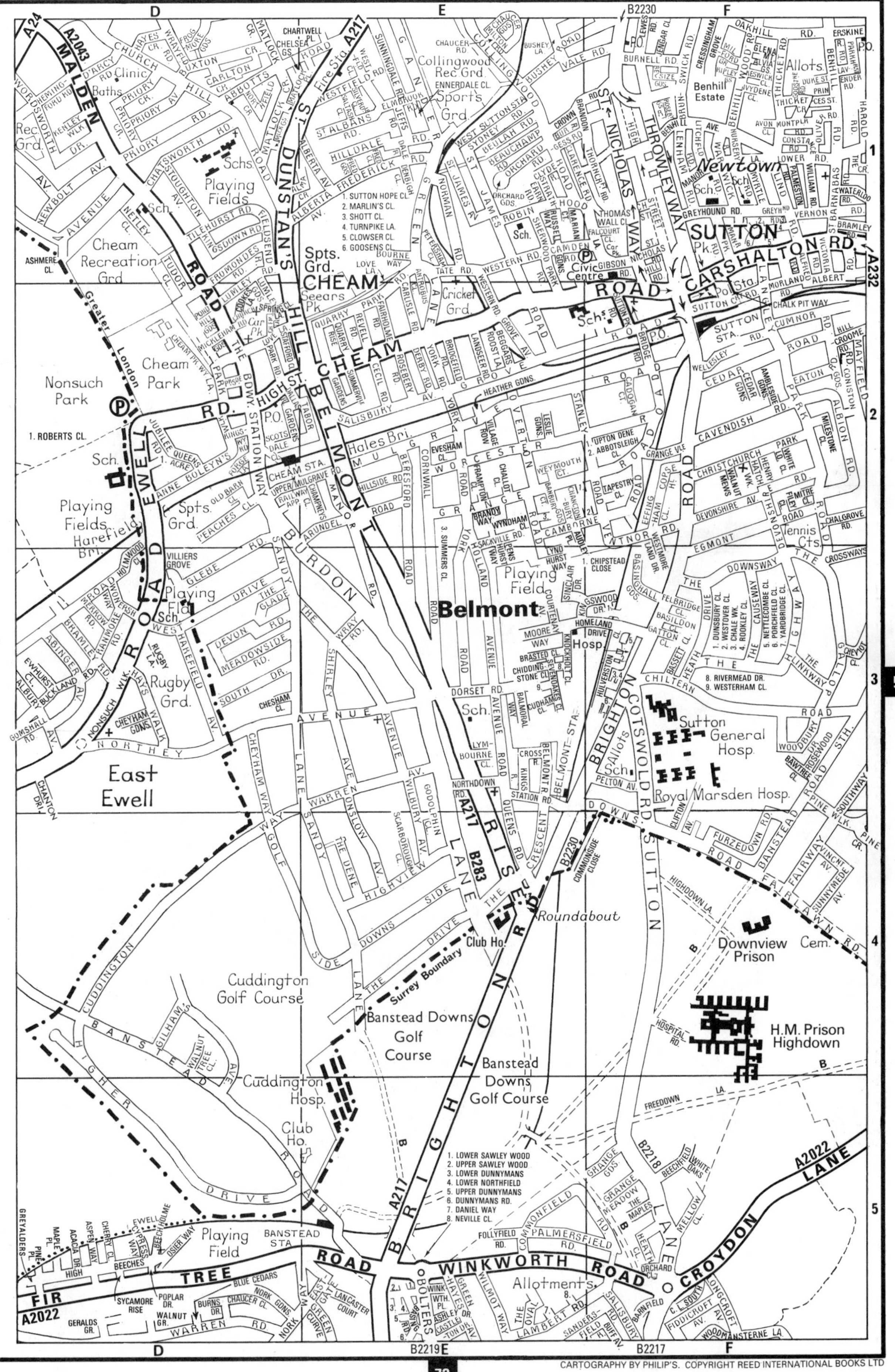

CARTOGRAPHY BY PHILIP'S. COPYRIGHT REED INTERNATIONAL BOOKS LTD.

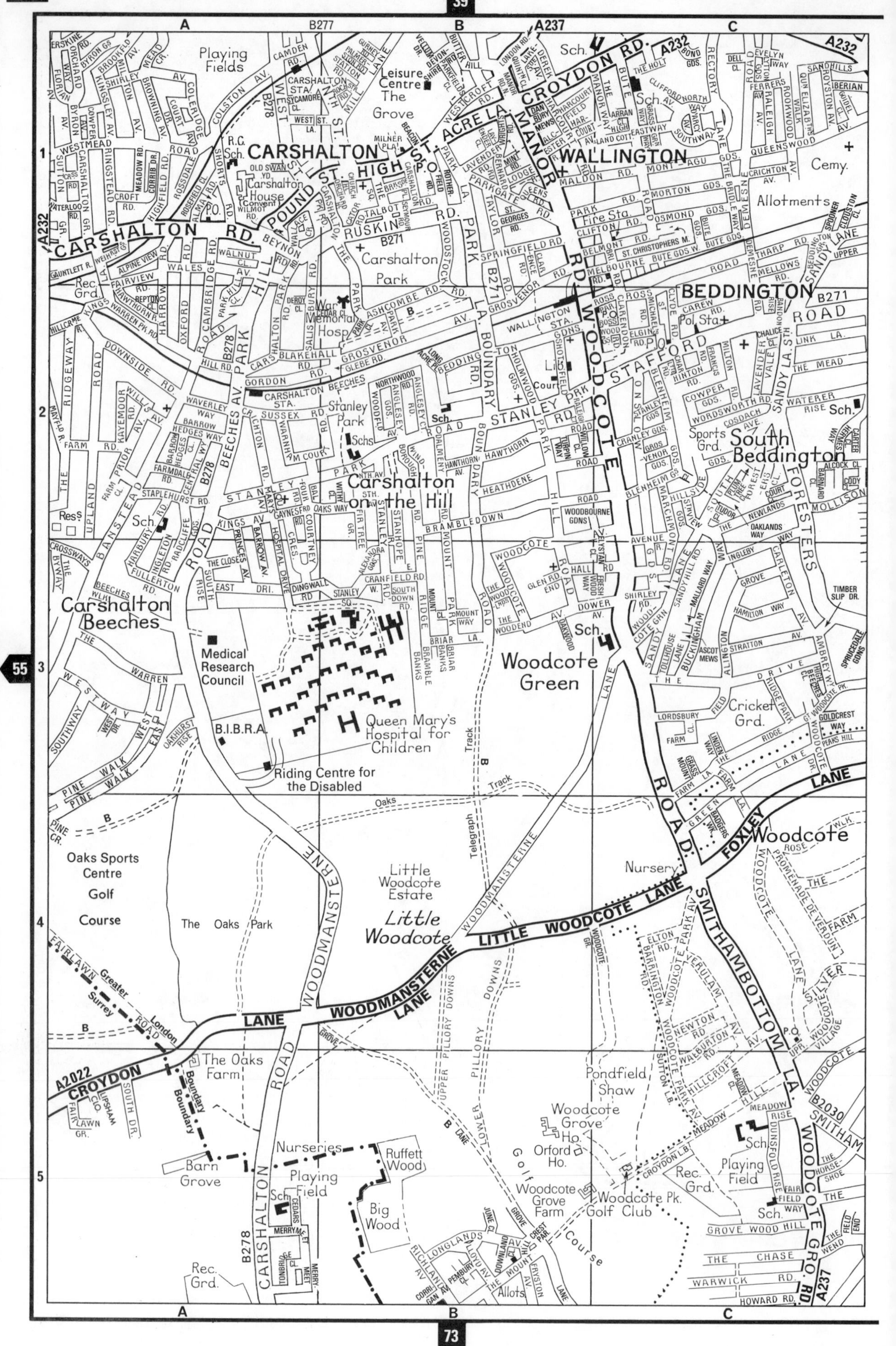
39
A
B
C
B277
A237
A232
1
2
3
4
5
55
73
Playing Fields
CARSHALTON
WALLINGTON
BEDDINGTON
South Beddington
Carshalton on the Hill
Carshalton Beeches
Carshalton Park
Carshalton House
Leisure Centre
The Grove
Stanley Park
War Memorial Hosp.
Medical Research Council
B.I.B.R.A.
Queen Mary's Hospital for Children
Riding Centre for the Disabled
Woodcote Green
Woodcote
Little Woodcote Estate
Little Woodcote
Oaks Sports Centre
Golf Course
The Oaks Park
The Oaks Farm
Barn Grove
Nurseries
Ruffett Wood
Big Wood
Playing Field
Rec. Grd.
Pondfield Shaw
Woodcote Grove Ho.
Orford Ho.
Woodcote Grove Farm
Woodcote Pk. Golf Club
Cricket Grd.
Sports Grd.
Cemy.
Allotments
Nursery
Allots
Greater London
Surrey
Boundary
CARSHALTON RD.
CROYDON RD.
MANOR RD.
WOODCOTE RD.
STAFFORD RD.
LITTLE WOODCOTE LANE
WOODMANSTERNE LANE
WOODMANSTERNE RD.
CARSHALTON RD.
CROYDON RD.
A2022
B278
B271
B2030
FOXLEY LANE
SMITHAMBOTTOM LA.
WOODCOTE GRO. RD.
PARK HILL
BEECHES AV.
BANSTEAD RD.
BOUNDARY RD.
PARK LA.
HIGH ST.
POUND ST.
ACRE LA.
STANLEY PARK RD.
GROSVENOR AV.
FORESTERS DR.
TELEGRAPH TRACK
UPPER PILLORY DOWNS
LOWER PILLORY DOWNS

B272 D A23 A232 A235 A212 F

CROYDON RD.

PURLEY WAY

DENNING AV

WADDON

Duppas Hill Park

DUPPAS HILL RD.

SOUTHBRIDGE RD.

STH. END

COOMBE

A2039

Coombe Cliff

PARK HILL RD.

A212 ROAD

1

Sports Grd.

WARHAM ROAD

Swan & Sugar Loaf P.H.

Playing Fields

SOUTH CROYDON STA.

Mellows Pk.

STAFFORD ROAD

Sch.

Water Works

Haling Park

South Croydon

2

Sports Grounds

Roundshaw

Purley Way Playing Fields

Allots. Sch.

Haling Grove

Red Deer P.H.

Rec. Grd.

Works

Allot. Gdns.

1. WESTLAND WAY
2. SOPWITH WAY
3. FARMAN WAY
4. SWIFT WAY
5. BARLOW CL.
6. OLLEY CL.
7. McINTOSH CL.
8. BRACKLEY CL.
9. DOUGLAS CL.

B272

DRIVE

PLOUGH LANE

Sports Ground

Sports Ground

RES.

CHANCELLOR CL. Sch.

KINGSDOWN

BLENHEIM

BRIGHTON

SANDERSTEAD ROAD

SANDERSTEAD STA.

B269

3

HILLCREST

HIGHFIELD

Russell Hill

Rec. Grd.

Hosp.

MONTPELIER

PURLEY PARK

Purley Beeches

Allots.

THE RIDGE WAY

EAST HILL

BOOK HILL

A2022 **FOXLEY LANE**

Lib.

High St.

PURLEY

Super Store

Purley STA.

SELCROFT

RIDDLESDOWN

Purley Downs Golf Club

Purley Downs

Golf Course

P.O.

4

MANOR VALLEY

Council Offices

Fire Sta.

REEDHAM STA.

Playing Field

GODSTONE RD.

DOWNSCOURT RD.

Partridge Knoll

RIDDLESDOWN STA.

MITCHLEY AVENUE A2022

WESTFIELD

DOWNS RD.

BRIGHTON RD.

A23

B2030 D

Sch.

WOODLAND WAY

Rec. Grd.

St. JAMES'S RD.

The Pins

CRANFORD RD.

Riddlesdown

RIDDLESDOWN

HONISTER HEIGHTS

5

KENLEY STA.

Pol. Sta.

RD. A22

School

CARTOGRAPHY BY PHILIP'S. COPYRIGHT REED INTERNATIONAL BOOKS LTD

41

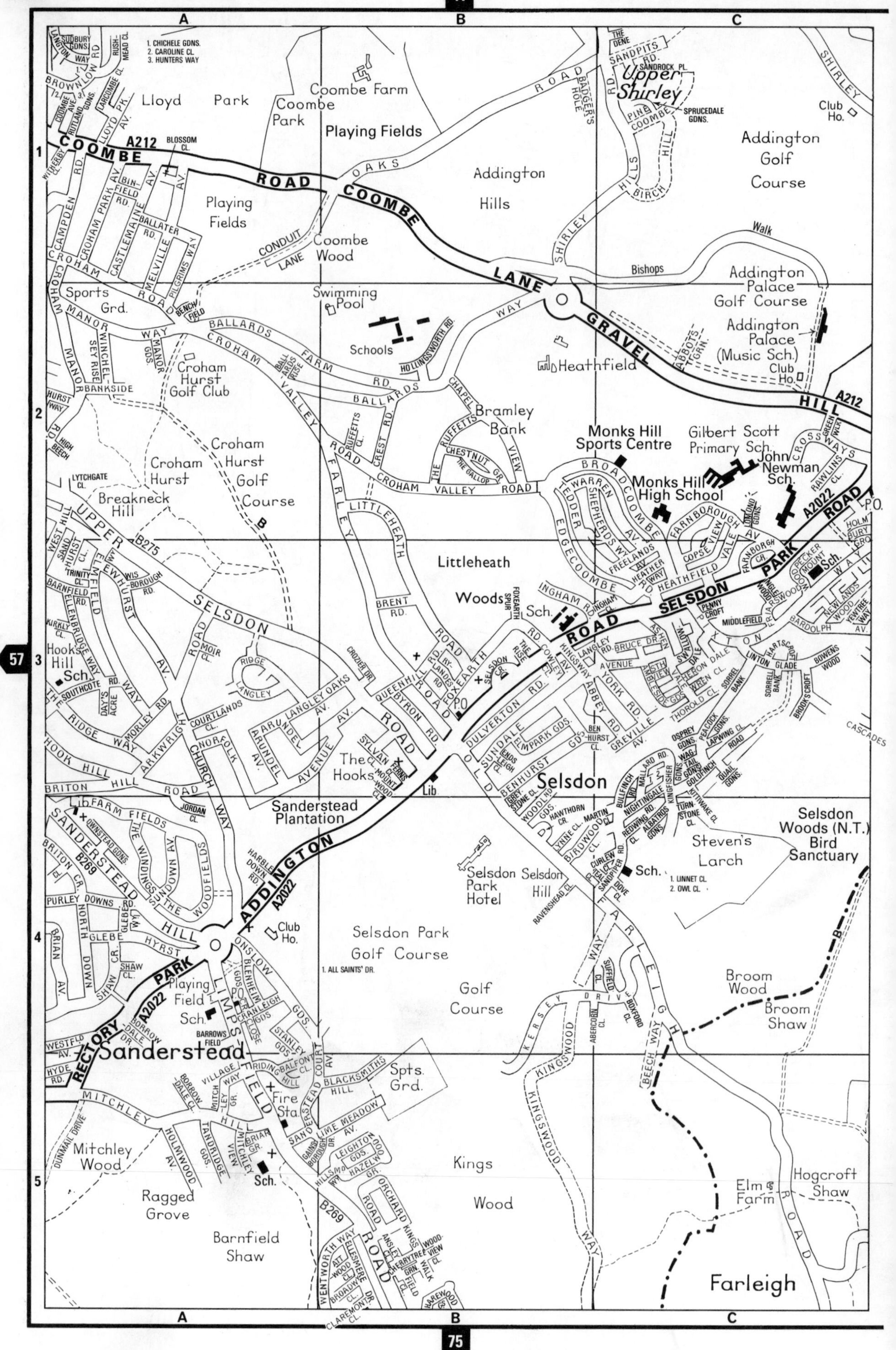
A
B
C
1
2
3
4
5
1. CHICHELE GDNS.
2. CAROLINE CL.
3. HUNTERS WAY
Lloyd Park
Coombe Farm
Coombe Park
Playing Fields
COOMBE ROAD
A212
BLOSSOM CL.
Addington Hills
Upper Shirley
THE DENE
SANDPITS RD.
SANDROCK PL.
SPRUCEDALE GDNS.
PINE COOMBE
BADGER'S HOLE
OAKS ROAD
Club Ho.
Addington Golf Course
Playing Fields
COOMBE LANE
CONDUIT LANE
Coombe Wood
SHIRLEY HILLS RD.
BIRCH HILL
Walk
Bishops
Addington Palace Golf Course
Addington Palace (Music Sch.)
Club Ho.
GRAVEL HILL
Sports Grd.
Swimming Pool
Schools
HOLLINGSWORTH RD.
Heathfield
ABBOTS GRN.
CROHAM ROAD
CROHAM MANOR RD.
CROHAM PARK AV.
CAMPDEN RD.
CASTLEMAINE AV.
BALLATER RD.
MELVILLE AV.
PILGRIMS WAY
BENCHFIELD
BALLARDS FARM RD.
BALLARDS RISE
BALLARDS WAY
CROHAM VALLEY ROAD
MANOR WAY
WINCHELSEY RISE
BANKSIDE
Croham Hurst Golf Club
Bramley Bank
CHAPEL VIEW
RUFFETTS CL.
THE RUFFETTS
CHESTNUT GR.
THE GALLOP
CREST RD.
Monks Hill Sports Centre
Gilbert Scott Primary Sch.
John Newman Sch.
Monks Hill High School
BROADCOOMBE
CROSSWAYS
RAWLINS CL.
A2022
P.O.
HURST WAY
HIGH BEECH
LYTCHGATE CL.
Croham Hurst
Breakneck Hill
Croham Hurst Golf Course
FARLEY ROAD
LITTLEHEATH RD.
Littleheath Woods
WARREN AV.
SHEPHERDS WY.
EDGECOOMBE
FREELANDS AV.
HEATHER WAY
FARNBOROUGH AV.
COPSE VIEW
HEATHFIELD VALE
FARNBOROUGH CR.
SELSDON PARK ROAD
PECKER MOUNT
Sch.
UPPER SELSDON ROAD
B275
WEST HILL
SANDHURST CL.
TRINITY CL.
ELMFIELD
EWHURST AV.
BOROUGH RD.
BARNFIELD RD.
ELLENBRIDGE WAY
KIRKLY CL.
Hooks Hill
Sch.
SOUTHCOTE RD.
BRENT RD.
FOXEARTH SPUR
Sch.
INGHAM RD.
SELSDON ROAD
MIDDLEFIELD
PENNY CROFT
FRIARSWOOD
NEWLANDS WOOD
YEWTREE WAY
BARDOLPH AV.
LINTON GLADE
HARTSCROFT
BOWENS WOOD
SORRELL BANK
BROOK'S CROFT
CASCADES
MOIR CL.
RIDGE LANGLEY
CROZIER DR.
QUEENHILL RD.
RYLANDS RD.
SELSDON CR.
THE RISE
COWLEY AV.
KINGSWAY AVENUE
LANGLEY RD.
BRUCE DR.
ASHEN VALE
SWALLOWDALE
HEBDON DALE
WREN CL.
THOROLD CL.
SORREL BANK
THE RIDGE WAY
DAY'S ACRE
MORLEY RD.
COURTLANDS CL.
LANGLEY OAKS AV.
ARUNDEL AV.
AVENUE
BYRON RD.
FOXEARTH ROAD
P.O.
DULVERTON RD.
ABBEY RD.
YORK RD.
GREVILLE AV.
OSPREY GDNS.
PEACOCK GDNS.
LAPWING CL.
QUAIL GDNS.
HOOK HILL
ARKWRIGHT RD.
NORFOLK
CHURCH WAY
SYLVAN CL.
FERNS CL.
MOUNTWOOD CL.
The Hooks
Lib
OLD FARLEIGH ROAD
SUNDALE AV.
ELMPARK GDS.
BEN HURST CL.
BENHURST GDS.
Selsdon
BRITON HILL ROAD
JORDAN CL.
Lib
FARM FIELDS
ADDINGTON ROAD
Sanderstead Plantation
HAWTHORN CR.
MARTIN CR.
BULLFINCH RD.
MALLARD RD.
NIGHTINGALE RD.
KINGFISHER GDS.
REDWING CL.
ALBATROS GDNS.
TURNSTONE CL.
KITTIWAKE CL.
Selsdon Woods (N.T.) Bird Sanctuary
Steven's Larch
SANDERSTEAD HILL
B269
BRITON CR.
THE WINDINGS
SUNDOWN AV.
THE WOODFIELDS
HARBLE DOWN RD.
Selsdon Park Hotel
Selsdon Hill
RAVENSHEAD CL.
CURLEW CL.
SANDPIPER RD.
DOVE CL.
Sch.
1. LINNET CL.
2. OWL CL.
PURLEY DOWNS RD.
NORTH DOWN
BRIAN AV.
GLEBE HYRST
SHAW CR.
SHAW CL.
Club Ho.
Selsdon Park Golf Course
1. ALL SAINTS' DR.
FARLEIGH
WAY
SUFFIELD CL.
Broom Wood
RECTORY PARK
A2022
Playing Field
Sch.
LIMPSFIELD
ONSLOW GDS.
BLENHEIM
CRANLEIGH GDS.
P.O.
Golf Course
KERSEY DRIVE
ABERCORN CL.
BOXFORD CL.
Broom Shaw
BORROWDALE DR.
BARROWS FIELD
WESTFLD AV.
Sanderstead
STANLEY GDS.
BALFONT CL.
RIDING HILL
BLACKSMITHS HILL
SANDERSTEAD COURT AV.
Spts. Grd.
KINGSWOOD
BEECH WAY
HYDE RD.
MITCHLEY HILL
VILLAGE WAY
MITCHLEY GR.
Fire Sta.
LIME MEADOW AV.
BOROUGH DR.
DUNMAIL DRIVE
Mitchley Wood
HOLMWOOD AV.
TANDRIDGE GDS.
MITCHLEY VIEW
BRIAR GR.
Sch.
LEIGHTON GDS.
HAZELWOOD GR.
Kings Wood
KINGSWOOD WAY
Elm Farm
Hogcroft Shaw
Ragged Grove
Barnfield Shaw
ORCHARD ROAD
KINGS WOOD
WOODVIEW CL.
WENTWORTH WAY
ELLESMERE DR.
ATTWOOD CL.
BROADWAY CL.
ANSLEY CL.
CHERRYTREE GRN.
FIELD CL.
HAREWOOD GDS.
CLAREMONT CL.
ROAD
Farleigh

57

75

D   E   F

Shirley Heath

PALACE VIEW

LAUREL CR.
FIR TREE GDNS.
ERICA GDNS.
CORSE RD.
BORDER GDNS.
SHRUBLANDS AV.
BRAMBLE CL.
BRIAR
CORSEHILL
WOODLND. WAY

Spring Park

ADDINGTON RD. A2022

Wickham Court
St. John Rigby School

LAYHAMS

SYLVAN WAY
HAWTHORN DR.
CHESTNUT AV.
BIRCH TREE RD.
CHERRY TREE AV.
QUEENSWAY
LIME TREE WLK.
CHERRY TREE WLK.
MONARCH

CHURCH RD.
FULLER'S WOOD
BRIDLE WAY
THE WICKET
BOUNDARY WAY

Threehalfpenny Wood

BROMLEY L.B.
CROYDON L.B.

Fox Hill

Well Wood

ROXTON GDNS.
SPOUT HILL
TITH HILL
LODGE

ADDINGTON
GATE WAY

VILLAGE
THE PADDOCKS

Addington Park Rec. Grd.

KENT

P.O.
P.H.
Police Station

Rowdown Fields

Schs.

FIELD
NORTH WALK
LIND ENS
UNDERWOOD WAY

Birch Wood

The Larches

Long Shaw

Cooper's Wood

NORTH POLE LA.

Sch.

ELMSIDE
ELMSIDE
COPPINS
P.O.
FOXCOMBE
BRIERLY
APPLE GARTH
BYGROVE
IVERS WAY
HEADLEY
DUNLEY
LEIGH CR.
DANESBURY
ASHWOOD GDS.
CHESNEY
R.C.
RIPLEY

Castle Hill Sch.

NETLEY CL.
P.O.
WITLEY
WALTON GREEN
WOOD
MERROW WAY
DRIVE
CLAYGATE
WRIGHTS
FRIMLEY CR.
FRENSHAM
HORSLEY DR.
FRIMLEY
THURSLEY CR.
BROCKHAM
MICKLEHAM WAY
GOLDCREST
DRIVE
AVENUE

Bradmanshill Wood

Bushfield Shaw

Fire Sta.

HUNTINGFIELD
FALCONWOOD RD.
PALACE GREEN
HEATHER BED
SILVER WOOD
CROFTERS MEAD
THE GREEN

1. Westcott Cl.
2. Unity Cl.
3. Betchworth Way
4. Lomas Cl.

St. Francis Centre
Club Ho.

Sch.

HOLLY WOODS
OSWARD
MARKFIELD
COURT WOOD

North Down

DUNSFOLD WAY
CASTLE HILL
KING
PARKWAY
NORTH DOWNS
NTH. DOWNS CR.

Sch.

New Addington

Rowdown Wood

Works

ROWDOWN AV.
STONE PK.
VULCAN WAY
WINDHAM
CALLEY DOWN
RED START

WOLSEY CR.
MONTACUTE
ALDRICH CR.
SHAXTON CR.
GRENVILLE RD.
PROTHWELL RD.
HENEAGE RD.
WALSH
GINGHAM RD.
GODRIC
QUEEN ELIZABETH'S DR.
HARES BANK

Lib.
Sch.
P.O.
SALCOT
GOWNSTER
HILL
Central Parade
Swim. Baths

Sch.
Red

Sch.

Dog Training Kennels

Addington Court Golf Course

Playing Field
Sch.

OVERBURY CRES.
CHERTSEY CRES.
HOMESTEAD
FARLEIGH DEAN CR.
CUDHAM DRIVE

Hall

ARNHEM DRIVE
CLEVES
MILNE PARK WEST
MILNE PARK EAST
EDWARDS
LEVERET
WARBANK CL.
WARBANK CR.
CATOR CL.

Milne Park

UVEDALE CRES.
POWAY
COM.
WALSH CR.
PORT GDN. AV.
FAIRCHILDES

Schools
Playing Fields

SHEEPBARN LA.

Frith Wood

Haggler's Dean

Farleigh Dean

Frylands Wood

GREATER LONDON BOUNDARY
SURREY BOUNDARY

Hutchingsons Bank

THORPE CL.
FLORA CL.
FLORA GDS.
KENNEL WOOD CR.
CORBETT

Crab Wood

Chapel Hill

Coldblow Shaw

Fairchildes House

Beechfield Wood

White Bear (P.H.)

Fairchildes Farm

PARK RD.
BLACKMAN'S LA.
SKIDHILL LA.

Sch.

Limekiln Shaw

FARLEIGH COURT ROAD

Little Farleigh Green Farm

Little Farleigh Green

Fickleshole Farm

Fickleshole

Farleigh Court

Great Park Wood

1   2   3   4   5

not continued, see key diagram

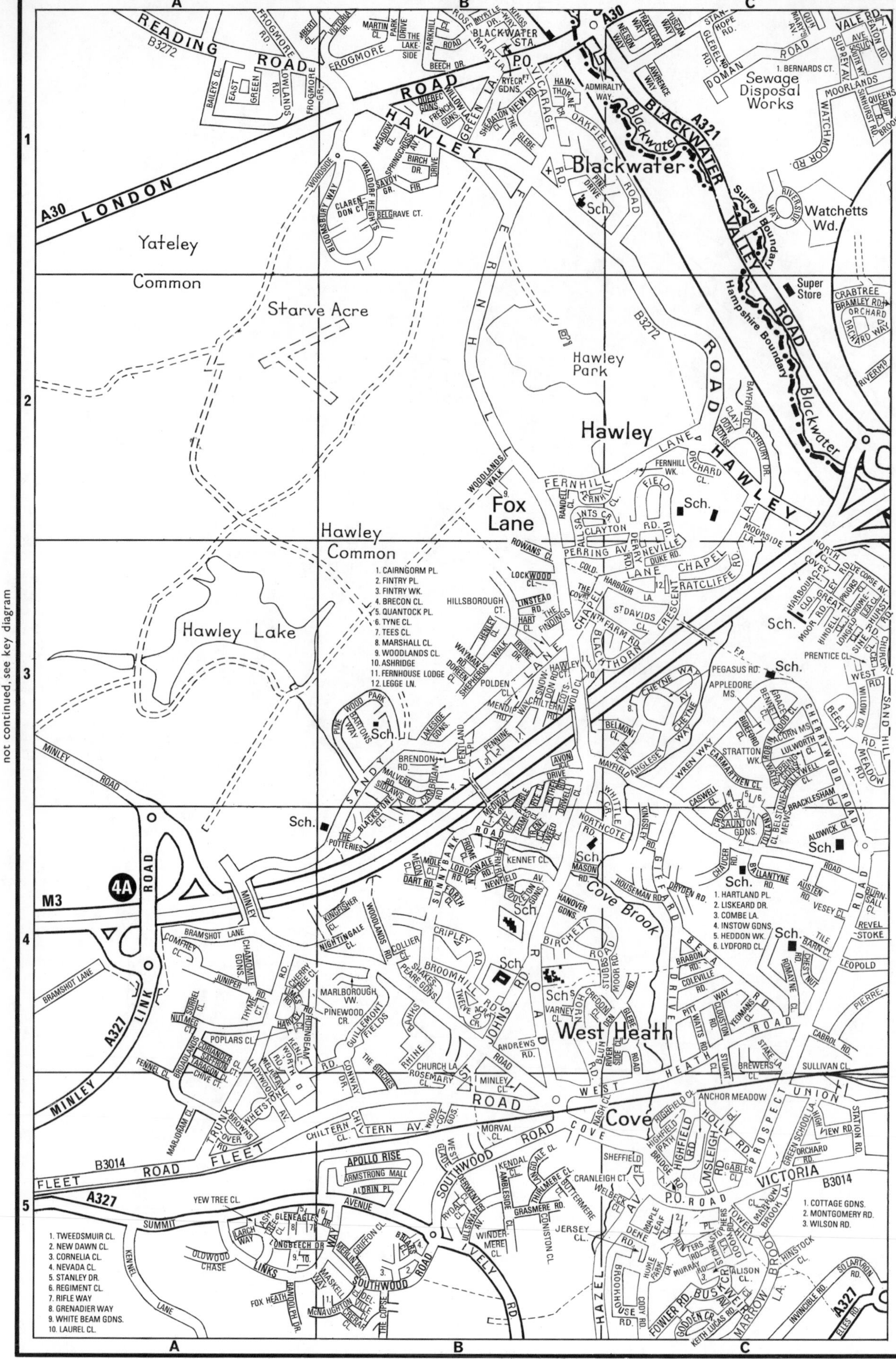

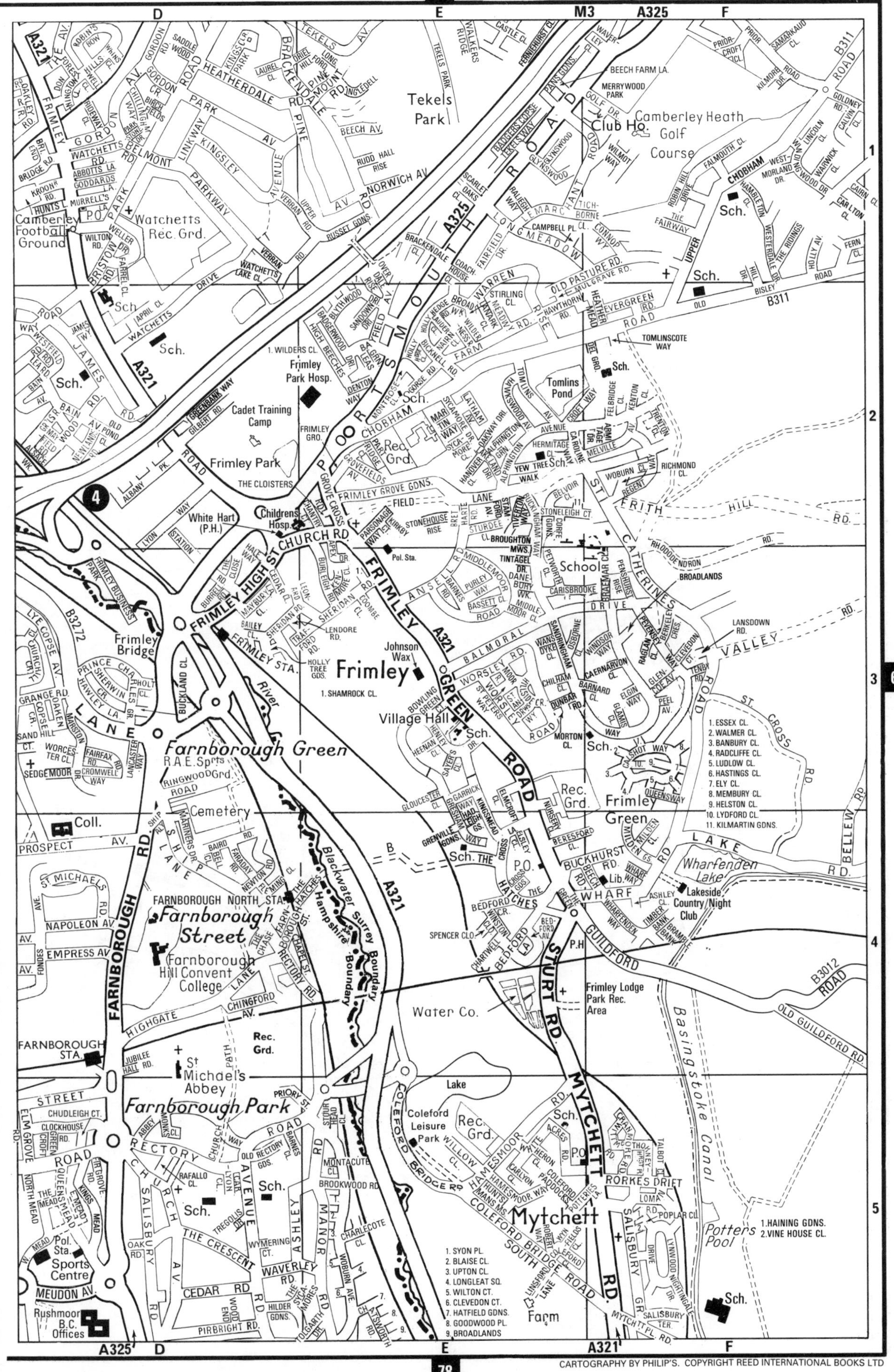

CARTOGRAPHY BY PHILIP'S. COPYRIGHT REED INTERNATIONAL BOOKS LTD

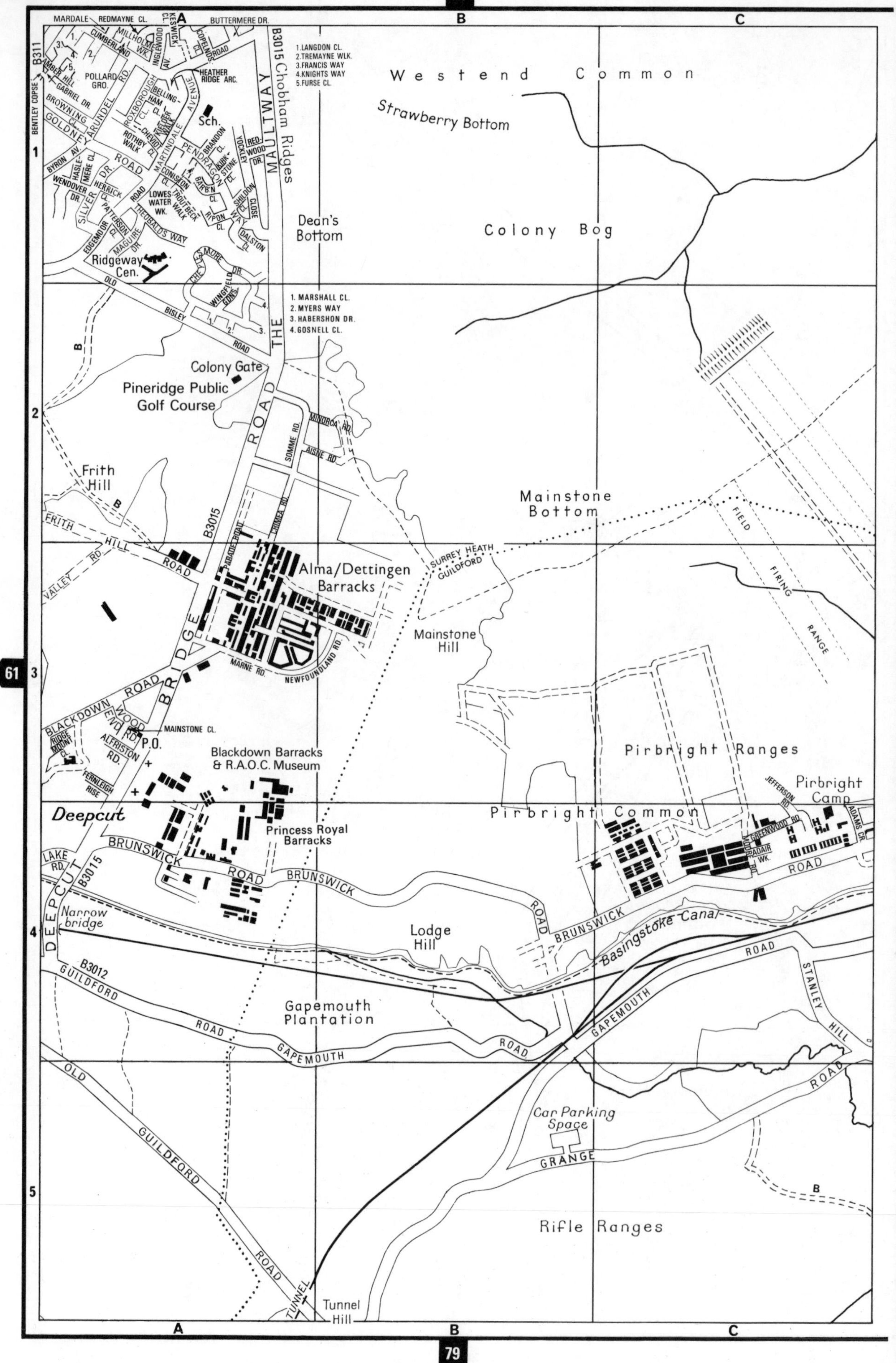
45
61
79
A
B
C
1
2
3
4
5
MARDALE
REDMAYNE CL.
BUTTERMERE DR.
KESWICK CL.
MILLHOLME WK.
INGLEWOOD AV.
COPELNDS
ROAD
CUMBERLAND
B311
AMBER HILL
GABRIEL DR
POLLARD GRO.
ARUNDEL RD.
HEATHER RIDGE ARC.
BENTLEY COPSE
BROWNING CL.
GOLDNEY
ROXBOROUGH CL.
BELLINGHAM CL.
AVENUE
Sch.
CHEVIOT
ROTHBY WALK
MARTINDALE
BRANDON
REDWOOD DR.
YOCKLEY CL.
BYRON AV.
HASLEMERE CL.
ROAD
PENDRAGON
KIRKSTONE
WENDOVER DR.
HERRICK CL.
CONISTON CL.
SILVER DR.
LOWES WATER WK.
TROUTBECK WALK
SHILDON CLOSE
RIPON CL.
PATTERSON CL.
EDGEMOOR RD.
MAGUIRE DR.
THEOBALDS WAY
DALSTON CL.
Ridgeway Cen.
WINGFIELD GDNS.
OLD
BISLEY
ROAD
THE MAULTWAY
B3015 Chobham Ridges
1.LANGDON CL.
2.TREMAYNE WLK.
3.FRANCIS WAY
4.KNIGHTS WAY
5.FURSE CL.
Westend Common
Strawberry Bottom
Dean's Bottom
Colony Bog
1. MARSHALL CL.
2. MYERS WAY
3. HABERSHON DR.
4. GOSNELL CL.
Colony Gate
Pineridge Public Golf Course
ROAD
MINORCA RD.
SOMME RD.
AISNE RD.
Frith Hill
B3015
CRIMEA RD.
FRITH HILL ROAD
VALLEY RD.
Mainstone Bottom
FIELD FIRING RANGE
SURREY HEATH
GUILDFORD
Alma/Dettingen Barracks
Mainstone Hill
BRIDGE
MARNE RD.
NEWFOUNDLAND RD.
BLACKDOWN ROAD
WOOD END RD.
MAINSTONE CL.
P.O.
RIDGE MOUNT CL.
ALFRISTON RD.
FERNLEIGH RISE
Blackdown Barracks
& R.A.O.C. Museum
Pirbright Ranges
Pirbright Camp
JEFFERSON RD.
GREENWOOD RD.
ADAMS CR.
Deepcut
Pirbright Common
Princess Royal Barracks
LAKE RD.
BRUNSWICK
B3015
ROAD
BRUNSWICK
RADAIR WK.
ROAD
DEEPCUT
Narrow bridge
BRUNSWICK
ROAD
Basingstoke Canal
Lodge Hill
ROAD
STANLEY HILL
B3012
GUILDFORD
ROAD
Gapemouth Plantation
GAPEMOUTH
ROAD
GAPEMOUTH
ROAD
OLD
GUILDFORD
ROAD
Car Parking Space
GRANGE
B
Rifle Ranges
TUNNEL
Tunnel Hill

D E F

FORD ROAD
GUILDFORD RD.
A322
CHURCH
School
PO
Bisley
Sch.
CEDAR DR.
SCHOOLS DR.
GREY CORBETTS
ROAD
LOBELIA RD.
CHURCH LANE
LANE
ROMANY RD.
Golf Course
SANDPIT LANE
ROMANY RD.
WARBURY LANE
Hill Place
BARRS LA.

1. NASTURTIUM DR.
2. ORCHID DR.
3. MARIGOLD DR.
4. JUNIPER DR.
5. KINGCUP DR.
6. HOLLYHOCK DR.
7. GERMANDER DR.
8. YELLOWCRESS DR.
9. FREESIA DR.
10. DAFFODIL DR.
11. ROSEBURY DR.
12. QUINCE DR.
13. ZINNIA DR.
14. STRAWBERRY FIELDS
15. STRAWBERRY RISE
16. PRIMROSE DR.

ELM GR.
OAKWOOD
PILGRIMS WAY
HAWTHORN
WILCOT
WILCOT CT.
WS.
SHAFTESBURY RD.
METHUSA WAY
SOUTH RD.
MAINS
Westend Common
LUCAS GREEN RD.
PRIEST LA.

Bullhousen Farm
Coldingley Prison
PORT WAY
QUEENS WAY
QUEENS RD.
SNOWDROP WAY
CLIFTON ROW
QUEENS WAY

ROAD
BAGSHOT ROAD
KILN LA.
The Fox (P.H.)
WOKING SURREY HEATH.
LIMECROFT RD.
Knaphill
CHOBHAM RD.
SURREY HEATH.
MAYTREES
SUSSEX
LANE END DR.
HIGHCLERE RD.
RAVENS
LARKSWAY
BARLEY MOW CL.
MEADOW RISE
CLERE GDNS.
WATERERS RISE
HILLSIDE
HIGHCLERE
P.O.
Lib.

Bisley Ranges
Bisley Common
B
Bisley Common
STAFFORD LANE
IVYDENE RD.
TRINITY RD.
Sch.
HIGH ST.
SUSSEX RD.
ALAN BROOKE
QUEEN'S RD.
POWDERHAM CT.
PARVELL RD.

Bisley Camp
Cowshot Common
Sheet's Heath
BENWELL RD.
THE RIDGEWAY
OAKWOOD GDNS.
THE SPUR
OAK RD.
SPARVELL RD.
Police Office
BIRDS GROVE
Cricket Grd.
Brookwood Hospital
A324

Tele. Ex.
The Lye
BROOKWOOD LYE RD.
64

BEECH GROVE
COOPERS HILL DR.
SLADE RD.
ROAD
BRUNSWICK CL.
LOOKSHOT
MANOR CRES.
HERONS MANOR
PLOVER LA.
Brookwood
Hill's Gdn.
ST. JOHNS CL.
RIVERSIDE CL.
CONNAUGHT CRES.
SHEET'S HEATH
P.O.
HEATH DR.
Brookwood Bridge
ROAD
LOCKSWOOD
WEST HILL CL.
Club House
BROOKWOOD

The Slade
CONNAUGHT
A324
CHURCH
BROOKWOOD STA.
PALES
West Hill
BAGSHOT

GOLE ROAD
B3012
Narrow Bridge
DAWNEY HILL
THE GARDENS
Memorial Grounds
CEMETERY LANE
Brookwood Cemetery
HEATH HOUSE RD.
ROUGH ROAD

VAPERY LA.
CATERHAM RD.
DAWNEY RD.
Pirbright Common
B3405
SCHOOL RD.
West Heath
CHURCH LANE
St. Michael
Hodge Brook
AV. DE CAGNEY
CEMETERY
The Cricketers (P.H.)
P.O.
CHAPEL LANE
Golf Course

Pirbright
GUILDFORD RD.
LANE
MILL LANE
White Hart Inn
Cove Bridge
Manor Fm.
RAPLEYS FIELD
COLLENS FIELD
Swallow Corner
BORNERS HEATH
GUILDFORD
ROWE
B3032
ROAD
WOKING GUILDFORD
THE FAIRWAY
STORRS LA.
LAWFORDS HILL RD.
A322
BERRY LA.
B3380
A324 ALDERSHOT RD.

D E F

CARTOGRAPHY BY PHILIP'S. COPYRIGHT REED INTERNATIONAL BOOKS LTD

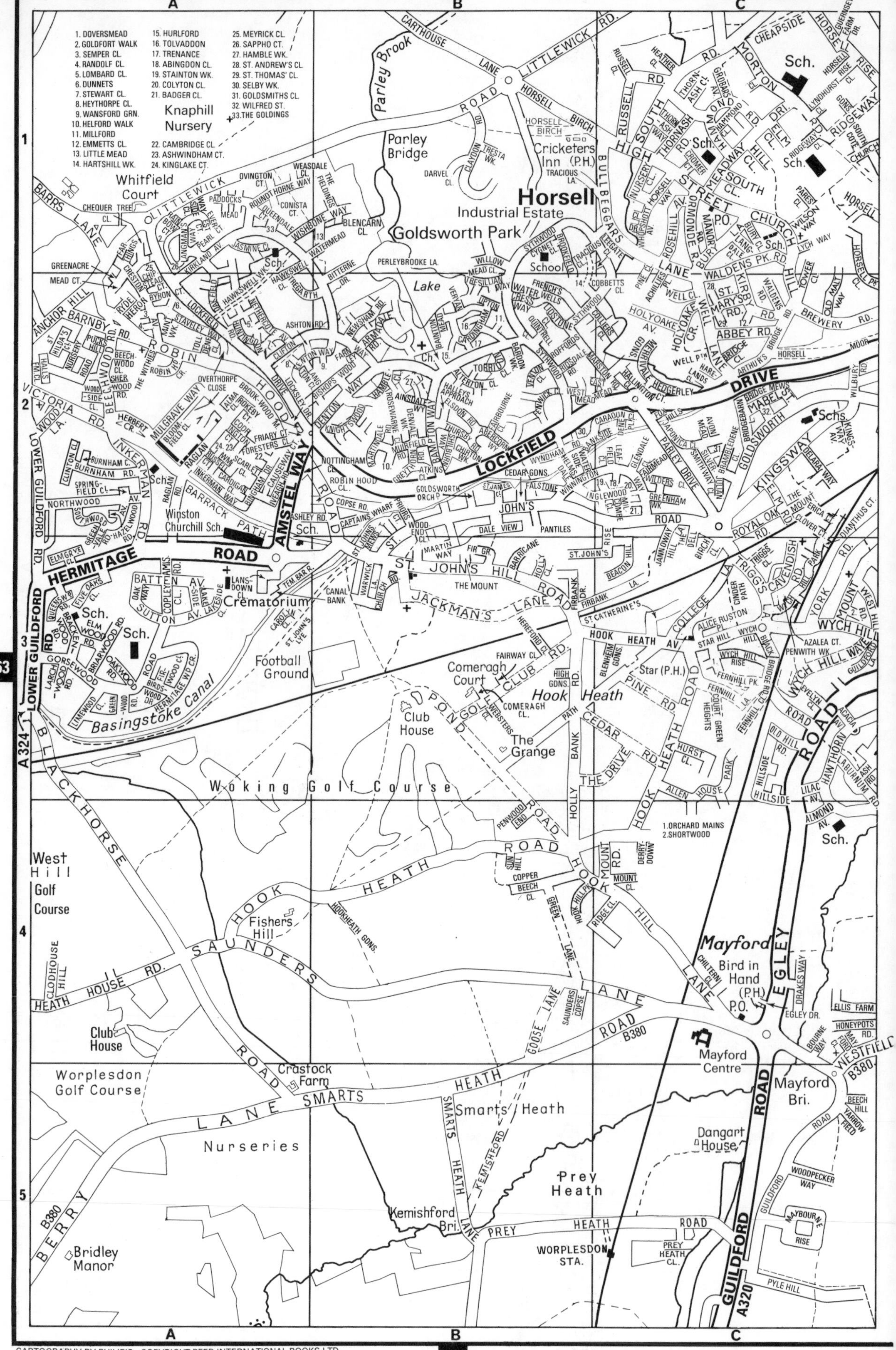

1. DOVERSMEAD
2. GOLDFORT WALK
3. SEMPER CL.
4. RANDOLF CL.
5. LOMBARD CL.
6. DUNNETS
7. STEWART CL.
8. HEYTHORPE CL.
9. WANSFORD GRN.
10. HELFORD WALK
11. MILLFORD
12. EMMETTS CL.
13. LITTLE MEAD
14. HARTSHILL WK.

15. HURLFORD
16. TOLVADDON
17. TRENANCE
18. ABINGDON CL.
19. STAINTON WK.
20. COLYTON CL.
21. BADGER CL.

22. CAMBRIDGE CL.
23. ASHWINDHAM CT.
24. KINGLAKE CT.

25. MEYRICK CL.
26. SAPPHO CT.
27. HAMBLE WK.
28. ST. ANDREW'S CL.
29. ST. THOMAS' CL.
30. SELBY WK.
31. GOLDSMITHS CL.
32. WILFRED ST.
33. THE GOLDINGS

Knaphill Nursery

Horsell
Horsell Industrial Estate
Goldsworth Park

Whitfield Court

Parley Bridge
Parley Brook

Cricketers Inn (P.H.)

Sch.

Lake

School

LOCKFIELD

AMSTEL WAY

HERMITAGE ROAD

Winston Churchill Sch.

Crematorium

Football Ground

Basingstoke Canal

Woking Golf Course

St. John's Hill
The Mount

Comeragh Court

Club House

Hook Heath

The Grange

Star (P.H.)

GOLDSWORTH ROAD

KINGSWAY

WYCH HILL

West Hill Golf Course

Club House

Fishers Hill

SAUNDERS ROAD

Worplesdon Golf Course

HEATH LANE
SMARTS

Crastock Farm

Nurseries

Smarts Heath

Mayford
Bird in Hand (P.H.)

Mayford Centre

Mayford Bri.

Dangart House

Prey Heath

Kemishford Bri.

WORPLESDON STA.

Bridley Manor

1. ORCHARD MAINS
2. SHORTWOOD

63
81

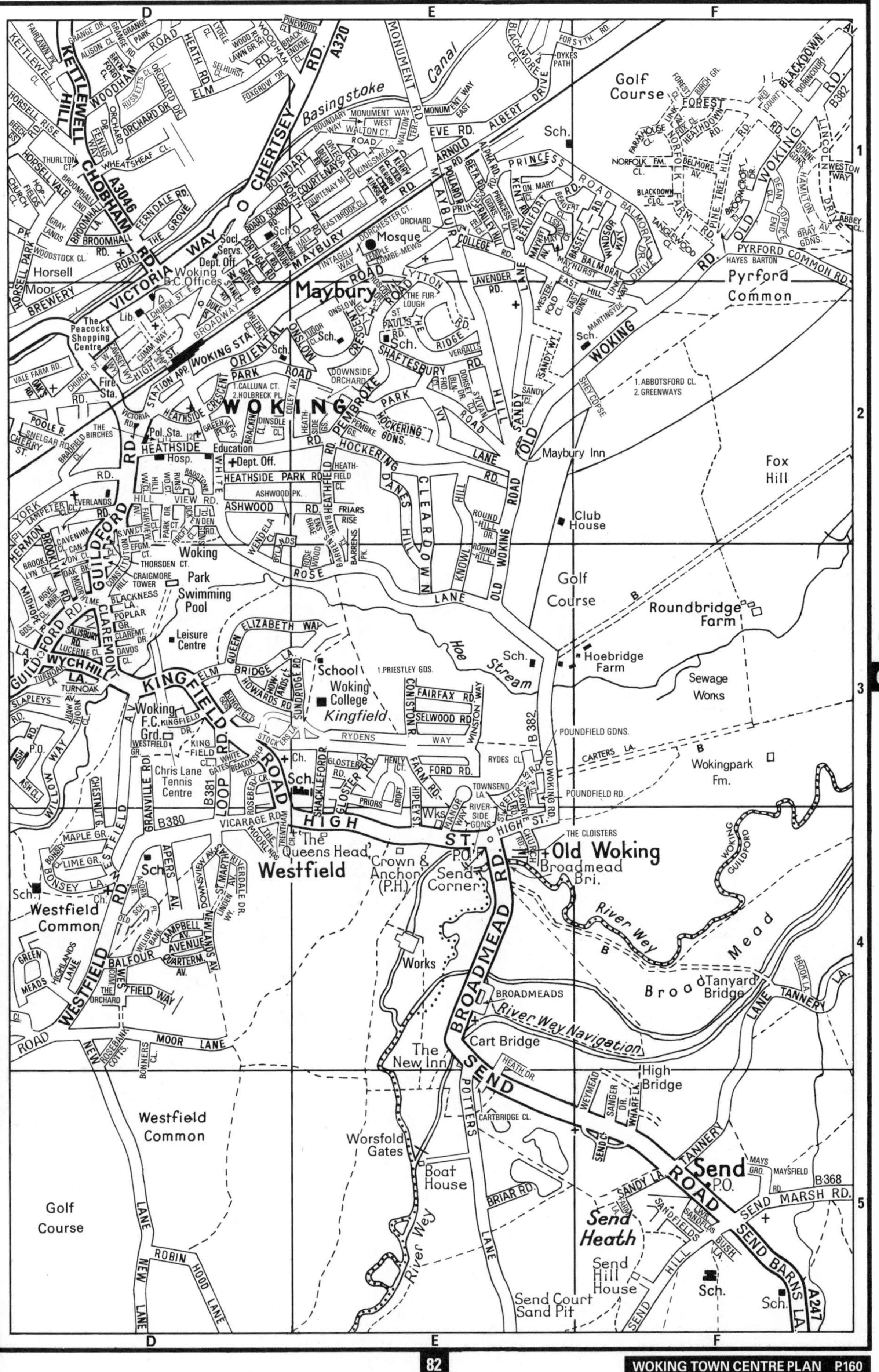

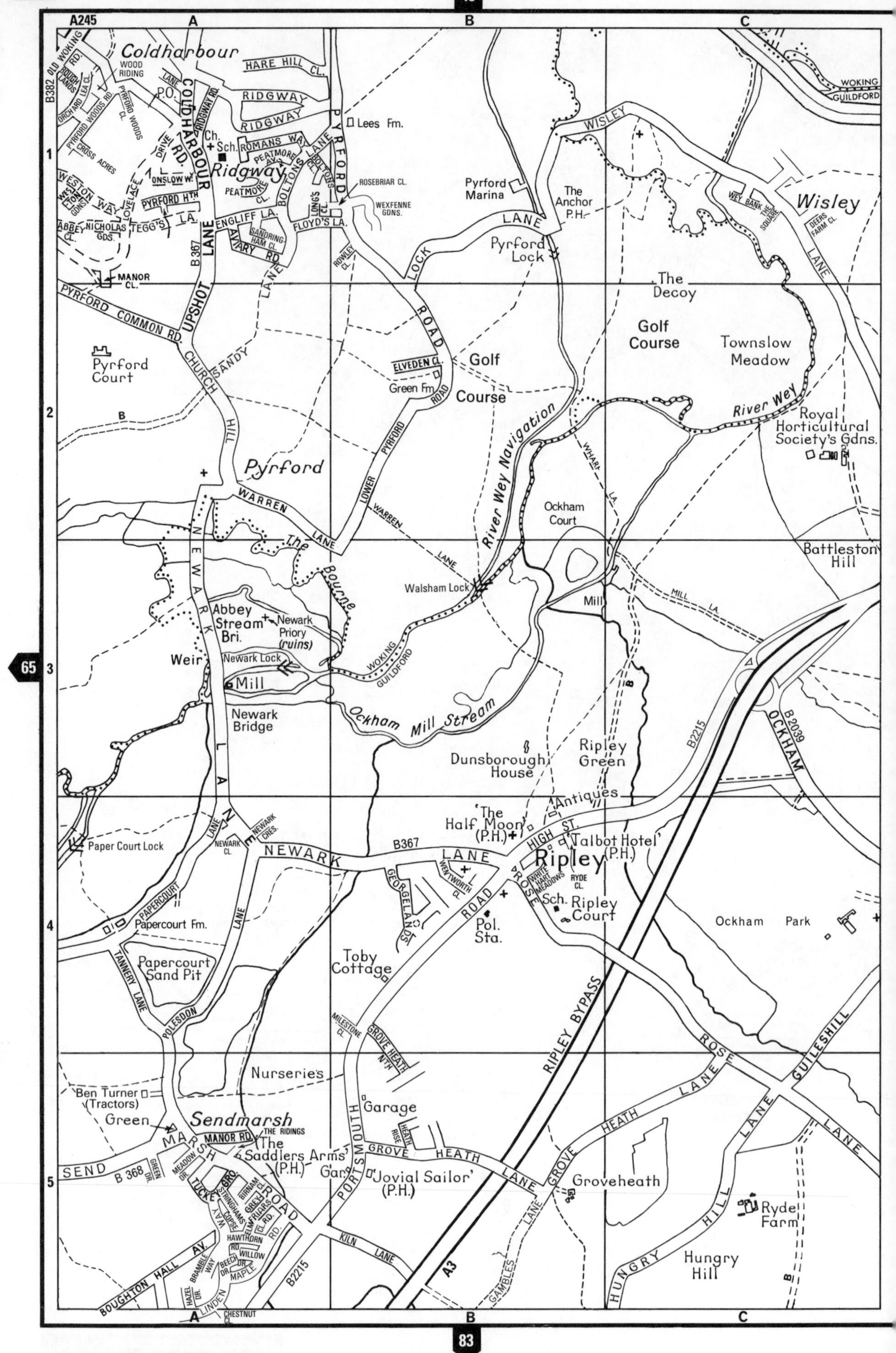
49
Coldharbour
Ridgway
Pyrford
Wisley
Pyrford Marina
The Anchor P.H.
Pyrford Lock
The Decoy
Golf Course
Townslow Meadow
Pyrford Court
Green Fm.
Royal Horticultural Society's Gdns.
River Wey Navigation
River Wey
Ockham Court
Battleston Hill
Walsham Lock
Mill
The Bourne
Abbey Stream Bri.
Newark Priory (ruins)
Weir
Newark Lock
Newark Bridge
Ockham Mill Stream
Dunsborough House
Ripley Green
Antiques
'The Half Moon' (P.H.)
'Talbot Hotel' (P.H.)
Ripley
Sch.
Ripley Court
Pol. Sta.
Ockham Park
Paper Court Lock
Papercourt Fm.
Papercourt Sand Pit
Toby Cottage
Nurseries
Ben Turner (Tractors)
Green
Sendmarsh
Garage
The Saddlers Arms' (P.H.)
'Jovial Sailor' (P.H.)
Groveheath
Ryde Farm
Hungry Hill
RIPLEY BYPASS
A3
B367
B2215
B2039
B 368
83
65

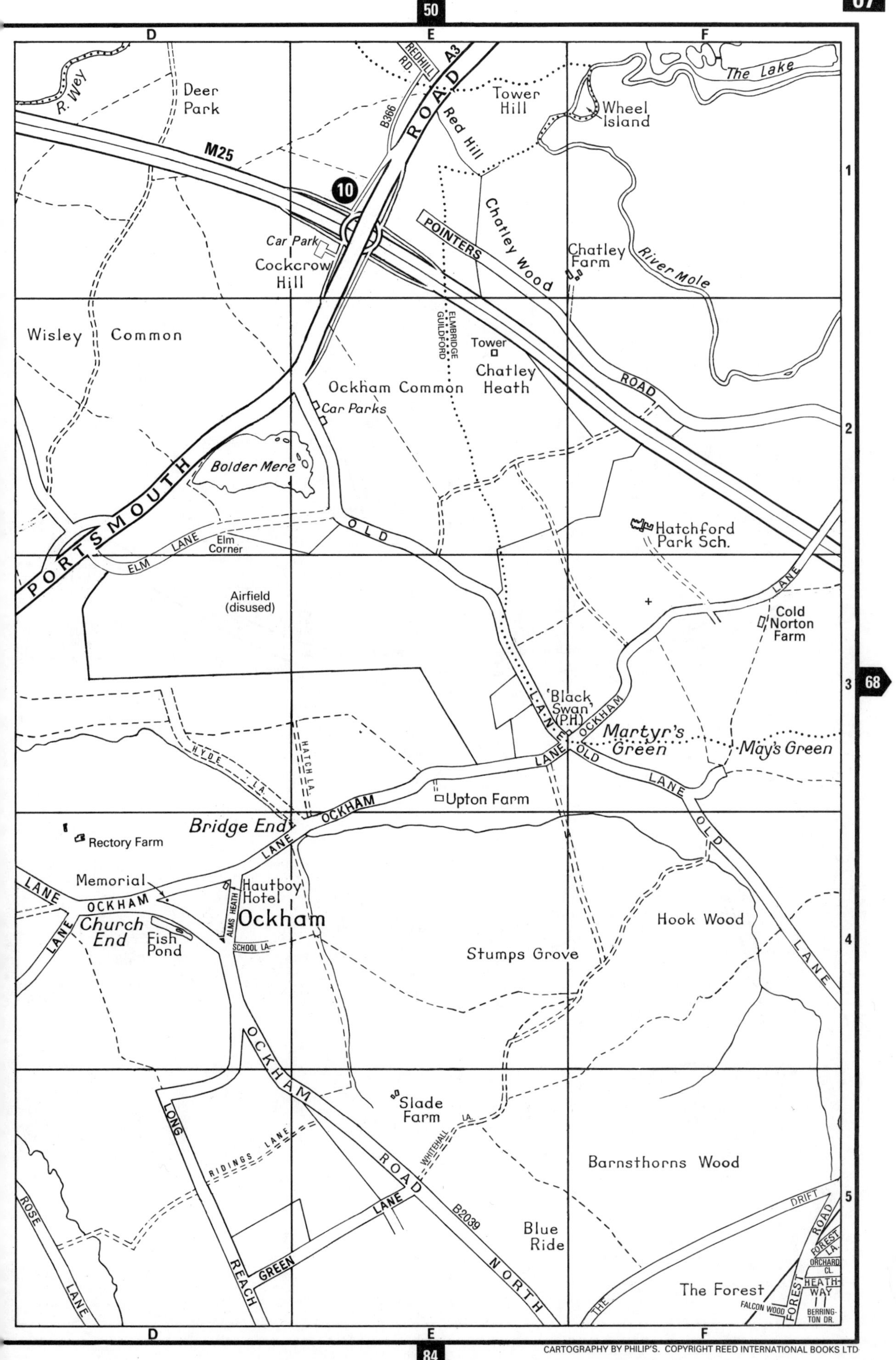

D

E

A3

F

R. Wey

Deer Park

The Lake

M25

REDHILL RD

Tower Hill

Wheel Island

ROAD

Red Hill

River Mole

10

Chatley Wood

Chatley Farm

1

Car Park

POINTERS

Cockcrow Hill

B366

Chatley Heath

Wisley Common

ELMBRIDGE GUILDFORD

Tower

ROAD

Ockham Common

Car Parks

2

Bolder Mere

OLD

Hatchford Park Sch.

PORTSMOUTH

ELM   LANE

Elm Corner

LANE

Cold Norton Farm

Airfield (disused)

+

3   68

'Black Swan' (P.H.)

Martyr's Green

May's Green

LANE

OCKHAM

OLD

HYDE LA.

HATCH LA.

LANE

LANE

Upton Farm

Bridge End

OCKHAM

Rectory Farm

Hook Wood

LANE

Memorial

ADAMS HEATH

Hautboy Hotel

OCKHAM

LANE

Ockham

Stumps Grove

4

Church End

Fish Pond

SCHOOL LA.

OCKHAM

LANE

ROAD

Slade Farm

WHITEHALL LA.

Barnsthorns Wood

DRIFT

LONG

RIDINGS LANE

ROAD

FOREST

5

ROSE   LANE

GREEN

REACH   LANE

LANE

B2039

NORTH

Blue Ride

THE

The Forest

FOREST LA.

ORCHARD CL.

HEATH WAY

FALCON WOOD

FOREST ROAD

BERRINGTON DR.

D

E

F

51

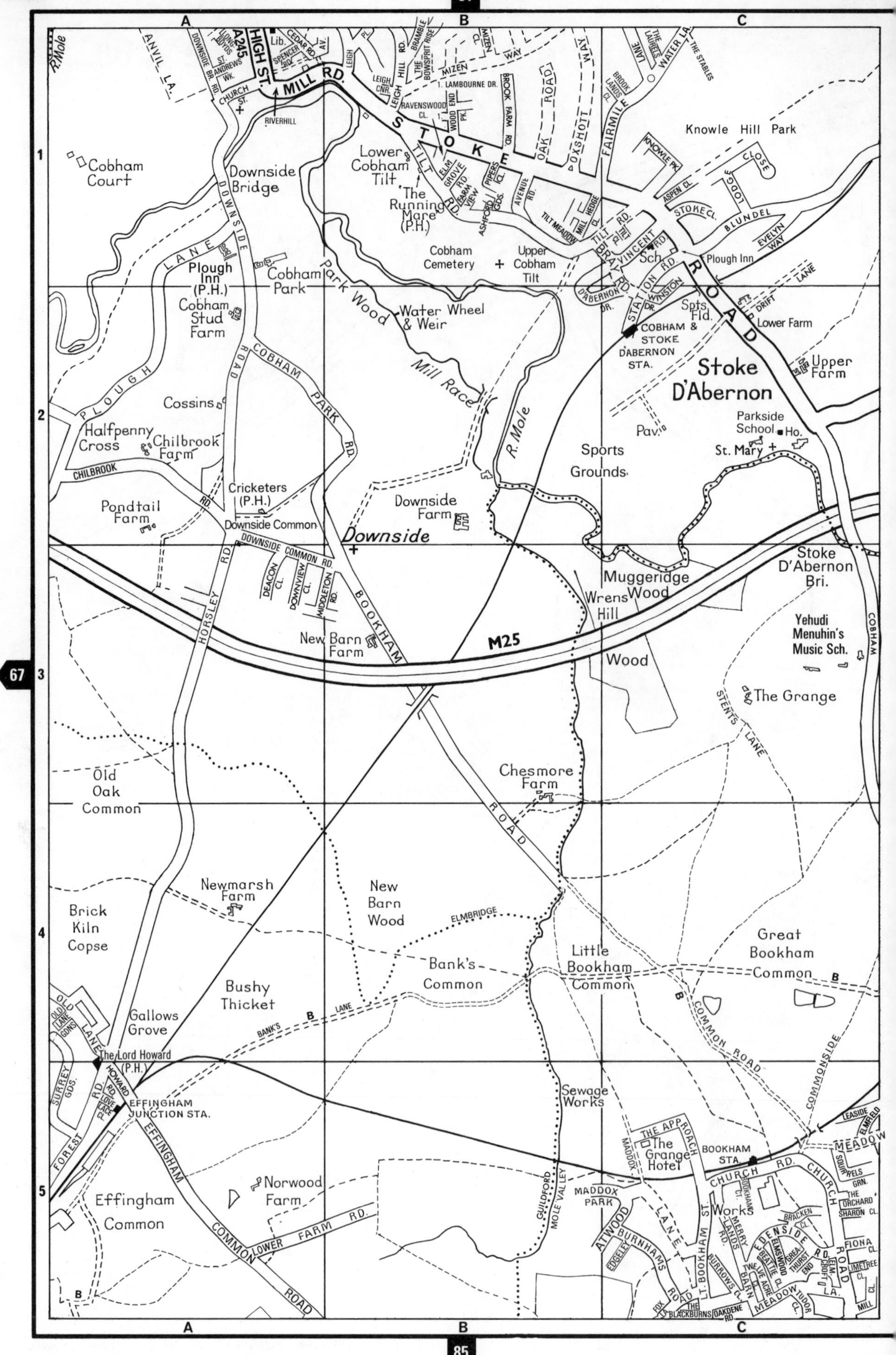
Cobham Court
Downside Bridge
Lower Cobham Tilt
The Running Mare (P.H.)
Cobham Cemetery
Upper Cobham Tilt
Knowle Hill Park
Plough Inn (P.H.)
Cobham Park
Cobham Stud Farm
Park Wood
Water Wheel & Weir
Mill Race
COBHAM & STOKE D'ABERNON STA.
Stoke D'Abernon
Lower Farm
Upper Farm
Cossins
Halfpenny Cross
Chilbrook Farm
Parkside School
St. Mary
Sports Grounds
Pav.
Cricketers (P.H.)
Pondtail Farm
Downside Common
Downside Farm
Downside
Muggeridge Wood
Wrens Hill
Stoke D'Abernon Bri.
Yehudi Menuhin's Music Sch.
New Barn Farm
M25
Wood
The Grange
Old Oak Common
Chesmore Farm
Newmarsh Farm
New Barn Wood
Brick Kiln Copse
Bank's Common
Little Bookham Common
Great Bookham Common
Bushy Thicket
Gallows Grove
The Lord Howard (P.H.)
EFFINGHAM JUNCTION STA.
Sewage Works
The Grange Hotel
BOOKHAM STA.
Norwood Farm
Effingham Common
MADDOX PARK
Works
HIGH ST.
A245
MILL RD.
STOKE ROAD
DOWNSIDE RD.
PLOUGH LANE
COBHAM PARK RD.
BOOKHAM ROAD
HORSLEY RD.
CHILBROOK RD.
DOWNSIDE COMMON RD.
STENTS LANE
COMMON ROAD
COMMONSIDE
EFFINGHAM COMMON ROAD
LOWER FARM RD.
BANK'S LANE
ELMBRIDGE
GUILDFORD
MOLE VALLEY
CHURCH RD.
EDENSIDE ROAD
LT. BOOKHAM ST.
MADDOX LANE
ANVIL LA.
R. Mole
FAIRMILE LANE
OXSHOTT WAY
OAK ROAD
STATION RD.
BLUNDEL LANE
DRIFT LANE
EVELYN WAY
COBHAM

67

85

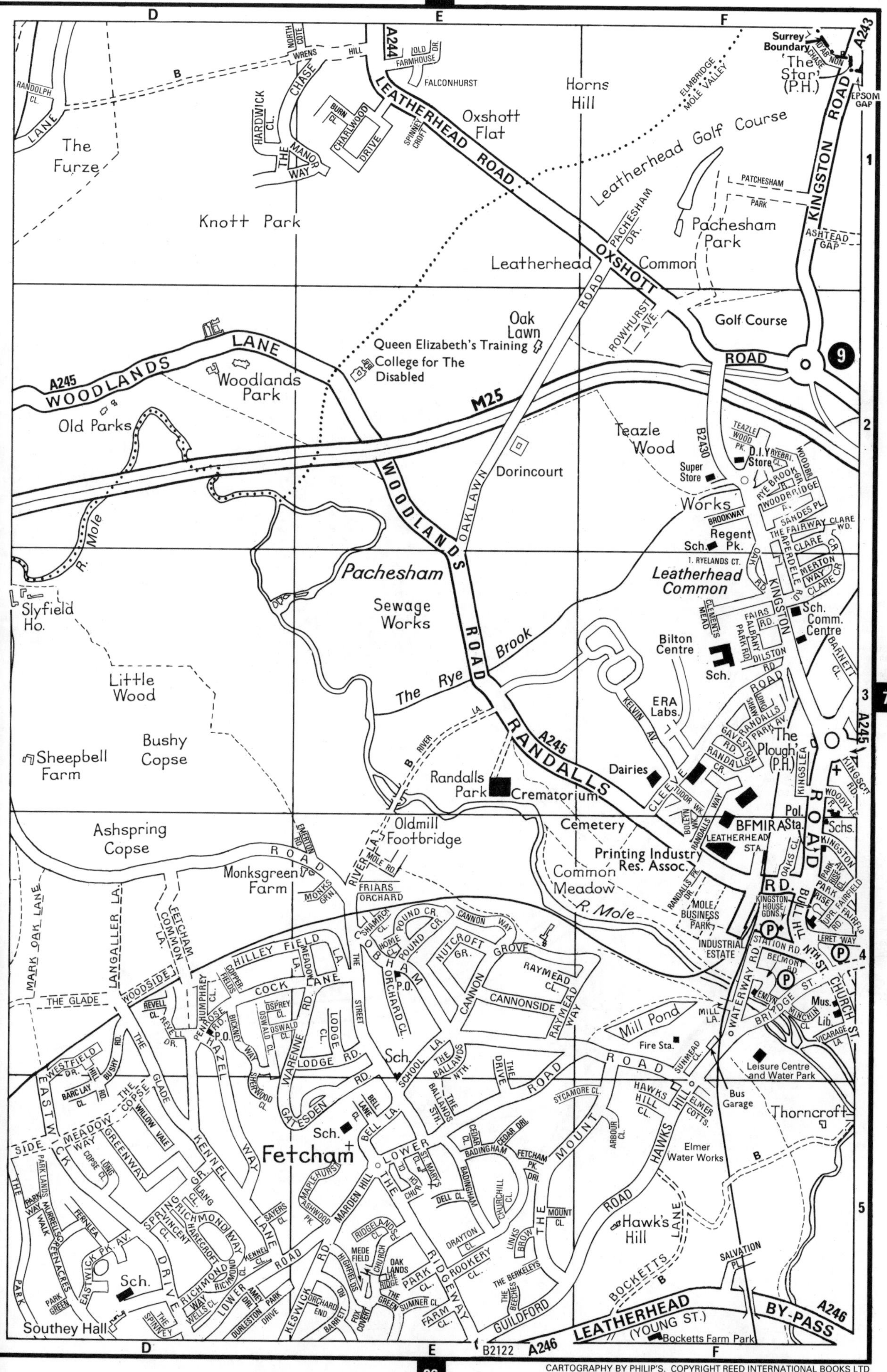

CARTOGRAPHY BY PHILIP'S. COPYRIGHT REED INTERNATIONAL BOOKS LTD

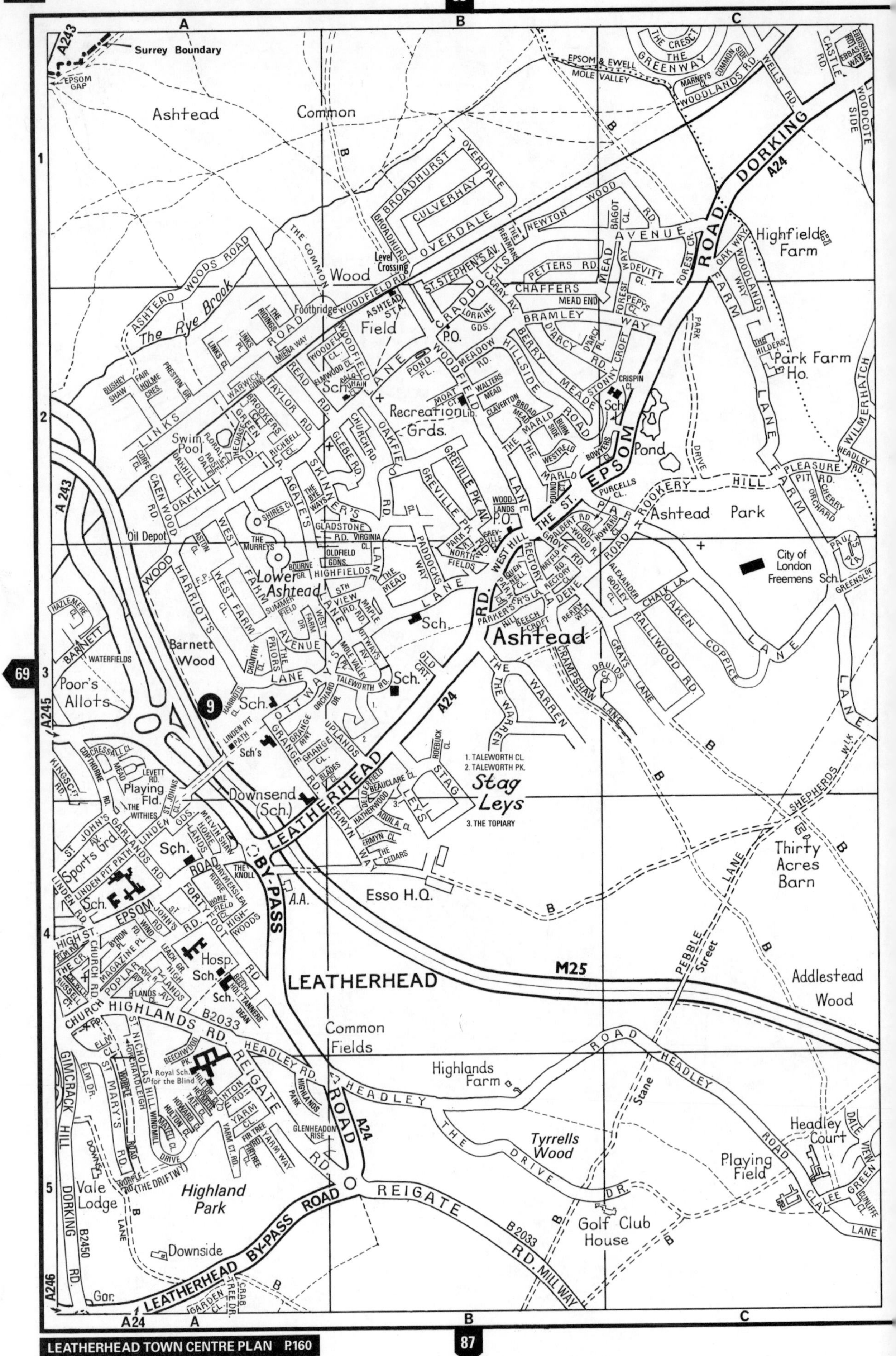
53
A
B
C
1
2
3
4
5
69
87
Surrey Boundary
EPSOM GAP
A243
Ashtead
Common
Wood
Level Crossing
Footbridge
ASHTEAD STA.
Field
The Rye Brook
ASHTEAD WOODS ROAD
THE COMMON
WOODFIELD RD.
BROADHURST
OVERDALE
CULVERHAY
NEWTON WOOD RD.
AVENUE
BAGOT CL.
MEAD
DEVITT CL.
PETTERS RD.
CHAFFERS
MEAD END
BRAMLEY
WAY
PEPYS CL.
FOREST WAY
FOREST CR.
CRADDOCKS
ST. STEPHEN'S AV.
GRAY AV.
LORAINE GDS.
P.O.
Sch.
Recreation Grds.
Lib.
Pond
Swim Pool
LINKS RD.
TAYLOR RD.
READ RD.
OAKHILL
CAEN WOOD RD.
Oil Depot
WEST FARM AV.
Lower Ashtead
HARRIOT'S LA.
Barnett Wood
WATERFIELDS
Poor's Allots
A245
A 243
HIGHFIELDS
SKINNER'S LANE
AGATE'S LANE
GLADSTONE RD.
OTTWAY'S LA.
TALEWORTH RD.
GREVILLE PK. AV.
PADDOCKS WAY
PARK LANE
WEST HILL
RECTORY LA.
THE ST.
EPSOM
DORKING
ROAD
A24
Highfield Farm
FARM LANE
Park Farm Ho.
WILMERHATCH
PLEASURE PIT RD.
ROOKERY HILL
Ashtead Park
City of London Freemens Sch.
ALEXANDER GODLEY CL.
CHALK LA.
OAKEN COPPICE
RALLIWOOD RD.
GRAYS LANE
Ashtead
CRAMPSHAW LANE
DRUIDS CL.
THE WARREN
STAG LEYS
Stag Leys
1. TALEWORTH CL.
2. TALEWORTH PK.
3. THE TOPIARY
ROEBUCK CL.
LEATHERHEAD RD.
Downsend (Sch.)
Sch's
Playing Fld.
Sports Grd.
Sch.
BY-PASS
A.A.
Esso H.Q.
M25
SHEPHERDS WLK.
Thirty Acres Barn
PEBBLE LANE
Street
Addlestead Wood
LEATHERHEAD
Hosp.
Common Fields
HIGHLANDS RD.
B2033
CHURCH RD.
HIGH ST.
REIGATE RD.
HEADLEY RD.
Royal Sch. for the Blind
Highlands Farm
HEADLEY ROAD
Stane
THE DRIVE
Tyrrells Wood
Golf Club House
Headley Court
Playing Field
CLAY LANE
GIMCRACK HILL
DORKING RD.
B2450
Vale Lodge
Highland Park
Downside
LEATHERHEAD BY-PASS ROAD
A246
A24
Gor.
MILL WAY
B

Woodcote

Epsom Dist. Hosp.
Sports Grds.
The Durdans
Berkeley Pl.
Sanatorium
Club Ho.
Stables
Stables
Stables
EPSOM DOWNS STA.

REIGATE
A240 ROAD
YEW TREE BOTTOM RD.

Fish Ponds
Tennis Courts
Woodcote Park (R.A.C.) (Club Ho.)
Golf Course
Golf Course
Buckle's Gap
Grandstand
The Rubbing House (P.H.)
Grandstand

EPSOM RACE COURSE
Epsom Downs
Metropolitan Course
Tattenham Corner
Tattenham Corner Sta.

The Hill
Oaks Way

Fairways
Spindles
Little Copse
Spinneys
Meridian
Langley Bottom Wood
Racing Stables
"Derby" Start

Sch.
P.O.
Langley Vale
The Warren
Rec. Grd.

Walton Downs

Langley Bottom Farm

South Tadworth Farm

Pit Wood
Football Ground
Community Centre
Sports Centre

1. BRIER RD.
2. MALLOW CL.
3. GORSE CL.
4. CAMPION DRIVE
5. LORDSGROVE CL.

1. THE KNOWLE

Gilletts Cottages
Nohome Farm
Downs View Wood

Shelvers Hill
Kingswood Road

Tadworth
TADWORTH STA.
THE AVENUE
P.O.

Little Hurst Wood
Round Wood

Fourfield Close
The Hurst

Rough Dale
St. Cross
Withybed Corner
Pond
NEW RD.
B290

M25
Headley Park
Hook Wood
Great Hurst Wood
Sandhill Wood

Walton
Blue Ball (P.H.)
MEADOW WALK

△ 612 ft.

CARTOGRAPHY BY PHILIP'S. COPYRIGHT REED INTERNATIONAL BOOKS LTD

BANSTEAD

Park Wood

Nork

Great Burgh

Nork Park

Tumble Beacon

Tattenham Way Rec. Grd.

Council Offices

CHIPSTEAD

Wood Lodge

Canons Wood

Ruffett Wood

Holly Hill

New Place

Little Haugh

Park Downs

Merton

Belvedere Ho.

Banstead Place

Apsley

Cricket Grd

Rosehill Farm Meadow

Hosp.

'Surrey Yeoman' (P.H.)

1. Broome Court
2. Gardenfields
3. Tinefields

Council Depot.

The Queen Elizabeth Hospital for Children

Banstead Wood

Perrotts Farm

Lunch Wood

Fames Rough

Pond Burgh Heath

Burgh Heath

REST LA.

READS REST LA.

Chipstead Bottom

Chiphouse Wood

Garden Farm

Furze Hill

'Kingswood Arms' (P.H.)

'Red Ho. Arms' (P.H.)

Tadworth Court Hosp

Out Wood

Kingswood Sta.

WATERHOUSE LANE

THE OUTWOOD LANE

Eyhurst Farm

Eyhurst Court

Longcroft Shaw

Farm

Banstead Newton

Kingswood Warren Res. Centre

Tadorne

The Warren

Avalon

Club Ho.

Kingswood Golf Course

Morrey Shaw

'Blue Anchor' (P.H.)

Car Park

Northfield Shaw

Westfield Shaw

Kingswood

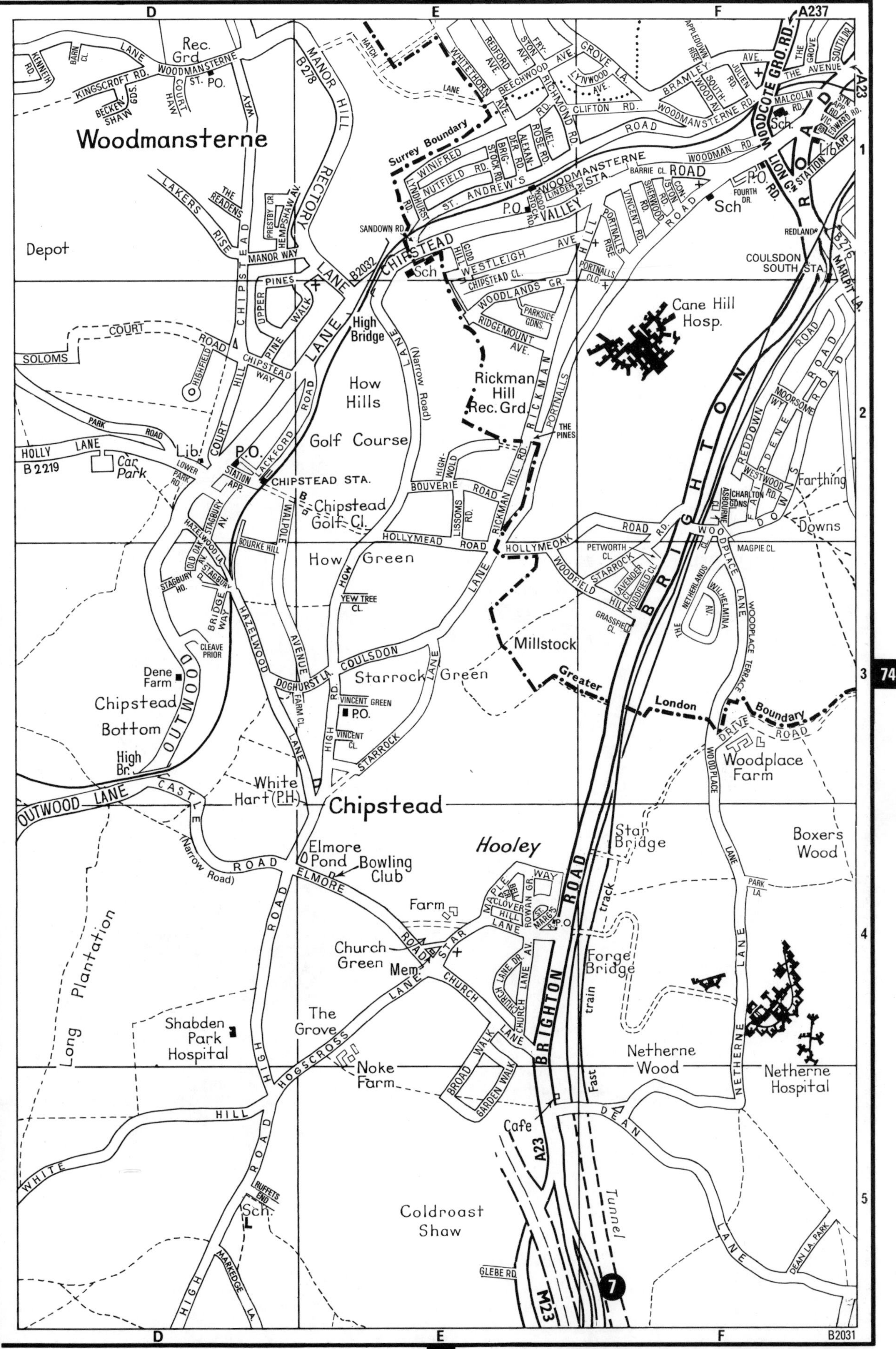

56
Woodmansterne
Rec. Grd
Depot
Surrey Boundary
Cane Hill Hosp.
Coulsdon South Sta.
How Hills
Golf Course
Chipstead Sta.
Chipstead Golf Cl.
How Green
Rickman Hill Rec. Grd.
Millstock
Starrock Green
Greater London Boundary
Chipstead Bottom
Dene Farm
White Hart (P.H.)
Chipstead
Hooley
Elmore Pond
Bowling Club
Star Bridge
Woodplace Farm
Farthing Downs
Boxers Wood
Church Green
The Grove
Shabden Park Hospital
Noke Farm
Long Plantation
Forge Bridge
Netherne Wood
Netherne Hospital
Coldroast Shaw
Brighton Road
Outwood Lane
Hazelwood Lane
Rickman Hill Rd.
Woodmansterne Road
Chipstead Valley Road
Woodplace Lane
Netherne Lane
Dean Lane
High Road
Hogscross Lane
Elmore Road
Castle Road
White Hill
Holly Lane
Hollymead Road
Coulsdon Lane
Starrock Lane
A23
M23
Fast train track
Tunnel
Cafe
74
90

57

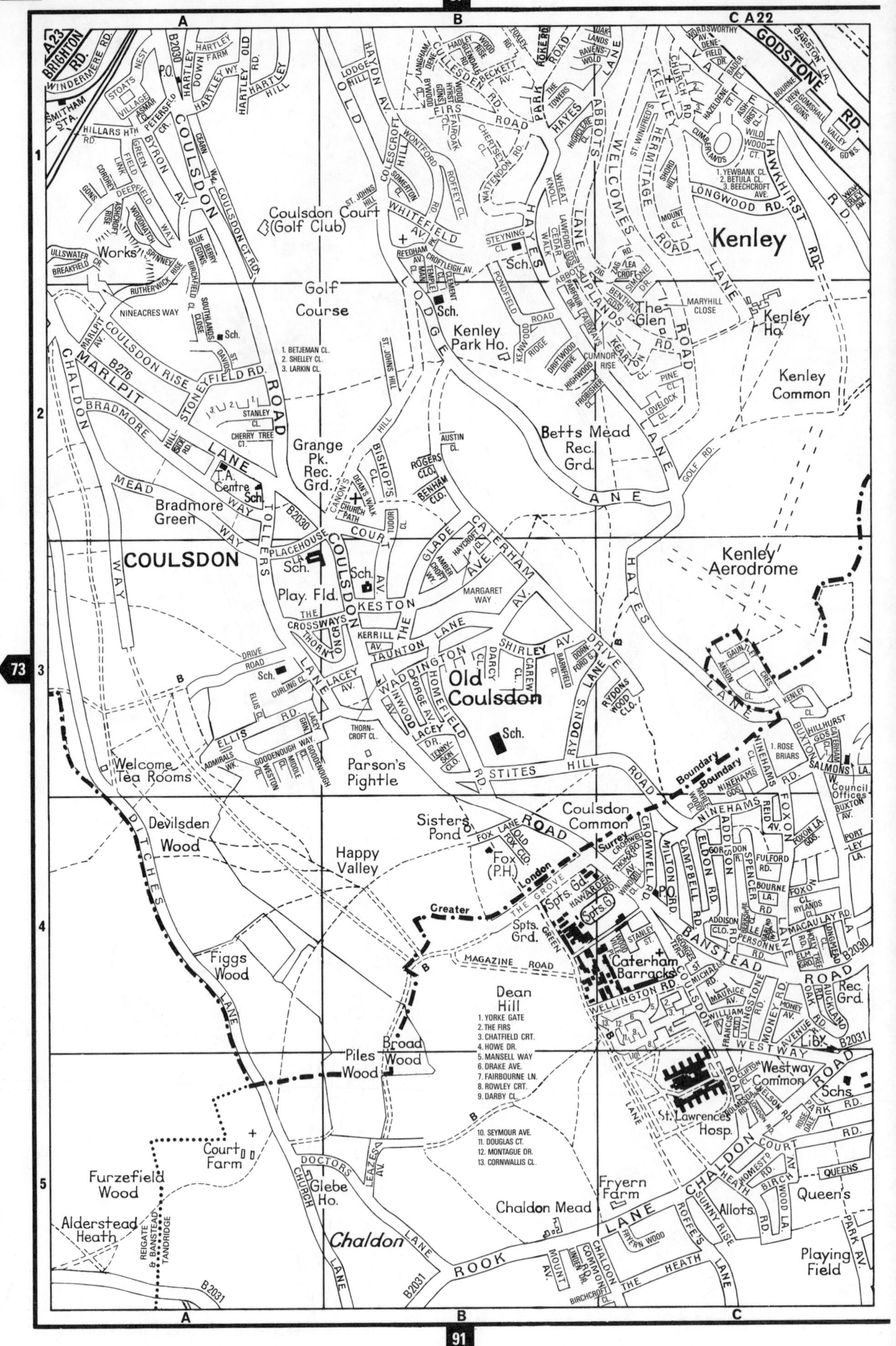
Kenley
Golf Course
Coulsdon Court (Golf Club)
Kenley Park Ho.
Kenley Common
Kenley Ho.
Betts Mead Rec. Grd.
Grange Pk. Rec. Grd.
Bradmore Green
COULSDON
Kenley Aerodrome
Old Coulsdon
Play. Fld.
Parson's Pightle
Welcome Tea Rooms
Devilsden Wood
Happy Valley
Sisters Pond
Coulsdon Common
Fox (P.H.)
Figgs Wood
Dean Hill
Caterham Barracks
Piles Wood
Broad Wood
Court Farm
Furzefield Wood
Alderstead Heath
Glebe Ho.
Chaldon
Chaldon Mead
Fryern Farm
St. Lawrence's Hosp.
Westway Common
Allots.
Queen's
Playing Field
Boundary
Greater London
Surrey
Works
Sch.
Schs.
Lib.
Rec. Grd.
Council Offices
T.A. Centre
SMITHAM STA.
BRIGHTON RD.
GODSTONE RD.
COULSDON RD.
MARLPIT LANE
CHALDON WAY
DITCHES LANE
CATERHAM DRIVE
STITES HILL RD.
BANSTEAD ROAD
ROOK LANE
HAYES LANE
WELCOMES ROAD
KENLEY LANE
HAWKHIRST RD.
LODGE LANE
1. BETJEMAN CL.
2. SHELLEY CL.
3. LARKIN CL.
1. YEWBANK CL.
2. BETULA CL.
3. BEECHCROFT AVE.
1. ROSE BRIARS
1. YORKE GATE
2. THE FIRS
3. CHATFIELD CRT.
4. HOWE DR.
5. MANSELL WAY
6. DRAKE AVE.
7. FAIRBOURNE LN.
8. ROWLEY CRT.
9. DARBY CL.
10. SEYMOUR AVE.
11. DOUGLAS CT.
12. MONTAGUE DR.
13. CORNWALLIS CL.
REIGATE & BANSTEAD
TANDRIDGE
A23
A22
B2030
B2031
B276

73

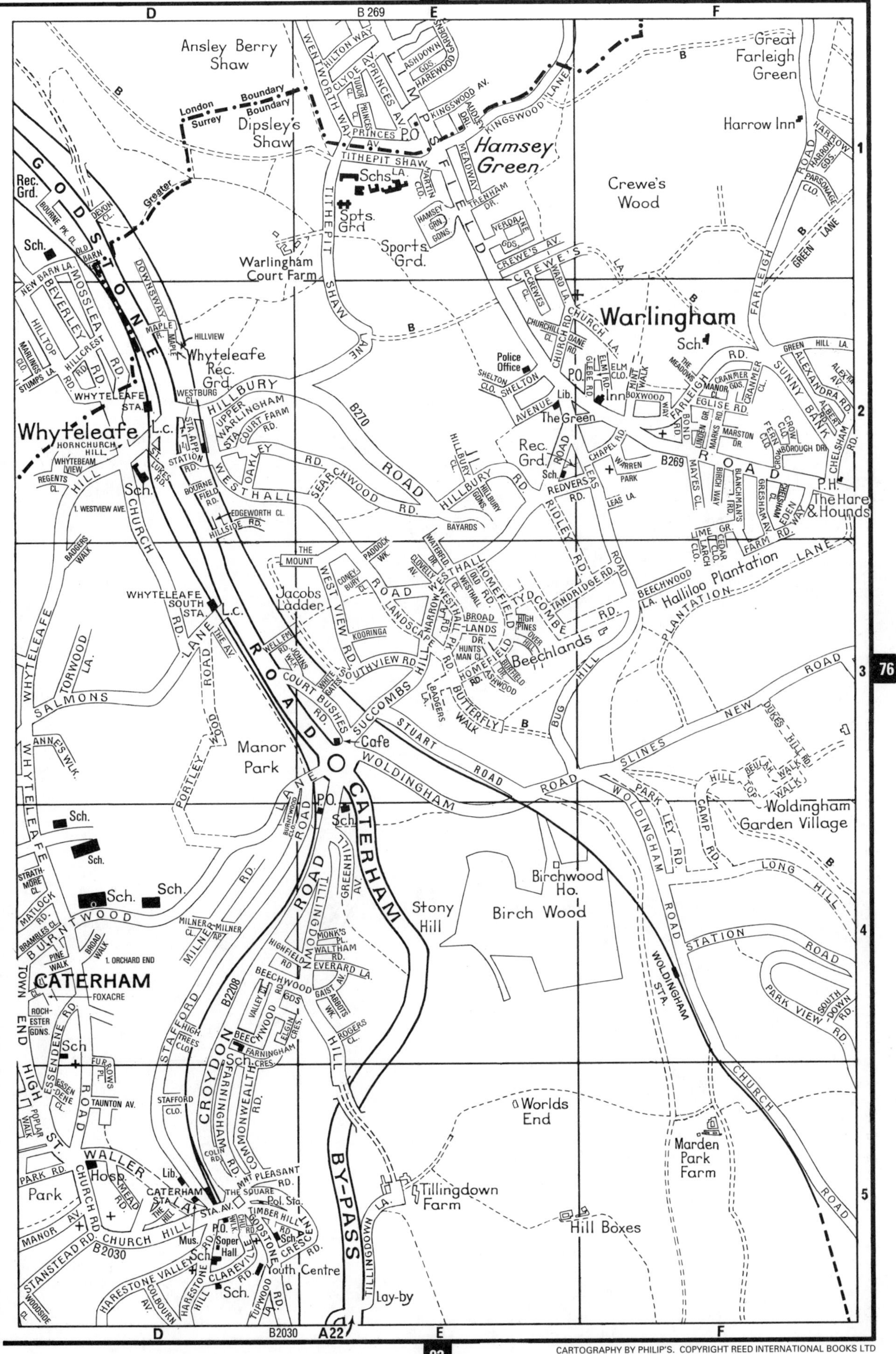

CARTOGRAPHY BY PHILIP'S. COPYRIGHT REED INTERNATIONAL BOOKS LTD

75

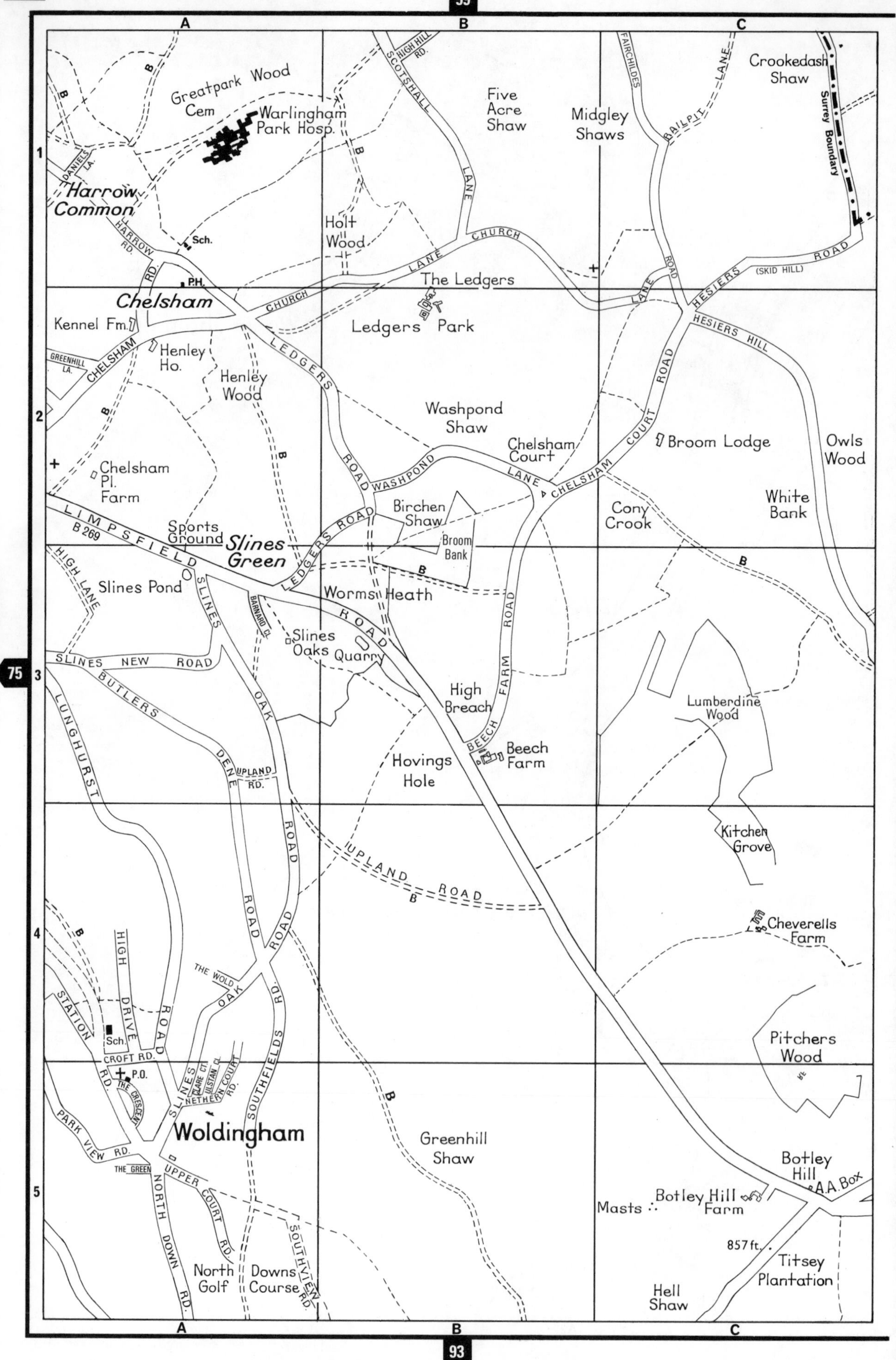

A — B — C

1

Greatpark Wood
Cem
Warlingham
Park Hosp.

Five
Acre
Shaw

Midgley
Shaws

Crookedash
Shaw

Surrey Boundary

*Harrow
Common*

Holt
Wood

SCOTSHALL LANE

HIGH HILL RD.

FAIRCHILDES LANE

BAILPIT LANE

The Ledgers

CHURCH LANE

(SKID HILL)

HESIERS ROAD

Sch.

P.H.

Chelsham

Kennel Fm.

DANIELS LA.

HARROW RD.

GREENHILL LA.

Chelsham LA.

Henley
Ho.

Henley
Wood

LEDGERS

Ledgers Park

CHURCH

HESIERS HILL

2

Washpond
Shaw

Chelsham
Court

CHELSHAM COURT ROAD

Broom Lodge

Owls
Wood

Chelsham Pl.
Farm

ROAD

WASHPOND LANE

Birchen
Shaw

Broom
Bank

Cony
Crook

White
Bank

LIMPSFIELD
B 269

Sports
Ground

*Slines
Green*

LEDGERS ROAD

Wormsy Heath

HIGH LANE

Slines Pond

SLINES

Slines
Oaks Quarry

BARNARD CL.

FARM ROAD

75 3

SLINES NEW ROAD

BUTLERS

DENE

OAK ROAD

UPLAND RD.

High
Breach

BEECH

Beech
Farm

Lumberdine
Wood

LUNGHURST

Hovings
Hole

Kitchen
Grove

4

HIGH DRIVE

THE WOLD

OAK ROAD

SOUTHFIELDS RD.

UPLAND ROAD

Cheverells
Farm

Pitchers
Wood

STATION RD.

Sch.

CROFT RD.

P.O.

THE CRESCENT

SLINES

CLARE CT.

TRISTAN CT.

NETHERN COURT RD.

Greenhill
Shaw

PARK VIEW RD.

Woldingham

THE GREEN

UPPER COURT RD.

NORTH DOWN RD.

SOUTHVIEW RD.

Botley
Hill
A.A.Box

5

North
Golf

Downs
Course

Masts

Botley Hill
Farm

857 ft.

Hell
Shaw

Titsey
Plantation

A — B — C

BIGGIN HILL
AIRFIELD

Skid Hill
House

Leasons
Wood

CROSSLEY CL.
HAWTHORN AV.
DOWDING RD.
JAIL
SOPWITH

BLACKTHORN RD.

MAGNOLIA DR.
ACER RD.
SPRUCE RD.
Cem

KINGSMEAD

Biggin
Hill
F.S.

OLD TYE AV.

JAIL LANE

LANE

Mollards
Wood

Sch.
GDNS
VICTORIA GDNS
SUNNINGVALE
CHRISTY RD.
ARTHUR RD.
CAMELOT RD.
LAMBERT CL.
MELROSE RD.
JUG HILL
LUNAR CL.

VIEW CL.
GRAND VW.
AV.
HIGHFIELD
LANE
KINGS ROAD
CHALLOCK CL.
P.O.
Roundway
SUNNINGVALE
STOCK HILL
CREST RD.
POLES HILL
MERRY HILL RD.
MT. PLEASANT
RUSHGROVE WK.
MT. PLEASANT
DAWELL DR.

CHURCH
THE RIDINGS
ALLENBY ROAD
NELSON RD.
MALAN CL.
FOX RD.
SUTHERLAND GDNS
LEBANON GDNS
HAIG AV.

APERFIELD RD.
JUNIPER CL.
VILLAGE GREEN AV.

Aperfield

CHERRY TREE WK.
NORHEADS LANE
BEECH ROAD
KINGS
SPRING RD.
KEMBLE SIDE RD.
ILLINGSDALE RD.
HILL MELODY
SCARBOROUGH DR.
SPRINGHAM
UPPER
 ROAD
WAKELY RD.
WOOD RD.
ST. MARY'S
GREENWAY RD.
ROSE AV.
ROSE HILL
TREE BOURNE RD.
TIMBERTOP RD.
STEEPLE HEIGHTS
CHARLTON
EVER GLADE
VALLEY RD.
POLES LANE
LILLIE RD.
AVENUE
ROAD
HALL
THE RICKETTS
EAGLES DR.
LUSTED LANE

MOSELLE RD.
EDWARD RD.
EARL RD.
BELVEDERE RD.
WOOD RD.
ST. WINIFRED RD.
CLARENCE RD.
AVENUE
WOODSIDE RD.
BURY RD.
WOODSY RD.

Westerham
Hill

Fox & Hounds
Inn

P.O.

WESTERHAM ROAD

South
Street

A233

ALEXANDRA RD.
RICHMOND RD.
FILEY CL.
SWEVELANDS
BRIDLINGTON
1. FLAMBOROUGH CL.

LUSTED HALL LANE

Lusted
Hall
Farm

Greater London Boundary
Surrey Boundary

RD.
ROAD
HILL ROAD
GROVE ROAD

CUDHAM RD.

B

BEDDLESTEAD

Tatsfield

GOATSFIELD RD.
SHAW RD.
GREENWAY
KEMSLEY
JOHN'S RD.
GEORGES RD.
CROSSWAYS

Manor
Ho.

MANOR ROAD
CUDHAM RD.
AVENUE RD.

Surrey Boundary

Greater
London Boundary
TATSFIELD LANE

PALACE RD.
THE AVENUE

WHITE COTTAGES
GROVE RD.
RED HOUSE
WESTMORE RD.
PAYNESFIELD RD.
THE SQUARE
RAYNESFIELD
GRANGEFIELD
OLD LANE
RICKETTS HILL RD.
RAG HILL RD.
RAG HILL CL.
Fm.

RAG HILL
PARKWOOD RD.

Kent Boundary

CHESTNUT AV.

CROYDON ROAD

Westmore
Green
P.O.
WEDGEWOODS
The Old Ship
(P.H.)
THE SHIP
NINEHAMS
MAESMAUR RD.
EDGAR RD.
BOROUGH HILL

Sch.

Furze Corner

ROAD
APPROACH
CLARKS
LANE
Width restriction

B

CHESTNUT AV.
THE AVENUE

B2024
CLARKS
TITSEY
LANE
LANE
HILL
B269
WHITE

CHURCH HILL
LANE

RECTORY LA.

Tatsfield
Court
Farm

PILGRIMS LANE

B

Titsey
Place

Pilgrims'
Farm

(PILGRIMS LANE)

CLACKETTS LANE

B2024

not continued, see key diagram

A B C

not continued, see key diagram

Airfield

Tech. Coll.

King George V Playing Field

BOUNDARY RD.

CANTERBURY

Aircraft Esplanade

South Farnborough

THE GROVE

FELLOWS RD.

WHITE'S RD.

SOUTH ST.

READING

CAMBRIDGE

ALEXANDRA RD.

ALBERT RD.

FARNBOROUGH ROAD

LYNCHFORD ROAD

Sewage Disposal

Level Crossing

STRATFORD RD.

FRIMLEY RD.

MYTCHETT RD.

Camping Grd.

Mytchett Place

Mytchett Lake

Keogh Barracks

Furze Hill

Keogh

CROSS ST.

MAITLAND RD.

GOVT. HOUSE RD.

Govt. Ho.

A3011

A3012

LYSONS AV.

ASH RD.

North Camp Sta.

ASH VALE STA.

STATION VIEW

P.O.

Rec. Gd.

Barracks

CONNAUGHT'S RD.

KITCHENER RD.

Mus.

HAMMERSLEY RD.

Blenheim Park

DUKE OF CONNAUGHT'S RD.

Queen's Parade

Stadium

PRINCE'S

QUEEN'S

FOWLER'S RD.

Basingstoke Canal

Barracks

Aldershot Stubs

R. Blackwater

Hampshire Boundary

Surrey Boundary

BUSH LANE

HOLLY LANE

Range

Range

Ash Vale

WOOD ST.

ST. MARY'S RD.

Heathvale Br. Rd.

HEATHVALE

WENTWORTH CRES.

The Gold

LAKESIDE ROAD

Lakeside

Spring Lakes

ASH ROAD

ASH HILL RD.

Ash Wharf

A321

GOVERNMENT ROAD

CAMP FARM ROAD

BULLERS RD.

MAIDA RD.

ALISONS RD.

THORNHILL RD.

Military Cem.

HURST RD.

GALWEY RD.

Hospital

Hosp.

Falaise

AINGER CL.

P.O.

Hosp.

ALDERSHOT

DEADBROOK LANE

PEGASUS AV.

Greenway

BROOKFIELD

North Town

Sch.

WINCHESTER RD.

Sch.

GRANGE FARM

ASH

St. Peters Ch.

CHURCH STREET

Sch.

LONG ACRE

A3014

SHAWFIELD LANE

ALDERSHOT RD.

ASH

Library

A323

Pol. Sta.

P.O.

East End

HIGH ST.

Cemy

VICTORIA RD.

ALBERT RD.

Rosedale

CONNAUGHT RD.

BELLEVUE RD.

ST. AUGUSTINES CL.

NELSON CL.

ANGLESEY RD.

ASH RD. A323

NEWPORT RD.

NORTH CL.

Greyhound

MANOR FARM LANE

OAKTREES

ASH LODGE DR.

6. SOUTHLANDS CL.
7. NEW POPLARS CT.

1. KOHIMA CL.
2. ARNHEM CL.
3. BLUFF COVE
4. DARWIN GRO.

1. VENTNOR TER.
2. SHANKLIN CT.
3. RAGLAN CL.
4. PEMBURY PL.
5. BOULTERS RD.

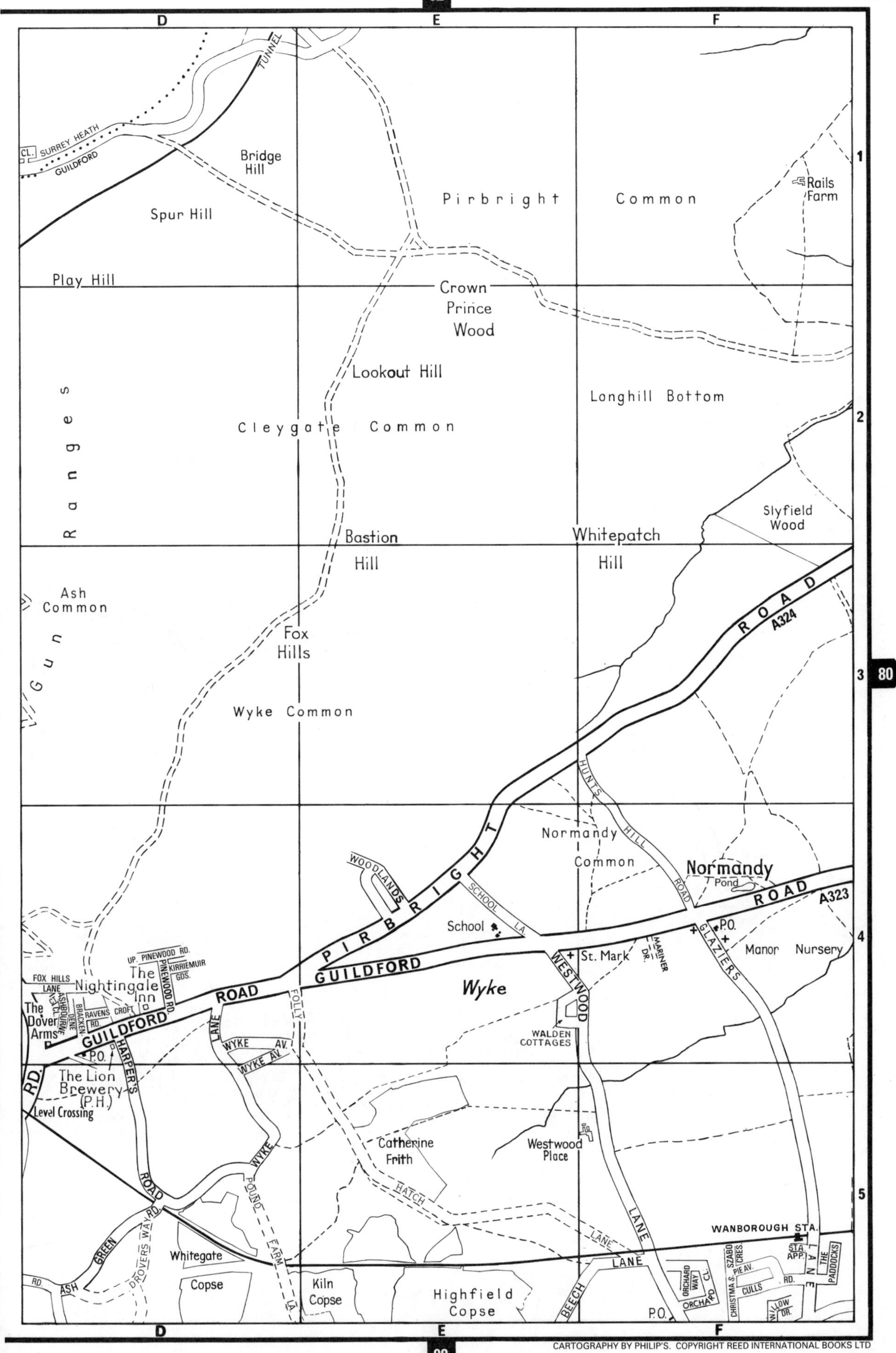

CARTOGRAPHY BY PHILIP'S. COPYRIGHT REED INTERNATIONAL BOOKS LTD

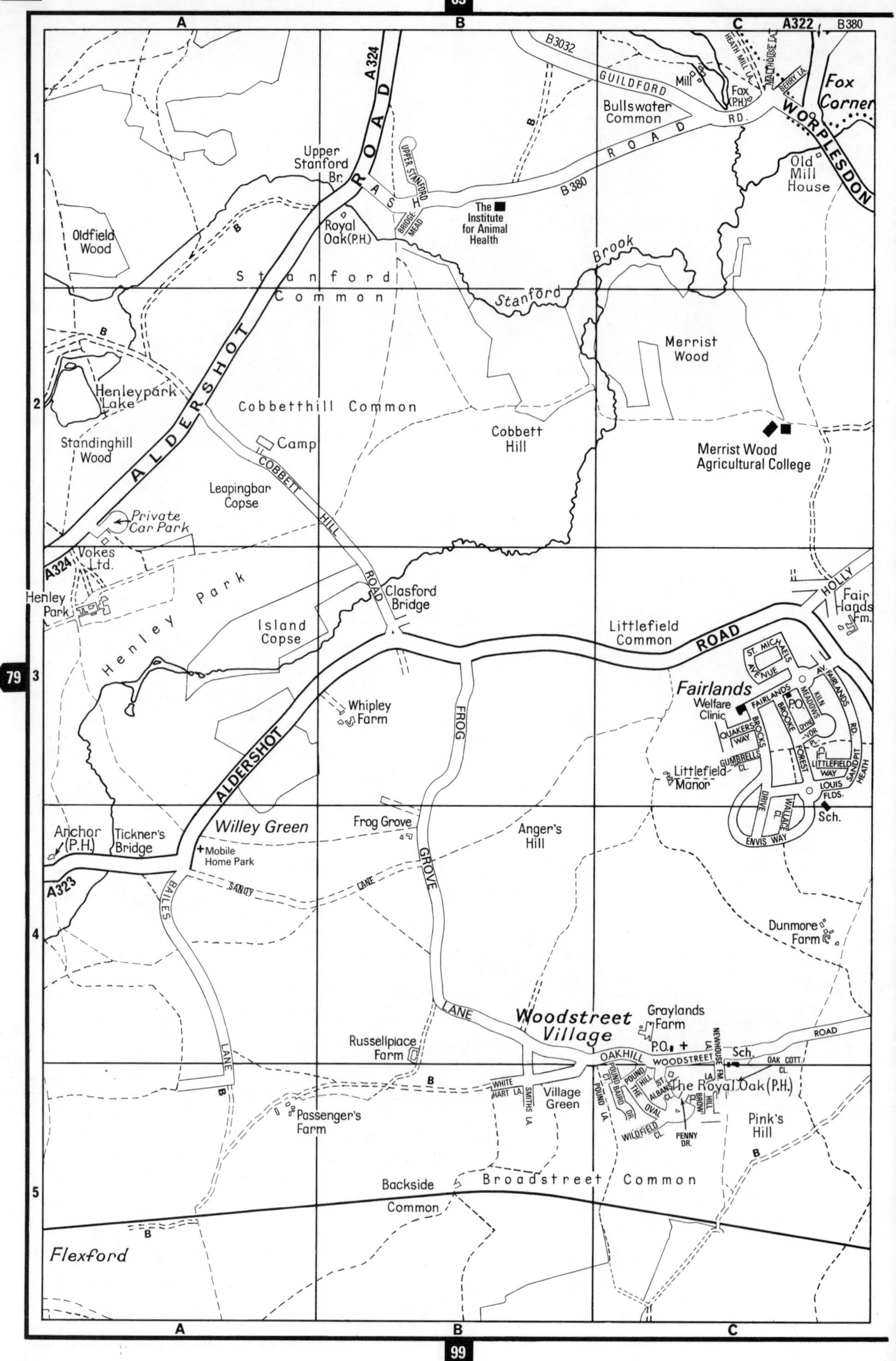

A   B   C

1

Oldfield
Wood

UPPER STANFORD
Upper
Stanford
Br.

Royal
Oak (P.H.)

BRIDGE
MEAD

The ■
Institute
for Animal
Health

A 324

ROAD

STANFORD

ALDERSHOT

B 3032

GUILDFORD

B 380

Bullswater
Common

ROAD

Mill

Fox
(PH)

HEATH MILL LA.

LIGHTHOUSE LA.

BERRY LA.

MALTHOUSE LA.

Fox
Corner

WORPLESDON

Old
Mill
House

A 322   B 380

2

Henleypark
Lake

Standinghill
Wood

B

S t a n f o r d
C o m m o n

Stanford

Brook

Merrist
Wood

Camp

Cobbetthill Common

Cobbett
Hill

◆ ■
Merrist Wood
Agricultural College

COBBETT

Leapingbar
Copse

HILL

Private
Car Park

3

A 324

Vokes
Ltd.

Henley Park

H e n l e y   P a r k

ROAD

Clasford
Bridge

Island
Copse

Whipley
Farm

Littlefield
Common

ROAD

HOLLY

Fair
Hands
Fm.

ST. MICHAELS
AVENUE

FAIRLANDS RD.

Fairlands

Welfare
Clinic

QUAKERS
WAY

BROCKS

KILN
MEADOWS

FAIRLANDS

LYDLING
BROOKE

FOREST

Littlefield
Manor

GUMBRELLS
CL.

DRIVE

WALLACE
CL.

LITTLEFIELD
WAY

LOUIS
FLDS.

SANDPIT
HEATH

Sch.

ENVIS WAY

FROG

4

Anchor
(P.H.)

Tickner's
Bridge

Willey Green

Mobile
Home Park

A 323

BAILES

SANDY

LANE

Frog Grove

GROVE

LANE

Anger's
Hill

Dunmore
Farm

5

LANE

Russellplace
Farm

Woodstreet
Village

Graylands
Farm

P.O. +

OAKHILL

WOODSTREET

NEWHOUSE FM. LA.

Sch.

ROAD

OAK COTT.

Passenger's
Farm

WHITE
HART LA.

SMITHS LA.

Village
Green

POUND
HILL

POUND
BARD DR.

POUND LA.

ST.
ALBANS

THE
OVAL

WOODSTREET
HILL LA.

The Royal Oak (P.H.)

WILDFIELD
CL.

PENNY
DR.

BROW

Pink's
Hill

Backside
Common

B r o a d s t r e e t   C o m m o n

Common

Flexford

A   B   C

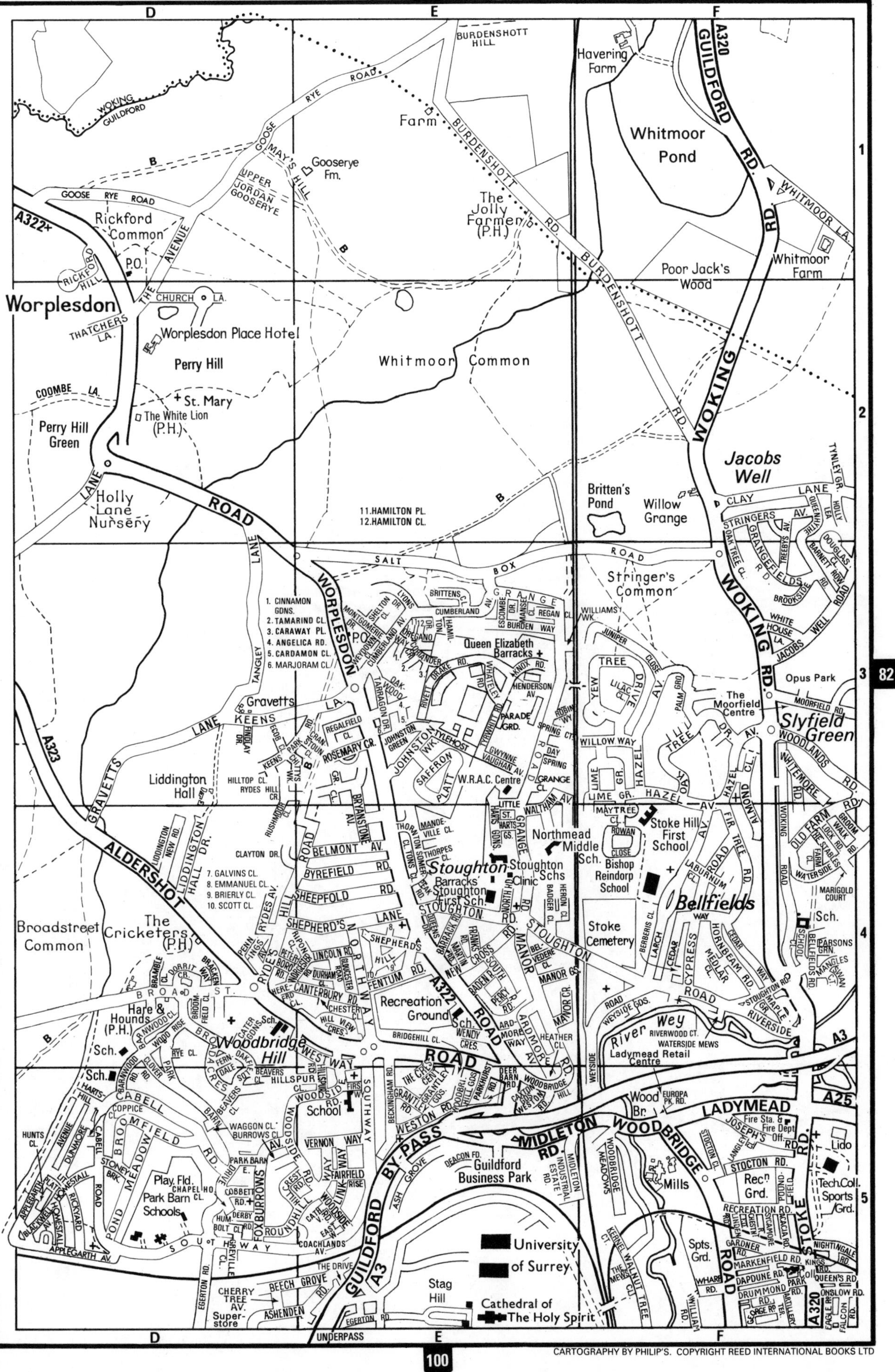

BURDENSHOTT HILL

Havering Farm

Whitmoor Pond

A320 GUILDFORD RD.

WHITMOOR LA.

1

RYE ROAD

WOKING GUILDFORD

May's Hill

Gooserye Fm.

Upper Jordan Gooserye

THE AVENUE

GOOSE RYE ROAD

A322+

Rickford Common

P.O.

RICKFORD HILL

Farm

BURDENSHOTT RD.

The Jolly Farmers (P.H.)

Poor Jack's Wood

Whitmoor Farm

WOKING RD.

Worplesdon

THATCHERS LA.

CHURCH LA.

Worplesdon Place Hotel

Perry Hill

St. Mary

The White Lion (P.H.)

Whitmoor Common

Jacobs Well

TYNLEY GR.

HOLLY

QUEENS

CLAY LANE

STRINGERS

GRANGEFIELDS RD.

OAK TREE LA.

TREBYS AV.

BARNETT

DOUGLAS

2

COOMBE LA.

Perry Hill Green

LANE

Holly Lane Nursery

ROAD

SALT

BOX

Britten's Pond

Willow Grange

Stringer's Common

WHITE HOUSE LA.

JACOBS WELL RD.

BROOKSIDE

11.HAMILTON PL.
12.HAMILTON CL.

ROAD

WOKING RD.

Opus Park

MOORFIELD RD.

The Moorfield Centre

Slyfield Green

82

3

A323

GRAVETTS

LANE

WORPLESDON

P.O.

1. CINNAMON GDNS.
2. TAMARIND CL.
3. CARAWAY PL.
4. ANGELICA RD.
5. CARDAMON CL.
6. MARJORAM CL.

Gravetts

KEENS

REGALFIELD CL.

ROSEMARY CR.

TANGLEY

LA.

BRITTENS CL.

CUMBERLAND

BURDEN DR.

LYONS CL.

SHELON DR.

MONTGOMERIE DR.

OREGANO

TARRAGON DR.

OAK WOOD

RIVETT

DRAKE

TOM

WHATELY

REGAN

WILLIAMS WK.

GRANGE

Queen Elizabeth Barracks

KNYOX RD.

HENDERSON AV.

ROBIN

TREE

JUNIPER

YEW

LILAC

DRIVE

PALM GR.

WOODLANDS RD.

WHITMORE

WOKING RD.

OLD FARM

GROOM

 A323

Liddington Hall

HILLTOP CL.
RYDES HILL CR.

BRYANSTONE AV.

JOHNSTON GREEN

SAFFRON

PLATT

TYLEHOST

WK.

PARADE GDNS.

DAY SPRING

SPRING CT.

WILLOW WAY

GRANGE

LIME GR.

HAZEL

LIME GR.

HAZEL AV.

FIR TREE

MAYTREE

HAZEL

WOODY

Stoke Hill First School

LABURNUM

OLD FARM LA.

WALK

MARIGOLD COURT

Sch.

4

Broadstreet Common

The Cricketers (P.H.)

Woodbridge Hill

7. GALVINS CL.
8. EMMANUEL CL.
9. BRIERLY CL.
10. SCOTT CL.

ALDERSHOT

RYDES HILL

CLAYTON DR.

BELMONT AV.

BYREFIELD RD.

SHEEPFOLD

SHEPHERD'S

LANE

THORNTON

MANDEVILLE CL.

THORPES CL.

STOUGHTON

Stoughton First Sch.

Stoughton Clinic

Stoughton Schs

W.R.A.C. Centre

Northmead Middle Sch.

Bishop Reindorp School

Stoke Cemetery

BERBERIS CL.

LARCH

CEDAR

CYPRESS

HORNBEAM RD.

MEDLAR

Bellfields

MANGLES

PARSONS GRN.

SCHOOL

BELLFIELDS RD.

Sch.

PENN RD.

LINCOLN

FENTUM RD.

Recreation Ground

Sch.

WENDY CRES.

BADGER

MANOR GS.

ARDMORE WAY

HEATHER

WEYSIDE GDNS.

River Wey

RIVERWOOD CT.

WATERSIDE MEWS

Ladymead Retail Centre

Riverside

A3

Hare & Hounds (P.H.)

Sch.

BRAMBLE

DORRIT WAY

BROOM

RYE CL.

WOOD RISE

BRIDGEFIELD

CANTERBURY RD.

CHESTER

HILL VIEW CRES.

BRIDGEHILL

Recreation Ground

DEER BARN

Woodbridge

Wood Br.

EUROPA RD.

JOSEPH'S CL.

Fire Sta. & Fire Dept.

LADYMEAD

A25

Lido

Sch.

HARTS

COPPICE

BROOMFIELD

WAGGON CL.

BURROWS

Sch.

School

WESTWAY

HILLSPUR

BEAVERS

FIRS

WOODSIDE

SOUTHWAY

WESTON

BECKINGHAM RD.

GRANTLEY RD.

PARKWAY

Guildford Business Park

MIDLETON RD.

WOODBRIDGE

Mills

WOODBRIDGE MEADOWS

STOCTON RD.

Rec. Grd.

RECREATION RD.

Tech. Coll. Sports Grd.

STOKE RD.

A320

HUNTS CL.

APPLEGARTH AV.

CABELL RD.

STONEY BRK.

Park Barn Schools

CHAPEL HO.

COBBETT

DERBY

FOXBURROWS

VERNON

FAIRFIELD RISE

LINK WAY

WINDSOR WAY

ROUNDHILL

EAST

COACHLANDS AV.

GUILDFORD BY-PASS

A3

ASH GROVE

DEACON FD.

MIDLETON INDUSTRIAL ESTATE

RECREATION RD.

GARDNER RD.

MARKENFIELD RD.

DAPDUNE RD.

KINGS

COLLEGE

Spts. Grd.

WALNUT TREE CL.

WHARF

DRUMMOND RD.

NIGHTINGALE RD.

QUEEN'S RD.

APPLEGARTH AV.

EGERTON RD.

CHERRY TREE AV.

BEECH GROVE

ASHENDEN

Superstore

THE DRIVE

EGERTON RD.

Stag Hill

University of Surrey

Cathedral of The Holy Spirit

GORSE RD.

WILLIAM RD.

ONSLOW RD.

FALCON

A320

UNDERPASS

100

CARTOGRAPHY BY PHILIP'S. COPYRIGHT REED INTERNATIONAL BOOKS LTD

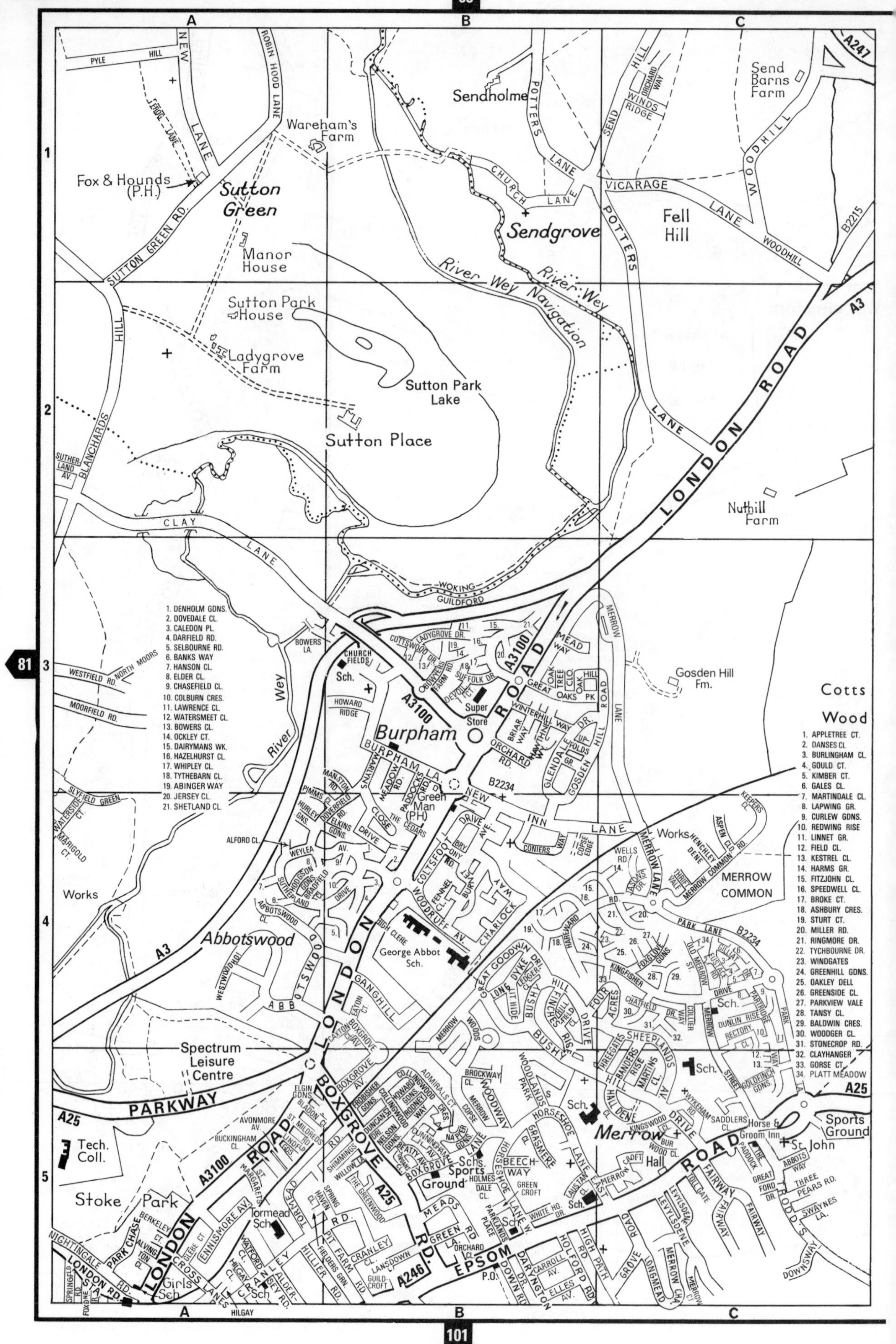

A B C

1

2

3

4

5

PYLE HILL

NEW LANE

ROBIN HOOD LANE

B3032

Fox & Hounds (P.H.)

Sutton Green

SUTTON GREEN RD.

Wareham's Farm

Sendholme

SEND HILL WAY

WINDS RIDGE

Send Barns Farm

POTTERS LANE

WOODHILL

A247

B215

CHURCH LANE

VICARAGE LANE

Sendgrove

Manor House

Fell Hill

WOODHILL

HILL

SUTTON GREEN RD.

Sutton Park House

River Wey

River Wey Navigation

A3

Ladygrove Farm

Sutton Park Lake

POTTERS LANE

SUTHERLAND AV.

BLANCHARDS

Sutton Place

Nuthill Farm

LONDON ROAD

CLAY LANE

WOKING GUILDFORD

1. Denholm Gdns.
2. Dovedale Cl.
3. Caledon Pl.
4. Darfield Rd.
5. Selbourne Rd.
6. Banks Way
7. Hanson Cl.
8. Elder Cl.
9. Chasefield Cl.
10. Colburn Cres.
11. Lawrence Cl.
12. Watersmeet Cl.
13. Bowers Cl.
14. Ockley Ct.
15. Dairymans Wk.
16. Hazelhurst Cl.
17. Whipley Cl.
18. Tythebarn Cl.
19. Abinger Way
20. Jersey Cl.
21. Shetland Cl.

WESTFIELD RD.

NORTH MOORS

MOORFIELD RD.

SLYFIELD GREEN

WATERSIDE RD.

MARGOLD CT.

Works

BOWERS LA.

CHURCH FIELDS

Sch.

HOWARD RIDGE

River Wey

A3100

SUPER STORE

Burpham

BURPHAM LA.

LADYGROVE DR.

COTTSWOOD DR.

ORCHARDS

SUFFOLK DR.

A3100

MEAD WAY

MERROW

GREAT OAKS

OAK TREE CLO.

HILL

Gosden Hill Fm.

Cotts Wood

1. Appletree Ct.
2. Danses Cl.
3. Burlingham Cl.
4. Gould Ct.
5. Kimber Ct.
6. Gales Cl.
7. Martindale Cl.
8. Lapwing Gr.
9. Curlew Gdns.
10. Redwing Rise
11. Linnet Gr.
12. Field Cl.
13. Kestrel Cl.
14. Harms Gr.
15. Fitzjohn Ct.
16. Speedwell Cl.
17. Broke Ct.
18. Ashbury Cres.
19. Sturt Ct.
20. Miller Rd.
21. Ringmore Dr.
22. Tychbourne Dr.
23. Windgates
24. Greenhill Gdns.
25. Oakley Dell
26. Greenside Cl.
27. Parkview Vale
28. Tansy Cl.
29. Baldwin Cres.
30. Woodger Cl.
31. Stonecrop Rd.
32. Clayhanger
33. Gorse Ct.
34. Platt Meadow

BRIAR WYTHE WINTERHILL WAY

GLENDALE GOSDEN HILL

ORCHARD RD.

B2234

NEW INN LANE

Green Man (PH)

MANSTON RD.

PIMMS

HURLEY GDNS.

WEYLEA

ALFORD CL.

Works

MERROW COMMON

KEEPERS RD.

ASPEN CLO.

MERROW LANE

HENCHLEY DENE

WELLS RD.

PARK LANE B2234

Abbotswood

A3

LONDON ROAD

GANGHILL

George Abbot Sch.

WOODRUFF AV.

FENNEL CL.

CHARLOCK WAY

BURPHAM

CONIERS WAY

COTTESLOE

HIGH CLERE

KINGFISHER

GREAT GOODWIN DR.

LONG BUSHY RISE

FINCHS RISE

HILL

DYKE RD.

CHATFIELD DR.

FOXGLOVE

LONGFIELD GDNS.

DUNLIN RISE

RECTORY

PARTRIDGE

Sch.

A25

Spectrum Leisure Centre

Tech. Coll.

Stoke Park

PARKWAY

A25

LONDON ROAD

BOXGROVE ROAD

A3100

ST. MARGARETS

ELGIN GDNS.

BLAGON CT.

AVONMORE AV.

BUCKINGHAM CL.

MILLBRED RD.

BOXGROVE AV.

SHIMMINGS

WILLOW CL.

BROCKWAY CL.

WOODLANDS PARK

MERROW WOODS

HORSESHOE LANE

WYCHAM CLOSE

Sch.

Sch.

GOLDFINCH GDNS.

STREET

Merrow

SADDLERS CL.

Horse & Groom Inn

St. John Hall

Sports Ground

A25

MERROW ROAD

Sports Ground

BEECHWAY

GREEN CROFT

HOLMES DALE CL.

Sch.

GUILDFORD

PARSONS GREEN

WHITE HO. LANE

WOOD CL.

KINGSWOOD

GREAT FORD

THREE PEARS RD.

ABBOTS WAY

SWAYNES LA.

FAIRWAY

LEVYLSDENE

MERROW CH.

DOWNSWAY

Tormead Sch.

ENNISMORE AV.

BERKELEY CT.

PARK CHASE

ALVINGTON

CROSS LANES

NIGHTINGALE RD.

LONDON RD.

FOXHE

SPRINGFIELD RD.

Girls Sch.

HILGAY

THE GREENWAY

SPRING RD.

RAVENS

CRANLEY RD.

HILLIER RD.

ALDER RD.

WATFORD CL.

PIT FARM RD.

A246

EPSOM ROAD

LANSDOWN RD.

GUILD CROFT

ORCHARD CL.

P.O.

CARROLL RD.

ELLES AV.

HIGH PATH RD.

HOLFORD RD.

GROVE RD.

LONGMEAD

DARLINGTON

A B C

D E F

SEND BARNS LA.
KEVAN DR.
LAMBERLEY CL.
BOUGHTON HALL AV.
BIRCH
PATH WAY
CLANDON WAY
PL.
FIELD WAY
BURNTCOMMON LA.
Burntcommon
GAMBLES LANE
Nursery
HUNGRY HILL LANE
Nursery
B
1

B2215
Garden Centre Nursery
RIPLEY
BYPASS
A3
CLANDON RD.
Highcotts Wd.
TITHEBARNS LANE
Sussex Farm
Holride Farm
B

HIGHCOTTS LA.
B
RIPLEY
THE SPINNEY
H.M. Prison
B
Inwood Cottage
B
2

Dedswell Manor
FELIX DR.
LIME GROVE
LIME CLOSE
WOODSTOCK
MALACCA FARM RD.
ROAD
B
Gason Wd.
CROCKERY LA.

Frythys Wood
BEDSWELL DRIVE
THE STREET
BENNETT WAY
OAK GRANGE
STA. APP.
CLANDON STA.
Tel. Ex.
Onslow Arms (P.H.)
Village Hall
West Clandon
Pol. Sta.
MEADOW LANDS
Norcote Wood
ROAD
Home Farm
84 3

Clandon Park
Sch.
Bulls Head (P.H.)
A247
STREET
Clandon Regis Golf Club
East Clandon
SAWPIT LA.
BACK LA.
Queens Head (P.H.)
New Manor Farm
NEW RD.
THE STREET
Sch.
ROAD A246
BLAKES LA.
4

Temple Court
St. Peter & St. Paul
Clandon House (N.T.)
Regimental Museum
EPSOM RD.
GLEBE COTTAGES
STAPLE ROAD
High Clandon
B

Quarry
SHERE RD.
A25
Clandon Downs
5

Wellhouse Farm
B
B
B

D E F

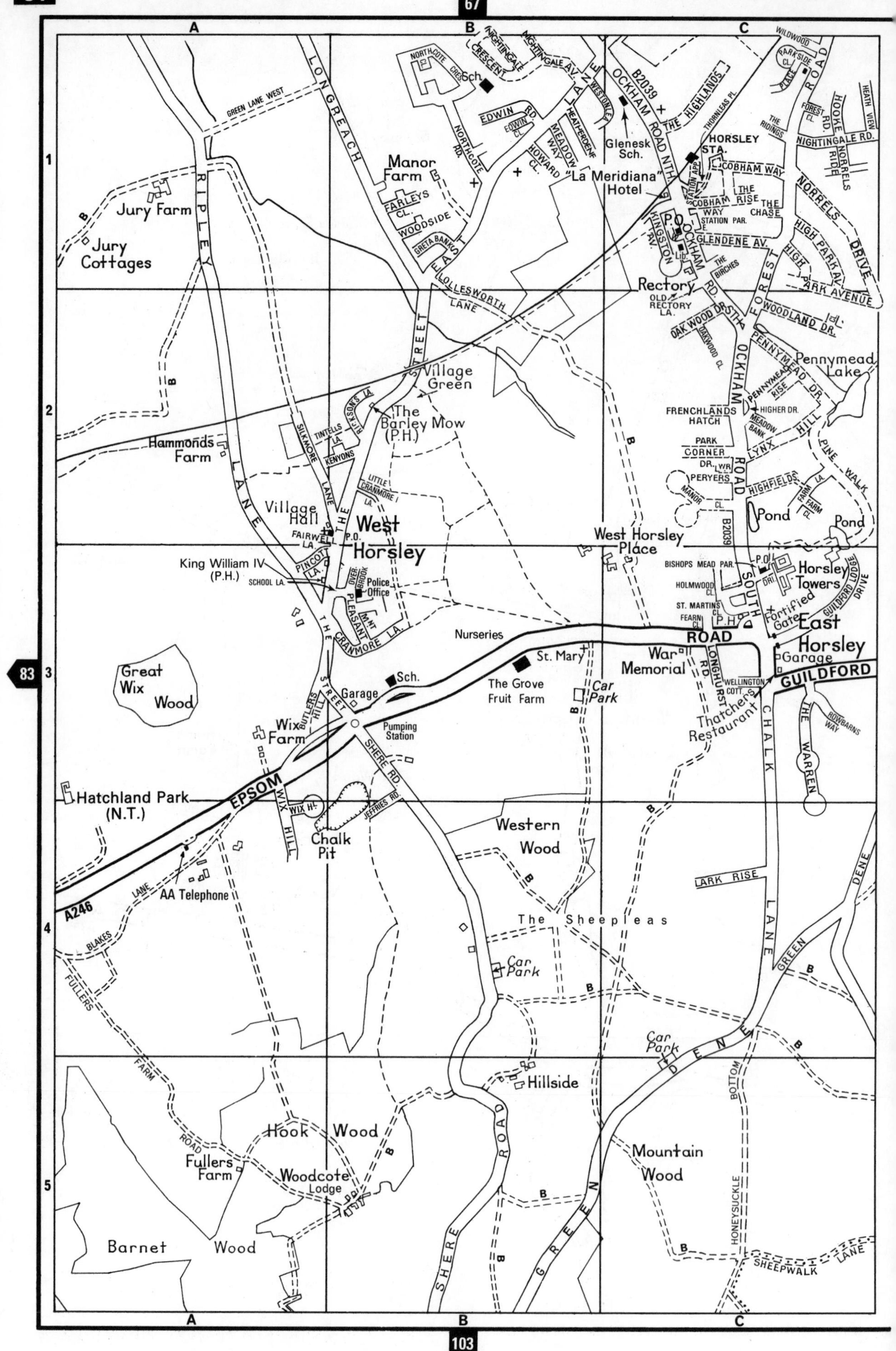
67
103
83
Jury Farm
Jury Cottages
Hammonds Farm
Manor Farm
Village Green
The Barley Mow (P.H.)
Village Hall
West Horsley
King William IV (P.H.)
Police Office
Nurseries
St. Mary
The Grove Fruit Farm
Great Wix Wood
Wix Farm
Garage
Sch.
Pumping Station
Hatchland Park (N.T.)
EPSOM
A246
AA Telephone
Chalk Pit
Western Wood
The Sheepleas
Car Park
Hillside
Hook Wood
Fullers Farm
Woodcote Lodge
Barnet Wood
Mountain Wood
Glenesk Sch.
"La Meridiana" Hotel
HORSLEY STA.
Rectory
Pennymead Lake
West Horsley Place
Pond
Horsley Towers
Fortified Gate
East Horsley
War Memorial
Thatchers Restaurant
GUILDFORD
ROAD
OCKHAM ROAD NTH.
OCKHAM ROAD STH.
B2039
RIPLEY LANE
LONGREACH
EAST LANE
THE STREET
SHERE RD.
SHERE ROAD
CHALK LANE
GREEN DENE
NORRELS DRIVE
FOREST ROAD
SHEEPWALK LANE

68

D E F

Indian Fm

Thornet Wood

Little Bookham

P.O. FAIRLAWN

SOLE FARM

THE GARSTONS

MEAD CR.

CHURCH RD.

SOLEGATE

STONEHILL CL.

VICARAGE CL.

Greatlee Wood

Lee Wood Farm

LITTLE BOOKHAM ST.

CHILDS HALL

LONG MEADOW

MIDDLEMEAD FARM

AV.

GLEBE RD.

THE LORNE

1

Littlelee Wood

EFFINGHAM COMMON

Windsor Castle (P.H.)

Great Bookham

Great Ridings Plantation

Dunglass Farm

Preston Cross Hotel

WATER LANE

ROAD

RECTORY LANE

MANORHOUSE LA.

SWANNS MEADOW

HAWKS HILL

HAWKWOOD

HAWKWOOD DELL

Ridings Wood

Nursery

Sch.

Sch. Sch.

The Grange

GUILDFORD RD.

A246

'The Plough' (P.H.)

LEEWOOD WAY

LOWER ROAD

CHURCH ST.

The Lodge

Effingham

Nursery

2

Orestan Farm

ORESTAN LANE

MIDDLE FARM

YEW TREE WK.

PL.

BROWNS LA.

Rec. Grd.

ROAD

WOODLANDS RD.

CHALKPIT LANE

"The Sir Douglas Haig" (P.H.)

P.O.

STREET

MANOR GREEN

PIXHOLME RD.

ORCHARD GDNS.

LINDEN CL.

MT. PLEASANT

MEAD

LINKS WAY

WAY

Park Wood

DIRTHAM LANE

CALVERT ROAD

CHESTER RD.

Sch.

BEECH ROAD

Club Ho.

BEECH CL.

NORWOOD RD.

NORWOOD

STRATHCONA AV.

SALMONS ROAD

GUILDFORD ROAD

Standard Hill

Effingham Golf Course

Warren Farm

Reservoir (Underground)

AVENUE

HIGH BARN ROAD

MOLE VALLEY GUILDFORD

Big High Grove

3

86

Park Horsley

DIRTHAM LANE

A246 ROAD

GREEN DENE

LONDON LANE

Rowbarns Grange

Oldlands Plantation

Stars Wood

BEECH LANE

White Hill

High Barn

B

Black Bush Plantation

Oldlands Copse

Six Acre Copse

Round Lions Copse

Yewtree Farm

4

Northfield Plantation

Hazel Bucket

Stonyrock Copse

ROAD

Ranmore House Farm

RANMORE

Chippens Copse

Burrows Wood

CRITTEN LANE

St. Teresa's Convent

CROCKNORTH ROAD

Crocknorth Farm

5

Birchett Plantation

Dogkennel Green

RANMORE COMMON ROAD

Lillies Copse

GUILDFORD MOLE VALLEY

Dunley Hill Farm

D E F

104

A B C

B2122

YOUNG ST. A246

LEATHERHEAD RD.

Eastwick

Playing Field

Park View
THE PARK
PARK AV.
EASTWICK PARK AV.
CHURCH RD.
LIFE RD.
POSTHSE.
I.A.P.O.
Lib.
Sch.
Car Pk.
HIGH ST.
LOWER RD.
DORKING
Rec. Grd.

DURLESTON PARK DR.
BOSTOCK
OSRIDGE AV.
EASTWICK
BURNEY CL.
GILMAIS WAY

A246
GROVESIDE
NEWENHAM RD.
DOWLANS
STYLES END
WEST
DOWN
DOWLANS CL.
KIDBOROUGH DOWN

Great Bookham

CHAPEL ROAD

Kenilworth Riding Stables

Roaringhouse Farm

Fetcham Downs

Updown Wood

Walnut Tree Clump

Denshire Hill

Norbury Park

Norbury Park

Swanworth Farm

MICKLEHAM

Bookham Wood

Druids Grove

Goldstone Farm

POLESDEN
CONNICUT LANE

HOGDEN LA.

Connicut Wood

Phœnice Farm

Beechy Wood

CRABTREE LANE

River

Preserve Copse

Polesden Lacey (N.T.)

Chapelhill Wood

Chapel Wood

Chapel Hill

Chapel Farm

Camilla Lacey

CAMILLA DR.

BAGDEN HILL

Freehold Wood

CHAPEL

Old Dene

COMMON ROAD

Polesden Farm

Tanner's Hatch (Youth Hostel)

Long Bottom

Bagden Wood

Dorking Wood

Ashcombe Wood

Ashleigh

BURNEY ROAD
ADLERS LA.
PILGRIMS

Gravel Pit Plantat.

Fort (Dismantled)

Denbies Wine Est.
BRADLEY LA.

Ranmore Common

Denbies Farm

North Downs Way

Ranmore Common

RANMORE COMMON RD.

Ranmore Roundabout The Spains

St. Barnabas

Sch. Denbies

RANMORE ROAD

KEPPEL RD.

YEW-TREE RD.

ASHCOMBE
A2003

A B C

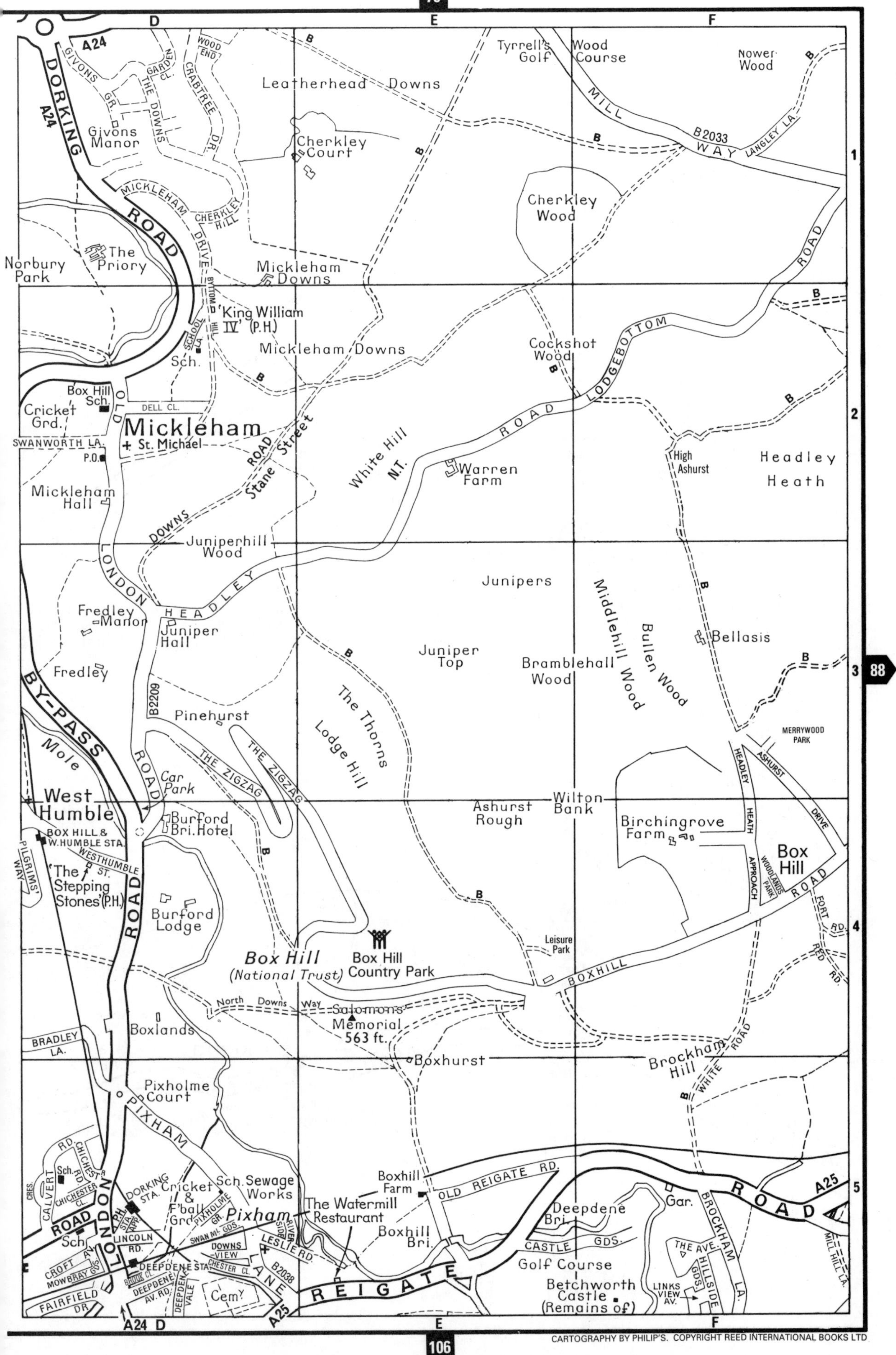

CARTOGRAPHY BY PHILIP'S. COPYRIGHT REED INTERNATIONAL BOOKS LTD

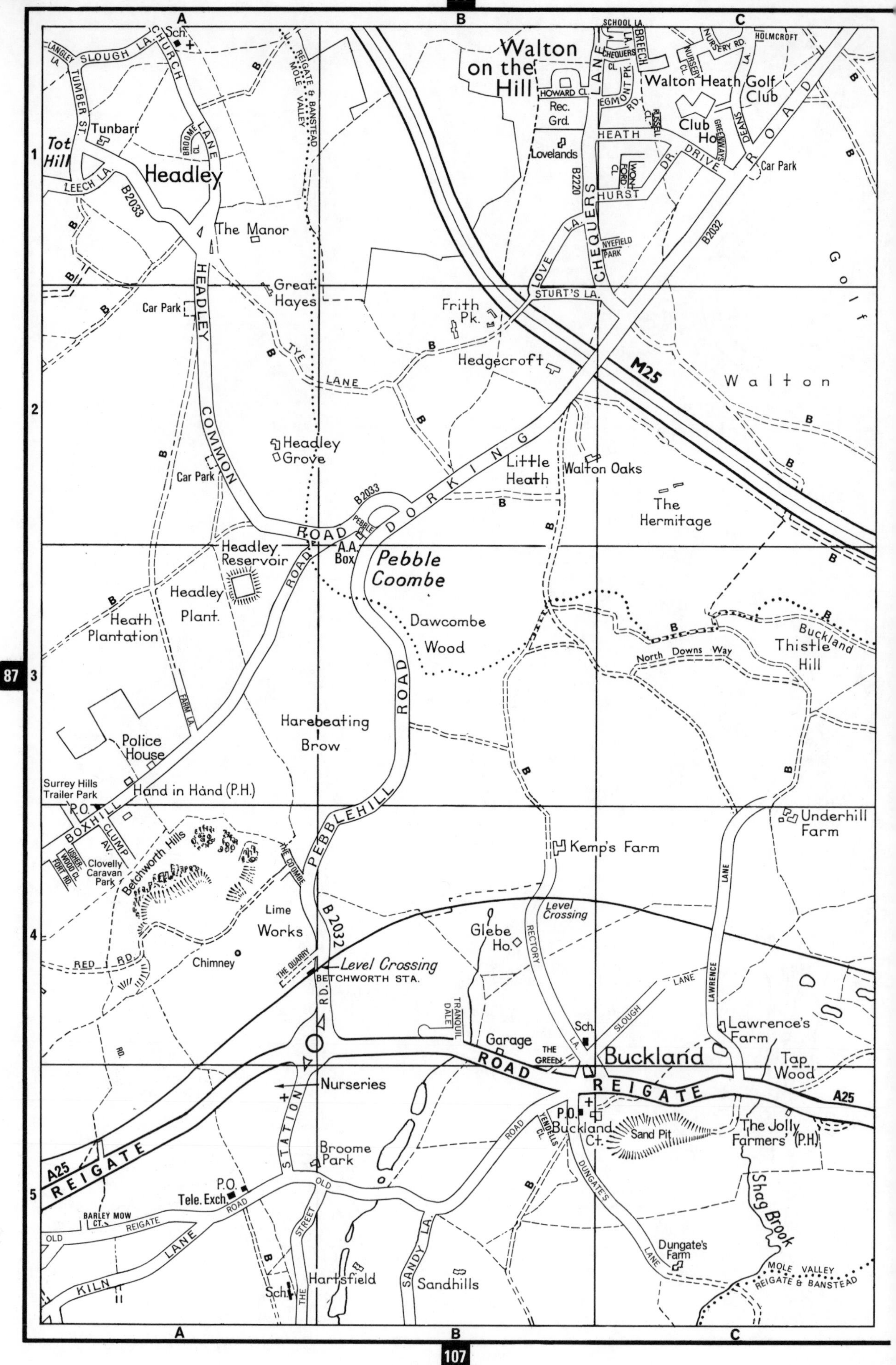
71
107
87
Walton on the Hill
Headley
Tot Hill
Tunbarr
The Manor
Great Hayes
Car Park
Frith Pk.
Hedgecroft
Walton Heath Golf Club
Club Ho
Rec. Grd.
Lovelands
M25
Walton
Golf
Headley Grove
Little Heath
Walton Oaks
The Hermitage
Headley Reservoir
A.A. Box
Pebble Coombe
Dawcombe Wood
Headley Plant.
Heath Plantation
North Downs Way
Buckland Thistle Hill
Harebeating Brow
Police House
Surrey Hills Trailer Park
Hand in Hand (P.H.)
P.O.
Underhill Farm
Kemp's Farm
Clovelly Caravan Park
Betchworth Hills
Lime Works
Chimney
Level Crossing
Glebe Ho.
BETCHWORTH STA.
Garage
Sch.
Buckland
Lawrence's Farm
Tap Wood
Nurseries
Buckland Ct.
Sand Pit
The Jolly Farmers' (P.H.)
Broome Park
Tele. Exch.
Shag Brook
Dungate's Farm
Hartsfield
Sandhills
MOLE VALLEY
REIGATE & BANSTEAD
HEADLEY COMMON ROAD
DORKING ROAD
PEBBLEHILL ROAD
REIGATE ROAD
A25
B2033
B2032
B2220
TYE LANE
SLOUGH LA.
CHURCH LA.
TUMBER ST.
LEECH LA.
BOXHILL RD.
STATION RD.
SANDY LA.
KILN LANE
OLD REIGATE ROAD
BARLEY MOW CT.
DUNGATE'S LANE
RECTORY LA.
SLOUGH LANE
LAWRENCE LANE
CHEQUERS LANE
LOVE LA.
STURT'S LA.
HEATH DRIVE
DEANS LA.
NURSERY RD.
HOLMCROFT
SCHOOL LA.
BREECH LA.
EGMONT PK. RD.
HOWARD CL.
HURST
NYEFIELD PARK
THE QUARRY
THE COOMBE
THE GREEN
TRANQUIL DALE
RED RD.
FARM LA.
CLUMP AV.
YENDELLS CL.
A
B
C
1
2
3
4
5

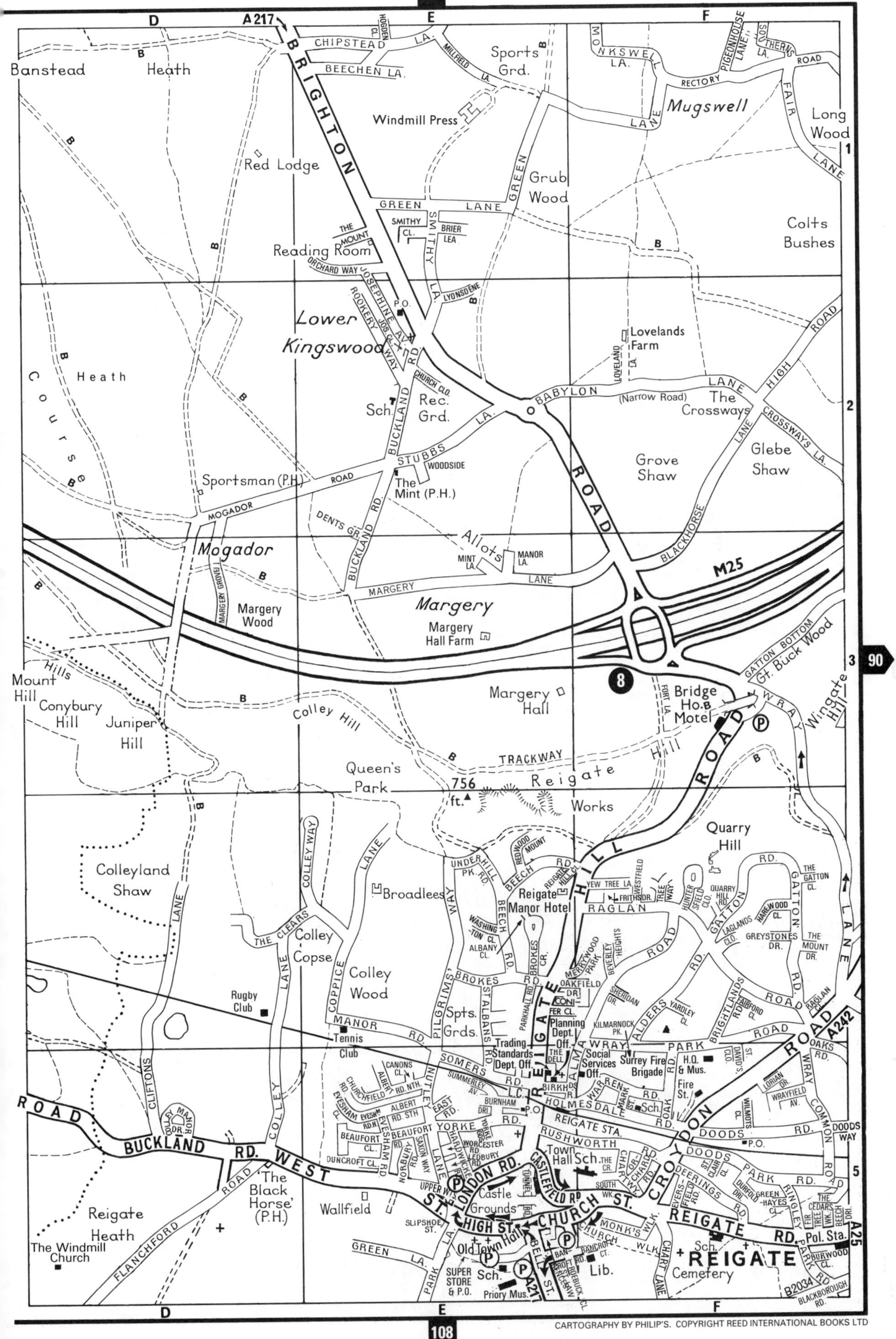
Banstead
Heath
Red Lodge
Reading Room
Lower Kingswood
Heath
Course
Sportsman (P.H.)
Mogador
Margery Wood
Margery
Margery Hall Farm
Margery Hall
Mount Hill
Conybury Hill
Juniper Hill
Colley Hill
Queen's Park
Reigate Hill
Reigate Works
Colleyland Shaw
Colley Copse
Colley Wood
Broadlees
Reigate Manor Hotel
Rugby Club
Tennis Club
Reigate Heath
The Windmill Church
The Black Horse (P.H.)
Wallfield
Sports Grd.
Windmill Press
Grub Wood
Mugswell
Long Wood
Colts Bushes
Lovelands Farm
The Crossways
Grove Shaw
Glebe Shaw
Bridge Ho. Motel
Quarry Hill
REIGATE
Cemetery
Castle Grounds
Old Town Hall
Priory Mus.
Town Hall
BRIGHTON ROAD
REIGATE HILL
CROYDON ROAD
BUCKLAND RD.
WEST ST.
HIGH ST.
CHURCH ST.
REIGATE RD.
M25
A217
A242
A25
B2034
CARTOGRAPHY BY PHILIP'S. COPYRIGHT REED INTERNATIONAL BOOKS LTD

72
90
108

73

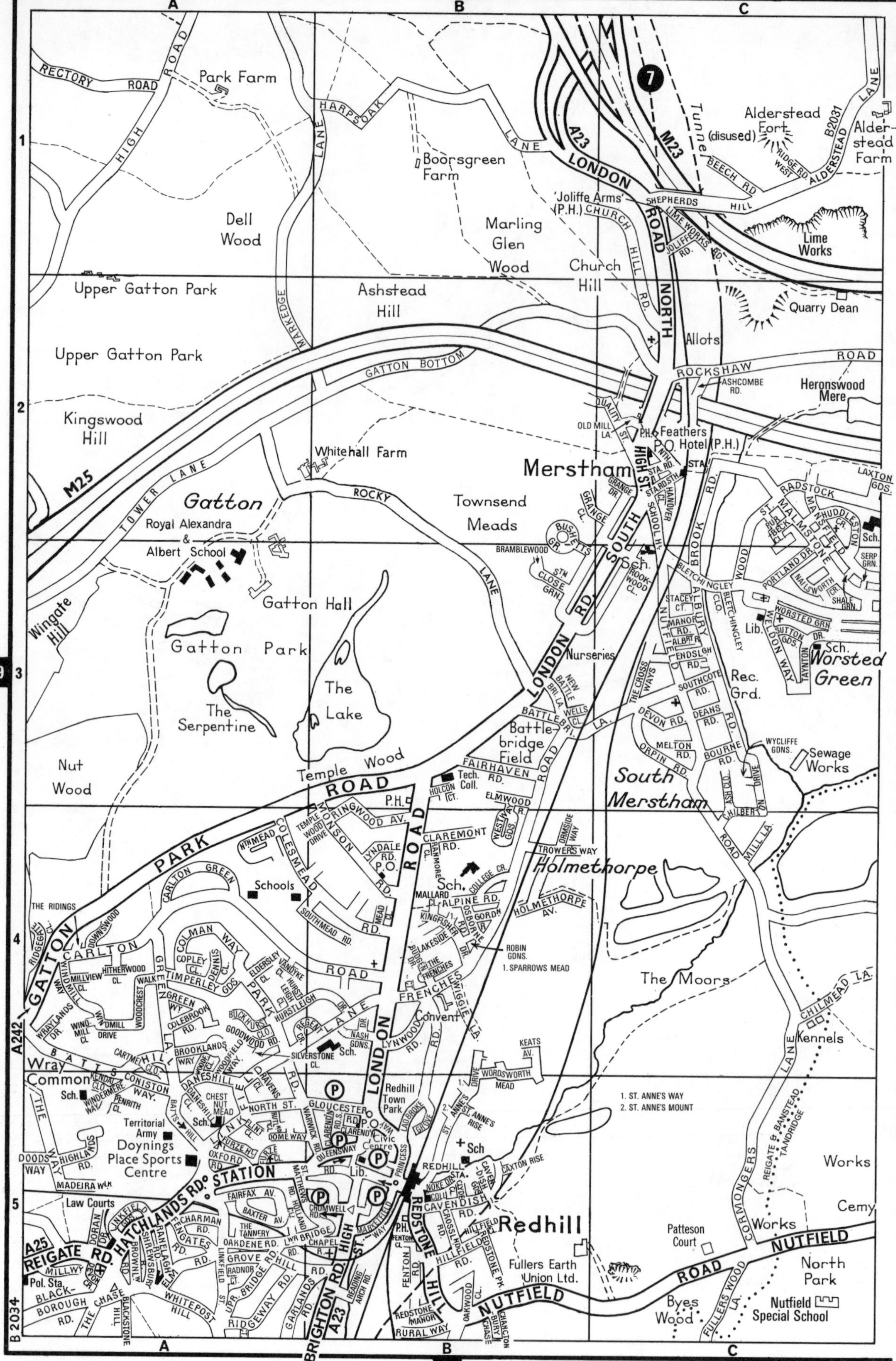

A
B
C
1
2
3
4
5
RECTORY ROAD
HIGH ROAD
Park Farm
HARPSOAK LANE
Boorsgreen Farm
Dell Wood
Marling Glen Wood
Church Hill
Upper Gatton Park
Ashstead Hill
MARKEDGE LANE
Alderstead Fort (disused)
Alderstead Farm
ALDERSTEAD LANE
B2031
BEECH RD
RIDGE RD. WEST
Lime Works
M23
A23
LONDON ROAD NORTH
Tunnel
'Joliffe Arms' (P.H.)
CHURCH HILL RD.
SHEPHERDS HILL
LIME WORKS RD.
JOLIFFE RD.
Quarry Dean
Allots
M25
GATTON BOTTOM
ROCKSHAW ROAD
ASHCOMBE RD.
Heronswood Mere
Kingswood Hill
QUALITY ST.
OLD MILL LA.
P.H.
Feathers Hotel (P.H.)
P.O.
Whitehall Farm
Merstham
HIGH ST.
STA.
TOWER LANE
Gatton
ROCKY LANE
Townsend Meads
Royal Alexandra & Albert School
LAXTON GDS.
RADSTOCK
MALMSTONE
MANSFIELD
HUDDLESTON
Sch.
BROOK RD.
SOUTH RD.
GRANGE CL.
BUSHETTS GR.
BRAMBLEWOOD
Sch.
Wingate Hill
Gatton Hall
Gatton Park
LONDON RD.
Nurseries
BLETCHINGLEY
PORTLAND DR.
NAILSWORTH CR.
SHALE GRN.
SERP GRN.
WORSTED GRN
WELDON WAY
SUTTON GDS.
TAYNTON DR.
Lib.
Sch.
Worsted Green
The Serpentine
The Lake
NUTFIELD
ALBURY
STACEY CT.
MANOR RD.
ALBERT RD.
ENDSLEIGH RD.
THE CROSS WAYS
SOUTHCOTE RD.
Rec. Grd.
NEW BATTLE BRI. LA.
WELLS CL.
BATTLE BRI. LA.
Battlebridge Field
DEVON RD.
DEANS RD.
MELTON RD.
ORPIN RD.
BOURNE RD.
WYCLIFFE GDNS.
Sewage Works
Nut Wood
Temple Wood
FAIRHAVEN RD.
Tech. Coll.
HOLCON CT.
ELMWOOD
South Merstham
ASH CL.
CHILBERTON
DRIVE
ROAD
MILL LA.
PARK ROAD
P.H.
MORINGWOOD AV.
TEMPLE WOOD DRIVE
MONSON
LYNDALE RD.
P.O.
COLESMEAD
CLAREMONT RD.
WESTWAY GDS.
ORMSIDE WAY
TROWERS WAY
Holmethorpe
CARLTON GREEN
Schools
Sch.
MALLARD CL.
ALPINE RD.
COLLEGE CR.
HOLMETHORPE AV.
THE RIDINGS
SOUTHMEAD RD.
KINGFISHER
LAKESIDE
OSBORNE
GORDON
ROBIN GDNS.
1. SPARROWS MEAD
GATTON
CARLTON
HITHERWOOD CL.
MILLVIEW CL.
COLMAN WAY
COPLEY CL.
DENNIS CL.
TIMPERLEY GDS.
ELDERSLEY CL.
HURSTLEIGH
ROAD
THE FRENCHES
FRENCHES
WIGGIE LA.
The Moors
CHILMEAD LA.
A242
WRAYLANDS DR.
WINDMILL DRIVE
COLEBROOK RD.
BUCKHURST CL.
GOODWOOD RD.
REGENT CR.
LANE
NASH GDNS.
Sch.
SILVERSTONE CL.
LONDON ROAD
LYNWOOD RD.
Convent
KEATS AV.
Kennels
Wray Common
BATTS HILL
CONISTON WAY
BROOKLANDS WAY
DANESHILL
DRIVE
WORDSWORTH MEAD
Sch.
KENDAL CLO.
WINDERMERE WAY
PENRITH CL.
CHESTNUT MEAD
NORTH ST.
GLOUCESTER RD.
Redhill Town Park
Civic Centre
1. ST. ANNE'S WAY
2. ST. ANNE'S MOUNT
ST. ANNE'S RISE
Territorial Army
Doynings Place Sports Centre
Sch.
HIGHLANDS RD.
DOODS WAY
MADEIRA WLK
OXFORD RD.
STATION
QUEENSWAY
PRINCESS WAY
Lib.
REDHILL STA.
Sch
CAXTON RISE
Works
REIGATE & BANSTEAD
TANDRIDGE
Law Courts
HATCHLANDS RD.
FAIRFAX AV.
BAXTER AV.
CHARMAN RD.
FENGATES RD.
CROMWELL
HOLLAND
CAVENDISH RD.
NOKE DR.
Redhill
CORMONGERS LANE
Works
Cemy
A25
REIGATE RD.
MILLWAY
Pol. Sta.
BLACKBOROUGH RD.
OAKDENE RD.
THE TANNERY
CHAPEL
LWR BRIDGE
HIGH ST.
MARKETFIELD WAY
HILLFIELD
REDSTONE HILL
REDSTONE PK.
Fullers Earth Union Ltd.
Patteson Court
NUTFIELD ROAD
North Park
GROVE HILL RD.
RADNOR CT.
UPR. BRIDGE RD.
RIDGEWAY RD.
GARLANDS RD.
BRIGHTON RD.
A23
READING ARCH RD.
FENTON CL.
OAKWOOD CL.
REDSTONE MANOR
RURAL WAY
BURY CHASE
CHANCTON
NUTFIELD
Byes Wood
FULLERS WOOD LA.
Nutfield Special School
B 2034
THE CHASE
BLACKSTONE HILL
WHITEPOST HILL

89

109

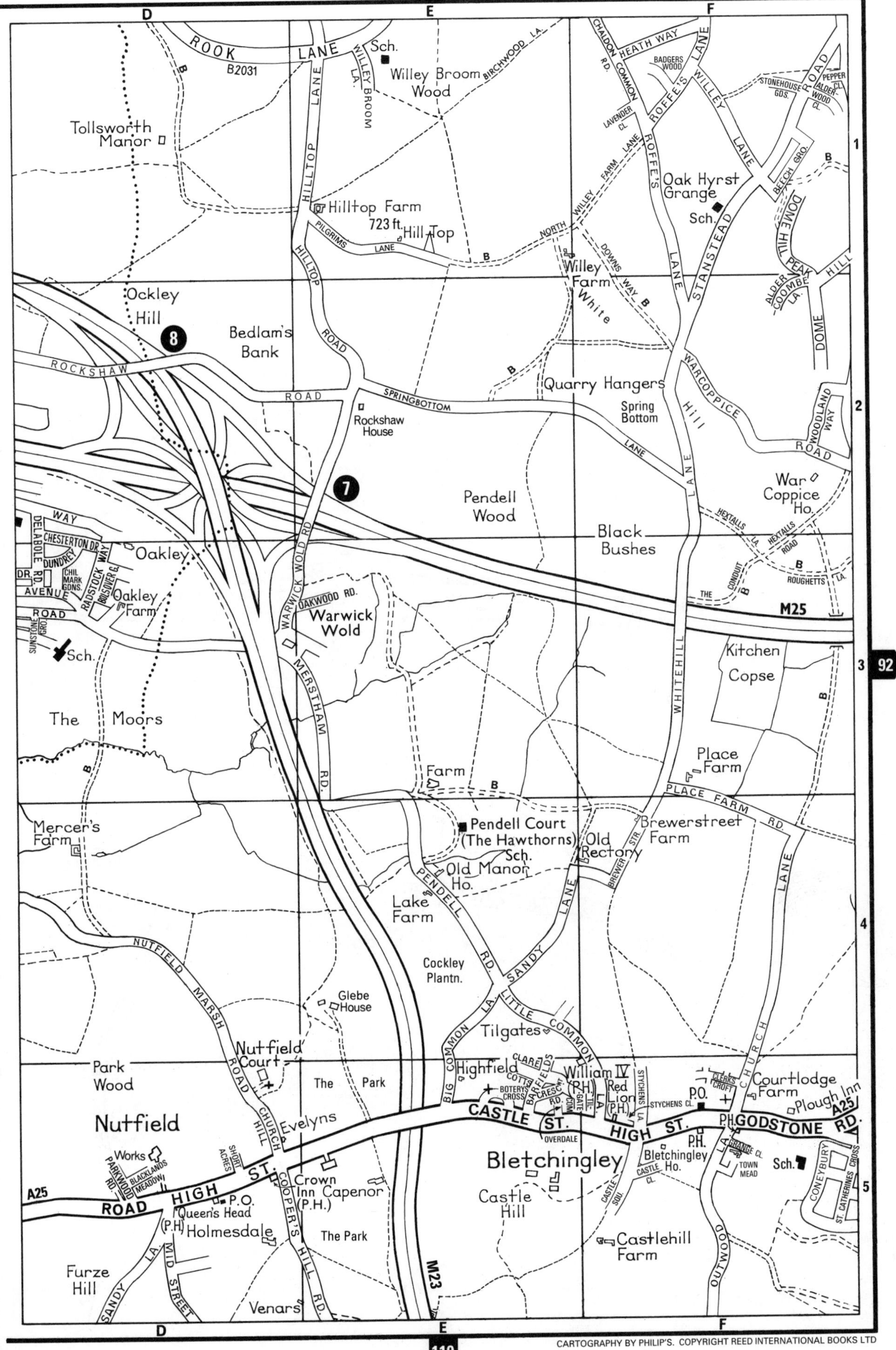

CARTOGRAPHY BY PHILIP'S. COPYRIGHT REED INTERNATIONAL BOOKS LTD

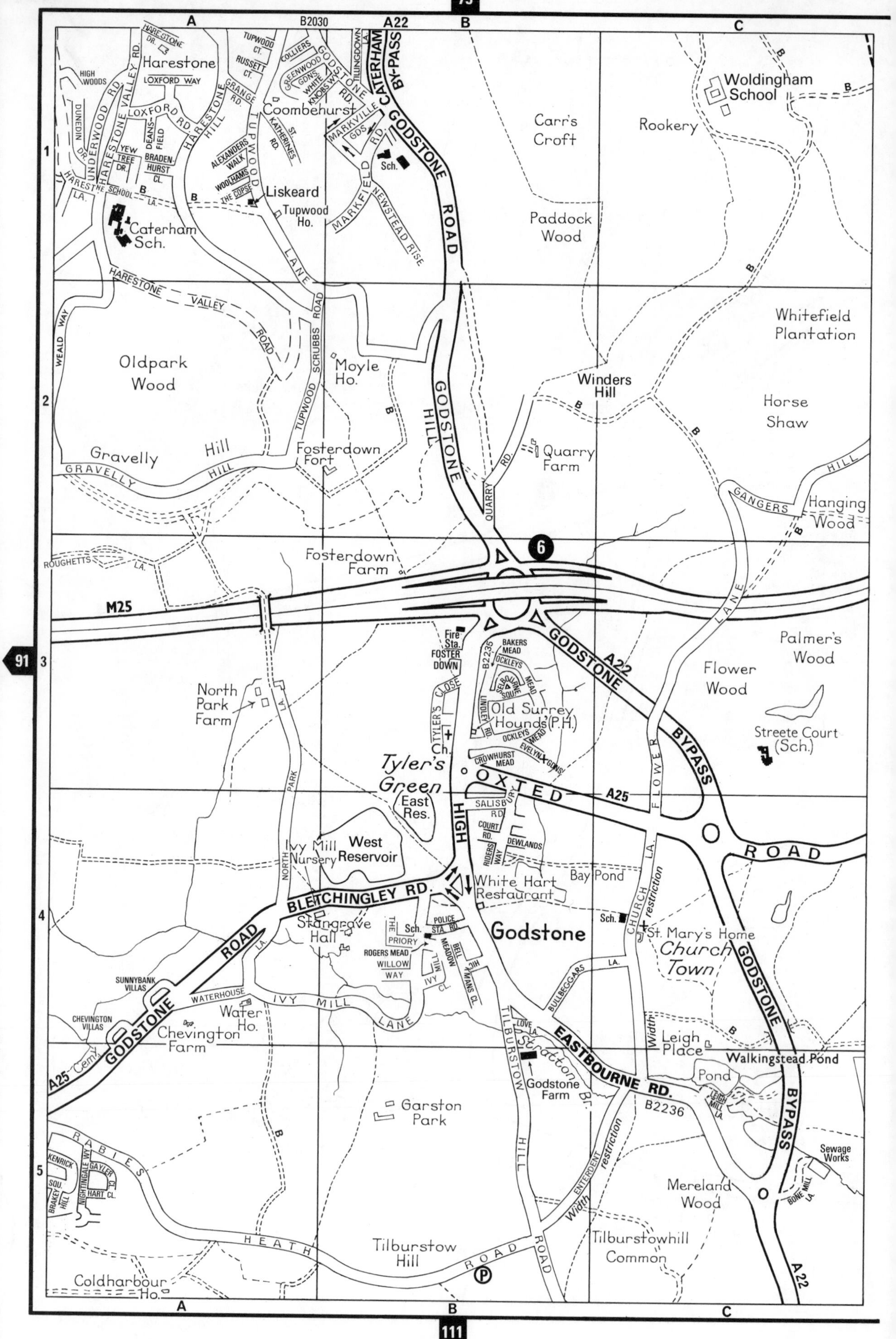

A   B2030   A22   B   C

HARESTONE
HIGH WOODS
Harestone
LOXFORD WAY
UNDERWOOD DR.
DUNEDIN
HARESTONE VALLEY RD.
LOXFORD RD.
ORANGE RD.
HARESTONE HILL
TUPWOOD CT.
COLLIERS
RUSSETT CT.
GREENWOOD GDNS.
WHITE KNOBS WAY
ST. KATHERINES RD.
MARKVILLE GDS.
TILLINGDOWN
GODSTONE RD.
CATERHAM BY-PASS

Coombehurst
YEW TREE DR.
BRADEN HURST CL.
DEANS FIELD
ALEXANDERS WALK
WOOLHAMS
THE COPSE
Sch.
Liskeard
Tupwood Ho.

HARESTONE LA.
HARESTONE SCHOOL
B
B

Caterham Sch.

HARESTONE VALLEY ROAD

WEALD WAY

Oldpark Wood

Moyle Ho.

TUPWOOD LANE
SCRUBBS ROAD

Fosterdown Fort

Gravelly Hill

GRAVELLY HILL

ROUGHETTS LA.

M25

GODSTONE HILL

QUARRY RD.

Quarry Farm

Winders Hill

Carr's Croft

Paddock Wood

Rookery

Woldingham School

Whitefield Plantation

Horse Shaw

GANGERS HILL

Hanging Wood

Fosterdown Farm

6

GODSTONE

A22

BYPASS

Palmer's Wood

Flower Wood

Streete Court (Sch.)

Fire Sta.
FOSTER DOWN
TYLER'S CLOSE
B2235
BAKERS MEAD
OCKLEYS
LINDLEY
DUNKIRK SQUARE
OCKLEYS MEAD
EVELYN GDNS.
Old Surrey Hounds (P.H.)
CROWHURST MEAD
Ch.

North Park Farm

NORTH PARK LA.

Tyler's Green
East Res.

West Reservoir
Ivy Mill Nursery

HIGH
OXTED
SALISBURY RD.
COURT RD.
ROGERS WAY
DEWLANDS
A25

ROAD

FLOWER LA.

Bay Pond

Sch.
restriction
CHURCH LA.
St. Mary's Home
Church Town

BLETCHINGLEY RD.

Stangrove Hall

GODSTONE ROAD
A25 Cem.
SUNNYBANK VILLAS
CHEVINGTON VILLAS
Chevington Farm
Water Ho.
WATERHOUSE

IVY MILL LANE

THE PRIORY
Sch.
ROGERS MEAD
WILLOW WAY
BELL MEADOW
POLICE STA. RD.
HIGH ST.
MILL
IVY
White Hart Restaurant

Godstone

BULLBEGGARS

LOVE LA.
Godstone Farm
TILBURSTOW HILL
Stratton Br.
EASTBOURNE RD.
B2236

LEIGH MILL LA.
Leigh Place
Pond
Walkingstead Pond

Width restriction
Width restriction
ENTERDENT restriction

Garston Park

RABIES
KENRICK SQU.
BRACEY HILL
NIGHTINGALE WY.
GAYLER CL.
HART CL.

HEATH

Tilburstow Hill

TILBURSTOW HILL ROAD

P

Coldharbour Ho.

Mereland Wood

Tilburstowhill Common

Sewage Works
BONE MILL LA.

BYPASS

A22

A   B   C

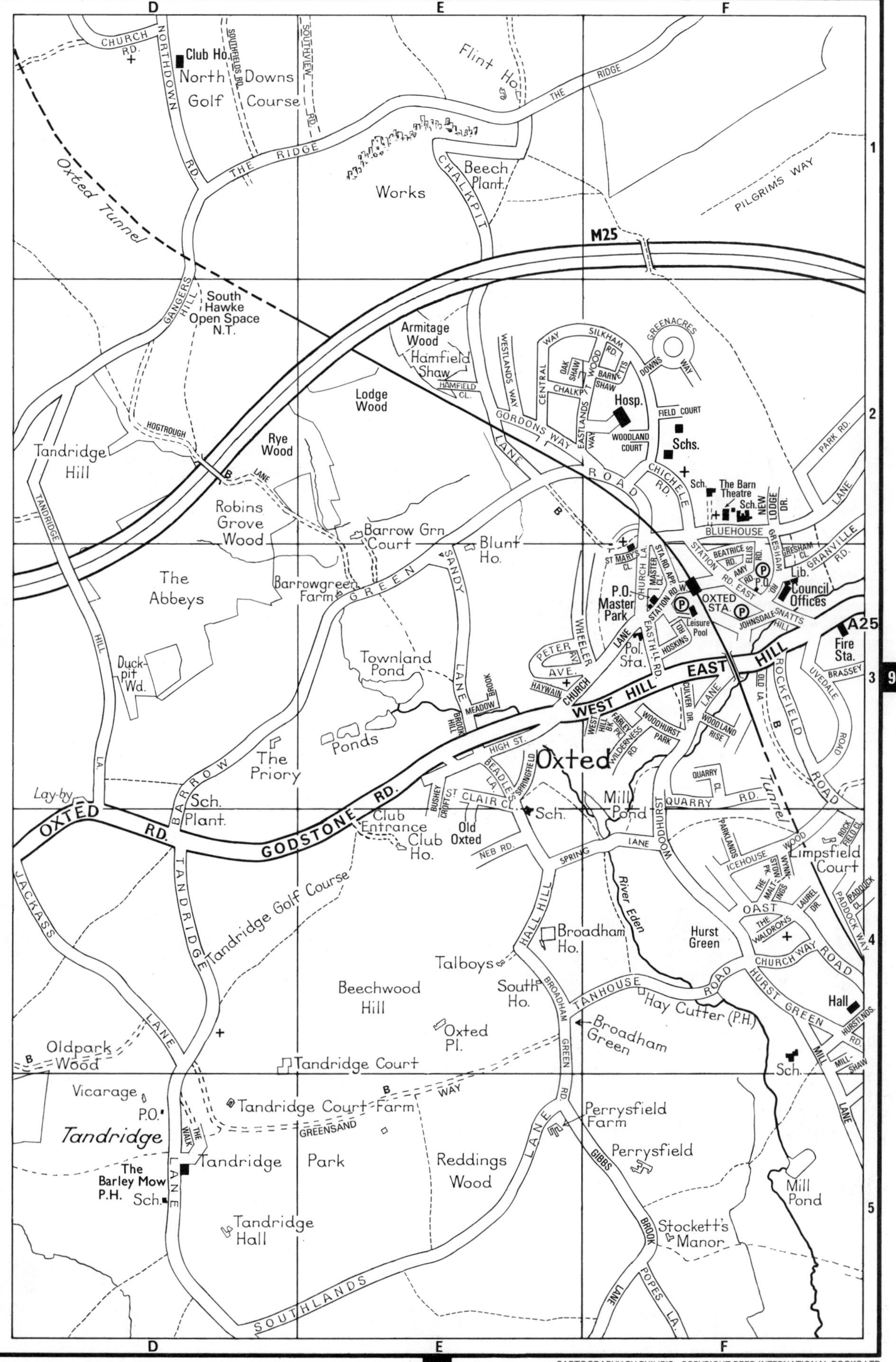

76
D
E
F
Club Ho.
North Downs Golf Course
Flint Ho.
THE RIDGE
Works
Beech Plant.
CHALKPIT
Oxted Tunnel
PILGRIM'S WAY
M25
South Hawke Open Space N.T.
Armitage Wood
Hamfield Shaw
Lodge Wood
Rye Wood
Tandridge Hill
Robins Grove Wood
Barrow Grn Court
Blunt Ho.
The Abbeys
Barrowgreen Farm
Duckpit Wd.
Townland Pond
Ponds
The Priory
Hosp.
Schs.
The Barn Theatre
P.O. Master Park
OXTED STA.
Lib.
Council Offices
Leisure Pool
Pol. Sta.
Fire Sta.
A25
WEST HILL
EAST HILL
Oxted
Mill Pond
Lay-by
OXTED RD.
GODSTONE RD.
Sch. Plant.
Club Entrance
Club Ho.
Old Oxted
Limpsfield Court
Tandridge Golf Course
River Eden
Hurst Green
Broadham Ho.
Talboys
Beechwood Hill
South Ho.
Hay Cutter (P.H.)
Broadham Green
Hall
Oxted Pl.
Oldpark Wood
Tandridge Court
Vicarage
P.O.
Tandridge
Tandridge Court Farm
Perrysfield Farm
Perrysfield
The Barley Mow P.H.
Tandridge Park
Reddings Wood
Mill Pond
Tandridge Hall
Stockett's Manor
SOUTHLANDS
1
2
3
4
5
94
112

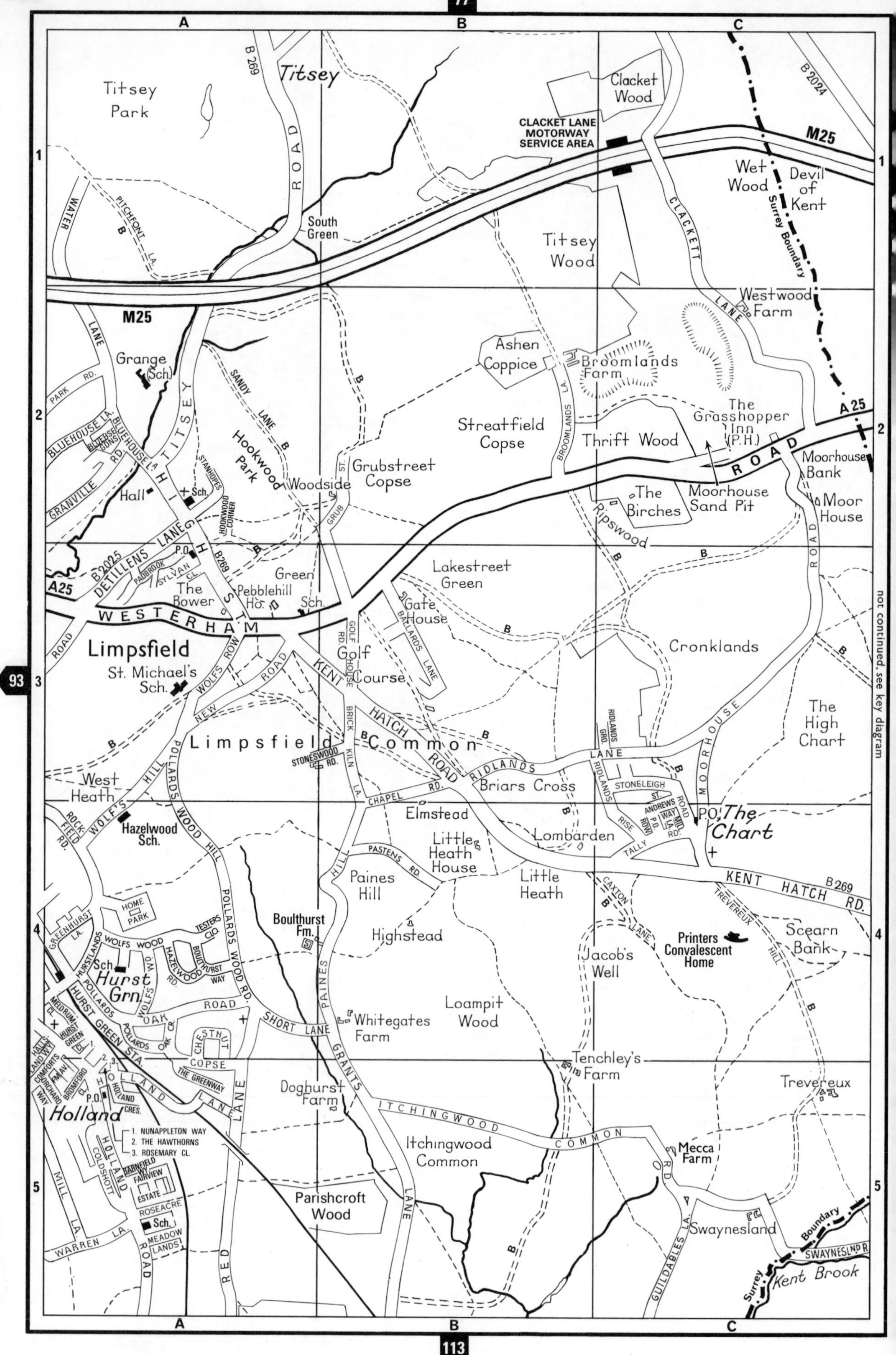
77
Titsey Park
Titsey
South Green
Clacket Wood
CLACKET LANE MOTORWAY SERVICE AREA
M25
Wet Wood
Devil of Kent
Surrey Boundary
Titsey Wood
Westwood Farm
Grange (Sch.)
Ashen Coppice
Broomlands Farm
Hookwood Park
Streatfield Copse
Thrift Wood
The Grasshopper Inn (P.H.)
Grubstreet Copse
Woodside
The Birches
Moorhouse Sand Pit
Moorhouse Bank
Moor House
Hall
Lakestreet Green
The Bower
Pebblehill Ho.
Green
Sch.
Gate House
Limpsfield
St. Michael's Sch.
Golf Course
Cronklands
Limpsfield Common
The High Chart
West Heath
Briars Cross
Hazelwood Sch.
Elmstead
Little Heath House
Lombarden
The Chart
Paines Hill
Little Heath
Boulthurst Fm.
Highstead
Printers Convalescent Home
Scearn Bank
Hurst Grn
Jacob's Well
Loampit Wood
Whitegates Farm
Tenchley's Farm
Trevereux
Doghurst Farm
Holland
Itchingwood Common
Mecca Farm
Parishcroft Wood
Swaynesland
Kent Brook
1. NUNAPPLETON WAY
2. THE HAWTHORNS
3. ROSEMARY CL.
not continued, see key diagram
93
113

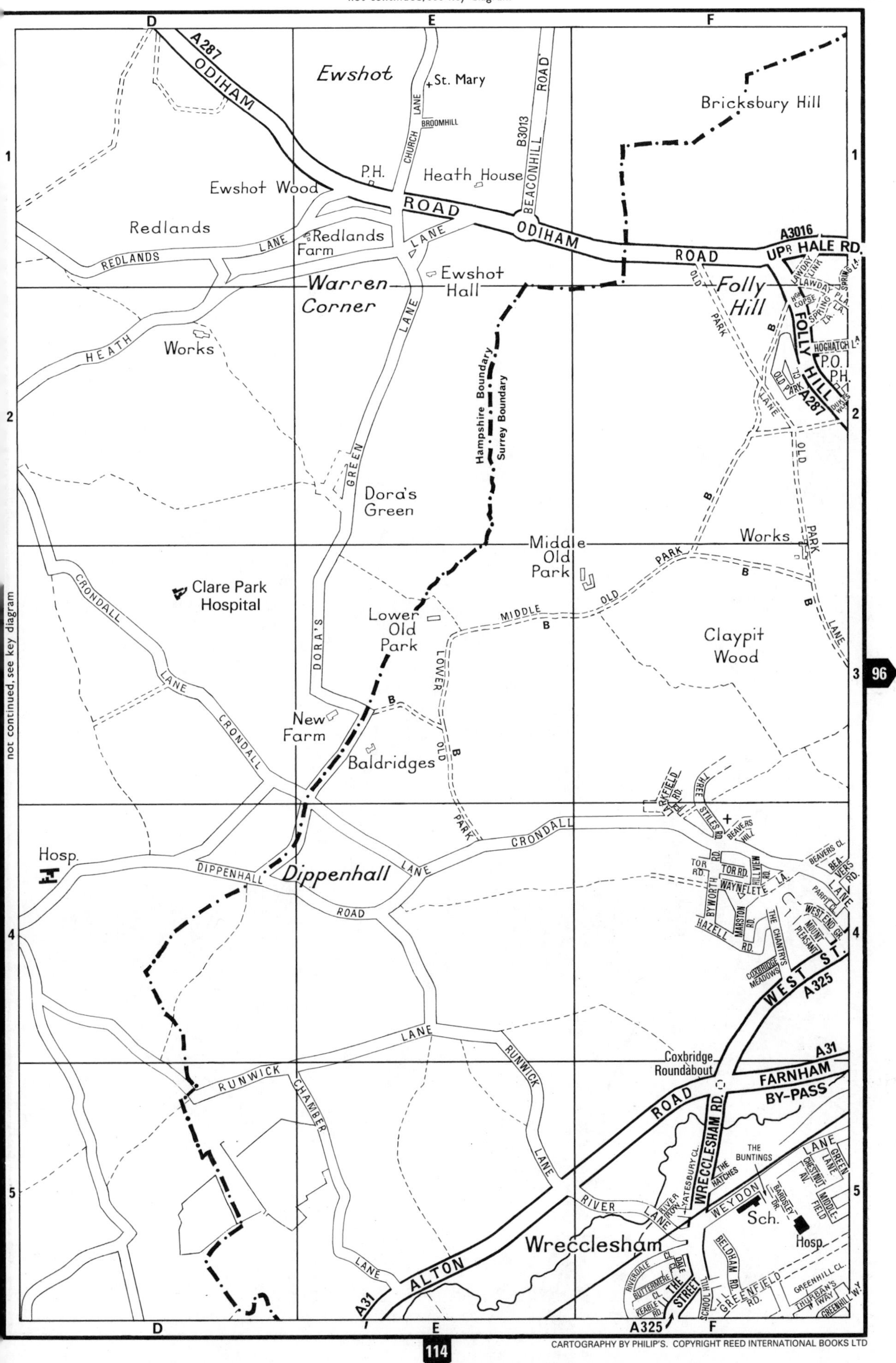

D   A287   ODIHAM

Ewshot   + St. Mary   Bricksbury Hill

CHURCH LANE   BROOMHILL

B3013

BEACONHILL ROAD

Ewshot Wood   Heath House

P.H.   ROAD   ODIHAM   ROAD   UPR HALE RD.

A3016

Redlands   Redlands Farm   A287   FOLLY HILL

REDLANDS   LANE   LANE   Folly Hill

Warren Corner   Ewshot Hall   P.O.   PH.

HEATH   Works   HOGHATCH LA.

Hampshire Boundary   Surrey Boundary

GREEN   Dora's Green   OLD PARK A287   Works

OLD PARK LANE   B

Clare Park Hospital   Middle Old Park   B

DORA'S   Claypit Wood

Lower Old Park   MIDDLE   B

CRONDALL   LOWER   96

LANE   New Farm   B   B   3

CRONDALL   Baldridges   OLD   B

PARK LANE   CRONDALL   Hosp.   DIPPENHALL   Dippenhall

WAYNFLETE

HAZELL   WEST ST.   A325

ROAD   A31   FARNHAM BY-PASS

LANE   Coxbridge Roundabout   THE BUNTINGS

RUNWICK   WRECCLESHAM RD.   WEYDON LANE   Sch.   Hosp.

CHAMBER LANE   Road   RIVER LANE   BELDHAM RD.   GREENFIELD RD.

RUNWICK   THE STREET

ALTON   Wrecclesham

A31   A325

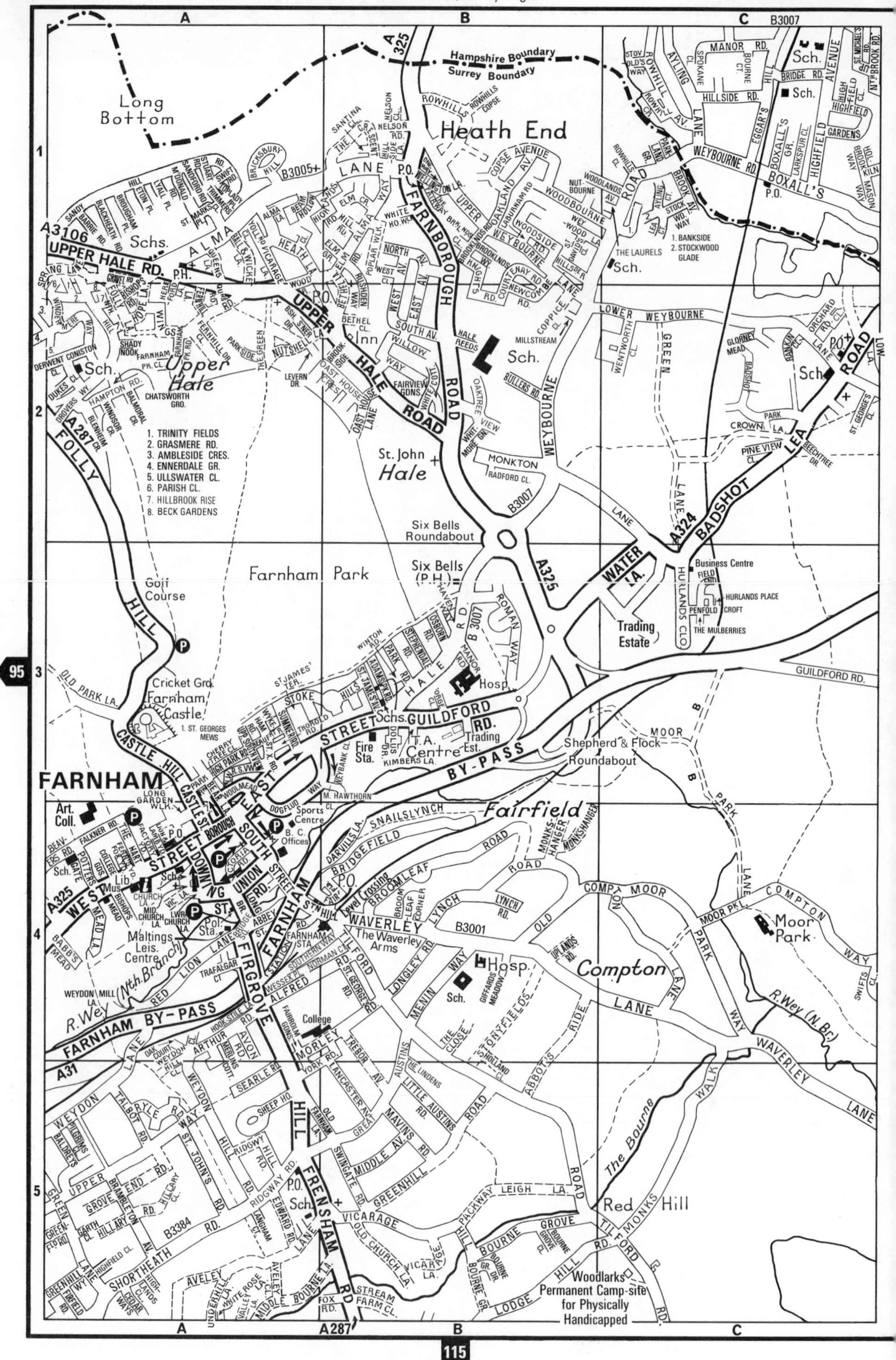

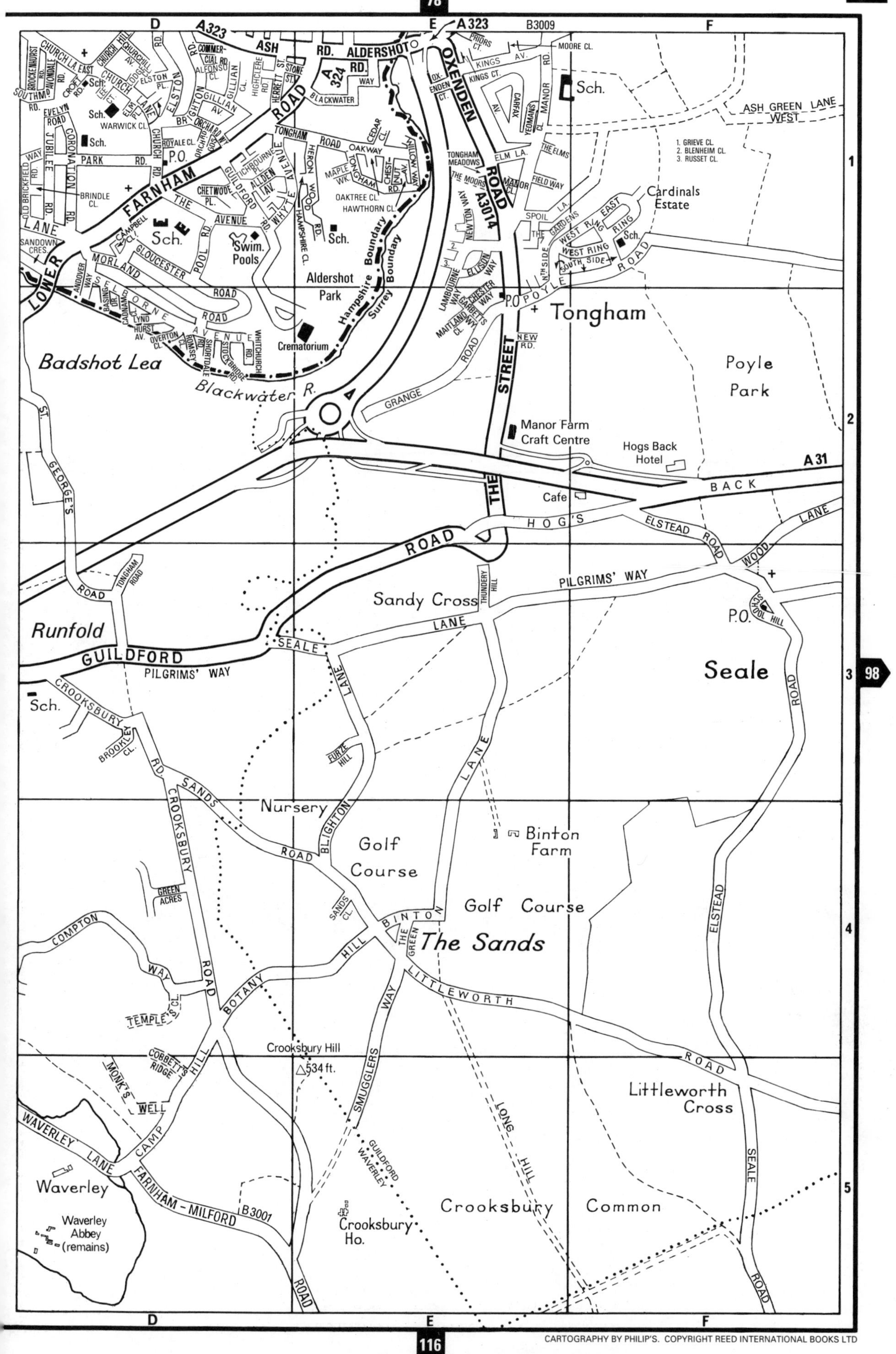

CARTOGRAPHY BY PHILIP'S. COPYRIGHT REED INTERNATIONAL BOOKS LTD

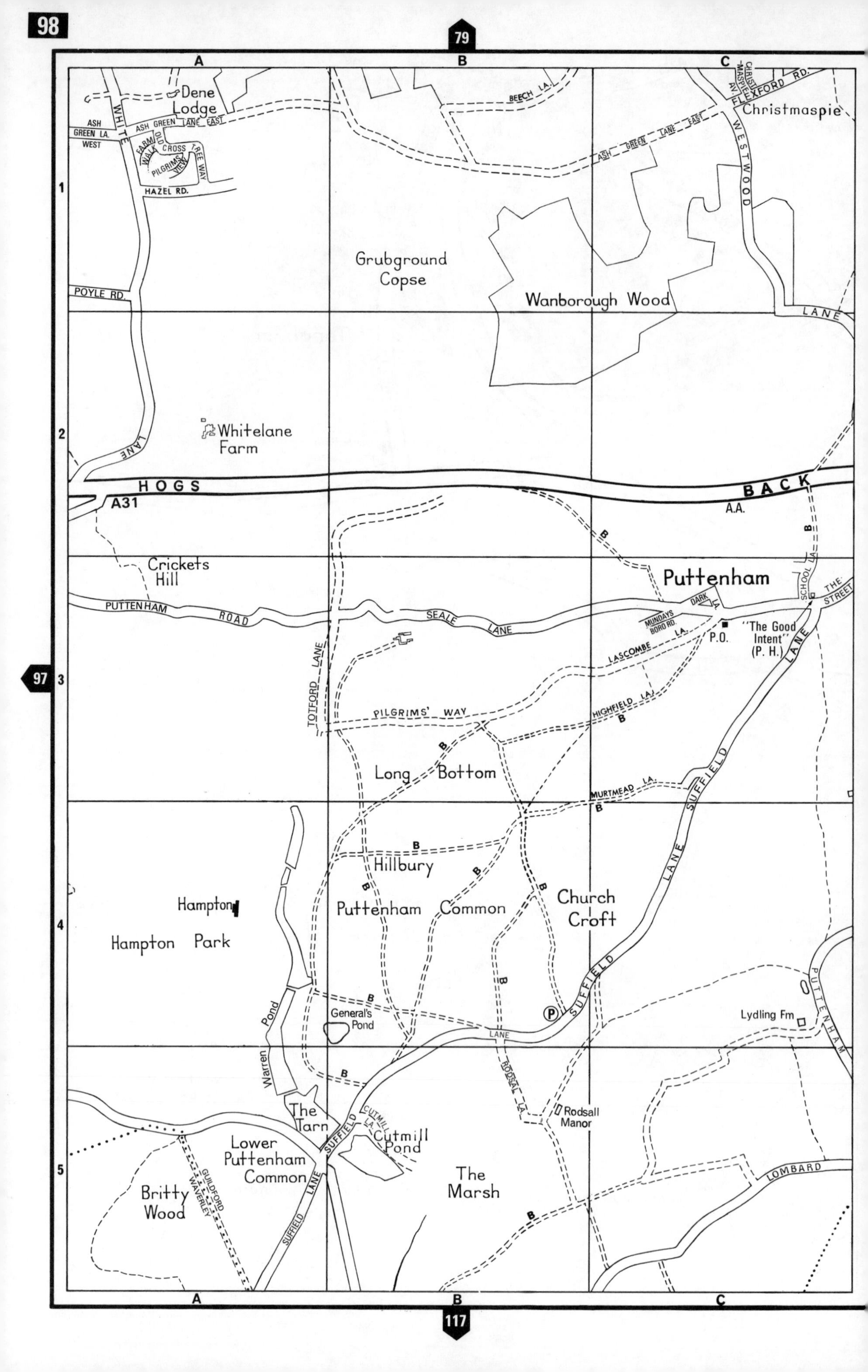

A   B   C

Dene Lodge

ASH GREEN LA. WEST

FARM WALK

ASH GREEN LANE EAST

PILGRIMS VIEW

CROSS TREE WAY

HAZEL RD.

CHRISTMASPIE AV.

FLEXFORD RD.

Christmaspie

ASH GREEN LANE EAST

WESTWOOD

LANE

1

POYLE RD

Grubground Copse

Wanborough Wood

LANE

Whitelane Farm

2

H O G S   B A C K

A31

A.A.

Crickets Hill

Puttenham

SCHOOL LA.

THE STREET

PUTTENHAM   ROAD

SEALE   LANE

DARK LA.

MUNDAYS BORO RD.

P.O.

"The Good Intent" (P. H.)

TOTFORD LANE

LASCOMBE

LA.

3

PILGRIMS' WAY

HIGHFIELD LA.

B

Long   Bottom

B

B

MURTMEAD LA.

B

Hillbury

B

B

Hampton

SUFFIELD   LANE

Puttenham   Common

B

Church Croft

Hampton Park

4

PUTTENHAM

Pond

B

B

General's Pond

P

SUFFIELD

Lydling Fm

LANE

RODSAL LA.

Warren

B

Rodsall Manor

The Tarn

CUTMILL LA.

Cutmill Pond

LOMBARD

5

Lower Puttenham Common

The Marsh

B

Britty Wood

GUILDFORD WAVERLEY

SUFFIELD LANE

A   B   C

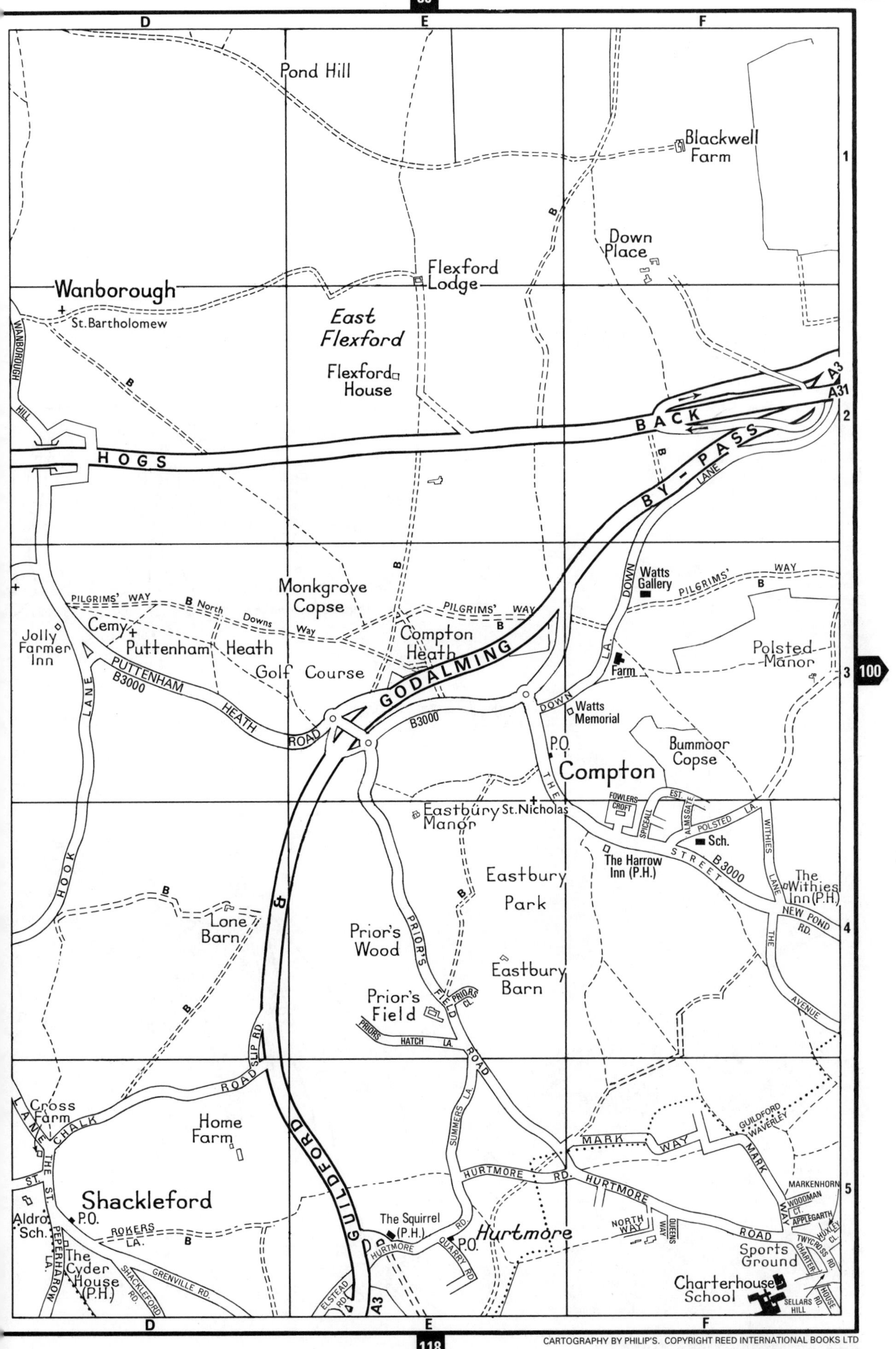

D · E · F

1

2

3

4

5

Pond Hill

Blackwell Farm

Down Place

Wanborough
+ St.Bartholomew

Flexford Lodge

East Flexford

Flexford House

A3
A31

HOGS   BACK   BY-PASS

LANE

Monkgrove Copse

Watts Gallery

PILGRIMS'   WAY

Polsted Manor

Jolly Farmer Inn

PILGRIMS' WAY   North   Downs   Way

Cemy
+ Puttenham   Heath

Compton Heath
Golf Course

GODALMING

DOWN   LA.

Farm

LANE

Watts Memorial

PUTTENHAM   HEATH   ROAD   B3000

B3000

P.O.

Bummoor Copse

Compton

HOOK   LANE

Eastbury St.Nicholas
Manor

FOWLERS CROFT
SPICEALL
EST
ALMSGATE
POLSTED   LA.
WITHIES   LANE

Sch.

The Withies Inn (P.H.)

The Harrow Inn (P.H.)

STREET   B 3000

NEW POND RD.

THE

Lone Barn

Eastbury Park

Prior's Wood

Eastbury Barn

PRIOR'S FIELD

PRIORS ROAD

AVENUE

Prior's Field

PRIORS   HATCH LA.

ROAD SLIP RD.

GUILDFORD

SUMMERS LA.

MARK   WAY

GUILDFORD WAVERLEY

Cross Farm

Home Farm

CHALK   LANE   THE ST.   ST. PETERHAROW

HURTMORE RD.   HURTMORE

MARK   WAY

MARKENHORN
WOODMAN CT.
APPLEGARTH
TWYCROSS RD.
HUXLEY CL.
CHARTER RD.
HOUSE RD.

Shackleford

ROKERS LA.

The Squirrel (P.H.)

HURTMORE RD.

QUARRY RD.

P.O.

Hurtmore

NORTH WAY   QUEENS WAY

Sports Ground

Aldro Sch.
P.O.

GRENVILLE RD.

SHACKLEFORD RD.

ELSTEAD RD.

A3

Charterhouse School

SELLARS HILL

The Cyder House (P.H.)

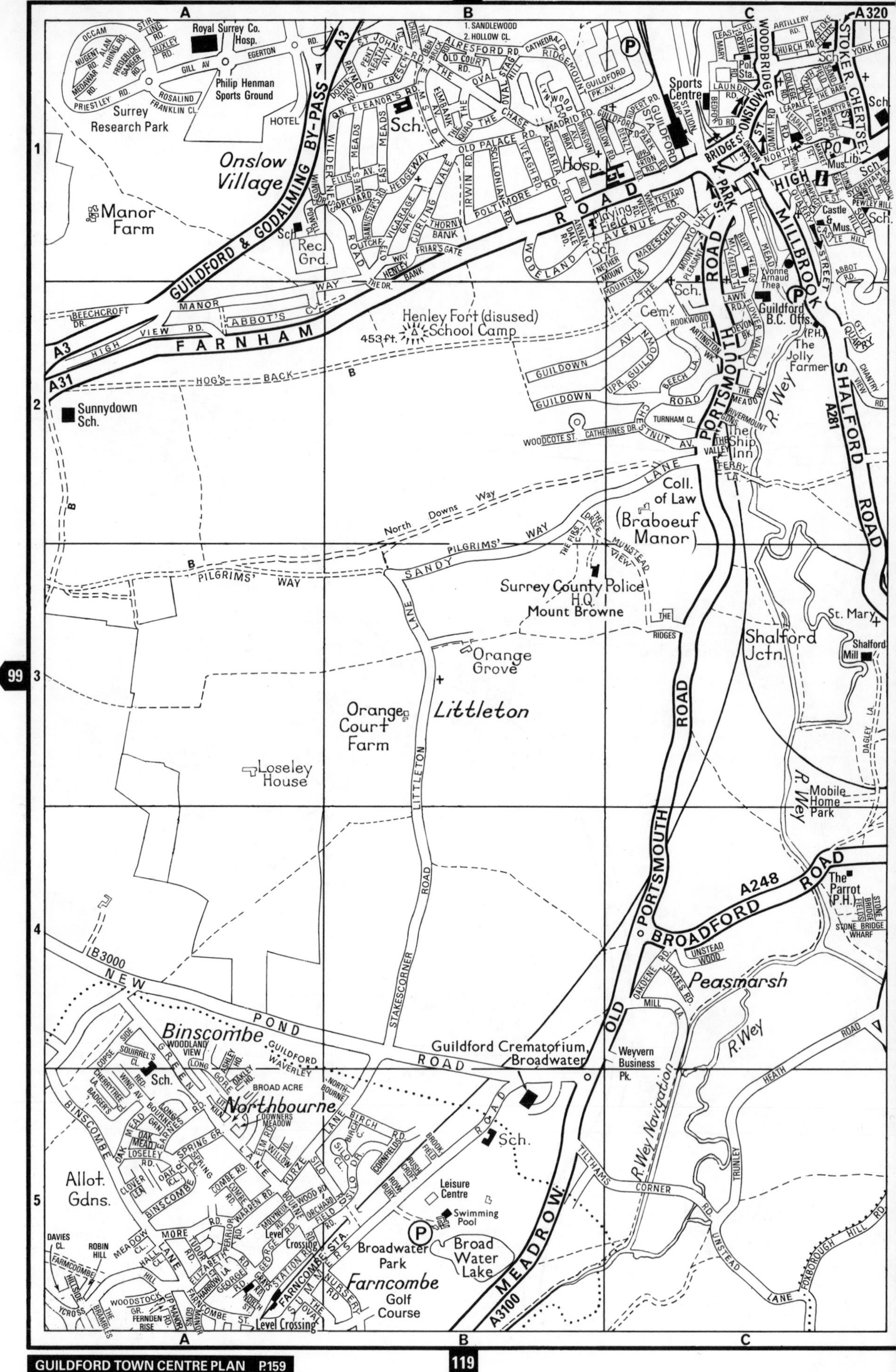
81
A
B
C
1
2
3
4
5
99
Royal Surrey Co. Hosp.
Philip Henman Sports Ground
Surrey Research Park
Onslow Village
Manor Farm
GUILDFORD & GODALMING BY-PASS
A3
A31
FARNHAM ROAD
HOG'S BACK
HIGH VIEW RD.
BEECHCROFT DR.
MANOR WAY
ABBOT'S CL.
Henley Fort (disused) School Camp
453 ft.
Sunnydown Sch.
Rec. Grd.
Sch.
Hosp.
Playing Field
Sports Centre
GUILDFORD STA.
ONSLOW ST.
BRIDGE ST.
PARK ST.
HIGH ST.
MILLBROOK
PORTSMOUTH ROAD
SHALFORD ROAD
A281
A320
STOKE RD.
CHERTSEY ST.
Pol. Sta.
P.O.
Lib.
Mus.
Castle & Mus.
Yvonne Arnaud Thea.
Guildford B.C. Offs.
The Jolly Farmer (P.H.)
R. Wey
The Ship Inn
Cem.
GUILDOWN AV.
GUILDOWN ROAD
CHESTNUT AV.
WOODCOTE ST. CATHERINES DR.
TURNHAM CL.
North Downs Way
PILGRIMS' WAY
SANDY LANE
Coll. of Law (Braboeuf Manor)
Surrey County Police H.Q. Mount Browne
Orange Grove
Littleton
Orange Court Farm
Loseley House
LITTLETON LANE
STAKESCORNER ROAD
Shalford Jctn.
St. Mary
Shalford Mill
Mobile Home Park
A248
BROADFORD ROAD
The Parrot (P.H.)
STONE BRIDGE WHARF
OLD PORTSMOUTH ROAD
Peasmarsh
R. Wey Navigation
Weyvern Business Pk.
Guildford Crematorium, Broadwater
B 3000
NEW POND ROAD
Binscombe
Northbourne
Sch.
Allot. Gdns.
Leisure Centre
Swimming Pool
Broadwater Park
Broad Water Lake
Farncombe Golf Course
Level Crossing
MEADROW
A3100
TILTHAMS CORNER RD.
UNSTEAD LANE
FOXBOROUGH HILL RD.
HEATH ROAD
TRUNLEY
119

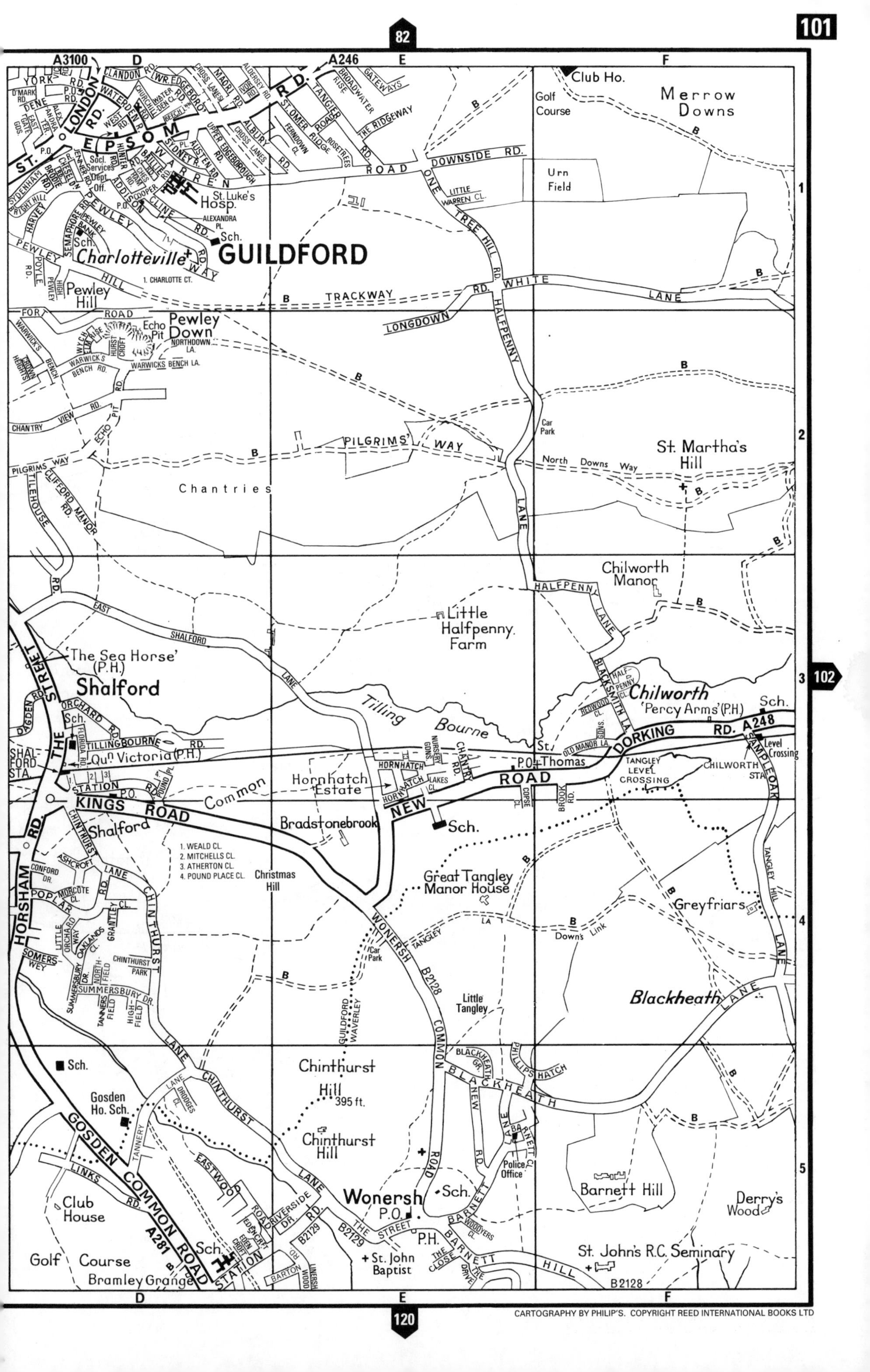
82
GUILDFORD
Charlotteville
Pewley Hill
Pewley Down
Chantries
St. Luke's Hosp.
Merrow Downs
Urn Field
Golf Course
Club Ho.
St. Martha's Hill
North Downs Way
PILGRIMS' WAY
TRACKWAY
WHITE LANE
Chilworth Manor
Little Halfpenny Farm
Shalford
'The Sea Horse' (P.H.)
Qu^n Victoria (P.H.)
Tilling Bourne
Chilworth
'Percy Arms' (P.H.)
DORKING RD. A248
NEW ROAD
KINGS ROAD
Hornhatch Estate
Bradstonebrook
Common
Christmas Hill
Great Tangley Manor House
Greyfriars
Blackheath
Little Tangley
Chinthurst Hill
395 ft.
Wonersh
St. John Baptist
Barnett Hill
Derry's Wood
St. John's R.C. Seminary
Club House
Golf Course
Bramley Grange
Gosden Ho. Sch.
GOSDEN COMMON ROAD
A281
HORSHAM RD.
WONERSH COMMON ROAD
B2128
B2129
1. WEALD CL.
2. MITCHELLS CL.
3. ATHERTON CL.
4. POUND PLACE CL.
1. CHARLOTTE CT.
102
120

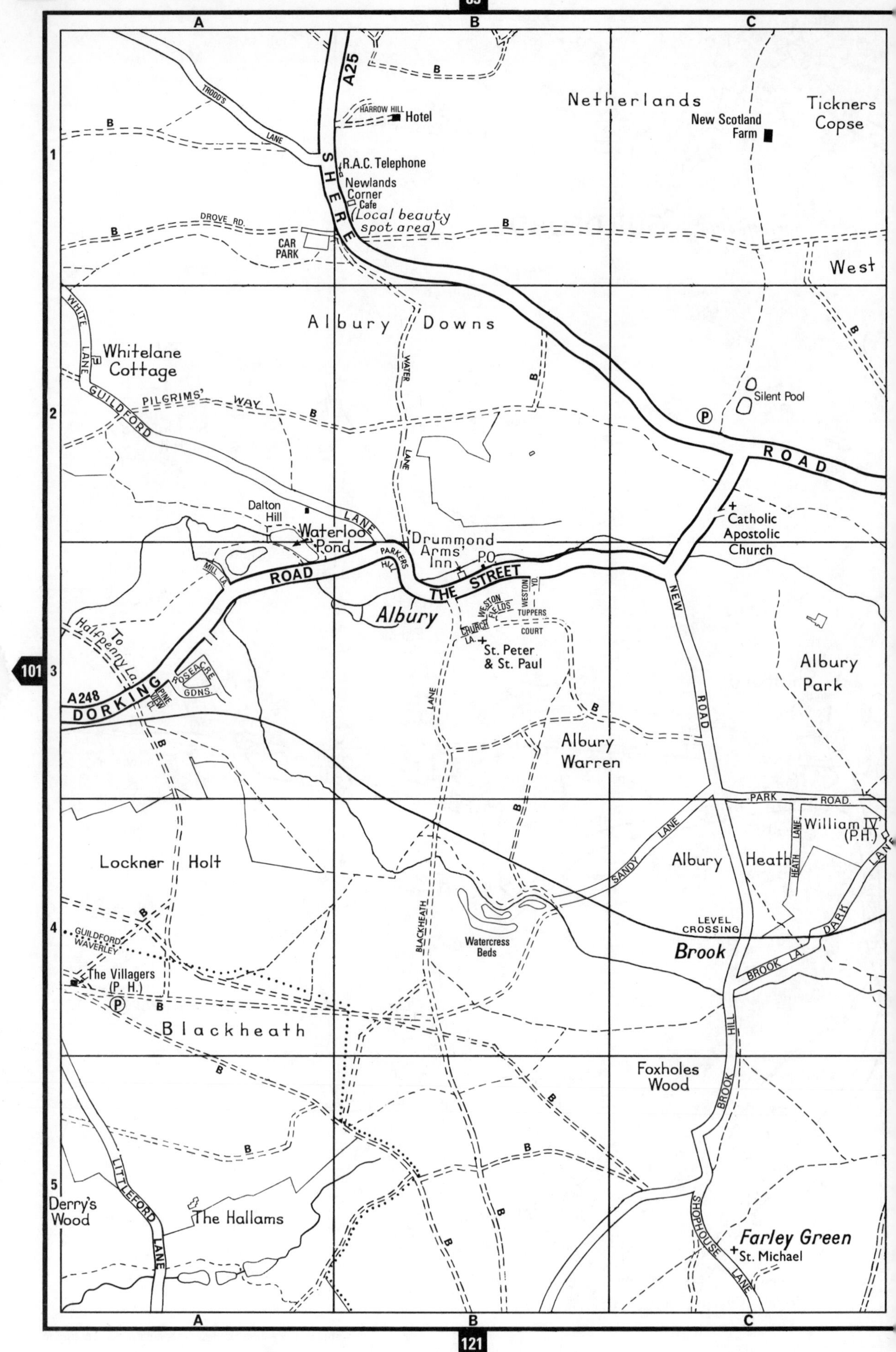

A25

TRODD'S LANE

B

B

Netherlands

Tickners Copse

New Scotland Farm

HARROW HILL ■ Hotel

R.A.C. Telephone

Newlands Corner Cafe

(Local beauty spot area)

DROVE RD.

B

SHERE

CAR PARK

West

B

1

Albury Downs

WHITE LANE

Whitelane Cottage

GUILDFORD

PILGRIMS' WAY

B

WATER LANE

B

Silent Pool

P

ROAD

2

Dalton Hill

Waterloo Pond

MILL LA.

GUILDFORD ROAD

PARKERS HILL

Drummond Arms' Inn

PO

THE STREET

Albury

WESTON FIELDS

WESTON YD.

TUPPERS COURT

CHURCH LA.

St. Peter & St. Paul

Catholic Apostolic Church

NEW ROAD

Albury Park

3

To Halfpenny La.

DORKING

A248

ROSEACRE GDNS.

PINE VIEW

B

LANE

B

Albury Warren

B

PARK ROAD

William IV (P.H.)

HEATH LANE

DARK LANE

Lockner Holt

B

SANDY LANE

Albury Heath

LEVEL CROSSING

BLACKHEATH

Watercress Beds

Brook

BROOK LA.

4

GUILDFORD WAVERLEY

The Villagers (P. H.)

P

B

Blackheath

BROOK HILL

B

B

Foxholes Wood

B

5

Derry's Wood

LITTLEFORD LANE

The Hallams

WATER LANE

B

B

SHOPHOUSE LANE

Farley Green

St. Michael

A

B

C

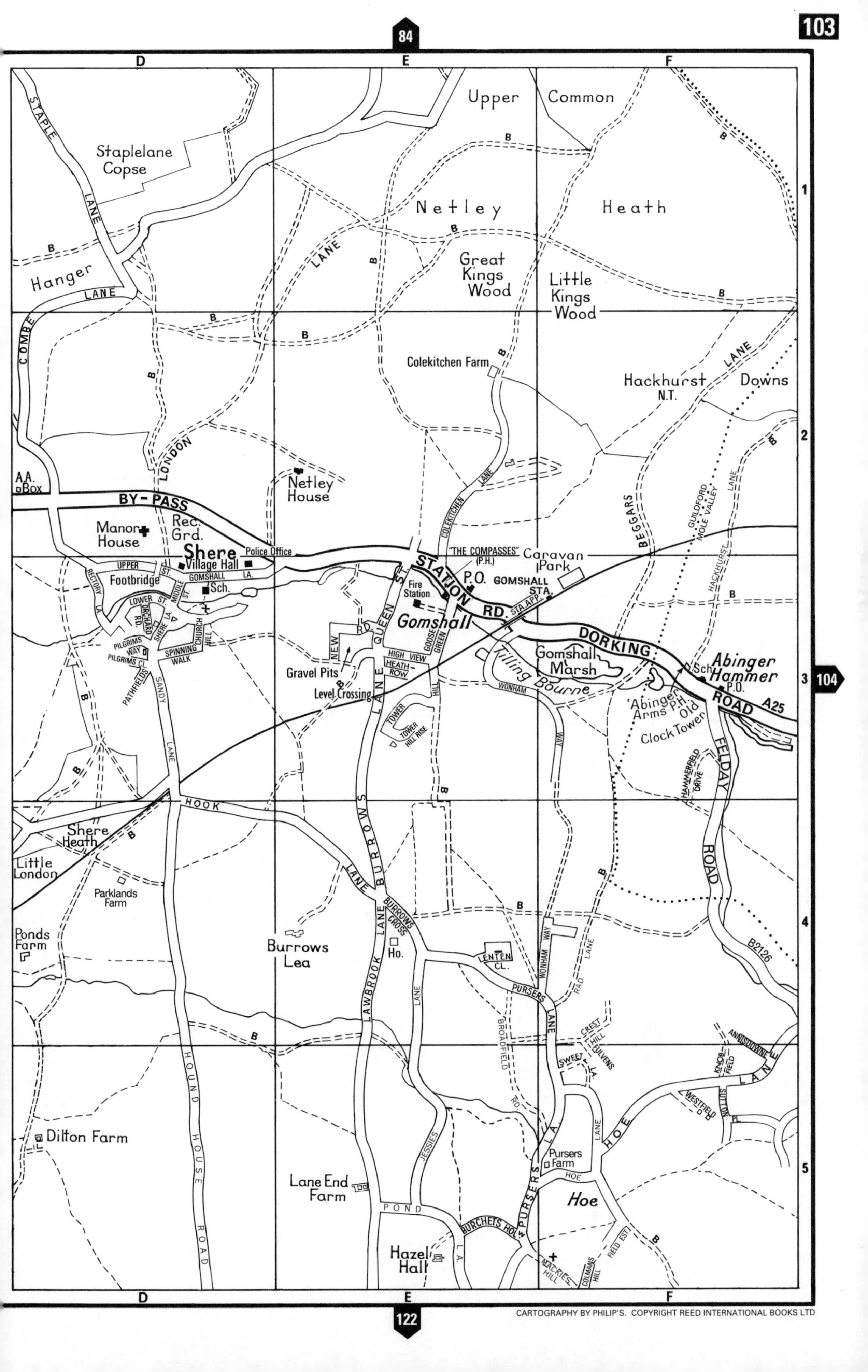

CARTOGRAPHY BY PHILIP'S. COPYRIGHT REED INTERNATIONAL BOOKS LTD

Effingham Upper Common

GUILDFORD
MOLE VALLEY

Great
Copse

Oaken Grove

Pickett's
Hole

SHEEPWALK LANE

Rifle Range

Coomb
Farm

Blindoak
Gate

Old Simm's
Copse

Dunley
Wood

North Downs Way

Coomb
Copse

WHITE DOWN LANE

New
Barn

Park
Farm

Rectory

COAST
HILL LANE

Leasers
Barn

Deerleap Wood

COAST HILL

THE HUXERY

Fish
Pond

The
Rough

Eversheds
Rough

Car Park

The
Paddock

WEST LANE

St. John's +
Ch.

Wotton

Broomy Downs

Westlane
Barn

Sch.
The
Wotton
Hatch(P.H.)

SHEEPHOUSE LANE

Abinger
Hall

The Crossways

GUILDFORD

ROAD

Horsley
Copse

A25

Paddington
Farm

ABINGER LANE

THE DENE

Abinger
Mill

Tilling Bourne

BRICKYARD LA.

Manor
Farm

Firtree
Plat

HOLLOW LANE

Wotton House

Damphurst
Wood

Townhurst
Wood

Whitings
Wood

Fish
Ponds

Ellix
Wood

Chandlers
Wood

High
Copse

Bushy
Wood

RAIKES

HOLLOW RAIKES

Stone Age
Farm

Mundies
Plantation

Kempslade
Farm

Sutton

The
'Volunteer'
(P.H.)

HORSHAM

WATER LA.

Sch.

St. James
+

Abinger
Hatch(P.H.)

Millpond
Copse

Noons
Corner

Suttonplace
Farm

Frolbury

Abinger
Manor
Farm

ABINGER LANE

LANE

FRIDAY STREET

Stephen
Langton
Inn

Friday
Street

SUTTON

MOLE VALLEY
GUILDFORD

EVELYN
COTT.

GLEBE LA.

Abinger

WOODHOUSE LA.

RADNOR LA.

ROAD

B2126

Pasture Wood

Abinger
Common

Youth
Hostel

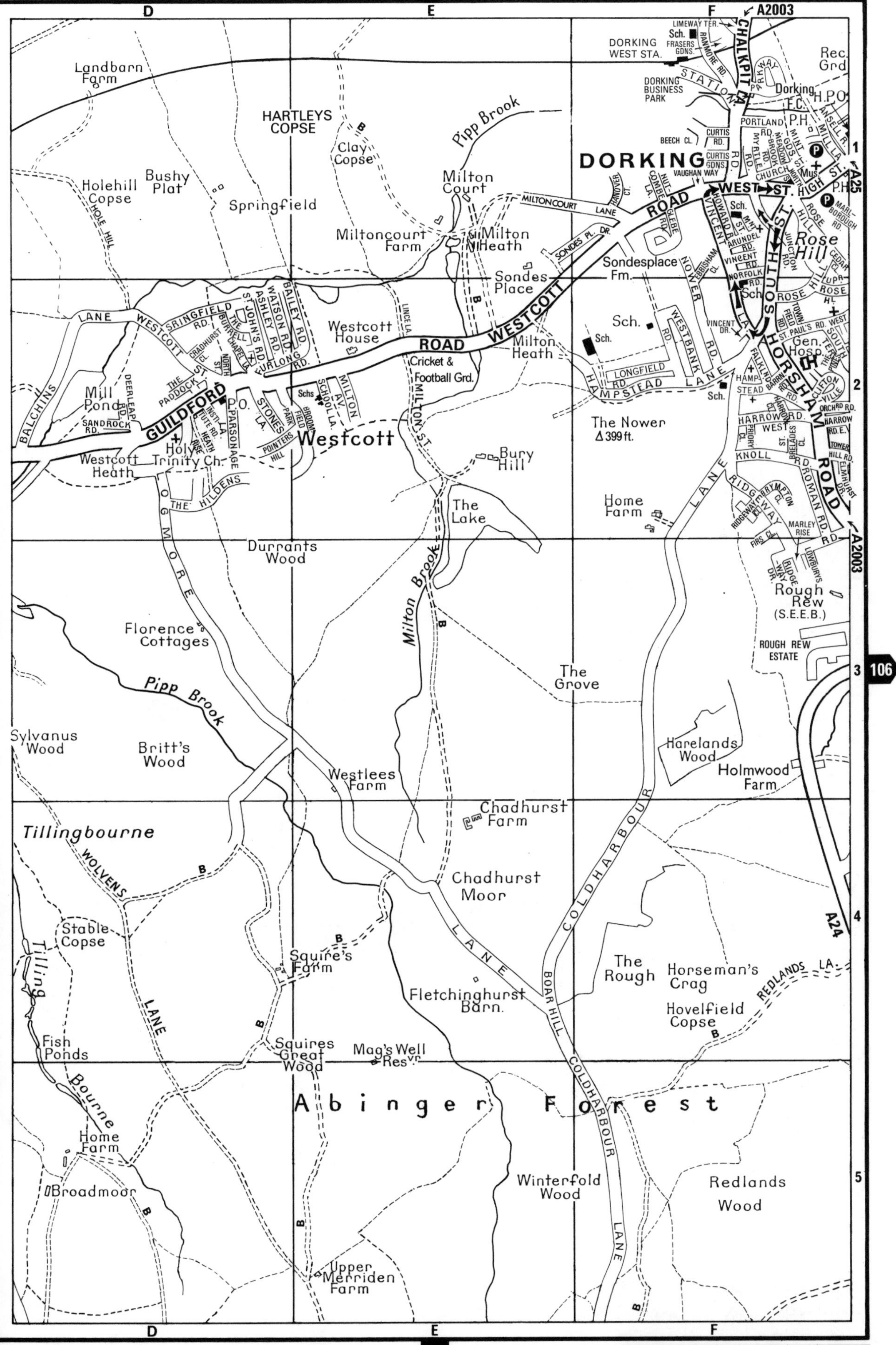

DORKING TOWN CENTRE PLAN P.160

86
Westcott
Abinger Forest
Landbarn Farm
HARTLEYS COPSE
Clay Copse
Pipp Brook
Milton Court
Holehill Copse
Bushy Plat
Springfield
Miltoncourt Farm
Milton Heath
Sondes Place
Sondesplace Fm.
Westcott House
Mill Pond
Holy Trinity Ch.
Westcott Heath
Cricket & Football Grd.
The Nower
Bury Hill
The Lake
Home Farm
Durrants Wood
Milton Brook
Florence Cottages
Rough Rew (S.E.B.)
ROUGH REW ESTATE
The Grove
Sylvanus Wood
Britt's Wood
Westlees Farm
Harelands Wood
Holmwood Farm
Tillingbourne
Chadhurst Farm
Chadhurst Moor
Stable Copse
Squire's Farm
The Rough
Horseman's Crag
Fletchinghurst Barn
Hovelfield Copse
Fish Ponds
Squires Great Wood
Mag's Well Resʳ
Home Farm
Broadmoor
Winterfold Wood
Redlands Wood
Upper Merriden Farm
DORKING WEST STA.
DORKING BUSINESS PARK
Rose Hill
GUILDFORD ROAD
WESTCOTT ROAD
COLDHARBOUR LANE
BOAR HILL
WOLVENS LANE
A2003
A25
A24
106
124

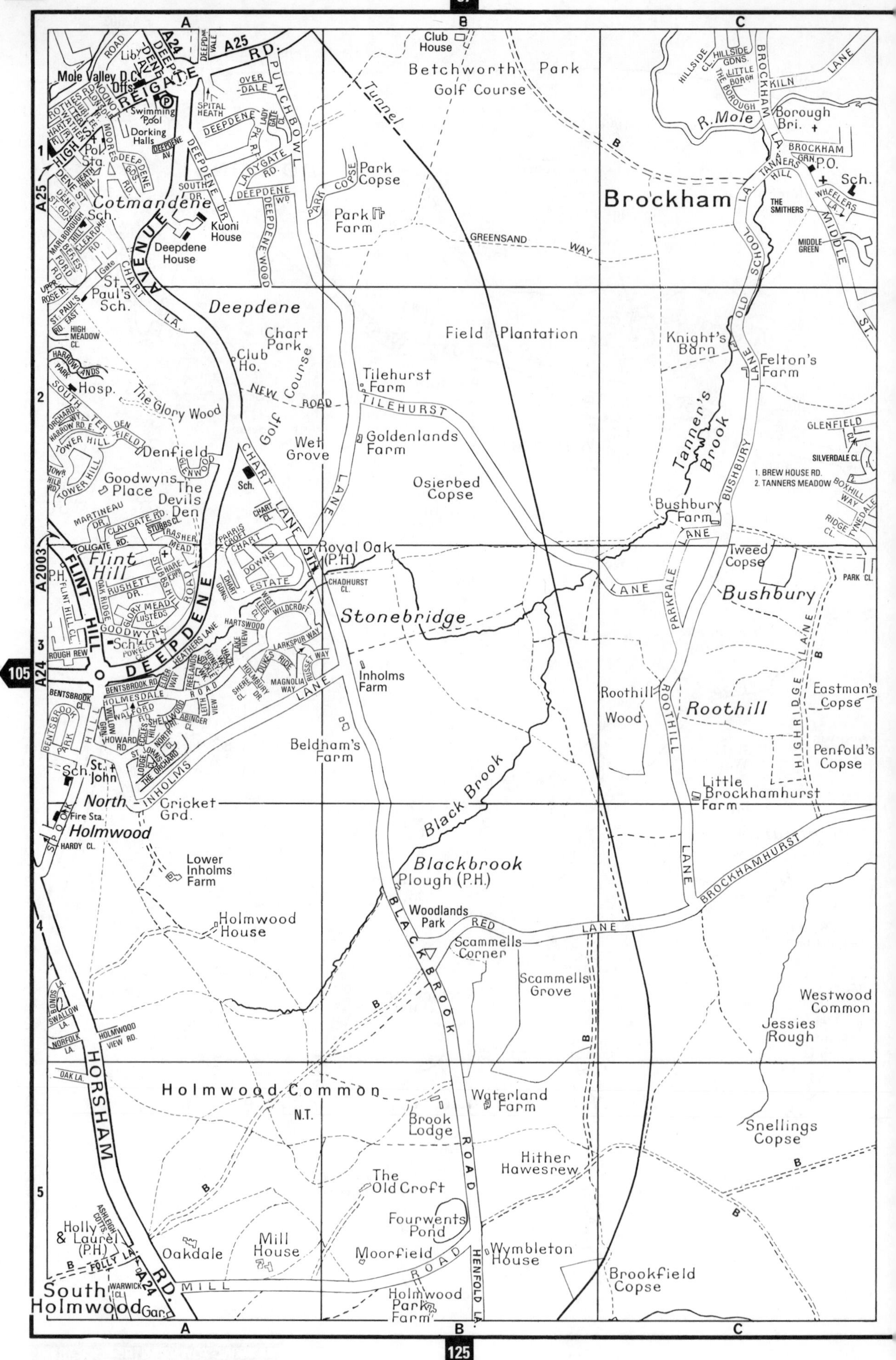
87
125
105
Betchworth Park
Golf Course
Club House
Tunnel
Brockham
R. Mole
Borough Bri.
Cotmandene
Deepdene
Deepdene House
Kuoni House
Mole Valley D.C. Offs.
Dorking Halls
Swimming Pool
Field Plantation
Park Copse
Park Farm
GREENSAND WAY
Knight's Barn
Felton's Farm
Tanner's Brook
Chart Park
Golf Course
Tilehurst Farm
Goldenlands Farm
Wet Grove
Osierbed Copse
The Glory Wood
Denfield
Goodwyns Place
The Devils Den
Flint Hill
Royal Oak (P.H.)
Stonebridge
Bushbury Farm
Tweed Copse
Bushbury
Inholms Farm
Beldham's Farm
Roothill Wood
Roothill
Eastman's Copse
Penfold's Copse
Little Brockhamhurst Farm
North Holmwood
Cricket Grd.
Black Brook
Blackbrook
Plough (P.H.)
Lower Inholms Farm
Holmwood House
Woodlands Park
Scammells Corner
Scammells Grove
Westwood Common
Jessies Rough
Holmwood Common
N.T.
Waterland Farm
Brook Lodge
Snellings Copse
Hither Hawesrew
The Old Croft
Fourwents Pond
Moorfield
Wymbleton House
Brookfield Copse
Mill House
Oakdale
Holly & Laurel (P.H.)
South Holmwood
Holmwood Park Farm
1. BREW HOUSE RD.
2. TANNERS MEADOW
HORSHAM RD.
BLACKBROOK ROAD
MILL ROAD
RED LANE
BROCKHAMHURST
ROOTHILL LANE
HIGHRIDGE LANE
TILEHURST LANE
CHART LANE
DEEPDENE AVENUE
INHOLMS LANE
REIGATE RD.

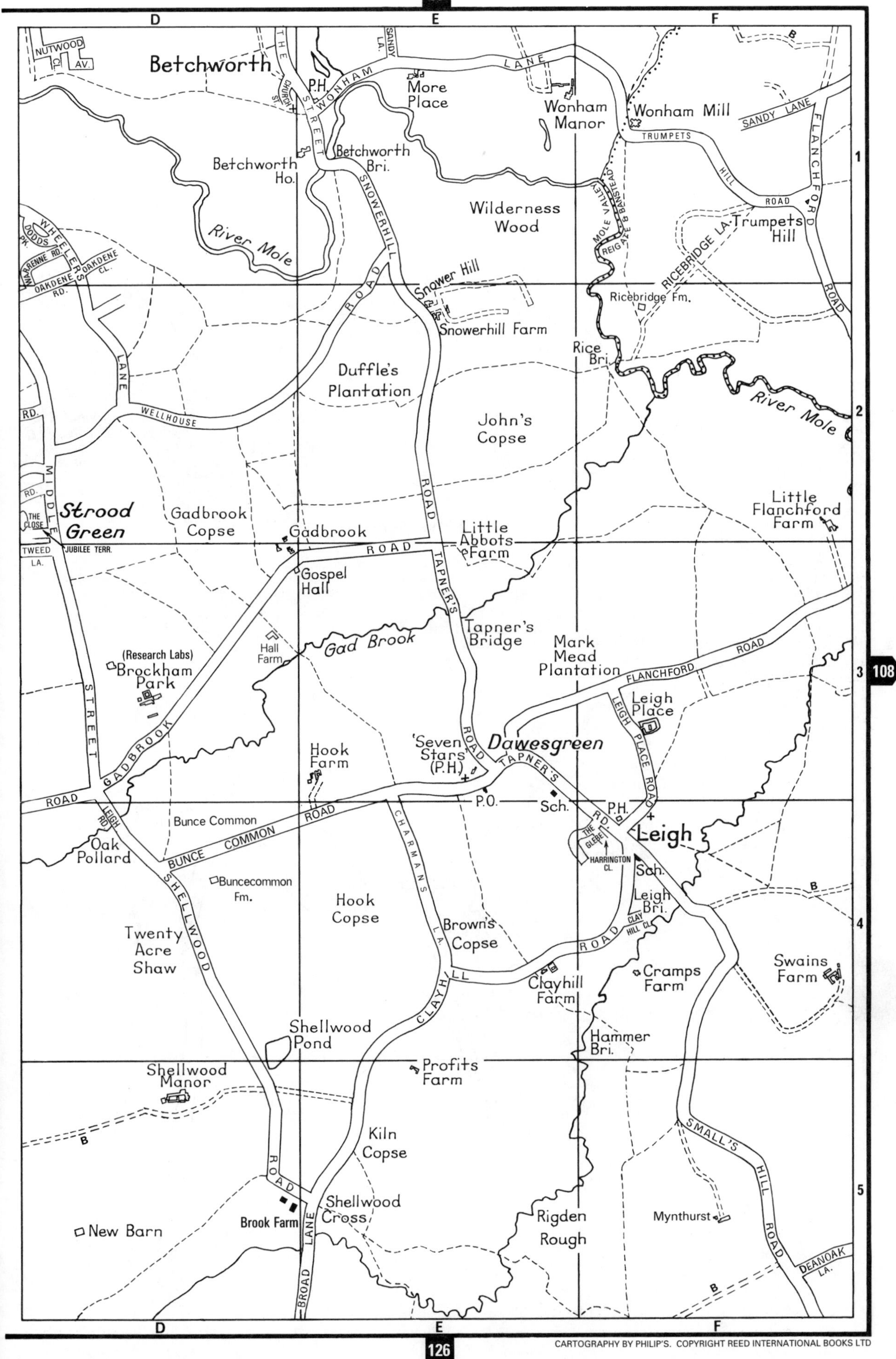

D E F

Betchworth

NUTWOOD AV.

THE CHURCH STREET

WONHAM LANE

SANDY LA.

P.H.

More Place

LANE

Wonham Manor

Wonham Mill

SANDY LANE

TRUMPETS

FLANCHFORD

1

Betchworth Ho.

Betchworth Bri.

SNOWERHILL

Wilderness Wood

MOLE VALLEY

REIGATE B. BENSTEAD

RICEBRIDGE LA.

Trumpets Hill

ROAD

WHEELER'S PK.

DODDS

MARENNE RD. CL.

OAKDENE RD.

OAKDENE CL.

River Mole

ROAD

Snawer Hill

Snowerhill Farm

Ricebridge Fm.

Rice Bri.

River Mole

Little Flanchford Farm

2

RD.

LANE

MIDDLE RD.

WELLHOUSE

Duffle's Plantation

John's Copse

Strood Green

THE CLOSE

TWEED LA.

JUBILEE TERR.

Gadbrook Copse

Gadbrook

ROAD

TAPNER'S

Little Abbots Farm

Little Flanchford Farm

Gospel Hall

ROAD

Tapner's Bridge

Mark Mead Plantation

FLANCHFORD

ROAD

3

STREET

GADBROOK

(Research Labs)

Brockham Park

Hall Farm

Gad Brook

Tapner's Bridge

Leigh Place

LEIGH PLACE ROAD

ROAD

LEIGH

Hook Farm

'Seven Stars' (P.H.)

Dawesgreen

P.O.

Sch.

P.H.

Leigh

THE GLEBE

HARRINGTON CL.

Sch.

Leigh Bri.

Bunce Common

ROAD

CHARMANS LA.

CLAY HILL CL.

Oak Pollard

BUNCE COMMON ROAD

Hook Copse

Brown's Copse

ROAD

Cramps Farm

Swains Farm

4

SHELLWOOD

Buncecommon Fm.

CLAYHILL LL.

Clayhill Farm

Twenty Acre Shaw

ROAD

Shellwood Pond

Hammer Bri.

SMALL'S HILL ROAD

Shellwood Manor

Profits Farm

Kiln Copse

Rigden Rough

Mynthurst

5

B

ROAD

BROAD LANE

Shellwood Cross

DEANOAK LA.

New Barn

Brook Farm

B

D E F

A   B   C

FLANCHFORD RD.

Heathfield

1

Reigate Park

Littleton Farm

431ft.

Park Hill

LESBOURNE RD.

Mead Vale

A217 BELL ST.

South Park

Clayhall Farm

Sch.

Sandcross Hall

COCKSHOT HILL

Woodhatch

WOODHATCH ROAD A2044

2

Flanchford Farm

Doversgreen

The Beehive (P.H.)

Mill Pond

3

Hilly Furze Field

Hartswood Manor

Dovers Farm

Sidlow

REIGATE & BANSTEAD MOLE VALLEY

Sidlow Br.

Bury's Court

Birchett Copse

R. Mole

LONESOME LANE

Bures Manor

Sch.

4

Bell Copse

Dabden Bri.

Irons Bottom

Three Horse Shoes (P.H.)

Kinnersley Manor

Dene Farm

Stumblehole Farm

R. Mole

5

Dulands Copse

DEANOAK LANE

Deanoak Bri.

Moor Copse

Naiderswood

Duxhurst Estate

Lower Duxhurst Cafe

Grove Farm

Groves Cottage

REIGATE ROAD A217

A   B   C

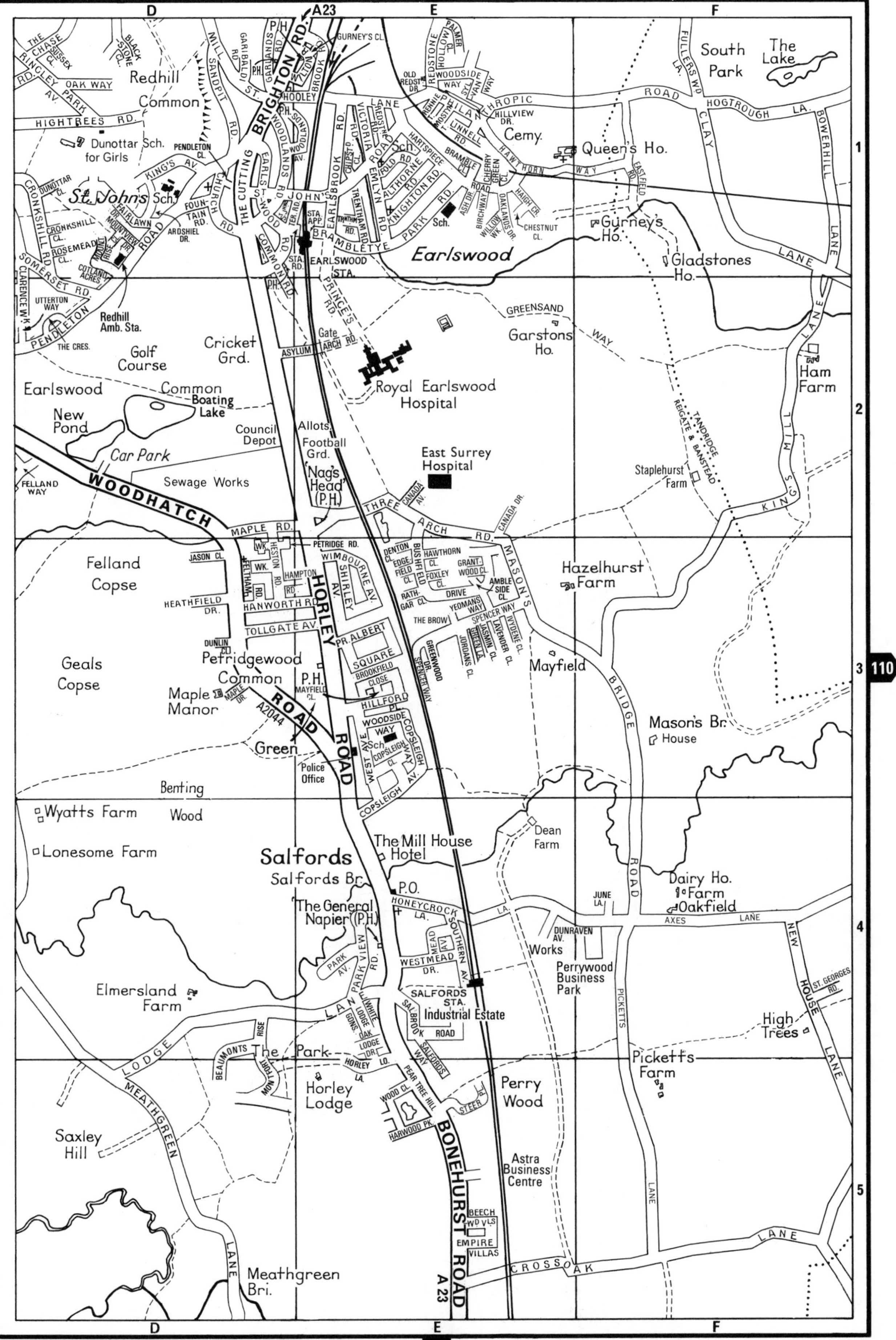

CARTOGRAPHY BY PHILIP'S. COPYRIGHT REED INTERNATIONAL BOOKS LTD

91

A
B
C
1
2
3
4
5
M23
Sandhills
SANDY LANE
MID STREET
BRAES MEAD
KENTWYNS RISE
Sch.
Hall
Allot. Gdns.
South Nutfield
TRINDLES RD.
HOLMESDALE RD.
NUTFIELD STA.
THE COPSE
OAKWOOD CL.
MORRIS RD.
CRICKET HILL
KING'S MEAD
POWERHILL CL.
NETHERLEIGH PK.
THE AVENUE
KINGSCROSS LANE
RIDGEGREEN CL.
THEPPS CL.
Ridgegreen House
Ridge Green
Lyttel Hall
(Brewing Industry Research Foundation)
COOPER'S HILL RD.
Crabhill Ho.
(Winged Fellowship Holiday Home)
Crabhill Farm
CRABHILL LANE
Henhaw Farm
Home Farm
OUTWOOD ROAD
B
Kennels
Old Kiln
Bransland Wood
Poundhill Wood
Temple Wood
Redhill Aerodrome
Lawn Hill
Pond
Burstow Park
MOATS LANE
South Hale Farm
PRINCE OF WALES' ROAD
Furzefield Wood
GREEN LANE
HATCH LANE
Shepheards Hurst
The Orchards
Harewoods
BRICKFIELD ROAD
DAYSEYS
Dog & Duck (P.H.)
Rectory
WASP GREEN LA.
Outwood Common
Torvcross Shaw
HATCH LA.
Outwood
Cricket Grd.
P.O.
Bell Inn (P.H.)
Windmill
Gay Ho.
GAYHOUSE LANE
REIGATE & BANSTEAD
TANDRIDGE
HATHERSHAM LANE
HILL
BELL WEATHER LA.
MILLERS LANE
B.H.
MILLERS COPSE
LITTLE COLLINS
Lodge
Marl Pond
ROOKERY HILL
SCOTT'S HILL

109

129

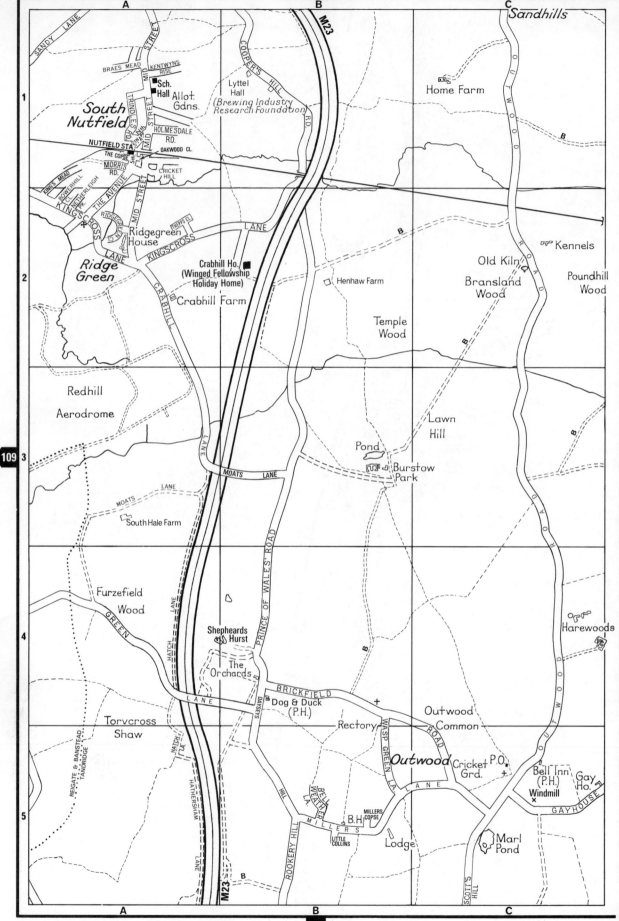

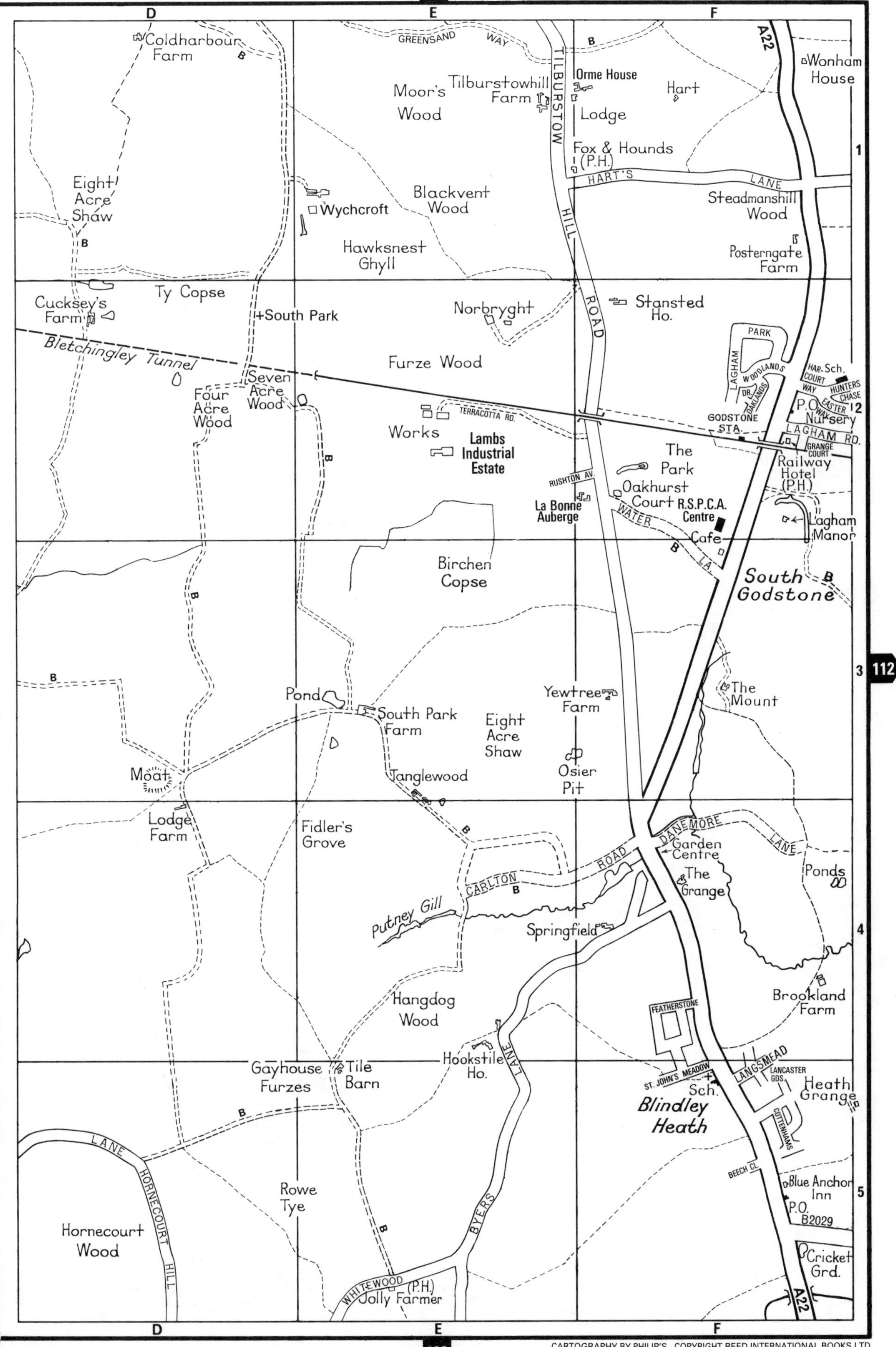

92
D
E
F
Coldharbour Farm
GREENSAND WAY
Moor's Wood
Tilburstowhill Farm
Orme House
Hart
Lodge
Wonham House
A22
TILBURSTOW HILL ROAD
Fox & Hounds (P.H.)
HART'S LANE
Eight Acre Shaw
Wychcroft
Blackvent Wood
Hawksnest Ghyll
Steadmanshill Wood
Posterngate Farm
1
Ty Copse
Cucksey's Farm
South Park
Norbryght
Stansted Ho.
Bletchingley Tunnel
Furze Wood
Seven Acre Wood
Four Acre Wood
PARK
LAGHAM
WOODLANDS
DR.
OAKLANDS
HAR COURT
Sch.
WAY
HUNTERS CHASE
EASTER WAY
P.O.
Nursery
2
TERRACOTTA RD.
Works
Lambs Industrial Estate
GODSTONE STA.
LAGHAM RD.
GRANGE COURT
The Park
Railway Hotel (P.H.)
RUSHTON AV.
Oakhurst Court
R.S.P.C.A. Centre
La Bonne Auberge
WATER LA
Cafe
Lagham Manor
Birchen Copse
South Godstone
3
112
Yewtree Farm
The Mount
Pond
South Park Farm
Eight Acre Shaw
Moat
Osier Pit
Tanglewood
Lodge Farm
Fidler's Grove
DANEMORE LANE
Garden Centre
The Grange
Ponds
CARLTON ROAD
Putney Gill
Springfield
4
Hangdog Wood
FEATHERSTONE
Brookland Farm
Gayhouse Furzes
Tile Barn
Hookstile Ho.
LANE
ST. JOHN'S MEADOW
Sch.
LANGSMEAD
LANCASTER GDS.
Heath Grange
Blindley Heath
COTTENHAMS
LANE
HORNECOURT HILL
BEECH CL.
Blue Anchor Inn
5
Rowe Tye
BYERS
P.O.
B2029
Hornecourt Wood
Cricket Grd.
WHITEWOOD
(P.H.)
Jolly Farmer
A22
B
130

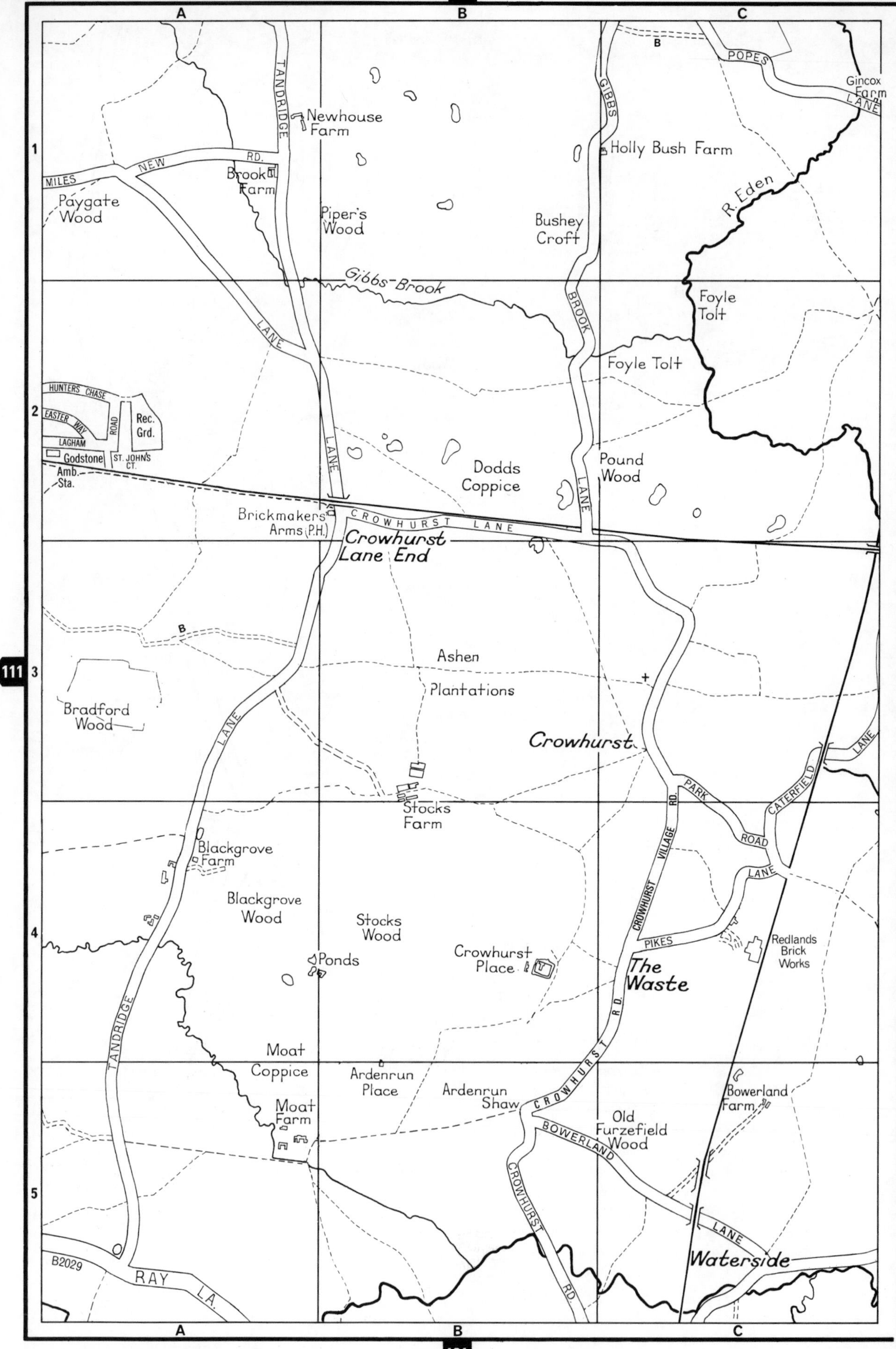
93
A
B
C
1
2
3
4
5
111
131
Newhouse Farm
Holly Bush Farm
Gincox Farm
POPES LANE
GIBBS BROOK LANE
TANDRIDGE LANE
NEW RD.
MILES
Brook Farm
Paygate Wood
Piper's Wood
Bushey Croft
R. Eden
Gibbs Brook
Foyle Tolt
Foyle Tolt
HUNTERS CHASE
EASTER WAY
LAGHAM ROAD
Rec. Grd.
Godstone
ST. JOHN'S CT.
Amb. Sta.
Dodds Coppice
Pound Wood
Brickmakers Arms (P.H.)
CROWHURST LANE
Crowhurst Lane End
Ashen Plantations
Bradford Wood
Crowhurst
Stocks Farm
PARK ROAD
CATERFIELD LANE
CROWHURST VILLAGE RD.
Blackgrove Farm
Blackgrove Wood
Stocks Wood
Ponds
Crowhurst Place
PIKES LANE
The Waste
Redlands Brick Works
Moat Coppice
Ardenrun Place
Ardenrun Shaw
CROWHURST RD.
Bowerland Farm
Moat Farm
Old Furzefield Wood
BOWERLAND LANE
B2029
RAY LA.
Waterside

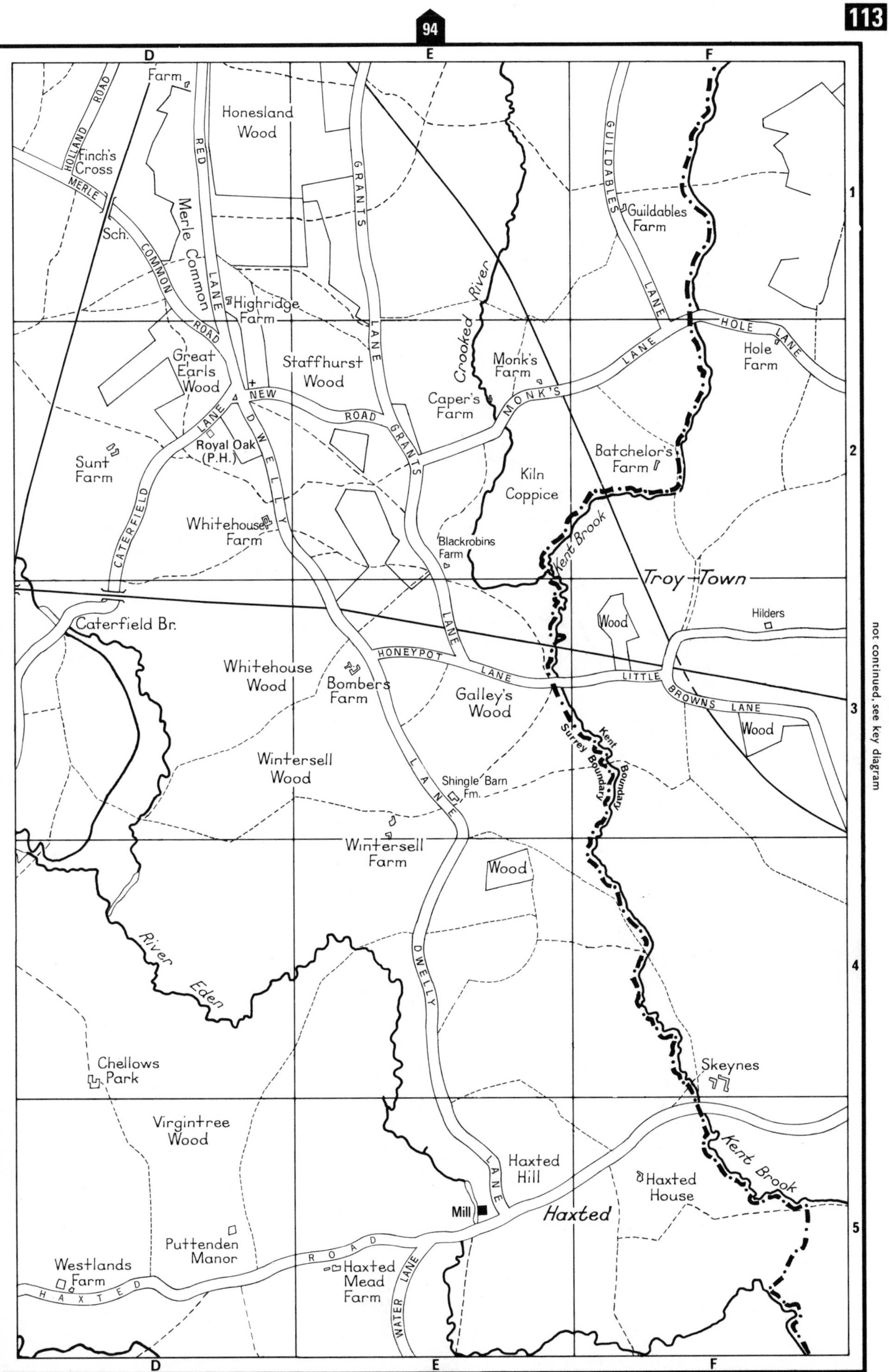

D E F

Farm

Honesland
Wood

Finch's
Cross

MERLE

Sch.

Highridge
Farm

Great
Earls
Wood

Staffhurst
Wood

Monk's
Farm

Caper's
Farm

Guildables
Farm

HOLE LANE

Hole
Farm

1

Sunt
Farm

Royal Oak
(P.H.)

Kiln
Coppice

Batchelor's
Farm

2

Whitehouse
Farm

Blackrobins
Farm

Troy Town

Hilders

Caterfield Br.

Whitehouse
Wood

Bombers
Farm

Galley's
Wood

HONEYPOT LANE

LITTLE BROWNS LANE

Wood

Wood

3

Wintersell
Wood

Shingle Barn
Fm.

Wood

Kent Boundary

Surrey Boundary

Wintersell
Farm

River Eden

4

Chellows
Park

Skeynes

Virgintree
Wood

Haxted
Hill

Haxted
House

Kent Brook

Mill

Haxted

5

Westlands
Farm

Puttenden
Manor

Haxted
Mead
Farm

D E F

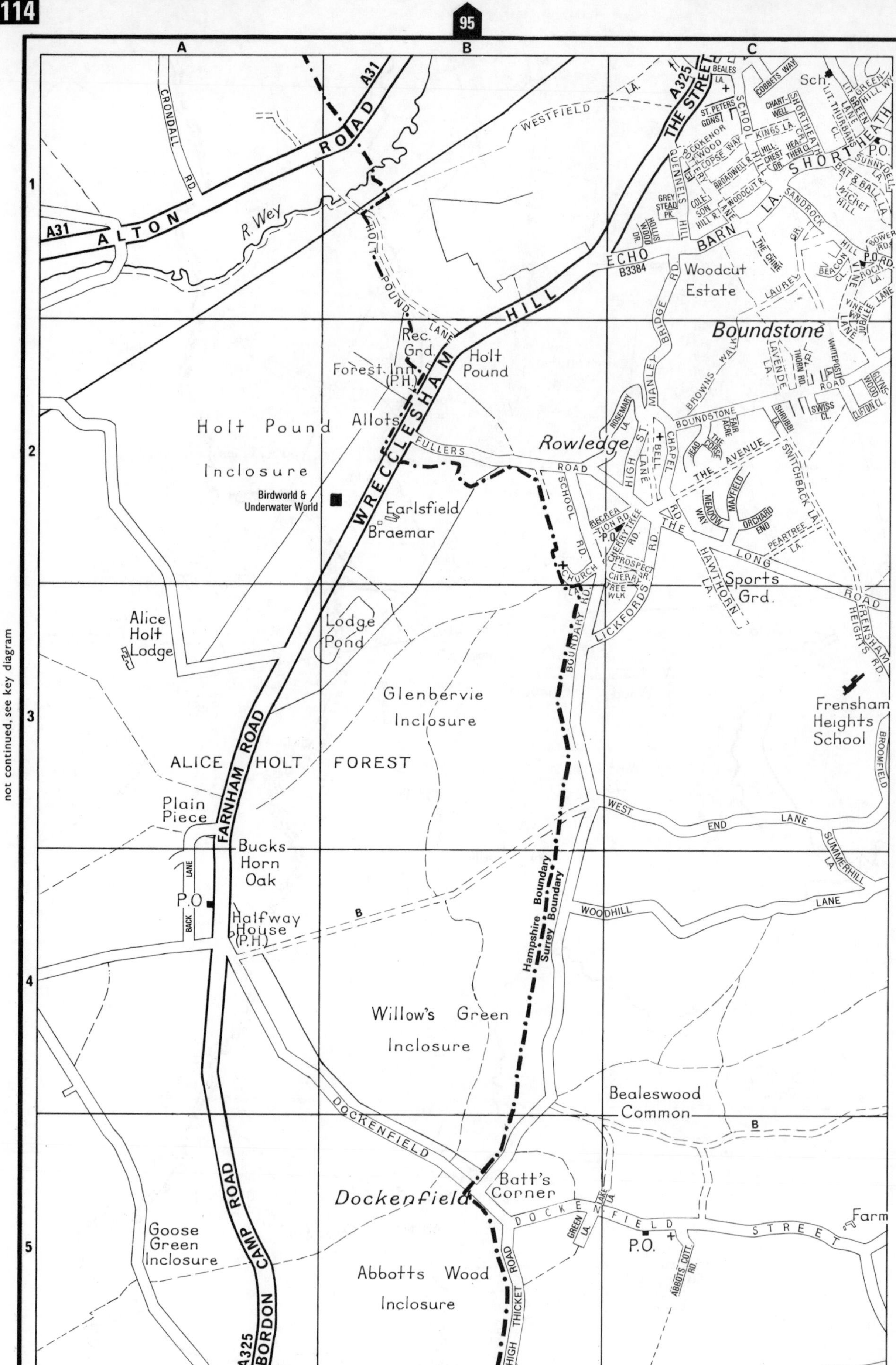

A   B   C

CRONDALL RD.

A31

A31 ALTON ROAD

R. Wey

HOLT POUND LANE

WESTFIELD

THE STREET

A325

ST. PETERS GDNS.

BEALES LA.

LIT. THURBANS

GREEN HILL LA.

Sch.

CORBETS WAY

CHART-
WELL

SCHOOL LA.

SHORTHEATH

KINGS LA.

SOCKENOR WOOD

COPSE WAY

BROADWELL R.

HILL CREST DR.

WOODCUT R.

HEATHER DL.

SHORT HEATH

PAT & BALLA

SANDROCK HILL

SUNNY LA.

COLE SON HILL R.

GREY STEAD PK.

B3384

ECHO

BARN

GREY STEAD PK.

MANLEY BRIDGE RD.

QUENNELS HILL

LAUREL

Woodcut Estate

THE CHINE

BERCOT

VINE LA.

WICKET HILL

BOWER RD.

VINEHALL RD.

Rec. Grd.

Forest Inn (P.H)

Holt Pound

WRECCLESHAM HILL

Allots.

FULLERS

Holt Pound
Inclosure

Rowledge

CHAPEL LANE

HIGH ST.

BELL LA.

ROSEMARY

BROWNS WALK

Boundstone

WHITEPOST

LAVENDE LA.

THORN RD.

Boundstone

FAIR ACRE

SHRUBB LA.

SWISS CL.

CLIFTON CL.

GLENS WOOD

Boundstone

Birdworld &
Underwater World

Earlsfield

Braemar

ROAD

Alice
Holt
Lodge

Lodge
Pond

Glenbervie
Inclosure

SCHOOL RD.

CHURCH RD.

BOUNDARY RD.

RECREA-
TION RD.

P.O.

CHERRYTREE RD.

PROSPECT DR.

CHERRY TREE WLK.

LICKFORDS

THE HAWTHORNS

THE AVENUE

MEADOW WAY

MAYFIELD

ORCHARD END

PEARTREE LA.

LONG ROAD

SWITCHBACK LA.

Sports
Grd.

HEIGHTS RD.

FRENSHAM RD.

Frensham
Heights
School

BROOMFIELD

ALICE HOLT FOREST

FARNHAM ROAD

Plain
Piece

Bucks
Horn
Oak

LANE

P.O

BACK LANE

Halfway
House
(P.H)

B

WEST END LANE

WOODHILL

SUMMERHILL LA.

LANE

Willow's Green

Inclosure

Hampshire Boundary

Surrey Boundary

Bealeswood
Common

B

DOCKENFIELD

Dockenfield

Batt's
Corner

DOCKENFIELD ROAD

GREEN LA.

STREET

Farm

P.O.

ABBOTS COTT. RD.

Goose
Green
Inclosure

A325

BORDON CAMP ROAD

Abbotts Wood

Inclosure

HIGH THICKET ROAD

A   B   C

not continued, see key diagram

1

2

3

4

5

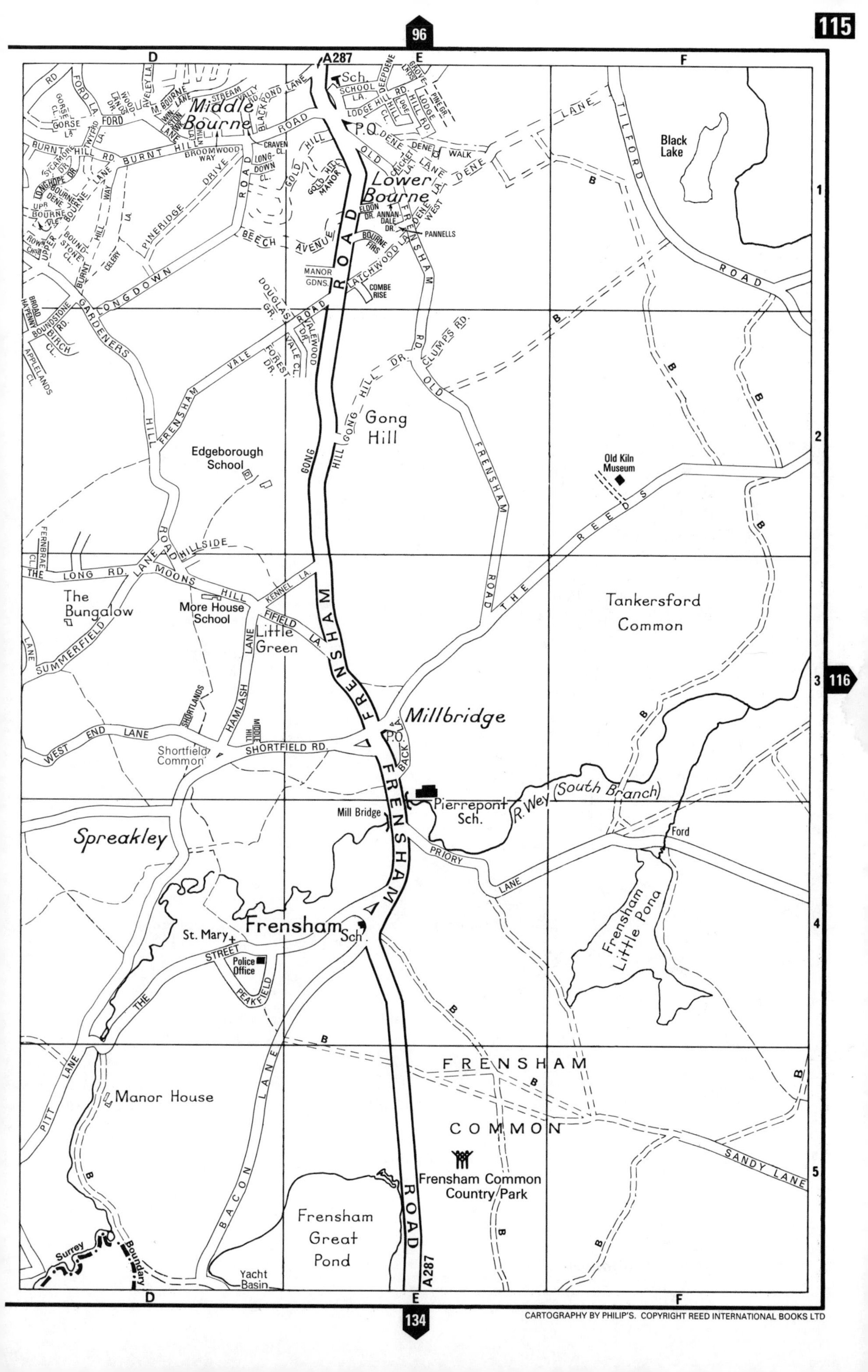

CARTOGRAPHY BY PHILIP'S. COPYRIGHT REED INTERNATIONAL BOOKS LTD

A   B   C

1

SHEPHATCH LANE

GREEN LANE

B3001

Monks Hill

B

B

Uplands

Charleshill Court

The Donkey (PH)

Charleshill

School

R. Wey (North Branch)

SQUIRES HILL LA.

SHEPHERDS WAY

Normanswood

THE STREET

WHITMEAD

2

TILFORD

THE REEDS

Barley Mow (P.H.)

P.O.

Whitmead

River Wey

Home Wood

Westbrook

Inst

Sch.

All Saints +

Tilford

B

B

Stockbridge Pond

ROAD

B

B

B

115 **3**

B

Tilford Common

Golf Course

Yagden Hill

Westbrook Moor

WOOLFORD LANE

B

TILFORD ROAD

B

4

GRANGE ROAD

Little Pond House

Hankley Common

Lion's Mouth

B

B

Golden Acres

THURSLEY ROAD

WINCHESTER RD.

EGLINTON ROAD

EGLINTON RD.

CARLISLE RD.

WELLESLEY RD. +

LOWICKS RD.

5

GLEBE LA.

Kettlebury Hill

Houndown

B

SANDY LANE

TILFORD RD.

P.O.

Rushmoor

A   B   C

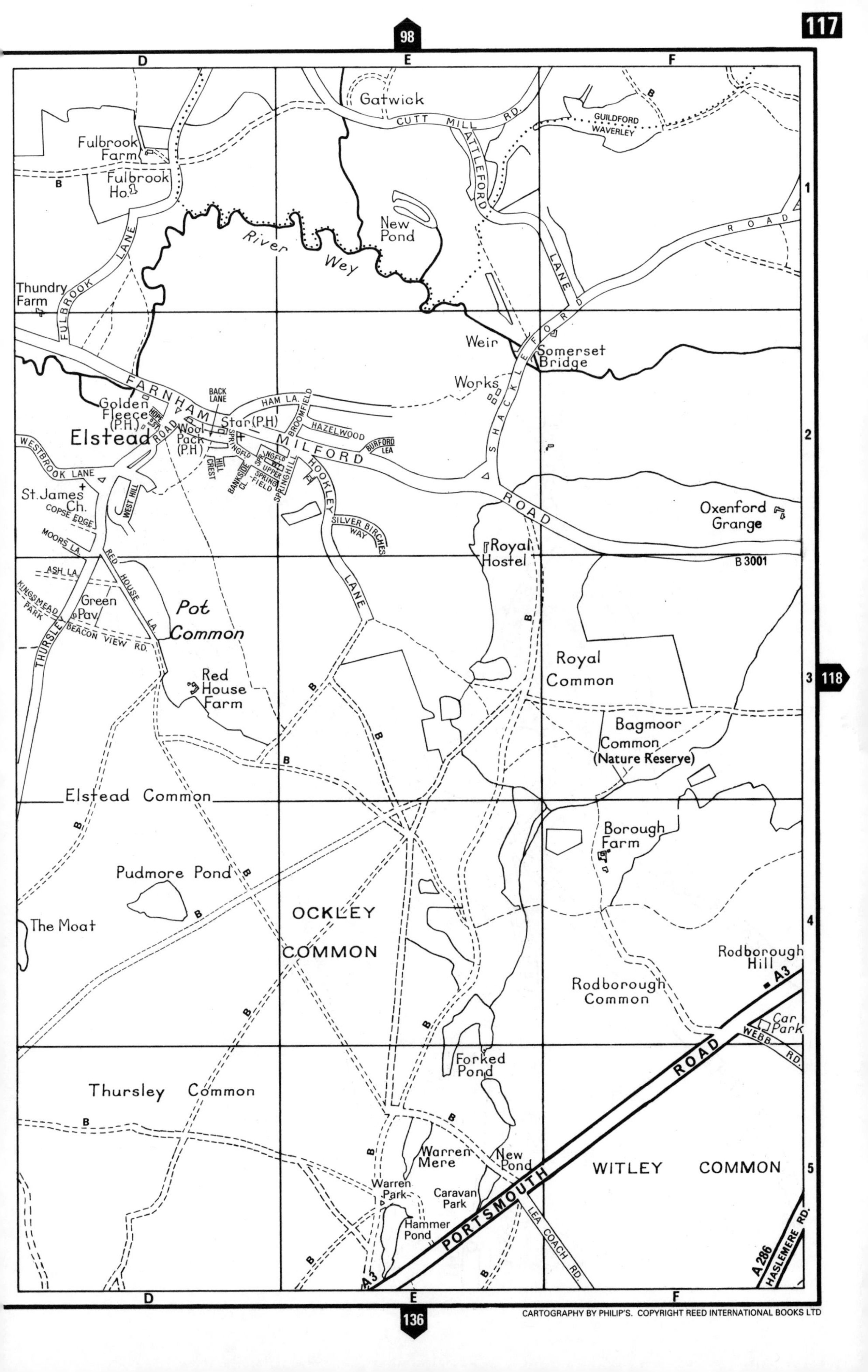

CARTOGRAPHY BY PHILIP'S. COPYRIGHT REED INTERNATIONAL BOOKS LTD

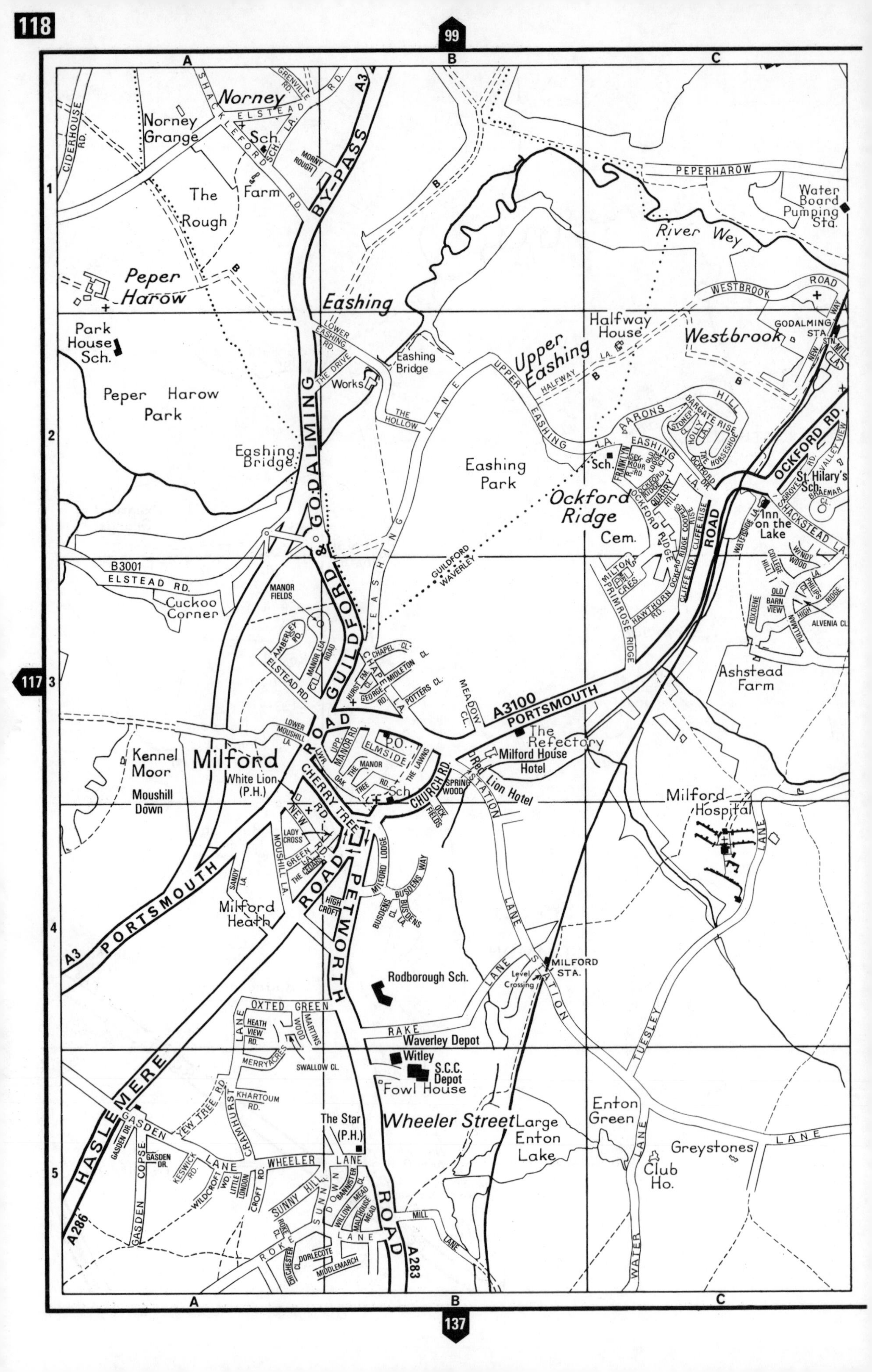
99
Norney
Norney Grange
Sch.
Farm
The Rough
Peper Harow
Eashing
BY-PASS
PEPERHAROW
Water Board Pumping Sta.
River Wey
WESTBROOK ROAD
Halfway House
Upper Eashing
Westbrook
GODALMING STA.
Park House Sch.
Peper Harow Park
Eashing Bridge
Works
GODALMING
Eashing Park
Ockford Ridge
Cem.
OCKFORD RD.
St. Hilary's Sch.
Inn on the Lake
B3001
ELSTEAD RD.
Cuckoo Corner
GUILDFORD
MANOR FIELDS
Ashstead Farm
A3100
PORTSMOUTH
The Refectory
Milford House Hotel
Lion Hotel
Milford
Kennel Moor
White Lion (P.H.)
Moushill Down
Milford Hospital
CHERRY TREE
CHURCH RD.
Milford Heath
PORTSMOUTH
PETWORTH
MILFORD STA.
Rodborough Sch.
OXTED GREEN
Waverley Depot
Witley
S.C.C. Depot
Fowl House
HASLEMERE
The Star (P.H.)
Wheeler Street
Large Enton Lake
Enton Green
Greystones
Club Ho.
A286
A283
ROAD
137
117

100

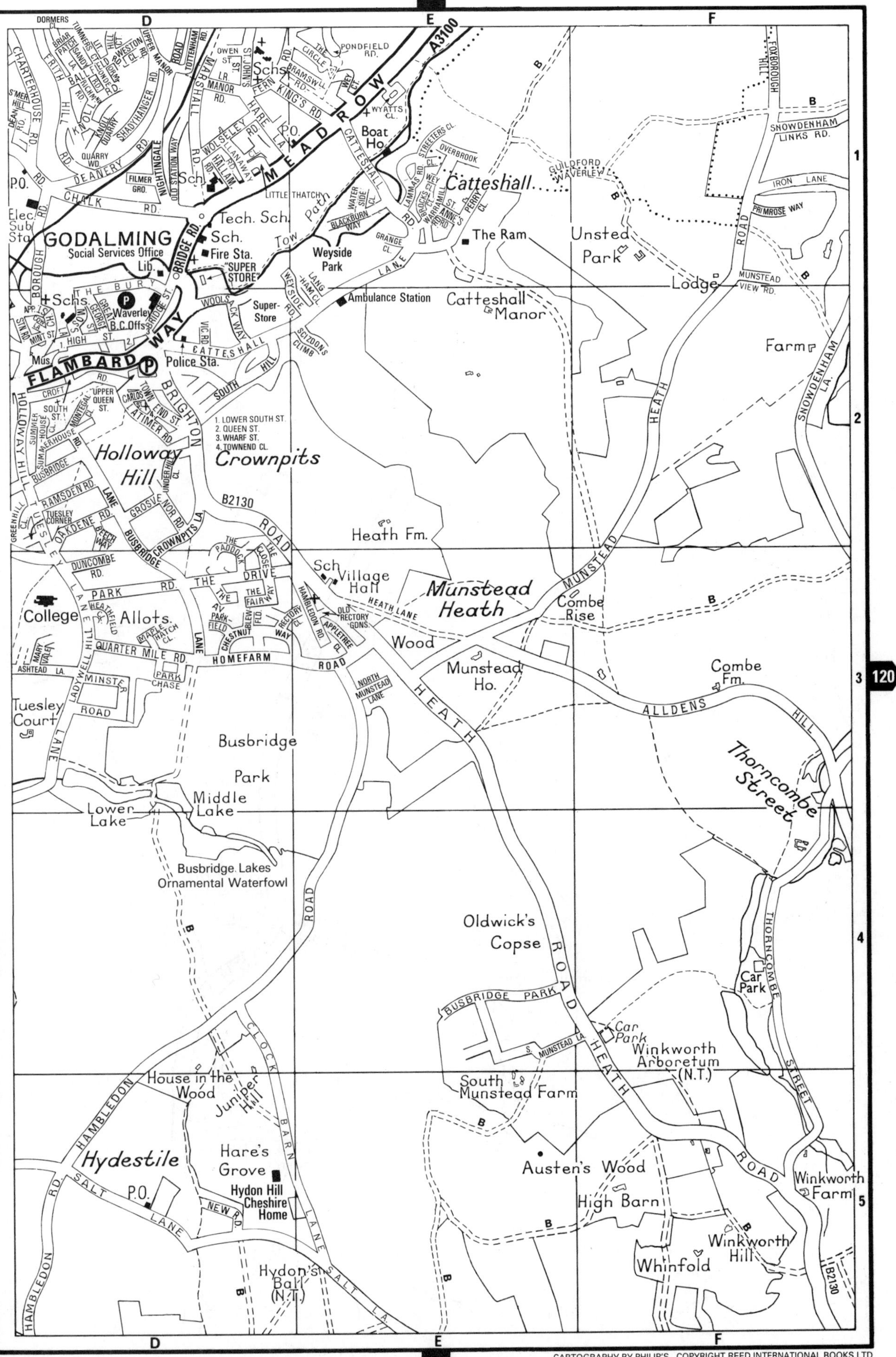
GODALMING
Catteshall
Unsted Park
Holloway Hill
Crownpits
Munstead Heath
Busbridge Park
Thorncombe Street
Hydestile
Oldwick's Copse
Winkworth Arboretum (N.T.)
Austen's Wood
Winkworth Hill
Whinfold
Hydon's Ball (N.T.)
Hydon Hill Cheshire Home
Busbridge Lakes Ornamental Waterfowl
Middle Lake
Lower Lake
Catteshall Manor
Heath Fm.
Munstead Ho.
Combe Fm.
Combe Rise
The Ram
Tuesley Court
College
Allots.
South Munstead Farm
Winkworth Farm
House in the Wood
Juniper Hill
Hare's Grove
High Barn
Weyside Park
Ambulance Station
Police Sta.
Waverley B.C. Offs
Social Services Office
Tech. Sch.
Fire Sta.
Boat Ho.
Village Hall
A3100
B2130
MEADROW
FLAMBARD WAY
HEATH ROAD
ALLDENS HILL
HAMBLEDON RD.
SALT LANE
CLOCK BARN LANE
HOMEFARM ROAD
BRIGHTON ROAD
1. LOWER SOUTH ST.
2. QUEEN ST.
3. WHARF ST.
4. TOWNEND CL.

120

138

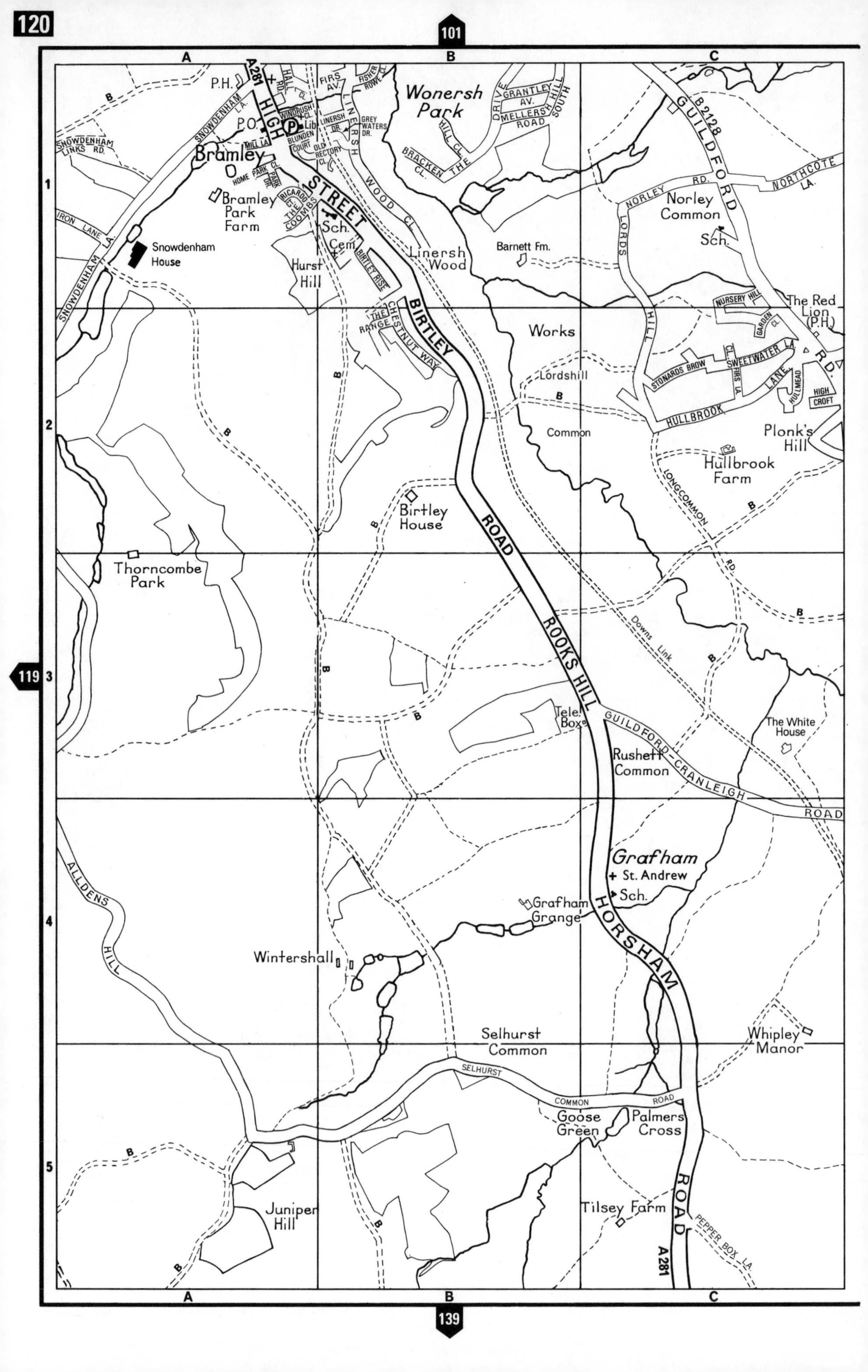
101
A
B
C
1
2
3
4
5
119
139
Bramley
P.H.
P.O.
Lib
A281
HIGH
STREET
SNOWDENHAM LA.
SNOWDENHAM LINKS RD.
IRON LANE
SNOWDENHAM LA.
Snowdenham House
Bramley Park Farm
HOME PARK CL.
PARK DR.
MILL LA.
WINDRUSH CL.
BLUNDEN COURT
OLD RECTORY CL.
LINERSH DR.
GREY WATERS DR.
HALL RD.
HALL CL.
FIRS AV.
FISHER ROWE CL.
RICARDO CT.
THE COOMBS
Sch.
Cem.
BIRTLEY RISE
Hurst Hill
LINERSH WOOD CL.
Linersh Wood
Wonersh Park
GRANTLEY AV.
MELLERSH HILL ROAD
SOUTH DRIVE
THE HILL CL.
BRACKEN CL.
Barnett Fm.
B2128
GUILDFORD RD.
NORTHCOTE LA.
NORLEY RD.
Norley Common
LORDS HILL
Sch.
The Red Lion (P.H.)
NURSERY HILL
GARDEN CL.
SWEETWATER LA.
STONARDS BROW
FIRS LA.
CL.
HULLBROOK LANE
HULLMEAD
HIGH CROFT
Plonk's Hill
Hullbrook Farm
LONGCOMMON RD.
Works
Lordshill
Common
THE RANGE
CHESTNUT WAY
BIRTLEY
ROAD
Birtley House
Thorncombe Park
ROOKS HILL
Downs Link
Tele. Box
GUILDFORD-CRANLEIGH ROAD
Rushett Common
The White House
Grafham
St. Andrew
Sch.
Grafham Grange
HORSHAM ROAD
ALLDENS HILL
Wintershall
Selhurst Common
SELHURST COMMON ROAD
Whipley Manor
Goose Green
Palmers Cross
Juniper Hill
Tilsey Farm
PEPPER BOX LA.
A281
B

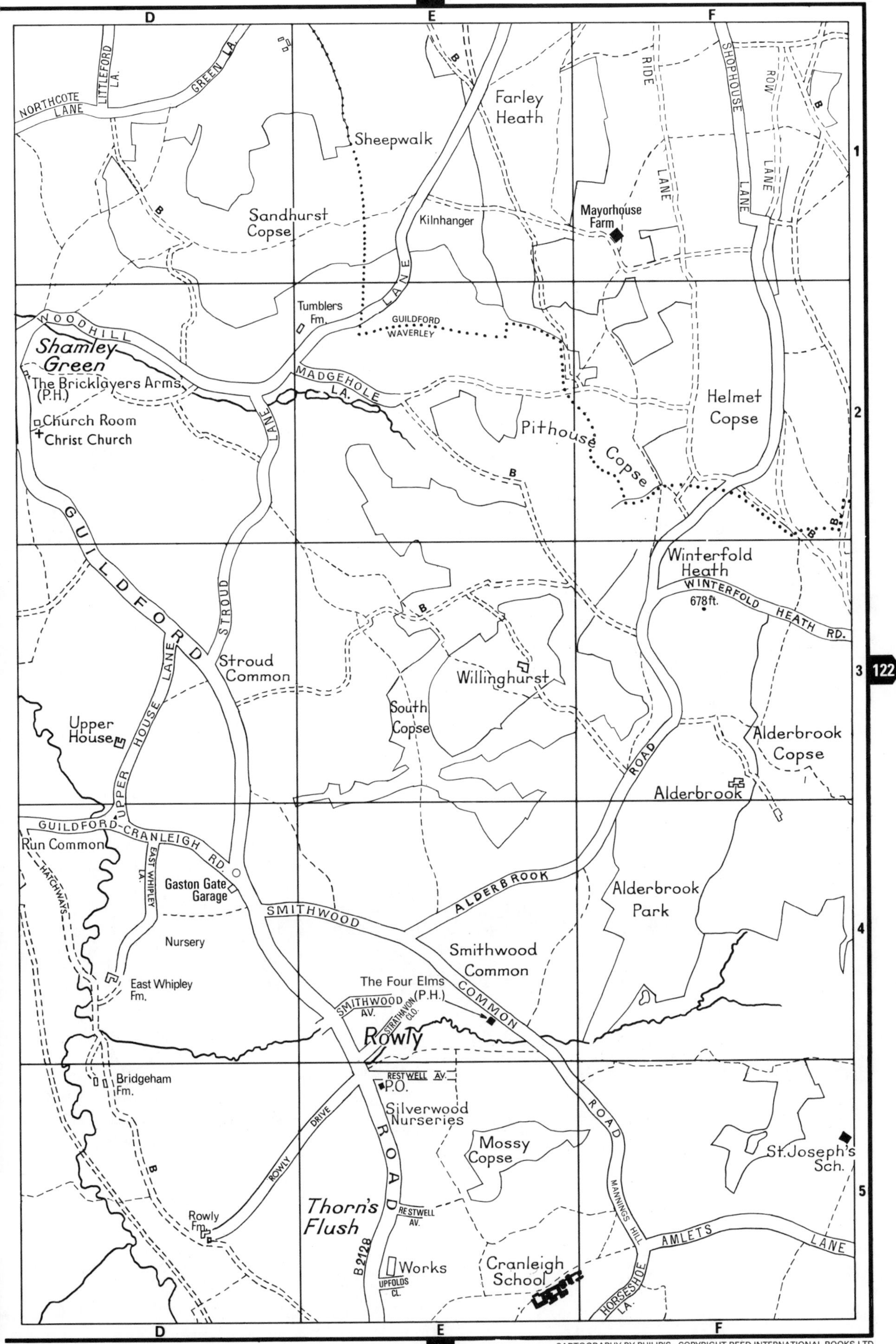

CARTOGRAPHY BY PHILIP'S. COPYRIGHT REED INTERNATIONAL BOOKS LTD

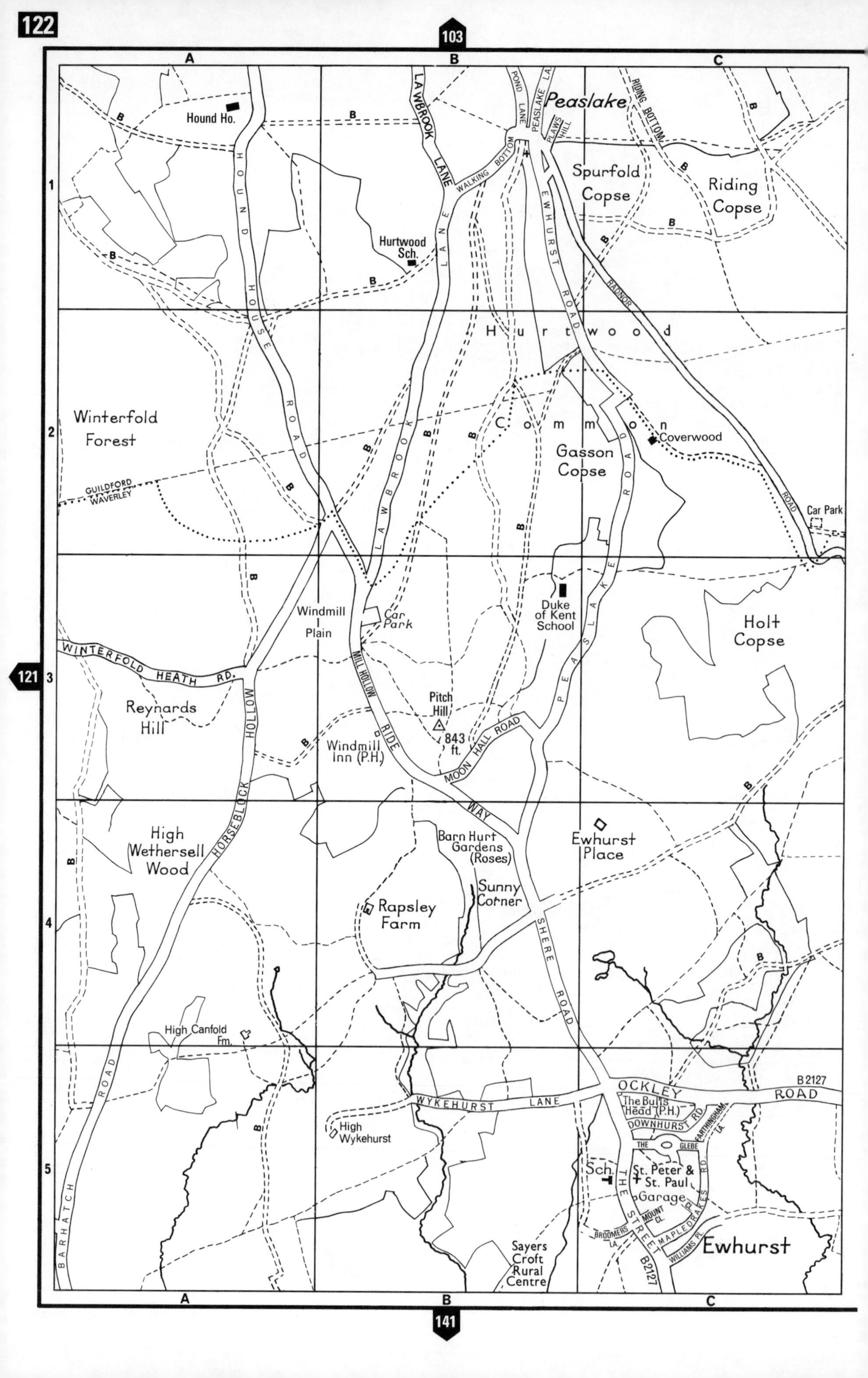
103
A
B
C
Peaslake
Hound Ho.
LAWBROOK LANE
POND LANE
PEASLAKE LA.
PLAWS HILL
RIDING BOTTOM
WALKING BOTTOM
Spurfold Copse
Riding Copse
Hurtwood Sch.
HOUND HOUSE ROAD
EWHURST ROAD
RADNOR ROAD
Hurtwood Common
Winterfold Forest
Gasson Copse
Coverwood
GUILDFORD
WAVERLEY
Car Park
Windmill Plain
Duke of Kent School
Holt Copse
WINTERFOLD HEATH RD.
MILL HOLLOW RIDE WAY
Reynards Hill
Pitch Hill
843 ft.
MOON HALL ROAD
PEASLAKE ROAD
Windmill Inn (P.H.)
HORSEBLOCK HOLLOW
High Wethersell Wood
Barn Hurt Gardens (Roses)
Ewhurst Place
Sunny Corner
Rapsley Farm
SHERE ROAD
High Canfold Fm.
WYKEHURST LANE
OCKLEY ROAD
B2127
The Bulls Head (P.H.)
DOWNHURST RD.
FARTHINGHAM LA.
THE GLEBE
High Wykehurst
Sch.
St. Peter & St. Paul
Garage
MOUNT CL.
MAPLEDRAKES RD.
BROOMERS LA.
THE STREET
WILLIAMS PL.
Ewhurst
Sayers Croft Rural Centre
BARHATCH ROAD
121
1
2
3
4
5
141

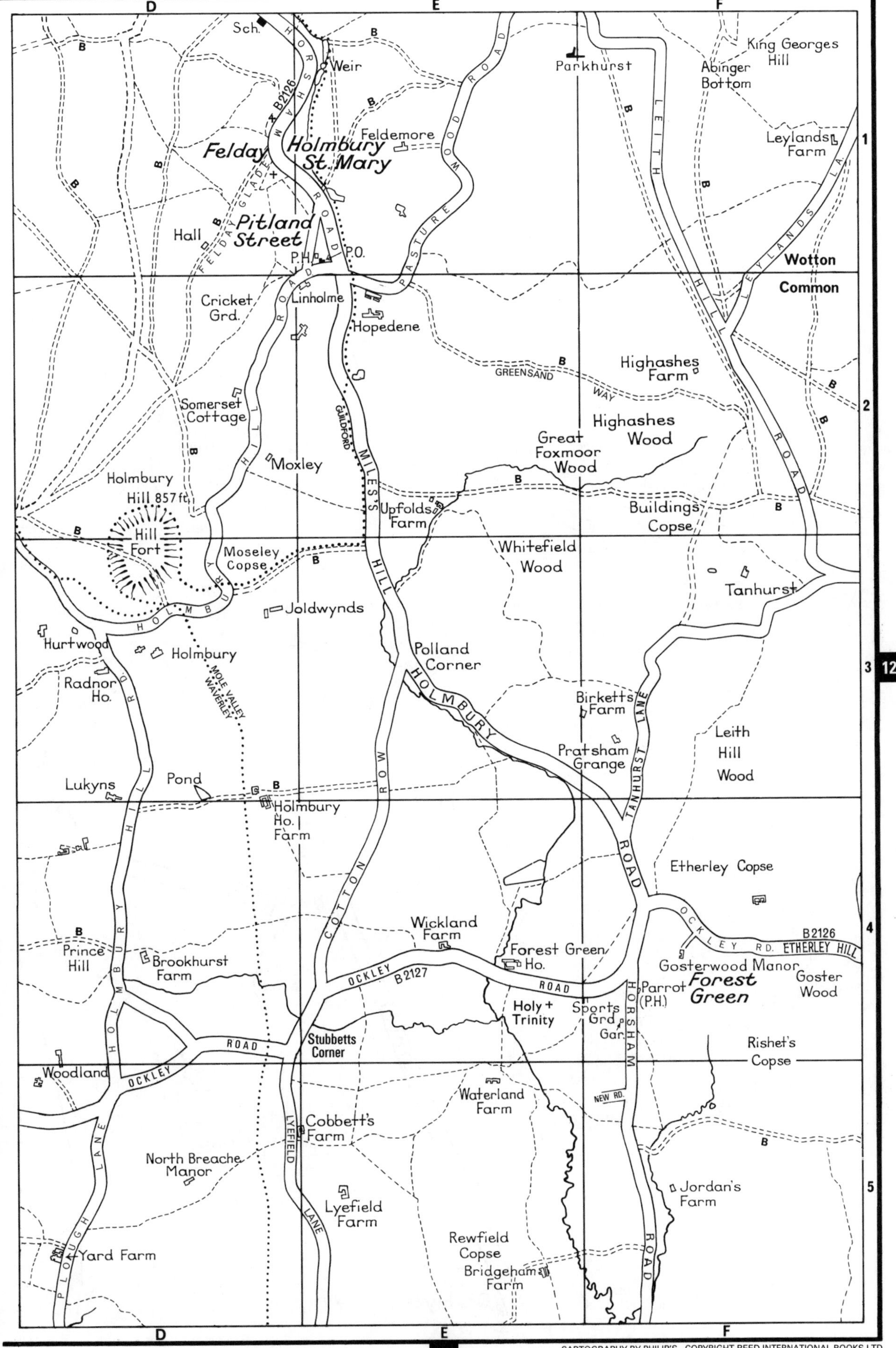

D E F

Sch.
Weir
Feldemore
King Georges Hill
Abinger Bottom
Leylands Farm
1

Felday
Holmbury St. Mary
Pitland Street
Parkhurst

Hall
P.H.
P.O.
Cricket Grd.
Linholme
Hopedene
Wotton Common
Highashes Farm
GREENSAND WAY
2
Highashes Wood

Somerset Cottage
Moxley
Great Foxmoor Wood
Buildings Copse

Holmbury Hill 857 ft.
Hill Fort
Moseley Copse
Upfolds Farm
Whitefield Wood
Tanhurst

Hurtwood
Holmbury
Joldwynds
Polland Corner
Birketts Farm
Leith Hill Wood
3

Radnor Ho.
MOLE VALLEY WAVERLEY
Pratsham Grange

Lukyns
Pond
Holmbury Ho. Farm
Etherley Copse

Prince Hill
Brookhurst Farm
Wickland Farm
Forest Green Ho.
B 2126 ETHERLEY HILL
4
OCKLEY RD.
Gosterwood Manor
Goster Wood

Forest Green
Parrot (P.H.)
Holy + Trinity
Sports Grd. Gar.
Rishet's Copse

Woodland
OCKLEY
ROAD
B 2127
Stubbetts Corner
NEW RD.

Cobbett's Farm
Waterland Farm
Jordan's Farm
5

North Breache Manor
Lyefield Farm

Yard Farm
Rewfield Copse
Bridgeham Farm

D E F

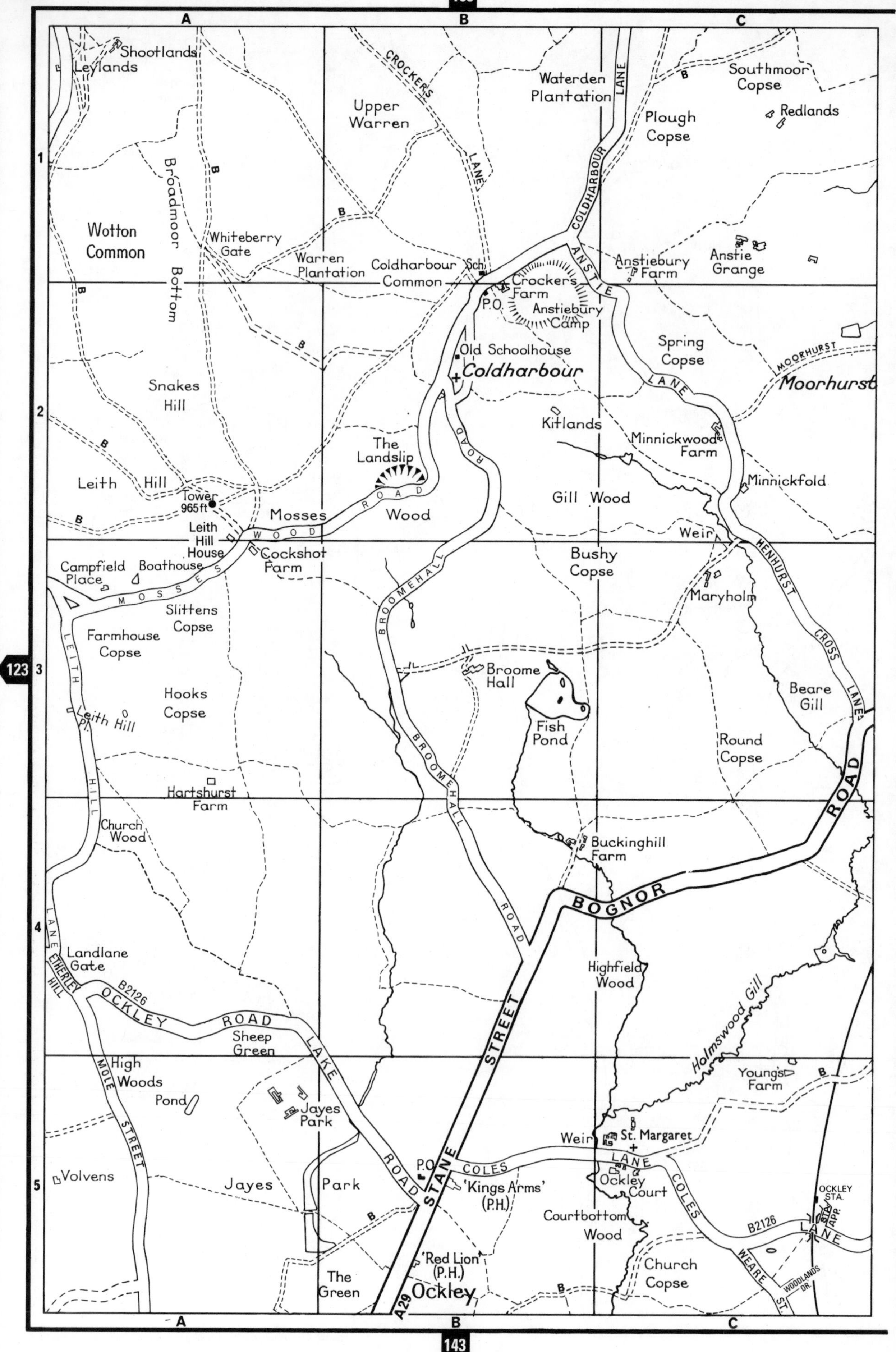

A   B   C

Shootlands
Leylands

Upper
Warren

Waterden
Plantation

Southmoor
Copse

Redlands

Plough
Copse

1

Broadmoor Bottom

Whiteberry
Gate

Warren
Plantation

Coldharbour Sch.

Coldharbour Common

Anstiebury
Farm

Anstie
Grange

Wotton
Common

Crockers
Farm

P.O.

Anstiebury
Camp

Spring
Copse

Moorhurst

Snakes
Hill

Old Schoolhouse

✛ Coldharbour

Kitlands

Minnickwood
Farm

2

Leith Hill

The
Landslip

Gill Wood

Minnickfold

Tower
965ft ●

Mosses   Wood

Weir

Leith
Hill
House

Cockshot
Farm

Bushy
Copse

Maryholm

Campfield
Place

Boathouse

Slittens
Copse

Broome
Hall

Beare
Gill

3

Farmhouse
Copse

Hooks
Copse

Fish
Pond

Round
Copse

Leith Hill

Hartshurst
Farm

Buckinghill
Farm

Church
Wood

4

Landlane
Gate

BOGNOR

Highfield
Wood

Holmswood Gill

B2126

OCKLEY ROAD

Sheep
Green

Young's
Farm

High
Woods

Pond

Jayes
Park

Weir

St. Margaret

Volvens

Jayes   Park

P.O

COLES

'Kings Arms'
(P.H.)

Ockley
Court

OCKLEY
STA.

5

Courtbottom
Wood

B2126

'Red Lion
(P.H.)

The
Green

Ockley

Church
Copse

A   B   C

123

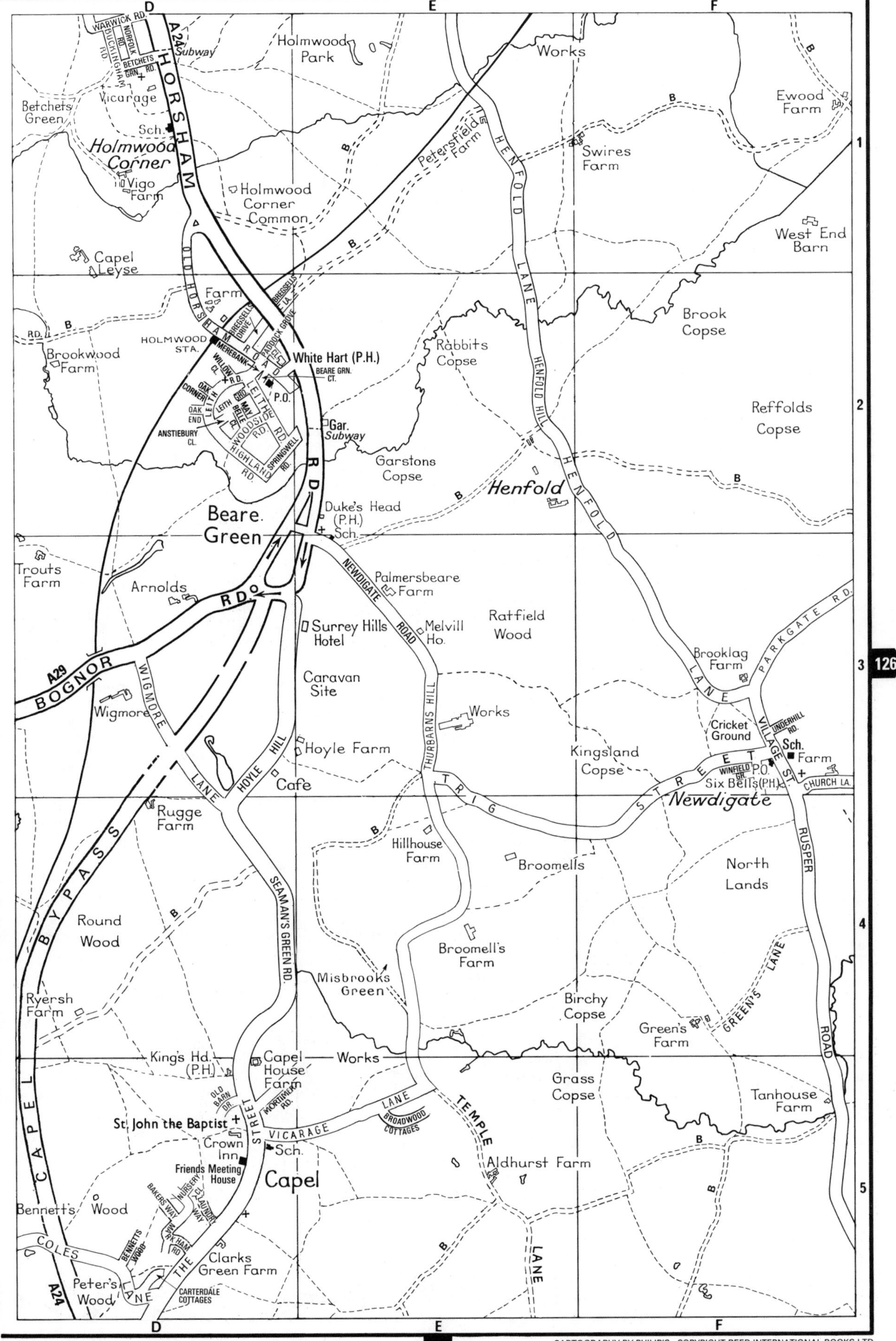

CARTOGRAPHY BY PHILIP'S. COPYRIGHT REED INTERNATIONAL BOOKS LTD

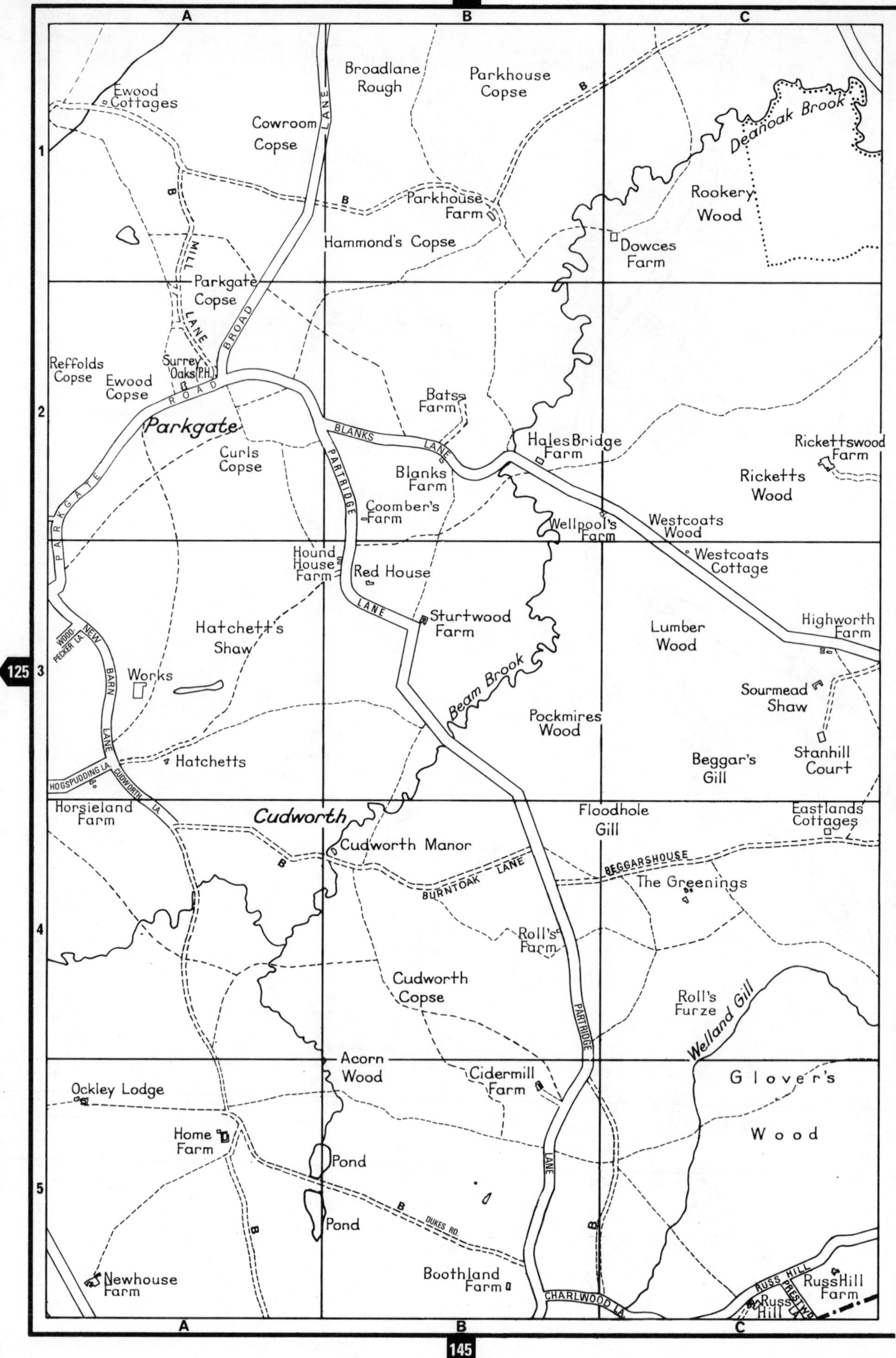

A   B   C

Ewood
Cottages

Broadlane
Rough

Parkhouse
Copse

B

Deanoak Brook

Cowroom
Copse

1

Rookery
Wood

B

Parkhouse
Farm

Hammond's Copse

Dowces
Farm

Parkgate
Copse

Reffolds
Copse

Surrey
Oaks (P.H.)

Bats
Farm

Ewood
Copse

ROAD

Ricketts wood
Farm

2

Parkgate

BLANKS LANE

Hales Bridge
Farm

Ricketts
Wood

Curls
Copse

Blanks
Farm

Coomber's
Farm

Wellpool's
Farm

Westcoats
Wood

Westcoats
Cottage

Hound
House
Farm

Red House

Sturtwood
Farm

Lumber
Wood

Highworth
Farm

125 3

WOOD-PECKER LA.

Hatchett's
Shaw

Works

Beam Brook

Sourmead
Shaw

Pockmires
Wood

Beggar's
Gill

Stanhill
Court

Hatchetts

HOGSPUDDING LA.

CUDWORTH LA.

Horsieland
Farm

Cudworth

Floodhole
Gill

Eastlands
Cottages

B

Cudworth Manor

BEGGARSHOUSE

The Greenings

BURNTOAK LANE

Roll's
Farm

4

Cudworth
Copse

Roll's
Furze

Welland Gill

Acorn
Wood

Cidermill
Farm

Glover's

Ockley Lodge

Wood

Home
Farm

Pond

PARTRIDGE LANE

5

Pond

B

DUKES RD.

Newhouse
Farm

Boothland
Farm

CHARLWOOD LA.

Russ Hill

RussHill
Farm

A   B   C

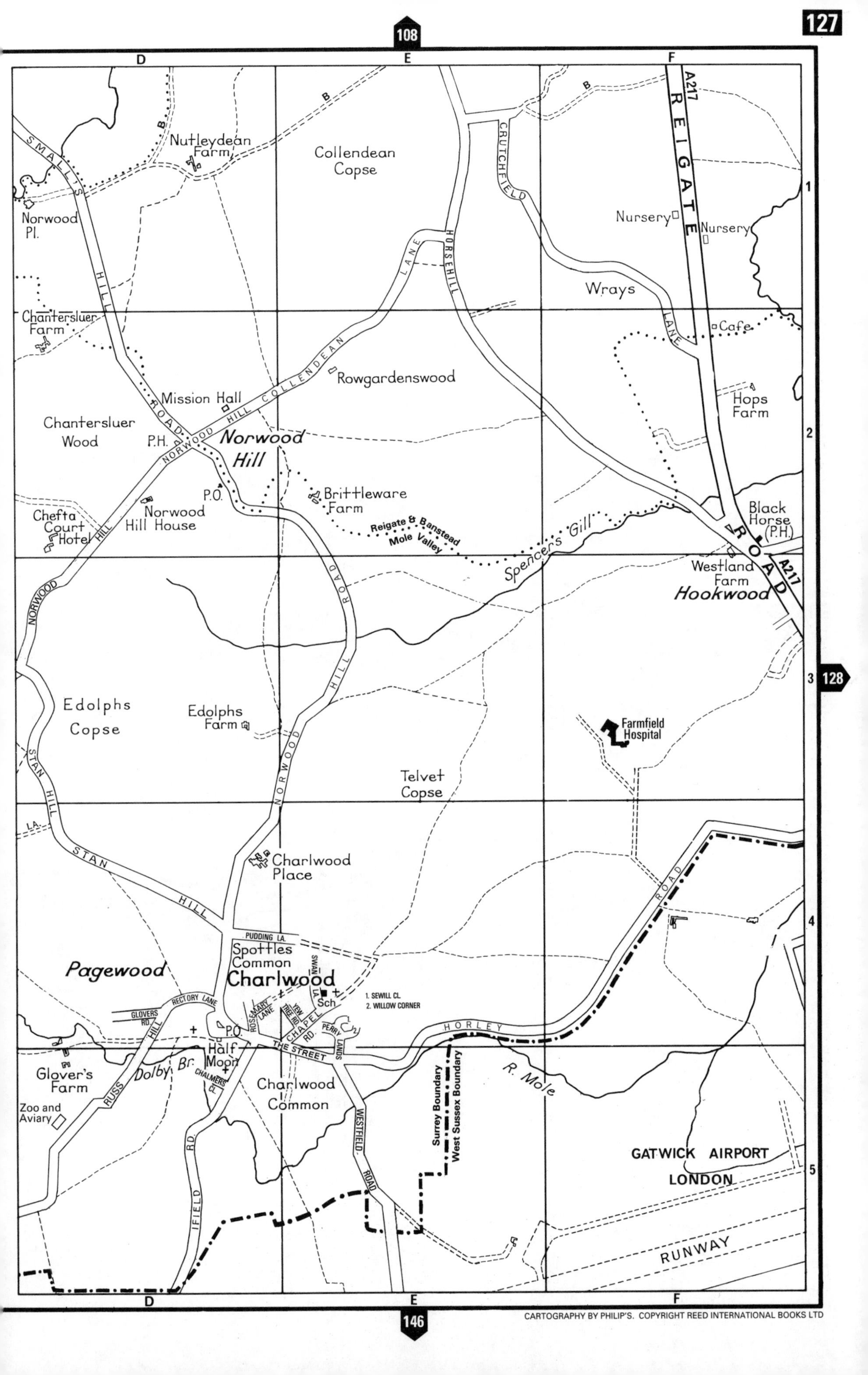

D E F

SMALLS

B Nutleydean Farm

Collendean Copse

CRUTCHFIELD

B

A217

REIGATE

Norwood Pl.

Nursery

Nursery

Wrays

Chantersluer Farm

HORSEHILL LANE

Cafe

LANE

Chantersluer Wood

Mission Hall

COLLENDEAN HILL

NORWOOD ROAD

Rowgardenswood

Hops Farm

Norwood Hill

P.H.

P.O.

Brittleware Farm

Reigate & Banstead Mole Valley

Spencers Gill

Black Horse (P.H.)

ROAD A217

Westland Farm

Hookwood

Chefta Court Hotel Hill

Norwood Hill House

Edolphs Copse

NORWOOD HILL ROAD

Edolphs Farm

Farmfield Hospital

STAN HILL LA.

Telvet Copse

STAN HILL

Charlwood Place

PUDDING LA.

Spottles Common

Charlwood

SWAIN LA.

ROAD

Pagewood

RECTORY LANE

GLOVERS RD.

ROSEMARY LANE

NEW RD

CHAPEL RD

Sch

1. SEWILL CL.
2. WILLOW CORNER

HORLEY

R. Mole

RUSS RD

HILL

P.O.

THE STREET

PERRY LANDS

Glover's Farm

Dolby Br.

CHALMERS CL.

Half Moon

Charlwood Common

IFIELD RD.

WESTFIELD ROAD

Surrey Boundary

West Sussex Boundary

GATWICK AIRPORT

LONDON

Zoo and Aviary

RUNWAY

D E F

CARTOGRAPHY BY PHILIP'S. COPYRIGHT REED INTERNATIONAL BOOKS LTD

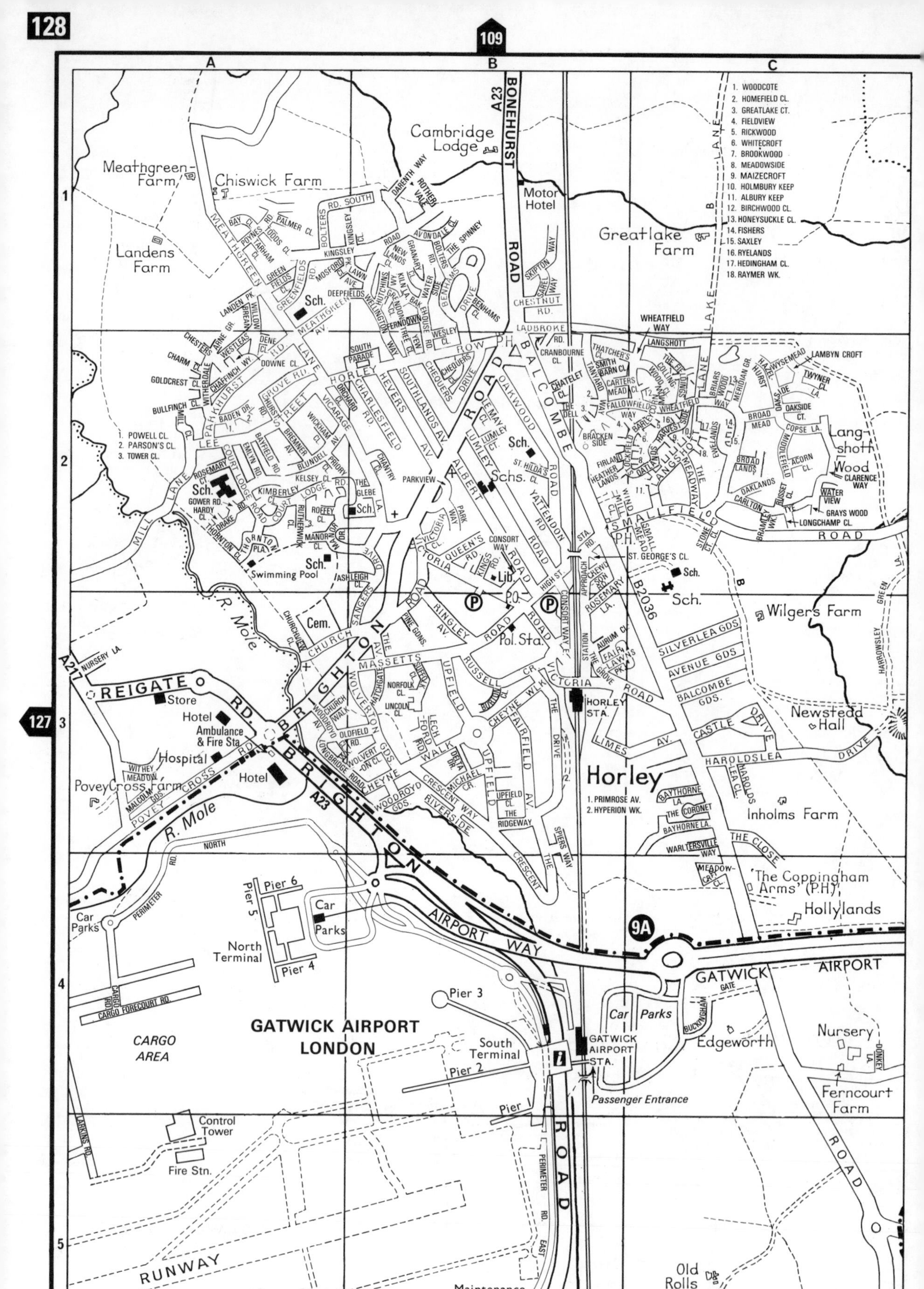

1. WOODCOTE
2. HOMEFIELD CL.
3. GREATLAKE CT.
4. FIELDVIEW
5. RICKWOOD
6. WHITECROFT
7. BROOKWOOD
8. MEADOWSIDE
9. MAIZECROFT
10. HOLMBURY KEEP
11. ALBURY KEEP
12. BIRCHWOOD CL.
13. HONEYSUCKLE CL.
14. FISHERS
15. SAXLEY
16. RYELANDS
17. HEDINGHAM CL.
18. RAYMER WK.

Meathgreen Farm

Chiswick Farm

Cambridge Lodge

Motor Hotel

Greatlake Farm

Landens Farm

1. POWELL CL.
2. PARSON'S CL.
3. TOWER CL.

Wilgers Farm

Newstedd Hall

REIGATE

Store

Hotel

Ambulance & Fire Sta.

Hospital

Hotel

Povey Cross Farm

R. Mole

Horley

1. PRIMROSE AV.
2. HYPERION WK.

Inholms Farm

The Coppingham Arms (P.H.)

Hollylands

Pier 6

Pier 5

Car Parks

North Terminal

Pier 4

Car Parks

Pier 3

GATWICK AIRPORT LONDON

South Terminal

Pier 2

GATWICK AIRPORT STA.

Passenger Entrance

GATWICK   AIRPORT

Car Parks

Edgeworth

Nursery

Ferncourt Farm

CARGO AREA

Control Tower

Fire Stn.

Pier 1

RUNWAY

Lowfield Heath

Gatwick Gate

Maintenance Area

Sewage Works

Old Rolls Farm

Upr. Pickett's

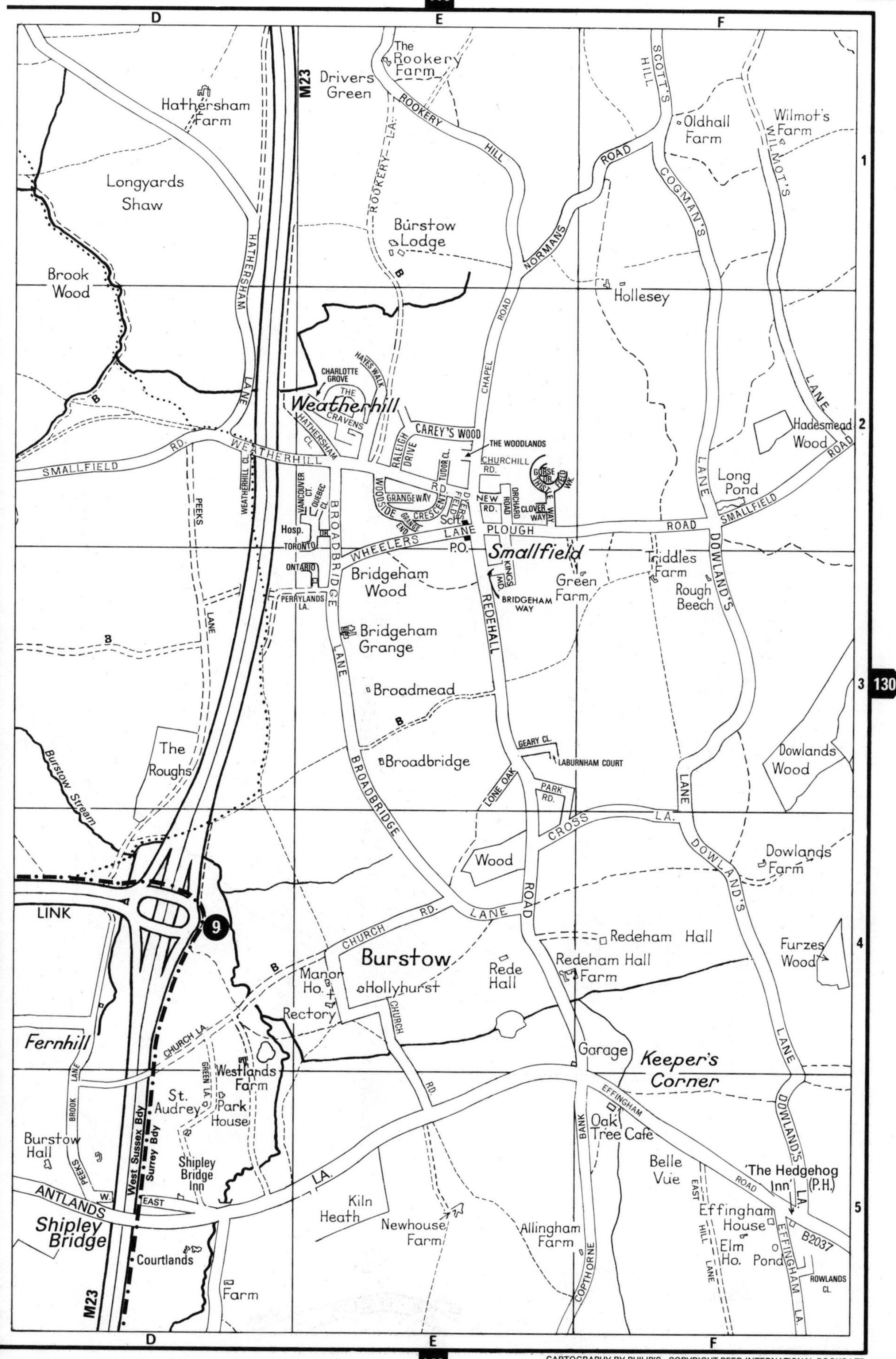

CARTOGRAPHY BY PHILIP'S. COPYRIGHT REED INTERNATIONAL BOOKS LTD

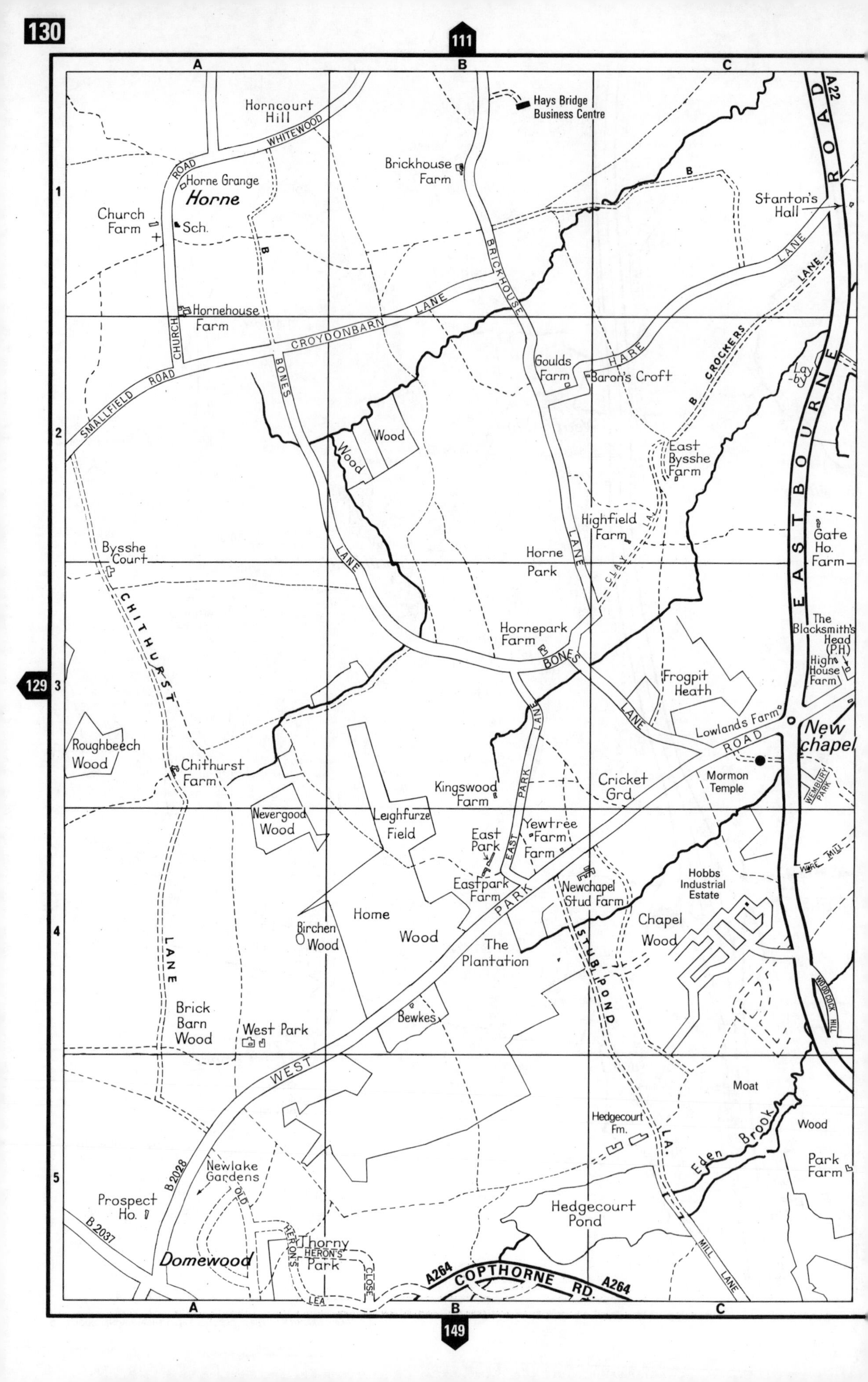

A B C

Horncourt Hill
WHITEWOOD
Hays Bridge Business Centre
Horne Grange
Horne
Church Farm
Sch.
Brickhouse Farm
Stanton's Hall
ROAD
Hornehouse Farm
CROYDONBARN LANE
BONES LANE
BRICKHOUSE LANE
HARE LANE
Goulds Farm
Baron's Croft
CROCKERS LANE
SMALLFIELD ROAD
CHURCH ROAD
Wood
Wood
East Bysshe Farm
EASTBOURNE ROAD
A22
Bysshe Court
CHITHURST
BONES LANE
Highfield Farm
Horne Park
CLAY LA.
Gate Ho. Farm
LANE
The Blacksmith's Head (P.H.)
High House Farm
Roughbeech Wood
Chithurst Farm
Hornepark Farm
BONES LANE
PARK LANE
Frogpit Heath
Lowlands Farm
New chapel
Mormon Temple
WEMBURY PARK
Nevergood Wood
Leighfurze Field
Kingswood Farm
East Park
Yewtree Farm
Cricket Grd.
WIRE MILL
LANE
Birchen Wood
Home Wood
Eastpark Farm
EAST PARK LANE
Newchapel Stud Farm
Hobbs Industrial Estate
Chapel Wood
WOODCOCK HILL
Brick Barn Wood
West Park
The Plantation
STUB POND
West PARK LANE
Bewkes
B 2028
Moat
Hedgecourt Fm.
Eden Brook
Wood
Park Farm
Newlake Gardens
Prospect Ho.
B 2037
HERON'S LEA
OLD HOUSE LA.
Thorny Park
HERON'S
Hedgecourt Pond
MILL LANE
Domewood
A264
COPTHORNE RD.
A264

A B C

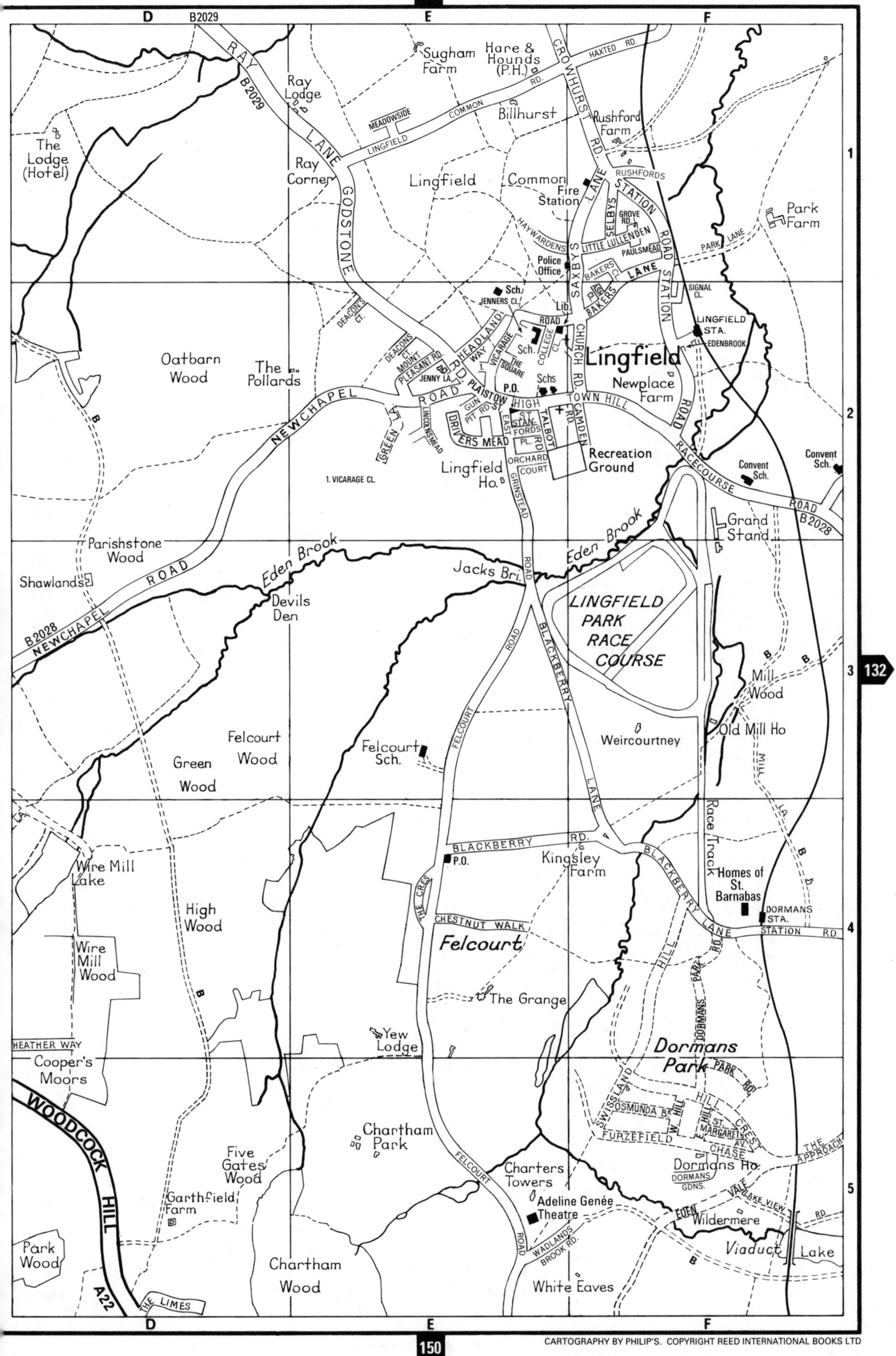

CARTOGRAPHY BY PHILIP'S. COPYRIGHT REED INTERNATIONAL BOOKS LTD

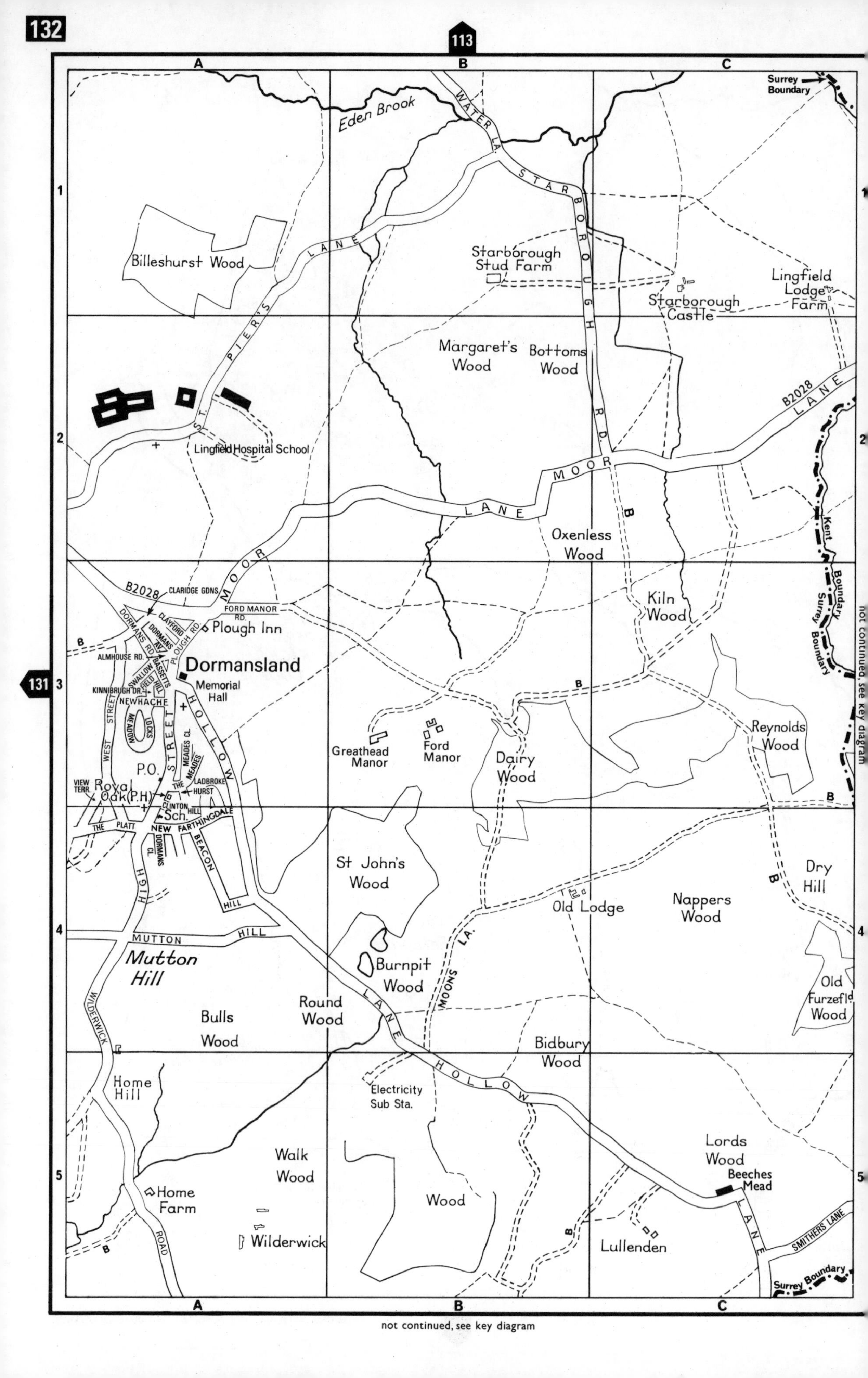

Surrey Boundary

Eden Brook

WATER LA

STARBOROUGH

Billeshurst Wood

Starborough Stud Farm

Starborough Castle

Lingfield Lodge Farm

B2028 LANE

Margaret's Wood

Bottoms Wood

ST. PIERS LANE

Lingfield Hospital School

MOOR LANE

Oxenless Wood

Kiln Wood

Kent Boundary Surrey Boundary

not continued, see key diagram

B2028 CLARIDGE GDNS.

FORD MANOR RD.

CLAYTON RD.

DORMANS RD.

DORMANS AV.

ASSETTS

Plough Inn

ALMHOUSE RD.

SWALLOW FIELD

Dormansland

KINNIBRUGH DR.

NEWHACHE

MEADOW

Memorial Hall

WEST STREET

STREET

HOLLOW

Greathead Manor

Ford Manor

Dairy Wood

Reynolds Wood

P.O.

MEADES CL.

THE MEADES

LADBROKE HURST

VIEW TERR.

Royal Oak (P.H)

CLINTON HILL

Sch.

THE PLATT

NEW DORMANS

FARTHINGDALE

CL.

BEACON HILL

St John's Wood

Old Lodge

Nappers Wood

Dry Hill

HIGH

MUTTON HILL

Mutton Hill

Bulls Wood

Round Wood

LANE

MOONS LA.

Burnpit Wood

Old Furzefld Wood

WILDERWICK

Home Hill

Bidbury Wood

HOLLOW

Electricity Sub Sta.

Walk Wood

Wood

Lords Wood

Beeches Mead

LANE

SMITHERS LANE

Home Farm

Wilderwick

Lullenden

ROAD

Surrey Boundary

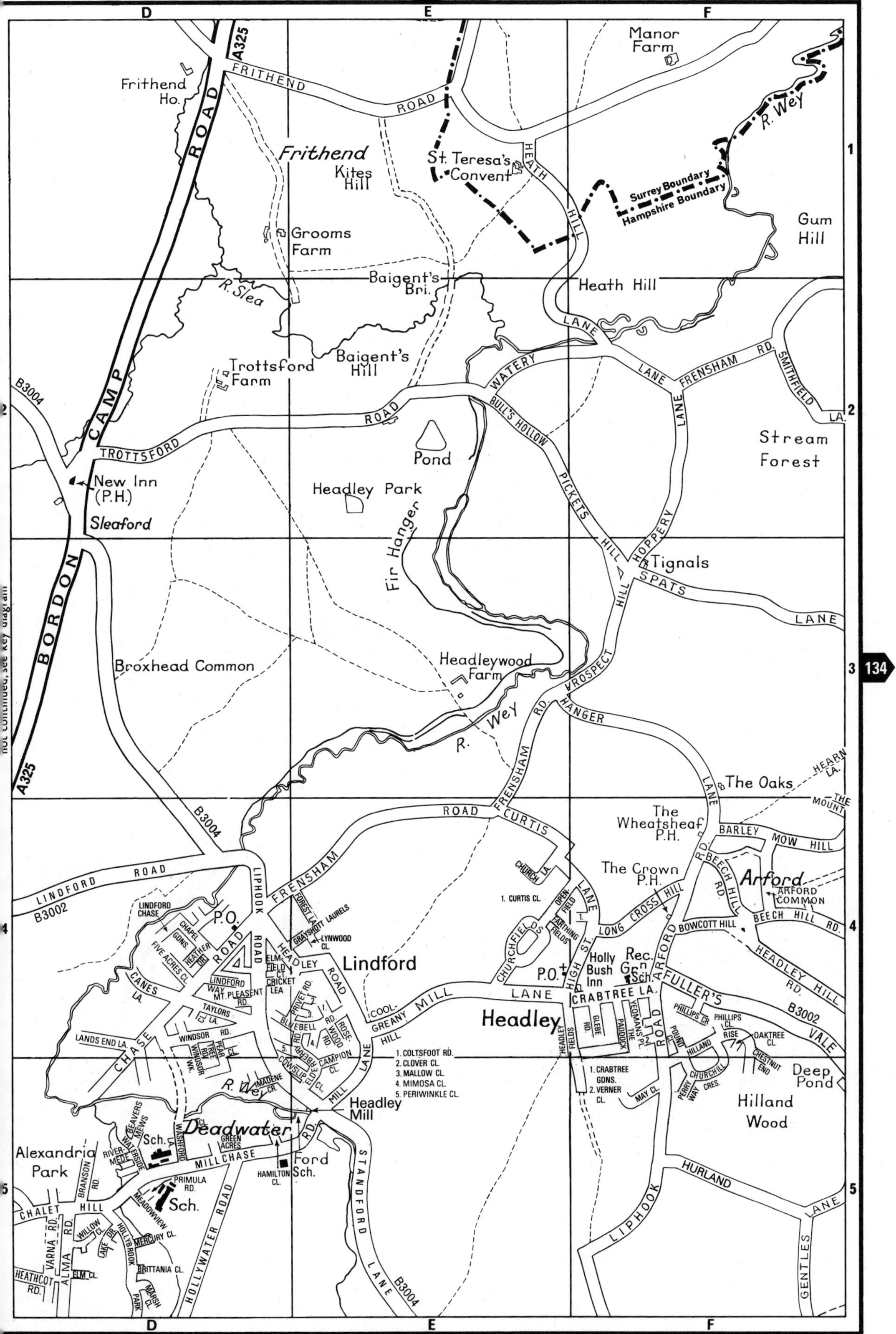

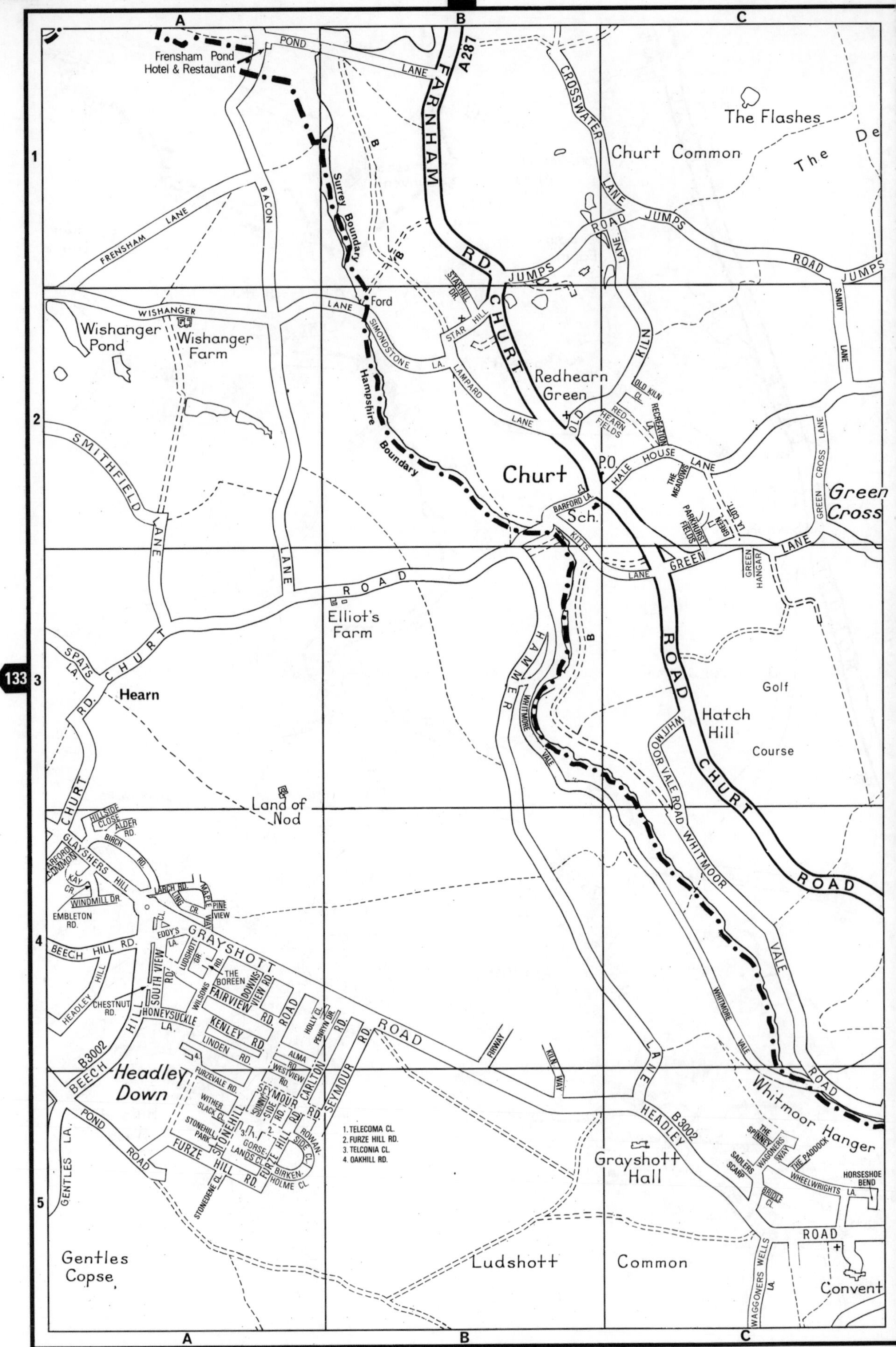

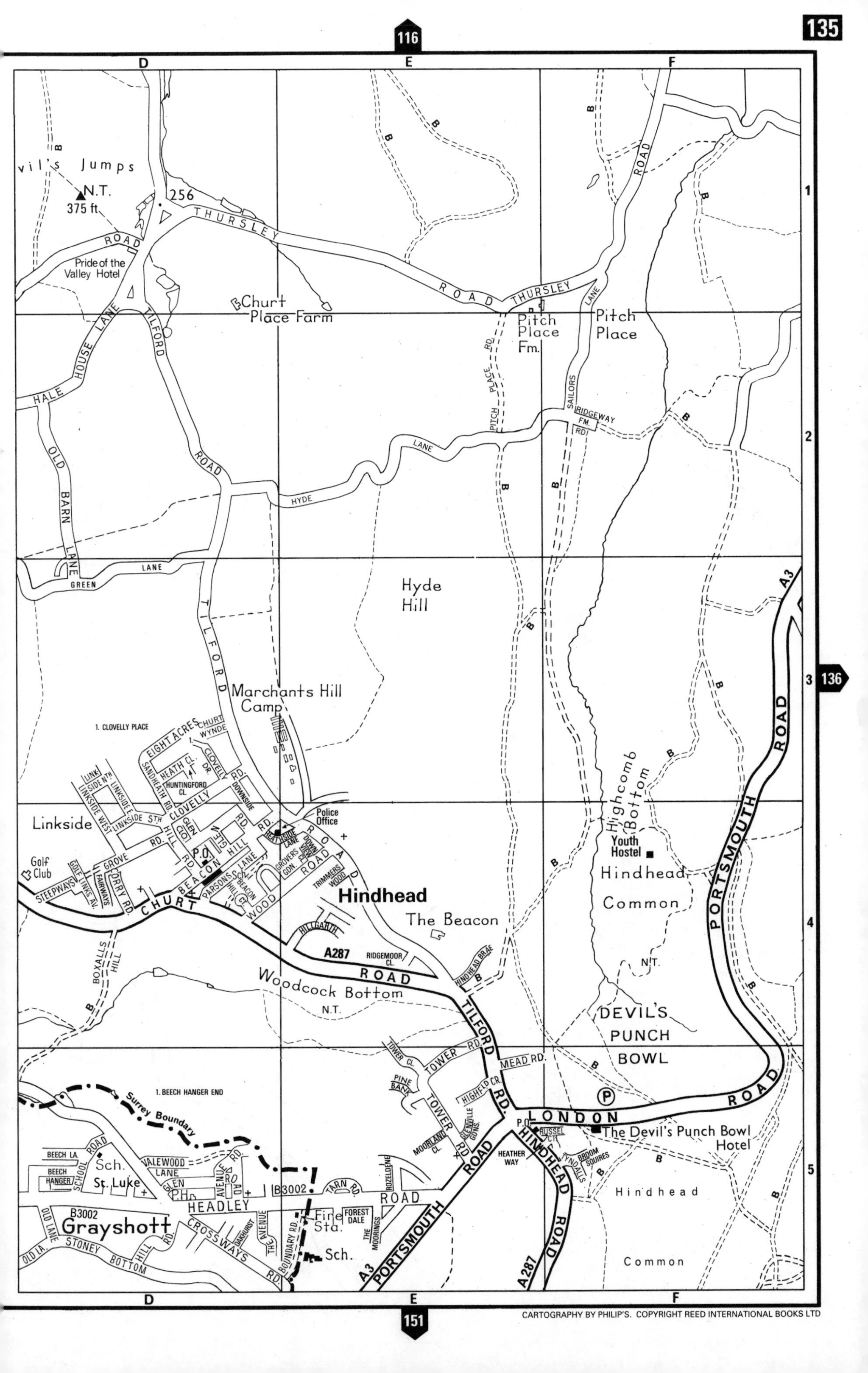
116
D
E
F
1
2
3
4
5
136
vil's Jumps
N.T.
375 ft
256
THURSLEY ROAD
Pride of the Valley Hotel
Churt Place Farm
Pitch Place Fm.
Pitch Place
HALE HOUSE LANE
TILFORD ROAD
OLD BARN LANE
GREEN LANE
HYDE LANE
SAILORS LANE
PITCH PLACE RD.
RIDGEWAY FM. RD.
Hyde Hill
Marchants Hill Camp
1. CLOVELLY PLACE
EIGHT ACRES
CHURT WYNDE
CLOVELLY DR.
HEATH CL.
SANDHEATH RD.
HUNTINGFORD CL.
CLOVELLY RD.
DOWNSIDE
LINKSIDE NTH.
LINKSIDE WEST
LINKSIDE STH.
LINKSIDE E.
Linkside
Golf Club
GROVE RD.
GLEN CLO.
HILL RD.
P.O.
BEACON HILL RD.
PARSONS LANE
Sch.
BEACON HILL CT.
HEATHSIDE LANE
GROVERS GDN.
DOWN VIEW CL.
Police Office
TRIMMERS WOOD
Hindhead
WOOD RD.
STEEPWAYS
GOLF LINKS AV.
FAIRWAYS
CHURT ROAD
A287
HILLGARTH
RIDGEMOOR CL.
The Beacon
HINDHEAD BRAE
Woodcock Bottom
N.T.
BOXALLS HILL
Highcomb Bottom
Youth Hostel
Hindhead Common
N.T.
DEVIL'S PUNCH BOWL
PORTSMOUTH ROAD
A3
TILFORD RD.
TOWER CL.
TOWER RD.
MEAD RD.
PINE BANK
HIGHFLD CR.
GLENVILLE GDNS.
MOORLAND CL.
LONDON ROAD
P.O.
RUSSEL CT.
The Devil's Punch Bowl Hotel
HEATHER WAY
HINDHEAD ROAD
TYNDALLS
BROOM SQUIRES
1. BEECH HANGER END
Surrey Boundary
BEECH LA.
BEECH HANGER
SCHOOL ROAD
Sch.
St. Luke
VALEWOOD LANE
GLEN
P.H.
AVENUE RD.
B3002
TARN RD.
ROZELDENE
HEADLEY ROAD
B3002
Grayshott
OLD LANE
OLD LA.
STONEY BOTTOM
HILL RD.
CROSSWAYS RD.
OAKHURST
THE AVENUE
BOUNDARY RD.
Fire Sta.
FOREST DALE
THE MOORINGS
Sch.
Hindhead Common
151

A B C

ROAD

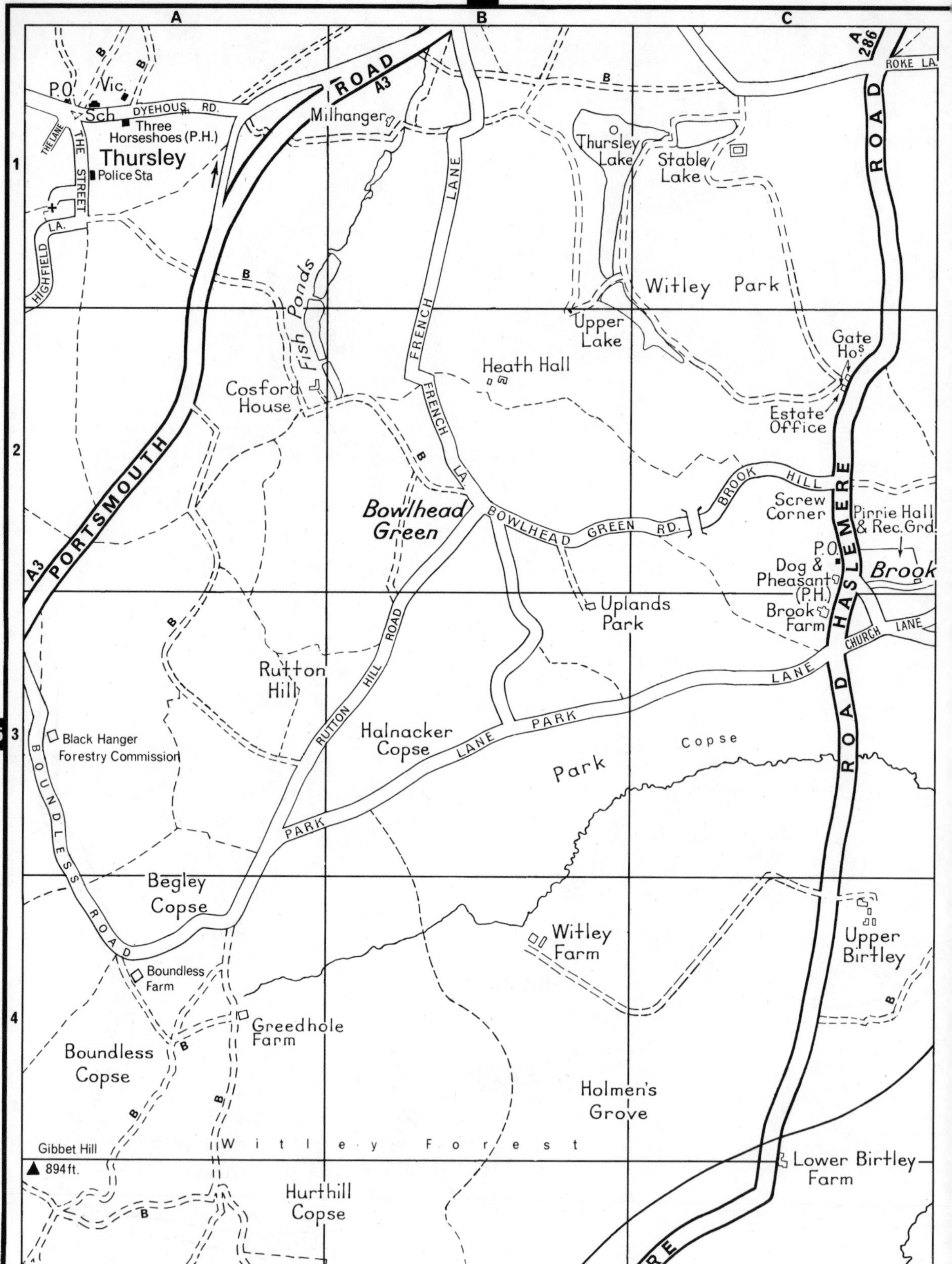

A3

P.O.
Vic.
B
B

DYEHOUS RD.

Sch

Milhanger

Three
Horseshoes (P.H.)

Thursley

Police Sta

THE STREET

THE LANE

HIGHFIELD LA.

1

Thursley
Lake

Stable
Lake

Witley   Park

FRENCH LANE

Fish Ponds

B

Upper
Lake

Gate
Ho^s

Heath Hall

A 286

ROKE LA.

A 286

Cosford
House

Estate
Office

ROAD

PORTSMOUTH

A.3

FRENCH LA.

2

B

Bowlhead
Green

Bowlhead   Green   Rd.

BROOK   HILL

Screw
Corner

Pirrie Hall
& Rec. Grd.

P.O.
Dog &
Pheasant
(P.H.)

Brook

HASLEMERE

B

Uplands
Park

Brook
Farm

LANE

RUTTON HILL ROAD

Rutton
Hill

CHURCH LANE

3

Black Hanger
Forestry Commission

Halnacker
Copse

LANE   PARK

Park

Copse

PARK

BOUNDLESS   ROAD

ROAD

B

Begley
Copse

Witley
Farm

Upper
Birtley

B

4

Boundless
Farm

Boundless
Copse

B

Greedhole
Farm

Holmen's
Grove

B

B

Lower Birtley
Farm

Gibbet Hill
▲ 894 ft.

W   i   t   l   e   y   F   o   r   e   s   t

B

Hurthill
Copse

HASLEMERE

5

B

B

B

Invall

B

A286

Stroud

A B C

118

D
E
F
1
2
3
4
5
138
153
ROKE LANE
Barrow Hills
NEWLANDS
GEORGE ELIOT CL.
NORTH FIELD
A283
Witley Manor
Witley
White Hart (P.H.)
Sch.
LANE
PETWORTH
Ponds
LANE
WATER
Fish Pond
Enton Hall Nursing Home
Parson's Hanger
Culmer
Sweetwater Pond
Foot Grd.
P.O.
Bryony Hill
Wormley
Hambledon
LANE
King Edward's Sch.
Sch.
Inst.
MALTHOUSE
PADDOCK CL.
BEECH HILL
LA.
Nat. Inst. of Oceanography
GURDON'S
ROAD
BROOK
CHURCH
Sandhills
Leybourne
The Hill
WORMLEY
ROAD
Hambledon Common
LANES END
VANN
LANE
WITLEY STA.
CAR PARK
The Wood Pigeon (P.H.)
Oakhurst Cott. (N.T.)
SANDHILLS
Sandhills Common
NEW
ROAD
COMBE
PETWORTH
Factory
Kiln Copse
Minepit Copse
Red Lands
Hambledon Hurst
LANE
ROAD
Winterton Arms (P.H.)
Northbridge
Combe Court
Fish Ponds
WOODBERRY CL.
PINCKARDS
HARTSGROVE
Combe Court Farm
Mont Colline
ROAD
COMBE VIEW
WOODSIDE
ASH
VALE
YEWENS
CROFT CL.
Granthams
Combe Common
WOODSIDE CL.
ROSENEATH DR.
ROAD
QUEENS MEAD
LANE
POOK
Langhurst House
ST. STEPHENS FIELD
OAK
ASHCOOMBE
BEECH CL.
PATHFIELD CL.
COXCOMBE
THE WILLOWS
RIDGELEY
ROAD
Sch.
Chiddingfold
BALLSDOWN
Green
P.O.
RD.
Pook Hill Cottages
HILL
LANE
POCKFORD
The Knipp
PRESTWICK
Langhurst Manor
Crown (P.H.)
PLAISTOW
Oaklands Park
Prestwick
MILL LANE
PETWORTH
A283
Swan (P.H.)
TURNERS MEAD
RD.
Little Prestwick Farm

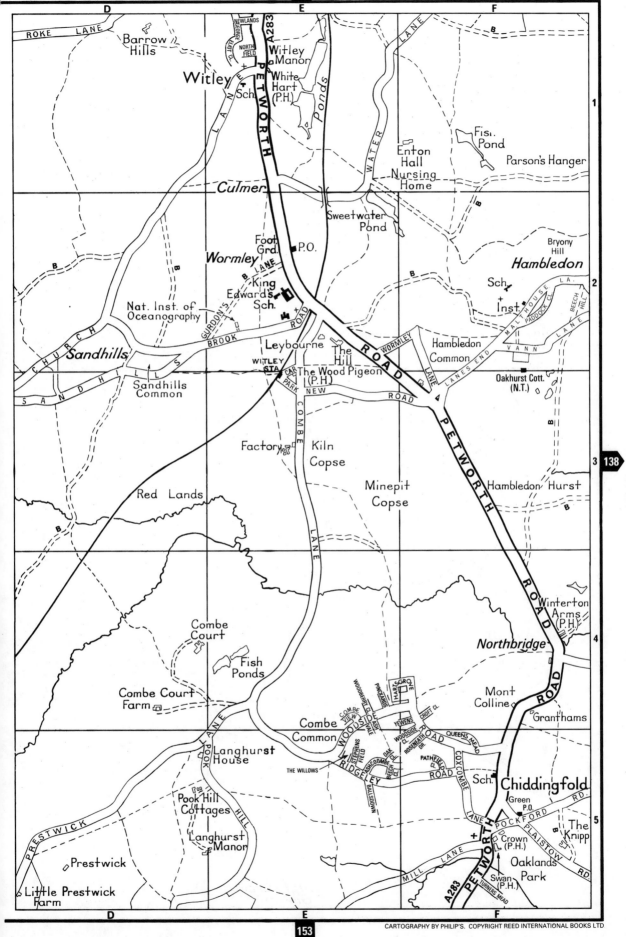

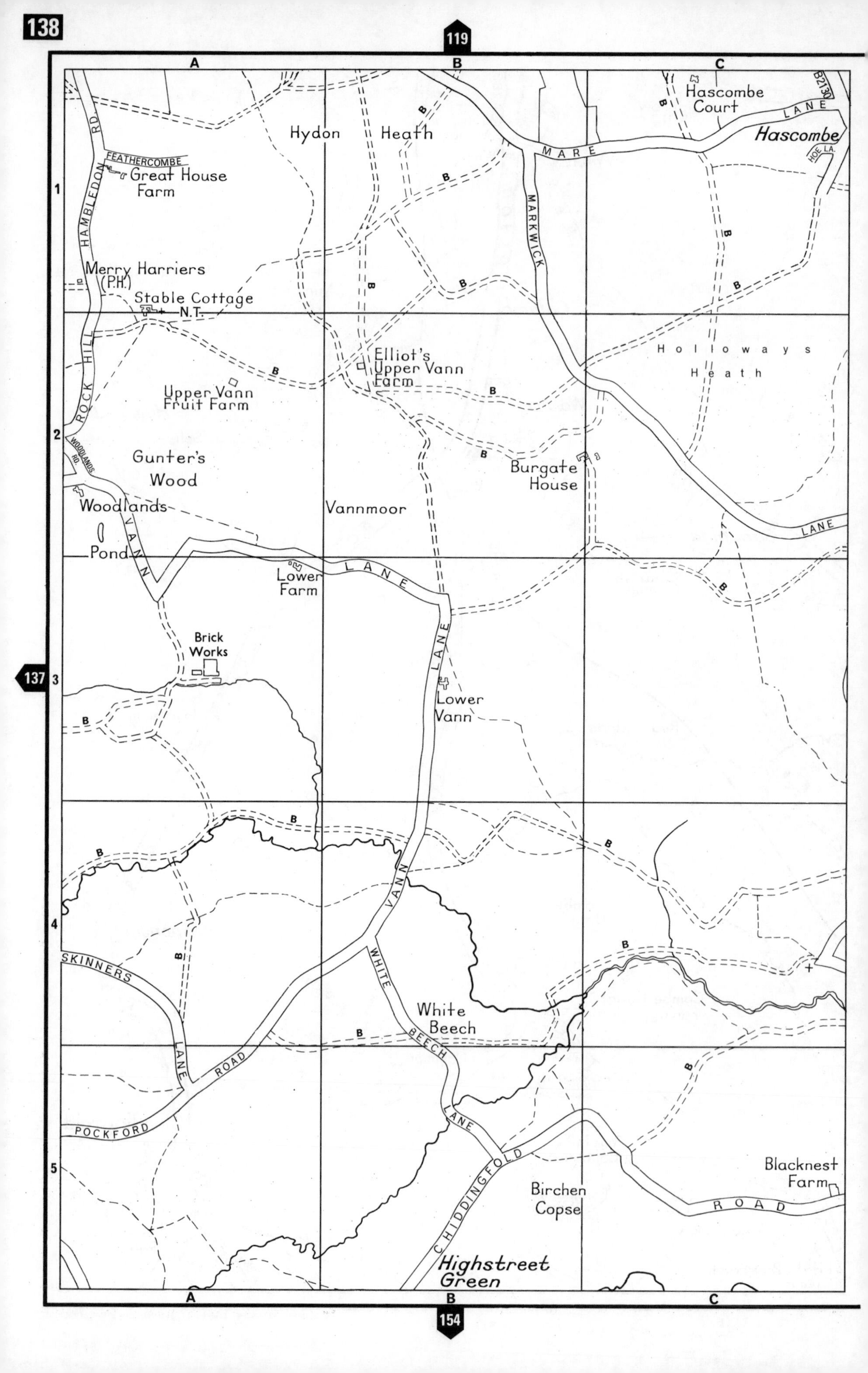
119
A
B
C
Hydon
Heath
Hascombe
Court
B2130
LANE
Hascombe
MARE
HOE LA.
FEATHERCOMBE
Great House
Farm
HAMBLEDON RD.
MARKWICK
Merry Harriers
(P.H.)
Stable Cottage
N.T.
1
ROCK HILL
Elliot's
Upper Vann
Farm
Holloways
Heath
Upper Vann
Fruit Farm
2
WOODLANDS RD.
Gunter's
Wood
Burgate
House
Woodlands
Vannmoor
LANE
Pond
VANN
Lower
Farm
LANE
Brick
Works
LANE
137
3
Lower
Vann
VANN
4
SKINNERS
WHITE
White
Beech
BEECH
LANE
ROAD
POCKFORD
LANE
5
CHIDDINGFOLD
Birchen
Copse
Blacknest
Farm
ROAD
Highstreet
Green
A
B
C
154

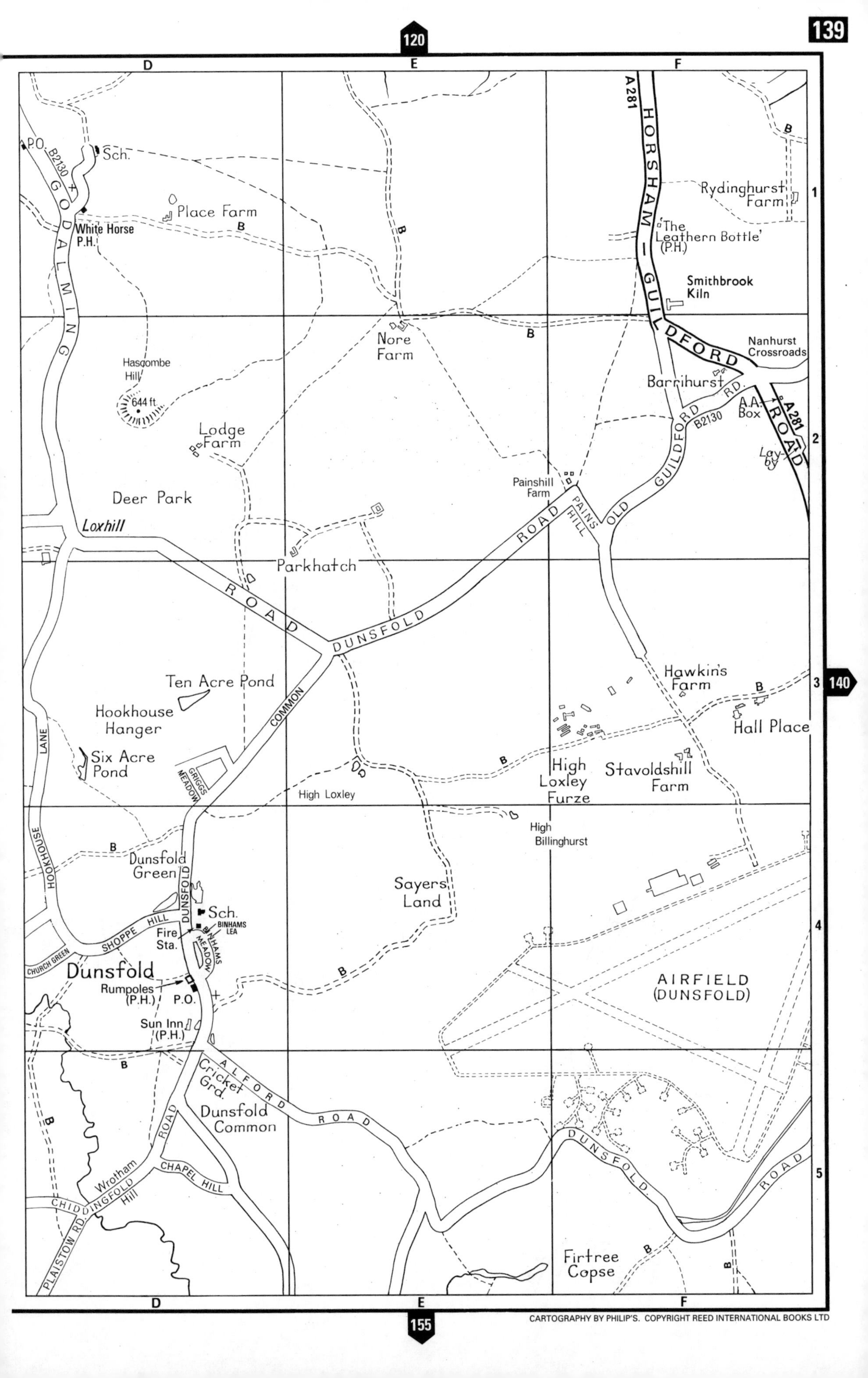

D   E   F

P.O. B2130

Sch.

Place Farm

White Horse P.H.

B

A281

HORSHAM — GUILDFORD

Rydinghurst Farm

1

'The Leathern Bottle' (P.H.)

Smithbrook Kiln

Nanhurst Crossroads

Nore Farm

B

B

Barrihurst

GODALMING

Hasgombe Hill

644 ft

Lodge Farm

Deer Park

Loxhill

Guildford RD.

B2130

A.A. Box

A281 ROAD

Lay-by

2

Painshill Farm

PAINS HILL

OLD GUILDFORD ROAD

Parkhatch

ROAD

DUNSFOLD

Ten Acre Pond

Hookhouse Hanger

Hawkin's Farm

B

Hall Place

3

Six Acre Pond

GRIGGS MEADOW

COMMON

High Loxley

B

High Loxley Furze

Stavoldshill Farm

LANE

High Billinghurst

B

Dunsfold Green

DUNSFOLD HILL

Sch.

Fire Sta.

BINHAMS LEA

BINHAMS MEADOW

Sayers Land

AIRFIELD (DUNSFOLD)

4

HOOKHOUSE

SHOPPE

CHURCH GREEN

Dunsfold

Rumpoles (P.H.)

P.O.

Sun Inn (P.H.)

B

Cricket Grd.

ALFORD ROAD

Dunsfold Common

ROAD

DUNSFOLD ROAD

5

B

Wrotham Hill

CHAPEL HILL

CHIDDINGFOLD RD.

PLAISTOW RD.

Firtree Copse

B

B

D   E   F

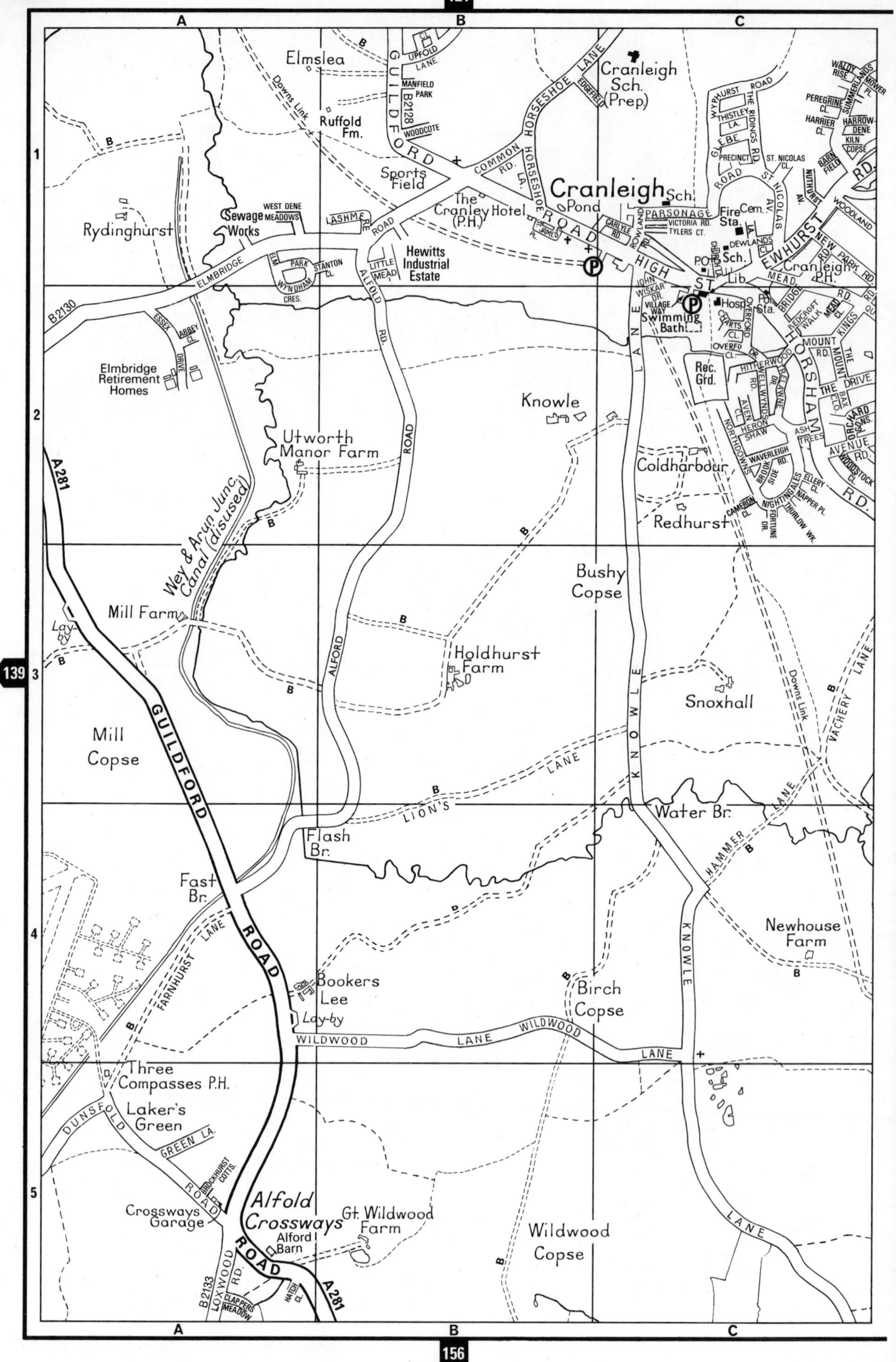
121
A
B
C
1
2
3
4
5
139
156
Elmslea
Ruffold Fm.
Sports Field
Cranleigh Sch. (Prep)
Cranleigh
The Cranley Hotel (P.H.)
Pond
Sch.
Fire Sta.
Cem.
Sch.
P.O.
Lib.
Hosp.
Pol. Sta.
Swimming Bath
Cranleigh P.H.
Rec. Grd.
Rydinghurst
Sewage Works
West Dene Meadows
Ashmere
Hewitts Industrial Estate
Elmbridge
B2130
Essex Drive
Abbey Cl.
Park
Stanton Cl.
Wyndham Cres.
Little Mead
Elm
Guildford Road
B2128
Upfold Lane
Manfield Park
Woodcote
Downs Link
Common Rd.
Horseshoe Lane
Horseshoe La.
Edgefield
High St.
Parsonage
Carlyle Rd.
Rowland Rd.
Victoria Rd.
Tylers Ct.
Dewlands
Church
John Wiskar Dr.
Village Way
Knowle Lane
Wyphurst Road
Thistley La.
Glebe
The Ridings Rd.
Precinct
Glebe Road
St. Nicolas Av.
St. Nicolas Cl.
Ewhurst Road
Waldy Rise
Summerlands
Mower Pl.
Peregrine Cl.
Harrier Cl.
Harrowdene
Kiln Copse
Barnfield
Nuthurst Av.
Woodland
New Park Rd.
Mead
Bridge
Redcroft Walk
Mead Cl.
Kings Rd.
Mount Rd.
The Mount
The Drive
Horsham Rd.
Overford Dr.
Overford Cl.
Courts Cl.
Hitherwood
Wellwynds Rd.
Orelane
Aven Cl.
Heron Shaw
Northdowns
Waverleigh Rd.
Brookside
Ash Trees
Bax Clo.
Orchard Gdns.
Avenue Rd.
Woodstock Cl.
Ellery Cl.
Napper Pl.
Nightingales
Fortune Dr.
Cameron Cl.
Thurlow Wk.
Knowle
Coldharbour
Redhurst
Utworth Manor Farm
Alford Road
Wey & Arun Junc. Canal (disused)
A281
Mill Farm
Lay-by
Bushy Copse
Holdhurst Farm
Snoxhall
Vachery Lane
Mill Copse
Guildford Road
Lion's Lane
Knowle Lane
Water Br.
Flash Br.
Hammer Lane
Fast Br.
Farnhurst Lane
Newhouse Farm
Bookers Lee
Lay-by
Birch Copse
Wildwood Lane
Three Compasses P.H.
Laker's Green
Dunsfold Road
Green La.
Brickhurst Cotts.
Crossways Garage
Alfold Crossways
Gt. Wildwood Farm
Alford Barn
Wildwood Copse
Loxwood Rd.
B2133
Clappers Meadow
Hatch Cl.
Lane
B

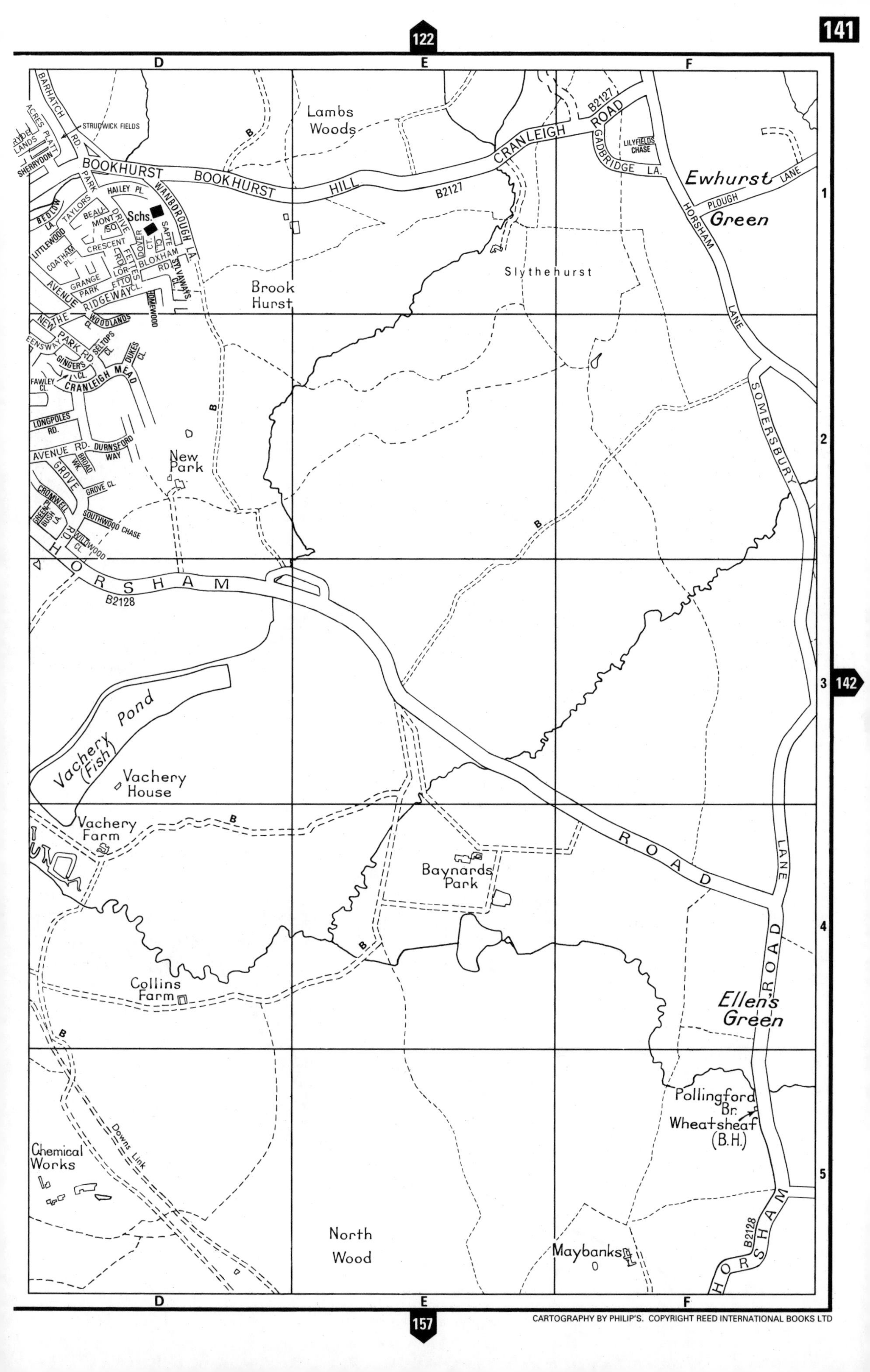

D · E · F

BARHATCH RD.
ACRES PLATT
2nd LANDS
SHERRYDON
BEDLOW LA.
TAYLORS
LITTLEWOOD
COATHAM PL.
GRANGE PARK
AVENUE
NETHE
RIDGEWAY

BOOKHURST

STRUDWICK FIELDS

Lambs Woods

BOOKHURST HILL
B2127

CRANLEIGH
B2127 ROAD
GADBRIDGE LA.
LILYFIELDS CHASE

Ewhurst Green

PLOUGH LANE

HORSHAM LANE

1

HAILEY PL.
BEAU MONT DRIVE
50
CRESCENT
LOR-
FETTO
BLOXHAM RD.
SAPTE CL.
WANBOROUGH LA.
STRUWWAYS
Schs.
HAILEY PL.
FETTES
CLOVER CT.
SOMERWOOD
WOODLANDS

Brook Hurst

Slythehurst

NEW PARK RD.
GREENSWAY
GINGERS CL.
FAWLEY CL.
LONGPOLES RD.
AVENUE RD.
GROVE
CRUMWELL
GREEN BUSH RD.
SOUTHWOOD
RULLWOOD CL.

SELTOPS CL.
DUKES CL.
CRANLEIGH MEAD
BROAD WK.
DURNSFORD WAY
GROVE CL.
SOUTHWOOD CHASE

New Park

B

SOMERSBURY LANE

2

HORSHAM
B2128

B

3

142

Vachery (Fish) Pond

Vachery House

ROAD

Vachery Farm

B

Baynards Park

HORSHAM ROAD

LANE

Collins Farm

B

Ellen's Green

4

B

Chemical Works

Downs Link

Pollingford Br.
Wheatsheaf (B.H.)

B2128

5

North Wood

Maybanks
0

HORSHAM

D · E · F

CARTOGRAPHY BY PHILIP'S. COPYRIGHT REED INTERNATIONAL BOOKS LTD

141

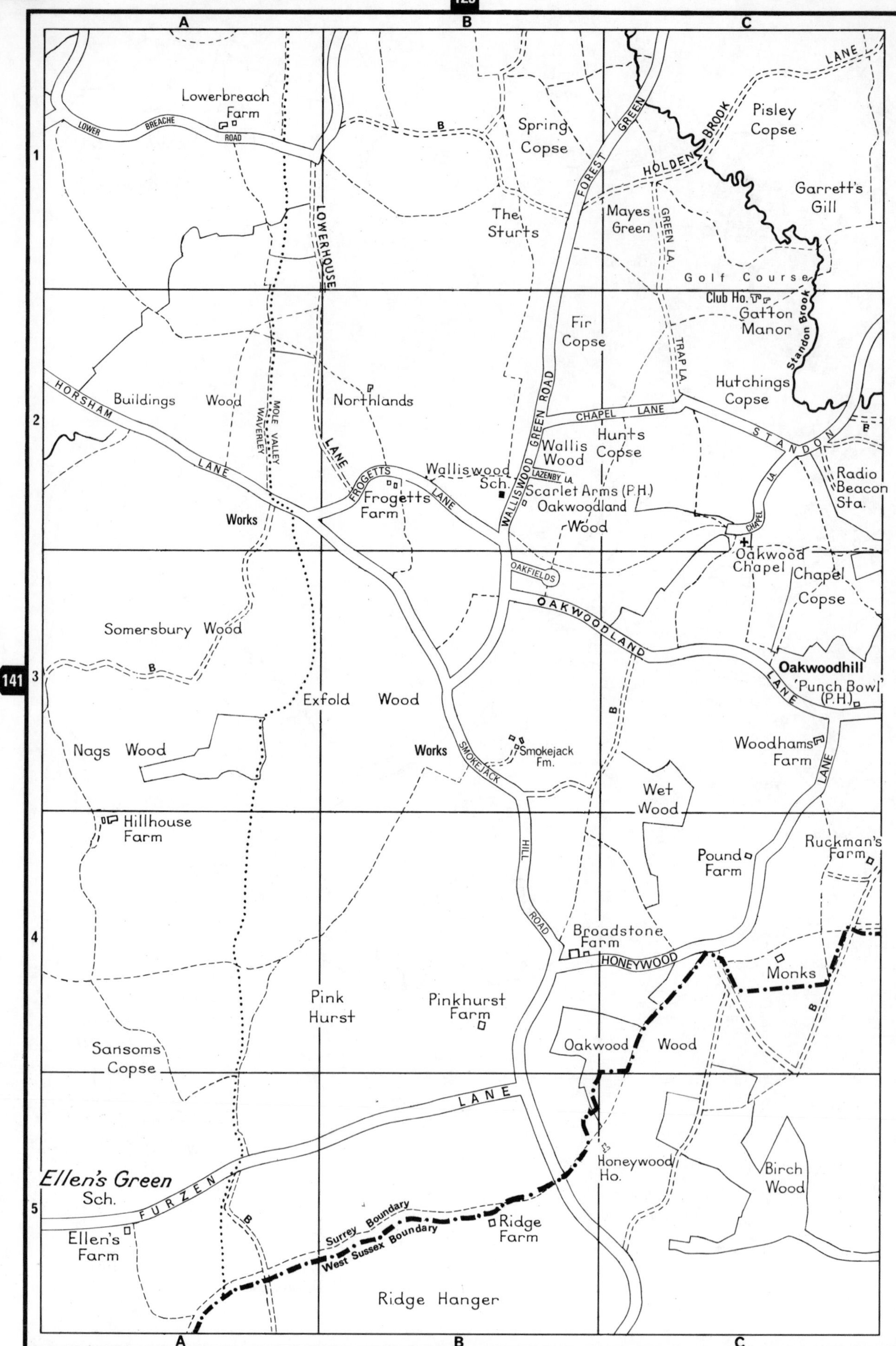

not continued, see key diagram

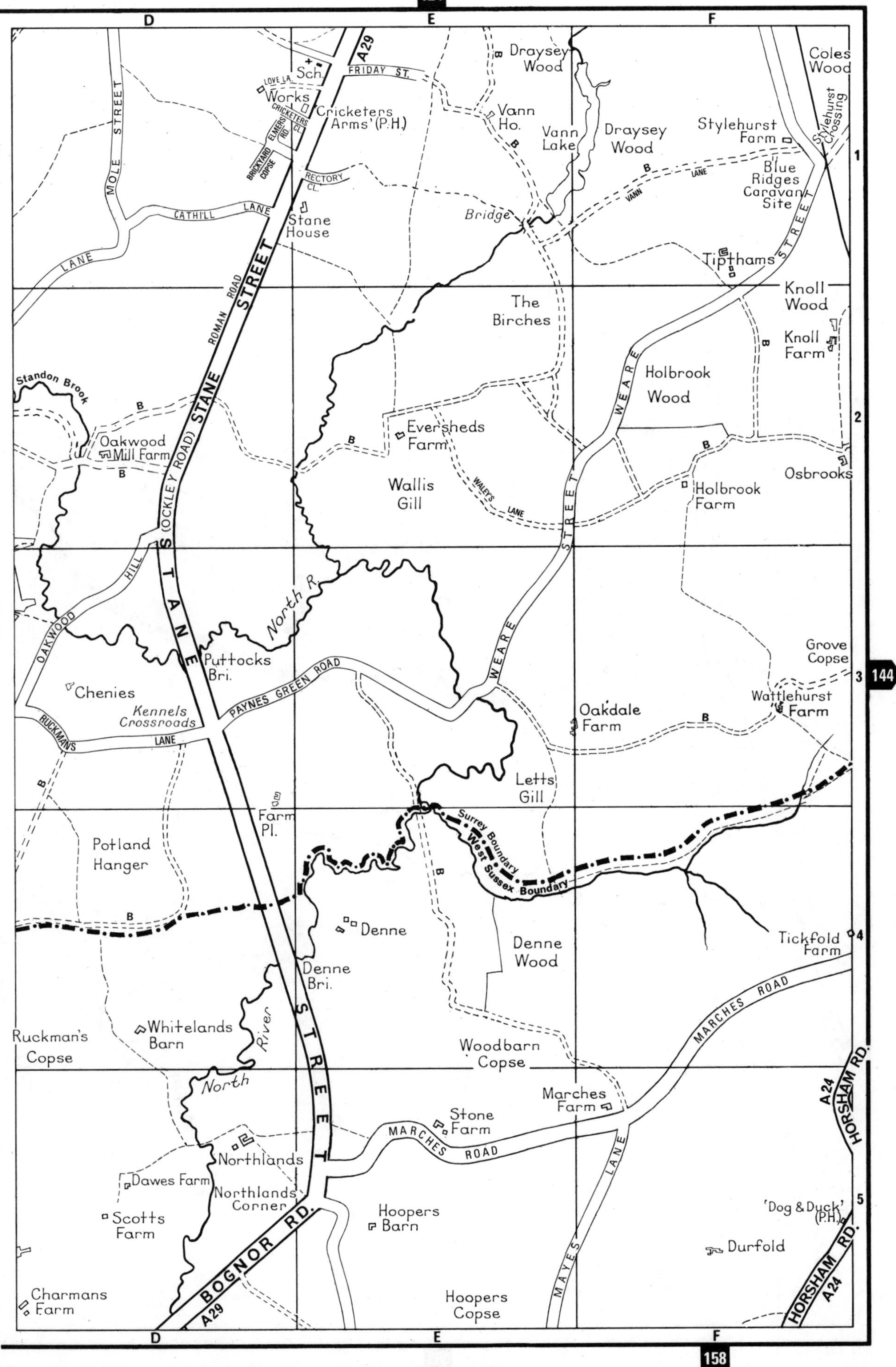

124
D
E
F
A29
Sch.
FRIDAY ST.
LOVE LA.
Works
Cricketers Arms' (P.H.)
CRICKETERS CL.
ELMERS RD.
BRICKYARD COPSE
RECTORY CL.
MOLE STREET
CATHILL LANE
LANE
Stane House
Draysey Wood
Vann Ho.
Vann Lake
Draysey Wood
Bridge
VANN LANE
Stylehurst Farm
Stylehurst Crossing
Coles Wood
Blue Ridges Caravan Site
Tipthams
STREET
Knoll Wood
Knoll Farm
The Birches
ROMAN ROAD
STANE STREET
(OCKLEY ROAD)
Standon Brook
Oakwood Mill Farm
Evershed's Farm
Holbrook Wood
WEARE
Wallis Gill
WALEY'S LANE
Holbrook Farm
Osbrooks
STREET
HILL
OAKWOOD
North R.
WEARE
Grove Copse
Puttocks Bri.
PAYNES GREEN ROAD
Chenies
Kennels Crossroads
RUCKMANS LANE
Oakdale Farm
Wattlehurst Farm
Letts Gill
Farm Pl.
Potland Hanger
Surrey Boundary
West Sussex Boundary
Denne
Denne Wood
Tickfold Farm
Denne Bri.
Whitelands Barn
River
Ruckman's Copse
Woodbarn Copse
MARCHES ROAD
North
Marches Farm
Stone Farm
MARCHES ROAD
Northlands
Dawes Farm
Northlands Corner
Scotts Farm
Hoopers Barn
MAYES LANE
A24
HORSHAM RD.
'Dog & Duck' (P.H.)
Durfold
BOGNOR RD.
A29
Charmans Farm
Hoopers Copse
1
2
3
144
4
5
158

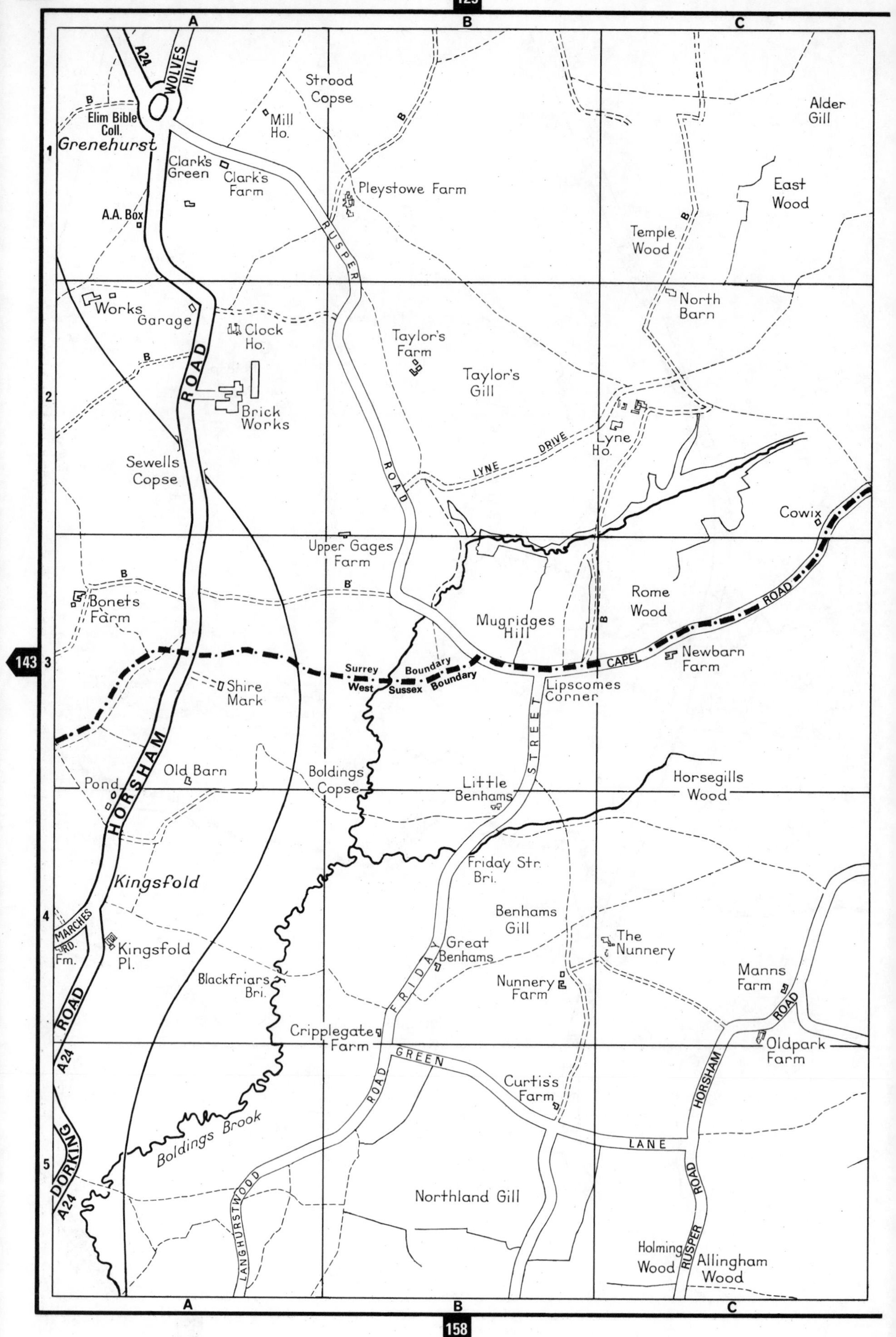

143 3

A24 WOLVES HILL

Elim Bible Coll.
Grenehurst

Clark's Green
Clark's Farm

A.A. Box

Mill Ho.

Strood Copse

Pleystowe Farm

RUSPER

Alder Gill

East Wood

Temple Wood

North Barn

Works
Garage

Clock Ho.

Brick Works

ROAD

Taylor's Farm

Taylor's Gill

LYNE DRIVE

Lyne Ho.

Sewells Copse

ROAD

Upper Gages Farm

Cowix

Bonets Farm

Shire Mark

B'

Surrey West
Boundary Sussex Boundary

Mugridges Hill

Rome Wood

Newbarn Farm

ROAD

CAPEL

Lipscomes Corner

HORSHAM

Pond

Old Barn

Boldings Copse

Little Benhams

STREET

Horsegills Wood

Kingsfold

Friday Str. Bri.

Benhams Gill

The Nunnery

MARCHES RD. Fm.

Kingsfold Pl.

Blackfriars Bri.

Great Benhams

Nunnery Farm

Manns Farm

ROAD

ROAD

A24

Cripplegate Farm

FRIDA

GREEN ROAD

Curtis's Farm

Oldpark Farm

HORSHAM ROAD

DORKING

A24

Boldings Brook

LANGHURSTWOOD

LANE

Northland Gill

RUSPER ROAD

Holming Wood

Allingham Wood

A B C

1

2

3

4

5

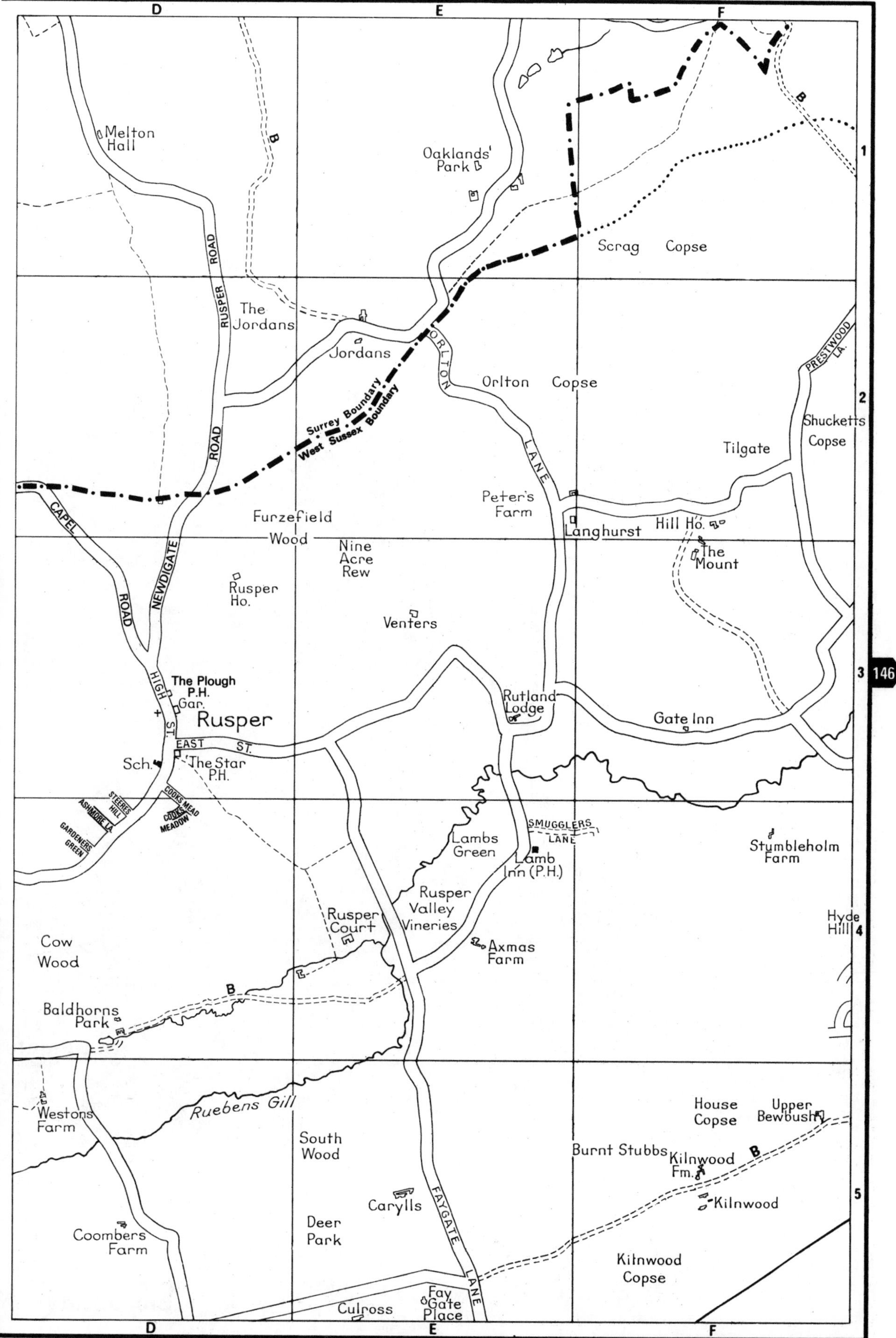

D   E   F

Melton
Hall

Oaklands'
Park

Scrag   Copse

B

1

The
Jordans

Jordans

ORLTON

Orlton   Copse

PRESTWOOD   LA.

Shucketts
Copse

2

RUSPER   ROAD

Surrey Boundary

West Sussex Boundary

Tilgate

LANE

CAPEL   ROAD

Furzefield
Wood

Nine
Acre
Rew

Peter's
Farm

Langhurst

Hill Ho.

The
Mount

NEWDIGATE

Rusper
Ho.

Venters

146

3

The Plough
P.H.
Gar.

Rusper

Rutland
Lodge

Gate Inn

HIGH ST.

EAST   ST.

Sch.

The Star
P.H.

ASHMORE LA.

STEERS
HILL

COOKS MEAD

COOKS
MEAD
MEADOW

SMUGGLERS
LANE

Stumbleholm
Farm

GARDENER'S
GREEN

Lambs
Green

Lamb
Inn (P.H.)

Hyde
Hill   4

Rusper
Valley
Vineries

Cow
Wood

Rusper
Court

Axmas
Farm

B

Baldhorns
Park

Ruebens   Gill

House
Copse

Upper
Bewbush

Westons
Farm

South
Wood

Burnt Stubbs

Kilnwood
Fm.

B

Kilnwood

5

Carylls

Coombers
Farm

Deer
Park

FAYGATE   LANE

Fay
Gate
Place

Kilnwood
Copse

Culross

D   E   F

not continued, see key diagram

CARTOGRAPHY BY PHILIP'S. COPYRIGHT REED INTERNATIONAL BOOKS LTD

A   B   C

1

Littlepark Farm

LOWFIELD HEATH RD.

CHARLWOOD ROAD

CRAWLEY

POLES LANE

B

Red Gable

PRESTWOOD LANE

Manor Ho. Farm

IFIELD ROAD

Ifield Wood

BONNETTS LANE

The Brook

Playing Fields

Langley Green

MULBERRY RD.

2

Ifield Court Farm

Ifield Crt.

Ifieldwood Farm

Ifieldwood

Rivermead

Ifield Village

STRATH RD.

The Rectory

P.O.

Ifield Green

Sch.

Sch.

Ifield

Sch.

Play Flds

Playing

Bonwycks Place Farm

RUSPERS KEEP

Sch.

Sch.

Playing Flds.

CRAWLEY

Subway

The Grove

Lower Barn

Sch.

West Green

Hosp.

IFIELD

3

Club Ho.

Sch.

Ifield Sta.

Cemetery

Footbridge

Level Crossing

Goff's Park Public Playing Fields

Southgate

4

Ifield Golf Course

Pond

Comm. Centre

School

Playing Field

Sch.

Gossops Green

Mill Pond

School

HORSHAM RD.

PARK ROAD

5

School

Bewbush

BEWBUSH

HORSHAM

AVENUE A23

Broadfield

A2220

not continued, see key diagram

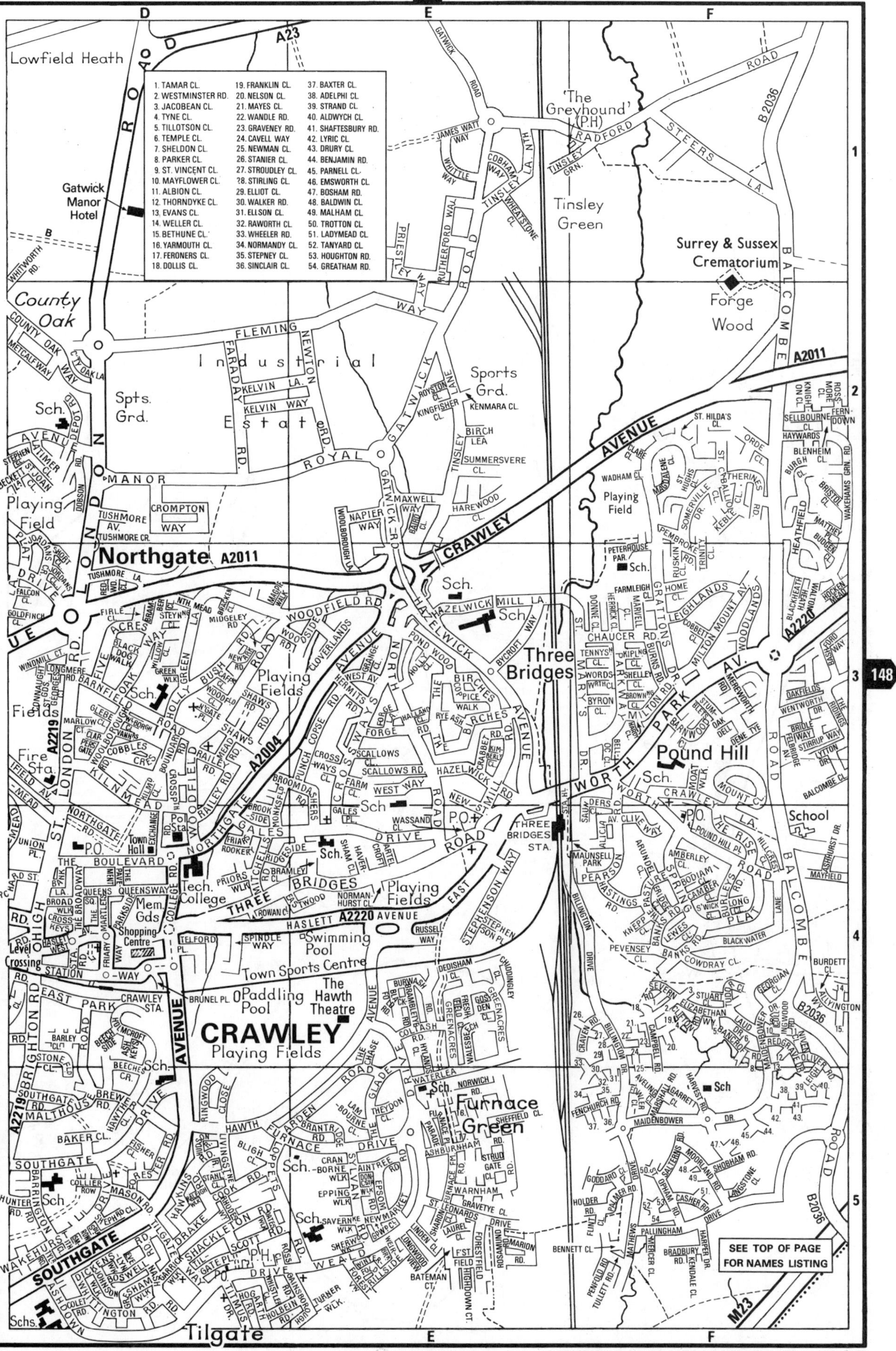

Street name index:

1. TAMAR CL.
2. WESTMINSTER RD.
3. JACOBEAN CL.
4. TYNE CL.
5. TILLOTSON CL.
6. TEMPLE CL.
7. SHELDON CL.
8. PARKER CL.
9. ST. VINCENT CL.
10. MAYFLOWER CL.
11. ALBION CL.
12. THORNDYKE CL.
13. EVANS CL.
14. WELLER CL.
15. BETHUNE CL.
16. YARMOUTH CL.
17. FERONERS CL.
18. DOLLIS CL.
19. FRANKLIN CL.
20. NELSON CL.
21. MAYES CL.
22. WANDLE RD.
23. GRAVENEY RD.
24. CAVELL WAY
25. NEWMAN CL.
26. STANIER CL.
27. STROUDLEY CL.
28. STIRLING CL.
29. ELLIOT CL.
30. WALKER RD.
31. ELLSON CL.
32. RAWORTH CL.
33. WHEELER RD.
34. NORMANDY CL.
35. STEPNEY CL.
36. SINCLAIR CL.
37. BAXTER CL.
38. ADELPHI CL.
39. STRAND CL.
40. ALDWYCH CL.
41. SHAFTESBURY RD.
42. LYRIC CL.
43. DRURY CL.
44. BENJAMIN RD.
45. PARNELL CL.
46. EMSWORTH CL.
47. BOSHAM RD.
48. BALDWIN CL.
49. MALHAM CL.
50. TROTTON CL.
51. LADYMEAD CL.
52. TANYARD CL.
53. HOUGHTON RD.
54. GREATHAM RD.

SEE TOP OF PAGE
FOR NAMES LISTING

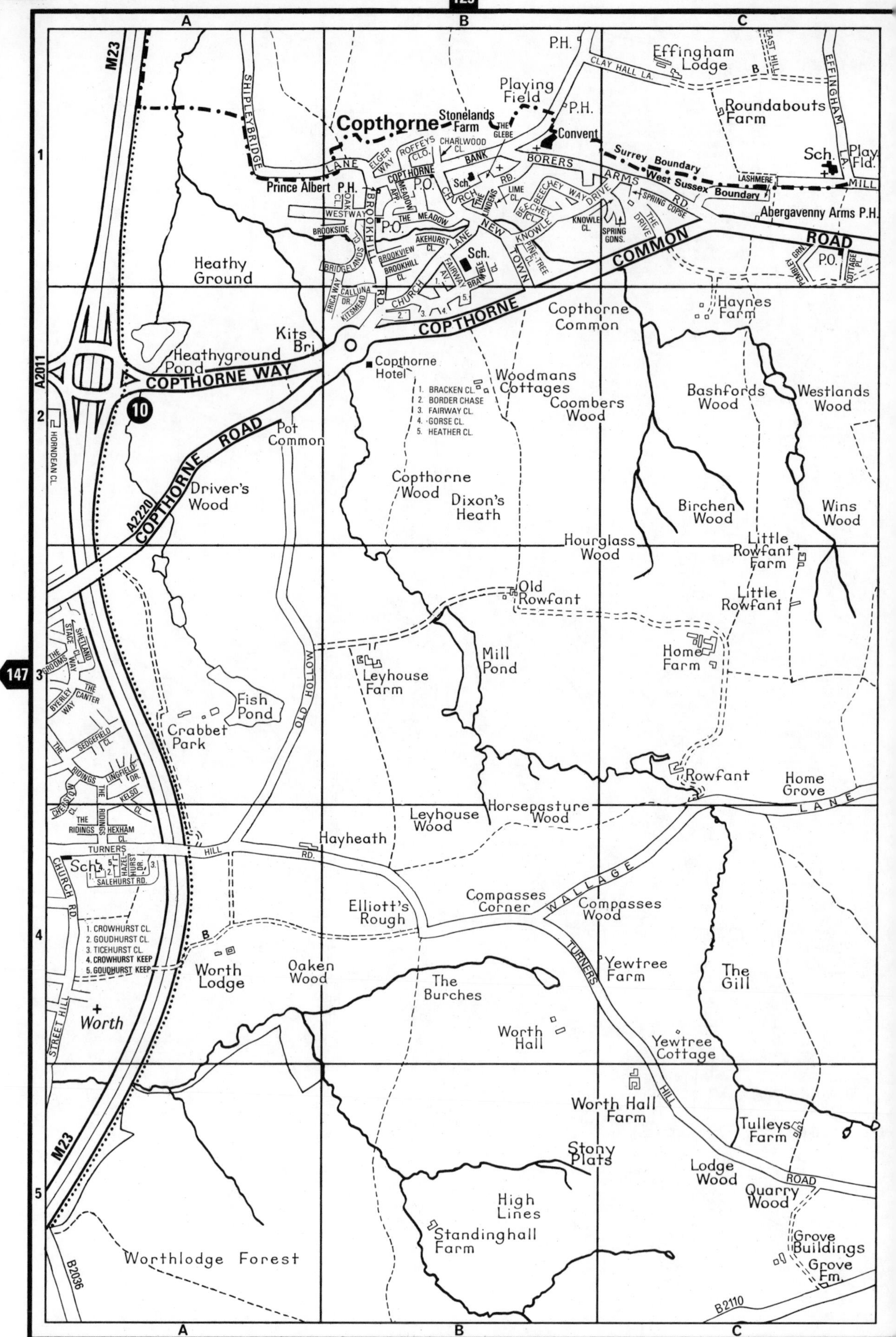

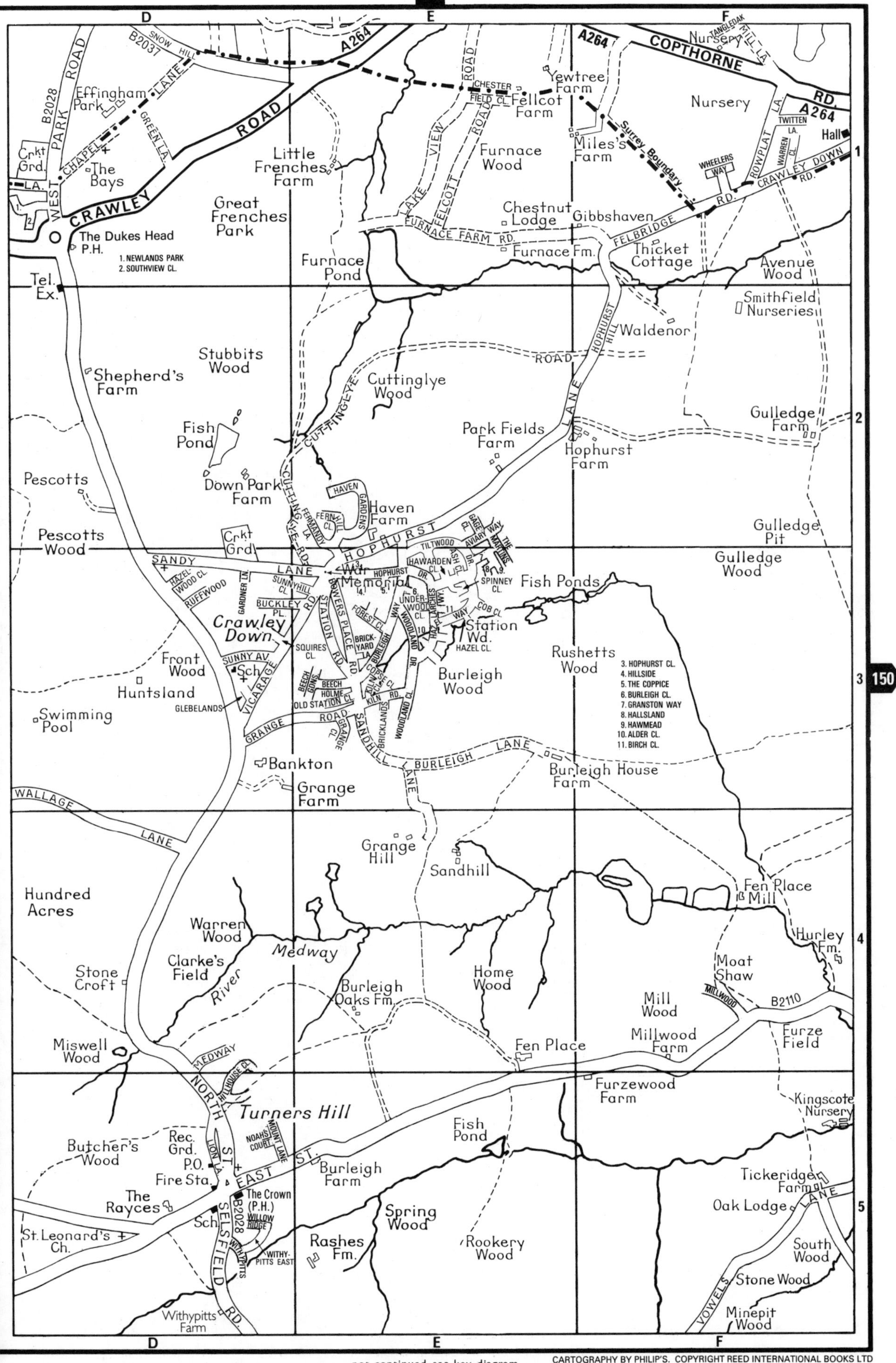

CARTOGRAPHY BY PHILIP'S. COPYRIGHT REED INTERNATIONAL BOOKS LTD

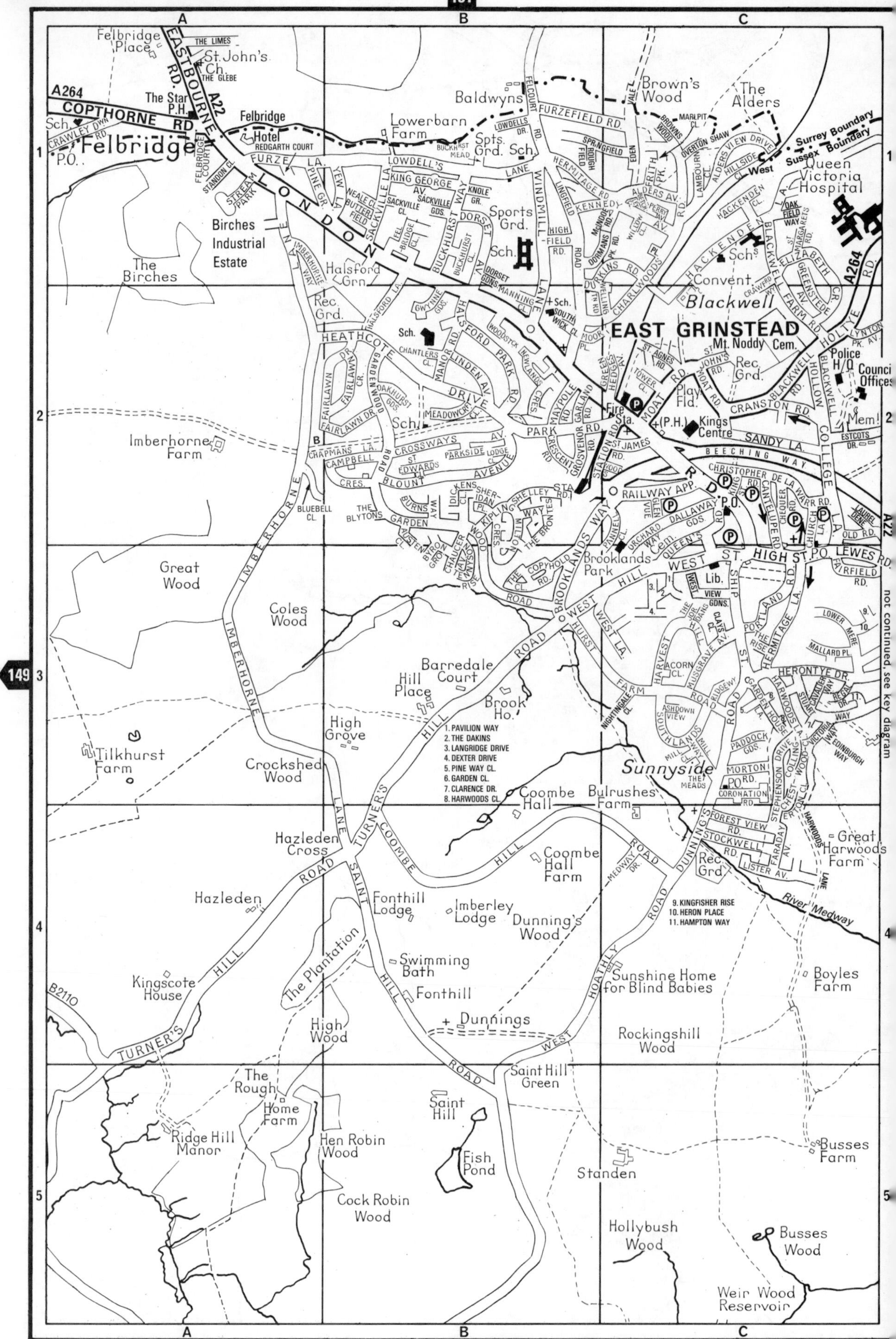

not continued, see key diagram

D   **E**   **F**

Hunters Moon

MOWATT RD.

KINGSWOOD FIRS

CYPRESS WAY

THE ROWANS

R.N. Sch.

Tudor House

KINGSWOOD LANE

HIGH ROAD

A3

A287

B

B

1

Surrey Hampshire Boundary

BRAMSHOTT LODGE DR.

Nutcombe

PITFOLD

HAZEL

GLEN LEA

GROVE

Sch.

Sch.

Sch.

POLECAT HILL

POLECAT VALLEY

LANE

STOATLEY RISE

1

Bramshott Common

Surrey Hampshire Boundary

NUTCOMBE LA.

POLECAT DR.

STOATLEY HOLLOW

2

A3 PORTSMOUTH

WOOLMER LANE

Woolmer Hill Sch.

Frensham Hall Farm

HINDHEAD

AZALEA DR.

BRAESIDE CL.

THE PADDOCK

STOATLEY RD.

WEYDOWN RD.

DERBY RD.

2

Woolmer Hill

St. Mary's Abbey

Critchmere

1. MALLARD CL.
2. DEEPDENE
3. ROE DEER COPSE
4. TROUT RD.
5. HERONDALE
6. FOX RD.
7. GLOVERS FIELD

Holy Cross Hospital

Sch.

CHERRY TREE AV.

THE WOODLANDS LA.

THE AVENUE

BUNCH WAY

HASLEMERE STA.

HATCHETTS DR.

RACKFIELD

LOWER HANGER

CRITCHMERE HILL

Sch.

CRITCHMERE LANE

PITFOLD AV.

CRITCHMERE RD.

DOLPHIN CL.

BUFF BEARDS LA.

ST. STEPHENS

PRIORSHOLT

VICARAGE LA.

Shottermill

B2131

P.O.

Lib.

WEYSPRINGS

CHURCH HILL

P

P

HASLEMERE STA.

LOWER ST.

CEDAR ST.

COURTS MT. RD.

HOLLY RIDGE

3   152

Hammer Bottom

SUNVALE AV.

Cem.

FIRTREE AV.

SUNVALE AV.

OAK TREE LANE

MANOR CL.

PITFOLD CL.

LIPHOOK RD.

P.O.

LUCAS FIELD

JUNCTION PLACE

LION GREEN WEY

MEAD WAY

Council Offices

THE MEADS

LION LA.

Dolmetsch Works

INDUSTRIAL SITE

KINGS RD.

SUN BROW

DALE VIEW

FOUNDRY LANE

LONGDENE RD.

COURTS

HASLE DR.

HEDGEHOG LA.

ARDS EST.

CHILTERN CL.

3

R. Wey

HAMMER VALE

MOOR RD.

P.O.

HEATH RD.

COPSE LANE

LINCHMERE RD.

PEGASUS CL.

PITTOCKS CL.

ROAD

SHOTTER MILL RD.

THE MILL STREAM

Ponds

CAMELSDALE RD.

NEW RD.

SICKLE RD.

Sch.

STURT RD.

MOOR FIELD AV.

STURT RD.

A287

Camelsdale

A286

Longdene

A286 MIDHURST ROAD

4

Hammer Coppice

GILHAM'S LA.

B2131

HAMMER HILL ESTATE

ROAD

Hammer

PENTWITH DR.

MARLEY LANE

SPRINGFARM RD.

HILLSIDE RD.

MARLEY COOMBE RD.

B2131

West Sussex Boundary

BELL RD.

Surrey Boundary

BELL

VALE LANE

MILLCROSS RD.

GREEN LA.

The Warren

MARLEY HANGER

FERNDEN LANE

4

Ridge Plantations

Linchmere Common

LINCHMERE ROAD

The Ridge

GLOVERS FIELD

Marley Common

BELL RD.

5

Linchmere House

Church Farm

Linchmere

LINCHMERE LANE

Cognor Wood

MARLEY LANE

Sch.

Kingsley Green

HATCH LA.

KINGSLEY GREEN ROAD

5

Linchmere Marsh

Marley Heights

SNIPE LN.

CHILCROFT RD.

SQUARE DR.

A286

D   **E**   **F**

CARTOGRAPHY BY PHILIP'S. COPYRIGHT REED INTERNATIONAL BOOKS LTD

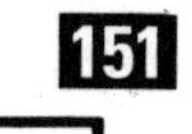

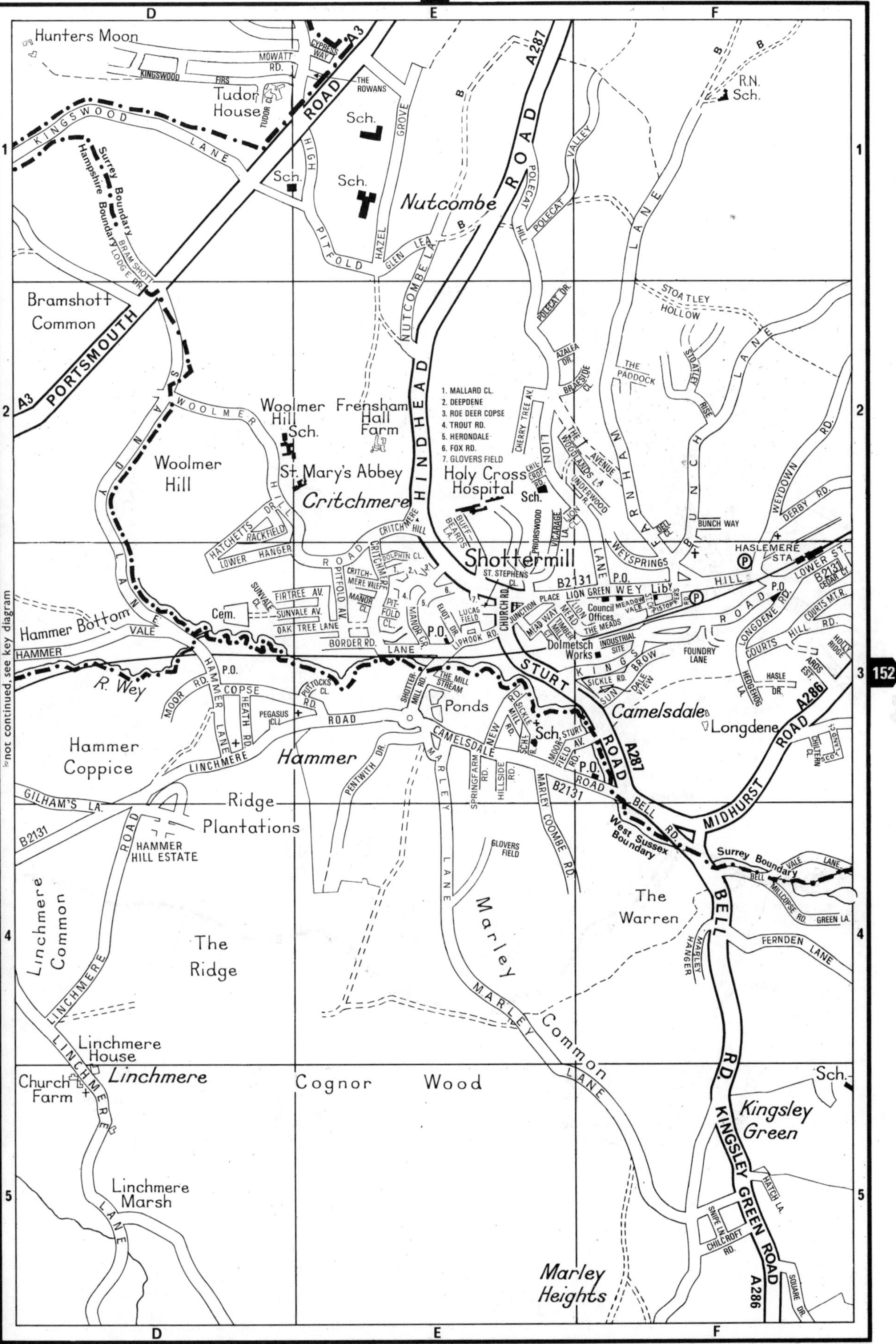

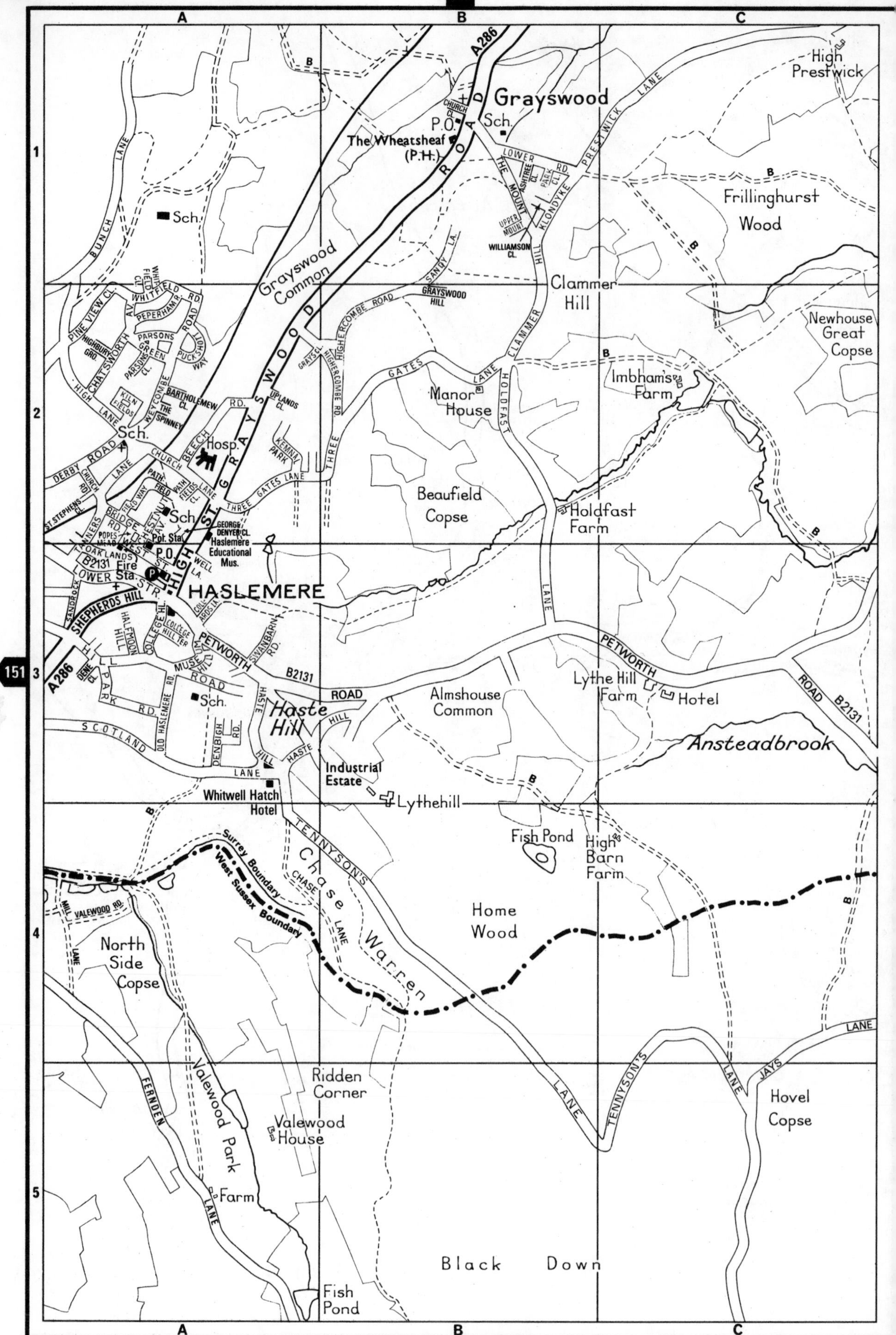

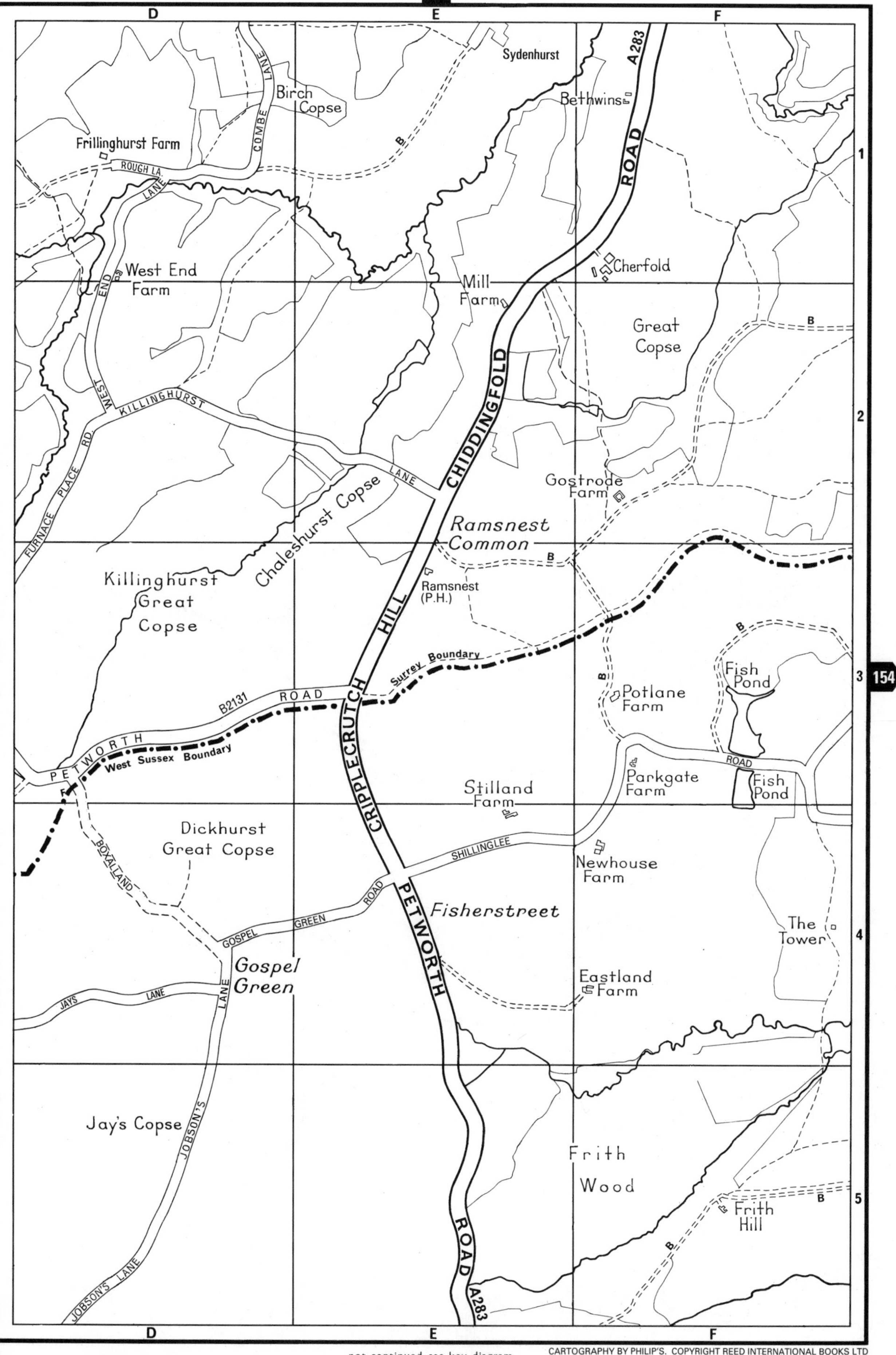

D E F

Sydenhurst

Bethwins

A 283 ROAD

Birch Copse

Frillinghurst Farm

ROUGH LA LANE

COMBE LANE

Cherfold

1

Mill Farm

West End Farm

Great Copse

B

WEST END

CHIDDINGFOLD

2

KILLINGHURST

FURNACE PLACE RD

LANE

Chaleshurst Copse

Gostrode Farm

Ramsnest Common

B

Killinghurst Great Copse

Ramsnest (P.H.)

CRIPPLECRUTCH HILL

Surrey Boundary

B

Fish Pond

B2131 ROAD

PETWORTH

West Sussex Boundary

Potlane Farm

B

3

ROAD

Fish Pond

Dickhurst Great Copse

Stilland Farm

Parkgate Farm

BOXALAND

SHILLINGLEE

Newhouse Farm

PETWORTH

Fisherstreet

The Tower

4

GOSPEL GREEN ROAD

Gospel Green

LANE

JAYS LANE

Eastland Farm

JOBSON'S LANE

Jay's Copse

Frith Wood

B

Frith Hill

5

ROAD

A 283

B

D E F

A   B   C

1

Botany
Bay

Lagfold Copse

B

PICKHURST HIGH STREET

Pickhurst

Tugley
Farm

Oaken Wood

Canterbury
Copse

The
Hatchetts

2

ROAD

HILL FISHER

Tugley
Wood

Oak
Wood

PLAISTOW ROAD

Fisherlane
Farm

FISHER   LANE

Durfold Hall Fm

PLAISTOW

3

WHITE'S PARK RD

SHILLINGLEE

Stick Factory

Shillinglee
Park

Downlands

Fisherlane
Wood

Durfold   Wood

B

Shortland
Copse

DURFOLD

WOOD

DUNSFOLD

B

Surrey Boundary
West Sussex Boundary

4

SHILLING

Newhouse
Farm

Eastend
Farm

ROAD

Shorts
Farm

ROAD

The
Lake

Haymans
Farm

Kingspark
Wood

Mill
Copse

5

Birchfold
Copse

Dale's
Farm

Chilsfold Farm

A   B   C

not continued, see key diagram

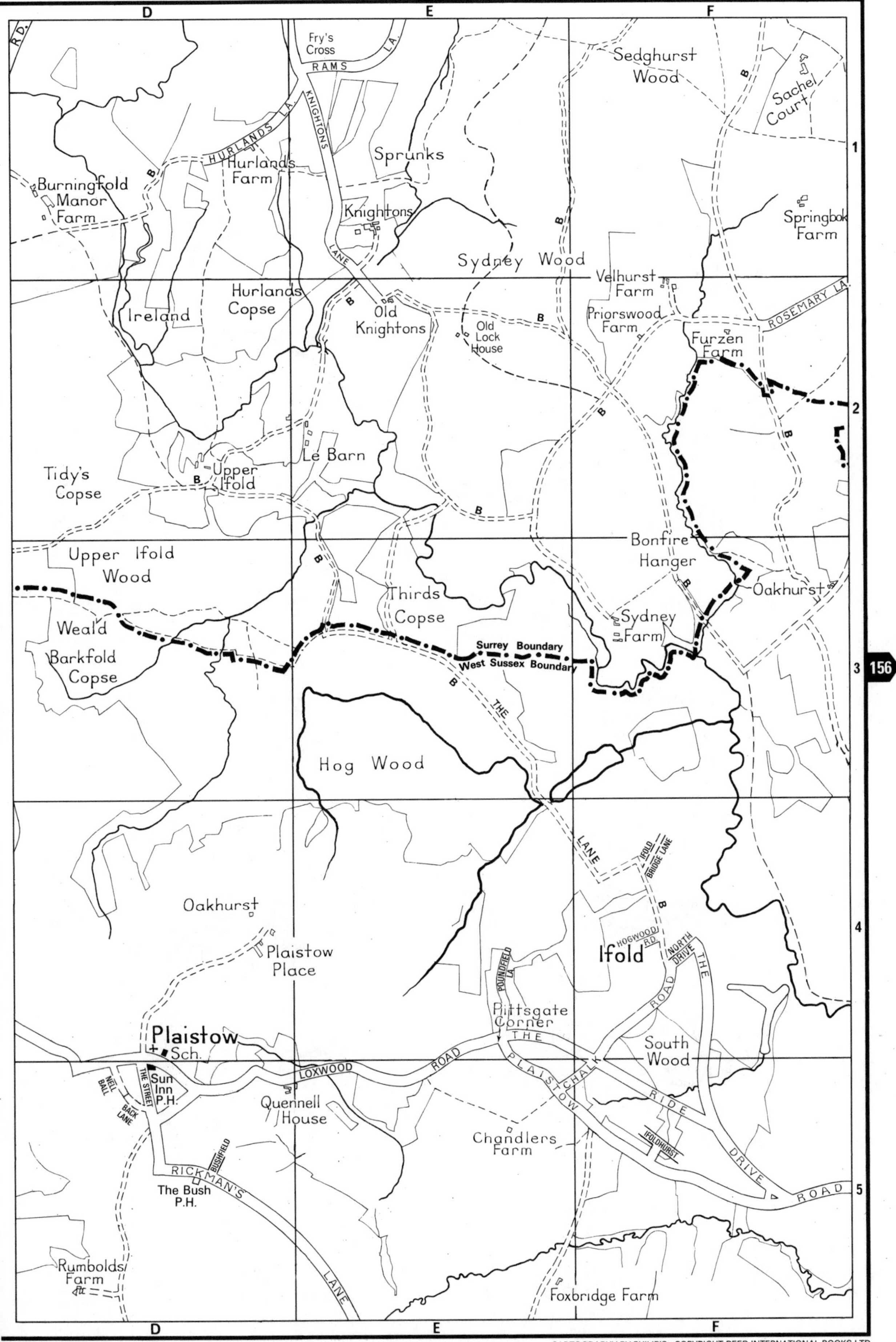

D E F

1

Fry's
Cross

RAMS LA.

Sedghurst
Wood

Sachel
Court

B

Burningfold
Manor
Farm

HURLANDS LA.
Hurlands
Farm

KNIGHTONS LA.

Sprunks

Knightons

Springbok
Farm

Ireland

Hurlands
Copse

LANE

Old
Knightons

Sydney Wood

Old
Lock
House

B

Velhurst
Farm

ROSEMARY LA.

Priorswood
Farm

Furzen
Farm

B

2

Tidy's
Copse

Le Barn

Upper
Ifold

B

B

Bonfire
Hanger

Oakhurst

Upper Ifold
Wood

B

Thirds
Copse

Sydney
Farm

B

Weald

Barkfold
Copse

Surrey Boundary
West Sussex Boundary

B

3

Hog Wood

THE

LANE

IFOLD
BRIDGE LANE

B

4

Oakhurst

Plaistow
Place

Ifold

HOGWOOD RD.

NORTH DRIVE

ROAD

THE

POUND FIELD LA.

Pittsgate
Corner

THE

South
Wood

Plaistow   Sch.

WELL
BALL

THE STREET

Sun
Inn
P.H.

BACK
LANE

LOXWOOD   ROAD

Quennell
House

PLAISTOW

CHALK   RIDE

DRIVE   ROAD

IFOLD HURST

5

RICKMAN'S

BUSHFIELD

The Bush
P.H.

Chandlers
Farm

LANE

Rumbolds
Farm

Foxbridge Farm

D E F

not continued, see key diagram   CARTOGRAPHY BY PHILIP'S. COPYRIGHT REED INTERNATIONAL BOOKS LTD

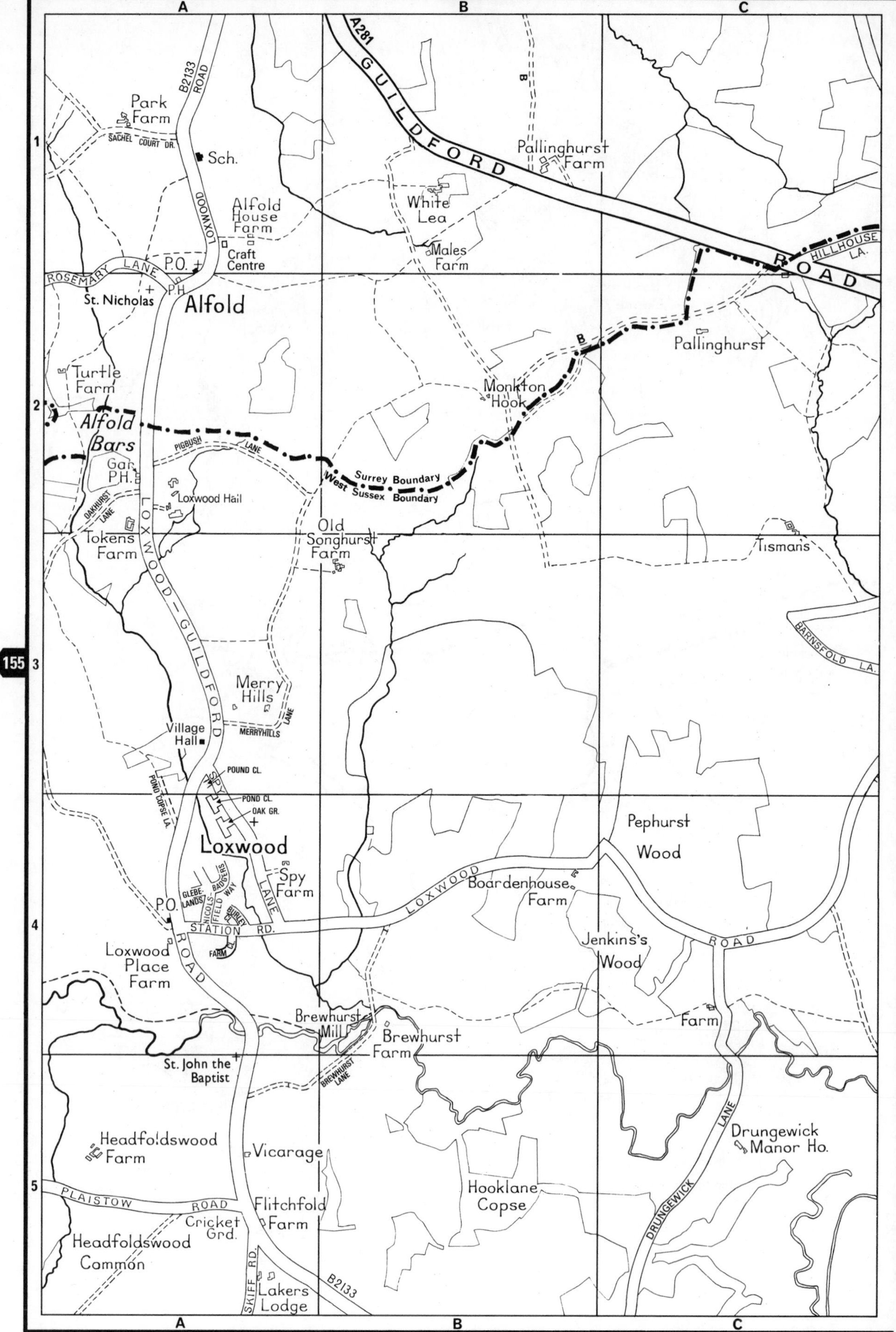

A281

GUILDFORD ROAD

HILLHOUSE LA.

1

Park
Farm

SACHEL COURT DR.

Sch.

Alfold
House
Farm

Craft
Centre

White
Lea

Pallinghurst
Farm

Males
Farm

B2133 ROAD

LOXWOOD

ROSEMARY LANE

P.O.

P.H.

St. Nicholas

Alfold

Pallinghurst

B

2

Turtle
Farm

**Alfold
Bars**

Gar.
P.H.

Monkton
Hook

PIGBUSH LANE

OAKHURST LANE

Loxwood Hall

West Sussex Boundary

Surrey Boundary

Old
Songhurst
Farm

Tismans

3

Tokens
Farm

LOXWOOD — GUILDFORD

Merry
Hills

MERRYHILLS LANE

BARNSFOLD LA.

Village
Hall

POND CL.

POND COPSE LA.

POND CL.

OAK GR.

SPY LANE

Pephurst
Wood

Loxwood

Spy
Farm

GLEBE-
LANDS

NICHOLS

BAKERS
WAY

FIELD WAY

BUREY

Boardenhouse
Farm

LOXWOOD ROAD

4

P.O.

STATION RD.

FARM

Loxwood
Place
Farm

ROAD

Jenkins's
Wood

Farm

Brewhurst
Mill

Brewhurst
Farm

BREWHURST LANE

St. John the
Baptist

Drungewick
Manor Ho.

5

Headfoldswood
Farm

Vicarage

Flitchfold
Farm

Hooklane
Copse

DRUNGEWICK LANE

PLAISTOW ROAD

Cricket
Grd.

SKIFF RD.

Headfoldswood
Common

Lakers
Lodge

B2133

A   B   C

not continued, see key diagram

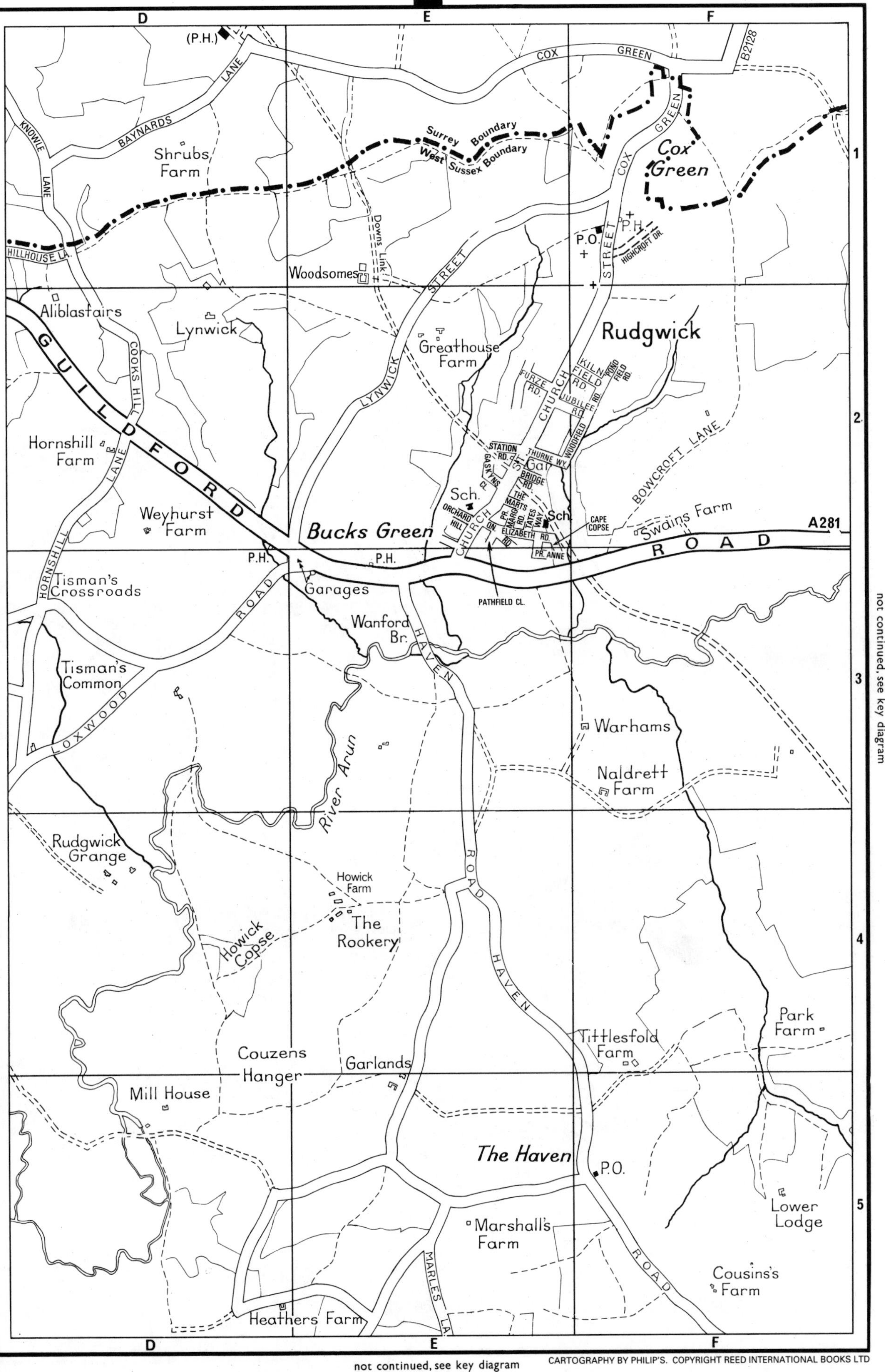

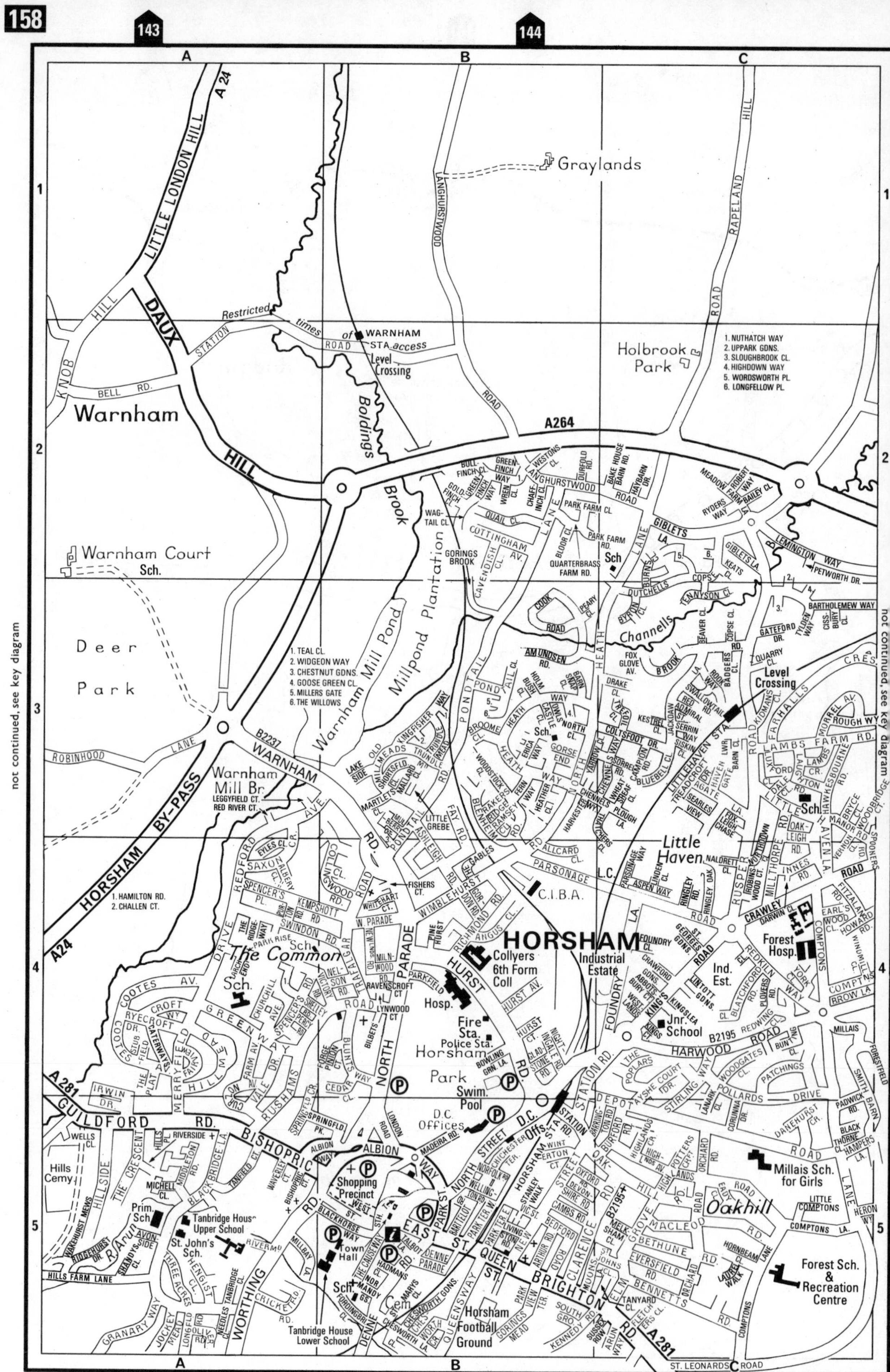

143　144

A　B　C

1　1

Graylands

LITTLE LONDON HILL
A 24

KNOB HILL
DAUX HILL
BELL RD.

Warnham

Restricted
times of access
Level Crossing
WARNHAM STA.

Boldings Brook

LANGHURSTWOOD ROAD

RAPELAND HILL
ROAD

Holbrook Park

1. NUTHATCH WAY
2. UPPARK GDNS.
3. SLOUGHBROOK CL.
4. HIGHDOWN WAY
5. WORDSWORTH PL.
6. LONGFELLOW PL.

2　A 264　2

Warnham Court Sch.

Millpond Plantation
Warnham Mill Pond

Gorings Brook

BULL FINCH CL.
GOLD FINCH CL.
WAG TAIL CL.
QUAIL CL.
COTTINGHAM AV.
CAVENDISH
COOK ROAD
PEARL CL.

GREEN FINCH WAY
CHAFF INCH CL.
WREN CL.
WESTONS CL.
LANGHURSTWOOD ROAD
DUFFIELD RD.
BAKE HOUSE BARN RD.
RYDERS WAY
Park Farm Cl.
Park Farm Rd.
QUARTERBRASS FARM RD.

MEADOW FARM
ROBERT WAY
BAILEY CL.
GIBLETS LA.
GIBLETS WAY
LEMINGTON WAY
PETWORTH DR.
KEATS CL.
COPSE
Sch.
TENNYSON CL.
BURNS
DUTCHELLS

3　Deer Park　3

B 2237

ROBINHOOD LANE

WARNHAM BY-PASS

1. TEAL CL.
2. WIDGEON WAY
3. CHESTNUT GDNS.
4. GOOSE GREEN CL.
5. MILLERS GATE
6. THE WILLOWS

PONDTAIL
POND TAIL ROAD
KINGFISHER WAY
OLD MARTLETS
MALLARD
TRUNDLE
BROOME
HEATH WAY
Channels

Channels Brook
FOX GLOVE AV.
BRAKES WAY
Sch.
GORSE END
ERICA
HEATHER WAY
FERN ROAD
CASTLE CL.
HEATH
DRAKE
COLTSFOOT DR.
KESTREL
SERRIN WAY
JACKDAW
SWALLOWTAIL
ADMIRAL
AMUNDSEN RD.
NORTH HEATH LA.

BARTHOLEMEW WAY
BURY CL.
GATEFORD DR.
GATEFORD RD.
QUARRY LA.
Level Crossing
BEAVER CL.
COPSE CL.
BADGERS
KIDMANS CL.
CRES.
ROUGH WY.
MURREL RD.
KENNEDY RD.
LITTLEHAVEN STA.
LWR. TREADCROFT FARM
HAVEN
GATE BARN
AGATE LA.
FORD
OAK CHASE
Sch.
LINTOTT
Little Haven
LAMBS FARM RD.
ROAD
SHELLEY RD.

4　A 24　4
HORSHAM

1. HAMILTON RD.
2. CHALLEN CT.

Warnham Mill Br.
LEGGYFIELD CT.
RED RIVER CT.

REDFORD DRIVE
BYLES CL.
SAXON
SPENCER'S PL.
THE RIDGE WAY
PARK RISE
KEMPSHOTT RD.
SWINDON RD.
AUBREY CL.
COLLINGWOOD RD.
WHITE HART CL.
FISHERS CT.
W. PARADE

The Common
Sch.
COOTES AV.
CROFT WY.
RAVENSCROFT
MILNWOOD CT.
RAVENSCROFT CT.

NORTH PARADE
WIMBLEHURST ROAD
RICHMOND RD.
ANGUS CL.
LITTLE GREBE
FAY RD.
BLENHEIM
CABLES
PARSONAGE
ALLCARD CL.

C.I.B.A.
L.C.
ASPEN WAY
RINGLEY OAK
RUSPER ROAD
CRAWLEY ROAD
Forest Hosp.
FOREST WAY
COMPTONS

HURST
HURST AV.
Collyers 6th Form Coll
Hosp.
Fire Sta.
Police Sta.
Horsham Park
Swim. Pool
D.C. Offices
BOWLING GRN. LA.

Industrial Estate
FOUNDRY LA.
ST. GEORGES GDNS.
CRAWFORD
ABBOTTS BURY
KINGS
Jnr. School
B 2195
HARWOOD ROAD
Ind. Est.

DARWIN CL.
REDKILN WAY
BLATCHFORD RD.
WADEY
PLOVERS RD.
BUNTING CL.
REDWING RD.
Millais

5　Horsham Football Ground　5

GUILDFORD RD.
A 281
IRWIN DR.
WELLS CL.
Hills Cemy.
BIRCHHURST MEWS
HILLSIDE
THE CRESCENT
MICHELL CL.
BLACKBRIDGE LA.
Prim. Sch.
Tanbridge House Upper School
St. John's Sch.
RIVERMEAD
MILLBAY LA.
Tanbridge House Lower School
GRANARY WAY
JOCKEY MEAD
LONGFIELD
NEEDLES
TANBRIDGE CL.
THREE ACRES
Hills Farm Lane

BISHOPRIC
WORTHING ROAD
Shopping Precinct
Town Hall
Sch.
DENNE RD.
Cem.

RUSHAMS ROAD
ALBION WAY
ALBION
SPRINGFIELD PK.
RIVERSIDE
LONDON ROAD
MADEIRA RD.
D.C. Offices
EAST ST.
NORTH ST.
PARK ST.
QUEEN ST.
STATION ROAD
WINTERTON
STANLEY WALK
OXFORD RD.
BEDFORD RD.
Horsham STA.
STATION RD.

BRIGHTON ROAD
A 281
GROVE RD.
MACLEOD RD.
BETHUNE RD.
CLARENCE RD.
EVERSFIELD RD.
BENNETTS RD.
TANYARD
SOUTH GRO.
ARUN RD.
KENNEDY RD.

Oakhill
Millais Sch. for Girls
LITTLE COMPTONS
COMPTONS LA.
HERON WY.
BLACK THORNE CL.
HAMPERS LA.
Forest Sch. & Recreation Centre

ST. LEONARDS ROAD
A　B　C

not continued, see key diagram

not continued, see key diagram
CARTOGRAPHY BY PHILIP'S. COPYRIGHT REED INTERNATIONAL BOOKS LTD.

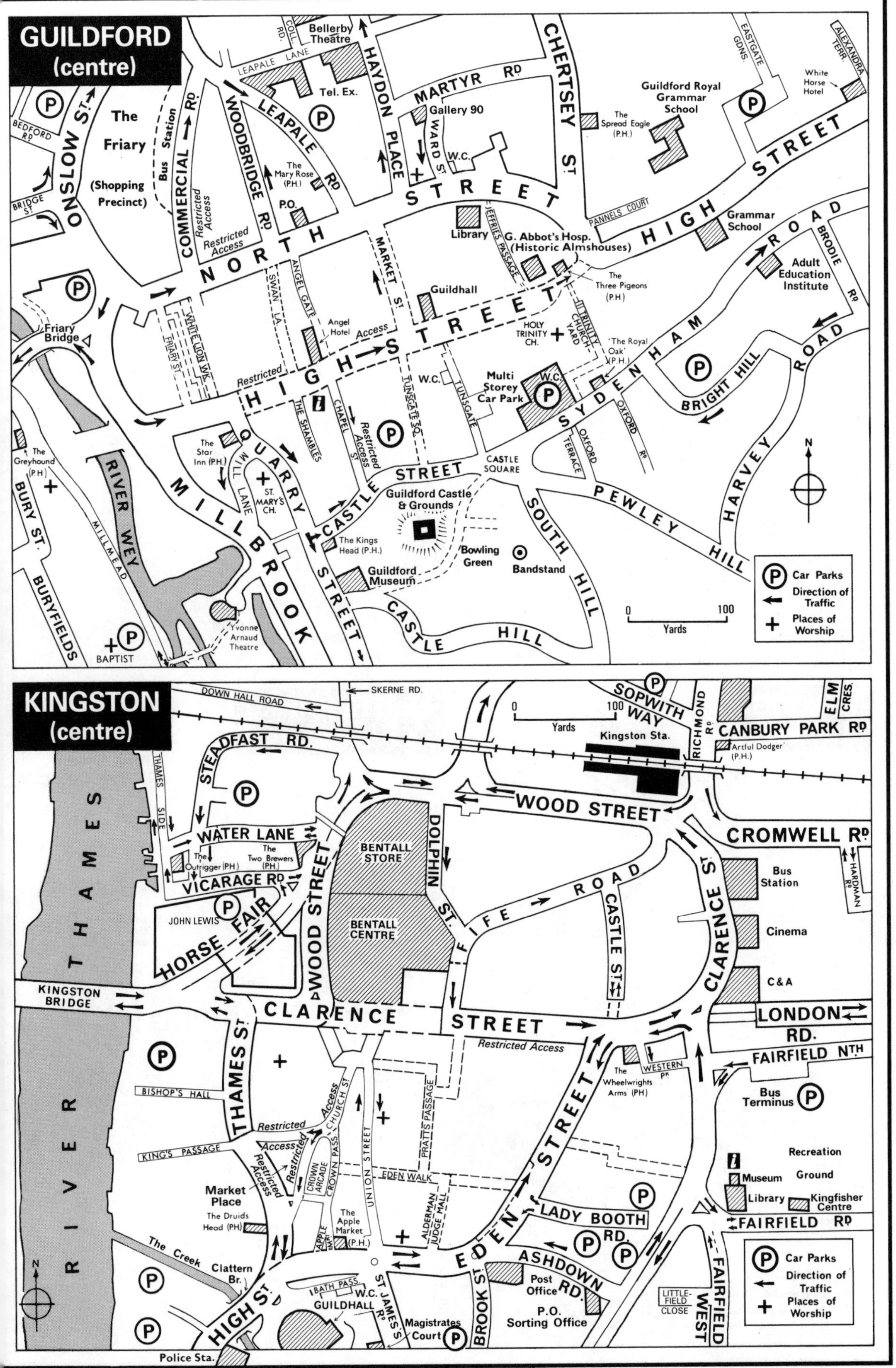

GUILDFORD (centre)

BEDFORD RD.
ONSLOW ST.
BRIDGE ST.
COLL. RD.
LEAPALE LANE
Bellerby Theatre
Tel. Ex.
HAYDON PLACE
MARTYR RD.
WARD ST.
Gallery 90
W.C.
CHERTSEY ST.
EASTGATE GDNS.
Guildford Royal Grammar School
White Horse Hotel
ALEXANDRA TERR.

The Friary (Shopping Precinct)
Bus Station
COMMERCIAL RD.
Restricted Access
WOODBRIDGE RD.
LEAPALE RD.
The Mary Rose (P.H.)
P.O.
MARKET ST.
Library
JEFFRIES PASSAGE
G. Abbot's Hosp. (Historic Almshouses)
The Spread Eagle (P.H.)
PANNELS COURT
HIGH STREET
Grammar School
BRODIE RD.
Adult Education Institute

NORTH STREET
SWAN LA.
ANGEL GATE
Angel Hotel
Guildhall
Access
The Three Pigeons (P.H.)
TRINITY CHURCHYARD
HOLY TRINITY CH.
'The Royal Oak' (P.H.)
SYDENHAM ROAD
BRIGHT HILL
HARVEY ROAD

Friary Bridge
WHITE LION WLK.
FRIARY ST.
HIGH STREET
Restricted
THE SHAMBLES
CHAPEL ST.
Restricted Access
TUNSGATE
W.C.
Multi Storey Car Park
W.C.
OXFORD RD.
OXFORD TERRACE
PEWLEY HILL
N

The Greyhound (P.H.)
BURY ST.
RIVER WEY
MILLMEAD
MILLBROOK
MILL LANE
The Star Inn (P.H.)
ST. MARY'S CH.
QUARRY ST.
CASTLE STREET
Access
CASTLE SQUARE
Guildford Castle & Grounds
SOUTH HILL
Bowling Green
Bandstand

BURYFIELDS
BAPTIST
Yvonne Arnaud Theatre
The Kings Head (P.H.)
Guildford Museum
CASTLE STREET
CASTLE HILL

P Car Parks
← Direction of Traffic
+ Places of Worship

0   100
Yards

KINGSTON (centre)

DOWN HALL ROAD
SKERNE RD.
STEADFAST RD.
THAMES SIDE
SOPWITH WAY
Kingston Sta.
RICHMOND RD.
CANBURY PARK RD.
ELM CRES.
'Artful Dodger' (P.H.)

Water Lane
The Outrigger (PH)
VICARAGE RD.
The Two Brewers (P.H.)
JOHN LEWIS
WOOD STREET
BENTALL STORE
BENTALL CENTRE
DOLPHIN ST.
WOOD STREET
FIFE ROAD
CASTLE ST.
CROMWELL RD.
Bus Station
HARDMAN RD.
Cinema
C&A

THAMES
RIVER
KINGSTON BRIDGE
HORSE FAIR
THAMES ST.
CLARENCE STREET
Restricted Access
The Wheelwrights Arms (PH)
WESTERN PL.
CLARENCE ST.
LONDON RD.
FAIRFIELD NTH.
Bus Terminus

BISHOP'S HALL
Restricted Access
KING'S PASSAGE
CHURCH ST.
CROWN PASS.
UNION STREET
PRATT'S PASSAGE
EDEN WALK
EDEN STREET
Recreation Ground
Museum
Library
Kingfisher Centre
FAIRFIELD RD.
FAIRFIELD WEST

The Creek
Clattern Br.
Market Place
The Druids Head (PH)
CROWN ARCADE
APPLE MKT.
The Apple Market (P.H.)
ALDERMAN JUDGE MALL
LADY BOOTH RD.
ASHDOWN RD.
BROOK ST.
Post Office
P.O. Sorting Office
LITTLEFIELD CLOSE

N
HIGH ST.
BATH PASS.
W.C.
GUILDHALL
ST. JAMES'S RD.
Magistrates Court
Police Sta.

P Car Parks
← Direction of Traffic
+ Places of Worship

0   100
Yards

CARTOGRAPHY BY PHILIP'S. COPYRIGHT REED INTERNATIONAL BOOKS LTD.

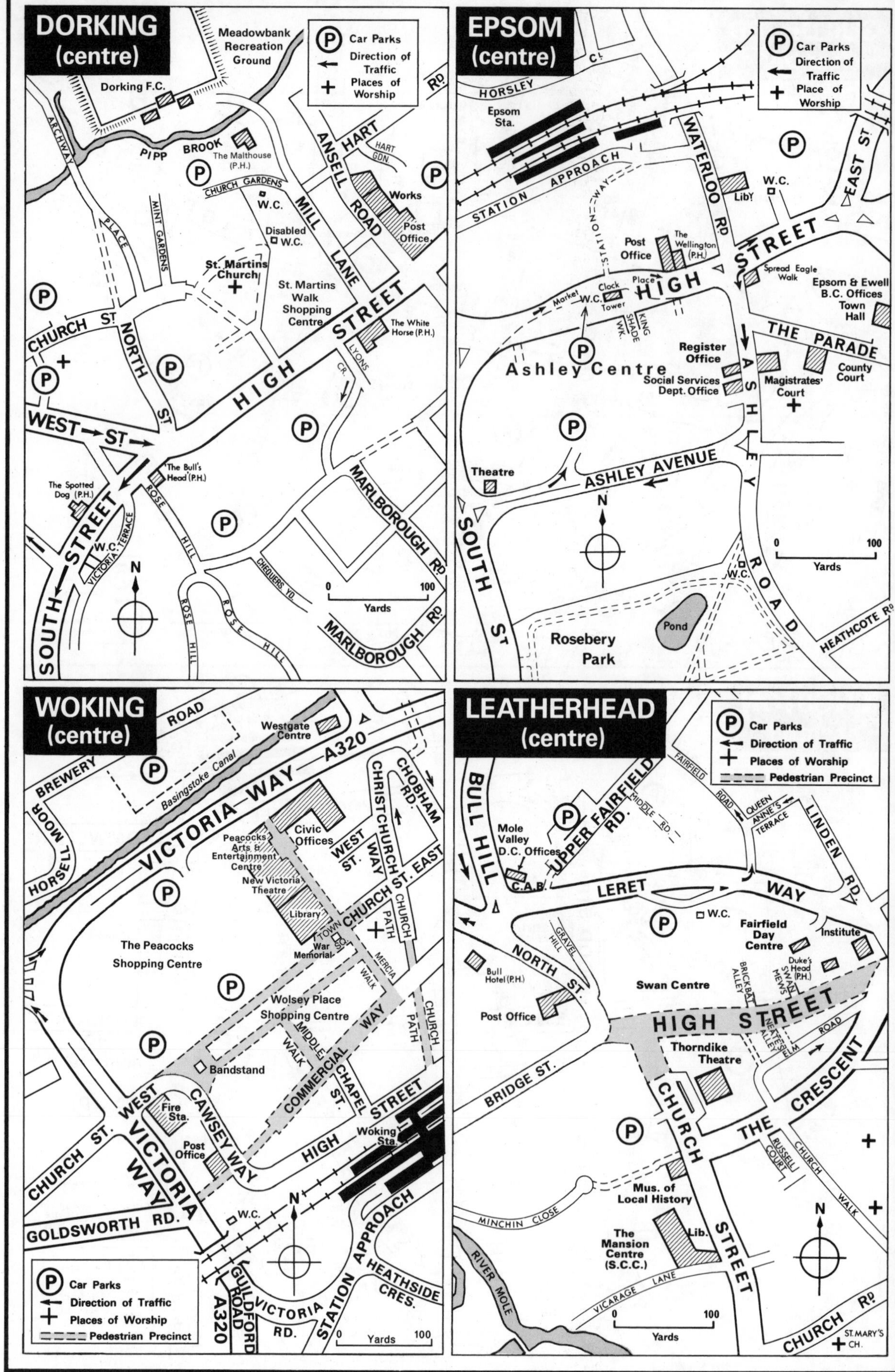

DORKING (centre)

P Car Parks
← Direction of Traffic
✠ Places of Worship

Meadowbank Recreation Ground
Dorking F.C.
ARCHWAY
PIPP BROOK
The Malthouse (P.H.)
P
CHURCH GARDENS
W.C.
Disabled W.C.
St. Martins Church
St. Martins Walk Shopping Centre
The White Horse (P.H.)
CHURCH ST.
NORTH ST.
MINT GARDENS
PLACE
P
P
✠
P
WEST → ST.
The Bull's Head (P.H.)
The Spotted Dog (P.H.)
W.C.
VICTORIA TERRACE
SOUTH STREET
ROSE HILL
ROSE HILL
CHEQUERS YD.
N
LYONS
CR.
HIGH STREET
MILL LANE
ANSELL ROAD
HART RD.
HART GDN.
Works
Post Office
MARLBOROUGH RD.
MARLBOROUGH RD.
P
P
0 100 Yards

EPSOM (centre)

P Car Parks
← Direction of Traffic
✠ Place of Worship

HORSLEY CL.
HORSLEY RD.
Epsom Sta.
STATION APPROACH
STATION WAY
WATERLOO RD.
Lib.
W.C.
EAST ST.
P
Post Office
The Wellington (P.H.)
HIGH STREET
Spread Eagle Walk
Epsom & Ewell B.C. Offices Town Hall
Market Place
Clock Tower
KING SHADE WK.
ASHLEY ROAD
THE PARADE
Register Office
Social Services Dept. Office
Magistrates' Court
County Court
Ashley Centre
P
P
Theatre
ASHLEY AVENUE
N
SOUTH ST.
W.C.
Rosebery Park
Pond
HEATHCOTE RD.
0 100 Yards

WOKING (centre)

ROAD
Westgate Centre
BREWERY ROAD
HORSELL
Basingstoke Canal
VICTORIA WAY A320
CHOBHAM RD.
CHRISTCHURCH RD.
Peacocks Arts & Entertainment Centre
Civic Offices
WEST ST.
CHURCH ST. EAST
New Victoria Theatre
Library
CHURCH ST.
P
P
P
P
P
The Peacocks Shopping Centre
TOWN SQ.
War Memorial
CHURCH PATH
MERCIA WALK
Wolsey Place Shopping Centre
Bandstand
MIDDLE WALK
CHAPEL ST.
COMMERCIAL WAY
CHURCH PATH
HIGH STREET
WEST
CAWSEY WAY
Fire Sta.
Post Office
VICTORIA WAY
Woking Sta.
GOLDSWORTH RD.
W.C.
N
CHURCH ST.
GUILDFORD ROAD A320
VICTORIA RD.
STATION APPROACH
HEATHSIDE CRES.

P Car Parks
← Direction of Traffic
✠ Places of Worship
▨ Pedestrian Precinct

0 100 Yards

LEATHERHEAD (centre)

P Car Parks
← Direction of Traffic
✠ Places of Worship
▨ Pedestrian Precinct

FAIRFIELD RD.
UPPER FAIRFIELD RD.
MIDDLE RD.
QUEEN ANNE'S TERRACE
LINDEN RD.
BULL HILL
Mole Valley D.C. Offices
C.A.B.
P
LERET WAY
W.C.
Fairfield Day Centre
Institute
NORTH ST.
GRAVEL HILL
Bull Hotel (P.H.)
Post Office
Swan Centre
BRICKBAT ALLEY
Duke's Head (P.H.)
SYNN MEWS
ELM
NEXTER
HIGH STREET
ROAD
Thorndike Theatre
BRIDGE ST.
CHURCH STREET
THE CRESCENT
CHURCH WALK
RUSSELL COURT
CHURCH RD.
P
MINCHIN CLOSE
Mus. of Local History
The Mansion Centre (S.C.C.)
Lib.
N
RIVER MOLE
VICARAGE LANE
ST. MARY'S CH.
0 100 Yards

CARTOGRAPHY BY PHILIP'S. COPYRIGHT REED INTERNATIONAL BOOKS LTD

INDEX OF STREET NAMES

Abbreviations

App.—Approach
Av.—Avenue
Br.—Bridge
Cl.—Close
Cres.—Crescent
Ct.—Court
Dri.—Drive
Fld.—Field
Gdns.—Gardens
Grn.—Green
Gro.—Grove
Gt.—Great
La.—Lane
Nth.—North
Pk.—Park
Pl.—Place
Rd.—Road
Sth.—South
Sq.—Square
St.—Street, Saint
Ter.—Terrace
Wk.—Walk

A

Name	Grid		Name	Grid		Name	Grid		Name	Grid
Aarons Hill	118 2C		Acacia Av., Woking	64 3C		Agraria Rd.	100 1B		Alcester Rd.	56 1B
Abbes Cl.	22 2B		Acacia Cl., Banstead	55 5D		Ailsa Av.	18 1F		Alcock Cl.	56 2C
Abbets La.	61 1D		Acacia Cl., Woodham	49 3D		Ailsa Cl.	146 5C		Alcocks Cl.	72 3A
Abbeville Rd.	21 1F		Acacia Dri., Banstead	55 5D		Ailsa Rd.	18 1A		Alcocks La.	72 3A
Abbey Cl., Cranleigh	140 2A		Acacia Dri., N. Cheam	38 4B		Ainger Cl.	78 4A		Alcorn Cl.	38 5B
Abbey Cl., Woking	65 1F		Acacia Dri., Woodham	49 3D		Ainsdale Way	64 2B		Aldenham Ter.	27 3D
Abbey Cl., Wokingham	25 1E		Acacia Gdns.	42 5B		Aintree Cl.	7 4A		Aldenholme	50 2C
Abbey Dri.	32 2B		Acacia Gro., New Malden	37 2D		Aintree Rd.	147 5E		Aldensley Rd.	9 1F
Abbey Gdns.	32 3A		Acacia Gro., W. Dulwich	22 3C		Aircraft Esplanade	78 1A		Alder Cl., Ash Vale	78 2C
Abbey La.	24 5A		Acacia Rd., Guildford	81 5F		Airdale Av.	9 2E		Alder Cl., Crawley Down	149 3E
Abbey Park Est.	24 5A		Acacia Rd., Hampton	17 5D		Airedale Rd., South Ealing	8 1A		Alder Cl., Egham	13 4D
Abbey Rd., Chertsey	32 4B		Acacia Rd., Mitcham	39 1E		Airedale Rd., Wandsworth			Alder Cl., Headley Down	134 4A
Abbey Rd., Croydon	40 5B		Acacia Rd., Norbury	40 1A		Common	21 2E		Alderbrook Rd., Clapham	
Abbey Rd., Horsell	64 2C		Acacia Rd., Sandhurst	43 3E		Airport Way, Gatwick	128 4B		Common	21 1E
Abbey Rd., Selsdon	58 3C		Acacia Rd., Staines	14 4A		Airport Way, Heathrow	7 5B		Alderbrook Rd., Rowly	121 4E
Abbey Rd., Shepperton	33 4D		Academy Cl.	44 4B		Aisne Rd.	62 2A		Alderbury Rd.	9 3F
Abbey Rd., South			Accommodation La., West			Aitken Rd.	24 3A		Aldercoombe La.	91 2F
Wimbledon	38 1C		Drayton	7 3C		Akehurst Cl	148 1B		Alderman Judge Mall,	
Abbey Rd., Virg. Water	30 3C		Accommodation La., West			Akehurst St.	19 1F		Kingston	159
Abbey St.	96 4A		Drayton	7 4B		Akerman Rd.	36 3A		Alders Av.	150 1C
Abbey Way	61 5D		Accommodation Rd.,			Alacross Rd.	8 1A		Alders Rd.	89 4F
Abbey Wk.	35 2D		Ottershaw	48 1A		Alamein Rd.	78 4A		Alders, The, Hanworth	16 4C
Abbey Wood	29 4E		Accorn Dri.	25 1D		Alan Brooke Cl.	63 2F		Alders, The, West	
Abbot Rd.	100 1C		Acer Rd.	77 1E		Alan Rd.	20 4A		Wickham	42 4A
Abbot's Cl.	100 2A		Achilles Pl.	64 2C		Alan Turing Rd.	100 1A		Alders View Dri.	150 1C
Abbots Cottage Rd.	114 5C		Ackroyd Rd.	23 2F		Alanbrook Rd.	78 3D		Aldersbrook Dri.	18 5B
Abbots Dri.	30 3B		Acorn Cl., East Grinstead	150 3C		Albacore Cres.	24 1A		Aldersey Rd.	82 5A
Abbots Green	58 2C		Acorn Cl., Horley	128 2C		Albain Cres.	14 3C		Aldersgrove	35 3E
Abbots La.	74 1B		Acorn Gdns.	41 1D		Albany Cl., East Sheen	8 5C		Aldershot	78 5A
Abbots Mede Cl.	17 3F		Acorn Grn.	72 5B		Albany Cl., Esher	51 3F		Aldershot Rd., Ash	78 5B
Abbots Pk.	22 3B		Acorn Gro.	65 4D		Albany Cl., Reigate	89 4E		Aldershot Rd., Guildford	81 4D
Abbot's Ride	96 5B		Acorn Mews	60 3C		Albany Cres.	52 2B		Aldershot Rd., Pirbright	80 2A
Abbots Tilt	34 5B		Acorn Way	23 3F		Albany Park	61 2D		Aldershot Rd., Willey Grn.	80 3A
Abbots Walk	75 4E		Acorns Way	52 1A		Albany Park Rd., Kingston	18 5B		Alderside Wk.	13 4D
Abbots Way, Elmers End	41 3F		Acre La.	56 1B		Albany Park Rd.,			Aldersmead Av.	41 3F
Abbots Way, Merrow	82 5C		Acre Rd., Colliers Wood	21 5D		Leatherhead	69 3F		Aldersmead Rd.	23 5F
Abbotsbury	26 3C		Acre Rd., Kingston	36 1B		Albany Pk.	7 4A		Alderstead La.	90 1C
Abbotsbury Court.	158 4D		Acres Gdns.	72 3A		Albany Pl.	13 4E		Alderton Rd.	41 4D
Abbotsbury Rd., Morden	38 3C		Acres Platt	141 1D		Albany Rd., Brentford	8 3B		Alderwood Cl.	91 1F
Abbotsbury Rd., West			Acris St.	20 1C		Albany Rd., Crawley	146 4C		Aldingbourne Cl.	146 3B
Wickham	42 5C		Acton La.	9 1D		Albany Rd., Hersham	51 1E		Aldis St.	21 4D
Abbotsfield Rd.	146 4A		Acuba Rd.	20 3B		Albany Rd., New Malden	37 2D		Aldren Rd.	20 3C
Abbotsford Cl.	65 2E		Adair Walk	62 4C		Albany Rd., Old Windsor	12 1B		Aldrich Cres.	59 3E
Abbotshall Rd.	24 2B		Adams Croft	62 4C		Albatross Gdns.	58 4C		Aldridge Rise	37 4E
Abbotsleigh Cl.	55 2F		Adams Park Rd.	96 3B		Albemarle Av.	16 2C		Aldrin Pl.	60 5B
Abbotsleigh Rd.	21 4F		Adams Rd.	41 3F		Albemarle Gdns.	37 2D		Aldrington Rd.	21 4F
Abbotswell Rd.	24 1A		Adams Way	41 3D		Albemarle Rd.	42 1B		Aldwick Cl.	60 4C
Abbotswood	82 4A		Adamsrill Rd.	23 4F		Albert Carr. Gdns.	22 4A		Aldwick Rd.	57 1D
Abbotswood Cl.	82 4A		Adare Walk	22 3A		Albert Dri., Sheerwater	48 5D		Aldworth Cl.	26 2C
Abbotswood Dri.	50 3C		Addington	59 2D		Albert Dri., Southfields	20 3A		Aldworth Grn.	24 1B
Abbotswood Rd.	21 3F		Addington Gro.	23 4F		Albert Gro.	38 1A		Aldwych Cl.	147 5F
Abbott Av.	38 1A		Addington Rd., Addington	59 1E		Albert Rd., Addlestone	49 1F		Alexander Cl.	17 3E
Abbott Cl., Hampton	16 5C		Addington Rd., Croydon	40 4B		Albert Rd., Aldershot	78 5A		Alexander Godley Cl.	70 3C
Abbott Cl., Staines	14 5C		Addington Rd.,			Albert Rd., Ashford	15 4D		Alexander Pl., Egham	13 4E
Abbotts Cl.	49 3F		Sanderstead	58 4A		Albert Rd., Ashstead	70 2B		Alexander Rd., Reigate	108 2B
Abbotts Rd.	30 2C		Addington Village Rd.	59 2D		Albert Rd., Bracknell	27 1D		Alexander Rd.,	
Abbotts Rd., Cheam	55 1D		Addiscombe Av.	41 4D		Albert Rd., Camberley	44 5A		Woodmansterne	73 1E
Abbotts Rd., Mitcham	39 2F		Addiscombe Court Rd.	41 4D		Albert Rd., Crowthorne	43 1D		Alexander Wk.	26 3C
Abelia Cl.	46 5A		Addiscombe Green	40 5C		Albert Rd., Englefield Green	12 5C		Alexanders Wk.	92 1A
Abercairn Rd.	39 1F		Addiscombe Rd.,			Albert Rd., Epsom	54 5B		Alexandra Av., Camberley	43 5F
Aberconway Rd.	38 2C		Addiscombe	41 5D		Albert Rd., Hampton Hill	17 4D		Alexandra Av., Chiswick	9 3D
Abercorn Cl.	58 4C		Addiscombe Rd.,			Albert Rd., Horley	128 2B		Alexandra Av., Sutton	38 5B
Abercorn Way	64 2B		Crowthorne	43 2D		Albert Rd., Kingston	36 1B		Alexandra Av., Warlingham	75 2F
Aberdare Cl.	42 5B		Addison Cl.	74 4C		Albert Rd., Merstham	90 3C		Alexandra Cl., Ashford	15 5F
Aberdeen Rd., Croydon	57 1F		Addison Gdns.	36 2C		Albert Rd., Mitcham	39 2E		Alexandra Cl., Staines	14 5C
Aberfoyle Rd.	21 5F		Addison Gro.	9 1E		Albert Rd., New Malden	37 2E		Alexandra Cl., Walton-on-	
Abernethy Manor La. Ter.	24 1C		Addison Rd., Caterham	74 4C		Albert Rd., Old Windsor	12 1B		Thames	34 5A
Abingdon Cl., Bracknell	27 2E		Addison Rd., Guildford	101 1D		Albert Rd., Penge	23 5F		Alexandra Court.	15 5F
Abingdon Cl., Wimbledon	20 5C		Addison Rd., Kingston	18 5A		Albert Rd., Richmond	18 1B		Alexandra Cres.	24 5C
Abingdon Cl., Woking	64 2C		Addison Rd., Norwood			Albert Rd., South			Alexandra Dr., Surbiton	36 4C
Abingdon Rd., Norbury	40 1A		Junction	41 2D		Farnborough	78 1A		Alexandra Dr., W.	
Abingdon Rd., Sandhurst	43 4D		Addison's Cl.	41 5F		Albert Rd., South Norwood	41 2E		Norwood	22 4C
Abinger	104 5B		Addlestone	49 1D		Albert Rd., Sutton	55 2F		Alexandra Gdns.,	
Abinger Av.	55 3D		Addlestone Moor	32 5B		Albert Rd., Teddington	17 5F		Carshalton on the Hill	56 3B
Abinger Cl., Croydon	57 1D		Addlestone Pk.	49 1E		Albert Rd., Twickenham	17 2F		Alexandra Lodge	50 1B
Abinger Cl., Dorking	106 3A		Addlestone Rd.	49 1F		Albert Rd., Warlingham	75 2F		Alexandra Pl.	101 1D
Abinger Hammer	103 3F		Addlestonemoor	32 5B		Albert Rd., Wokingham	25 2D		Alexandra Rd., Acton	9 1D
Abinger La.	104 5B		Adecroft Way	35 2D		Alberta Av., Cheam	55 1E		Alexandra Rd., Addlestone	49 1F
Abinger Rd.	9 1E		Adela Av.	37 3F		Alberta Av., Laleham	32 2B		Alexandra Rd., Ash	78 5B
Abinger Way	82 3B		Adelaide Av.	24 1A		Alberta Rd.	32 2B		Alexandra Rd., Biggin Hill	77 3D
Aboyne Dri.	37 1E		Adelaide Pl.	50 1B		Albertine Cl.	71 1F		Alexandra Rd., Brentford	8 3A
Aboyne Rd.	20 3C		Adelaide Rd., Ashford	14 4C		Albery Cl.	158 4A		Alexandra Rd., Deadwater	133 5D
Abury Rd.	27 3F		Adelaide Rd., Richmond	8 5B		Albion Cl.	147 4F		Alexandra Rd., East	
Acacia Av., Shepperton	33 3D		Adelaide Rd., Surbiton	36 3B		Albion Gdns.	9 2F		Croydon	40 4C
			Adelaide Rd., Teddington	17 5F		Albion Pl.	41 2D		Alexandra Rd., Englefield	
			Adelaide Rd., Walton	34 5A		Albion Rd., Coombe	37 1D		Green	12 5C
			Adeline Ms.	21 2F		Albion Rd., Horsham	158 1D		Alexandra Rd., Epsom	54 5B
			Adelphi Cl.	147 5F		Albion Rd., Reigate	108 1C		Alexandra Rd., Kew	8 4B
			Adelphi Rd.	54 5A		Albion Rd., Sutton	55 2F		Alexandra Rd., Kingston	18 5C
			Adie Rd.	9 1F		Albion Rd., Twickenham	17 2E		Alexandra Rd., Mortlake	9 5D
			Adlers La.	86 4D		Albion Rd., York Town	43 4D		Alexandra Rd., Penge	23 5F
			Admiral Rd.	146 5B		Albion St.	40 4B		Alexandra Rd., South	
			Admirals Court	82 5B		Albion Ter.	158 5B		Farnborough	78 1A
			Admiral's Rd.	86 2A		Albion Villas Rd.	23 3E		Alexandra Rd., Sunbury	15 5F
			Admirals Walk	74 3A		Albion Way	158 5B		Alexandra Rd., Thames	
			Admiralty Rd.	17 E5		Albury	102 3B		Ditton	35 3F
			Adolf St.	24 4A		Albury Av.	55 3D		Alexandra Rd., Tooting	21 5D
			Advance Rd.	22 4C		Albury Cl., Hampton Hill	17 5D		Alexandra Rd.,	
			Agate La., Horsham	158 3C		Albury Cl., Longcross	30 5B		Twickenham	18 1A
			Agate Rd.	9 1F		Albury Keep	128 2C		Alexandra Rd., Warlingham	75 2F
			Agate's La., Lower			Albury Rd., Chessington	53 1E		Alexandra Rd., Wimbledon	20 5B
			Ashtead	70 2A		Albury Rd., Guildford	101 1D		Alexandra Sq.	38 3B
			Agnew Rd.	23 2F		Albury Rd., Merstham	90 3C		Alexandra Ter.	101 1D
						Albury Rd., Weybridge	50 2C		Alfold La.	140 3B

162

Alfold Rd Arragon Rd

Alfold Rd., Cranleigh 140 1B
Alfonso Cl. 97 1D
Alford 156 2A
Alford Cl. 82 4A
Alford Crossways 140 5A
Alford Grn. 59 2E
Alford Rd., Dunsfold 139 5D
Alfred Rd., Farnham 96 4A
Alfred Rd., Feltham 16 3B
Alfred Rd., Kingston 36 2B
Alfred Rd., Norwood Junction 41 3D
Alfred Rd., Sutton 55 1F
Alfreton Cl. 20 3A
Alfriston 36 3B
Alfriston Av., 40 4A
Alfriston Rd., Clapham Common 21 1E
Alfriston Rd., Deepcut 62 3A
Algarve St. 20 2C
Alicia Av. 147 4F
Alington Gro. 56 3C
Alison Cl., Cove 60 5C
Alison Cl., Shirley 41 4F
Alison Cl., Woking 65 1D
Alison Dri. 44 5B
Alison's Rd. 78 4A
All Saints Cl. 25 1E
All Saints Cres. 60 2B
All Saints Dri. 58 4A
All Saints Rd., Acton 9 1D
All Saints' Rd., Lightwater 45 3F
All Saints Rd., Merton 20 5C
All Saints Rd., Sutton 38 5C
All Souls Rd. 28 2C
Allan Cl. 37 3D
Allbrook Cl. 17 4E
Allcard Cl. 158 4B
Allcot Court 15 2F
Allden Av. 97 1D
Alldens Hill 119 3F
Allen House Park 64 3C
Allen Rd., Croydon 40 4A
Allen Rd., Elmers End 41 1F
Allen Rd., Great Bookham 86 1A
Allen Rd., Sunbury 34 1A
Allenby Av. 57 3F
Allenby Rd., Biggin Hill 77 2E
Allenby Rd., Forest Hill 23 3F
Allenby Rd., York Town 43 5F
Allendale Cl. 23 4F
Allerford Rd. 24 4B
Alleyn Pk. 22 3C
Alleyn Rd. 22 3C
Allfarthing La. 20 1C
Allgood Cl. 38 3A
Allingham Rd. 108 2B
Allington Gdns. 52 1B
Allison Gro. 23 2D
Allwood Cl. 23 4F
Allyington Way 147 4F
Allyn Cl. 14 5A
Alma Cl., Aldershot 78 4B
Alma Cl., Woking 64 2A
Alma Cres. 55 1D
Alma La. 96 1A
Alma Pl., Sunbury 16 5A
Alma Pl., Sunbury 16 5A
Alma Pl., Thornton Heath 40 3B
Alma Rd., Carshalton 56 1A
Alma Rd., Deadwater 133 5D
Alma Rd., Esher 35 4E
Alma Rd., Headley Down 134 4A
Alma Rd., Reigate 89 5E
Alma Rd., Wandsworth 20 1C
Alma Sq. 78 2A
Alma Ter. 21 2D
Alma Way 96 1B
Almer Rd. 19 5F
Almhouse Rd. 132 3A
Almners Rd. 31 4E
Almond Av., South Ealing 8 1B
Almond Av., Sutton 39 5D
Almond Av., Woking 64 4C
Almond Cl., Englefield Green 12 5B
Almond Cl., Littleton 33 2E
Almond Cl., Slyfield Green 81 4F
Almond Rd. 54 4A
Almond Way 39 2F
Alms Heath 67 4D
Almsgate 99 4F
Almshouse La. 53 3D
Alpha Rd., Addiscombe 40 4C
Alpha Rd., Chobham 47 3D
Alpha Rd., Crawley 146 4C
Alpha Rd., Surbiton 36 4B
Alpha Rd., Twickenham 17 4E
Alpha Rd., Woking 65 1E
Alpha Way 31 1F
Alphia Cl. 21 5D
Alphington Av. 61 2E
Alphington Grn. 61 2E
Alpine Av. 37 5D
Alpine Rd., Redhill 90 4B
Alpine Rd., Walton 34 4A
Alpine View 56 1A
Alresford Rd. 100 1B
Alric Av. 37 2E
Alsace Wk. 61 2D
Alsford Cl. 45 4E
Alsom Av. 54 1B
Alston Cl. 36 4A
Alston Rd. 21 4D
Altenburg Av. 8 1A
Alterton Cl. 64 2B
Althorne Rd. 109 1E
Althorp Rd. 21 2D
Alton Court 31 1F
Alton Gdns. 17 2E
Alton Rd., Bentley 114 1A
Alton Rd., Richmond 8 5B
Alton Rd., Roehampton 19 2F
Alton Rd., Waddon 40 5B
Alton Rd., Wrecclesham 95 5E
Alton Ride 43 5D
Altyre Rd. 40 5C
Altyre Way 41 3F
Alvenia Cl. 118 3C
Alverston Gdns. 41 3D
Alverston Gdns. 41 3D
Alverstone Av. 20 3B
Alverstone Rd. 37 2E
Alvia Gdns. 55 1F
Alvington Cl. 82 5A
Alway Av. 54 1A
Alwyn Av. 9 2D
Alwyn Cl. 59 2E
Alwyne Rd. 20 5B
Alwyns Cl. 32 3A
Alwyns La. 32 3A
Ambassador 26 3C
Amber Hill 62 1A
Ambercroft Way 74 3B
Amberley Cl., Burntcommon 83 1D
Amberley Cl., Crawley 147 4F
Amberley Dri. 49 3D
Amberley Gdns. 54 1B
Amberley Green 41 4D
Amberley Gro. 23 4E
Amberley Rd. 118 3A
Amberley Way 38 4B
Amberwood Dri. 44 4B
Amberwood Rise 37 3D
Amblecote 51 4E
Ambleside 24 5C
Ambleside Av., Streatham 21 4F
Ambleside Av., Walton-on-Thames 34 4B
Ambleside Cl., Cove 60 5B
Ambleside Cl., Mytchett 78 1C
Ambleside Cl., Salfords 109 3E
Ambleside Cres. 96 2A
Ambleside Dri. 15 3F
Ambleside Gdns., Selsdon 58 3C
Ambleside Gdns., Sutton 55 2F
Ambleside Rd. 45 4E
Ambleside Way 13 5E
Ambrey Way 56 3C
Ambridge Kennels 13 2F
Amerland Rd. 20 1B
Amesbury Av. 22 3A
Amesbury Cl. 38 4A
Amesbury Rd. 16 3B
Amey Dri. 69 5D
Amis Av., Chessington 53 2F
Amis Av., Woodham 49 3D
Amis Rd. 64 3A
Amity Gro. 37 1F
Amlets La. 121 5F
Amner Rd. 21 1E
Ampere Way 40 4A
Amroth Cl. 23 2E
Amstel Way 64 2A
Amundsen Rd. 158 3B
Amy Rd. 93 3F
Amyand Park Gdns. 17 2F
Amyand Park Rd. 17 2F
Amyruth Rd. 24 1A
Ancaster Cres. 37 3E
Ancaster Rd. 41 2F
Anchor Hill 64 2A
Anchor Meadow 60 5C
Anderson Cl. 53 4F
Anderson Dri. 15 4E
Anderson Pl. 45 2E
Anderson Rd. 33 5E
Andover Cl. 54 4A
Andover Rd., Darby Grn. 43 5D
Andover Rd., Twickenham 17 2E
Andover Way 97 1D
Andrew Cl. 25 2E
Andrewartha Rd. 78 1B
Andrew's Cl., Epsom 54 5B
Andrews Cl., N. Cheam 38 5A
Andrews Rd. 60 4B
Andromeda Cl. 146 5A
Anerley Gro. 23 5D
Anerley Hill 23 5D
Anerley Pk. 23 5E
Anerley Rd. 41 1E
Anerley Station Rd. 41 1E
Anerley Vale 23 5D
Anfield Cl. 21 2F
Angas Court 50 1B
Angel Gate, Guildford 159
Angel Gro. 9 2F
Angel Hill 38 5C
Angel Hill Dri. 38 5C
Angel Rd. 35 4F
Angelica Gdns. 41 4F
Angelica Rd. 63 1E
Anglers Cl. 18 4A
Angles Rd. 22 4A
Anglesea Rd. 36 2B
Anglesey Av. 60 3C
Anglesey Cl. 15 3D
Anglesey Court Rd. 56 2B
Anglesey Gdns. 56 2B
Anglesey Rd. 78 5A
Angus Cl., Chessington 53 1F
Angus Cl., Horsham 158 4B
Anlaby Rd. 17 4E
Annandale Dri. 115 1E
Annandale Rd., Addisc'be 41 5D
Annandale Rd., Chiswick 9 2E
Annandale Rd., Guildford 100 1B
Anne Boleyn Wk., Kingston 18 4B
Anne Boleyn's Wk., Cheam 55 2D
Anne Way 35 2D
Anners Cl. 31 2E
Anne's Wk. 75 3D
Annesley Dri. 42 5A
Annett Rd. 34 4A
Annisdowne 103 5F
Annsworth Av. 40 2C
Ansell Gro. 39 4E
Ansell Rd., Dorking 105 1F
Ansell Rd., Frimley 61 3E
Ansell Rd., Upper Tooting 21 3D
Anselm Cl. 41 5D
Anselm Cl. 41 5D
Ansford Rd. 24 4B
Ansley Cl. 58 5B
Anson Cl. 74 3C
Anstice Cl. 9 3E
Anstie La. 124 1B
Anstiebury Cl. 125 2D
Anthony Rd. 41 3D
Antlands La. 129 5D
Anton Cres. 38 5B
Antrobus Cl. 55 1E
Antrobus Rd. 9 2D
Anvil La. 51 5D
Anvil Rd. 34 2A
Anyards Rd. 51 5D
Apeldorn Dri. 57 3D
Aperdele Rd. 69 2F
Aperfield Rd. 77 2F
Apers Av. 65 4D
Apex Cl., Beckenham 42 1B
Apex Cl., Weybridge 33 5E
Apex Dri. 61 3E
Apley Rd. 108 2B
Aplin Way 45 3F
Apollo Rise 60 5B
Appach Rd. 22 1A
Apple Market 36 1B
Apple Tree Way 43 3E
Appleby Cl. 17 3E
Appleby Gdns. 15 3F
Appledore, Easthampstead 26 3C
Appledore, Upper Tooting 21 3D
Appledore Mews 60 3C
Appledown Rise 73 1F
Applegarth, Addington 59 2D
Applegarth, Claygate 52 1C
Applegarth, Godalming 99 5F
Applegarth Av. 81 5D
Applelands Cl. 115 2D
Appleton Gdns. 37 3E
Appletree Cl. 119 3E
Appletree Court 82 4C
Appletree Pl. 26 1C
Appley Court 44 5A
Appley Dri. 44 5A
Approach Rd., Ashford 15 5E
Approach Rd., Raynes Park 37 1F
Approach Rd., Tatsfield 77 5D
Approach Rd., West Molesey 34 3C
Approach, The, Dormans Pk. 131 5F
Approach, The, Little Bookham 68 5C
April Cl., Camberley 61 2D
April Cl., Feltham 16 3A
April Cl., Horsham 158 4B
April Glen 23 3F
Aprilwood Cl. 49 4D
Apsley Cl. 37 2D
Apsley Rd. 41 2E
Aquila Cl. 70 4B
Arabella Dri. 9 5E
Aragon Av., Ewell 54 3C
Aragon Av., Thames Ditton 35 3F
Aragon Cl. 59 5F
Aragon Pl. 59 3F
Aragon Rd., Kingston 18 4B
Aragon Rd., Merton 38 3A
Aran Court. 33 5F
Arbour Cl. 69 5F
Arbrook La. 52 2B
Arbury Ter. 23 3B
Arbutus Cl. 108 1C
Arbutus Rd. 108 2C
Arch Rd. 34 5B
Archbishops Pl. 22 1A
Archer Cl. 18 5B
Archer Rd. 41 2E
Archway Cl., Summerstown 20 4C
Archway Cl., Wallington 39 5F
Archway Pl., Dorking 160
Archway St. 9 5E
Arcturus Rd. 146 5A
Arcus Rd. 24 5C
Ardbeg Rd. 22 1C
Arden Cl., Bracknell 27 1E
Arden Cl., Reigate 108 2C
Arden Rd. 147 5E
Ardent Cl. 40 2C
Ardfern Rd. 40 2A
Ardfillan Rd. 24 3C
Ardgowan Rd. 24 2C
Ardingley 26 3C
Ardingley Cl 146 3C
Ardleigh Gdns. 38 4B
Ardley Cl. 23 3F
Ardlui Rd. 22 3B
Ardmere Rd. 24 1B
Ardmore Av. 81 4E
Ardmore Way 81 4E
Ardoch Rd. 24 3B
Ardrossan Av. 44 5C
Ardrossan Gdns. 37 5E
Ardshiel Dri. 109 1D
Ardsley Wood 50 1C
Ardui Rd. 22 3B
Ardway Gdns. 36 3B
Arenal Dri. 43 2D
Arethusa Way 63 1E
Arford Common 133 4F
Arford Rd. 133 4F
Argosy Gdns. 14 5A
Argosy La. 14 2C
Argus Way 8 1C
Argyle Av. 17 1D
Argyle Pl. 9 2F
Argyle Rd., Hounslow 17 1D
Argyle Rd., Twickenham 17 4E
Arkell Gdns. 22 5B
Arkindale Rd. 24 3B
Arkwright Dri. 26 1B
Arkwright Rd., Poyle 7 4A
Arkwright Rd., Sanderstead 58 3A
Arlesley Cl. 20 1A
Arlingford Rd. 22 1B
Arlington Cl., Bracknell 26 1C
Arlington Cl., Nth. Cheam 38 5B
Arlington Dri. 39 5D
Arlington Gdns. 9 2D
Arlington Rd., Ashford 15 4D
Arlington Rd., Ham 18 3A
Arlington Rd., St. Margaret's 18 1A
Arlington Rd., Twick. 17 4F
Arlington Rd. Surb. 36 4B
Arlington Sq. 26 1C
Armadale Rd., Feltham 16 1A
Armadale Rd., Woking 64 2B
Armfield Cl. 34 3C
Armfield Cres. 39 1E
Armitage Dri. 61 2F
Armoury Way 20 1B
Armstrong Cl. 34 3A
Armstrong Mall 60 5B
Armstrong Rd., Englefield Green 12 5C
Armstrong Rd., Hanworth 16 4B
Arnal Cres. 20 2A
Arncliffe 26 2C
Arndale Way 13 4E
Arne Grn. 128 2A
Arnewood Pl. 19 2E
Arnewood Rd. 52 5A
Arneys Rd. 39 3E
Arnfield Cl. 146 4A
Arngask Rd. 24 2B
Arnhem Cl. 78 4A
Arnhem Dri. 59 4E
Arnison Rd. 35 2E
Arnold Cres. 17 1E
Arnold Rd., Colliers Wood 21 5E
Arnold Rd., Staines 14 5B
Arnold Rd., Woking 65 1E
Arnot Rd. 9 2D
Arnulf St. 24 4A
Arnulls Rd. 22 5B
Arodene Rd. 22 1A
Aros Estate 151 3F
Arpley Rd. 23 5E
Arragon Gdns., Streatham 22 5A
Arragon Gdns., West Wickham 42 5A
Arragon Rd. 17 2F

Arran Cl
163
Avondale Rd

Arran Cl. 146 5C
Arran Rd. 24 3B
Arran Way 35 5D
Arras Av. 38 3C
Arrol Rd. 41 2E
Arrow Rd. 56 1C
Artel Cres. 147 4E
Arterberry Rd. 38 1A
Arthur Cl. 45 3D
Arthur Rd., Biggin Hill 77 1E
Arthur Rd., Farnham 96 4A
Arthur Rd., Horsham 158 5B
Arthur Rd., Kingston 18 5C
Arthur Rd., Motspur Pk. 37 3F
Arthur Rd., Wimbledon Park 20 4B
Arthur Rd., Wokingham 25 2D
Arthurdon Rd. 24 1A
Arthur's Bridge Rd. 64 2C
Artillery Rd., Aldershot 78 2B
Artillery Rd., Guildford 100 1C
Artillery Ter. 81 5F
Artington Wk. 100 2C
Arun Way 158 5C
Arundel Av., Ewell 54 3C
Arundel Av., Morden 38 2B
Arundel Av., Sanderstead 58 3A
Arundel Cl., Crawley 147 4F
Arundel Cl., Croydon 40 5B
Arundel Court 17 4D
Arundel Rd., Cheam 55 2E
Arundel Rd., Dorking 105 1F
Arundel Rd., Heatherside 62 1A
Arundel Rd., Norbiton 36 1C
Arundel Rd., Selhurst 40 3C
Arundel Ter. 9 3F
Aschurch Rd. 41 4D
Ascot 28 2C
Ascot Ms. 56 3C
Ascot Rd., E. Bedfont 15 2D
Ascot Rd., Tooting 21 5E
Ascott Av. 8 1B
Ash 78 5C
Ash Church Rd. 78 5C
Ash Cl., Anerley 41 1E
Ash Cl., Ash 78 4C
Ash Cl., Blackwater 43 5D
Ash Cl., Crawley Down 149 3E
Ash Cl., Kingston 37 1D
Ash Cl., Lingfield 131 2F
Ash Cl., Merstham 90 3C
Ash Cl., Sutton 39 5D
Ash Cl., Woking 65 3D
Ash Court 54 1A
Ash Dri., Earlswood 109 1E
Ash Green 41 1E
Ash Green Lane East 98 1A
Ash Green Lane W. 97 1F
Ash Green Rd. 79 5D
Ash Gro., Beckenham 41 1E
Ash Gro., East Bedfont 15 2F
Ash Gro., Guildford 81 5E
Ash Gro., South Ealing 8 1B
Ash Gro., Staines 14 5B
Ash Gro., West Wickham 42 5B
Ash Hill Rd. 78 4C
Ash Keys 147 4A
Ash La. 117 3D
Ash Lodge Cl. 78 5C
Ash Lodge Dri. 78 5C
Ash Rd., Aldershot 97 1D
Ash Rd., Littleton 33 2D
Ash Rd., North Cheam 38 4B
Ash Rd., Pirbright 80 1B
Ash Rd., West Wickham 42 5A
Ash Rd., Woking 65 3D
Ash St. 78 5B
Ash Tree Cl. 60 5A
Ash Tree Way 41 3F
Ash Vale 78 3C
Ash Vale, Chiddingfold 137 4E
Ash Vale Rd. 78 2C
Ashbourne 26 3C
Ashbourne Cl. 79 4D
Ashbourne Ct. 79 4D
Ashbourne Gdns. 73 2F
Ashbourne Gro. 9 2E
Ashbourne Rd. 21 5E
Ashbrook Rd. 12 2B
Ashburnham Pk. 52 1A
Ashburnham Rd., Crawley 147 5E
Ashburnham Rd., Ham 18 3A
Ashburton Av. 41 4E
Ashburton Gdns. 41 5D
Ashburton Rd. 41 5D
Ashbury Cres. 82 4B
Ashbury Dri. 60 2C
Ashby Av. 53 2F
Ashchurch Gro. 9 1E
Ashchurch Park Villas 9 1E
Ashchurch Ter. 9 1E
Ashcombe Av. 36 4B
Ashcombe Rd., Carshalton 56 2B
Ashcombe Rd., Dorking 86 5C
Ashcombe Rd., Merstham 90 2C
Ashcombe Rd., Merton 20 4B
Ashcombe Ter. 71 3F
Ashcoombe 137 5E
Ashcroft 101 4D
Ashcroft Park Estate 51 4E
Ashcroft Rd. 36 5B
Ashcroft Rise 74 1A
Ashdale 86 1A
Ashdene Cl. 15 5E
Ashdene Cres. 78 4C
Ashdene Rd., Ash 78 4C
Ashdene Rd., Guildford 81 5D
Ashdown Av. 78 1B
Ashdown Cl., Bracknell 27 1F
Ashdown Cl., Reigate 108 2C
Ashdown Dri. 147 5D
Ashdown Gdns. 75 1E
Ashdown Pl. 35 4F
Ashdown Rd., Epsom 54 5B
Ashdown Rd., Kingston 36 1B
Ashdown Rd., Reigate 108 2C
Ashdown View 150 3C
Ashen Gro. 20 3B
Ashen Vale 150 3C
Ashenden Rd., 81 5D
Ashfield Av. 16 2A
Ashfield Cl. 18 2B
Ashford 15 4D
Ashford Av. 15 5D
Ashford Cl. 14 4C
Ashford Cres. 14 3C
Ashford Gdns. 68 1B
Ashford Rd., Ashford 15 4E
Ashford Rd., Staines 14 5C
Ashgrove Rd., Ashford 15 4E
Ashgrove Rd., Downham 24 5C
Ashlake Rd. 22 4A
Ashlea Cl. 78 4C
Ashleigh Av. 13 5E
Ashleigh Cl. 128 2B
Ashleigh Cotts. 106 5A
Ashleigh Gdns. 38 5C
Ashleigh Rd., Elmers End 41 2E
Ashleigh Rd., Horsham 158 4B
Ashleigh Rd., Mortlake 9 5D
Ashley Av., Epsom 54 5A
Ashley Av., Morden 38 3B
Ashley Cl., Frimley Green 61 4F
Ashley Cl., Gt. Bookham 85 1F
Ashley Cl., Walton 33 4F
Ashley Dri., Banstead 55 5E
Ashley Dri., Frogmore Pk. 60 1B
Ashley Dri., Walton 34 5A
Ashley Dri., Whitton 17 2D
Ashley Gdns. 18 3A
Ashley Ho. 100 5A
Ashley La. 57 1E
Ashley Park Av. 33 5F
Ashley Park Cres. 34 4A
Ashley Park Rd. 34 5A
Ashley Rd., Dorking 105 2D
Ashley Rd., Epsom 54 5A
Ashley Rd., Farnborough Park 61 5D
Ashley Rd., Goldsworth 64 2A
Ashley Rd., Hampton 35 1D
Ashley Rd., Merton 20 5C
Ashley Rd., Thames Ditton 35 3F
Ashley Rd., Thornton Heath 40 2A
Ashley Rd., Walton 34 5A
Ashley Rd., Weybridge 50 1C
Ashley Rise 34 5A
Ashley Way 46 5A
Ashling Rd. 41 4D
Ashlyns Pk. 51 5F
Ashlyns Way 53 2D
Ashmead Rd. 16 2A
Ashmere Av. 42 1B
Ashmore La. 145 4D
Ashness Rd. 21 1D
Ashridge 60 3B
Ashridge Green 27 1D
Ashridge Rd. 25 1E
Ashridge Way, Morden 38 2B
Ashridge Way, Sunbury-on-Thames 16 5A
Ashtead 70 3B
Ashtead Gap 69 1F
Ashtead La. 119 3D
Ashtead Woods Rd. 70 2A
Ashton Cl. 51 2D
Ashton Rd. 64 2A
Ashtree Av. 39 1D
Ashtree Cl., Croydon 41 3F
Ashtree Cl., Grayswood 152 1B
Ashtrees 140 2C
Ashurst Cl. 74 1C
Ashurst Dri., Laleham 32 3C
Ashurst Dri., West Humble 87 3F
Ashurst Rd., Ash Wharf 78 4B
Ashurst Rd., Tadworth 71 4F
Ashurst Walk 41 5E
Ashvale Rd. 21 4D
Ashview Cl. 14 4C
Ashview Gdns. 14 4C
Ashville Way 25 3D
Ashwell Dri. 44 5B
Ashwindham Court 64 2A
Ashwood 75 3E
Ashwood Gdns. 59 2E
Ashwood Pk., Fetcham 69 5E
Ashwood Pk., Woking 65 2D
Ashwood Rd., Englefield Green 12 5B
Ashwood Rd., Woking 65 2D
Askew Cres. 9 1E
Askew Rd. 9 1E
Askill Dri. 20 1B
Aslett St. 20 2C
Asmar Cl. 74 1A
Aspen Cl., Banstead 55 5D
Aspen Cl., Ealing 8 1B
Aspen Cl., Guildford 82 4C
Aspen Cl., Stoke D'Abernon 68 1C
Aspen Gdns. 39 3E
Aspen Sq. 33 5E
Aspen Way 158 4C
Aspley Rd. 20 1C
Assembly Wk. 39 4D
Assher Rd. 34 5B
Aston Cl. 70 2A
Aston Rd., Claygate 52 1B
Aston Rd., Raynes Pk. 38 1A
Aston Way 71 1E
Astonville St. 20 2B
Astor Cl., Addlestone 49 1F
Astor Cl., Kingstone 18 5C
Asylum Arch Rd. 109 2E
Atbara Rd. 18 5A
Atchison Rd. 23 1E
Atfield Grn. 46 2A
Athelden Rd. 20 2C
Athelney St. 24 3A
Athelstan Rd. 36 2B
Athenlay Rd. 23 1F
Atherfield Rd. 108 2C
Atherley Way 16 2C
Atherton Cl., Shalford 101 4D
Atherton Cl., Stanwell 14 1B
Atherton Rd. 9 3E
Athlone 52 2B
Athlone Rd. 22 2A
Atirebatti Rd. 43 4D
Atkins Cl. 64 2B
Atkins Dr. 42 5B
Atkins Rd. 21 2F
Attfield Cl. 78 5B
Attleford La. 117 1E
Attwood Cl. 58 5B
Atwater Cl. 22 2B
Atwood 68 5C
Atwood Av. 8 4C
Atwood Rd. 9 2F
Aubyn Sq. 19 1F
Aubyns Hill 22 4C
Aubyn's Rd. 23 5D
Auckland Cl. 41 1D
Auckland Gdns. 41 1D
Auckland Hill 22 4B
Auckland Rd., Caterham 74 4C
Auckland Rd., Kingston 36 2B
Auckland Rd., Penge 23 5D
Auckland Rise 41 1D
Audley Cl., Addlestone 49 1E
Audley Dri. 75 1E
Audley Firs 51 1D
Audley Pl., Cheam 55 2E
Audley Rd. 18 1B
Audley Way 28 2A
Audrey Cl. 42 3A
Augur Cl. 14 4A
Augusta Cl. 34 2C
Augusta Rd. 17 3D
Augustine Cl. 7 5A
Augustus Cl., Brentford 8 3A
Augustus Cl., Camberley 45 5D
Augustus Gdns. 45 5D
Augustus Rd. 20 2A
Aultone Way, Hackbridge 39 5D
Aultone Way, Sutton 38 5C
Aurelia Gdns. 40 3A
Aurelia Rd. 40 3A
Auriol Cl. 37 4E
Auriol Park Rd. 37 4E
Aurum Cl. 128 3B
Austen Cl. 150 2B
Austen Rd., Guildford 101 1D
Austen Rd., West Heath 60 4C
Austin Cl., Coulsdon 74 2B
Austin Cl., Lewisham 23 2F
Austin Cl., Richmond 18 1A
Austyn Gdns. 36 4C
Av. de Cagney 63 4E
Avarn Rd. 21 5D
Avebury 26 3C
Avebury Rd. 38 1B
Aveley Cl. 96 5A
Aveley La. 96 5A
Aveling Cl. 57 5D
Aven Cl. 140 2C
Avening Rd. 20 2B
Avenue Cl. 71 4F
Avenue Cres. 8 1C
Avenue Gdns., Acton 8 1C
Avenue Gdns., East Sheen 9 5D
Avenue Gdns., Horley 128 3C
Avenue Gdns., South Norwood 41 2D
Avenue Gdns., Twick. 17 5F
Avenue Park Rd. 22 3B
Avenue Rd., Acton 8 1C
Avenue Rd., Banstead 72 1C
Avenue Rd., Beddington 56 2C
Avenue Rd., Belmont 55 3E
Avenue Rd., Brentford 8 2A
Avenue Rd., Caterham 74 4C
Avenue Rd., Cobham 68 1B
Avenue Rd., Cranleigh 140 2C
Avenue Rd., Egham 13 4F
Avenue Rd., Elmers End 41 1E
Avenue Rd., Epsom 54 5A
Avenue Rd., Farnborough Park 61 5D
Avenue Rd., Feltham 15 3F
Avenue Rd., Grayshott 135 5D
Avenue Rd., Hampton 35 1D
Avenue Rd., Kingston 36 2B
Avenue Rd., Merton 39 1F
Avenue Rd., New Malden 37 2E
Avenue Rd., Raynes Park 37 1F
Avenue Rd., S. Norwood 41 1D
Avenue Rd., Tatsfield 77 3F
Avenue Rd., Teddington 17 5F
Avenue South 36 4C
Avenue Sucy 60 1C
Avenue Ter. 37 2D
Avenue, The, Aldershot 97 1D
Avenue, The, Ascot 10 5B
Avenue, The, Beckenham 42 1B
Avenue, The, Bedford Pk. 9 1D
Avenue, The, Belmont 55 3E
Avenue, The, Brockham 87 5F
Avenue, The, Camberley 44 5A
Avenue, The, Chobham 47 3E
Avenue, The, Clapham Common 21 1E
Avenue, The, Claygate 52 2B
Avenue, The, Compton 99 4F
Avenue, The, Coulsdon North 73 1F
Avenue, The, Crowthorne 43 1D
Avenue, The, Croydon 40 5C
Avenue, The, Easthampstead 26 4B
Avenue, The, Easthampstead 26 4B
Avenue, The, Egham 13 4E
Avenue, The, Farnham 114 2C
Avenue, The, Godalming 119 3D
Avenue, The, Grayshott 135 5D
Avenue, The, Hanworth 16 4C
Avenue, The, Haslemere 151 2F
Avenue, The, Horley 128 3B
Avenue, The, Hounslow 17 1D
Avenue, The, Kew 8 4B
Avenue, The, Laleham 32 1B
Avenue, The, Lightwater 45 3E
Avenue, The, Old Windsor 12 1B
Avenue, The, Richmond 18 1A
Avenue, The, Shottermill 151 2E
Avenue, The, South Nutfield 110 2A
Avenue, The, Sunbury 34 1A
Avenue, The, Surbiton 36 3C
Avenue, The, Tadworth 71 4F
Avenue, The, Tooting Bec 21 2E
Avenue, The, Whyteleafe 75 3D
Avenue, The, Woodham 49 3D
Avenue, The, Worcester Park 37 5E
Avenue, The, Worplesdon 81 2D
Avenue, The, W. Wickham 42 4C
Averil Gro. 22 5B
Avern Gdns. 35 2D
Avern Rd. 35 3D
Aviary Rd. 66 1A
Aviary Way 149 2E
Aviemore Cl. 41 3F
Aviemore Way 41 3F
Avington Gro. 23 5E
Avoca Rd. 21 4E
Avon Cl., Addlestone 49 2D
Avon Cl., Ash 78 5C
Avon Cl., Hawley 60 3B
Avon Cl., Sutton 55 1F
Avon Cl., Worcester Pk. 37 5E
Avon Mead 64 2C
Avon Path 57 2F
Avon Rd., Farnham 96 4A
Avon Rd., Sunbury 15 5F
Avon Wk. 146 4B
Avondale, Ash Vale 78 2C
Avondale Av., Hinchley Wood 35 5F
Avondale Av., Staines 14 5A
Avondale Av., Worcester Pk. 37 4E
Avondale Cl., Hersham 51 1E
Avondale Cl., Horley 128 2B
Avondale Gdns. 16 1C
Avondale Rd., Aldershot 97 1D
Avondale Rd., Ashford 14 3C

Avondale Rd., Bromley 24 5C
Avondale Rd., Merton 20 4C
Avondale Rd., Mortlake 9 5D
Avondale Rd., South Croydon 57 2F
Avonmore Av. 82 5A
Avonside 158 5A
Avro Way, Byfleet 49 3F
Avro Way, Roundshaw 57 2D
Axbridge 27 3E
Axes La. 109 4E
Axwood 71 1D
Aycliff Cl. 36 1C
Ayebridges Av. 13 5E
Aylesford Av. 41 3F
Aylesworth Spur 12 2B
Ayling La. 96 1C
Aylmer Rd. 9 1E
Aylward Rd., Forest Hill 23 3F
Aylward Rd., Merton 38 1B
Aymer Cl. 31 1F
Aymer Dri. 31 1F
Aysgarth 26 3C
Aysgarth Rd. 22 2C
Ayshe Court Dri. 158 4C
Azalea Cl. 133 1D
Azalea Ct. 64 3C
Azalea Dri. 151 2E
Azalea Way 44 5C

B

Babb's Mead 96 4A
Baber Dri. 16 1A
Babercomb Cl. 53 1D
Babington Rd. 21 4F
Babylon La. 89 2E
Back Alley, Dorking 160
Back Green 51 2E
Back La., Bucks Horn Oak 114 4A
Back La., E. Clandon 83 4F
Back La., Elstead 117 2D
Back La., Forest Grn. 123 4E
Back La., Ham 18 3A
Back La., Hawley 60 3B
Back La., Millbridge 115 3E
Back La., Plaistow 155 5D
Back La., Reigate 89 3F
Bacon Cl. 43 5E
Bacon La. 134 1A
Baden Cl. 14 5B
Baden Dri. 128 2A
Baden Rd. 81 4E
Bader Cl. 74 1C
Badger Cl., Lower Feltham 16 3A
Badger Cl., Stoughton 81 4E
Badger Cl., Woking 64 2C
Badger Dri. 45 3E
Badgers 37 1E
Badgers Bridge Ride 10 2C
Badgers Cl., Godalming 100 5A
Badgers Cl., Horsham 158 3C
Badgers Copse, Camberley 61 1E
Badgers Copse, Worcester Park 37 5E
Badgers Hill 30 3C
Badger's Hole 58 1B
Badgers La. 75 3E
Badgers Walk, Whyteleafe 75 3D
Badgers Walk, Woodcote 56 4C
Badgers Way, Bracknell 27 1E
Badgers Way, Loxwood 156 4A
Badgers Wood 91 1F
Badgerwood Dri. 61 2E
Badingham Dri. 69 5E
Badminton Rd. 21 1E
Badshot Lea Rd. 96 2C
Badshot Pk. 96 2C
Bagden Hill 86 3B
Bagot Cl. 70 1C
Bagshot 45 2E
Bagshot Green 45 2E
Bagshot Rd., Bracknell 27 2D
Bagshot Rd., Brookwood 63 2F
Bagshot Rd., Englefield Grn. 12 5C
Bagshot Rd., Sunninghill 29 3D
Bagshot Rd., West End 46 4A
Bagshot-Bracknell Rd. 27 3D
Bahram Rd. 54 3A
Baigents La. 46 2A
Bailes La. 80 4A
Bailey Cl., Frimley 61 3D
Bailey Cl., Horsham 158 2C
Bailey Rd. 105 2D
Baileys Cl. 60 1A
Baillie Rd. 101 1D
Bain Av. 61 2D
Bainton Mead 64 2B
Baird Cl. 147 2E
Baird Dri. 80 5C
Baird Gdns. 22 4C
Baird Rd. 61 4D
Bakeham La. 12 5C
Bakehouse Barn Rd. 158 2C
Bakehouse Rd. 128 1B
Baker Cl. 147 5D
Baker La. 39 1E
Baker St. 50 1A
Bakers Cl. 131 1F
Bakers End 38 1A
Bakers La. 131 2F
Bakers Mead 92 3B
Bakers Way 125 5D
Bakewell Way 37 1D
Balaclava Rd. 36 4A
Balcher Rd. 23 1E
Balchins La. 105 2D
Balcombe Cl. 147 3F
Balcombe Gdns. 128 3C
Balcombe Rd., Horley 128 2B
Balcombe Rd., Three Bridges 147 2F
Baldreys 96 5A
Baldry Gdns. 22 5A
Baldwin Cl. 147 5F
Baldwin Cres. 82 4C
Balfern Gro. 9 2E
Balfont Cl. 58 5A
Balfour Av. 65 4D
Balfour Cres. 27 3D
Balfour Pl. 9 5F
Balfour Rd., Carshalton 56 2A
Balfour Rd., Merton 20 5C
Balfour Rd., S. Norwood 41 2D
Balfour Rd., Weybridge 50 1A
Balgents La. 46 2A
Balgowan Rd. 41 1F
Balham Gro. 21 2E
Balham High Rd. 21 3E
Balham Hill 21 2E
Balham New Rd. 21 2E
Balham Park Rd. 21 2D
Balham Station Rd. 21 2E
Balintore Court 43 4E
Ball & Wicket La. 96 1A
Ballands North, The 69 4E
Ballands South, The 69 5E
Ballantyne Dri. 72 4B
Ballantyne Rd. 60 4C
Ballard Cl. 19 5D
Ballard Rd. 44 4C
Ballards Farm Rd. 58 2A
Ballards Green 72 3A
Ballards La. 94 3B
Ballards Rise 58 2A
Ballards Way 58 2B
Ballater Rd. 58 1A
Ballencrief Rd. 29 4E
Ballfield Rd. 119 1D
Ballina St. 23 2F
Ballingdon Rd. 21 1E
Balliol Cl. 147 2F
Balliol Way 43 3E
Ballock Rd. 24 2B
Ballsdown 137 5E
Balmoral Av. 41 2F
Balmoral Cl. 20 1A
Balmoral Cres., Upper Hale 96 2A
Balmoral Cres., W. Molesey 34 2C
Balmoral Dri. 65 1F
Balmoral Mews 9 1E
Balmoral Rd., Ash 78 4C
Balmoral Rd., Frimley 61 3E
Balmoral Rd., Kingston 36 2B
Balmoral Rd., Worcester Park 37 5F
Balmoral Way 55 3E
Balmuir Gdns. 9 5F
Balquwain Cl. 70 2B
Baltic Cl. 21 5D
Balvernie Gro. 20 2B
Bamford Rd. 24 4B
Bampfylde Cl. 39 5F
Bampton Rd. 23 3F
Bampton Way 64 2B
Banavie Gdns. 42 1B
Banbury 27 3E
Banbury Cl. 61 3F
Banbury Court 55 2E
Bancroft Cl. 15 4D
Bancroft Court 89 5F
Bancroft Rd., Crawley 147 4F
Bancroft Rd., Reigate 89 5E
Band La. 13 4D
Banders Rise 82 5C
Bandon Rise 56 2C
Bank Av. 39 1D
Bank La., Crawley 147 4D
Bank La., Kingston 18 5B
Bank La., Roehampton 19 1E
Bankfoot Rd. 24 4C
Bankhurst Rd. 24 2A
Bank's La. 68 4A
Banks Rd. 147 4F
Banks Way 82 4A
Bankside, Heath End 96 1C
Bankside, S. Croydon 58 2A
Bankside, Woking 64 2C
Bankside Cl. 117 2D
Bankside Dri. 35 4F
Bannister Cl. 118 5B
Bannister's Rd. 100 1B
Banstead 72 1C
Banstead Rd., Carshalton 56 3A
Banstead Rd., Caterham 74 4C
Banstead Rd., Ewell 54 4C
Banstead Rd., Purley 57 4D
Banstead Rd., Sutton 55 4D
Banstead Road South 55 4F
Banstead Way 57 1D
Barbara Cl. 33 3E
Barbican Cl. 62 1A
Barchard St. 20 1C
Barclay Cl. 69 5D
Barclay Rd. 40 5C
Barcombe Av. 22 3A
Bardney Rd. 38 2C
Bardolph Av. 58 3C
Bardon Wk. 64 2B
Bardsley Dri. 95 5F
Barfields 91 5E
Barford La. 134 2B
Barfreston Way 41 1E
Bargate Cl. 37 4E
Bargate Rise 118 2C
Barge Walk 35 2E
Bargery Rd. 24 2B
Bargrove Cl. 23 5D
Bargrove Cres. 24 2A
Barham Cl. 50 1B
Barham Rd., Croydon 57 1F
Barham Rd., Wimbledon 19 5E
Barhatch Rd. 141 1D
Baring Rd. 41 4D
Barker Green 27 3D
Barker Rd. 32 4A
Barkham Rd. 25 2D
Barkhart Dr. 25 1E
Barkhart Dri. 25 1E
Barkis Mead 43 3E
Barley Cl. 147 4D
Barley Mow Cl. 63 2F
Barley Mow Hill 133 4F
Barley Mow La. 63 1F
Barley Mow Rd. 12 4C
Barley Mow Way 33 2D
Barleycorn Meadow 128 2C
Barleydene 28 4C
Barleymow Court 88 5A
Barlow Cl. 57 2D
Barlow Rd., Crawley 146 5A
Barlow Rd., Hampton 17 5D
Barmeston Rd. 24 3A
Barmouth Rd., Shirley 41 5F
Barmouth Rd., Wandsworth 20 1C
Barn Cl., Ashford 15 4D
Barn Cl., Bracknell 27 1E
Barn Cl., Camberley 44 5B
Barn Cl., Woodmansterne 73 1D
Barn Cres. 57 5F
Barn Hill Av. 42 3C
Barn Lea Cl. 16 3C
Barn Mead 47 3D
Barn Meadow La. 68 5C
Barnacres Pl. 57 3E
Barnard Cl., Beddington 56 2C
Barnard Cl., Frimley 61 3E
Barnard Cl., Sunbury on Thames 16 5A
Barnard Gdns. 37 2F
Barnard Rd., Mitcham 39 2E
Barnard Rd., Slines Green 76 3A
Barnato Cl. 49 4F
Barnby Rd. 64 2A
Barnes 9 4F
Barnes Av. 9 3E
Barnes Cl. 61 5D
Barnes High St. 9 4E
Barnes Rd., Farncombe 100 5A
Barnes Rd., Frimley 61 3E
Barnes Wallis Dri. 49 4F
Barnet Wood La. 70 3A
Barnett Cl., Leatherhead 69 3F
Barnett Cl., Wonersh 101 5E
Barnett Hill 101 5E
Barnett La., Lightwater 45 4E
Barnett La., Wonersh 101 5E
Barnett Row 81 3F
Barnetts Shaw 93 2F
Barnfield, Banstead 55 5F
Barnfield, Cranleigh 140 1C
Barnfield, Malden 37 3D
Barnfield Av., Ham 18 4B
Barnfield Av., Shirley 41 5E
Barnfield Cl., Old Coulsdon 74 3B
Barnfield Cl., Parklangley 42 3B
Barnfield Gdns. 18 4B
Barnfield Rd., Crawley 147 3D
Barnfield Rd., Sanderstead 58 3A
Barnfield Rd., Tatsfield 77 3E
Barnfield Way 94 5A
Barnfield Woods Rd. 42 3B
Barnmead Rd. 41 1F
Barnsbury Cl. 37 2D
Barnsbury Cres. 37 4D
Barnsbury La. 37 4D
Barnsfold La. 156 3C
Barnsford Cres. 46 4B
Barnsley Cl. 78 1C
Barnsnap Cl. 158 3B
Barnway 12 4C
Barnwell Rd. 22 1B
Barnwood Cl. 147 3F
Barnwood Rd. 81 5D
Barnyard, The 71 5F
Baron Gro. 39 2D
Barons Court 39 5F
Baron's Hurst 71 1D
Barons, The 18 1A
Barons Walk 41 3F
Baron's Way, Doversgreen 108 2B
Barons Way, Egham 13 5F
Baronsfield Rd. 18 1A
Baronsmead Rd. 9 4F
Baronsmede 8 1B
Barossa Rd. 44 4A
Barr Hill Rd. 22 3A
Barracaine Dri. 43 1D
Barrack Path 64 2A
Barrack Rd. 81 4E
Barracks, The 32 5B
Barrens Brae 65 2E
Barrens Cl. 65 3E
Barrens Pk. 65 3E
Barrett Cres. 25 2E
Barrett Rd. 69 5E
Barricane 64 3B
Barrie Cl. 73 1F
Barrie Rd. 96 1A
Barringer Sq. 21 3E
Barrington Lo. 50 1B
Barrington Rd., Crawley 147 5D
Barrington Rd., Dorking 105 2F
Barrington Rd., Horsham 158 5C
Barrington Rd., Sutton 38 4B
Barrington Rd., Woodcote 56 4C
Barrosa Dri. 34 3C
Barrow Av. 56 2A
Barrow Green Rd. 93 4D
Barrow Hedges Cl. 56 2A
Barrow Hedges Way 56 2A
Barrow Hill Cl. 37 5E
Barrow Rd., Clapham 21 2F
Barrow Rd., Croydon 57 2E
Barrow Rd., Streatham 22 5A
Barrowdale 45 5D
Barrowgate Rd. 9 2D
Barrows Field 58 4A
Barrs La. 63 1F
Barry Rd. 23 1D
Bars, The 100 1C
Barston Rd. 22 3C
Barstow Cl. 22 2A
Bartelot Rd. 158 5B
Bartholemew Way 158 3C
Bartholomew Cl. 152 2A
Barton Cl., Addlestone 49 2D
Barton Cl., Shepperton 33 3D
Barton Cl., Windlesham 46 2A
Barton Green 37 1D
Barton Rd. 101 5E
Barton, The 51 4E
Bartons Way 60 3B
Bartram Rd. 23 1F
Barttelot Rd. 158 5B
Barwood Cl. 15 4F
Basden Gro. 16 3C
Basemoor 27 1E
Bashford Way 147 3F
Basil Gdns. 41 4F
Basildon Cl. 55 3F
Basing Cl. 35 4F
Basing Dri. 97 2D
Basing Rd. 55 5E
Basing Way 35 4F
Basingfield Rd. 35 4F
Basinghall Gdns. 55 3F
Baskerville Rd. 21 2D
Bassano St. 23 1D
Bassein Park Rd. 9 1E
Basset Cl. 49 3E
Bassett Cl., Belmont 55 3F
Bassett Cl., Frimley 61 3E
Bassett Rd. 65 1E
Bassetts Hill 132 3A
Bassingham Rd. 20 2C
Bat & Ball La. 114 1C
Batavia Cl. 34 1A
Batavia Rd. 34 1A
Batcombe Mead 27 4E
Bateman Court 147 5E
Bates Cres., Sth. Croydon 57 2E
Bates Cres., Streatham Vale 21 5F
Bates Wk. 49 2E
Bateson Way 48 5B
Bath Rd., Camberley 44 5A
Bath Rd., Colnbrook 7 4A
Bath Rd., Turnham Green 9 2E
Bathgate Rd. 20 3A
Bathhouse Rd. 40 4A
Bathhurst Wk. 7 1B
Batram Rd. 23 1F
Batson St. 9 1E
Batsworth Rd. 39 2D
Batten Av. 64 3A

Battersby Rd.	24 3C	Beaulieu Cl., Bracknell	27 2F	Beech Dri., Reigate	89 5F	Beechwood Cl., Long	
Battersea Rise	21 1D	Beaulieu Cl., Richmond	18 1A	Beech Dri., Sendmarsh	66 5A	Ditton	36 4A
Battle Cl.	20 5C	Beaulieu Gdns.	43 5D	Beech Farm La.	61 1E	Beechwood Cl., Weybridge	50 1C
Battlebridge La.	90 3B	Beaumont Av.	8 5B	Beech Farm Rd.	76 3B	Beechwood Gdns.	75 4D
Batts Hill	90 4A	Beaumont Cl.	146 4A			Beechwood Gro.	60 4A
Battys Barn Cl.	25 2E	Beaumont Dri.	15 4E	Beech Gdns., Crawley		Beechwood La.	75 3F
Baudwin Rd.	24 3C	Beaumont Gdns.	27 2E	Down	149 3E	Beechwood Manor	50 1C
Bavant Rd.	40 1A	Beaumont Rd., Acton		Beech Gdns., S. Ealing	8 1B	Beechwood Pk.,	
Bawdale Rd.	23 1D	Green	9 1D	Beech Gdns., Woking	65 1D	Leatherhead	70 4A
Bawtree Cl.	55 3F	Beaumont Rd., Purley	57 5D	Beech Gro., Addlestone	49 1E	Beechwood Rd., Caterham	75 4D
Bax Cl.	140 2C	Beaumont Rd., Southfields	20 2A	Beech Gro., Banstead	71 2F	Beechwood Rd., Knaphill	64 2A
Baxter Av.	90 5A	Beaumont Rd., Upper		Beech Gro., Caterham	91 1F	Beechwood Rd., S.	
Baxter Cl.	147 5F	Norwood	22 5B	Beech Gro., Guildford	81 5D	Croydon	57 3F
Bay Cl.	128 1A	Beaumont Sq.	141 1D	Beech Gro., Mayford	64 5C	Beechwood Rd., Virginia	
Bay Dri.	27 1E	Beaumonts	109 5D	Beech Gro., Mitcham	39 2F	Water	30 4B
Bay Rd.	27 1E	Beauval Rd.	23 1D	Beech Gro., New Malden	37 2D	Beechwood Villas	109 5E
Bayards	75 2E	Beaver Cl., Hampton	35 1D	Beech Grove Cl.	29 2D	Beecot La.	34 5B
Baye Cl.	43 3D	Beaver Cl., Horsham	158 3C	Beech Hall, Ottershaw	48 2B	Beecroft	23 1F
Bayeaux	72 4A	Beaver Cl., Penge	23 5D	Beech Hanger	135 5D	Beedon Dri.	26 3B
Bayes Cl.	23 4E	Beavers Cl., Farnham	95 4F	Beech Hanger End	135 5D	Beehive La.	26 1B
Bayfield Av.	61 2E	Beavers Cl., Guildford	81 5D	Beech Hill, Hambledon	137 2F	Beehive Rd., Bracknell	26 1B
Bayfield Rd.	128 2A	Beavers Hill	95 4F	Beech Hill, Woking	64 5C	Beehive Rd., Staines	14 4A
Bayford Cl.	60 2C	Beavers Mews	133 5D	Beech Hill Rd., Arford	133 4F	Beehive Way	108 2C
Bayham Rd.	38 2C	Beavers Rd.	95 4F	Beech Hill Rd., Sunningdale	29 3E	Beeleigh Rd.	38 2C
Baylin Rd.	20 1C	Beavor La.	9 3F	Beech Holt	70 4A	Beeston Way	16 1B
Baynards La.	157 1D	Beck Gdns.	96 2A	Beech House Rd.	40 5C	Beetons Av.	78 4C
Baythorne La.	128 3C	Beck La.	41 2E	Beech La., Grayshott	135 5D	Beggar's Hill	54 2B
Bazalgette Cl.	37 3D	Beckenham	42 1A	Beech La., Guildford	100 2C	Beggars La., Camberley	46 4C
Bazalgette Gdns.	37 3D	Beckenham Gro.	42 1B	Beech La., Wanborough	79 5E	Beggars La., Gomshall	103 2F
Beach Gro.	16 3C	Beckenham Hill Est.	24 4A	Beech Lawn	101 1D	Beggars Roost	55 2E
Beachborough Rd.	24 4B	Beckenham Hill Rd.	24 4B	Beech Meads	51 5E	Beggarshole Rd.	126 4C
Beacon Cl., Boundstone	114 1C	Beckenham La.	42 1C	Beech Rd., Biggin Hill	77 2D	Beira St.	21 2F
Beacon Cl., Nork	72 1A	Beckenham Place Pk.	24 5A	Beech Rd., Epsom	71 1E	Beldham Bridge Rd.	46 5B
Beacon Grn.	56 1B	Beckenham Rd.,		Beech Rd., Frimley	61 4F	Beldham Gdns.	35 2D
Beacon Hill, Dormans Land	132 4A	Beckenham	41 1F	Beech Rd., Haslemere	152 2A	Beldham Rd.	95 5F
Beacon Hill, Woking	64 3C	Beckenham Rd., West		Beech Rd., Hawley	60 3C	Belfast Rd.,	41 2E
Beacon Hill Court	135 4D	Wickham	42 4B	Beech Rd., Merstham	90 1C	Belfield Rd.	54 3A
Beacon Hill Rd.	135 4D	Beckenshaw Gdns.	72 1D	Beech Rd., Norbury	40 1A	Belgrade Rd.	35 1D
Beacon Rd., E. Bedfont	15 1D	Becket Cl.	41 3D	Beech Rd., Reigate	89 4E	Belgrave Cl.	51 1D
Beacon Rd., Hither Green	24 1B	Beckett Av.	74 1B	Beech Rd., Southville	15 2F	Belgrave Court	60 1B
Beacon View Rd.	117 3D	Beckett Cl., Streatham	21 3F	Beech Rd., Weybridge	50 1B	Belgrave Cres.	34 1A
Beacon Way	72 1A	Beckett Cl., Wokingham	25 2F	Beech Ride	43 3D	Belgrave Manor	65 3D
Beaconhill La.	95 1E	Beckett La.	147 2D	Beech Row	18 4B	Belgrave Rd., Morden	38 2C
Beaconhill Rd.	95 1E	Beckett Walk	23 5F	Beech Tree La.	32 1B	Belgrave Rd., Norwood	
Beaconsfield Pl.	54 4B	Becketts Cl.	16 1A	Beech Tree Pl.	55 1F	Junction	41 2D
Beaconsfield Rd., Acton Gr.	9 1D	Beckett's Pl.	36 1A	Beech Way, Epsom	71 1E	Belgrave Rd., Sunbury-on-	
Beaconsfield Rd., Claygate	52 2B	Beckford Av.	26 3C	Beech Way, Godalming	119 2D	Thames	34 1A
Beaconsfield Rd., Epsom	71 3D	Beckford Rd.	41 3D	Beech Way, Selsdon	58 5C	Belgrave Wk.	39 2D
Beaconsfield Rd., Lammas		Beckingham Rd.	81 5E	Beech Wk., Ewell	54 4B	Belgravia Gdns.	24 5C
Park	8 1A	Becklow Rd.	9 1E	Beech Wk., Windlesham	46 2A	Belgravia Ms.	36 2B
Beaconsfield Rd., New		Beckway	42 2A	Beechcroft	26 2C	Bell Bridge Rd.	32 4A
Malden	37 1D	Beckway Rd.	39 1F	Beechcroft, Ashtead	70 3B	Bell Cl.	61 4D
Beaconsfield Rd.,		Beckwith Rd.	22 1C	Beechcroft Av., Kenley	74 1C	Bell Cres.	75 4E
Richmond	18 1A	Beclands Rd.	21 5E	Beechcroft Av., Kingston	37 1D	Bell Dri.	20 2A
Beaconsfield Rd., Selhurst	40 3C	Becmead Av.	21 4F	Beechcroft Dri.	29 2D	Bell Foundry Rd.	25 1E
Beaconsfield Rd., Surbiton	36 4B	Becondale Rd.	22 4C	Beechcroft Dri.	100 2A	Bell Green	23 4F
Beaconsfield Rd., Woking	65 3D	Bedale Cl.	146 5C	Beechcroft Manor	33 5E	Bell Green La.	23 4F
Beadle's La.	93 3E	Beddicott	20 3A	Beechcroft Rd., Hook	36 5B	Bell La., Blackwater	43 5D
Beadnell Rd.	23 2F	Beddington Farm Rd.	40 4A	Beechcroft Rd.,		Bell La., Fetcham	69 5E
Beadon Rd.,	9 2F	Beddington Gdns.	56 2B	Wandsworth	21 3D	Bell La., Rowledge	114 2C
Beaford Gro.	38 2B	Beddington Gro.	56 1C	Beechdale Rd.	22 1A	Bell La., Twickenham	17 2F
Beagle Cl.	16 4A	Beddington La.	39 3F	Beechdene	71 4F	Bell Lane Cl.	69 5E
Beale's La.	33 5D	Beddlestead La.	77 3D	Beeche Holme	149 3E	Bell Meadow	92 4B
Beales La., Farnham	114 1C	Bedfont Cl.	15 2E	Beechen La.	89 1E	Bell Meadows	23 4D
Beales Rd.	86 2A	Bedfont Court	7 5C	Beeches Avenue, The	56 2A	Bell Pl.	45 2E
Beam Hollow	96 1A	Bedfont Green Cl.	15 2E	Beeches Cl.	72 5B	Bell Rd., East Molesey	35 3E
Beamore Cl.	19 2F	Bedfont La.	15 2F	Beeches Cres.	147 5D	Bell Rd., Hammersmith	151 4F
Bean Oak Rd.	25 2F	Bedfont Rd.	15 2E	Beeches La.	45 3F	Bell Rd., Horsham	158 2A
Bear La.	96 3A	Bedfont Rd., E. Bedfont	15 3E	Beeches Rd., North Cheam	38 4A	Bell Rd., Shottermill	151 4F
Bear Rd.	16 4B	Bedfont Rd., Stanwell	14 1C	Beeches Rd., Wandsworth	21 3D	Bell St., Reigate	89 5E
Beard Rd.	18 4B	Bedford Av., Frimley Green	61 4E	Beeches, The, Ash Vale	78 2C	Bell Vale La.	151 4F
Beardell St.	23 5D	Bedford Av., Roundshaw	57 2D	Beeches, The, Banstead	72 1A	Bell Weather La.	110 5B
Beard's Hill	35 1D	Bedford Cres.	61 4E	Beeches, The, Fetcham	69 5E	Bellamy St.	21 2E
Beard's Rd.	15 5F	Bedford Hill	21 2E	Beeches Wk.	56 3A	Bellasis Av.	22 3A
Beare Grn. Ct.	125 2D	Bedford La., Frimley Green	61 4E	Beeches Wood	72 4B	Bellever Hill	44 5B
Bearfield Rd.	18 5B	Bedford La., Sunningdale	29 3F	Beechey Cl.	148 1B	Belleville Rd.	21 1D
Bears Den	72 4B	Bedford Pk.	40 4C	Beechey Way	148 1B	Bellevue Cl., Aldershot	78 5B
Bearstead Rise	23 1F	Bedford Pl.	40 4C	Beechfield	55 5F	Bellevue Pk.	40 2B
Bearwood Cl.	49 2D	Bedford Rd., Bedford Pk.	9 1D	Beechfield Rd.	24 2A	Bellevue Rd., Aldershot	78 5A
Beasley's La.	33 3F	Bedford Rd., Guildford	100 1C	Beechhill Rd.	134 4A	Bellevue Rd., Barnes	9 4E
Beatrice Av.	40 2A	Bedford Rd., Horsham	158 5B	Beeching Cl.	78 4C	Bellevue Rd., Kingston	36 2B
Beatrice Rd.	93 3F	Bedford Rd., N. Cheam	37 3F	Beeching Way	150 2C	Bellevue Rd., Wandsw'th	21 2D
Beattie Cl.	68 5C	Bedford Rd., Twickenham	17 3E	Beechmont Av.	30 3C	Bellew Rd., Frimley Green	61 4F
Beatty Av.	82 5B	Bedgbury Gdns.	20 2B	Beechmont Cl.	24 4C	Bellew Rd., Summerstown	20 3C
Beauchamp Rd., Beulah Hill	40 1C	Bedlow La.	141 1D	Beechmore Gdns.	38 5A	Bellfields	81 4F
Beauchamp Rd., Cheam	55 1E	Bedster Gdns.	35 1D	Beechnut Dri.	43 5D	Bellfields Rd.	81 4F
Beauchamp Rd., E. Molesey	35 3D	Bedwardine Rd.	22 5C	Beechnut Rd.	78 5A	Bellingham Cl.	62 1A
Beauchamp Rd.,		Beech Av., Brentford	8 3A	Beecholme	55 5D	Bellingham Green	24 3A
Twickenham	17 2F	Beech Av., Effingham	85 2E	Beecholme Av.	39 1E	Bellingham Rd.	24 3B
Beauclare Cl.	70 3B	Beech Av., Farnham	115 1D	Beechside	147 4A	Bello Clo.	22 2B
Beauclerc Rd.	9 1F	Beech Av., Frimley	61 1E	Beechtree Av.	12 5B	Belloc Cl.	147 3F
Beaufort Cl., Reigate	89 5E	Beech Av., Purley Oaks	57 4F	Beechtree Dri.	96 2C	Belltrees Gro.	22 4A
Beaufort Cl., Roehampton	19 2F	Beech Cl., Blindley Heath	111 5F	Beechway, Guildford	82 5B	Bellvue Cl., Staines	32 1A
Beaufort Cl., Woking	65 1E	Beech Cl., Byfleet	49 4F	Beechway, Twickenham	17 3D	Bellweir Cl.	13 3E
Beaufort Court	18 4A	Beech Cl., Chiddingfold	137 5E	Beechwood, Cobham	51 4F	Belmarsh Rd.	49 1E
Beaufort Gdns.	22 5A	Beech Cl., Dorking	105 1F	Beechwood Av., Banstead	72 4B	Belmont Av., Guildford	81 4E
Beaufort Rd., Farnham	96 3A	Beech Cl., Effingham	85 2E	Beechwood Av., Kew	8 4C	Belmont Av., Motspur Park	37 3F
Beaufort Rd., Ham	18 4A	Beech Cl., Hersham	51 1D	Beechwood Av., Staines	14 5B	Belmont Cl.	60 3C
Beaufort Rd., Kingston	36 2B	Beech Cl., Oxshott	51 4F	Beechwood Av., Sunbury	16 5A	Belmont Gro.	9 2D
Beaufort Rd., Reigate	89 5E	Beech Cl., Roehampton	19 2E	Beechwood Av., Thornton		Belmont Rd., Beckenham	41 1F
Beaufort Rd., Richmond	18 2A	Beech Cl., Stanwell	14 2C	Heath	40 2B	Belmont Rd., Belmont	55 3E
Beaufort Rd., Woking	65 1E	Beech Cl., Wimbledon	19 5F	Beechwood Av.,		Belmont Rd., Camberley	61 1D
Beaufort Way	54 2C	Beech Cl., The Wrythe	39 5D	Weybridge	50 1C	Belmont Rd., Carshalton	56 1B
Beauforts	12 4C	Beech Close Court	51 4F	Beechwood Av.,		Belmont Rd., Chiswick	9 2D
Beaufront Cl.	44 4C	Beech Copse	57 1F	Woodmansterne	73 1E	Belmont Rd., Crowthorne	43 1D
Beaufront Rd.	44 4C	Beech Dri., Blackwater	60 1B	Beechwood Cl., Ascot		Belmont Rd., Leatherhead	69 4F
Beaulieu Av.	23 4E	Beech Dri., Kingswood	72 4B	Heath	10 5B	Belmont Rd., Mead Vale	108 1C
				Beechwood Cl., Knaphill	64 2A		

Name	Ref		Name	Ref		Name	Ref		Name	Ref
Belmont Rd., Twickenham	17 3E		Berkeleys, The	69 5E		Biggin Av.	39 1D		Birds Hill Rise	52 5B
Belmont Rd., Woodside	41 3E		Berkshire Cl.	74 4C		Biggin Cl.	146 5C		Birdswood Dri.	64 3A
Belmont Rise	55 2E		Berkshire Rd.	44 4B		Biggin Hill	77 1E		Birdwood Cl.	58 4B
Belmore Av.	65 1F		Berkshire Way, Bracknell	26 2B		Biggin Hill, Upper Norwood	22 5B		Birkbeck Gro.	9 1D
Beloe Cl.	9 5F		Berkshire Way, Mitcham	40 2A		Biggin Way	22 5B		Birkbeck Hill	22 3B
Belsize Av.	8 1A		Bernard Av.	8 1A		Bigginwood Rd.	22 5B		Birkbeck Pl., Sandhurst	43 3E
Belsize Gdns.	55 1F		Bernard Gdns.	20 4B		Bilbets	158 4B		Birkbeck Pl., Tulse Hill	22 3B
Belstone Mews	60 3C		Bernard Rd.	56 1B		Billet Rd.	14 3A		Birkbeck Rd., Anerley	41 1E
Beltane Dri.	20 3A		Bernards Court	60 1C		Billington Dr.	147 4F		Birkbeck Rd., Wimbledon	20 4C
Belthorn Cres.	21 2F		Berne Rd.	40 3B		Billockby Cl.	53 2E		Birkdale	26 4B
Belton Rd.	44 5B		Bernel Dri.	42 5A		Bilton Cl.	7 4B		Birkdale Dri.	146 4A
Belvedere Av.	20 4A		Berney Rd.	40 4C		Binden Rd.	9 1E		Birkenhead Av.	36 1B
Belvedere Cl., Esher	52 1A		Berridge Rd.	22 4C		Binfield Rd., Byfleet	49 4F		Birkenholme Cl.	134 5A
Belvedere Cl., Guildford	81 4E		Berrington Dri.	67 5F		Binfield Rd., Croydon	58 1A		Birkhall Rd.	24 2B
Belvedere Cl., Teddington	17 4E		Berry Bank	43 5E		Binfield Rd., Priestwood			Birkheads Rd.	89 5E
Belvedere Dri.	20 4A		Berry La., Hersham	51 1E		Common	26 1C		Birkwood Cl.	21 2F
Belvedere Gdns.	34 3C		Berry La., Worplesdon	80 1C		Binfield Rd., Wokingham	25 2E		Birnam Cl.	66 5A
Belvedere Gro.	20 4A		Berry Meade	70 2B		Bingham Dr., Ashford	14 5C		Birtley Rd.	120 2B
Belvedere Rd., Penge	23 5D		Berry Way	8 1B		Bingham Dri., Knaphill	64 2A		Birtley Rise	120 1B
Belvedere Rd., S.			Berry Wk.	70 3B		Bingham Rd.	41 4D		Bisenden Rd.	40 5C
Farnborough	78 1A		Berrylands, Raynes Park	38 2A		Bingley Rd.	16 5A		Bisham Cl.	39 4D
Belvedere Rd., Westerham			Berrylands, Surbiton	36 3C		Binhams Lea	139 4D		Bishop Duppas Pk.	33 4F
Hill	27 2F		Berrylands Rd.	36 3B		Binhams Meadow	139 4D		Bishop Fox Way	34 2C
Belvoir Cl.	61 2E		Berrymead Gdns.	9 1D		Binns Rd.	9 2D		Bishopdale	26 2C
Belvoir Rd.	23 2D		Berrymead Rd.	9 1D		Binscombe Cres.	100 5A		Bishopric	158 5A
Benbow Rd.	9 1F		Berry's Croft Rd.	14 5B		Binscombe La.	100 5A		Bishopric Court.	158 5A
Benbrick Rd.	100 1B		Berry's La.	49 4F		Binstead Dri.	43 5E		Bishop's Cl., Coulsdon	74 2B
Benbury Cl.	24 4B		Berryscroft Court.	14 5B		Binton La.	97 4E		Bishop's Cl., Ham	18 3B
Bence, The	31 5E		Bert Rd.	40 3B		Birbeck Rd.	8 2A		Bishops Cl., Sutton	38 5B
Bench Field	58 2A		Bertal Rd.	20 4C		Birch Av.	74 5C		Bishop's Dri.	25 1E
Bencombe Rd.	57 5D		Bertie Rd.	23 5F		Birch Circle, Godalming	100 5B		Bishop's Gro., Hampton	16 4C
Bencroft Rd.	21 5F		Bertram Rd.	18 5C		Birch Cl., Byfleet	49 3F		Bishops Gro., Windlesham	46 2A
Bendon Valley	20 2C		Berwyn Rd., Sheen	8 5C		Birch Cl., Camberley	44 5D		Bishops Hill	34 4A
Benedict Dri.	15 3C		Berwyn Rd., Tulse Hill	22 2B		Birch Cl., Crawley Down	149 3E		Bishops Mead	96 4A
Benedict Rd.	39 2D		Berystede	18 5C		Birch Cl., Farnham	115 2D		Bishops Mead Par.	84 3C
Benenstock Rd.	14 1A		Besley St.	21 5F		Birch Cl., Send Barns	83 1D		Bishop's Park Rd.	40 1A
Benett Gdns.	40 1A		Bessborough Rd.	19 2F		Birch Cl., Teddington	17 4F		Bishops Rd., Croydon	40 4B
Benfleet Cl., Cobham	51 4E		Beswick Gdns.	27 1F		Birch Cl., Woking	64 3C		Bishops Rd., Upper Hale	96 2A
Benfleet Cl., Sutton	38 5C		Beta Rd., Chobham	47 3D		Birch Cres.	39 4D		Bishops Sumner Dri.	96 2A
Benham Cl.	74 2B		Beta Rd., West Heath	60 4C		Birch Dri.	60 1B		Bishops Walk	58 1C
Benhams Cl.	128 1B		Beta Rd., Woking	65 1E		Birch Gate	71 4F		Bishops Way	13 5F
Benhams Dri.	128 1B		Beta Way	31 1F		Birch Green	14 4A		Bishops Wood	64 2B
Benhill Av.	55 1F		Betchets Grn. Rd.	125 1D		Birch Gro., Bracknell	27 2D		Bishopsford Rd.	38 4C
Benhill Estate	55 1F		Betchley Cl.	150 1C		Birch Gro., Cobham	51 5E		Bishopsgate Rd.	12 3B
Benhill Rd.	55 1F		Betchworth	107 1D		Birch Gro., Hither Green	24 2C		Bishopsmead Dri.	84 3C
Benhill Wood Rd.	55 1F		Betchworth Way	59 3E		Birch Gro., Kingswood	72 5B		Bishopsthorpe Rd.	23 4F
Benhilton Gdns.	38 5C		Bethany Waye	15 2F		Birch Gro., Pyrford Com.	65 1F		Bisley	63 1E
Benhurst Cl.	58 3B		Bethel Cl.	96 2B		Birch Gro., Sunbury	33 1F		Bisley Cl.	38 4A
Benhurst Court	22 4B		Bethel La.	96 2B		Birch Hill	58 1C		Bitmead Cl.	146 4A
Benhurst Gdns.	58 3B		Betherden Cl.	24 5A		Birch Hill Rd.	26 4C		Bittams La.	48 1C
Benin St.	24 2C		Bethune Cl.	147 4F		Birch La., Bracknell	27 1E		Bittern Cl., Ifield	146 4A
Benjamin Rd.	147 5F		Bethune Rd.	158 5C		Birch La., Purley	57 4D		Bittern Cl., Sandhurst	43 4E
Benner La.	46 4B		Betjeman Cl.	74 2A		Birch La., West End	46 4A		Bitterne Dri.	64 2B
Bennerley Rd.	21 1D		Betony Cl.	41 4F		Birch Lea	147 2E		Bittoms, The	36 2B
Bennet Cl.	36 1A		Betts Way	36 4A		Birch Platt	46 5A		Black Cap Cl.	146 5C
Bennett Cl.	147 5F		Betula Rd.	74 1C		Birch Rd., Bagshot	46 5A		Black Dog Wk.	147 3D
Bennett Way	83 2E		Between Streets	51 5D		Birch Rd., Godalming	100 5B		Black Horse Way	158 5A
Bennetts Av.	41 5F		Beulah Cres.	40 1C		Birch Rd., Hanworth	16 4B		Black Lake Cl.	31 1E
Bennetts Cl.	51 5D		Beulah Green	40 3C		Birch Rd., Headley Down	134 4A		Black Lion La.	9 2E
Bennetts Rd.	158 5C		Beulah Hill	22 5B		Birch Rd., Wick Hill	25 5D		Black Meadows	27 3D
Bennetts Way	41 5F		Beulah Rd., Cheam	55 1E		Birch Rd., Windlesham	46 2A		Black Prince Cl.	49 5F
Bennetts Wood	125 5D		Beulah Rd., Thornton Heath	40 2B		Birch Tree Av.	59 1F		Blackberry Cl.	33 2F
Bensbury Cl.	19 2F		Beulah Rd., Wimbledon	20 5B		Birch Tree Way	41 5E		Blackberry La.	131 3E
Bensham Cl.	40 2C		Beulah Wk.	75 3F		Birch Vale	52 5A		Blackberry Rd.	131 4E
Bensham Green	40 1B		Bevan Court	57 1E		Birch View Dri.	45 3F		Blackbird Cl.	43 4E
Bensham La., Croydon	40 4B		Beverley Av.	37 1E		Birch Walk	39 1E		Blackborough Cl.	108 1C
Bensham La., Thornton			Beverley Cl., Addlestone	49 1F		Birch Way, Ash Vale	78 2C		Blackborough Rd.	108 1C
Heath	40 2B		Beverley Cl., Ash	78 5C		Birch Way, Warlingham	75 2F		Blackbridge La.	158 5A
Bensham Manor Rd.	40 2C		Beverley Cl., Barnes	9 4E		Birchanger Rd.	41 3D		Blackbridge Rd.	64 3C
Benson Rd., Croydon	40 5B		Beverley Cl., Camberley	45 5D		Birchdale Cl.	49 4E		Blackbrook Rd.	106 4B
Benson Rd., Forest Hill	23 2E		Beverley Cl., Chessington	53 1D		Birchend Cl.	57 2F		Blackburn Way	119 1E
Benthall Gdns.	74 2C		Beverley Cl., Ewell	54 4C		Birches Cl.	71 1E		Blackburns, The	68 5C
Bentham Av.	48 5B		Beverley Cl., Weybridge	33 5F		Birches, The, Farnborough	60 5B		Blackcap Cl.	43 4E
Bentley Copse	62 1A		Beverley Gdns.	37 4F		Birches, The, Horsley	84 1C		Blackdown Av.	65 1F
Bentley Dri.	50 3A		Beverley Heights	89 4F		Birches, The, Three Bridges	147 3E		Blackdown Cl., W. Heath	60 3B
Bentons La.	22 4C		Beverley La., Kingston	19 5E		Birches, The, Woking	65 2D		Blackdown Cl., Woking	65 1F
Bentons Rise	22 4C		Beverley Rd., Cheam	37 5F		Birchett Rd.	60 4B		Blackdown Rd.	62 3A
Bentsbrook Cl.	106 3A		Beverley Rd., Chiswick	9 2E		Birchetts Cl., Bracknell	26 1C		Blackett Cl.	32 1A
Bentsbrook Pk.	106 3A		Beverley Rd., Hampton			Birchfield Cl., Addlestone	49 1E		Blackfold Rd.	147 4E
Bentsbrook Rd.	106 3A		Wick	36 1A		Birchfield Cl., Coulsdon	74 1A		Blackheath	147 3F
Benwell Court	34 1A		Beverley Rd., Mill Hill	9 5E		Birchfield Gro.	54 3C		Blackheath Gro.	101 5E
Benwell Rd.	63 3E		Beverley Rd., Mitcham	39 2F		Birchfields	61 1D		Blackheath La., Brook	102 4B
Berberis Cl.	81 4F		Beverley Rd., New Malden	37 2E		Birchington Rd.	36 4C		Blackheath La., Wonersh	101 5E
Bere Rd.	27 3E		Beverley Rd., Sunbury-on-			Birchlands Av.	21 2E		Blackheath Rd., Upper Hale	96 1A
Beresford Av., Tolworth	36 4C		Thames	33 1F		Birchway	109 1E		Blackhills	51 3F
Beresford Av.,			Beverley Rd., Whyteleafe	15 2D		Birchwood Av., Eden Park	42 2A		Blackhorse La.,	
Twickenham	18 1A		Beverley Way	37 1E		Birchwood Av., Hackbri'.	39 5E		Addiscombe	41 4D
Beresford Cl.	61 4E		Beverstone Rd.	40 2B		Birchwood Cl., Horley	128 2C		Blackhorse La., Lower	
Beresford Gdns.	16 1C		Bevington Rd.	42 1A		Birchwood Cl., Morden	38 2C		Kingswood	89 3F
Beresford Rd., Cheam	55 2E		Bewbush Dri.	146 5B		Birchwood Dri., Lightwater	46 3A		Blackhorse Rd.	64 3A
Beresford Rd., Dorking	106 1A		Bewlys Rd.	22 4B		Birchwood Dri., W. Byfleet	49 4D		Blacklands Meadow	91 5D
Beresford Rd., Kingston	36 1B		Bexhill Cl.	16 3B		Birchwood Gro.	17 5D		Blacklands Rd.	24 4B
Beresford Rd., New Malden	37 2D		Bexhill Rd., Ladywell	24 1A		Birchwood La., Caterham	91 1E		Blackman's La.	59 5F
Bergenia Court	46 5B		Bexhill Rd., Mortlake	9 5D		Birchwood La., Esher	52 3B		Blackmoor Wood	28 1A
Berkeley Cl.	13 3F		Beynon Rd.	56 1A		Birchwood Rd., Tooting			Blackmore Cres.	48 5B
Berkeley Court, Guildford	82 5A		Bicester Rd.	8 5C		Bec	21 4E		Blackmores Gro.	17 5F
Berkeley Court, Oatlands			Bickersteth Rd.	21 5D		Birchwood Rd., W. Byfleet	49 4D		Blackness La.	65 3D
Park	33 5F		Bickley St.	21 4D		Bird Wk.	16 2C		Blacknest Rd.	30 2A
Berkeley Cres.	61 3F		Bicknell Rd.	61 2E		Birdhurst Av.	57 1F		Blackpond La.	115 1D
Berkeley Gdns., Claygate	52 2C		Bickney Way	69 4D		Birdhurst Gdns.	57 1F		Blackshaw Rd.	20 4C
Berkeley Gdns., Walton-			Bidborough Cl.	42 3C		Birdhurst Rd., Croydon	57 1F		Blacksmith La.	101 3F
on-Thames	33 4F		Biddulph Rd.	57 3E		Birdhurst Rd., Merton	21 5D		Blacksmiths Hill	58 5B
Berkeley Gdns., W. Byfleet	49 5D		Bideford Cl., Hanworth	16 3C		Birdhurst Rd., Wandsworth	20 1C		Blacksmiths La., Chertsey	32 4A
Berkeley Pl., Epsom	71 1D		Bideford Cl., W. Heath	60 3C		Birdhurst Rise	57 1F		Blacksmith's La., Lale'm	32 2B
Berkeley Pl., Wimbledon	20 5A		Bideford Rd.	24 3C		Birds Grove	63 2F		Blackstone Cl., Hawley	60 3B
Berkeley Rd.	9 4E		Bidhams Cres.	71 4F		Birds Hill Dri.	52 5B		Blackstone Cl., Redhill	109 1D
			Big Common La.	91 5E		Birds Hill Rd.	52 4B		Blackstone Hill	90 5A

167
Blackstroud La
Bracondale

Blackstroud La. 46 4A
Blackthorn Cl., Crawley 146 3C
Blackthorn Cl., Reigate 108 1C
Blackthorn Cres. 60 3C
Blackthorn Dri. 45 4F
Blackthorn Rd., Biggin Hill 77 1E
Blackthorn Rd., Woodhatch 108 1C
Blackthorne Av. 41 4E
Blackthorne Cl. 158 5C
Blackthorne Cres., Colnbrook 7 4B
Blackthorne Rd., Great Bookham 86 1A
Blackthorne Rd., Poyle 7 5A
Blackwater La. 147 4F
Blackwater Valley Rd. 60 1C
Blackwater Way 97 1E
Blackwell Av. 81 5D
Blackwell Farm Rd. 150 1C
Blackwell Hollow 150 2C
Blackwell Rd. 150 2C
Blackwood Cl., Byfleet 49 4E
Blackwood Cl., Hanworth 16 4B
Bladen Cl. 50 2C
Blades Cl., Leatherhead 70 3A
Blades Cl., Upper Hale 96 2A
Bladon Cl. 82 5A
Blagdon Rd., Hither Green 24 1B
Blagdon Rd., New Malden 37 2E
Blagdon Walk 18 5A
Blair Av. 35 5D
Blairderry Rd. 22 3A
Blaise Cl. 61 5E
Blake Cl. 25 1E
Blake Cl., Crowthorne 43 2D
Blake Cl., Hackbridge 39 4D
Blake Cres. 25 1E
Blake Rd., Croydon 40 5C
Blake Rd., Mitcham 39 2D
Blakeden Dri. 52 2C
Blakehall Rd. 56 2A
Blakemore Rd. 40 3A
Blakeney Av. 42 1A
Blakeney Cl. 54 4A
Blakeney Rd. 42 1A
Blakenham Rd. 21 4D
Blakes Av. 37 3E
Blakes La., E. Clandon 84 4A
Blakes La., Motspur Pk. 37 3E
Blakes Ter. 37 3E
Blanchards Hill 82 2A
Blanchland Rd. 38 3C
Blanchman's Rd. 75 2F
Blandfield Rd. 21 1E
Blandford Av., Beckenham 41 1F
Blandford Av., Whitton 17 2D
Blandford Cl., Beddington 40 5A
Blandford Cl., Woking 65 2E
Blandford Rd., Elmers End 41 2E
Blandford Rd., Lammas Park 8 1A
Blandford Rd., Twickenham 17 4E
Blane's La. 27 4F
Blanford Rd. 108 1C
Blanks La. 126 2B
Blashford St. 24 2C
Blatchford Rd. 158 4C
Blays Cl. 12 5C
Blay's La. 12 5B
Blean Grn. 23 5E
Blegborough Rd. 21 4F
Blencarn Cl. 64 1A
Blenheim Cl., Beddington 56 4F
Blenheim Cl., Crawley 147 2F
Blenheim Cl., Raynes Park 37 2F
Blenheim Cl., Tongham 97 1E
Blenheim Cl., W. Byfleet 49 5D
Blenheim Cres., S. Croydon 57 2E
Blenheim Cres., Upper Hale 96 2A
Blenheim Gdns., Beddington 56 2C
Blenheim Gdns., Brixton 22 1A
Blenheim Gdns., Kingston Hill 18 5C
Blenheim Gdns., Sanderstead 58 4A
Blenheim Gdns., Woking 64 3C
Blenheim Park, Aldershot 78 2A
Blenheim Park Rd. 57 3E
Blenheim Rd., Bedford Pk. 9 1E
Blenheim Rd., Epsom 54 4A
Blenheim Rd., Horsham 158 3B
Blenheim Rd., Penge 23 5E
Blenheim Rd., Raynes Park 37 2F
Blenheim Rd., Sutton Common 38 5B
Blenkarne Rd. 21 1D
Bletchingley 91 5F
Bletchingley Cl. 90 3C
Bletchingley Rd., Godstone 92 4B
Bletchingley Rd., Merstham 90 3C
Blewburton Wk. 27 2E
Blewfield 119 3D
Bligh Cl. 147 5D
Blighton La. 97 4E
Blincoe Cl. 20 3A
Blind La. 46 3B
Blomfield Dale 26 1B
Blondin Av. 8 2A
Bloom Grn. 22 3B
Bloomfield Cl. 64 2A
Bloomfield Rd. 36 2B
Bloomhall Rd. 22 4C
Bloomsbury Cl. 54 3A
Bloomsbury Court 60 1B
Bloomsbury Way 60 1B
Bloor Cl. 158 2B
Blossom Cl., S. Croydon 58 1A
Blossom Cl., S. Ealing 8 1B
Blount Av. 150 2B
Bloxham Cres. 34 1C
Bloxham Rd. 141 1D
Bloxworth Cl. 39 5F
Blue Ball La. 13 4D
Blue Barn La. 50 4A
Blue Cedars 55 5D
Blue Coat Wk. 27 3E
Bluebell Cl., E. Grinstead 150 2A
Bluebell Cl., Hackbridge 39 4E
Bluebell Cl., Horsham 158 3C
Bluebell Hill 27 1E
Bluebell Rd. 133 4E
Bluebell Rise, Lightwater 45 4F
Blueberry Gdns. 74 1A
Bluefield Cl. 16 4C
Bluegates 54 2C
Bluehouse Gdns. 94 2A
Bluehouse La. 93 2F
Bluethroat Cl. 43 4E
Bluff Cove 78 4A
Blundel La., Oxshott 52 5A
Blundel La., Stoke D'Aber. 68 1C
Blundell Av. 128 2A
Blunden Court 120 1A
Blunden Rd. 60 4C
Blunt Rd. 57 1F
Blunts Way 158 4B
Blyth Rd. 42 1C
Blythe Cl. 23 2F
Blythe Hill 24 2A
Blythe Hill La. 24 2A
Blythe Vale 24 2A
Blythewood La. 28 1B
Blythwood Dri. 61 2E
Blytons The 150 2B
Boar Hill 105 4E
Board School Rd. 65 1D
Bocketts La. 69 5F
Bockhampton Rd. 18 5C
Bodens Ride 28 4A
Bodiam Cl. 147 4F
Bodiam Rd. 21 5F
Bodley Cl. 37 3E
Bodley Rd. 37 3D
Bodmin Gro. 38 3C
Bodmin St. 20 2B
Bodnant Gdns 37 2F
Bog La. 27 2F
Bognor Rd. 124 4B
Boileau Rd. 9 3F
Bois Hall Rd. 49 1F
Bolderwood Way 42 5A
Bolding House La. 46 4B
Boleyn Av. 54 3C
Boleyn Cl. 13 4F
Boleyn Dri. 34 2C
Boleyn Gdns. 42 5A
Boleyn Wk. 69 4F
Bolingbroke Gro. 21 1D
Bollo Bridge Rd. 8 1C
Bollo La. 8 1C
Bolney Way 16 3C
Bolsover Gro. 91 3D
Bolstead Rd. 39 1E
Bolters La. 55 5E
Bolters Rd. 128 1B
Bolters Rd. South 128 1A
Bolton Cl. 53 2E
Bolton Gdns. 17 5F
Bolton Rd., Chessington 53 2E
Bolton Rd., Chiswick 9 3D
Boltons Cl. 66 1A
Boltons La. 66 1A
Bond Gdns. 56 1C
Bond Rd., Mitcham 39 1D
Bond Rd., Surbiton 36 5B
Bond Rd., Warlingham 75 2F
Bond St. 12 4B
Bonds La. 106 4A
Bone Mill La. 92 5C
Bonehurst Rd. 109 4E
Bones La. 130 2A
Bonham Rd. 22 1A
Bonner Hill Rd. 36 1B
Bonners Cl. 65 5D
Bonnetts La. 146 2B
Bonneville Gdns. 21 1F
Bonser Rd. 17 3F
Bonsey Cl. 65 4D
Bonsey La. 65 4D
Bonsor Dri. 72 4A
Bookham Court 68 5C
Bookham Rd. 68 2B
Bookhurst Hill 141 1D
Bookhurst Rd., Cranleigh 141 1D
Booth Dri. 14 5C
Booth Rd. 146 5A
Border Chase 148 2B
Border Cres. 23 4E
Border Gate 39 1D
Border Gdns. 59 1D
Border Rd., Crystal Palace 23 4E
Border Rd., Shottermill 151 3E
Bordesley Rd. 38 2C
Bordon Camp Rd. 133 3D
Boreen, The 134 4A
Borer's Arms Rd. 148 1B
Borland Rd. 18 5A
Borners Heath 63 5E
Borough 96 4A
Borough Hill 40 5B
Borough Rd., Godalming 119 1D
Borough Rd., Mitcham 39 1D
Borough Rd., Tatsfield 77 4E
Borough, The 106 1C
Borrodale Rd. 20 1C
Borrowdale Cl., Crawley 146 5C
Borrowdale Cl., Egham 13 5E
Borrowdale Cl., Sanderstead 58 5A
Borrowdale Dri. 58 4A
Borrowdale Gdns. 45 5D
Bosbury Rd. 24 3B
Boscombe Cl. 31 1E
Boscombe Rd., Hammersmith 9 1F
Boscombe Rd., Merton 38 1B
Boscombe Rd., North Cheam 38 4A
Boscombe Rd., Tooting 21 5E
Bosham Rd. 147 5F
Bosmam Dri. 45 1F
Boston Gdns. 9 3E
Boston Manor Rd. 8 2A
Boston Park Rd. 8 2A
Boston Rd. 40 3A
Boswell Rd., Crawley 147 5D
Boswell Rd., Thornton H'th 40 2B
Botany Hill 97 4D
Botery Cross 91 5B
Botford Rd. 38 1A
Bothwell Rd. 59 3E
Botleys 31 5E
Boughton Av. 42 4C
Boughton Hall Av. 83 1D
Bouldish Farm Rd. 28 2B
Boulevard, The 147 4D
Boulogne Rd. 40 3C
Boulters Rd. 78 5A
Boulthurst Way 94 4A
Boundaries Rd., Balham 21 2E
Boundaries Rd., Feltham 16 2B
Boundary Cl. 36 2C
Boundary Rd., Ashford 14 4B
Boundary Rd., Carshalton 56 2B
Boundary Rd., Grayshott 135 5E
Boundary Rd., Northgate 147 3D
Boundary Rd., Rowledge 114 3B
Boundary Rd., South Farnborough 78 1A
Boundary Rd., Tooting 21 5D
Boundary Rd., Woking 65 1D
Boundary Way 65 1E
Boundary Way, Addington 59 1D
Boundfield Rd. 24 3C
Boundstone Cl. 115 1D
Boundstone Rd. 114 2C
Bourdon Rd. 41 1E
Bourke Cl. 22 1A
Bourke Hill 73 2D
Bourne Court 96 1C
Bourne Cres. 49 5E
Bourne Dene 115 1D
Bourne Firs 115 1E
Bourne Gro., Farnham 96 5B
Bourne Gro., Leatherhead 70 3A
Bourne Grove Cl. 96 5B
Bourne Grove Dri. 96 5B
Bourne Lane 74 4C
Bourne Meadow 31 2E
Bourne Pk. Cl. 75 1D
Bourne Rd., Farncombe 100 5A
Bourne Rd., Merstham 90 3C
Bourne Rd., Virginia Water 30 3C
Bourne Vale 42 4C
Bourne View 74 1C
Bourne Way, Addlestone 49 1E
Bourne Way, Cheam 55 1E
Bourne Way, Ewell 54 1A
Bourne Way, West Wickham 42 5C
Bourne Way, Woking 64 4C
Bournefield Rd. 75 2D
Bournemouth Rd. 38 1B
Bourneside 30 4B
Bourneside Rd. 49 1F
Bournevale Rd. 22 4A
Bourneville Rd. 24 2A
Bournside Gdns. 24 4B
Bousley Rise 48 2C
Bouverie Rd. 73 2E
Boveney Rd. 23 2F
Bovill Rd. 23 2F
Bow La. 38 3A
Bowan Ms. 20 2B
Bowater Cl. 22 1A
Bowater Ridge 50 3B
Bowcott Hill 133 4F
Bowcroft La. 157 2F
Bowden Cl. 15 2F
Bowden Rd. 29 3D
Bowen Dri. 22 3C
Bowens Wood 58 3C
Bower Rd. 114 1C
Bowerhill Cl. 110 2A
Bowerhill La. 109 1F
Bowerland La. 112 5B
Bowers Cl. 82 3B
Bowers Farm Rd. 82 3B
Bowers La. 82 3A
Bowers Place Rd. 149 3E
Bowes Rd., Hythe 13 4F
Bowes Rd., Walton 34 5A
Bowie Cl. 21 2F
Bowland Dri. 27 4E
Bowland Grn. 23 3E
Bowlhead Green Rd., Bowlhead Green 136 2B
Bowling Green Court 61 3E
Bowling Green La. 158 4B
Bowling Green. Rd., Chobham 47 3D
Bowling Grn. Cl. 19 2F
Bowmans Lea 23 2E
Bowmans Meadow 39 5E
Bowness Cl. 146 4A
Bowness Cres. 19 4D
Bowness Rd. 24 2B
Bowry Dri. 43 1D
Bowsprit, The 68 1B
Bowyer Cres. 25 1E
Bowyers Cl. 70 2C
Box And Donkey Rd. 157 1D
Box Ridge Av. 57 4D
Boxall Rd. 22 1C
Boxalland 153 4D
Boxall's Gro. 96 1C
Boxalls Hill 135 4D
Boxall's La. 96 1C
Boxford Cl. 58 4C
Boxford Ridge 27 2D
Boxgrove Av. 82 4B
Boxgrove La. 82 5B
Boxgrove Rd. 82 5A
Boxhill Rd. 87 4F
Boxhill Way 106 2C
Boxley Rd. 38 2C
Boxwood Way 75 2F
Boyd Cl. 68 5C
Boyd Ct. 26 1C
Boyd Rd. 21 5D
Boyland Rd. 24 4C
Boyle Farm Rd. 35 3F
Brabazon Av. 57 2D
Brabon Rd. 60 4C
Brabourne Rise 42 3B
Bracebridge 43 5F
Bracewood Gdns. 41 5D
Bracken Av., Clapham 21 1E
Bracken Av., Shirley 42 5A
Bracken Bank 28 1A
Bracken Cl., Bookham 68 5C
Bracken Cl., Copthorne 148 1B
Bracken Cl., Crawley 147 3D
Bracken Cl., Whitton 16 2C
Bracken Cl., Woking 65 2D
Bracken Cl., Wonersh 120 1B
Bracken Gdns. 9 4E
Bracken Hill La. 42 1C
Bracken Path 53 5F
Bracken Way, Chobham 47 3D
Bracken Way, Guildford 81 4D
Brackenbury Rd. 9 1F
Brackendale Cl. 61 1E
Brackendale Rd. 44 5A
Brackendene 79 4D
Brackendene Cl. 65 1D
Brackenhill 52 4A
Brackenhill La. 42 1C
Brackens, The 25 5F
Brackens, The 25 5F
Brackenside 128 2B
Brackenwood, Camberley 45 5D
Brackenwood, Sunbury on Thames 34 1A
Brackenwood Rd. 64 3A
Bracklesham Cl. 60 3C
Brackley 50 1C
Brackley Cl. 57 2D
Brackley Rd., Beckenham 24 5A
Brackley Rd., Chiswick 9 2E
Brackley Ter. 9 2E
Bracknell 27 2D
Bracknell Cl. 44 3C
Bracknell Rd., Bagshot 45 1D
Bracknell Rd., Camberley 44 3C
Bracknell Rd., Crowthorne 26 5B
Bracondale 52 1A

Name		
Bradbourne Rise	42	3B
Bradbury Rd.	147	5F
Braddon Rd.	8	5B
Bradenhurst Cl.	92	1A
Bradfield Cl., Guildford	82	4A
Bradfield Cl., Woking	65	2D
Bradfields	27	2E
Bradford Dri.	54	2B
Bradford Rd.	23	4E
Bradgate Rd.	24	1A
Brading Rd., Brixton	22	2A
Brading Rd., Thornton Heath	40	3A
Bradley La.	86	4C
Bradley Rd.	22	5B
Bradmore Park Rd.	9	2F
Bradmore Way	74	2A
Bradshaws Cl.	41	2D
Bradstock Rd.	54	1C
Braemar Av., Sanderstead	57	3F
Braemar Av., Sanderstead	57	3F
Braemar Av., Thornton Heath	40	2B
Braemar Av., Wimbledon Park	20	3B
Braemar Cl.	118	2C
Braemar Court	61	3F
Braemar Gdns.	42	4B
Braemar Rd., Brentford	8	3B
Braemar Rd., Cheam	37	5F
Braes Mead	110	1A
Braeside, Beckenham	24	4A
Braeside, Woodham	49	4E
Braeside Cl.	151	2E
Braeside Rd.	21	5F
Braid Cl.	16	3C
Braidwood Rd.	24	2B
Brailsford Cl.	21	5D
Brailsford Rd.	22	1B
Brainton Av.	16	2A
Brakey Hill	92	5A
Bramber Cl.	147	3D
Bramble Bank	61	4F
Bramble Banks	56	3B
Bramble Cl., Addington	59	1D
Bramble Cl., Copthorne	148	1B
Bramble Cl., Earlswood	109	1E
Bramble Cl., Guildford	81	4D
Bramble Gdns.	40	2A
Bramble Rise	68	1B
Bramble Walk	53	5F
Bramble Way	66	5A
Brambledene Cl.	64	2C
Brambledown	32	1B
Brambledown Cl.	42	3C
Brambledown Rd., South Croydon	57	2F
Brambledown Rd., Wallington	56	2B
Brambles Cl., Bramley	120	1A
Brambles Cl., Caterham	75	4D
Brambles Cl., Upp. Halliford	33	2F
Brambles, The	100	5A
Brambleton Av.	96	5A
Brambletye Park Rd.	109	1E
Brambletye Rd.	147	4E
Bramblewood	90	3B
Bramblewood Cl.	39	4D
Bramcote	45	5D
Bramcote Av.	39	2D
Bramcote Rd.	9	5F
Bramely	120	1A
Bramerton Rd.	42	2A
Bramfield Rd.	21	1D
Bramham Gdns.	53	1E
Bramley Av.	73	1F
Bramley Cl., Chertsey	32	4B
Bramley Cl., Crawley	147	4E
Bramley Cl., Croydon	57	1E
Bramley Cl., Staines	14	5B
Bramley Cl., Whitton	17	1D
Bramley Hill	57	1E
Bramley La.	43	5D
Bramley Rd., Ewell	55	3D
Bramley Rd., Frimley	60	2C
Bramley Rd., Sutton	55	1F
Bramley Way, Ashstead	70	2B
Bramley Way, Hounslow	16	1C
Bramley Way, Whitton	16	1C
Bramley Way, W. Wickham	42	5A
Bramley Wk.	128	2C
Brampton Gdns.	51	1D
Brampton Rd.	41	4D
Bramshaw Rise	37	3E
Bramshot La.	60	4A
Bramshott Lodge Dri.	151	1D
Bramswell Rd.	119	1E
Bramwell Close	34	1B
Brancaster La.	57	3E
Brancaster Rd.	22	3A
Brancker Way	57	2D
Brandon Cl.	62	1A
Brandon Rd.	55	1E
Brandreth Rd.	21	3E
Brandsland	108	2C
Brandy Way	55	2E
Brangbourne Rd.	24	4B
Brangwyn Cres.	38	1C
Branksmere Rd.	38	1B
Branksome Cl., Camberley	44	5B
Branksome Cl., Walton-on-Thames	34	5B
Branksome Hill Rd., York Tn.	43	4E
Branksome Park Rd.	44	5B
Branksome Rd., Brixton	22	1A
Branksome Way	37	1D
Bransby Rd.	53	2E
Branson Rd., Deadwater	133	5D
Branston Rd., Kew	8	4B
Brantridge Rd.	147	5E
Brants Bridge	27	1E
Brantwood Cl.	49	5D
Brantwood Gdns.	49	5D
Brantwood Rd., Herne Hill	22	1B
Brantwood Rd., Sanderstead	57	3F
Brassey La.	94	3A
Brassey Rd.	93	3F
Brasted Cl.	55	3E
Brathway Rd.	20	2B
Bravington Cl.	33	3D
Braxted Park	22	5A
Bray Gardens	65	1F
Bray Rd., Guildford	100	1B
Bray Rd., Stoke D'Aber.	68	1C
Braycourt Av.	34	4A
Braywood Av.	13	5D
Braziers La.	10	4A
Brazil Cl.	40	4A
Breakfield	74	1A
Breamwater Gdns.	18	3A
Breasley Cl.	9	5F
Brecon Cl., Croydon	40	2A
Brecon Cl., Hawley	60	3B
Bredon Rd.	41	4D
Breech La.	88	1C
Breezehurst Dri.	146	5B
Bregsells Dri.	125	2D
Bregsells La.	125	2D
Bremer Rd.	14	3A
Bremner Av.	128	2A
Brenchley Gdns.	23	1E
Brenda Rd.	21	3D
Brende Gdns.	35	2D
Brendon Cl.	52	2A
Brendon Dri.	52	2A
Brendon Rd.	60	3B
Brent Lea	8	3A
Brent Rd., Brentford	8	3A
Brent Rd., Selsdon	58	3B
Brentford	8	2B
Brentmoor Rd.	46	5C
Brentside	8	3A
Brentway	8	3A
Brentwick Gdns.	8	2B
Brentwood Court	49	5D
Bretharte Rd.	61	2E
Bretlands Rd.	31	5F
Brettgrave	54	3A
Brew House Rd.	106	2C
Brewer Rd.	147	5D
Brewer St.	91	4F
Brewers Cl.	60	4C
Brewery La.	49	5F
Brewery Rd.	65	2C
Brewhurst Lane	156	5B
Brian Av.	58	4A
Briane Rd.	54	3A
Briar Av., Lightwater	45	4E
Briar Av., Norbury	22	5A
Briar Banks	56	3B
Briar Cl., Byfleet	49	4E
Briar Cl., Hanworth	16	4C
Briar Cl., Isleworth	17	1F
Briar Court	146	2C
Briar Grn.	58	5A
Briar Hill	57	4D
Briar La., Addington	59	1D
Briar La., Woodcote Grn.	56	3B
Briar Patch	119	1D
Briar Rd., Norbury	40	2A
Briar Rd., Send	65	5E
Briar Rd., Shepperton	33	3D
Briar Rd., Twickenham	17	2E
Briar Way	82	3B
Briar Wk., Roehampton	9	5F
Briar Wk., W. Byfleet	49	4D
Briars Cl.	60	5B
Briars Court	52	5B
Briars Wood	128	2C
Briarwood Cl.	15	4F
Briarwood Rd., Brookwood	64	3A
Briarwood Rd., Clapham	21	1F
Briarwood Rd., Stoneleigh	54	2B
Brick Field Cl.	8	3A
Brick Kiln La.	94	3B
Brickbat Alley, Leatherhead	160	
Brickfield Rd., Merton	20	4C
Brickfield Rd., Norbury	40	1B
Brickfield Rd., Outwood	110	4B
Brickhouse La.	130	1B
Bricklands	149	3E
Bricksbury Hill	96	1A
Brickwood Rd.	40	5C
Brickyard Copse	143	1D
Brickyard La., Crawley Down	149	3E
Brickyard La., Wotton	104	3B
Bridalway Cl.	54	3C
Bridge Av.	9	2F
Bridge Barn La.	64	2C
Bridge Cl., Byfleet	50	4A
Bridge Cl., Horsell	64	2C
Bridge Cl., Walton-on-Thames	33	4F
Bridge End	61	1D
Bridge Gdns., E. Molesey	35	2E
Bridge Gdns., Sunbury	15	5E
Bridge La., Vir. Water	31	3D
Bridge Mews	64	2C
Bridge Rd., Aldershot	96	1C
Bridge Rd., Bagshot	45	2E
Bridge Rd., Beckenham	24	5A
Bridge Rd., Camberley	61	1D
Bridge Rd., Chertsey	32	4B
Bridge Rd., Chessington	53	1E
Bridge Rd., Cove	60	5C
Bridge Rd., Cranleigh	140	2C
Bridge Rd., East Molesey	35	3E
Bridge Rd., Epsom	54	4B
Bridge Rd., Godalming	119	1D
Bridge Rd., Haslemere	152	2A
Bridge Rd., Rudgwick	157	2E
Bridge Rd., Sunninghill	29	3D
Bridge Rd., Sutton	55	2F
Bridge Rd., Twickenham	18	1A
Bridge Rd., Wallington	56	1C
Bridge Rd., Weybridge	50	1A
Bridge Row	40	4C
Bridge St., Colnbrook	7	3A
Bridge St., Godalming	119	1D
Bridge St., Guildford	100	1C
Bridge St., Leatherhead	69	4F
Bridge St., Staines	13	4F
Bridge St., Turnham Green	9	2D
Bridge St., Walton	33	4F
Bridge Sq., Farnham	96	4A
Bridge View	29	4F
Bridge Way, Chipstead	73	3D
Bridge Way, Cobham	51	5D
Bridge Way, Whitton	17	2D
Bridgefield	96	4B
Bridgefield Cl.	72	1A
Bridgefield Rd.	55	2E
Bridgeham Cl.	50	1A
Bridgeham Way	129	3E
Bridgehill Cl.	81	4E
Bridgelands Cl.	148	1B
Bridgeman Rd.	17	5F
Bridgemead	80	1B
Bridges Cl.	20	5C
Bridges La.	57	1D
Bridgewater Rd.	50	2B
Bridgewood Rd., Stoneleigh	54	1C
Bridgewood Rd., Worcester Pk.	37	5F
Bridgham Cl.	50	1A
Bridgman Rd.	9	1D
Bridle Cl., Epsom	54	5B
Bridle Cl., Grayshott	134	5C
Bridle Cl., Kingston-upon-Thames	36	2B
Bridle Cl., Sunbury	34	2A
Bridle Cl., West Ewell	54	1A
Bridle Cl., Claygate	52	2C
Bridle Rd., Epsom	54	5B
Bridle Rd., Shirley	42	5A
Bridle Road, The	57	3D
Bridle Way, Crawley	147	3F
Bridle Way, Croydon	59	1D
Bridle Way, The	56	1C
Bridlepath Way	15	2F
Bridport Rd.	40	2B
Brier Lea	89	1E
Brier Rd.	71	3F
Brierley	59	2D
Brierly Cl.	81	4E
Bright Hill	101	1D
Brightfield Rd.	24	1C
Brightlands Rd.	89	4F
Brightling Rd.	24	1A
Brightman Rd.	20	2C
Brighton Cl.	49	1E
Brighton Rd., Addlestone	49	1E
Brighton Rd., Aldershot	97	1D
Brighton Rd., Burgh Heath	72	3A
Brighton Rd., Coulsdon	73	2F
Brighton Rd., Godalming	119	2D
Brighton Rd., Hooley	73	4E
Brighton Rd., Horley	128	3A
Brighton Rd., Horsham	158	5B
Brighton Rd., Kingswood	89	1E
Brighton Rd., Purley	57	5D
Brighton Rd., Redhill	90	5B
Brighton Rd., Southgate	146	5C
Brighton Rd., Surbiton	36	3A
Brighton Rd., Sutton	55	3F
Brightside Av.	14	5B
Brightside Rd.	24	1B
Brightwell Cres.	21	4D
Brightwells Rd.	96	3A
Brigstock Rd., Thornton Heath	40	3B
Brigstock Rd., Woodmansterne	73	1E
Brimshot La.	47	3D
Brindles, The	72	2B
Brinkley Rd.	37	5F
Brinn's La.	43	5D
Brisbane Av.	38	1C
Briscoe Rd.	21	5D
Brisson Cl.	51	2F
Bristol Cl., Stanwell	14	1C
Bristol Cl., Three Bridges	147	2F
Bristol Gdns.	19	2F
Bristol Rd.	38	3C
Bristow Rd., Camberley	61	1D
Bristow Rd., Gypsy Hill	22	4C
Bristow Rd., Waddon	57	1D
Britannia Cl.	133	5D
Britannia Way	14	2C
British Grove	9	2E
Briton Cres.	58	4A
Briton Hill Rd.	58	3A
Brittain Court	43	4D
Brittain Rd.	51	1E
Brittania Rd.	36	3B
Britten Cl.	78	5C
Brittens Cl.	81	3E
Britton Cl.	58	4A
Brixton Hill	22	2A
Brixton Water La.	22	1A
Broad Acre	100	5A
Broad Cl.	34	5B
Broad Green Av.	40	4B
Broad Ha'penny	115	2D
Broad High Way	51	5E
Broad La., Borough Green	27	2D
Broad La., Hampton	17	5D
Broad Lane, Parkgate	126	2A
Broad Oaks	36	4C
Broad Oaks Way	42	3C
Broad St., Donkey Town	46	5A
Broad St., Guildford	81	4D
Broad St., Teddington	17	5F
Broad St., Wokingham	25	2D
Broad Walk, Burgh Heath	72	3A
Broad Walk, Camberley	61	2E
Broad Walk, Caterham	75	4D
Broad Walk, Cranleigh	141	2D
Broad Walk, Crawley	147	4D
Broad Walk, Hooley	73	5E
Broadacre	14	4A
Broadacres	81	4D
Broadbridge La.	129	2E
Broadcoombe	58	2C
Broadfield Cl., Croydon	40	5A
Broadfield Cl., Tadworth	71	3F
Broadfield Dri.	146	5C
Broadfield Rd., Catford	24	2C
Broadfield Rd., Hoe	103	4E
Broadfields	35	3E
Broadford La.	47	4D
Broadford Rd.	100	4C
Broadham Green La.	93	4E
Broadhurst	70	1B
Broadhurst Gdns.	108	2C
Broadland Way	37	3E
Broadlands	61	5E
Broadlands, Frimley	61	3F
Broadlands, Horley	128	2C
Broadlands, The,	16	3C
Broadlands., W. Heath	60	5A
Broadlands Av., Shepperton	33	3E
Broadlands Av., Streatham	22	3A
Broadlands Cl.	22	3A
Broadlands Dri., Sunninghill	29	4D
Broadlands Dri., Whyteleafe	75	3E
Broadley Grn.	46	2A
Broadleys	15	3D
Broadmead, Ashtead	70	2B
Broadmead, Bellingham	24	3A
Broadmead, Horley	128	2C
Broadmead Av.	37	4E
Broadmead Rd.	65	4E
Broadmeads	65	4E
Broadoaks Cres.	49	5E
Broadview Rd.	21	5F
Broadwater Cl., Hersham	51	1D
Broadwater Cl., West Byfleet	43	4C
Broadwater Cl., Wraysbury	13	2D
Broadwater La.	119	1E
Broadwater Rd.	21	4D
Broadwater Rd. North	51	1D
Broadwater Rise	101	1E
Broadway, Bracknell	27	1D
Broadway, Brookwood	63	3F
Broadway, Hammersmith	9	2F
Broadway, Laleham	32	2B
Broadway, Stoneleigh	54	1B
Broadway, Thames Ditton	35	4E
Broadway, Tolworth	36	4C
Broadway, Woking	65	2D

Broadway Av

Burford Rd

Broadway Av., Richmond	18	1A
Broadway Av., Selhurst	40	3C
Broadway Cl.	58	5B
Broadway Gdns.	39	2D
Broadway Rd., Lightwater	45	3F
Broadway Rd., Windlesham	46	3A
Broadway, The, Cheam	55	2D
Broadway, The, Crawley	147	4D
Broadway, The, Wimbledon	20	5B
Broadway, The, Woodham	49	3D
Broadway, The, York Town	43	4D
Broadwell Rd.	114	1C
Broadwood Cotts.	125	5E
Brock Rd.	146	2C
Brockenhurst	34	3C
Brockenhurst Av.	37	4E
Brockenhurst Cl.	48	5A
Brockenhurst Rd., Addiscombe	41	4E
Brockenhurst Rd., Aldershot	97	1D
Brockenhurst Rd., Bracknell	27	2F
Brockenhurst Rd., South Ascot	28	3C
Brockenhurst Way	39	1F
Brockham	106	1C
Brockham Av.	74	3A
Brockham Cl.	20	4B
Brockham Cres.	59	2E
Brockham Green	106	1C
Brockham Lane	87	5F
Brockham Rise	24	4B
Brockhamhurst Rd.	106	4C
Brocklebank Rd.	20	2C
Brockley Gro.	24	1A
Brockley Hal Rd.	23	1F
Brockley Park	23	2F
Brockley Rd.	23	1F
Brockley Rise	23	2F
Brockley View	23	2F
Brockley Way	23	1F
Brockleycombe	50	1C
Brocks Cl.	119	1E
Brocks Dri., Guildford	80	3C
Brocks Dri., N. Cheam	38	5A
Brocks Way	30	3C
Brockway	30	2C
Brockway Cl.	82	5B
Brockwell Park Gdns.	22	2B
Broderick Grove	86	1A
Brodie Rd.	101	1D
Brodrick Rd.	21	3D
Broke Court	82	4B
Brokes Cres.	89	4E
Brokes Rd.	89	4E
Bromford Court	94	5A
Bromley Av.	24	5C
Bromley Cres.	42	2C
Bromley Gdns.	42	2C
Bromley Gro.	42	1B
Bromley Hill	24	5C
Bromley Rd., Beckenham	42	1B
Bromley Rd., Lammas Park	8	1C
Brompton Cl.	16	1C
Bronson Rd.	38	1A
Brontes, The	150	2B
Brook	136	2C
Brook Av.	96	1C
Brook Cl., Ash	78	4C
Brook Cl., Dorking	87	5D
Brook Cl., Matthewsgreen	25	1D
Brook Cl., Raynes Park	37	2F
Brook Cl., Sandhurst	43	3E
Brook Cl., West Bedfont	15	2D
Brook Dri., Ashford	15	5F
Brook Dri., Bracknell	27	2E
Brook Farm Rd.	68	1B
Brook Gdns., Kingston	37	1D
Brook Gdns., Roehampton	9	5E
Brook Hill, Albury Heath	102	4C
Brook Hill, Brook	136	2C
Brook Hill, Oxted	93	3E
Brook La., Brook	102	4C
Brook La., Chobham	47	4D
Brook La., Old Woking	65	4F
Brook Lane North	8	2A
Brook Rd., Bagshot	45	2E
Brook Rd., Camberley	60	1C
Brook Rd., Chilworth	101	3F
Brook Rd., Earlswood	109	1E
Brook Rd., Horsham	158	3C
Brook Rd., Merstham	90	3C
Brook Rd., South	8	3A
Brook Rd., Surbiton	36	5B
Brook Rd., Thornton Heath	40	2B
Brook Rd., Twickenham	17	1F
Brook Rd., Wormley	137	2E
Brook St.	36	1B
Brookdale Rd.	24	2A
Brooke Forest	80	3C
Brookehowse Rd.	24	3A
Brookers Cl.	70	2A
Brookers Corner	43	1D
Brookers Row	43	1D
Brookfield	64	1B

Brookfield, Godalming	100	5B
Brookfield Av., Carshalton	56	1A
Brookfield Av., The Wrythe	39	5D
Brookfield Cl., Ottershaw	48	2C
Brookfield Cl., Salfords	109	3E
Brookfield Gdns.	52	2C
Brookfield Rd., Aldershot	78	4B
Brookfield Rd., Bedford Park	9	1D
Brookfields Av.	39	3D
Brookhill Cl.	148	1B
Brookhill Rd.	148	1B
Brookhouse Rd.	60	5C
Brookhurst Rd., Addlestone	49	2E
Brooklands Av.	20	3C
Brooklands Cl., Heath End	96	1B
Brooklands Cl., Sunbury	33	1F
Brooklands La.	50	1A
Brooklands Rd., Byfleet	50	4A
Brooklands Rd., H'th End	96	1B
Brooklands Rd., Thames Ditton	35	4F
Brooklands Way, E. Grinstead	150	3B
Brooklands Way, H'th End	96	1B
Brooklands Way, Redhill	90	4A
Brookley Cl.	97	3D
Brookleys	47	3E
Brooklyn Av.	41	2E
Brooklyn Cl., Woking	65	3D
Brooklyn Cl., The Wrythe	39	5D
Brooklyn Rd., S. Norwood	41	2E
Brooklyn Rd., Woking	65	2D
Brookmead	54	2B
Brookmead Rd.	39	3F
Brooks Cl.	50	3A
Brooks Rd., Brentford	8	2C
Brookscroft	58	3C
Brookside, Carshalton	56	1B
Brookside, Chertsey	32	4A
Brookside, Colnbrook	7	3A
Brookside, Copthorne	148	1B
Brookside, Cranleigh	140	2C
Brookside, Crawley	147	4D
Brookside, Heath End	96	2B
Brookside, Jacobs Well	81	3F
Brookside, Matthewsgreen	25	1D
Brookside, Sandhurst	43	4D
Brookside Av.	14	4B
Brookside Cl.	16	3A
Brookside Cres.	37	4F
Brookside Way	41	3F
Brookview	148	1B
Brookview Rd.	21	4F
Brookway	69	2F
Brookwood	63	3E
Brookwood, Horley	128	2C
Brookwood Av.	9	4E
Brookwood Lye Rd.	63	3F
Brookwood Mews	64	2A
Brookwood Rd., Farnborough	61	5E
Brookwood Rd., Southfields	20	2B
Broolmhall Rd.	57	3F
Broom Acres	43	4D
Broom Cl., Esher	52	1A
Broom Cl., Guildford	81	5D
Broom Cl., Hampton Wick	18	5A
Broom La.	47	2D
Broom Park	18	5A
Broom Rd., Kingston	18	4A
Broom Rd., Shirley	42	5A
Broom Squires	135	5F
Broom Water	18	4A
Broom Water West	18	4A
Broom Way	50	1C
Broomcroft Dri.	65	1F
Broomdashers Rd.	147	3E
Broome Cl., Headley	88	1A
Broome Cl., Horsham	158	3B
Broome Court	72	3A
Broome Rd.	34	1C
Broomehall Rd.	124	3B
Broomers La.	122	5C
Broomfield	117	2E
Broomfield, Elmers End	41	2F
Broomfield, Elstead	117	2E
Broomfield, Guildford	81	5D
Broomfield, Lightwater	45	4F
Broomfield, Sunbury	34	1A
Broomfield Cl., Broomhall	29	4F
Broomfield Cl., Guildford	81	4D
Broomfield Court	50	2A
Broomfield Dri.	29	3F
Broomfield Gdns.	8	4B
Broomfield La.	114	3C
Broomfield Pk., Sunningdale	29	4F
Broomfield Pk., Westcott	105	2E
Broomfield Rd., Surbiton	36	4C
Broomfield Rd., Teddington	18	5A
Broomfield Rd., Woodham	49	4E
Broomfield Ride	52	4B
Broomfield Way	81	4D
Broomfields	52	1B

Broomhall Dri.	52	5B
Broomhall End	65	1D
Broomhall La., Sunningdale	29	3E
Broomhall La., Woking	65	1D
Broomhall Rd., S. Croydon	57	3F
Broomhall Rd., Woking	65	1D
Broomhill Rd., Wandsworth	20	1B
Broomhill Rd., West Heath	60	4B
Broomlands La.	94	2B
Broomleaf Corner	96	4B
Broomleaf Rd.	96	4B
Broomloan La.	38	5B
Broomsquires Rd.	45	3E
Broomwood Rd.	21	1D
Broomwood Way	115	1D
Broseley Gro.	23	4F
Brougham Pl.	96	1A
Broughton Av.	18	4A
Broughton Mews	61	2E
Broughton Rd.	40	3A
Brouncker Rd.	9	1D
Brow, The	109	3E
Browell's La.	16	3A
Brown Cl.	57	2D
Brownhill Rd.	24	2B
Browning Av., Carshalton	56	1A
Browning Av., Worcester Park	37	4F
Browning Cl., Camberley	62	1A
Browning Cl., Crawley	147	3F
Browning Cl., Hanworth	16	4C
Browning Rd.	86	1B
Brownlow Rd., Redhill	90	5A
Brownlow Rd., S. Croydon	58	1A
Brownrigg Cres.	27	1E
Brownrigg Rd.	15	4D
Browns La.	85	2E
Browns Rd.	36	4B
Browns Wk.	114	2C
Brownsover Rd.	60	5A
Brownswood	150	1C
Brox La.	48	3C
Brox Rd.	48	2C
Broxash Rd.	21	1E
Broxholm Rd.	22	3B
Broxted Rd.	23	3F
Bruce Av.	33	3E
Bruce Cl.	49	5F
Bruce Dri.	58	3C
Bruce Rd., Selhurst	40	2C
Bruce Rd., Tooting	21	5E
Brudenell Rd.	21	3E
Brumana Cl.	50	2A
Brumfield Rd.	54	1A
Brunel Cl.	23	5D
Brunel Pl.	147	4D
Brunner Court.	48	1B
Brunswick	26	4C
Brunswick Cl., Thames Ditton	35	4F
Brunswick Cl., Walton-on-Thames	34	5B
Brunswick Dri.	63	3D
Brunswick Grn.	51	5E
Brunswick Ms.	21	5F
Brunswick Pl.	23	5D
Brunswick Rd., Deepcut	62	4A
Brunswick Rd., Kingston	36	1C
Brunswick Rd., Sandhurst	63	4D
Brunswick Rd., Sutton	55	1F
Brunswick Rd., Twickenham	17	3E
Bruton Rd.	38	2C
Bruton Way	27	4E
Bryan Cl.	16	5A
Bryanston Av.	17	2D
Bryanstone Av.	81	3E
Bryanstone Cl.	81	3E
Bryanstone Grn.	81	3E
Bryce Cl.	158	3C
Bryden Cl.	23	4F
Brympton Cl.	105	2F
Bryne Rd.	21	2E
Brynford Cl.	65	1D
Bryony Rd.	82	4B
Bryony Way	16	5A
Buchan, The	44	4C
Bucharest Rd.	20	2C
Buckfast Rd.	38	2C
Buckhold Rd.	20	1B
Buckhurst Av.	39	4D
Buckhurst Cl., East Grinstead	150	1B
Buckhurst Cl., Redhill	90	4A
Buckhurst Gro.	25	2F
Buckhurst Hill	27	2E
Buckhurst La.	29	2E
Buckhurst Mead	150	1B
Buckhurst Rd., Cheapside	29	1E
Buckhurst Rd., Frimley Grn.	61	4E
Buckhurst Way	150	1B
Buckingham Av., Hounslow	16	1A
Buckingham Av., Molesey	35	1D
Buckingham Av., Norbury	40	1B
Buckingham Cl., Guildford	82	5A
Buckingham Cl., Hampton	16	4C

Buckingham Gate	128	4C
Buckingham Gdns., Molesey	35	1D
Buckingham Gdns., Norbury	40	1B
Buckingham La.	23	2F
Buckingham Rd., Ham	18	3A
Buckingham Rd., Hanworth	16	4C
Buckingham Rd., Kingston	36	2B
Buckingham Rd., South Holmwood	125	1D
Buckingham Way, Frimley	61	3E
Buckingham Way, Wallington	56	3C
Buckland	88	4C
Buckland Cl.	61	3D
Buckland Rd., Chessington	53	1E
Buckland Rd., Ewell	55	3D
Buckland Rd., Lwr. Kingswood	89	2E
Buckland Rd., Reigate	89	5D
Buckland St.	88	5A
Buckland Way	37	4F
Buckland Wk.	38	2C
Bucklands Rd.	18	5A
Bucklebury	26	4C
Buckleigh Av.	38	2B
Buckleigh Rd.	22	5A
Buckles Way	72	1A
Buckley Pl.	149	3D
Buckmans Rd.	146	4C
Bucknills Cl.	54	5A
Bucks Cl.	49	5E
Bucks Green	157	2E
Buckstone Cl.	23	1E
Buckswood Dri.	146	5B
Buckthorn Cl.	25	1F
Buckthorne Rd.	23	1F
Buckthornes	26	1B
Budebury Rd.	14	4A
Budgen Dri.	90	4B
Budges Gdns.	25	1E
Budges Rd.	25	1E
Buff Av., Banstead	55	5F
Buff-Beards La.	151	2E
Bug Hill	75	3E
Buisbridge La.	119	3D
Bulbeggars La., Godstone	92	4B
Bulbeggars La., Horsell	64	1C
Bulcanak Rd.	40	2B
Bulkeley Cl.	12	4C
Bull Hill	69	4F
Bull La.	27	1D
Bullbrook Dri.	27	1E
Buller La., Aldershot	78	2A
Buller Rd., Thornton	40	2C
Bullers Rd., Alderston	78	4A
Bullers Rd., Hale	96	2B
Bullfinch Cl., Horley	128	2A
Bullfinch Cl., Horsham	158	2B
Bullfinch Cl., Sandhurst	43	4E
Bullfinch Rd.	58	4C
Bull's Hollow	133	2E
Bunbury Way	71	1F
Bunce Common Rd.	107	4D
Bunch La.	151	2F
Bunch Way	151	2F
Bundys Way	14	5A
Bungalow Rd.	41	2D
Bungalows, The	21	5E
Bungalows, The	21	5E
Bunting Cl.	158	4C
Buntings, The	95	5F
Bunyan Cl.	146	5A
Bunyans La.	46	5C
Bunyard Dri.	48	5B
Burbage Grn.	27	3F
Burbage Rd.	22	1C
Burberry Cl.	37	1D
Burbridge Rd.	33	2D
Burchets Hollow	103	5E
Burchett's Way	33	3E
Burcote	50	2C
Burcote St.	21	2D
Burcott Gdns.	49	2E
Burcott Rd.	57	5D
Burden Way	81	3E
Burdenshott Av.	8	5C
Burdenshott Hill	81	1E
Burdenshott Rd.	81	1E
Burdett Av.	37	1E
Burdett Cl.	147	4F
Burdett Rd., North Sheen	8	4C
Burdett Rd., Selhurst	40	3C
Burdock Cl., Croydon	41	4F
Burdock Cl., Lightwater	45	4F
Burdon La.	55	2D
Burfield Dri.	75	3E
Burfield Rd.	12	2B
Burford La.	54	4C
Burford Lea	117	2E
Burford Rd., Bellingham	24	3A
Burford Rd., Blackwater	60	1C
Burford Rd., Brentford	8	2B
Burford Rd., Horsham	158	5C
Burford Rd., North Cheam	38	5B

Burford Rd., Worcester
Park 37 4E
Burford Way 59 2E
Burgess Rd. 55 1E
Burgess Way 14 4A
Burgh Cl. 147 2F
Burgh Heath 72 3A
Burgh Heath Rd. 71 1E
Burgh Mount 72 1B
Burgh Wood 72 1A
Burghead Cl. 43 4E
Burghfield 71 1E
Burghill Rd. 23 4F
Burghley Av. 37 1D
Burghley Rd. 20 4A
Burgoyne Rd., Camberley 44 5C
Burgoyne Rd., S. Norwood 41 2D
Burgoyne Rd., Sunbury 15 5F
Burhill Rd. 51 2D
Burke Cl. 9 5E
Burland Rd. 21 1E
Burlands 146 2B
Burlea Cl. 51 1D
Burleigh Av. 39 5E
Burleigh Cl., Addlestone 49 1E
Burleigh Cl., Crawley Down 149 3E
Burleigh Gdns. 15 4E
Burleigh La. 149 3E
Burleigh Pk. 51 4F
Burleigh Rd., Addlestone 49 1E
Burleigh Rd., Ascot 28 1B
Burleigh Rd., Frimley 61 3E
Burleigh Rd., N. Cheam 38 4A
Burleigh Way 149 3E
Burleigh Wk. 24 2B
Burley Cl., Loxwood 156 4A
Burley Cl., Mitcham 39 1F
Burley Orchard 32 3A
Burley Way 43 5D
Burleys Rd. 147 4E
Burlingham Cl. 82 4C
Burlings, The 28 1B
Burlington Av. 8 4C
Burlington Cl. 15 2E
Burlington Gdns. 9 2D
Burlington La. 9 3D
Burlington Rd., Beaulah Hill 40 1C
Burlington Rd., Chiswick 8 2C
Burlington Rd., New Malden 37 2E
Burlsdon Way 27 1E
Burma Rd. 30 5A
Burmester Rd. 20 3C
Burn Cl., Addlestone 49 1F
Burn Cl., Oxshott 69 1E
Burnaby Cres. 8 3C
Burnaby Gdns. 8 3C
Burnbury Rd. 21 2F
Burne-Jones Dri. 43 5E
Burnell Av. 18 4A
Burnell Rd. 55 1F
Burnet Av. 82 4B
Burnet Cl. 46 5A
Burnet Gro. 54 5A
Burney Av. 36 3B
Burney Cl. 86 1A
Burney Rd. 86 4C
Burnham Cl. 64 2A
Burnham Dri., N. Cheam 38 5A
Burnham Dri., Reigate 89 5E
Burnham Rd., Morden 38 2C
Burnham Rd., Woking 64 2A
Burnhams Rd. 68 5C
Burnhill Rd. 42 1A
Burnmoor Chase 27 4E
Burns Av. 16 1A
Burns Cl. 158 2C
Burns Pl. 55 5D
Burns Rd. 147 3F
Burns Way 150 2A
Burnsall Cl. 60 4C
Burnside 70 2B
Burnside Cl. 17 1F
Burnt Ash Rd. 24 1C
Burnt Hill Rd. 115 1D
Burnt Hill Way 115 1D
Burntcommon Cl. 83 1D
Burntcommon La. 83 1D
Burntoak La. 126 4B
Burntpollard La. 46 3A
Burntwood Cl. 75 4D
Burntwood Grange Rd. 21 2D
Burntwood La., Caterham 75 4D
Burntwood La., Earlsfield 20 3C
Burntwood Rd. 81 5D
Burpham 82 3B
Burpham La. 82 3B
Burr Hill La. 47 3D
Burr Rd. 20 2B
Burrel Rd. 61 3D
Burrell Row 42 1A
Burrell, The 105 2D
Burrow Grn. 47 3D
Burrowhill 47 2D
Burrows Cl., Guildford 81 5D
Burrows Cl., Little Bookham 68 5C
Burrows Cross 103 4E
Burrows Hill Cl. 7 5C

Burrows Hill La. 7 5C
Burrows La. 103 4E
Burrwood Gdns. 78 3C
Burstead Cl. 51 5E
Burstow 129 4E
Burstow Rd. 38 1A
Burtenshaw Rd. 35 4F
Burton Cl., Chessington 53 2D
Burton Cl., Horley 128 3B
Burton Rd., Kingston 18 5B
Burton's Rd. 17 4D
Burtwell La. 22 4C
Burwood Av. 57 5E
Burwood Cl., Hersham 51 2E
Burwood Cl., Merrow 82 5C
Burwood Cl., Reigate 89 5F
Burwood Park Rd. 51 1D
Burwood Rd. 50 2C
Bury Cl. 64 1C
Bury Fields 100 1C
Bury Gro. 38 3C
Bury La. 64 1C
Bury St., Guildford 159
Burys, The 119 2D
Burywood Hill 124 5B
Busbridge La. 119 3D
Busbridge Pk. 119 4E
Busdens Cl. 118 4B
Busdens La. 118 4B
Busdens Way 118 4B
Bush Cl. 49 1E
Bush La. 65 5F
Bush Rd., Kew 8 3B
Bush Rd., Shepperton Grn. 33 3D
Bushbury La. 106 2C
Bushetts Gro. 90 2B
Bushey Court 37 1F
Bushey Croft 93 3E
Bushey La. 55 1E
Bushey Rd., Cheam 55 1E
Bushey Rd., Raynes Park 38 1A
Bushey Rd., Shirley 42 5A
Bushey Shaw 70 2A
Bushey Way 42 3B
Bushfield 155 5D
Bushfield Dri. 109 3E
Bushnell Rd. 21 3E
Bushwood Rd. 8 3C
Bushy Hill Dri. 82 4B
Bushy Park Gdns. 17 4E
Bushy Park Rd. 18 5A
Bushy Rd., Fetcham 69 4D
Bushy Rd., Teddington 17 5E
Busk Cres. 60 5C
Bute Av. 18 3B
Bute Gardens West 56 1C
Bute Gdns. 56 1C
Bute Rd., Croydon 40 4B
Bute Rd., Wallington 56 1C
Butler Rd., Bagshot 45 3E
Butler Rd., Crowthorne 43 1D
Butlers Dene Rd. 76 3A
Butlers Hill 84 3A
Butter Hill 56 1B
Buttercup Cl. 25 2F
Buttercup Sq. 14 2C
Butterfield 150 1B
Butterfly Walk 75 3E
Buttermere Cl., Cove 60 5B
Buttermere Cl., Feltham 15 2F
Buttermere Cl.,
Wrecclesham 95 5F
Buttermere Dri. 45 5D
Buttermere Gdns.,
Bracknell 27 2D
Buttermere Gdns.,
Riddlesdown 57 5F
Buttermere Way 13 5E
Buttermoere Dri. 20 1B
Butts Cl. 146 3C
Butts Cottages 16 3C
Butts Cres. 16 3C
Butts, The, Brentford 8 3A
Butts, The, Sunbury-on-
Thames 34 2B
Buxton Av. 74 4C
Buxton Cres. 55 1D
Buxton Dri. 37 1D
Buxton La. 74 3C
Buxton Rd., Ashford 14 4C
Buxton Rd., Barnes 9 5E
Buxton Rd., Thornton H'th 40 3B
Bycroft Way 147 3E
Byegrove Rd. 21 5D
Byerley Way 148 3A
Byers La. 111 5E
Byeway, The, Mortlake 9 5D
Byeways 17 3D
Byeways, The, Ashtead 70 2A
Byeways, The, Stoneleigh 54 1B
Byeways, The, Surbiton 36 3C
Byfeld Gdns. 9 4E
Byfleet 49 4F
Byfleet Corner 49 5D
Byfleet Rd., Byfleet 50 4A
Byfleet Rd., New Haw 49 2F
Bygrove 59 2D

Bylands 65 3D
Byne Rd., Penge 23 5E
Byne Rd., Sutton 39 5D
Bynes Rd. 57 2F
By-pass Rd. 27 1D
Byrd Rd. 146 5B
Byrefield Rd. 81 4E
Byron Av., Carshalton 56 1A
Byron Av., Coulsdon 74 1A
Byron Av., Heatherside 62 1A
Byron Av., Motspur Park 37 3F
Byron Cl., Crawley 147 3F
Byron Cl., Hampton Hill 16 4C
Byron Cl., Horsham 158 3C
Byron Cl., Knaphill 64 2A
Byron Cl., Walton-on-
Thames 34 4C
Byron Dri. 43 2D
Byron Gdns. 56 1A
Byron Gro. 150 2B
Byron Pl. 70 4A
Byron Rd., Selsdon 58 3B
Byron Rd., Weybridge 49 1F
Byton Rd. 21 5E
Byttom Hill 87 2D
Byward Av. 16 1A
Byway, The, Carshalton 56 3A
Bywood 26 4C
Bywood Av. 41 3E
Bywood Cl. 74 1B
Byworth Rd. 95 4F

C

Cabell Rd. 81 5D
Cabinmoss 27 4E
Cabrera Av. 30 3C
Cabrera Cl. 30 3C
Cabrol Rd. 60 4C
Caburn Heights 146 5C
Cadbury Cl. 15 5F
Cadbury Rd. 15 5F
Caddy Cl. 13 5E
Cader Rd. 20 1C
Cadley Ter. 23 3E
Cadnam Cl. 97 2D
Cadogan Cl. 17 4E
Cadogan Court 55 2F
Cadogan Rd. 36 3A
Caen Wood Rd. 70 2A
Caens Hill Rd. 50 2A
Caenwood Cl. 50 2A
Caernavon Cl., Frimley 61 3F
Caernavon Cl., Mitcham 40 2A
Caesar's Camp Rd. 44 4C
Caesar's Close 44 4C
Caesar's Way 33 3E
Caesars Wk. 39 3E
Caffins Cl. 147 3D
Caillard Rd. 49 4F
Cain Rd. 26 1B
Cains La. 15 1F
Cairn Cl. 61 1F
Cairngorm Pl. 60 3B
Caister Rd. 21 2E
Caithness Rd. 21 5E
Calbourne Rd. 21 2E
Caldbeck Av. 37 5F
Calder Rd. 38 3C
Calder Way 7 5B
Calderdale Cl. 146 5C
Caldervale Rd. 21 1F
Caldwell Rd. 46 1A
Caledon Rd. 82 4B
Caledonia Rd. 14 2C
Calfridus Way 27 2E
California Rd. 37 2D
Callander Rd. 24 3B
Calley Down Cres. 59 3E
Callow Field 57 5E
Callow Hill 30 2C
Calluna Ct. 65 2D
Calluna Dri. 148 2B
Calmont Rd. 24 5C
Calonne Rd. 20 4A
Calthorpe Gdns. 38 5C
Calton Av. 22 1C
Calverley Cl. 24 5A
Calverley Rd. 54 2B
Calvert Cl. 78 5B
Calvert Rd., Dorking 87 5D
Calvert Rd., Effingham 85 2D
Calvin Cl. 61 1F
Camac Rd. 17 2E
Cambalt Rd. 20 1A
Camber Cl. 147 4F
Camberley 44 5A
Camberley Av. 37 1F
Camberley Cl. 38 5A
Camberwell 22 1C
Camborne Rd., Morden 38 3A
Camborne Rd., Sutton 55 2E
Cambourne Av. 8 1A
Cambourne Rd. 20 2B
Cambray Rd. 21 2F
Cambria Court 16 2A

Cambria Gdns. 14 2C
Cambrian Cl., Camberley 44 5A
Cambrian Cl., Streatham 22 3B
Cambrian Rd., Fox La. 60 3B
Cambrian Rd., Richmond 18 1B
Cambrian Way 25 5D
Cambridge Av. 37 2E
Cambridge Cl., Horsell 64 2A
Cambridge Cl., Raynes Park 37 1F
Cambridge Cotts. 8 3C
Cambridge Cres. 17 4F
Cambridge Gdns. 36 1C
Cambridge Green 9 2F
Cambridge Grove Rd. 36 2C
Cambridge Pk. 18 1A
Cambridge Rd., Anerley 41 2E
Cambridge Rd., Barnes 9 4E
Cambridge Rd., Carshalton 56 2A
Cambridge Rd., Cottenham
Park 37 1F
Cambridge Rd.,
Crowthorne 43 2D
Cambridge Rd., Hampton 16 5C
Cambridge Rd., Horsham 158 5B
Cambridge Rd., Kew 8 3C
Cambridge Rd., Kingston 36 1C
Cambridge Rd., Mitcham 39 2F
Cambridge Rd., New
Malden 37 2D
Cambridge Rd., Owlsmoor 43 3E
Cambridge Rd., Richmond 18 1A
Cambridge Rd., Sandhurst 43 3E
Cambridge Rd., South
Farnborough 78 1A
Cambridge Rd., Sunbury 15 5E
Cambridge Rd., Teddington 17 4F
Cambridge Rd., Walton 34 3A
Cambridge Rd., West
Molesey 34 2C
Cambridge Wk. 44 5A
Cambury Promenade 18 5B
Camden Av. 16 2A
Camden Gdns. 40 2B
Camden Hill Rd. 23 5D
Camden Rd., Carshalton 56 1A
Camden Rd., Cheam 55 1E
Camden Rd., Lingfield 131 2F
Camden Way 40 2B
Camelia Pl. 17 2D
Camelot Cl., Biggin Hill 77 1E
Camelot Cl., Wimbledon 20 4B
Camelsdale Rd. 151 3E
Cameron Cl. 140 2C
Cameron Rd., Aldershot 78 2B
Cameron Rd., Bellingham 24 3A
Cameron Rd., Thornton
Heath 40 3B
Cameron Sq. 39 1D
Camilla Cl. 86 1A
Camilla Dri. 86 3C
Camille Cl. 41 2D
Camlin Rd. 24 4C
Camm Gdns. 35 4E
Camp End Rd. 50 4B
Camp Farm Rd. 78 3B
Camp Hill 97 5D
Camp Pl., Wimbledon 19 4F
Camp Rd., South
Farnborough 78 2A
Camp Rd., Woldingham 75 4F
Camp View 19 4F
Campbell Av. 65 4D
Campbell Cl., Aldershot 97 1D
Campbell Cl., Streatham 21 4F
Campbell Cl., Twickenham 17 2E
Campbell Cres. 150 2B
Campbell Pl. 61 1E
Campbell Rd., Caterham 74 4C
Campbell Rd., Crawley 147 4F
Campbell Rd., Croydon 40 4B
Campbell Rd., Twickenham 17 3E
Campbell Rd., Weybridge 50 2A
Campden Rd. 58 1A
Campen Cl. 20 3A
Campfield Wk. 38 1C
Camphill Court 49 4E
Camphill Rd. 49 4D
Campin Cl. 57 1F
Campion Dri. 71 3F
Campion Rd., Horsham 158 3C
Campion Rd., Roehampton 19 1F
Campion Way 25 1F
Campshill Rd. 24 1B
Camrose Av. 16 4A
Camrose Cl., Croydon 41 4F
Camrose Cl., Morden 38 2B
Can Hatch 72 2A
Canada Av. 109 2E
Canada Dri. 109 2E
Canada Rd., Byfleet 49 4F
Canada Rd., Cobham 51 5D
Canadian Av. 24 3A
Canal Bank 64 3A
Canal Wk. 41 3D
Canbury Av. 36 1B
Canbury Park Rd. 36 1B
Candy Croft 86 1A

Canes La. 133 4D
Canewden Cl. 65 3D
Canford Dri. 32 5B
Canford Gdns. 37 3D
Canford Rd. 21 1E
Canham Rd., Bedford Park 9 1D
Canham Rd., South Norwood 40 2C
Canmore Gdns. 21 5F
Canning Rd., Addiscombe 41 5D
Canning Rd., Aldershot 78 5A
Cannizaro Rd. 20 4A
Cannon Cl., Hampton Hill 17 5D
Cannon Cl., Raynes Park 38 2A
Cannon Cl., Sandhurst 43 4F
Cannon Cres. 47 4D
Cannon Gro. 69 4E
Cannon Hill 27 3D
Cannon Hill La. 38 3A
Cannon Way, Fetcham 69 4E
Cannon Way, W. Molesey 35 2D
Cannonside 69 4E
Canonbie Rd. 23 2E
Canons Cl. 89 5E
Canon's Hill 74 2B
Canons La. 72 2A
Canons Wk. 41 5F
Canons Wk. 41 5F
Canopus Way 14 2C
Cansbury Av. 16 1A
Cantelope Rd. 150 2C
Canter, The 148 3A
Canterbury Cl. 42 1A
Canterbury Gro. 22 4B
Canterbury Rd., Ash 78 4C
Canterbury Rd., Croydon 40 4A
Canterbury Rd., Guildford 81 4E
Canterbury Rd., Hanworth 16 3C
Canterbury Rd., S. Farnborough 78 1A
Canterbury Rd., St. Helier 38 4C
Cantley Cres. 25 1D
Cantley Gdns. 41 1D
Canvey Cl. 146 5C
Cape Copse 157 2E
Capel 125 5D
Capel Av. 57 1D
Capel Bypass 125 5D
Capel Rd. 145 3D
Capella 146 4B
Capital Interchange Way 8 2C
Capitol Pl. 57 1D
Capri Rd. 41 4D
Capsey Rd. 146 4A
Capstone Rd. 24 4C
Captains Wharf 64 2B
Caradon Cl. 64 2C
Caraway Pl. 81 3E
Carberry Av. 8 1B
Carberry Rd. 23 5D
Carbery La. 28 2C
Cardamon Cl. 81 3E
Cardigan Cl. 64 2A
Cardigan Rd., Barnes 9 4E
Cardigan Rd., Richmond 18 1B
Cardigan Rd., Wimbledon 20 5C
Cardinal Av., Kingston 18 4B
Cardinal Av., Morden 38 3A
Cardinal Cl., Morden 38 3A
Cardinal Cl., Stoneleigh 54 1B
Cardinal Cres. 37 1D
Cardinal Dri. 34 4B
Cardinal Rd. 16 2A
Cardinals 97 1F
Cardinals, The 27 2D
Cardinals, The 27 2D
Cardinals Wk., Ashford 15 5F
Cardinals Wk., Hampton 17 5D
Cardingham 64 2B
Cardross St. 9 1F
Cardwell Cres. 28 3C
Carew Cl. 74 3B
Carew Rd., Ashford 15 5E
Carew Rd., Beddington 56 2C
Carew Rd., Lammas Park 8 1A
Carew Rd., Mitcham 39 1E
Carew Thornton Heath 40 2B
Carey Rd. 25 2D
Carey's Wood 129 2E
Carfax Av. 97 1E
Cargill Rd. 20 2C
Cargo Forecourt Rd., Gatwick 128 4A
Cargo Rd., Gatwick 128 4A
Cargreen Rd. 41 2D
Carholme Rd. 24 2A
Carina Ms. 22 4B
Carisbrook Rd. 40 2A
Carisbrooke 61 3E
Carleton Av. 56 3C
Carleton Cl. 35 4E
Carlin Walk Dri. 44 4B
Carlingford Rd. 38 3A
Carlisle Cl. 36 1C
Carlisle Rd., Cheam 55 2E
Carlisle Rd., Hampton Hill 17 5D
Carlisle Rd., Rushmoor 116 5A
Carlisle Way 21 4E
Carlos St. 119 2D
Carlton Av., Hounslow 16 1B
Carlton Av., Selsdon 57 2F
Carlton Cl., Camberley 61 1F
Carlton Cl., Chessington 53 2E
Carlton Cl., Woking 48 5A
Carlton Cres. 55 1D
Carlton Dri. 20 1A
Carlton Green 90 4A
Carlton Park Av. 38 1A
Carlton Rd., Acton Green 9 1D
Carlton Rd., Godstone 111 4F
Carlton Rd., Headley Down 134 5A
Carlton Rd., Kingston 37 1D
Carlton Rd., Redhill 90 4A
Carlton Rd., Selsdon 57 2F
Carlton Rd., Sheen 8 5C
Carlton Rd., Sunbury 15 5F
Carlton Rd., Walton 34 4A
Carlton Rd., Woking 48 5A
Carlton Ter. 23 3E
Carlton Tye 128 2C
Carlwell St. 21 4D
Carlyle Cl. 35 1D
Carlyle Rd., Addiscombe 41 5D
Carlyle Rd., Brentford 8 2A
Carlyle Rd., Cranleigh 140 1C
Carlyle Rd., Staines 14 5A
Carlyon Cl., Mytchett 61 5E
Carlyon Cl., Woking 65 2D
Carlyon Rd. 61 5D
Carmalt Gdns. 51 1D
Carmarthen Cl. 60 3C
Carmichael Rd. 41 3D
Carminia Rd. 21 3E
Carnac St. 22 4C
Carnegie Cl. 20 3A
Carnforth Cl. 53 2F
Carnforth Rd. 21 5F
Carnoustie 26 4B
Carolina Rd. 40 1B
Caroline Cl., Addiscombe 58 1A
Caroline Cl., Streatham 22 3A
Caroline Court 15 5D
Carolinè Dri. 25 1D
Caroline Rd. 20 5B
Caroline St. 9 2F
Caroline Way 61 2E
Carolyn Cl. 64 3A
Carrick Gate 35 5D
Carrington Av. 17 1D
Carrington La. 78 2C
Carrington Pl. 52 1A
Carrington Rd. 8 5C
Carroll Av. 82 5B
Carroll Cres. 28 2B
Carrow Rd. 34 5B
Carshalton 56 1A
Carshalton Gro. 56 1A
Carshalton Park Rd. 56 2A
Carshalton Pl. 56 1B
Carshalton Rd., Camb. 44 3C
Carshalton Rd., Carshalton 56 1A
Carshalton Rd., Mitcham 39 3E
Carshalton Rd., Woodmansterne 56 5A
Carslake Rd. 19 1F
Carson Rd. 22 3C
Carstairs Rd. 24 3B
Carswell Rd. 24 2B
Cartbridge Cl. 65 5E
Carter Cl. 56 2C
Carter Rd. 21 5D
Carterdale Cottages 125 5D
Carters Cl. 38 5A
Carters Lane 65 3E
Carters Mead 128 2B
Carters Rd. 71 1E
Carthew Rd. 9 1F
Carthouse La. 47 5D
Cartmel Cl. 90 4A
Cartmel Gdns. 38 3C
Carver Rd. 22 1B
Carville Cres. 8 2B
Cascades 58 3C
Caseldon Cl. 49 1E
Casewick Rd. 22 4B
Casher Rd. 147 5F
Casino Av. 22 1C
Casino Cl. 78 5A
Cassilis Rd. 18 1A
Cassiobury Av. 15 2F
Casslee Rd. 24 2A
Castello Av. 19 1F
Castelnau 9 3F
Castelnau Row 9 3F
Castillon Rd. 24 3C
Castlands Rd. 24 3A
Castle Av., Ewell 54 3C
Castle Av., Wimbledon 42 2C
Castle Cl., Bletch. 91 5F
Castle Cl., Camberley 61 1E
Castle Cl., Reigate 108 2C
Castle Cl., Sunbury 15 5F
Castle Cl., Wimbledon 20 3A
Castle Craig Court 43 4E
Castle Dri., Doversgreen 108 2C
Castle Dri., Horley 128 3C
Castle Gdns. 87 5E
Castle Green 33 5F
Castle Grove Rd. 47 4D
Castle Hill, Farnham 96 3A
Castle Hill, Guildford 100 1C
Castle Hill Rd. 12 3C
Castle Parade 54 3C
Castle Rd., Camberley 44 5B
Castle Rd., Chipstead 73 3D
Castle Rd., Epsom 70 1C
Castle Rd., Walton 33 5F
Castle Rd., Woking 48 5A
Castle St., Bletch. 72 1B
Castle St., Farnham 96 3A
Castle St., Guildford 100 1C
Castle St., Kingston 159
Castle St., Kingston-upon-Thames 36 1B
Castle Sq. 91 5F
Castle View 53 5F
Castle Way, Ewell 54 3C
Castle Way, Hanworth 16 4B
Castle Way, Wimbledon 20 3A
Castlecombe Dri. 20 2A
Castledine Rd. 23 5E
Castlefield Rd. 89 5E
Castlegate 8 5B
Castlemaine Av., Ewell 54 3C
Castlemaine Av., S. Croydon 58 1A
Castleton Cl. 72 1B
Castleton Dri. 55 5E
Castleton Rd. 39 2F
Castleview Rd. 50 1B
Caswell Cl 60 3C
Cat Hill 143 1D
Catena Rise 45 3F
Caterbury Cl. 42 1A
Caterfield La. 113 2D
Caterham 75 4D
Caterham By-Pass 75 4E
Caterham Cl., Brookwood 63 4D
Caterham Cl., Caterham 74 3C
Caterham Dri. 74 2B
Caterways 158 4A
Catford 24 2B
Catford Broadway 24 2A
Catford Hill 24 3A
Catford Rd. 24 2A
Cathedral View 81 5E
Catherine Cl. 49 5F
Catherine Dri. 15 5F
Catherine Rd. 36 3A
Catherine Wheel Yard 8 3A
Cathill La. 143 1D
Cathles Rd. 21 1E
Cathnor Rd. 9 1F
Catlin Cres. 33 3E
Catling Cl. 23 3F
Cator Cl. 59 4F
Cator Cres. 59 4F
Cator La. 42 1A
Cator Rd., Carshalton 56 1B
Cator Rd., Penge 23 5F
Catteshall La. 119 2D
Catteshall Rd. 119 1E
Causeway Court 64 2A
Causeway, The, Claygate 52 2C
Causeway, The, Hackbridge 39 5E
Causeway, The, Hook 53 1E
Causeway, The, Horsham 158 5B
Causeway, The, Staines 13 4F
Causeway, The, Sutton 55 3F
Causeway, The, Wimbledon 20 4A
Cautley Av. 21 1F
Cavalier Way 150 3C
Cavans Rd. 78 3A
Cave Rd. 18 4A
Cavell Way 147 4F
Cavendish Av. 37 3F
Cavendish Cl., Horsham 158 2B
Cavendish Cl., Sunbury 15 5F
Cavendish Court 15 5F
Cavendish Gdns. 90 5B
Cavendish Meads 29 3D
Cavendish Park 43 5E
Cavendish Rd., Colliers Wood 21 5D
Cavendish Rd., Redhill 90 5B
Cavendish Rd., Sunbury 15 5F
Cavendish Rd., Weybridge 50 2B
Cavendish Rd., Woking 64 3C
Cavenham Cl. 65 3D
Caverleigh Way 37 4F
Caversham Rd. 36 1B
Cawsey Way, Woking 160
Caxton Av. 49 2D
Caxton Cl. 82 4B
Caxton Gdns. 81 5E
Caxton Lane 94 4C
Caxton Rd. 20 4C
Caxton Rise 90 5B
Caygill Cl. 42 2C
Cayley Cl. 57 2D
Cearn Way 74 1A
Cecil Cl., Ashford 15 5E
Cecil Cl., Hook 53 1E
Cecil Pl. 39 3E
Cecil Rd., Cheam 55 2E
Cecil Rd., Croydon 40 3A
Cecil Rd., South Wimbledon 20 5C
Cecil Rd., Sunbury 15 5E
Cedar Av., Cobham 68 1A
Cedar Av., Whitton 17 1D
Cedar Cl., Aldershot 97 1E
Cedar Cl., Bagshot 45 2E
Cedar Cl., Carshalton 56 2B
Cedar Cl., Claremont 51 2F
Cedar Cl., Coombe 19 4D
Cedar Cl., Dorking 105 1F
Cedar Cl., East Molesey 35 2E
Cedar Cl., Epsom 54 5B
Cedar Cl., Fetcham 69 5E
Cedar Cl., Horsham 158 4B
Cedar Cl., Laleham 32 2B
Cedar Cl., Langley 146 2C
Cedar Cl., Reigate 108 1C
Cedar Cl., Warlingham 75 3F
Cedar Cl., Wimbledon 20 3A
Cedar Cl., Wokingham 25 2D
Cedar Court, Egham 13 4E
Cedar Court, Haslemere 151 3F
Cedar Dri. 69 5E
Cedar Gdns., Horsell 64 2B
Cedar Gdns., Sutton 55 2F
Cedar Grn., Bisley 63 1E
Cedar Gro., Ealing 8 1B
Cedar Gro., Weybridge 50 1B
Cedar Heights 18 2B
Cedar Hill 71 1D
Cedar La. 61 3D
Cedar Rd., Bromhall 29 4E
Cedar Rd., Cobham 51 5D
Cedar Rd., Croydon 40 5C
Cedar Rd., East Bedfont 15 2E
Cedar Rd., East Molesey 35 2E
Cedar Rd., Farnborough Park 61 5D
Cedar Rd., Sutton 55 2F
Cedar Rd., Teddington 17 4F
Cedar Rd., Weybridge 50 1A
Cedar Rd., Woking 64 3C
Cedar Ter. 8 5B
Cedar Tree Grn. 22 4B
Cedar Walk, Burgh Heath 72 3A
Cedar Walk, Kenley 74 1B
Cedar Way, Bellfields 81 4F
Cedar Way, Sunbury 15 5F
Cedarcroft Rd. 36 5B
Cedars 56 5A
Cedars Av., Mitcham 39 2E
Cedars Av., Waddon 40 5A
Cedars Rd., Barnes 9 4E
Cedars Rd., Beckenham 42 1A
Cedars Rd., Chiswick 9 3D
Cedars Rd., Hampton Wick 36 1A
Cedars Rd., Morden 38 2B
Cedars Rd., Waddon 57 1D
Cedars, The, Byfleet 50 4A
Cedars, The, Guildford 82 4B
Cedars, The, Milford 118 4A
Cedars, The, Reigate 89 5F
Cedars, The, Teddington 17 5F
Cedarville Gdns. 22 5A
Cedarways 96 5A
Celandine Cl. 43 1D
Celandine Rd. 51 1E
Celery La. 115 1D
Celia Cres. 14 5C
Cell Farm Av. 12 1B
Celtic Av. 42 2C
Celtic Rd. 49 5F
Cemetery La. 33 4D
Cemetery Pales 63 4E
Central Av., Isleworth 17 1E
Central Av., W. Molesey 34 2C
Central Hill 22 4C
Central Parade 59 3E
Central Rd., Morden 38 3B
Central Rd., Worcester Park 37 5F
Central Way, Carshalton Beeches 56 2A
Central Way, Feltham 16 1A
Central Way, Oxted 93 2E
Centurion Cl. 43 4E
Century Rd. 13 4F
Cerotus Pl. 32 4A
Chadacre Rd. 54 2C
Chadhurst Cl. 106 3A
Chadmore Cl. 25 3E
Chadwick Cl. 17 5F
Chadworth Way 52 1B
Chaffers Mead 70 2B
Chaffinch Av. 41 3F
Chaffinch Cl., Elmers End 41 3F
Chaffinch Cl., Horsham 158 2B
Chaffinch Cl., Sandhurst 43 4E
Chaffinch Cl., Tolworth 36 5C
Chaffinch Rd. 41 1F

172
Chaffinch Way
Chestnut Av

Chaffinch Way 128 2A
Chailey Pl. 51 1F
Chalcot Cl. 55 2E
Chalcot Mews 22 3A
Chalcott Gdns. 36 4A
Chalcroft Rd. 24 1C
Chaldon Common Rd. 91 1F
Chaldon La. 74 5A
Chaldon Rd. 74 5C
Chaldon Way 74 2A
Chale Rd. 22 1A
Chale Walk 55 3F
Chalet Hill 133 5D
Chalfont Dri. 78 1A
Chalfont Rd. 41 2D
Chalford Cl. 34 2C
Chalford Rd. 22 4C
Chalgrove Av. 38 3B
Chalgrove Rd. 55 2F
Chalice Cl. 56 2C
Chalk La., Ashtead 70 3C
Chalk La., East Horsley 84 3C
Chalk La., Epsom 71 1D
Chalk Paddocks 71 1A
Chalk Pit Rd., Banstead 72 2B
Chalk Pit Rd., Epsom Downs 71 3D
Chalk Pit Way 55 2F
Chalk Rd., Godalming 119 1D
Chalk Rd., Ifold 155 5F
Chalk Rd., Shackleford 99 5D
Chalkpit La., Dorking 105 1F
Chalkpit La., Effingham 85 2F
Chalkpit La., Oxted 93 1E
Chalkpit Ter. 86 5C
Chalkpit Wood 93 2E
Chalky La. 53 3D
Challen Court. 158 4A
Challenge Rd. 15 4E
Challice Way 22 2A
Challis Pl. 26 1B
Challis Rd. 8 2A
Challock Cl. 77 1E
Challoners Cl. 35 2E
Chalmers Cl. 127 5D
Chalmers Rd., Ashford 15 4E
Chalmers Rd., Banstead 72 1C
Chalmers Rd. East 15 4E
Chalmers Way 16 1A
Chamber La. 95 5E
Chamberlain Cres. 42 4A
Chambers Rd. 78 3C
Chamomile Gdns. 60 4A
Champion Cres. 23 4F
Champion Rd. 23 4F
Champness Cl. 22 4C
Champneys Cl. 55 2E
Chancellor Gro. 22 3C
Chancellor's Rd. 9 2F
Chancellors St. 9 2F
Chancery La. 42 1B
Chanctonbury Chase 90 5B
Chanctonbury Dri. 29 4D
Chanctonbury Gdns. 55 2E
Chanctonbury Way 146 5C
Chandlers Rd. 78 4C
Chandos Av. 8 2A
Chandos Rd. 13 4F
Chantlers Cl. 150 2B
Chanton Dri. 55 3D
Chantry Cl., Horley 128 2B
Chantry Cl., Lwr. Ashstead 70 3A
Chantry Court 61 2E
Chantry Hurst 71 1D
Chantry Rd., Bagshot 45 3D
Chantry Rd., Chertsey 32 4B
Chantry Rd., Chessington 53 1F
Chantry Rd., Guildford 101 3E
Chantry View Rd. 100 2C
Chantrys, The 95 4F
Chapel Av. 49 1E
Chapel Cl. 118 3B
Chapel Gdns. 133 4D
Chapel Gro., Addlestone 49 1E
Chapel Gro., Bagshot 45 3D
Chapel Gro., Burgh Hth. 71 3F
Chapel Hill 139 5D
Chapel House Cl. 81 5D
Chapel La., Bagshot 45 3D
Chapel La., Effingham 149 1D
Chapel La., Hawley 60 3B
Chapel La., Leatherhead 86 2A
Chapel La., Milford 118 3B
Chapel La., Oakwoodhill 142 2C
Chapel La., Pirbright 63 5E
Chapel La., Westcott 105 2D
Chapel Park Rd 49 1E
Chapel Rd., Ban. Newton 72 5A
Chapel Rd., Camberley 44 5A
Chapel Rd., Charlwood 127 4E
Chapel Rd., Limpsfield 94 3B
Chapel Rd., Mitcham 39 2D
Chapel Rd., Redhill 90 5B
Chapel Rd., Rowledge 114 2C
Chapel Rd., Smallfield 129 2E
Chapel Rd., Twickenham 18 2A
Chapel Rd., Warlingham 75 2F
Chapel Rd., West Norwood 22 4B
Chapel St., Frimley 61 4D
Chapel St., Guildford 100 1C
Chapel View 58 2B
Chapel Way 71 3F
Chaplains Rd. 43 2E
Chaplin Cres. 15 5F
Chapman Rd. 40 4A
Chapmans La. 150 2B
Chapter Way 16 4C
Chargate Cl. 50 2C
Charlecote Cl. 61 5E
Charles Rd. 14 5C
Charles St., Chertsey 32 4A
Charles St., Mortlake 9 4E
Charles Sq. 27 1D
Charlesfield Rd. 128 2B
Charleville Circus 23 4E
Charlmont Rd. 21 5D
Charlock Way 82 4B
Charlotte Ct. 101 1D
Charlotte Grn. 129 2E
Charlotte Rd., Barnes 9 4E
Charlotte Rd., Beddington 56 2C
Charlton 33 1E
Charlton Av. 51 1D
Charlton Dri. 77 2E
Charlton Gdns. 73 2F
Charlton Kings, Oatlands Park 33 5F
Charlton Kings, Weybridge 50 1C
Charlton La. 33 2E
Charlwood 127 4D
Charlwood Cl. 148 1B
Charlwood Dri. 69 1E
Charlwood La. 126 5B
Charlwood Rd. 146 1C
Charlwood Walk 146 2C
Charlwoods Pl. 150 1C
Charlwoods Rd. 150 1C
Charm Cl. 128 2A
Charman Rd. 90 5A
Charmans La. 107 4E
Charminster Av. 38 1B
Charminster Court 36 4A
Charminster Rd. 38 4A
Charnwood 29 3E
Charnwood Av. 38 1B
Charnwood Cl. 37 2E
Charnwood Rd. 40 3C
Charsly Rd. 24 3A
Chart Cl., Croydon 41 3E
Chart Cl., Dorking 106 2A
Chart Downs Estate 106 3A
Chart Gdns. 106 3A
Chart La., Dorking 106 1A
Chart La., Reigate 89 5F
Chart La., South 106 2A
Chart La. Sth. 106 2A
Chart, The 94 4C
Charta Rd., South 13 5E
Charta Rd., West 13 5E
Charta Rd. East 13 5E
Charter House Cl. 27 3E
Charter Rd. 36 2C
Charter Sq. 36 1C
Charterhouse Rd. 119 1D
Charters Cottages 29 3D
Charters Rd. 29 4E
Charters Way 29 4E
Chartfield Av. 20 1A
Chartfield Rd. 108 1C
Chartham Rd. 41 2E
Charthouse Rd. 78 2C
Charts Cl. 140 2C
Charts Rd. 29 4D
Chartway 89 5F
Chartwell 114 1C
Chartwell, Frimley 61 4E
Chartwell Cl. 40 4C
Chartwell Gdns. 78 2A
Chartwell Pl., Cheam 55 1E
Chartwell Pl., Epsom 54 5B
Chartwell Way 41 1E
Chartwood Rd. 25 2F
Charwood 22 4A
Chase End 54 4A
Chase Gdns. 17 2E
Chase La. 152 4A
Chase Rd., Epsom 54 4A
Chase Rd., Lindford 133 4D
Chase Side Av. 38 1A
Chase, The, Ashtead 70 2A
Chase, The, Crawley 147 4E
Chase, The, Frimley 61 4D
Chase, The, Guildford 100 1B
Chase, The, Horsely 84 1C
Chase, The, Kingswood 72 4B
Chase, The, Norwood 22 5A
Chase, The, Oxshott 69 1D
Chase, The, Reigate 90 5A
Chase, The, Sunbury 34 1A
Chase, The, Waddon 57 1D
Chase, The, Wimbledon 38 1A
Chase, The, Woodcote 56 5C
Chasefield Cl. 82 4B
Chasefield Rd. 21 4E
Chasemore Gdns. 57 1E
Chaseside Gdns. 32 4B
Chatelet Cl. 128 2B
Chatfield Cl. 78 1A
Chatfield Court. 74 4C
Chatfield Dri. 82 4C
Chatfield Rd. 40 4B
Chatfields 146 5C
Chatham Av. 42 4C
Chatham Cl. 38 4B
Chatham Rd., Kingston 36 1C
Chatham Rd., Wandsworth 21 1D
Chatsfield 54 3C
Chatsworth Av., Haslemere 152 2A
Chatsworth Av., Merton 38 1A
Chatsworth Cl. 42 5C
Chatsworth Gdns. 37 3E
Chatsworth Gro. 96 2A
Chatsworth Heights 44 4C
Chatsworth Pl. 39 2D
Chatsworth Rd., Cheam 55 1D
Chatsworth Rd., Chiswick 9 3D
Chatsworth Rd., Croydon 57 1F
Chatsworth Rd., Mytchett 61 5E
Chatsworth Way 22 3B
Chattern Hill 15 4D
Chattern Rd. 15 4E
Chatto Rd. 21 1E
Chatton Row 63 2E
Chaucer Av., E. Grinst'd 150 2B
Chaucer Av., N. Sheen 8 5C
Chaucer Av., Weybridge 50 2A
Chaucer Cl., Banstead 55 5D
Chaucer Cl., Wokingham 25 2F
Chaucer Gdns. 55 1E
Chaucer Green 41 4E
Chaucer Rd., Ashford 14 4C
Chaucer Rd., Cheam 55 1E
Chaucer Rd., Crowthorne 43 2D
Chaucer Rd., Herne Hill 22 1B
Chaucer Rd., Three Bri's 147 3F
Chaucer Rd., W. Heath 60 4C
Chaucer Way 49 2D
Chaworth Rd. 48 2B
Chawridge Lane 10 2A
Cheam 55 1E
Cheam Cl., Bracknell 27 3E
Cheam Cl., Tadworth 71 4F
Cheam Common Rd. 37 5F
Cheam Park Way 55 2D
Cheam Rd., Cheam 55 2E
Cheam Rd., Ewell 54 3B
Cheap Side 47 5F
Cheapside Rd. 29 2D
Cheeseman Cl. 25 1F
Chelford Rd. 24 4B
Chelsea Cl. 17 4D
Chelsea Gdns. 55 1D
Chelsfield Gdns. 23 3E
Chelsham 76 2A
Chelsham Av. 17 2F
Chelsham Cl. 75 2F
Chelsham Common Rd. 76 1A
Chelsham Court Rd. 76 2B
Chelsham Rd., Chelsham 76 2A
Chelsham Rd., S. Croydon 57 2F
Cheltenham Av. 17 2F
Cheltenham Rd. 23 1E
Cheltenham Villas 14 1A
Chelwood Cl. 54 4B
Chelwood Gdns. 8 4C
Chelysmore Dri. 62 1A
Cheniston Cl. 49 5D
Cheniston Court 29 4E
Chennels Way 158 3B
Chepstow Cl. 20 1A
Chepstow Rd. 41 5D
Chepstow Rise 41 5D
Chequer Rd. 150 2C
Chequer Tree Cl. 64 1A
Chequers Cl., Horley 128 2B
Chequers Cl., Walton-on-the-Hill 88 1C
Chequers Dri. 128 2B
Chequers La. 88 1C
Chequers Yd., Dorking 160
Cherbury Cl. 27 2E
Cherimoya Gdns. 35 2D
Cherington Way 28 1A
Cheriton Rd. 21 3E
Cherkley Hill 87 1D
Cherry Cl., Banstead 55 5D
Cherry Cl., Brentford 8 1A
Cherry Cl., Morden 38 2A
Cherry Cl., The Wrythe 39 5D
Cherry Green Cl. 109 1E
Cherry Hill Gdns. 57 1D
Cherry La. 146 2C
Cherry Orchard, Ashtead 70 2C
Cherry Orchard, Staines 14 4A
Cherry Orchard Gdns. 34 2C
Cherry Orchard Rd., Croydon 40 5C
Cherry Orchard Rd., W. Molesey 34 2C
Cherry St. 65 2D
Cherry Tree Av., Guildford 81 5D
Cherry Tree Av., Shottermill 151 2E
Cherry Tree Av., Staines 14 5B
Cherry Tree Cl. 43 3E
Cherry Tree Cl., Farnham 96 3A
Cherry Tree Cl., West Heath 60 4A
Cherry Tree Court 74 2A
Cherry Tree Dri. 22 3A
Cherry Tree Dri. 27 2D
Cherry Tree Green 58 5B
Cherry Tree Rd., Milford 118 3A
Cherry Tree Rd., Rowledge 114 2C
Cherry Tree Wk., Eden Park 42 2A
Cherry Tree Wk, Rowledge 114 2C
Cherry Tree Wk., West Wickham 59 1F
Cherry Way, Ewell 54 2A
Cherry Way, Sunbury 33 2F
Cherrydale Rd. 45 5D
Cherrytree La. 100 5A
Cherrytree Wk., Biggin Hill 77 2D
Cherrywood Av. 12 5B
Cherrywood Cl. 18 5C
Cherrywood Dri. 20 1A
Cherrywood La. 38 2A
Cherrywood Rd. 60 3C
Cherston Cl. 148 3A
Chertsey 32 4A
Chertsey Bridge Rd. 32 4B
Chertsey Cl. 74 1B
Chertsey Cres. 59 3E
Chertsey Dri. 38 5A
Chertsey La. 13 4F
Chertsey Rd., Addlestonemoor 32 5B
Chertsey Rd., Byfleet 49 4F
Chertsey Rd., Chobham 47 3E
Chertsey Rd., Feltham 15 4F
Chertsey Rd., Shepperton 32 4C
Chertsey Rd., Sunbury 15 5E
Chertsey Rd., Twickenham 17 2E
Chertsey Rd., Updown Hill 46 2A
Chertsey Rd., Woking 65 1D
Chertsey St., Guildford 100 1C
Chertsey St., Tooting 21 4E
Cherwell Court 54 1A
Cherwell Wk. 146 4B
Cheseldon Rd. 101 1D
Cheseman St. 23 3E
Chesfield Rd. 18 5B
Chesham Cl. 55 3D
Chesham Cres. 41 1E
Chesham Rd., Anerley 41 1E
Chesham Rd., Guildford 101 1D
Chesham Rd., Kingston 36 1C
Chesham Rd., Mitcham 21 5D
Cheshire Cl., Mitcham 40 2A
Cheshire Cl., Ottershaw 48 2C
Cheshire Gdns. 53 2D
Chesney Cres. 59 2E
Chessholme Rd., Ashford 15 5E
Chessholme Rd., Guildford 101 1D
Chessington 53 1F
Chessington Cl. 54 2A
Chessington Hill Park 53 1F
Chessington Rd. 53 2F
Chessington Way 42 5A
Chessman Cl. 16 5C
Chester Av., Richmond 18 1B
Chester Av., Whitton 16 2C
Chester Blade La. 27 4E
Chester Cl., Ashford 15 4E
Chester Cl., Cheam 38 5B
Chester Cl., Dorking 87 5D
Chester Cl., Guildford 81 4E
Chester Gdns. 38 3C
Chester Rd., Ash 78 5C
Chester Rd., Effingham 85 2D
Chester Rd., Wimbledon 19 5F
Chester Way 97 2E
Chesterblade La. 17 4E
Chesterfield Cl. 149 1E
Chesterfield Dri. 35 5F
Chesterfield Gro. 23 1D
Chesterfield Mews 14 4C
Chesterfield Rd., Ashford 14 4C
Chesterfield Rd., Chiswick 9 3D
Chesterfield Rd., Ewell 54 2A
Chesters, Horley 128 2A
Chesters, Kingston 37 1E
Chesters Rd. 44 5C
Chesterton Cl. 150 3C
Chesterton Dri., West Bedfont 15 2D
Chesterton Dri., Worsted Green 91 2D
Chesterton Ter. 36 1C
Chestnut Av., Aldershot 97 1E
Chestnut Av., Brentford 8 2A
Chestnut Av., Bushy Park 35 1F
Chestnut Av., Camberley 44 5C
Chestnut Av., Ewell 54 1A
Chestnut Av., Guildford 100 2C
Chestnut Av., Hampton 16 5C
Chestnut Av., Haslemere 152 2A
Chestnut Av., Sunningdale 30 2A

Chestnut Av., Tatsfield	77	4F
Chestnut Av., Thames Ditton	35	4E
Chestnut Av., West Wickham	59	1F
Chestnut Av., Weybridge	50	2B
Chestnut Av., Whiteley Village	50	3C
Chestnut Av., Wrecclesham	95	5F
Chestnut Cl., Addlestone	49	1F
Chestnut Cl., Ashford	15	4D
Chestnut Cl., Englefield Green	12	5C
Chestnut Cl., Hackbridge	39	4D
Chestnut Cl., Hanworth	16	5C
Chestnut Cl., Kingswood	72	5B
Chestnut Cl., Redhill	109	1E
Chestnut Cl., Sendmarsh	66	5A
Chestnut Cl., Southend	24	4B
Chestnut Cl., Streatham	22	4A
Chestnut Cl., Sunbury	15	5F
Chestnut Copse	94	4A
Chestnut Dri.	12	5C
Chestnut End	133	4F
Chestnut Gdns.	158	3B
Chestnut Gro., Balham	21	2E
Chestnut Gro., Bramley Bank	58	2B
Chestnut Gro., Lammas Park	8	1A
Chestnut Gro., Malden	37	2D
Chestnut Gro., Mitcham	39	2F
Chestnut Gro., Staines	14	5B
Chestnut Gro., Westfield	65	3D
Chestnut La., Valley End	46	1C
Chestnut La., Weybridge	50	1B
Chestnut Manor Cl.	14	4B
Chestnut Mead	90	5A
Chestnut Rd., Ashford	15	4D
Chestnut Rd., Guildford	81	5F
Chestnut Rd., Headley Down	134	4A
Chestnut Rd., Horley	128	1B
Chestnut Rd., Kingston	18	5B
Chestnut Rd., Raynes Park	38	1A
Chestnut Rd., Twickenham	17	3E
Chestnut Rd., West Dulwich	22	3B
Chestnut Rd., West Heath	60	4C
Chestnut Walk, Felcourt	131	4E
Chestnut Walk, Upper Halliford	33	3F
Chestnut Way, Bramley	120	2B
Chestnut Way, Feltham	16	3A
Chestnut Way, Godalming	119	3D
Chestnut Wk.	146	2C
Chestnuts, The	34	4A
Cheston Av.	41	5F
Chesworth Cres.	158	5B
Chesworth Gdns.	158	5B
Chesworth La.	158	5B
Chetwode Cl.	25	2E
Chetwode Dri.	72	2A
Chetwode Pl.	97	1D
Chetwode Rd., Tadworth	71	3F
Chetwode Rd., Tooting	21	3E
Chevening Rd.	22	5C
Chevington Villas	92	4A
Cheviot Cl., Banstead	72	1C
Cheviot Cl., Belmont	55	3F
Cheviot Cl., Heatherside	61	2A
Cheviot Rd.	22	4B
Chewter Cl.	45	2E
Chewter La.	28	5C
Cheyham Gdns.	55	3D
Cheyham Way	55	3D
Cheylesmore Dri.	62	1A
Cheyne Av.	16	2C
Cheyne Hill	36	2B
Cheyne Rd.	15	5E
Cheyne Walk, Addiscombe	41	5D
Cheyne Walk, Horley	128	3B
Cheyne Way	60	3C
Chichele Gdns.	58	1A
Chichele Rd.	93	2F
Chichester Cl., Dorking	87	5D
Chichester Cl., Wheeler Street	118	5A
Chichester Ct.	54	3B
Chichester Dri.	57	4D
Chichester Mews	22	4B
Chichester Rd., Ash	78	4C
Chichester Rd., Croydon	41	5D
Chichester Rd., Dorking	87	5D
Chichester Ter.	158	5B
Chichester Way	16	2A
Chiddingfold	137	5F
Chiddingfold Rd., Dunsfold	139	5D
Chiddingfold Rd., Highstreet Green	138	5B
Chiddingfold Rd., Ramsnest Common	153	2E
Chiddingley Cl.	147	4E
Chiddingstone Cl.	55	3E
Chilberton Dri.	90	3C
Chilbrook Rd.	68	2A
Chilcroft Rd., Kingsley Grn.	151	5F
Chilcroft Rd., Shottermill	151	2E
Childebert Rd.	21	3E
Childs Hall Rd.	85	1F
Childs La.	23	5D
Chilham Cl.	61	3E
Chillerton Rd.	21	4E
Chillingham Way	61	1D
Chilmans Dri.	86	1A
Chilmark Gdns., Malden	37	3E
Chilmark Gdns., Merstham	91	3D
Chilmark Rd.	39	1F
Chilmead La.	90	4C
Chilsey Green Rd.	32	3A
Chiltern Av., South Ealing	8	2A
Chiltern Av., West Heath	60	5B
Chiltern Av., Whitton	16	2C
Chiltern Cl., Addiscombe	41	5D
Chiltern Cl., Crawley	146	4C
Chiltern Cl., Haslemere	151	3F
Chiltern Cl., Mayford	64	4C
Chiltern Cl., W. Heath	60	5B
Chiltern Dri.	36	3C
Chiltern Gdns.	42	2C
Chiltern Rd., Hawley	60	3B
Chiltern Rd., Sutton	55	3F
Chilthorne Cl.	24	2A
Chilton Court	51	1D
Chilton Rd.	8	5C
Chiltons Cl.	72	1C
Chilworth Gdns.	38	5C
Chine, The	114	1C
Chingford Av.	61	4D
Chingley Cl.	24	5C
Chinthurst La.	101	4D
Chinthurst Park	101	4D
Chipstead	73	3E
Chipstead Av.	40	2B
Chipstead Cl., Belmont	55	3F
Chipstead Cl., Earlswood	109	1E
Chipstead Cl., Knaphill	64	2A
Chipstead Cl., Penge	23	5D
Chipstead Cl., Woodmansterne	73	2E
Chipstead La.	72	5B
Chipstead Rd.	72	2B
Chipstead Valley Rd.	73	1E
Chipstead Way	73	2D
Chirton Walk	64	2B
Chisbury Cl.	27	3E
Chisholm Rd., Croydon	40	5C
Chisholm Rd., Richmond	18	1B
Chislehurst Rd.	18	1B
Chiswick	9	3D
Chiswick Cl.	40	5A
Chiswick Common Rd.	9	2D
Chiswick Flyover	8	2C
Chiswick High Rd.	8	2C
Chiswick La.	9	2E
Chiswick La. Sth.	9	3E
Chiswick Mall	9	3E
Chiswick Quay	9	4D
Chiswick Rd.	9	2D
Chiswick Village	8	2C
Chiswick Wharf	9	3E
Chithurst La.	130	3A
Chiton Court	51	1D
Chittys Wk.	81	3D
Chivalry Rd.	21	1D
Chive Cl.	41	4F
Chive Court	60	4A
Chobham	47	4D
Chobham Cl.	48	2B
Chobham Gdns.	20	3A
Chobham La.	30	5B
Chobham Rd., Brookwood	63	2F
Chobham Rd., Chobham	47	5F
Chobham Rd., Frimley	61	2E
Chobham Rd., Ottershaw	48	2B
Chobham Rd., Sunningdale	29	4F
Chobham Rd., Woking	65	1D
Cholmley Rd.	36	3A
Cholmondeley Wk.	18	1A
Chrislane Cl.	14	1C
Christ Church Mount	53	4F
Christchurch Av.	17	4F
Christchurch Cl.	21	5D
Christchurch Drive	43	5D
Christchurch Gdns.	53	4F
Christchurch Pk.	55	2F
Christchurch Rd., Colliers Wood	21	5D
Christchurch Rd., East Sheen	18	1C
Christchurch Rd., Epsom	53	4E
Christchurch Rd., Purley	57	4E
Christchurch Rd., Sheen	19	1D
Christchurch Rd., Surbiton	36	3C
Christchurch Rd., Tulse Hill	22	2A
Christchurch Rd., Virginia Water	30	2B
Christian Fields	22	5B
Christie Cl.	45	3F
Christine Cl., Ash	78	5B
Christine Cl., Stanwell	14	1C
Christmas Av.	78	5A
Christmas Pl.	78	5A
Christmaspie	98	1C
Christmaspie Av.	79	5F
Christopher Cl.	71	5F
Christopher Rd.	150	2C
Christy La.	86	1A
Christy Rd.	77	1E
Chuck's La.	71	5F
Chudleigh Court	61	5D
Chudleigh Gdns.	38	5C
Chudleigh Rd., Ladywell	24	1A
Chudleigh Rd., Twickenham	17	1E
Chulsa Rd.	23	4E
Chumleigh Wk.	36	2B
Church App.	22	3C
Church Av., Beckenham	42	1A
Church Av., Farnborough Park	61	5D
Church Av., Sheen	9	5D
Church Circle	78	1A
Church Cl., Addlestone	49	1E
Church Cl., Brookwood	63	4E
Church Cl., Fetcham	69	5E
Church Cl., Grayswood	152	1B
Church Cl., Haslemere	152	2A
Church Cl., Laleham	32	3D
Church Cl., Lwr. Kingsw'd	89	2E
Church Cl., Woking	65	1D
Church Dri.	42	5C
Church Farm La.	55	2D
Church Fields, Guildford	82	3B
Church Fields, West Molesey	35	2D
Church Gdns., Dorking	160	
Church Gdns., Ealing	8	1A
Church Grn., Dunsfold	139	4D
Church Grn., Hersham	51	2E
Church Gro.	36	1A
Church Hill, Aldershot	97	1D
Church Hill, Camberley	44	5B
Church Hill, Carshalton	56	1B
Church Hill, Caterham	75	5D
Church Hill, Horsell	64	1C
Church Hill, Nutfield	91	5D
Church Hill, Purley	57	3D
Church Hill, Pyrford	66	2A
Church Hill, Reigate	90	1B
Church Hill, Shere	103	3D
Church Hill, Tatsfield	77	4E
Church Hill, Wimbledon	20	4B
Church Hill Dri.	50	1B
Church Hill Rd., Cheam	55	1D
Church Hill Rd., Surbiton	36	3B
Church La., Albury	102	3B
Church La., Aldershot	97	1D
Church La., Ash	78	5C
Church La., Banstead	72	2A
Church La., Bisley	63	1E
Church La., Bletch.	91	5F
Church La., Brook	136	3C
Church La., Burstow	129	4D
Church La., Chelsham	76	2A
Church La., Chessington	53	2E
Church La., Copthorne	148	2B
Church La., Cranleigh	140	1C
Church La., East Grinstead	150	2C
Church La. Ewshot	95	1E
Church La., Godstone	92	4C
Church La., Gt. Bookham	86	1A
Church La., Haslemere	152	2A
Church La., Headley	88	1A
Church La., Headley	133	4E
Church La., Hooley	73	4E
Church La., Lammas Park	8	1A
Church La., Merton	38	1B
Church La., Newdigate	125	4F
Church La., Oxted	93	3F
Church La., Pirbright	63	5D
Church La., Rowledge	114	2B
Church La., Sendgrove	82	1B
Church La., Sunningdale	29	3F
Church La., Sunninghill	29	2D
Church La., Sutton	55	1F
Church La., T. Ditton	35	3F
Church La., Teddington	17	4F
Church La., Tooting Bec	21	4E
Church La., Wallington	39	5F
Church La., Warlingham	75	2E
Church La., Warlingham	75	2F
Church La., West Heath	60	5B
Church La., Worplesdon	81	2D
Church Lane Av.	73	4E
Church Lane Dri.	73	4E
Church Lane East	97	1D
Church Ley Rd.	23	4E
Church Meadow	36	5A
Church Path, Acton Green	9	1D
Church Path, Ash Wharf	78	4C
Church Path, Coulsdon	74	2B
Church Path, Farnborough Park	61	5D
Church Path, Merton	38	1B
Church Path, Sunninghill	29	2D
Church Path, Woking	160	
Church Pl., Mitcham	39	2D
Church Pl., South Ealing	8	1A
Church Rd., Acton	9	1D
Church Rd., Addington	59	1D
Church Rd., Addlestone	49	1D
Church Rd., Aldershot	97	1D
Church Rd., Ascot	27	1F
Church Rd., Ashford	15	4D
Church Rd., Ashtead	70	2B
Church Rd., Bagshot	45	2D
Church Rd., Barnes	9	4E
Church Rd., Beckenham	42	1A
Church Rd., Beulah Hill	40	1C
Church Rd., Biggin Hill	77	2E
Church Rd., Bookham	68	5C
Church Rd., Bracknell	27	1D
Church Rd., Brookwood	64	3B
Church Rd., Burstow	129	4E
Church Rd., Byfleet	49	5F
Church Rd., Caterham	75	5D
Church Rd., Cheam	55	2D
Church Rd., Claygate	52	2C
Church Rd., Copthorne	148	1B
Church Rd., Crowthorne	43	2D
Church Rd., Croydon	40	5B
Church Rd., Crystal Palace	23	5D
Church Rd., Earlswood	109	1D
Church Rd., East Molesey	35	2E
Church Rd., Egham	13	4E
Church Rd., Ewell	54	2A
Church Rd., Farleigh	59	5D
Church Rd., Frimley	61	2D
Church Rd., Guildford	100	1C
Church Rd., Hanworth	16	4B
Church Rd., Haslemere	152	2A
Church Rd., Hook	36	4A
Church Rd., Horley	128	3A
Church Rd., Horne	130	2A
Church Rd., Kenley	74	1C
Church Rd., Kingston	36	1B
Church Rd., Leatherhead	70	4A
Church Rd., Lingfield	131	2F
Church Rd., Lit. Bookham	85	1F
Church Rd., Lowfield Heath	128	5A
Church Rd., Milford	118	3B
Church Rd., Mitcham	39	1D
Church Rd., Old Windsor	12	1B
Church Rd., Owlsmoor	43	3E
Church Rd., Purley	57	3D
Church Rd., Reigate	108	1B
Church Rd., Richmond	18	1B
Church Rd., Richmond Park	18	4B
Church Rd., Sandhurst	43	3E
Church Rd., Shepperton	33	4D
Church Rd., Shortlands	42	2C
Church Rd., Shottermill	151	3E
Church Rd., South Farnborough	78	1A
Church Rd., Sunningdale	29	3E
Church Rd., Teddington	17	4E
Church Rd., Twickenham	17	2F
Church Rd., Wallington	39	5F
Church Rd., Warlingham	75	2E
Church Rd., West End	46	4B
Church Rd., Whyteleafe	75	2D
Church Rd., Wimbledon	20	4A
Church Rd., Windlesham	45	2F
Church Rd., Winkfield	10	3A
Church Rd., Woking	64	1C
Church Rd., Woldingham	75	5F
Church Rd., Woldingham	75	5F
Church Rd., Worcester Park	37	4E
Church Rd., Worth	148	4A
Church Rise, Chessington	53	2E
Church Rise, Forest Hill	23	3F
Church Row	28	3C
Church St., Betchworth	107	1D
Church St., Bucks Green	157	2E
Church St., Chiswick	9	3E
Church St., Cobham	68	1A
Church St., Crowthorne	43	1D
Church St., Croydon	40	5B
Church St., Dorking	105	1F
Church St., Effingham	85	2D
Church St., Epsom	54	5B
Church St., Esher	52	1A
Church St., Ewell	54	3B
Church St., Godalming	119	2D
Church St., Hampton	35	1D
Church St., Kingston	36	1B
Church St., Leatherhead	69	4F
Church St., Old Woking	65	4E
Church St., Reigate	89	5E
Church St., Staines	13	4F
Church St., Sunbury	34	2A
Church St., Sutton	55	1F
Church St., Twickenham	17	2F
Church St., Walton	34	4A
Church St., Weybridge	50	1A
Church St., Woking	65	2D
Church St. E., Woking	160	
Church St. West	65	2D
Church Side	53	5F
Church Sq.	33	4D
Church Vale	23	3E
Church View	78	5C
Church View Rd.	17	2E
Church Walk, Horley	128	3A
Church Way, Oxted	93	4F

Church Way, Sanderstead 58 3A
Church Wk., Brentford 8 3A
Church Wk., Caterham 75 5D
Church Wk., Leatherhead 70 4A
Church Wk., Raynes Park 37 2F
Church Wk., Reigate 89 5F
Church Wk., Thames Ditton 35 3F
Church Wk., Walton 34 4A
Church Wk., Weybridge 33 5D
Churchcroft Cl. 21 2E
Churchdown 24 4C
Churchfield Av. 50 1A
Churchfield Rd., Reigate 89 5E
Churchfield Rd., Walton 34 4A
Churchfield Rd., Weybridge 50 1A
Churchfields 133 4E
Churchfields Av. 16 3C
Churchfields Rd. 41 1F
Churchill Av., Aldershot 97 1D
Churchill Av., The Common 158 4A
Churchill Cl., Fetcham 69 5E
Churchill Cl., Frimley 61 3D
Churchill Cl., Warlingham 75 2E
Churchill Cres., Farnborough Grn. 61 3D
Churchill Cres., Headley 133 5F
Churchill Rd., Guildford 101 1D
Churchill Rd., S. Croydon 57 3F
Churchill Rd., Smallfld 129 2E
Churchill Way 16 4A
Churchmore Rd. 39 1F
Churchview Cl. 128 3A
Churston Dri. 38 3A
Churt 134 2B
Churt Rd. 134 2B
Churt Wynde 135 3D
Chuters Cl. 49 4F
Chuters Gro. 54 4B
Cibber Rd. 23 3F
Cicada Rd. 20 1C
Ciderhouse Rd. 118 1A
Cinder Path 64 3C
Cinderford Way 24 4C
Cinnamon Gdns. 81 3E
Cintra Pk. 23 5D
Circle Gdns., Byfleet 49 5F
Circle Gdns., Merton 38 2B
Circle Hill Rd. 43 1D
Circle Rd. 50 3C
Circle, The 119 1E
Cissbury Cl. 158 3C
Cissbury Hill 146 5C
Clacket La. 94 1C
Clacketts La. 77 5F
Clairview Rd. 21 4E
Clammer Hill 152 2B
Clandia 20 2A
Clandon Av. 31 1E
Clandon Cl. 54 2B
Clandon Rd., Burntcommon 83 1D
Clandon Rd., Guildford 101 1D
Clandon Way 83 1D
Clapham 21 1F
Clapham Common South Side 21 1F
Clapham Common West Side 21 1E
Clappers Gate 147 3D
Clappers La. 46 4C
Clappers Meadow 140 5A
Clare Av. 25 1E
Clare Cl., Crawley 147 2F
Clare Cl., W. Byfleet 49 5D
Clare Cotts. 91 5E
Clare Court 76 5A
Clare Cres. 69 2F
Clare Gdns. 13 4E
Clare Hill 52 2A
Clare Lawn Av. 19 1D
Clare Mead 114 2C
Clare Rd. 14 2C
Clare Wood 69 2F
Clarefield Court 29 4E
Claremont Av., Camberley 44 5B
Claremont Av., Esher 51 2F
Claremont Av., Hersham 51 1E
Claremont Av., Motspur Pk. 37 3F
Claremont Av., Sunbury 34 1A
Claremont Av., Woking 65 3D
Claremont Cl., Hersham 51 1E
Claremont Cl., Sanderstead 58 5B
Claremont Cl., Tulse Hill 22 2A
Claremont Dri., Shepperton 33 3E
Claremont Dri., Woking 65 3D
Claremont Gdns. 72 2A
Claremont La. 52 1A
Claremont Park Rd. 52 2A
Claremont Rd., Addiscombe 41 4D
Claremont Rd., Claygate 52 2B
Claremont Rd., Egham 13 4F
Claremont Rd., Redhill 90 4B
Claremont Rd., Richmond 18 1A
Claremont Rd., Surbiton 36 3B
Claremont Rd., Teddington 17 4F
Claremont Rd., West Byfleet 49 4D
Claremount Cl. 72 2A
Clarence Av., Clapham 21 1F
Clarence Av., Malden 37 1D
Clarence Cl., Aldershot 78 5A
Clarence Cl., Hersham 51 1D
Clarence Cres. 21 1F
Clarence Dri., E. Grinstead 150 3C
Clarence Dri., Englefield Grn. 12 4C
Clarence La. 19 1E
Clarence Rd., Cheam 55 1E
Clarence Rd., Croydon 40 4C
Clarence Rd., Horsham 158 5B
Clarence Rd., Kew 8 4C
Clarence Rd., Reigate 108 2C
Clarence Rd., Teddington 17 5F
Clarence Rd., Wallington 56 1B
Clarence Rd., Walton 51 1D
Clarence Rd., Westerham Hill 77 2F
Clarence Rd., Wimbledon 20 5B
Clarence St., Egham 13 5D
Clarence St., Kingston 36 1B
Clarence St., Staines 14 4A
Clarence Way 128 2C
Clarence Wk. 109 1D
Clarendon Court 60 1B
Clarendon Cres. 17 3E
Clarendon Dri. 9 5F
Clarendon Gro. 39 2E
Clarendon Rd., Ashford 14 4C
Clarendon Rd., Beddingt'n 56 2C
Clarendon Rd., Croydon 40 5B
Clarendon Rd., Mitcham 21 5D
Clarendon Rd., Redhill 90 5B
Clarendon Rd. South 90 5B
Clarens Rd. 24 3A
Clareville Rd. 75 5D
Clarewood Dri. 44 5B
Clarice Way 57 3D
Claridge Gdns. 132 3A
Clarkes Av. 38 4A
Clarks La. 77 5D
Claudia Jones Way 22 1A
Claverdale Rd. 22 2A
Claverdon 26 4C
Clavering Av. 9 3F
Clavering Cl. 17 4F
Claverton 70 2B
Clay Hall La., Copthorne 148 1B
Clay Hill Cl. 107 4F
Clay La., Headley 70 5C
Clay La., Jacobs Well 81 2F
Clay La., New Chapel 130 2C
Clay La., Redhill 109 1F
Clay La., West Bedfont 15 1D
Clay La., Wokingham 25 2F
Claydon Gdns. 60 2C
Claydon Rd. 64 1B
Clayford 132 3A
Claygate 52 2B
Claygate Cres. 59 2E
Claygate La. 35 5F
Claygate Lodge Cl. 52 2B
Claygate Rd. 106 2A
Clayhall La., Old Windsor 12 1B
Clayhall La., Reigate 108 2A
Clayhanger 82 4C
Clayhill 36 3C
Clayhill La. 27 2F
Clayhill Rd. 107 4E
Claymore Cl. 38 4B
Clayponds Av. 8 2B
Clayponds Gdns. 8 2B
Claypords La. 8 2B
Clays Cl. 150 3C
Clayton Cres. 8 2A
Clayton Dri. 81 4D
Clayton Gro. 27 1E
Clayton Hill 146 5C
Clayton Rd., Epsom 54 5B
Clayton Rd., Hawley 60 2C
Clayton Rd., Hook 53 1D
Clear Springs 45 4E
Cleardene Rd. 106 1A
Cleardown 65 2E
Clears, The 89 4D
Cleave Prior 73 3D
Cleaveland Rd. 36 3A
Cleeve Hill 23 2E
Cleeve Rd. 69 3F
Cleeves Way 16 5C
Clement Cl., Acton Green 9 2D
Clement Cl., Kenley 74 1B
Clement Rd., Elmers End 41 1F
Clement Rd., Wimbledon 20 4A
Clements Mead 69 3F
Clements Rd. 34 5A
Clerks Croft 91 5F
Clevedon 50 1B
Clevedon Court, Frimley 61 3F
Clevedon Court, Mytchett 61 5E
Clevedon Rd., Kent House 41 1F
Clevedon Rd., Richmond 18 1A
Cleveland Av., Hampton 16 5C
Cleveland Av., Merton 38 1B
Cleveland Av., Turn. Grn. 9 2E
Cleveland Cl. 34 5A
Cleveland Dri. 32 1B
Cleveland Gdns., Barnes 9 4E
Cleveland Gdns., Worcester Park 37 5E
Cleveland Pk. 14 1C
Cleveland Rd., Barnes 9 4E
Cleveland Rd., New Malden 37 2E
Cleveland Rd., Worcester Park 37 5E
Cleveland Rise 38 4A
Cleveland Ter. 78 2A
Cleves Av. 54 3C
Cleves Cl. 51 5D
Cleves Cres. 59 4E
Cleves Rd. 18 3A
Cleves Way 15 5F
Cleves Wood 50 1C
Clewborough Dri. 44 5C
Clew's La. 63 1E
Clifden Rd., Brentford 8 3A
Clifden Rd., Twickenham 17 2F
Cliff End 57 4E
Cliffe Rd., Ockford Ridge 118 3C
Cliffe Rd., S. Croydon 57 1F
Cliffe Rise 118 2C
Clifford Av., Sheen 8 5C
Clifford Av., Wallington 56 1C
Clifford Gro. 15 4D
Clifford Manor Rd. 101 2D
Clifford Rd., Ham 18 3B
Clifford Rd., Norwood 41 2D
Clifford Rd., Sheen 8 5C
Clifton Av., Belmont 55 4F
Clifton Av., Feltham 16 3A
Clifton Cl., Caterham 74 5C
Clifton Cl., Chertsey 32 5B
Clifton Cl., Farnham 114 2C
Clifton Gdns. 9 2D
Clifton La. 89 5D
Clifton Park Av. 37 1F
Clifton Pl. 72 1B
Clifton Rd., Crawley 147 4F
Clifton Rd., Kingston 36 1C
Clifton Rd., Matthewsgreen 25 1D
Clifton Rd., Selhurst 40 2C
Clifton Rd., Twickenham 17 4E
Clifton Rd., Wallington 56 1B
Clifton Rd., Wimbledon 20 5A
Clifton Rd., Woodmansterne 73 1F
Clifton Way 64 2A
Cliftonville 105 2F
Climping Rd. 146 3C
Cline Rd. 101 1D
Clinton Av. 35 2D
Clinton Cl. 64 2A
Clinton Green 26 1C
Clinton Hill 132 3A
Clinton Rd. 70 5A
Clitherow Rd. 8 2A
Clive Green 27 3D
Clive Rd., Esher 52 1A
Clive Rd., Feltham 16 1A
Clive Rd., Strawberry Hill 17 4F
Clive Rd., Tooting 21 5D
Clive Rd., West Dulwich 22 3C
Clive Way, Thorpe 31 1F
Clive Way, Three Bridges 147 4F
Cliveden Pl. 33 4E
Cliveden Rd. 38 1B
Clock Barn La. 119 4D
Clock House Cl. 50 4A
Clock House Rd., Byfleet 50 4A
Clock House Rd., Elmers End 41 2F
Clockhouse La., Ashford 15 4D
Clockhouse La., Egham 13 5E
Clockhouse Mead 52 5A
Clockhouse Rd. 61 5D
Clodhouse Hill 64 4A
Cloisters, The, Frimley 61 2E
Cloisters, The, Woking 65 4E
Clonmel Rd. 17 4E
Clonmore St. 20 2B
Close, The, Ascot 28 1A
Close, The, Bracknell 27 2D
Close, The, Carshalton Beeches 56 3A
Close, The, East Grinstead 150 3B
Close, The, Farnham 96 4B
Close, The, Frimley 61 3D
Close, The, Godalming 119 3D
Close, The, Horley 128 3C
Close, The, Kingston 37 1D
Close, The, Lightwater 45 3E
Close, The, Mitcham 39 2D
Close, The, Morden Park 38 4B
Close, The, Purley 57 3D
Close, The, Purley 57 3E
Close, The, Reigate 108 1C
Close, The, Strood Grn. 107 2D
Close, The, Virginia Water 30 3C
Close, The, West Byfleet 49 5D
Close, The, Wonersh 101 5E
Close, The, York Town 43 4E
Closeworth Rd. 78 2B
Cloudesdale Rd. 21 3E
Clouston Cl. 56 1C
Clouston Rd. 60 4C
Clovelly Av. 75 3E
Clovelly Dri. 135 3D
Clovelly Pl. 135 3D
Clovelly Rd., Acton 9 1D
Clovelly Rd., Hindhead 135 4D
Clovelly Rd., Lammas Park 8 1A
Clover Cl. 133 1E
Clover Court 64 2C
Clover Hill 73 4E
Clover Lea 100 5A
Clover Rd. 81 5D
Clover Way 129 2E
Cloverlands 147 3E
Clowders Rd. 24 3A
Clowser Cl. 55 1F
Club La. 60 1B
Clump Av. 88 4A
Clumps Rd. 115 2E
Clumps, The 15 4E
Clyde Av. 75 1E
Clyde Cl. 90 5B
Clyde Rd., Addiscombe 41 5D
Clyde Rd., Beddington 56 2C
Clyde Rd., Cheam 55 1E
Clyde Rd., Stanwell 14 2C
Clyde Vale 23 3E
Clydesdale Gdns. 8 5C
Clymping Dene 16 2A
Coach House Cl. 20 3A
Coach House Mews 23 2E
Coach Rd. 48 2B
Coach-house Cl. 61 1E
Coachlands Av. 81 5E
Coast Hill 104 3C
Coast Hill La. 104 3C
Coast Hill Rd. 104 3C
Coatham Pl. 141 1D
Cob Cl. 149 3E
Cob Wk. 146 4B
Cobbett Cl. 147 3F
Cobbett Hill Rd. 80 2A
Cobbett Rd., Guildford 81 5D
Cobbett Rd., Whitton 17 2D
Cobbetts Cl. 64 2C
Cobbetts Hill 50 2A
Cobbett's Ridge 97 4D
Cobbetts Way 114 1C
Cobbetts Wk. 63 1E
Cobbles Cres. 147 3D
Cobbold Rd. 9 1E
Cobden Rd. 41 3D
Cobham 51 5D
Cobham Av. 37 3E
Cobham Cl. 57 2D
Cobham Gate 51 5D
Cobham Park Rd. 68 2A
Cobham Rd., Fetcham 69 4E
Cobham Rd., Kingston 36 1C
Cobham Way, E. Horsley 84 1C
Cobham Way, Northgate 147 1E
Cobnor Cl. 146 5B
Cobs Way 49 3E
Coburg Cres. 22 2A
Cochran Pl. 46 1A
Cochrane Rd. 20 5B
Cock La. 69 4D
Cockpit Path 25 2E
Cocks Cres. 37 2E
Cockshot Hill 108 1C
Cockshot Rd. 108 1C
Codrington Hill 23 2F
Cody Cl. 56 2C
Cody Rd 60 5C
Coe Av. 41 3D
Cogman's La. 129 1F
Cogmore Farm Cl. 32 3A
Cokenor Wood 114 1C
Colborne Way 37 5F
Colburn Av. 75 5D
Colburn Cres. 82 4B
Colburn Way 39 5D
Colby Rd., Gypsy Hill 23 4D
Colby Rd., Walton-on-Thames 34 4A
Colcokes Rd. 72 1B
Cold Blows 39 2D
Coldborough Rise 26 1C
Coldharbour 124 2B
Coldharbour Cl. 31 2F
Coldharbour La., Coldharbour 124 1B
Coldharbour La., Dorking 105 4F
Coldharbour La., Hawley 60 3B
Coldharbour La., Purley 57 3E
Coldharbour La., Thorpe 31 2F
Coldharbour La., W. End 46 4B
Coldharbour Rd., Coldharbour 66 1A
Coldharbour Rd., S. Croydon 57 1E
Coldharbour Rd., West Byfleet 49 5D
Coldharbour Way 57 1E
Coldshott 94 5A

175
Coldstream Gdns
Copthorne Way

Coldstream Gdns. 20 1B
Cole Bank Rd. 40 1A
Cole Park Gdns. 17 1F
Cole Park Rd. 17 1F
Cole Rd. 17 1F
Colebrook 48 2C
Colebrook Cl. 20 1A
Colebrook Rd. 90 4A
Colebrooke Rise 42 1C
Colefield Rd. 20 1C
Coleford Bridge Rd. South 61 5E
Coleford Cl. 61 5E
Coleford Paddocks 61 5E
Colekitchen La. 103 2E
Coleman Rd. 78 5A
Coleridge Av. 56 1A
Coleridge Cres. 7 4B
Coleridge Rd., Ashford 14 4C
Coleridge Rd., Woodside 41 3E
Coles La. 124 5B
Colesburgh Rd. 41 1F
Colescroft Hill 74 1B
Coleshill Rd. 17 5E
Colesmead Rd. 90 4A
Coleson Hill Rd. 114 1C
Colet Rd. 147 5D
Coleville Rd. 60 4C
Coley Av. 65 2D
Colfe Rd. 23 2F
Colfin Cl. 41 5F
Colin Cl. 42 5C
Colin Rd. 75 5D
Colinette Rd. 9 5E
Collamore Av. 21 2D
Collards La. 152 3A
College Av., Egham 13 5E
College Av., Epsom 54 5B
College Cl., Camberley 44 4B
College Cl., Lingfield 131 2E
College Cl., Twickenham 17 2E
College Cres., Redhill 90 4B
College Cres., Sandhurst 43 4E
College Gdns., Camberwell 22 2C
College Gdns., Farnham 96 4A
College Gdns., Malden 37 3E
College Gdns., Wandsworth 21 3D
College Green 22 5C
College Hill, Godalming 118 3C
College Hill, Haslemere 152 3A
College Hill Ter. 152 3A
College La., E. Grinstead 150 2C
College La., Woking 64 3C
College Rd., Ash Wharf 78 4C
College Rd., Bracknell 27 2D
College Rd., Colliers Wood 21 5D
College Rd., Crawley 147 4D
College Rd., Croydon 40 5C
College Rd., Epsom 54 5B
College Rd., Guildford 100 1C
College Rd., Hither Green 24 1B
College Rd., West Dulwich 22 2C
College Rd., Woking 65 1E
College Rd., York Town 43 4E
College Ride 44 3C
College Way 15 4D
Collendean La. 127 2E
Collens Field 63 5E
Collesden Rd. 74 1B
Colley La. 89 5D
Colley Manor Dri. 89 5D
Colley Way 89 4E
Collier Cl., West Ewell 53 2F
Collier Cl., West Heath 60 4B
Collier Row 147 5D
Collier Way 82 4C
Colliers 92 1A
Colliers Cl. 64 2C
Colliers Water La. 40 3B
Collingtree Rd. 23 4E
Collingwood Av. 37 4D
Collingwood Cl., E. Grin. 150 3C
Collingwood Cl., Horley 128 2C
Collingwood Cl., Horsham 158 4B
Collingwood Cl., Whitton 17 2D
Collingwood Cres. 82 5B
Collingwood Grange Cl. 44 4C
Collingwood Rd., Crawley 147 4F
Collingwood Rd., Mitcham 39 2D
Collingwood Rd., West Sutton 55 1E
Collingwood Rise 44 4C
Collins Rd. 146 5A
Collinswood Pl. 34 5A
Colliston Rd. 20 2B
Collyer Av. 57 1D
Collyer Rd. 57 1D
Colman Cl. 71 2F
Colmans Hill 103 5F
Colmans Way 90 4A
Colmer Rd. 40 1A
Colnbrook 7 3A
Colnbrook By-Pass 7 3A
Colndale Rd. 7 4A
Colne Court 54 1A
Colne Dri. 34 5B
Colne Rd. 17 2E
Colne Reach 14 1A
Colne Ridge 14 1A
Colne Way, Ash 78 5C
Colne Way, Hythe End 13 3E
Colonel's La. 32 3A
Colonial Av. 17 1D
Colonial Rd. 15 2F
Colonsay Rd. 146 5C
Colson Rd. 40 5C
Colson Way 21 4F
Colston Av. 56 1A
Colston Rd. 9 5D
Coltash Rd. 147 4E
Coltsfoot Cl. 133 1E
Coltsfoot Dri., Guildford 82 4B
Coltsfoot Dri., Horsham 158 3C
Columbia Av. 37 4E
Columbine Av. 57 2E
Colville Gdns. 45 4F
Colville Rd. 8 1C
Colvin Cl. 23 4E
Colvin Rd. 40 3B
Colwell Rd. 23 1D
Colwood Gdns. 21 5D
Colworth Rd. 41 4D
Colwyn Cl., Broadfield 146 5B
Colwyn Cl., Tooting Bec 21 4F
Colyton Cl. 64 2C
Colyton Rd. 23 1E
Combe La., Albury 103 2D
Combe La., Chiddingfold 153 1D
Combe La., West Heath 60 4C
Combe La., Whiteley Village 50 3C
Combe La., Wormley 137 3E
Combe Rd. 100 5A
Combe Rise 115 1E
Combe View 137 4E
Combemartin Rd. 20 2B
Combermere Rd. 38 3C
Comeragh Cl. 64 3B
Comet Rd. 14 2C
Comforts Farm La. 94 5A
Comfrey Cl., West Heath 60 4A
Comfrey Cl., Wokingham 25 1F
Commerce Rd. 8 3A
Commerce Way 40 5A
Commercial Rd., Badshot Lea 97 1D
Commercial Rd., Guildf'd 100 1C
Commercial Rd., Staines 14 5A
Commercial Way 65 2D
Common Cl. 47 5F
Common La., Claygate 52 2C
Common La., New Haw 49 3E
Common Rd., Barnes 9 5F
Common Rd., Bookham 68 4C
Common Rd., Claygate 52 2C
Common Rd., Cranleigh 140 1B
Common Rd., Redhill 109 1D
Common Side 70 1C
Common, The, Ashstead 70 1A
Common, The, Ham 18 3A
Commondale 9 4F
Commonfield Rd. 55 5E
Commonfields 46 5B
Commonside, Bookham 68 5C
Commonside, East 39 2E
Commonside, West 39 2E
Commonside Cl. 55 4F
Commonwealth Rd. 75 5D
Como Rd. 23 3F
Comper Cl. 146 5A
Comport Cl. 59 4F
Comport Green 59 4F
Comport Green Cl. 59 4F
Compton 99 3F
Compton Cl. 43 3D
Compton Cl., Easthampstead 26 3B
Compton Cl., Esher 52 2A
Compton Cl., Sandhurst 43 3D
Compton Cres., Chessington 53 2E
Compton Cres., Chiswick 9 3D
Compton Gdns. 49 1E
Compton Rd., Addiscombe 41 4E
Compton Rd., Wimbledon 20 5B
Compton Way 96 4C
Comptons Brow La. 158 4C
Comptons La. 158 5C
Comsaye Walk 27 3D
Conaways Cl. 54 3C
Condor Rd. 32 2B
Conduit La. 58 1A
Conduit, The 91 3F
Coney Berry 108 2C
Coney Cl. 146 3C
Coney Hill Rd. 42 5C
Coneybury 91 5F
Coneybury Cl. 75 3E
Conford Dri. 101 4D
Coniers Way 82 4B
Conifer Cl. 89 4E
Conifer Dri. 44 5C
Conifer Gdns., Streatham 22 3A
Conifer Gdns., Sutton 38 5C
Conifer Pk. 54 4B
Conifers, Weybridge 50 1C
Conifers Cl. 18 5A
Conifers La. 13 4E
Conifers, The, Crowthorne 25 5F
Coningham Rd. 9 1F
Coningsby 27 2D
Coningsby Rd., Lammas Park 8 1A
Coningsby Rd., Purley Oaks 57 3E
Conisborough Cres. 24 3B
Conista Court 64 1A
Coniston Cl., Camberley 62 1A
Coniston Cl., Morden 38 3A
Coniston Cl., West Heath 60 5B
Coniston Court 45 3F
Coniston Dri. 96 2A
Coniston Gdns. 55 2F
Coniston Rd., Addiscombe 41 4D
Coniston Rd., Bromley Hill 24 5C
Coniston Rd., Whitton 17 1D
Coniston Rd., Woking 65 3E
Coniston Rd., Woodmansterne 73 1F
Coniston Way, Hook 36 5B
Coniston Way, Reigate 90 5A
Connaught Av., Ashford 14 4C
Connaught Av., E. Sheen 9 5D
Connaught Cl. 39 5D
Connaught Cres. 63 3E
Connaught Gdns. 147 3D
Connaught Rd., Aldershot 78 5A
Connaught Rd., Bagshot 45 2D
Connaught Rd., Brookwood 63 4E
Connaught Rd., Camberley 44 5B
Connaught Rd., New Malden 37 2E
Connaught Rd., Teddington 17 5F
Connaught Rd., The Wrythe 39 5D
Connicut La. 86 3A
Connington Rd. 78 1B
Connop Way 61 1F
Conquest Rd. 49 1E
Conrad Dri. 38 4A
Consfield Av. 37 3F
Consort Mews 17 1E
Consort Way 128 2B
Consort Way East 128 3B
Constable Way 43 5E
Constance Cres. 42 4C
Constance Rd., Croydon 40 4B
Constance Rd., Sutton 55 1F
Constance Rd., Whitton 17 2D
Constitution Hill 65 3D
Convent Gdns. 8 2A
Convent Hill 22 5C
Convent La. 50 4C
Convent Rd. 15 4D
Conway Dri., Ashford 15 5E
Conway Dri., W. Heath 60 5B
Conway Gdns. 40 2A
Conway Rd., Hanworth 16 4B
Conway Rd., Raynes Park 38 1A
Conway Rd., Whitton 16 2C
Conway Walk 16 5C
Conyers Cl. 51 1E
Conyer's Rd. 21 4F
Cook Rd., Crawley 147 5D
Cook Rd., Horsham 158 3B
Cookes La. 55 2D
Cookham Cl. 43 4D
Cookham Rd. 26 1B
Cooks Hill 157 2D
Cooks Mead 145 3D
Cooks Meadow 145 4D
Coolarne Rise 44 5C
Coolgardie Rd. 15 4E
Coolgreany Hill 133 4E
Coombe Av. 58 1A
Coombe Bank 37 1E
Coombe Cl., Crawley 146 3C
Coombe Cl., Frimley 61 3E
Coombe Cres. 16 5C
Coombe Dri. 49 2D
Coombe End 19 5D
Coombe Gdns., Cottenham Park 37 1E
Coombe Gdns., New Malden 37 2E
Coombe Hill Rd., East Grinstead 150 3C
Coombe Hill Rd., Kingston 19 5E
Coombe House 37 1D
Coombe La., Croydon 58 1B
Coombe La., Raynes Park 37 1E
Coombe La., Sunninghill 28 2C
Coombe La., Worplesdon 81 2D
Coombe Lane West 19 5E
Coombe Neville 19 5D
Coombe Park 19 4D
Coombe Pine 27 3E
Coombe Rd., Chiswick 9 2E
Coombe Rd., Croydon 58 1A
Coombe Rd., Hampton 16 5C
Coombe Rd., Kingston 36 1C
Coombe Rd., Malden 37 1E
Coombe Rd., Upper Sydenham 23 4E
Coombe Ridings 19 4D
Coombe Rise 37 1D
Coombe, The 88 4A
Coombe Wk. 38 5C
Coombe Wood Hill 57 5F
Coombe Wood Rd. 19 4D
Coombefield Cl. 37 3E
Coombelands La. 49 2D
Coomber Way 39 4F
Coombs, The 120 1A
Cooper Cres. 39 5D
Cooper Mill Rd. 7 5A
Cooper Rd., Croydon 57 1E
Cooper Rd., Guildford 101 1D
Cooperfield Av. 43 3E
Coopers Cl. 14 4A
Coopers Hill Dri. 63 4D
Coopers Hill La. 12 3C
Cooper's Hill Rd. 91 5D
Coopers Rd. 46 2A
Coopers Rise 118 2C
Cootes Av. 158 4A
Copelands Cl. 62 1A
Copeman Cl. 23 4E
Copenhagen Gdns. 9 1D
Copenhagen Way 34 5A
Copenhagen Wk. 43 2D
Copers Cope Rd. 42 1A
Copleigh Dri. 72 3A
Copley Cl., Reigate 90 4A
Copley Cl., Woking 64 3A
Copley Park 22 5A
Copley Way 72 3A
Copne Cl. 14 4C
Copped Hall 22 3C
Copped Hall Dri. 45 5D
Copped Hall Way 45 5D
Copper Beech Cl. 64 4B
Copper Mill La. 20 4C
Copperfield Cl. 57 4F
Copperfield Rise 49 1D
Copperfields 69 4D
Coppermill Rd. 13 1E
Coppice Cl., Hale 96 2B
Coppice Cl., Raynes Park 37 2F
Coppice Cl., Woodbridge Hill 81 5D
Coppice Dri., Old Windsor 12 2C
Coppice Dri., Roehampton 19 1F
Coppice End 65 1F
Coppice La. 89 4E
Coppice, The 149 3E
Coppice Wk. 147 3A
Coppins, The 59 2E
Copps Field 34 2C
Copse Av., Heath End 96 1B
Copse Av., W. Wickham 42 5A
Copse Cl., Ashtead 70 2A
Copse Cl., Camberley 44 5C
Copse Cl., Chilworth 101 3E
Copse Cl., Horsham 158 3C
Copse Cres. 146 3C
Copse Edge, Burpham 82 4B
Copse Edge, Elstead 117 2D
Copse Edge Av. 54 5B
Copse End 44 5C
Copse Glade 36 4A
Copse Hill, Cottenham Park 19 5F
Copse Hill, Purley 57 5D
Copse Hill, Sutton 55 2F
Copse La. 128 2C
Copse Rd., Cobham 51 5D
Copse Rd., Hammer 151 3D
Copse Rd., Matthewsgreen 25 1D
Copse Rd., Reigate 108 1C
Copse Rd., Woking 64 2B
Copse Side 100 4A
Copse, The, Boundstone 114 2C
Copse, The, Caterham 92 1A
Copse, The, Farnborough 60 5B
Copse, The, Fetcham 69 5D
Copse, The, S. Nutfield 110 1A
Copse View 58 3C
Copse Way 114 1C
Copseel 149 3E
Copsem Dri. 52 2A
Copsem La. 52 2A
Copsleigh Av. 109 4E
Copsleigh Cl. 109 3E
Copsleigh Way 109 3E
Copthall Gdns. 17 2F
Copthall Way 49 3D
Copthill La. 72 3A
Copthorne 148 1B
Copthorne Av. 21 2F
Copthorne Bank 148 1B
Copthorne Cl. 33 3E
Copthorne Common Rd. 148 2B
Copthorne Dri. 45 3F
Copthorne Rd., Copthorne 148 2A
Copthorne Rd., Felbridge 149 1F
Copthorne Rd., Leatherhead 70 3A
Copthorne Rise 57 5F
Copthorne Way 148 2A

Copyhold Rd. 150 3B
Corbet Rd., 54 3B
Corbett Cl. 59 4E
Corbett Way 45 4E
Corby Dri. 12 5C
Cordelia Gdns. 14 2C
Cordelia Rd. 14 2C
Corderoy Pl. 32 3A
Cordrey Gdns. 74 1A
Cordwalles Rd. 44 4B
Corfe Gdns. 61 2E
Coriander Cl. 60 4A
Coriander Cres. 81 3E
Corinthian Way 14 2C
Corkran Rd. 36 4B
Corkscrew Hill 42 5B
Cormongers La. 90 5C
Cormorant Cl. 43 4E
Cornelia Cl. 60 5B
Corney Rd. 9 3E
Cornfield 100 5B
Cornfields Rd. 108 1C
Cornflower Cl. 41 4F
Cornflower La. 41 4F
Cornflower Ter. 23 1E
Cornford Gro. 21 3E
Cornhill Cl. 32 5B
Cornwall Av., Byfleet 49 5F
Cornwall Av., Claygate 52 2C
Cornwall Cl. 44 4B
Cornwall Gro. 9 2E
Cornwall Rd., Cheam 55 2E
Cornwall Rd., Croydon 40 5B
Cornwall Rd., Twickenham 17 2F
Cornwall Way 13 5F
Cornwallis Cl. 74 4C
Cornwell Rd. 12 1B
Coronation Rd., Aldershot 97 1D
Coronation Rd., East Grinstead 150 3C
Coronation Rd., South Ascot 28 4B
Coronation Square 25 2E
Coronet, The 128 3C
Corporation Rd. 41 3E
Corrib Dri. 56 1A
Corrie Gdns. 30 4C
Corrie Rd., Addlestone 49 1F
Corrie Rd., Old Woking 65 3E
Corrigan Av. 56 5B
Corry Rd. 135 4D
Corsair Cl. 14 2C
Corsair Rd. 14 2C
Corscombe Cl. 19 4D
Corsehill St. 21 5F
Corsham Way 43 1D
Cortis Rd. 19 1F
Corunna Dri. 158 5C
Cosdach Av. 56 2C
Cosedge Cres. 57 1E
Cosmur Cl. 9 1E
Coteford St. 21 4E
Cotelands 40 5C
Cotenham Dri. 19 5F
Cotford Rd. 40 2C
Cotham Cl. 20 1A
Cotheritone Rd. 54 3A
Cotherstone Rd. 22 2A
Cotland Acres 109 1D
Cotsford Av. 37 3D
Cotswold Cl., Crawley 146 4C
Cotswold Cl., Hawley 60 3B
Cotswold Cl., Kingston Hill 18 5C
Cotswold Cl., Staines 14 4A
Cotswold Rd. 55 3F
Cotswold St. 22 4B
Cottage Cl. 48 2B
Cottage Farm Way 31 2E
Cottage Gdns. 60 5C
Cottage Gro. 36 3A
Cottage Pl. 148 1C
Cottage Rd. 54 2A
Cottenham Cl. 19 5F
Cottenham Park Rd. 19 5F
Cottenhams 111 5F
Cotterill Rd. 36 5B
Cottesbrook Cl. 7 4A
Cottesmore 26 4C
Cottimore Av. 34 4A
Cottimore Cres. 34 4A
Cottimore La. 34 4A
Cottimore Ter. 34 4A
Cottingham Av. 158 2B
Cottingham Rd. 23 5F
Cottington Rd. 16 4B
Cotton Hill 24 4B
Cotton Row 123 4E
Cottswood Dri. 82 3B
Couchmore Av. 35 5E
Coulsdon 74 3A
Coulsdon Court Rd. 74 1A
Coulsdon La. 73 3E
Coulsdon Rd., Caterham 74 4C
Coulsdon Rd., Coulsdon 74 1A
Coulsdon Rise 74 2A
Coulter Rd. 9 1F
Country Way 16 4A
County Oak La. 147 2D
County Rd. 40 1B
Courland Rd. 32 5B
Course Rd. 28 2C
Court Av. 74 3B
Court Bushes Rd. 75 3D
Court Cl., Beddington 56 2C
Court Cl., Twickenham 17 3D
Court Cl. Av. 17 3D
Court Cres. 53 2D
Court Downs Rd. 42 1A
Court Dri., Carshalton 56 1A
Court Dri., Waddon 57 1D
Court Farm Av. 54 1A
Court Farm Gdns. 54 4A
Court Farm Rd. 75 2D
Court Gdns. 44 5A
Court Green Heights 64 3C
Court Haw 73 1D
Court Hill, Chipstead 73 2D
Court Hill, Sanderstead 57 4F
Court La. 23 2D
Court Lane Gdns. 23 2D
Court Lodge Rd. 128 2A
Court Rd., Banstead 72 1B
Court Rd., Caterham 74 5C
Court Rd., Godstone 92 4B
Court Rd., S. Norwood 41 2D
Court Way 17 2F
Court Wood La. 59 4D
Courtenay Rd., Cheam 38 5A
Courtenay Rd., Heath End 96 2B
Courtenay Rd., Maybury 65 1E
Courtenay Rd., Mitcham 21 5D
Courtfield Rd. 15 5E
Courtfield Rise 42 5B
Courthill Rd. 24 1B
Courthorpe Rd. 20 4A
Courthorpe Villas Rd. 20 5B
Courtland Av. 22 5A
Courtlands Av., Esher 51 2F
Courtlands Av., Hampton 16 5C
Courtlands Av., North Sheen 8 4C
Courtlands Av., West Wickham 42 4C
Courtlands Cl. 58 3A
Courtlands Cres. 72 1B
Courtlands Dri. 54 2B
Courtlands Rd. 36 4C
Courtleas 51 5F
Courtney Cres. 56 2A
Courtney Mews 65 1E
Courtney Rd. 40 5B
Courtrai Rd. 23 1F
Courts Hill Rd. 151 3F
Courts Mount Rd. 151 3F
Courts, The 22 5A
Coutts Av. 53 1E
Coval La. 8 5C
Coval Rd. 8 5C
Cove Rd. 60 5B
Coveham Cres. 51 5D
Coventry Rd. 41 2D
Coverack Cl. 41 4F
Coverdale Rd. 9 1F
Covert La. 27 2D
Covert, The, Hawley 60 3B
Covert, The, S. Ascot 28 4C
Coverton Rd. 21 4D
Coverts Rd. 52 3C
Covey Cl. 60 3C
Covington Gdns. 22 5B
Covington Way 22 5A
Cow La. 119 2D
Cowden Rd. 24 4A
Cowdray Cl. 147 4F
Cowdrey Rd. 20 4C
Cowey Cl. 146 3C
Cowfold Cl. 146 5B
Cowick Rd. 21 4E
Cowix Rd. 145 3D
Cowleaze Rd. 36 1B
Cowley Av. 32 4A
Cowley Cl., Selsdon 58 3B
Cowley Cres., Hersham 51 1E
Cowley La. 32 4A
Cowley Rd. 9 5D
Coworth Cl. 29 3F
Coworth Rd. 29 3E
Cowper Av. 56 1A
Cowper Cl. 32 3A
Cowper Gdns. 56 2C
Cowper Rd., Kingston 18 4B
Cowper Rd., Wimbledon 20 5C
Cowshot 63 4D
Cowslip Cl. 133 5E
Cowslip La. 47 5E
Cox Green, Rudgwick 157 1F
Cox Green, Sandhurst 43 5E
Cox La. 53 1F
Coxbridge Meadows 95 4F
Coxcombe La. 137 5F
Coxdean 72 3A
Coxley Dr. 57 5E
Coxwell Rd. 23 5D
Crab Hill 24 5B
Crabbet Rd. 147 3E
Crabhill La. 110 2A
Crabtree Cl. 86 1A
Crabtree Dri. 87 1D
Crabtree Gdns. 133 4F
Crabtree La., Bookham 86 1A
Crabtree La., Headley 133 4F
Crabtree Rd., Crawley 146 3C
Crabtree Rd., Frimley 60 2C
Crabtree Rd., Leatherhead 70 5A
Crabtree Rd., Thorpe 31 1E
Craddock Ac. 70 2B
Cradhurst Cl. 105 2D
Craig Rd. 18 4A
Craigen Av. 41 4E
Craigmore Tower 65 3D
Craignair Rd. 22 2A
Craignish Av. 40 1A
Craigwell Av. 16 3A
Craigwell Court 14 5A
Crail Cl. 25 3D
Crake Pl. 43 4E
Crakell Rd. 108 1C
Cramhurst La. 118 5A
Crampshaw La. 70 3B
Crampton Rd. 23 5E
Cranborne Av. 36 5C
Cranborne Wk. 147 5E
Cranbourne Cl. 128 2B
Cranbrook Dri., Esher 35 5D
Cranbrook Dri., Whitton 17 2D
Cranbrook Rd., Beulah Hill 40 1C
Cranbrook Rd., Chiswick 9 2E
Cranbrook Rd., Wimbledon 20 5A
Crane Av. 17 1F
Crane Court 54 1A
Crane Park Rd. 17 3D
Crane Rd., Twickenham 17 2E
Crane Way 17 2D
Craneford Cl. 17 2F
Craneford Way 17 2F
Cranes Dri. 36 2B
Cranes Park Av. 36 2B
Cranes Park Cres. 36 2B
Cranes Pk. 36 2B
Cranfield Rd., E. & W. 56 3B
Cranford Av. 14 2C
Cranford Cl., Purley 57 5F
Cranford Cl., Stanwell 14 2C
Cranford Cl., Wimbledon 19 5F
Cranford Rise 52 1A
Cranleigh 140 1C
Cranleigh Cl. 58 4A
Cranleigh Court 60 5C
Cranleigh Gdns., Kingston 18 5B
Cranleigh Gdns., Rose Hill 38 5C
Cranleigh Gdns., Sanderstead 58 4A
Cranleigh Mead 141 2D
Cranleigh Rd., Esher 35 4D
Cranleigh Rd., Ewhurst 141 1E
Cranleigh Rd., Felthamhill 15 4F
Cranleigh Rd., S. Merton 38 2B
Cranley Cl. 82 5B
Cranley Gdns. 56 2C
Cranley Rd., Guildford 82 5A
Cranley Rd., Weybridge 50 1C
Cranmer Av. 8 1A
Cranmer Cl., Morden 38 3A
Cranmer Cl., Warlingham 75 2F
Cranmer Cl., Weybridge 50 2A
Cranmer Gdns. 75 2F
Cranmer Rd., Hampton Hill 17 4D
Cranmer Rd., Mitcham 39 2E
Cranmer Ter. 21 4D
Cranmore La. 84 3B
Cranmore Rd., Catford 24 3C
Cranmore Rd., Mytchett 61 5F
Cranston Cl., Guildford 81 3E
Cranston Pl. 108 1C
Cranston Rd., East Grinstead 150 2C
Cranston Rd., Lewisham 23 2F
Crantock Rd. 24 3B
Cranwell Grn., Lightwater 45 4E
Cranwell Grn., Littleton 33 2D
Craster Rd. 22 2A
Cravan Av. 16 3A
Craven Cl. 115 1D
Craven Gdns. 20 4B
Craven Rd., Addiscombe 41 4E
Craven Rd., Kingston 36 1B
Cravens, The 129 2E
Crawford Gdns., Horsham 158 4C
Crawford Gdns., York Town 43 5F
Crawford Way 150 2C
Crawley 147 4D
Crawley Av. 146 3C
Crawley Down Rd. 149 1F
Crawley Dri. 44 5B
Crawley Hill 44 5B
Crawley La. 147 3F
Crawley Rd., Horsham 158 4C
Crawley Rd., Snow Hill 149 1D
Crawley Ridge 44 5B
Crawley Wood Cl. 44 5B
Crawshaw Rd. 48 2C
Cray Av. 70 2B
Crayke Hill 53 2E
Crayonne Court 33 1F
Crealock St. 20 1C
Crebor St. 23 1D
Credenhill St. 21 5F
Crediton Way 52 1C
Credon Cl. 60 4B
Creek Rd. 35 2E
Creek, The 34 3A
Creeland Gro. 24 3A
Crees Meadow 46 2A
Creighton Rd. 8 1A
Cremorne Gdns. 54 3A
Crerar Cl. 60 5B
Crescent Cl. 18 5C
Crescent Gdns., The 20 3B
Crescent Gro. 39 2D
Crescent La., Ash Vale 78 3C
Crescent La., Clapham 21 1F
Crescent Rd., Beckenham 42 1B
Crescent Rd., Bletch. 91 5E
Crescent Rd., Caterham 75 5D
Crescent Rd., East Grinstead 150 2B
Crescent Rd., Kingston Hill 18 5C
Crescent Rd., Reigate 108 1B
Crescent Rd., Shepperton 33 3E
Crescent Rd., Wimbledon 38 1A
Crescent Rd., Wokingham 25 2E
Crescent, The, Ashford 14 4C
Crescent, The, Barnes 9 4E
Crescent, The, Belmont 55 4E
Crescent, The, Earlswood 109 2D
Crescent, The, Egham 13 5D
Crescent, The, Epsom 53 5F
Crescent, The, Epsom 70 1C
Crescent, The, Felcourt 131 4E
Crescent, The, Guildford 81 5E
Crescent, The, Heath End 96 1B
Crescent, The, Horley 128 3B
Crescent, The, Horsham 158 5A
Crescent, The, Kingston 37 2D
Crescent, The, Leatherh'd 70 4A
Crescent, The, Parklangley 42 3C
Crescent, The, Reigate 89 5F
Crescent, The, Selhurst 40 3C
Crescent, The, Streatham 22 5A
Crescent, The, Surbiton 36 3B
Crescent, The, Sutton 55 1F
Crescent, The, Weybridge 33 5D
Crescent, The, Wimbledon Park 20 3B
Crescent, The, W. Molesey 34 2C
Crescent, The, Woldingham 76 5A
Crescent Way 128 3B
Crescent Wood Rd. 23 3D
Cressall Cl. 70 3A
Cressall Mead 70 3A
Cressingham Grn. 55 1F
Cresswell Rd., Richmond 18 1A
Cresswell Rd., South Norwood 41 2D
Crest Rd., Croham Hurst 58 2B
Crest Rd., West Wickham 42 4C
Crest, The 36 3C
Cresta Dri. 49 3D
Creston Av 64 2A
Creston Way 38 5A
Crestway 19 1F
Creswell Rd. 16 4B
Crewdson Rd. 128 2B
Crewe's Av. 75 1E
Crewe's Cl. 75 1E
Crewe's La. 75 1E
Crichton Av. 56 1C
Crichton Rd. 56 2A
Cricket Field Gr. 43 2E
Cricket Green 39 2D
Cricket Hill 110 1A
Cricket La., Beckenham 23 5F
Cricket La., Lower Bourne 115 1E
Cricket Lea 133 4D
Cricket Way 33 5F
Cricketers Cl., Capel 143 1E
Cricketers Cl., Hook 53 1D
Cricketers La. 46 1A
Cricketfield Rd. 158 5A
Cricklade Av. 22 3A
Crieff Court 18 5A
Crieff Rd. 20 1C
Criffel Av. 22 2A
Crimea Rd., Deepcut 62 3A
Crimp Hill Rd. 12 2B
Cripley Rd. 60 4B
Cripplecrutch Hill 153 4E
Crisp Rd. 9 2F
Crispin Cl. 70 2C
Crispin Cres. 39 5F
Critchmere Hill 151 2E
Critchmere La. 151 3E
Critchmere Vale 151 3E
Critten La. 85 5E
Crockers La., Coldharbour 124 1B
Crockers La., New Chapel 130 2C

Crockerton Rd.	21	3D
Crockery La.	83	3F
Crockford Cl.	49	1E
Crockford Park Rd.	49	1E
Crockham Cl.	146	5C
Crocknorth Rd.	85	5D
Croffets	72	4A
Croft Av., Dorking	87	5D
Croft Av., W. Wickham	42	4B
Croft Cl., Chiddingfold	137	4F
Croft Cl., Eastheath	25	4D
Croft Rd., Aldershot	97	1D
Croft Rd., Carshalton	56	1A
Croft Rd., Godalming	119	2D
Croft Rd., South Wimbledon	20	5C
Croft Rd., Upper Norwood	22	5B
Croft Rd., Wheeler St.	118	5A
Croft Rd., Woldingham	76	4A
Croft Sq.	9	2E
Croft, The	146	4B
Croft Way, Frimley	61	2E
Croft Way, Horsham	158	4A
Crofters Cl.	17	1E
Crofters Mead	59	3D
Crofters, The	12	1B
Croftleigh Av.	74	1B
Crofton Av., Walton-on-Thames	34	5A
Crofton Ave., Chiswick	9	3D
Crofton Cl., Bracknell	27	3E
Crofton Cl., Ottershaw	48	2B
Crofton Gate Way	23	1F
Crofton Park Rd.	24	1A
Crofton Ter.	8	5B
Crofts, The	33	2F
Croham Cl.	57	2F
Croham Manor Rd.	58	2A
Croham Mount	57	2F
Croham Park Av.	58	1A
Croham Rd.	58	1A
Croham Valley Rd.	58	2A
Cromer Court	64	1C
Cromer Rd., Norwood	41	2E
Cromer Rd., Tooting	21	5E
Cromford Rd.	20	1B
Cromford Way	37	1D
Crompton Way	147	2D
Cromwell Av.	37	3E
Cromwell Cl.	34	4A
Cromwell Gro.	74	4C
Cromwell Pl.	141	2D
Cromwell Rd., Ascot	28	2C
Cromwell Rd., Camberley	44	4A
Cromwell Rd., Caterham	74	4C
Cromwell Rd., Elmers End	41	1F
Cromwell Rd., Feltham	16	2A
Cromwell Rd., Hounslow	16	1C
Cromwell Rd., Kingston	36	1B
Cromwell Rd., Redhill	90	5A
Cromwell Rd., Teddington	17	5F
Cromwell Rd., Walton-on-Thames	34	4A
Cromwell Rd., Wimbledon	20	4B
Cromwell Rd., Worcester Park	37	5D
Cromwell Way	61	3D
Crondall La.	95	3D
Crondall Rd.	114	1A
Cronks Hill	108	1C
Cronkshill Cl.	109	1D
Cronkshill Rd.	109	1D
Crooksbury Rd.	97	3D
Crosby Cl.	16	4B
Crosby Hill Dri.	44	4B
Crosby Walk	22	2B
Cross Acres	66	1A
Cross Deep	17	3F
Cross Deep Gdns.	17	3F
Cross Fell	26	2C
Cross Gdns.	61	4E
Cross La., Burstow	129	4E
Cross La., Frimley	61	4E
Cross La., Green Cross	135	3D
Cross La., Ottershaw	48	2B
Cross Lanes	101	1D
Cross Rd., Ash Hill	78	4C
Cross Rd., Belmont	55	3E
Cross Rd., Carshalton	56	1A
Cross Rd., Croydon	40	4C
Cross Rd., Hanworth	16	4C
Cross Rd., Purley	57	5E
Cross Rd., Sunningdale	29	4E
Cross Rd., Tadworth	71	4F
Cross Rd., Wimbledon	20	5B
Cross St., Barnes	9	4E
Cross St., Hampton Hill	17	4D
Cross St., South Farnborough	78	2A
Cross St., Wokingham	25	2E
Cross Ways	78	5A
Cross Ways, The	90	3C
Crossfield Pl.	50	2A
Crossgates Cl.	27	2E
Crosskeys	147	4D
Crossland Rd., Redhill	90	5B

Crossland Rd., Thornton Heath	40	3B
Crosslands	48	1C
Crosslands Rd.	54	2A
Crossley Cl.	77	1E
Crossoak La.	109	5E
Crosspath	147	3D
Crossroads, The	85	2E
Crosswater La.	134	1B
Crossway, Raynes Park	37	2F
Crossway, Walton-on-Thames	34	5A
Crossway Rd.	135	5D
Crossways, Addington	58	2C
Crossways, Ashford	15	5F
Crossways, Carshalton Beeches	56	3A
Crossways, Tatsfield	77	3E
Crossways, Thorpe Lea	13	5F
Crossways, Three Bridges	147	3E
Crossways, Tolworth	36	4C
Crossways Av.	150	2B
Crossways Cl.	147	3E
Crossways La.	89	2F
Crossways Rd., Beckenham	42	2A
Crossways Rd., Grayshott	135	5D
Crossways Rd., Mitcham	39	2E
Crossways, The	74	3A
Crosswell Cl.	33	2E
Crouch La.	10	2B
Crouch Oak La.	49	1E
Crowborough Cl. & Dri.	75	2F
Crowborough Rd.	21	5E
Crowhurst Cl.	148	4A
Crowhurst Keep	148	4A
Crowhurst La.	112	2B
Crowhurst Mead	92	3B
Crowhurst Rd.	112	5B
Crowhurst Village Rd.	112	4C
Crowland Wk.	38	3C
Crowley Cres.	57	1E
Crown Cl.	34	4A
Crown Dale	22	4B
Crown Heights	101	2D
Crown Hill	40	5B
Crown La., Badshot Lea	96	2C
Crown La., Morden	38	2B
Crown La., Virginia Wat.	30	3C
Crown La., West Norwood	22	4B
Crown Pl.	43	3E
Crown Rd., Croydon	40	4C
Crown Rd., Malden	37	1D
Crown Rd., Morden	38	2B
Crown Rd., Richmond	18	1A
Crown Rd., Sutton	55	1E
Crown Rd., Virginia Water	30	3C
Crown Row	27	3E
Crown St.	13	4D
Crown Ter.	8	5B
Crownpits La.	119	2D
Crownstone Rd.	22	1A
Crowther Av.	8	2B
Crowther Rd.	41	2D
Crowthorne	43	2D
Crowthorne, Southfields	20	2B
Crowthorne Rd., Easthampstead	26	3C
Crowthorne Rd., Long Down	43	4D
Crowthorne Rd. North	27	2D
Croxden Wk.	38	3C
Croxted Rd.	22	1B
Croyde Cl.	60	4C
Croydon	40	5B
Croydon La.	55	5F
Croydon Rd., Anerley	41	1E
Croydon Rd., Beckenham	42	1A
Croydon Rd., Caterham	75	5D
Croydon Rd., Mitcham	39	2E
Croydon Rd., Reigate	89	5F
Croydon Rd., Tatsfield	77	5F
Croydon Rd., Waddon	57	1D
Croydon Rd., Wallington	56	1B
Croydon Rd., West Wickham	42	5C
Croydonbarn La.	130	2A
Croysdale Av.	34	2A
Crozier Dri.	58	3B
Cruckshank Lea	43	5E
Crunden Rd.	57	2F
Crusoe Rd.	21	5D
Crutchfield La., Hookwood	127	1E
Crutchfierld La., Walton	34	5A
Crutchley Rd., Catford	24	3C
Crutchley Rd., Wokingham	25	1E
Crystal Palace Parade	23	5D
Crystal Palace Park Rd.	23	4D
Crystal Palace Rd.	23	1D
Crystal Palace Sta. Rd.	23	5D
Crystal Terr.	22	5C
Cubitt St.	57	1D
Cuckfield Cl.	146	5B
Cuckmere Cres.	146	4B
Cuckoo La.	46	5A
Cuckoo Pound	33	3F
Cuckoo Vale	46	5A

Cudas Cl.	54	1B
Cuddington Av.	37	5E
Cuddington Cl.	72	3A
Cuddington Way	55	4D
Cudham Cl.	55	3E
Cudham Dri.	59	4E
Cudham Rd.	77	3F
Cudworth La.	126	3A
Cullerne Cl.	54	3B
Cull's Rd.	79	5F
Culmington Rd., Lammas Park	8	1A
Culmington Rd., South Croydon	57	2E
Culmstock Rd.	21	1E
Culsac Rd.	36	5B
Culver Dri.	93	3F
Culver Rd.	43	3E
Culverden Rd.	21	3F
Culverden Terr.	33	5F
Culverhay	70	1B
Culverhouse Gdns.	22	3A
Culverlands Cres.	78	4C
Culverley Rd.	24	2A
Culvers Av.	39	5D
Culvers Retreat	39	5E
Culvers Way	39	5D
Culverstone Cl.	42	3C
Cumberland Av., South Norwood	41	2D
Cumberland Av., Stoughton	81	3E
Cumberland Cl.	54	3A
Cumberland Dri.	27	1E
Cumberland Dri., Hinchley Wood	35	5F
Cumberland Dri., Hook	36	5B
Cumberland Pl., Catford	24	2C
Cumberland Pl., Sunbury	34	2A
Cumberland Pl., Wimbledon	20	5A
Cumberland Rd., Barnes	9	4E
Cumberland Rd., Camberley	62	1A
Cumberland Rd., Kew	8	3C
Cumberland Rd., Shortlands	42	2C
Cumberland Rd., Staines	14	3C
Cumberland Rd., Woodside	41	3E
Cumberland St.	13	4F
Cumberlands	74	1C
Cumbernauld Gdns.	15	4F
Cumbrae Gdns.	36	4A
Cumnor Gdns.	54	2C
Cumnor Rd.	55	2F
Cumnor Rise	74	2C
Cumnor Way	27	2E
Cunliffe Cl.	70	5C
Cunliffe Rd.	54	1B
Cunliffe St.	21	5F
Cunningham Av.	82	5B
Cunningham Cl.	42	5A
Cunningham Rd.	72	1C
Cunnington Rd.	78	1B
Cunnington St.	9	2D
Cunworth Cl.	26	3B
Curfew Bell Rd.	32	4A
Curl Way	25	2D
Curlew Cl.	58	4C
Curlew Gdns.	82	4C
Curleyhill Rd.	45	4E
Curling Cl.	74	3A
Curling Vale	100	1B
Curran Av.	39	5E
Currie Hill Cl.	20	4B
Curtis Cl.	133	4F
Curtis Field Rd.	22	4A
Curtis Gdns.	105	1F
Curtis La.	133	4E
Curtis Rd., Dorking	105	1F
Curtis Rd., West Ewell	54	1A
Curtis Rd., Whitton	16	2C
Curvan Cl.	54	3B
Curwen Rd.	9	1E
Curzon Av.	158	4A
Curzon Cl.	50	1A
Curzon Rd., Thornton Heath	40	3A
Curzon Rd., Weybridge	50	1A
Cusack Cl.	17	4E
Cuthbert Gdns.	40	2C
Cuthbert Rd., Ash Vale	78	3C
Cuthbert Rd., Croydon	40	5B
Cutmill La.	98	5B
Cutt Mill Rd.	117	1E
Cutting, The	109	1D
Cuttinglye Rd.	149	2E
Cutts Rd.	78	2A
Cyclamen Way	54	1A
Cygnet Av.	16	2B
Cygnet Cl.	64	1B
Cypress Av.	17	2O
Cypress Cl.	25	5D
Cypress Cres.	78	2C
Cypress Rd., Guildford	81	4F
Cypress Rd., Norwood	41	1D
Cypress Walk, Englefield Gn.	12	5C

Cypress Way, Banstead	55	5D
Cypress Way, Nutcombe	151	1E
Cyprus Row	33	1F

D

D'Abernon Chase	69	1F
D'Abernon Cl.	52	1A
D'Abernon Dri.	68	2B
Dacre Rd.	40	4A
Dacres Rd.	23	3F
Daffodil Cl.	41	4F
Daffodil Dri.	63	1E
Dafforne Rd.	21	3E
Dagden Rd.	101	3D
Dagley La.	100	3C
Dagmar Rd.	18	5C
Dagnall Pk.	40	3C
Dagnan Rd.	21	1F
Dahlia Gdns.	39	2F
Dahomey Rd.	21	5F
Daimler Way	57	2D
Dainford Cl.	24	4B
Dairy Cl.	40	1C
Dairymans Wk.	82	3B
Daisy Cl.	41	4F
Dakins, The	150	3C
Dalberg Rd.	22	1B
Dalcross	27	3E
Dale Cl., Addlestone	49	1E
Dale Cl., Horsham	158	3C
Dale Cl., Sunningdale	29	3E
Dale Park Av.	39	5E
Dale Park Rd.	40	1C
Dale Rd., Cheam	55	1E
Dale Rd., Purley	57	4E
Dale Rd., Sunbury	15	5F
Dale Rd., Walton	33	4F
Dale St.	9	2D
Dale View, Camelsdale	151	3F
Dale View, Headley Park	70	5C
Dale View, Woking	64	2B
Dalebury Rd.	21	3D
Dalegarth Gdns.	57	5F
Daleham Av.	13	5D
Dalekeith Rd.	22	2C
Daleside Rd., Ewell	54	2A
Daleside Rd., Tooting Bec	21	4E
Dalewood Gdns.	37	5F
Dallas Rd., Cheam	55	2D
Dallas Rd., Upper Sydenham	23	3E
Dallaway Gdns.	150	2C
Dalling Rd.	9	1F
Dallinger Rd.	24	1C
Dallington Cl.	51	2E
Dalmain Rd.	23	2F
Dalmally Rd.	41	4D
Dalmeny Av.	40	1B
Dalmeny Rd., Carshalton on the Hill	56	2B
Dalmeny Rd., Worc. Pk.	37	5F
Dalmore Av.	52	2B
Dalmore Rd.	22	3C
Dalston Cl.	62	1A
Dalton Av.	39	1D
Dalton Cl.	57	4F
Dalton St.	22	3B
Damask Cl.	46	5A
Danbrook Rd.	22	5A
Dancer Rd.	8	5C
Dane Court	49	5D
Dane Gdns.	41	5D
Dane Rd., Ashford	15	5E
Dane Rd., Warlingham	75	2E
Dane Rd., Wimbledon	38	1C
Danebury Av.	19	1E
Danebury Walk	61	3E
Daneby Rd.	24	3B
Danecroft Rd.	22	1C
Danehurst Cres.	158	5C
Danemore La.	111	4F
Danes Cl.	52	5A
Danes Hill	65	2E
Danesbury	59	2E
Danesbury Rd.	16	2A
Danescourt Cres.	38	5C
Daneshill	90	5A
Daneshill Cl.	90	5A
Danesway	52	5B
Daneswood Av.	24	3B
Daneswood Cl.	50	1B
Danetree Cl.	54	2B
Danetree Rd.	54	2A
Daniel Way	55	5E
Daniels La.	76	1A
Danses Cl.	82	4C
Dapdune Rd.	81	5F
Daphne St.	20	1C
Darby Cl.	74	4C
Darby Cres.	34	2B
Darby Gdns.	34	1B
Darby Green La.	43	5D
Darby Green Rd.	43	5D
D'Arcy Av.	56	1C
D'Arcy Cl.	70	2B

D'Arcy Rd., Ashtead 70 2B
D'Arcy Rd., Cheam 55 1D
Darcy Cl. 74 3B
Darcy Rd., Norbury 40 1A
Darell Rd. 8 5C
Darenth Way 128 1B
Darfield Rd., Guildford 82 4B
Darfield Rd., Lewisham 23 1F
Darfold Rd. 24 1A
Dark La., Putenham 98 3C
Dark La., Windlesham 45 2F
Darkhole Ride 10 1C
Darlaston Rd. 20 5A
Darley Cl., Addlestone 49 1E
Darley Cl., Croydon 41 3F
Darley Dri. 37 1D
Darley Gdns. 38 3C
Darleydale 146 5C
Darleydale Cl. 43 3E
Darlington Rd. 22 4B
Darnley Pk. 33 5D
Darrell Rd. 23 1D
Dart Rd. 60 4B
Dartmouth Av. 48 5C
Dartmouth Cl. 27 2E
Dartmouth Grn. 48 5C
Dartmouth Pl. 9 3E
Dartmouth Rd. 23 3E
Dartnell Av. 49 4E
Dartnell Cl. 49 4E
Dartnell Cres. 49 4E
Dartnell Park Rd. 49 4E
Dartnell Pl. 49 4E
Dartnell Rd. 41 4D
Darvel Cl. 64 1B
Darvills La. 96 4B
Darwell Dri. 28 1A
Darwin Cl. 158 4C
Darwin Grove 78 4A
Darwin Rd. 8 2A
Daryngton Dri. 82 5B
Dashwood Cl., Bracknell 27 1D
Dashwood Cl., Byfleet 49 4E
Dassett Rd. 22 4B
Datchet Rd. 24 3A
Dault Rd. 20 1C
Daux Hill 158 2A
Davell Cl. 64 1B
Davenport Cl. 17 5F
Davenport Rd., Bullbrook 27 1E
Davenport Rd., Hither Grn. 24 1B
Daventry Cl. 7 4B
Daventry Court. 27 1D
David Rd. 7 4B
Davids Rd. 23 2E
Davidson Rd. 41 4D
Davies Cl., Croydon 41 3D
Davies Cl., Godalming 100 5A
Davies Way 13 4F
Davis Gdns. 43 4E
Davis Rd., Chessington 53 1F
Davis Rd., Hammersmith 9 1E
Davisville Rd. 9 1E
Davos Cl. 65 3D
Davy Cl. 25 2D
Dawell Dri. 77 2E
Dawes Av. 17 1F
Dawley Ride 7 4A
Dawlish Av. 20 3C
Dawnay Rd. 20 3C
Dawnay Rd., Camberley 44 4A
Dawnay Rd., Gt. Bookham 86 1A
Dawney Gdns. 20 3C
Dawney Hill 63 4E
Dawney Rd. 63 4D
Dawsmere Cl. 45 5D
Dawson Rd., Byfleet 49 4F
Dawson Rd., Kingston 36 2B
Day Spring 81 3E
Daybrook Rd. 38 1C
Daylesford Av. 9 5E
Daymerselea Ridge 70 4A
Day's Acre 58 3A
Daysbrook Rd. 22 2A
Dayseys Hill 110 5B
De Burgh Pk. 72 1C
De Haviland Way 14 1C
De Havilland Dri. 49 4F
De Havilland Rd. 57 2D
De La Mere Rd. 8 1B
De La Warr Rd. 150 2C
De Montfort Rd. 22 3A
De Ros Pl. 13 5E
Deacon Cl., Downside 68 3A
Deacon Cl., Purley 57 3D
Deacon Cl., Wokingham 25 1E
Deacon Fld. 81 5E
Deacon Rd. 36 1B
Deacons Court 131 2E
Deadbrook La. 78 4B
Deadwater Rd. 133 5D
Deal Rd. 21 5E
Dean Cl., Woking 65 1F
Dean Gr. 25 1E
Dean La. 73 5F
Dean Lane Pk. 73 4F
Dean Rd., Croydon 57 1F
Dean Rd., Godalming 119 1D
Dean Rd., Hanworth 16 4C
Dean Rd., Whitton 17 1D
Dean Walk 86 1A
Deanery Rd. 119 1D
Deanoak La. 108 5A
Deans Cl., Croydon 41 5D
Deans Cl., Tadworth 71 4F
Deans Court 46 2A
Deans La. 88 1C
Deans Rd., Merstham 90 3C
Deans Rd., Sutton 38 5C
Dean's Walk 74 2B
Deansfield 92 1A
Deansgate Cl. 23 3F
Dearn Gdns. 39 2D
Deburgh Rd. 20 5C
Dedisham Cl. 147 4E
Dedswell Dri. 83 3D
Dee Way 54 3B
Deedman Cl. 78 5C
Deep Pool 47 5E
Deepcut 62 4A
Deepcut Bridge Rd. 62 4A
Deepdale, Bracknell 26 2C
Deepdale, Wimbledon 20 4A
Deepdale Av. 42 3C
Deepdene, Lower Bourne 115 1E
Deepdene, Shottermill 151 2E
Deepdene Av., Croydon 41 5D
Deepdene Av., Dorking 106 1A
Deepdene Avenue Rd. 87 5D
Deepdene Dri. 106 1A
Deepdene Gdns., Dorking 106 1A
Deepdene Gdns., Tulse Hill 22 2A
Deepdene Park Rd. 106 1A
Deepdene Vale 87 5D
Deepdene Wood 106 1A
Deepfield Rd. 27 1D
Deepfield Way 74 1A
Deepfields 128 1B
Deeprock Hill 27 3D
Deepwell Dri. 44 5B
Deer Barn Rd. 81 5E
Deer Leap 45 4F
Deer Park 42 5C
Deer Park Cl. 18 5C
Deer Park Gdns. 39 2D
Deer Park Rd. 38 1C
Deer Rock Rd. 44 4B
Deerbrook Rd. 22 2B
Deerhurst Rd. 22 4A
Deering Rd. 89 5F
Deerleap Rd. 105 2D
Deers Farm Cl. 66 1C
Deerswood Cl. 146 3C
Deerswood Rd. 146 3C
Deeside Rd. 20 3C
Defiant Way 57 2D
Defoe Av. 8 3C
Defoe Cl. 21 5D
Defrene Rd. 23 4F
Dekker Rd. 22 1C
Delabole Rd. 91 2D
Delamare Cres. 41 3E
Delamere Rd., Raynes Park 38 1A
Delamere Rd., Reigate 108 2C
Delara Way 64 2C
Delawyk Cres. 22 1C
Delcombe Av. 37 4F
Delderfield 70 4B
Delia St. 20 2C
Dell Cl., Fetcham 69 5E
Dell Cl., Mickleham 87 2D
Dell Cl., Shottermill 151 2F
Dell Cl., Sutton 56 1C
Dell Gro. 61 2F
Dell La. 54 1B
Dell Rd., Stoneleigh 54 2C
Dell, The, Brentford 8 3A
Dell, The, Feltham 16 2A
Dell, The, Goldsworth 64 3C
Dell, The, Horley 128 2B
Dell, The, Reigate 89 5E
Dell, The, Tadworth 72 4A
Dell Walk 37 1E
Dellbow Rd. 16 1A
Delmey Cl. 41 5D
Delta Cl., Chobham 47 3D
Delta Cl., Worcester Pk. 37 5E
Delta Dri. 128 3B
Delta Rd., Chobham 47 3D
Delta Rd., Woking 65 1E
Delta Rd., Worcester Park 37 5E
Delta Way 31 1F
Delves 72 4A
Delville Cl. 60 5B
Demesne Rd. 56 1C
Dempster Cl. 36 4A
Dempster Rd. 20 1C
Den Cl. 42 2B
Den Rd. 42 2B
Denbigh Cl. 55 1E
Denbigh Gdns. 18 1B
Denbigh Rd, * 152 3A
Denby Rd. 51 5D
Denchers Plat 146 2C
Dendy St. 21 2E
Dene Cl., Haslemere 152 3A
Dene Cl., Hayes 42 4C
Dene Cl., Horley 128 2A
Dene Cl., Lower Bourne 115 1E
Dene Cl., Worcester Pk. 37 5E
Dene Gdns. 35 5F
Dene Lane 115 1E
Dene Lane West 115 1E
Dene Pl. 64 2C
Dene Rd., Ashtead 70 3B
Dene Rd., Farnborough 60 5C
Dene Rd., Guildford 101 1D
Dene St. 106 1A
Dene Street Gdns. 106 1A
Dene, The, Abinger 104 3A
Dene, The, Belmont 55 4E
Dene, The, Shirley 58 1C
Dene, The, W. Molesey 34 3C
Dene Tye 147 3F
Dene Wk. 115 1E
Denefield Dri. 74 1C
Denehurst Gdns., North Sheen 8 5C
Denehurst Gdns., Twickenham 17 2E
Denfield 106 2A
Denham Cres. 39 2D
Denham Gro. 27 3D
Denham Rd., Egham 13 4E
Denham Rd., Epsom 54 4B
Denham Rd., Feltham 16 2B
Denholm Gdns. 82 4B
Denison Rd. 15 4F
Denistoun Cl. 44 5B
Denleigh Gdns. 35 3E
Denley Way 45 3F
Denman Dri., Ashford 15 5D
Denman Dri., Claygate 52 1C
Denmark Av. 20 5A
Denmark Gdns. 39 5E
Denmark Rd., Guildford 101 1D
Denmark Rd., Hackbridge 39 5E
Denmark Rd., Kingston 36 2B
Denmark Rd., Norwood 41 3E
Denmark Rd., Twickenham 17 3E
Denmark Rd., Wimbledon 20 5A
Denmark St., Aldershot 78 5B
Denmark St., Wokingham 25 2D
Denmark Sq. 78 5B
Denmead Court 27 3E
Denmead Rd. 40 4B
Dennan Rd. 36 4B
Denne Parade 158 5B
Denne Rd., Horsham 158 5B
Denne Rd., West Green 146 4C
Dennett Rd. 40 4B
Denning Av. 57 1E
Denning Cl. 16 4C
Denningtons, The 37 5E
Denningtons, The 37 5E
Dennis Cl., Redhill 90 4A
Dennis Cl., Sunbury 15 5E
Dennis Park Cres. 38 1A
Dennis Rd. 35 2D
Dennison Rd. 21 5D
Denton Cl. 109 3E
Denton Gro. 34 5B
Denton Rd., Richmond 18 1A
Denton Rd., Wokingham 25 2E
Denton St. 20 1C
Denton Way, Frimley 61 2E
Denton Way, Knaphill 64 2B
Dents Grn. 89 2E
Dents Rd. 21 1D
Denvale Walk 64 2B
Denzil Rd. 100 1C
Depot Rd., Epsom 54 5B
Depot Rd., Horsham 158 5C
Depot Rd., Northgate 147 2D
Derby Arms Rd. 71 2E
Derby Cl. 71 3F
Derby Hill 23 3E
Derby Hill Cres. 23 3E
Derby Rd., Cheam 55 2E
Derby Rd., Croydon 40 4B
Derby Rd., Guildford 81 5D
Derby Rd., Haslemere 152 2A
Derby Rd., North Sheen 8 5C
Derby Rd., Tolworth 36 4C
Derby Rd., Wimbledon 20 5B
Derby Stables Rd. 71 2B
Derek Av., Wallington 56 1B
Derek Av., West Ewell 53 2F
Derek Cl. 53 1F
Derek Horn Court 44 5A
Deridene Cl. 14 1C
Dering Pl. 57 1E
Dering Rd. 57 1F
Derinton Rd. 21 4E
Dermody Rd. 24 1B
Dernhurst Cl. 16 4A
Deronda Rd. 22 2B
Deroy Cl. 56 2A
Derrick Av. 57 3F
Derrick Rd. 41 2F
Derry Rd., Hawley 60 3C
Derry Rd., Waddon 40 5A
Derrydown 64 4C
Derwent Av., Ash Wharf 78 4C
Derwent Av., Kingston Vale 19 4D
Derwent Cl., Addlestone 49 1F
Derwent Cl., Claygate 52 2B
Derwent Cl., Crawley 146 4B
Derwent Cl., Hook 15 2F
Derwent Cl., Upper Hale 96 2A
Derwent Cl., W. H'th. 60 5B
Derwent Dri. 57 5F
Derwent Quadrant 78 4C
Derwent Rd., Anerley 41 1E
Derwent Rd., Egham 13 5E
Derwent Rd., Lammas Park 8 1A
Derwent Rd., Lightwater 45 4F
Derwent Rd., Whitton 17 1D
Desborough Cl. 33 4D
Desenfans Rd. 22 1C
Desford Way 15 3D
Dessington Av. 24 1A
Detillens La. 94 3A
Devas Rd. 38 1A
Devenish La. 29 4D
Devenish Rd. 29 4D
Devereux Rd. 21 1E
Devil's Highway, The, Broadmoor 43 1F
Devil's Highway, The, Rapley Lake 44 1C
Devil's La. 13 5F
De-Vitre Gn. 25 1F
Devitt Cl. 70 1C
Devoil Cl. 82 3B
Devoke Way 34 5B
Devon Av. 17 2D
Devon Bank 100 2C
Devon Cl., Kenley 75 1D
Devon Cl., Sandhurst 43 4E
Devon Cres. 90 5A
Devon Rd., Ewell 55 3D
Devon Rd., Hersham 51 1E
Devon Rd., South Merstham 90 3C
Devon Way, Hook 53 1D
Devon Way, West Ewell 53 1F
Devonport Rd. 9 1F
Devonshire Av., Sheerwater 48 5C
Devonshire Av., Sutton 55 2F
Devonshire Cl. 44 4C
Devonshire Dri., Long Ditton 36 4A
Devonshire Gdns. 9 3D
Devonshire Pl. 9 2D
Devonshire Rd., Carshalton 56 1B
Devonshire Rd., Chiswick 9 2D
Devonshire Rd., Croydon 40 4C
Devonshire Rd., Forest Hill 23 2E
Devonshire Rd., Hanworth 16 4C
Devonshire Rd., Horsham 158 5B
Devonshire Rd., Lammas Park 8 1A
Devonshire Rd., Sutton 55 2F
Devonshire Rd., Tooting 21 5D
Devonshire Rd., Weybridge 50 1A
Devonshire St. 9 2E
Devonshire Way 42 5A
Dewey St. 21 4D
Dewlands 92 4B
Dewsbury Gdns. 37 5E
Dexter Drive 150 3C
Diamedes Av. 14 2C
Diamedes Cres. 14 2C
Diamond Hill 44 4B
Diamond Ridge 44 4B
Diana Gdns. 36 5B
Dianthus Cl. 31 4F
Dianthus Court 64 3C
Dibdin Cl. 38 5B
Dibdin Rd. 38 5B
Diceland Rd. 72 1B
Dickens Cl., E. Grinstead 150 2B
Dickens Cl., Petersham 18 3B
Dickens Dri. 49 2D
Dickens Rd. 147 5D
Dickenson Rd. 16 4B
Dickensons La. 41 3D
Dickerage La. 37 2D
Dickerage Rd. 37 1D
Digby Pl. 41 5D
Digdens Rise 71 1D
Dillwyn Cl. 23 4F
Dillwyn Rd. 23 4F
Dilston Rd. 69 3F
Dilton Gdns. 19 2F
Dingle Rd. 15 4D
Dingle, The 146 3C
Dingley La. 21 3F
Dingwall Av. 40 5C
Dingwall Rd., Carshalton Beeches 56 3A
Dingwall Rd., Croydon 40 5C
Dingwall Rd., Earlsfield 20 2C
Dinsdale Cl. 65 2D
Dinsdale Gdns. 41 3D
Dinsmore Rd. 21 2E

179
Dinton Rd
Dundee Rd

Dinton Rd., Kingston 18 5B
Dinton Rd., Mitcham 21 5D
Dippenhall Rd. 95 4E
Dirdene Cl. 54 4B
Dirdene Gdns. 54 4B
Dirdene Gro. 54 4B
Dirtham La. 85 3D
Ditches La. 74 4A
Ditchling 26 4C
Ditchling Hill 146 5C
Ditton Cl. 35 4F
Ditton Grange Cl. 36 4A
Ditton Grange Dri. 36 4A
Ditton Hill 36 4A
Ditton Hill Rd. 36 4A
Ditton Lawn 35 4F
Ditton Pl. 41 1E
Ditton Rd. 36 4B
Ditton Reach 36 3A
Divis Way 19 1F
Dixon Pl. 42 4A
Dixon Rd. 41 2D
Dobbins Pl. 146 4A
Dobson Rd. 147 2D
Dock Rd. 8 3A
Dockenfield 114 5B
Dockenfield St. 114 5C
Dockett Eddy La. 32 4C
Doctors Cl. 23 4E
Doctors La. 74 5A
Dodbroke Rd. 22 3B
Dodd's Cres. 49 5E
Dodd's La. 49 5E
Dodds Park Rd. 107 1D
Dogflud Way 96 3A
Doggett Rd. 24 2A
Doghurst La. 73 3D
Dollis Cl. 147 4F
Dolman Rd. 9 2D
Dolphin Cl., Kingston 36 3B
Dolphin Cl., Shottermill 151 3E
Dolphin Court 14 3A
Dolphin Rd. 33 1F
Dolphin Rd., N. 33 1F
Dolphin Rd., S. 33 1F
Dolphin Rd., W. 33 1F
Dolphin St., Kingston 36 1B
Dolus Dri. 96 3B
Doman Rd. 60 1C
Dome Hill 91 2F
Dome Hill Peak 91 1F
Dome Way 90 5A
Domehill Pk. 23 4D
Domewood 130 5A
Dominion Rd. 41 4D
Donald Rd. 40 3A
Doncaster Wk. 147 5E
Doncastle Rd. 26 2B
Donington Cl. 61 1D
Donkey Alley 23 2E
Donkey La. 128 4C
Donne Cl. 147 3F
Donne Gdns. 65 1F
Donnington Rd. 37 5F
Donnybrook 26 4C
Donnybrook Rd. 21 5F
Donovan Cl. 54 3A
Doods Park Rd. 89 5F
Doods Rd. 89 5F
Doods Way 89 5F
Dora Rd. 20 4B
Doran Dri. 90 5A
Dora's Green La. 95 3E
Dorchester Court 65 1E
Dorchester Dri., East Bedfont 15 1F
Dorchester Dri., Herne Hill 22 1B
Dorchester Gro. 9 3E
Dorchester Rd., Cheam 38 4A
Dorchester Rd., St. Helier 38 4C
Dorchester Rd., Weybridge 33 5D
Dore Gdns. 38 4C
Doreen Cl. 60 3B
Doric Dri. 72 3B
Dorien Rd. 38 1A
Dorincourt 65 1F
Doris Rd. 15 5E
Dorking 105 1F
Dorking Business Park 105 1F
Dorking By-Pass 106 3A
Dorking Cl. 38 5A
Dorking Rd., Chilworth 101 3F
Dorking Rd., Epsom 54 5A
Dorking Rd., Gomshall 103 3E
Dorking Rd., Gt. Bookham 86 1A
Dorking Rd., Kingsfold 144 5A
Dorking Rd., Leatherhead 70 5A
Dorking Rd., Mickleham 87 1D
Dorking Rd., Pebble Coombe 88 2B
Dorking Rd., Tadworth 72 5A
Dorking Rd., Westcott 105 2D
Dorlcote Rd. 21 2D
Dorlectote 118 5A
Dorling Dri. 54 4B
Dorly Cl. 33 3F
Dormans 146 5B
Dormans Av. 132 3A
Dormans Cl. 132 4A
Dormans Gdns. 131 5F
Dormans Land 132 3A
Dormans Mark 131 5F
Dormans Park Rd., Dormans Park 131 4F
Dormans Park Rd., E. Grinstead 150 1B
Dormans Rd. 132 3A
Dormay St. 20 1B
Dormers Cl. 119 1D
Dorney Gro. 33 5D
Dorney Way 16 1C
Dornford Gdns. 74 3B
Dornton Rd., Selsdon 57 2F
Dornton Rd., Tooting Bec 21 3F
Dorrington Court 40 1C
Dorrit Cres. 81 4D
Dorset Av. 150 1B
Dorset Court. 44 4B
Dorset Dri. 65 2E
Dorset Gdns. 150 1B
Dorset Rd., Ashford 14 3C
Dorset Rd., Ash Vale 78 3C
Dorset Rd., Belmont 55 3E
Dorset Rd., Ealing 8 1A
Dorset Rd., Elmers End 41 2F
Dorset Rd., Lammas Park 8 1A
Dorset Rd., Merton 38 1B
Dorset Rd., Mitcham 39 1D
Dorset Way, Byfleet 49 3F
Dorset Way, Twickenham 17 2E
Dorsten Pl. 146 5B
Dorville Cres. 9 1F
Douai Gro. 35 1D
Douglas Av. 37 2F
Douglas Cl., Jacobs Well 81 2F
Douglas Cl., Roundshaw 57 2D
Douglas Ct. 74 4C
Douglas Dri. 42 5A
Douglas Gro. 115 1D
Douglas La. 13 1D
Douglas Rd., Kingston 36 1C
Douglas Rd., Lwr. Green 35 5D
Douglas Rd., Stanwell 14 1C
Douglas Rd., Tolworth 36 5B
Dounesforth Gdns. 20 2C
Dove Cl., Northgate 146 3C
Dove Cl., Selsdon 58 4C
Dovecote Cl. 33 5E
Dovedale Cl. 43 3E
Dovedale Cl., Guildford 82 4B
Dovedale Cl., Sandhurst 43 3E
Dovedale Cres. 146 5C
Dovedale Rd. 23 1E
Dovedale Rise 21 5D
Dovehouse Grn. 50 1C
Dover Gdns. 39 5E
Dover Park Dri. 19 1F
Dover Rd. 22 5C
Dovercourt 141 1D
Dovercourt Av. 40 3B
Dovercourt La. 38 5C
Dovercourt Rd. 23 1D
Doverfield Rd. 82 4A
Doverford Rd. 22 1A
Doverhouse Rd. 19 1F
Doversgreen 108 3C
Doversgreen Rd. 108 2C
Doversmead 64 1A
Dowanhill Rd. 24 2B
Dowding Rd. 77 1E
Dower Av. 56 3B
Dower Walk 146 4B
Dowlands La. 129 3F
Dowlans Cl. 86 2A
Dowlans Rd. 86 2A
Down Hall Rd., Kingston 36 1B
Down Hall Rd., Kingston 159
Down La., Compton 99 3E
Down La., Headley Down 134 5A
Down Rd., Guildford 82 5B
Down Rd., Hammersmith 9 2F
Down Rd., Teddington 18 5A
Down St. 34 3C
Down View Cl., Hindhead 135 4E
Downderry Rd. 24 4C
Downe Cl. 128 2A
Downers Meadow 100 5A
Downham Way 24 4C
Downhurst Rd. 122 5C
Downing Av. 100 1B
Downing St. 96 4A
Downland Cl., Great Burgh 71 2F
Downland Cl., Woodmansterne 56 5B
Downland Dri. 146 5C
Downland Gdns. 71 2F
Downland Pl. 146 5C
Downland Way 71 2F
Downlands Rd. 57 5D
Downmill Rd. 26 1C
Downs Av. 71 1E
Downs Bridge Rd. 42 1B
Downs Court Rd. 57 4E
Downs Hill 42 1B
Downs La. 70 5A
Downs Rd., Beckenham 42 1A
Downs Rd., Belmont 55 3E
Downs Rd., Coulsdon 73 2F
Downs Rd., Epsom 54 5B
Downs Rd., Epsom Downs 71 3D
Downs Rd., Mickleham 87 2D
Downs Rd., Purley 57 4E
Downs Side, Belmont 55 4E
Downs Side, Epsom 54 5B
Downs, The, Leatherhead 87 1D
Downs, The, Raynes Park 38 1A
Downs View 71 4F
Downs View Court 81 3F
Downs View Rd. 86 2B
Downs Way, Barrow Green 93 2F
Downs Way, Caterham 91 1F
Downs Way, Epsom 71 1E
Downs Way, Leatherhead 86 1A
Downs Way, Tadworth 71 4F
Downs Way Cl. 71 4F
Downs Wood, Banstead 71 2F
Downshill Rd. 54 5B
Downshire Way 26 1C
Downside 68 2B
Downside, Hindhead 135 3D
Downside, Sunbury 34 1A
Downside Bridge Rd. 68 1A
Downside Common Rd. 68 3A
Downside Gdns. 17 3F
Downside Orchard 65 2E
Downside Rd., Carshalton 56 2A
Downside Rd., Guildford 101 1E
Downside Rd. Cobham 68 1A
Downsview 87 5D
Downsview Av. 65 4D
Downsview Rd., Upper Norwood 22 5B
Downsview Rd. Headley Down 134 4A
Downsway, Guildford 82 5C
Downsway, Purley 57 4F
Downsway, Whyteleafe 75 1D
Downsway, The 3F 5S
Downswood, Redhill 90 4A
Downton Av. 22 3A
Downview Cl., Downside 68 3A
Downview Cl., Hindhead 135 4E
Doyle Rd. 41 2D
Dr. Johnsons Av. 21 3E
Dragon La. 50 3A
Drake Av., Caterham 74 4C
Drake Av., Mytchett 78 1C
Drake Cl., Bracknell 27 3D
Drake Cl., Horsham 158 3C
Drake Rd., Chessington 53 1F
Drake Rd., Croydon 40 4A
Drake Rd., Horley 128 2A
Drake Rd., Tilgate 147 5D
Drakefield Rd. 21 3E
Drakes Av. 14 4A
Drakes Cl. 51 1F
Drakes Gro 51 1F
Drakes Rd. 39 3E
Drakes Way 64 4C
Drakewood Pl. 21 5F
Drax Av. 19 5E
Draycot Rd. 36 4C
Draycott 27 3E
Drayhorse Dri. 45 3E
Drayton Cl., Bracknell 27 1D
Drayton Cl., Fetcham 69 5E
Drayton Rd. 40 5B
Dresden Way 50 1B
Dressington Av. 24 1A
Drewstead Rd. 22 3A
Drift La. 68 2C
Drift Rd. 10 1B
Drift, The 67 5F
Drift Way, Banstead 72 1A
Drift Way, Colnbrook 7 4A
Driftway 39 1E
Driftway, The 70 5A
Driftwood Dri. 74 2B
Drill Hall Rd. 32 4A
Drive Mead 57 5D
Drive Rd. 73 3F
Drive Spur 72 4C
Drive, The, Beckenham 42 1A
Drive, The, Cobham 51 5F
Drive, The, Coombe 19 5D
Drive, The, Copthorne 148 1C
Drive, The, Cottenham Park 19 5F
Drive, The, Coulsdon 57 5D
Drive, The, Cranleigh 140 2C
Drive, The, Eashing 118 2B
Drive, The, Esher 35 4D
Drive, The, Ewell 54 2B
Drive, The, Feltham 16 2B
Drive, The, Fetcham 69 4E
Drive, The, Godalming 119 3D
Drive, The, Guildford 100 2B
Drive, The, Hooley 73 3F
Drive, The, Horley 128 3B
Drive, The, Ifold 155 5F
Drive, The, Leatherhead 70 5B
Drive, The, Morden 38 3C
Drive, The, Sunbury 15 5E
Drive, The, Surbiton 36 4B
Drive, The, Sutton 55 4E
Drive, The, Thornton Heath 40 2C
Drive, The, Virginia Water 31 3D
Drive, The, West Wickham 42 4B
Drive, The, Wimbledon 20 5A
Drive, The, Woking 64 3C
Drive, The, Wonersh 101 5E
Drive, The, Woodbridge Hill 81 5E
Drive, The, Woodcote Grn. 56 3C
Drive, The, Wraysbury 12 1C
Drivers Mead 131 2E
Drodges Cl. 101 5D
Droitwich Cl., Bracknell 27 2E
Droitwich Cl., Dulwich 23 3D
Dromore Rd. 20 1A
Drove Rd. 102 1A
Drovers' Rd. 57 1F
Drovers Way, Ash 79 5D
Drovers Way, Bracknell 27 2E
Drovers Way, Upper Hale 96 2A
Druce Rd. 23 1D
Druids Cl. 70 3B
Druids Way 42 2C
Drumaline Ridge 37 5E
Drummond Cl. 27 1E
Drummond Gdns. 53 4F
Drummond Rd., Crawley 146 4A
Drummond Rd., Croydon 40 5B
Drummond Rd., Guildford 81 5F
Drungewick La. 156 5C
Drury Cl. 147 5F
Dryarch Rd. 29 3E
Dryburgh Rd. 9 5F
Dryden 26 4C
Dryden Rd., Merton 20 5C
Dryden Rd., W. Heath 60 4C
Drynham Pk. 33 5F
Ducks Wk. 18 1A
Dudley Cl. 32 5B
Dudley Dri. 38 4A
Dudley Grns. 8 1A
Dudley Gro. 54 5A
Dudley Rd., Ashford 15 4D
Dudley Rd., East Bedfont 15 2E
Dudley Rd., Kingston 36 2B
Dudley Rd., North Sheen 8 4C
Dudley Rd., Walton 34 3A
Dudley Rd, Wimbledon 20 5B
Duffield Rd. 71 5F
Duffins Orchard 48 2B
Duke Of Connaught's Rd. 78 2A
Duke Of Cornwall Av. 44 3A
Duke Of Edinburgh Rd. 38 5C
Duke Rd. 9 2D
Duke St., Richmond 8 5B
Duke St., Sutton 55 1F
Duke St., Woking 65 2D
Duke's Av., Chiswick 9 2D
Dukes Av., Ham 18 4A
Dukes Av., Malden 37 2E
Dukes Cl., Ashford 15 4E
Dukes Cl., Cranleigh 141 2D
Dukes Cl., Hampton 16 4C
Dukes Cl., Upper Hale 96 2A
Dukes Covert 45 1E
Dukes Dri. 43 1D
Dukes Green Av. 16 1A
Dukes Hill Rd. 75 3F
Duke's La. 11 5E
Dukes Rd., Hersham 51 1E
Dukes Rd., Russ Hill 126 5B
Dukes Ride 106 3A
Dukes Way 42 5C
Dukes Wk. 95 2F
Duke's Wood 43 1D
Dukeshill Rd. 26 1C
Dukesthorpe Rd. 23 4F
Dulverton Rd. 58 3B
Dulwich Common 23 2D
Dulwich Gate 23 2D
Dulwich Rd. 22 1B
Dulwich Village 22 1C
Dulwich Wood Av. 22 4C
Dulwich Wood Pk. 23 4D
Dumbarton Rd. 22 1A
Dumfield Rd. 24 4B
Dunally Pk. 33 4E
Dunbar Av., Elmers End 41 2F
Dunbar Av., Norbury 40 1B
Dunbar Pla. 22 3B
Dunbar Rd. 61 3E
Dunbar St. 22 3B
Dunboe Pl. 33 4E
Duncan Dri., Guildford 82 5B
Duncan Dri., Wokingham 25 2E
Duncan Rd., Burgh Heath 72 3A
Duncan Rd., Richmond 8 5B
Duncombe Hill 23 2F
Duncombe Rd. 119 3D
Duncrievie Rd. 24 1C
Duncroft Cl. 89 5E
Dundaff Cl. 44 5C
Dundas Cl. 27 2D
Dundas Gdns. 35 2D
Dundee Rd. 41 3E

Dundela Gdns. 54 1C
Dundonald Rd. 20 5B
Dundrey Cres. 91 3D
Dunear Rd. 37 2D
Dunedin Dri. 92 1A
Dunelm Grn. 22 3B
Dunfee Way 49 4F
Dunfield Gdns. 24 4B
Dungarvan Av. 9 5E
Dungate's La. 88 5B
Dunheved Road North 40 3B
Dunheved Road South 40 3B
Dunheved Road West 40 3B
Dunkland Rd. 40 2C
Dunleary Cl. 16 2C
Dunley Dri. 59 2E
Dunlin Cl. 109 3D
Dunlin Rise 82 4C
Dunmail Dri. 58 5A
Dunmail Rd. 58 5A
Dunmore 81 5D
Dunmore Rd. 38 1A
Dunnets 64 2A
Dunning's Rd. 150 3C
Dunnymans Rd. 55 5E
Dunoon Rd. 23 2E
Dunottar Cl. 109 1D
Dunraven Av. 109 4E
Dunsbury Cl. 55 3F
Dunsdon Av. 100 1B
Dunsfold 139 4D
Dunsfold Cl. 146 2C
Dunsfold Common 139 4D
Dunsfold Rd. 139 5F
Dunsfold Rd. 154 3C
Dunsfold Rise 56 5C
Dunsfold Way 59 2E
Dunsmore Rd. 34 3A
Dunstable Rd., Richmond 8 5B
Dunstable Rd., West
    Molesey 34 2C
Dunstall Rd. 19 5F
Dunstall Way 35 2D
Dunstan's Grn. 23 1E
Dunstans Rd. 23 2D
Dunster Av. 38 4A
Dunton Cl. 36 4B
Duntshill Rd. 20 2C
Dunvegan Cl. 35 2D
Dupont Rd. 38 1A
Duppas Av. 57 1E
Duppas Cl. 33 3E
Duppas Hill 57 1E
Duppas Hill Rd. 57 1E
Duppas Rd. 40 5B
Duppas Ter. 40 5B
Duraden Cl. 24 5A
Durand Cl. 39 4D
Durban Rd., Beckenham 42 1A
Durban Rd., West Norwood 22 4C
Durbin Rd. 53 1E
Durfield Cres. 19 2F
Durfold Dri. 89 5F
Durfold Rd. 158 2B
Durham Av. 42 2C
Durham Cl. 81 4E
Durham Rd., Feltham 16 2B
Durham Rd., Lammas Park 8 1A
Durham Rd., Raynes Park 37 1F
Durham Rd., Sandhurst 43 3E
Durham Rd., Shortlands 42 2C
Durkins Rd. 150 1C
Durleston Park Dri. 86 1A
Durleston Pk. Av. 69 5D
Durley Mead 27 3E
Durlston Rd. 18 5B
Durning Rd. 22 4C
Durnsford Av. 20 3B
Durnsford Rd. 20 3B
Durnsford Way 141 2D
Durrell Way 33 3E
Dutch Barn Cl. 14 1C
Dutchells Copse 158 3C
Duval Pl. 45 2E
Dwelly La. 113 2D
Dyehouse La. 136 1A
Dyers Field 129 2E
Dyer's La. 9 5F
Dykes Path 65 1E
Dymes 20 3A
Dynevor Pl. 80 3C
Dynevor Rd. 18 1B
Dysart Av. 18 4A

E

Eady Cl 158 5C
Eagle Rd. 81 5F
Eagles Dri. 77 2E
Ealing Park Gdns. 8 2A
Ealing Rd. 8 2B
Eardley Rd. 21 4F
Earle Gdns. 18 5B
Earles Wood 51 4E
Earleydene 28 4C
Earls Grove 44 5B

Earlsbrook Rd. 109 1E
Earlsfield Rd. 20 2C
Earlsthorpe Rd. 23 4F
Earlswood 109 1E
Earlswood, Easthampstead 26 4C
Earlswood Av. 40 3B
Earlswood Cl. 158 4C
Earlswood Rd. 109 1D
Easby Cres. 38 3C
Eashing 118 1B
Eashing La. 118 3B
East Av., Beddington 57 1D
East Av., Farnham 96 2B
East Av., Whiteley Village 50 3C
East Clandon 83 3E
East Dri., Carshalton 56 3A
East Dri., Virginia Water 30 4B
East Dulwich Gro. 22 1C
East Ewell 55 3D
East Gdns. 65 2F
East Green 60 1A
East Grinstead 150 2B
East Grinstead Rd.,
    Copthorne 148 2A
East Grinstead Rd.,
    Lingfield 131 2E
East Hill, Biggin Hill 77 2D
East Hill, Copthorne 129 5F
East Hill, Dormans Pk. 131 5F
East Hill, Oxted 93 3F
East Hill, Sanderstead 57 3F
East Hill, Wandsworth 20 1C
East Hill, Woking 65 2F
East Hill Rd. 93 3F
East Horsley 84 3C
East La. 84 1B
East Mead, Farnb'h Pk. 61 5D
East Mead, Woking 64 2C
East Meads 100 1B
East Molesey 35 3D
East Pk. 147 4D
East Pk. La. 130 4B
East Rd., East Bedfont 15 2E
East Rd., Kingston 36 1B
East Rd., Reigate 89 5E
East Rd., S. Wimbledon 20 5C
East Rd., Weybridge 50 2B
East Ring 97 1F
East St., Bookham 86 1A
East St., Epsom 54 5A
East St., Farnham 96 3A
East St., Horsham 158 5B
East St., Rusper 143 3D
East St., Turners Hill 149 5D
East Shalford La. 101 3D
East Sheen Av. 9 5D
East Stratton Cl. 27 3E
East Way, Frimley 60 1C
East Way, Guildford 81 5E
East Way, Shirley 41 5F
East Whipley, La. 121 4D
Eastbank Rd. 17 4D
Eastbourne Rd., Brentford 8 2A
Eastbourne Rd., Chiswick 9 3D
Eastbourne Rd., Godstone 92 5C
Eastbourne Rd., Hanworth 16 3B
Eastbourne Rd., Newchapel 130 3C
Eastbourne Rd., Tooting 21 5E
Eastbrook Cl. 65 1E
Eastbury Rd. 18 5B
Eastcote Av. 34 3C
Eastcroft Rd. 54 2B
Eastdean Av. 53 5F
Easter Way 111 2F
Eastern Av. 32 2B
Eastern La. 43 2E
Eastern Rd., Bulbrook 27 1E
Eastern Rd., North Town 78 5B
Eastern View 77 2E
Eastfield Rd. 109 1F
Eastfields Rd. 39 1E
Eastgate 55 5E
Eastgate Gdns. 101 1D
Easthampstead, Holme
    Grn. 26 3C
Easthampstead Rd. 26 4A
Easthampstead Rd.,
    Priestwood Common 26 1C
Easthampstead Rd.,
    Wokingham 25 2E
Eastheath Av. 25 3D
Eastheath Cl. 25 3D
Eastlands Cres. 23 1D
Eastlands Way 93 2E
Eastman Rd. 9 1D
Eastmearn Rd. 22 3C
Eastmont Rd. 35 5E
Eastney Rd. 40 4B
Eastnor Rd. 108 2B
Eastry Av. 42 3C
Eastway, Cannon Hill 38 3A
Eastway, Epsom 54 4A
Eastway, Wallington 56 1C
Eastwick 86 1A
Eastwick Dri 69 5D
Eastwick Park Av. 86 1A
Eastwick Rd., Gt. Bookham 86 1A

Eastwick Rd., Hersham 51 2D
Eastwood 147 4D
Eastwood Rd. 101 5D
Eastwood St. 21 5F
Eastworth 32 4A
Eastworth Rd. 32 4A
Eaton Court 82 4B
Eaton Park Rd. 51 5F
Eaton Pk. 51 5F
Eaton Rd., Camberley 60 1C
Eaton Rd., Sutton 55 2F
Eatonville Rd. 21 3E
Ebbas Way 70 1C
Ebbisham La. 71 5E
Ebbisham Rd., Cheam 37 5F
Ebbisham Rd., Epsom 70 1C
Ebenezer Wk. 39 1F
Ebsworth St. 23 2F
Ebury Mews 22 3B
Ecclebourne Rd. 40 3B
Eccles Hill 106 3A
Echelforde Dri. 15 4D
Echo Barn La. 114 1C
Echo Pit Rd. 101 2D
Ecob Cl. 81 3D
Ecton Rd. 49 1E
Ector Rd. 24 3C
Eddington Rd. 26 3B
Eddy's Cl. 134 4A
Eddy's La. 134 4A
Eddystone Rd. 23 1F
Eden Cl. 49 3E
Eden Croft 101 5D
Eden Grove Rd. 49 5F
Eden Park Av. 42 2A
Eden Rd., Crawley 146 5B
Eden Rd., Elmers End 41 2F
Eden Rd., South Croydon 57 1F
Eden Rd., West Norwood 22 4B
Eden St. 36 1B
Eden Vale 150 1C
Eden Walk, Kingston 159
Eden Way, Eden Park 42 3A
Eden Way, Warlingham 75 2F
Edenbrook 131 2F
Edencourt Rd. 21 5E
Edencroft 101 5D
Edenfield Gdns. 37 5E
Edenside 68 5C
Edensor Gdns. 9 2E
Edensor Rd. 9 3D
Edenvale Rd. 21 5E
Ederline Av. 40 2A
Edes Field 108 1A
Edgar Rd., Purley Oaks 57 3F
Edgar Rd., Tatsfield 77 4E
Edgar Rd., Whitton 16 2C
Edge Cl. 50 3A
Edge Hill 20 5A
Edge Point Cl. 22 4B
Edgecombe 58 2C
Edgecombe Cl. 19 5D
Edgefield 140 1B
Edgefield Cl. 109 3E
Edgehill Rd., Mitcham 39 1E
Edgehill Rd., Purley 57 3E
Edgeley 68 5C
Edgell Cl. 31 2D
Edgell Rd. 14 4A
Edgemoor Rd. 62 1A
Edgepoint Cl. 22 4B
Edgewood Gdns. 41 4F
Edgeworth Cl. 75 2D
Edginton Rd. 21 5F
Edinburgh Cl. 78 3C
Edinburgh Dri. 14 5B
Edinburgh Rd. 38 5C
Edinburgh Way 150 3C
Edith Gdns. 36 4C
Edith Rd., Selhurst 40 3C
Edith Rd., Wimbledon 20 5C
Edmund Rd. 39 2D
Edmund St. 146 2C
Edna Rd. 38 1A
Edridge Rd., East Croydon 40 5C
Edridge Rd., South Croydon 57 1F
Edward Av., Camberley 43 5F
Edward Av., Morden 38 3C
Edward Cl. 14 5B
Edward II Av. 49 5F
Edward Rd., Addiscombe 41 4D
Edward Rd., Aperfield 77 2D
Edward Rd., East Bedfont 15 1F
Edward Rd., Farnham 96 5A
Edward Rd., Hampton Hill 17 4D
Edward Rd., Penge 23 5F
Edward Rd., Windlesham 46 2A
Edward Rd.,
    Woodmansterne 73 1F
Edward Way 15 3D
Edwards Cl. 38 5A
Edwin Cl. 84 1B
Edwin Rd., Horsley 84 1B
Edwin Rd., Twickenham 17 2E
Effingham 85 2E
Effingham Cl. 55 2F
Effingham Common Rd. 68 5A

Effingham Court 65 3D
Effingham La. 148 1C
Effingham Rd., Croydon 40 4A
Effingham Rd., Hither Green 24 1C
Effingham Rd., Keeper's
    Corner 129 5F
Effingham Rd., L. Ditton 36 4A
Effingham Rd., Reigate 108 1C
Effort St. 21 4D
Effra Parade 22 1B
Effra Rd., Brixton Hill 22 1A
Effra Rd., Wimbledon 20 5B
Egerton Pl. 50 2B
Egerton Rd., Guildford 100 1A
Egerton Rd., New Malden 37 2E
Egerton Rd., Selhurst 40 2C
Egerton Rd., Twickenham 16 2C
Egerton Rd., Weybridge 50 2B
Eggar's Hill 96 1C
Egham 13 4E
Egham By-Pass 13 4D
Egham Cl. 38 5A
Egham Cres. 38 5A
Egham Hill 13 5D
Eglantine Rd. 20 1C
Egleston Rd. 38 3C
Egley Dri. 64 4C
Egley Rd. 64 4C
Eglington Rd. 116 5A
Eglise Rd. 75 2F
Egliston Ms. 9 5F
Egmont Av. 36 4C
Egmont Park Rd. 88 1C
Egmont Rd., New Malden 37 2E
Egmont Rd., Sutton 55 3F
Egmont Rd., Tolworth 36 4C
Egmont Rd., Walton-on-
    Thames 34 4A
Egmont Way 72 3A
Egremont Rd. 22 3B
Eight Acres 135 3D
Eileen Rd. 40 3C
Eland Rd., Aldershot 78 5A
Eland Rd., Waddon 40 5B
Elberon Av. 39 3F
Elborough St. 20 2B
Elbow Meadow 7 4B
Elder Cl. 82 4A
Elder Rd., Bisley 63 1E
Elder Rd., W. Norwood 22 4C
Elder Way, Flint Hill 106 3A
Elder Way, Mitcham 39 1F
Elderberry Rd., Ealing 8 1B
Elderberry Rd., Lindford 133 4E
Eldersley Cl. 90 4A
Elderslie Cl. 42 3A
Elderton Rd. 23 4F
Eldon Av. 41 5E
Eldon Dri. 115 1E
Eldon Pk. 41 2E
Eldon Rd. 74 4C
Eldridge Cl. 16 2A
Eleanor Av. 54 3A
Eleanor Gro. 9 5E
Elers Rd. 8 1A
Elfindale Rd. 22 1C
Elfrida Cres. 24 4A
Elgar Av., Brentford 8 1B
Elgar Av., Crowthorne 26 5A
Elgar Av., Norbury 40 2A
Elgar Av., Tolworth 36 4C
Elger Way 148 1B
Elgin Av. 15 5E
Elgin Cres. 75 4D
Elgin Gdns. 82 5A
Elgin Rd., Beddington 56 2C
Elgin Rd., Rose Hill 38 5C
Elgin Rd., Weybridge 50 1A
Elgin Rd,. Addiscombe 41 5D
Elgin Way 61 3F
Eliot Bank 23 3E
Eliot Dri. 151 3E
Eliot Gdns. 9 5E
Elizabeth Av., Ashford 14 5B
Elizabeth Av., Bagshot 45 3E
Elizabeth Cl. 27 2D
Elizabeth Court. 100 5A
Elizabeth Cres. 150 1C
Elizabeth Gdns., Ascot 28 3C
Elizabeth Gdns., Sunbury-
    on-Thames 34 2B
Elizabeth Gdns., Upper
    Norwood 22 5C
Elizabeth Rd., Guildford 100 5A
Elizabeth Rd., Wokingham 25 2E
Elizabeth Way 16 4B
Elizabethan Cl. 14 2C
Elizabethan Way, Crawley 147 4F
Elizabethan Way, Stanwell 14 2C
Elkins Gdns. 82 4B
Ellenborough Cl. 27 1D
Ellenbridge Way 58 3A
Elleray Court 78 3C
Elleray Rd. 17 5F
Ellerdine Rd. 17 1E
Ellerker Gdns. 18 1B
Ellerman Av. 16 2C

Name		
Ellerslie Sq.	22	1A
Ellerton Rd., Surbiton	36	5B
Ellerton Rd., Wandsworth	21	2D
Ellerton Rd., Wimbledon	19	5E
Ellery Cl.	140	2C
Ellery Rd.	22	5C
Elles Av.	82	5B
Elles Rd.	60	5C
Ellesfield Av.	26	2B
Ellesmere Dri.	58	5B
Ellesmere Rd., Chiswick	9	3D
Ellesmere Rd., Twickenham	18	1A
Ellesmere Rd., Weybridge	50	2C
Ellingham Rd., Chessington	53	2E
Ellingham Rd., Shepherd's Bush	9	1F
Ellington Rd.	15	4F
Elliot Cl.	147	4F
Elliot Gdns.	33	2D
Elliott Rd., Thornton Heath	40	2B
Elliott Rd., Turnham Green	9	2D
Ellis Av.	100	1B
Ellis Cl.	74	3A
Ellis Farm Cl.	64	4C
Ellis Rd., Coulsdon	74	3A
Ellis Rd., Crowthorne	43	1D
Ellis Rd., Oxted	93	3F
Ellison Rd., Barnes	9	4E
Ellison Rd., Streatham Vale	22	5A
Ellison Way	97	1E
Ellman Rd.	146	5B
Ellora Rd.	21	4F
Ellson Cl.	147	4F
Elm Bridge La.	65	3D
Elm Cl., Deadwater	133	5D
Elm Cl., Hackbridge	39	4D
Elm Cl., Horsell	64	1C
Elm Cl., Leatherhead	70	4A
Elm Cl., Raynes Park	37	2F
Elm Cl., Sendmarsh	66	5A
Elm Cl., South Croydon	57	2F
Elm Cl., Stanwell	14	2C
Elm Cl., Tolworth	37	4D
Elm Cl., Twickenham	17	3D
Elm Cl., Warlingham	75	2F
Elm Cres., Heath End	96	1B
Elm Cres., Kingston	36	1B
Elm Croft	68	5C
Elm Dri., Chobham	47	3E
Elm Dri., Leatherhead	70	5A
Elm Dri., Sunbury	34	1B
Elm Gdns., Burgh Heath	71	3F
Elm Gdns., Claygate	52	2C
Elm Gdns., Mitcham	39	2F
Elm Gro., Bisley	63	1E
Elm Gro., Caterham	74	4C
Elm Gro., Horsham	158	5C
Elm Gro., Sutton	55	1F
Elm Gro., Wimbledon	20	5A
Elm Grove, Epsom	54	5A
Elm Grove, Farnham	96	1B
Elm Grove Parade	39	5E
Elm Grove Rd., Barnes	9	4F
Elm Grove Rd., Cobham	68	1B
Elm Grove Rd., North Farnborough	61	5D
Elm Grove Rd., South Ealing	8	1B
Elm La., Catford	24	2A
Elm La., Tongham	97	1E
Elm La., Wisley	67	3D
Elm Mews	18	1B
Elm Park	29	4D
Elm Pk., Brixton Hill	22	1A
Elm Pk., Cranleigh	140	1A
Elm Pk., South Norwood	41	2D
Elm Pl.	97	1D
Elm Rd., Beckenham	41	1F
Elm Rd., Chessington	53	1E
Elm Rd., Claygate	52	2C
Elm Rd., East Bedfont	15	2E
Elm Rd., Ewell	54	2B
Elm Rd., Farncombe	100	5A
Elm Rd., Hackbridge	39	4E
Elm Rd., Heath End	96	1B
Elm Rd., Horsell	65	1D
Elm Rd., Kingston	36	1B
Elm Rd., Leatherhead	70	4A
Elm Rd., Malden	37	1D
Elm Rd., Mortlake	9	5D
Elm Rd., Purley	57	5E
Elm Rd., Reigate	90	5A
Elm Rd., Selhurst	40	2C
Elm Rd., Warlingham	75	2F
Elm Rd., Woking	64	2C
Elm Road West	38	4B
Elm Tree Av.	35	4E
Elm Treet Cl.	31	5F
Elm View	78	4C
Elm Walk, Raynes Pk.	38	2A
Elm Walk, West Ewell	54	1A
Elm Way, Worcester Pk.	37	5F
Elmbank Av., Egham Wick	12	5B
Elmbank Av., Guildford	100	1B
Elmbourne Rd.	21	3E
Elmbridge Av.	37	3D
Elmbridge Rd.	140	1A
Elmbrook Cl.	34	1A
Elmbrook Rd.	55	1E
Elmcourt Rd.	22	3B
Elmcroft Cl., Feltham	15	1F
Elmcroft Cl., Frimley	61	3E
Elmcroft Cl., Hook	36	5B
Elmcroft Dri., Ashford	15	4D
Elmcroft Dri., Hook	36	5B
Elmdene	37	4D
Elmdene Cl.	41	3F
Elmer Cottages	69	5F
Elmer Rd.	24	2B
Elmers Av.	36	3B
Elmers End Rd.	41	1E
Elmers Rd., Addiscombe	41	4D
Elmers Rd., Ockley	143	1D
Elmfield	68	5C
Elmfield Av.	17	4F
Elmfield Court	133	3D
Elmfield Rd.	21	3E
Elmfield Way	58	3A
Elmgate Av.	16	3A
Elmgrove Cl.	64	3A
Elmgrove Rd., Addiscombe	41	4E
Elmgrove Rd., Weybridge	33	5D
Elmhurst Av.	21	5E
Elmhurst Dri.	105	2F
Elmore Rd.	73	4E
Elmpark Gdns.	58	3B
Elms Cres.	21	1F
Elms Rd., Clapham	21	1F
Elms Rd., Wokingham	25	2D
Elms, The, Roehampton	9	5E
Elms, The, Tongham	97	1E
Elmscott Rd.	24	4C
Elmshaw Rd.	19	1F
Elmshorn	71	1F
Elmside, Addington	59	2D
Elmside, Guildford	100	1D
Elmside, Milford	118	3B
Elmsleigh Rd., Staines	14	4A
Elmsleigh Rd., Twickenham	17	3E
Elmslie Cl.	54	5A
Elmstead Cl.	54	1B
Elmstead Gdns.	37	5E
Elmstead Rd.	49	5D
Elmsway	15	4D
Elmswood	68	5C
Elmtree Cl., Ashford	15	4D
Elmtree Cl., Byfleet	49	5F
Elmtree Rd.	17	4E
Elmwood Av.	16	3A
Elmwood Cl., Ashtead	70	2B
Elmwood Cl., Hackbridge	39	5E
Elmwood Dri.	54	2B
Elmwood Gro.	22	3C
Elmwood Rd., Brookwood	64	3A
Elmwood Rd., Camberwell	22	1C
Elmwood Rd., Chiswick	9	3D
Elmwood Rd., Croydon	40	4B
Elmwood Rd., Mitcham	39	2D
Elmwood Rd., Redhill	90	3B
Elmworth Grove	22	3C
Elsdon Rd.	64	2B
Elsenham St.	20	2B
Elsenwood Cres.	44	4C
Elsenwood Dri.	44	4C
Elsiemaud Rd.	24	1A
Elsinore Av.	14	2C
Elsinore Rd.	23	2F
Elsley Cl.	61	4E
Elsrick Av.	38	3B
Elstan Way	41	4F
Elstead	117	2D
Elstead Rd., Milford	118	3A
Elstead Rd., Norney	118	1A
Elstead Rd., Seale	97	2F
Elsted Cl.	146	3C
Elston Pl.	97	1D
Elston Rd.	97	1D
Elstree Hill	24	5C
Elsworth Cl.	15	2F
Elsworthy	35	3E
Elthorne Court	16	2B
Elthruda Rd.	24	1C
Elton Cl.	18	5A
Elton Rd., Kingston	36	1C
Elton Rd., Woodcote	56	4C
Elveden Cl.	66	2B
Elveden Rd.	51	4D
Elvino Rd.	23	4F
Elwell Cl.	13	4E
Elwill Way	42	2B
Ely Cl., Frimley	61	3F
Ely Cl., New Malden	37	1E
Ely Rd.	40	3C
Elystan Cl.	56	3C
Embankment, The, Runnymede	12	2C
Embankment, The, Twickenham	17	2F
Ember Cl.	49	1F
Ember Farm Av.	35	3E
Ember Farm Way	35	3E
Ember Gdns.	35	4E
Ember La.	35	4E
Embercourt Rd.	35	3E
Embleton Rd.	134	4A
Emerton Rd.	69	1E
Emerydown Cl.	27	2F
Emley Rd.	32	5B
Emlyn La., Earlswood	69	4F
Emlyn Rd.	9	1E
Emlyn Rd., Earlswood	109	1E
Emlyn Rd., Horley	128	2A
Emmanuel Cl.	81	4E
Emmanuel Rd.	21	2F
Emmetts Cl.	64	2C
Empire Villas	109	5E
Empress Av.	61	4D
Emsworth Cl.	147	5F
Emsworth St.	22	3A
Ena Rd.	40	2A
Endale Cl.	39	5E
Endeavour Way, Croydon	40	4A
Endeavour Way, Summerstown	20	4C
Endlesham Rd.	21	2E
Endsleigh Cl.	58	3B
Endsleigh Gdns., Hersham	51	1D
Endsleigh Gdns., Surbiton	36	3A
Endsleigh Rd.	90	3C
Endway	36	4C
Endymion Rd.	22	1A
Enelby Rd.	36	4C
Enerdals Cl.	15	2F
Enfield Rd., Acton	8	1C
Enfield Rd., Ash Vale	78	3C
Enfield Rd., Brentford	8	2A
Engadine Cl.	41	5D
Engadine St.	20	2B
Englefield Green	12	4B
Englefield Rd.	63	2F
Engleheart Rd.	24	2B
Englehurst	12	5C
Englesfield	45	5D
Englewood Rd.	21	1F
Engliff La.	66	1A
Enmore Gdns.	19	1D
Enmore Rd.	41	3D
Ennerdale	26	2C
Ennerdale Cl., Cheam	55	1E
Ennerdale Cl., Southgate	146	5C
Ennerdale Rd.	8	4B
Ennersdale Rd.	24	1B
Ennismore Av., Guildford	82	5A
Ennismore Av., Turnham Green	9	2E
Ennismore Gdns.	35	3E
Ensign Cl.	14	2C
Ensign Way	14	2C
Enterdent	92	5F
Envis Way	80	4C
Epping Walk	147	5E
Epping Way	27	2E
Epsom	54	5A
Epsom Cl.	44	4A
Epsom Gap	69	1F
Epsom Lane North	71	2F
Epsom Lane South	71	4F
Epsom Rd., Ashtead	70	2B
Epsom Rd., Crawley	147	5E
Epsom Rd., East Horsley	84	3B
Epsom Rd., Ewell	54	4B
Epsom Rd., Guildford	101	1D
Epsom Rd., Leatherhead	70	4A
Epsom Rd., Merrow	82	5A
Epsom Rd., Morden Pk.	38	4B
Epsom Rd., Waddon	40	5B
Eresby Cres.	42	4A
Erica Cl., Copthorne	148	2B
Erica Cl., West End	46	5A
Erica Court	64	2C
Erica Dr.	25	2E
Erica Gdns.	59	1D
Erica Way, Horsham	158	3B
Eridge Cl.	147	4F
Eriswell Cres.	50	2C
Eriswell Rd.	50	2C
Erkenwald Cl.	32	3A
Ermyn Cl.	70	4B
Ermyn Way	70	4B
Erncroft Way	17	1F
Ernest Av.	22	4B
Ernest Gdns.	8	3C
Ernest Gro.	42	3A
Ernest Rd.	36	1C
Ernie Rd.	19	5F
Erpingham Rd.	9	5F
Erridge Rd.	38	1B
Errol Gdns.	37	2F
Erskine Cl.	39	5D
Erskine Rd., Carshalton	56	1A
Erskine Rd., The Wrythe	39	5D
Erviston Gdns.	22	5B
Esam Way	22	4B
Escombe Dri.	81	3E
Escott Pl.	48	2C
Escourt Rd.	41	3E
Esher	52	1A
Esher Av., Cheam	38	5A
Esher Av., Walton-on-Thames	34	4A
Esher Cl.	52	1A
Esher Gdns.	20	3A
Esher Green	52	1A
Esher Ms.	39	2E
Esher Park Av.	52	1A
Esher Place Av.	52	1A
Esher Rd., Camberley	44	3C
Esher Rd., East Molesey	35	3E
Esher Rd., Hersham	51	1E
Eskdale Gdns.	57	5F
Eskdale Way	45	5D
Eskmont Ridge	22	5C
Esmond Rd.	9	2D
Essenden Rd.	57	2F
Essendene Cl.	75	5D
Essendene Rd.	75	5D
Essex Cl., Addlestone	49	1E
Essex Cl., Frimley	61	3F
Essex Cl., Morden	38	4A
Essex Court	9	4E
Essex Dri.	140	2A
Essex Gro.	22	5C
Essex Pl.	9	2D
Estcots Dri.	150	2C
Estella Av.	37	2F
Estreham Rd.	21	5F
Eswyn Rd.	21	4D
Ethel Rd.	14	4C
Ethelbert Rd.	38	1A
Ethelbert St.	21	2F
Etherley Hill	123	4F
Etherow St.	23	2D
Etherstone Grn.	22	4A
Etherstone Rd.	22	4A
Eton Av.	37	3D
Eton Pl.	96	1A
Eureka Rd.	36	1C
Europa Pk Rd.	81	5F
Eustace Cres.	25	1E
Eustace Rd.	82	4C
Euston Rd.	40	4A
Evans Cl.	147	4F
Evans Gro.	16	3C
Evans Rd.	24	3C
Eve Rd.	65	1E
Evedon	27	4D
Evelina Rd.	23	5E
Eveline Rd.	39	1D
Evelyn Cl., Whitton	17	2D
Evelyn Cl., Woking	64	3C
Evelyn Cott.	104	5B
Evelyn Cres.	33	1F
Evelyn Gdns., Godstone	92	3B
Evelyn Gdns., Richmond	8	5B
Evelyn Rd., Aldershot	97	1D
Evelyn Rd., Ham	18	3A
Evelyn Rd., Merton	20	4C
Evelyn Rd., Richmond	8	5B
Evelyn Ter.	8	5B
Evelyn Walk	147	5D
Evelyn Way, Carshalton	56	1C
Evelyn Way, Stoke D'Abernon	68	1C
Evelyn Way, Sunbury	33	1F
Evelyn Woods Rd.	78	2A
Evendons Cl.	25	3D
Evendons La.	25	3D
Evenlode Way	43	4E
Evenwood Cl.	20	1A
Everard La.	75	4E
Everdon Rd.	9	3E
Everest Court	64	1A
Everest Rd., Camberley	44	4A
Everest Rd., Crowthorne	43	1D
Everest Rd., Stanwell	14	2C
Evergreen Rd.	61	2F
Evergreen Way	14	2C
Everlands Cl.	65	2D
Eversfield Rd., Horsham	158	5C
Eversfield Rd., Kew	8	4B
Eversfield Rd., Reigate	89	5F
Eversley Rd., Kingston	36	2B
Eversley Rd., Upper Norwood	22	5C
Eversley Way, Thorpe	31	1E
Eversley Way, W. Wickham	42	5A
Everton Rd.	41	4D
Evesham Cl., Cheam	55	5E
Evesham Cl., Reigate	89	5E
Evesham Green	38	3C
Evesham Rd., Feltham	16	2B
Evesham Rd., Reigate	89	5E
Evesham Rd., St. Helier	38	3C
Evesham Road North	89	5E
Evesham Walk	43	3E
Ewart Rd.	23	2F
Ewelands	128	2C
Ewell	54	3B
Ewell By-Pass	54	2B
Ewell Court Av.	54	1B
Ewell Downs Rd.	54	4B
Ewell House Cres.	54	3B
Ewell Park Way	54	2B
Ewell Rd., Cheam	55	2D
Ewell Rd., Surbiton	36	3B
Ewell Rd., Tolworth	36	4C
Ewelme Rd.	23	2E
Ewen Cres.	22	2B

Ewhurst	122	5C
Ewhurst Av.	58	3A
Ewhurst Cl.	55	3D
Ewhurst Rd., Cranleigh	140	1C
Ewhurst Rd., Lewisham	24	1A
Ewhurst Rd., Peaslake	122	1B
Ewhurst Rd., West Green	146	4C
Ewins Cl.	78	5C
Exbury Rd.	24	3A
Exchange Rd., Crawley	147	4D
Exchange Rd., Sunninghill	28	3C
Exeford Av.	15	4D
Exeter Rd., Addiscombe	41	4D
Exeter Rd., Ash Vale	78	4C
Exeter Rd., Hanworth	16	3C
Explorer Av.	14	2C
Eyebright Cl.	41	4F
Eyhurst Cl.	72	5B
Eyhurst Spur	72	5B
Eyles Cl.	158	4A
Eylewood Rd.	22	4C
Eynalla Rd.	23	2D
Eyot Gdns.	9	2E
Eyston Dr.	50	3A

F

Factory La.	40	4B
Factory Path	14	4A
Factory Yard	96	4A
Fagg's Rd.	16	1A
Fair La.	89	1F
Fair Lawn, Chertsey	49	4D
Fair Lawn, Little Bookham	85	1D
Fairacre, Boundstone	114	2C
Fairacre, New Malden	37	2D
Fairacres, Cobham	51	4E
Fairacres, Roehampton	9	5E
Fairbourne	51	5E
Fairbourne Cl.	64	2B
Fairbourne La.	74	4C
Faircare, Kingswood	72	4A
Fairchildes Av.	59	5F
Fairchildes Rd.	76	1C
Fairdale Gdns.	9	5F
Fairdene Rd.	73	2F
Fairfax	26	1C
Fairfax Av., Ewell	54	3C
Fairfax Av., Redhill	90	5A
Fairfax Cl.	34	4A
Fairfax Gro.	9	1E
Fairfax Rd., Farnborough Green	61	3D
Fairfax Rd., Teddington	18	5A
Fairfax Rd., Woking	65	3E
Fairfield, Eastwick	86	1A
Fairfield, Farnham	96	4A
Fairfield App.	12	1C
Fairfield Av., Horley	128	3B
Fairfield Av., Staines	14	4A
Fairfield Av., Whitton	17	2D
Fairfield Cl., Mitcham	21	5D
Fairfield Cl., Stoneleigh	54	1B
Fairfield Dri., Dorking	87	5D
Fairfield Dri., Frimley	61	1E
Fairfield Dri., Wandsworth	20	1C
Fairfield East	36	1B
Fairfield Lane	46	4B
Fairfield North	36	1B
Fairfield Pk.	51	5E
Fairfield Pl.	36	2B
Fairfield Rd., East Croydon	40	5C
Fairfield Rd., East Grinstead	150	3C
Fairfield Rd., Hampton Wick	36	1B
Fairfield Rd., Leatherhead	69	4F
Fairfield Rd., Wraysbury	12	1C
Fairfield Rise	81	5E
Fairfield St.	20	1C
Fairfield South	36	1B
Fairfield Way, Coulsdon	56	5C
Fairfield Way, Stoneleigh	54	1B
Fairfield West	36	1B
Fairford Av.	41	3F
Fairford Cl., Reigate	89	4F
Fairford Cl., W. Byfleet	49	5D
Fairford Gdns.	37	5E
Fairgreen Rd.	40	3B
Fairhaven	13	4D
Fairhaven Av.	41	3F
Fairhaven Rd.	90	3B
Fairholme	15	2F
Fairholme Cl.	70	2A
Fairholme Cres.	70	2A
Fairholme Rd., Ashford	14	4C
Fairholme Rd., Cheam	55	2E
Fairholme Rd., Croydon	40	4B
Fairlands Av., Guildford	80	3C
Fairlands Av., Rose Hill	38	5B
Fairlands Av., Thornton Heath	40	2A
Fairlands Rd.	80	3C
Fairlawn	50	1C
Fairlawn Av.	9	2D
Fairlawn Cl., Claygate	52	2C
Fairlawn Cl., Hanworth	16	4C

Fairlawn Cl., Kingston Hill	19	5D
Fairlawn Cres.	150	2B
Fairlawn Dri., East Grinstead	150	2B
Fairlawn Dri., Redhill	109	1D
Fairlawn Gro., Banstead	56	5A
Fairlawn Gro., Chiswick	9	2D
Fairlawn Pk., Horley	128	3B
Fairlawn Pk., Sydenham	23	4F
Fairlawn Pk., Woking	65	1D
Fairlawn Rd., Banstead	56	4A
Fairlawn Rd., Wimbledon	20	5B
Fairlawns, Richmond	18	1A
Fairlawns, Sunbury-on-Thames	34	2A
Fairlawns Cl.	14	5B
Fairlie Gdns.	23	2E
Fairlight Cl.	54	1C
Fairlight Rd.	21	4D
Fairmead Cl.	37	2D
Fairmead Cl.	43	4E
Fairmead Rd.	40	4A
Fairmeads	51	5F
Fairmile Av., Cobham	51	5F
Fairmile Av., Streatham	21	4F
Fairmile La.	51	4E
Fairmile Park Copse	51	4F
Fairmile Park Rd.	51	5F
Fairmount Rd.	22	1A
Fairoak Cl., Kenley	74	1B
Fairoak Cl., Oxshott	52	4B
Fairoak La.	52	4A
Fairrolm Gdns.	96	4A
Fairs Rd.	69	3F
Fairview, Ewell	54	4C
Fairview, Horsham	158	4A
Fairview Av.	65	2D
Fairview Court	15	4D
Fairview Dri.	33	3D
Fairview Estate	94	5A
Fairview Gdns.	96	2B
Fairview Rd., Ash	78	4C
Fairview Rd., Carshalton	56	1A
Fairview Rd., Epsom	54	4B
Fairview Rd., Headley Down	134	4A
Fairview Rd., Norbury	40	1A
Fairview Rd., Wokingham	25	2E
Fairwater Dri.	49	3F
Fairway, Banstead	55	4F
Fairway, Chertsey	32	4B
Fairway, Copthorne	148	1B
Fairway, Crawley	146	4A
Fairway, Merrow	82	5C
Fairway, Raynes Park	37	2F
Fairway Cl., Ewell	54	1A
Fairway Cl., Woking	64	3B
Fairway, The, Byfleet	50	4A
Fairway, The, Camberley	61	1F
Fairway, The, Godalming	119	3D
Fairway, The, Heath End	96	1B
Fairway, The, Kingston	37	1D
Fairway, The, Leatherh'd	69	2F
Fairway, The, Molesey	35	2D
Fairway, The, Woking	63	5F
Fairways, Ashford	15	5D
Fairways, Coulsdon	74	2B
Fairways, Hindhead	135	4D
Fairways, Teddington	18	5A
Fairways Heights	44	5C
Fairways, The	30	3C
Fairwell La.	84	2A
Fairwyn Rd.	23	4F
Fakenham Way	43	3E
Falaise Cl., Aldershot	78	4A
Falaise Cl., Egham	13	4D
Falcon Cl.	147	3D
Falcon Court	48	5C
Falcon Dri.	14	1C
Falcon Rd., Guildford	81	5F
Falcon Rd., Hampton	16	5C
Falcon Way, Lightwater	45	4E
Falcon Way, Upper Halliford	33	1F
Falcon Wood	13	4D
Falconhurst	69	1E
Falconwood	67	5F
Falconwood Rd.	59	2D
Falcourt Cl.	55	1F
Falkland Court	78	2B
Falkland Park Av.	40	2C
Falkland Rd.	105	2F
Falkner Rd.	96	4A
Fallowfield Way	128	2C
Fallsbrook Rd.	21	5F
Falmouth Cl., Heatherside	61	1F
Falmouth Cl., Hither Green	24	1C
Falmouth Rd.	51	1E
Falstaff Mews	17	4E
Fambridge Cl.	24	4A
Famet Av.	57	5E
Famet Cl.	57	5E
Famet Walk	57	5E
Fanes Cl.	26	1C
Fanny Rd.	9	3F
Fanshawe Rd.	18	4A
Fanthorpe St.	9	5F

Faraday Av.	150	4C
Faraday Rd., Crawley	147	2D
Faraday Rd., Farnboro'	61	4D
Faraday Rd., Wimbledon	20	5B
Faraday Rd., W. Molesey	34	2C
Faraday Way	40	4A
Farcrosse Cl.	43	4D
Fareham Rd.	16	2B
Farewell Pl.	39	1D
Farhalls Cres.	158	3C
Faringdon Cl.	43	4D
Faringdon Dri.	27	3E
Farington Acres	33	5E
Faris Barn Dri.	49	4D
Faris La.	49	4D
Farleigh	58	5C
Farleigh Av.	42	3C
Farleigh Court Rd.	59	5D
Farleigh Dean Cres.	59	4E
Farleigh Rd., Warlingham	75	2F
Farleigh Rd., Woodham	49	4D
Farleton Cl.	50	2C
Farley Copse	26	1B
Farley Pk.	93	3F
Farley Rd., Hither Green	24	2B
Farley Rd., Selsdon	58	2B
Farleys Cl.	84	1B
Farling Pl.	19	2F
Farlton Rd.	20	2C
Farm Av., Streatham	22	4A
Farm Av., The Common	158	4A
Farm Cl., Byfleet	49	4F
Farm Cl., Carshalton Beeches	56	2A
Farm Cl., Chipstead	73	3D
Farm Cl., Crawley	147	3E
Farm Cl., Crowthorne	26	5A
Farm Cl., E. Horsley	84	2C
Farm Cl., Fetcham	69	5E
Farm Cl., Guildford	81	4F
Farm Cl., Loxwood	156	4A
Farm Cl., Priestwood Common	26	1C
Farm Cl., Shepperton	33	4D
Farm Cl., Staines	13	4F
Farm Cl., Thorpe	31	3E
Farm Cl., West Wickham	42	5C
Farm Cl., Woodcote	56	3C
Farm Dri., Shirley	42	5A
Farm Dri., Woodcote	56	4C
Farm Fields	58	4A
Farm Gro.	42	5A
Farm La., Ashtead	70	1C
Farm La., E. Horsley	84	2C
Farm La., Pebble Coombe	88	3A
Farm La., S. Beddington	56	3C
Farm La., Send	65	5F
Farm La., Shirley	42	5A
Farm Rd., Aldershot	78	4B
Farm Rd., Carshalton Beeches	56	2A
Farm Rd., Frimley	61	2E
Farm Rd., Hanworth	16	2C
Farm Rd., Lower Green	35	5D
Farm Rd., Morden	38	3C
Farm Rd., Old Woking	65	3E
Farm Rd., Staines	14	5B
Farm Rd., Warlingham	75	3F
Farm View	68	1B
Farm Way, Cheam	38	5A
Farm Way, Stanwellmoor	14	1A
Farm Wk.	98	1A
Farman Way	57	2D
Farmdale Rd.	56	2A
Farmers Rd.	13	4F
Farmfield Rd.	24	4C
Farmhouse Cl.	65	1F
Farmhouse Rd.	21	5F
Farmington Av.	39	5D
Farmleigh Cl.	147	3F
Farmleigh Gro.	50	2C
Farmstead Rd.	24	4A
Farnaby Rd.	42	1C
Farnborough	61	5D
Farnborough Av.	58	2C
Farnborough Cres.	58	3C
Farnborough Cres., Hayes	42	4C
Farnborough Rd., Farnborough	61	5D
Farnborough Rd., Heath End	96	1B
Farnborough St.	61	4D
Farncombe	100	5B
Farncombe Hill	100	5A
Farncombe St.	100	5A
Farnell Rd.	14	3A
Farnham	96	4A
Farnham By-Pass	95	5F
Farnham Cl.	27	1D
Farnham Gdns.	37	1F
Farnham La.	151	2F
Farnham Park Cl.	96	2A
Farnham Park Rd.	96	2A
Farnham Rd., Churt	134	1B
Farnham Rd., Dockenfield	114	3A
Farnham Rd., Guildford	100	2A
Farnham-Milford Rd.	97	5D

Farnhurst La.	140	4A
Farningham	27	3E
Farningham Cres.	75	4D
Farningham Rd.	75	5D
Farnley	64	2B
Farnley Rd.	40	2C
Farquhar Rd., Crystal Palace	23	4D
Farquhar Rd., Wimbledon Park	20	3B
Farquharson Rd.	40	4B
Farran Rd.	22	4A
Farrel Cl.	61	1D
Farren Rd.	23	3F
Farrier Cl.	34	2A
Farriers Cl.	55	4B
Farriers Rd.	54	4B
Farrington Acres	33	5B
Farthing Fields	133	4E
Farthingham La.	122	5C
Farwig La.	42	1C
Fassett Rd.	36	2B
Fathings	64	1A
Fauconberg Rd.	9	3D
Faulkner Pl	45	2E
Faulkners Rd.	51	1E
Faversham Rd.	43	3E
Faversham Rd., Beckenham	42	1A
Faversham Rd., Catford	24	2A
Faversham Rd., Morden	38	3C
Fawcus Cl.	52	2B
Fawler Mead.	27	2F
Fawnbrake Av.	22	1B
Fawns Manor Cl.	15	2E
Fawns Manor Rd.	15	2E
Fay Rd.	158	3B
Faygate La.	143	5E
Faygate Rd.	22	3A
Fayland Av.	21	4F
Fearn Cl.	84	3C
Fearnley Cres.	16	4C
Fearsden Cl.	48	2C
Featherbed La.	59	2D
Feathercombe	138	1A
Feathers La.	13	3E
Featherstone Av.	23	3E
Feathstone	111	4F
Fee Farm Rd	52	2C
Felbridge Av.	147	3F
Felbridge Cl., East Grinstead	150	1B
Felbridge Cl., Sutton	55	3F
Felbridge Cl., West Norwood	22	4B
Felbridge Court	150	1A
Felbridge Rd.	149	1F
Felcott Cl.	34	5B
Felcott Rd., Crawley Down	149	1E
Felcott Rd., Walton-on-Thames	34	5A
Felcourt	131	4E
Felcourt Rd., Felbridge	150	1B
Felcourt Rd., Felcourt	131	3E
Felday Glade	123	1D
Felday Rd., Abinger	103	3F
Felday Rd., Ladywell	24	1A
Felix Dri.	83	2D
Felix La.	33	3F
Felix Rd.	34	3A
Fell Rd.	40	5C
Felland Way	109	2D
Fellbridge	150	1A
Fellbrigg Rd.	23	1D
Fellbrook	18	3A
Fellow Green Rd.	46	5B
Fellowes Rd., The Wrythe	39	5D
Fellows Rd., South Farnborough	78	1B
Felmingham Rd.	41	1E
Felsberg Rd.	22	1A
Felstead Rd.	54	4A
Feltham	16	3A
Feltham Av.	35	2E
Feltham Hill Rd.	15	4D
Feltham Rd., Ashford	15	4D
Feltham Rd., Mitcham	39	1E
Feltham Rd., Reigate	109	3D
Feltham Wk.	109	3D
Felthambrook Way	16	4A
Felthamhill Rd.	16	4A
Fencote	27	3E
Fendall Rd.	54	1A
Fengates Rd.	90	5A
Fennel Cl., Farnborough	60	5A
Fennel Cl., Guildford	82	4B
Fennel Cl., Shirley	41	4F
Fennel Cres.	146	5C
Fennel's Mead	54	3B
Fenns La.	46	5A
Fenns Way	65	1D
Fenn's Yard	96	4A
Fenton Av.	14	5B
Fenton Cl.	90	5B
Fenton Rd.	90	5B
Fentum Rd.	81	4E
Fenwick Cl.	64	2B
Ferguson Av.	36	3B

183
Fermandy La
Foss Rd

Fermandy La. 149 2E
Fermor Rd. 23 2F
Fern Av. 39 2F
Fern Bank Rd. 49 1E
Fern Cl. Camberley 61 1F
Fern Cl. Warlingham 75 2F
Fern Gro. 16 2A
Fern Hill 52 5B
Fern Hill La. 64 3C
Fern Hill Pk. 64 3C
Fern Rd. 119 1D
Fern Walk 14 4C
Fern Way 158 3B
Fernbank Av. 34 4C
Fernbank Cres. 28 1A
Fernbank Place 28 1A
Fernbank Rd. 28 1A
Fernbrae Cl. 115 2D
Fernbrook Rd. 24 1C
Ferndale 81 4D
Ferndale Av. 31 5F
Ferndale Rd., Banstead 72 2B
Ferndale Rd., Staines 14 4C
Ferndale Rd., Woking 65 1D
Ferndale Rd., Woodside 41 3E
Fernden La. 151 4F
Fernden Lane 152 5A
Fernden Rise 100 5A
Ferndown, Horley 128 1B
Ferndown, Three Bridges 147 2F
Ferndown Cl. 101 1E
Fernery, The 13 4F
Ferney Court 49 4F
Ferney Rd. 49 4F
Fernham Rd. 40 2B
Fernhill Cl., Crawley Down 149 2E
Fernhill Cl., Hawley 60 2B
Fernhill Cl., Woking 64 3C
Fernhill Dri. 96 2A
Fernhill Gdns. 18 4B
Fernhill La., Hawley 60 2B
Fernhill La., Upper Hale 96 2A
Fernhill Rd. 60 2B
Fernhill Wk. 60 2C
Fernholme Rd. 23 1F
Fernhouse Lodge 60 3B
Fernhurst Cl. 146 3C
Fernhurst Rd., Addiscombe 41 4E
Fernhurst Rd., Ashford 15 4E
Ferniehurst Cl. 61 1E
Fernihough Cl. 50 4A
Fernlands Cl. 31 5F
Fernlea 69 5D
Fernlea Rd., Balham 21 2E
Fernlea Rd., Mitcham 39 1E
Fernleigh 57 1E
Fernleigh Rise 62 3A
Ferns Cl. 58 3B
Fernside Av. 16 3A
Fernside Rd. 21 2E
Fernthorpe Rd. 21 5F
Fernwood Av. 21 4F
Feroners Cl. 147 5E
Ferrard Cl. 28 1A
Ferrers Av. 56 1C
Ferrers Rd. 21 4F
Ferriers Way 72 3A
Ferris Av. 41 5E
Ferry Av. 13 5F
Ferry La., Guildford 100 2C
Ferry La., Hythe End 13 3E
Ferry La., Kew 8 3B
Ferry La., Laleham 32 2B
Ferry La., Shepperton 33 4D
Ferry Rd., Barnes 9 3E
Ferry Rd., Teddington 17 4F
Ferry Rd., Thames Dit'n 35 3F
Ferry Rd., West Molesey 35 2D
Ferry Sq. 33 4D
Ferrymoor 18 3A
Fetcham 69 5D
Fetcham Common La. 69 4D
Fetcham Park Dri. 69 5E
Fettes Rd. 141 1D
Fickleshole 59 5F
Fiddicroft Av. 55 5F
Field Cl., Chessington 53 1D
Field Cl., E. Moseley 35 3D
Field Cl., Merrow 82 5C
Field Cl., Sanderstead 58 5B
Field Court 93 2F
Field End, Coulsdon 56 5C
Field End, Farnham 96 3C
Field End, Twickenham 17 4F
Field End, West End 46 5B
Field La., Brentford 8 3A
Field La., Frimley 61 2E
Field Pk. 27 1E
Field Pl. 37 3E
Field Rd., Feltham 16 1A
Field Rd., Hawley 60 2C
Field Stores App. 78 4A
Field View, Egham 13 4F
Field View, Feltham 15 4E
Field Way, Addington 59 2D
Field Way, Burntcommon 83 1D
Field Way, Haslemere 152 2A
Field Wk. 129 2E
Fieldcommon La. 34 4C
Fielden Pl. 27 1D
Fielders Grn. 82 5A
Fieldhouse Cl. 28 4B
Fieldhouse Rd. 21 2F
Fieldhurst Cl. 49 1E
Fielding Av. 17 3D
Fielding Gdns. 43 2D
Fielding Rd., Bedford Park 9 1D
Fielding Rd., Sandhurst 43 5E
Fielding Rd., Streatham Vale 39 1F
Fieldings, The, Forest Hill 23 2E
Fieldings, The, Horley 128 2C
Fieldings, The, Woking 64 1B
Fieldsend Rd. 55 1D
Fieldside Rd. 24 4B
Fieldview, Earlsfield 20 2C
Fieldview, Horley 128 2B
Fieldview, Horley 128 2C
Fieldway, Aldershot 78 4B
Fife Rd., East Sheen 19 1D
Fife Rd., Kingston 36 1B
Fife Way 86 1A
Fifehead Cl. 14 5C
Fifield La. 115 3D
Fifth Cross Rd. 17 3E
Filbert Cres. 146 4B
Filby Rd. 53 2F
Filey Cl., Biggin Hill 77 3D
Filey Cl., Sutton 55 2F
Filmer Gro. 119 1D
Finborough Rd. 21 5E
Finch Av. 22 4C
Finch Dri. 16 2B
Finchampstead Rd. 25 4D
Finches Rise 82 4B
Findhorn Cl. 43 4E
Findings, The 60 3B
Findlay Dri. 81 3D
Findon Rd., Hammersmith 9 1F
Findon Rd., Ifield 146 3C
Finlay Gdns. 49 1E
Finlays Cl. 53 1F
Finmere 27 4D
Finnart Cl. 33 5E
Finney Dri. 46 2A
Finstock Grn. 27 2F
Fintry Pl. 60 3B
Fintry Walk 60 3B
Fiona Cl. 68 5C
Fir Acre Rd. 78 3C
Fir Cl. 34 4A
Fir Dr. Blackwater 60 1B
Fir Grange Av. 50 1B
Fir Gro., Malden 37 3E
Fir Grove, Woking 64 3B
Fir Grove Rd. 61 5D
Fir Rd., Hanworth 16 4B
Fir Rd., North Cheam 38 4B
Fir St. 23 3E
Fir Tree Cl., Esher 52 1A
Fir Tree Cl., Stoneleigh 54 1B
Fir Tree Cl., Tooting Bec 21 4F
Fir Tree Gdns., Addington 59 1D
Fir Tree Gro. 56 2B
Fir Tree Pl. 15 4D
Fir Tree Rd., Banstead 55 5D
Fir Tree Rd., Bellfields 81 4F
Fir Tree Rd., Epsom Downs 71 1F
Fir Tree Rd., Highland Park 70 5A
Fir Tree Walk 89 5F
Firbank Dri. 64 3B
Firbank La. 64 3C
Firbank Pl. 12 5B
Fircroft Cl. 65 2D
Fircroft Rd., Chessington 53 1E
Fircroft Rd., Upper Tooting 21 3D
Firdene 37 4D
Fireball Hill 29 4D
Firfield Rd., Addlestone 49 1E
Firfield Rd., Farnham 96 5A
Firfields 50 2B
Firgrove Hill 96 4A
Firhill Rd. 24 4A
Firlands, Bracknell 27 3D
Firlands, Horley 128 2B
Firlands, Weybridge 50 2C
Firlands Av. 44 5A
Firle Cl. 147 3D
Firs Av. 120 1B
Firs Cl., Dorking 105 2F
Firs Cl., Esher 52 2B
Firs Cl., Lewisham 23 2F
Firs Cl., Merrow 82 5C
Firs Cl., Mitcham 39 1E
Firs Cl., South Farnbor'h 78 1A
Firs La. 120 2C
Firs Rd. 74 1B
Firs, The 100 2B
Firs, The, Caterham 74 4C
Firs Way 81 5F
Firsby Av. 41 4F
First Av., Epsom 54 3A
First Av., Mortlake 9 5E
First Av., Walton 34 3A
First Av., West Molesey 34 2C
First Cl. 35 2D
First Cross Rd. 17 3E
First Rd. 40 2A
First Slip 69 2F
Firstway 37 1F
Firswood Av. 54 1B
Firtree Av., Mitcham 39 1E
Firtree Av., Shottermill 151 3D
Firtree Cl., Epsom Downs 71 1F
Firtree Cl., Langley Green 146 2C
Firtree Cl., Leatherhead 70 5A
Firway 134 4B
Firwood Cl. 64 3A
Firwood Dri. 44 5A
Firwood Rd. 30 3A
Fisher Cl., Crawley 147 5D
Fisher Cl., Weybridge 51 1D
Fisher La. 154 2A
Fisher Rowe Cl. 120 1B
Fisherman Cl. 18 4A
Fishers 128 2C
Fishers Court. 158 4B
Fisher's La. 9 2D
Fishers Wood 29 4F
Fishersdene 52 2C
Fishponds Rd., Tooting 21 4D
Fishponds Rd., Wokingham 25 3D
Fitchet Cl. 146 3C
Fitzalan Rd., Claygate 52 2B
Fitzalan Rd., Horsham 158 4C
Fitzgeorge Av. 37 1D
Fitzgerald Rd. 35 3F
Fitzgerard Av. 9 5E
Fitzhugh Gro. 21 1D
Fitzjames Av. 41 5D
Fitzjohn Cl. 82 4B
Fitzrobert Pl. 13 5E
Fitzroy Cres. 9 3D
Fitzroy Gdns. 23 5D
Fitzwilliam Av. 8 4B
Five Acre Cl., Lindford 133 4D
Five Acre Cl., Thornton Heath 40 3B
Five Acres 147 3D
Five Oaks Cl., Addlestone 49 2D
Five Oaks Cl., Woking 64 3A
Flag Cl. 41 4F
Flambard Way 119 2D
Flamborough Cl. 77 3D
Flanchford La. 107 3F
Flanchford Rd., Bedford Park 9 1E
Flanchford Rd., Reigate 89 5D
Flanders Court 13 4E
Flanders Rd. 9 2E
Flaxley Rd. 38 4C
Fleece Rd. 36 4A
Fleet Cl. 34 3C
Fleet Rd. 60 5A
Fleet Sq. 36 2C
Fleet Way 31 2E
Fleetside 34 3C
Fleetwood Cl., Chessington 53 2D
Fleetwood Cl., Tadworth 72 4A
Fleetwood Court 49 5D
Fleetwood Rd. 36 2C
Fleming Cl. 61 4D
Fleming Mead 21 5D
Fleming Way 147 2D
Flemish Fields 32 4A
Fletcher Cl. 48 2C
Fletcher Gdns. 26 1B
Fletcher Rd., Ealing 9 1D
Fletcher Rd., Ottershaw 48 2C
Fletchers Cl. 158 5C
Fleur Gates 20 2A
Flexford Grn. 26 3B
Flexford Rd. 98 1C
Flimwell Cl. 24 4C
Flint Cl., Crawley 147 5F
Flint Cl., Leatherhead 86 1A
Flint Cl., Redhill 90 5A
Flint Gro. 27 1D
Flint Hill 106 3A
Flint Hill Cl. 106 3A
Flintlock Cl. 7 5B
Flora Cl. 59 4E
Flora Gdns. 59 4E
Floral Court 70 2A
Florence Av., Morden 38 3C
Florence Av., Woodham 49 4D
Florence Cl. 34 4A
Florence Gdns. 14 5B
Florence Rd., Feltham 16 2A
Florence Rd., Kingston 18 5B
Florence Rd., Sanderstead 57 3F
Florence Rd., Walton-on-Thames 34 4A
Florence Rd., Wimbledon 20 5B
Florence Rd., York Town 43 4E
Florian Av. 56 1A
Florida Rd. 40 1B
Florida Row 101 3D
Flower Cres. 48 2B
Flower La. 92 3C
Flower Wk. 100 2C
Floyd's La. 66 1A
Foley Mews 52 2B
Foley Rd., Biggin Hill 77 2E
Foley Rd., Claygate 52 2B
Follet Cl. 12 1B
Folly Hill 96 2A
Folly La., Farnham 96 2A
Folly La., South Holmwood 106 5A
Follyfield Rd. 55 5E
Follyhatch La. 79 5E
Fontaine Rd. 22 5A
Fontenoy Rd. 21 3F
Fontley Way 19 2E
Fontmell Cl. 15 4D
Fontmell Pk. 15 4D
Ford Cl., Ashford 14 5C
Ford Cl., Shepperton Grn. 33 3D
Ford La. 115 1D
Ford Manor Rd. 132 3A
Ford Rd., Ashford 14 4C
Ford Rd., Bisley 63 1E
Ford Rd., Chertsey 32 4B
Ford Rd., Chobham 46 3C
Ford Rd., Old Woking 65 3E
Fordbridge Cl. 32 4B
Fordbridge Rd., Ashford 15 4D
Fordbridge Rd., Lower Halliford 33 3F
Fordel Rd. 24 2B
Fordingbridge Cl. 158 5B
Fordmill Rd. 24 3A
Fordwater Rd. 32 4B
Fordwater Trading Estate 32 4B
Fordwell Rd. 27 2F
Fordyce Rd. 24 1B
Foremans Pk. 78 5C
Foreman's Rd. 78 5C
Forest Cl., Ascot Heath 28 2A
Forest Cl., Crawley Down 149 3E
Forest Cl., Horsley 84 1C
Forest Cl., Woking 65 1F
Forest Cres. 70 1C
Forest Dale 135 5E
Forest Dri., Farnham 115 2D
Forest Dri., Kingswood 72 4B
Forest Green 123 4F
Forest Green, Bracknell 27 1E
Forest Hill Rd. 23 1E
Forest Hills 61 1D
Forest La., Effingham Junction 67 5F
Forest La., Lindford 133 4E
Forest Rd., Ascot 10 5B
Forest Rd., Cranbourne 11 3D
Forest Rd., Crowthorne 43 1D
Forest Rd., Effingham Junction 67 5F
Forest Rd., Feltham 16 3A
Forest Rd., Horsley 84 2C
Forest Rd., Kew 8 3C
Forest Rd., St. Helier 38 4B
Forest Rd., Woking 65 1F
Forest Ridge 42 2A
Forest Side 37 4E
Forest View 147 5E
Forest View Rd. 150 3C
Forest Way 70 2C
Forester Rd. 147 5D
Foresters Cl., Beddington 56 2C
Foresters Cl., Woking 64 2A
Foresters Dri. 56 2C
Foresters Sq. 27 2E
Foresters Way 43 2F
Forestfield, Crawley 147 5E
Forestfield, Horsham 158 4C
Forestholme Cl. 23 3E
Forge Av. 74 3B
Forge Cl., Farnham 96 3B
Forge Dri., Claygate 52 2C
Forge La., Cheam 55 2D
Forge La., Hanworth 16 4B
Forge La., Sunbury-on-Thames 34 2A
Forge La., Three Bridges 147 3E
Forge Pinion Court 158 4B
Forge Rd. 147 3E
Forman Pk. 78 5C
Forrest Gdns. 40 2A
Forster Rd., Brixton Hill 22 2A
Forster Rd., Elmers End 41 2F
Forsyth Path 48 5C
Forsyth Rd. 48 5C
Forsythe Cres. 40 1C
Fort La. 89 3F
Fort Rd., Guildford 101 2D
Fort Rd., West Humble 87 4F
Fortescue Av. 17 3D
Fortescue Rd., Mitcham 21 5D
Fortescue Rd., Weybridge 50 1A
Forth Cl. 60 4B
Fortrose Cl. 43 4E
Fortrose Gdns. 22 2A
Fortune Dri. 140 2C
Fortyfoot Rd. 70 4A
Forum, The 35 2D
Foss Av. 57 1E
Foss Rd. 20 4C

184

Fossewood Dri — Garden Wood Rd

Fossewood Dri. 44 4B
Foster Down 92 3B
Foster La. 63 2F
Fosters Green 45 1F
Fosters Grove 45 1F
Fosters Rd. 9 2D
Foulser Rd. 21 3E
Foulsham Rd. 40 2C
Foundary Cl. 158 4C
Foundary La. 158 4C
Founders Gdns. 22 5C
Foundry La. 151 3F
Fountain Cl. 146 5B
Fountain Dri. 23 4D
Fountain Rd., Mitcham 39 1D
Fountain Rd., Norbury 40 1B
Fountain Rd., Redhill 109 1D
Fountain Rd., Tooting 21 4D
Fountains Av. 16 3C
Fountains Cl. 16 3C
Fountains Garth 26 2C
Four Acres, Merrow 82 4B
Four Acres, Oxshott 51 5F
Four Seasons Cres. 38 5B
Four Wents 51 5D
Fourth Cross Rd. 17 3E
Fourth Dri. 73 1F
Fowler Rd. 60 5C
Fowlers Croft 99 4F
Fowlers La. 26 1C
Fowlers Mead 47 3D
Fowler's Rd. 78 3A
Fox Cl., Crawley 146 2C
Fox Cl., Oatlands Pk. 50 1C
Fox Cl., Woking 65 1F
Fox Covert, Fetcham 69 5E
Fox Covert, Lightwater 45 3F
Fox Covert La. 29 3D
Fox Glove Av. 158 3C
Fox Heath 60 5A
Fox Hill 23 5A
Fox Hill Gdns. 23 5D
Fox Hills La. 79 4D
Fox La., Lit. Bookham 68 5C
Fox Lane, Caterham 74 4B
Fox Lane North 32 4A
Fox Lane South 32 4A
Fox Leigh Chase 158 3C
Fox Rd., Bracknell 27 2D
Fox Rd., Farnham 96 5B
Fox Rd., Shottermill 151 2E
Fox Yard 96 4A
Foxacre 75 4D
Foxborough Gdns. 24 1A
Foxborough Hill 119 1F
Foxborough Hill Rd. 100 5C
Foxbourne Rd. 21 3E
Foxburrows Av. 81 5D
Foxcombe 59 2E
Foxcombe Rd. 19 1F
Foxcote 25 5D
Foxdene 118 3C
Foxdene Rd. 82 5A
Foxdown Cl. 44 5A
Foxearth Cl. 77 2F
Foxearth Rd. 58 3B
Foxearth Spur 58 3B
Foxes Dale 42 2B
Foxglove Cl. 14 2C
Foxglove Gdns. 82 4C
Foxglove La. 53 1F
Foxglove Way 39 4E
Foxgrove Av. 24 5B
Foxgrove Dri. 65 1D
Foxgrove Rd. 24 5A
Foxhill Cres. 44 4C
Foxhills 64 2C
Foxhills Cl. 48 2B
Foxhills Rd. 48 1B
Foxholes 50 1C
Foxhurst Rd. 78 4C
Foxlake Rd. 49 4F
Foxley Cl., Blackwater 43 5D
Foxley Cl., Salfords 109 3E
Foxley Gdns. 57 5E
Foxley Hill Rd. 57 4E
Foxley La. 57 3D
Foxley Rd., Kenley 57 5E
Foxley Rd., Thornton H'th. 40 2B
Foxon Cl. 74 4C
Foxon La. 74 4C
Foxon Lane Gdns. 74 4C
Foxwarren 52 3C
Foxwood Cl. 16 3A
Frailey Cl. 65 1E
Frailey Hill 65 1E
Framfield Cl. 146 3B
Framfield Rd. 39 1E
Frampton Cl. 55 2E
Frampton Rd. 16 1C
France Hill Dri. 44 5A
Francemary Rd. 24 1A
Franche Court Rd. 20 3C
Francis Av. 16 3A
Francis Chichester Cl. 28 3C
Francis Cl., Ewell 54 1A
Francis Cl., Littleton 33 2D
Francis Rd., Beddington 56 2C
Francis Rd., Caterham 74 4C
Francis Rd., Croydon 40 4B
Francis Way 62 1A
Franciscan Rd. 21 4D
Franconia Rd. 21 1F
Frank Cl. 36 2C
Frank Dixon Way 22 2C
Frankfurt Rd. 22 1C
Franklands Dri. 49 2D
Franklin Cl. 147 4F
Franklin Cres. 39 2F
Franklin Gdns. 40 4A
Franklyn Rd., Ockford Ridge 118 2C
Franklyn Rd., Penge 23 5E
Franklyn Rd., Walton-on-Thames 34 3A
Franks Av. 37 2D
Frank's Field Estate 103 5F
Franks Rd. 81 4E
Fransfield Gro. 23 3E
Frant Rd. 40 3B
Franthorne Way 24 3A
Fraser Gdns. 86 5C
Fraser Mead 43 5E
Fraser Rd. 27 1D
Fraser St. 9 2D
Frasers Gdns. 105 1F
Frederick Cl. 55 1E
Frederick Gdns. 55 1E
Frederick Pl. 25 2D
Frederick Rd. 55 1E
Frederick Sanger Rd. 100 1A
Free Prae Rd. 32 4A
Freeborn Way 27 1E
Freedown La. 55 5F
Freelands Av. 58 3C
Freelands Rd. 51 5D
Freeman Cl. 33 2F
Freeman Rd. 38 3C
Freemantle Rd. 45 2E
Freemasons Rd. 40 4C
Freesia Dri. 63 1E
French Gdns., Blackwater 60 1B
French Gdns., Cobham 51 5E
French La. 136 2B
French St. 34 1B
Frenchaye 49 1E
Frenches Av. 49 1E
Frenches Court 90 4B
Frenches Rd. 90 4B
Frenches, The 90 4B
Frenchlands Hatch 84 2C
French's Wells 64 2B
Frensham 115 4E
Frensham, Bracknell 27 3D
Frensham Dri., New Addington 59 2E
Frensham Dri., Roehampton Vale 19 3E
Frensham Heights Rd. 114 3C
Frensham La. 134 1A
Frensham Rd., Crowthorne 43 1D
Frensham Rd., Farnham 96 5A
Frensham Rd., Frensham 115 4E
Frensham Rd., Headley 133 4E
Frensham Rd., Hearn 133 2F
Frensham Rd., Kenley 57 5E
Frensham Vale Rd. 115 2D
Frensham Way 71 1F
Freshford St. 20 3C
Freshmount Gdns. 53 4F
Freshwater Cl. 21 5E
Freshwater Rd. 21 5E
Freshwood Way 56 3C
Frewin Rd. 21 2D
Friar Mews 22 3B
Friars Av. 19 3E
Friar's Gate 100 1B
Friars Keep 27 2D
Friars La. 18 1A
Friars Orchard 69 4E
Friars Rd. 30 2C
Friars Rise 65 2E
Friars Rookery 147 4D
Friars Stile Rd. 18 1B
Friars Way 32 3A
Friarswood 58 3C
Friary Court. 64 2A
Friary Rd., S. Ascot 28 3C
Friary Rd., Wraysbury 12 1C
Friary St., Guildford 159
Friary, The, Guildford 159
Friary, The, Old Windsor 12 1C
Friary Way 147 4D
Friday Rd. 21 5D
Friday St., Ockley 143 1E
Friday Street 104 5C
Friday Street, Abinger 104 5B
Friday Street, Kingsfold 144 4B
Friend Av. 78 5B
Friends Rd., E. Croydon 40 5C
Friends Rd., Purley 57 4E
Friern Rd. 23 2D
Frimley 61 3E
Frimley Av. 57 1D
Frimley Business Park 61 3D
Frimley Cl. 59 2E
Frimley Cres. 59 2E
Frimley Gdns. 39 2D
Frimley Green Rd. 61 3E
Frimley Grove 61 2E
Frimley Grove Gdns. 61 2E
Frimley Hall Dri. 44 5B
Frimley High St. 61 3D
Frimley Rd., Ash Vale 78 1C
Frimley Rd., Camberley 43 5F
Frimley Rd., Chessington 53 1E
Frinton Rd. 21 5E
Friston Wk. 146 3B
Frith Hill Rd., Frimley 61 2F
Frith Hill Rd., Godalming 119 1D
Frith Knoll 51 1D
Frith Pk. 150 1C
Frith Rd. 40 5B
Frithend Rd. 133 1D
Friths Dri. 89 4F
Frithwald Rd. 32 4A
Frobisher 27 4D
Frobisher Cl. 74 2C
Frobisher Cres. 14 2C
Frobisher Gdns. 82 5B
Frodsham Way 43 3E
Frog Grove La. 80 3B
Frog La. 26 2C
Frogetts La. 142 2B
Froghall Dri. 25 2F
Frogmore 20 1B
Frogmore Cl. 38 5A
Frogmore Gdns. 55 1D
Frogmore Green 60 1A
Frogmore Park Dri. 60 1B
Frogmore Rd. 60 1A
Frome Cl. 60 4B
Fromondes Rd. 55 1D
Fromow Gdns. 46 2A
Froxfield Down 27 3F
Fruen Rd. 15 2F
Fryern Wood 74 5C
Fry's La. 45 3D
Fryston Av., Addiscombe 41 5E
Fryston Av., Woodmansterne 73 1E
Fulbrook Av. 49 4D
Fulbrook La. 117 2D
Fulford Rd., Caterham 74 4C
Fulford Rd., W. Ewell 54 3A
Fullbrooks Av. 37 4E
Fullers Av. 36 5B
Fullers Farm Rd. 84 4A
Fullers Rd. 114 2B
Fuller's Vale 133 4F
Fullers Way 36 5B
Fullers Way Nth. 36 5B
Fullers Way Sth. 36 5B
Fuller's Wood 59 1D
Fullers Wood La. 109 1F
Fullerton Cl. 50 5A
Fullerton Dri. 49 5F
Fullerton Rd., Addiscombe 41 4D
Fullerton Rd., Byfleet 49 5F
Fullerton Rd., Carshalton 56 3A
Fullerton Rd., Wandsworth 20 1C
Fullerton Way 49 5F
Fullmer Way 49 3D
Fulmar Cl., Crawley 146 4A
Fulmer Cl., Hanworth 16 4C
Fulvens 103 5F
Fulwell Park Av. 17 3D
Fulwell Rd. 17 4E
Fulwood Gdns. 17 1F
Fulwood Walk 20 2A
Furlong Cl. 39 4E
Furlong Rd. 105 2D
Furlough, The 65 2E
Furlough, The 65 2E
Furmage St. 20 2C
Furnace Dri. 147 5E
Furnace Farm Rd., Snowhill 149 1E
Furnace Farm Rd., Tilgate 147 5E
Furnace Parade 147 5E
Furnace Pl. 147 5E
Furnace Place Rd. 153 2D
Furneaux Av. 22 4B
Furness Rd. 38 3C
Furnival Cl. 30 3C
Furrows Pl. 75 5D
Furrows, The 34 5B
Furse Cl. 62 1A
Further Green Rd. 24 2C
Furze Cl., Furze Hill 78 2C
Furze Cl., Redhill 90 5A
Furze Field 52 5B
Furze Gro. 72 4B
Furze Hill, Kingswood 72 3B
Furze Hill, Purley 57 4D
Furze Hill, Redhill 90 5A
Furze Hill, Sandy Cross 97 3E
Furze Hill Cres. 43 2D
Furze Hill Rd. 134 5A
Furze La., Farncombe 100 5A
Furze La., Felbridge 150 1A
Furze La., Purley 57 4D
Furze Rd., Addlestone 49 2D
Furze Rd., Rudgwick 157 2E
Furze Rd., Thornton Heath 40 2C
Furzedown Dri. 21 4E
Furzedown Rd., Belmont 55 4F
Furzedown Rd., Tooting Bec 21 4E
Furzefield 146 3C
Furzefield Chase 131 5F
Furzefield Cres. 108 1C
Furzefield Rd., Felcourt 150 1B
Furzefield Rd., Mead Vale 108 1C
Furzemoors 27 3D
Furzen La. 142 5A
Furzevale Rd. 134 5A
Furzewood 34 1A
Fuscia Way 46 5A
Fydlers Cl. 10 5C

G

Gable Ct. 23 4E
Gables Av. 15 4D
Gables Cl., Ash Vale 78 3C
Gables Cl., West Heath 60 5C
Gables, The, Banstead 72 2B
Gables, The, Horsham 158 4B
Gables, The, Horsham 158 4B
Gables, The, Oxshott 52 5A
Gabriel Dri. 62 1A
Gabriel St. 23 2F
Gadbrook Rd. 107 3D
Gadesden Rd. 54 2A
Gaffney Cl. 78 2B
Gage Cl. 149 2E
Gainsborough 27 4D
Gainsborough Cl., Beckenham 24 5A
Gainsborough Cl., Camberley 44 5B
Gainsborough Cl., South Farnborough 78 1A
Gainsborough Cl., Thames Ditton 35 4E
Gainsborough Court 51 1D
Gainsborough Dri., Ascot 28 1A
Gainsborough Dri., Sanderstead 58 5B
Gainsborough Gdns. 17 1E
Gainsborough Rd., Crawley 147 5D
Gainsborough Rd., Ewell 54 3A
Gainsborough Rd., Kew 8 4B
Gainsborough Rd., Malden Manor 37 4D
Gainsborough Rd., Turnham Green 9 2E
Gaist Av. 75 4E
Galatia Rd. 9 3E
Gale Cl. 16 5C
Gale Cres. 72 2B
Gale Dri. 45 3F
Gales Cl. 82 4C
Gales Dri. 147 4D
Gales Pl. 147 4E
Galgate Cl. 20 2A
Gallery Rd. 22 2C
Galleymead Rd. 7 4B
Gallop, The, Bramley Bank 58 2B
Gallop, The, Sutton 55 3F
Gallop, The, Windsor Great Park 11 2F
Galpin's Rd. 40 3A
Galsworthy Rd., Chertsey 32 4A
Galsworthy Rd., Kingston 36 1C
Galvani Way 40 4A
Galveston Rd. 20 1B
Galvins Cl. 81 4E
Galwey Rd. 78 4A
Gambles La., Sendmarsh 66 5B
Gambole Rd. 21 4D
Gander Green La. 55 1E
Gane Cl. 57 2D
Gangers Hill 92 2C
Ganghill 82 4B
Gap Rd. 20 4B
Gapemouth Rd. 62 4A
Garbetts Way 97 2E
Garbrand Wk. 54 3B
Garden Av. 21 5E
Garden Cl., Addlestone 49 1F
Garden Cl., Ashford 15 5E
Garden Cl., Banstead 72 1B
Garden Cl., E. Grinstead 150 3C
Garden Cl., Hanworth 16 4C
Garden Cl., Leatherhead 70 5A
Garden Cl., Roehampton 19 2F
Garden Cl., Shamley Grn. 120 2C
Garden Cl., Waddon 57 1D
Garden Cottages 54 4A
Garden House La. 150 3C
Garden La. 22 2A
Garden Rd., Anerley 41 1E
Garden Rd., Nth. Sheen 8 5C
Garden Rd., Walton-on-Thames 34 3A
Garden Wk. 73 5E
Garden Wood Rd. 150 2B

Gardeners Green 145 4D
Gardeners Hill Rd. 115 1D
Gardeners Rd. 40 4B
Gardeners Wk. 86 1A
Gardenfields 72 3A
Gardens, The, E. Bedfont 15 1E
Gardens, The, Eden Park 42 1B
Gardens, The, Esher 51 1F
Gardens, The, Pirbright 63 4E
Gardens, The, Tongham 97 1E
Gardenwood La. 150 2B
Gardner La. 149 3D
Gardner Rd., Guildford 81 5F
Gardner Rd., Hanworth 16 3C
Garendon Gdns. 38 4B
Garendon Rd. 38 4B
Gareth Cl. 38 5A
Garfield Rd., Addlestone 49 1E
Garfield Rd., Camberley 44 5A
Garfield Rd., Twickenham 17 2F
Garfield Rd., Wimbledon 20 4C
Garibaldi Rd. 109 1D
Garland Rd. 150 2B
Garland Way 74 4C
Garlands Rd., Leatherhead 70 4A
Garlands Rd., Redhill 90 5A
Garlichill Road 71 2F
Garlies Rd. 23 3F
Garnet Rd. 40 2C
Garrads Rd. 21 3F
Garrard Rd. 72 1B
Garratt Cl. 57 1D
Garratt La. 20 1C
Garratt Ter. 21 4D
Garratts La. 72 1B
Garrick Cl., Hersham 51 1D
Garrick Cl., Staines 14 5A
Garrick Gdns., W. Moseley 34 2C
Garrick Gro. 40 5C
Garrick Rd., N. Sheen 8 4C
Garrick Way 61 3E
Garrick Wk. 147 5D
Garrison La. 53 2D
Garside Cl. 17 5D
Garson La. 12 2C
Garson Rd. 51 2F
Garston La. 74 1C
Garstons, The 85 1F
Garswood 27 3D
Garth Cl., Cheam 38 4A
Garth Cl., Farnham 96 5A
Garth Rd., Kingston 18 4B
Garth Rd., North Cheam 38 4A
Garth, The, Ash 78 5B
Garth, The, Hampton Hill 17 5D
Garth, The, Oxshott 51 5F
Garthorne Rd. 23 2F
Garthside 18 4B
Gartmoor Gdns. 20 2B
Gascoigne Rd., New
  Addington 59 3E
Gascoigne Rd., Weybridge 33 5D
Gasden Copse 118 5A
Gasden Dri. 118 5A
Gasden La. 118 5A
Gaskarth Rd. 21 1E
Gaskyns Cl. 157 2E
Gassiot Rd. 21 4E
Gassiot Way 39 5D
Gasson Wood Rd. 146 5A
Gaston Bell Cl. 8 5B
Gaston Bridge Rd. 33 3F
Gaston Rd. 39 2E
Gaston Way 33 3E
Gateford Dri. 158 3C
Gatehouse Cl. 19 5D
Gates Green Rd. 42 5C
Gatesden Rd,. 69 5E
Gateside Rd. 21 3D
Gatestone Rd. 22 5C
Gateway 33 5E
Gateway, The 48 5B
Gateways 101 1E
Gatfield Gro. 16 3C
Gatley Av. 53 1F
Gatton 90 2A
Gatton Cl., Belmont 55 3F
Gatton Cl., The Reigate 89 4F
Gatton Park Rd. 90 4A
Gatton Rd., Reigate 89 4F
Gatton Rd., Tooting 21 4D
Gatwick Airport 128 4B
Gatwick Airport Link 128 4C
Gatwick Gate 128 5A
Gatwick Rd., Crawley 147 2E
Gatwick Rd., Southfields 20 2B
Gauntlet Cres. 74 3C
Gauntlett Rd. 56 1A
Gavell Rd. 51 5D
Gaveston Cl. 49 5F
Gaveston Rd. 69 3F
Gaydon 57 1D
Gayfere Rd. 54 1C
Gayford Rd. 9 1E
Gayhouse La. 110 5C
Gayler Cl. 92 5A

Gaynesford Rd., Carshalton
  on the Hill 56 2A
Gaynesford Rd., Forest Hill 23 3F
Gayville Rd. 21 1E
Gaywood Court 22 2D
Gaywood Rd. 70 2B
Geary Cl. 129 3E
Geneva Cl. 33 1F
Geneva Rd., Kingston 36 2B
Geneva Rd., Thornton
  Heath 40 3B
Genoa Av 20 1A
Genoa Rd. 41 1E
Gentles La. 133 5F
George Denyer Cl. 152 2A
George Eliot Cl. 137 1E
George Grove Rd. 41 1D
George La. 24 1B
George Rd., Farncombe 100 5A
George Rd., Guildford 81 5F
George Rd., Kingston Hill 18 5C
George Rd., Malden 37 2E
George Rd., Milford 118 3B
George St., Croydon 40 5C
George St., Richmond 18 1B
George St., Staines 14 4A
George St., Sutton 55 1F
Georgeham Rd. 43 3E
Georgelands 66 4B
George's Av. 8 1A
George's Rd. 77 3E
Georges Terr. 74 4C
Georgetown Cl. 22 4C
Georgia Rd., Kingston 37 2D
Georgia Rd., Norbury 40 1B
Georgian Cl., Camberley 44 4B
Georgian Cl., Staines 14 4B
Georgian Court 22 4A
Geraldine Rd., Brentford 8 3C
Geraldine Rd., Wandsworth 20 1C
Geralds Grn. 55 5D
Gerard Av. 16 2C
Gerard Rd. 9 4E
Germander Dri. 63 1E
Gerotus Pl. 32 4A
Gerrards Mead 72 1B
Ghent St. 24 3A
Gibbet La. 44 4C
Gibbon Rd. 36 1B
Gibbons Cl. 43 4D
Gibbs Av. 22 4C
Gibbs Brook La. 112 1C
Giblets La. 158 2C
Gibraltar Cres. 54 3B
Gibson Cl. 53 1D
Gibson Ct. 35 5F
Gibson Pl. 14 1B
Gibson Rd. 55 1F
Gibsons Hill 22 5B
Gidd Hill 73 1E
Giffard Rd. 60 4C
Gigghill Rd. 35 4F
Giggshill Gdns. 35 4F
Giggshill Rd. 35 4F
Gilbert Rd., Frimley 61 2D
Gilbert Rd., Wimbledon 20 5C
Gilbey Rd. 21 4D
Gilders Rd. 53 2E
Giles Cop 23 4D
Giles Travers Cl. 31 2E
Gilham's Rd. 55 4D
Gilham's La. 151 3D
Gilkes Cres. 22 1C
Gill Av. 100 1A
Gillett Rd. 40 2C
Gilliam Grn. 57 3E
Gillian Av. 97 1D
Gillian Cl. 97 1D
Gillian Park Rd. 38 4B
Gillian St. 24 1A
Gilliat Dri. 82 4C
Gilmais 86 1A
Gilmore Cres. 15 4D
Gilpin Av. 9 5D
Gilpin Cres. 17 2D
Gilsland Rd. 40 2C
Gilton Rd. 24 3C
Gimcrack Hill 70 4A
Gingers Cl. 141 2D
Ginhams Rd. 146 4C
Gipsy La., Bracknell 27 1D
Gipsy La., Wokingham 25 3E
Gipsy Rd. 22 4C
Gipsy Road Gdns. 22 4C
Girdwood Rd. 20 2A
Girton Cl. 43 3E
Girton Gdns. 42 5A
Girton Rd. 23 4F
Givons Gro. 87 1D
Glade Gdns. 41 4F
Glade Spur 72 4C
Glade, The, Ascot 28 3C
Glade, The, East Ewell 55 3D
Glade, The, Fetcham 69 4D
Glade, The, Furnace Green 147 5E
Glade, The, Kingswood 72 4B
Glade, The, Monks Orchard 41 3F

Glade, The, Old Coulsdon 74 3B
Glade, The, Staines 14 5B
Glade, The, Stoneleigh 54 2C
Glade, The, West Wickham 42 5B
Glade, The Sheerwater 48 5C
Gladeside 41 3F
Gladeside Cl. 53 2D
Gladiator St. 23 2F
Gladioli Cl. 16 5C
Gladsmuir Cl. 34 5A
Gladstone Av. Feltham 16 1A
Gladstone Av. Twickenham 17 2E
Gladstone Ms. 23 5E
Gladstone Rd., Acton
  Green 9 1D
Gladstone Rd., Ashtead 70 2B
Gladstone Rd., Croydon 40 4C
Gladstone Rd., Hook 36 5B
Gladstone Rd., Horsham 158 4B
Gladstone Rd., Kingston 36 2C
Gladstone Rd., Wimbledon 20 5B
Glamis Cl. 61 3F
Glamorgan Cl. 40 2A
Glamorgan Rd. 18 5A
Glanfield Rd. 42 2A
Glanty 13 4E
Glanty, The 13 4E
Glanville Rd. 22 1A
Glasbrook Av. 16 2C
Glasford St. 21 5E
Glassonby Wk. 45 5D
Glastonbury Rd. 38 4B
Glayshers Hill 134 4A
Glazebrook Cl. 22 3C
Glazebrook Rd. 17 5E
Glazier Rd. 134 4A
Glaziers La. 79 4F
Glebe Av. 39 1D
Glebe Cl., Crawley 147 3D
Glebe Cl., Gt. Bookham 85 1F
Glebe Cl., Lightwater 46 3A
Glebe Cottages 83 5E
Glebe Court, Guildford 82 5A
Glebe Court, Mitcham 39 2D
Glebe Gdns., Byfleet 49 5F
Glebe Gdns., Malden 37 4E
Glebe Hyrst 58 4A
Glebe La., Abinger 104 5B
Glebe La., Rushmoor 116 5A
Glebe Path 39 2D
Glebe Rd., Arford 133 4F
Glebe Rd., Ashtead 70 2B
Glebe Rd., Barnes 9 4E
Glebe Rd., Carshalton 56 2B
Glebe Rd., Cranleigh 140 1C
Glebe Rd., Dorking 105 1F
Glebe Rd., East Ewell 55 3D
Glebe Rd., Egham 13 5F
Glebe Rd., Hooley 73 5E
Glebe Rd., Old Windsor 12 1B
Glebe Rd., Staines 14 4B
Glebe Rd., Warlingham 75 2F
Glebe Rd., West Heath 60 4C
Glebe St., Chiswick 9 2D
Glebe St., Twickenham 17 1F
Glebe, The, Blackwater 60 1B
Glebe, The, Copthorne 148 1B
Glebe, The, Ewhurst 122 5C
Glebe, The, Felbridge 150 1A
Glebe, The, Horley 128 2B
Glebe, The, Leigh 107 4F
Glebe, The, Malden 37 4E
Glebe Way, Hanworth 16 3C
Glebe Way, Sanderstead 58 4A
Glebe Way, W. Wickham 42 5B
Glebelands, Claygate 52 3C
Glebelands, Crawley Down 149 3D
Glebelands, East Molesey 35 2D
Glebelands, Loxwood 156 4A
Glebelands Gdns. 33 3E
Glebelands Rd., Camberley 60 1C
Glebelands Rd., Feltham 16 2A
Glebelands Rd.,
  Wokingham 25 1D
Glebewood 27 3D
Gledhow Wood 72 4C
Glen Albyn Rd. 20 3A
Glen Av. 15 4D
Glen Cl., Hindhead 135 4D
Glen Cl., Kingswood 72 5A
Glen Cl., Littleton 33 2D
Glen Gdns. 57 1E
Glen Innes 43 3E
Glen Lea 151 1E
Glen Rd., Grayshott 135 5D
Glen Rd., Hindhead 135 4D
Glen Rd., Hook 53 1E
Glen Road End 56 3B
Glen, The, Addlestone 49 1D
Glen, The, Shirley 41 5F
Glen, The, Shortlands 42 1C
Glen Vue 150 2C
Glena Mount 55 1F
Glenavon Cl. 52 2C
Glenbow Rd. 24 5C
Glenbuck Rd. 36 3B
Glenburnie Rd. 21 3D

Glencairn Rd. 22 5A
Glenco Cl. 61 3F
Glencoe 61 3F
Glencoe Rd. 33 5D
Glendale 64 2C
Glendale Dri., Burpham 82 3B
Glendale Dri., Wimbledon 20 4B
Glendale Gro. 82 3B
Glendale Rd. 74 1B
Glendene Av. 84 1C
Glendower Rd. 9 5D
Gleneagle Rd. 21 4F
Gleneagles Cl. 14 1B
Gleneagles Dri. 60 5A
Gleneldon Rd. 22 4A
Glenelg Rd. 22 1A
Glenfarg Rd. 24 2B
Glenfield 8 1A
Glenfield Cl. 106 2C
Glenfield Rd., Banstead 72 1B
Glenfield Rd., Streatham 21 2F
Glenfield Rd., Strood Grn. 106 2C
Glenfield Rd., Sunbury 15 5E
Glengarry Rd. 23 1D
Glenheadon Rise 70 5B
Glenhurst 45 1F
Glenhurst Rd. 8 3A
Glenhurst Rise 22 5C
Glenister Park Rd. 21 5F
Glenlion Court. 33 5F
Glenmore Cl. 32 5B
Glenmount Rd. 78 1C
Glenn Av. 57 4E
Glennie Rd. 22 3B
Glentham Rd. 9 3F
Glenthorne Av. 41 4E
Glenthorne Cl. 38 4B
Glenthorne Gdns. 38 4B
Glenthorne Rd.,
  Hammersmith 9 2F
Glenthorne Rd., Kingston 36 2B
Glenthorpe Rd. 38 3A
Glenville Gdns. 135 5E
Glenville Ms. 20 2B
Glenville Rd. 36 1C
Glenwood, Bracknell 27 2E
Glenwood, Dorking 106 2A
Glenwood Rd., Catford 24 2A
Glenwood Rd., Ewell 54 2B
Glenwood Way 41 3F
Globe Farm La. 43 5D
Glorney Mead 96 2C
Glory Mead 106 3A
Glossop Rd. 57 3F
Gloster Rd., Malden 37 2E
Gloster Rd., Woking 65 3E
Gloucester Cl., Frimley 61 3E
Gloucester Cl., Thames
  Ditton 35 4F
Gloucester Court 8 3C
Gloucester Cres. 14 5C
Gloucester Dri. 13 3F
Gloucester Gdns., Bagshot 45 2E
Gloucester Gdns., Sutton 38 5C
Gloucester Rd., Aldershot 97 1D
Gloucester Rd., Bagshot 45 2E
Gloucester Rd., Croydon 40 4C
Gloucester Rd., Feltham 16 2A
Gloucester Rd.,
  Hammersmith 9 1D
Gloucester Rd., Hampton
  Hill 17 5D
Gloucester Rd., Kew 8 3C
Gloucester Rd., Kingston 36 1C
Gloucester Rd., Lammas
  Park 8 1A
Gloucester Rd., Redhill 90 5B
Gloucester Rd.,
  Twickenham 17 4E
Gloucester Rd., Whitton 17 2D
Gloucester Rd.,
  Woodbridge Hill 81 4E
Glovers Field 151 3E
Glovers Rd., Charlwood 127 4D
Glover's Rd., Reigate 108 1C
Glyn Cl. 54 3B
Glyn Rd. 38 5A
Glynswood, Camberley 61 1E
Glynswood, Upper Bourne 114 2C
Goat Rd. 39 4E
Goaters Rd. 28 1A
Goatsfield Rd. 77 3E
Godalming 119 1D
Godalming Av. 57 1D
Godalming Rd. 139 1D
Goddard Cl., Crawley 147 5F
Goddard Cl., Shepperton
  Grn. 33 2D
Goddard Rd. 41 2F
Goddards La. 61 1D
Godden Cres. 60 5C
Godfrey Av. 17 2E
Godfrey Way 16 2C
Godley Rd., Byfleet 50 5A
Godley Rd., Earlsfield 20 2D
Godolphin Cl. 55 3E

Godolphin Rd., Hammersmith	9 1F	Gordon Cres.	61 1D
Godolphin Rd., Weybridge	50 2B	Gordon Dri., Chertsey	32 5A
Godric Cres.	59 3E	Gordon Dri., Shepperton	33 4E
Godson Rd.	40 5B	Gordon Rd., Ashford	14 3C
Godstone	92 4B	Gordon Rd., Camberley	44 5A
Godstone Bypass	92 3B	Gordon Rd., Carshalton Beeches	56 2A
Godstone Hill	92 2B	Gordon Rd., Caterham	74 4C
Godstone Rd., Bletchingley	91 5F	Gordon Rd., Chiswick	8 3C
Godstone Rd., Caterham	75 5D	Gordon Rd., Claygate	52 2B
Godstone Rd., Kenley	74 1C	Gordon Rd., Crowthorne	43 2E
Godstone Rd., Lingfield	131 1E	Gordon Rd., Eden Park	42 2A
Godstone Rd., Oxted	93 4D	Gordon Rd., Egham	13 4E
Godstone Rd., Purley	57 4E	Gordon Rd., Elmers End	41 2F
Godstone Rd., Sutton	55 1F	Gordon Rd., Horsham	158 4B
Godstone Rd., Twickenham	17 1F	Gordon Rd., Kingston	36 1B
Godstone Rd., Whyteleafe	75 1D	Gordon Rd., North Sheen	8 4C
Godwin Cl.	54 2A	Gordon Rd., Redhill	90 4B
Goffs Cl.	146 4C	Gordon Rd., S. Farnboro'	78 2B
Goffs Lane	146 4C	Gordon Rd., Shepperton	33 3E
Goffs Park Rd.	146 5C	Gordon Rd., Surbiton	36 4B
Goff's Rd.	15 5E	Gordonbrock Rd.,	24 1A
Gogmore Farm Cl.	32 4A	Gordondale	20 3B
Gogmore La.	32 4A	Gordons Way	93 2E
Goidel Cl.	56 1C	Gore Rd.	37 1F
Gold Cup La.	28 1A	Goring Rd.	13 4F
Gold Hill	115 1E	Goring Sq.	14 4A
Gold Hill Manor	115 1E	Gorings Brook	158 3B
Goldcliff Cl.	38 4B	Gorings Mead	158 5B
Goldcrest Cl.	128 2A	Gorling Cl.	146 4A
Goldcrest Way, New Addington	59 2E	Gorrick Sq.	25 3D
Goldcrest Way, Woodcote	56 3C	Gorringe Park Av.	21 5E
Golden Orb Wood	26 1B	Gorse Bank Cl.	45 4F
Goldfinch Cl.	158 2B	Gorse Cl.	71 3F
Goldfinch Cl., Northgate	147 3D	Gorse Cl., Copthorne	148 2B
Goldfinch Gdns.	82 5C	Gorse Cl., Lower Bourne	115 1D
Goldfinch Rd.	58 3C	Gorse Court	82 4C
Goldfort Wk.	64 1A	Gorse Dri.	129 2E
Goldings, The	64 1A	Gorse End	158 3B
Goldney Rd.	61 1F	Gorse Hill La.	31 2D
Goldrings Rd.	52 5A	Gorse Hill Rd.	30 2C
Goldsmith Way	43 2D	Gorse La., Chobham	47 2D
Goldsmiths Cl.	64 2C	Gorse La., Farnham	115 1D
Goldsworth Orchard	64 2B	Gorse Rd., Frimley	61 2E
Goldsworth Rd.	64 2C	Gorse Rd., Shirley	42 5A
Goldwell Rd.	40 2A	Gorse Rise	21 4E
Gole Rd.	63 4D	Gorselands Cl., Ash Vale	78 3C
Golf Cl.	49 5D	Gorselands Cl., Byfleet	49 4E
Golf Club Dri.	19 5D	Gorselands Cl., Headley Down	134 5A
Golf Club Rd., Weybridge	50 3B	Gorsewood Rd.	64 3A
Golf Club Rd., Woking	64 3B	Gorst Rd.	21 1D
Golf Dri.	61 1F	Gosburton Rd.	21 2E
Golf House Rd., Limpsfield	94 3B	Gosbury Hill	53 1E
Golf Links Av.	135 4D	Gosden Cl., Bramley	101 5D
Golf Rd., Kenley	74 2C	Gosden Cl., Crawley	147 4E
Golf Side, Belmont	55 4D	Gosden Common Rd.	101 5D
Golf Side, Twickenham	17 3E	Gosden Hill Rd.	82 3B
Golfside Cl.	37 1E	Gosden Rd.	46 5B
Goliath Cl.	57 2D	Gosfield Rd.	54 4A
Gomer Gdns.	17 5F	Gosnell Cl.	62 2A
Gomer Pl.	17 5F	Gospel Green Rd.	153 4D
Gomshall	103 3E	Gossops Dri.	146 4B
Gomshall Av.	57 1D	Gossops Green La.	146 4B
Gomshall Gdns.	74 1C	Gostling Rd.	17 2D
Gomshall La.	103 3D	Goston Gdns.	40 2B
Gomshall Rd.	55 3D	Gothic Rd.	17 3E
Gong Hill	115 2E	Goudhurst Cl.	148 4A
Gong Hill Dri.	115 2E	Goudhurst Keep	148 4A
Gonston Cl.	20 3A	Goudhurst Rd.	24 4C
Gonville Rd.	40 3A	Gough's La.	27 1D
Goodchild Rd.	25 2E	Goughs Meadow	43 4D
Goodenough Cl.	74 3A	Gould Court	82 4C
Goodenough Rd.	20 5B	Gould Rd., East Bedfont	15 2F
Goodenough Way	74 3A	Gould Rd., Twickenham	17 2E
Goodhart Way	42 4C	Government Ho. Rd.	78 2A
Goodhew Rd.	41 3D	Government Rd.	78 4B
Goodings Grn.	25 2F	Govett Av.	33 3E
Goodman Pl.	14 4A	Govett Grn.	46 1A
Goodrich Rd.	23 1D	Gower Cl.	21 1F
Goodways Dri.	27 1D	Gower Pk.	43 4E
Goodwin Gdns.	57 2E	Gower Rd., Horley	128 2A
Goodwin Rd., Hammersmith	9 1F	Gower Rd., Weybridge	50 2B
Goodwin Rd., South Croydon	57 1E	Gower, The	31 2E
Goodwood Cl., Camberley	44 5A	Graburn Way	35 2E
Goodwood Cl., Morden	38 2B	Grace Bennett Cl.	60 3C
Goodwood Close, Tilgate	147 5E	Grace Reynolds Wk.	44 5A
Goodwood Pl.	61 5E	Gracedale Rd.	21 4E
Goodwood Rd.	90 4A	Gracefield Gdns.	22 3A
Goodwyns Rd.	106 3A	Graciouspond Rd.	47 2E
Goose Green Cl.	158 3B	Gradient, The	23 4D
Goose Grn., Downside	68 3A	Graemesdyke Rd.	8 5C
Goose Grn., Gomshall	103 3E	Graffham Cl.	146 3B
Goose La.	64 4B	Grafton Cl., W. Byfleet	49 5D
Goose Pl.	32 4A	Grafton Cl., Whitton	16 2C
Goose Rye Rd.	81 1D	Grafton Cl., Worcester Park	37 5E
Goosens Cl.	55 1F	Grafton Park Rd.	37 5E
Gordon Av., Camberley	61 1D	Grafton Rd., Croydon	40 4B
Gordon Av., East Sheen	9 5D	Grafton Rd., New Malden	37 2E
Gordon Av., Purley	57 3F	Grafton Rd., Worcester Park	37 5D
Gordon Av., Richmond	17 1F	Grafton Way	34 2C
Gordon Cl., Chertsey	32 5A	Graham Av., Lammas Park	8 1A
Gordon Cl., Staines	14 4B	Graham Av., Mitcham	39 1E
		Graham Cl.	42 5A
		Graham Gdns.	36 4B
		Graham Rd., Acton	9 1D

Graham Rd., Hampton	16 4C	Granville Av., Hounslow	16 1C
Graham Rd., Mitcham	39 1E	Granville Cl., Croydon	40 5C
Graham Rd., Purley	57 5E	Granville Cl., Weybridge	50 2B
Graham Rd., Wimbledon	20 5B	Granville Gdns.	22 5A
Graham Rd., Windlesham	46 2A	Granville Rd., Limpsfield	93 3F
Graigans	146 4B	Granville Rd., Southfields	20 2B
Granada St.	21 4D	Granville Rd., Weybridge	50 2B
Granard Av.	19 1F	Granville Rd., Woking	65 4D
Granard Rd.	21 2D	Grasmere Av., Cove	60 5B
Granary Cl.	128 1B	Grasmere Av., Kingston Vale	19 4D
Granary Way	158 5A	Grasmere Av., Morden	38 2B
Grand Av., Camberley	44 5A	Grasmere Av., Whitton	17 1D
Grand Av., Surbiton	36 3C	Grasmere Cl., East Bedfont	15 2F
Grand Dri.	38 3A	Grasmere Cl., Egham	13 5E
Grand View Av.	77 2E	Grasmere Cl., Guildford	82 5B
Granden Rd.	40 1A	Grasmere Rd.	96 2A
Grandford Rd.	158 5B	Grasmere Rd., Lightwater	45 3F
Grandison Rd., Clapham	21 1E	Grasmere Rd., Purley	57 4E
Grandison Rd., N. Cheam	37 5F	Grasmere Rd., Streatham	22 4A
Grandstand Rd.	71 2E	Grasmere Rd., Woodside	41 3E
Grange Av., Beulah Hill	40 1C	Grasmere Way	50 4A
Grange Av., Crowthorne	43 1D	Grass Mount	23 3E
Grange Av., Surbiton	36 3C	Grass Way	56 1C
Grange Av., Twickenham	17 3E	Grassfield Cl.	73 3E
Grange Cl., Ashtead	70 3A	Grassmount	56 3C
Grange Cl., Bellfields	81 3E	Grattons Dri.	147 3F
Grange Cl., Bletchingley	91 5F	Gravel Hill, Addington	58 2C
Grange Cl., Crawley Down	149 3E	Gravel Hill, Leatherhead	69 4F
Grange Cl., Godalming	119 1E	Gravel Rd., South Farnborough	78 2B
Grange Cl., Merstham	90 2B	Gravel Rd., Twickenham	17 2C
Grange Cl., Three Bridges	147 3E	Gravel Rd., Upper Hale	96 1A
Grange Cl., Wraysbury	13 1D	Gravelley Ride	19 4F
Grange Court, S. Godstone	111 2F	Gravelly Hill	92 2A
Grange Court, Walton	34 5A	Graveney Grn.	23 5E
Grange Dri., Merstham	90 2C	Graveney Rd.	21 4D
Grange Dri., Woking	65 1D	Graveney Rd.	147 4F
Grange End	129 2E	Gravetts La.	81 3D
Grange Farm Rd.	78 4C	Gravetye Cl.	147 5E
Grange Gdns., Banstead	55 5F	Gray Cl.	49 1E
Grange Gdns., Norwood	40 1C	Grayham Rd.	37 2D
Grange Hill	40 1C	Graylands	65 1D
Grange La.	23 3D	Grays Cl.	152 2A
Grange Meadow	55 5F	Grays La., Ashford	15 4D
Grange Mill Way	24 3A	Grays La., Ashtead	70 3C
Grange Mount	70 3A	Grays Rd.	100 5A
Grange Ms.	54 2B	Grays Wood	128 2C
Grange Park, Cranleigh	141 4D	Grayshot Dri.	43 5D
Grange Park, Woking	65 1D	Grayshott	135 5D
Grange Park Cl.	19 5E	Grayshott Laurels	133 4E
Grange Park Rd.	40 2C	Grayshott Rd.	134 4A
Grange Pl.	32 1B	Grayswood	152 1B
Grange Rd., Ash	78 5C	Grayswood Dri.	78 1C
Grange Rd., Ashtead	70 3A	Grayswood Gdns.	37 2F
Grange Rd., Barnes	9 4E	Grayswood Hill	152 2B
Grange Rd., Bellfields	81 4E	Grayswood Rd.	152 2A
Grange Rd., Beulah Hill	40 2C	Great Austins	96 5B
Grange Rd., Bracknell	27 1D	Great Bookham	85 1F
Grange Rd., Camberley	44 5B	Great Chertsey Rd., Grove Park	9 4D
Grange Rd., Caterham	92 1A	Great Chertsey Rd. Hanworth	16 3C
Grange Rd., Cheam	55 2E	Great Ellshams	72 1B
Grange Rd., Chiswick	8 2C	Great George St.	119 2D
Grange Rd., Crawley Down	149 3D	Great Goodwin Dri.	82 4B
Grange Rd., Egham	13 4D	Great Hollands Rd.	26 3B
Grange Rd., Farnborough Green	61 3D	Great Oaks Pk.	82 3B
Grange Rd., Farnham	81 3E	Great Quarry	100 5A
Grange Rd., Hersham	51 1E	Great South-West Rd.	15 1E
Grange Rd., Hook	53 1E	Great Tattenhams	71 2F
Grange Rd., Kingston	36 2B	Great West Rd., Brentford	8 3A
Grange Rd., Molesey	35 3D	Great West Rd., Chiswick	9 3E
Grange Rd., New Haw	49 3D	Great Woodcote Pk.	57 3D
Grange Rd., Pirbright	62 5B	Greatfield Rd.	60 3C
Grange Rd., Sanderstead	57 3F	Greatford Dri.	82 5C
Grange Rd., Tilford	116 4A	Greatham Rd.	147 5F
Grange Rd., Tongham	97 2E	Greathearst End	68 5C
Grange Rd., Woking	48 5A	Greatlake Court	128 2B
Grange, The, Chobham	47 3D	Greatwood Cl.	48 3B
Grange, The, Redhill	90 4B	Greaves Pl.	21 4D
Grange, The, Shirley	41 3F	Grecias Crescent	22 5B
Grange, The, Walton-on-Thames	34 5A	Green Acres, Deadwater	133 5D
Grange, The, Walton-on-Thames	34 5A	Green Acres, The Sands	97 4D
Grange, The, Wimbledon	20 5A	Green Av.	8 1A
Grange, The, Worc. Pk.	54 1A	Green Cl., East Bedfont	15 2F
Grange Vale	55 2F	Green Cl., Hanworth	16 4B
Grangecliffe Gdns.	40 1C	Green Cl., Shortlands	42 2C
Grangefields Rd.	81 2F	Green Cl., The Wrythe	39 5D
Grangemill Rd.	24 3A	Green Croft	82 5B
Grangeway	129 2E	Green Cross La.	134 2C
Grangewood Dri.	15 5F	Green Curve	55 5E
Granston Way	149 3E	Green Dale	22 1C
Grant Cl.	33 3E	Green Dene	84 4C
Grant Pl.	41 4D	Green Dragon La.	8 3A
Grant Rd., Addiscombe	41 4D	Green Dri., Sendmarsh	66 5A
Grant Rd., Crowthorne	43 2D	Green Dri., Wokingham	25 3E
Grantham Cl.	43 3E	Green End	53 1E
Grantham Rd.	9 3D	Green Farm Rd.	45 2E
Grantley Av.	120 1B	Green Hangar	134 3C
Grantley Cl.	101 4D	Green Hedges Av.	150 5E
Grantley Gdns.	81 5E	Green Hill Cl., Camberley	45 5D
Grantley Rd.	81 5E	Green Hill La.	75 2F
Granton Rd.	21 5F	Green Hill Rd., Camberley	45 5D
Grants La.	94 4B	Green Hill Way	114 1C
Grants Walk	29 4D	Green La., Alford Crossways	140 5A
Grantwood Cl.	109 3E	
Granville Av., Feltham	16 3A	

Green La., Bagshot	45	3E
Green La., Binscombe	100	4A
Green La., Blackwater	60	1B
Green La., Byfleet	50	4A
Green La., Caterham	74	4B
Green La., Cheapside	29	1D
Green La., Chertsey	31	5F
Green La., Chessington	53	3E
Green La., Chobham	47	3E
Green La., Churt	134	3C
Green La., Cobham	51	4E
Green La., Dockenfield	114	5B
Green La., East Molesey	35	3D
Green La., Egham	13	4E
Green La., Farnham	96	2C
Green La., Forest Green	142	1C
Green La., Guildford	82	5B
Green La., Hanworth	16	4B
Green La., Hersham	51	2D
Green La., Kingsfold	144	5B
Green La., Kingsley Green	151	4F
Green La., Leatherhead	70	4A
Green La., Lingfield	131	2E
Green La., Lower Ashtead	70	2A
Green La., Lower Kingswood	89	1E
Green La., Malden	37	3D
Green La., Milford	118	4A
Green La., Norbury	40	1B
Green La., Northgate	147	3D
Green La., Ockham	67	5D
Green La., Outwood	110	4A
Green La., Penge	23	5F
Green La., Rapley Lake	27	5F
Green La., Redhill	90	4A
Green La., Reigate	89	5E
Green La., Salfords	109	3E
Green La., Shamley Grn.	121	1D
Green La., Shepperton	33	3E
Green La., Shipleybridge	129	4D
Green La., Shottermill	151	4F
Green La., Snow Hill	149	1D
Green La., St. Helier	38	3B
Green La., Sunbury	15	5F
Green La., Thorpe	31	1F
Green La., Tilford	116	1B
Green La., Warlingham	75	1F
Green La., Woking	64	4B
Green La., Woodcote	56	4C
Green La., Worcester Park	37	4F
Green La., Wrecclesham	95	5F
Green Lane Av.	51	1D
Green Lane Cl., Byfleet	50	4A
Green Lane Cl., Camberley	44	4A
Green Lane Cl., Chertsey	31	5F
Green Lane Cott.	134	2C
Green Lane East, Christmaspie	98	1C
Green Lane Gdns.	40	1B
Green Lane West	98	1A
Green Lane West., W. Horsley	84	1A
Green Lanes	54	3B
Green Law Gdns.	37	4E
Green Leas, Ashford	15	5F
Green Leas, Frimley	61	2E
Green Leas Cl.	15	5F
Green Mead	51	2F
Green Meads	65	4D
Green Park	13	3F
Green Rd.	31	2E
Green Ride	27	4E
Green St.	34	1A
Green, The, Addington	59	3D
Green, The, Borough Green	27	2D
Green, The, Buckland	88	4B
Green, The, Burgh Heath	72	3A
Green, The, Cannon Hill	38	2A
Green, The, Ewell	54	4B
Green, The, Feltham	16	3A
Green, The, Fetcham	69	5E
Green, The, Frimley Green	61	4E
Green, The, Hersham	51	1E
Green, The, New Malden	37	2D
Green, The, The Sands	97	4E
Green, The, Twickenham	17	3E
Green, The, Upper Hale	96	2A
Green, The, Upper Halliford	33	2F
Green, The, Warlingham	75	2F
Green, The, Woldingham	76	5A
Green, The, Wraysbury	13	1D
Green, The, Sutton	38	5C
Green View	53	2E
Green Way, Aldershot	78	4B
Green Way, Reigate	90	4A
Green Way, Sunbury	34	2A
Green Way, Wallington	56	1C
Green Wk., Addington	58	2C
Green Wk., Northgate	147	3D
Green Wood, Ascot	28	1A
Greenacre	64	1A
Greenacres, Crawley	147	4E
Greenacres, Fetcham	69	5D
Greenacres, Oxted	93	2F
Greenbank Way	61	2D
Greenbush La.	141	2D
Greencourt Av.	41	5E

Greencourt Gdns.	41	4E
Greencroft, Farnborough Park	61	5D
Greencroft, Wokingham	25	1E
Greenefielde End	14	5C
Greenend Rd.	9	1D
Greenfield Av.	36	3C
Greenfield Link	74	1A
Greenfield Rd.	95	5F
Greenfields Cl.	128	1A
Greenfields Rd.	128	1A
Greenfinch Way	158	2B
Greenfinch Way	158	2B
Greenford Rd.	55	1F
Greenham Walk	64	2C
Greenhayes Av.	72	1B
Greenhayes Cl.	89	5F
Greenhayes Gdns.	72	1B
Greenheyes Pl.	65	2D
Greenhill	38	5C
Greenhill Av.	75	4E
Greenhill Cl., Godalming	119	2D
Greenhill Cl., Wrecclesham	95	5F
Greenhill Gdns.	82	4B
Greenhill La.	76	2A
Greenhill Rd., Farnham	96	5B
Greenhill Way	95	5F
Greenhow	26	2C
Greenhurst La.	94	4A
Greenhurst Rd.	22	4B
Greenlands Rd., Portmore Pk.	33	5E
Greenlands Rd., Staines	14	4A
Greeno Cres.	33	3D
Greenoak Rise	77	2E
Greenock Rd., Acton Green	8	1C
Greenock Rd., Streatham Vale	39	1F
Green's La.	125	4F
Greens School La.	60	5C
Greenside	18	1A
Greenside Cl.	82	4C
Greenside Rd., Croydon	40	4B
Greenside Rd., Hammersmith	9	1F
Greenside Rd., Weybridge	33	5D
Greenslade Av.	70	3C
Greenstede Av.	150	2C
Greenvale Rd.	64	3A
Greenview Av.	41	3F
Greenville Gdns.	61	4E
Greenway, Fetcham	69	5D
Greenway, Horsham	158	4A
Greenway, Raynes Park	37	2F
Greenway Av.	41	3F
Greenway Cl.	49	5D
Greenway Dri.	32	1C
Greenway Gdns.	41	5F
Greenway Tatsfield	77	3E
Greenway, The, Epsom	70	1C
Greenway, The, Hurst Green	94	5A
Greenways, Beckenham	42	1A
Greenways, Hinchley Wood	52	1B
Greenways, Sandhurst	43	3D
Greenways, Walton on the Hill	88	1C
Greenways, Woking	65	2E
Greenways Court, Egham	13	4D
Greenways Dri.	29	4D
Greenwood Cl., Long Ditton	35	4F
Greenwood Cl., Morden	38	2A
Greenwood Cl., Woodham	49	4D
Greenwood Dri.	109	3E
Greenwood Gdns.	92	1A
Greenwood La.	17	4D
Greenwood Pk.	19	5E
Greenwood Rd., Brookwood	64	3A
Greenwood Rd., Crowthorne	43	1D
Greenwood Rd., Croydon	40	4B
Greenwood Rd., Long Ditton	35	4F
Greenwood Rd., Mitcham	39	2F
Greenwood Rd., Pirbright	62	4C
Greenwood, The	82	5B
Greenwrythe Cres.	39	4D
Greenwrythe Gdns.	39	4D
Greenwrythe La.	39	3D
Gregory Dri.	12	1B
Grena Gdns.	8	5B
Grena Rd.	8	5B
Grenaby Av.	40	4C
Grenaby Rd.	40	4C
Grenadier Rd.	78	4C
Grenadier Way	60	5A
Grendon Cl.	128	1B
Grenfell Rd.	21	5E
Grennell Cl.	38	5C
Grennell Rd.	38	5C
Grenville Cl., Cobham	51	5E
Grenville Cl., Tolworth	37	4D
Grenville Cl., New Addington	59	3E
Grenville Rd., Shackleford	99	5D

Gresham Av.	75	2F
Gresham Cl.	93	3F
Gresham Rd., Hanworth	16	5C
Gresham Rd., Limpsfield	93	2F
Gresham Rd., Staines	14	4A
Gresham Way, Frimley	61	3E
Gresham Way, Wimbledon	20	3B
Gresham Wk.	147	5D
Gressenhall Rd.	20	1B
Greta Bank	84	1B
Greville Av.	58	3C
Greville Cl., Ashtead	70	2B
Greville Cl., Guildford	81	5D
Greville Cl., Richmond	17	2F
Greville Court	86	1A
Greville Park Av.	70	2B
Greville Park Rd.	70	2B
Greville Rd.	18	1B
Grey Fields Cl.	57	5E
Grey Friars Dri.	63	1E
Greyalders	55	5D
Greycott Rd.	24	4A
Greyfriars Dri.	28	3C
Greyfriars Rd.	66	5A
Greyhound Cl.	78	5B
Greyhound La.	22	5A
Greyhound Rd.	55	1F
Greyhound Ter.	39	1F
Greyshot Dri.	43	5D
Greystead Pk.	114	1C
Greystead Rd.	23	2E
Greystoke Court	43	2D
Greystone Cl.	58	4B
Greystones Cl.	108	1C
Greystones Dri.	89	4F
Greyswood St.	21	5E
Greythorne Rd.	64	2B
Greywaters Dri.	120	1B
Grier Cl.	146	4A
Grierson Rd.	23	2F
Grieve Cl.	97	1E
Griffin Way, Gt. Bookham	86	1A
Griffin Way, Sunbury	34	1A
Griffiths Cl.	37	5F
Griffiths Rd.	20	5B
Griffon Cl.	60	5B
Griggs Meadow	139	3D
Grimwade Av.	41	5D
Grimwood Rd.	17	2F
Grindstone Cres.	63	2E
Grisedale Cl.	57	5F
Grisedale Gdns.	57	5F
Grizedale Ter.	23	3E
Grobars Av.	64	1C
Grogan Cl.	16	5C
Groom Cres.	20	2C
Groom Walk	81	4F
Groombridge Gdns.	51	1D
Grooms, The	148	3A
Grosvenor Av., Carshalton Beeches	56	2B
Grosvenor Av., Mortlake	9	5D
Grosvenor Court	82	3B
Grosvenor Gdns., Beddington	56	2C
Grosvenor Gdns., Kingston	18	5B
Grosvenor Gdns., Mortlake	9	5D
Grosvenor Hill	20	5A
Grosvenor Pl.	33	5E
Grosvenor Rd., Brentford	8	3B
Grosvenor Rd., Chiswick	8	2C
Grosvenor Rd., Chobham	47	4D
Grosvenor Rd., East Grinstead	150	2B
Grosvenor Rd., Epsom	71	3D
Grosvenor Rd., Holloway Hill	119	2D
Grosvenor Rd., Richmond	18	1B
Grosvenor Rd., Shirley	42	5A
Grosvenor Rd., Staines	14	5A
Grosvenor Rd., Twickenham	17	2F
Grosvenor Rd., Wallington	56	2B
Groton Rd.	20	3C
Grotto Rd.	33	5D
Grove Av., Cheam	55	2E
Grove Av., Epsom	54	5B
Grove Av., Twickenham	17	2F
Grove Barns	14	5A
Grove Cl., Gt. Bookham	86	2A
Grove Cl., Kingston	36	2B
Grove Cl., Lewisham	23	2F
Grove Cl., Old Windsor	12	2C
Grove Cl., Wick Hill	25	5E
Grove Cres., Hanworth	16	4B
Grove Cres., Kingston	36	2B
Grove Cres., Walton-on-Thames	34	4A
Grove Crescent Rd.	36	2B
Grove Cross Rd.	61	2E
Grove End	45	1E
Grove End La.	35	4E
Grove End Rd.	96	5A
Grove Gdns.	17	4F
Grove Heath La.	66	5B
Grove Heath North	66	4B
Grove Hill Rd.	90	5A

Grove La., Kingston	36	2B
Grove La., Woodmansterne	73	1F
Grove Mews	9	1F
Grove Park Br.	9	3D
Grove Park Gdns.	8	3C
Grove Park Rd.	8	3C
Grove Park Ter.	8	3C
Grove Pass.	17	4F
Grove Pl.	50	1B
Grove Rd., Ashtead	70	2B
Grove Rd., Ash Wharf	78	4C
Grove Rd., Barnes	9	4E
Grove Rd., Brentford	8	2A
Grove Rd., Camberley	44	5B
Grove Rd., Chertsey	32	3A
Grove Rd., Cranleigh	141	2D
Grove Rd., East Molesey	35	2E
Grove Rd., Epsom	54	5B
Grove Rd., Godalming	118	2C
Grove Rd., Hindhead	135	4D
Grove Rd., Horley	128	2A
Grove Rd., Lingfield	131	1F
Grove Rd., Merrow	82	5C
Grove Rd., Merton	38	1C
Grove Rd., Mitcham	39	2E
Grove Rd., Richmond	18	1B
Grove Rd., Shepperton	33	3E
Grove Rd., South Wimbledon	20	5C
Grove Rd., Surbiton	36	3A
Grove Rd., Sutton	55	2E
Grove Rd., Tatsfield	77	3E
Grove Rd., Thornton H'th	40	2A
Grove Rd., Twickenham	17	3E
Grove Rd., Woking	65	1D
Grove Shaw	72	5B
Grove Side	86	2A
Grove Stile Ways	15	2E
Grove Ter.	17	4F
Grove, The, Addlestone	49	1E
Grove, The, Aperfield	77	2F
Grove, The, Ascot	28	1A
Grove, The, Caterham	74	4B
Grove, The, Coulsdon	56	5C
Grove, The, Egham	13	4E
Grove, The, Epsom	54	5B
Grove, The, Ewell	54	3B
Grove, The, Horley	128	3B
Grove, The, Teddington	17	4F
Grove, The, Walton	34	4A
Grove, The, West Green	146	4C
Grove, The, West Wickham	42	5B
Grove, The, Woking	65	1D
Grove, The, Woodmansterne	73	1F
Grove Way	35	5D
Grove Wood Hill	56	5C
Grovefields Av.	61	2E
Groveland Av.	22	5A
Groveland Rd.	42	2A
Groveland Way	37	3D
Grovelands, Lower Bourne	115	1E
Grovelands, W. Molesey	34	2C
Grovelands Rd.	57	4D
Groveley Rd.	15	4F
Grover's Gdns.	135	4D
Groveside	86	2A
Groveside Cl.	39	5D
Grub St.	94	2B
Guards Ct.	29	4F
Gubyon Av.	22	1B
Guernsey Farm Dri.	64	1C
Guernsey Gro.	22	2B
Guidables La.	94	5C
Guild Croft	82	5B
Guildersfield Rd.	22	5A
Guildford	101	1D
Guildford & Godalming By-Pass	99	5E
Guildford Av., Feltham	16	3A
Guildford Business Park	81	5E
Guildford La., Albury	102	2A
Guildford La., Woking	64	3C
Guildford Lodge Dri.	84	3C
Guildford Park Av.	100	1B
Guildford Park Rd.	100	1C
Guildford Rd., Aldershot	97	1D
Guildford Rd., Alfold	140	3A
Guildford Rd., Bagshot	45	2E
Guildford Rd., Bagshot	45	2E
Guildford Rd., Bucks Grn.	157	2D
Guildford Rd., Chertsey	32	4A
Guildford Rd., Cranleigh	140	1B
Guildford Rd., East Horsley	84	3C
Guildford Rd., Effingham	85	2F
Guildford Rd., Farnham	96	3B
Guildford Rd., Farnham	96	3C
Guildford Rd., Frimley Green	61	4F
Guildford Rd., Horsham	158	5A
Guildford Rd., Leatherhead	69	5D
Guildford Rd., Mayford	64	5C
Guildford Rd., Normandy	79	4E
Guildford Rd., Ottershaw	48	3B
Guildford Rd., Pirbright	80	1B

Guildford Rd., Selhurst	40	3C
Guildford Rd., Shamley Green	121	3D
Guildford Rd., South Farnborough	78	1A
Guildford Rd., Westcott	105	2D
Guildford Rd., West End	46	5B
Guildford Rd., Woking	65	3D
Guildford Rd., Wotton	104	3A
Guildford Rd. Castle Green	47	5D
Guildford St., Chertsey	32	4A
Guildford St., Staines	14	5A
Guildford Way	57	1D
Guildford-Cranleigh Rd.	120	3C
Guildown Av.	100	2B
Guildown Rd.	100	2B
Guileshill La.	66	5C
Guilford Av.	36	3B
Guillemont Fields	60	4B
Gull Cl.	57	2D
Gumbrells Cl.	80	3C
Gumleigh Rd.	8	2A
Gun Pit Rd.	131	2E
Gunners Rd.	21	3D
Gunnersbury Av.	8	1B
Gunnersbury Cres.	8	1B
Gunnersbury Dri.	8	1B
Gunnersbury Gdns.	8	1C
Gunnersbury La.	8	1C
Gunns Grn.	134	4B
Gunsite, The	51	5E
Gunton Rd.	21	5E
Gurdon's La.	137	2E
Gurney Cres.	40	4A
Gurney Rd.	56	1B
Gurney's Cl.	109	1E
Guy Rd.	39	5F
Guyscroft Rd.	24	1B
Gwendolen Av.	20	1A
Gwydor Rd.	41	2F
Gwydyr Rd.	42	2C
Gwynne Av.	41	4F
Gwynne Gdns.	150	2B
Gwynnes Cl.	29	2D
Gypsy Hill	22	4C
Gypsy La.	9	5F

H

H. Jones Cres.	78	4A
Habershon Dri.	62	2A
Hackbridge Park Gdns.	39	5E
Hackbridge Rd.	39	5E
Hackenden Cl.	150	1C
Hackenden La.	150	1C
Hacketts La.	49	5D
Hackhurst La.	103	3F
Hackington Cres.	24	5A
Haddington Rd.	24	4C
Haddon Cl., Malden	37	3E
Haddon Cl., Oatlands Park	50	1C
Haddon Rd.	55	1F
Hadfield Rd.	14	2C
Hadleigh Cl.	53	1D
Hadleigh Gdns.	61	4E
Hadley Gdns.	9	2D
Hadley Rd.	39	2F
Hadley Wood Rise	74	1B
Hadlow Pl.	23	5D
Hadmans Cl.	158	5B
Hadrian Cl., Roundshaw	57	2D
Hadrian Cl., Stanwell	14	2C
Hadrian Way	14	2C
Haggard Rd.	17	2F
Haig Rd., Biggin Hill	77	2E
Haig Rd., East End	78	5A
Haig Rd., York Town	43	5F
Hailey Pl.	141	1D
Hailsham Av.	22	3A
Hailsham Cl.	36	4B
Hailsham Rd.	21	5E
Haines Court	50	1B
Haining Gdns.	61	5F
Hainthorpe Rd.	22	3B
Haldane Pl.	20	2C
Haldon Rd.	20	1B
Hale	96	2B
Hale End	27	2E
Hale House La.	134	2C
Hale Pit Rd.	86	1A
Hale Rd.	96	3B
Hale Reeds	96	2B
Hale St.	14	4A
Hale Way	61	3D
Halebourne La.	46	4B
Hales Oak	86	1B
Halesowen Rd.	38	4B
Haleswood	51	5D
Halewood	26	3C
Half Acre	8	3A
Half Moon La.	22	1B
Half Moon St.	45	2E
Half Penny La.	29	4E
Halfmoon Hill	152	3A
Halford Rd.	18	1B
Halfpenny Cl.	101	3F

Halfpenny La.	101	3F
Halfway La.	118	2B
Haliburton Rd.	17	1F
Halifax St.	23	4E
Haling Grn.	57	2F
Haling Park Gdns.	57	2E
Haling Park Rd.	57	1E
Haling Rd.	57	2F
Hall Cl., Camberley	44	5B
Hall Cl., Farncombe	100	5A
Hall Dene Cl.	82	5C
Hall Dri.	23	4E
Hall Farm Dri.	17	2E
Hall Hill	93	4E
Hall Park	65	1E
Hall Place Dri.	50	1C
Hall Rd., Bramley	120	1A
Hall Rd., Isleworth	17	1E
Hall Rd., Woodcote Green	56	3B
Hall Way	57	5E
Hallam Rd.	119	1D
Halland Cl.	147	3E
Halley Dri.	28	1A
Halleys App.	64	2B
Halliards, The	34	3A
Halliards, The	34	3A
Halliford Cl.	33	2F
Halliford Rd.	33	3F
Hallington Pl.	64	2C
Halliwell Rd.	22	1A
Hallmead Rd.	38	5C
Hallowell Av.	57	1D
Hallowell Cl.	39	2E
Halls Farm Cl.	64	2A
Hallsland	149	3E
Hallsland Way	94	4A
Halsford La.	150	2B
Halsford Park Rd.	150	2B
Halsham Cl.	43	3E
Ham Cl.	18	3A
Ham Farm Rd.	18	4A
Ham Gate Av.	18	4B
Ham La., Elstead	117	2D
Ham La., Englefield Grn.	12	4B
Ham Lane, Old Windsor	12	1C
Ham Ridings	18	4B
Ham St.	18	3A
Ham, The	8	3A
Ham View	41	3F
Hambalt Rd.	21	1F
Hamble Cl.	64	2B
Hamble View	43	5E
Hamble Wk.	64	2B
Hambledon	137	2F
Hambledon Hill	71	1D
Hambledon Rd., Hambledon	138	1A
Hambledon Rd., Hydestile	119	5D
Hambledon Rd., Southfields	20	2B
Hambledon Vale	71	1D
Hambleton Cl.	61	1F
Hambro Av.	21	4F
Hambrook Rd.	41	2E
Hamesmoor Rd.	61	5E
Hamesmoor Way	61	5E
Hamfield Cl.	93	2E
Hamilton Av., Cobham	51	5D
Hamilton Av., N. Cheam	38	5A
Hamilton Av., Tolworth	36	5C
Hamilton Av., Woking	65	1F
Hamilton Cl., Deadwater	133	5D
Hamilton Cl., Epsom	54	4A
Hamilton Cl., Guildford	81	3E
Hamilton Cres.	17	1D
Hamilton Dri.	81	3E
Hamilton Pl., Guildford	81	3E
Hamilton Pl., Sunbury	16	5A
Hamilton Rd., Acton Green	9	1D
Hamilton Rd., Beulah Hill	40	2C
Hamilton Rd., Brentford	8	3A
Hamilton Rd., Felthamhill	15	4F
Hamilton Rd., Gypsy Hill	22	4C
Hamilton Rd., Horsham	158	4A
Hamilton Rd., Purley	57	4E
Hamilton Rd., Twickenham	17	2E
Hamilton Rd., Wimbledon	20	5C
Hamilton Way	56	3C
Hamlash	115	3D
Hamlash La.	115	3D
Hamlet Gdns.	9	2E
Hamlet Rd.	23	5D
Hamlyn Gdns.	22	5C
Hamm Ct.	33	5D
Hamm Moor La.	49	1F
Hammer Bottom La.	151	3D
Hammer Hill Estate	151	4D
Hammer La., Churt	134	3B
Hammer La., Cranleigh	140	4C
Hammer La., Hammer	151	3D
Hammer Vale	151	3D
Hammerfield Dri.	103	3F
Hammersley Rd.	78	2A
Hammersmith	9	2F
Hammersmith Flyover	9	2F
Hammersmith Gro.	9	1F
Hammersmith Ter.	9	2E

Hammond Av.	39	1E
Hammond Cl., Hampton	34	1C
Hammond Cl., Horsell	64	1C
Hammond Rd.	64	1C
Hammond Way	45	3F
Hampden Av.	41	1F
Hampden Rd., Elmers End	41	1F
Hampden Rd., Kingston	36	2C
Hampers La.	158	5C
Hampshire Cl.	97	1E
Hampshire Rd.	44	4B
Hampstead La.	105	2F
Hampstead Rd.	105	2F
Hampton Court Av.	35	3E
Hampton Court Rd.	36	2A
Hampton Court Way	35	5E
Hampton Gro.	54	4B
Hampton La., Hanworth	16	4C
Hampton Rd., Farnham	96	2A
Hampton Rd., Hampton Hill	17	4E
Hampton Rd., Selhurst	40	3C
Hampton Rd., Twickenham	17	3E
Hampton Rd., Woodhatch	109	3D
Hampton Rd., Worcester Park	37	5F
Hampton Road East	16	4C
Hampton Road West	16	3C
Hampton Way	150	3C
Hamsey Green Gdns.	75	1E
Hamsey La.	75	1E
Hanbury Path	48	5C
Hanbury Rd., Acton	8	1C
Hanbury Rd., Crawley	146	4A
Hancock Rd.	22	5C
Hancocks Mt.	29	3D
Handcroft Rd.	40	4B
Handen Rd.	24	1C
Handside Cl.	38	4A
Hanford Cl.	20	2B
Hanger Hill	50	2A
Hanger La.	133	3F
Hanley Court	60	3B
Hannen Rd.	22	3B
Hannibal Rd.	14	2C
Hannibal Way	57	2D
Hanover Av.	16	3A
Hanover Cl., Englefield Green	12	5C
Hanover Cl., Frimley	61	2E
Hanover Cl., Merstham	90	2C
Hanover Court	105	1F
Hanover Gdns.	60	4B
Hanover Rd.	20	5C
Hanover Wk.	33	5F
Hansler Gro.	35	2E
Hansler Rd.	23	1D
Hanson Cl., Burpham	82	4A
Hanson Cl., Wandsworth	21	2E
Hanworth Cl., Bracknell	27	3D
Hanworth Cl., Chertsey	32	4A
Hanworth La.	32	4A
Hanworth Rd., Bracknell	26	4C
Hanworth Rd., Feltham	16	2A
Hanworth Rd., Hanworth	16	4C
Hanworth Rd., Hounslow	17	1D
Hanworth Rd., Reigate	109	3D
Hanworth Rd., Sunbury	16	5A
Hanworth Trading Estate	32	4A
Harberson Rd.	21	2E
Harble Down Rd.	58	4A
Harborough Rd.	22	4A
Harbourfield Rd.	72	1B
Harbridge Av.	19	2E
Harbury Rd.	56	3A
Harcourt Av.	56	1B
Harcourt Cl.	13	5C
Harcourt Field	56	1B
Harcourt Rd., Camberley	43	5F
Harcourt Rd., Easthampstead	27	3D
Harcourt Rd., Thornton Heath	40	3A
Harcourt Rd., Wallington	56	1B
Harcourt Way	111	2F
Hardcastle Cl.	41	3D
Hardel Wk.	22	2B
Hardell Cl.	13	4E
Hardell Rise	22	2B
Hardham Cl.	146	3B
Harding Rd.	71	3D
Hardings La.	23	5F
Hardman Rd.	36	1B
Hardwell Way	27	2E
Hardwick La.	31	4F
Hardwick Rd.	18	4A
Hardwicke Cl.	69	1D
Hardwicke Rd., Acton Green	9	2D
Hardwicke Rd., Mead Vale	108	1C
Hardwicke Rd., Reigate	89	5E
Hardwicks Way	20	1B
Hardy Cl., Dorking	106	4A
Hardy Cl., Horley	128	2A
Hardy Cl., Three Bridges	147	3F
Hardy Grn.	43	2D
Hardy Rd.	20	5C
Hare Hill	49	1D

Hare Hill Cl.	66	1A
Hare La., Blindley Heath	130	2C
Hare La., Claygate	52	5D
Hare La., Crawley	146	2C
Hare La., Godalming	119	1D
Harebell Hill	51	5E
Harecroft, Dorking	106	3A
Harecroft, Fetcham	69	5D
Haredon Cl.	23	2E
Harefield	35	5E
Harefield Av.	55	3D
Harefield Rd., Streatham Vale	22	5A
Harefield Rd., Sunbury	34	1B
Harelands Cl.	64	2C
Harelands La.	64	2C
Harendon	72	4A
Hares Bank	59	3E
Harestone Dri.	92	1A
Harestone Hill	92	1A
Harestone La.	92	1A
Harestone Valley	92	1A
Harestone Valley Rd.	75	5D
Hareward Rd.	82	4B
Harewood Cl., Crawley	147	2E
Harewood Cl., Reigate	89	4F
Harewood Gdns	58	5B
Harewood Rd., Mitcham	21	5D
Harewood Rd., South Croydon	57	2F
Harkness Cl.	71	1F
Harland Av.	41	5D
Harlequin Cl.	17	1E
Harlington Road East	16	2A
Harlington Road West	16	1A
Harman Pl.	57	4E
Harmans Water Rd.	27	3D
Harmar Cl.	25	2F
Harmony Cl., Beddington	57	3D
Harmony Cl., Crawley	146	5A
Harms Grn.	82	4C
Harold Rd., Sutton	55	1F
Harold Rd., Upper Norwood	22	5C
Haroldslea Cl.	128	3C
Haroldslea Dri.	128	3C
Harpenden Rd.	22	3B
Harper Dr.	147	5F
Harper's Rd.	79	4D
Harpesford Rd.	30	3C
Harpsoak La.	90	1B
Harpurs	72	4A
Harrier Cl.	140	1C
Harrington Cl., Beddington	40	5A
Harrington Cl., Leigh	107	4F
Harrington Rd.	41	2E
Harriot's Cl.	70	3A
Harriot's La.	70	3A
Harris Cl.	146	5C
Harris Way	33	1F
Harrison Cl.	108	1C
Harrisons Rise	40	5B
Harrow Bottom Rd.	31	3D
Harrow Cl., Addlestonemoor	32	5B
Harrow Cl., Chessington	53	2D
Harrow Cl., Dorking	105	2F
Harrow Common	76	1A
Harrow Gdns.	75	1F
Harrow Hill	102	2B
Harrow La.	100	5A
Harrow Lands	106	3A
Harrow Rd., Carshalton	56	2A
Harrow Rd., Har. Common	76	1A
Harrow Rd., West Bedfont	15	2D
Harrow Road East	105	2F
Harrow Road West	105	2F
Harrow Way	33	2E
Harrowdene	140	1C
Harrowlands Pk.	106	2A
Harrowsley Green La.	128	3C
Hart Cl., Bletchingley	92	5A
Hart Cl., Fox Lane	60	3B
Hart Dyke Cl.	25	3D
Hart Rd., Byfleet	49	5F
Hart Rd., Dorking	106	1A
Hart, The	96	4A
Hartfield Cl.	41	1E
Hartfield Cres.	20	5B
Hartfield Rd., Chessington	53	1D
Hartfield Rd., Wimbledon	20	5B
Hartford Rd.	53	2F
Hartford Rise	44	4A
Hartington Rd., Grove Pk.	8	3C
Hartington Rd., Richmond	18	1A
Hartland Cl.	49	3E
Hartland Pl.	60	4C
Hartland Rd., Addlestone	49	2D
Hartland Rd., Morden	38	4B
Hartland Way, Morden Pk.	38	4B
Hartland Way, Shirley	41	5F
Hartley Cl.	43	5D
Hartley Copse	12	1B
Hartley Down	74	1A
Hartley Farm	74	1A
Hartley Hill	74	1A
Hartley Old Rd.	74	1A
Hartley Rd.	40	4B

Street	Page	Grid
Hartley Way	74	1A
Harts Gdns.	81	4E
Hart's La.	111	1F
Harts Leap Cl.	43	4D
Harts Leap Rd.	43	4D
Hartscroft	58	3C
Hartsgrove	137	4E
Hartshill	81	5D
Hartshill Wk.	64	2C
Hartspiece Rd.	109	1E
Hartswood	106	3A
Hartswood Av.	108	2B
Hartswood Rd.	9	1E
Harvard Rd., Chiswick	8	2C
Harvard Rd., Hither Green	24	1B
Harvard Rd., Sandhurst	43	3E
Harvest Hill, East Grinstead	150	3C
Harvest Hill, Godalming	119	2D
Harvest La.	35	3F
Harvest Rd., Crawley	147	5F
Harvest Rd., Englefield Green	12	4C
Harvest Rd., Feltham	16	3A
Harvest Ride	27	1F
Harvester Rd.	54	3A
Harvesters	158	3B
Harvestside	128	2C
Harvey Rd., Guildford	101	1D
Harvey Rd., Walton-on-Thames	34	4A
Harvey Rd., West Heath	60	4A
Harvey Rd., Whitton	16	2C
Harwood Av.	39	2D
Harwood Gdns.	12	2B
Harwood Pk.	109	5E
Harwood Rd.	158	4C
Harwoods Cl.	150	3C
Harwoods La.	150	4C
Hascombe	138	1C
Haseley End	23	2E
Haslam Av.	38	4A
Hasle Dri., Haslemere	151	3F
Haslemere	152	3A
Haslemere Av., Earlsfield	20	3C
Haslemere Av., Mitcham	39	1D
Haslemere Cl., Croydon	57	1D
Haslemere Cl., Hampton	16	4C
Haslemere Cl., Heatherside	62	1A
Haslemere Rd., Graysw'd	136	3C
Haslemere Rd., Merton	38	1C
Haslemere Rd., Milford	118	5A
Haslemere Rd., Thornton Heath	40	3B
Haslett Av. East	147	4E
Haslett Rd.	33	1F
Hassocks Cl.	23	3E
Hassocks Rd.	39	1F
Haste Hill	152	3A
Hastings Cl.	61	3F
Hastings Rd., Addiscombe	41	4D
Hastings Rd., Three Bridges	147	4F
Hatch Cl., Addlestonemoor	32	5B
Hatch Cl., Alfold Crossways	140	5A
Hatch End	46	2A
Hatch Gdns.	72	3A
Hatch La., Kingsley Grn.	151	5F
Hatch La., Ockham	67	3E
Hatch La., Outwood	110	5A
Hatch La., Woodmansterne	73	1E
Hatch Pl.	18	4B
Hatch Rd.	40	1A
Hatch Ride	26	5A
Hatches, The	61	4D
Hatchet La.	10	4C
Hatchett	15	2E
Hatchetts Dri.	151	3D
Hatchgate	128	3B
Hatchgate Copse	26	3B
Hatchlands Rd.	90	5A
Hatchways	121	4D
Hatfield Cl.	38	2C
Hatfield Gdns.	61	5E
Hatfield Mead	38	3B
Hatfield Rd., Ashtead	70	3B
Hatfield Rd., Ealing	9	1D
Hathaway Rd.	40	4B
Hatherleigh Cl.	38	2B
Hatherley Rd.	8	4B
Hatherop Rd.	16	5C
Hathersham Cl.	129	2E
Hathersham La.	110	5A
Hathersham Rd.	129	1D
Hatherwood	70	4B
Hathesham Cl.	129	2E
Hatton Gdns.	39	3E
Hatton Hill Rd.	45	1F
Hatton Rd.	15	2E
Havana Rd.	20	3B
Havelock Rd., Addiscombe	41	5D
Havelock Rd., Wimbledon	20	4C
Havelock Rd., Wokingham	25	2D
Haven Gate	158	3C
Haven Gdns.	149	2E
Haven Rd., Ashford	15	4D
Haven Rd., Bucks Green	157	3E
Haven, The	8	5C
Haven Way	96	3B
Haverfield Rd.	8	3C
Haverhill Rd.	21	2F
Havers Av.	51	1E
Haversham Cl.	18	1B
Haversham Cl.	147	4E
Haversham Dri.	27	3D
Havisham Pl.	22	5B
Hawarden Cl.	149	3E
Hawarden Gro.	22	2B
Hawarden Rd.	74	4B
Hawes Lane	42	4B
Hawk La.	27	2E
Hawke Rd.	22	5C
Hawke Rise	85	1F
Hawker Cl.	57	2D
Hawkes Cl.	25	1D
Hawkes Leap	45	1F
Hawkes Rd.	39	1D
Hawkesbourne Rd.	158	3C
Hawkesbury Rd.	19	1F
Hawkesfield Rd.	23	3F
Hawkesley Cl.	17	4F
Hawkesmoor Rd.	146	5A
Hawkeswood Rd.	34	2A
Hawkesworth Dri.	45	3D
Hawkhirst Rd.	74	1C
Hawkhurst	52	5A
Hawkhurst Gdns.	53	1E
Hawkhurst Way, Malden	37	3D
Hawkhurst Way, W. Wickham	42	5A
Hawkins Cl.	27	1F
Hawkins Rd., Crawley	147	5D
Hawkins Rd., Kingston	18	5A
Hawkins Way	25	2E
Hawkley Gdns.	22	3B
Hawks Hill	69	5F
Hawks Hill Cl.	69	5F
Hawks Rd.	36	1B
Hawks Way	14	3A
Hawkshaw Cl.	22	2A
Hawkshead Cl.	24	5C
Hawkshill Cl.	51	2F
Hawkshill Way	51	2F
Hawkslade Rd.	23	1F
Hawksview	51	5F
Hawkswell Cl.	64	1A
Hawkswell Wk.	64	1A
Hawkswood Av.	61	2E
Hawkswood Dell	85	1F
Hawkswood Rise	85	1F
Hawley	60	2C
Hawley Cl.	16	5C
Hawley La.	60	2C
Hawley Rd.	60	1B
Hawley Way	15	4D
Hawmead	149	3E
Haws La.	14	1A
Hawstead Rd.	24	1A
Hawth Av.	147	5D
Hawth Cl.	147	5D
Hawthorn Av., Biggin Hill	77	1E
Hawthorn Av., Carshalton on the Hill	56	2B
Hawthorn Av., Norbury	40	1B
Hawthorn Cl., Crawley	146	2C
Hawthorn Cl., Hanworth	16	4C
Hawthorn Cl., Salfords	109	3E
Hawthorn Cl., Woking	65	3D
Hawthorn Cres., Blackwater	60	1B
Hawthorn Cres., Selsdon	58	4B
Hawthorn Dri.	59	1F
Hawthorn Gdns.	8	1B
Hawthorn Green	41	1E
Hawthorn Hatch	8	3A
Hawthorn La.	114	2C
Hawthorn Pl.	54	4B
Hawthorn Rd., Brentford	8	3A
Hawthorn Rd., Carshalton	56	2B
Hawthorn Rd, Carshalton on the Hill	56	2B
Hawthorn Rd., Frimley	61	2E
Hawthorn Rd., Glantly	13	4E
Hawthorn Rd., Ockford Ridge	118	3C
Hawthorn Rd., Sendmarsh	66	5A
Hawthorn Rd., Woking	64	3C
Hawthorn Way, Bisley	63	1E
Hawthorn Way, Earlswood	109	1F
Hawthorn Way, New Haw	49	3E
Hawthorn Way, Shepperton	33	2E
Hawthorn Way, Upper Halliford	33	2E
Hawthorn Way, Walton on Thames	34	4B
Hawthorne Av.	39	1D
Hawthorne Cl., Aldershot	97	1E
Hawthorne Cl., Morden	38	5C
Hawthorne Cl., Priestwood	26	1C
Hawthorne Cres., Selsdon	58	4B
Hawthorne Cres., Tooting Beck	21	4E
Hawthorne Rd., West Wickham	42	5C
Hawthorne Way	14	2C
Hawthorne Way, Burpham	82	3B
Hawthorns	94	5A
Hawthorns, The	7	4B
Haxted	113	5E
Haxted Rd., Haxted	113	5D
Haxted Rd., Lingfield	131	1F
Haybarn Dri.	158	2C
Haycroft Cl.	74	3B
Haycroft Rd., Brixton Hill	22	1A
Haycroft Rd., Hook	36	5B
Haydn Av.	74	1B
Haydn Park Rd.	9	1E
Haydon Court	49	4E
Haydon Park Rd.	20	4B
Haydon Pl.	100	1C
Haydons Rd.	20	4C
Hayes Barton	65	1F
Hayes Chase	42	3C
Hayes Cres.	55	1D
Hayes Hill	42	4C
Hayes Hill Rd.	42	4C
Hayes La., Kenley	74	1B
Hayes La., Parklangley	42	2B
Hayes Mead	42	4C
Hayes Rd.	74	1B
Hayes, The	71	3D
Hayes Walk	129	2E
Hayes Way	42	2B
Hayesford Park Dri.	42	3C
Haygarth Pl.	20	4A
Haygreen Cl.	18	5C
Hayling Av.	16	3A
Haymeads	52	2A
Haymer Gdns.	37	5F
Hayne Rd.	42	1A
Haynes La.	23	5D
Haynt Wk.	38	2A
Hays Walk	55	3D
Haysleigh Gdns.	41	1D
Hayter Rd.	22	1A
Haywain	93	3E
Hayward Dri.	23	5D
Haywardens	131	1E
Haywards	147	2F
Haywards Gdns.	20	1A
Haywood	27	4D
Hazel Av.	81	3F
Hazel Bank	37	4D
Hazel Cl., Brentford	8	3A
Hazel Cl., Crawley	149	3E
Hazel Cl., Croydon	41	4F
Hazel Cl., Englefield Green	12	5B
Hazel Cl., Langley Green	146	3C
Hazel Cl., Reigate	108	1C
Hazel Cl., Whitton	17	2E
Hazel Dri., Sendmarsh	66	5A
Hazel Gro., Nutcombe	151	1E
Hazel Gro., Staines	14	5B
Hazel Gro., Sydenham	23	4F
Hazel Hill	27	2D
Hazel La.	18	3B
Hazel Mead	54	3B
Hazel Rd., Ash	98	1A
Hazel Rd., Mychett	78	1C
Hazel Rd., West Byfleet	49	5D
Hazel Rd., Woodhatch	108	1C
Hazel Walk	106	3A
Hazel Way, Crawley Down	149	3E
Hazel Way, Fetcham	69	4D
Hazelbank Rd., Catford	24	3C
Hazelbank Rd., Chertsey	32	4B
Hazelbourne Rd.	21	1E
Hazeldean Rd.	40	5C
Hazeldene	49	1E
Hazeldene Court	74	1C
Hazeldene Rd.	9	3D
Hazeldon Rd.	23	1F
Hazelhurst, Beckenham	42	1B
Hazelhurst, Horley	128	2C
Hazelhurst Cl.	82	3B
Hazelhurst Rd.	20	4C
Hazell Rd.	95	4F
Hazelmere Cl., East Bedfont	15	1F
Hazelmere Cl., Leatherhead	70	3A
Hazelthorne Rd.	23	4F
Hazelwell Rd.	20	1A
Hazelwick Av.	147	3E
Hazelwick Mill La.	147	3E
Hazelwick Rd.	147	3E
Hazelwood, Crawley	146	4B
Hazelwood, Elstead	117	2E
Hazelwood Av.	38	2C
Hazelwood Cl., Crawley Down	149	3D
Hazelwood Cl., Surbiton	36	3B
Hazelwood Gro.	58	5B
Hazelwood Lane	73	2D
Hazelwood Rd., Brookw'd	64	2A
Hazelwood Rd., Hurst Grn.	94	4A
Hazlemere Gdns.	37	4F
Hazlewell Rd.	19	1F
Hazon Way	54	4A
Headcorn Rd.	40	2A
Headington Dri.	25	1E
Headington Rd.	20	2C
Headlam Rd.	21	1F
Headland Way	131	2E
Headley, Hampshire	133	4E
Headley, Surrey	88	1A
Headley Av.	57	1D
Headley Cl.	53	2F
Headley Common Rd.	88	1A
Headley Down	134	5A
Headley Dri., New Addington	59	2D
Headley Dri., Tadworth	71	3F
Headley Fields	133	4E
Headley Heath App.	87	3F
Headley Hill Rd.	133	4F
Headley Rd., Deadwater	133	5D
Headley Rd., Epsom	71	3D
Headley Rd., Grayshott	134	5C
Headley Rd., Leatherhead	70	4A
Headley Rd., Lindford	133	4E
Headley Rd., Mickleham	87	3D
Headley View	71	3F
Headway Cl.	18	4A
Headway, The	54	3B
Hearn La.	133	3F
Hearn Wk.	27	1E
Hearne Rd.	8	3C
Hearnville Rd.	21	2E
Hearsley Gdns.	43	5D
Heath Cl., Banstead	55	5F
Heath Cl., Heath End	96	1A
Heath Cl., Hindhead	135	3D
Heath Cl., Stanwell	14	1B
Heath Cl., Virginia Water	30	2C
Heath Cl., Wokingham	25	3D
Heath Dri., Brookwood	63	3E
Heath Dri., Raynes Pk.	38	2A
Heath Dri., Send	65	5E
Heath Dri., Sutton	55	3F
Heath Dri., Walton on the Hill	88	1C
Heath End	96	1B
Heath Gdns.	17	2F
Heath Grn.	23	5E
Heath Gro.	15	5F
Heath Grove Est.	24	1B
Heath Hill	106	1A
Heath Hill La.	133	1E
Heath Hill Rd.	43	1D
Heath House Rd.	63	4F
Heath Hurst Rd.	57	3F
Heath La., Brook	102	4C
Heath La., Ewshot	95	2D
Heath La., Heath End	96	1A
Heath La., Munstead Heath	119	3E
Heath Mill La.,	80	1C
Heath Moors	27	3D
Heath Park Dri.	46	2A
Heath Rd., Bagshot	45	2E
Heath Rd., Caterham	74	5C
Heath Rd., Chobham	47	3D
Heath Rd., Hammer	151	3D
Heath Rd., Munstead Heath	119	3E
Heath Rd., Oxshott	52	4A
Heath Rd., Thornton H'th	40	2C
Heath Rd., Twickenham	17	2F
Heath Rd., Weybridge	50	1A
Heath Rd., Woking	65	1D
Heath Ridge Green	51	5F
Heath Rise, Sendmarsh	66	5B
Heath Rise, Virginia Water	30	2C
Heath Rise, Westcott	105	2D
Heath Rise, West Hill	20	1A
Heath, The	74	5C
Heath View	84	1C
Heath Way, Caterham	91	1F
Heath Way, Horsham	158	3B
Heatham Pk.	17	2F
Heathbridge	50	2A
Heathcot Rd.	133	5D
Heathcote	72	4A
Heathcote Cl.	78	4C
Heathcote Dri.	150	2B
Heathcote Rd., Ash Wharf	78	4C
Heathcote Rd., Camberley	44	5A
Heathcote Rd., Epsom	54	5A
Heathcote Rd., Richmond	18	1A
Heathcroft Av.	15	5F
Heathdene Rd., Norbury	22	5A
Heathdene Rd., South Beddington	56	2B
Heathdown Rd.	65	1F
Heathedge	23	3E
Heather Cl., Ash Vale	78	3C
Heather Cl., Copthorne	148	2B
Heather Cl., Farnham	114	1C
Heather Cl., Guildford	81	4E
Heather Cl., Hampton	34	1C
Heather Cl., Horsham	158	3B
Heather Cl., Horsham	158	3B
Heather Cl., Kingswood	72	4A
Heather Cl., Woking	64	1C
Heather Cl., Woodham	49	3E
Heather Dri., Broomhall	29	4F
Heather Dri., Lindford	133	4D
Heather Gdns.	55	2E
Heather Mead	59	2F
Heather Mount	27	2E
Heather Ridge Arcade	62	1A

Heather Walk, Pirbright	63 4D	Henchley Dene	82 4C	Herrett St.	97 1D	·High St., Croydon	40 5C
Heather Way, Chobham	47 2D	Henderson Av.	81 3E	Herrick Cl., Heatherside	62 1A	High St., Dorking	105 1F
Heather Way, Hindhead	135 5E	Henderson Rd., Selhurst	40 3C	Herrick Cl., Three Bridges	147 3F	High St., Dormans Land	132 4A
Heather Way, New Chap.	131 4D	Henderson Rd.,		Herrings La., Chertsey	32 3A	High St., East Grinstead	150 3C
Heather Way, Selsdon	58 3C	Wandsworth Common	21 2D	Herrings La., Windlesham	46 1A	High St., Egham	13 4D
Heatherdale Cl.	18 5C	Hendham Rd.	21 3D	Herschell Rd.	23 2F	High St., Epsom	54 5A
Heatherdale Rd.	61 1D	Hendon Way	14 1C	Hersham	51 1E	High St., Esher	52 1A
Heatherdene	84 1B	Hendrick Av.	21 1E	Hersham Bypass	51 1E	High St., Ewell	54 3B
Heatherdene Cl.	39 2D	Heneage Cres.	59 3E	Hersham Cl.	19 2F	High St., Feltham	16 3A
Heatherfield Ave.	21 2D	Henfield Rd.	38 1B	Hersham Gdns.	51 1D	High St., Godalming	119 2D
Heatherfields Rd.	95 2F	Henfold	125 2E	Hersham Rd.	34 4A	High St., Godstone	92 4B
Heatherlands, Horley	128 2B	Henfold Hill	125 2E	Hertford Av.	9 5D	High St., Guildford	100 1C
Heatherlands, Sunbury	16 5A	Henfold Lane	125 1E	Hertford Way	40 2A	High St., Hampton	35 1D
Heatherley Cl.	44 5A	Hengelo Gdns.	38 2C	Hesiers Hill	76 2C	High St., Hampton Hill	17 5D
Heatherley Rd.	44 5A	Hengist Cl.	158 5A	Hesiers Rd.	76 2C	High St., Hampton Wick	36 1A
Heathers La.	106 3A	Hengist Way	42 2C	Heslop Rd.	21 2E	High St., Haslemere	152 3A
Heathers, The	14 2C	Hengrave Rd.	23 2E	Hessle Grove	54 4B	High St., Headley	133 4F
Heatherset Gdns.	22 5A	Hengrove Cres.	14 3C	Heston Rd.	109 3D	High St., Highstreet Grn.	154 1A
Heatherside Dri.	30 3B	Henhurst Cross Lane	124 3C	Heston Wk.	109 3D	High St., Horley	128 2B
Heatherside Rd.	54 2A	Henley Av.	38 5A	Hethergrove Estate	24 1B	High St., Horsell	64 1C
Heathervale Rd.	49 3E	Henley Bank	100 1B	Hetherington Rd.	33 2E	High St., Kingston	36 2B
Heathfield, Cobham	51 5F	Henley Cl.	60 3B	Hetley Gdns.	23 5D	High St., Knaphill	63 2F
Heathfield, Three Bridges	147 2F	Henley Court	65 3E	Hetley Rd.	9 1F	High St., Leatherhead	70 4A
Heathfield Av.	29 3D	Henley Dri., Frimley	61 3E	Hevers Av.	128 2B	High St., Limpsfield	94 2A
Heathfield Cl., Godalming	119 3D	Henley Dri., Kingston	19 5E	Hewers Way	71 3F	High St., Lingfield	131 2E
Heathfield Cl., Woking	65 2E	Henley Way	16 4B	Hewlett Pl.	45 2E	High St., Malden	37 2E
Heathfield Dri.	109 3D	Hennel Cl.	23 3E	Hexal Rd.	24 3C	High St., Merstham	90 2C
Heathfield Gdns.	9 2D	Henry Hatch Walk	55 2F	Hexham Cl., Crawley	148 4A	High St., Merton	20 5C
Heathfield North	17 2F	Henry Prince Est.	20 2C	Hexham Cl., Sandhurst	43 3E	High St., Nutfield	91 5D
Heathfield Rd., Acton	8 1C	Henryson Rd.	24 1A	Hexham Rd., St. Helier	38 4B	High St., Old Woking	65 4E
Heathfield Rd., Bromley		Hensford Gdns.	23 4E	Hexham Rd., West Dulwich	22 3C	High St., Oxshott	52 5B
Park	24 5C	Henshaw Cl.	146 5B	Hextalls La.	91 2F	High St., Oxted	93 3E
Heathfield Rd., Hersham	51 1E	Henslow Way	48 5C	Hextalls Rd.	91 3F	High St., Penge	23 5E
Heathfield Rd., S. Croydon	57 1F	Henslowe Rd.	23 1D	Heybridge Av.	22 5A	High St., Purley	57 4E
Heathfield Rd.,		Hensworth Rd.	14 4C	Heyford Av.	38 2B	High St., Redhill	90 5B
Wandsworth	20 1C	Hently Wk.	19 1F	Heyford Rd.	39 1D	High St., Reigate	89 5E
Heathfield Rd., Woking	65 2E	Hepburn Gdns.	42 4C	Heymead	70 5A	High St., Ripley	66 4B
Heathfield South	17 2F	Heppleston Cl.	19 1F	Heythorp St.	20 2B	High St., Rowledge	114 2C
Heathfield Squ.	20 2C	Hepworth Rd.	22 5A	Heythorpe Cl.	64 2A	High St., Rusper	145 3D
Heathfield Ter.	9 2D	Hepworth Way	33 4F	Hibernia Gdns.	17 1D	High St., Shepperton	33 3E
Heathfield Vale	58 3C	Heracles Cl.	57 2D	Hichisson Rd.	23 1E	High St., South
Heathland Cl.	34 1A	Herald Gdns.	39 5E	Hickmans Cl.	92 4B	Farnborough	78 2A
Heathlands	72 4A	Herbert Cl.	26 3C	Hidcot Gdns.	37 2F	High St., South Norwood	41 2D
Heathlands Cl.	17 2F	Herbert Cres.	64 2A	Higgs La.	45 2D	High St., Staines	14 4A
Heathlands Rd.	25 4F	Herbert Rd., Kingston	36 2B	High Alham	27 4E	High St., Stanwell	14 1C
Heathlands Way	16 1C	Herbert Rd., Wimbledon	20 5B	High Barn Rd.	85 3E	High St., Sunningale	29 3E
Heathrise, Camberley	44 5B	Hereford Cl., Epsom	54 5A	High Beech	58 2A	High St., Sunninghill	29 3D
Heathrow	103 3E	Hereford Cl., Laleham	32 1B	High Beeches, Banstead	55 5D	High St., Sutton	55 1F
Heathrow Airport	15 1E	Hereford Cl., Woking	64 3B	High Beeches, Frimley	61 2E	High St., Tadworth	71 5F
Heathrow Cl.	7 4C	Hereford Cl., Woodbridge		High Beeches Cl.,		High St., Teddington	17 4F
Heathside, Hinchley Wood	35 5E	Hill	81 4D	Woodcote	56 3C	High St., Thames Ditton	35 4F
Heathside, Weybridge	50 1A	Hereford Gdns.	17 2D	High Cedar Dri.	19 5F	High St., Thornton Heath	40 2C
Heathside, Whitton	16 2C	Hereford La.	96 2A	High Clere	29 3D	High St., Tooting	21 5D
Heathside Cl.	35 5E	Hereford Rd., Feltham	16 2B	High Coombe Pl.	19 5D	High St., Walton	34 4A
Heathside Cres.	65 2D	Hereford Rd., Lammas Pk.	8 1A	High Copse	95 2F	High St., West End	46 4B
Heathside Gdns.	65 2E	Hereford Way	53 1D	High Croft, Godalming	118 4B	High St., West Molesey	35 3D
Heathside La.	135 4D	Hereward Av.	57 3E	High Croft, Shamley Green	120 2C	High St., West Wickham	42 4A
Heathside Park Rd.	65 2D	Hereward Rd.	21 4D	High Dri., Kingston	37 1D	High St., Weybridge	50 1A
Heathside Rd.	65 2D	Heriot Rd.	32 4A	High Dri., Oxshott	52 5B	High St., Whitton	17 2D
Heathvale Bridge Rd.	78 3C	Hermes Way	56 2C	High Dri., Woldingham	76 4A	High St., Wimbledon	20 4A
Heathview Gdns.	19 2F	Hermitage Cl., Camberley	61 2E	High Fields	16 2A	High St., Woking	65 3D
Heathview Rd., Milford	118 4A	Hermitage Cl., Claygate	52 2C	High Foleys	52 2C	High St., Wraysbury	13 1D
Heathview Rd., Thornton		Hermitage Cl., Shepperton	33 2D	High Garth	52 2A	High Thicket Rd.	114 5B
Heath	40 2B	Hermitage Cl., South		High Gdns.	64 3B	High Trees, Shirley	41 4F
Heathway, Ascot Heath	28 1A	Farnborough	78 1A	High Hill Rd.	76 1B	High Trees, Tulse Hill	22 2B
Heathway, Camberley	44 5B	Hermitage Dri.	28 1B	High La., Haslemere	152 2A	High Trees Cl.	75 4D
Heathway, Effingham		Hermitage Gdns.	22 5C	High La., Slines Grn.	76 3A	High View	103 3E
Junction	67 5F	Hermitage La.,		High Level Dri.	23 4D	High View Av.	57 1D
Heathway, Shirley	42 5A	Addiscombe	41 4D	High Mead	42 5C	High View Rd., Bagshot	45 4E
Heathway Cl.	44 5B	Hermitage La., East		High Meadow Cl.	106 2A	High View Rd., Guildford	100 2A
Heaton Rd.	21 5E	Grinstead	150 3C	High Oaks	146 5C	High View Rd., Lightwater	45 4E
Hebdon Rd.	21 3D	Hermitage La., Norbury	22 5A	High Park Rd., Farnham	96 3A	High View Rd., North
Heber Rd.	23 1D	Hermitage Rd., Beulah Hill	22 5C	High Park Rd., N. Sheen	8 4C	Farnborough	60 5C
Hebron Rd.	9 1F	Hermitage Rd., Brookwood	64 3A	High Path Rd.	82 5B	High Woods	92 1A
Heddon Walk	60 3C	Hermitage Rd., Felcourt	150 1B	High Path Station Rd.	38 1C	Highams Hill	146 4B
Hedgehog La.	151 3F	Hermitage Rd., Kenley	74 1C	High Pewley	101 1D	Highams La.	46 2B
Hedgerley Court	64 2C	Hermitage, The	18 1B	High Pine Cl.	50 1B	Highbarrow Rd.	41 4D
Hedgeway	100 1B	Hermitage Wood Cres.	64 3A	High Pines	75 3E	Highbeech	27 2E
Hedgley St.	24 1C	Hermits Rd.	147 3E	High Pitfold	151 1E	Highbroom Cres.	42 4A
Hedingham Cl.	128 2C	Herndon Cl.	13 4E	High Pk. Av.	84 1C	Highbury Av.	40 1B
Hedley Rd.	16 2C	Herndon Rd.	20 1C	High Point	50 1A	Highbury Cl., Malden	37 2D
Heelas Rd.	25 2D	Herne Hill	22 1B	High Rd., Byfleet	49 4F	Highbury Cl., West
Heenan Cl.	61 3E	Herne Pl.	22 1B	High Rd., Chipstead	73 3E	Wickham	42 5B
Heighton Gdns.	57 1E	Herne Rd.	36 5B	High Ridge	118 3C	Highbury Cres.	44 4C
Heights Cl., Banstead	72 2A	Heron Cl., Ascot	28 1A	High St., Addlestone	49 1E	Highbury Grn.	152 4C
Heights Cl., Wimbledon	19 5F	Heron Cl., Crawley	146 3C	High St., Aldershot	78 5A	Highbury Rd.	20 4A
Helby Rd.	21 1F	Heron Cl., Guildford	81 4E	High St., Ascot	28 2B	Highclere.	82 4B
Helder Gro.	24 2C	Heron Cl., Mytchett	61 5E	High St., Bagshot	45 2D	Highclere Cl.	74 1B
Helder St.	57 2F	Heron Court, Richmond	18 1A	High St., Banstead	72 1B	Highclere Court	63 2F
Helen Av.	16 2A	Heron Dale	49 1F	High St., Beckenham	42 1A	Highclere Dri.	44 4C
Helen Cl.	35 2D	Heron Fields	12 5C	High St., Bletchingley	91 5D	Highclere Gdns.	63 2F
Helena Cl.	57 2D	Heron Pl.	150 3C	High St., Bletchingley	91 5F	Highclere Rd., Aldershot	97 1D
Helford Wk.	64 2B	Heron Shaw	140 2C	High St., Bookham	86 1A	Highclere Rd., Knaphill	63 2F
Helgiford Gdns	15 5F	Heron Way	158 5C	High St., Bracknell	27 1D	Highclere Rd., Malden	37 2D
Helix Gdns.	22 1A	Heron Wk., Sheerwater	48 5B	High St., Bramley	120 1A	Highclere St.	23 4F
Helix Rd.	22 1A	Heron Wood Rd.	97 1E	High St., Brentford	8 3A	Highcliffe Dri.	19 1E
Helmsdale, Bracknell	27 3E	Herondale, Bracknell	27 4D	High St., Camberley	44 5A	Highcotts La.	83 1D
Helmsdale, Woking	64 2B	Herondale, Selsdon	58 3C	High St., Carshalton	56 1B	Highcroft Dri.	157 1F
Helmsdale Rd.	39 1F	Herondale, Shottermill	151 2E	High St., Caterham	75 5D	Highdaun Dri.	40 2A
Helston Cl.	61 3F	Herondale Rd.	21 2D	High St., Cheam	55 2D	Highdown	37 5E
Helvellyn Cl.	13 5E	Heronry, The	51 2D	High St., Chobham	47 4D	Highdown Court	147 5E
Helvetia St.	24 3A	Heron's Cl.	130 5B	High St., Claygate	52 2C	Highdown Rd.	19 1F
Hemingford Rd.	55 1D	Herons Court	45 4F	High St., Cobham	68 1A	Highdown Way	158 3C
Hemlock Cl.	72 5B	Herons Croft	50 2B	High St., Colnbrook	7 3A	Higher Dri., Banstead	55 4D
Hempshaw Av.	73 1D	Herons Way, Brookwood	63 4D	High St., Cranleigh	140 1C	Higher Dri., Purley	57 5E
Hemsby Rd.	53 2E	Herons Way, Wokingham	25 1E	High St., Crawley	147 4D	Higher Dri., West Horsley	84 2B
Henbit Cl.	71 3F	Herontye Dri.	150 3C	High St., Crowthorne	43 2D	Higher Green	54 5C

Highercombe Rd. 152 2B
Highfield, Chipstead 73 2D
Highfield, Easthampstead 26 3C
Highfield, Feltham 16 2A
Highfield, Shalford 101 4D
Highfield Av. 96 1C
Highfield Cl., Aldershot 96 1C
Highfield Cl., Cove 60 5C
Highfield Cl., Englefield Green 12 5C
Highfield Cl., Farnham 96 5A
Highfield Cl., Long Ditton 36 4A
Highfield Cl., Oxshott 52 4B
Highfield Cl., W. Byfleet 49 5D
Highfield Cl., Wokingham 25 2D
Highfield Cres. 135 5E
Highfield Dri., Ewell 54 2B
Highfield Dri., West Wickham 42 5B
Highfield Gdns. 96 1C
Highfield Hill 22 5C
Highfield La., Puttenham 98 3C
Highfield La., Thursley 136 1A
Highfield Path 60 5C
Highfield Rd., Biggin Hill 77 2E
Highfield Rd., Caterham 75 4D
Highfield Rd., Chertsey 32 4A
Highfield Rd., Cove 60 5C
Highfield Rd., Feltham 16 2A
Highfield Rd., North End 150 1B
Highfield Rd., Purley 57 3D
Highfield Rd., Shortlands 42 2C
Highfield Rd., Sutton 56 1A
Highfield Rd., Tolworth 37 4D
Highfield Rd., Upper Halliford 33 3F
Highfield Rd., Walton 34 4A
Highfield Rd., W. Byfleet 49 5D
Highfields, East Horsley 84 2C
Highfields, Fetcham 69 5E
Highfields, Lower Ashtead 70 3A
Highfields, Sunninghill 29 3E
Highgate La. 61 4D
Highland Cottages 56 1C
Highland Croft 24 5A
Highland Rd., Aldershot 78 5A
Highland Rd., Beare Green 125 2D
Highland Rd., Bromley Park 42 1C
Highland Rd., Camberley 44 4B
Highland Rd., Coulsdon 57 5E
Highland Rd., Gypsy Hill 22 5C
Highlands Av., Horsham 158 5C
Highlands Av., Leatherhead 70 4A
Highlands Cl., Leatherh'd 70 4A
Highlands Cl., Wrecclesham 96 5A
Highlands Cres. 158 5C
Highlands Heath 19 2F
Highlands La. 65 4D
Highlands Park 70 5A
Highlands Rd., Heath End 96 1A
Highlands Rd., Horsham 158 5C
Highlands Rd., Leatherh'd 70 4A
Highlands Rd., Redhill 90 5A
Highlands, The 84 1C
Highridge Cl. 54 5B
Highridge La. 106 3C
Hightown La. 55 4F
Hightree Cl. 49 1D
Hightrees Rd. 108 1C
Highview 55 4E
Highview Cl. 41 1D
Highview Cres. 44 3B
Highview Rd., Beulah Hill 22 5C
Highway, The 55 3F
Highwaymans Ridge 45 1F
Highwold 73 2E
Highwood 74 2B
Highwoods 70 4A
Hilary Av. 39 2E
Hilbert Rd. 28 5A
Hilbury Rd. 21 3E
Hildenborough Gdns. 24 5C
Hildenlea Pl. 42 1C
Hildens, The 105 2D
Hilder Gdns. 61 5D
Hilders, The 70 2C
Hilgay Cl. 82 5A
Hill Barn 57 4F
Hill Brow Cl. 80 5C
Hill Cl., Horsell 64 1C
Hill Cl., Riddlesdown 57 5F
Hill Cl., Wonersh Park 120 1B
Hill Copse View 27 1E
Hill Court 119 1D
Hill Cres., Cheam 38 5A
Hill Cres., Kingston 36 2C
Hill Crest, Dormans Park 131 5F
Hill Crest, Weybridge 50 1A
Hill Crest Dri. 114 1C
Hill Crest Par. 56 5B
Hill Crest Rd., Biggin Hill 77 1E
Hill Crest Rd., Lewisham 23 4D
Hill Dri., Norbury 40 2A
Hill Drive, Heatherside 61 1F
Hill House Dri., Reigate 108 1C
Hill House Dri., Weybridge 50 4A
Hill House Rd. 22 4A
Hill La. 72 4B
Hill Rd., Carshalton Beeches 56 2A
Hill Rd., Fetcham 69 5D
Hill Rd., Grayshott 135 5D
Hill Rd., Grayshott 135 5D
Hill Rd., Haslemere 152 3A
Hill Rd., Heath End 96 1B
Hill Rd., Hindhead 135 4D
Hill Rd., Purley 57 4D
Hill Rd., Streatham 21 5F
Hill Rd., Sutton 55 1F
Hill Rise, Dorking 86 5C
Hill Rise, Hinchley Wood 35 5F
Hill Rise, Richmond 18 1B
Hill Rise, Walton-on-Thames 33 4F
Hill Row 23 2E
Hill St. 18 1B
Hill, The 75 5D
Hill Top 38 4B
Hill Top Walk 75 3F
Hill View 19 5F
Hill View, Raynes Park 19 5F
Hill View Cl., Tadworth 71 4F
Hill View Cl., Woking 65 2D
Hill View Rd., Claygate 52 2C
Hill View Rd., Farnham 95 4F
Hill View Rd., Woking 65 2D
Hilland Rise 133 4F
Hillars Heath Rd. 74 1A
Hillary Cl. 96 5A
Hillary Cres. 34 4A
Hillary Dri. 43 1D
Hillary Rd. 96 5A
Hillberry 27 4D
Hillbrook Gdns. 50 2A
Hillbrook Rd. 21 3E
Hillbrook Rise 96 2A
Hillbrow 37 2E
Hillbrow Rd., Esher 52 1A
Hillbrow Rd., Southend 24 5C
Hillbury Cl. 75 2E
Hillbury Gdns. 75 2E
Hillbury Rd., Tooting 21 3E
Hillbury Rd., Whyteleafe 75 2D
Hillcote Av. 22 5A
Hillcourt Rd. 23 1E
Hillcrest 117 2D
Hillcrest Av. 31 5F
Hillcrest Cl., Epsom 71 1E
Hillcrest Cl., Three Bridges 147 4F
Hillcrest Gdns. 35 5F
Hillcrest Rd., Camberley 44 4C
Hillcrest Rd., Guildford 81 5D
Hillcrest Rd., Purley 57 3D
Hillcrest Rd., Whyteleafe 75 2D
Hillcrest View 41 3F
Hillcroft Av. 56 5C
Hillcroome Rd. 56 2A
Hillcross Av. 38 3A
Hilldale Rd. 55 1E
Hilldown Rd., Hayes 42 4C
Hilldown Rd., Streatham Common 22 5A
Hillersdon Av. 9 4E
Hilley Field La. 69 4D
Hillfield Av. 39 3D
Hillfield Cl., Merrow 82 4B
Hillfield Cl., Redhill 90 5B
Hillfield Rd. 90 5B
Hillfield Rd., Hampton 16 5C
Hillford Pl. 109 3E
Hillgarth 135 4E
Hillgate Pl. 21 1E
Hillhouse Cl. 149 5D
Hillhouse La. 157 1D
Hillhurst Gdns. 74 3C
Hillier Gdns. 57 1E
Hillier Rd., Guildford 82 5A
Hillier Rd., Wandsworth 21 1E
Hillier's La. 40 5A
Hillingdon Av. 14 2C
Hillingsdale 77 2D
Hillmead, Crawley 146 4B
Hillmead, Horsham 158 4A
Hillmore Gro. 23 4F
Hillmount Rd. 35 5E
Hills Farm La. 158 5A
Hills Pl. 158 5A
Hillsboro Rd. 23 1D
Hillsborough Court 60 3B
Hillsborough Pk. 45 5D
Hillside, Crawley Down 149 3E
Hillside, Esher 52 1A
Hillside, Farnham 115 2D
Hillside, Horsham 158 5A
Hillside, Nork 72 1A
Hillside, Virginia Water 30 3C
Hillside, Wimbledon 20 5A
Hillside, Woking 64 3C
Hillside Av. 57 5E
Hillside Cl., Brockham 106 1C
Hillside Cl., Crawley 146 5C
Hillside Cl., Headley Down 134 4A
Hillside Cl., Knaphill 63 2F
Hillside Cl., Nork 72 1A
Hillside Cl., Raynes Pk. 38 2A
Hillside Cres. 61 3E
Hillside Gdns., Addlestone 49 1D
Hillside Gdns., Brockham 87 5F
Hillside Gdns., Wallington 56 2C
Hillside La., Heath End 96 1B
Hillside La., West Wickham 42 5C
Hillside Park 29 4E
Hillside Rd., Aldershot 96 1C
Hillside Rd., Ashtead 70 2B
Hillside Rd., Ash Wharf 78 4C
Hillside Rd., Cheam 55 2E
Hillside Rd., Coulsdon 74 2A
Hillside Rd., Ewell 54 3C
Hillside Rd., Heath End 96 1B
Hillside Rd., Kingston 36 2C
Hillside Rd., Shortlands 42 2C
Hillside Rd., Shottermill 151 3E
Hillside Rd., Streatham 22 3A
Hillside Rd., Tatsfield 77 3F
Hillside Rd., Waddon 57 1E
Hillside Rd., Whyteleafe 75 2D
Hillside Way 100 5A
Hillsmead Way 58 5B
Hillsour Cl. 81 5D
Hillspur Road 81 5E
Hilltop Cl., Cheapside 29 1D
Hilltop Cl., Guildford 81 3D
Hilltop Cl., Leatherhead 70 5A
Hilltop La. 91 1E
Hilltop Rd., Caterham 91 1E
Hilltop Rd., Reigate 108 1C
Hilltop Rd., Whyteleafe 75 2D
Hilltop Rise 86 1A
Hillview, Whyteleafe 75 2D
Hillview Cl., Purley 57 4E
Hillview Cl., Tadworth 71 4F
Hillview Cres. 81 4E
Hillview Dri. 109 1E
Hillview Rd. 12 1C
Hillview Rd., The Wrythe 38 5C
Hillview Rd., Twickenham 17 1F
Hillworth Rd. 22 2B
Hilton Way 75 1E
Himley Rd. 21 4D
Hinchley Cl. 35 5F
Hinchley Dri. 35 5F
Hinchley Way 35 5F
Hinchley Wood 35 5F
Hinchliffe Cl. 57 2D
Hindell Cl. 60 3C
Hindhead 135 4D
Hindhead Brae 135 4E
Hindhead Rd. 135 5E
Hindhead Way 57 1D
Hindmans Rd. 23 1D
Hindsley Pl. 23 3E
Hinkler Cl. 57 2D
Hinstock Cl. 60 5C
Hinton Cl. 26 5A
Hinton Dri. 26 5A
Hinton Rd. 56 2C
Hipley St. 65 3E
Hitchcock Cl. 33 2D
Hitching's Way 108 2B
Hither Green La. 24 1B
Hitherfield Rd. 22 3A
Hithermoor Rd. 14 1A
Hitherwood 140 2C
Hitherwood Cl. 90 4A
Hitherwood Dri. 23 4D
Hoadly Rd. 21 3F
Hobart Pl. 18 2B
Hobart Rd. 37 5F
Hobbes Wk. 19 1F
Hobbs Cl. 49 5E
Hobbs Rd. 22 4C
Hockenmead 147 3F
Hockering Gdns. 65 2E
Hockering Rd. 65 2E
Hodge La. 10 4C
Hodges Cl. 45 3D
Hodgson Gdns. 82 4A
Hoe 103 5F
Hoe Bridge Rd. 65 3E
Hoe La., Hascombe 138 1C
Hoe La., Hoe 103 5F
Hogarth Av. 15 5E
Hogarth Cl. 43 5E
Hogarth Cres. 39 1D
Hogarth La. 9 3E
Hogarth Rd. 147 5D
Hogarth View 35 1D
Hogden Cl. 89 1E
Hogden La. 86 3A
Hoghatch La. 95 2F
Hogs Back 99 2D
Hogscross La 73 5D
Hogshill La. 51 5D
Hogsmill Way 54 1A
Hogspudding La. 126 3A
Hogtrough La., Earlswood 109 1F
Hogtrough La., Oxted 93 2D
Hogwood Rd. 155 4F
Holbeach Rd. 24 2A
Holbeck 26 3C
Holbein Rd. 147 5D
Holbreck Pl. 65 2D
Holbrook Way 96 1C
Holcon Court 90 3B
Holdenbrook La. 142 1C
Holdenby Rd. 23 1F
Holder Rd., Aldershot 78 5B
Holder Rd., Crawley 147 5F
Holderness Way 22 4B
Holderness Rd. 21 3E
Holdfast La. 152 2B
Hole Hill 105 1D
Hole La. 113 2F
Holford Rd. 82 5B
Holland Av., Belmont 55 3E
Holland Av., Cottenham Park 37 1E
Holland Cl., Farnham 96 4B
Holland Cl., West Wickham 42 5C
Holland Cres., Hurst Grn. 94 5A
Holland Cres., Reigate 90 5A
Holland Dri. 23 3F
Holland Gdns. 32 1A
Holland La. 94 5A
Holland Park 15 4F
Holland Pines 26 4C
Holland Rd., Holland 94 5A
Holland Rd., Woodside 41 3D
Holland Way 42 5C
Hollands, The, 37 4E
Holley Rd. 9 1E
Hollies Av. 49 5D
Hollies Cl., Fulwell 17 4D
Hollies Cl., Twickenham 17 3F
Hollies Cl., Upper Norwood 22 5B
Hollies Court 49 1E
Hollies Rd. 8 2A
Hollingbourne Rd. 22 1C
Hollingsworth Rd. 58 2B
Hollington Cres. 37 3E
Hollis Wood Dri. 114 1C
Hollman Gdns. 22 5B
Hollow Cl. 100 1B
Hollow La., Abinger 104 4B
Hollow La., Dormans Land 132 3A
Hollow La., Stroude 30 2C
Hollow, The, Eashing 118 2B
Holloway Hill, Chertsey 31 5F
Holloway Hill, Godalming 119 2D
Holly Av., Camberley 61 1F
Holly Av., Walton 34 4B
Holly Av., Woodham 49 3D
Holly Bank Rd., West Byfleet 49 5D
Holly Bank Rd., Woking 64 4B
Holly Bush La., Aldershot 78 3B
Holly Bush La., Hampton 16 5C
Holly Bush Ride, Kingston 18 5B
Holly Cl., Ash 78 5A
Holly Cl., Cove 60 5C
Holly Cl., Englefield Green 12 5B
Holly Cl., Hanworth 16 4B
Holly Cl., Headley Down 134 4A
Holly Cl., Longcross 30 5B
Holly Cl., Three Bridges 147 3E
Holly Cl., Woking 64 3B
Holly Cres. 42 3A
Holly Dri. 12 1A
Holly Grn. 50 1C
Holly Hedge Cl. 61 2E
Holly Hedge Rd., Cobham 51 5D
Holly Hedge Rd., Frimley 61 2E
Holly Hill Dri. 72 2B
Holly La., Banstead 72 1B
Holly La., Ockford Ridge 118 2C
Holly La., Worplesdon 80 3C
Holly Lane East 72 1B
Holly Lane West 72 2B
Holly Lea 81 2F
Holly Rd., Aldershot 78 5A
Holly Rd., Hampton 17 5D
Holly Rd., North Farnborough 60 5C
Holly Rd., Reigate 108 1C
Holly Rd., Turnham Green 9 2D
Holly Rd., Twickenham 17 2F
Holly Spring La. 27 1D
Holly Tree Rd. 74 4C
Holly Trees Gdns. 61 3E
Holly Way, Blackwater 43 5E
Holly Way, Mitcham 39 2F
Holly Wk. 11 4E
Hollybank 46 5B
Hollybank Cl. 16 4C
Hollybrook Park 133 5D
Hollybush Rd., Bagshot 28 5B
Hollybush Rd., Crawley 147 3D
Hollybush Ride 25 5E
Hollycombe 12 4C
Hollyfield Rd. 36 4B
Hollyfields Cl. 44 5A
Hollyhock Dri. 63 1E
Hollymead Rd. 73 2E
Hollymeoak Rd. 73 3E
Hollymoor La. 54 3A
Hollyridge 151 3F
Hollytree Cl. 20 2A
Hollywater Rd. 133 5D

192

Hollywell Cl — Hurst Rd

Hollywell Cl. 60 3C
Hollywoods 59 3D
Holm Cl. 48 4C
Holm Oak Cl. 20 1B
Holman Rd. 54 1A
Holmbank Dri. 33 2F
Holmbury Dri. 106 3A
Holmbury Grn. 58 2C
Holmbury Hill Rd. 123 3D
Holmbury Keep 128 2C
Holmbury Rd. 123 3E
Holmbury St. Mary 123 1E
Holmbush Cl. 158 3B
Holmbush Rd. 20 1A
Holmcroft, Crawley 147 4D
Holmcroft, Walton on Thames 88 1C
Holmdene Av. 22 1C
Holme Chase 50 2B
Holme Lacey Rd. 24 1C
Holmefield Cl. 128 2B
Holmes Cres. 25 3D
Holmes Rd., 17 3F
Holmesdale 82 5B
Holmesdale Av. 8 5C
Holmesdale Rd., Caterham 74 5C
Holmesdale Rd., Kew 8 4B
Holmesdale Rd., Kingston 18 5A
Holmesdale Rd., North Holmwood 106 3A
Holmesdale Rd., Reigate 89 5E
Holmesdale Rd., Selhurst 40 3C
Holmesdale Rd., South Norwood 41 2D
Holmesdale Rd., South Nutfield 110 1A
Holmesley Rd., 23 1F
Holmethorpe Av. 90 4B
Holmewood Gdns. 22 2A
Holmewood Rd., Brixton Hill 22 2A
Holmewood Rd., South Norwood 41 2D
Holmoak Mews 22 1A
Holmshaw Cl. 23 4F
Holmside Rd. 21 1E
Holmsley Cl. 37 4E
Holmwood Av. 58 5A
Holmwood Cl., Addlestone 49 1D
Holmwood Cl., Eastheath 25 4C
Holmwood Cl., E. Ewell 55 3D
Holmwood Cl., E. Horsley 84 3C
Holmwood Gdns. 56 2B
Holmwood Rd., Chessington 53 1E
Holmwood Rd., Ewell 54 3C
Holmwood View Rd. 106 4A
Holne Chase 38 3B
Holroyd Cl. 52 3C
Holroyd Rd. 52 3C
Holstein Av. 50 1A
Holsworthy Way 53 1D
Holt Cl. 61 3D
Holt La. 25 1D
Holt Pound La. 114 1B
Holt, The 56 1C
Holtwood Rd. 52 5A
Holtye Rd. 150 2C
Holwood Cl. 34 5B
Holybank Rd., Woking 64 4B
Holybourne Av. 19 2F
Holyoake Av. 64 2C
Holyoake Cres. 64 2C
Holywell Cl. 14 2C
Holywell Way 14 2C
Home Cl., Fetcham 69 4E
Home Cl., Pound Hill 147 3F
Home Cl., The Wrythe 39 5D
Home Court 16 2A
Home Farm Cl., Esher 52 2A
Home Farm Cl., Gt. Burgh 72 2A
Home Farm Cl., Ottershaw 48 2B
Home Farm Cl., Thames Ditton 35 4F
Home Farm Cl., Upper Halliford 33 2F
Home Farm Cres. 60 5C
Home Farm Gdns. 34 5B
Home Meadow 72 1B
Home Park 96 4A
Home Park Cl. 120 1A
Home Park Rd. 20 4B
Home Park Walk 36 2B
Homebrook Dri. 26 1B
Homebury Av. 25 5F
Homecroft Rd. 23 4E
Homefarm Rd. 119 3D
Homefield 51 1E
Homefield Cl., Leatherhead 70 4A
Homefield Cl., Woodham 49 4D
Homefield Gdns., Mitcham 38 1C
Homefield Gdns., Tadworth 71 3F
Homefield Rd., Hersham 34 4C
Homefield Rd., Old Coulsdon 74 3B
Homefield Rd., Stamford Brook 9 2E
Homefield Rd., Warlingham 75 3E
Homefield Rd., Wimbledon 20 4A
Homeland Dri. 55 3F
Homelands 70 4A
Homelands Dri. 22 5C
Homelea Cl. 60 3C
Homeleigh Rd. 23 1F
Homemead Rd. 39 3F
Homer Cl., Sandhurst 43 3E
Homer Cl., Wokingham 25 1F
Homer Rd. 41 3F
Homersham Rd. 36 1C
Homestall 81 5D
Homestall Rd. 23 1E
Homestead Gdns. 52 1B
Homestead Rd., Caterham 74 5C
Homestead Rd., Staines 14 5B
Homestead Way 59 4E
Homewater Av. 33 1F
Homewood 141 1D
Homewood Cl. 16 5C
Homewood Rd. 39 2D
Hone Hill 43 4D
Honey Hill Rd. 25 4F
Honeybrook Rd. 21 2F
Honeycrock La. 109 4E
Honeyhill Rd. 26 1C
Honeypot La. 113 3E
Honeypots Rd. 64 4C
Honeysuckle Bottom 84 5C
Honeysuckle Cl., Crowthorne 26 5A
Honeysuckle Cl., Horley 128 2C
Honeysuckle Gdns. 41 4F
Honeysuckle La., Headley Down 134 4A
Honeysuckle La., Langley Green 146 2C
Honeysuckle La., N. Holmwood 106 3A
Honeywell Rd. 21 1D
Honeywood La. 142 4C
Honister Heights 57 5F
Honley Rd. 24 2B
Honnor Rd. 14 5C
Honor Oak Pk. 23 1E
Honor Oak Rd. 23 2E
Honor Oak Rise 23 1E
Hood Av. 19 1D
Hood Rd. 19 5E
Hook Heath Av. 64 3D
Hook Heath Gdns. 64 4B
Hook Heath Rd. 64 4C
Hook Hill 58 3A
Hook Hill Park 64 4B
Hook La., Puttenham H'th 99 4D
Hook La., Shere 103 4D
Hook Mill La. 46 3A
Hook Rd., Ewell 54 2A
Hook Rd., Hook 36 5B
Hook Rise 36 5B
Hooke Rd. 84 1C
Hookfield 54 5A
Hookhill La. 64 4B
Hookhouse La. 139 3D
Hookley La. 117 2E
Hookstile La. 96 4A
Hookstone La. 46 4B
Hookwood 127 3F
Hookwood Corner 94 2A
Hooley 73 4E
Hooley La., Earlswood 109 1D
Hope Av. 27 4E
Hope Cl. 55 1F
Hope La. 96 2A
Hope Park 24 5C
Hope St. 117 2D
Hopeman Cl. 43 4E
Hopfield Av. 49 4F
Hopfields 65 1D
Hophurst Cl. 149 3E
Hophurst Dri. 149 3E
Hophurst Hill 149 2F
Hophurst La. 149 2E
Hoppery La. 133 2F
Hoppetty, The 72 5A
Hoppingwood Av. 37 2E
Hopton Gdns. 37 3E
Hopton Rd. 22 4A
Horace Rd. 36 2B
Horatious Way 57 2D
Horewood Rd. 27 3D
Horley 128 3B
Horley Lodge La. 109 4E
Horley Rd., Charlwood 127 4E
Horley Rd., Earlswood 109 1D
Horley Row 128 2A
Horman Rd. 15 5E
Horn Rd. 60 4B
Hornbeam Cl., Horsham 158 5C
Hornbeam Cl., Sandhurst 43 3E
Hornbeam Cl., West Heath 60 4A
Hornbeam Cres. 8 3A
Hornbeam Rd., Bellfields 81 4F
Hornbeam Rd., Woodhatch 108 2C
Hornchurch Hill 75 2D
Horndeam Cl. 148 2A
Horndean Rd. 27 3F
Horne Rd. 33 2D
Horne Way 9 4F
Hornecourt Hill 111 5D
Hornhatch 101 3E
Hornhatch Cl. 101 3E
Horniman Dri. 23 2E
Hornshill La. 157 3D
Horse Croft 72 2B
Horse Fair, Kingston 159
Horse Shoe Green 38 5C
Horseblock Hollow 122 4A
Horsefair 36 1B
Horsefield Rd. 22 1A
Horsegate Rde, Ascot 28 3C
Horsegate Ride, Bracknell 27 3F
Horsehill 127 1E
Horsell 64 1B
Horsell Birch 64 1B
Horsell Common Rd. 47 5F
Horsell Court 32 4B
Horsell Moor 64 2C
Horsell Park Cl. 64 1C
Horsell Pk. 64 1C
Horsell Rise 64 1C
Horsell Vale 65 1D
Horsell Way 64 1C
Horseshoe Cl. 44 4B
Horseshoe Cres. 44 4B
Horseshoe La., Ash Vale 78 2C
Horseshoe La., Cranleigh 140 1B
Horseshoe Lane East 82 5B
Horseshoe Lane West 82 5B
Horseshoe, The, Banstead 72 1B
Horseshoe, The, Godalming 118 2C
Horseshoe, The, Purley 56 5C
Horsford Rd. 22 1A
Horsham 158 4B
Horsham By-Pass 158 3A
Horsham La., Ewhurst Green 142 2A
Horsham Rd. 43 3E
Horsham Rd., Beare Green 125 1D
Horsham Rd., Bramley 120 4C
Horsham Rd., Cranleigh 140 2C
Horsham Rd., Dorking 105 2F
Horsham Rd., E. Bedfont 15 1E
Horsham Rd., Ellen's Green 141 5F
Horsham Rd., Forest Green 123 4F
Horsham Rd., Kingsfold 143 5F
Horsham Rd., Rusper 144 5C
Horsham Rd., Shalford 101 4D
Horsham Rd., Southgate 146 5C
Horsham Rd., Sutton 104 5A
Horsham-Guildford Rd. 139 1F
Horsley Cl. 54 5A
Horsley Dri. 59 2E
Horsley Rd. 68 3A
Horsneile La. 27 1D
Horton Gdns. 54 4A
Horton Hill 54 4A
Horton La. 53 3F
Horton Rd., Poyle 7 5A
Horton Rd., Stanwell Moor 14 1A
Horvath Cl. 50 1C
Hosack Rd. 21 3E
Hoskins Rd. 93 3F
Hospital Bridge Rd. 17 2D
Hospital Dri. 56 3A
Hospital Rd., Aldershot 78 4A
Hotham Rd., Roehampton 9 5F
Hotham Rd., S. Wimbledon 20 5C
Houblon Rd. 18 1B
Houghton Cl. 16 5C
Houghton Rd. 147 5F
Houlder Cres. 57 2E
Houlton Court 45 3E
Hound House Rd. 122 1A
Hounslow Av. 17 1D
Hounslow Gdns. 17 1D
Hounslow Rd., Feltham 16 2A
Hounslow Rd., Hanworth 16 3B
Hounslow Rd., Whitton 17 1D
Houseman Rd. 60 4C
Houston Pl. 35 4E
Houston Rd. 23 3F
Hove Gdns. 38 4C
How La. 73 3E
Howard Av. 54 3C
Howard Cl., Ashtead 70 2C
Howard Cl., Hampton Hill 17 5D
Howard Cl., Highland Park 70 5A
Howard Cl., Horsley 84 1B
Howard Cl., Sunbury 15 5F
Howard Cl., Walton on the Hill 88 1B
Howard Gdns. 82 5B
Howard Rd., Anerley 41 1E
Howard Rd., Dorking 105 1F
Howard Rd., Effingham Junction 68 5A
Howard Rd., Gt. Bookham 86 2A
Howard Rd., Horsham 158 4C
Howard Rd., New Malden 37 2E
Howard Rd., N. Holmwood 106 3A
Howard Rd., Reigate 108 1C
Howard Rd., Surbiton 36 3B
Howard Rd., Wokingham 25 2E
Howard Rd., Woodmansterne 56 5C
Howard Rd., Woodside 41 3D
Howard Ridge 82 3B
Howards Cl. 65 3D
Howards La., Addlestone 49 2D
Howard's La., Roehampton 9 5F
Howards Rd. 65 3D
Howards St. 36 4A
Howberry Rd. 40 1C
Howden Rd. 41 1D
Howe Dri. 74 4C
Howell Cl. 54 4C
Howell Hill Cl. 54 4C
Howell Hill Gro. 54 3C
Howletts Rd. 22 1C
Howley Rd. 40 5B
Howsman Rd. 9 3E
Howson Ter. 18 1B
Hoxbear St. 24 1A
Hoylake Cl. 146 4A
Hoyle Hill 125 3D
Hoyle Rd. 21 4D
Hubbard Rd. 22 4C
Hubberholme 26 2C
Huddleston Cres. 90 2C
Hudson Rd. 147 5D
Hughenden Rd. 37 4F
Hughes Rd., Ashford 15 5E
Hughes Rd., Wokingham 25 1E
Hullbrook La. 120 2C
Hullmead 120 2C
Hulton Cl. 70 5A
Hulverston Cl. 55 3F
Humber Way 43 4E
Humbolt Cl. 81 5D
Hummer Rd. 13 4E
Humphrey Cl. 69 4D
Hungerford Cl. 43 4D
Hungerford Sq. 50 1C
Hungry Hill La. 83 1E
Hunstanton Cl., Caterham 75 3E
Hunstanton Cl., Crawley 146 4A
Hunston Rd. 38 4C
Hunter Cl. 21 2E
Hunter Rd., Crawley 147 5D
Hunter Rd., Guildford 101 1D
Hunter Rd., Raynes Park 37 1F
Hunter Rd., Thornton Heath 40 2C
Hunters Chase 111 2F
Hunters Cl. 54 5A
Hunters Meadow 23 4D
Hunters Rd., Cove 60 5C
Hunters Rd., Hook 53 1E
Hunters Way 58 1A
Huntersfield Cl. 89 4F
Hunting Cl. 52 1A
Hunting Gate Mews 38 5C
Huntingate Dri. 53 2E
Huntingdon Cl. 40 2A
Huntingdon Gdns. 37 5F
Huntingdon Rd. 64 2A
Huntingfield 59 2D
Huntingfield Rd. 19 1F
Huntingfield Way 13 5F
Huntingford Cl. 135 3D
Huntly Rd. 41 2D
Huntly Way 37 1E
Hunts Cl. 81 5D
Hunts Hill Rd. 79 3F
Hunts La. 59 1D
Hunts Slip Rd. 22 3C
Huntsman's Cl., Fetcham 86 1B
Huntsmans Cl., Hanworth 16 4A
Huntsmans Mews 61 5E
Huntsmoor Rd. 54 1A
Huntspill St. 20 3C
Hurland La. 133 5F
Hurlands Cl. 96 3C
Hurlands La. 155 1D
Hurlands Pl. 96 3C
Hurlestone Rd. 40 3C
Hurley Cl. 34 5A
Hurley Gdns. 82 4A
Hurlford 64 2B
Hurnford Cl. 57 3F
Huron Rd. 21 3E
Hurst Av. 158 4B
Hurst Cl., Chessington 53 1F
Hurst Cl., Crawley 146 5B
Hurst Cl., Hayes 42 4C
Hurst Cl., Woking 64 3C
Hurst Court 158 4B
Hurst Croft 101 2D
Hurst Dri. 88 1C
Hurst Farm Cl. 118 3B
Hurst Farm Rd. 150 3C
Hurst Green Cl. 94 4A
Hurst Green Rd. 93 4F
Hurst Grn. 94 4A
Hurst Gro. 33 4F
Hurst La., East Molesey 35 2D
Hurst La., Headley 71 5D
Hurst Rd., Aldershot 78 4A
Hurst Rd., Epsom 54 4A

Hurst Rd., Hawley	60	3C		Inchmery Rd.	24	3B		James Rd., Frimley	61	2D
Hurst Rd., Horley	128	2A		Inchwood	27	4D		James Rd., Peasmarsh	100	4C
Hurst Rd., Horsham	158	4B		Ingham Cl.	58	3B		James Watt Way	147	1E
Hurst Rd., South Croydon	57	1F		Ingham Rd.	58	3B		James Way	61	2D
Hurst Rd., Walton on the Hill	71	5D		Ingle Glen, Wick Hill	25	5D		James's Cotts.	8	3C
Hurst Rd., West Molesey	34	3B		Ingleboro Dri.	57	5F		Jameston	27	4D
Hurst St.	22	1B		Ingleby Way	56	3D		Jamnagar Cl.	14	5A
Hurst View Rd.	57	2F		Ingledell	61	1E		Jannoway Hill La.	64	2C
Hurst Way, S. Croydon	58	2A		Inglehurst	49	3E		Japonica Cl.	64	2C
Hurst Way, W. Byfleet	49	5D		Inglemere Rd.	23	3F		Japonica Ct.	78	5B
Hurst Wood	28	3C		Ingleside	7	4C		Jarrow Cl.	38	3C
Hurstbourne	52	2C		Ingleside Cl.	24	5A		Jarvis Rd.	57	2F
Hurstbourne Rd.	23	2F		Ingleton	26	2C		Jasmin Cl.	109	3E
Hurstcourt Rd.	38	5B		Ingleton Rd.	56	3A		Jasmin Gdns.	42	5A
Hurstdene Av., Hayes	42	4C		Inglewood, Chertsey	32	4A		Jasmin Rd.	53	2F
Hurstdene Av., Staines	14	5B		Inglewood, Woking	64	2B		Jasmine Cl.	64	1A
Hurstfield Rd.	34	2C		Inglewood Av.	45	5D		Jasmine Green	41	1E
Hurstlands	94	4A		Inglis Rd.	41	4D		Jason Cl., Salfords	109	3D
Hurstleigh Cl.	90	4A		Ingram Rd.	40	1B		Jason Cl., Weybridge	50	1B
Hurstleigh Dri.	90	4A		Ingrams Cl.	51	1E		Jasons Dri.	82	4C
Hurtmore Rd.	99	5E		Inholms La.	106	3A		Jasper Rd.	23	4D
Hurtwood Rd.	34	4C		Inkerman Rd.	64	2A		Jebb Av.	22	1A
Hutchins Way	128	2C		Inman Rd.	20	2C		Jeddo Rd.	9	1E
Hutsons Cl.	25	1E		Inner Park Rd.	20	2A		Jeffers Ride	28	1B
Hutton Cl.	46	2A		Inner Staithe	9	4D		Jefferson Cl.	8	1A
Hutton Rd.	78	3C		Innes Gdns.	19	1F		Jefferson Rd.	62	4C
Huxley Cl.	99	5F		Innes Rd.	158	4C		Jeffries Passage, Guildford	159	
Huxley Rd.	100	1A		Institute Rd., Aldershot	78	5A		Jeffries Rd.	84	4B
Hyacinth Cl.	16	5C		Institute Rd., S. Farnboro	78	2A		Jeffs Rd.	55	1E
Hyacinth Rd.	19	2F		Institute Rd., Westcott	105	2D		Jelf Rd.	22	1B
Hyde Cl.	15	5F		Instone Cl.	57	2D		Jengar Cl.	55	1F
Hyde Dri.	146	4A		Instow Gdns.	60	3C		Jenkins' Hill	45	3D
Hyde La., Hindhead	135	2E		Inveresk Gdns.	37	5E		Jenner Dri.	46	4B
Hyde La., Ockham	67	3D		Inverness Rd.	38	4A		Jenner Rd.	101	1D
Hyde Rd.	58	5A		Inverness Way	43	4E		Jenners Cl.	131	2E
Hyde Ter.	15	5F		Invincible Rd.	60	5C		Jennett Rd.	40	5B
Hyde Wk.	38	4B		Inwood Av.	74	3B		Jennings Cl.	49	3E
Hydestile	119	5D		Inwood Cl.	41	5F		Jennings Rd.	23	1D
Hydethorpe Rd.	21	2F		Inwood Court	34	5A		Jenny La.	131	2C
Hylands	70	1C		Iona Cl., Catford	24	2A		Jenson Way	23	5D
Hylands Cl., Crawley	147	4E		Iona Cl., Crawley	146	5C		Jephtha Rd.	20	1B
Hylands Cl., Woodcote	71	1D		Ipswich Rd.	21	5E		Jeppo's La.	39	2D
Hylands Mews	71	1D		Irene Rd.	52	5A		Jersey Cl., Burpham	82	3B
Hylands Rd.	71	1D		Ireton Av.	33	5F		Jersey Cl., Chertsey	32	5A
Hylton Cl.	51	1E		Iris Cl., Shirley	41	4F		Jersey Cl., Farnborough	60	5C
Hymans Gdns.	37	2F		Iris Cl., Surbiton	36	4B		Jersey Rd.	21	5E
Hyndewood	23	3F		Iris Rd., Bisley	63	1E		Jerviston Gdns.	22	5B
Hyperion Pl.	54	3A		Iris Rd., West Ewell	53	1F		Jesmond Rd.	41	4D
Hyperion Walk	128	3B		Iron La.	119	1F		Jessamy Rd.	33	5D
Hyrstdene	57	1E		Irons Bottom	108	5B		Jessica Rd.	20	1C
Hythe	13	5F		Irvine Dri.	60	3B		Jessies La.	103	5E
Hythe Cl.	27	3F		Irvine Pl.	31	3D		Jessiman Terr.	33	3D
Hythe End Rd.	13	3E		Irwin Dri.	158	4A		Jessops Way	39	3F
Hythe Field Av.	13	5F		Irwin Rd.	100	1B		Jevington	27	4D
Hythe Park Rd.	13	4F		Isbells Rd.	108	1C		Jews Wk.	23	4E
Hythe Rd., Staines	13	4F		Isham Rd.	40	1A		Jeypore Rd.	20	2C
Hythe Rd., Thornton Heath	40	1C		Isis Way	43	4E		Jig's La. Sth.	27	1E
Hythe, The	13	4F		Island Cl.	13	4F		Jillian Cl.	16	5C
				Island Farm Av.	34	3C		Jobson's La.	153	5D
				Island Farm Rd.	34	3C		Jocelyn Rd.	8	5B
I				Island Rd.	21	5D		Jockey Mead	158	5A
				Itchingwood Common Rd.	94	5C		Jock's La.	26	1B
Iberian Av.	56	1C		Iveagh Court	27	3D		John Ashby Cl.	22	1A
Iberian Way	44	5C		Iveagh Rd., Guildford	100	1B		John Cobb Rd.	50	2A
Ibis La.	9	4D		Iveagh Rd., Woking	64	2A		John Nike Way	26	1B
Ibsley Gdns.	19	2F		Ively Dri.	60	5B		John St.	41	2D
Ice House Wood	93	4F		Iverna Gdns.	15	1F		John Wiskar Dri.	140	2C
Icehouse Hill	27	3F		Ivers Way	59	2D		Johns Cl.	15	4E
Icklingham Gate	51	4E		Ivy Cl.	34	1B		Johns La.	38	3C
Icklingham Rd.	51	4E		Ivy Cres.	8	2C		John's Rd.	77	3E
Iden Cl.	42	2C		Ivy Dri.	45	4E		Johns Walk	75	3D
Idlecombe Rd.	21	5E		Ivy Gdns.	39	2F		Johnsdale	93	3F
Idmiston Rd., West Dulwich	22	3B		Ivy La.	65	2E		Johnson Dri.	35	1D
Idmiston Rd., Worcester Park	37	4E		Ivy Mill Cl.	92	4B		Johnson Rd.	40	4C
Idmiston Sq.	37	4E		Ivy Mill La.	92	4A		Johnson Wk.	147	5D
Ifield Av.	146	2B		Ivy Pl.	36	3B		Johnsons Cl.	39	5E
Ifield Dri.	146	3B		Ivy Rd.	24	1A		Johnston Green	81	3E
Ifield Green	146	2B		Ivy Rd., Aldershot	78	5B		Johnston Wk.	81	3E
Ifield Rd., Charlwood	127	5D		Ivy Rd., Tolworth	36	4C		Joinville Cl.	49	1F
Ifield Rd., Crawley	146	4C		Ivybridge Cl.	17	2F		Joliffe Rd.	90	1C
Ifield Rd., Ifield	146	2B		Ivydale Rd., Hackbridge	39	5E		Jonquil Gdns.	16	5C
Ifield St.	146	3B		Ivydale Rd., Nunhead	23	1F		Jonson Cl.	39	2F
Ifley Rd.	9	1F		Ivyday Gro.	22	3A		Jordan Cl., Sanderstead	58	4A
Ifold Bridge Lane	155	4F		Ivydene, Knaphill	63	2F		Jordans Cl., Crawley	147	3D
Ifold Rd.	109	1E		Ivydene, W. Molesey	34	3C		Jordan's Cl., Guildford	82	5B
Ifoldhurst	155	5F		Ivydene Cl., Salfords	109	3E		Jordans Cl., Salfords	109	3E
Ikona Cl.	50	1B		Ivydene Cl., Sutton	55	1F		Jordans Cl., Stanwell	14	2B
Ildersly Gro.	22	3C		Ivymount Rd.	22	3B		Jordans Cres.	147	3D
Ilex Cl., Englefield Grn.	12	5B						Jordans, The	150	3C
Ilex Cl., Sunbury-on-Thames	34	1B		**J**				Joseph Locke Way	34	5C
Ilex Way	22	4B						Josephine Av., Lwr. Kingswood	89	2E
Ilfracombe Rd.	24	3C		Jackass La.	93	4D		Josephine Av., Tulse Hill	22	1A
Illingworth Gro.	27	1E		Jackdaw Cl.	146	3C		Josephine Court	89	2E
Imadene Cl.	133	5D		Jackdaw La.	158	3C		Joseph's Rd.	81	5F
Imadene Cres.	133	5D		Jackman's La.	64	3B		Jubilee Av., Ascot	28	1B
Imber Cl.	35	4E		Jacks Bridge Rd.	131	2E		Jubilee Av., Whitton	17	2D
Imber Gro.	35	4E		Jackson Cl., Bracknell	27	3D		Jubilee Cl., Wokingham	25	1D
Imber Park Rd.	35	4E		Jackson Cl., Epsom	54	5A		Jubilee Cl., Ascot Heath	28	1B
Imberhorne La.	150	2A		Jacob Cl.	26	1B		Jubilee Cl., Stanwell	14	2B
Imberhorne Way	150	1A		Jacob Rd.	43	4F		Jubilee Cres.	49	1F
Imjin Cl.	78	4A		Jacobean Cl.	147	4F		Jubilee Dri.	78	3C
Imperial Rd.	15	2F		Jacobs Well Rd.	82	2A		Jubilee Hall Rd.	61	4D
Imperial Way	57	2D		Jaggard Way	21	2D		Jubilee La.	114	2C
Ince Rd.	50	2C		Jail La.	77	1F		Jubilee Rd., Aldershot	97	1D
				Jamaica Rd.	40	3B		Jubilee Rd., Cheam	55	2D
				James Rd., Farnborough	78	2A		Jubilee Rd., Mytchett	78	1C

Jubilee Rd., Rudgwick	157	2F
Jubilee St.	119	2D
Jubilee Terr., Dorking	106	1A
Jubilee Terr., Grayshott	135	5D
Jubilee Terr., Strood Green	107	2D
Jubilee Way, Merton	38	1C
Jubilee Way, Tolworth	36	5C
Jug Hill	77	1E
Julian Cl.	64	2C
Julien Rd., South Ealing	8	2A
Julien Rd., Woodmansterne	73	1F
Jumps Rd.	134	1B
Junction Pl.	151	3E
Junction Rd., Ashford	15	4E
Junction Rd., Dorking	105	1F
Junction Rd., Lightwater	45	3F
Junction Rd., Little Ealing	8	2A
Junction Rd., S. Croydon	57	1F
June Cl., Coulsdon	56	5B
June La., Salfords	109	4F
Junewood Cl.	49	4D
Juniper	27	4D
Juniper Cl., Biggin Hill	77	2F
Juniper Cl., Guildford	81	3F
Juniper Cl., Reigate	108	1C
Juniper Dri.	63	1E
Juniper Gdns.	15	5F
Juniper Gdns.	39	1F
Juniper Rd., Crawley	146	2C
Juniper Rd., Reigate	108	1C
Juniper Rd., West Heath	60	4A
Jura Cl.	146	5C
Justin Cl.	8	3A
Jutland Pl.	13	4E
Jutland Rd.	24	2B
Juxon Cl.	146	5B

K

Kangley Bridge Rd.	24	4A
Kashmir Court	49	3F
Katherine Cl.	49	1D
Katherine St.	40	5C
Kay Cres.	134	4A
Kaye Don Way	50	3A
Kayemoor Rd.	56	2A
Keable Rd.	95	5F
Kearton Cl.	74	2C
Keats Av.	90	4B
Keats Cl.	158	2C
Keats Green	27	1D
Keats Way, Crowthorne	43	1D
Keats Way, Shirley	41	3E
Keble Cl., Old Malden	37	4E
Keble Cl., Three Bridges	147	2C
Keble St.	20	3C
Keeble Way	43	3E
Keedonwood Rd.	24	4C
Keeley Rd.	40	5A
Keens Lane	81	3D
Keens Park Rd.	81	3D
Keens Rd.	57	1F
Keep Hatch Rd.	25	1E
Keep, The	18	5B
Keepers Coombe	27	3D
Keeper's Corner	129	4F
Keepers Cott.	82	4C
Keepers Wk.	30	3C
Keevil Dri.	20	2A
Keldholme	26	2C
Kellerton Rd.	24	1C
Kellino St.	21	4D
Kelly Cl.	33	1F
Kelmscott Rd.	21	1D
Kelsey Cl.	128	2A
Kelsey La.	42	1A
Kelsey Park Av.	42	2A
Kelsey Way	42	2A
Kelso Cl.	148	3A
Kelso Rd.	38	4C
Kelvedon Av.	50	2C
Kelvedon Cl.	18	5C
Kelvin Av., Leatherhead	69	3F
Kelvin Av., Teddington	17	5E
Kelvin Cl.	53	2F
Kelvin Gro., Hook	36	5B
Kelvin Gro., Upper Sydenham	23	3E
Kelvin La.	147	2D
Kelvin Way	147	2D
Kelvinbrook	35	2D
Kelvington Cl.	41	4F
Kelvington Rd.	23	1F
Kemara Cl.	147	2E
Kemble Cl.	50	1B
Kemble Rd., Croydon	40	5B
Kemble Rd., Forest Hill	23	2F
Kemerton Rd., Addiscombe	41	4D
Kemerton Rd., Beckenham	42	1B
Kemishford La.	64	5B
Kemnal Pk.	152	2A
Kemp Court	45	3E
Kempshott Rd., Horsham	158	4A

194
Kempshott Rd
Kingston Rd

Kempshott Rd., Streatham Vale 22 5A
Kempton Av. 34 1A
Kempton Court 34 1A
Kemsing Cl. 40 2C
Kemsing Cl. 42 5C
Kemsley Rd. 77 3E
Kemton Rd. 34 1C
Kemton Walk 41 3F
Kencrick Cl. 25 2D
Kendal Cl., Farnborough 60 5B
Kendal Cl., Feltham 15 3F
Kendal Cl., Redhill 90 5A
Kendal Gro. 45 5D
Kendale Cl. 147 5F
Kendale Rd. 24 4C
Kendall Av., Elmers End 41 1F
Kendall Av., Sanderstead 57 3F
Kendall Avenue South 57 3F
Kendall Rd. 41 1F
Kendor Av. 54 4A
Kendra Hall Rd. 57 2E
Kendrey Gdns. 17 2E
Kenil Rd. 21 2F
Kenilworth Av., Bracknell 27 1D
Kenilworth Av., Oxshott 52 5A
Kenilworth Av., Wimbledon 20 4B
Kenilworth Cl. 72 1C
Kenilworth Dri. 34 5B
Kenilworth Gdns. 14 4B
Kenilworth Rd., Kent House 41 1F
Kenilworth Rd., Staines 14 3C
Kenilworth Rd., Stoneleigh 54 2B
Kenilworth Rd., West Heath 60 4A
Kenley 74 1C
Kenley Cl. 74 3C
Kenley Gdns. 40 2B
Kenley La. 74 1C
Kenley Rd., Headley Down 134 4A
Kenley Rd., Kingston 36 1C
Kenley Rd., Morden 38 1B
Kenley Rd., Twickenham 17 1F
Kenley Wk. 55 1D
Kenlor Rd. 21 4D
Kenmara Cl. 147 2E
Kenmare Dri. 21 5D
Kenmare Rd. 40 3A
Kenmore Cl. 61 3E
Kenmore Rd. 57 5E
Kennedy Av. 150 1B
Kennedy Rd. 158 5B
Kennel Av. 28 1B
Kennel Cl., Ascot Heath 10 5B
Kennel Cl., Fetcham 69 5D
Kennel Grn. 28 1B
Kennel La., Cove 60 5A
Kennel La., Fetcham 69 5D
Kennel La., Millbridge 115 3D
Kennel La., Windlesham 45 1F
Kennel Ride 10 5B
Kennel Wood 28 1B
Kennel Wood Cres. 59 4E
Kennet Cl., Ash 78 5C
Kennet Cl., Farnborough 60 4B
Kennet Sq. 39 1D
Kenneth Rd. 73 1D
Kenrick Sq. 92 5A
Kensham Way 43 3E
Kensington Av. 40 1B
Kenston Rd. 40 3A
Kent Cl., Mitcham 40 2A
Kent Cl., Staines 14 5C
Kent Dri. 17 4E
Kent Gate Way 59 2D
Kent Hatch Rd. 94 3B
Kent House La. 23 5F
Kent House Rd. 23 4F
Kent Rd., Ackton Green 9 1D
Kent Rd., East Molesey 35 2E
Kent Rd., Kew 8 3C
Kent Rd., West Wickham 42 4B
Kent Rd., Windlesham 46 1A
Kent Rd., Woking 65 1E
Kent Way 36 5B
Kentigern Dr. 43 1E
Kenton Av. 34 1B
Kenton Cl., Bracknell 27 1D
Kenton Cl., Frimley Green 61 2F
Kenton Way 64 2A
Kentwode Grn. 9 3E
Kentwyns Rise 110 1A
Kenwood Dri., Beckenham 42 2B
Kenwood Dri., Hersham 51 2D
Kenwood Dri., Sunbury 16 5A
Kenwood Dri., Weybridge 50 2B
Kenwood Park 50 2B
Kenwood Ridge 74 2B
Kenwyn Rd. 37 1F
Kenyngton Court 16 4A
Kenyngton Dri. 16 4A
Kenyons 84 2B
Keogh Cl. 78 1C
Keppel Rd. 86 5C
Keppel Spur 12 2B
Kepple Pl. 45 2E
Kerria Way 46 5A
Kerrill Av. 74 3B
Kerry Ter. 65 1E
Kersey Dri. 58 4C
Kersfield Rd. 20 1A
Kershaw Cl. 20 1C
Keston Av., Old Coulsdon 74 3B
Keston Av., Woodham 49 4D
Kestrel Av., Herne Hill 22 1B
Kestrel Av., Staines 14 4A
Kestrel Cl., Guildford 82 5C
Kestrel Cl., Horsham 158 3C
Kestrel Way 59 4E
Keswick Av., Coombe 19 4D
Keswick Av., Merton 38 1B
Keswick Cl., Camberley 62 1A
Keswick Cl., Crawley 146 5A
Keswick Cl., Sutton 55 1F
Keswick Rd., Egham 13 5E
Keswick Rd., Fetcham 69 5E
Keswick Rd., Lightwater 45 4F
Keswick Rd., Milford 118 5A
Keswick Rd., West Hill 20 1A
Keswick Rd., West Wickham 42 5C
Keswick Rd., Whitton 17 1D
Kettering St. 21 5F
Kettlewell Cl. 65 1D
Kettlewell Dri. 48 5A
Kettlewell Hill 48 5A
Kevan Dri. 83 1D
Kew 8 3C
Kew Bridge Court 8 2C
Kew Bridge Rd. 8 3B
Kew Cres. 38 5B
Kew Foot Rd. 8 5B
Kew Gardens Rd. 8 3C
Kew Grn. 8 3B
Kew Rd. 8 5B
Keymer Rd. 22 3A
Khama Rd. 21 4D
Khartoum Rd., Tooting 21 4D
Khartoum Rd., Wheeler St. 118 5A
Kibble Green 27 3D
Kidborough 146 5B
Kidborough Down 86 2A
Kidderminster Rd. 40 4B
Kidmans Cl. 158 3C
Kielder Walk 62 1A
Kier Park 28 2C
Kilcorral Cl. 54 5B
Kildoran Rd. 22 1A
Kilgour Rd. 23 1F
Killarne Rd. 20 1C
Killasser Court 71 5F
Killearn Rd. 24 2B
Killester Gdns. 54 1C
Killieser Av. 22 3A
Killinghurst La. 153 2D
Killy Hill 47 2D
Kilmarnock Park 89 4F
Kilmartin Av. 40 2A
Kilmartin Gdns. 61 2E
Kilmington Cl. 27 4E
Kilmington Rd. 9 3E
Kilmiston Av. 33 3E
Kilmore Dri. 61 1F
Kilmorie Rd. 23 2F
Kiln Cl. 149 3E
Kiln Copse 140 1C
Kiln Fields 152 2A
Kiln La., Brockham 106 1C
Kiln La., Burntcommon 66 5B
Kiln La., Epsom 54 4B
Kiln La., Horley 128 1B
Kiln La., Middle Bourne 115 1D
Kiln La., Priestwood 26 1C
Kiln La., Sunningdale 29 3E
Kiln La., Woodside 10 5C
Kiln Meadow 80 3C
Kiln Rd 149 3E
Kiln Ride 25 5D
Kiln Way, Aldershot 96 1C
Kiln Way, Grayshott 134 5B
Kilnfield Rd. 157 2F
Kilnmead 147 3D
Kilnmead Cl. 147 3D
Kilnside 52 2C
Kilross Rd. 15 2F
Kilrue La. 51 1D
Kilrush Ter. 65 1E
Kilsha Rd. 34 3A
Kimber Court 82 4C
Kimber Rd. 20 2B
Kimberley 27 4D
Kimberley Cl., Crawley 147 3E
Kimberley Cl., Horley 128 2A
Kimberley Rd., Elmers End 41 1F
Kimberley Rd., Thornton Heath 40 3B
Kimberley Ride 52 5A
Kimberley Wk. 34 4A
Kimbers La. 96 3B
Kimble Rd. 21 4D
Kimble Side Rd. 77 2D
Kimbolton Cl. 24 1C
Kimmeridge 27 3E
Kimpton Rd. 38 5B
Kinfauns Rd. 22 3B
Kinfisher Court 48 5C
King Acre Court 13 3F
King Alfred Av. 24 4A
King Charles Cres. 36 4C
King Charles Rd. 36 3B
King Charles Wk. 20 2A
King Cl. 50 2A
King Edward Dri. 36 5B
King Edward Ms. 9 4E
King Edwards Cl. 28 1B
King Edward's Gro. 18 5A
King Edward's Rd. 28 1B
King Edwards Rise. 28 1B
King Gdns. 22 1A
King George Av., East Grinstead 150 1B
King George Av., Walton-on-Thames 34 4B
King George Cl. 15 4F
King George Sq. 18 1B
King George VI Av. 39 2E
King George's Driv. 49 3D
King Henry's Dri. 59 3E
King Henry's Rd. 36 2C
King St., East Grinstead 150 2C
King St., Hammersmith 9 2F
King St., Richmond 18 1A
King St., Twickenham 17 2F
King St. Chertsey 32 4A
King Shade Wk., Epsom 160
Kingbury Dri. 12 2B
Kingcup Dri., 63 1E
Kingfield Cl. 65 3D
Kingfield Dri. 65 3D
Kingfield Gdns. 65 3D
Kingfield Rd. 65 3D
Kingfisher Cl., Crawley 147 2E
Kingfisher Cl., Hersham 51 1E
Kingfisher Court 48 5C
Kingfisher Dri., Ham 18 4A
Kingfisher Dri., Merrow 82 4C
Kingfisher Dri., Redhill 90 4B
Kingfisher Dri., Staines 14 4A
Kingfisher Gdns. 58 3C
Kingfisher Rise 150 3C
Kingfisher Way, Elmers End 41 3F
Kingfisher Way, Horsham 158 3B
Kingfisher Wk. 78 4B
Kingham Cl. 20 2C
Kinglake Court 64 2A
Kings Av., Balham 21 2F
Kings Av., Beckenham 24 5C
Kings Av., Brixton Hill 22 1A
Kings Av., Byfleet 49 4F
Kings Av., Carshalton Beeches 56 2A
Kings Av., New Malden 37 2E
King's Av., St. Johns 109 1D
King's Av., Sunbury 15 4F
Kings Av., Tongham 97 1E
Kings Chase 35 2D
Kings Cl., Staines 14 5C
Kings Cl., Walton-on-Thames 34 4A
Kings Court, Horsham 158 4C
Kings Court, Tadworth 71 4F
Kings Court, Tongham 97 1E
Kings Cres. 44 4A
Kings Dri., Surbiton 36 4C
Kings Dri., Thames Ditton 35 4F
King's Farm Av. 8 5C
Kings Hall Rd. 41 1F
Kings Head La. 49 4F
Kings Keep 43 3D
Kings La., Carshalton 56 2A
Kings La., Englefield Green 12 4B
Kings La., Farnham 114 1C
Kings La., Updown Hill 46 1A
Kings Mead, Smallfield 129 3E
Kings Mead, S.Nutfield 110 1A
Kings Mead Cl. 17 5F
King's Mill La. 109 3F
King's Rd., Belmont 55 3E
King's Rd., Biggin Hill 77 2D
Kings Rd., Cranleigh 140 2C
King's Rd., Crowthorne 43 2D
King's Rd., Egham 13 4E
King's Rd., Feltham 16 2A
King's Rd., Fulwell 17 4E
King's Rd., Godalming 119 1D
Kings Rd., Guildford 81 5F
King's Rd., Horley 128 2B
King's Rd., Horsham 158 4C
King's Rd., Kingston 18 5B
Kings Rd., Maybuiry 65 1E
King's Rd., Mitcham 39 2E
King's Rd., Mortlake 9 5D
King's Rd., Richmond 18 1B
Kings Rd., Shalford 101 4D
Kings Rd., Shottermill 151 3F
King's Rd., S. Norwood 41 2D
Kings Rd., Southborough 36 4A
King's Rd., Sunninghill 29 3D
King's Rd., Twickenham 18 1A
Kings Rd., Walton 34 5A
Kings Rd., West End 46 5B
King's Rd., Wimbledon 20 5B
Kings Rd., Woodham 49 3E
Kings Ride 44 5A
King's Ride Court 8 5C
Kings Way, Haddon 57 1D
King's Wk., Sanderstead 58 5B
King's Wk., York Town 43 5F
Kingsbridge Av. 8 1B
Kingsbridge Rd., Morden 38 4A
Kingsbridge Rd., Walton-on-Thames 34 4A
Kingsbury Cres. 13 4F
Kingsclear Pk. 61 1D
Kingsclere Cl. 19 2E
Kingscliffe Gdns. 20 2B
Kingscote Hill 146 5C
Kingscote Rd., Acton Green 9 1D
Kingscote Rd., Addiscombe 41 4E
Kingscote Rd., New Malden 37 2D
Kingscourt Rd. 22 3A
Kingscroft Rd., Leatherhead 69 3F
Kingscroft Rd., Woodmansterne 73 1D
Kingscross La. 110 2A
Kingscup Cl. 41 4F
Kingsdale Rd. 23 5F
Kingsdene 71 4F
Kingsdown Av., Lammas Park 8 1A
Kingsdown Av., Purley 57 3E
Kingsdown Rd., Cheam 55 1D
Kingsdown Rd., Epson 54 5B
Kingsdowne Rd. 36 4B
Kingsford Av. 57 2D
Kingsgate Rd. 36 1B
Kingshill Av. 37 4F
Kingskeep Est. 18 5B
Kingslea, Horsham 158 4C
Kingslea, Leatherhead 69 3F
Kingsleigh Pl. 39 2D
Kingsley Av., Banstead 72 1B
Kingsley Av., Camberley 61 1D
Kingsley Av., Carshalton 56 1A
Kingsley Av., Englefield Green 12 5B
Kingsley Cl., Crowthorne 43 2D
Kingsley Cl., Horley 128 1A
Kingsley Dri. 37 5E
Kingsley Green Rd. 151 5F
Kingsley Gro. 108 2B
Kingsley Rd., Crawley 146 5B
Kingsley Rd., Croydon 40 4B
Kingsley Rd., Horley 128 1A
Kingsley Rd., W. H'th 60 4C
Kingsley Rd., Wimbledon 20 4C
Kingslyn Cres. 40 1C
Kingsmead, Biggin Hill 77 1E
Kingsmead, Farnborough 61 5D
Kingsmead, Frimley 61 3E
Kingsmead, Richmond 18 1B
Kingsmead, Weybridge 50 2C
Kingsmead, Woking 65 1E
Kingsmead Av., Mitcham 39 1F
Kingsmead Av., Sunbury-on-Thames 34 2A
Kingsmead Av., Tolworth 36 5C
Kingsmead Av., Worcester Park 37 5F
Kingsmead Cl. 54 3A
Kingsmead Pk., Claygate 52 2B
Kingsmead Pk., Elstead 117 3D
Kingsmead Rd., St. Helier 38 4C
Kingsmead Rd., Tulse Hill 22 3B
Kingsmere Rd., Priestwood Common 26 1C
Kingsmere Rd., Wimbledon 20 3A
Kingsnympton Park 18 5C
Kingsthorpe Rd. 23 4F
Kingston Av., Feltham 15 1F
Kingston Av., Horsley 84 1C
Kingston Av., Leatherhead 69 4F
Kingston Av., North Cheam 38 5A
Kingston Br. 36 1A
Kingston By-Pass, Hinchley Wood 35 5E
Kingston By-Pass, Hook 36 5B
Kingston By-Pass, Kingston Vale 19 4E
Kingston By-Pass, Malden 37 4D
Kingston Cl. 17 5F
Kingston Cres. 14 4B
Kingston Gdns. 40 5A
Kingston Hall Rd. 36 2B
Kingston Hill 19 4D
Kingston Hill Pl. 19 4D
Kingston Ho. Gdns. 69 4F
Kingston La. 17 4F
Kingston Rd., Camberley 44 4C
Kingston Rd., Ewell 54 1A
Kingston Rd., Leatherhead 69 2F
Kingston Rd., Merton 20 5B
Kingston Rd., New Malden 37 2D
Kingston Rd., Raynes Park 38 1A
Kingston Rd., Roehampton 19 2F
Kingston Rd., Staines 14 4A
Kingston Rd., Teddington 18 5A

Kingston Rd., Tolworth 36 5C
Kingston Rise 49 3D
Kingston Vale 19 4D
Kingston-upon-Thames 36 2C
Kingsway, Blackwater 60 1B
Kingsway, Goldsworth 64 2C
Kingsway, Mortlake 8 5C
Kingsway, Motspur Park 37 3F
Kingsway, Staines 14 2C
Kingsway, West Wickham 42 5C
Kingsway Av., Selsdon 58 3B
Kingsway Av., Woking 64 2C
Kingsway Rd. 55 2D
Kingsway, The 54 4B
Kingswick Cl. 29 2E
Kingswick Dri. 29 2D
Kingswood 72 5A
Kingswood Av., Croydon 75 1E
Kingswood Av., Hampton 17 5D
Kingswood Av., Shortlands 42 2C
Kingswood Av., Thornton
    Heath 40 3B
Kingswood Cl., Englefield
    Green 12 4C
Kingswood Cl., Malden 37 3E
Kingswood Cl., Merrow 82 5C
Kingswood Cl., Weybridge 50 2A
Kingswood Court 72 5B
Kingswood Creek 12 1C
Kingswood Dri., Gypsy Hill 23 4D
Kingswood Dri.,
    Hackbridge 39 4E
Kingswood Dri., Sutton 55 3F
Kingswood Firs 151 1D
Kingswood La., Hamsey
    Green 75 1E
Kingswood La., Nutcombe 151 1D
Kingswood Rd., Acton Grn. 9 1D
Kingswood Rd., Brixton Hill 22 1A
Kingswood Rd., Merton 38 1D
Kingswood Rd., Penge 23 5E
Kingswood Rd., Shortlands 42 2C
Kingswood Rd., Tadworth 71 4F
Kingswood Rd.,
    Wimbledon 20 5B
Kingswood Rise 12 4C
Kingswood Way, Selsdon 58 4B
Kingswood Way, Waddon 57 1D
Kingsworthy Cl. 36 2B
Kinloss Rd. 38 4C
Kinnaird Av., Chiswick 9 3D
Kinnaird Av., Plaistow 24 5C
Kinnaird Cl. 24 5C
Kinnersley Wk. 108 3B
Kinniard Cl. 24 5C
Kinniburgh Dri. 132 3A
Kinross Av., Ascot 28 3B
Kinross Av., Worcester
    Park 37 5E
Kinross Cl. 15 4F
Kinross Dri. 15 4F
Kintyre Cl. 40 2A
Kipings 72 4A
Kipling Cl. 147 3F
Kipling Way 150 2B
Kirby Cl. 54 1B
Kirby Rd. 64 2C
Kirby Way 34 3B
Kirdford Cl. 146 3B
Kirk Rd. 38 5C
Kirk Rise 38 5C
Kirkby Court. 61 2E
Kirkdale 23 3E
Kirkham Cl. 43 3E
Kirkland Av. 64 1A
Kirklees Rd., Surbiton 36 4B
Kirklees Rd., Thornton
    Heath 40 2A
Kirkley Rd. 38 1B
Kirkly Cl. 58 3A
Kirkstall Gdns. 22 2A
Kirkstall Rd. 22 2A
Kirkstand Rd. 38 4B
Kirkstone Cl. 62 1A
Kirkstone Way 24 5C
Kirremuir Gdns. 79 4D
Kirtley Rd. 23 4F
Kirton Cl. 9 2D
Kitchener Rd., Aldershot 78 3A
Kitchener Rd., Thornton
    Heath 40 2C
Kites Cl. 146 4C
Kithurst Cl. 146 5C
Kitley Gdns. 41 1D
Kitsmead 148 2B
Kitsmead La. 30 4C
Kitson Rd. 9 4E
Kittiwake Cl. 58 3C
Kitts La. 134 3B
Klea Av. 21 1F
Klondyke 152 1B
Knapdale Cl. 23 3E
Knaphill Rd. 63 1F
Knapmill Rd. 24 3A
Knapmill Way 24 3A
Knappe Rd. 15 4D
Kneller Gdns. 17 1E

Kneller Rd., Malden Manor 37 4D
Kneller Rd., Whitton 17 1D
Knepp Cl. 147 4F
Knighton Cl., Crawley 147 4F
Knighton Cl., S. Croydon 57 2E
Knighton Park Rd. 23 4F
Knighton Rd. 109 1E
Knightons La. 155 1E
Knight's Av. 8 1B
Knights Cl. 13 5F
Knight's Hill 22 4B
Knights Park 36 2B
Knights Rd. 96 1B
Knights Way 62 1A
Knightsbridge Cres. 14 5B
Knightsbridge Grn. 44 4B
Knightsbridge Rd. 44 4B
Knightswood, Bracknell 27 4D
Knightswood, Woking 64 2B
Knightswood Cl. 108 1B
Knightwood Cres. 37 3E
Knipp Hill 51 5F
Knob Hill 158 2A
Knobfield 103 5F
Knockholt Cl. 55 3E
Knole Cl. 41 3E
Knole Gro., East Grinstead 150 1B
Knole Wood 29 4D
Knoll Quarry 119 1D
Knoll Rd., Camberley 44 5A
Knoll Rd., Dorking 105 2F
Knoll Rd., Godalming 119 1D
Knoll Rd., Wandsworth 20 1C
Knoll, The, Beckenham 42 1A
Knoll, The, Cobham 51 5F
Knoll, The, Leatherhead 70 4A
Knoll Walk 44 5A
Knollmead 37 4D
Knolls Cl. 37 5F
Knolls, The 71 1F
Knollys Cl. 22 3B
Knolly's Rd. 22 3A
Knowl Hill 65 3E
Knowle Cl. 148 1B
Knowle Dri. 148 1B
Knowle Gdns. 49 5D
Knowle Green 14 4B
Knowle Gro. 30 4C
Knowle Grove Cl. 30 4C
Knowle Hill, Knowlehill 30 4C
Knowle La. 140 3C
Knowle Park Av. 14 5B
Knowle Pk. 68 1C
Knowle Rd. 17 2E
Knowle, The 71 4F
Knowles Hill Cres. 24 1B
Kohat Rd. 20 4C
Kohima Cl. 78 4A
Kooringa 75 3E
Korda Cl. 33 2D
Kreisel Wk. 8 3B
Krooner Rd. 61 1D
Kuala Gdns. 40 1A
Kyle Cl. 26 2C
Kynaston Av. 40 3B
Kynaston Cres. 40 3C
Kynaston Rd. 40 3C
Kyre Rd. 21 1E

L

Laburnam Cres. 34 1A
Laburnam Pl. 12 5B
Laburnam Rd., Chertsey 32 4A
Laburnam Rd., Heath End 96 1B
Laburnam Rd., Wimbledon 20 5C
Laburnham Court. 129 3E
Laburnham Gdns. 41 4E
Laburnum Cl. 81 4F
Laburnum Gro. 37 1D
Laburnum Rd., Epsom 54 5A
Laburnum Rd., Mitcham 39 1E
Laburnum Rd., Woking 64 3C
Laburnum Way 14 2C
Lacey Av. 74 3B
Lacey Cl. 13 5F
Lacey Dri. 74 3B
Lackford Rd. 73 2D
Lacock Cl. 20 5C
Lacy Green 74 3A
Ladas Rd. 22 4B
Ladbroke Gro. 90 5B
Ladbroke Hurst 132 3A
Ladbroke Rd., Epsom 54 5A
Ladbroke Rd., Horley 128 1B
Ladbroke Rd., Redhill 90 5B
Ladbrook Rd., Selhurst 40 2C
Lady Booth Rd. 36 1B
Lady Hay 37 5E
Lady Margaret Rd.,
    Broomhall 29 4E
Lady Margaret Rd., Ifield 146 3B
Ladybank 27 4D
Ladycross 118 4B
Ladygate Cl. 106 1A
Ladygate Rd. 106 1A

Ladygrove Dri. 82 3B
Ladymead 81 5F
Ladymead Cl. 147 5F
Ladythorpe Cl. 49 1E
Ladywell Hill 119 3D
Ladywell Rd. 24 1A
Ladywood Av. 60 5A
Ladywood Rd. 36 5C
Lafone Av. 16 3B
Lagham Rd. 111 2F
Laglands Cl. 89 4F
Lahore Rd. 40 3C
Laing's Av. 39 1D
Laird Cl. 45 3E
Lairdale Cl. 22 2B
Laitwood Rd. 21 2E
Lake Cl. 49 4F
Lake Dri. 133 5D
Lake End Way 43 2D
Lake Gdns., Ham 18 3A
Lake Gdns., Wallington 39 5E
Lake La., Dockenfield 114 5B
Lake La., Horley 128 1C
Lake Rd., Deepcut 61 4F
Lake Rd., Ockley 124 4A
Lake Rd., Shirley 42 5A
Lake Rd., Virginia Water 30 2B
Lake Rd., Wimbledon 20 4B
Lake View 106 3A
Lake View Rd., Dormans
    Park 131 5F
Lake View Rd., Felbridge 149 1E
Lakehall Gdns. 40 3B
Lakehall Rd. 40 3B
Lakehurst Rd. 54 1A
Lakeland Dri. 61 2E
Laker Pl. 20 1B
Lakers Rise 73 1D
Lakes Cl. 101 3E
Lakeside, Ewell 54 2B
Lakeside, Horsham 158 3B
Lakeside, Kingston upon
    Thames 56 1B
Lakeside, Redhill 90 4B
Lakeside, Walton 33 5F
Lakeside, Woking 64 3A
Lakeside Cl., Ash Vale 78 4B
Lakeside Cl., Norwood 41 1D
Lakeside Cl., Woking 64 3A
Lakeside Dri. 52 2A
Lakeside Gdns. 60 3B
Lakeside Grange 33 5E
Lakeside Rd. 78 4B
Lakeside, The, 60 1B
Lakeview Rd. 22 4B
Laleham 32 2B
Laleham Rd., Catford 24 2B
Laleham Rd., Shepperton 32 2C
Laleham Rd., Staines 14 5A
Lamberhurst Rd. 22 4B
Lambert Av. 8 5C
Lambert Cl. 77 1E
Lambert Cres. 60 1B
Lambert Rd., Banstead 55 5E
Lambert Rd., Brixton 22 1A
Lamberts Rd. 36 3B
Lambeth Rd. 40 4B
Lambly Hill 31 2D
Lamborn Gro. 27 1E
Lambourne Av. 20 4B
Lambourne Cl. 147 5E
Lambourne Cres. 48 5C
Lambourne Dri., Bagshot 45 3D
Lambourne Dri., Cobham 68 1B
Lambourne Way 97 1E
Lambs Cres. 158 3C
Lambs Farm Rd. 158 3C
Lambton Rd. 37 1F
Lambyn Croft 128 2C
Lamerock Rd. 24 4C
Lamma Rd. 21 2F
Lammas Av. 39 1E
Lammas Cl. 119 1E
Lammas Dri. 13 4F
Lammas Green 23 3E
Lammas La. 51 1F
Lammas Park Rd. 8 1A
Lammas Rd., Godalming 119 1E
Lammas Rd., Ham 18 4A
Lampard La. 134 2B
Lampeter Cl. 65 2D
Lampton House Cl. 20 4A
Lanark Cl., Frimley 61 2E
Lanark Cl., Horsham 158 4C
Lancaster 17 2F
Lancaster Av., Farnham 96 5B
Lancaster Av., Thornton
    Heath 40 3A
Lancaster Av., Tulse Hill 22 3B
Lancaster Av., Wimbledon 20 4A
Lancaster Cl. 12 4C
Lancaster Cl., Kingston 18 4B
Lancaster Cl., Shortlands 42 2C
Lancaster Cl., Walton 40 5A
Lancaster Court, Banstead 55 5E
Lancaster Court, Walton-
    on-Thames 34 4A

Lancaster Gdns., Blindley
    Heath 111 5F
Lancaster Gdns., Kingston 18 4B
Lancaster Park 18 1B
Lancaster Rd., Anerley 41 1D
Lancaster Rd., Wimbledon 20 4A
Lancaster Way 61 3D
Lancelot Cl. 146 4A
Lancing Cl. 146 3B
Lancing Rd., Croydon 40 3A
Lancing Rd., Feltham 15 3F
Landalls Rd. 23 1D
Landcroft Rd. 23 1D
Landen Ct. 25 3D
Landen Pk. 128 1A
Landford Rd. 9 5F
Landgrove Rd. 20 4B
Landon Way 15 5E
Lands End La. 133 4D
Landscape Rd. 75 3E
Landseer Cl., Merton 38 1C
Landseer Cl., Sandhurst 43 5E
Landseer Rd., Cheam 55 2E
Landseer Rd., Malden
    Manor 37 4D
Lane Cl. 49 1E
Lane End, Bletchingley 91 4E
Lane End, Epsom 53 5F
Lane End Dri. 63 2F
Lane, The, Ifold 155 4F
Lane, The, Laleham 32 2A
Lane, The, Thursley 136 1A
Lane, The, Virginia Water 31 2D
Lanercost Rd. 22 3B
Lanes End 137 2F
Lang Cl., Crawley 146 4A
Lang Cl., Fetcham 69 5D
Langaller La. 69 4D
Langborough Rd. 25 2E
Langbourne Way 52 2C
Langcroft Cl. 39 5E
Langdale Av. 39 2E
Langdale Cl., E. Sheen 8 5C
Langdale Cl., Farnborough 60 5B
Langdale Cl., Woking 64 1C
Langdale Dri. 28 1A
Langdale Rd. 40 2B
Langdon Cl. 62 1A
Langdon Rd. 38 3C
Langham Cl. 119 1E
Langham Dene 74 1B
Langham Gdns. 18 4A
Langham House Cl. 18 4A
Langham Pl. 13 4D
Langham Rd., Teddington 17 4F
Langham Rd., Wimbledon 38 1A
Langhome Cl. 21 2F
Langhurstwood Rd. 158 2B
Langland Gdns. 42 5A
Langlands Rise 54 5A
Langley Av., N. Cheam 38 5A
Langley Av., Surbiton 36 4B
Langley Cl., Guildford 81 5F
Langley Cl., Langley Vale 71 3D
Langley Dri., Camberley 44 5B
Langley Dri., Crawley 146 3C
Langley Gro. 37 1D
Langley La., Crawley 146 3B
Langley La., Headley 87 1F
Langley Oaks Av. 58 3A
Langley Park Rd. 55 1F
Langley Pl. 146 2C
Langley Rd., Elmers End 41 2F
Langley Rd., Merton 38 1B
Langley Rd., Selsdon 58 3B
Langley Rd., Staines 14 5A
Langley Rd., Surbiton 36 4B
Langley Vale 71 3D
Langley Vale Rd. 71 3D
Langley Way 42 4B
Langley Wk. 146 2C
Langmans Way 64 1A
Langport Court 34 4B
Langridge Drive 150 3C
Langroyd Rd. 21 3D
Langshot Cl. 49 4D
Langshott La. 128 2C
Langside Av. 9 5E
Langsmead 111 5F
Langstone Cl. 147 5F
Langton Av. 54 4B
Langton Cl.,
    Addlestonemoor 32 5B
Langton Cl., Woking 64 2B
Langton Rd. 35 3D
Langton Rise 23 2E
Langton Way, S. Croydon 58 1A
Langton Way, Thorpe Lea 13 5F
Langwood Chase 18 5A
Lanier Rd. 24 1B
Lankton Cl. 42 1B
Lansbury Av. 16 1A
Lansdell Rd. 39 1E
Lansdown Cl., Walton-on-
    Thames 34 4A
Lansdown Cl., Woking 64 3A
Lansdown Rd. 61 3F

Lansdowne Cl., Wimbledon	20	5A
Lansdowne Ct.	37	5E
Lansdowne Hill	22	3B
Lansdowne La.	82	5B
Lansdowne Pl.	23	5D
Lansdowne Rd., Croydon	40	5C
Lansdowne Rd., Ewell	54	2A
Lansdowne Rd., Purley	57	4D
Lansdowne Rd., Staines	14	5B
Lansdowne Rd., Wimbledon	20	5A
Lansdowne Wood Cl.	22	3B
Lapsewood Walk	23	3E
Lapwing Grn.	82	4C
Lapwing Rd.	58	3C
Lara Cl., Chessington	53	2E
Lara Cl., Hither Green	24	1B
Larbert Rd.	21	5F
Larby Pl.	54	3B
Larch Av., Guildford	81	4F
Larch Av., Sunninghill	29	3D
Larch Av., Wokingham	25	1D
Larch Cl., Camberley	44	3B
Larch Cl., Chipstead	72	4C
Larch Cl., Mead Vale	108	1C
Larch Cl., Warlingham	75	3F
Larch Cres., West Ewell	53	2F
Larch Dri.	8	2C
Larch End	158	4A
Larch Rd., Balham	21	2B
Larch Rd., Headley Down	134	4A
Larch Tree Way	42	5A
Larch Way	60	5A
Larches Way	149	3E
Larchwood Cl.	72	1A
Larchwood Dri.	12	5B
Larchwood Glade	44	4C
Larchwood Rd.	64	3A
Larcombe Cl.	58	1A
Larden Rd.	9	1E
Larford Cl.	96	2B
Larges Bridge Dri.	27	2D
Larges La.	27	1D
Largewood Av.	36	5C
Lark Av.	14	3A
Lark Rise, Crawley	146	3C
Lark Rise, East Horsley	84	4C
Larkbere Rd.	23	4F
Larkfield	51	5D
Larkfield Rd., Farnham	95	4F
Larkfield Rd., Richmond	8	5B
Larkhall	51	2E
Larkham Cl.	15	4F
Larkin Cl.	74	2A
Larkins Rd., Gatwick	128	4A
Larksfield	12	5C
Larkspur Cl.	96	1C
Larkspur Way, Dorking	106	3A
Larkspur Way, West Ewell	54	1A
Larksway	63	2F
Larkswood Cl.	43	3D
Larkswood Dri.	43	1D
Larpent Av.	19	1F
Lascombe La.	98	3C
Lashmere, Capthorne	148	1C
Lashmere, Cranleigh	140	1B
Lasswade Rd.	32	4A
Latchmere Cl.	18	4B
Latchmere La.	18	5B
Latchmere Rd.	18	5B
Latchwood La.	115	1E
Lateward Rd.	8	3A
Latham Av.	61	2E
Latham Cl.	17	2F
Latham Rd.	17	2F
Lathams Way	40	4A
Latimer	27	4D
Latimer Cl., Northgate	147	2D
Latimer Cl., Stoneleigh	54	1C
Latimer Hanover St.	40	5B
Latimer Rd., Godalming	119	2D
Latimer Rd., Teddington	17	4F
Latimer Rd., Wimbledon	20	5C
Latimer Rd., Wokingham	25	2D
Latton Cl., Esher	52	1A
Latton Cl., Walton-on-Thames	34	4C
Latymer Cl.	50	1B
Laud Dri.	147	4F
Laud St.	40	5C
Laud Way	25	2F
Lauder Cl.	61	2E
Lauderdale Dri.	18	3A
Laughton Rd.	158	3C
Laundry La.	43	5F
Laundry Rd.	100	1C
Laundry Way	125	5D
Lauradale	26	2C
Laurel Av.	12	4B
Laurel Cl., Camberley	61	1D
Laurel Cl., Cove	60	5A
Laurel Cl., Crawley	147	5E
Laurel Cl., Poyle	7	3A
Laurel Cres., Addington	59	1D
Laurel Cres., Sheerwater	48	5C
Laurel Cres., Shirley	42	5A
Laurel Dene	150	2C
Laurel Dri.	93	4F
Laurel Gro., Boundstone	114	1C
Laurel Gro., Sydenham	23	4F
Laurel La.	17	2F
Laurel Rd., Barnes	9	4E
Laurel Rd., Cottenham Park	37	1F
Laurel Rd., Fulwell	17	4E
Laurel Walk	158	5C
Laurels, The, Aldershot	96	1C
Laurels, The, Banstead	72	2B
Laurels, The, Cobham	50	1B
Laurels, The, Cobham	68	1C
Laurels, The, Cobham	68	1C
Laurier Rd.	41	4D
Lauriston Rd.	20	5A
Lauser Rd.	14	2B
Laustan Cl.	82	5B
Lavant Cl.	146	4B
Lavender Av., Mitcham	39	1D
Lavender Av., Worcester Park	37	5F
Lavender Cl., Carshalton	56	1B
Lavender Cl., Caterham	91	1F
Lavender Cl., Coulsdon	73	3F
Lavender Cl., Salfords	109	3E
Lavender Gro.	39	1D
Lavender La.	114	2C
Lavender Park Rd.	49	4D
Lavender Rd., Byfleet	49	4D
Lavender Rd., Croydon	40	3A
Lavender Rd., Maybury	65	1E
Lavender Rd., Sutton	55	1F
Lavender Rd., Wallington	56	1B
Lavender Rd., West Ewell	53	1F
Lavender Vale	56	2C
Lavender Way	41	3F
Lavengro Rd.	22	3C
Lavenham Rd.	20	3B
Laverstoke Gdns.	19	2E
Lavington Cl.	146	3B
Lavington Rd.	57	1D
Lawbrook La.	103	4E
Lawday Link	95	1F
Lawday Pl.	95	1F
Lawdon Gdns.	57	1E
Lawford Cl.	57	3D
Lawford Rd.	9	3D
Lawfords Hill Rd.	63	5F
Lawn Cres.	8	4B
Lawn Rd., Beckenham	24	5A
Lawn Rd., Guildford	100	2C
Lawnford Gdns.	74	1B
Lawns, The, Ascot	28	2A
Lawns, The, Ascot	28	2A
Lawns, The, Milford	118	3B
Lawns, The, Norwood	40	1C
Lawrence Av.	37	3D
Lawrence Cl.	25	2E
Lawrence Court	82	3B
Lawrence Cres.	46	2A
Lawrence Grn.	26	1B
Lawrence La.	88	4C
Lawrence Pk. Gdns.	23	4E
Lawrence Rd., Brentford	8	2A
Lawrence Rd., Ham	18	4A
Lawrence Rd., Hampton	16	5C
Lawrence Rd., South Norwood	41	2D
Lawrence Way	60	1C
Lawrie Park Av.	23	4E
Lawrie Park Cres.	23	4E
Lawrie Park Gdns.	23	4E
Lawrie Park Rd.	23	5E
Lawson Way	29	3F
Laxton Gdns.	90	2C
Layhams Rd.	59	1F
Layton Court	50	1B
Layton Cres.	57	1E
Layton Rd.	8	2A
Layton's La.	33	1F
Lazenby La.	142	2B
Le May Cl.	128	2B
Le Personne Rd.	74	4C
Lea Cl., Ash	78	5C
Lea Cl., Crawley	146	4B
Lea Coach Rd.	117	5F
Lea Court	96	1C
Lea Croft, Crowthorne	43	1D
Lea Croft, Kenley	74	1C
Lea Rd., Beckenham	42	1A
Lea Rd., Camberley	61	2D
Lea, The	13	5E
Leach Grn.	70	4A
Leacroft	29	3D
Leacroft Av.	21	2E
Leacroft Cl.	14	4B
Leacroft Rd.	14	4B
Leaf Cl.	35	3E
Leaf Field Cl.	64	2C
Leaf Gro.	22	4B
Leafield Cl.	22	5B
Leafield Copse	27	2F
Leafield Rd., South Merton	28	2B
Leafield Rd., Sutton Common	38	5B
Leafy Way	41	5D
Leahurst Rd.	24	1B
Leamington Av.	38	2B
Leamington Cl.	17	1D
Leamore St.	9	2F
Leander Rd., Brixton Hill	22	1A
Leander Rd., Thornton Heath	40	2A
Leapale La.	100	1C
Leapale Rd.	100	1C
Leas Cl.	53	2E
Leas Lane	75	2F
Leas Rd., Guildford	100	1C
Leas Rd., Warlingham	75	2F
Leaside	68	5C
Leather Cl.	39	1E
Leatherhead	70	4A
Leatherhead By-Pass Rd.	69	5F
Leatherhead Rd., Chessington	53	3D
Leatherhead Rd., Eastwick	86	1A
Leatherhead Rd., L'head	70	4A
Leatherhead Rd., Oxshott	52	5B
Leathwaite Rd.	21	1E
Leaveland Cl.	42	2A
Leaves Grn.	27	3E
Leavesden Rd.	50	1B
Leazes Av.	74	5B
Lebanon Av.	16	4B
Lebanon Dri.	51	5F
Lebanon Gdns., Biggin Hill	77	2E
Lebanon Gdns., Wandsworth	20	1B
Lebanon Park	18	2A
Lebanon Rd., Croydon	40	2A
Lebanon Rd., Wandsworth	20	1B
Lechford Rd.	128	3B
Leckford St.	20	2C
Leconfield Av.	9	5E
Ledbury Rd., Reigate	89	5E
Ledbury Rd., South Croydon	57	1F
Ledger Cl.	82	4B
Ledger Dri.	49	1D
Ledgers Rd.	76	2A
Ledrington Rd.	23	5D
Lee Court	97	1D
Lee Green La.	70	5C
Lee Rd.	38	1C
Lee St.	128	2A
Leech La.	88	1A
Leechcroft Rd.	39	5E
Leefern Rd.	9	1F
Leegate Cl.	64	1C
Lees, The	42	5A
Leeward Gdns.	20	4B
Leewood Way	85	1E
Lefroy Rd.	9	1E
Legge La.	60	3C
Legge St.	24	1B
Leggyfield Court.	158	3A
Leicester	27	3E
Leicester Cl.	54	1C
Leicester Rd.	41	4D
Leigh	107	4F
Leigh Cl., Addlestone	49	2D
Leigh Cl., New Malden	37	2D
Leigh Corner	68	1B
Leigh Court	51	5E
Leigh Cres.	59	2E
Leigh Hill Rd.	68	1B
Leigh La.	96	5B
Leigh Mill La.	92	5C
Leigh Orchard Cl.	22	3A
Leigh Pl.	68	1B
Leigh Place Rd.	107	3F
Leigh Rd.	51	5D
Leigham Av.	22	3A
Leigham Court Rd.	22	3A
Leigham Vale	22	3A
Leighlands	147	3F
Leighton Gdns.	58	5B
Leighton St. East	40	4B
Leighton Way	54	5A
Leinster Av.	9	5D
Leisure La.	49	4E
Leith Cl.	26	5A
Leith Gro., Beare Green	125	2D
Leith Hill La.	124	5A
Leith Hill Rd.	123	1F
Leith Rd., Beare Green	125	2D
Leith Rd., Epsom	54	4B
Leith View	106	3A
Leithcote Gdns.	22	4A
Lemarchant Rd.	61	1E
Lemington Gro.	27	3D
Lemington Way	158	2C
Lena Gdns.	9	1F
Lendore Rd.	61	3E
Lenelby Rd.	36	4C
Lenham Rd., Beulah Hill	40	1C
Lenham Rd., Sutton	55	1F
Lennard Av.	42	5C
Lennard Cl.	42	5C
Lennard Rd., Croydon	40	4B
Lennard Rd., Penge	23	5F
Lennox Gdns.	57	1E
Lenten Cl.	103	4E
Lentmead Rd.	24	3C
Lenton Rise	8	5B
Leof Cres.	24	4A
Leominster Rd.	38	3C
Leonard Av.	38	3C
Leonard Cl.	61	3E
Leonard Rd.	39	1F
Leonards Rd.	9	5D
Leopold Av., Farnborough Street	60	4C
Leopold Av., Wimbledon	20	4B
Leopold Rd., West Green	146	4C
Leopold Rd., Wimbledon	20	4B
Leppington	27	4D
Leppoc Rd.	21	1F
Leret Way	69	4F
Lesbourne Rd.	108	1C
Lescombe Cl.	23	3F
Lescombe Rd.	23	3F
Leslie Gdns.	55	2E
Leslie Gro.	40	4C
Leslie Park Rd.	40	4C
Leslie Rd., Chobham	47	3D
Leslie Rd., Dorking	87	5D
Lessar Av.	21	1F
Lessing St.	23	2F
Lessingham Av.	21	4E
Lessness Rd.	38	3C
Letchworth Av.	15	2F
Letchworth St.	21	4D
Letcombe Sq.	27	2E
Levana Cl.	20	2A
Levendale Rd.	23	3F
Leveret Cl.	59	4E
Leveret La.	146	3C
Levern Dri.	96	2A
Leverson St.	21	5F
Levett Rd.	70	3A
Levylsdene	82	5C
Lewes Cl.	147	4F
Lewes Rd.	150	3C
Lewesdon	20	2A
Lewin Rd., East Sheen	9	5D
Lewin Rd., Streatham	21	5F
Lewins Rd.	53	5F
Lewis Cl.	49	1E
Lewis Rd., Mitcham	39	1D
Lewis Rd., Richmond	18	1B
Lewis Rd., Sutton	55	1F
Lewisham	23	2F
Lewisham High St.	24	1B
Lewisham Park	24	1B
Lewisham Way	43	3E
Lexden Rd.	39	2F
Lexington Court	57	3F
Lexton Gdns.	21	2F
Ley Rd.	60	3C
Leyborne Av.	8	1A
Leyborne Park	8	4C
Leybourne Av.	49	5F
Leybourne Cl.	49	5F
Leycester Cl.	45	1F
Leyfield	37	4E
Leylands La., Abinger	123	1F
Leyland's La., Longford	7	5B
Leys Rd.	52	4B
Leythe Rd.	9	1D
Leyton Rd.	20	5C
Liberty Av.	38	1C
Liberty Hall Rd.	49	1D
Liberty La.	49	1E
Liberty Ms.	21	1E
Liberty Rise	49	2D
Lichfield Rd.	8	4B
Lichfields	27	1E
Lickfords Rd.	114	3B
Licks Ride	10	5A
Liddington Dri.	81	4D
Liddington Hall New Rd.	81	4D
Lidiard St.	20	3C
Lidstone Cl.	64	2B
Lightwater	45	3F
Lightwater Bypass	45	3F
Lightwater Meadow	45	4F
Lightwater Rd.	45	4F
Lightwood	27	3D
Lilac Av.	64	3C
Lilac Cl.	81	3F
Lilac Gdns., Ealing	8	1A
Lilac Gdns., Shirley	42	5A
Lilian Rd.	39	1F
Lilleshall Rd.	38	3C
Lilley Rd.	72	4C
Lillian Av.	8	1C
Lillian Rd.	9	3F
Lillie Rd.	77	2E
Lily Hill Dri.	27	1E
Lily Hill Rd.	27	1E
Lilyfields Chase	141	1F
Lime Av., Bracknell	27	3F
Lime Av., Camberley	44	5C
Lime Av., Tooting Bec	21	3F
Lime Av., Windsor Great Park	11	3E
Lime Cl., Copthorne	148	1B
Lime Cl., Langley Grn.	146	2C
Lime Cl., The Wrythe	39	5D
Lime Cl., W. Clandon	83	2E

Street	Pg	Ref
Lime Cl., Woodhatch	108	2C
Lime Cres.	34	1B
Lime Gdns.	17	1F
Lime Gro., Hammersmith	9	1F
Lime Gro., New Malden	37	2D
Lime Gro., Slyfield Grn.	81	3F
Lime Gro., Warlingham	75	2F
Lime Gro., West Clandon	83	2E
Lime Gro., Westfield	65	4D
Lime Meadow Av.	58	5B
Lime Rd.	8	5B
Lime Tree Av.	35	4E
Lime Tree Cl.	68	5C
Lime Tree Gro.	42	5A
Lime Tree Pl.	39	1E
Lime Tree Wk.	59	1F
Lime Wk.	27	2D
Lime Works Rd.	90	1C
Limebush Cl.	49	3E
Limecroft Cl.	54	2A
Limecroft Rd.	63	2F
Limerick Cl., Bracknell	26	1C
Limerick Cl., Clapham	21	2F
Limes Av., Barnes	9	4E
Limes Av., Horley	128	3B
Limes Av., Penge	23	5E
Limes Av., St. Helier	39	4D
Limes Av., Waddon	40	5A
Limes Cl.	15	4D
Limes Gdns.	20	1B
Limes Gro.	49	1E
Limes Rd., Beckenham	42	1B
Limes Rd., Egham	13	4D
Limes Rd., Selhurst	40	3C
Limes Rd., West Heath	60	4A
Limes Rd., Weybridge	50	1A
Limes, The, Felbridge	131	5D
Limetree La.	22	2A
Limeway Ter., Dorking	86	5C
Limewood Cl.	64	3A
Limpsfield	94	3A
Limpsfield Av., Southfields	20	2A
Limpsfield Av., Thornton Heath	40	3A
Limpsfield Rd., Sanderstead	58	4A
Limpsfield Rd., Warlingham	75	1E
Lince La.	105	2E
Linchmere La.	151	5D
Linchmere Pl.	146	3B
Linchmere Rd., Hammer	151	3D
Linchmere Rd., Hither Green	24	2C
Lincoln Av., Twickenham	17	3D
Lincoln Av., Wimbledon	20	3A
Lincoln Cl., Camberley	61	1F
Lincoln Cl., Horley	128	3B
Lincoln Dri.	65	1F
Lincoln Rd., Dorking	87	5D
Lincoln Rd., Elmers End	41	2E
Lincoln Rd., Feltham	16	3C
Lincoln Rd., Kingston	37	2D
Lincoln Rd., Woodbridge Hill	81	4E
Lincoln Rd., Worcester Park	37	4F
Lincoln Walk	54	3A
Lincoln Way	33	1F
Lincolns Mead	131	2E
Lincombe Rd.	24	3C
Lind Rd.	55	1F
Lind Way	22	4B
Lindal Rd.	24	1A
Lindale Cl.	30	2A
Lindbergh Rd.	57	2D
Linden Av., East Grinstead	150	2B
Linden Av., Thornton Heath	40	2B
Linden Av., Woodmansterne	73	1E
Linden Cl., Crawley	147	5E
Linden Cl., Horsham	158	4C
Linden Cl., Thames Ditton	35	4F
Linden Cl., Woodham	49	4D
Linden Court, Camberley	44	4B
Linden Court, Englefield Green	12	5B
Linden Cres.	36	1C
Linden Dri.	74	5B
Linden Gdns., Chiswick	9	2D
Linden Gdns., Leatherhead	70	4A
Linden Gro., Walton-on-Thames	33	5F
Linden Gro., Warlingham	75	2F
Linden Leas	42	5B
Linden Pit Path	70	4A
Linden Pl.	54	4B
Linden Rd., Guildford	81	5F
Linden Rd., Hampton	34	1C
Linden Rd., Headley Down	134	4A
Linden Rd., Leatherhead	70	4A
Linden Rd., Weybridge	50	3B
Linden Way, Sendmarsh	66	5A
Linden Way, Shepperton	33	3E
Linden Way, Sutton	56	3C
Linden Way, Westfield	65	4D
Lindenhill Rd.	26	1C
Lindens	59	2E
Lindens, The, Copthorne	148	1B
Lindens, The, Farnham	96	5B
Lindfield Gdns.	82	5A
Lindford Chase	133	4D
Lindford Rd.	133	4D
Lindford Way	133	4D
Lindisfarne Rd.	19	5F
Lindley Rd., Tyler's Green	92	3B
Lindley Rd., Walton-on-Thames	34	5B
Lindon Cl.	85	2F
Lindon Rd.	134	4A
Lindores Rd.	38	4C
Lindsay Cl., Chessington	53	2E
Lindsay Cl., Epsom	54	5A
Lindsay Cl., Stanwell	14	1C
Lindsay Dri.	33	3E
Lindsay Rd., Fulwell	17	4D
Lindsay Rd., Woodham	49	3E
Lindsay Rd., Worcester Park	37	5F
Lindsey Cl., E. Bedfont	15	2E
Lindsey Cl., Mitcham	40	2A
Lindum Rd.	18	5A
Linersh Dri.	120	1B
Linersh Wood Cl.	120	1B
Linfield Cl.	51	1D
Linfold Rd.	41	3D
Ling Cres.	134	4A
Ling Dri.	45	4E
Lingfield	131	2F
Lingfield Av.	36	2B
Lingfield Common Rd.	131	1E
Lingfield Dri.	148	3A
Lingfield Rd., East Grinstead	150	1B
Lingfield Rd., Wimbledon	20	4A
Lingfield Rd., Worcester Park	37	5F
Lingwell Rd.	21	3D
Lingwood	27	3D
Link Av.	65	1F
Link La.	57	2D
Link Rd., E. Bedfont	15	2F
Link Rd., Hackbridge	39	4E
Link Rd., Weybridge	49	1F
Link, The	146	4C
Link Way, Ham	18	3A
Link Way, Staines	14	5B
Link Way, Woking	65	2F
Linkfield	35	2D
Linkfield Gdns.	90	5A
Linkfield La.	90	5A
Linkfield St.	90	5A
Links Av.	38	2B
Links Brow	69	5E
Links Cl.	70	2A
Links Green Way	51	5F
Links Pl.	70	2A
Links Rd., Ashford	14	4C
Links Rd., Bramley	101	5D
Link's Rd., Epsom	54	5B
Links Rd., Lower Ashtead	70	2A
Links Rd., Tooting	21	5E
Links Rd., W. Wickham	42	4B
Links, The, Ascot	28	1B
Links, The, Walton-on-Thames	34	5A
Links View Av.	87	5F
Links View Rd., Croydon	42	5A
Links View Rd., Hampton	17	4E
Links Way, Beckenham	42	3A
Links Way, Effingham	85	2F
Links Way, West Heath	60	5A
Linkscroft Av.	15	5D
Linkside	37	1E
Linkside East	135	3D
Linkside North	135	3D
Linkside South	135	4D
Linkside West	135	3D
Linkway, Camberley	61	1D
Linkway, Raynes Park	37	2F
Linkway, The	55	3F
Linkway, Woodbridge Hill	81	5E
Linnell Rd.	109	1E
Linnet Cl.	58	3C
Linnet Grn.	82	4C
Linstead Rd.	60	3B
Linton Glade	58	3C
Linton Gro.	22	4B
Linton's La.	54	4B
Lintott Cl.	14	1C
Lintott Gdns.	158	4C
Lion & Lamb Yard	96	4A
Lion Cl., Shepperton Grn.	33	2D
Lion Cl., Shottermill	151	2E
Lion Gate Gdns.	8	5B
Lion Green Rd.	73	1F
Lion La., Shottermill	151	2E
Lion La., Turners Hill	149	5D
Lion Mead	151	3F
Lion Park Av.	53	1F
Lion Rd., Thornton Heath	40	3C
Lion Rd., Twickenham	17	2F
Lion Way	8	3A
Lionel Rd.	8	1B
Lions Cl.	24	1A
Lion's La.	140	3B
Liphook Cres.	23	2E
Liphook Rd., Headley	133	5F
Liphook Rd., Lindford	133	4D
Liphook Rd., Shottermill	151	3E
Lipsham Cl.	56	5A
Lisbon Av.	17	3D
Liscombe	27	4D
Liskeard Dri.	60	4C
Lismore Cres.	146	5C
Lismore Rd.	57	2F
Lissoms Rd.	73	2E
Lister Av.	150	4C
Litchfield Av.	38	4B
Litchfield Rd.	55	1F
Litchfield Way	100	1B
Little Acre	42	2A
Little Austins Rd.	96	5B
Little Birch Court	49	3F
Little Bookham	85	1F
Little Bookham St.	85	1F
Little Borough	106	1C
Little Brownings	23	3E
Little Browns La.	113	3F
Little Collins	110	5B
Little Common La.	91	4E
Little Comptons	158	5C
Little Court	42	5C
Little Crabtree	146	3C
Little Cranmore La.	84	2B
Little Ealing La.	8	2A
Little Field Close, Kingston	159	
Little Green	8	5B
Little Green La., Upper Bourne	114	1C
Little Green La. Addlestone	31	5F
Little Halliards	34	3A
Little Haven La.	158	3C
Little Heath Rd.	47	3D
Little Hide	82	4B
Little Kiln	100	5A
Little London	118	5A
Little London Hill	158	1A
Little Lullenden	131	1F
Little Mead, Cranleigh	140	1D
Little Mead, Horsell	64	1B
Little Orchard, Woking	48	5B
Little Orchard, Woodham	49	4D
Little Orchard Way	101	4D
Little Paddocks	44	4C
Little Park Dri.	16	3B
Little Platt	81	5D
Little Queen's Rd.	17	5F
Little Ringdale	27	2E
Little Roke Av.	57	5E
Little Roke Rd.	57	5E
Little St.	81	4E
Little Thatch	119	1D
Little Thurbans Cl.	114	1C
Little Turners Court	119	1D
Little Warren Cl.	101	1E
Little Woodcote La.	56	4B
Littlebrook Cl.	41	3F
Littlecombe Cl.	20	1A
Littlecote Cl.	20	2A
Littlecroft Rd.	13	4D
Littledale Cl.	27	2E
Littlefield Cl., Ash	78	5C
Littlefield Cl., Guildford	80	3C
Littlefield Gdns.	78	5C
Littlefield Way	80	3C
Littleford La.	102	5A
Littleheath La.	52	5A
Littleheath Rd.	58	2B
Littlemead	52	1B
Littlemoor	43	3D
Littlers Cl.	38	1C
Littleton	33	2D
Littleton La., Laleham	32	4C
Littleton La., Littleton	100	3B
Littleton La., Reigate	108	1A
Littleton Rd.	15	5E
Littleton St.	20	3C
Littlewick Rd., Horsell	47	5F
Littlewick Rd., Knaphill	64	1A
Littlewood	141	1D
Littlewood Cl.	8	1A
Littlewood Rd.	24	1B
Littleworth Av.	52	1B
Littleworth Common Rd.	35	5E
Littleworth La.	52	1B
Littleworth Pl.	52	1B
Littleworth Rd., Esher	52	2B
Littleworth Rd., The Sands	97	4E
Liverpool Rd., Brentford	8	1B
Liverpool Rd., Kingston	18	5C
Liverpool Rd., Selhurst	40	2C
Livingstone Rd., Beulah Hill	40	1C
Livingstone Rd., Caterham	74	4C
Livingstone Rd., Crawley	147	5D
Livingstone Rd., Horsham	158	5B
Llanaway Cl.	119	1D
Llanaway Rd.	119	1D
Llantony Rd.	38	3C
Llanvair Cl.	28	3B
Llanvair Dri.	28	3B
Lloyd Av., Norbury	40	1A
Lloyd Av., Woodmansterne	56	5B
Lloyd Park Av.	58	1A
Lloyd Rd.	38	5A
Lloyds Way	41	3F
Loats Rd.	22	1A
Lobelia Rd.	63	1E
Lochinvar St.	21	2E
Lochinver	27	4D
Lock La.	66	1B
Lock Rd., Guildford	81	4F
Lock Rd., Ham	18	4A
Locke King Cl.	50	2A
Locke King Rd.	50	2A
Lockfield Dri.	64	2B
Lockhart Rd.	51	5E
Lock's La.	39	1E
Locks Meadow	132	3A
Locks Ride	10	5A
Locksley Dri.	64	2A
Locksmeade Rd.	18	4A
Lockswood	63	3F
Lockton Chase	28	2A
Lockwood Cl., Fox Lane	60	3B
Lockwood Cl., Lwr. Sydenham	23	4F
Lockwood Path	48	5C
Lockwood Way	53	1F
Loddon Cl., Camberley	44	5C
Loddon Cl., West Heath	60	4B
Loddon Way	78	5C
Loder Cl.	48	5C
Lodge Av.	40	5A
Lodge Cl., Aldershot	97	1D
Lodge Cl., Dorking	106	3A
Lodge Cl., East Ewell	54	3C
Lodge Cl., East Grinstead	150	2B
Lodge Cl., Englefield Grn.	12	4C
Lodge Cl., Fetcham	69	4E
Lodge Cl., Hackridge	39	4E
Lodge Cl., Stoke D'Abernon	68	1C
Lodge Cl., West Green	146	4C
Lodge Gdns.	42	3A
Lodge Hill	74	1B
Lodge Hill Cl.	115	1E
Lodge Hill Rd.	96	5B
Lodge La., Addington	59	2D
Lodge La., Salfords	109	5D
Lodge La., Fetcham	69	4E
Lodge Rd., Wallington	56	1B
Lodge Way, Ashford	14	3C
Lodge Way, Charlton	33	2E
Lodgebottom Rd.	87	2F
Loggetts, The	22	3C
Logmore La.	105	2D
Lois Dri.	33	3E
Lollesworth La.	84	2B
Loman Rd.	61	5F
Lomas Cl.	59	2E
Lombard Cl.	64	2A
Lombard Rd.	38	1C
Lombard St.	98	5C
Lomond Gdns.	58	2C
Loncin Mead Av.	49	3E
London La., Bromley	24	5C
London La., Shere	103	2D
London Rd., Ascot	28	2A
London Rd., Bagshot	45	1E
London Rd., Blackwater	60	1A
London Rd., Bracknell	27	1D
London Rd., Brentford	8	3A
London Rd., Burpham	82	4A
London Rd., Camberley	44	5A
London Rd., Caterham	74	5C
London Rd., Dorking	106	1A
London Rd., East Grinstead	150	1A
London Rd., Ewell	54	3B
London Rd., Forest Hill	23	2E
London Rd., Guildford	101	1D
London Rd., Hackbridge	39	3E
London Rd., Hindhead	135	5F
London Rd., Horsham	158	5B
London Rd., Kingston	36	1B
London Rd., Mitcham	39	2D
London Rd., Morden	38	3B
London Rd., Norbury	40	1A
London Rd., North Cheam	38	5A
London Rd., Northgate	147	2D
London Rd., Redhill	90	5B
London Rd., Reigate	89	5E
London Rd., Shortlands	42	1C
London Rd., Staines	14	4A
London Rd., Sunningdale	29	3F
London Rd., Sunninghill	29	2D
London Rd., Tooting	21	5E
London Rd., Twickenham	17	2F
London Rd., Wallington	56	1B
London Rd., Windlesham	28	5C
London Rd., Wokingham	25	2E
London Rd., York Town	43	5F
London Rd. N., Merstham	90	1B
London Rd. S., Merstham	90	3B
London St.	32	4A
Lone Acre	46	2A
Lone Oak	129	3E
Lonesome La.	108	3C
Long Acre	78	5C
Long Acre Rd.	56	2B

Long Bourne Green 100 5A
Long Bridge 96 4A
Long Cl. 147 4F
Long Copse Cl. 69 5D
Long Cross Hill 133 4F
Long Ditton 36 4A
Long Dyke 82 4B
Long Garden Walk 96 4A
Long Gore 100 4A
Long Grove Rd. 53 3F
Long Hill, The Sands 97 5E
Long Hill, Woldingham 75 4F
Long Hill Rd., Bracknell 27 1F
Long La., Ashford 14 3C
Long La., Woodside 41 3E
Long Lodge Dri. 34 5A
Long Meadow, Great
  Bookham 85 1F
Long Meadow,
  Windlesham 45 1F
Long Meadow Cl. 42 4B
Long Mickle 43 3D
Long Rd., The 114 2C
Long Reach 67 5D
Long Shaw 69 3F
Long Walk, The 12 2A
Long Wk., Burgh Heath 72 3A
Long Wk., New Malden 37 3D
Long Wk., West Horsley 84 3A
Longbeech Dri. 60 5A
Longbourne Way 32 3A
Longboyds 68 1A
Longbridge Rd. 128 3A
Longbridge Way 24 1B
Longchamp Cl. 128 2C
Longcommon Rd. 120 2C
Longcroft Av. 55 5F
Longcross Rd.,
Longdene Rd. 151 3F
Longdown Cl. 115 1D
Longdown La. North 54 5C
Longdown La. South 71 1F
Longdown Rd., Bellingham 24 4A
Longdown Rd., Epsom 54 5B
Longdown Rd., Guildford 101 2E
Longdown Rd., Lower
  Bourne 115 1D
Longdown Rd., Sandhurst 43 3D
Longfellow Pl. 158 2C
Longfellow Rd. 37 4F
Longfield 42 1C
Longfield Av. 39 4E
Longfield Cl. 60 3C
Longfield Cres., Sydenham 23 3E
Longfield Cres., Tadworth 72 3A
Longfield Dri., East Sheen 18 1C
Longfield Dri., Mitcham 21 5D
Longfield Rd., Ash 78 5C
Longfield Rd., Dorking 105 2F
Longfield Rd., Horsham 158 5A
Longfield St. 20 2B
Longford 7 4C
Longford Av., Feltham 15 1F
Longford Av., Stanwell 14 2C
Longford Cl., Camberley 61 1E
Longford Cl., Hampton 16 4C
Longford Court 54 1A
Longford Gdns. 38 5C
Longford Rd. 17 2D
Longford Way 14 2C
Longheath Gdns. 41 3E
Longhill Rd., Catford 24 3B
Longhope Dri. 115 1D
Longhurst Gdns. 41 3E
Longhurst Rd., E. Horsley 84 3C
Longhurst Rd., Hither Green 24 1C
Longlands Av. 56 5B
Longleat Sq. 61 5E
Longleat Way 15 2E
Longley Rd., Croydon 40 4B
Longley Rd., Farnham 96 4B
Longley Rd., Tooting 21 5D
Longmead 82 5C
Longmead Cl. 74 4C
Longmead Rd., Epsom 54 4A
Longmead Rd., Esher 35 4E
Longmead Rd., Tooting 21 4D
Longmeadow 61 1E
Longmere Gdns. 72 3A
Longmere Rd., Crawley 147 3D
Longmoors 26 1B
Longmore Rd., Hersham 51 1E
Longpoles Rd. 141 2D
Longreach 84 1A
Longridge Grove 49 5D
Long's Cl. 66 1A
Longs Way, Wokingham 25 1E
Longshot La. 26 1B
Longside Cl. 31 1E
Longstaff Cres. 20 1B
Longstaff Rd. 20 1B
Longstone Rd. 21 4E
Longthornton Rd. 39 1F
Longton Av. 23 4D
Longton Gro. 23 4E
Longwater Rd. 27 3D
Longways 32 1A

Longwood Dri. 19 1F
Longwood Rd. 74 1C
Longwood View 147 5E
Lonsdale Gdns. 40 2A
Lonsdale Rd., Barnes 9 4E
Lonsdale Rd., Dorking 106 1A
Lonsdale Rd., Norwood 41 2E
Lonsdale Rd., Turnham
  Green 9 2E
Lonsdale Rd., Weybridge 50 2A
Loop Rd., Epsom 71 1D
Loop Rd., Westfield 65 4D
Loppets Rd. 147 5D
Loraine Gdns. 70 2B
Loraine Rd. 8 3C
Lord Chancellor Cl. 37 1D
Lord Knyvetts Cl. 14 1C
Lords Cl., Feltham 16 3C
Lords Cl., Tulse Hill 22 3C
Lords Grove Cl. 71 3F
Lords Hill 120 1C
Lordsbury Field 56 3C
Lordship La. 23 1D
Loretto Cl. 141 1D
Lorian Dri. 89 5F
Lorne Av. 41 4F
Lorne Gdns. 41 4F
Lorne, The 85 1F
Lorraine Rd. 44 4B
Loseberry Rd. 52 1B
Loseley Rd. 100 5A
Lothair Rd. 8 1A
Lothian Wood 71 4F
Lotus Rd. 77 2F
Loubet St. 21 5E
Loudwater Cl. 34 2A
Loudwater Rd. 34 2A
Loughborough 27 3E
Louis Fields 80 3C
Louise Margaret Rd. 78 4A
Louisville Rd. 21 3E
Love La., Ash 78 5C
Love La., Cheam 55 2D
Love La., Godstone 92 4B
Love La., Long Ditton 36 5A
Love La., Mitcham 39 2D
Love La., Ockley 143 1D
Love La., S. Norwood 41 2E
Love La., St. Helier 38 4B
Love La., Walton on the Hill 88 1B
Loveday Rd. 8 1A
Lovedean Court 27 3E
Lovel La. 10 4C
Lovelace Cl. 68 5A
Lovelace Dri. 66 1A
Lovelace Gdns., Hersham 51 1D
Lovelace Gdns., Surbiton 36 4A
Lovelace Rd., Bracknell 26 2B
Lovelace Rd., Surbiton 36 4A
Lovelace Rd., Tulse Hill 22 3B
Loveland La. 89 2F
Lovelands La. 46 5C
Lovell Rd., Ham 18 3A
Lovell Rd., Woodside 10 4B
Lovells Cl. 45 3F
Lovelock Cl. 74 2C
Lovett Rd. 13 4E
Low La. 96 2C
Lowbury 27 2E
Lowburys 105 3F
Lowcross La. 23 3D
Lowdells Dri. 150 1B
Lowdell's La. 150 1B
Lower Addiscombe Rd. 41 4D
Lower Barn La. 158 3C
Lower Barn Rd. 57 4F
Lower Breache Rd. 142 1A
Lower Bridge Rd. 90 5A
Lower Broadmoor Rd. 43 2D
Lower Charles St. 44 5A
Lower Church La. 96 4A
Lower Common South 9 5F
Lower Coombe St. 57 1F
Lower Court Rd. 54 4A
Lower Downs Rd. 38 1A
Lower Dunnymans 55 5E
Lower Eashing La. 118 2B
Lower Edgeboro' Rd. 101 1D
Lower Farm Rd. 68 5A
Lower Farnham Rd. 97 1D
Lower Green Rd. 35 5D
Lower Green West 39 2D
Lower Grove Rd. 18 1C
Lower Guildford Rd. 64 3A
Lower Halliford 33 3F
Lower Hampton Rd. 34 2B
Lower Hanger 151 3D
Lower Hill Rd. 53 4F
Lower Kingswood 89 2E
Lower Mall 9 2F
Lower Manor Rd. 119 1D
Lower Marsh La. 36 2B
Lower Mere 150 3C
Lower Morden La. 38 3A
Lower Mortlake Rd. 8 5B
Lower Moushill Lane 118 3A
Lower Newport Rd. 78 5B

Lower Northfield 55 5E
Lower Nursery 29 3D
Lower Oak Tree Rd. 118 3B
Lower Old Pk. 95 3E
Lower Peryers 84 2C
Lower Pillory Downs 56 5B
Lower Pyrford Rd. 66 2B
Lower Rd., Effingham 85 2C
Lower Rd., Fetcham 69 5D
Lower Rd., Grayswood 152 1B
Lower Rd., Little Bookham 85 1F
Lower Rd., Mead Vale 108 1C
Lower Rd., Purley 57 5D
Lower Rd., Sutton 55 1F
Lower Richmond Rd.,
  Barnes 9 5F
Lower Richmond Rd., N.
  Sheen 8 5C
Lower St., Haslemere 152 3A
Lower St., Shere 103 3D
Lower Sandfields 65 5F
Lower Sawley Wood 55 5E
Lower Shott 86 1A
Lower South St. 119 2D
Lower South View 96 3A
Lower Staithe 9 4D
Lower Sunbury Rd. 34 1C
Lower Teddington Rd. 36 1A
Lower Village Rd. 28 3C
Lower Weybourne La. 96 2C
Lower Wood Rd. 52 2C
Lowerhouse La. 142 1A
Loweswater Wk. 62 1A
Lowfield Cl. 45 4F
Lowfield Heath Rd. 146 1B
Lowicks Rd. 116 5A
Lowlands Dri. 14 1C
Lowlands Rd. 60 1A
Lowry Cl. 43 5E
Lowther Hill 23 2F
Lowther Rd., Barnes 9 4E
Lowther Rd., Kingston 36 1B
Loxford Rd. 92 1A
Loxford Way 92 1A
Loxley Cl. 23 4F
Loxley Rd., Hanworth 16 4C
Loxley Rd., Wandsworth 21 2D
Loxton Rd. 23 3E
Loxwood 156 4A
Loxwood Cl. 15 2F
Loxwood Rd., Alford 156 1A
Loxwood Rd., Loxwood 156 4B
Loxwood Rd., Plaistow 155 5D
Loxwood Wk. 146 3B
Loxwood-Guildford Rd. 156 3A
Lt. Bornes 22 4C
Lucan Dri. 14 5C
Lucas Field 151 3E
Lucas Green Rd., Bisley 63 1D
Lucas Green Rd., Donkey
  Town 46 5A
Lucas Rd., Farnborough 60 5C
Lucas Rd., Penge 23 5E
Lucerne Cl. 65 3D
Lucerne Rd. 40 3B
Lucie Av. 15 5D
Lucien Rd., Tooting 21 4E
Lucien Rd., Wimbledon Pk. 20 3B
Luckley Rd. 25 3D
Luckley Wood. 25 3D
Lucorn Cl. 24 1C
Luddington Av. 31 1D
Ludlow 27 4D
Ludlow Cl. 61 3F
Ludlow Rd., Feltham 15 3F
Ludlow Rd., Guildford 100 1B
Ludovick Wk. 9 5E
Ludshott Grn. 134 4A
Lullingston Garth 24 5C
Lullington Rd. 23 5D
Lulworth Cl. 60 3C
Lumley Court 128 2B
Lumley Gdns. 55 2D
Lumley Rd., Cheam 55 2D
Lumley Rd., Horley 128 2B
Luna Rd. 40 2C
Lunar Cl. 77 1E
Lunghurst Rd. 76 3A
Lunham Rd. 22 5C
Lupin Cl., Bagshot 45 3D
Lupin Cl., Shirley 41 4F
Lushington Dri. 51 5D
Lushington Rd. 24 4A
Lusted Hall La. 77 2E
Lusteds Cl. 106 3A
Luther Rd. 17 4F
Luttens Cl. 146 5A
Luttrell Av. 19 1F
Lutwyche Rd. 23 3F
Luxford Cl. 158 3C
Lyall Av. 23 3D
Lyall Pl. 96 1A
Lych Way 64 1C
Lydden Gro 20 2C
Lydden Rd. 20 2C
Lydele Cl. 65 1D
Lydford Cl., Farnborough 60 3C

Lydford Cl., Frimley 61 3F
Lydhurst Av. 22 3A
Lye, The 72 4A
Lyecopse Av. 61 3D
Lyefield La. 123 5D
Lyfield Rd. 52 5A
Lyford Rd. 21 2D
Lygonby Gdns. 41 4F
Lyham Cl. 22 1A
Lyham Rd. 22 1A
Lyle Cl. 39 4E
Lymbourne Cl. 55 3E
Lymden Gdns. 108 1C
Lyme Gro. 49 1E
Lyme Regis Rd. 72 2B
Lymer Av. 23 4D
Lymescote Gdns. 38 5B
Lymington Cl. 39 1F
Lymington Gdns. 54 1B
Lynch Rd. 96 4B
Lynchford La. 78 1B
Lynchford Rd. 78 2A
Lyncroft Gdns., Ewell 54 3B
Lyncroft Gdns., Lammas
  Park 8 1A
Lyncroft Gdns., Whitton 17 1D
Lyndale Court 49 5D
Lyndale Rd. 90 4B
Lyndhurst Av., Aldershot 97 2D
Lyndhurst Av., Darby Grn. 43 5D
Lyndhurst Av., Mitcham 39 1F
Lyndhurst Av., Sunbury-
  on-Thames 34 2A
Lyndhurst Av., Tolworth 36 4C
Lyndhurst Av., Whitton 16 2C
Lyndhurst Cl., Bracknell 27 2F
Lyndhurst Cl., Crawley 146 4C
Lyndhurst Cl., Guildford 64 1C
Lyndhurst Dri. 37 4E
Lyndhurst Rd., Ascot 28 2B
Lyndhurst Rd., Reigate 108 2B
Lyndhurst Rd., Thornton
  Heath 40 2B
Lyndhurst Rd.,
  Woodmansterne 73 1E
Lyndhurst Way, Belmont 55 3E
Lyndhurst Way, Chertsey 31 5F
Lyndon Av. 39 5E
Lyndwood Cres. 29 3D
Lyne 31 4E
Lyne Cl. 31 3D
Lyne Crossing Rd. 31 3D
Lyne Dri. 144 2B
Lyne La. 31 3D
Lyne Rd. 30 3C
Lyneham Rd. 43 1D
Lynette Av. 21 1F
Lyngrove Av. 15 4E
Lynmouth Av. 38 4A
Lynn Cl. 15 4E
Lynn Rd. 21 2E
Lynn Way 60 3C
Lynn Wk. 108 2C
Lynne Cl. 58 4B
Lynne Wk. 52 1A
Lynsted Ct. 41 1F
Lynton Cl. 53 1E
Lynton Park Av. 150 2C
Lynton Rd., Malden 37 3D
Lynton Rd., Thornton Heath 40 3B
Lynwick St. 157 2E
Lynwood 100 1B
Lynwood Av., Cousdon 73 1F
Lynwood Av., Egham 13 5D
Lynwood Av., Epsom 54 5B
Lynwood Cl., Lindford 133 4E
Lynwood Dri., Mytchett 61 5F
Lynwood Dri., Old Windsor 12 1B
Lynwood Dri., Worcester
  Park 37 5F
Lynwood Gdns. 57 1D
Lynwood Rd., Epsom 54 5B
Lynwood Rd., Hinchley
  Wood 35 5F
Lynwood Rd., Redhill 90 4B
Lynwood Rd., Tooting 21 3E
Lynx Hill 84 2C
Lyobury 27 2E
Lyon Rd., Crowthorne 43 1D
Lyon Rd., Merton 38 1C
Lyon Rd., Walton-on-
  Thames 34 5C
Lyon Way 61 2D
Lyons Court, Dorking 160
Lyons Cres., Dorking 160
Lyons Dri. 81 3E
Lyonsdene 89 2E
Lyric Cl. 147 5E
Lyric Rd. 9 4E
Lysander Rd. 57 2D
Lysias Rd. 21 1E
Lysons Av. 78 2B
Lytchgate Cl. 58 2A
Lytcott Dr. 34 2C
Lytcott Gro. 23 1D

Lytham	26 3B	Malham Fell	26 2C
Lytton Dri.	147 3F	Malham Rd.	23 2F
Lytton Gdns.	56 1C	Mall	9 2F
Lytton Gro	20 1A	Mall, The, Roehampton	19 1D
Lytton Rd.	65 1E	Mall, The, Surbiton	36 3A
Lyveden Rd.	21 5D	Mallard Cl., Ash	78 4C
Lywood Cl	71 4F	Mallard Cl., Horsham	158 3B
		Mallard Cl., Redhill	90 4B
M		Mallard Cl., Shottermill	151 2E
		Mallard Cl., Whitton	16 2C
Maberley Cres.	23 5D	Mallard Pl., East Grinstead	150 3C
Maberley Rd., Elmers End	41 2F	Mallard Pl., Twickenham	17 3F
Maberley Rd., Penge	23 5D	Mallard Rd.	58 3C
Mable St.	64 2C	Mallard Way	56 3C
Macaulay Av.	35 5E	Mallard Wk.	41 3F
Macaulay Rd.	74 4C	Mallards Reach	33 5F
Macclesfield Rd.	41 3E	Mallards, The	32 1B
Macdonald Rd.	45 4E	Mallards Way	45 4E
Mackay Cl.	78 4A	Mallett Rd.	24 1B
Mackenzie Rd.	41 1E	Malling Cl.	41 3E
Mackie Rd.	22 2B	Malling Gdns.	38 3C
Mackies Hill	103 5F	Malling Way	42 4C
Mackrells	108 2C	Mallinson Rd., Croydon	39 5F
Maclean Rd.	23 1F	Mallinson Rd., Waddon	21 1D
Macleod Rd.	158 5C	Mallinson Rd.,	
Macphail Cl.	25 1F	Wandsworth	21 1D
Madans Wk.	71 1D	Mallow Cl., Frith End	133 1E
Maddin Rd.	23 4F	Mallow Cl., Shirley	41 4E
Maddison Cl.	17 5F	Mallow Cl., Tadworth	71 3F
Maddox La.	68 5C	Mallowdale Rd.	27 4E
Maddox Pk.	68 5B	Malmains Cl.	42 2B
Madeira Av.	42 1C	Malmains Way	42 2B
Madeira Cl.	49 5D	Malmesbury Rd.	38 4C
Madeira Cres.	49 5D	Malmstone Av.	90 2C
Madeira Rd., Horsham	158 5B	Malt Hill	13 4D
Madeira Rd., Mitcham	39 2E	Malt House Cl.	12 2C
Madeira Rd., Streatham	22 4A	Maltby Rd.	53 2F
Madeira Rd., W. Byfleet	49 5D	Malthouse La., Hambledon	137 2F
Madeira Wk.	90 5A	Malthouse La., West End	46 4B
Madeline Rd.	23 5D	Malthouse La., Worplesdon	80 1C
Madely	74 1B	Malthouse Mead	118 5B
Madgehole La.	121 2E	Malthouse Rd., Crawley	147 5D
Madingley	27 4D	Malthouse Rd., Hanworth	16 4B
Madison Gdns.	42 2C	Maltings, The, Byfleet	49 5F
Madrid Rd., Barnes	9 4E	Maltings, The, Oxted	93 4F
Madrid Rd., Guildford	100 1B	Malus Cl.	49 2D
Maesmaur Rd.	77 4E	Malus Dri.	49 2D
Mafeking Av.	8 3B	Malva Cl.	20 1C
Mafeking Rd.	13 3E	Malvern Cl., Ottershaw	48 2B
Magazine Pl.	70 4A	Malvern Cl., Surbiton	36 4B
Magazine Rd.	74 4B	Malvern Dri.	16 4B
Magdalen Cl.	49 5F	Malvern Rd., Crawley	146 4C
Magdalen Cres.	49 5F	Malvern Rd., Fox La.	60 3B
Magdalen Rd.	20 2C	Malvern Rd., Hampton	16 5C
Magdalene Cl.	147 2F	Malvern Rd., Thornton	
Magdalene Rd.,		Heath	40 2B
Shepperton Grn.	33 2D	Malvern Rd., Tolworth	36 5B
Magdalene Rd. Sandhurst	43 3F	Malwood Rd.	21 1E
Magna Carta La.	13 2D	Malyons Rd.	24 1A
Magnolia Cl.	43 3E	Manchester Rd.	40 2C
Magnolia Court	18 5C	Manchuria Rd.	21 1E
Magnolia Dri.	77 1E	Manderville Court	13 4E
Magnolia Rd.	8 3C	Mandeville Cl., Guildford	81 4E
Magnolia Way, Dorking	106 3A	Mandeville Cl., Wimbledon	20 5A
Magnolia Way, West Ewell	54 1A	Mandeville Dri.	36 4A
Magpie Cl.	73 2F	Mandeville Rd.	33 3D
Magpie Wk.	147 3D	Mandora Rd.	78 4A
Maguire Dri., Ham	18 4A	Mandrake Rd.	21 3D
Maguire Dri., Heatherside	62 1A	Mandrell Rd.	22 1A
Maida Rd.	78 4A	Manfield Pk.	140 1B
Maiden La.	146 3C	Manfred Rd.	20 1B
Maidenbower Dri.	147 4F	Mangles Rd.	81 4F
Maidenshaw Rd.	54 4A	Manley Bridge Rd.	114 2C
Main Rd.	77 1E	Mannamead	71 3D
Main St.	16 4B	Mannamead Cl.	71 3D
Mainprize Rd.	27 1E	Manning Cl.	150 2B
Mainstone Cl.	62 3A	Mannings Hill	121 5F
Mainstone Cres.	63 4D	Manningtree	20 2A
Mainstone Rd.	63 1E	Manns Cl.	17 1F
Maise Webster Cl.	14 2B	Manoel Rd.	17 3D
Maitland Cl., Tongham	97 2E	Manon Pl.	55 1F
Maitland Cl. W. Byfleet	49 5D	Manonia Cl.	46 5A
Maitland Rd., Farnborough	78 2A	Manor Av.	75 5D
Maitland Rd., Penge	23 5F	Manor Chase	50 1A
Maizecroft	128 2C	Manor Cl., East Horsley	84 2C
Malacca Farm Rd.	83 3E	Manor Cl., Horley	128 2A
Malan Cl.	77 2F	Manor Cl., Malden	37 4E
Malbrook Rd.	19 1F	Manor Cl., Pyrford	66 1A
Malcolm Rd.	36 4B	Manor Cl., Shottermill	151 3E
Malcolm Gdns.	128 3A	Manor Cl., Tongham	97 1E
Malcolm Rd., Wimbledon	20 5A	Manor Cl., Warlingham	75 2F
Malcolm Rd.,		Manor Court	50 1B
Woodmansterne	73 1F	Manor Cres., Brookwood	63 4D
Malcolm Rd., Woodside	41 3D	Manor Cres., Byfleet	50 5A
Malden Av.	41 2E	Manor Cres., Guildford	81 4E
Malden Court	37 2F	Manor Cres., Shottermill	151 3E
Malden Green Av.	37 4E	Manor Cres., Staines	36 3C
Malden Hill	37 2E	Manor Dri., Hanworth	16 4B
Malden Hill Gdns.	37 2E	Manor Dri., Hinchley Wood	35 5F
Malden Pk.	37 3E	Manor Dri., Surbiton	36 3C
Malden Rd., Cheam	55 1D	Manor Dri., West Ewell	54 2B
Malden Rd., Malden	37 3E	Manor Dri., Woodham	49 3D
Maldon Rd.	56 1B	Manor Drive North	37 4E
Malet Cl.	13 5F	Manor Drive Sunbury	34 1A
Maley Av.	22 3B	Manor Drive, The	37 4E
Malham Cl.	147 5F	Manor Farm Av.	33 3D
		Manor Farm Cl.	78 5B

Manor Farm La.	13 4E	Mantlet Cl.	21 5F
Manor Fields, Milford	118 3A	Manville Rd.	21 3E
Manor Fields, Roehampton	20 1A	Manwood Rd.	24 1A
Manor Fields, Seale	97 2F	Manygate La.	33 4E
Manor Gate Rd.	36 1C	Maori Rd.	101 1D
Manor Gdns., Effingham	85 2E	Maple Cl., Ash Vale	78 2C
Manor Gdns., Farncombe	100 5A	Maple Cl., Clapham	21 1F
Manor Gdns., Farnham	115 1E	Maple Cl., Hampton	16 5C
Manor Gdns., Guildford	81 4E	Maple Cl., Langley Green	146 2C
Manor Gdns., Gunnersbury	8 2C	Maple Cl., Mitcham	39 1E
Manor Gdns., Hampton Hill	17 5D	Maple Cl., Whyteleafe	75 2D
Manor Gdns., Merton	38 1B	Maple Court, Englefield	
Manor Gdns., Selsdon	58 2A	Green	12 5B
Manor Gdns., Sunbury	34 1A	Maple Court, New Malden	37 2D
Manor Green Rd.	53 5F	Maple Dri., Crowthorne	26 5A
Manor Gro., Beckenham	42 1A	Maple Dri., Lightwater	45 4E
Manor Gro., North Sheen	8 5C	Maple Dri., Salfords	109 3D
Manor Gro., Richmond	8 5B	Maple Gdns.	14 3C
Manor Hill	73 1E	Maple Gro., Bellfields	81 4F
Manor House Court	33 4E	Maple Gro., Brentford	8 3A
Manor House Dri.	10 5B	Maple Gro., Lammas Park	8 1A
Manor La., Feltham	16 3A	Maple Gro., Westfield	65 4D
Manor La., Hither Green	24 1C	Maple Hatch Cl.	119 3D
Manor La., Lwr. Kingswood	89 3E	Maple Leaf Cl.	60 5C
Manor La., Sunbury	34 1A	Maple Pl.	55 5D
Manor La., Sutton	55 1F	Maple Rd., Anerley	41 1E
Manor Lea Cl.	118 3A	Maple Rd., Ashtead	70 3B
Manor Leaze	13 4E	Maple Rd., Earlswood	109 2D
Manor Mount	23 2E	Maple Rd., Penge	23 5E
Manor Park Rd., Sutton		Maple Rd., Sendmarsh	66 5A
West	55 1F	Maple Rd., Surbiton	36 3A
Manor Park Rd., West		Maple Rd., Whyteleafe	75 2D
Wickham	42 4A	Maple Walk	97 1E
Manor Pk.	24 1C	Maple Way, Feltham	16 3A
Manor Pk. Cl.	42 4A	Maple Way, Hooley	73 4E
Manor Pl., Feltham	16 2A	Mapledale Av.	41 5D
Manor Pl., Mitcham	39 2F	Mapledrakes Cl.	122 5C
Manor Pl., Staines	14 4B	Mapledrakes Rd.	122 5C
Manor Rd., Aldershot	96 1C	Maplehurst	69 5E
Manor Rd., Ashford	15 4D	Maplehurst Cl.	36 2B
Manor Rd., Beckenham	42 1A	Maples, The, Banstead	55 5F
Manor Rd., Cheam	55 2E	Maples, The, Ottershaw	48 2B
Manor Rd., East Grinstead	150 2B	Maplestead Rd.	22 2A
Manor Rd., Eastheath	25 4D	Maplethorpe Rd.	40 2B
Manor Rd., East Molesey	35 2E	Mapleton Cres.	20 1C
Manor Rd., Farnham	96 3B	Marble Hill Cl.	18 2A
Manor Rd., Guildford	81 4E	Marble Hill Gdns.	18 2A
Manor Rd., Hanworth	16 4B	Marbles Way	72 3A
Manor Rd., Horley	128 2A	March Rd., Twickenham	17 2F
Manor Rd., Horsell	64 1C	March Rd., Weybridge	50 1A
Manor Rd., Horsham	158 3C	Marches Rd.	143 5E
Manor Rd., Merstham	90 3C	Marchmont Rd.,	
Manor Rd., Merton	38 1B	Beddington	56 2C
Manor Rd., Mitcham	39 2F	Marchmont Rd., Richmond	18 1B
Manor Rd., Mytchett	61 5E	Marco Rd.	9 1F
Manor Rd., North Sheen	8 5C	Mardale	62 1A
Manor Rd., Reigate	89 4E	Mardell Rd.	41 3F
Manor Rd., South Norwood	41 2D	Marden Cres.	40 3A
Manor Rd., Tatsfield	77 3E	Marden Hill	69 5E
Manor Rd., Teddington	17 4F	Marden Rd.	40 3A
Manor Rd., Tongham	97 1E	Mardens, The	146 3C
Manor Rd., Twickenham	17 3E	Mare La.	138 1B
Manor Rd., Wallington	56 1B	Mareschal Rd.	100 1C
Manor Rd., Walton	33 4F	Mareth Cl.	78 5A
Manor Rd., West Wickham	42 5A	Marfleet Cl.	39 5D
Manor Rd. North	35 4F	Margaret Cl.	14 5C
Manor Rd. South	52 1B	Margaret Rd.	100 1C
Manor Royal	147 2D	Margaret Way	74 3B
Manor, The, Milford	118 3B	Margate Rd.	22 1A
Manor Vale	8 2A	Margery Grn.	89 3D
Manor Walk	50 1A	Margery La.	89 3E
Manor Way, Bagshot	45 3E	Margin Dri.	20 4A
Manor Way, Beckham	42 1A	Marham Gdns., Morden	38 3C
Manor Way, Egham	13 5D	Marham Gdns.,	
Manor Way, Mitcham	39 2F	Wandsworth	21 2D
Manor Way, Old Woking	65 4E	Marian Court	55 1E
Manor Way, Onslow Vill.	100 2A	Marian Rd.	39 1F
Manor Way, Oxshott	69 1D	Marie Therese Cl.	37 3D
Manor Way, Purley	57 4D	Marigold Court.	81 4F
Manor Way, Selsdon	58 2A	Marigold Court	82 4A
Manor Way,		Marigold Dri.	63 1E
Woodmansterne	73 1D	Marigold Way	41 4F
Manor Way, Worcester Pk.	37 4E	Marina Av.	37 3F
Manor Way, The	56 1C	Marina Way	18 5A
Manor Wood Rd.	57 5D	Mariner Dri.	79 4F
Manorcroft Rd.,	13 5E	Mariner Gdns.	18 3A
Manordene Cl.	35 4F	Mariners Dri.	61 4D
Manorhouse La.	85 1F	Marion Av.	33 3E
Manorlea Rd.	118 3A	Marion Rd., Crawley	147 5E
Mansel Cl.	81 3E	Marion Rd., Thorn.H'th	40 3C
Mansel Rd.	20 5B	Marius Rd.	21 3E
Mansell Rd.	9 1D	Marjoram Cl., Farnborough	60 5A
Mansell Way	74 4C	Marjoram Cl., Guildford	81 3E
Mansfield Cl., Ascot	28 1A	Mark Oak La.	69 4D
Mansfield Cl., Weybridge	50 1A	Mark St.	89 5F
Mansfield Cres.	27 3D	Mark Way	99 5F
Mansfield Dri.	90 2C	Markedge La., Chipstead	73 5D
Mansfield Pl.	28 1A	Markedge La., Gatton	90 2B
Mansfield Rd., Chessington	53 1D	Markenfield Rd.	81 5F
Mansfield Rd., South		Markenhorn	99 5F
Croydon	57 2F	Market Pl.	25 2E
Manship Rd.	21 5E	Market Rd.	8 5C
Manston Cl.	41 1E	Market St., Bracknell	27 1D
Manston Dri.	27 3D	Market St., Guildford	100 1C
Manston Rd.	82 3B	Market Sq.	14 4A
Mantilla Rd.	21 4E	Marketfield Rd.	90 5B
		Marketfield Way	90 5B

Markfield 59 4D
Markfield Rd. 92 1B
Markham Rd. 125 5D
Markhole Cl. 16 5C
Marks Rd., Warlingham 75 2F
Marks Rd., Wokingham 25 1D
Marksbury Av. 8 5C
Markville Gdns. 92 1B
Markway 34 1B
Marlborough Cl. 34 5B
Marlborough Cres. 9 1D
Marlborough Dri. 33 5E
Marlborough Hill 106 1A
Marlborough Rd., Ashford 14 4C
Marlborough Rd., Chiswick 9 2D
Marlborough Rd., Colliers Wood 21 5D
Marlborough Rd., Cotmandene 106 1A
Marlborough Rd., Gunnersbury 8 1B
Marlborough Rd., Hampton 16 5C
Marlborough Rd., Hanworth 16 3B
Marlborough Rd., Maybury 65 1D
Marlborough Rd., Richmond 18 1B
Marlborough Rd., South Croydon 57 2F
Marlborough Rd., Sutton 38 5B
Marlborough Rise 44 5B
Marlborough View 60 4B
Marlbrook Rd. 9 5F
Marld, The 70 2B
Marler Rd. 23 2F
Marles La. 157 5E
Marley Cl. 49 2D
Marley Coombe Rd. 151 3E
Marley Hanger 151 4F
Marley La. 151 4E
Marley Rise 105 3F
Marlingdene Cl. 16 5C
Marlings Cl. 75 2D
Marlin's Cl. 55 1F
Marlow Cl. 41 2E
Marlow Court 147 3D
Marlow Cres. 17 1F
Marlow Dri. 38 5A
Marlow Rd. 41 2E
Marlowe Way 40 5A
Marlpit Av. 74 2A
Marlpit Cl. 150 1C
Marlpit La. 74 2A
Marlyns Cl. 82 3B
Marlyns Dri. 82 4B
Marmora Rd. 23 1E
Marne Rd. 62 3A
Marneys Cl. 70 1C
Marnham Pl. 49 1E
Marnock Rd. 23 1F
Maroons Way 24 4A
Marrick Cl. 9 5F
Marriot Cl. 15 1F
Marriot Lodge Cl. 49 1E
Marrow Brook La. 60 5C
Marrow Brook Rd. 60 5C
Marrowells 33 5F
Marryat Rd. 20 4A
Marsh Av., Ewell 54 3B
Marsh Av., Mitcham 39 1E
Marsh Cl. 133 5D
Marsh Farm Rd. 17 2E
Marsh La. 49 1E
Marshall Cl., Farnborough 60 3C
Marshall Cl., Heatherside 62 2A
Marshall Cl., Isleworth 16 1C
Marshall Parade 66 1A
Marshall Pl. 49 3E
Marshall Rd., Godalming 119 1D
Marshall Rd., Sandhurst 43 5E
Marshall's Rd. 55 1F
Marshals Cl. 54 5A
Marshwood Dri. 46 4A
Marston Av. 53 2E
Marston Court 34 4A
Marston Dri., Farnborough Green 61 3D
Marston Dri., Warlingham 75 2F
Marston Rd., Farnham 95 4F
Marston Rd., Teddington 18 4A
Marston Rd., Woking 64 2B
Marston Way 22 5B
Martell Rd. 22 3C
Martin Cl., Blackwater 60 1B
Martin Cl., Crawley 146 3C
Martin Cl., Hamsey Grn. 75 1E
Martin Cl., Selsdon 58 4C
Martin Cres. 40 4A
Martin Gro. 38 2B
Martin Rd., Balham 21 2F
Martin Rd., Guildford 81 4E
Martin Way, Frimley 61 2E
Martin Way, Morden 38 2A
Martin Way, Woking 64 3B
Martindale Av. 62 1A
Martindale Cl. 82 4C
Martindale Rd. 64 2B
Martineau Cl. 52 1B
Martineau Dri. 106 2A
Martingale Cl. 34 2A
Martingales Cl. 18 3A
Martins Cl., Guildford 82 5C
Martins Dri. 25 1D
Martin's La. 27 2E
Martin's Rd. 42 1C
Martins, The 149 2E
Martins Wood 118 4A
Martinsyde 65 2F
Martlets Cl. 158 3B
Martlets, The 147 4D
Marton Cl. 24 3A
Marts, The 157 2E
Martyr Rd. 100 1C
Martyrs Av. 146 2C
Martyr's Grn. 67 3F
Martyr's La. 48 4B
Marvell Cl. 147 3F
Marwick La. 138 1B
Mary Adelaide Cl. 19 3D
Mary Rd. 100 1C
Maryhill Cl. 74 2C
Maryland Rd. 40 1B
Maryland Way 34 1A
Marys Ter. 17 2F
Maryvale 119 3D
Masefield Rd. 16 4C
Masefield Way 15 2D
Maskall Cl. 22 2B
Maskell Rd. 20 3C
Maskell Way 60 5B
Mason Cl. 34 1C
Mason Rd., Crawley 147 5D
Mason Rd., Farnborough 60 4B
Mason Way 96 1C
Masonic Hall Rd. 32 3A
Mason's Bridge Rd. 109 3E
Mason's Paddock 86 5C
Massets Rd. 128 3B
Master Cl. 93 3F
Maswell Park Cres. 17 1D
Maswell Park Rd. 17 1D
Matham Rd. 35 3E
Mathews Dr. 147 5F
Mathias Cl. 54 5A
Mathisen Way 7 4B
Matlock Cres. 55 1D
Matlock Gdns. 55 1D
Matlock Pl. 55 1D
Matlock Rd. 75 4D
Matlock Way 37 1D
Matthew Arnold Cl. 51 5D
Matthew St. 108 2B
Matthew Ter. 78 5A
Matthews Cl. 78 2B
Matthews Rd. 44 4A
Matthewsgreen Rd. 25 1D
Matthey Pl. 147 2F
Mauleverer Rd. 22 1A
Maultway Cl. 44 4C
Maultway Cres. 44 4C
Maultway, The 45 5D
Maunsell Park 147 4F
Maurice Av. 74 4C
Mavins Rd. 96 5B
Mavis Av. 54 1B
Mavis Cl. 54 1B
Mawbey Rd. 48 2C
Mawson Cl. 38 1A
Mawson La. 9 3E
Maxine Cl. 43 3D
Maxwell Cl. 40 4A
Maxwell Dri. 49 4E
Maxwell Rd. 15 5E
Maxwell Way 147 2E
May Cl., Chessington 53 2F
May Cl., Headley 133 5F
May Cl., Ockford Ridge 118 3C
May Cl., Sandhurst 43 4E
May Cres. 78 5B
May Rd. 17 2E
May Tree Cl. 81 4F
Maybelle Cl. 125 2D
Mayberry Cl. 36 4B
Maybourne Cl. 23 4E
Maybourne Rise 64 5C
Maybury 65 2E
Maybury Cl., Burgh Heath 72 3A
Maybury Cl., Frimley 61 3D
Maybury Hill 65 1E
Maybury Rd. 65 1E
Maybury St. 21 4D
Maycross Av. 38 2B
Mayday Rd. 40 3B
Mayell Cl. 70 5A
Mayes Cl., Three Bridges 147 4F
Mayes Cl., Warlingham 75 2F
Mayes La. 143 5E
Mayfair Av., Whitton 17 2D
Mayfair Av., Worcester Pk. 37 4E
Mayfair Cl., Beckenham 42 1A
Mayfair Cl., Surbiton 36 4B
Mayfield, Rowledge 114 2C
Mayfield, Three Bridges 147 4F
Mayfield Av., Turnham Green 9 2E
Mayfield Av., Woodham 49 3E
Mayfield Cl., Ashford 15 5D
Mayfield Cl., Clapham 21 1F
Mayfield Cl., Esher 35 4F
Mayfield Cl., Hersham 51 1D
Mayfield Cl., Woodham 49 3E
Mayfield Cres. 40 2A
Mayfield Gdns., Hersham 51 1D
Mayfield Gdns., Hythe 14 5A
Mayfield Rd., Ash 78 5C
Mayfield Rd., Carshalton Beeches 56 2A
Mayfield Rd., Frimley 61 2D
Mayfield Rd., Hammersmith 9 1E
Mayfield Rd., Hawley 60 3C
Mayfield Rd., Merton 38 1B
Mayfield Rd., Mitcham 40 2A
Mayfield Rd., Sanderstead 57 3F
Mayfield Rd., Walton 51 1D
Mayfield Rd., Weybridge 50 1A
Mayflower Cl. 147 4F
Mayford Cl. 64 4C
Mayford Rd. 21 2E
Mayhurst Av. 65 1E
Mayhurst Cl. 65 1E
Mayhurst Cres. 65 1E
Mayle Way 134 4A
Maynorth Gdns. 39 4D
Mayo Rd., Selhurst 40 3C
Mayo Rd., Walton-on-Thames 34 4A
Mayow Rd. 23 4F
Maypole Rd. 150 2B
Mayroyd Av. 36 5C
May's Green 67 3F
Mays Gro. 65 5F
May's Hill 81 1D
Mays Hill Rd. 42 1C
Mays Rd., Twick'm. 17 4E
Mays Rd., Wokingham 25 2F
Maysfield Rd. 65 5F
Maytree Cl. 81 4F
Maytree Wk. 22 3B
Maytrees 63 2F
Maywater Cl. 57 4F
Maywood Cl. 24 5A
Maywood Dri. 44 4C
Maze Rd. 8 3C
McCarthy Rd. 16 4B
McDonough Cl. 53 1E
McIndoe Rd. 150 1C
McIntosh Cl. 57 2D
McKay Rd. 19 5F
McNaughton Cl. 60 5B
Mead Av. 109 4E
Mead Cl., Brentford 8 3C
Mead Cl., Cranleigh 140 2C
Mead Cl., Egham 13 5E
Mead Cl., Redhill 90 4B
Mead Court. 64 2A
Mead Cres., Bookham 85 1F
Mead Cres., Carshalton 56 1A
Mead End 70 2B
Mead La., Chertsey 32 4B
Mead La., Farnham 96 4A
Mead Pk. 20 5C
Mead Pl. 40 4B
Mead Rd., Caterham 75 5D
Mead Rd., Cranleigh 140 1C
Mead Rd., Crawley 147 3D
Mead Rd., Ham 18 3A
Mead Rd., Hersham 51 1E
Mead Rd., Hindhead 135 5E
Mead, The, Ashtead 70 3B
Mead, The, Beckenham 42 1B
Mead, The, Beddington 56 2C
Mead, The, Farnborough 61 5D
Mead, The, West Wickham 42 4B
Mead Way, Burpham 82 3B
Mead Way, Coulsdon 74 2A
Mead Way, Effingham 85 2F
Mead Way, Parklangley 42 3C
Mead Way, Raynes Park 37 2F
Mead Way, Shirley 41 5E
Mead Way, Shottermill 151 3E
Mead Way Cl. 14 5A
Meades Cl. 132 3A
Meades, The, Dormans Land 132 3A
Meadhurst Rd. 32 4B
Meadlands Dri. 18 3A
Meadow Approach 148 1B
Meadow Bank, East Horsley 84 2C
Meadow Bank, Surbiton 36 3B
Meadow Bank Rd. 45 3F
Meadow Brook 93 3E
Meadow Cl., Blackwater 60 1B
Meadow Cl., Cannon Hill 38 2A
Meadow Cl., Esher 51 1F
Meadow Cl., Farncombe 100 5A
Meadow Cl., Hinchley Wood 35 5F
Meadow Cl., Milford 118 3B
Meadow Cl., Mytchett 78 1B
Meadow Cl., Old Windsor 12 1B
Meadow Cl., Purley 56 5C
Meadow Cl., Richmond 18 2B
Meadow Cl., Rose Hill 38 5C
Meadow Cl., Whitton 16 1C
Meadow Court, Epsom 54 5A
Meadow Court, Staines 13 3F
Meadow Dri. 66 5A
Meadow Farm La. 158 2C
Meadow Gdns. 13 4F
Meadow Hill, Malden 37 3D
Meadow Hill, Woodcote 56 5C
Meadow La., Fetcham 69 4E
Meadow La., Staines 14 4A
Meadow Lands, Oxted 94 5A
Meadow Lands Rd. 83 3E
Meadow Pl. 9 3E
Meadow Rd., Ashford 15 4E
Meadow Rd., Ashtead 70 2B
Meadow Rd., Burpham 82 3B
Meadow Rd., Carshalton 56 1A
Meadow Rd., Claygate 52 2B
Meadow Rd., Hanworth 16 3B
Meadow Rd., Hawley 60 3C
Meadow Rd., Shortlands 42 1C
Meadow Rd., South Wimbledon 20 5C
Meadow Rd., Wentworth 30 3A
Meadow Rd., Wokingham 25 2D
Meadow Rise, Knaphill 63 2F
Meadow Rise, Woodmansterne 56 5C
Meadow Vale, Camelsdale 151 3F
Meadow Vale, Wokingham 25 2D
Meadow View, Shepperton 33 4E
Meadow View., Stanwellmoor 14 1A
Meadow View, Thornton Heath 40 3B
Meadow View Rd. 54 3B
Meadow Way, Addlestone 49 1E
Meadow Way, Aldershot 78 4B
Meadow Way, Blackwater 43 5D
Meadow Way, Burgh Heath 72 2A
Meadow Way, Chessington 53 1E
Meadow Way, Fetcham 69 5D
Meadow Way, Horsley 84 1B
Meadow Way, Old Windsor 12 1B
Meadow Way, Rowledge 14 2C
Meadow Way, Rowledge 114 2C
Meadow Way, West End 46 4B
Meadow Way, Wokingham 25 2D
Meadow Way, Woodhatch 108 2C
Meadow Wk., Hackbridge 39 5E
Meadow Wk., Stoneleigh 54 2B
Meadow Wk., Walton on the Hill 71 5F
Meadowbrook Cl. 7 4B
Meadowbrook Rd. 105 1F
Meadowcroft Cl., East Grinstead 150 2B
Meadowcroft Cl., Horley 128 4C
Meadowlands, Cobham 51 5D
Meadowlands, Crawley 146 4C
Meadows End 34 1A
Meadows Leigh Cl. 33 5E
Meadows, The, Catford 24 4B
Meadows, The, Catford 24 4B
Meadows, The, Churt 134 2C
Meadows, The, Guildford 100 2C
Meadows, The, Sandhurst 43 5E
Meadows, The, Warlingham 75 2F
Meadowside, Bookham 68 5C
Meadowside, Horley 128 2C
Meadowside, Lingfield 131 1E
Meadowside, Walton 34 5B
Meadowside Rd. 55 3D
Meadowview 133 5D
Meadowview Cl. 24 4A
Meadowview Rd. 24 4A
Meadrow, Farncombe 100 5B
Meadrow, Godalming 119 1D
Meads Rd. 82 5B
Meads, The, East Grinstead 150 3C
Meads, The, Haslemere 151 3F
Meads, The, North Cheam 38 5A
Meads, The, Weybridge 50 2B
Meads, The, Weybridge 50 2B
Meadvale Rd. 41 4D
Meadway, Ashford 15 4D
Meadway, Beckenham 42 1B
Meadway, Epsom 54 4A
Meadway, Esher 52 3A
Meadway, Frimley 61 2E
Meadway, Hamsey Green 75 1E
Meadway, Oxshott 52 5B
Meadway, Staines 14 5A
Meadway, Tolworth 37 4D
Meadway, Twickenham 17 2E
Meadway Cl. 41 3E
Meadway Dri., Horsell 64 1C
Meadway Dri., New Haw 49 2E
Meadway, The 128 2C
Mears Cl. 72 5A
Meathgreen Av. 128 1A
Meathgreen La., Lee St. 128 1A

Meathgreen La., Salfords 109 5D
Medawar Rd. 100 1A
Mede Cl. 12 2C
Mede Field 69 5E
Medfield St. 19 2F
Medhurst Cl. 47 3E
Medina Av. 35 5E
Medlake Rd. 13 5E
Medland Cl. 39 4E
Medlar Cl., Crawley 146 2C
Medlar Cl., Guildford 81 4F
Medusa Rd. 24 1A
Medway 149 4D
Medway Dri., E. Grinstead 150 4C
Medway Dri., W. Heath 60 3B
Medway Rd. 146 4B
Melbourne Gro. 23 1D
Melbourne Mews 24 2B
Melbourne Rd., Kingston 18 5A
Melbourne Rd., Merton 38 1B
Melbourne Rd., Wallington 56 1C
Melbury Cl., Chertsey 32 4B
Melbury Cl., Claygate 52 2C
Melbury Cl., W. Byfleet 49 5D
Melbury Gdns. 37 1F
Meldrum Cl. 94 4A
Melford Rd. 23 2D
Melfort Rd. 40 2B
Melina Rd. 9 1F
Meliot Rd. 24 3C
Melksham Cl., Oakhill 158 5C
Melksham Cl., Owlsmoor 43 3E
Mellersh Hill Rd. South 120 1B
Mellison Rd. 21 4D
Mellor Cl. 34 4C
Mellow Cl. 55 5F
Mellows Rd. 56 1C
Melody Rd., Biggin Hill 77 2D
Melody Rd., Wandsworth 20 1C
Melrose 27 4D
Melrose Av., Mitcham 21 5E
Melrose Av., Norbury 40 2A
Melrose Av., West Heath 60 5A
Melrose Av., Whitton 17 2D
Melrose Av., Wimbledon Park 20 3B
Melrose Gdns., Hammersmith 9 1F
Melrose Gdns., Hersham 51 1E
Melrose Gdns., Malden 37 2D
Melrose Rd., Biggin Hill 77 1E
Melrose Rd., Merton 38 1B
Melrose Rd., West Hill 20 1B
Melrose Rd., Weybridge 50 1A
Melrose Rd., Woodmansterne 73 1E
Melrose Ter. 9 1F
Melsa Rd. 38 3C
Melton Fields 54 3A
Melton Pl. 54 3A
Melton Rd. 90 3C
Melville Av., Cottenham Park 19 5E
Melville Av., Frimley 61 2F
Melville Av., South Croydon 58 1A
Melville Rd. 9 4E
Melvin Rd. 41 1E
Melvin Shaw 70 4A
Membury Cl. 61 3F
Membury Walk 27 2E
Mendip Cl. 20 3A
Mendip Rd., Bracknell 27 3E
Mendip Rd., Farnborough 60 3B
Menin Way 96 4B
Menlo Gdns. 22 5C
Meon Cl., Farnborough 60 4B
Meon Cl., Tadworth 71 4F
Meon Rd. 9 1D
Meopham Rd. 39 1F
Merantun Way 38 1C
Merbury Cl. 24 1B
Mercer Cl., Crawley 147 5F
Mercer Cl., Thames Ditton 35 4F
Merchiston Rd. 24 3B
Mercia Way 65 2D
Mercier Rd. 20 1A
Mercury Cl. 133 5D
Mercury Rd. 8 2A
Mere Cl. 20 2A
Mere End 41 4F
Mere Rd., Portmore Park 33 5E
Mere Rd., Shepperton 33 3E
Mere Rd., Tadworth 71 5F
Merebank 125 2D
Merebank La. 57 1D
Meredyth Rd. 9 4E
Merefield 69 5E
Merefield Gdns. 72 3A
Mereside 30 3C
Mereside Pl. 30 4B
Merevale Cres. 38 3C
Mereway Rd. 17 2E
Mereworth Cl. 42 3C
Mereworth Rd. 147 3D
Meridan Grove 128 2C
Merland Cl. 71 3F
Merland Green 71 3F
Merland Rise 71 3F
Merle Common Rd. 113 1D
Merlewood 27 3D
Merlewood Cl. 74 4C
Merlin Gro. 42 2A
Merlin Way 48 5B
Merlins Cl. 75 2D
Merrilands Rd. 37 4F
Merrilyn Cl. 52 2C
Merritt Rd. 24 1A
Merrivale Gdns. 64 2C
Merrow 82 5C
Merrow Chase 82 5C
Merrow Common 82 4C
Merrow Copse 82 5B
Merrow Court 82 5C
Merrow Croft 82 5C
Merrow La. 82 3C
Merrow Rd. 55 3D
Merrow St. 82 4C
Merrow Way 59 2E
Merrow Woods 82 4B
Merryacres 118 5A
Merryfield Dri. 158 4A
Merryhill Rd. 26 1C
Merryhills Cl. 77 1E
Merryhills Lane 156 3A
Merrylands 32 5A
Merrylands Rd. 68 5C
Merrymeet 56 5A
Merrywood Pk., Box Hill 87 3F
Merrywood Pk., Heatherside 61 1F
Merrywood Pk., Reigate 89 4E
Merryworth Cl. 78 5B
Mersham Pl. 41 1E
Mersham Rd. 40 2C
Merstham 90 2C
Merstham Rd. 91 3E
Merthyr Ter. 9 3F
Merton 38 1B
Merton Av. 9 2E
Merton Cl. 43 3F
Merton Gdns. 72 3A
Merton Hall Gdns. 38 1A
Merton Hall Rd. 38 1A
Merton Rd., Southfields 20 1B
Merton Rd., South Wimbledon 20 5C
Merton Rd., Woodside 41 3D
Merton Way, East Molesey 35 2D
Merton Way, Leatherhead Common 69 3F
Mervyn Rd. 33 4E
Metcalf Rd. 15 4D
Metcalf Way 147 2D
Meteor Way 57 2D
Meudon Av. 61 5D
Mews, The 81 5F
Mexfield Rd. 20 1B
Meyrick Cl. 64 1A
Miall Wk. 23 4F
Michael Cres. 128 3B
Michael Rd. 40 2C
Micheldever Rd. 24 1C
Micheldever Way 27 3F
Michelet Cl. 45 3F
Michelham Gdns. 71 3F
Michell Cl. 158 5A
Michels Row 8 5B
Mickle Hill 43 3D
Mickleham 87 2D
Mickleham By-Pass 86 2C
Mickleham Dri. 87 1D
Mickleham Gdns. 55 2D
Mickleham Way 59 2E
Mid St. 91 5D
Middle Av. 96 5B
Middle Bourne 115 1D
Middle Bourne La. 96 5A
Middle Church La. 96 4A
Middle Cl., Camberley 45 5D
Middle Cl., Coulsdon 74 3A
Middle Farm Pl. 85 2E
Middle Gordon Rd. 44 5A
Middle Green, Brockham 106 1C
Middle Green, Staines 14 5C
Middle Hill, Egham 12 4C
Middle Hill, Millbridge 115 3D
Middle La., Epsom 54 4B
Middle La., Teddington 17 5F
Middle Old Pk. 95 3E
Middle Rd., Leatherhead 160
Middle Rd., Mitcham 39 1F
Middle St., Brockham 106 1C
Middle St., Shere 103 3D
Middle St., Strood Green 107 2D
Middle Way 39 1F
Middle Wk. 65 2D
Middlefield, Horley 128 2C
Middlefield, Selsdon 58 3C
Middlefield, Wrecclesham 95 5F
Middlemarch 118 5B
Middlemead Cl. 85 1F
Middlemeads Rd. 85 1F
Middlemoor Cl. 61 3E
Middlemoor Rd. 61 3E
Middlesex Rd. 40 3A
Middleton Cl. 118 3B
Middleton Rd., Camberley 44 5B
Middleton Rd., Downside 68 3A
Middleton Rd., Ewell 54 3A
Middleton Rd., Horsham 158 5A
Middleton Rd., Morden 38 3C
Middleton Way 146 4A
Midgeley Rd. 147 3D
Midholm Rd. 41 5F
Midhope Cl. 65 3D
Midhope Gdns. 65 3D
Midhope Rd. 65 3D
Midhurst Av. 40 4B
Midhurst Cl. 146 3B
Midhurst Rd. 151 4F
Midleton Cl. 118 3B
Midleton Gdns. 60 4B
Midleton Industrial Estate Rd. 81 5E
Midleton Rd. 81 5E
Midmoor Rd., Balham 21 2F
Midmoor Rd, Wimbledon 38 1A
Midway, Cheam 38 4B
Midway, Walton-on-Thames 34 5A
Midway Av. 31 2E
Miena Way 70 2A
Mike Hawthorn Dri. 96 3B
Milbanke Ct. 26 1C
Milbanke Way 26 1C
Milborough Cres. 24 1C
Milbourne La. 52 2A
Milbrook, Esher 52 2A
Milburn Wk. 71 1E
Milcombe Cl. 64 2C
Milden Cl. 61 4F
Milden Gdns. 61 4F
Mile Path 64 3B
Mile Rd. 39 4E
Mile's Hill 123 2E
Miles La., Crowhurst 112 1A
Miles La., Oxshott 51 5F
Miles New Rd. 112 1A
Miles Pl., Kingston 36 2B
Miles Pl., Lightwater 45 4E
Miles Rd., Ash Wharf 78 4C
Miles Rd., Epsom 54 4A
Milestone Cl., Ripley 66 4B
Milestone Cl., Sutton 55 2F
Milestone Rd. 23 5D
Milford 118 3A
Milford Grn. 47 4E
Milford Gro. 55 1F
Milford Lodge 118 4B
Milford Mews 22 3A
Milford Rd. 117 2E
Milkwood Rd. 22 1B
Mill Bay La., Horsham 158 5A
Mill Cl., Bookham 68 5C
Mill Cl., East Grinstead 150 3C
Mill Cl., Hackbridge 39 5E
Mill Cl., Horley 128 2A
Mill Copse Rd. 151 4F
Mill Farm Av. 15 5F
Mill Farm Cres. 16 2C
Mill Hedge Cl. 68 1B
Mill Hill Gro. 8 1C
Mill Hill La. 87 5F
Mill Hill Rd., Acton 8 1C
Mill Hill Rd., Barnes 9 4E
Mill Hollow 122 3B
Mill House La. 31 2E
Mill La., Bramley 120 1A
Mill La., Byfleet 50 5A
Mill La., Carshalton 56 1B
Mill La., Chiddingfold 137 5F
Mill La., Chilworth 102 3A
Mill La., Domewood 148 1C
Mill La., Dorking 105 1F
Mill La., Easthampstead 26 2C
Mill La., Ewell 54 3B
Mill La., Felbridge 149 1F
Mill La., Godalming 118 2C
Mill La., Guildford 159
Mill La., Headley 133 4E
Mill La., Holland 95 5A
Mill La., Ifield Village 146 3B
Mill La., Kingsley Grn. 152 4A
Mill La., Leatherhead 69 4F
Mill La., Lee Street 128 2A
Mill La., Lingfield 131 3F
Mill La., Oxted 94 5A
Mill La., Parkgate 126 1A
Mill La., Peasmarsh 100 4C
Mill La., Pirbright 63 5D
Mill La., Ripley 66 3C
Mill La., South Merstham 90 4C
Mill La., The Chart 94 4C
Mill La., Thorpe 31 2E
Mill La., Virginia Water 29 1E
Mill La., Waddon 40 5A
Mill La., Wheeler Street 118 5B
Mill Pl. 36 2B
Mill Rd., Banstead Newton 72 5A
Mill Rd., Cobham 68 1A
Mill Rd., Epsom 54 4B
Mill Rd., Hersham 34 5C
Mill Rd., South Holmwood 106 5A
Mill Rd., South Wimbledon 20 5C
Mill Rd., Three Bridges 147 3E
Mill Rd., Twickenham 17 3D
Mill Ride 28 1A
Mill St., Colnbrook 7 3A
Mill St., Kingston 36 2B
Mill St., Redhill 109 1D
Mill Stream 96 2B
Mill Vale 42 1C
Mill View Cl. 54 2B
Mill View Gdns. 41 5E
Mill Way, East Grinstead 150 3C
Mill Way, Feltham 16 1A
Mill Way, Headley 87 1F
Mill Way, Tyrell's Wood 70 5B
Millais 158 4C
Millais Rd. 37 4D
Millais Way 54 1A
Millars Cl. 25 3D
Millbank, The 146 4B
Millbourne Rd. 16 4C
Millbrook, Guildford 100 1C
Millbrook, Weybridge 50 1C
Millbrook Way 7 4A
Millchase 133 5D
Millen Cl. 49 3E
Miller Rd., Croydon 40 4A
Miller Rd., Guildford 82 4C
Miller Rd., Tooting 21 5D
Millers Cl. 14 4B
Millers Copse, Langley Vale 71 3D
Millers Copse, Outwood 110 5B
Millers Gate. 158 3B
Miller's La. 110 5B
Millfield, Bagshot 45 2D
Millfield, Sunbury 33 1F
Millfield La. 89 1E
Millfield Rd. 16 2C
Millford 64 2B
Millgreen Rd. 39 4E
Millholme Wk. 62 1A
Millins Cl. 43 3E
Millmead, Byfleet 50 4A
Millmead, Guildford 100 1C
Millmead, Staines 14 4A
Millmead Terrace 100 1C
Millmeads 158 3B
Millpond Court 49 1F
Millpond Rd. 45 1F
Mills Rd., Hersham 51 1E
Mills Spur 12 2B
Millshaw 93 4F
Millside 39 5E
Millstream, The 151 3E
Millthorpe Rd. 158 4C
Millview Cl. 90 4A
Millway 90 5A
Millwood 149 4F
Millwood Rd. 17 1D
Milman Cl. 27 1F
Milne Park East 59 4E
Milne Park West 59 4E
Milner Approach 75 4D
Milner Close 75 4D
Milner Dri., Cobham 51 4F
Milner Dri., Whitton 17 2E
Milner Pl. 56 1B
Milner Rd., Caterham 75 4D
Milner Rd., Kingston 36 2B
Milner Rd., Merton 38 1C
Milner Rd., Mitcham 39 3D
Milnthorpe Rd. 9 3D
Milnwood Rd. 158 4B
Milo Rd. 23 1D
Milton Av., Carshalton 56 1A
Milton Av., Croydon 40 4C
Milton Av., Westcott 105 2E
Milton Cl., Easthampstead 26 3C
Milton Cl., Feltham 16 1A
Milton Cl., The Wrythe 39 5D
Milton Cres. 150 2B
Milton Dri. 32 3C
Milton Gdns., Epsom 54 5B
Milton Gdns., West Bedfont 15 2D
Milton Gdns., Wokingham 25 1D
Milton Mount Av. 147 3F
Milton Rd., Beddington 56 2C
Milton Rd., Caterham 74 4C
Milton Rd., Cheam 55 1E
Milton Rd., Croydon 40 4C
Milton Rd., Egham 13 4D
Milton Rd., Hampton 17 5D
Milton Rd., Herne Hill 22 1B
Milton Rd., Mortlake 9 5D
Milton Rd., Pound Hill 147 3F
Milton Rd., Row Town 49 2D
Milton Rd., Tooting 21 5E
Milton Rd., Walton on Thames 34 5B
Milton Rd., Wimbledon 20 5C
Milton Rd., Wokingham 25 1D
Milton St. 105 2E
Milton Way 86 1A

Miltoncourt La. 105 1E
Miltons Cres. 118 3C
Miltons Yd. 137 1E
Milward Gdns. 25 1B
Mimosa Cl. 133 1E
Mina Rd. 38 1B
Minard Rd. 24 2C
Minchin Cl. 69 4F
Mincing La. 47 3E
Minden Rd., Anerley 41 1E
Minden Rd., Nth. Cheam 38 5B
Minehead Rd. 22 4A
Minerva Rd. 36 1B
Minley Cl. 60 5B
Minley Link Rd. 60 4A
Minley Rd. 60 3A
Minniedale 36 3B
Minorca Rd., Frimley 62 2A
Minorca Rd., Weybridge 50 1A
Minstead Cl. 27 2F
Minstead Gdns. 19 2E
Minstead Way 37 3D
Minster Dri. 57 1E
Minster Gdns. 34 3C
Minster Rd., Godalming 119 3D
Minster Rd., Sutton 38 5B
Minsterley Av. 33 2F
Minstral Gdns. 36 2C
Mint Gdns. 105 1F
Mint La. 89 3E
Mint Rd., Banstead 72 1C
Mint Rd., Wallington 56 1B
Mint St. 119 2D
Mint Walk, Croydon 40 5C
Mint Walk, Warlingham 75 2F
Missenden Gdns. 38 3C
Mistletoe Cl. 41 4F
Misty's Field 34 4B
Mitcham 39 1D
Mitcham Garden Village 39 3E
Mitcham La. 21 5F
Mitcham Pk. 39 2D
Mitcham Rd., Camberley 44 3C
Mitcham Rd., Croydon 40 3A
Mitcham Rd., Tooting 21 4D
Mitchells Cl. 101 4D
Mitchells Rd. 147 4D
Mitchley Av. 57 5F
Mitchley Green 58 5A
Mitchley Hill 58 5A
Mitchley View 58 5A
Mitre Cl. 55 2F
Mixbury Grn. 50 2B
Mixnams La. 32 2A
Mizen Cl. 68 1B
Mizen Way 51 5E
Moat Court 70 2B
Moat Rd. 150 2C
Moat Side 16 4B
Moat, The 37 1E
Moat Walk 147 3F
Moats Lane 110 3A
Moffat Rd., Beulah Hill 40 1C
Moffats Dri. 43 4D
Moffatt Rd., Colliers W'd. 21 4D
Mogador Rd. 89 2D
Mogden La. 17 1E
Moir Cl. 58 3A
Mole Abbey Gdns. 35 2D
Mole Cl., Crawley 146 3C
Mole Cl., West Heath 60 4B
Mole Court 54 1A
Mole Rd., Fetcham 69 4E
Mole Rd., Hersham 51 1E
Mole St., Ockley 124 5A
Mole Valley Pl. 70 3B
Molember Court 35 2E
Molember Rd. 35 3E
Moles Cl. 25 2E
Moles Hill 52 4B
Molesey Av. 34 3C
Molesey Cl. 51 1E
Molesey Dri. 38 5A
Molesey Park Rd. 35 3D
Molesey Pk. Av. 35 3D
Molesey Pk. Cl. 35 3D
Molesey Rd., Hersham 51 1E
Molesey Rd., Walton-on-Thames 34 5B
Molesham Cl. 35 2D
Molesham Way 35 2D
Molesworth Rd. 51 5D
Mollison Dri. 57 2D
Molly Huggins Cl. 21 2F
Molly Miller's La. 25 3D
Molyneaux Rd., Farncombe 100 5A
Molyneaux Rd., Weybridge 50 1A
Molyneux Rd., Windlesham 46 2A
Monahan Av. 57 4D
Monarch Cl., Crawley 146 5B
Monarch Cl., E. Bedfont 15 2F
Monarch Cl., W. Wickham 59 1F
Monarch Mews 22 4B
Monaveen Gdns. 35 2D
Money Av. 74 4C
Money Rd. 74 4C
Mongers La. 54 3B
Monk Leigh Rd. 38 2A
Monks Av. 34 3C
Monks Cl., Farnborough 61 5D
Monks Cl., Sunninghill 28 3C
Monks Cl., Walton-on-Thames 34 4A
Monks Cres. 49 1E
Monks Dri. 28 3C
Monks Green 69 4E
Monk's La. 113 2E
Monks Orchard Rd. 42 4A
Monk's Place 75 4E
Monks Rd., Banstead 72 2B
Monks Rd., Virginia Water 30 2C
Monks Way, Eden Park 42 3A
Monks Way, Staines 14 5C
Monk's Well 97 5D
Monks Wk., Farnham 96 5C
Monk's Wk., Reigate 89 5F
Monks Wk, S. Ascot 28 3C
Monksdene Gdns. 38 5C
Monksfield 147 4D
Monkshanger 96 4B
Monkswell La. 72 5C
Monkton La. 96 2B
Monlieu Gdns. 19 1F
Monmouth Av. 18 5A
Monmouth Cl. 40 2A
Mono La. 16 3A
Mons Wk. 13 4E
Monsell Gdns. 13 4F
Monson Rd. 90 4B
Montacute Cl. 61 5E
Montacute Rd., Catford 24 2A
Montacute Rd., New Addington 59 3E
Montacute Rd., Surbiton 38 3C
Montagu Gdns. 56 1C
Montague Av. 57 4F
Montague Cl., Camberley 43 5F
Montague Cl., Walton-on-Thames 34 4A
Montague Dri. 74 4C
Montague Rd., Croydon 40 4B
Montague Rd., Richmond 18 1B
Montague Rd., Wimbledon 20 5B
Montana Cl. 57 3F
Montana Rd., Tooting Bec 21 3E
Montana Rd., Wimbledon 38 1A
Montegal Cl. 119 2D
Montem Rd., Lewisham 23 2F
Montem Rd., New Malden 37 2D
Montford Rd. 34 2A
Montfort Rise 109 5D
Montgomerie Dri. 81 3E
Montgomerry Cl. 43 4D
Montgomery Av. 35 5E
Montgomery Rd., Chiswick 9 2D
Montgomery Rd., Farnborough 60 5C
Montholme Rd. 21 1D
Montpelier Rd., Purley 57 3E
Montpelier Rd., Sutton 55 1F
Montpelier Row 18 2A
Montrell Rd. 22 2A
Montrose Av. 17 2D
Montrose Cl., Ashford 15 5E
Montrose Cl., Frimley 61 2E
Montrose Gdns., Mitcham 39 2E
Montrose Gdns., Oxshott 52 4B
Montrose Gdns., Rose Hill 38 5C
Montrose Rd. 15 1E
Montrose Walk 33 5D
Montrose Way 23 2F
Montrouge Cres. 71 1F
Montserrat Cl. 22 4C
Monument Hill 50 1A
Monument Rd., Maybury 48 5B
Monument Rd., Weybridge 33 5E
Monument Way East And West 65 1E
Moon Hall Rd. 122 3B
Moons Hill 115 3D
Moons La., Dormans Land 132 4B
Moons La., Horsham 158 5C
Moor Cl., Owlsmoor 43 3E
Moor Cl., Whitton 16 2C
Moor La., Chessington 53 1E
Moor La., Dorman's Land 132 3A
Moor La., Harmondsworth 7 3C
Moor La., Poyle 7 5A
Moor La., Staines 13 3F
Moor La., Westfield 65 4D
Moor Mead Rd. 17 1F
Moor Park Cres. 145 4F
Moor Park La. 96 3C
Moor Park Way 96 4C
Moor Pl., E. Grinstead 150 2B
Moor Pl., Windlesham 45 1F
Moor Rd., Frimley 61 3E
Moor Rd., Hammer 151 3D
Moor Rd., Hawley 60 3C
Moordale Av. 26 1B
Moore Cl., Addlestone 49 1E
Moore Cl., Sutton 57 2D
Moore Cl., Tongham 97 1E
Moore Grove Cres. 13 5D
Moore Rd., Brookwood 62 4C
Moore Rd., Upper Norwood 22 5B
Moore Way 55 3E
Moores Rd. 106 1A
Moorfield Cl. 31 1F
Moorfield Rd., Camelsdale 151 3E
Moorfield Rd., Chessington 53 1E
Moorfield Rd., Guildford 82 3A
Moorhayes Dri. 32 2B
Moorholme 65 3D
Moorhouse Rd. 94 3C
Moorhurst Rd. 124 2C
Moorings, The 135 5E
Moorland Cl. 135 5E
Moorland Rd., Crawley 147 5F
Moorlands Rd. 60 1C
Moorlands, The 65 4D
Moormead Dri. 54 1B
Moormede Cres. 14 4A
Moors La. 117 2D
Moors, The 97 1E
Moorside La. 60 2C
Moorside Rd. 24 3C
Moorsome Way 73 2F
Moray Av. 43 4E
Morcoombe Cl. 18 5C
Morcote Cl. 101 4D
Morden 38 2B
Morden Cl. 72 3A
Morden Court 38 2B
Morden Gdns. 39 2D
Morden Hall Rd. 38 2C
Morden Rd. 38 1C
Morden Way 38 4B
Mordred Rd. 24 3C
More Cl. 57 4D
More La., Esher 52 1A
More La., Lower Green 35 5D
More Rd. 100 5A
Morecambe Cl. 146 5B
Moreland Av. 7 3A
Morella Cl. 30 2C
Morella Rd. 21 2D
Moremead Rd. 24 4A
Morena St. 24 2A
Moresby Av. 36 4C
Moretaine Rd. 14 3C
Moreton Rd., South Croydon 57 1F
Moreton Rd., Worcester Park 37 5F
Moring Rd. 21 4E
Morkyns Walk 22 3C
Morland Av. 40 4C
Morland Cl. 16 4C
Morland Rd., Addiscombe 41 4D
Morland Rd., Aldershot 97 1D
Morland Rd., Penge 23 5F
Morland Rd., Sutton 55 2F
Morlands Rd. 78 3A
Morley Rd., Farnham 96 4A
Morley Rd., Hither Green 24 1B
Morley Rd., Richmond 18 1A
Morley Rd., Selsdon 58 3A
Morley Rd., St. Helier 38 4B
Morney Rough 118 1B
Morningside Rd. 37 5F
Mornington Rd. 15 4E
Mornington Walk 18 4A
Morrel Av. 158 3C
Morris Gdns. 20 2B
Morris Rd., S. Farnborough 78 2B
Morris Rd., S. Nutfield 110 1A
Morrish Rd. 22 2A
Morston Cl. 71 3F
Morten Cl. 21 1F
Mortimer Cl. 21 3F
Mortimer Cres. 37 5D
Mortimer Rd., Capel 125 5D
Mortimer Rd., Mitcham 39 1D
Mortlake Cl. 40 5A
Mortlake Dri. 39 1D
Mortlake High St. 9 4D
Mortlake Rd. 8 3C
Morton 72 4A
Morton Cl. 61 3E
Morton Gdns. 56 1C
Morton Rd., East Grinstead 150 3C
Morton Rd., Mitcham 39 3D
Morton Rd., Woking 64 1C
Morval Cl. 60 5B
Morval Rd. 22 1B
Moselle Rd. 77 2F
Mosford Cl. 128 1A
Mospey Cres. 71 1E
Moss La. 119 2D
Mosses Wood Rd. 124 3A
Mossfield 51 5D
Mosslea Rd., Penge 23 5E
Mosslea Rd., Whyteleafe 75 2D
Mossville Gdns. 38 2B
Mostyn Rd. 38 1B
Mostyn Ter. 109 1E
Motspur Pk. 37 3E
Motts Hill La. 71 5F
Mount Adon Pk. 23 2D
Mount Angelus Rd. 19 2E
Mount Ararat Rd. 18 1B
Mount Ash Rd. 23 3E
Mount Av. 74 5B
Mount Cl., Carshalton 56 3B
Mount Cl., Ewhurst 122 5C
Mount Cl., Fetcham 69 5E
Mount Cl., Kenley 74 1C
Mount Cl., Mayford 64 4C
Mount Cl., Pound Hill 147 3F
Mount Cl., West Wickham 42 5C
Mount Cl., The 30 3C
Mount Dri., The 89 4F
Mount Ephraim La. 21 3F
Mount Ephraim Rd. 21 3F
Mount Felix 33 4F
Mount Gdns. 23 3E
Mount Hermon Cl. 65 2D
Mount Hermon Rd. 64 3C
Mount La., Bracknell 27 2D
Mount La., Turners Hill 149 5D
Mount Lee 13 4D
Mount Nod Rd. 22 3A
Mount Park 56 3B
Mount Park Av. 57 3E
Mount Park Cl. 56 3B
Mount Pleasant, Biggin Hill 77 2E
Mount Pleasant, Bracknell 27 2D
Mount Pleasant, Effingham 85 2F
Mount Pleasant, Ewell 54 3B
Mount Pleasant, Farnham 95 4F
Mount Pleasant, Guildford 100 1C
Mount Pleasant, Weybridge 33 5D
Mount Pleasant, W. Horsley 84 3B
Mount Pleasant, Wokingham 25 2D
Mount Pleasant Cl. 45 3F
Mount Pleasant Rd., Aldershot 78 5A
Mount Pleasant Rd., Caterham 75 5D
Mount Pleasant Rd., Hither Green 24 1B
Mount Pleasant Rd., Lindford 133 4D
Mount Pleasant Rd., New Malden 37 2D
Mount Pleasant Rd., Plaistow Street 131 2E
Mount Rd., Chessington 53 1E
Mount Rd., Chobham 47 4E
Mount Rd., Cranleigh 140 2C
Mount Rd., Earlsfield 20 3B
Mount Rd., Hanworth 16 3B
Mount Rd., Mayford 64 4C
Mount Rd., Mitcham 39 1D
Mount Rd., New Malden 37 2D
Mount Rd., Sunninghill 29 3D
Mount Rise 109 1D
Mount St. 105 1F
Mount, The, Cranleigh 140 2C
Mount, The, Esher 51 2F
Mount, The, Ewell 54 3B
Mount, The, Fetcham 69 5E
Mount, The, Grayswood 152 1B
Mount, The, Guildford 100 1C
Mount, The, Headley 133 4F
Mount, The, Kingswood 89 1E
Mount, The, New Malden 37 2E
Mount, The, Stoneleigh 54 1C
Mount, The, Walton 33 5F
Mount, The, Whyteleafe 75 3E
Mount, The, Woking 64 2C
Mount, The, Woodmansterne 56 5B
Mount View Rd. 52 2C
Mount Way 56 3B
Mountacre Cl. 23 4D
Mountbatten Cl. 22 4C
Mountcombe Cl. 36 4B
Mountearl Gdns. 22 3A
Mountfield Cl. 14 1A
Mounthurst Rd. 42 4C
Mounts Hill 10 3C
Mountsfield Court. 24 1B
Mountside 100 2C
Mountview Cl. 109 1D
Mountview Dri. 109 1D
Mountwood 35 2D
Mountwood Cl. 58 3B
Moushill La. 118 4A
Mowatt Rd. 151 1D
Mowbray Av. 49 5F
Mowbray Cres. 13 4E
Mowbray Dri. 146 5B
Mowbray Gdns. 87 5D
Mowbray Rd., Anerley 41 1D
Mowbray Rd., Ham 18 3A
Mower Pl. 140 1C
Moys Cl. 40 3A
Moyser Rd. 21 4E
Muchelney Rd. 38 3C
Mucies Mews 24 3B
Muckhatch La. 31 2E
Muirdown Av. 9 5D
Muirfield Cl. 146 4A

203
Muirfield Rd
Nork Rise

Muirfield Rd. 64 2B
Muirkirk Rd. 24 2B
Mulberries, The 96 3C
Mulberry Av. 14 2C
Mulberry Cl., Ash 78 4C
Mulberry Cl., Tooting Bec 21 4F
Mulberry Cl., Weybridge 50 1B
Mulberry Cl., Woking 48 5A
Mulberry Court 158 3B
Mulberry La. 41 5D
Mulberry Rd. 146 2C
Mulberry Trees 33 4E
Mulgrave Rd., Cheam 55 2E
Mulgrave Rd., Croydon 40 5C
Mulgrave Rd., Frimley 61 2E
Mulgrave Way 64 2A
Mullens Rd. 13 4E
Mullins Path 9 5D
Mulroy Dri. 44 5C
Mulion Rd. 21 2D
Muncaster Cl. 15 4D
Muncaster Rd., Ashford 15 4D
Muncaster Rd., Clapham 21 1E
Mundania Rd. 23 1E
Mundays Boro Rd. 98 3C
Munnings Dri. 43 5E
Munstead 119 3E
Munstead Heath Rd. 119 2F
Munstead Hth. 119 3E
Munstead View 100 3C
Munstead View Rd. 119 1F
Munster Rd. 18 5A
Murcia Walk, Woking 160
Murdoch Cl. 14 4A
Murdoch Rd. 25 2E
Murfett Cl. 20 3A
Murray Av. 17 1D
Murray Grn. 48 5C
Murray Rd., Aldershot 78 3A
Murray Rd., Brentford 8 2A
Murray Rd., Cove 60 5C
Murray Rd., Ham 18 3A
Murray Rd., Ottershaw 48 2C
Murray Rd., Wimbledon 20 5A
Murray Rd., Wokingham 25 2D
Murrelhill La. 26 1A
Murrell Rd. 78 4C
Murrell's La. 61 1D
Murrell's Wk. 69 5D
Murreys, The 70 2A
Murtmead La. 98 3C
Muschamp Rd. 39 5D
Museum Hill 152 3A
Musgrave Av. 150 3C
Mustard Mill Rd. 14 4A
Mutton Hill 132 4A
Mutton Oaks 26 1B
Muybridge Rd. 37 1D
Mychett Rd. 61 5E
Myers Way 62 2A
Mylls Cl. 23 4E
Mylne Sq. 25 2E
Mylor Cl. 48 5A
Mynns Cl. 53 5F
Myrna Cl. 21 5D
Myrtle Ave. 15 1F
Myrtle Cl., Lightwater 45 4F
Myrtle Cl., Poyle 7 4A
Myrtle Dri. 60 1B
Myrtle Gro., Lower Sydenham 23 4F
Myrtle Gro., New Malden 37 1D
Myrtle Rd., Dorking 105 1F
Myrtle Rd., Hampton 17 5D
Myrtle Rd., Shirley 42 5A
Myrtle Rd., Sutton 55 1F
Mytchett 61 5E
Mytchett Lake Rd. 78 1C
Mytchett Place Rd. 78 1C
Mytchett Rd., Ash Vale 78 1C
Mytchett Rise 78 1C
Myton Rd. 22 3C

N

Nailsham Cl. 36 4B
Nailsworth Cres. 90 3C
Nairn Cl. 61 2E
Nairne Gro. 22 1C
Naldrett Cl. 158 4C
Nallhead Rd. 16 4B
Namton Dri. 40 2A
Napier Cl. 43 2E
Napier Dri. 44 4C
Napier Gdns. 82 5B
Napier La. 78 4C
Napier Rd., Ashford 15 5E
Napier Rd., Crowthorne 43 2D
Napier Rd., South Croydon 57 2F
Napier Way 147 2E
Napoleon Av. 61 4D
Napoleon Rd. 18 2A
Napper Cl. 28 1A
Napper Pl. 140 2C
Narbonne Av. 21 1F
Narow La. 75 3E
Naseby 26 4C
Naseby Court 34 5A
Naseby Rd. 22 5C
Nash Cl. 60 5B
Nash Dri. 90 4B
Nash Gdns., Ascot 28 1A
Nash Gdns., Redhill 90 4B
Nash Rd., Crawley 147 5D
Nash Rd., Lewisham 23 1F
Nassau Rd. 9 4E
Nasturtium Dri. 63 1E
Natal Rd., Streatham 22 4A
Natal Rd., Streatham Vale 21 5F
Natal Rd., Thornton Heath 40 2C
Natalie Cl. 15 2E
Neale Cl. 150 1B
Neate's Alley, Leatherhead 160
Neath Gdns. 38 3C
Neb Rd. 93 4E
Needles Cl. 158 5A
Neil Cl. 15 4E
Neil Wates Cres. 22 2B
Nelgarde Rd. 24 2A
Nell Ball 155 5D
Nell Gwyn Av. 33 3E
Nell Gwynne's Av. 29 2D
Nelson Cl., Aldershot 78 5A
Nelson Cl., Biggin Hill 77 2F
Nelson Cl., Bracknell 27 1E
Nelson Cl., Heath End 96 1B
Nelson Cl., Three Bridges 147 4F
Nelson Cl., Walton 34 4A
Nelson Gdns., Guildford 82 5B
Nelson Gdns., Whitton 16 1C
Nelson Rd., Ashford 14 4C
Nelson Rd., Caterham 74 5C
Nelson Rd., Heath End 96 1B
Nelson Rd., Horsham 158 4B
Nelson Rd., Malden 37 3D
Nelson Rd., Merton 20 5C
Nelson Rd., Whitton 17 1D
Nelson Way 60 1C
Nene Gdns. 16 3C
Nepean St. 19 1F
Neptune Cl. 146 5A
Nether Mount 100 1B
Netheravon Rd. 9 2E
Netherbury Rd. 8 1A
Netherby Pk. 50 1C
Netherby Rd. 23 2E
Nethercote Av. 64 2A
Netherlands, The 73 3F
Netherleigh Park 110 2A
Nethern Court Rd. 76 5A
Netherne La. 73 4F
Netherton 26 2C
Netherton Rd. 17 1F
Netherwood 146 5B
Netley Cl., Cheam 55 1D
Netley Cl., New Addington 59 2E
Netley Dri. 34 4C
Netley Gdns 38 4C
Netley Rd., Brentford 8 3B
Netley Rd., St. Helier 38 4C
Netley St. 78 2A
Nettlecombe 27 3E
Nettlecombe Cl. 55 3F
Nettlewood Rd. 21 5F
Neuchatel Rd. 24 3A
Nevada Cl. 60 5B
Nevelle Cl. 26 1B
Neville Av. 37 1D
Neville Cl., Banstead 55 5E
Neville Cl., Crawley 146 5B
Neville Cl., Esher 51 2F
Neville Duke Rd. 60 3C
Neville Gill Cl. 20 1B
Neville Rd., Croydon 40 4C
Neville Rd., Ham 18 3A
Neville Rd., Norbiton 36 1C
Neville Wk. 39 4D
Nevis Rd. 21 3E
New Addington 59 3E
New Barn La., Kenley 75 1D
New Barn La., Newdigate 126 3A
New Barnes Av. 39 2F
New Battlebridge La. 90 3B
New Berry La. 51 1E
New Causeway 108 2C
New Chapel 130 3C
New Cl. 38 2C
New Court 32 5B
New Cross Rd. 81 4E
New Dawn Cl. 60 5B
New England Hill 46 4A
New Farthingale 132 4A
New Forest Dri. 27 4E
New Forest Ride 27 2F
New Haven Rd. 40 3C
New Haw 49 2E
New Haw Rd. 49 1E
New House La. 109 4F
New Inn La. 82 4B
New La. 65 4D
New Lodge Dri. 93 2F
New Malden 37 2E
New Meadow 28 1A
New Mile Rd. 28 1C
New North Rd. 108 2B
New Park Rd., Ashford 15 4E
New Park Rd., Cranleigh 140 1C
New Park Rd., Streatham 22 2A
New Pond Rd. 100 4A
New Poplars Court. 78 5C
New Rd., Albury Park 102 3C
New Rd., Ascot 10 5B
New Rd., Bagshot 45 2E
New Rd., Banstead Newton 72 5A
New Rd., Blackwater 60 1B
New Rd., Bracknell 27 1E
New Rd., Brentford 8 3A
New Rd., Chilworth 101 4E
New Rd., Crowhurst 113 2D
New Rd., Crowthorne 43 1D
New Rd., Deepdene 106 2A
New Rd., East Bedfont 15 1E
New Rd., E. Clandon 83 4F
New Rd., Esher 52 1B
New Rd., Feltham 16 2A
New Rd., Forest Green 123 5F
New Rd., Glanty 13 4F
New Rd., Gomshall 103 3E
New Rd., Hackbridge 39 4E
New Rd., Ham 18 4A
New Rd., Hanworth 16 4B
New Rd., Hydestile 119 5D
New Rd., Kingston 18 5C
New Rd., Limpsfield 94 3A
New Rd., Littleton 33 2D
New Rd., Milford 118 4A
New Rd., Shottermill 151 3E
New Rd., Smallfield 129 2E
New Rd., South Godstone 112 1A
New Rd., Tongham 97 2E
New Rd., West Molesey 35 2D
New Rd., Weybridge 50 1B
New Rd., Wonersh 101 5E
New Rd., Wormley 137 3E
New St., Horsham 158 5B
New St., Staines 14 4A
New St., Three Bridges 147 3E
New Sq. 15 2E
New Town 148 1B
New Way 118 2C
New Wickham La. 13 5E
New Wokingham Rd. 25 5F
New Zealand Av. 33 4F
Newark Cl. 66 4A
Newark Court 34 4B
Newark Cres. 66 4A
Newark La. 66 3A
Newark Rd., Northgate 147 3D
Newark Rd., S. Croydon 57 2F
Newark Rd., Windlesham 45 1F
Newbolt Av. 55 1D
Newbolt Cl. 39 4D
Newbury Gdns. 54 1B
Newchapel Rd. 131 3D
Newcombe Rd. 96 2B
Newdigate 125 3F
Newdigate Rd., Beare Green 125 3F
Newdigate Rd., Rusper 145 3D
Newenham Rd. 86 1A
Newfield Av. 60 4B
Newfield Rd. 78 3C
Newfoundland Rd. 62 3A
Newgate Cl. 16 3C
Newhache 132 3A
Newhaven Cres. 15 4E
Newhaven Rd. 40 3C
Newholme Gdns. 22 3A
Newhouse Cl. 37 4E
Newhouse Farm La. 80 5C
Newhouse Wk. 38 4C
Newlands 137 1E
Newlands Av., T. Ditton 35 4E
Newlands Av., Westfield 65 4D
Newlands Cl., Hersham 51 1F
Newlands Cl., Horley 128 1B
Newlands Corner 102 1A
Newlands Cres. 150 2B
Newlands Dri., Ash Wharf 78 4C
Newlands Dri., Poyle 7 5B
Newlands Park 149 1D
Newlands Pk. 23 4E
Newlands Rd., Camberley 61 2D
Newlands Rd., Horsham 158 4B
Newlands Rd., Norbury 40 1A
Newlands Rd., Southgate 146 4C
Newlands, The 56 2C
Newlands Way 53 1D
Newlands Wood 58 3C
Newman Cl. 147 4F
Newman Rd. 40 4A
Newmarket Rd. 147 5E
Newminster Rd. 38 3C
Newnham Cl. 40 1B
Newport Rd., Aldershot 78 5A
Newport Rd., Chiswick 20 4F
Newquay Rd. 24 3B
Newry Rd. 17 1F
Newsham Rd. 64 2B
Newstead Rd. 24 2C
Newstead Rise 92 1B
Newstead Way 20 3A
Newstead Wk. 38 4C
Newton Av. 9 1D
Newton Court 12 1B
Newton Gro. 9 2D
Newton La. 12 1B
Newton Rd., Crawley 147 2E
Newton Rd., Farnborough 61 4D
Newton Rd., Wimbledon 20 5B
Newton Rd., Woodcote 56 4C
Newton Way 97 1E
Newton Woods Rd. 70 1B
Newtown Rd. 43 4D
Niagara Av. 8 2A
Nicholas Gdns., Lammas Pk. 8 1A
Nicholas Gdns., Ridgway 66 1A
Nicholas Rd. 57 1D
Nicholson Rd. 41 4D
Nicol Cl. 18 1A
Nicola Cl. 57 2E
Nicolsfield 156 4A
Nicosia Rd. 21 2D
Niederwold Rd. 23 4F
Nightingale Av. 84 1B
Nightingale Cl., Cobham 51 4E
Nightingale Cl., Crawley 146 3C
Nightingale Cl., E. Grinstead 150 3C
Nightingale Cl., Hackbridge 39 5E
Nightingale Cl., West Heath 60 4B
Nightingale Cres., Bracknell 27 3D
Nightingale Cres., Horsley 84 1B
Nightingale Cres., Sandhurst 43 4D
Nightingale Dri., Mytchett 61 5F
Nightingale Dri., West Ewell 53 2F
Nightingale Gro. 24 1C
Nightingale La., Clapham 21 2D
Nightingale La., Richmond 18 2B
Nightingale Rd., Claremont 51 2F
Nightingale Rd., E. Molesey 35 3D
Nightingale Rd., Godalming 119 1D
Nightingale Rd., Guildford 82 5A
Nightingale Rd., Hanworth 16 5C
Nightingale Rd., Horsham 158 4B
Nightingale Rd., Horsley 84 1C
Nightingale Rd., Selsdon 58 4C
Nightingale Rd., Walton-on-Thames 34 4A
Nightingale Rd. Hackbridge 39 5E
Nightingale Sq. 21 2E
Nightingale Way 92 5A
Nightingale Wk. 21 1E
Nightingales, Cranleigh 140 2C
Nightingales, The, West Bedfont 15 2D
Nimbus Rd. 54 3A
Nimrod Rd. 21 5E
Ninehams Cl. 74 3C
Ninehams Gdns. 74 3C
Ninehams Rd., Caterham 74 4C
Ninehams Rd., Tatsfield 77 4E
Ninemile Ride 26 5A
Niton Rd. 8 5C
Niven Cl. 147 4F
Niven Ct. 29 3D
Noah's Court 149 5D
Nobles Way 13 5D
Noke Dri. 90 5B
Nonsuch Court Av. 54 3C
Nonsuch Wk. 55 3D
Noons Corner 104 5C
Norbiton Av. 36 1C
Norbiton Common Rd. 36 2C
Norbury Av. 40 1A
Norbury Cl. 40 1B
Norbury Court Rd. 40 2A
Norbury Cres. 40 1A
Norbury Cross 40 2A
Norbury Hill 22 5B
Norbury Rd., Reigate 89 5E
Norbury Rd., Thornton Heath 40 1C
Norbury Rise 40 2A
Norbury Way 86 1B
Norcroft Gdns. 23 2D
Norcutt Rd. 17 2E
Norfolk Av. 58 3A
Norfolk Cl. 128 3B
Norfolk Farm Cl. 65 1F
Norfolk Farm Rd. 65 1F
Norfolk House Rd. 22 3A
Norfolk La. 106 4A
Norfolk Rd., Claygate 52 1B
Norfolk Rd., Colliers W'd 21 5D
Norfolk Rd., Dorking 105 1F
Norfolk Rd., Feltham 16 2B
Norfolk Rd., Holmwood 125 1D
Norfolk Rd., Horsham 158 5B
Norfolk Rd., Thornton Heath 40 2C
Norheads La. 77 2D
Norhyrst Av. 41 2D
Nork 72 1A
Nork Gdns. 55 5D
Nork Rise 72 1A

204
Nork Way
Oakhurst

Nork Way 72 1A
Norlands La. 31 2F
Norley View 92 2F
Norman Av., Epsom 54 4B
Norman Av., Feltham 16 3C
Norman Av., Purley 57 3E
Norman Av., Richmond 18 2A
Norman Court 96 4A
Norman Rd., Cheam 55 1E
Norman Rd., South Wimbledon 20 5C
Norman Rd., Thornton Heath 40 3B
Normanby Cl. 20 1B
Normandy 79 4F
Normandy Cl. 147 5F
Normandy Gdns., Horsham 158 5B
Normandy Wk. 13 4E
Normanhurst 15 4D
Normanhurst Cl. 147 4E
Normanhurst Dri. 17 1F
Normanhurst Rd. 34 5B
Normans Rd. 129 1E
Normansfield Av. 18 5A
Normanton Av. 20 3B
Normanton Rd. 57 2F
Normanton St. 23 3F
Norrels Dri. 84 1C
Norrels Ride 84 1C
Norreys Av. 25 2E
Norris Rd. 14 4A
Norstead Pl. 19 3E
North Acre 72 1B
North Albert Rd. 89 5E
North Av., Carlshalton 56 2B
North Av., Heath End 96 1B
North Av., Whiteley Village 50 3C
North Bourne 100 5B
North Brook Rd., Aldershot 96 1C
North Cheam 38 5A
North Cl., Aldershot 78 5B
North Cl., Cannon Hill 38 2A
North Cl., Dorking 106 3A
North Cl., East Bedfont 15 1E
North Cl., Hawley 60 3C
North Cl., Horsham 158 3B
North Cliffe Cl. 37 4E
North Common 50 1B
North Cott. 26 4C
North Cross Rd. 23 1D
North Down 58 4A
North Downs Cres. 59 3E
North Downs Rd. 59 3E
North Dri., Ifold 155 4F
North Dri., Streatham 21 4F
North Dri., Virginia Water 30 3A
North End 40 5B
North End La. 29 4F
North Farm Rd. 60 3C
North Green 27 1E
North Gro. 32 3A
North Heath La. 158 3B
North Holmwood 106 4A
North Kinver Rd. 23 4E
North La., Aldershot 78 5B
North La., Teddington 17 5F
North Lodge Dri. 28 1A
North Mead, Crawley 147 3D
North Mead, Farnborough 61 5D
North Mead, Redhill 90 4A
North Moors 82 3A
North Parade, Chessington 53 1E
North Parade, Horsham 158 4B
North Park 7 1A
North Park La. 92 4A
North Pl., Mitcham 21 5D
North Pl., Mitcham 21 5D
North Pole La. 59 2F
North Rd., Ash Vale 78 3C
North Rd., Bracknell 27 1F
North Rd., Brentford 8 3B
North Rd., East Bedfont 15 1E
North Rd., Hersham 51 1E
North Rd., Lammas Park 8 1A
North Rd., North Sheen 8 5C
North Rd., South Farnborough 78 2A
North Rd., South Park 108 2B
North Rd., Stoughton 81 4E
North Rd., Surbiton 36 3B
North Rd., Three Bridges 147 3E
North Rd., Waddon 57 1D
North Rd., West Wickham 42 4B
North Rd., Wimbledon 20 5C
North Rd., Woking 65 1D
North St., Carshalton 56 1B
North St., Dorking 105 1F
North St., Egham 13 4D
North St., Farncombe 100 5A
North St., Guildford 100 1C
North St., Horsham 158 5B
North St., Leatherhead 69 4F
North St., Redhill 90 5A
North St., Turners Hill 149 5D
North St., Westcott 105 2D
North St., Winkfield 10 4B
North Side, Tongham 97 1E
North Side, Wandsworth 20 1C
North Spur Rd. 38 5B
North View 19 4F
North View Cres. 71 2F
North Way, Godalming 99 5F
North Way, Wallington 56 1C
North Willey Farm La. 91 1F
North Wk. 59 2E
North Worple Way 9 5D
Northampton Cl. 27 2E
Northampton Rd. 41 5D
Northanger Rd. 22 5A
Northborough Rd. 40 1A
Northbrook Copse 27 3E
Northbrook Rd., Hither Green 24 1C
Northbrook Rd., Selhurst 40 3C
Northcote 49 1F
Northcote Av., Tolworth 36 4C
Northcote Av., Twickenham 17 1F
Northcote Cl. 84 1B
Northcote Cres. 84 1B
Northcote La. 120 1C
Northcote Rd., Ash Vale 78 2C
Northcote Rd., Horsley 84 1B
Northcote Rd., New Malden 37 2D
Northcote Rd., Selhurst 40 3C
Northcote Rd., Twickenham 17 1F
Northcote Rd., Wandsworth 21 1D
Northcote Rd., West Heath 60 4B
Northcroft Cl. 12 4B
Northcroft Gdns. 12 4C
Northcroft Rd., Ealing 8 1A
Northcroft Rd., Englefield Green 12 4B
Northcroft Rd., West Ewell 54 2A
Northcroft Villas 12 4B
Northdown Cl. 158 4C
Northdown La. 101 2D
Northdown Rd., Belmont 55 3E
Northdown Rd., Woldingham 76 5A
Northdowns 140 2C
Northernhay Wk. 38 2A
Northey Av. 55 3D
Northfield, Lightwater 45 4F
Northfield, Witley 137 1E
Northfield Av. 8 1A
Northfield Cl. 78 5B
Northfield Cres. 55 1D
Northfield Pl. 50 2A
Northfield Rd., Cobham 51 5D
Northfield Rd., Laleham 32 1B
Northfields, Ashtead 70 3B
Northfields, Epsom 54 4B
Northfields, Shalford 101 4D
Northgate Av. 147 3E
Northgate Dri. 44 4C
Northgate Pl. 147 3D
Northgate Rd. 147 4D
Northington Cl. 27 3F
Northlands Rd. 158 2C
Northover 24 3C
Northstead Rd. 22 3B
Northumberland Cl. 14 1C
Northumberland Cres. 15 1F
Northumberland Gdns. 39 3F
Northway, Cannon Hill 38 2A
Northway, Guildford 81 4E
Northway Rd. 41 3D
Northwood Av., Purley 57 5E
Northwood Av., Woking 64 2A
Northwood Rd., Carshalton 56 2B
Northwood Rd., Lewisham 23 2F
Northwood Rd., Norbury 40 1B
Northwood Way 22 5C
Norton Av. 36 4C
Norton Gdns. 40 1A
Norton Pk. 28 3C
Norton Rd., Camberley 45 5D
Norton Rd., Wokingham 25 2D
Norwich Av. 61 1E
Norwich Rd., Crawley 147 5E
Norwich Rd., Thorn. H'th. 40 2C
Norwood Cl. 85 2E
Norwood High St. 22 4B
Norwood Hill 127 2D
Norwood Hill Rd. 127 3E
Norwood Park Rd. 22 4C
Norwood Rd., Effingham 85 2E
Norwood Rd., Tulse Hill 22 3B
Nottingham Cl. 64 2A
Nottingham Rd., Waddon 57 1E
Nottingham Rd., Wandsworth 21 2D
Nova Rd. 40 4B
Nowell Rd. 9 3E
Nower Rd. 105 1F
Noyna Rd. 21 3E
Nuffield Dri. 43 3E
Nugee Ct. 43 1D
Nugent Rd., Guildford 100 1A
Nugent Rd., S. Norwood 41 2D
Nunappleton Way 94 4A
Nuneaton 27 3E
Nuns Wk. 30 3C
Nursery Av. 41 5F
Nursery Cl., Capel 125 5D
Nursery Cl., Ewell 54 3B
Nursery Cl., Feltham 16 2A
Nursery Cl., Frimley 61 3E
Nursery Cl., Horsell 64 1C
Nursery Cl., Shirley 41 5F
Nursery Cl., Walton-on-the-Hill 88 1C
Nursery Cl., Woodham 49 3D
Nursery Gdns., Chilworth 101 3E
Nursery Gdns., Staines 14 5B
Nursery Gdns., Upp. Halliford 33 1F
Nursery Hill 120 1C
Nursery La., Ascot Heath 28 1B
Nursery La., Horley 128 3A
Nursery Rd., Farncombe 100 5B
Nursery Rd., Merton 38 1C
Nursery Rd., Mitcham 39 2D
Nursery Rd., Sunbury 33 1F
Nursery Rd., Sutton 55 1F
Nursery Rd., Walton-on-the-Hill 88 1C
Nursery Rd., Wimbledon 20 5A
Nursery Rd., Woking 64 2A
Nursery Way 12 1C
Nurserylands 146 4B
Nutbourne 96 1B
Nutcombe 151 2E
Nutcombe La. 105 1F
Nutcroft Gro. 69 4E
Nutfield 91 5D
Nutfield Marsh Rd. 91 4D
Nutfield Rd., Redhill 90 5B
Nutfield Rd., South Merstham 90 5B
Nutfield Rd., Thornton Heath 40 2B
Nutfield Rd., Woodmansterne 73 1E
Nuthatch Cl. 15 2D
Nuthatch Gdns. 108 2C
Nuthatch Way 158 2B
Nuthurst 27 3E
Nuthurst Av., Cranleigh 140 1C
Nuthurst Av., Streatham 22 3A
Nuthurst Cl. 146 3B
Nutley 26 4C
Nutley La. 89 5E
Nutmeg Court 60 4A
Nutshell La. 96 2A
Nutty La. 33 2E
Nutwell St. 21 4D
Nutwood Av. 107 1D
Nutwood Cl. 107 1D
Nyefield Park Cl. 88 1C
Nylands Av. 8 4C
Nymans Gdns. 37 1F
Nyon Gro. 23 3F

O

Oak Av., Crowthorne 43 3E
Oak Av., Hanworth 16 4C
Oak Av., Sandhurst 43 3E
Oak Av., Shirley 42 5A
Oak Av., Thorpe Lea 13 5F
Oak Bank 65 3D
Oak Cl., Chiddingfold 137 5E
Oak Cl., Copthorne 148 1B
Oak Cl., Morden 38 5C
Oak Cl., Northbourne 100 5A
Oak Corner 125 2D
Oak Cot. Cl. 24 2C
Oak Cottage Cl. 80 5C
Oak Ct. 96 4A
Oak Dell 147 3F
Oak End 125 2D
Oak End Way 49 4D
Oak Farm Cl. 43 5D
Oak Field Gdns. 23 4D
Oak Gdns. 42 5A
Oak Glade 53 4F
Oak Grange Rd. 83 3E
Oak Grn. 156 4A
Oak Gro., Sunbury-on-Thames 16 5A
Oak Gro., W. Wickham 42 5B
Oak Grove Rd. 41 1E
Oak Hill, Burpham 82 3B
Oak Hill, Woodcote 71 1D
Oak La., Englefield Green 12 3C
Oak La., Isleworth 17 1E
Oak La., S. Holmwood 106 5A
Oak La., Twickenham 17 2F
Oak La., Woking 65 1E
Oak Lands 69 5E
Oak Leaf Cl. 54 4A
Oak Lodge Cl. 51 1E
Oak Lodge Dri., Salfords 109 4E
Oak Lodge Dri., W. Wickham 42 4B
Oak Mead 100 5A
Oak Park 49 5D
Oak Pk. Gdns. 20 2A
Oak Rd., Caterham 74 4C
Oak Rd., Cobham 68 1B
Oak Rd., Farnborough Pk. 61 5D
Oak Rd., Farnborough Pk. 61 5D
Oak Rd., Leatherhead Common 69 2F
Oak Rd., New Malden 37 1D
Oak Rd., Reigate 89 5F
Oak Rd., West Green 146 4C
Oak Rd., West Green 146 4C
Oak Ridge 106 3A
Oak Row 39 1F
Oak Shaw 93 2E
Oak Tree Cl., Bisley Common 63 2F
Oak Tree Cl., Burpham 82 3B
Oak Tree Cl., Jacobs Well 81 2F
Oak Tree Cl., Knowlehill 30 4C
Oak Tree Dri., Englefield Grn. 12 4C
Oak Tree Dri., Guildford 81 3F
Oak Tree La. 151 3D
Oak Tree Rd., Bisley 63 3F
Oak Tree Rd., Milford 118 3B
Oak Way, Ashtead 70 1C
Oak Way, Brookwood 64 3A
Oak Way, East Bedfont 15 2F
Oak Way, Northgate 147 3D
Oak Way, Reigate 109 1D
Oak Way, Southborough 36 4A
Oakbank 59 2E
Oakbank Av. 34 4C
Oakcombe Cl. 37 1D
Oakcroft Cl. 49 5D
Oakcroft Rd., Hook 53 1E
Oakcroft Rd., W. Byfleet 49 5D
Oakcroft Villas 53 1E
Oakdale 27 3D
Oakdale Rd., Ewell 54 3A
Oakdale Rd., Streatham 22 4A
Oakdale Rd., Weybridge 33 5D
Oakdale Way 39 4E
Oakdene 29 3D
Oakdene, Burgh H'th 72 3A
Oakdene, Chobham 47 3E
Oakdene Av. 35 4F
Oakdene Cl., Brockham 107 1D
Oakdene Cl., Gt. Bookham 86 2A
Oakdene Cl., Nth. Cheam 38 4B
Oakdene Dri., 37 4D
Oakdene Rd., Brockham 107 2D
Oakdene Rd., Cobham 51 5D
Oakdene Rd., Holloway Hill 119 2D
Oakdene Rd., Lt. Bookham 68 5C
Oakdene Rd., Peasmarsh 100 4C
Oakdene Rd., Redhill 90 5A
Oaken Coppice 70 3C
Oaken Copse Cres. 61 3D
Oaken Dri. 52 2C
Oaken Lane 52 1B
Oakengates 26 4C
Oakfield 64 2A
Oakfield Cl. 37 3E
Oakfield Dri., Reigate 89 4E
Oakfield Dri., Wimbledon 20 3A
Oakfield Gdns., Eden Park 42 3A
Oakfield Gdns., St. Helier 39 4D
Oakfield Glade 50 1B
Oakfield Rd., Ashford 15 4D
Oakfield Rd., Ashtead 70 2B
Oakfield Rd., Blackwater 60 1B
Oakfield Rd., Cobham 51 5D
Oakfield Rd., Croydon 40 4B
Oakfield Rd., Penge 23 5E
Oakfield Way 150 1C
Oakfields, Camberley 43 5F
Oakfields, Crawley 147 3F
Oakfields, Guildford 81 4D
Oakfields, Oakwoodhill 142 3B
Oakfields, Walton-on-Thames 34 4A
Oakfields, West Byfleet 49 5E
Oakhall Dri. 15 4F
Oakham Cl. 24 3A
Oakham Dri. 42 2C
Oakhill, Claygate 52 2C
Oakhill, Surbiton 36 4B
Oakhill, Woodstreet Village 80 4C
Oakhill Cl. 70 2A
Oakhill Cres. 36 4B
Oakhill Dri. 36 4B
Oakhill Gro. 36 3B
Oakhill Path 36 3B
Oakhill Rd., Beckenham 42 1B
Oakhill Rd., Handley Down 134 4A
Oakhill Rd., Horsham 158 5C
Oakhill Rd., Lower Ashtead 70 2A
Oakhill Rd., Mead Vale 108 1C
Oakhill Rd., Norbury 40 1A
Oakhill Rd., Rowhill 49 2D
Oakhill Rd., Surbiton 36 3B
Oakhill Rd., Sutton 55 1F
Oakhill Rd., Wandsworth 20 1B
Oakhurst, Burrowhill 47 3D
Oakhurst, Grayshott 135 5D

Oakhurst Gdns.	150	2B
Oakhurst Lane	156	2A
Oakhurst Rd.	54	2A
Oakhurst Rise	56	3A
Oakington Dri.	34	1B
Oakland Av.	96	1B
Oakland Way	54	2A
Oaklands, Haslemere	152	3A
Oaklands, Horley	128	2C
Oaklands, Kenley	74	1B
Oaklands, S. Godstone	111	2F
Oaklands Av., Esher	35	4E
Oaklands Av., Thornton Heath	40	2A
Oaklands Av., West Wickham	42	5A
Oaklands Cl., Ascot	10	5B
Oaklands Cl., Chessington	53	1D
Oaklands Cl., Shalford	101	4D
Oaklands Court	32	5B
Oaklands Dri., Ascot	10	5B
Oaklands Dri., Earlswood	109	1E
Oaklands Dri., Wokingham	25	2D
Oaklands Gdns.	57	5E
Oaklands La., Biggin Hill	77	1E
Oaklands La., Oaklands	26	5A
Oaklands Pk.	25	3D
Oaklands Rd.	24	5C
Oaklands Way, South Beddington	56	2C
Oaklands Way, Tadworth	72	4A
Oaklawn Rd.	69	2E
Oaklea	78	3C
Oakleigh Av.	36	4C
Oakleigh Rd.	158	3C
Oakleigh Way	39	1E
Oakley Av.	57	1D
Oakley Cl.	49	1E
Oakley Dell	82	4C
Oakley Gdns.	72	1C
Oakley Ho.	100	5A
Oakley Rd., Camberley	61	1D
Oakley Rd., Whyteleafe	75	1D
Oakley Rd., Woodside	41	3E
Oakmead Pl.	39	1D
Oakmead Rd., Balham	21	2E
Oakmead Rd., Beddington	39	3F
Oakridge	46	3A
Oakridge Rd.	24	4C
Oaks Av., Gypsy Hill	22	4C
Oaks Av., Hanworth	16	3B
Oaks Av., Stoneleigh	54	1C
Oaks Av., Worcester Park	37	5F
Oaks Cl.	69	4F
Oaks La.	41	5E
Oaks Rd., Purley	57	5E
Oaks Rd., Reigate	89	5F
Oaks Rd., Stanwell	14	1C
Oaks Rd., Upper Shirley	58	1B
Oaks Rd., Woking	65	2D
Oaks, The, Bracknell	27	1D
Oaks, The, Epsom	54	5B
Oaks, The, West Byfleet	49	5E
Oaks Track	56	4B
Oaks Way, Carshalton Beeches	56	2A
Oaks Way, Epsom	71	3F
Oaks Way, Long Ditton	36	4A
Oaks Way, Purley	57	5E
Oaksford Av.	23	3E
Oakshade Rd., Oxshott	52	5A
Oakshade Rd., Southend	24	4C
Oakshaw Rd.	20	2C
Oakside Court	128	2C
Oakside La.	128	2C
Oaktree Cl., Aldershot	97	1E
Oaktree Cl., Headley	133	4F
Oaktree Cl., Mytchett	78	1C
Oaktree View	96	2B
Oaktree Way	43	3D
Oaktrees	78	5B
Oakview Grove	41	4F
Oakview Rd.	24	4A
Oakway, Aldershot	97	1E
Oakway, Beckenham	42	1B
Oakway, Raynes Park	38	2A
Oakway Dri.	61	2E
Oakwood, Carshalton	56	3B
Oakwood, Guildford	81	3E
Oakwood Av., Beckenham	42	1B
Oakwood Av., Mitcham	39	1D
Oakwood Av., Purley	57	4E
Oakwood Cl., E. Horsley	84	2C
Oakwood Cl., Redhill	90	5B
Oakwood Cl., S. Nutfield	110	1A
Oakwood Court	63	1E
Oakwood Dri., East Horsley	84	2C
Oakwood Dri., Upper Norwood	22	5C
Oakwood Gdns., Bagshot	45	2E
Oakwood Gdns., Knaphill	63	2E
Oakwood Hill	143	3D
Oakwood Rd., Bracknell	27	1E
Oakwood Rd., Brookwood	64	3A
Oakwood Rd., Cottenham Park	37	1F
Oakwood Rd., Horley	128	2B
Oakwood Rd., Virginia Water	30	3C
Oakwood Rd., Warwick Fold	91	3E
Oakwood Rd., Windlesham	46	2A
Oakwoodhill	142	3C
Oakwoodland La.	142	3C
Oareborough	27	2E
Oast House Cl.	13	2D
Oast House Cres.	96	2B
Oast House La.	96	2B
Oast Rd.	93	4F
Oates Wk.	147	5D
Oatfield Rd.	71	4F
Oatlands	146	4B
Oatlands, Horley	128	2C
Oatlands Av.	50	1B
Oatlands Chase	33	5F
Oatlands Cl.	50	1B
Oatlands Dri., Oatlands Park	33	5E
Oatlands Dri., Weybridge	50	1B
Oatlands Grn.	33	5E
Oatlands Mere	33	5E
Oatlands Park	33	5F
Oatlands Rd.	72	3A
Oban Rd.	40	2C
Obelisk Way	44	5A
Oberon Way	146	5A
Observatory Rd.	9	5D
Occam Rd.	100	1A
Occupation La., Ealing	8	2A
Oceansgate	26	4C
Ockenden Cl.	65	2D
Ockenden Gdns.	65	2D
Ockenden Rd.	65	2D
Ockfields	118	4B
Ockford Dri.	118	2C
Ockford Rd.	118	2C
Ockford Ridge	118	2C
Ockham	67	4D
Ockham La.	66	3C
Ockham Road North	67	4D
Ockham Road South	84	1C
Ockley	124	5B
Ockley Court	82	3B
Ockley Rd., Beare Grn.	125	3D
Ockley Rd., Croydon	40	4A
Ockley Rd., Ewhurst	122	5C
Ockley Rd., Ockley	124	4A
Ockley Rd., Streatham	22	4A
Ockleys Mead	92	3B
O'Connor Rd.	78	2B
Octagon Rd.	50	3C
Octavia	26	4C
Octavia Way	14	5A
Odak Dell	147	3F
Odakdale Rd.	22	4A
Odakdene Dri.	37	4D
Odard Rd.	34	2C
Odiham Rd.	95	1E
Okeburn Rd.	21	4E
Okingham Cl.	43	3E
Olave's Wk.	39	1F
Old Acre, W. Byfleet	49	5D
Old Acre, West End	46	4B
Old Av., Sheerwater	48	5C
Old Av., West Byfleet	48	5C
Old Av., Weybridge	50	1B
Old Avenue Cl.	48	5C
Old Barn Cl.	55	2D
Old Barn Dri.	125	5D
Old Barn La., Hindhead	135	2D
Old Barn La., Kenley	75	1D
Old Barn Rd.	71	2D
Old Barn View	118	3C
Old Bisley Rd.	61	2F
Old Bracknell La.	26	2C
Old Bracknell Rd. West	27	2D
Old Brickfield Rd	97	1D
Old Bromley Rd.	24	4B
Old Building St.	36	1A
Old Charlton Rd.	33	3E
Old Chertsey La.	13	4F
Old Chestnut Av.	52	2A
Old Church La.	96	5B
Old Claygate La.	52	2C
Old Common Rd.	51	5D
Old Compton La.	96	4B
Old Court	70	3B
Old Court Rd.	100	1B
Old Cross Tree Way	98	1A
Old Dean Rd.	44	4A
Old Deer Park Gdns.	8	5B
Old Devonshire Rd.	21	2E
Old Dock Cl.	8	3C
Old Esher Rd.	51	1E
Old Farleigh Rd.	58	4B
Old Farm Rd., Guildford	81	4F
Old Farm Rd., Hampton	16	5C
Old Farnham La.	96	5B
Old Ferry Dri.	12	1C
Old Forge Cres.	33	3E
Old Fox Cl.	74	4B
Old Frensham Rd.	115	1E
Old Green La.	44	4A
Old Guildford Rd., Frimley	61	4F
Old Guildford Rd., West Cranleigh	139	2F
Old Haslemere Rd.	152	3A
Old Heron's Lea	130	5A
Old Hill Rd.	64	3C
Old Hollow	148	3A
Old Horsham Rd., Beare Green	125	2D
Old Horsham Rd., Crawley	146	5C
Old House Cl.	54	3B
Old House Gdns.	18	1A
Old Kiln Rd.	134	2B
Old Kingston Rd.	37	5D
Old La., Aldershot	78	5B
Old La., Grayshott	135	5D
Old La., Ockham	67	2E
Old La., Oxted	93	3F
Old La., Tatsfield	77	4E
Old Lane Gdns.	68	4A
Old Lodge Cl.	118	2C
Old Lodge La.	74	1B
Old London Rd., Epsom Downs	71	2F
Old London Rd., Mickleham	87	2D
Old Malden La.	37	5D
Old Malt Way	64	2C
Old Manor Cl.	146	3B
Old Manor Drive	17	1E
Old Manor Gdns.	101	3F
Old Manor La.	101	3F
Old Merrow St.	82	4C
Old Mill La.	90	2C
Old Oak Av.	73	3D
Old Oak Ct.	26	4B
Old Orchard, Byfleet	50	4A
Old Orchard, Sunbury	34	1A
Old Palace La.	18	1A
Old Palace Rd., Croydon	40	5B
Old Palace Rd., Guildford	100	1B
Old Palace Rd., Weybridge	33	5D
Old Park Av.	21	1E
Old Park Cl.	95	2F
Old Park La.	95	1F
Old Pasture Rd.	61	2E
Old Pond Cl.	61	2D
Old Portsmouth Rd.	100	4C
Old Pottery Cl.	108	1B
Old Rd., East Grinstead	150	2C
Old Rd., Row Town	49	2D
Old Rectory Cl., Bramley	120	1A
Old Rectory Cl., Walton-on-the-Hill	71	5F
Old Rectory Dri.	78	5C
Old Rectory Gdns., Farnborough	61	5D
Old Rectory Gdns., Godalming	119	3E
Old Rectory La., E. Hors.	84	2C
Old Redstone Dri.	109	1E
Old Reigate Rd., Dorking	87	5E
Old Reigate Rd., Dorking	88	5A
Old Road, Buckland	88	5B
Old Sawmill La.	43	1D
Old School Cl.	41	1F
Old School Cl.	78	4C
Old School Court	13	2D
Old School La.	106	2C
Old School Mews	50	1B
Old School Pl.	65	4D
Old Schools La.	54	3B
Old Slade La.	7	1B
Old Station Cl.	149	3E
Old Station La.	13	1D
Old Station Way	119	1D
Old Swan Yard	56	1A
Old Town	40	5B
Old Tye Av.	77	1F
Old Westhall Cl.	75	3A
Old Windsor	12	1B
Old Woking	65	4E
Old Woking Rd.	65	2E
Old Wokingham Rd.	26	5A
Oldbury	26	2C
Oldbury Cl., Chertsey	31	4F
Oldbury Cl., Frimley	61	3E
Oldbury Rd.	31	4F
Olde Farm Cl.	43	5D
Olden La.	57	4E
Oldfield Gdns.	70	3B
Oldfield Rd., Hampton	34	1C
Oldfield Rd., Horley	128	3A
Oldfield Rd., Wimbledon	20	5A
Oldfields Rd.	38	5B
Oldham Ter.	9	1D
Oldhouse La., Bisley	46	5B
Oldhouse La., Windlesham	45	2F
Oldlands Hill	27	1D
Oldridge Rd.	21	2E
Oldstead	27	3E
Oldstead Rd.	24	4B
Oldwood Chase	60	5A
Olive Rd.	8	1A
Oliver Av.	41	2D
Oliver Cl., Addlestone	49	1E
Oliver Cl., Brentford	8	3C
Oliver Grove	41	2D
Oliver Rd., Ascot	28	2C
Oliver Rd., Horsham	158	5A
Oliver Rd., New Malden	37	1D
Oliver Rd., Sutton	55	1F
Olivier Rd.	147	4C
Ollerton	26	4C
Olley Cl.	57	2D
Olveston Wk.	39	3D
Omega Rd.	65	1E
Omega Way	31	1F
One Tree Hill Rd.	101	1E
Onetree Cl.	23	1E
Ongar Cl.	49	2D
Ongar Hill	49	2D
Ongar Pl.	49	2D
Ongar Rd.	49	1D
Onslow Av., Cheam	55	3E
Onslow Av., Richmond	18	1B
Onslow Cl., Hinchley Wood	35	4E
Onslow Cl., Woking	65	2E
Onslow Cres.	65	2E
Onslow Dri.	10	5B
Onslow Gdns., Sanderstead	58	4A
Onslow Gdns., Thames Ditton	35	4E
Onslow Gdns., Wallington	56	2C
Onslow Mews	32	3A
Onslow Rd., Burwood Pk.	51	1D
Onslow Rd., Guildford	81	5F
Onslow Rd., New Malden	37	2C
Onslow Rd., Richmond	18	1B
Onslow Rd., Sanderstead	40	4A
Onslow Rd., Sunningdale	29	4F
Onslow St.	100	1C
Onslow Way	66	1A
Ontario Cl.	129	3E
Openfields	133	4E
Openview	20	2C
Opham Rd.	147	5E
Opladen Way	27	3E
Opus Park	81	3F
Orange Court.	43	4E
Orangery, The	18	3A
Orangery, The	18	3A
Orchard Av., Ashford	15	5E
Orchard Av., East Bedfont	15	1E
Orchard Av., Hackbridge	39	4E
Orchard Av., Long Ditton	35	4F
Orchard Av., New Malden	37	2E
Orchard Av., Shirley	41	4F
Orchard Av., Woodham	49	4D
Orchard Cl., Ashford	15	5E
Orchard Cl., Ash Vale	78	3C
Orchard Cl., Badshot Lea	96	2C
Orchard Cl., Banstead	55	5F
Orchard Cl., Effingham Com.	67	5F
Orchard Cl., Egham	13	4E
Orchard Cl., Fetcham	69	4E
Orchard Cl., Hawley	60	2C
Orchard Cl., Horley	128	2A
Orchard Cl., Long Ditton	36	4A
Orchard Cl., West End	46	5B
Orchard Cl., West Ewell	53	2F
Orchard Cl., Woking	65	1E
Orchard Court	37	4E
Orchard Dri., Ashtead	70	3A
Orchard Dri., Woking	65	1D
Orchard End, Caterham	75	4D
Orchard End, Fetcham	69	5E
Orchard End, Rowledge	114	5C
Orchard End, Walton-on-Thames	33	5F
Orchard Field Rd.	100	5A
Orchard Gate, Sandhurst	43	4D
Orchard Gate, Thames Ditton	35	4E
Orchard Gdns., Aldershot	97	1D
Orchard Gdns., Cheam	55	1E
Orchard Gdns., Chessington	53	1E
Orchard Gdns., Cranleigh	14	2C
Orchard Gdns., Cranleigh	140	2C
Orchard Gdns., Effingham	85	2F
Orchard Gdns., Epsom	54	5A
Orchard Gro.	23	5E
Orchard Hill, Bucks Green	157	2E
Orchard Hill, Carlshalton	56	1B
Orchard Hill, Windlesham	46	2A
Orchard La., East Molesey	35	3E
Orchard La., Raynes Park	37	1F
Orchard Lea	66	1A
Orchard Mains	64	3C
Orchard Rd., Badshot Lea	96	2C
Orchard Rd., Brentford	8	3A
Orchard Rd., Burpham	82	3B
Orchard Rd., Cheam	55	1E
Orchard Rd., Chessington	53	1E
Orchard Rd., Dorking	105	2F
Orchard Rd., Hackbridge	39	4E
Orchard Rd., Hampton	16	5C
Orchard Rd., Horsham	158	5C
Orchard Rd., Kingston	36	1B
Orchard Rd., North Farnborough	60	5C
Orchard Rd., North Sheen	8	5C
Orchard Rd., Old Windsor	12	1B

Orchard Rd., Onslow
  Village 100 1B
Orchard Rd., Reigate 89 5F
Orchard Rd., Richmond 17 1F
Orchard Rd., Sanderstead 58 5B
Orchard Rd., Shalford 101 3D
Orchard Rd., Shere 103 3D
Orchard Rd., Smallfield 129 2E
Orchard Rd., Sunbury 16 5A
Orchard Rd., Whitton 16 1C
Orchard Rise, New Malden 37 1D
Orchard Rise, N. Sheen 8 5C
Orchard Rise, Shirley 41 4F
Orchard St. 147 4D
Orchard, The, Bedford Pk. 9 2D
Orchard, The, Bookham 68 5C
Orchard, The, Dorking 106 3A
Orchard, The, Ewell 54 2B
Orchard, The, Gt. Bookham 68 5C
Orchard, The, Ifield 146 4A
Orchard, The, Lightwater 45 4F
Orchard, The, Virginia
  Water 31 3D
Orchard, The, Woking 65 4D
Orchard Way, Addlestone 49 2E
Orchard Way, Aldershot 97 1D
Orchard Way, Camberley 60 2C
Orchard Way, Carshalton 56 1A
Orchard Way, East
  Grinstead 150 2C
Orchard Way, Esher 52 2A
Orchard Way, Lwr.
  Kingswood 89 1E
Orchard Way, Monks
  Orchard 41 4F
Orchard Way, Oxted 94 5A
Orchard Way, Sendgrove 82 1C
Orchard Way, Staines 15 3D
Orchard Way, Wanborough 79 5F
Orchard Way, Woodhatch 108 2C
Orchardleigh 70 4A
Orchid Dri. 63 1E
Orde Cl. 147 2F
Ordnance Cl. 16 3A
Ordnance Rd. 78 4A
Oregano Way 81 3E
Oregon Cl. 37 2D
Orena Rd. 8 5B
Orestan La. 85 2D
Orewell Gdns. 108 1C
Orford Gdns. 17 3F
Oriel Hill 61 1E
Oriental Cl. 65 2D
Oriental Rd., Sunninghill 29 2D
Oriental Rd., Woking 65 2D
Orion 26 4C
Orlands Gdns. 54 3A
Orleans Cl. 35 5E
Orleans Rd., Twickenham 18 2A
Orleans Rd., Upper
  Norwood 22 5C
Orlton La. 143 2E
Ormanton Rd. 23 4E
Orme Rd. 36 1C
Ormeley Rd. 21 2E
Ormond Av. 35 1D
Ormond Cres. 35 1D
Ormond Dri. 17 5D
Ormond Rd., Richmond 18 1B
Ormonde Av. 54 3A
Ormonde Rd., Godalming 119 1D
Ormonde Rd., Horsell 64 1C
Ormonde Rd., Mortlake 9 5D
Ormonde Rd., Wokingham 25 2D
Ormside Way 90 4B
Orpin Rd. 90 3C
Orpwood Cl. 16 5C
Orton Wk. 45 5D
Orwan Cl. 37 2D
Orwell Cl. 60 3B
Osborn La. 23 2F
Osborn Rd., Farnham 96 3B
Osborne Cl., Elmers End 41 2F
Osborne Cl., Frimley 61 3E
Osborne Cl., Hanworth 16 4B
Osborne Dri. 45 4F
Osborne Gdns. 40 1C
Osborne Rd., Acton 8 1C
Osborne Rd., Egham 13 5D
Osborne Rd., Kingston 18 5B
Osborne Rd., Norbury 40 1B
Osborne Rd., Redhill 90 4B
Osborne Rd., South
  Farnborough 78 2A
Osborne Rd., Walton 34 4A
Osborne Rd., Wokingham 25 2E
Osbourne Av. 14 2C
Osbourne Cl. 16 4B
Osier Way 55 5D
Oslac Rd. 24 4B
Osmond Gdns. 56 1C
Osmunda Bank 131 5F
Osnaburgh Hill 43 5F
Osney Wk. 39 3D
Osprey Cl. 69 4D
Osprey Gdns. 58 3C
Ostade Rd. 22 2A

Osterley Cl. 25 2F
Osterley Gdns. 40 1B
Oswald Cl. 69 4D
Osward 59 3D
Osward Rd. 21 3E
Otford Cres. 23 1F
Otter Cl. 48 2B
Otter Mead La. 48 2C
Otterburn St. 21 5E
Otterden St. 24 4A
Ottershaw 48 2B
Otto Cl. 23 3E
Ottways Av. 70 3B
Ottway's La. 70 3A
Otway Cl. 146 5B
Ouseley Rd., Balham 21 2B
Ouseley Rd., Wraysbury 12 2C
Outram Pl. 50 1B
Outram Rd. 41 5D
Outwood 110 5C
Outwood La., Bletchingley 91 5F
Outwood La., Chipstead 73 4D
Outwood Rd. 110 1C
Oval Rd. 40 5C
Oval, The, Banstead 55 5E
Oval, The, Farncombe 100 5A
Oval, The, Guildford 100 1B
Oval, The, West End 46 4B
Oval, The, Woodstreet
  Village 80 5C
Overbrae 24 5A
Overbrook, Godalming 119 1E
Overbrook, W. Horsley 84 3B
Overbury Av. 42 2B
Overbury Cres. 59 3E
Overdale, Ashtead 70 1B
Overdale, Bletchingley 91 5E
Overdale, Dorking 106 1A
Overdale, Goldsworth 64 2B
Overdale Av. 37 1D
Overdale Rd. 8 1A
Overdale Rise 61 1E
Overdene Dri. 146 4B
Overdown Rd. 24 4A
Overford Cl. 140 2C
Overford Dri. 140 2C
Overhill 75 3E
Overhill Rd., Dulwich 23 2D
Overhill Rd., Purley 57 3D
Overhill Way 42 3B
Overland Cl. 44 4A
Oversland Cl. 42 3A
Overstone Gdns. 41 4F
Overstone Rd. 9 2F
Overthorpe Cl. 64 2A
Overton Cl. 97 2D
Overton Rd. 55 2E
Overton Shaw 150 1C
Overton Way 86 1A
Overton's Yd. 40 5B
Ovett Cl. 23 5D
Ovington Court 64 1A
Owen Rd. 46 1A
Owen St. 119 1D
Owens Way 23 2F
Owl Cl. 58 3C
Owlcastle Cl. 158 3B
Owlsmoor La. 27 2E
Owlsmoor Rd. 43 4E
Owlstead Gdns. 58 4A
Ownsted Hill 59 3E
Ox La. 54 3C
Oxdowne Cl. 52 5A
Oxenden Court 97 1E
Oxenden Rd. 97 1E
Oxenhope 26 2C
Oxford Av. 38 1A
Oxford Cl., Feltham 15 5E
Oxford Cl., Mitcham 39 2F
Oxford Cottages 15 3F
Oxford Cres. 37 3D
Oxford Gdns. 8 3C
Oxford Rd., Carshalton
  Beeches 56 2A
Oxford Rd., Fulwell 17 4E
Oxford Rd., Guildford 100 1C
Oxford Rd., Gunnersbury 8 2C
Oxford Rd., Horsham 158 5B
Oxford Rd., Norwood 22 5C
Oxford Rd., Redhill 90 5A
Oxford Rd., South
  Farnborough 78 1A
Oxford Rd., Wokingham 25 1D
Oxford Ter. 100 1C
Oxford Way 16 4B
Oxlip Cl. 41 4F
Oxshott 52 5A
Oxshott Rd. 69 1F
Oxshott Rise 51 5E
Oxshott Way 68 1B
Oxted 93 3F
Oxted Green 118 4A
Oxted Rd. 92 3B
Oyster La. 49 4F

P

Pachesham Dri. 69 1F
Packington Rd. 8 1C
Packway 96 5B
Padbrook 94 3A
Padbury Cl. 15 2F
Paddenswick Rd. 9 1F
Paddock Cl., Camberley 44 5C
Paddock Cl., Cobham 51 5E
Paddock Cl., Hambledon 137 2F
Paddock Cl., Lower
  Sydenham 23 4E
Paddock Cl., Old Malden 37 4E
Paddock Cl., Oxted 93 4F
Paddock Gdns. 23 5D
Paddock Gdns. 150 3C
Paddock Grn., 125 2D
Paddock Grn. Cl. 125 2D
Paddock, The, Bracknell 27 2D
Paddock, The, Bracknell 27 2D
Paddock, The, Godalming 119 3D
Paddock, The, Grayshott 134 5C
Paddock, The, Headley 133 4F
Paddock, The, Merrow 82 5C
Paddock, The, Shottermill 151 2F
Paddock, The, Westcott 105 2D
Paddock Way, Oxted 93 4F
Paddock Way, Sheerwater 48 5B
Paddock Wk. 75 3C
Paddockhurst Rd. 146 4B
Paddocks Cl. 70 2B
Paddocks Mead 64 1A
Paddocks Rd. 82 4B
Paddocks, The, Addington 59 2D
Paddocks, The, Flexford 79 5F
Paddocks, The, Gt.
  Bookham 86 1A
Paddocks, The, Weybridge 33 5F
Paddocks Way, Ashtead 70 3B
Paddocks Way, Chertsey 32 4B
Padua Rd. 41 1E
Padwich Rd. 158 4C
Page Cl. 16 5C
Page Cres. 57 1E
Page Rd. 15 1F
Pageant Walk 40 5C
Pagehurst Rd. 41 4E
Pagerine Gdns. 41 4F
Pages Croft 25 2F
Paget Av. 39 5D
Paget Cl. 17 4E
Paget Pl. 19 5D
Pagoda Av. 8 5D
Paice Green 25 1E
Paines Hill Rd. 94 4B
Pains Hill 139 2F
Paisley Rd. 39 4D
Palace Dri. 33 5E
Palace Green 59 2D
Palace Rd., Crystal Palace 23 5D
Palace Rd., E. Molesey 35 2E
Palace Rd., Kingston 36 2B
Palace Rd., Tulse Hill 22 2A
Palace Sq. 23 5D
Palace View 59 1D
Palestine Gro. 38 1C
Palewell Common Dri. 19 1D
Palewell Pk. 19 1D
Palgrave Rd. 9 1E
Pallingham Dr. 147 5F
Palm Grn. 8 1B
Palm Gro. 81 3F
Palmer Av. 54 1C
Palmer Cl., Earlswood 109 1E
Palmer Cl., Horley 128 1A
Palmer Cl., West Wickham 42 5B
Palmer Cres., Kingston 36 2B
Palmer Cres., Ottershaw 48 2C
Palmer Rd. 147 5F
Palmers Grn. 34 2C
Palmers Rd. 40 1A
Palmersfield Rd. 55 5E
Palmerston Cl. 48 5A
Palmerston Rd., Acton Grn. 9 1D
Palmerston Rd., Carshalton 56 1B
Palmerston Rd., East Sheen 9 5D
Palmerston Rd., Sutton 55 1F
Palmerston Rd.,
  Twickenham 17 1E
Palmerston Rd.,
  Wimbledon 20 5B
Pampisford Rd. 57 4E
Pams Way 54 1A
Pankhurst Dri. 27 3D
Pankhurst Rd. 34 4B
Panmuir Rd. 37 1F
Panmure Rd. 23 3E
Pannell Cl. 150 2C
Pannells 115 1E
Pannells Court, Guildford 159
Pans Gdns. 61 1E
Pantile Rd. 50 1B
Pantiles 64 2B
Papercourt La. 66 1A
Papworth Way 22 2B
Parade Rd. 62 3A

Parade, The, Claygate 52 2B
Parade, The, Epsom 54 5A
Paradise Rd. 18 1B
Paragon Gro. 36 3B
Parbury Rd. 23 1F
Parbury Rise 53 2E
Parchmore Rd. 40 1B
Parchmore Way 40 1B
Pares Cl. 64 1C
Parfour Dri. 74 2B
Parham Rd. 146 3B
Parish Cl. 96 2A
Parish La. 23 5F
Parish Rd. 78 2A
Park Av., Bromley Hill 24 5C
Park Av., Camberley 61 1D
Park Av., Carshalton 56 2B
Park Av., Caterham 74 5C
Park Av., East Sheen 9 5D
Park Av., Salfords 109 4E
Park Av., Staines 14 5A
Park Av., Thorpe Lea 13 5E
Park Av., Tooting 21 5E
Park Av., West Wickham 42 5B
Park Av., Whitton 17 1D
Park Av., Windsor 12 1C
Park Av., Wokingham 25 2D
Park Avenue East 54 2C
Park Avenue West 54 2B
Park Barn Dri. 81 5D
Park Chase, Godalming 119 3D
Park Chase, Guildford 82 5A
Park Cl., Carshalton 56 2B
Park Cl., Claremont 51 2F
Park Cl., Fetcham 69 5E
Park Cl., Grayswood 152 1B
Park Cl., Hampton 35 1D
Park Cl., Isleworth 17 1D
Park Cl., Strood Green 106 3C
Park Cl., Walton 33 5F
Park Cl., Woodham 49 3E
Park Copse 106 1A
Park Corner Dri. 84 2C
Park Court, Hampton Wick 36 1A
Park Court, Hanworth 16 4B
Park Court, Woking 65 2D
Park Cres., Sunningdale 29 3E
Park Cres., Whitton 17 2E
Park Dri., Acton 8 1C
Park Dri., Ashtead 70 2C
Park Dri., Bramley 120 1A
Park Dri., Bromley 42 3C
Park Dri., Cranleigh 141 1D
Park Dri., East Sheen 9 5D
Park Dri., Sunningdale 29 3E
Park Dri., Weybridge 50 1A
Park Dri., Woking 65 2D
Park End 42 1C
Park Farm Cl. 158 2B
Park Farm Rd., Horsham 158 2B
Park Farm Rd., Kingston 18 5B
Park Gdns. 18 4C
Park Green Dri. 69 5D
Park Hall Rd. 22 3C
Park Hill, Carshalton
  Beeches 56 2A
Park Hill, Clapham 21 1F
Park Hill, Richmond 18 1B
Park Hill Cl., Blackwater 60 1B
Park Hill Cl., Carshalton
  Beeches 56 2A
Park Hill Rd., Carshalton 56 2B
Park Hill Rd., Croydon 40 5C
Park Hill Rd., Epsom 54 4B
Park Hill Rd., Shortlands 42 1C
Park Hill Rd., South
  Croydon 57 1F
Park Hill Rise 41 5D
Park Horsley 85 3D
Park House Dri. 108 1B
Park House Gdns. 18 1A
Park La., Ashtead 70 2C
Park La., Brook 136 3A
Park La., Camberley 44 5A
Park La., Carshalton 56 1B
Park La., Cheam 55 2D
Park La., Croydon 40 5C
Park La., Hooley 73 4F
Park La., Lingfield 131 1F
Park La., Merrow 82 4C
Park La., Reigate 89 5E
Park La., Richmond 8 5A
Park La., South Croydon 57 1F
Park La., South Park 108 1B
Park La., Teddington 17 5F
Park La., W. Wickham 42 4A
Park Lane East 108 2B
Park Lawn Av., Horley 128 1B
Park Lawn Rd. 50 1B
Park Leigh Rd. 38 1C
Park Ley Rd. 75 3F
Park Pl., Farnborough Pk. 61 5D
Park Pl., Gunnersbury 8 2C
Park Pl., Hampton 17 5D
Park Rise, Horsham 158 4A
Park Rise, Leatherhead 69 4F
Park Rise Cl. 69 4F

Park Rd., Aldershot 97 1D
Park Rd., Ashford 15 4E
Park Rd., Ashtead 70 3B
Park Rd., Banstead 72 1C
Park Rd., Beckenham 24 5A
Park Rd., Bracknell 27 1D
Park Rd., Brook 102 3C
Park Rd., Burstow 129 3E
Park Rd., Camberley 44 5A
Park Rd., Caterham 74 5C
Park Rd., Cheam 55 2D
Park Rd., Chipstead 73 2D
Park Rd., Chiswick 9 3D
Park Rd., Crowhurst 112 3C
Park Rd., Dormans Park 131 5F
Park Rd., East Grinstead 150 2B
Park Rd., East Molesey 35 2D
Park Rd., Egham 13 4D
Park Rd., Esher 52 1A
Park Rd., Farnham 96 3B
Park Rd., Fickleshole 59 5F
Park Rd., Godalming 119 3D
Park Rd., Guildford 81 5F
Park Rd., Hackbridge 39 5E
Park Rd., Hampton Wick 36 1A
Park Rd., Hanworth 16 4B
Park Rd., Haslemere 152 3A
Park Rd., Isleworth 8 4A
Park Rd., Kempton Park 16 5A
Park Rd., Kenley 74 1B
Park Rd., Kingston 36 1C
Park Rd., Limpsfield 94 2A
Park Rd., New Malden 37 2D
Park Rd., Redhill 90 4A
Park Rd., Richmond 18 1B
Park Rd., Sandhurst 43 4D
Park Rd., Shepperton 33 4D
Park Rd., S. Norwood 40 2C
Park Rd., South Farnborough 78 1B
Park Rd., Stanwell 14 1B
Park Rd., Surbiton 36 3B
Park Rd., Teddington 17 5F
Park Rd., Tooting 21 5D
Park Rd., Twickenham 18 1A
Park Rd., Wallington 56 1B
Park Rd., West 65 2D
Park Rd., Whitton 17 1D
Park Rd., Wimbledon 20 4B
Park Rd., Woking 65 2E
Park Rd., Wokingham 25 2D
Park Road East 8 1C
Park Road North 8 1C
Park Row, Farnham 96 3A
Park Row, Lewisham 23 2F
Park Row Rd. 23 2F
Park St., Bagshot 45 2D
Park St., Camberley 44 5A
Park St., Croydon 40 5C
Park St., Guildford 100 1C
Park St., Horsham 158 5B
Park St., Poyle 7 3A
Park St., Teddington 17 5E
Park Side 49 3E
Park Ter. 37 4E
Park Terrace East 158 5B
Park Terrace West 158 5B
Park, The, Carlshalton 56 1B
Park, The, Eastwick 86 1A
Park, The, Forest Hill 23 3E
Park View, Bagshot 45 2D
Park View, Eastwick 86 1A
Park View, Horley 128 2B
Park View, New Malden 37 2E
Park View Rd., Salfords 109 4E
Park View Rd., Woldingham 75 4F
Park View Ter. 158 5B
Park Way, East Molesey 35 2D
Park Way, Feltham 16 2A
Park Way, Fetcham 69 5D
Park Way, Weybridge 33 5E
Park Wood View 72 1A
Parkcroft Rd. 24 2C
Parkdale Cres. 37 5D
Parke Rd., Barnes 9 4E
Parke Rd., Sunbury-on-Thames 34 2A
Parker Cl. 147 4F
Parker Rd. 57 1F
Parker's Cl. 70 3B
Parkers Hill, Albury 102 3B
Parker's Hill, Ashtead 70 3B
Parker's La. 70 3B
Parkfield, Godalming 119 3D
Parkfield, Ham 18 4B
Parkfield, Horsham 158 4B
Parkfield Av., Feltham 16 3A
Parkfield Av., Mortlake 9 5D
Parkfield Cres. 16 3A
Parkfield Rd. 16 3A
Parkfields, Barnes 9 5F
Parkfields, Crawley 146 4B
Parkfields, Oxshott 52 4B
Parkfields, Shirley 42 4A
Parkfields Cl., Carshalton 56 1B
Parkfields Cl., Ham 18 4B
Parkgate 126 2A
Parkgate Gdns. 19 1D
Parkgate Rd., Parkgate 126 2A
Parkgate Rd., Reigate 108 1C
Parkgate Rd., Wallington 56 1B
Parkhall Rd. 89 4E
Parkhill 23 3E
Parkhill Rd., Blackwater 60 1B
Parkhurst 54 3A
Parkhurst Fields 134 2C
Parkhurst Rd., Guildford 81 5E
Parkhurst Rd., Lee Street 128 2A
Parkhurst Rd., Sutton 55 1F
Parkland Dri. 27 1E
Parkland Gdns. 20 2A
Parkland Gro., Ashford 15 4D
Parkland Gro., Heath End 96 1C
Parkland Rd. 15 4D
Parkland Way 37 5E
Parklands, Addlestone 49 1E
Parklands, Fetcham 69 5D
Parklands, Oxted 93 4F
Parklands, Surbiton 36 3B
Parklands Cl. 19 1D
Parklands Pl. 82 5B
Parklands Rd. 21 4E
Parklawn Av., Epsom 53 5F
Parkleys 18 4B
Parkmead 19 1F
Parkpale La. 106 3C
Parkshot 8 5B
Parkside, Cheam 55 2D
Parkside, Crawley 147 4D
Parkside, East Grinstead 150 2B
Parkside, Hampton 17 4E
Parkside Av. 20 4A
Parkside Cl. 84 1C
Parkside Court 50 1A
Parkside Cres. 37 3D
Parkside Gdns., Chipstead 73 2E
Parkside Gdns., Wimbledon 20 4A
Parkside Pl. 84 1C
Parkside Rd., Hounslow 17 1D
Parkside Rd., Sunningdale 29 3E
Parkstead Rd. 19 1F
Parkstone Dri. 61 1D
Parkthorne Rd. 21 2F
Parkview Rd. 41 4D
Parkview Vale 82 4C
Parkway, Abbotswood 82 5A
Parkway, Camberley 61 1D
Parkway, Cannon Hill 38 2A
Parkway, Dorking 105 1F
Parkway, Horley 128 2B
Parkway, New Addington 59 3E
Parkway, Pound Hill 147 3F
Parkway, Weybridge 50 1B
Parkwood Av. 35 4E
Parkwood Cl. 72 1A
Parkwood Gro. 34 2A
Parkwood Rd., Banstead 72 1A
Parkwood Rd., Nutfield 91 5D
Parkwood Rd., Tatsfield 77 4F
Parkwood Rd., Wimbledon 20 4B
Parley Dri. 64 2C
Parnell Cl. 147 5F
Parnham Av. 46 4A
Parr Av. 54 3C
Parr Cl., Leatherhead 69 3F
Parr Court 16 4B
Parr Dri. 70 2C
Parris Croft 106 3A
Parrs Cl. 57 3F
Parry Cl. 54 2C
Parry Dri. 50 3A
Parry Rd. 40 2C
Parsley Gdns. 41 4E
Parsonage Cl. 75 1F
Parsonage La. 105 2D
Parsonage Rd., Cranleigh 140 1C
Parsonage Rd., Englefield Green 12 4C
Parsonage Rd., Horsham 158 4B
Parsonage Way 61 2E
Parsonage Way 158 4C
Parsonfield Cl. 72 1A
Parsonfield Rd. 72 1A
Parsons Cl., Aldershot 78 5A
Parson's Cl., Haslemere 152 2A
Parsons Cl., Horley 128 2A
Parsons Field 43 4D
Parsons Grn., Guildford 81 4F
Parsons Grn, Haslemere 152 2A
Parsons La. 135 4D
Parson's Mead, Croydon 40 4B
Parsons Mead, Hampton Court 35 2E
Parsons Rd. 81 4F
Parthia Cl. 71 3F
Partridge Cl. 61 2E
Partridge Knoll 57 5E
Partridge La. 126 4B
Partridge Mead 72 1A
Partridge Rd. 16 5C
Partridge Way 82 5C
Partrington Cl. 146 5B
Parvis Rd. 49 5E
Paschal Rd. 44 4C
Pascoe Rd. 24 1B
Pastens Rd. 94 4B
Pasture, The 147 4F
Pasture Rd. 24 2C
Pasture Wood Rd. 123 1E
Patchesham Pk. 69 1F
Patching Cl. 146 3B
Patchings 158 4C
Paterson Rd. 14 4C
Path Fields Cl. 152 2A
Path, The 38 1C
Pathfield 152 2A
Pathfield Cl., Bucks Green 157 2E
Pathfield Cl., Chiddingfold 137 5F
Pathfield Rd., Rudgwick 157 2E
Pathfield Rd., Streatham 22 5A
Pathfields 103 3D
Pathway, The, 83 1D
Patmore La. 50 2C
Patrol Cl. 21 1F
Patten Ash Dri. 25 1E
Patten Rd. 21 2D
Pattenden Rd. 24 2A
Patterdale 49 5D
Patterdale Cl. 146 5C
Patterson Cl. 62 1A
Patterson Ct. 23 5D
Patterson Rd. 23 5D
Paul Gdns. 41 5D
Pauline Cres. 17 2D
Paul's Pl. 70 3C
Paulsmead 131 1F
Pavement, The 147 4D
Pavilion Gdns. 14 5B
Pavilion Way 150 3C
Pawlyne Rd. 23 5E
Pawson's Rd. 40 3B
Pax Cl. 146 5A
Paxton Cl. 34 4B
Paxton Gdns. 48 4C
Paxton Pl. 22 4C
Paxton Rd., Chiswick 9 3D
Paxton Rd., Forest Hill 23 3F
Payley Dr. 25 1F
Paynes Green Rd. 143 3D
Paynesfield Rd. 77 4E
Peabody Estate 22 2B
Peabody Hill 22 2B
Peabody Rd. 78 1A
Peacemaker Cl. 146 5A
Peach St. 25 2E
Peaches Cl. 55 2D
Peacock Av. 15 2E
Peacock Gdns. 58 3C
Peacock La. 26 2B
Peak Hill 23 4E
Peak Rd. 81 4E
Peak, The 23 3E
Peakfield 115 4D
Peaks Hill 56 3C
Peall Rd. 40 3A
Pear Tree Cl., Addlestone 49 1D
Pear Tree Cl., Chessington 53 1F
Pear Tree Cl., Lindford 133 4D
Pear Tree Cl., Mitcham 39 1D
Pear Tree Hill 109 4E
Pear Tree Rd., Addlestone 49 1D
Pear Tree Rd., Ashford 15 4E
Pearce Field 23 2E
Pearce Rd. 35 2D
Pearfield Rd. 23 3F
Pearl Court 64 1A
Pearmain Cl. 33 3E
Pearson Rd. 147 4F
Peartree La. 114 2C
Peary Cl. 158 3B
Peaslake 122 1A
Peaslake La. 122 1B
Peaslake Rd. 122 3B
Peatmore Av. 66 1A
Peatmore Cl. 66 1A
Pebble Coombe 88 3B
Pebble La. 70 4C
Pebblehill Rd. 88 4A
Peckarmans Wood 23 3D
Peckham Rye 23 1E
Peek Cres. 20 4A
Peeks Brook La. 129 5D
Peeks La. 129 2D
Peel Av. 61 3F
Peel Court. 78 2A
Pegasus Av. 78 5B
Pegasus Cl. 151 3D
Pegasus Rd. 57 2E
Pegasus Rd. 60 3C
Pegotty Place 43 3E
Pegwell Cl. 146 5B
Peket Cl. 31 1F
Peldon Court. 18 1B
Peldon Pass. 18 1B
Peleham Rd. 20 5B
Pelham Rd. 41 1E
Pelham Way 86 1A
Pelhams Cl. 51 1F
Pelhams Wk. 34 5C
Pelhams Wk. 51 1F
Pelinore Rd. 24 3C
Pellatt Rd. 23 1D
Pelling Hill 12 2B
Pelton Av. 55 3F
Pemberton Pl. 35 5D
Pemberton Rd. 35 2D
Pembley Grn. 148 1C
Pembroke 26 4C
Pembroke Av., Hersham 51 1E
Pembroke Av., Surbiton 36 3C
Pembroke Broadway 44 5A
Pembroke Cl., Banstead 72 2C
Pembroke Cl., Sunninghill 29 3D
Pembroke Gdns. 65 2E
Pembroke Lodge 29 3D
Pembroke Rd., Crawley 147 2F
Pembroke Rd., Thorn. H. 40 2C
Pembroke Rd., Woking 65 2E
Pembroke Villas 8 5A
Pembury Av. 37 4F
Pembury Cl., Coulsdon 56 5B
Pembury Cl., Hayes 42 4C
Pembury Pl. 78 5A
Pembury Rd. 41 2D
Pemdevon Rd. 40 4B
Penates 52 1B
Penberth Rd. 24 2B
Pendarves Rd. 37 1F
Pendell Rd. 91 4E
Pendennis Cl. 49 5D
Pendennis Rd. 22 4A
Penderel Rd. 16 1C
Penderry Rise 24 3B
Pendle Rd. 21 5E
Pendlebury 26 4C
Pendleton Cl. 109 1D
Pendleton Rd. 108 2C
Pendragon Rd. 24 3C
Pendragon Way 62 1A
Penerley Rd. 24 2A
Penfold Rd. 147 5F
Penge 23 5E
Penge La. 23 5E
Penge Rd. 41 2D
Penhurst 48 5A
Peninsula Cl. 15 1F
Penistone Rd. 22 5A
Pennard Rd. 9 1F
Pennards, The 34 2B
Penner Cl. 20 3A
Pennine Way 60 3B
Pennings Av. 81 4D
Pennington Dri. 33 5F
Penns Wood 78 1A
Penny Croft 58 3C
Penny Dri. 80 5C
Penny La. 33 4F
Pennyfield 51 5D
Pennymead Dri. 84 2C
Pennymead Rise 84 2C
Pennypot La. 46 5C
Penrhyn Rd. 36 2B
Penrith Cl., Putney 20 1A
Penrith Cl., Redhill 90 5A
Penrith Rd., Beulah Hill 40 1C
Penrith Rd., New Malden 37 2D
Penrith St. 21 5F
Penrose Rd. 69 4D
Penryn Dr. 134 4B
Pensfold Av 8 4C
Penshurst 27 3E
Penshurst Grn. 42 3C
Penshurst Rd. 40 3B
Penshurst Rise 61 3F
Penshurst Way 55 3E
Pentelow Gdns. 16 1A
Pentland Av. 33 3D
Pentland Pl. 60 3B
Pentland St. 20 1C
Pentlow St. 9 4F
Pentney Rd. 21 2F
Penton Av. 14 5A
Penton Hall Dri. 32 1A
Penton Hook Rd. 14 5A
Penton Rd. 14 5A
Pentreath Av. 100 1B
Pentwith Dri. 151 3E
Penwith Rd. 20 3B
Penwith Wk. 64 3C
Penwood End 64 4B
Penwood Gdns. 26 3B
Penwortham Rd., Sanderstead 57 3F
Penwortham Rd., Streatham Vale 21 5F
Peperham Rd. 152 2A
Peperharow La. 99 5D
Peperharow Rd. 118 1C
Pepper Box La. 120 5C
Pepper Cl. 91 1F
Pepys Cl. 70 2C
Pepys Rd. 38 1A
Percival Rd., Felthanm 15 3F
Percival Rd., Mortlake 9 5D
Percival Way 54 1A
Percy Av. 15 4D

Percy Bryant Rd. 15 5F
Percy Gdns. 37 4D
Percy Rd., Anerley 41 1E
Percy Rd., Guildford 81 4E
Percy Rd., Hackbridge 39 4E
Percy Rd., Hammersmith 9 1E
Percy Rd., Hampton 16 5C
Percy Rd., Horsham 158 4A
Percy Rd., Whitton 17 2D
Percy Rd., Woodside 41 3D
Percy Way 17 2D
Peregrine Cl. 26 3C
Peregrine Cl., Bracknell 27 3D
Peregrine Cl., Cranleigh 140 1C
Peregrine Rd. 33 1F
Perimeter Rd. East, Gatwick 128 5B
Perimeter Rd. North, Gatwick 128 4A
Periwinkle Cl. 133 4D
Perkins Court 14 4C
Perkins Way 25 2D
Perleybrooke La. 64 2B
Perran Rd. 22 3B
Perrin Cl. 14 4C
Perring Av. 60 3B
Perrings 23 3D
Perrior Rd. 100 5A
Perry Av. 150 1C
Perry Cl. 119 1E
Perry Hill 24 3A
Perry Oaks 27 1E
Perry Rise 23 3F
Perry Vale 23 3E
Perry Way, Bracknell 27 1E
Perry Way, Headley 133 5F
Perry Way, Lightwater 45 4E
Perryfield Rd. 146 4C
Perryfield Way 18 3A
Perryhow 37 4E
Perryland La. 129 3D
Perrylands 127 5E
Perrywood Business Pk. 109 4E
Persant Rd. 24 3C
Persfield Cl. 54 3B
Pershore Gro. 39 3D
Perth Cl. 37 1E
Perth Rd. 42 1B
Peter Av. 93 3E
Peterborough Rd., Carshalton 39 3D
Peterborough Rd., Guildford 81 4D
Peterhouse Cl. 43 3F
Peterhouse Par. 147 3F
Petersfield Av. 14 5B
Petersfield Cres. 74 1A
Petersfield Rd., Ealing 9 1D
Petersfield Rd., Staines 14 4B
Petersham Av. 49 4F
Petersham Cl., Byfleet 49 4F
Petersham Cl., Cheam 55 1E
Petersham Cl., Ham 18 3B
Petersham Rd. 18 1B
Peterwood Way 40 5A
Petridge Rd. 109 3D
Petters Rd. 70 1B
Pettiward Cl. 9 5F
Petts La. 33 2D
Petworth Cl., Coulsdon 73 3F
Petworth Cl., Frimley 61 3E
Petworth Dri. 158 2C
Petworth Gdns. 37 2F
Petworth Rd., Chiddingfold 137 5F
Petworth Rd., Fisherstreet 153 4E
Petworth Rd., Haslemere 152 3A
Petworth Rd., Milford 118 4B
Petworth Rd., Witley 137 1E
Pevensey Cl. 147 1F
Pevensey Rd., Tooting 21 4D
Pevensey Way 61 3F
Peverel Rd. 146 4A
Peveril Dri. 17 4C
Pewley Bank 101 1D
Pewley Hill 100 1C
Pewley Way 101 1D
Pewsey Vale 27 3F
Pheasant Cl. 57 5E
Philanthropic Rd. 109 1E
Philip Gdns. 41 5F
Philip Rd. 14 5C
Phillips Cl., Godalming 118 3C
Phillips Cl., Lindford 133 4D
Phillips Cres. 133 4F
Phillips Hatch 101 5E
Philpot La. 47 4F
Phipps Bridge Rd. 38 1C
Phoenix Cl. 42 5C
Phoenix Rd. 23 5E
Phyllis Av. 37 3F
Pickering 26 2C
Picket Post Cl. 27 2F
Pickets Hill 133 2F
Picketts La. 109 4F
Pickhurst Green 42 4C
Pickhurst La. 42 3C
Pickhurst Mead 42 4C
Pickhurst Pk. 42 3C

Pickhurst Rd. 154 1A
Pickhurst Rise 42 4B
Pickwick Rd. 22 2C
Picquets Way 72 2B
Pier Rd. 16 1A
Piermont Rd. 23 1E
Pierre-Fondes Av. 61 4D
Pigbush La. 156 2A
Pigeon La. 16 4C
Pigeonhouse La., Coulsdon 72 5C
Pigeonhouse La., Winkfield 10 3A
Piggot Rd. 25 1E
Pikes Hill 54 5B
Pikes La. 112 4C
Pilgrims Cl., Farnham 96 5A
Pilgrims Cl., Shere 103 3D
Pilgrim's Cl., West Humble 86 4C
Pilgrims La., Caterham 91 1E
Pilgrims La., Titsey 77 5E
Pilgrims View 98 1A
Pilgrims Way, Bisley 63 1E
Pilgrims Way, Guildford 101 2D
Pilgrim's Way, Puttenham 98 3B
Pilgrim's Way, Reigate 89 4E
Pilgrims' Way, S. Croydon 58 2A
Pilgrims' Way, Shere 103 3D
Pilgrims' Way, West Humble 87 4D
Pilsden Cl. 20 2A
Pimms Cl. 82 4B
Pinckards 137 4E
Pincott La. 84 3A
Pine Av., Camberley 61 1E
Pine Av., West Wickham 42 4A
Pine Bank 135 5E
Pine Cl., Ash Vale 78 3C
Pine Cl., Coulsdon 74 2C
Pine Cl., Crawley 146 2C
Pine Cl., Woking 64 2C
Pine Cl., Woodham 49 4E
Pine Coombe 58 1C
Pine Cres. 55 4F
Pine Dri. 60 1B
Pine Gdns., Horley 128 3B
Pine Gdns., Surbiton 36 3C
Pine Grn., Felbridge 150 1A
Pine Grn., Wimbledon 20 4B
Pine Gro., Farnham 115 1E
Pine Gro., Updown Hill 46 2A
Pine Gro., Weybridge 50 1B
Pine Grove Mews 50 1B
Pine Hill 71 1D
Pine Hurst 158 4B
Pine Mount Rd. 61 1E
Pine Pl. 55 5D
Pine Rd. 64 3C
Pine Ridge 56 3B
Pine Tree Hill Rd. 65 1F
Pine View 134 4A
Pine View Cl., Albury 102 3A
Pine View Cl., Haslemere 152 2A
Pine View Cl., Badshot Lea Rd., Farnham 96 2C
Pine Way 12 5B
Pine Way Cl. 150 3C
Pine Wk., Carshalton Beeches 56 4A
Pine Wk., Caterham 75 4D
Pine Wk., Chipstead 73 2D
Pine Wk., Cobham 51 5E
Pine Wk., East Horsley 84 2C
Pine Wk., Great Bookham 86 1A
Pine Wk., Surbiton 36 3C
Pinecote Dri. 29 4E
Pinecroft Rd. 25 4D
Pinedean 86 1A
Pinedean 86 1A
Pinefields Cl. 43 2D
Pinehill Rd. 43 2D
Pinehurst, S. Farnborough 78 1A
Pinehurst, Sunninghill 29 3D
Pineridge Dri. 115 1D
Pines Dri. 25 5D
Pines, The, Coulsdon 73 2E
Pines, The, Dorking 105 2F
Pines, The, Sunbury-on-Thames 34 2A
Pines, The, Woking 48 5A
Pine-Tree Cl. 148 1B
Pinewood 34 1A
Pinewood Av., Crowthorne 43 1D
Pinewood Av., New Haw 49 3E
Pinewood Cl., Shirley 41 5F
Pinewood Cl., Woking 65 1E
Pinewood Cres. 60 4A
Pinewood Dri. 14 4A
Pinewood Gdns. 45 2D
Pinewood Gro. 49 3E
Pinewood Pk., Hawley 60 3B
Pinewood Pk., Woodham 49 4E
Pinewood Pl. 54 1A
Pinewood Rd., Virginia Water 30 2B
Pinewood Rd., Wyke 79 4D
Pinfold Rd. 22 4A
Pink Walk, Bookham 86 1A
Pinkcoat Cl. 16 3A

Piper Rd. 36 2C
Pipers Cl. 68 1B
Pipers End 30 2C
Pipers Gdns. 41 4F
Pipewell Rd. 39 3D
Pippins Ct., Ashford 15 5D
Piquet Rd. 41 1E
Pirbright 63 5D
Pirbright Cres. 59 2E
Pirbright Rd., Farnborough Park 61 5D
Pirbright Rd., Southfields 20 2B
Pirbright Rd., Wyke 79 4E
Pit Farm Rd. 82 5B
Pit Wood Green 71 3F
Pitcairn Rd. 21 5D
Pitch Place Rd. 135 2E
Pitchfont La. 94 1A
Pitfold Av. 151 3E
Pitfold Cl. 151 3E
Pitlake 40 5B
Pitson Cl. 49 1F
Pitt Cres. 20 4B
Pitt La. 115 5D
Pitt Rd., Epsom 54 5B
Pitt Rd., Thornton Heath 40 3C
Pitt Way 60 4C
Pitville Gdns. 41 2D
Pitwood Pk. 71 3F
Pixham 87 5D
Pixham La. 87 5D
Pixholme Gro. 87 5D
Pixton Way 58 3C
Place Farm Rd. 91 3F
Placehouse La. 74 3A
Plain Ride 11 2D
Plaistow 155 4D
Plaistow Rd., Chiddingfold 137 5F
Plaistow Rd., Dunsfold 139 5D
Plaistow St. 131 2E
Plane Tree Cres. 16 3A
Planes, The 32 4B
Plantagenet Cl. 54 1A
Plantain Cres. 146 5C
Plantation La. 75 3F
Plantation Row 43 5F
Plassy Rd. 24 2B
Plat, The 158 4A
Platt Meadow 82 4C
Platt, The 132 4A
Plaws Hill 122 1B
Plawsford Rd. 41 1F
Playfield Cres. 23 1D
Playgreen Way 24 4A
Pleasance Rd. 19 1F
Pleasance, The 9 5F
Pleasant Gro. 42 5A
Pleasant Pl. 51 2E
Pleasure Pit Rd. 70 2C
Plesman Way 57 3D
Plevna Rd. 35 1D
Pleydell Av., Penge 23 5D
Pleydell Av., Stamford B'k 9 2E
Plough Cl. 146 3B
Plough La., Cobham 68 2A
Plough La., Erwell 23 1D
Plough La., Ewhurst 123 5D
Plough La., Ewhurst Green 141 1F
Plough La., Horsham 158 3C
Plough La., Purley 57 3D
Plough La., Waddon 57 1D
Plough La., Wimbledon 20 4C
Plough La., Wokingham 25 1F
Plough Lands 26 1C
Plough Rd., Dormans Land 132 3A
Plough Rd., Ewell 54 3A
Plough Rd., Smallfield 129 2E
Ploughmans End 17 1E
Plover Cl., Crawley 146 3C
Plover Cl., Staines 14 3A
Plover La. 63 4D
Plover Rd. 158 4C
Plumgarth 8 2B
Plummer La. 39 1D
Plummer Rd. 21 1F
Plumptom Way 39 5D
Pockford Rd. 138 5A
Pointers Hill 105 2D
Pointers Rd. 67 1E
Polden Cl. 60 3B
Polecat Alley 42 5C
Polecat Dri. 151 2E
Polecat Hill 151 1E
Polecat Valley 151 1E
Polecroft La. 24 3A
Poles La. 146 1C
Polesden Gdns 37 1F
Polesden Lacey 86 3A
Polesden Rd. 86 2A
Polesden View 86 2A
Polesdon La. 66 4A
Polesteeple Hill 77 2E
Police Station Rd., Godstone 92 4B
Police Station Rd., Hersham 51 2E
Pollard Grn. 62 1A
Pollard Rd., Morden 39 3D

Pollard Rd., Woking 65 1E
Pollardrow Av. 26 1C
Pollards Cross 40 2A
Pollards Dri. 158 4C
Pollards Hill East 40 2A
Pollards Hill North 40 2A
Pollards Hill South 40 2A
Pollards Hill West 40 2A
Pollards Oak Cres. 94 4A
Pollards Oak Rd. 94 4A
Pollards Wood Hill 94 3A
Pollards Wood Rd., Hurst Green 94 4A
Pollards Wood Rd., Norbury 40 2A
Polsted La. 99 4F
Polsted Rd. 24 2A
Poltimore Rd. 100 1B
Polworth Rd. 22 4A
Pond Cl., Loxwood 156 3A
Pond Cl., Weybridge 50 2C
Pond Copse La. 156 3A
Pond Cottage Rd. 42 4A
Pond Field Rd. 157 2F
Pond Head 22 1C
Pond Hill Gdns. 55 2D
Pond Hotel Rd. 115 5D
Pond La., Frensham 134 1A
Pond La., Peaslake 122 1B
Pond Meadow 81 5D
Pond Piece 52 5A
Pond Pl. 70 2B
Pond Rd., Egham 13 5E
Pond Rd., Headley Down 134 5A
Pond Rd., Woking 64 3B
Pond Way 18 5A
Pond Wood Rd. 147 3E
Pondfield La. 155 4E
Pondfield Rd., Coulsdon 74 2B
Pondfield Rd., Goldalming 119 1E
Pondfield Rd., W. Wickham 42 4C
Pondhead La. 50 3C
Pondmoor Rd. 27 3D
Ponds, The 50 2C
Ponds, The 50 2C
Pondtail Cl. 158 3B
Pondtail La. 158 3B
Pondtail Rd. 158 3B
Ponsonby Rd. 19 2F
Pontefract Rd. 24 4C
Pony Chase 51 5F
Pook Hill 137 5E
Pool Cl., Bellingham 24 4A
Pool Cl., W. Molesey 34 3C
Pool Rd., Aldershot 97 1D
Pool Rd., W. Molesey 34 3C
Poole End Cl. 33 3D
Poole Rd., West Ewell 54 2A
Poole Rd., Woking 65 2D
Pooley Av. 13 4E
Pooley Green Cl. 13 4E
Pooley Green Rd. 13 4E
Pope Cl. 15 2F
Popes Av. 17 3E
Pope's Grove 17 3E
Pope's La., Ealing 8 1A
Popes La., Oxted 112 1C
Popes Mead 152 2A
Popeswood Rd. 26 1B
Popham Cl., Bracknell 27 3E
Popham Cl., Hanworth 16 3C
Popham Gdns. 8 5C
Poplar Av., Leatherhead 70 4A
Poplar Av., Mitcham 39 1E
Poplar Av., Windlesham 45 1F
Poplar Cl., Crawley 146 2C
Poplar Cl., Mytchett 61 5F
Poplar Cl., Poyle 7 4B
Poplar Court 20 4B
Poplar Cres. 53 2F
Poplar La., Banstead 55 5D
Poplar Farm Cl. 54 2A
Poplar Gdns. 37 1D
Poplar Gro., New Malden 37 2D
Poplar Gro., Woking 65 3D
Poplar Rd., Ashford 15 4E
Poplar Rd., Leatherhead 70 4A
Poplar Rd., Merton 38 1B
Poplar Rd., North Cheam 38 4B
Poplar Rd., Shalford 101 4D
Poplar Road South 38 2B
Poplar Way 16 3A
Poplar Wk., Caterham 75 5D
Poplar Wk., Croydon 40 5B
Poplar Wk., Heath End 96 1B
Poplars Cl. 60 4A
Poplars, The 158 4C
Poppy Cl. 39 4E
Poppy La. 41 4E
Poppyhills Rd. 44 4B
Porchester Mead. 24 5A
Porchester Rd., Ascot 28 2C
Porchester Rd., Kingston 36 1C
Porchfield Cl. 55 3F
Port Way 63 2E
Portal Cl. 22 3B
Portesbery Hill Dri. 44 5B

Portesbery Rd.	44	5A
Porthcawe Rd.	23	4F
Portinscale Rd.	20	1A
Portland Av.	37	4E
Portland Cres.	15	4E
Portland Dri.	90	3C
Portland Pl.	54	4B
Portland Rd., Ashford	14	3C
Portland Rd., Dorking	105	1F
Portland Rd., East Grinstead	150	3C
Portland Rd., Kingston	36	2B
Portland Rd., Mitcham	39	1D
Portland Rd., South Norwood	41	2D
Portland Ter.	8	5A
Portley La.	74	4C
Portley Wood Rd.	75	3D
Portman Av.	9	5D
Portman Pl.	26	1C
Portman Rd.	36	1C
Portmore Park Rd., Portmore Park	33	5D
Portmore Park Rd., Weybridge	50	1A
Portmore Pk.	33	5E
Portmore Quays	50	1A
Portmore Way	33	5D
Portnall Dri.	30	3A
Portnall Rd.	30	3A
Portnall Rise	30	3A
Portnalls Cl.	73	1F
Portnalls Rd.	73	2E
Portnalls Rise	73	1F
Portsmouth Av.	35	4F
Portsmouth Rd., Camberley	44	5C
Portsmouth Rd., Cobham	51	4E
Portsmouth Rd., Esher	35	5D
Portsmouth Rd., Frimley	61	2D
Portsmouth Rd., Guildford	100	2C
Portsmouth Rd., Hindhead	135	5E
Portsmouth Rd., Long Ditton	36	3A
Portsmouth Rd., Milford	118	4A
Portsmouth Rd., Ripley	66	5B
Portsmouth Rd., Roehampton	19	2F
Portsmouth Rd., Witley	117	5E
Portugal Gdns.	17	3D
Portugal Rd.	65	1D
Portway	54	3B
Portway Cres.	54	3B
Post La.	17	2E
Post Office Row	94	4C
Posthouse La.	86	1A
Postmill Cl.	41	5F
Poteries La.	61	5E
Potteries, The	60	4B
Potterne Cl.	20	2A
Potters Cl.	118	3B
Potters Cres.	78	5C
Potters Croft	158	5C
Potters Gate	96	4A
Potters Gro.	37	2D
Potters La., Sendgrove	65	5E
Potters La., Send Heath	82	1B
Potters Way	108	2C
Pottery Court	114	1C
Pottery La.	114	1C
Pottery Rd.	8	3B
Poulcott	13	1D
Poulett Gdns.	17	2F
Poulton Av.	39	5D
Pound Cl., Loxwood	156	3A
Pound Cl., Southborough	36	4A
Pound Court, Ashtead	70	2B
Pound Court, Woodstreet Village	80	5C
Pound Cres.	69	4E
Pound Farm La.	79	5D
Pound Hill	80	5C
Pound Hill Place	147	4F
Pound La., Epsom	54	4A
Pound La., Updown Hill	46	2A
Pound La., Woodstreet	80	5C
Pound Pl.	101	4D
Pound Place Cl.	101	3D
Pound Rd., Aldershot	78	5A
Pound Rd., Banstead	72	2B
Pound Rd., Chertsey	32	4B
Pound St.	56	1A
Poundfield	81	5F
Poundfield Gdns.	65	3E
Poundfield La.	155	4E
Poundfield Rd.	65	3E
Povey Cross Rd.	128	3A
Powder Mill La.	16	2C
Powell Cl., Guildford	100	1A
Powell Cl., Horley	128	2A
Powell Cl., Roundshaw	57	2D
Powells Cl.	106	3A
Power Rd.	8	2C
Powers Ct.	18	2A
Poyle	7	4A
Poyle Rd., Colnbrook	7	5A
Poyle Rd., Guildford	101	1D
Poyle Rd., Tongham	97	2E
Poynders Gdns.	21	2F
Poynders Rd.	21	1F
Poynes Rd.	128	1A
Poynings Rd.	146	4A
Poynings, The	7	2B
Prairie Cl.	32	5B
Prairie Rd.	32	5B
Pratts La.	51	1E
Prebend Gdns.	9	2E
Prentice Cl.	60	3C
Prentis Rd.	21	4F
Presburg Rd.	37	3E
Prescot Rd.	7	4A
Prescott	26	4C
Prestbury Cres.	73	1D
Preston Cl.	17	3E
Preston Dri.	54	2B
Preston Gro.	70	2A
Preston La.	71	4F
Preston Pl.	18	1B
Preston Rd., Cottenham Park	19	5E
Preston Rd., Shepperton	33	3D
Preston Rd., Upper Norwood	22	5B
Prestwick Cl.	146	4A
Prestwick La.	137	5D
Prestwood Cl.	146	2C
Prestwood La., Ockley	145	2F
Prestwood La., Rusper	146	1A
Pretoria Rd., Chertsey	32	4A
Pretoria Rd., Tooting	21	5F
Prey Heath Cl.	64	5C
Prey Heath Rd.	64	5B
Price Cl.	21	3D
Price Rd.	57	1E
Price's La.	108	2B
Prickley Wood	42	5C
Prides Crossing	10	5B
Pridham Rd.	40	2C
Priest Av.	25	2F
Priest Hill	12	3C
Priest La.	63	1D
Priestcroft Cl.	146	4B
Priestfield Rd.	23	3F
Priestley Gdns.	65	3E
Priestley Rd., Guildford	100	1A
Priestley Rd., Mitcham	39	1E
Priestley Way	147	1E
Priests Bridge	9	5E
Priestwood Av.	26	1C
Priestwood Court	26	1C
Primrose Av.	128	3B
Primrose Cl., Hackbridge	39	4E
Primrose Cl., Southend	24	4B
Primrose Dri.	63	1E
Primrose La.	41	4F
Primrose Rd.	51	1E
Primrose Ridge	118	3C
Primrose Way, Bramley	119	1F
Primrose Way, Sandhurst	43	3D
Primrose Wk., Bracknell	27	3D
Primrose Wk., Ewell	54	2B
Primula Rd.	133	5D
Prince Albert Dri.	28	2A
Prince Albert Sq.	109	3E
Prince Andrew Way	28	1A
Prince Charles Rd.	61	3D
Prince Charles Way	39	5E
Prince Consort Dri., Ascot	28	2A
Prince Consorts Dri., Windsor	11	2E
Prince Georges Av.	38	1A
Prince George's Rd.	39	1D
Prince Of Wales' Rd., Outwood	110	4B
Prince Of Wales Rd., Sutton	39	5D
Prince Rd.	40	3C
Princes Av., Acton	8	1C
Prince's Av., Aldershot	78	3A
Princes Av., Carshalton Beeches	56	2A
Princes Av., Hamsey Green	75	1E
Princes Av., Tolworth	36	4C
Princes Cl.	75	1E
Princes Rd., Ashford	15	4D
Princes Rd., Brentford	8	4B
Prince's Rd., Earlswood	109	2E
Princes Rd., Egham	13	5D
Princes Rd., Feltham	15	3F
Princes Rd., Fulwell	17	4E
Princes Rd., Penge	23	5F
Prince's Rd., Weybridge	50	1B
Prince's Rd., Wimbledon	20	5B
Princes St.	55	1F
Princes Way, Bagshot	45	3D
Princes Way, Southfields	20	2A
Princes Way, Waddon	57	1D
Princess Anne Rd.	157	3F
Princess Cl.	17	4E
Princess Dri.	52	4B
Princess Gdns.	65	1E
Princess Margaret Rd.	157	2E
Princess Mary's Rd.	49	1E
Princess Rd., Richmond	18	1B
Princess Rd., Thornton Heath	40	3B
Princess Rd., West Green	146	4C
Princess Rd., Woking	65	1E
Princess Sq.	27	1D
Princess Way, Camberley	44	5A
Princess Way, Redhill	90	5B
Princethorpe Rd.	23	4F
Pringle Gdns.	21	4F
Prior Av.	56	2A
Prior Croft Cl.	61	1F
Prior End	44	5C
Prior Rd.	44	5C
Prioress Rd.	22	3B
Priors Cl., Compton	99	4E
Priors Cl., Farnborough	60	3C
Priors Court, Tongham	97	1E
Priors Court, Woking	64	2B
Priors Croft	65	3E
Prior's Field Rd.	99	4E
Prior's Hatch La.	99	4E
Priors Mead	86	1A
Priors, The	70	3A
Priors Wk.	147	4D
Priorswood	151	3E
Priory Av., Bedford Park	9	2E
Priory Av., Cheam	55	1D
Priory Cl., Broomhall	29	4E
Priory Cl., Dorking	105	2F
Priory Cl., Elmers End	41	2F
Priory Cl., Kempton Park	16	5A
Priory Cl., Lee Street	128	2A
Priory Cl., Walton	34	5A
Priory Cl., West Byfleet	48	5C
Priory Cres.	55	1D
Priory Dri.	108	1B
Priory Gdns., Hampton	34	1C
Priory Gdns., Upper Norwood	21	5D
Priory Grn.	14	4B
Priory La., Frensham	115	4E
Priory La., Kew	8	3C
Priory La., Molesey	35	2D
Priory La., Roehampton	9	5E
Priory Rd., Acton Green	9	1D
Priory Rd., Bracknell	27	1F
Priory Rd., Cheam	55	1D
Priory Rd., Croydon	40	4B
Priory Rd., Hampton	16	5C
Priory Rd., Hook	36	5B
Priory Rd., Kew	8	3C
Priory Rd., South Park	108	1B
Priory Rd., Sunningdale	29	4E
Priory Rd., Tooting	21	5D
Priory Rd., Whitton	17	1D
Priory St.	61	5D
Priory Ter.	16	5A
Priory, The,	92	4B
Priory Wk.	27	2E
Privet Rd.	133	1E
Probyn Rd.	22	3B
Proctor Gdns.	86	1A
Proctor Rd.	25	2F
Profumo Rd.	51	1E
Progress Way	40	5A
Promenade Approach Rd.	9	3D
Promenade de Verdun	56	4C
Prospect Av.	61	4D
Prospect Cl.	23	4E
Prospect Cres.	17	1D
Prospect Hill	133	3F
Prospect La.	12	4B
Prospect Pl., Epsom	54	4B
Prospect Pl., Staines	14	4A
Prospect Rd., Ash Vale	78	3C
Prospect Rd., Long Ditton	36	3A
Prospect Rd., Rowledge	114	2C
Prospect Rd., West Heath	60	4C
Prossers	72	4A
Providence Pl.	54	4B
Prune Hill	13	5D
Prunus Cl.	46	5B
Pucks Hill	64	2A
Puckshott Way	152	2A
Pudding Hill	27	5E
Pudding La.	127	4D
Puffin Cl.	41	3F
Puffin Rd.	146	4A
Pulborough Rd.	20	2B
Pullman Gdns.	19	1F
Pullman La.	118	3C
Pump La.	29	1E
Pumping Station Rd.	9	3E
Punch Copse Rd.	147	3E
Punchbowl La.	106	1A
Purbeck Av.	37	3E
Purbeck Cl.	90	2C
Purbeck Dri.	48	5A
Purberry Gro.	54	3B
Purbrook Court	27	3E
Purcell Rd.	43	1D
Purcells Cl.	70	2C
Purley	57	4E
Purley Bury Av.	57	4E
Purley Bury Cl.	57	4F
Purley Downs Rd., Purley	57	3E
Purley Downs Rd., Sanderstead	58	4A
Purley Hill	57	4E
Purley Knoll	57	4D
Purley Oaks Rd.	57	3F
Purley Park Rd.	57	4E
Purley Rd., Purley	57	4E
Purley Rd., South Croydon	57	2F
Purley Rise	57	4D
Purley Vale	57	5E
Purley Way, Croydon	40	4A
Purley Way, Frimley	61	3E
Purley Way, Waddon	57	1D
Pursers La.	103	4E
Purslane	25	2E
Purton Rd.	158	4A
Putney Bridge Rd.	20	1B
Putney Heath	20	1A
Putney Heath La.	20	1A
Putney Hill	20	1A
Putney Park La.	19	1F
Putney Pk.	9	5F
Puttenham	98	3C
Puttenham Heath Rd.	99	3D
Puttenham La., Shackleford	98	4C
Puttenham Rd., Seale	98	3A
Puttocks Cl.	151	3E
Pyegreen Chase	27	3F
Pylbrook Rd.	38	5B
Pyle Hill	64	5C
Pylon Way	40	5A
Pymers Mead	22	2C
Pyne Rd.	36	4C
Pyrcroft La.	50	1B
Pyrcroft Rd., Chertsey	32	4A
Pyrcroft Rd., Twynersh	31	4F
Pyrford	66	2A
Pyrford Common Rd.	65	1F
Pyrford Heath	66	1A
Pyrford Rd.	49	5D
Pyrford Wood Cl.	66	1A
Pyrford Woods Rd.	66	1A
Pyrland Rd.	18	1B
Pyrmont Rd.	8	3C
Pytchley Cres.	22	5C

Q

Quad, The	100	1B
Quadrant Ct.	27	2E
Quadrant Rd.	40	2B
Quadrant, The, Ash Wharf	78	4C
Quadrant, The, Richmond	8	5B
Quadrant, The, Wimbledon	38	1A
Quail Cl.	158	2B
Quail Gdns.	58	3C
Quakers Way	80	3C
Qualitas	26	4C
Quality St.	90	2B
Quantock Pl.	60	4B
Quarr Rd.	39	3D
Quarry Bank	45	4E
Quarry Cl., Horsham	158	3C
Quarry Cl., Oxted	93	3F
Quarry Hill	118	2C
Quarry Hill Rd.	89	4F
Quarry Park Rd.	55	2E
Quarry Rise	55	2E
Quarry Rd., Godstone	92	2B
Quarry Rd., Hurtmore	99	5E
Quarry Rd., Oxted	93	3F
Quarry Rd., Wandsworth	20	1C
Quarry St.	100	1C
Quarry, The	88	4A
Quarter Mile Rd.	119	3D
Quarterbrass Farm Rd.	158	2B
Quartermain Av.	65	4D
Quebec Cl.	129	2E
Quebec Gdns.	60	1B
Queen Adelaide Rd.	23	5E
Queen Anne Av.	42	2C
Queen Anne Dri.	52	2B
Queen Anne's Cl.	17	3E
Queen Anne's Gdns., Bedford Park	9	1E
Queen Anne's Gdns., Gunnersbury	8	1B
Queen Anne's Gdns., Mitcham	39	2D
Queen Anne's Gro., Bedford Park	9	1D
Queen Anne's Gro., Gunnersbury	8	1B
Queen Anne's Ride	11	3F
Queen Caroline St.	9	2F
Queen Eleanor's Rd.	100	1B
Queen Elizabeth Gdns.	59	3E
Queen Elizabeth Rd., Camberley	44	3A
Queen Elizabeth Rd., Kingston	36	1B
Queen Elizabeth Rd., Rudgwick	157	2E
Queen Elizabeth Way	65	3D
Queen Elizabeth's Dri.	59	3E
Queen Elizabeth's Wk.	56	1C
Queen Mary Av.	38	3A

210
Queen Mary Cl — Redbarn Cl

Queen Mary Cl. 65 1E
Queen Mary Rd., Charlton 33 1E
Queen Mary Rd., Streatham 22 5B
Queen Mary's Av., Camberley 60 1C
Queen Marys Av., Carshalton 56 2A
Queen Mary's Dri. 49 3D
Queen St., Aldershot 78 5B
Queen St., Chertsey 32 4A
Queen St., Godalming 119 2D
Queen St., Gomshall 103 3E
Queen St., Horsham 158 5B
Queen Victoria's Av. 12 5A
Queendale Court 64 1A
Queenhill Rd. 58 3B
Queenhythe Rd. 81 2F
Queens Acre 55 2D
Queens Av., Byfleet 49 4F
Queens Av., Lower Feltham 16 4A
Queen's Av., South Farnborough 78 3A
Queens Cl., Old Windsor 12 1B
Queens Cl., Walton-on-the Hill 71 5E
Queens Court, Forest Hill 23 3E
Queens Court, Richmond 18 1B
Queens Court, Weybridge 50 2C
Queens Court Ride 51 5D
Queens Cres. 18 1B
Queens Dri., Esher 52 4A
Queens Dri., Guildford 81 4E
Queens Dri., Surbiton 36 4C
Queens Dri., Thames Ditton 35 4F
Queens Gate 51 4E
Queens Hill Rise 28 2C
Queens La., Ashford 14 4C
Queens La., Upper Hale 96 1A
Queens Mead 137 5F
Queen's Mead Rd. 42 1C
Queen's Park Rd. 74 5C
Queens Pine 27 3F
Queens Pk. 17 1E
Queens Pl. 50 1C
Queens Rd., Belmont 55 3E
Queens Rd., Bisley 63 2E
Queens Rd., Camberley 60 1C
Queens' Rd., East Grinstead 150 2C
Queen's Rd., Egham 13 4D
Queens Rd., Elmers End 41 1F
Queen's Rd., Feltham 16 2A
Queen's Rd., Fulwell 17 4D
Queen's Rd., Guildford 81 5F
Queen's Rd., Hersham 51 1D
Queen's Rd., Horley 128 2B
Queen's Rd., Kingston 18 5C
Queen's Rd., Knaphill 63 2F
Queens Rd., Morden 38 2B
Queens Rd., Mortlake 9 5D
Queens Rd., Raynes Park 38 1C
Queen's Rd., Richmond 18 1B
Queen's Rd., South Farnborough 78 2A
Queen's Rd., Sunninghill 29 3D
Queen's Rd., Teddington 17 5E
Queen's Rd., Thames Ditton 35 3F
Queens Rd., Thornton Heath 40 3B
Queen's Rd., Twickenham 17 2F
Queens Rd., Upper Hale 96 2A
Queen's Rd., Wallington 56 1B
Queens Rd., Weybridge 50 1B
Queen's Rd., Wimbledon 20 5B
Queens Reach 35 2E
Queen's Ride 9 5F
Queens Rise 18 1B
Queens Sq. 147 4D
Queens Way, Godalming 99 5F
Queens Way, Hanworth 16 4B
Queens Way, Hersham 51 1E
Queens Way, Waddon 57 2D
Queens Wk. 14 4C
Queensland Av. 38 1C
Queensmead 61 5D
Queensmead Av. 54 3C
Queensmere Rd. 20 3A
Queensthorpe Rd. 23 4F
Queensville Rd. 21 2F
Queensway, Cranleigh 141 2D
Queensway, Crawley 147 4D
Queensway, Frimley Grn. 61 3F
Queensway, Horsham 158 5B
Queensway, Redhill 90 5B
Queensway, Sunbury 34 1A
Queensway, West Wickham 42 5C
Queenswood Av., Hampton 17 5D
Queenswood Av., Thornton Heath 40 3B
Queenswood Av., Wallington 56 1C
Queenswood Rd., Lewisham 23 3F
Queenswood Rd., Woking 64 3A
Quennell Cl. 70 3B
Quennels Hill 114 1C
Quentin Way 30 2B
Quick Rd. 9 2D
Quicks Rd. 20 5C
Quiet Cl. 49 1E
Quillot, The 50 1C
Quince Dri. 63 1E
Quince Rd. 29 2D
Quincy Rd. 13 4E
Quintilis 26 4C
Quintin Av. 38 1B
Quinton Cl., Beckenham 42 2B
Quinton Cl., Wallington 56 1B
Quinton Rd. 35 4F
Quinton St. 20 3C
Quintrel Cl. 64 2B

R

Rabbit La. 51 2D
Rabies Heath Rd. 92 5A
Raby Rd. 37 2D
Racecourse Rd. 131 2F
Rackfield 151 2D
Rackham Cl. 146 5C
Rad La. 103 4F
Radbourne Av. 8 2A
Radbourne Rd. 21 2F
Radcliffe Cl., 61 3F
Radcliffe Gdns. 56 3A
Radcliffe Rd. 41 5D
Radcliffe Squ. 20 1A
Radcliffe Way 26 1B
Radford Cl. 96 2B
Radford La. 147 1E
Radford Rd., Crawley 147 1F
Radford Rd., Lewisham 24 1B
Radlett Av. 23 3E
Radnor Cl. 40 2A
Radnor Court 90 5A
Radnor Gdns. 17 3F
Radnor La. 104 5A
Radnor Rd., Bracknell 27 2E
Radnor Rd., Peaslake 122 1C
Radnor Rd., Twickenham 17 3F
Radnor Rd., Walton-on-Thames 33 5D
Radnor Walk 41 4F
Radolphs 72 4A
Radstock Way 90 2C
Radstone Court 65 2D
Rae Rd. 78 1A
Raeburn Av. 36 3C
Raeburn Cl. 18 5A
Raeburn Way 43 5E
Rag Hill 77 4F
Rag Hill Cl. 77 4E
Rag Hill Rd. 77 4E
Raglan Cl., Aldershot 78 5A
Raglan Cl., Frimley 61 3F
Raglan Cl., Reigate 89 4F
Raglan Court 57 1E
Raglan Rd., Knaphill 64 2A
Raglan Rd., Reigate 89 4F
Raikes Hollow 104 4A
Raikes La. 104 4A
Railey Rd. 147 3D
Railton Rd. 22 1B
Railway App., Cheam 55 2D
Railway App., East Grinstead 150 2C
Railway App., Twickenham 17 2F
Railway Rd. 17 4E
Railway Side 9 5E
Railway Ter., Feltham 16 2A
Railway Ter., Staines 13 4F
Rainbow Court 64 1A
Rainham Cl. 21 1D
Rake La. 118 4B
Rakers Ridge 158 3B
Raleigh Av. 56 1C
Raleigh Court, Staines 14 4B
Raleigh Court, Wallington 56 2B
Raleigh Ct., Beckenham 42 1B
Raleigh Dri., Claygate 52 1B
Raleigh Dri., Smallfield 129 2E
Raleigh Dri., Tolworth 37 4D
Raleigh Gdns. 39 2D
Raleigh Rd., Feltham 15 3F
Raleigh Rd., Penge 23 5F
Raleigh Rd., Richmond 8 5B
Raleigh Way, Feltham 16 4A
Raleigh Way, Frimley 61 1E
Raleigh Wk. 147 5D
Ralliwood Rd. 70 3C
Ralph's Ride 27 2E
Ram St. 20 1C
Rambler Cl. 21 4F
Ramillies Cl. 22 1A
Ramillies Rd., Chiswick 9 2D
Ramillies Rd., South Farnborough 78 2A
Rams La. 155 1E
Ramsay Rd. 9 1D
Ramsbury Cl. 26 3B
Ramsdale Rd. 21 4E
Ramsden Rd., Godalming 119 2D
Ramsden Rd., Wandsworth 21 1E
Ramsey Cl.,Horley 128 2A
Ramsey Cl., Horsham 158 3B
Ramsey Rd., Thornton Heath 40 3A
Ramsey Rd., Windlesham 46 1A
Ramslade Rd. 27 2D
Rances La. 25 2F
Randal Cres. 108 1B
Randalls Cres. 69 3F
Randalls Park Av. 69 3F
Randalls Pk Dri. 69 4F
Randalls Rd. 69 3E
Randalls Way 69 4F
Randell Cl. 60 2B
Randle Rd. 18 4A
Randlesdown Rd. 24 4A
Randolph Cl., Coombe 19 4D
Randolph Cl., Woking 64 2A
Randolph Dri. 60 5A
Randolph Rd. 54 5B
Ranelagh Av. 9 4E
Ranelagh Cres. 28 1A
Ranelagh Dri., Bracknell 27 2D
Ranelagh Dri., Richmond 18 1A
Ranelagh Ms. 8 1A
Ranelagh Pl. 37 3D
Ranelagh Rd., Ealing 8 1A
Ranelagh Rd., Redhill 90 5A
Ranfurley Rd. 38 5B
Range Rd., Wick Hill 25 5D
Range, The 120 2B
Range Way 33 4D
Rangefield Rd. 24 4C
Ranger Walk 49 1E
Ranklin Cl. 96 2C
Ranmore Av. 41 5D
Ranmore Cl., Hersham 51 1F
Ranmore Cl., Redhill 90 4B
Ranmore Common Rd. 85 5F
Ranmore Rd., Dorking 105 1F
Ranmore Rd., East Ewell 55 3D
Ranmore Rd., Ranmore Common 86 5B
Ransome Cl. 146 5A
Rapallo Cl. 61 5D
Rapeland Hill 158 1C
Rapley Cl. 44 4B
Rapley Green 27 3D
Rapleys Field 63 5E
Rastell Rd. 21 3F
Ratcliffe Rd. 60 3C
Rathfern Rd. 34 2A
Rathgar Cl. 109 3E
Rathlin Rd. 146 5C
Raven La. 146 3C
Ravendale Mews 14 5B
Ravendale Rd. 33 1F
Ravenfield 12 5C
Ravens Cl., Knaphill 63 2F
Ravens Cl., Redhill 90 5A
Ravensbourne Av., Beckenham 42 1B
Ravensbourne Av., Stanwell 14 2C
Ravensbourne Est. 24 4B
Ravensbourne Park Cres. 24 2A
Ravensbourne Pk. 24 1A
Ravensbourne Rd., Catford 24 2A
Ravensbourne Rd., Lewisham 23 2F
Ravensbourne Rd., Richmond 18 1A
Ravensburg Path 39 2D
Ravensbury Av. 38 3C
Ravensbury Gro. 38 2C
Ravensbury La. 39 2D
Ravensbury Rd. 20 3B
Ravenscar Rd., Downham 24 4C
Ravenscar Rd., Tolworth 36 4B
Ravenscourt 33 1F
Ravenscourt Gdns. 9 2E
Ravenscourt Pk. 9 1E
Ravenscourt Rd. 9 2F
Ravenscourt Sq. 9 1E
Ravenscroft Ct. 158 4B
Ravenscroft Rd., Anerley 41 1E
Ravenscroft Rd., Ash 79 4D
Ravenscroft Rd., Weybridge 50 4B
Ravensdale Gdns. 22 5C
Ravensdale Rd. 28 3C
Ravensfield Gdns. 54 1B
Ravenshead Cl. 58 4B
Ravenslea Rd. 21 2D
Ravensmead Rd. 24 5B
Ravensmede Way 9 2E
Ravenstone Rd. 45 5D
Ravenstone St. 21 2E
Ravenswold 74 1B
Ravenswood 21 2E
Ravenswood Av., Tolworth 36 5C
Ravenswood Av., West Wickham 42 4B
Ravenswood Court, Kingston 18 5C
Ravenswood Court, Woking 65 2D
Ravenswood Cres. 42 4B
Ravenswood Dri. 44 5C
Ravenwood Cl. 68 1B
Rawchester Cl. 20 2B
Rawlins Cl. 58 2C
Raworth Cl. 147 4F
Ray La. 112 5A
Ray Rd. 35 3D
Rayford Av. 24 2C
Rayleigh Av. 17 5E
Rayleigh Court 36 1C
Rayleigh Rd. 38 1B
Raymead Av. 40 3B
Raymead Cl. 69 4E
Raymead Way 69 4E
Raymer Wk. 128 2C
Raymond Cl., Poyle 7 4B
Raymond Cl., Sydenham 23 4E
Raymond Cres. 100 1B
Raymond Rd., Elmers End 41 2F
Raymond Rd., Wimbledon 20 5A
Raymond Way 52 2C
Rayners Rd. 20 1A
Raynham Rd. 9 2F
Rays Rd. 42 4B
Read Rd. 70 2A
Readens, The 73 1D
Reading Arch Rd. 90 5B
Reading Rd., Blackwater 60 1A
Reading Rd., South Farnborough 78 1A
Reading Rd., Wokingham 25 1D
Reads Rest La. 72 3B
Reaper Way 17 1E
Reckitt Rd. 9 2D
Recreation La. 134 2C
Recreation Rd., Guildford 81 5F
Recreation Rd., Lower Sydenham 23 4E
Recreation Rd., Rowledge 114 2C
Recreation Rd., Shortlands 42 1C
Recreation Way 40 2A
Rectory Cl., Ashtead 70 3B
Rectory Cl., Bracknell 27 2D
Rectory Cl., Byfleet 49 5F
Rectory Cl., Godalming 119 3D
Rectory Cl., Littleton 33 2D
Rectory Cl., Long Ditton 36 4A
Rectory Cl., Merrow 82 4C
Rectory Cl., Ockley 143 1E
Rectory Cl., Raynes Pk. 37 2F
Rectory Cl., Wokingham 25 2E
Rectory Green 42 1A
Rectory Gro., Croydon 40 5B
Rectory Gro., Hampton 16 4C
Rectory La., Ashstead 70 3B
Rectory La., Buckland 88 4B
Rectory La., Byfleet 49 5F
Rectory La., Charlwood 127 4D
Rectory La., Easthampstead 26 3C
Rectory La., Great Bookham 85 1F
Rectory La., Ifield 146 3B
Rectory La., Long Ditton 36 4A
Rectory La., Shere 103 3D
Rectory La., Titsey 77 5E
Rectory La., Tooting 21 5E
Rectory La., Wallington 56 1C
Rectory La., Windlesham 45 2F
Rectory La., Woodmansterne 73 1E
Rectory Orchard 20 4A
Rectory Pk. 58 4A
Rectory Rd., Barnes 9 4E
Rectory Rd., Beckenham 42 1A
Rectory Rd., Farnborough Park 61 5D
Rectory Rd., Farnborough St. 61 4D
Rectory Rd., Mugswell 89 1F
Rectory Rd., Sutton 38 5B
Rectory Rd., Wokingham 25 2D
Red Admiral St. 158 3C
Red House La., Elstead 117 3D
Red House La., Walton-on-Thames 34 5A
Red House Rd. 77 4E
Red La., Blackbrook 106 4B
Red La., Claygate 52 2C
Red La., Hurst Green 94 5A
Red Leaves Av. 15 4E
Red Lion La., Farnham 96 4A
Red Lion Rd., Chobham 47 3D
Red Lion Rd., Tolworth 36 5B
Red Lion St. 18 1B
Red Lodge Rd. 42 4B
Red Post Hill 22 1C
Red Rd., Bagshot Heath 45 5D
Red Rd., Betchworth 88 4A
Red River Court. 158 3A
Redan Gdns. 78 5A
Redan Rd. 78 5A
Redbarn Cl. 57 4E

211

Redberry Grn **Riverside Av**

Redberry Grn. 23 3E
Redclose Av. 38 3B
Redcourt 65 1F
Redcrest Gdns 44 5B
Redcroft Wk. 140 2C
Redditch 27 3E
Reddons Rd. 23 5F
Reddown Rd. 73 2F
Redehall Rd. 129 3E
Redfern Av. 16 2C
Redfern Rd. 24 2B
Redford Av., Horsham 158 4A
Redford Av., Roundshaw 57 2D
Redford Av., Thornton Heath 40 2A
Redford Av., Woodmansterne 73 1E
Redgarth Ct. 150 1A
Redgate Ter. 20 1A
Redgrave Cl. 41 3D
Redgrave Ct. 78 5C
Redgrave Dri. 147 4F
Redhearn Fields 134 2C
Redhill 90 5B
Redhill Rd., Byfleet 50 4B
Redhill Rd., Nutfield 90 5C
Redhouse Rd. 39 3F
Redkiln Way 158 4C
Redlands 73 1F
Redlands La., Dorking 105 4F
Redlands La., Warren Corner 95 1D
Redlands Way 22 2A
Redmayne Cl. 62 1A
Redmore Rd. 9 2F
Redroofs Cl. 42 1A
Redstart Cl. 59 3F
Redstone Hill 90 5B
Redstone Hollow 109 1E
Redstone Manor 90 5B
Redstone Pk. 90 5B
Redstone Rd. 109 1E
Redvers Buller Rd. 18 2A
Redvers Rd., Easthampstead 27 3D
Redvers Rd., Warlingham 75 2E
Redway Dri. 17 2D
Redwing Av. 100 5A
Redwing Cl., Horsham 158 4C
Redwing Cl., Selsdon 58 4C
Redwing Rise 82 4C
Redwood Cl., Chilworth 101 3F
Redwood Cl., Crawley 147 3D
Redwood Cl., Kenley 57 5F
Redwood Dri., Broomhill 29 3F
Redwood Dri., Heatherside 62 1A
Redwood, Egham 32 1A
Redwood Mount 89 4E
Redwood, Roehampton 19 2E
Reed Pl. 48 5C
Reedfield Cl. 15 4D
Reedham Dri. 57 5D
Reedham Pk. Av. 74 1B
Reeds Hill 26 3C
Reeds, The 115 3E
Reedsfield Rd. 15 4D
Rees Gdns. 41 3D
Reeve Rd. 108 2C
Reeves Rd. 78 5A
Reeves Way 25 3D
Regal Cres. 39 5E
Regal Dri. 150 3C
Regalfield Cl. 81 3E
Regan Cl. 81 3E
Regency Cl. 16 4C
Regency Dri. 49 5D
Regency Gdns. 34 4B
Regency Mews 17 1E
Regency Wk. 41 3F
Regent Cl., Byfleet 49 3F
Regent Court 45 3E
Regent Cres. Reigate 90 4B
Regent Rd., Herne Hill 22 1B
Regent Rd., Surbiton 36 3C
Regent St. 8 2C
Regent Way 61 2F
Regents Cl. 75 2D
Regents Pl. 43 4D
Regents Walk 28 3C
Regiment Cl. 60 5B
Regina Rd. 41 2D
Reid Av. 74 4C
Reigate 89 5F
Reigate Av. 38 4B
Reigate Hill Cl. 89 4E
Reigate Hill Rd. 89 5E
Reigate Rd., Buckland 88 5C
Reigate Rd., Dorking 106 1A
Reigate Rd., Ewell 54 3B
Reigate Rd., Hookwood Common 127 1F
Reigate Rd., Leatherhead 70 4A
Reigate Rd., Lewisham 24 3C
Reigate Rd., Reigate 89 5F
Reigate Rd., Sidlowbridge 108 4C
Reigate Rd., Tyrell's Wood 70 5B
Reigate Way 57 1D
Relko Court 54 3A
Rembrant Way 34 5A
Renfree Way 33 4D
Renfrew Rd. 19 5D
Renmans, The 70 1B
Renmuir St. 21 5E
Rennie Cl. 14 3C
Rennie Ter. 109 1E
Renown Cl. 40 4B
Replingham Rd. 20 2B
Repton Cl. 56 2A
Repton Court 42 1B
Restmor Way 39 5E
Restwell Av. 121 5E
Retreat, The, Englefield Green 12 4C
Retreat, The, Surbiton 36 3B
Retreat, The, Thornton Heath 40 2C
Retreat, The, Worcester Park 37 5F
Revell Cl. 69 4D
Revell Dri. 69 4D
Revell Rd., Cheam 55 2E
Revell Rd., Kingston 36 1C
Revelstoke Av. 60 4C
Revelstoke Rd. 20 3B
Revesby Cl. 46 5A
Revesby Rd. 39 3D
Rewley Rd. 39 3D
Rex Av. 15 4D
Reynolds Av. 53 2E
Reynolds Cl. 39 4E
Reynolds Grn. 43 5E
Reynolds Pl., Crawley 146 3C
Reynolds Pl., Richmond 18 1B
Reynolds Rd., Crawley 146 3C
Reynolds Rd., Malden Manor 37 4D
Reyward Dri. 23 5D
Rhine Banks 60 4B
Rhodes Cl. 13 4E
Rhodes Moorhouse Wk. 38 3B
Rhodes Way 147 5D
Rhododendron Rd. 61 3F
Rhododendron Ride 12 4A
Rhododendron Walk 10 5B
Rhodrons Av. 53 1E
Rialto Rd. 39 1E
Ribble Pl. 60 3B
Ribblesdale Rd. 21 5E
Ricardo Court 120 1A
Ricardo Rd. 12 1B
Ricebridge La. 107 1F
Richards Rd. 52 5A
Richbell Cl. 70 2A
Richford St. 9 1F
Richings Park 7 1B
Richings Way 7 1B
Richland Av. 56 5B
Richlands Av. 54 1C
Richmond Av., East Bedfont 15 1F
Richmond Av., Merton 38 1B
Richmond Cl., Biggin Hill 77 3D
Richmond Cl., Epsom 54 5B
Richmond Cl., Fetcham 69 5D
Richmond Cl., Frimley 61 2F
Richmond Cres. 14 4A
Richmond Dri. 33 3E
Richmond Green 40 5A
Richmond Gro. 36 3B
Richmond Hill 18 1B
Richmond Park Rd., East Sheen 9 5D
Richmond Park Rd., Kingston 18 5B
Richmond Rd., Cottenham Park 37 1F
Richmond Rd., Godalming 119 1D
Richmond Rd., Gunnersbury 8 1B
Richmond Rd., Horsham 158 4B
Richmond Rd., Kingston 18 5B
Richmond Rd., Richmond 18 1A
Richmond Rd., Staines 14 4A
Richmond Rd., Thornton Heath 40 2B
Richmond Rd., Waddon 40 5A
Richmond Rd., Woodmansterne 73 1E
Richmond Rd., York Town 43 4E
Richmond Way 69 5D
Richmond Wood 29 4F
Richmond-upon-Thames 18 1A
Rickard Cl. 22 2A
Rickards Cl. 36 4B
Ricketts Hill 77 4E
Ricketts Hill Rd. 77 2E
Rickfield 146 4B
Rickford Hill 81 2D
Rickman Cl. 27 3D
Rickman Cres. 32 5B
Rickman Hill Rd. 73 2E
Rickman Rd. 73 2E
Rickman's La. 155 5D
Rickson's La. 84 2B
Rickwood 128 2C
Rickyard 81 5D
Riddlesdown Av. 57 4E
Riddlesdown Rd., Purley 57 3E
Ride La. 121 1F
Ride, The, Brentford 8 2A
Ride, The, Ifold 155 5F
Ride Way 122 3B
Riders Way 92 4B
Rideway Cl. 61 1D
Ridge Cl., Brockham 106 2C
Ridge Cl., Woking 64 4C
Ridge Langley 58 3A
Ridge Mount 23 5E
Ridge Mount Rd. 29 4E
Ridge Pk. 56 3C
Ridge Rd., North Cheam 38 4A
Ridge Rd., Tooting 21 5E
Ridge Road West 90 1C
Ridge, The, Coulsdon 57 5D
Ridge, The, Epsom 71 2D
Ridge, The, Fetcham 69 5E
Ridge, The, Fetcham 69 5E
Ridge, The, Surbiton 36 3C
Ridge, The, Whitton 17 2E
Ridge, The, Woking 65 2E
Ridge, The, Woldingham 93 1D
Ridge, The, Woodcote 56 3C
Ridge Way, Hanworth 16 3B
Ridge Way, The, Horsham 158 4A
Ridge Way, The, Sanderstead 57 3F
Ridge Way, The, Waddon 40 5A
Ridgegate Cl., 90 4A
Ridgegreen Cl. 110 2A
Ridgehurst Dri. 158 5A
Ridgelands 69 5E
Ridgeley Rd. 137 5E
Ridgemead Rd. 12 3B
Ridgemoor Cl. 135 4E
Ridgemount, Guildford 100 1B
Ridgemount, Walton-on-Thames 33 5F
Ridgemount Av., Chipstead 73 2E
Ridgemount Av., Shirley 41 5F
Ridgemount Cl. 62 3A
Ridges, The 100 3C
Ridgeside 147 4D
Ridgeway, East Grinstead 150 3C
Ridgeway, Epsom 54 4A
Ridgeway, Walton on Thames 33 4F
Ridgeway, Wimbledon 20 5A
Ridgeway, Woking 64 1C
Ridgeway Cl., Dorking 105 2F
Ridgeway Cl., Lightwater 45 4F
Ridgeway Cl., Oxshott 52 5A
Ridgeway Cl., Woking 64 1C
Ridgeway Dri. 105 3F
Ridgeway Farm Rd. 135 2F
Ridgeway Gdns. 20 5A
Ridgeway Rd., Dorking 105 2F
Ridgeway Rd., Farnham 96 5A
Ridgeway Rd., Redhill 90 5A
Ridgeway, The, Acton 8 1C
Ridgeway, The, Bracknell 27 2D
Ridgeway, The, Carshalton Beeches 56 2A
Ridgeway, The, Cranleigh 141 2D
Ridgeway, The, Guildford 101 1E
Ridgeway, The, Horley 128 3B
Ridgeway, The, Lightwater 45 3F
Ridgeway, The, Oxshott 52 5A
Ridgway Hill Rd. 96 5A
Ridgway Pl. 20 5A
Ridgway Rd., Ridgway 66 1A
Ridgway, The, Brookwood 63 3E
Riding Bottom 122 1C
Riding Hill 58 5A
Riding, The, Maybury 48 5B
Ridings La. 67 5D
Ridings, The, Ashtead 70 2A
Ridings, The, Biggin Hill 77 2E
Ridings, The, Burgh Heath 72 3B
Ridings, The, Camberley 61 1F
Ridings, The, Cobham 52 4A
Ridings, The, Cranleigh 140 1C
Ridings, The, Crawley 147 3F
Ridings, The, Epsom 71 1E
Ridings, The, Ewell 54 3B
Ridings, The, Horsley 84 1C
Ridings, The, Redhill 90 4A
Ridings, The, Rowhill 49 2D
Ridings, The, Sendmarsh 66 5A
Ridings, The, Sunbury 34 1A
Ridings, The, Surbiton 36 3C
Ridings, The, Three Bridges 148 3A
Ridlands Cl. 94 3C
Ridlands Gro. 94 3C
Ridlands La. 94 3B
Ridlands Rise 94 4C
Ridley Rd., Lammas Pk. 8 1A
Ridley Rd., Warlingham 75 2E
Ridley Rd., Wimbledon 20 5C
Ridsdale Rd., Penge 23 5E
Ridsdale Rd., Woking 64 2B
Rifle Butts Alley 71 1E
Rifle Way 60 5A
Rigby Cl. 40 5B
Riggindale Rd. 21 4F
Rillside 147 5E
Rimbault Cl. 78 2B
Rinaldo Rd. 21 2E
Ring, The 27 1D
Ringford Rd. 20 1B
Ringley Av. 128 3B
Ringley Oak 158 4C
Ringley Park Av. 109 1D
Ringley Park Rd. 89 5F
Ringmead, Bracknell 26 3B
Ringmore Dri. 82 4C
Ringmore Rd. 34 5B
Ringmore Rise 23 2E
Ringstead Rd., Carshalton 56 1A
Ringstead Rd., Catford 24 2B
Ringwold Cl. 23 5F
Ringwood Av., Croydon 40 4A
Ringwood Av., Redhill 90 4B
Ringwood Cl., Ascot 28 2C
Ringwood Cl., Crawley 147 5D
Ringwood Gdns. 19 2F
Ringwood Rd., Blackwater 43 5D
Ringwood Rd., Farnboro' 61 3D
Ringwood Way 16 4C
Ripley 66 4B
Ripley Av. 13 5D
Ripley Bypass 83 1D
Ripley Cl. 59 2E
Ripley Gdns., Mortlake 9 5D
Ripley Gdns., Sutton 55 1F
Ripley La. 84 1A
Ripley Rd., East Clandon 83 2E
Ripley Rd., Hampton 16 5C
Ripley Way 16 4C
Ripon Cl., Camberley 62 1A
Ripon Cl., Guildford 81 4D
Ripon Gdns. 53 1D
Ripplesmere 27 2E
Ripplesmoor Cl. 43 4D
Ripston Rd. 15 4E
Risborough Dri. 37 4F
Rise Rd. 29 3E
Rise, The, E. Grinstead 150 3C
Rise, The, Ewell 54 3B
Rise, The, Horsley 84 1C
Rise, The, Pound Hill 147 4F
Rise, The, Selsdon 58 3B
Rise, The, Tadworth 72 4A
Riseldine Rd. 23 1F
Ritchie Rd. 41 3E
Ritherdon Rd. 21 3E
River Av. 35 4F
River Bank 35 2E
River Court Rd. 9 2F
River Gdns., Feltham 16 1A
River Gdns., Hackbridge 39 5E
River La., Leatherhead 69 4E
River La., Richmond 18 2B
River La., Wrecclesham 95 5F
River Meads Av. 17 3D
River Mount 33 4F
River Park Av. 13 4F
River Park Gdns. 24 5B
River Rd 32 1A
River Reach 18 4A
River Row 95 5F
River Way, Twickenham 17 3D
River Way, West Ewell 54 2A
River Wk. 34 3A
Riverbank 35 3F
Riverbank Way 8 3A
Riverdale 18 1A
Riverdale Cl. 95 5F
Riverdale Dri. 65 4D
Riverdale Rd., Hanworth 16 4C
Riverdale Rd., Richmond 18 1A
Riverford Rd. 14 5A
Riverhead Dr. 55 3E
Riverholme Dri. 54 3A
Rivermead, Byfleet 50 5A
Rivermead, E. Molesey 35 1D
Rivermead, Horsham 158 5A
Rivermead, Ifield 146 2B
Rivermead Cl., Ham 18 4A
Rivermead Cl., New Haw 49 2E
Rivermead Rd. 60 2C
Rivermede 133 5D
Rivermount Gdns 100 2C
Rivernook Cl. 34 3A
Rivers Cl. 78 1B
Riversdale Rd. 35 3F
Riversdell Cl. 32 4A
Riverside,Bellfields 81 4F
Riverside,Horley 128 3B
Riverside, Horsham 158 5A
Riverside, Laleham 32 1A
Riverside,Lower Halliford 33 4F
Riverside,Old Windsor 12 2C
Riverside,Pixham 87 5D
Riverside, Richmond 18 2A
Riverside,Runnymede 13 3E
Riverside, Sunbury 34 2B
Riverside,Twickenham 17 2F
Riverside Av., E. Molesey 35 3E

212

Riverside Av **Rowhills Cl**

Riverside Av., Lightwater 46 3A
Riverside Cl., Brookwood 63 3E
Riverside Cl., Farnborough 60 4C
Riverside Cl., Hackbridge 39 5E
Riverside Cl., Kingston 36 2B
Riverside Cl., Staines 32 1A
Riverside Dri., Chiswick 9 3D
Riverside Dri., Ham 18 3A
Riverside Dri., Hythe 14 4A
Riverside Dri., Mitcham 39 3D
Riverside Dri., Staines 32 1A
Riverside Dri., West End 51 1F
Riverside Dri., Wonersh 101 5E
Riverside Gdns. 65 4E
Riverside Pl. 14 1C
Riverside Rd., Hersham 51 1E
Riverside Rd., Staines 14 5A
Riverside Rd., Stanwell 14 1C
Riverside Rd., Summerstown 20 3C
Riverside Way 60 1C
Riverview Gdns., Barnes 9 3F
Riverview Gdns., Twickenham 17 3F
Riverview Gro. 8 3C
Riverview Pk. 24 3A
Riverview Rd., Chiswick 8 3C
Riverview Rd., West Ewell 54 1A
Riverway, Laleham 32 1B
Riverwood Ct. 81 4F
Rivey Cl. 49 5D
Roakes Av. 32 5B
Robert Cl., Hersham 51 1D
Robert Way 158 2C
Robert Way, Mytchett 61 5E
Roberts All. 8 1A
Roberts Cl., Cheam 55 2D
Roberts Cl., Cheam 55 2D
Roberts Cl., Stanwell 14 1B
Roberts Rd., Aldershot 78 5A
Roberts' Rd., Camberley 43 5F
Roberts Way 12 5C
Robertsbridge Rd. 38 4C
Robertson Way 78 5B
Robin Cl., Addlestone 49 1F
Robin Cl., Ash Vale 78 3C
Robin Cl., Crawley 146 3C
Robin Gdns. 90 4B
Robin Grn. 8 3A
Robin Hill 100 5A
Robin Hill Dri. 61 1F
Robin Hood Cl., Hawley 60 3C
Robin Hood Cl., Mitcham 39 2F
Robin Hood Cl., Woking 64 2B
Robin Hood Cres. 64 2A
Robin Hood La., Cheam 55 1E
Robin Hood La., Guildford 82 1A
Robin Hood La., Kingston Vale 19 4E
Robin Hood La., Mitcham 39 2F
Robin Hood Pl. 19 4D
Robin Hood Rd., Wimbledon 19 4F
Robin Hood Rd., Woking 64 2A
Robin Hood Way 19 5E
Robin La. 43 4D
Robin Way,Guildford 81 3E
Robin Way,Staines 14 3A
Robinhood La., Warnham 158 3A
Robin's Row 61 1D
Robinson Rd., Crawley 146 4C
Robinson Rd., Tooting 21 5D
Robinsway 51 1E
Robinswood Court. 158 4C
Robson Rd. 22 3B
Rochdale Rd. 27 1D
Roche Rd. 40 1A
Roche Wk. 38 3C
Rochester Av. 16 3A
Rochester Gdns. 75 4D
Rochester Rd., Carshalton 56 1B
Rochester Rd., Hythe 13 4F
Rochester Walk 108 3B
Rochford Way 40 3A
Rock Av. 9 5D
Rock Hill,Hambledon 138 2A
Rock Hill,Sydenham 23 4D
Rock La. 114 1C
Rockbourne Rd. 23 2F
Rockell's Pl. 23 1E
Rockfield Cl. 93 4F
Rockfield Rd. 93 3F
Rockfield Way 43 4E
Rockhampton Rd., South Croydon 57 2F
Rockhampton Rd., West Norwood 22 4B
Rockingham Cl. 9 5E
Rockmount Rd. 22 5C
Rocks La. 9 5E
Rockshaw Rd. 90 2C
Rockwell Gdns. 23 4D
Rocky La. 90 2B
Roden Gdns. 40 3C
Rodenhurst Rd. 21 1F
Rodney Cl., Malden 37 3E
Rodney Cl., Walton-on-Thames 34 4B
Rodney Rd., Malden 37 3D
Rodney Rd., Mitcham 39 1D
Rodney Rd., Walton-on-Thames 34 5B
Rodney Way,Guildford 82 5B
Rodney Way,Poyle 7 4B
Rodona Rd. 50 4B
Rodsal La. 98 5B
Rodway Rd. 19 2F
Rodwell Rd. 23 1D
Roe Deer Copse 151 2E
Roe Way 57 2D
Roebuck Cl., Ashtead 70 3B
Roebuck Cl., Feltham 16 3A
Roebuck Cl., Reigate 89 5F
Roebuck Rd. 53 1F
Roedean Cres. 19 1E
Roehampton 19 2F
Roehampton Cl. 9 5E
Roehampton Gate 19 1E
Roehampton High St. 19 2F
Roehampton La. 19 1E
Roehampton Vale 19 3E
Roffe's La. 74 5C
Roffey Cl., Horley 128 2A
Roffey Cl., Kenley 74 1B
Roffeys Cl., Copthorne 148 1B
Roffords 64 2B
Rogers Cl., Caterham 75 4E
Rogers Cl., Coulston 74 2B
Rogers Mead 92 4B
Rogers Rd. 21 4D
Rojack Rd. 23 2F
Roke Cl., Purley 57 5E
Roke Cl., Wheeler Street 118 5A
Roke La. 118 5A
Roke Rd. 74 1B
Rokeby Cl. 27 1D
Rokeby Court 64 2A
Rokelo Rd. 57 5E
Rokers La. 99 5D
Roland Way 37 5E
Rollesby Rd. 53 2F
Rolleston Rd. 57 2F
Rollit Cres. 17 1D
Rollscourt Av. 22 1B
Roman Cl. 16 1A
Roman Gdns. 38 4B
Roman Rd., Dorking 105 2F
Roman Rd., Turnham Green 9 2E
Roman Rise 22 5C
Roman Way,Croydon 40 5B
Roman Way,Farnham 96 3B
Romanhurst Av. 42 2C
Romanhurst Gdns. 42 2C
Romans Way 66 1A
Romany Rd. 63 1F
Romayne Cl. 60 4C
Romborough Way 24 1B
Romburgh Rd. 21 3E
Romeyn Rd. 22 3A
Rommany Rd. 22 4C
Romney Cl., Ashford 15 4E
Romney Cl., Chessington 53 1E
Romney Rd. 37 3D
Romola Rd. 22 2B
Romsborough Gdns. 24 1B
Romsey Cl., Badshot Lea 97 2D
Romsey Cl., Blackwater 43 5D
Romsey Cl., Hampton 16 5C
Rona Cl. 146 5C
Ronald Cl. 42 2A
Ronce La. 46 5A
Ronelean Rd. 36 5B
Ronneby Cl. 33 5F
Ronson Way 69 4F
Ronver Rd. 24 2C
Rook La. 74 5B
Rook Way 158 3C
Rookeries Cl. 16 3A
Rookery Cl. 69 5E
Rookery Dri. 104 2C
Rookery Hill,Ashtead 70 2C
Rookery Hill,Outwood 110 5B
Rookery La. 129 1E
Rookery Rd. 14 4B
Rookery, The 104 3C
Rookery Way 89 2E
Rookley Cl. 55 3F
Rooks Hill 120 3B
Rooksmead Rd. 34 1A
Rookstone Rd. 21 4D
Rookwood Av., New Malden 37 2E
Rookwood Av., Sandhurst 43 3E
Rookwood Av., Wallington 56 1C
Rookwood Cl. 90 3C
Rookwood Court 100 2C
Roothill La. 106 3C
Rope Wk. 34 2A
Rorkes Drift 61 5F
Rosa Av. 15 4D
Rosalind Franklin Cl. 100 1A
Rosamund Rd. 147 5E
Rosary Gdns. 15 4D
Rosary, The,Croydon 41 3E
Rosary, The,Thorpe 31 1F
Roscoe Dri. 65 2E
Rose Av., Mitcham 39 1D
Rose Av., Morden 38 3C
Rose Bank 54 5A
Rose Briars 74 3C
Rose Bushes 71 1F
Rose Cres. 14 2C
Rose Croft Gdns. 17 2E
Rose Dale 74 5C
Rose End 38 4A
Rose Gdns., Brentford 8 1B
Rose Gdns., Feltham 16 3A
Rose Gdns., S. Ealing 8 1B
Rose Heath Rd. 16 1C
Rose Hill, Dorking 105 1F
Rose Hill, Rose Hill 38 5C
Rose La. 66 4B
Rose Park 49 3D
Rose St. 25 2E
Rose Wk., Purley 57 4D
Rose Wk., Surbiton 36 3C
Rose Wk., West Wickham 42 5B
Roseacre 94 5A
Roseacre Cl. 33 3D
Roseacre Gdns. 102 3A
Rosebank 23 5E
Rosebank 54 5A
Rosebank Cottages 65 4D
Rosebay 25 1F
Roseberry Av., New Malden 37 2E
Roseberry Av., Norwood 40 1C
Roseberry Cl. 38 3A
Roseberry Gdns. 55 1F
Roseberry Rd., Brixton 22 1A
Roseberry Rd., Cheam 55 2E
Roseberry Rd., Isleworth 17 1E
Roseberry Rd., Kingston 36 1C
Rosebery Av. 54 5B
Rosebery Cres. 65 4D
Rosebery Rd. 71 3D
Rosebine Av. 17 2E
Rosebriar Cl. 66 1B
Rosebury Dri. 63 1E
Rosecourt Rd. 40 3A
Rosedale, Aldershot 78 5A
Rosedale, Ashtead 70 2A
Rosedale Cres. 146 5B
Rosedale Gdns. 26 3C
Rosedale Rd., Richmond 8 5B
Rosedale Rd., Stoneleigh 54 1B
Rosedene Av., Morden 38 3B
Rosedene Av., Streatham 22 3A
Rosedene La. 43 4E
Rosefield Cl. 56 1A
Rosefield Gdns. 48 2C
Rosefield Rd. 14 4A
Rosehill,Hampton 35 1D
Rosehill Av., St. Helier 38 4C
Rosehill Av., Woking 64 1C
Rosehill Cl. 52 2C
Rosehill Farm Meadow 72 1C
Rosehill Gdns., Feltham 38 5C
Rosehill Park West 38 4C
Rosehill Rd., Biggin Hill 77 2E
Rosehill Rd., Wandsworth 20 1C
Roseleigh Cl. 18 1A
Rosemary Av., Ash Vale 78 2C
Rosemary Av., West Molesey 34 2C
Rosemary Cl., Holland 94 5A
Rosemary Cl., West Heath 60 5B
Rosemary Court 128 2A
Rosemary Cres. 81 3E
Rosemary Gdns. 43 5E
Rosemary La., Alford 156 2A
Rosemary La., Blackwater 43 5D
Rosemary La., Charlwood 127 4D
Rosemary La., Farnham 114 2C
Rosemary La., Horley 128 3B
Rosemary La., Thorpe 31 2E
Rosemary Rd. 20 3C
Rosemead Av., Feltham 15 3F
Rosemead Av., Mitcham 39 1F
Rosemead Cl. 109 1D
Rosemont Av. 49 5D
Rosemont Rd., New Malden 37 2D
Rosemount Rd., Richmond 18 1B
Rosendale Rd. 22 2B
Rosenheath Dri. 137 5F
Rosenheath Rd. 21 1E
Rosenthal Rd. 24 1B
Rosenthorpe Rd. 23 1F
Rosethorn Cl. 21 2F
Rosetrees 101 1E
Roseville Av. 16 1C
Rosevine Rd. 37 1F
Rosewarne Cl. 64 2B
Roseway 22 1C
Rosewood, Belmont 55 3F
Rosewood, Old Woking 65 3E
Rosewood, West End 46 5B
Rosewood Dri. 33 3D
Rosewood Grove 38 5C
Rosewood Rd. 133 4E
Roslin Rd. 8 1C
Roslyn Cl. 39 1D
Ross Cl. 147 5D
Ross Parade 56 2C
Ross Rd., Beddington 56 2C
Ross Rd., Cobham 51 5E
Ross Rd., South Norwood 40 2C
Ross Rd., Whitton 17 2D
Ross Wood Gdns. 56 2C
Rossdale 56 1A
Rosset Cl. 26 2C
Rossignol Gdns. 39 5E
Rossindel Rd. 16 1C
Rossiter Rd. 21 2E
Rosslyn Av., Barnes 9 5E
Rosslyn Av., Feltham 16 1A
Rosslyn Park 50 1C
Rosslyn Rd. 18 1A
Rossmore Cl. 147 2F
Rostella Rd. 21 4D
Rostrevor Rd. 20 4B
Rosy Bottom 29 1E
Rothby Walk 62 1A
Rother Cres. 146 4B
Rother Rd. 60 3B
Rother Vale 128 1B
Rotherfield Av. 25 1D
Rotherfield Rd. 56 1B
Rotherhill Rd. 21 5F
Rothermere Rd. 57 1D
Rothes Rd. 106 1A
Rothesay Av., N. Sheen 8 5C
Rothesay Av., Wimbledon Chase 38 1A
Rothesay Rd. 40 2C
Rothschild St. 22 4B
Rougemont Av. 38 3B
Rough Field 150 1B
Rough La. 153 1D
Rough Rd. 63 4F
Rough Rew 106 3A
Rough Rew Estate 105 3F
Rough, The 84 1B
Rough Way 158 3C
Roughetts La. 92 3A
Rounce La. 46 5A
Round Grn. 41 4F
Round Hill 23 3E
Round Oak Rd. 33 5D
Roundhay Cl. 23 3F
Roundhill 65 3E
Roundhill Dri. 65 2E
Roundhill Way,Cobham 52 4A
Roundhill Way,Woodbridge Hill 81 5D
Roundshaw 57 2D
Roundtable Rd. 24 3C
Roundthorn Way 64 1A
Roundway, Biggin Hill 77 1E
Roundway,Camberley 45 5D
Roundway,Egham 13 4F
Roundway Cl. 45 5D
Roundway, The 52 2C
Roundwood View 72 1A
Roundwood Way 72 1A
Roupell Rd. 22 2A
Rouse Gdns. 22 4E
Routh Rd. 21 2D
Row La. 121 1F
Row Town 49 2D
Rowan Av. 13 4E
Rowan Chase 115 1D
Rowan Cl., Camberley 44 4B
Rowan Cl., Crawley 147 4D
Rowan Cl., Ealing 8 1B
Rowan Cl., Feltham 16 1A
Rowan Cl., Guildford 81 4F
Rowan Cl., Mead Vale 108 1C
Rowan Cl., Mitcham 39 1F
Rowan Cl., New Malden 37 1E
Rowan Cres. 39 1F
Rowan Dri. 43 1D
Rowan Gdns. 41 5D
Rowan Grn. 50 1C
Rowan Gro. 73 4E
Rowan Rd., Brentford 8 3A
Rowan Rd., Mitcham 39 1F
Rowan Tree Rd. 17 2E
Rowans Cl. 60 3B
Rowans, The, Grayshott 151 1E
Rowans, The, Grayshott 151 1E
Rowans, The, Sunbury 15 4F
Rowans, The, Sunbury 15 4F
Rowanside Cl. 134 5A
Rowbarns Way 84 3C
Rowbury 100 5B
Rowcroft Cl. 78 3C
Rowden Rd., Beckenham 41 1F
Rowden Rd., West Ewell 53 1F
Rowdown Cres. 59 3F
Rowe La. 63 5E
Rowfant Rd. 21 2E
Rowhill 49 2D
Rowhill Av. 96 1C
Rowhill Cres. 96 1C
Rowhills 96 1B
Rowhills Cl. 96 1C

Rowhills Copse 96 1B
Rowhurst Av., Addlestone 49 2E
Rowhurst Av., Leatherhead 69 2F
Rowland Cres. 23 4E
Rowland Rd. 140 1C
Rowland Way 15 5E
Rowlands Cl., Domewood 129 5F
Rowledge 114 2C
Rowley Cl. 66 1B
Rowley Court. 74 4C
Rowlls Rd. 36 2C
Rowly 121 4E
Rowly Dri. 121 5D
Rowplat La. 149 1F
Rowtown 49 2D
Roxborough Cl. 62 1A
Roxburgh Rd. 22 4B
Roxeth Court 15 4D
Roxford Cl. 33 3F
Roxley Rd. 24 1B
Roxton Gdns. 59 1D
Roxwell Rd. 9 1E
Roy Grove 17 5D
Royal Av. 37 5E
Royal Circus 22 3B
Royal Cl. 37 5E
Royal Dri. 71 2F
Royal Oak Pl. 23 1E
Royal Oak Rd. 64 2C
Royal Rd. 17 4E
Royal Victoria Gdns. 28 2B
Royal Wk. 39 5E
Royale Cl. 97 1D
Roydon Ct. 51 1D
Royston Av., Byfleet 49 4F
Royston Av.,The Wrythe 39 5D
Royston Av., Wallington 56 1C
Royston Cl., Crawley 147 2E
Royston Cl., Walton-on-
Thames 34 4A
Royston Rd., Beckenham 41 1F
Royston Rd., Byfleet 49 4F
Royston Rd., Richmond 18 1B
Roystons, The 36 3C
Rozeldene 135 5E
Rubens St. 24 3A
Rubus Cl. 46 5A
Ruckmans La. 143 3D
Rudd Hall Rise 61 1E
Ruden Way 71 1F
Rudge Rd. 49 1D
Rudgwick Rd. 146 3B
Rudloe Rd. 21 2F
Ruffets Cl. 58 2B
Ruffets End 73 5D
Ruffets, The 58 2B
Ruffetts Way 72 2A
Ruffwood 149 3D
Rugby Cl. 43 3E
Rugby La. 55 3D
Rugby Rd., Acton Green 9 1D
Rugby Rd., Isleworth 17 1E
Ruggles Brise Rd. 14 4C
Rugosa Rd. 46 5A
Ruislip St. 21 4D
Runnemede Rd. 13 4D
Runnymede 13 3D
Runnymede Bridge 13 4E
Runnymede Cl. 17 2D
Runnymede Court 13 4E
Runnymede Cres. 40 1A
Runnymede Gdns. 17 2D
Runnymede Rd., Merton 38 1C
Runnymede Rd., Whitton 17 1D
Runwick La. 95 5D
Rupert Rd., Guildford 100 1C
Rupert Rd., Turnham Green 9 1E
Rural Way, Mitcham 21 5F
Rural Way, Redhill 90 5B
Ruscombe Way 15 2F
Rush Croft 100 5B
Rusham Park Av. 13 5D
Rusham Rd., Egham 13 5D
Rusham Rd., Wandsworth 21 1E
Rushams Rd. 158 4A
Rushden Cl. 22 5C
Rushden Way 96 2B
Rushdene Walk 77 2E
Rushen Wk. 39 4D
Rushett Cl. 36 4A
Rushett Dri. 106 3A
Rushett La. 53 4D
Rushett Rd. 36 4A
Rushetts Rd., Crawley 146 2C
Rushetts Rd., Woodhatch 108 2C
Rushey Green 24 2A
Rushey Mead 24 1A
Rushford Rd. 24 1A
Rushfords 131 1F
Rushley Cl. 37 3D
Rushmead Cl. 58 1A
Rushmere Ct. 37 5E
Rusholme Grn. 23 4D
Rusholme Rd. 20 1A
Rushtall Av. 9 2D
Rushton Av. 111 2F
Rushworth Rd. 89 5E

Ruskin Av., East Bedfont 15 1F
Ruskin Av., Feltham 16 2A
Ruskin Av., Kew 8 3C
Ruskin Cl. 147 3F
Ruskin Dri. 37 5F
Ruskin Rd., Carshalton 56 1B
Ruskin Rd., Croydon 40 5B
Ruskin Rd., Staines 14 5A
Ruskin Wk. 22 1C
Rusper Rd., Capel 144 1B
Rusper Rd., Gossops Green 146 4B
Rusper Rd., Horsham 158 4C
Rusper Rd., Newdigate 125 4F
Ruspers Keep 146 3B
Russ Hill 126 5C
Russell Cl., Beckenham 42 2B
Russell Cl., Horsell 64 1C
Russell Cl., Walton 88 1C
Russell Court, Hindhead 135 5F
Russell Court, Leatherhead 70 4A
Russell Dri. 14 1C
Russell Green Cl. 57 3E
Russell Hill 57 3D
Russell Hill Rd. 57 3E
Russell Rd., Horsell 64 1C
Russell Rd., Shepperton 33 4E
Russell Rd., The Wrythe 39 2D
Russell Rd., Walton 34 3A
Russell Rd., Wimbledon 20 5B
Russell Way, Crawley 147 4E
Russell Way, Sutton 55 1F
Russells Cres. 128 3B
Russells 72 4A
Russet Cl., Horley 128 2C
Russet Cl., Stanwellmoor 14 1A
Russet Cl., Walton-on-
Thames 34 4B
Russet Way 106 3A
Russett Cl., Tongham 97 1C
Russett Ct., Caterham 92 1A
Russett Dri. 41 4F
Russett Gdns. 61 1E
Russington Rd. 33 3E
Rusthall Cl. 41 3E
Rustic Av. 21 5F
Rustington Wk. 38 4D
Ruston Av. 36 4C
Rutford Rd. 22 4A
Ruthen Cl. 53 5F
Rutherford Way 147 1E
Rutherwick Cl. 128 2A
Rutherwick Rise 74 2A
Rutherwyck Cl. 54 2C
Rutherwyke Rd. 31 4F
Rutland Cl., Chessington 53 2E
Rutland Cl., Ewell 54 3A
Rutland Cl., Redhill 90 5A
Rutland Dri., North Cheam 38 3B
Rutland Dri., Richmond 18 2B
Rutland Gate 42 2C
Rutland Gdns. 58 1A
Rutland Gro. 9 2F
Rutland Park 24 3A
Rutland Rd. 17 3E
Rutland Wk. 24 3A
Rutlish Rd. 38 1B
Rutson Rd. 49 5F
Rutton Hill Rd. 136 3B
Ruxbury Rd. 31 3F
Ruxley Cl. 53 1F
Ruxley Cres. 53 2D
Ruxley La. 53 2F
Ruxley Mews 53 1F
Ruxley Ridge 52 2C
Rycott Path 23 2D
Rycroft Av. 17 2D
Rycroft Rd., Lewisham 24 1B
Rycroft Rd., Streatham 22 5B
Rydal Cl., Camberley 45 5D
Rydal Cl., Crawley 146 5A
Rydal Cl., Farnborough 60 5B
Rydal Cl., Purley 57 5F
Rydal Dri. 42 5C
Rydal Gdns., Coombe 19 4E
Rydal Gdns., Whitton 17 1D
Rydal Pl. 45 4F
Rydal Rd. 21 4F
Rydal Way 13 5E
Ryde Cl. 66 4B
Ryde Heron 64 2A
Ryde Pl. 18 1A
Ryde, The 32 1B
Ryde Vale Rd. 21 3E
Rydelands 141 1D
Rydens Av., Guildford 81 4D
Rydens Av., Walton-on-
Thames 34 5A
Rydens Cl. 34 5B
Rydens Gro. 51 1E
Rydens Pk. 34 5B
Rydens Rd. 34 5A
Rydens Way 65 3E
Ryders Way 158 2C
Rydes Cl. 65 3E
Rydes Hill Cres. 81 3D
Ryde's Hill Rd. 81 4D
Rydevale Rd. 21 3F

Rydon's La. 74 3B
Rydons Wood Cl. 74 3C
Rye Ash 147 3E
Rye Brook Rd. 69 2F
Rye Cl., Bracknell 27 1D
Rye Cl., Guildford 81 4D
Rye Cl., West Heath 60 3B
Rye Gro. 46 2B
Rye Walk 20 1A
Ryebridge Cl. 69 2F
Ryecotes Mead 23 2D
Ryecroft Dri. 158 4A
Ryecroft Gdns. 60 1B
Ryedale 23 1E
Ryefield Rd., Norwood 22 5C
Ryefield Rd., Selsdon 58 5B
Ryelands, Crawley 146 4B
Ryelands, Horley 128 2C
Ryelands Ct. 69 3F
Ryelands Pl. 33 5F
Ryemead La. 10 3A
Ryfold Rd. 20 3B
Ryland Cl. 15 4F
Rylandes Rd. 58 3B
Rylands Cl. 74 4C
Ryle Rd. 96 5A
Rylett Cres. 9 1E
Rylett Rd. 9 1E
Rymer Rd. 41 4D
Rymer St. 22 1B
Rythe Court 35 4F
Rythe Rd. 52 1B

S

Sachel Court Dri. 156 1A
Sackville Cl. 150 1B
Sackville Gdns. 150 1B
Sackville La. 150 1B
Sackville Rd. 55 2E
Saddleback Rd. 44 4B
Saddlers Cl. 82 5C
Saddlers Way 71 3D
Saddlewood 61 1D
Sadler Cl. 39 1D
Sadler Row 147 5D
Sadlers Ridge 35 2D
Sadlers Scarp 134 5C
Saffron Court. 60 4A
Saffron Platt 81 3E
Saffron Rd. 26 2C
Saffron Way 36 4A
Sailors La. 135 2F
Sainfoin Rd. 21 3E
Sainsbury Rd. 22 4C
St. Agatha Dri. 18 5B
St. Agatha's Green 39 4D
St. Agbury Cl. 73 3D
St. Agnes Rd. 150 2C
St. Aidans Rd., Camberwell 23 1E
St. Aidans Rd., Ealing 8 1A
St. Albans Av., Acton 9 1D
St. Albans Av., Hanworth 16 4B
St. Albans Av., Weybridge 33 5D
St. Albans Cl. 80 5C
St. Alban's Gdns. 17 4F
St. Albans Gro. 39 4D
St. Albans Rd., Cheam 55 1E
St. Albans Rd., Kingston 18 5B
St. Albans Rd., Reigate 89 4E
St. Amunds Cl. 24 4A
St. Andrews 26 3B
St. Andrew's Cl., Horsell 64 2C
St. Andrews Cl., Mead Vale 108 1C
St. Andrew's Cl., Old
Windsor 12 1B
St. Andrew's Cl., Upper
Halliford 33 2F
St. Andrews Cl.,
Wraysbury 13 2D
St. Andrew's Rd., Crawley 146 4A
St. Andrews Rd., Surbiton 36 3B
St. Andrews Rd., The
Wrythe 39 5D
St. Andrew's Rd.,
Woodmansterne 73 1E
St. Andrew's Sq. 36 3A
St. Andrews Walk 68 1A
St. Andrews Way, Frimley 61 3E
St. Andrews Way,
Limpsfield 94 3C
St. Anne's Av. 14 2C
St. Anne's Cl. 45 2D
St. Anne's Dri. 90 5B
St. Anne's Glade 45 2D
St. Anne's Mt. 90 5B
St. Annes Pk. Rd. 20 1C
St. Anne's Rd. 119 1E
St. Annes Rise 90 5B
St. Anne's Way 90 5B
St. Anns Cl. 32 3A
St. Ann's Cres. 20 1C
St. Ann's Hill 20 1C
St. Anns Hill Rd. 31 3F
St. Ann's Rd. 9 4E
St. Anns Rd., Chertsey 32 3A

St. Anns Way 57 2E
St. Anthonys Cl. 26 1C
St. Arvans Cl. 41 5D
St. Aubyn's Av., Whitton 16 1C
St. Aubyn's Av.,
Wimbledon 20 4B
St. Augustine's Av. 57 2E
St. Augustines Cl. 78 5A
St. Barnabas Rd., Sutton 55 1F
St. Barnabas Rd., Tooting 21 5E
St. Benet's Cl. 21 3D
St. Benet's Gro. 38 4C
St. Bernards Cl. 22 4C
St. Brelades Cl. 105 2F
St. Catherine's Cl. 21 3D
St. Catherines Cross 91 5F
St. Catherines Dri. 100 2C
St. Catherine's Estate 64 3C
St. Catherines Rd., Crawley 147 2F
St. Catherine's Rd., Frimley 61 2F
St. Chad's Cl. 36 4A
St. Charles Pl. 50 1A
St. Christopher's Gdns. 28 1A
St. Christopher's Mews 56 1C
St. Christopher's Rd., Cove 60 5C
St. Christopher's Rd.,
Shottermill 151 3F
St. Clair Cl., Oxted 93 3E
St. Clair Cl., Reigate 89 5F
St. Clair Dri. 37 5F
St. Cloud Rd. 22 4C
St. Crispins Way 48 3C
St. Cross Rd., Frimley 61 3F
St. Cuthbert's Cl. 12 5C
St. Davids 74 2A
St. Davids Cl., Hawley 60 3C
St. David's Cl., Heath End 96 1B
St. David's Cl., Reigate 89 5F
St. Davids Cl., W. Wickham 42 4A
St. Denis Rd. 22 4C
St. Denys Cl. 63 2F
St. Dunstan's Hill 55 1D
St. Dunstan's Rd., Feltham 15 3F
St. Dunstans Rd., South
Norwood 41 2D
St. Edmund Cl., Langley
Grn. 146 2C
St. Edmund's Cl. 21 3D
St. Edwards Cl., E.
Grinstead 150 2B
St. Edwards Cl., New
Addington 59 4E
St. Edward's Rd. 40 5B
St. Elmo Rd. 9 1E
St. Fillans Rd. 24 2B
St. Francis Wk. 146 5A
St. George's Av. 50 2A
St. George's Cl., Farnham 96 2C
St. George's Cl., Horley 128 2C
St. George's Cl.,
Weybridge 50 1B
St. George's Court 147 3D
St. George's Gdns., Epsom 54 5B
St. George's Gdns.,
Horsham 158 4C
St. George's La. 28 2C
St. George's Lo. 50 1B
St. George's Mews 96 4A
St. George's Rd.,
Addlestone 49 1E
St. Georges Rd.,
Beckenham 42 1A
St. George's Rd.,
Camberley 44 5A
St. George's Rd., East End 78 5A
St. George's Rd., Farnham 96 4B
St. George's Rd., Hanworth 16 4B
St. Georges Rd., Kingston 18 5C
St. George's Rd., Morden 39 2E
St. Georges Rd., Richmond 8 5B
St. Georges Rd., Salfords 109 4F
St. Georges Rd.,
Twickenham 18 1A
St. George's Rd.,
Weybridge 50 2B
St. George's Rd.,
Wimbledon 20 5B
St. George's Rd., Badshot
Lea Rd., Farnham 97 2D
St. Germans Rd. 23 2F
St. Gothard Rd. 22 4C
St. Helens Cres. 43 4D
St. Helens Rd. 40 1A
St. Helier Av. 38 4C
St. Helier Cl. 25 3D
St. Helier's Av. 16 1C
St. Hilda's Av. 14 4C
St. Hilda's Cl., Horley 128 2B
St. Hilda's Cl., Three
Bridges 147 2F
St. Hilda's Cl., Upper
Tooting 21 3D
St. Hilda's Cl., Woking 64 2A
Saint Hill Rd. 150 3C
St. Hughes Cl., Upper
Tooting 21 3D
St. Hughs Cl., Pound Hill 147 2F

St. Hugh's Rd.	23	5E
St. James Av., Cheam	55	1E
St. James Av., Elmers End	41	2F
St. James Av., Epsom	54	4B
St. James' Av., Farnham	96	3B
St. James Cl.	64	2B
St. James Mews	50	1A
St. James Rd., Cheam	55	1E
St. James Rd., East Grinstead	150	2C
St. James' Rd., Kingston	36	1B
St. James' Rd., Purley	57	5E
St. James' Rd., Surbiton	36	3B
St. James Rd., The Wrythe	39	5D
St. James Rd., Tooting	21	5E
St. James St.	9	2F
St. James' Ter.	96	3A
St. James Wk.	7	1B
St. James's Av., Hampton Hill	17	4D
St. James's Cl.	54	5A
St. James's Dri.	21	2D
St. James's Pk.	40	4B
St. James's Pl.	140	1B
St. James's Rd., Croydon	40	4B
St. James's Rd., Hampton Hill	17	4D
St. Joan Cl.	147	2C
St. Johns Av., Epsom	54	4B
St. John's Av., Leatherh'd.	70	4A
St. John's Av., Putney	20	1A
St. John's Cl., Guildford	100	1B
St. John's Cl., Horsham	158	5C
St. John's Cl., Leatherhead	70	4A
St. John's Court, Brookwood	63	4E
St. John's Court, S. Godstone	112	2A
St. John's Dri.	34	4B
St. Johns Gro.	8	5B
St. Johns Hill, Coulsdon	74	2B
St. Johns Hill, Purley	74	1B
St. Johns Hill, Wandsworth	20	1C
St. John's Hill Rd.	64	3B
St. John's Lye	64	3A
St. John's Meadow	111	5F
St. Johns Mews	64	3B
St. Johns Rd., Ascot	10	5B
St. John's Rd., Earlswood	109	1D
St. John's Rd., East Grinstead	150	2C
St. John's Rd., E. Molesey	35	2E
St. John's Rd., Goldsworth	64	2B
St. Johns Rd., Guildford	100	1B
St. Johns Rd., Hampton Wick	36	1A
St. Johns Rd., Hanworth	16	4C
St. Johns Rd., Kingston	37	2D
St. John's Rd., Leatherh'd	70	4A
St. John's Rd., N. Holmwood	106	3A
St. John's Rd., Penge	23	5E
St. John's Rd., Richmond	8	5B
St. John's Rd., Sandhurst	43	4D
St. John's Rd., Sutton Common	38	5B
St. John's Rd., The Wrythe	39	5D
St. John's Rd., Westcott	105	2D
St. Johns Rd., West Heath	60	4B
St. Johns Rd., Wimbledon	20	5A
St. John's Rd., Wrecclesham	96	5A
St. John's Rise	64	3B
St. John's St.	119	1D
St. John's Ter. Rd.	109	1D
St. Jude's Cl.	12	4C
St. Jude's Rd.	12	4C
St. Julians Cl.	22	4B
St. Julians Farm Rd.	22	4B
St. Katherines Rd.	92	1A
St. Kitts Ter.	22	4C
St. Lawrences Way	89	5E
St. Leonards Dri.	147	5E
St. Leonard's Rd., Burgh Heath	71	3F
St. Leonard's Rd., Claygate	52	2C
St. Leonard's Rd., Croydon	40	5B
St. Leonard's Rd., Hinchley Wood	35	3F
St. Leonards Rd., Horsham	158	5C
St. Leonards Rd., Long Ditton	36	3A
St. Leonards Rd., North Sheen	8	5C
St. Leonard's Rd., Winkfield	11	1D
St. Leonards Walk	7	1B
St. Louis Rd.	22	4C
St. Luke's Rd., Old Windsor	12	1B
St. Luke's Rd., Whyteleafe	75	2D
St. Margarets	82	5A
St. Margarets Av., Ashford	15	4E
St. Margaret's Av., Cheam	38	5A
St. Margaret's Av., Dormans Park	131	5F
St. Margarets Cres.	19	1F
St. Margaret's Gro.	17	1F
St. Margaret's Rd., Chipstead	73	4E
St. Margarets Rd., Coulsdon	73	4E
St. Margarets Rd., East Grinstead	150	1C
St. Margaret's Rd., Elmers End	41	2F
St. Margarets Rd., Richmond	17	1F
St. Marks Cl.	78	1A
St. Mark's Hill	36	3B
St. Marks Pl.	96	1A
St. Mark's Rd., Burgh Heath	72	2A
St. Mark's Rd., Mitcham	39	1E
St. Marks Rd., Popeswood	26	1B
St. Marks Rd., Teddington	18	5A
St. Martha's Av.	65	4D
St. Martin's Av.	54	5B
St. Martin's Cl., E. Horsley	84	3C
St. Martin's Cl., Epsom	54	5B
St. Martin's Dri.	34	5B
St. Martin's Place, Dorking	160	
St. Marys Av., Hackbridge	39	5E
St. Mary's Av., Shortlands	42	2C
St. Mary's Av., Stanwell	14	2C
St. Mary's Av., Teddington	17	5F
St. Mary's Cl., Chess'n	53	2E
St. Mary's Cl., Fetcham	69	5E
St. Marys Cl., Horsham	158	5B
St. Mary's Cl., Oxted	93	3F
St. Mary's Cl., Stanwell	14	2C
St. Mary's Cl., Upper Halliford	34	2A
St. Mary's Cl., West Ewell	54	2B
St. Mary's Cres.	14	2C
St. Mary's Dri., Crawley	147	3F
St. Mary's Dri., E. Bedfont	15	2C
St. Mary's Gdns.	45	2E
St. Mary's Grn.	77	2E
St. Mary's Gro., Barnes	9	5F
St. Mary's Gro., Biggin Hill	77	2C
St. Mary's Gro., Chiswick	8	3C
St. Mary's Gro., Richmond	8	5B
St. Mary's Hill	28	3C
St. Marys La.	10	3A
St. Mary's Rd., Ash Vale	78	3C
St. Mary's Rd., Camberley	44	5A
St. Mary's Rd., Ealing	8	1A
St. Mary's Rd., East Molesey	35	3E
St. Mary's Rd., Horsell	64	2C
St. Mary's Rd., Leatherhead	70	5A
St. Mary's Rd., Mead Vale	108	1C
St. Mary's Rd., Merton	38	1B
St. Mary's Rd., Sanderstead	57	3F
St. Mary's Rd., South Ascot	28	3C
St. Mary's Rd., Southborough	36	4A
St. Mary's Rd., South Norwood	40	2C
St. Marys Rd., Surbiton	36	3B
St. Mary's Rd., Weybridge	50	1B
St. Mary's Rd., Wimbledon	20	4A
St. Mary's Rd., Worcester Pk.	37	5E
St. Mathew La.	14	4A
St. Matthews Av.	36	4B
St. Matthew's Rd., Brixton Hill	22	1A
St. Matthews Rd., Redhill	90	5A
St. Michaels Av., Guildford	80	3C
St. Michaels Av., Walton-on-Thames	34	5B
St. Michaels Cl., Worcester Park	37	5E
St. Michaels Rd., Ashford	15	4D
St. Michael's Rd., Beddington	56	2C
St. Michael's Rd., Camberley	44	5A
St. Michaels Rd., Caterham	74	4C
St. Michaels Rd., East End	78	5A
St. Michaels Rd., Farnborough Street	61	4D
St. Michaels Rd., Woking	48	5C
St. Mildreds Rd., Guildford	82	5A
St. Mildreds Rd., Hither Green	24	2C
St. Monica's Rd.	72	4B
St. Nazaire Cl.	13	4E
St. Nicholas Av., Eastwick	86	1A
St. Nicholas Cl.	140	1C
St. Nicholas Dri.	33	4D
St. Nicholas Glebe	21	4E
St. Nicholas Hill	70	4A
St. Nicholas Rd., Sutton	55	1F
St. Nicholas Rd., Thames Ditton	35	3F
St. Nicholas Way	55	1F
St. Nicolas Av., Cranleigh	140	1C
St. Normans Way	57	2E
St. Olave's Cl.	14	5A
St. Omer Rd.	101	1E
St. Omer Ridge	101	1E
St. Oswald's Rd.	40	1B
St. Pauls Cl., Addlestone	49	1D
St. Paul's Cl., Ashford	15	4E
St. Paul's Cl., Chessington	53	1E
St. Pauls Cl., Ealing	8	1B
St. Paul's Gate	25	2D
St. Paul's Rd., Brentford	8	3A
St. Paul's Rd., Hythe	13	4F
St. Paul's Rd., Maybury	65	2E
St. Paul's Rd., Richmond	8	5B
St. Paul's Rd., Thornton Heath	40	2C
St. Paul's Rd. E.	106	2A
St. Paul's Rd. W., Dorking	105	2F
St. Peters Cl., Byfleet	49	4F
St. Peter's Cl., Old Windsor	12	1B
St. Peter's Cl., Old Woking	65	3E
St. Peter's Cl., Staines	14	5A
St. Peter's Ct.	35	2D
St. Peters Gdns.	114	1C
St. Peters Mead	78	5C
St. Peter's Rd., Hammersmith	9	2E
St. Peter's Rd., Kingston	36	1C
St. Peter's Rd., Richmond	18	1A
St. Peter's Rd., South Croydon	57	1F
St. Peters Rd., West Green	146	4C
St. Peter's Rd., Woking	65	4E
St. Peter's St.	57	1F
St. Peter's Sq.	9	2E
St. Peters Way, Addlestone	32	5A
St. Peters Way, Frimley	61	3E
St. Philip's Av.	37	5F
St. Philips Rd.	36	3B
St. Pier's La.	132	2A
St. Pinnock Av.	32	1A
St. Saviour's Rd., Brixton Hill	22	1A
St. Saviour's Rd., Thornton Heath	40	3B
St. Sebastian's Cl., Wick Hill	25	5F
St. Simons Av.	20	1A
St. Stephen Gdns.	18	1A
St. Stephen's Av., Ashtead	70	2B
St. Stephen's Av., Hammersmith	9	1F
St. Stephens Cl.	151	3E
St. Stephen's Gdns.	20	1B
St. Stephen's Rd.	17	1D
St. Swithuns Rd.	24	1B
St. Thomas' Cl.	64	2C
St. Thomas Dri.	83	4F
St. Thomas Rd.	8	3C
St. Vincent Cl.	147	4F
St. Vincent Rd., Walton-on-Thames	34	5A
St. Vincent Rd., Whitton	17	2D
St. Winifred Rd.	77	2F
St. Winifred's	74	1C
St. Winifred's Rd.	18	5A
Saints Cl.	22	4B
Salbrook Rd.	109	4E
Salcombe Dri.	38	4A
Salcombe Rd.	14	4C
Salcot Cres.	59	3E
Salcott Rd., Waddon	57	1D
Salcott Rd., Wandsworth	21	1D
Salehurst Rd.	24	1A
Salford Rd.	21	2F
Salfords	109	4E
Salfords Way	109	4E
Salisbury Av.	55	2E
Salisbury Cl., E. Heath	25	4D
Salisbury Cl., Worcester Park	37	5E
Salisbury Gro.	61	5F
Salisbury Pl.	49	4E
Salisbury Rd., Ash Wharf	78	4C
Salisbury Rd., Banstead	55	5F
Salisbury Rd., Carshalton Beeches	56	2A
Salisbury Rd., Farnborough Park	61	5D
Salisbury Rd., Feltham	16	2B
Salisbury Rd., Godstone	92	4B
Salisbury Rd., New Malden	37	2D
Salisbury Rd., Richmond	8	5B
Salisbury Rd., Wimbledon	20	5A
Salisbury Rd., Woking	65	3D
Salisbury Rd., Worc. Park	37	5E
Salisbury Ter.	61	5F
Salix Cl.	16	5A
Salmond Rd.	85	3D
Salmons La.	75	3D
Salmons Lane West	74	3C
Salmons Rd., Chessington	53	2E
Salmons Rd., Effingham	85	3D
Salt Box Rd.	81	3E
Salt La.	119	5D
Saltash Cl.	55	1E
Saltcoates Rd.	9	1D
Salterford Rd.	21	5E
Salterns Rd.	147	5F
Salter's Hill	22	4C
Saltram Rd.	78	1B
Salvation Pl.	69	5F
Salway Cl.	27	3D
Samaritan Cl.	146	5A
Samarkand Cl.	61	1F
Sambruck Mews	24	3B
Samos Rd.	41	1E
Sampleoak La.	101	3F
Sampson Pk.	26	1B
San Carlos App.	78	4A
Sand Hill	60	3C
Sand Hills	137	3D
Sandal Rd.	37	3D
Sandalwood	100	1B
Sandalwood Av.	31	5F
Sandalwood Rd.	16	3A
Sandbourne Av.	38	1C
Sandcross La.	108	2B
Sandell's Av.	15	4E
Sanders Cl.	17	4D
Sandersfield Gdns.	72	1B
Sandersfield Rd.	55	5E
Sanderstead	58	4A
Sanderstead Court Av.	58	5A
Sanderstead Hill	58	4A
Sanderstead Rd.	57	3D
Sandes Pl.	69	2F
Sandfield Gdns.	40	2B
Sandfield Rd.	40	2B
Sandfield Ter.	100	1C
Sandfields	65	5F
Sandford Down	27	2F
Sandford Rd., North Cheam	38	5B
Sandford Rd., Upper Hale	96	1A
Sandheath Rd.	135	3D
Sandhill Court	61	3D
Sandhill La.	149	3E
Sandhills	56	1C
Sandhills Court	31	3D
Sandhills La.	31	3D
Sandhills Rd.	108	1B
Sandhurst Av.	36	4C
Sandhurst Cl.	58	3A
Sandhurst La.	43	5D
Sandhurst Rd., Catford	24	2B
Sandhurst Rd., Crowthorne	43	2D
Sandhurst Rd., Wokingham	25	5D
Sandiford Rd.	38	5B
Sandiland Cres.	42	5C
Sandilands	41	5D
Sandlands Gro.	71	5F
Sandlands Rd.	71	5F
Sandon Cl.	35	4E
Sandown Av.	42	1A
Sandown Cres.	97	1D
Sandown Dri.	61	2E
Sandown Rd., Croydon	41	3E
Sandown Rd., Esher	52	1A
Sandown Rd., Woodmansterne	73	1E
Sandpiper Cl.	146	5A
Sandpiper Rd.	58	4C
Sandpit Hall Rd.	47	4E
Sandpit Heath	80	3C
Sandpit La., Bisley	46	5C
Sandpit La., Bisley	63	1F
Sandpit Rd., Redhill	109	1D
Sandpit Rd., Southend	24	4C
Sandpits Rd., Ham	18	3B
Sandpits Rd., Selsdon	58	1C
Sandra Cl.	17	1D
Sandringham Av.	38	1A
Sandringham Cl.	66	1A
Sandringham Dri.	14	4C
Sandringham Rd., Selhurst	40	3C
Sandringham Rd., Stanwell	14	1C
Sandringham Rd., Worcester Park	37	5F
Sandringham Way	61	3E
Sandrock	152	3A
Sandrock Hill Rd.	114	5A
Sandrock Pl.	58	1C
Sandrock Rd.	105	2D
Sandroyd Way	52	5A
Sands Cl.	97	4E
Sands Rd.	97	3D
Sandy Cl.	65	2E
Sandy Dri., Feltham	15	2F
Sandy Dri., Oxshott	52	4A
Sandy Hill Rd., Beddington	56	3C
Sandy Hill Rd., Upper Hale	96	1A
Sandy La., Albury	102	4C
Sandy La., Ascot Heath	28	1A
Sandy La., Beech Hill	134	4A
Sandy La., Betchworth	88	5B
Sandy La., Bletchingley	91	4E
Sandy La., Bracknell	27	1D
Sandy La., Camberley	44	5B
Sandy La., Cheam	55	2D
Sandy La., Chobham	47	3D
Sandy La., Churt	134	2C
Sandy La., Cobham	51	4F
Sandy La., Crawley Down	149	3D
Sandy La., Critchmere	151	2D
Sandy La., East Grinstead	150	2C
Sandy La., Godalming	119	1D
Sandy La., Ham	18	3A
Sandy La., Hampton Wick	36	1A

Sandy La., Haslemere 152 1B
Sandy La., Kingswood 72 5B
Sandy La., Limpsfield 94 2A
Sandy La., Littleton 100 3B
Sandy La., Milford 118 4A
Sandy La., Mitcham 39 1E
Sandy La., Nutfield 91 5D
Sandy La., Oxted 93 3E
Sandy La., Pyrford 66 2A
Sandy La., Reigate 107 1F
Sandy La., Rushmoor 115 5F
Sandy La., Send 65 5F
Sandy La., Shere 103 3D
Sandy La., Sunningdale 29 3E
Sandy La., Teddington 17 5F
Sandy La., Virginia Water 31 2D
Sandy La., Wallington 56 1C
Sandy La., Walton 34 3A
Sandy La., West Heath 60 3B
Sandy La., Willey Green 80 4A
Sandy La., Woking 65 2E
Sandy Lane South 56 2C
Sandy Rd., Addlestone 49 2E
Sandy Way, Oxshott 52 4A
Sandy Way, Shirley 41 5F
Sandy Way, Walton 33 4F
Sandy Way, Woking 65 2E
Sandycombe Rd., Feltham 16 2A
Sandycombe Rd., North Sheen 8 4C
Sandycombe Rd., Richmond 18 1A
Sandyride 29 2D
Sanger Av. 53 1E
Sanger Dri. 65 5F
Sangers Dri. 128 3B
Sangley Rd., Catford 24 2B
Sangley Rd., South Norwood 41 2D
Santina Cl. 96 1B
Santos Rd. 20 1B
Sanway Cl. 49 5F
Sanway Rd. 49 5F
Sappho Court 64 1A
Sapte Cl. 141 1D
Sarel Way 128 1B
Sarjant 20 3A
Sarsey Dri. 13 3E
Sarsfield Rd. 21 2D
Sarum 26 4B
Sarum Cres. 25 1E
Sarum Grn. 33 5F
Saunders Cl. 147 4F
Saunders Copse 64 4B
Saunders La. 64 4A
Saunton Gdns. 60 4C
Savernake 27 3E
Savernake Way 27 3F
Savernake Wk. 147 5E
Saville Cl. 37 3E
Saville Cres. 15 5E
Saville Gdns., Addiscombe 41 5D
Saville Gdns., Camberley 44 5C
Saville Gdns., Kingston 37 2F
Saville Rd., Acton 9 1D
Saville Rd., East Bedfont 15 2E
Saville Rd., Twickenham 17 2F
Saville Row 42 4C
Savona Cl. 20 5A
Savoy Grn. 60 1B
Sawkins Cl. 20 3A
Sawpit La. 83 3F
Sawtry Cl. 39 4D
Saxby Rd. 22 2A
Saxbys La. 131 2F
Saxley 128 2C
Saxon Av. 16 3C
Saxon Cres. 158 4A
Saxon Rd., Ashford 15 5E
Saxon Rd., Bromley Hill 24 5C
Saxon Rd., Selhurst 40 3C
Saxon Rd., Walton-on-Thames 34 5B
Saxon Way, Reigate 89 5E
Saxon Way, Wraysbury 12 1C
Saxonbury Av. 34 2A
Saxonbury Cl. 38 2C
Saxonby Gdns. 36 4A
Saxons 72 4A
Sayers Cl., Fetcham 69 5D
Sayers Cl., Frimley 61 3E
Sayes Court 49 1E
Sayes Court Farm Dri. 49 1E
Scallows Cl. 147 3E
Scallows Rd. 147 3E
Scampton Rd. 14 5C
Scarborough Cl., Belmont 55 4E
Scarborough Cl., Biggin Hill 77 2E
Scarbrook Rd. 40 5B
Scarlet Oaks Cl. 61 1E
Scarlet Rd. 24 3C
Scarlett Cl. 64 2A
Scarth Rd. 9 5E
Scholars Rd. 21 2F
School Allotment Ride 10 2C
School Cl. 81 4F
School Hill, Merstham 90 2C

School Hill, Seale 97 3F
School Hill, Wrecclesham 95 5F
School La., Addlestone 32 5A
School La., Ascot 28 1B
School La., Bagshot 45 2D
School La., Bisley 63 1E
School La., Copthorne 148 1B
School La., East Clandon 83 4F
School La., Egham 13 4E
School La., Fetcham 69 5E
School La., Forest Hill 23 3E
School La., Hampton 17 5D
School La., Hampton Wick 36 1A
School La., Lower Bourne 115 1E
School La., Mickleham 87 2D
School La., Norney 118 1A
School La., Ockham 67 4D
School La., Pirbright 63 4D
School La., Puttenham 98 3C
School La., Shepperton 33 3E
School La., Tolworth 36 4C
School La., Walton on the Hill 88 1C
School La., Westcott 105 2E
School La., W. Horsley 84 3B
School La., Windlesham 46 1A
School La., Wyke 79 4E
School Rd., Ashford 15 4D
School Rd., E. Molesey 35 2E
School Rd., Hindhead 135 5D
School Rd., Rowledge 114 2E
School Rd., Shottermill 151 3E
School Rd., Sunninghill 29 3D
School Rd., Windlesham 45 1F
School Rd., Wokingham 25 2E
School Road Av. 17 5D
School Wk. 33 2F
Schoolhouse La 18 5A
Schroder Court 12 4B
Schubert Rd. 20 1B
Scillonian Rd. 100 1B
Scizdons Climb 119 2E
Scotland Bridge Rd. 49 4D
Scotland Cl., Ash Vale 78 3C
Scotland Cl., Haslemere 151 3F
Scotland Farm Rd. 78 3C
Scotland La. 152 3A
Scots Cl. 14 2C
Scots Dale Cl. 55 2D
Scotshall La. 76 1B
Scotswood Cl. 78 3C
Scott Cl., Guildford 81 4E
Scott Cl., Norbury 40 1A
Scott Cl., Stoneleigh 54 1A
Scott Farm Cl. 35 4F
Scott Rd. 147 5D
Scott Ter. 27 1E
Scott's Av., Beckenham 42 1B
Scott's Av., Sunbury 15 5F
Scott's Dri. 17 5D
Scotts Farm Rd. 54 1A
Scott's Grove Cl. 46 5C
Scotts Grove Rd. 46 5C
Scott's Hill 110 5C
Scott's La., Beckenham 42 2B
Scotts La., Hersham 51 1E
Scott's Rd. 9 1F
Scott's Way 15 5F
Scrooby St. 24 1A
Scrutton Cl. 21 2F
Scutari Rd. 23 1E
Scutley La. 46 3A
Scylla Rd. 15 1E
Seabrook Dri 42 5C
Seaford Rd. 25 2E
Seaforth Av. 37 3F
Seaforth Gdns. 54 1B
Sealand Rd. 15 1D
Seale 97 3F
Seale Hill 108 1B
Seale La. 97 3D
Seale Rd. 97 5F
Seaman's Green Rd. 125 4D
Searchwood Rd. 75 2E
Searle Rd. 96 5A
Searles View 158 3C
Seaton Cl., Isleworth 17 1E
Seaton Cl., Roehampton 19 1C
Seaton Dri. 14 3C
Seaton Rd., Camberley 44 5A
Seaton Rd., Isleworth 17 1E
Seaton Rd., Mitcham 39 1D
Second Av., Mortlake 9 5D
Second Av., Walton-on-Thames 34 3A
Second Cl. 35 2D
Second Cross Rd. 17 3E
Second Rd. 40 2A
Seddon Rd. 38 3C
Sedgefield Cl. 148 3A
Sedgehill Rd. 24 4A
Sedgemoor 61 3D
Sedgeway 24 2C
Sedgeway Cres. 24 2C
Seeley Dri. 23 4D
Seeley Rd. 21 5E
Seething Wells La. 36 3A

Sefton Cl. 46 5B
Sefton Rd., Addiscombe 41 4E
Sefton Rd., Epsom 54 3A
Sefton St. 9 4F
Segal Cl. 23 2F
Segrave Cl. 50 2A
Segsbury Gro. 27 2E
Selborne Av. 97 2D
Selborne Rd., Croydon 41 5D
Selborne Rd., New Malden 37 1E
Selbourne Av., Woodham 49 3E
Selbourne Cl., Crawley 147 2F
Selbourne Cl., Frogmore 43 5D
Selbourne Cl., Woodham 49 3E
Selbourne Rd. 82 4B
Selbourne Sq. 92 3B
Selby Cl. 53 2E
Selby Green 39 4D
Selby Rd., Anerley 41 1D
Selby Rd., Ashford 15 5E
Selby Rd., St. Helier 39 4D
Selby Wk. 64 2B
Selbys 131 1F
Selcroft Rd. 57 4E
Selham Cl. 146 3B
Selhurst Cl. 65 1D
Selhurst Common Rd. 120 5B
Selhurst New Rd. 40 3C
Selhurst Pl. 40 3C
Selhurst Rd. 40 3C
Selkirk Rd., Tooting 21 4D
Selkirk Rd., Twickenham 17 3D
Sellars Hill 99 5F
Sellincourt Rd. 21 4D
Sellinge Cl. 24 5A
Selsdon 58 3B
Selsdon Cl. 36 3B
Selsdon Cres. 58 3B
Selsdon Park Rd. 58 3C
Selsdon Rd., South Croydon 57 1F
Selsdon Rd., West Norwood 22 4B
Selsdon Rd., Woodham 49 4D
Selsfield Rd. 149 5D
Seltops Cl. 141 2D
Selwood Cl. 14 1B
Selwood Gdns. 14 1B
Selwood Rd., Addiscombe 41 4E
Selwood Rd., Chessington 53 1D
Selwood Rd., North Cheam 38 4B
Selwood Rd., Woking 65 3E
Selworthy Rd. 24 3A
Selwyn Av. 8 5B
Selwyn Rd. 37 3D
Semaphore Rd. 101 1D
Semley Rd. 40 1A
Semper Cl. 64 2A
Send 65 5F
Send Barns La. 65 5F
Send Cl. 65 5F
Send Hill 65 5F
Send Marsh Rd. 65 5F
Send Rd. 65 4E
Sendmarsh 66 5A
Seneca Rd. 40 2B
Senga Rd. 39 4E
Senhouse Rd. 38 5A
Serpentine Green 90 3C
Serrin Way 158 3C
Seven Hills Cl. 50 3C
Seven Hills Rd. 50 5C
Sevenoakes Cl. 55 3E
Sevenoaks Rd. 23 1F
Severn Acres 39 5D
Severn Cl. 43 4D
Severn Dri., Hinchley Wood 35 5F
Severn Dri., Walton-on-Thames 34 5B
Severn Rd., Crawley 147 4E
Severn Rd., Farnborough 60 4B
Seward Rd. 41 1F
Sewell Av. 25 1D
Sewill Cl. 127 4E
Seymour Av., Caterham 74 5C
Seymour Av., Ewell 54 3C
Seymour Av., Morden 38 4A
Seymour Cl. 35 3D
Seymour Gdns., Hanworth 16 4A
Seymour Gdns., Surbiton 36 3B
Seymour Gdns., Twickenham 17 2F
Seymour Rd., Carshalton 56 1B
Seymour Rd., Chiswick 9 2D
Seymour Rd., Crawley 146 5C
Seymour Rd., East Molesey 35 3D
Seymour Rd., Hackbridge 39 4E
Seymour Rd., Hampton Hill 17 4D
Seymour Rd., Hampton Wick 36 1A
Seymour Rd., Headley Down 134 5A
Seymour Rd., Ockford Ridge 118 2C
Seymour Rd., Wandsworth 20 1B
Seymour Rd., Wimbledon 20 3A

Seymour Villas 41 1E
Seymour Way 15 5F
Shackleford 99 5D
Shackleford Rd., Elstead 117 2E
Shackleford Rd., Shackleford 99 5D
Shackleford Rd., Woking 65 4E
Shacklegate La. 17 4E
Shackleton Cl. 23 3E
Shackleton Rd. 147 5D
Shackstead La. 118 2C
Shackwood Way 96 1C
Shadbolt Cl. 37 5E
Shadyhanger Rd. 119 1D
Shaftesbury Av. 16 2A
Shaftesbury Cl., Bracknell 27 3D
Shaftesbury Cl., Crawley 147 5F
Shaftesbury Cres. 14 5C
Shaftesbury Rd., Beckenham 42 1A
Shaftesbury Rd., Bisley 63 1E
Shaftesbury Rd., Woking 65 2E
Shaftesbury Way 17 3E
Shaftsbury Rd., Richmond 8 5B
Shaftsbury Rd., The Wrythe 39 4D
Shakespeare Av. 16 1A
Shakespeare Gdns. 60 4B
Shakespeare Rd., Addlestone 49 1F
Shakespeare Rd., Herne Hill 22 1B
Shakespeare Way 16 4B
Shalbourne Rise 44 5B
Shaldon Dri. 38 3A
Shaldon Way 34 5B
Shale Green 90 3C
Shalford 101 3D
Shalford Rd. 100 2C
Shalston Villas 36 3B
Shalstone Rd. 8 5C
Shambles, The, Guildford 159 121 2D
Shamrock Cl., Fetcham 69 4E
Shamrock Cl., Frimley 61 3E
Shamrock Rd. 40 3A
Shandon Rd. 21 1F
Shandys Cl. 158 5A
Shanklin Court 78 5A
Shap Cres. 39 4D
Shardcroft Av. 22 1B
Sharon Cl., Bookham 68 5C
Sharon Cl., Crawley 147 5E
Sharon Cl., Epsom 54 5A
Sharon Cl., Long Ditton 36 4A
Shaw Cl., East Grinstead 58 4A
Shaw Cl., Ewell 54 4B
Shaw Cl., Ottershaw 48 2C
Shaw Court 12 1B
Shaw Cres. 58 4A
Shaw Dri. 34 4B
Shaw Pk. 43 2D
Shaw Rd., Southend 24 3C
Shaw Rd., Tatsfield 77 3E
Shaw Way 57 2D
Shawbury Rd. 23 1D
Shawfield La. 78 5B
Shawfield Rd. 78 5B
Shawford Rd. 54 2A
Shawley Cres. 72 2A
Shawley Way 71 2F
Shaws Rd. 147 3D
Shaxton Cres. 59 3E
Sheath's La. 52 5A
Sheen Common Dri. 18 1C
Sheen Court Rd. 8 5C
Sheen Gate Gdns. 9 5D
Sheen La. 19 1D
Sheen Pk. 8 5B
Sheen Rd. 18 1B
Sheen Way 57 1D
Sheendale Rd. 8 5B
Sheene Wood 23 4E
Sheenstone Cl. 25 5D
Sheep House 96 5A
Sheep Wk., Headley 71 4D
Sheep Wk., Shepperton Green 33 4D
Sheepbarn La. 59 4F
Sheepfold Rd. 81 4E
Sheephatch La. 116 1A
Sheephouse Green 104 3C
Sheephouse La. 104 3C
Sheephouse Way 37 4D
Sheeplands Av. 82 4C
Sheepwalk La. 84 5C
Sheerwater Av. 49 4D
Sheerwater Rd. 48 4C
Sheet Street Rd. 11 4D
Sheets Heath La. 63 3E
Sheffield Cl., Crawley 147 5E
Sheffield Cl., Farnborough 60 5C
Sheffield Cl., Stanwellmoor 14 1A
Shefford Cres. 25 1E
Shelbury Rd. 23 1E
Sheldon Cl., Crawley 147 4F
Sheldon Cl., Penge 41 1E
Sheldon Cl., Reigate 108 1C

Sheldrick Cl. 38 1C	Ship Alley 61 4D	Silo Rd. 100 5A	Smithy Cl. 89 1E
Shelford Rise 23 5D	Ship Hill 77 4E	Silver Birch Cl. 49 4D	Smithy La. 89 1E
Shelley Av. 27 1E	Ship La., Farnborough Street 61 4D	Silver Birches Way 117 2E	Smoke La. 108 1C
Shelley Cl., Banstead 72 1A	Ship La., Mortlake 9 4D	Silver Cres. 8 2C	Smokejack Hill Rd. 142 3B
Shelley Cl., Coulsdon 74 2A	Ship St. 150 3C	Silver Dri. 62 1A	Smugglers Way 97 5E
Shelley Cl., Three Bridges 147 3F	Shipfield Fl. 77 4E	Silver Hill 43 4E	Snailslynch 96 4B
Shelley Cl., E. Grinstead 150 2B	Shipka Rd. 21 2E	Silver La., West Wickham 42 5B	Snatts Hill 93 3F
Shelley Rd., Horsham 158 4A	Shipley Church Rd. 41 5F	Silver La., Woodcote 56 4C	Snelgar Rd. 65 2D
Shellwood Rd. 107 4D	Shipley Rd. 146 3B	Silver Tree Cl. 51 1D	Snell Hatch 146 4C
Shelson Av. 15 3F	Shipleybridge 129 5D	Silverdale 23 4E	Snellings Rd. 51 1E
Shelton Av. & Cl. Warlingham 75 2E	Shipleybridge La. 148 1A	Silverdale Av., Oxshott 52 5A	Snipe La. 151 5F
Shelton Cl., Guildford 81 3E	Shipman Rd. 23 3F	Silverdale Av., Walton 33 5F	Snow Hill 149 1D
Shelton Rd. 38 1B	Shirburn Cl. 23 2E	Silverdale Cl., Beckenham 24 5A	Snowdenham La. 120 1A
Shelvers Green 71 4F	Shire Cl. 45 3E	Silverdale Cl., Cheam 55 1E	Snowdenham Links Rd. 119 1F
Shelvers Grn. 71 4F	Shires Cl. 70 2A	Silverdale Cl., Strood Green 106 2C	Snowdon Rd. 60 3B
Shelvers Hill 71 4F	Shires Ho. 49 5F	Silverdale Court 14 4B	Snowdrop Way 63 2E
Shelvers Spur 71 4F	Shirley Av., Addiscombe 41 4E	Silverdale Dri. 34 1A	Snowerhill Rd. 107 1E
Shelvers Way 72 4A	Shirley Av., Belmont 55 3E	Silverlea Gdns. 128 3C	Snows Paddock 28 5C
Shelwood Dri. 106 3A	Shirley Av., Carshalton 56 1A	Silverleigh Rd. 40 2A	Snow's Ride 45 1F
Shenstone Park 29 2D	Shirley Av., Old Coulsdon 74 3B	Silvermere Rd. 24 2A	Soames Walk 37 1E
Shepherd Cl. 147 5D	Shirley Av., Salfords 109 3E	Silversmiths Way 64 2C	Soane Cl. 146 5A
Shepherd's Cl., Bagshot 45 3D	Shirley Church Rd. 58 1C	Silverstone Cl. 90 4A	Solartron 60 5C
Shepherds Cl., Shepperton 33 3D	Shirley Cl. 17 1D	Silverwood Cl. 59 3D	Soldiers Rise 25 5E
Shepherds Hill, Bracknell 27 1D	Shirley Cres. 41 2F	Silverwood Dri. 44 4C	Sole Farm Av. 85 1F
Shepherds Hill, Haslemere 152 3A	Shirley Dri. 17 1D	Silvery Sands 32 1A	Sole Farm Rd. 85 1F
Shepherds Hill, Merstham 90 1C	Shirley Hills Rd. 58 1B	Silvester Rd. 23 1D	Solecote 85 1F
Shepherd's Hill, Stoughton 81 4E	Shirley Oaks Rd. 41 5F	Silwood 26 4B	Solent Rd. 15 1D
Shepherd's La. 81 4E	Shirley Park Rd. 41 4E	Silwood Cl. 29 1D	Solom's Court Rd. 73 2D
Shepherds Walk, Fox Lane 60 3B	Shirley Pl. 63 2F	Silwood Rd. 29 2E	Somerfield Cl. 72 3A
Shepherds Way, Selsdon 58 2C	Shirley Rd., Addiscombe 41 4E	Simmil Rd. 52 1B	Somers Rd., Reigate 89 5E
Shepherds Way, Tilford 116 2A	Shirley Rd., Woodcote 56 3C	Simmonds Cl. 26 1B	Somers Rd., Tulse Hill 22 1A
Shepherds Wk., Ashtead 70 3C	Shirley Way 41 5F	Simms Cl. 39 5D	Somersbury La. 141 2F
Shepley Cl. 39 5E	Shobham Rd. 147 5F	Simondstone La. 134 2B	Somerset Av., Chessington 53 1D
Shepley Dri. 29 3F	Shophouse La. 121 1F	Simone Dri. 74 1C	Somerset Av., Raynes Pk. 37 1F
Shepley End 29 3F	Shoppe Hill 139 4D	Simons Cl. 48 2B	Somerset Cl., Ewell 54 3A
Sheppard Cl. 36 2B	Shord Hill 74 1C	Simons Walk 12 5C	Somerset Cl., Malden 37 3E
Shepperton 33 3E	Shore Cl. 16 2A	Simplemarsh Rd. 49 1D	Somerset Gdns. 40 2A
Shepperton Ct. Dri. 33 3D	Shore Gro. 16 3C	Simpson Rd., Ham 18 4A	Somerset Rd., Acton 9 1D
Shepperton Grn. 33 2D	Shoreham Cl., Croydon 41 3E	Simpson Rd., Whitton 16 1C	Somerset Rd., Brentford 8 3A
Shepperton Rd. 32 2B	Shoreham Cl., Wandsworth 20 1C	Sinclair Cl. 147 5F	Somerset Rd., Fulwell 17 4E
Sheraton Cl. 60 1B	Shoreham Rd. 14 1C	Sinclair Dri. 55 3E	Somerset Rd., Kingston 36 1C
Sheraton Dri. 54 4A	Shores Rd. 48 5A	Sine Cl. 60 3C	Somerset Rd., Redhill 109 1D
Sherborne Cl. 7 4B	Shorndean St. 24 2B	Sinhurst Rd. 60 1C	Somerset Rd., South Farnborough 78 1A
Sherborne Cres. 39 4D	Short Acres 91 5D	Sion Rd. 17 2F	Somerset Rd., Wimbledon 20 3A
Sherborne Rd., East Bedfont 15 2E	Short Cl. 147 5F	Siskin Cl. 158 3C	Somerset Way 7 1B
Sherborne Rd., South Farnborough 78 1A	Short La., Hurst Green 94 4A	Sispara Gdns. 20 1B	Somerswey 101 4D
Sherborne Rd., Sutton Common 38 5B	Short La., West Bedfont 15 2D	Sistova Rd. 21 2E	Somerton Av. 8 5C
Sherbourne Cl. 71 2F	Short Rd. 14 1C	Siward Rd. 20 3C	Somerton Cl. 74 1B
Sherbourne Dri. 30 3A	Short Way 17 2D	Sixth Cross Av. 17 3D	Somertons Cl. 81 4E
Sherbourne Rd. 53 1E	Shortcroft Rd. 54 2B	Skeena Hill 20 2A	Somerville Dri. 147 2F
Shere 103 2D	Shortdale Rd. 97 2D	Skelbrook St. 20 3C	Somerville Rd., Oxshott 52 5A
Shere Av. 54 3C	Shortfield Rd. 115 3D	Skerne Rd. 36 1B	Somerville Rd., Penge 23 5F
Shere Bypass 103 2D	Shortheath Cres. 114 1C	Skerne Rd., Kingston 159	Somme Rd. 62 2A
Shere Cl., Chessington 53 1E	Shortheath Rd. 96 5A	Skidhill La. 59 5F	Sommerfield La. 36 5A
Shere Cl., Dorking 106 3A	Shortlands 115 3D	Skiff Rd. 156 5A	Sondes Place Dri. 105 1E
Shere La. 103 3D	Shortlands Gdns. 42 1C	Skimpedhill La. 26 1C	Soning Rd. 41 3D
Shere Rd., Albury 102 1B	Shortlands Gro. 42 2B	Skinners La., Chiddingfold 138 4A	Sonning Gdns. 16 5C
Shere Rd., Ewhurst 122 4B	Shortlands Rd., Kingston 18 5C	Skinner's La., Lower Ashtead 70 2A	Sopwith Cl., Biggin Hill 77 1E
Shere Rd., W. Horsley 84 3B	Shortlands Rd., Shortlands 42 2B	Skipton Way 128 1B	Sopwith Cl., Kingston 18 4B
Sherfield Gdns. 19 1E	Shorts Rd. 56 1A	Slade Court 48 2C	Sopwith Dri. 49 4F
Sheridan Dri. 89 4F	Shortsfield Cl. 158 3B	Slade Rd., Brookwood 63 3D	Sopwith Way, Kingston 36 1B
Sheridan Pl. 150 2B	Shortwood 64 3C	Slade Rd., Ottershaw 48 2C	Sopwith Way, Kingston 159
Sheridan Rd., Eastwick 86 1A	Shortwood Av. 14 4B	Slagrove Pl. 24 1A	Sopwith Way, Roundshaw 57 2D
Sheridan Rd., Frimley 61 3D	Shotfield 56 2B	Slaidburn Grn. 27 4E	Sorrel Bank 58 3C
Sheridan Rd., Ham 18 3A	Shott Cl. 55 1F	Slapleys 64 3D	Sorrel Cl., West Heath 60 4A
Sheridan Rd., Merton 38 1B	Shottermill 151 3E	Slines Grn. 76 2A	Sorrel Cl., Wokingham 25 1F
Sheridans Rd. 86 1A	Shottermill Rd. 151 3E	Slines New Rd. 75 3F	Sorrel Dri. 45 4E
Sheriden Pl. 9 5E	Shrewsbury Cl. 36 5B	Slines Oak Rd. 76 3A	Sorrel Rd. 158 3C
Sheringham Av., Feltham 16 3A	Shrewsbury Rd., Elmers End 41 2F	Slinfold Wk. 146 4B	Sorrento Rd. 38 5B
Sheringham Av., Whitton 16 2C	Shrewsbury Rd., Redhill 90 5A	Slip Rd. 99 4D	South Albert Rd. 89 5E
Sheringham Rd. 41 2E	Shrewsbury Rd., St. Helier 39 4D	Slipshatch Rd. 108 2A	South Atlantic Dri. 78 4A
Sherland Rd. 17 2F	Shrivenham Cl. 43 4E	Slipshoe St. 89 5E	South Av., Carshalton 56 2B
Sherrydon 141 1D	Shroffold Rd. 24 4C	Sloane Walk 41 3F	South Av., Hale 96 2B
Sherwin Cres. 61 3D	Shrubbery Rd. 22 4A	Slougbrook Cl. 158 3C	South Av., Thorpe Lea 13 5F
Sherwood 60 5B	Shrubbs Hill 46 3C	Slough La., Buckland 88 4C	South Bank 36 3B
Sherwood Av. 21 5F	Shrubbs Hill La. 29 3F	Slough La., Headley 88 1A	South Border 57 4D
Sherwood Cl., Bracknell 27 1F	Shrubbs La. 114 2C	Slyfield 82 3A	South Cl., Twickenham 17 3D
Sherwood Cl., Fetcham 69 4D	Shrubland Gro. 37 5F	Slyfield Green 81 3F	South Cl., Woking 64 1C
Sherwood Cres. 108 2C	Shrubland Rd. 72 1B	Smallfield 129 3E	South Cl., Wokingham 25 2E
Sherwood Park Rd., Mitcham 39 2F	Shrublands Av. 42 5A	Smallfield Rd., Horley 128 2B	South Close Green 90 3B
Sherwood Park Rd., Sutton 55 1E	Shrublands Dri. 45 4F	Smallfield Rd., Horne 130 2A	South Croft Av. 42 5B
Sherwood Rd., Addiscombe 41 4E	Shute End 25 2D	Smallholdings Rd. 54 5C	South Croxted Rd. 22 3C
Sherwood Rd., Hampton Hill 17 4D	Sibthorp Rd. 39 1D	Smallmead 128 2C	South Dri., Banstead 56 5A
Sherwood Rd., Merton 20 5B	Sibton Rd. 39 4D	Small's Hill Rd., Leigh 107 5F	South Dri., Cheam 55 3D
Sherwood Rd., Woking 64 2A	Sickle Mill Rd. 151 3E	Small's Hill Rd., Norwood Hill 127 1D	South Dri., Cotmandene 106 1A
Sherwood Rd., Woodmasterne 73 1F	Sickle Rd. 151 3E	Smalls Mead 146 4C	South Dri., Virginia Water 30 4B
Sherwood Way 42 5B	Siddons Rd., Croydon 40 5B	Smallwood Rd. 20 4C	South Dri., Wokingham 25 2E
Sherwood Wk. 147 5E	Siddons Rd., Lewisham 23 3F	Smarts Heath La. 64 5B	South Dri., Woodmansterne 56 5A
Shetland Cl., Burpham 82 3B	Side View 128 5A	Smarts Heath Rd. 64 5B	South Ealing Rd. 8 1A
Shetland Cl., Crawley 148 3A	Sidings, The 14 4B	Smeaton Rd. 20 2B	South Eden Park Rd. 42 3A
Shey Copse 65 2F	Sidings, The 78 4A	Smith Barn Cl. 128 2B	South End, Bookham 86 1A
Shield Rd. 15 4E	Sidings, The 78 4A	Smith Cl. 147 5D	South End, South Croydon 57 1F
Shilburn Way 64 2B	Sidlaws Rd. 60 3B	Smith Rd. 108 2B	South Gdns. 21 5D
Shildon Cl. 62 1A	Sidney Rd., Beckenham 41 1F	Smith St. 36 3B	South Godstone 111 3F
Shilling Rd. 154 4A	Sidney Rd., Staines 14 4A	Smith Sq. 27 1D	South Gro., Chertsey 32 3A
Shillinglee Park Rd. 154 3A	Sidney Rd., Twickenham 17 1F	Smitham Downs Rd. 56 5C	South Grove, Horsham 158 5B
Shillinglee Rd. 153 4E	Sidney Rd., Walton 34 5A	Smithambottom La. 56 5C	South Hill, Godalming 119 2D
Shillinglee Rd. 153 4E	Sidney Rd., Woodside 41 3D	Smithbarn 158 4C	South Hill, Guildford 100 1C
Shimners Cl. 41 3D	Signal Cl. 131 2F	Smithers La. 132 5C	South Hill Rd., Easthampstead 27 3D
	Silbury Av. 39 1D	Smithers, The 106 1C	South Hill Rd., Shortlands 42 2C
	Silkham Rd. 93 2F	Smithfield La. 133 2F	South Holmwood 106 5A
	Silkmore La. 84 2A	Smiths La. 80 5B	South Kinver Rd. 23 4E
	Silo Cl. 100 5B	Smithwood Av. 121 4E	South La., Ash 78 5C
	Silo Dri. 100 5B	Smithwood Cl. 20 2A	South La., Kingston 36 2B
		Smithwood Common Rd. 121 4E	

South La., Malden 37 2D
South Lane West 37 2D
South Lodge Av. 40 2A
South Lynn Cres. 26 3C
South Meadow 43 2E
South Munstead La. 119 4E
South Norwood Hill 41 1D
South Nutfield 110 1A
South Oak Rd. 22 4A
South Parade, Bedford Park 9 2D
South Parade, Horley 128 2B
South Park Cres. 24 2C
South Park Gro. 37 2D
South Park Hill Rd. 57 1F
South Park Rd. 20 5B
South Pl. 36 4B
South Rd., Ash Wharf 78 4C
South Rd., Bisley 63 1E
South Rd., Bracknell 26 4B
South Rd., Brentford 8 2A
South Rd., Brooklands 50 3A
South Rd., Englefield Grn. 12 5C
South Rd., Hampton 16 5C
South Rd., Hanworth 16 4B
South Rd., Horsell 64 1C
South Rd., Lewisham 23 2F
South Rd., Mead Vale 108 1C
South Rd., Stoughton 81 4E
South Rd., Twickenham 17 3E
South Rd., Weybridge 50 1B
South Rd., Wimbledon 20 5C
South Ridge 50 3A
South Rise 56 3A
South St., Dorking 105 2F
South St., Epsom 54 5A
South St., Farnham 96 4A
South St., Godalming 119 2D
South St., Horsham 158 5B
South St., South Farnborough 78 1B
South St., Staines 14 4A
South Side, Stamford Brook 9 1E
South Side, Tongham 97 1E
South Ter., Surbiton 36 3B
South Terrace, Dorking 105 2F
South Vale 22 5C
South View, Selsdon 58 3C
South View Rd., Ashtead 70 3B
South View Rd., Beech Hill 134 4A
South Walk, Reigate 89 5F
South Way, Blackwater 60 1C
South Way, Shirley 41 5F
South Western Rd. 17 1F
South Wk., Aldershot 78 5B
South Wk., W. Wickham 42 5C
South Worple Way 9 5D
Southampton Cl. 43 5D
Southampton Rd. 15 1D
Southampton St. 78 2A
Southbank 36 4A
Southborough Cl. 36 4B
Southborough Rd. 36 4B
Southbridge Pl. 57 1E
Southbridge Rd. 57 1E
Southbrook Rd., Hither Green 24 1C
Southbrook Rd., Norbury 40 1A
Southcote 64 1C
Southcote Av., Feltham 16 3A
Southcote Av., Tolworth 36 4C
Southcote Dri. 44 5C
Southcote Rd., Merstham 90 3C
Southcote Rd., Selsdon 58 3A
Southcote Rd., Woodside 41 3E
Southcroft Rd. 21 5E
Southdean Gdns. 20 3B
Southdown Rd., Carshalton 56 3B
Southdown Rd., Hersham 51 1E
Southdown Rd., Wimbledon 38 1A
Southdown Rd., Woldingham 75 4F
Southend La. 24 4A
Southend Rd. 24 5A
Southerland Cl. 50 1B
Southern Av., Feltham 16 2A
Southern Av., Salfords 109 4E
Southern Av., Shortlands 41 2D
Southern Rd. 44 5A
Southern Way 96 4A
Southerns La. 72 5C
Southerton Rd. 9 2F
Southey Rd. 20 5B
Southey St. 23 5F
Southfield Gdns. 17 4F
Southfield Pl. 50 2A
Southfield Rd., Acton 9 1D
Southfield Rd., Wandsworth 20 1B
Southfields 35 3E
Southfields Av. 15 5E
Southfields Rd. 76 5A
Southgate Av., Ashford 15 4E
Southgate Av., Crawley 147 5D
Southgate Dri. 147 5D
Southgate Rd. 147 5D

Southland Way 17 1E
Southlands 150 3C
Southlands Av. 128 2B
Southlands Cl., Ash 78 5C
Southlands Cl., Coulsdon 74 2A
Southlands Cl., Wokingham 25 2E
Southlands La. 93 5D
Southlands Rd., Ash 78 5C
Southlands Rd., Wokingham 25 3E
Southly Cl. 38 5B
Southmead, Ewell 54 2B
Southmead Rd., Aldershot 97 1D
Southmead Rd., Redhill 90 4B
Southmead Rd., Southfields 20 2A
Southmont Rd. 35 5E
Southsea Rd., Croydon 40 4B
Southsea Rd., Kingston 36 2B
Southside Common 20 5A
Southview Cl. 149 1D
Southview Court 65 2D
Southview Gdns. 56 2C
Southview Rd., Downham 24 4B
Southview Rd., Whyteleafe 75 3E
Southview Rd., Woldingh'm 76 5A
Southville 15 2F
Southville Cl., Ewell 54 3A
Southville Cl., Feltham 15 2F
Southville Cres. 15 2F
Southville Rd., E. Bedfont 15 2F
Southville Rd., Long Ditton 35 4F
Southwater Cl. 24 5B
Southway, Cannon Hill 38 2A
Southway, Carshalton Beeches 56 3A
Southway, Wallington 56 1C
Southway, Woodbridge Hill 81 5E
Southwell Park Rd. 44 5A
Southwell Rd. 40 3B
Southwick Cl. 147 4F
Southwick Court 27 3E
Southwick Rd. 150 2B
Southwold 26 4B
Southwood Av., Coombe 37 1D
Southwood Av., Knaphill 64 2A
Southwood Av., Ottershaw 48 2C
Southwood Av., Woodmansterne 73 1F
Southwood Chase 141 2D
Southwood Cl. 38 4A
Southwood Dri. 37 4D
Southwood Gdns. 35 5F
Southwood Rd. 60 5B
Sovereign Ct. 34 2C
Spa Dri. 53 5F
Spa Hill 40 1C
Space Way 16 1A
Spalding Rd. 21 4E
Sparks Cl. 16 5C
Sparrow Farm Dri. 16 2B
Sparrow Farm Rd. 54 1C
Sparrow Row 46 2C
Sparrows Mead 90 4B
Sparvell Rd. 63 3F
Spats La. 133 3F
Speedwell Cl. 82 4B
Speer Rd. 35 4F
Speke Rd. 40 1C
Speldhurst Rd. 9 1D
Spelthorne Gro. 15 5F
Spelthorne La. 33 1E
Spence Av. 49 5F
Spence Pk. 21 1D
Spencer Cl., Frimley Grn. 61 4E
Spencer Cl., Langley Vale 71 3E
Spencer Cl., Sheerwater 48 5C
Spencer Gdns. 12 4C
Spencer Hill 20 5A
Spencer Pk. 35 3E
Spencer Pl. 40 4C
Spencer Rd., Bromley Hill 24 5C
Spencer Rd., Caterham 74 4C
Spencer Rd., Chiswick 9 3D
Spencer Rd., Cobham 68 1A
Spencer Rd., Croydon 57 1F
Spencer Rd., East Molesey 35 3E
Spencer Rd., Hackbridge 39 4E
Spencer Rd., Mitcham 39 2E
Spencer Rd., Priestwood 26 1C
Spencer Rd., Raynes Park 37 1F
Spencer Rd., Twickenham 17 3E
Spencer Way (Mason's Bridge Rd.) 109 3E
Spencer's Pl., Horsham 158 4A
Spencer's Rd., Horsham 158 4A
Spencer's Rd., West Green 146 4C
Spenser Av. 50 2A
Spenser Rd. 22 1B
Spiceall 99 4F
Spicer Cl. 34 3B
Spicers Field 52 5B
Spiers Cl. 37 3E
Spiers Way 128 3B
Spindle Way 147 4D

Spindlewoods Cl. 71 5F
Spinis 26 4B
Spinner Green 26 3C
Spinney Cl., Crawley Down 149 3E
Spinney Cl., Oxshott 52 4A
Spinney Croft 69 1E
Spinney Dri. 15 2E
Spinney Gdns. 23 4D
Spinney Hill 49 1D
Spinney, The, Camberley 45 5D
Spinney, The, Cheam 54 1C
Spinney, The, Crawley 146 5C
Spinney, The, Crawley Down 149 3E
Spinney, The, Fetcham 69 5D
Spinney, The, Grayshott 134 5C
Spinney, The, Guildford 83 2E
Spinney, The, Haslemere 152 2A
Spinney, The, Horley 128 1B
Spinney, The, Oxshott 52 4B
Spinney, The, Purley 57 4E
Spinney, The, Streatham 21 3F
Spinney, The, Sunbury 34 1A
Spinney, The, Sunningdale 29 3E
Spinney, The, Tatt. Corner 71 3F
Spinning Walk 103 3D
Spital Heath 106 1A
Spoil La. 97 1E
Spokane Cl. 96 1C
Spook Hill 106 4A
Spooner Wk. 56 1C
Spooners Rd. 158 3C
Sportsbank St. 24 2B
Spout Hill 59 1D
Spout La. 7 5C
Spratts Alley 48 2C
Spratts La. 48 2C
Spreighton Rd. 35 3D
Spring Av. 13 5D
Spring Cl., Northborne 100 5A
Spring Clears 45 4E
Spring Copse., Copthorne 148 1C
Spring Court 81 3E
Spring Cres. 8 2C
Spring Farm Rd. 151 3E
Spring Gdns., Biggin Hill 77 2D
Spring Gdns., Camberley 44 5C
Spring Gdns., Copthorne 148 1C
Spring Gdns., E. Molesey 35 3D
Spring Gdns., Farnborough 60 3C
Spring Gdns., South Ascot 28 3C
Spring Grn. 35 1D
Spring Gro., Fetcham 69 5D
Spring Gro., Northbourne 100 5A
Spring Grove Rd. 18 1B
Spring Haven Cl. 82 5B
Spring Hill 23 4E
Spring La., Cheam 55 2D
Spring La., Folly Hill 95 2F
Spring La., Oxted 93 4E
Spring La., Woodside 41 3E
Spring Meadow 27 1E
Spring Ms. 54 3B
Spring Park Av. 41 5F
Spring Park Rd., Beckenham 42 2B
Spring Park Rd., Shirley 41 5F
Spring Plat 147 4F
Spring Rd. 16 3A
Spring Rise 13 5D
Spring St. 54 3B
Spring Well Cl. 22 4A
Spring Woods, Sandhurst 43 3D
Spring Woods, Virginia Water 30 2B
Springbank Rd. 24 1C
Springbottom La. 91 2E
Springcopse Rd. 108 1C
Springcross Av. 60 1B
Springfield, Ashford 14 4C
Springfield, Camberley 44 4A
Springfield, E. Grinstead 150 1C
Springfield, Elstead 117 2D
Springfield, Lightwater 46 4A
Springfield, Oxted 93 3E
Springfield Av., Hampton Hill 17 5D
Springfield Av., Morden 38 2B
Springfield Cl. 64 2A
Springfield Cres. 158 5A
Springfield La. 50 1A
Springfield Meadow 50 1A
Springfield Park Rd. 158 5B
Springfield Pl. 37 2D
Springfield Rd., Ash Vale 78 3C
Springfield Rd., Bracknell 26 1B
Springfield Rd., Camberley 44 5C
Springfield Rd., East Ewell 54 3C
Springfield Rd., Guildford 82 5A
Springfield Rd., Horsham 158 5B
Springfield Rd., Kingston 36 2B
Springfield Rd., Norbury 40 1B
Springfield Rd., Sydenham 23 4E
Springfield Rd., Teddington 17 4F
Springfield Rd., Wallington 56 1B
Springfield Rd., Westcott 105 2D
Springfield Rd., West Grn. 146 4C

Springfield Rd., Whitton 17 2D
Springfield Rd., Wimbledon 20 4B
Springfield Rise 23 3E
Springfield Way 117 2D
Springfields Cl. 32 4B
Springhill 117 2E
Springholm Cl. 77 2E
Springrice Rd. 24 1B
Springvale Av. 8 2B
Springwell Rd., Beare Green 125 2D
Springwell Rd., Streatham 22 4A
Springwood 118 3B
Spruce Dri. 45 4E
Spruce Rd. 77 1E
Sprucedale Gdns., Upper Shirley 58 1C
Sprucedale Gdns., Wallington 56 3C
Spur Rd. 16 1A
Spur, The 63 2F
Spurfield 35 2D
Spurgeon Cl. 146 3C
Spurgeon Rd. 40 1C
Spy La. 156 3A
Square Dri. 151 5F
Square, The, Bagshot 45 2E
Square, The, Camberley 44 5A
Square, The, Carshalton 56 1B
Square, The, Caterham 75 5D
Square, The, Lightwater 45 3F
Square, The, Lingfield 131 2E
Square, The, Tatsfield 77 3E
Square, The, Weybridge 50 1B
Square, The, Wisley 66 1C
Squire Ct. 32 4B
Squire's Bridge Rd. 33 2D
Squires Cl. 149 3D
Squire's Hill La. 116 2A
Squire's Rd. 33 2D
Squires Wk. 15 5F
Squirrel Cl., Langley Grn. 146 2C
Squirrel Cl., Sandhurst 43 4D
Squirrel Wood 49 4E
Squirrel's Cl. 100 4A
Squirrels Grn., Fetcham 68 5C
Squirrels Grn., Wrc. Pk. 37 5E
Squirrels Nest La. 45 1F
Squirrels Way 71 1D
St Georges Rd. E. 78 5A
Stable Croft 45 3D
Stables, The 68 1C
Stace Way 148 3A
Stacey Court 90 3C
Stackfield Rd. 146 4A
Staff College Rd. 43 5F
Stafford Cl., Caterham 75 5D
Stafford Cl., Cheam 55 2D
Stafford Gdns. 57 1D
Stafford Lake 63 2F
Stafford Pl. 18 2B
Stafford Rd., Caterham 75 4D
Stafford Rd., Ifield Vill. 146 2D
Stafford Rd., Kingston 37 2D
Stafford Rd., Waddon 57 2D
Stag Hill 100 1B
Stag La. 19 3E
Stag Leys 70 3E
Stag Ride 19 3F
Stagbury Av. 73 2D
Stagbury Ho. 73 3D
Stagelands 146 3C
Stainash Cres. 14 4B
Stainbank Rd. 39 2E
Staines 14 4A
Staines Av. 38 5A
Staines By-Pass 13 3F
Staines La. 32 2A
Staines Rd., East Bedfont 15 2E
Staines Rd., Feltham 16 1A
Staines Rd., Laleham 32 1B
Staines Rd., Twickenham 17 3D
Staines Rd., Wraysbury 13 2D
Staines Road East 16 5A
Staines Road West 15 5D
Stainford Cl. 15 4E
Stainton Rd. 24 2B
Stainton Wk. 64 2C
Staithes Way 71 3F
Stake La. 60 4C
Stakescorner Rd. 100 4B
Stambourne Way, Norwood 41 1D
Stambourne Way, W. Wickham 42 5B
Stamford Av. 61 2E
Stamford Brook 9 1E
Stamford Brook Av. 9 1E
Stamford Dri. 42 2C
Stamford Green Rd. 53 5F
Stamford Rd. 34 5B
Stan Hill 127 2D
Standen Rd. 20 2B
Standford La. 133 5E
Standon La. 142 2C
Stane St., Mickleham 87 2D
Stane St., Ockley 124 5B
Stane Way 54 3B

Stanford Cl.	16	5C
Stanford Rd.	40	1A
Stanford Way	39	1F
Stanfords Pl.	131	2E
Stanger Rd.	41	2D
Stanhill Rd.	126	2B
Stanhope Gro.	42	3A
Stanhope Heath Way	14	1B
Stanhope Rd., Camberley	60	1C
Stanhope Rd., Carshalton	56	2B
Stanhope Rd., Croydon	40	5C
Stanhopes	94	2A
Stanier Cl.	147	4F
Stanley Av., Malden	37	3E
Stanley Av., Shortlands	42	2B
Stanley Cl., Coulsdon	74	2A
Stanley Cl., Crawley	147	5D
Stanley Dri.	60	5A
Stanley Gardens Rd.	17	4E
Stanley Gdns., Acton	9	1D
Stanley Gdns., Beddington	56	2C
Stanley Gdns., Hersham	51	2D
Stanley Gdns., Sanderstead	58	4A
Stanley Green	40	3B
Stanley Park Rd.	56	2A
Stanley Rd., Acton	8	1C
Stanley Rd., Ashford	14	4C
Stanley Rd., Carshalton	56	2B
Stanley Rd., Cheam	55	2E
Stanley Rd., Croydon	40	4B
Stanley Rd., Fulwell	17	4E
Stanley Rd., Morden	38	2B
Stanley Rd., North Sheen	8	5C
Stanley Rd., Tooting	21	5E
Stanley Rd., Wimbledon	20	5B
Stanley Rd., Woking	65	2D
Stanley Rd., Wokingham	25	2E
Stanley St.	74	4C
Stanley Sq.	56	3B
Stanley Walk	158	5B
Stanmore Cl.	28	2C
Stanmore Gdns., Richmond	8	5B
Stanmore Gdns., Sutton	38	5C
Stanmore Rd.	8	5B
Stanstead Cl.	42	3C
Stanstead Rd., Caterham	75	5D
Stanstead Rd., Lewisham	23	2F
Stanstead Rd., W. Bedfont	15	1D
Stanthorpe Rd.	22	4A
Stanton Av.	17	5E
Stanton Cl., Cheam	38	5A
Stanton Cl., Cranleigh	140	1B
Stanton Cl., Felbridge	150	1A
Stanton Cl., West Ewell	53	1F
Stanton Rd., Barnes	9	4E
Stanton Rd., Croydon	40	4B
Stanton Rd., Sydenham	23	4F
Stanton Rd., Wimbledon	38	1A
Stanton Way	23	4F
Stanwell	14	1C
Stanwell Cl.	14	1C
Stanwell Gdns.	14	1C
Stanwell Moor Rd., Longford	7	4C
Stanwell Moor Rd., Staines	14	3A
Stanwell New Rd.	14	3B
Stanwell Rd., Ashford	14	3C
Stanwell Rd., East Bedfont	15	2E
Stanwell Rd., Poyle	7	5A
Stanwellmoor	14	1A
Staple Hill Rd.	47	2D
Staple La.	103	1D
Staple Mews	22	4C
Staple Rd.	83	4F
Stapleford Cl., Southfields	20	2A
Stapleford Cl., Streatham	22	2A
Staplehurst	26	4B
Staplehurst Cl.	108	2C
Staplehurst Lane	109	3F
Staplehurst Rd., Carshalton	56	2A
Staplehurst Rd., Hither Green	24	1C
Staplehurst Rd., Woodhatch	108	2C
Stapleton Gdns.	57	1E
Stapleton Rd.	21	3E
Star and Garter Hill	18	2B
Star Hill, Churt	134	2B
Star Hill, Woking	64	3C
Star Hill Dri.	134	2B
Star La., Ash	78	5C
Star La., Hooley	73	4E
Star Post Rd.	44	4B
Starborough Rd.	132	1B
Starfield Rd.	9	1E
Starlings, The	52	5A
Starlings, The	52	5A
Starmead Dri.	25	2E
Starrock La.	73	3E
Starrock Rd.	73	3F
Starwood Cl.	49	4E
Statham Court	26	1B
Station App., Ashford	14	4C
Station App., Ash Vale	78	2C
Station App., Chipstead	73	2D
Station App., Coulsdon	73	1F
Station App., Dorking	87	5D

Station App., Earlswood	109	1E
Station App., Epsom	54	5A
Station App., Godalming	118	2C
Station App., Gomshall	103	3E
Station App., Guildford	100	1C
Station App., Hinchley W'd	35	5F
Station App., Horley	128	3B
Station App., Horsley	84	1C
Station App., Lower Sydenham	24	4A
Station App., New Oxted	93	3F
Station App., Ockley	124	5C
Station App., Shepperton	33	3E
Station App., Staines	14	4A
Station App., Sunbury	34	1A
Station App., Upper Warlingham	75	2D
Station App., Wanborough	79	5F
Station App., West Byfleet	49	4D
Station App., West Clandon	83	3E
Station App., West Wickham	42	4B
Station App., Woking	65	2D
Station App. Rd.	73	1F
Station Approach, Oxshott	52	4A
Station Approach North	110	1A
Station Approach Rd., Chiswick	9	3D
Station Approach Rd., Tadworth	71	4F
Station Approach South	110	1A
Station Av., Caterham	75	5D
Station Av., Ewell	54	3B
Station Av., New Malden	37	2E
Station Av., Walton	34	5A
Station Cres.	14	3C
Station Estate Rd.	16	2A
Station Gdns.	9	3D
Station Hill, Ascot	28	2B
Station Hill, Farnham	96	4A
Station La.	118	3B
Station Par., E. & W. Horsley	84	1C
Station Parade, Virginia Water	30	2C
Station Rd., Addlestone	49	1E
Station Rd., Ashford	14	4C
Station Rd., Ash Vale	78	2C
Station Rd., Bagshot	45	2E
Station Rd., Barnes	9	4E
Station Rd., Belmont	55	3E
Station Rd., Betchworth	88	5A
Station Rd., Bracknell	27	1D
Station Rd., Carshalton	56	1B
Station Rd., Chertsey	32	4A
Station Rd., Chessington	53	1E
Station Rd., Chobham	47	4D
Station Rd., Claygate	52	1B
Station Rd., Crawley	147	4D
Station Rd., Crawley Down	149	3E
Station Rd., Croydon	40	4B
Station Rd., Dorking	105	1F
Station Rd., Dormans Pk.	131	4F
Station Rd., Earlswood	109	1D
Station Rd., Egham	13	4D
Station Rd., E. Grinstead	150	2C
Station Rd., Esher	35	5E
Station Rd., Farncombe	100	5A
Station Rd., Farnham	96	4A
Station Rd., Frimley	61	2D
Station Rd., Godalming	119	2D
Station Rd., Gomshall	103	3E
Station Rd., Hampton	35	1D
Station Rd., Hampton Wick	36	1A
Station Rd., Horley	128	3B
Station Rd., Horsham	158	5B
Station Rd., Kenley	57	5F
Station Rd., Leatherhead	69	4F
Station Rd., Lingfield	131	1F
Station Rd., Loxwood	156	4A
Station Rd., Merton	38	1C
Station Rd., Mugswell	90	1A
Station Rd., North Farnborough	60	5C
Station Rd., Norwood	41	2D
Station Rd., Penge	23	5E
Station Rd., Redhill	90	5A
Station Rd., Rudgwick	157	2F
Station Rd., Shalford	101	3D
Station Rd., Shepperton	33	3E
Station Rd., Shortlands	42	1C
Station Rd., Stoke D'Abernon	68	2C
Station Rd., Sunbury	16	5A
Station Rd., Sunningdale	29	3E
Station Rd., Teddington	17	5F
Station Rd., Thames Diton	35	4F
Station Rd., Twickenham	17	2F
Station Rd., Warnham	158	2A
Station Rd., West Byfleet	49	4D
Station Rd., Whyteleafe	75	2D
Station Rd., Wokingham	25	2D
Station Rd., Woldingham	75	4F
Station Rd., Wonersh	101	5D
Station Rd., Wraysbury	13	1D
Station Road East, Ash Vale	78	2C

Station Road East, Oxted	93	3F
Station Road North	90	2C
Station Road South	90	2C
Station Road West	93	3F
Station View	78	2C
Station Way, Cheam	55	2D
Station Way, Claygate	52	2B
Station Way, Crawley	147	4D
Station Yard	17	2F
Staunton Rd.	18	5B
Staveley Gdns.	9	4D
Staveley Rd., Ashford	15	5F
Staveley Rd., Chiswick	9	3D
Staveley Way	64	2A
Staverton Cl.	25	2F
Stavordale Rd.	38	4C
Stayne End	30	2B
Stayton Rd.	38	5B
Steadfast Rd.	36	1B
Steadfast Rd., Kingston	159	
Steele Rd.	9	1D
Steels La.	52	5A
Steep Hill	46	2C
Steeple Cl.	20	4A
Steeple Gdns.	49	1E
Steeple Heights	77	2E
Steepways	135	4D
Steer Pl.	109	5E
Steerforth Copse	43	3E
Steerforth St.	20	3C
Steers Hill	145	4D
Steers La.	147	1F
Steers Mead	39	1D
Stella Rd.	21	5E
Stembridge Rd.	41	1E
Stents La.	68	3C
Stepgates	32	4B
Stephen Cl., Northgate	147	2D
Stephen Cl., Thorpe Lea	13	5F
Stephendale Rd.	96	3B
Stephens Field	137	5E
Stephenson Dri.	150	3C
Stephenson Pl.	147	4E
Stephenson Rd.	16	2C
Stephenson Way	147	4E
Stepney Cl.	147	5F
Sterling Pl.	8	2B
Sternhold Av.	21	3F
Sterry Dri., Thames Ditton	35	3E
Sterry Dri., Worcester Park	54	1A
Steucers La.	23	2F
Steve Biko La.	24	4A
Stevens Cl., Beckenham	24	5A
Stevens Cl., Epsom	54	4B
Stevens Cl., Hampton	16	4C
Stevens' Lane	52	2C
Stewards Cl.	95	5F
Stewart	72	4A
Stewart Av.	33	2D
Stewart Cl., Hanworth	16	4C
Stewart Cl., Woking	64	2A
Steyning Cl., Coulsdon	74	1B
Steyning Cl., Crawley	147	3D
Stile Hall Gdns.	8	2C
Stile Path	34	2A
Stillart Grn.	17	4E
Stillingfleet Rd.	9	3E
Stillness Rd.	24	1A
Stirling Cl., Banstead	72	2B
Stirling Cl., Frimley	61	2E
Stirling Cl., Three Bridges	147	4F
Stirling Rd., Acton	8	1C
Stirling Rd., Guildford	100	1A
Stirling Rd., Stanwell	14	1C
Stirling Rd., Whitton	17	2D
Stirling Walk	36	3C
Stirling Way, Croydon	40	4A
Stirling Way, Horsham	158	4C
Stites Hill Rd.	74	3B
Stoatley Hollow	151	2F
Stoatley Rise	151	2F
Stoats Nest Village	74	1A
Stock Hill	77	2E
Stockbridge Dri.	97	2D
Stockbury Rd.	41	3E
Stockers La.	65	3D
Stockfield	128	2C
Stockfield Rd., Esher	52	1B
Stockfield Rd., Streatham	22	3A
Stockhams Cl.	57	3F
Stockport Rd., Mitcham	39	1F
Stockton Rd., Reigate	108	2B
Stockwell Rd.	150	3C
Stockwood Glades	96	1C
Stockwood Rise	44	5C
Stocton Cl.	81	5F
Stocton Rd.	81	5F
Stodart Rd.	41	1E
Stoford Cl.	20	2A
Stoke Cl.	68	1C
Stoke D'Abernon	68	2C
Stoke Fields	100	1C
Stoke Hills	96	3B
Stoke Rd., Guildford	100	1C
Stoke Rd., Kingston	19	5D
Stoke Rd., Stoke D'Abernon	68	1B

Stoke Rd., Walton	34	5B
Stokes Rd.	41	3F
Stokes Ridings	72	5A
Stokesby Rd.	53	2E
Stokesheath Rd.	52	4A
Stompond La.	34	5A
Stonards Brow	120	2C
Stone Bridge Fields	100	4C
Stone Bridge Wharf	100	4C
Stone Court Cl.	128	2C
Stone Cres.	15	2F
Stone Gate	45	5D
Stone Hill Rd., Lightwater	45	3E
Stone Park Av.	42	2A
Stone Pl.	37	5F
Stone Rd.	42	3C
Stone St., Aldershot	97	1D
Stone St., Waddon	57	1D
Stonebanks	34	4A
Stonecot Cl.	38	4A
Stonecot Hill	38	4A
Stonecroft Way	40	4A
Stonecrop Rd.	82	4C
Stonedene Cl.	134	5A
Stonefield Cl.	147	4D
Stonehill Cl., Gt. Bookham	85	1F
Stonehill Cl., Richmond	19	1D
Stonehill Park	134	5A
Stonehill Rd., Botleys	31	5E
Stonehill Rd., Headley Down	134	5A
Stonehill Rd., Roehampton	19	1D
Stonehills Court	23	3D
Stonehouse Gdns.	91	1F
Stonehouse Rise	61	2E
Stoneleigh	54	1B
Stoneleigh Av.	54	1C
Stoneleigh Court	61	2E
Stoneleigh Cres.	54	1B
Stoneleigh Park Av.	41	3F
Stoneleigh Park Rd.	54	2B
Stoneleigh Pk.	50	2B
Stoneleigh Rd., Carshalton	39	4D
Stoneleigh Rd., Limpsfield	94	3C
Stonepit Cl.	118	2C
Stones La.	105	2D
Stone's Rd.	54	4B
Stoney Bottom	135	5D
Stoney Brook	81	5D
Stoney La.	23	5D
Stoney Rd.	26	1C
Stoneycroft Cl.	24	2C
Stoneycroft Wk.	146	4A
Stoneydeep	17	4F
Stoneyfield Rd.	74	2A
Stoneylands Court	13	4D
Stoneylands Rd.	13	4D
Stonny Croft	70	2B
Stonton Pk.	23	2F
Stony Hill	51	2F
Stonyfields	96	4B
Stonyrock Rd.	85	5F
Stoop Court	49	4E
Stopham Rd.	147	5F
Stormont Way	53	1D
Storrs La.	63	5F
Stoughton	81	4E
Stoughton Av.	55	1D
Stoughton Rd.	81	4E
Stourhead Cl.	61	5F
Stourhead Gdns.	37	2F
Stourmead	20	2A
Stourton Av.	16	4C
Stovold's Way	96	1C
Stowe Rd.	9	1F
Stowell Av.	59	3E
Stradella Rd.	22	1B
Strafford Rd., Acton	8	1C
Strafford Rd., Twickenham	17	2F
Straight Rd.	12	1B
Strand Cl., Crawley	147	5F
Strand Cl., Langley Vale	71	3D
Strand on the Green	8	3C
Stratfield	54	4B
Stratford Rd., Ash Vale	78	2B
Stratford Rd., Thornton Heath	40	2B
Strathavon Cl.	121	4E
Strathbrook Rd.	22	5A
Strathcona Av.	85	2F
Strathdon Dri.	21	3D
Strathearn Av.	17	2D
Strathearn Rd., Cheam	55	1E
Strathearn Rd., Wimbledon	20	4B
Strathleven Rd.	22	1A
Strathmore Cl.	75	4D
Strathmore Rd., Crawley	146	2B
Strathmore Rd., Croydon	40	4C
Strathmore Rd., Fulwell	17	4E
Strathmore Rd., Wimbledon Park	20	3B
Strathville Rd.	20	3B
Strathyre Av.	40	2A
Stratton Av.	56	3C
Stratton Cl., Merton	38	1B
Stratton Cl., Walton-on-Thames	34	4B

Stratton Rd.	38 1B	Sturt Rd., Shottermill	151 3E	Sunny Bank, Norwood	41 2D	Swallowtail Rd.	158 3C
Stratton Wk.	60 3C	Sturt's La.	88 2B	Sunny Bank, Warlingham	75 2F	Swan Cl.	16 4C
Strawberry Fields	63 1E	Stychens Cl.	91 5F	Sunny Bank, Woodcote	71 1D	Swan Court	81 4F
Strawberry Hill	17 3F	Stychens La.	91 5F	Sunny Down	118 5A	Swan La., Charlwood	127 4F
Strawberry Hill Cl.	17 3E	Styles End	86 2A	Sunny Hill	118 5A	Swan La., Guildford	100 1C
Strawberry La.	39 5E	Styles Way	42 2B	Sunny Rise	74 5C	Swan La., Sandhurst	43 4D
Strawberry Rise	63 1E	Styventon Pl.	32 4A	Sunny Side	34 3B	Swan Mews, Leatherhead	160
Strawberry Vale	17 3F	Succombs Hill	75 3E	Sunny View Cl.	78 5B	Swan Mill Gdns.	87 5D
Stream Cl.	49 4F	Sudbourne Rd.	22 1A	Sunnybank Rd.	60 4B	Swan Pl.	9 4E
Stream Farm Cl.	96 5B	Sudbrook Gdns.	18 3B	Sunnybank Villas	92 4A	Swan Rd.	16 4B
Stream Pk.	150 1A	Sudbrook La.	18 3B	Sunnycroft Rd.	41 2D	Swanage Rd.	20 1C
Stream Valley Rd.	115 1D	Sudbrooke Rd.	21 1E	Sunnydell La	114 1C	Swanbarn Rd.	152 3A
Streatham	22 3A	Suffield Cl.	58 4C	Sunnydene Rd.	57 5E	Swanns Meadow	85 1F
Streatham Common North	22 4A	Suffield La.	98 4B	Sunnydene St.	23 4F	Swanscombe Rd.	9 2E
Streatham Common South	22 5A	Suffield Rd., Anerley	41 2C	Sunnyhill Cl.	149 3E	Swanton Gdns.	20 2A
Streatham High Rd.	22 4A	Suffield Rd., Puttenham	98 5B	Sunnyhill Rd.	22 4A	Swanwick Cl.	19 2E
Streatham Hill	22 3A	Suffolk Cl., Bagshot	45 3D	Sunnyhurst Cl.	38 5B	Swanworth La.	87 2D
Streatham Pl.	22 2A	Suffolk Cl., Horley	128 3B	Sunnymead, Roehampton	19 1F	Swaynes La.	82 5C
Streatham Rd., Mitcham	39 1E	Suffolk Dri.	82 3B	Sunnymead, West Green	146 4C	Swaynesland Rd.	94 5C
Streatham Rd., Tooting	21 5E	Suffolk Rd., Barnes	9 3E	Sunnymead Av.	39 2F	Sweep's Ditch Cl.	14 5B
Streatham Vale	21 5F	Suffolk Rd., South		Sunnymede Av.,		Sweeps La.	13 4D
Streathbourne Rd.	21 3E	Norwood	41 2D	Carshalton	55 4F	Sweet Briar La.	54 5A
Street Hill	148 4A	Suffolk Rd., Worcester Park	37 5E	Sunnymede Av., Ewell	54 3A	Sweet La.	103 5F
Street, The, Albury	102 3B	Sugden Rd.	35 4F	Sunnyside	20 5A	Sweetwater Cl.	120 2C
Street, The, Ashtead	70 2B	Sulgrave Rd.	9 1F	Sunnyside Rd., Fulwell	17 4E	Sweetwater La.	120 2C
Street, The, Betchworth	107 1D	Sulina Rd.	22 2A	Sunnyside Rd., Headley		Sweetwell Rd.	26 1B
Street, The, Capel	125 5D	Sullivan Cl.	35 2D	Down	134 5A	Swievelands Rd.	77 3D
Street, The, Charlwood	127 5E	Sullivan Dri.	146 5B	Sunray Av., Camberwell	22 1C	Swift La., Bagshot	45 2E
Street, The, Compton	99 4F	Sullivan Rd.	43 5F	Sunray Av., Tolworth	36 5C	Swift La., Crawley	146 3C
Street, The, E. Clandon	83 4F	Sullivans Reach	33 4F	Sunrise Cl.	16 3C	Swift Rd., Hanworth	16 4B
Street, The, Effingham	85 2E	Sultan St.	41 1F	Sunset Gdns.	41 1D	Swift Rd., Upper Hale	96 1A
Street, The, Ewhurst	122 5C	Summer Av.	35 3E	Sunshine Way	39 1D	Swift Way	57 3D
Street, The, Fetcham	69 4E	Summer Gdns., Camberley	45 5D	Sunstone Gro.	91 3D	Swifts Cl.	96 4C
Street, The, Frensham	115 4D	Summer Gdns., Thames		Sunvale Av.	151 3D	Swiftsden Way	24 5C
Street, The, Plaistow	155 5D	Ditton	35 3E	Sunvale Cl.	151 3D	Swinburne Cres.	41 3E
Street, The, Puttenham	98 3C	Summer Hayes Cl.	48 5A	Surbiton	36 3C	Swinburne Rd.	9 5F
Street, The, Shalford	101 3D	Summer Hill	119 1D	Surbiton Court	36 3A	Swindon Rd.	158 4A
Street, The, Thursley	136 1A	Summer Rd.	35 3E	Surbiton Cres.	36 2B	Swingate Rd.	96 5B
Street, The, Tilford	116 2A	Summer Trees	34 1A	Surbiton Hill Pk.	36 3B	Swinley Rd.	28 2A
Street, The, Tongham	97 2E	Summerfield	70 3A	Surbiton Hill Rd.	36 2B	Swiss Cl.	114 2C
Street, The, W. Clandon	83 3D	Summerfield Cl.	49 1D	Surbiton Rd., Camberley	44 3C	Swissland Hill	131 5F
Street, The, West Horsley	84 2B	Summerfield La.	115 3D	Surbiton Rd., Kingston	36 2B	Switchback La.	114 2C
Street, The, Wonersh	101 5E	Summerfield Pl.	48 2C	Surrey Av.	60 1C	Swyncombe Av.	8 2A
Street, The, Wrecclesham	95 5F	Summerhayes	51 5E	Surrey Gdns.	68 5A	Sycamore Cl., Carshalton	56 1A
Street, The,	99 5D	Summerhill La.	114 3C	Surrey Gro.	39 5D	Sycamore Cl., Crawley	146 2C
Streeters Cl.	119 1E	Summerhouse Cl.	119 2D	Surrey Mount	23 2E	Sycamore Cl., Englefield	
Streeters La.	39 5F	Summerhouse Rd.	119 2D	Surrey Rd., Camberwell	23 1E	Grn.	12 5B
Streets Heath	46 4B	Summerlands	140 1C	Surrey Rd., W. Wickham	42 4B	Sycamore Cl., Feltham	16 3A
Stretton Rd., Addiscombe	41 4D	Summerlay Cl.	72 3A	Surrey Research Park	100 1A	Sycamore Cl., Frimley	61 2E
Stretton Rd., Ham	18 3A	Summerley Av.	89 5E	Surrey St.	40 5C	Sycamore Cl., Leatherhead	69 5F
Strickland Pl.	146 4A	Summerley St.	20 3C	Surridge Gdns.	22 5C	Sycamore Cl., Sandhurst	43 4D
Strickland Row	20 2C	Summers Cl., Belmont	55 1E	Sussex Cl., New Malden	37 2E	Sycamore Dri., Ash Vale	78 2C
Stringers Av.	81 2F	Summers Cl., Weybridge	50 4A	Sussex Cl., Reigate	109 1D	Sycamore Dri., Frimley	61 2E
Stringhams Copse	66 5A	Summers La., Hurtmore	99 5E	Sussex Court	63 2F	Sycamore Dri., Mid. Bourne	115 1D
Strode St.	13 4E	Summers Rd.	100 5A	Sussex Gdns.	53 2D	Sycamore Gdns.	9 1F
Strodes College La.	13 4D	Summersbury Dri.	101 4D	Sussex Pl.	37 2E	Sycamore Gro.	24 1B
Strodes Cres.	14 4B	Summersvere Cl.	147 2E	Sussex Rd., Carshalton		Sycamore Gro.	37 2D
Strood La.	10 5D	Summerville Gdns.	55 2E	Beeches	56 2A	Sycamore Rd., Cottenham	
Stroud Cres.	19 3E	Summerwood Rd.	17 1F	Sussex Rd., Knaphill	63 2F	Park	19 5F
Stroud Green Gdns.	41 4E	Summit Av.	60 5A	Sussex Rd., New Malden	37 2E	Sycamore Rd., Guildford	81 5F
Stroud Green Way	41 3E	Summit Way	23 5D	Sussex Rd., South Croydon	57 2F	Sycamore Rd., South	
Stroud La.	121 3D	Sumner Cl., Addlestone	49 1E	Sussex Row	158 5C	Farnborough	78 1A
Stroud Rd., Croydon	41 3D	Sumner Cl., Fetcham	69 5E	Sutherland Av., Biggin Hill	77 2E	Sycamore Rise, Banstead	55 5D
Stroud Rd., Wimbledon	20 3B	Sumner Rd., Croydon	40 4B	Sutherland Av., Guildford	82 2A	Sycamore Rise, Bracknell	27 2E
Stroud Water Pk.	50 2B	Sumner Rd., Farnham	96 3A	Sutherland Av., Sunbury	33 1F	Sycamore Way,	
Stroud Way	15 5E	Sumner Road South	40 4B	Sutherland Chase	28 1A	Teddington	18 5A
Stroude Rd.	31 2D	Sun Brow	151 3F	Sutherland Dri.	82 4A	Sycamore Way, Thornton	
Stroudes Cl.	37 4E	Sun Hill	64 4B	Sutherland Gdns., Sunbury	33 1F	Heath	40 3B
Stroudley Cl.	147 4F	Sunburgh Rd.	21 1E	Sutherland Gdns.,		Sycamores, The	61 5D
Strud Gate Cl.	147 5E	Sunbury Court Rd.	34 1B	Worcester Park	37 4F	Sydenham Av.	23 4E
Strudwicks Field	141 1D	Sunbury Cres.	15 4F	Sutherland Grove	20 1B	Sydenham Hill	23 3D
Stuart Av.	34 4A	Sunbury Ct. Ms.	34 1B	Sutherland Rd.	40 4B	Sydenham Park Rd.	23 3E
Stuart Cl., Crawley	147 4F	Sunbury La.	34 3A	Sutton	55 1F	Sydenham Pk.	23 3E
Stuart Cl., Farnborough	60 4C	Sunbury on Thames	33 1F	Sutton Av.	64 3A	Sydenham Rd., Croydon	40 4C
Stuart Cres., Reigate	108 2B	Sunbury Rd., Lower		Sutton Common Rd.	38 4B	Sydenham Rd., Guildford	100 1C
Stuart Cres., Shirley	42 5A	Feltham	15 3F	Sutton Court Rd., Sutton	55 2F	Sydenham Rd., Sydenham	23 4E
Stuart Rd., Caterham	75 3E	Sunbury Rd., North Cheam	38 5A	Sutton Court Rd., Turnham		Sydenham Rise	23 3E
Stuart Rd., Ham	18 3A	Sunbury Way	16 4B	Green	9 2D	Sydney Cl.	26 5A
Stuart Rd., Heath End	96 1A	Sundale Av.	58 3B	Sutton Gdns., Woodside	41 3D	Sydney Cres.	15 5D
Stuart Rd., South Park	108 2B	Sunderland Rd.	23 3F	Sutton Gdns., Worsted		Sydney Pl.	101 1D
Stuart Rd., Thornton Heath	40 2C	Sundew Cl., Lightwater	46 4A	Green	90 3C	Sydney Rd., Cheam	55 1E
Stuart Rd., Wimbledon Pk.	20 3B	Sundew Cl., Wokingham	25 1F	Sutton Green Rd.	82 1A	Sydney Rd., Feltham	16 2A
Stuart Way, East Grinstead	150 3C	Sundial Av.	41 2D	Sutton Gro.	56 1A	Sydney Rd., Guildford	101 1D
Stuart Way, Staines	14 5B	Sundon Cres.	30 3C	Sutton La., Abinger	104 5A	Sydney Rd., Raynes Park	38 1A
Stuart Way, Virginia Water	30 2B	Sundown Av.	58 4A	Sutton La., Belmont	55 4F	Sydney Rd., Richmond	8 5B
Stubbs Cl.	106 2A	Sundown Rd.	15 4E	Sutton La., Chiswick	9 2D	Sydney Rd., Teddington	17 4F
Stubbs Folly	43 4E	Sundridge Rd.,		Sutton La., Colnbrook	7 2A	Syke Ings	7 1B
Stubbs Hill	106 3A	Addiscombe	41 4D	Sutton Park Rd.	55 2F	Sykecluan	7 1B
Stubbs La.	89 2E	Sundridge Rd., Woking	65 3E	Sutton Pl.	103 2F	Sykes Dri.	14 4B
Stubbs Moor Rd.	60 4C	Sunkist Way	57 3D	Sutton Rd.	44 3C	Sylvan Cl., Limpsfield	94 3A
Stubbs Way	38 1C	Sunlow Rd.	20 1B	Swaby Rd.	20 2C	Sylvan Cl., Selsdon	58 3B
Stubfield	158 4A	Sunmead Cl.	69 4F	Swaffield Rd.	20 2C	Sylvan Cl., Woking	65 2E
Stubpond La.	130 4C	Sunmead Rd.	34 2A	Swain Rd.	40 3C	Sylvan Estate	41 1D
Studio Rd.	33 2D	Sunna Gdns.	34 1A	Swains Rd.	21 5D	Sylvan Gdns.	36 4A
Studland Rd., Byfleet	49 5F	Sunning Av.	29 4D	Swale Rd.	60 4B	Sylvan Hill	41 1D
Studland Rd., Kingston	18 5B	Sunningdale	29 3F	Swaledale	26 3C	Sylvan Rd., Penge	41 1D
Studland Rd., Lower		Sunningdale Av.	16 5C	Swaledale Cl.	146 4C	Sylvan Rd., Tilgate	147 5E
Sydenham	23 4F	Sunningdale Court	146 5C	Swallands Rd.	24 3A	Sylvan Way, Redhill	109 1E
Studland St.	9 2F	Sunningdale Rd.	55 1E	Swallow Cl., Milford	118 4A	Sylvan Way, W. Wickham	59 1F
Stumblets	147 3F	Sunninghill	29 3D	Swallow Cl., Staines	14 4A	Sylvanus	26 4B
Stumps Hill La.	24 5A	Sunninghill Rd., Camberley	28 5C	Swallow Field	132 3A	Sylvaways Cl.	141 1D
Stumps La.	75 2D	Sunninghill Rd., Sunninghill	29 2D	Swallow La.	106 4A	Sylverdale Rd.	40 5B
Sturdee Cl.	61 2E	Sunninghill Rd., Woodside	11 4D	Swallow Park	36 5C	Syon Pl.	61 5E
Sturges Rd.	25 2E	Sunningvale Av.	77 1E	Swallow Rd.	146 3C	Sythwood	64 1B
Sturt Av.	151 3E	Sunningvale Cl.	77 1E	Swallow Rise	63 2F	Szabo Cres.	79 5F
Sturt Court	82 4B	Sunny Av.	149 3D	Swallowdale	58 3C		
Sturt Rd., Frimley Green	61 4E			Swallowfield	12 5C		

T

Tabarin Way	71	1F
Tabor Gdns.	55	2E
Tabor Gro.	20	5B
Tabor Rd.	9	1F
Tachbrook Rd.	15	2F
Tadmor Cl.	33	3F
Tadorne Rd.	71	4F
Tadworth	71	4F
Tadworth Av.	37	3E
Tadworth Cl.	72	4A
Tadworth St.	72	5A
Taffys How	39	2D
Tait Rd.	40	4C
Talbot Cl., Horsham	158	5B
Talbot Cl., Mychett	61	5F
Talbot Cl., Reigate	108	1C
Talbot Pl.	45	2E
Talbot Rd., Ashford	14	4C
Talbot Rd., Carshalton	56	1B
Talbot Rd., Farnham	96	5A
Talbot Rd., Lingfield	131	2E
Talbot Rd., Selhurst	40	2C
Talbot Rd., Twickenham	17	2E
Taleworth Cl.	70	3B
Taleworth Pk.	70	3B
Taleworth Rd.	70	3B
Talisman Sq.	23	4D
Talisman Way	71	1F
Tall Elms Cl.	42	3C
Tall Trees, Mitcham	40	2A
Tall Trees, Poyle	7	4A
Tally Rd.	94	4C
Talma Gdns.	17	1E
Talmage Cl.	23	2E
Talman Cl.	146	4A
Tamar Cl.	147	4F
Tamarind Cl.	81	3E
Tamberts Pl.	40	4C
Tamesis Gdns.	37	5E
Tamworth	27	3E
Tamworth La.	39	1E
Tamworth Pk.	39	2E
Tamworth Rd.	40	5B
Tanbridge Cl.	158	5A
Tandridge	93	5D
Tandridge Gdns.	58	5A
Tandridge Hill La.	93	3D
Tandridge La.	93	4D
Tandridge Rd.	75	3E
Tanfield Court	158	5A
Tanfield Rd.	57	1E
Tangier Rd., Guildford	101	1E
Tangier Rd., North Sheen	8	5C
Tangier Way	72	2A
Tangier Wood	72	2A
Tangleoak	149	1F
Tanglewood, Wick Hill	25	5D
Tanglewood Cl.	16	3A
Tanglewood Cl., Longcross	30	5B
Tanglewood Cl., Shirley	41	5E
Tanglewood Cl., Woking	65	1F
Tanglewood Ride	46	4A
Tangley Dri.	25	3D
Tangley Gro.	19	2E
Tangley Hill	101	4F
Tangley La., Wonersh	101	4E
Tangley La., Worplesdon	81	3D
Tangley Park Rd.	16	4C
Tanglyn Av.	33	3D
Tangmere Rd.	146	4B
Tanhouse La.	25	2D
Tanhouse Rd.	93	4E
Tanhurst La.	123	4F
Tank Rd.	43	5F
Tankerton Rd.	36	5B
Tankervale Rd.	22	5A
Tankerville Rd.	21	5F
Tanners Cl.	34	3A
Tanners Dean	70	4A
Tanners Field	101	4D
Tanners Hill	106	1C
Tanners La., Haslemere	152	3A
Tanners Meadow	106	2C
Tannery Cl.	41	3F
Tannery La., Send	65	5F
Tannery La., Wonersh	101	5D
Tannery, The	90	5A
Tannsfield Rd.	23	4F
Tansy Cl.	82	4C
Tantallon Rd.	21	2E
Tanyard Cl., Crawley	147	5F
Tanyard Cl., Horsham	158	5C
Tanyard Way	128	2B
Tapestry Cl.	55	2F
Tapner's Rd	107	3E
Taragon Cl.	60	4A
Tarbat Court	43	4E
Tarbert Rd.	23	1D
Target Cl.	15	1F
Tarham Cl.	128	1A
Tarleton Gdns.	23	3E
Tarmac Way	7	3C
Tarn Rd.	135	5E
Tarnbrook	27	4E
Tarragon Dri.	81	3E

Tarrington Cl.	21	3F
Tartar Hill	51	5D
Tartar Rd.	51	5E
Tasman Court	15	5F
Tate Cl.	70	5A
Tate Rd.	55	1E
Tates Way	157	2E
Tatnell Rd.	23	1F
Tatsfield	77	3E
Tattenham Corner Rd.	71	2E
Tattenham Cres.	71	2E
Tattenham Gro.	71	3F
Tattenham Way	72	2A
Tattersall Cl.	25	2F
Taunton Av., Caterham	75	5D
Taunton Av., Raynes Park	37	1F
Taunton Cl.	38	4B
Taunton La.	74	3B
Taunton Rd.	24	1C
Tavistock Cl.	14	5C
Tavistock Cres.	40	2A
Tavistock Green	40	4C
Tavistock Rd., Croydon	40	4C
Tavistock Rd., Shortlands	42	2C
Tavistock Rd., St. Helier	39	4D
Tavistock Wk.	39	4D
Tawfield	26	4B
Tay Cl.	60	4B
Tayben Av.	17	1E
Taylor Av.	8	4C
Taylor Cl.	17	4D
Taylor Rd., Ashtead	70	2A
Taylor Rd., Tooting	21	5D
Taylor Rd., Wallington	56	1D
Taylor Walk	146	4C
Taylors Cres.	141	1D
Taylors La., Lindford	133	4D
Taylors La., Upper Sydenham	23	4E
Taymount Rise	23	3E
Taynton Dri.	90	3C
Teal Cl., Horsham	158	3B
Teal Cl., Selsdon	58	4C
Tealing Dri.	54	1A
Teasel Cl., Addiscombe	41	4E
Teasel Cl., Crawley	146	5C
Teazlewood Pk.	69	2F
Tebbit Cl.	27	1D
Tedder Cl.	53	1D
Tedder Rd.	58	2B
Teddington Cl.	54	3A
Teddington Park Rd.	17	4F
Teddington Pk.	17	4F
Tees Cl.	60	4B
Teesdale	146	5C
Teevan Rd.	41	4D
Tegg's La.	66	1A
Tekels Av.	44	5A
Tekels Pk.	61	1E
Tekels Way	61	1E
Telcoma Cl.	134	5A
Telconia Cl.	134	5A
Telegraph La.	52	2C
Telegraph Rd.	20	2A
Telegraph Track	56	4B
Telferscot Rd.	21	2F
Telford Av.	22	2A
Telford Cl.	23	5D
Telford Dri.	34	4B
Telford Pl.	147	4D
Telford Rd.	16	2C
Tellisford	52	1A
Temperley Rd.	21	2E
Tempest Rd.	13	5E
Templar Pl.	16	5C
Temple Av.	41	5F
Temple Bar Rd.	64	3A
Temple Cl., Crawley	147	4F
Temple Cl., Epsom	54	4A
Temple Combe Mews	65	1E
Temple Croft	15	5F
Temple Gdns.	32	1A
Temple La.	125	5E
Temple Rd., Acton	9	1D
Temple Rd., Croydon	57	1F
Temple Rd., Epsom	54	4A
Temple Rd., Kew	8	4B
Temple Rd., Lammas Park	8	1A
Temple Sheen Rd.	8	5C
Temple Way, Popeswood	26	1B
Temple Way, The Wrythe	39	5D
Temple Wood Dri.	90	4B
Templecombe Way	38	3A
Templedene Av.	14	5B
Templefield Cl.	49	2E
Templeman Cl.	74	1B
Templemere	33	5E
Temple's Cl.	97	4D
Templeton Cl.	40	1C
Ten Acre La.	31	1E
Ten Acres	86	1B
Tenbury Cl.	22	2A
Tenby Dri.	29	3D
Tenby Rd.	61	3F
Tenchley's La.	94	4B
Tenham Av.	21	3F
Tennison Rd.	41	2D

Tennyson Av., Motspur Park	37	3F
Tennyson Av., Twickenham	17	2F
Tennyson Cl., Horsham	158	3C
Tennyson Cl., Old Coulsdon	74	3B
Tennyson Cl., Pound Hill	147	3B
Tennyson Rd., Ashford	14	4C
Tennyson Rd., Penge	23	5F
Tennyson Rd., Weybridge	49	1F
Tennyson Rd., Wimbledon	20	4C
Tennyson Rise	150	2B
Tennyson's La.	152	4A
Tenterden Rd.	41	4D
Tern Rd.	146	4A
Terrace Gdns.	9	4E
Terrace La.	18	1B
Terrace Rd.	34	4A
Terrace, The, Addlestone	49	1F
Terrace, The, Barnes	9	4E
Terrace, The, Camberley	43	5F
Terrace, The, Crowthorne	43	2E
Terracotta Rd.	111	2E
Terrapin Rd.	21	3E
Testard Rd.	100	1C
Testers Cl.	94	4A
Tewkesbury Av.	23	2E
Tewkesbury Cl.	49	4F
Tewkesbury Rd.	39	4D
Thackeray Cl.	20	5A
Thakenam Cl.	23	4E
Thames Bank	9	4D
Thames Cl., Chertsey	32	4B
Thames Cl., Hampton	35	1D
Thames Cl., West Heath	60	4B
Thames Ditton	35	3F
Thames Mead	34	4A
Thames Meadow, Lwr. Halliford	33	4F
Thames Meadow, W. Molesey	35	1D
Thames Rd.	8	3C
Thames St., Hampton	35	1D
Thames St., Kingston	36	1B
Thames St., Portmore Pk.	33	5D
Thames St., Staines	14	4A
Thames St., Sunbury	34	2A
Thames St., Walton	33	4F
Thames Side, Kingston	36	1B
Thames Side, Laleham	32	2B
Thames Side, Teddington	18	5A
Thamesfield Court	33	4E
Thamesgate Cl.	18	4A
Thameside Rd.	14	5A
Thanescroft Gdns.	41	5D
Tharp Rd.	56	1C
Thatcher's Cl.	128	2B
Thatchers La.	81	2D
Thatchers Way	17	1E
Thayers Farm Rd.	41	1F
Theobald Rd.	40	5B
Theobalds Way	62	1A
Theodore Rd.	24	1B
Thepps Cl.	110	2A
Therapia La.	40	3A
Therapia Rd.	23	1E
Theresa Rd.	9	2E
Thesiger Rd.	23	5F
Thetford Rd., Ashford	14	4C
Thetford Rd., Malden	37	3D
Theydon Cl.	147	5E
Thibet Rd.	43	4D
Thicket Cres.	55	1F
Thicket Rd., Penge	23	5D
Thicket Rd., Sutton	55	1F
Thickhorne La.	14	5B
Third Cl.	35	2D
Third Cross Rd.	17	3E
Thirlmere Cl., Egham	13	5E
Thirlmere Cl., Farnborough	60	5B
Thirlmere Rd., Beckenham	24	5C
Thirlmere Rd., Tooting Bec	21	4F
Thirsk Rd., Selhurst	40	2C
Thirsk Rd., Tooting	21	5E
Thistle Way	129	2E
Thistlecroft Rd.	51	1E
Thistledene, Thames Ditton	35	3E
Thistledene, W. Byfleet	49	5D
Thistley La.	140	1C
Thomas Av.	74	4C
Thomas La.	24	2A
Thomas Rd.	9	3D
Thomas Wall Cl.	55	1F
Thompson Av.	8	5C
Thompson Rd.	23	1D
Thompsons La.	47	3D
Thomson Cres.	40	4A
Thorkhill Gdns.	35	4F
Thorkhill Rd.	35	4F
Thorley Cl.	49	5D
Thorley Gdns.	49	5D
Thorn Bank	100	1B
Thorn Cl.	114	2C
Thorn Rd.	114	2C
Thornash Cl.	64	1C
Thornash Rd.	64	1C
Thornash Way	64	1C

Thornbank Cl.	14	1A
Thornburn Way	38	1C
Thornbury Cl.	43	1D
Thornbury Rd.	22	1A
Thorncliffe Rd.	22	1A
Thorncombe Rd.	23	1D
Thorncombe St.	119	4F
Thorncroft	12	5C
Thorncroft Cl.	74	3B
Thorncroft Rd.	55	1F
Thorndon Gdns.	54	1B
Thorndown La.	46	2A
Thorndyke Cl.	147	4F
Thorne Cl., Ashford	15	5E
Thorne Cl., Crowthorne	26	5A
Thorne St.	9	5E
Thornes Cl.	42	2B
Thorney Hedge Rd.	8	2C
Thorney La. South	7	1B
Thorney Mill Rd.	7	1B
Thorneyhurst Rd.	61	5F
Thornfield Rd., Banstead	72	2B
Thornfield Rd., Hammersmith	9	1F
Thornford Rd.	24	1B
Thornhill, Bracknell	27	3E
Thornhill Av.	36	5B
Thornhill Rd., Aldershot	78	4B
Thornhill Rd., Croydon	40	4C
Thornhill Rd., Hook	36	5B
Thornhill Way	33	3D
Thornlaw Rd.	22	4B
Thornlease Pl.	84	1C
Thornloe Gdns.	57	1E
Thorns Flush	121	5E
Thornsbeach Rd.	24	2B
Thornsett Rd.	41	1E
Thornton Av., Croydon	40	3A
Thornton Av., Streatham	21	2F
Thornton Av., Turn. Green	9	2E
Thornton Cl., Guildford	81	4E
Thornton Cl., Horley	128	2A
Thornton Cres.	74	3A
Thornton Gdns.	21	2F
Thornton Hill	20	5A
Thornton Pl.	128	2A
Thornton Rd., Croydon	40	4A
Thornton Rd., Hackbridge	39	4D
Thornton Rd., Mortlake	9	5D
Thornton Rd., Streatham	21	2F
Thornton Rd., Wimbledon	20	5A
Thornwood Rd.	24	1C
Thornycroft Cl.	34	3B
Thorold Cl.	58	3C
Thorold Rd.	96	3A
Thoroughfare, The	71	5F
Thorpe	31	2E
Thorpe Bypass	31	2E
Thorpe Cl., East Heath	25	3D
Thorpe Cl., New Addington	59	4E
Thorpe Lea	13	5F
Thorpe Lea Rd.	31	1E
Thorpe Rd., Chertsey	31	3F
Thorpe Rd., Kingston	18	5B
Thorpe Rd., Staines	13	4F
Thorpes Cl.	81	4E
Thorpewood Av.	23	3E
Thorsden Cl.	65	3D
Thorsden Court	65	3D
Thrale Rd.	21	4F
Three Arch Rd.	109	2E
Three Bridges Rd.	147	4E
Three Gates La.	152	2A
Three Pears Rd.	82	5C
Three Stiles Rd.	95	3F
Threeacres	158	5A
Threegates	82	5C
Threshfield	26	3C
Thrift Wood	23	3E
Thrift Vale	82	4C
Thrigby Rd.	53	2F
Throwley Rd.	55	1F
Thrupps Av.	51	1E
Thrupps La.	51	1E
Thundery Hill	97	3E
Thurban's Way	95	5F
Thurbarn Rd.	24	4A
Thurbarns Hill	125	3E
Thurlby Rd.	22	4B
Thurleigh Rd.	21	2D
Thurleston Av.	38	3A
Thurlestone Rd.	22	3B
Thurlow Hill	22	2B
Thurlow Park Rd.	22	3B
Thurlow Walk	140	2C
Thurlstone Cl.	33	3E
Thurne Way	157	2E
Thurnham Way	72	4A
Thursby Rd.	64	2B
Thursley	136	1A
Thursley Cres.	59	2E
Thursley Gdns.	20	3A
Thursley Rd.	116	5C
Thurso St.	21	4D
Thurstan Rd.	19	5F
Thyme Court	60	4A
Tibbets Cl.	20	2A

Ticehurst Cl. 148 4A
Ticehurst Rd. 23 3F
Tichborne Cl., Blackwater 43 5E
Tichborne Cl., Camberley 61 1F
Tichbourne Pl. 97 1D
Tichmarsh 54 4A
Tichwell Rd. 21 2D
Tidenham Gdns. 41 5D
Tideswell Rd. 42 5A
Tideways Cl. 18 4A
Tiepigs La. 42 5C
Tierney Rd. 22 2A
Tilburstow Hill Rd., Godstone 92 5B
Tilburstow Hill Rd., S. Godstone 111 1E
Tildesley Rd. 19 1F
Tile Barn Cl. 60 4C
Tilehouse Rd. 101 2D
Tilehurst La. 106 2B
Tilehurst Rd., Cheam 55 1D
Tilehurst Rd., Wandsw'th 21 2D
Tilers Way 108 2C
Tilford 116 2A
Tilford Av. 59 3E
Tilford Gdns. 20 2A
Tilford Rd., Farnham 96 4B
Tilford Rd., Hindhead 135 3D
Tilford Rd., Tilford 116 2A
Tilgate Common 91 5E
Tilgate Dri. 147 5E
Tilgate Pl. 147 5D
Tilgate Way 147 5D
Tilley La. 71 5D
Tilley Rd. 71 5D
Tillingbourne 105 4D
Tillingbourne Rd. 101 3D
Tillingdown Hill 75 4E
Tillingdown La. 92 1B
Tillotson Cl. 147 4F
Tilly's La. 14 4A
Tilson Gdns. 22 2A
Tilt Cl. 68 1C
Tilt Meadow 68 1B
Tilt Rd. 68 1B
Tiltwood Dri. 149 3E
Timber Bank 61 4F
Timber Cl., Great Bookham 86 2A
Timber Cl., West Byfleet 49 5D
Timber Hill Rd. 75 5D
Timbercroft 54 1A
Timbermill Court 151 3E
Timberslip Dri. 56 3C
Timbertop Cl. 77 2E
Timline Green 27 1F
Timothy Cl. 21 1F
Timperley Gdns. 90 4A
Timsway 14 4A
Tindale Cl. 57 4F
Tinefields 72 3A
Tinglewood 58 3C
Tinsley Green 147 1F
Tinsley La. 147 2E
Tinsley Lane North 147 1E
Tintagel Dri. 61 3E
Tintagel Rd. 25 5D
Tintagel Way 65 1E
Tintells La. 84 2A
Tintern Cl. 20 1A
Tintern Rd., Crawley 146 5B
Tintern Rd., St. Helier 39 4D
Tippits Mead 26 1B
Tirle Mount Rd. 57 2E
Tirrell Rd. 40 3C
Tisbury Rd. 40 1A
Titchfield Rd. 39 4D
Titchfield Wk. 39 4D
Tite Hill 12 4C
Tithe Barn Cl. 36 1B
Tithe La. 13 1D
Tithe Meadows 30 3C
Tithebarns La. 83 1D
Tithepit Shaw La. 75 1E
Titlarks Hill Rd. 29 5F
Titmus Dri. 147 5D
Titmuss St. 9 1F
Titsey Hill 77 5D
Titsey Rd. 94 2A
Tiverton Way, Chessington 53 1D
Tiverton Way, Frimley 61 2E
Tivoli Rd. 22 4B
Todds Cl. 128 1A
Toland Sq. 19 1F
Tolgarth Dri. 61 5E
Toll Gdns. 27 2E
Tolldene Cl. 64 2A
Tollers La. 74 3A
Tollgate 82 5C
Tollgate Av. 109 3D
Tollgate Dri. 23 3D
Tollgate Rd. 106 3A
Tollhouse La. 56 3C
Tolvaddon 64 2B
Tolverne Rd. 37 1F
Tolworth Cl. 36 4C
Tolworth Park Rd. 36 5B
Tolworth Rd. 36 5B
Tolworth Rise North 37 4D
Tolworth Rise South 37 4D
Tomlin Cl. 54 4A
Tomlins Av. 61 2E
Tomlinscote Way 61 2F
Tomlinson Dr., Wick Hill 25 5D
Tonbridge Cl. 56 5A
Tonbridge Rd. 34 3C
Tonfield Rd. 38 4B
Tongham 97 2E
Tongham Meadows 97 1E
Tongham Rd., Aldershot 97 1D
Tongham Rd., Farnham 97 3D
Tonsley Hill 20 1C
Tonsley Pl. 20 1C
Tonsley Rd. 20 1C
Tonsley St. 20 1C
Tonstall Rd., Epsom 54 3A
Tonstall Rd., Mitcham 39 1E
Tooting Bec Gdns. 21 4F
Tooting Bec Rd. 21 3E
Tooting Gro. 21 4D
Tooting High St. 21 5D
Tootswood Rd. 42 2C
Top Park 42 2C
Topiary Sq. 8 5B
Topiary, The 70 3B
Toplady Pl. 96 1A
Topsham Rd. 21 3E
Tor La. 50 4B
Tor Rd. 95 4F
Torin Court 12 4C
Torland Dri. 52 5B
Tormead Cl. 24 5C
Tormead Rd. 82 5A
Toronto Dr. 129 2E
Torr Rd. 23 5F
Torre Wk. 39 4D
Torrens Rd. 22 1A
Torridge Rd. 40 3B
Torridon Cl. 64 2B
Torridon Rd. 24 2C
Torringdon Cl. 52 2B
Torrington Rd. 52 2B
Torrington Way 38 3B
Torwood La. 75 3D
Totford La. 98 3A
Totland Cl. 60 4C
Tottenham Rd. 119 1D
Tottenham Wk. 43 3E
Totterdown St. 21 4D
Totton Rd. 40 2B
Tovil Cl. 41 1E
Tower Av. 35 5D
Tower Cl., East Grinstead 150 2C
Tower Cl., Hindhead 135 5E
Tower Cl., Horley 128 2A
Tower Cl., Penge 23 5E
Tower Cl., Woking 64 2C
Tower Gro. 33 5F
Tower Hill, Dorking 106 2A
Tower Hill, Cove 60 5C
Tower Hill Rd., Dorking 105 2F
Tower Hill Rd., Gomshall 103 3E
Tower Hill Rise 103 3E
Tower La. 90 2A
Tower Rd., Hindhead 135 5E
Tower Rd., Tadworth 71 5F
Tower Rd., Twickenham 17 3F
Tower Rise 8 5B
Tower View 41 4F
Towers Dri. 43 2D
Towers, The 74 1B
Towers Wk. 50 2B
Towfield Av. 16 3C
Town Barn Rd. 146 3C
Town End 75 4D
Town End Cl. 119 2D
Town End St. 119 2D
Town Farm Way 14 2C
Town Hill 131 2F
Town La. 14 1B
Town Mead 91 5F
Town Meadow Wharf 8 3B
Town Sq. 160 –
Town Tree Rd. 15 4D
Townfield Rd. 105 2F
Townhend Ter. 8 5B
Townley Rd. 23 1D
Townmead 146 3C
Townmeade Rd. 8 4C
Townsend Cl. 27 3E
Townsend La. 65 3E
Townsend Rd. 14 4C
Townshend Rd. 8 5B
Townshott Cl. 86 1A
Towpath Way 41 3D
Towton Rd. 22 3C
Toynbee Rd. 38 1A
Tracery, The, 72 1C
Tracious Cl. 64 1B
Tracious La. 64 1B
Trafalgar Av. 38 4A
Trafalgar Court 96 4A
Trafalgar Dri. 34 5A
Trafalgar Rd., Horsham 158 4B
Trafalgar Rd., Twickenham 17 3E
Trafalgar Rd., Wimbledon 20 5C
Trafalgar Way 60 1C
Trafford Rd., Frimley 61 3D
Trafford Rd., Thornton Heath 40 3A
Tramway Path 39 2D
Tranmere Rd., Earlsfield 20 2C
Tranmere Rd., Whitton 17 2D
Tranquil Dale 88 4B
Transport Rd. 78 4A
Trap La. 142 2C
Traps La. 37 1D
Trasher Mead 106 2A
Travis Lane 43 4D
Treadcroft Dri. 158 3C
Treadwell Rd. 71 1E
Trebor Av. 96 4B
Tredenham Cl. 78 2A
Tree Cl., Malden 37 4E
Tree Cl., Richmond 18 2B
Tree Way 89 4F
Treebourne Rd. 77 2E
Treebys Av. 81 3F
Treedown Rd. 23 4E
Treelands 106 3A
Treen Av. 9 5E
Treetops Av. 44 4C
Trefoil Cl., Horsham 158 3C
Trefoil Cl., Wokingham 25 1F
Trefoil Rd. 20 1C
Tregarth Pl. 64 2A
Tregolls Dri. 61 5D
Trehaven Parade 108 2C
Trelawn Cl. 48 2C
Trelawn Rd. 22 1B
Trelawne Dri. 140 2C
Trelawny Gro. 50 2A
Treloar Gdns. 22 5C
Tremaine Rd. 41 1E
Tremayne Wk. 62 1A
Trenance 64 2B
Trenchard Cl. 51 1E
Trenham Dri. 75 1E
Trenholme Rd. 23 5E
Trent Cl., West H'th. 60 4B
Trent Cl., W. Wickham 146 5B
Trent Dri., Brixton Hill 22 1A
Trent Rd., Lammas Park 8 1A
Trentham Cres. 65 4D
Trentham Rd. 109 1E
Trentham St. 20 2B
Trentham Way 109 1E
Trentholme Rd. 23 5E
Trenton Cl. 61 2F
Treport St. 20 2C
Tresco Cl. 24 5C
Tresillian Way 64 2B
Tresta Walk 64 1B
Trevelyan 26 4B
Trevelyan Rd. 21 4D
Trevereux Hill 94 4C
Trevor Cl. 17 1F
Trevor Rd. 20 5A
Trevose Av. 49 5D
Trewin Rd. 21 2D
Trewince Rd. 37 1F
Trewinter St. 20 3C
Trewsbury Rd. 23 4F
Treyford Cl. 146 4B
Triangle, The 37 1D
Trig St. 125 3E
Triggs Cl. 64 3C
Trigg's La. 64 3C
Trigo Court 54 4A
Trilby Rd. 23 3F
Trimmers Cl. 96 1A
Trimmers Wood 135 4E
Trindles Rd. 110 1A
Tring Av. 8 1B
Tringham Cl. 48 1B
Trinity 43 3E
Trinity Church Rd. 9 3F
Trinity Church Yd., Guildford 159
Trinity Cl., Crawley 147 3F
Trinity Cl., Knaphill 63 2F
Trinity Cl., Sanderstead 58 3A
Trinity Cl., Stanwell 14 2B
Trinity Cres., Sunningdale 29 3E
Trinity Cres., Tooting Bec 21 3E
Trinity Hill 96 2A
Trinity Rd., Knaphill 63 2F
Trinity Rd., Richmond 8 5B
Trinity Rd., Stanwell 14 2B
Trinity Rd., Wandsworth 21 1D
Trinity Rd., Wimbledon 20 5B
Trinity Rise 22 2B
Tristram Rd. 24 4C
Tritton Av. 57 1D
Tritton Rd. 22 3C
Trittons 72 4A
Trodd's La. 102 1A
Trojan Way 40 5A
Troon Cl. 146 4A
Trossachs Rd. 23 1D
Trotsworth Av. 31 2D
Trotters La. 47 4E
Trotton Cl. 147 5F
Trottsford Rd. 133 2D
Trotwood Cl. 43 3E
Trout Rd. 151 3E
Troutbeck Walk 62 1A
Trouville Rd. 21 1F
Trower's Way 90 4B
Trowlock Av. 18 5A
Troy Cl. 71 3F
Troy Rd. 22 5C
Trumpets Hill Rd. 107 1F
Trumps Mill La. 31 3D
Trumpsgreen Av. 30 3C
Trumpsgreen Cl. 31 3D
Trumpsgreen Rd. 30 4C
Trumpsgreen Rd. 31 3D
Trundle Mead 158 3B
Trunk Rd. 60 5A
Trunley Heath Rd. 100 5C
Truslove Rd. 22 4B
Truss Hill Rd. 28 3C
Trys Hill 31 5D
Trystings Cl. 52 2C
Tucker Rd. 48 2C
Tuckey Gro. 66 5A
Tuckton Wk. 19 2E
Tudor Av., Hampton 16 5C
Tudor Av., Stoneleigh 54 1C
Tudor Cl., Ashford 14 4C
Tudor Cl., Bookham 68 5C
Tudor Cl., Cheam 55 1D
Tudor Cl., Chessington 53 1E
Tudor Cl., Coulsdon 74 2B
Tudor Cl., Crawley 147 4F
Tudor Cl., Ewell 54 3B
Tudor Cl., Grayshott 151 1D
Tudor Cl., Hamsey Green 75 1E
Tudor Cl., Nork 72 1A
Tudor Cl., Oxshott 51 5F
Tudor Cl., Smallfield 129 2E
Tudor Cl., Sutton 56 2C
Tudor Cl., Twickenham 17 2F
Tudor Cl., Woking 65 2E
Tudor Cl., Wokingham 25 2F
Tudor Court, Ash 78 5C
Tudor Court, Hanworth 16 4B
Tudor Dri., Kingston 18 4B
Tudor Dri., Lower Morden 38 3A
Tudor Dri., Walton-on-Thames 34 4B
Tudor Gdns., Twickenham 17 2F
Tudor Gdns., W. Wickham 42 5B
Tudor Pl. 21 5D
Tudor Rd., Ashford 15 5E
Tudor Rd., Beckenham 42 2B
Tudor Rd., Farncombe 100 5A
Tudor Rd., Hampton 17 5D
Tudor Rd., Kingston 18 5C
Tudor Rd., Penge 23 5D
Tudor Rd., Woodside 41 3E
Tudor Walk, Leatherhead 69 3F
Tudor Walk, Weybridge 33 5E
Tudor Way 8 1C
Tuesley Corner 119 2D
Tuesley La. 118 5C
Tufton Gdns. 35 1D
Tugela Rd. 40 3C
Tulip Cl., Hanworth 16 5C
Tulip Cl., Shirley 41 4E
Tullett Rd. 147 5F
Tulse Cl. 42 2B
Tulse Hill 22 1B
Tulsemere Rd. 22 3C
Tulyar Cl. 71 3F
Tumber St. 88 1A
Tumblewood Rd. 72 1A
Tumbling Bay 34 3A
Tummons Gdns. 40 1C
Tunley Rd. 21 2E
Tunnel Rd., Reigate 89 5E
Tunnel Rd., W. Bedfont 15 1D
Tunnmeade 146 4A
Tuns Gate 100 1C
Tunsgate Sq., Guildford 159
Tunstall Rd. 41 4D
Tunworth Cres. 19 1E
Tuppers Court 102 3B
Tupwood Ct. 92 1A
Tupwood La. 92 1A
Tupwood Scrubbs Rd. 92 2A
Turf Hill Rd. 44 4B
Turfhouse La. 47 3D
Turle Rd. 40 1A
Turnberry 26 4B
Turner Av., Mitcham 39 1D
Turner Av., Twickenham 17 3D
Turner Cl. 14 4B
Turner Pl. 43 5E
Turner Rd. 37 4D
Turner Wk. 147 5E
Turner's Hill Rd., E. Grinstead 150 3B
Turners Hill Rd., Worth 148 4A
Turners La. 51 2D
Turners Mead 137 5F
Turney Rd. 22 2C
Turnham Cl. 100 2C

Turnham Green Ter. 9 2E
Turnham Rd. 23 1F
Turnoak Av. 65 3D
Turnoak La. 65 3D
Turnpike La. 55 1F
Turnpike Link 40 5C
Turnpike Rd. 26 1B
Turnstone Cl. 58 4C
Turnville Cl. 45 3F
Turpin Rd. 15 1F
Turpin Way 56 2B
Turpins Rise 45 1F
Tuscan Way 60 1C
Tushmore Av. 147 2D
Tushmore Cres. 147 2D
Tushmore La. 147 3D
Tussock Cl. 146 5B
Tweed Cl. 66 4B
Tweed La., Crawley 146 2B
Tweed La., Strood Green 107 3D
Tweeddale Rd. 38 4C
Tweedsmuir Cl. 60 5B
Twelve Acre Cl. 68 5C
Twelve Acre Cres. 60 4B
Twickenham 17 3E
Twickenham Cl. 40 5A
Twickenham Rd., Hanworth 16 4C
Twickenham Rd., Richmond 18 1A
Twickenham Rd., Teddington 17 4F
Twickenham Rd., Twickenham 17 1F
Twilley St. 20 2C
Twining Av. 17 3D
Twinoaks 52 5A
Twitten La. 149 1F
Twycross Rd. 100 5A
Twyford La. 115 1D
Twyford Rd., St. Helier 39 4D
Twyford Rd., Wokingham 25 1D
Twyne Cl. 146 5B
Twyner Cl. 128 2C
Twynersh 31 3F
Twynham Rd. 44 5A
Tybenham Rd. 38 2B
Tychbourne Dri. 82 4C
Tydcombe Rd. 75 3E
Tye La. 88 2A
Tylden Way 158 3C
Tylecroft Rd. 40 1A
Tylehost 81 3E
Tyler Rd. 147 5D
Tyler's Cl. 92 3B
Tyler's Court 140 1C
Tyler's Grn. 92 3B
Tylner Cl. 23 4D
Tyndalls 135 5F
Tyne Cl., Crawley 147 4F
Tyne Cl., Farnborough 60 4B
Tynedale Rd. 106 2C
Tynemouth Rd. 21 5E
Tynley Gro. 81 2F
Tyrrell Sq. 39 1D
Tyson Rd. 23 2E
Tythebarn Cl. 82 3B
Tytheton 27 2D

U

Uckfield Gro. 39 1E
Udney Park Rd. 17 5F
Uffington Dri. 27 2E
Uffington Rd. 22 4B
Ullathorne Rd. 21 4F
Ullswater 26 4B
Ullswater Av. 60 5B
Ullswater Cl., Beckenham 24 5C
Ullswater Cl., Kingston Vale 19 4D
Ullswater Cl., Lightwater 45 3F
Ullswater Cl., Upper Hale 96 2A
Ullswater Cres., Coulsdon 74 1A
Ullswater Cres., King. Vale 19 4D
Ullswater Rd., Barnes 9 3E
Ullswater Rd., Lightwater 45 3F
Ullswater Rd., W. Norwood 22 3B
Ulstan Cl. 76 5A
Ulverscroft Rd. 23 1D
Ulwyn Av. 49 5F
Underhill Cl. 119 2D
Underhill La. 96 5A
Underhill Park Rd. 89 4E
Underhill Rd., Camberley 23 1D
Underhill Rd., Newdigate 125 3F
Undershaw Rd. 24 3C
Underswood 59 2E
Underwood 26 3B
Underwood Av. 78 5B
Underwood Cl. 149 3E
Underwood Rd., Caterham 92 1A
Underwood Rd., Shottermill 151 2F
Undine St. 21 4D
Unham Rd. 22 5C
Union Cl. 43 3E
Union Pl. 147 4D
Union Rd., Croydon 40 4C
Union Rd., Farnham 96 4A
Union St., Farnborough Park 60 5C
Union St., Kingston 36 1B
Unity Cl., New Addington 59 3E
Unity Cl., W. Norwood 22 4B
University Rd. 21 5D
Unstead La. 100 5C
Unstead Wood 100 4C
Unwin Av. 15 1F
Upavon Gdns. 27 3E
Upchurch Cl. 23 5E
Updown Hill 46 2A
Upfield, Addiscombe 41 5E
Upfield, Horley 128 3B
Upfield Cl., Horley 128 3B
Upfold Cl., and La. 140 1B
Upfold La. 40 1B
Upfolds 82 3B
Upfolds Cl. 121 5E
Upham Park Rd. 9 2E
Upland Rd., Camberley 44 4A
Upland Rd., Camberwell 23 1D
Upland Rd., Carshalton 56 2A
Upland Rd., South Croydon 57 1F
Upland Way 71 2F
Uplands, Beckenham 42 2A
Uplands, Leatherhead 70 3B
Uplands Cl., Haslemere 152 2A
Uplands Cl., Sandhurst 43 4D
Uplands Dri. 52 5B
Uplands Rd., Compton 96 4B
Uplands Rd., Kenley 74 2C
Uplands Rd., Woldingham 76 3A
Uppark Gdns. 158 3C
Upper Beulah Hill 40 1C
Upper Bourne La. 115 1D
Upper Bourne Vale 115 1D
Upper Bridge Rd. 90 5A
Upper Brighton Rd. 36 3B
Upper Broadmoor Rd. 43 1D
Upper Butts 8 3A
Upper Charles St. 44 5A
Upper Chobham Rd. 45 5D
Upper Church La. 96 4A
Upper College Ride 44 4B
Upper Court Rd., Epsom 54 4A
Upper Court Rd., Woldingham 76 5A
Upper Dri. 77 2E
Upper Dunnymans 55 5E
Upper Eashing La. 118 2B
Upper Edgeborough Rd. 101 1D
Upper Elmers End Rd. 42 3A
Upper Fairfield Rd. 69 4F
Upper Farm Rd. 34 2C
Upper Gordon Rd. 44 5A
Upper Green, E. & W. 39 1D
Upper Grotto Rd. 17 3F
Upper Grove 41 2D
Upper Guildown Rd. 100 2C
Upper Hale Rd. 96 1A
Upper Halliford 33 2F
Upper Halliford Bypass 33 3F
Upper Halliford Grn. 33 2F
Upper Halliford Rd. 33 3F
Upper Ham Rd. 18 4B
Upper High St. 54 5A
Upper House La. 121 3D
Upper Jordan Gooserye 81 1D
Upper Mall 9 2F
Upper Manor Rd., Farncombe 100 5A
Upper Manor Rd., Milford 118 3B
Upper Mount 152 1B
Upper Mulgrave Rd. 55 2D
Upper Nursery 29 3D
Upper Park Rd., Camberley 44 5B
Upper Park Rd., Kingston 18 5C
Upper Pillory Downs 56 5B
Upper Pines 73 2D
Upper Pinewood Rd. 79 4D
Upper Queen St. 119 2D
Upper Rd., Wallington 56 1C
Upper Richmond Rd. 9 5F
Upper Richmond Road W. 8 5C
Upper Rose Hill 105 2F
Upper St., Shere 103 3D
Upper St. Michael's Rd. 96 1C
Upper Sawley Wood 55 5E
Upper Selsdon Rd. 58 3A
Upper Shirley Rd. 41 5E
Upper South View 96 3A
Upper Springfield 117 2D
Upper Staithe 8 4C
Upper Stanford 80 1B
Upper Star Post Ride 26 5C
Upper Sunbury Rd. 34 1C
Upper Tooting Pk. 21 3E
Upper Tooting Rd. 21 4D
Upper Tulse Hill 22 2A
Upper Verran Rd. 61 1E
Upper Village Rd. 29 3D
Upper Way 96 5A
Upper West St. 89 5E
Upper Weybourne La. 96 1B
Upper Woodcote Village 56 4C
Upperton Rd. 100 1C
Upr. Elmer End Rd. 42 3A
Upshire Gdns. 27 2E
Upshot La. 66 2A
Upton 64 2B
Upton Cl. 61 5E
Upton Dene 55 2E
Upton Rd. 40 1C
Upwood Rd. 40 1A
Usherwood Cl. 88 4A
Uster Cl. 39 1D
Utterton Way 109 2D
Uvedale Cl. 59 4E
Uvedale Cres. 59 4E
Uvedale Rd. 93 3F
Uxbridge Rd., Hampton Hill 17 4D
Uxbridge Rd., Hanworth 16 3B
Uxbridge Rd., Kingston 36 2B

V

Vachery La. 140 3C
Vaillant Rd. 50 1B
Vale Cl., Lower Bourne 115 2E
Vale Cl., Purley 57 5D
Vale Cl., Weybridge 33 5E
Vale Cres. 19 4E
Vale Croft 52 3B
Vale Dri. 158 4A
Vale Farm Rd. 65 2D
Vale Gro. 9 1D
Vale Rd., Camberley 60 1C
Vale Rd., Cheam 55 1E
Vale Rd., Claygate 52 3B
Vale Rd., Mitcham 39 2F
Vale Rd., Stoneleigh 54 1B
Vale Rd., Weybridge 33 5E
Vale Rd., Worcester Park 37 5E
Vale Road North Cl. 36 5B
Vale Road South 36 5B
Vale St. 22 3C
Vale, The, Feltham 16 1A
Vale, The, Shirley 41 5F
Vale, The, Woodcote 56 5C
Valentyne Cl. 59 4F
Valeswood Rd. 24 4C
Valetta Rd. 9 1E
Valewood Dri. 115 2E
Valewood La. 135 5D
Valewood Rd. 152 4A
Valian Leas 42 2C
Valley Court 75 4D
Valley Cres. 25 1D
Valley End Rd. 46 2B
Valley La. 96 5A
Valley Mews 17 3F
Valley Rd., Frimley 61 3F
Valley Rd., Kenley 74 1C
Valley Rd., Shortlands 42 1C
Valley Rd., Streatham 22 4A
Valley, The, 100 2C
Valley View, Biggin Hill 77 2E
Valley View, Godalming 118 2C
Valley View Gdns. 74 1C
Valley Wk. 41 5E
Valleyfield Rd. 22 4A
Vallis Way 53 1D
Valnay St. 21 4D
Valonia Gdns. 20 1B
Valroy Cl. 44 5A
Van Dyck Av. 37 4D
Vanbrugh Dri. 34 3B
Vanbrugh Rd. 9 1D
Vancouver Cl. 129 2E
Vancouver Court 54 4A
Vancouver Rd. 23 3F
Vanderbilt Rd. 20 2C
Vandyke 26 3B
Vandyke Cl., Putney 20 1A
Vandyke Cl., Redhill 90 4A
Vanguard Cl. 40 4B
Vanguard Way 57 2D
Vann La., Chiddingfold 138 4B
Vann La., Grenehurst 143 1F
Vanners 147 3D
Vant Rd. 21 4E
Vapery La. 63 4D
Varley Way 39 1D
Varna Rd., Deadwater 133 5D
Varna Rd., Hampton 35 1D
Varney Cl. 60 4B
Varsity Dri. 17 1E
Varsity Row 9 4D
Vaughan Av. 9 2E
Vaughan Cl. 16 5C
Vaughan Rd. 36 4A
Vaughan Way 105 1F
Vaux Cres. 51 2D
Vauxhall Gdns. 57 2F
Veals Mead 39 1D
Vectis Rd. 21 5E
Vegal Cres. 12 4C
Vellum Dri. 56 1B
Venetia Rd. 8 1A
Venner Rd. 23 5E
Ventnor Rd. 55 2F
Ventnor Ter. 78 5A
Venton Cl. 64 2B
Verdant La. 24 2C
Verdayne Av. 41 5D
Verdayne Gdns. 75 1E
Verdun Rd. 9 3E
Vereker Dri. 34 2A
Vermont Rd., Sutton Common 38 5C
Vermont Rd., Upper Norwood 22 5C
Vermont St. 20 1C
Verner Cl. 133 4F
Vernon Av. 38 1A
Vernon Cl., Ewell 54 2A
Vernon Cl., Horsham 158 3C
Vernon Cl., Ottershaw 48 2C
Vernon Dri. 28 1A
Vernon Rd., Feltham 15 3F
Vernon Rd., Mortlake 9 5D
Vernon Rd., Sutton 55 1F
Vernon Way 81 5E
Vernon Wk. 72 3A
Verona Dri. 36 5B
Veronica Gdns. 39 1F
Veronica Rd. 21 3E
Verralls 65 2E
Verran Rd., Balham 21 2E
Verran Rd., Camberley 61 1D
Versailles Rd 23 5D
Verulam Av. 56 4C
Veryan 64 2B
Vesey Cl. 60 4C
Vespan Rd. 9 1E
Vestris Rd. 23 3F
Vevers Rd. 108 2C
Vevey St. 23 3F
Vibart Gdns. 22 2A
Viburnum Court 46 5B
Vicarage Av. 13 4E
Vicarage Cl., Egham 13 4E
Vicarage Cl., Gt. Bookham 85 1F
Vicarage Cl., Kingswood 72 5A
Vicarage Cl., Lingfield 131 2E
Vicarage Court, East Bedfont 15 2E
Vicarage Court, Egham 13 5E
Vicarage Fields 34 3A
Vicarage Gate 100 1B
Vicarage Gdns. 39 2D
Vicarage Hill 96 5B
Vicarage La., Bagshot 44 1C
Vicarage La., Capel 125 5D
Vicarage La., Ewell 54 3B
Vicarage La., Farnham 96 4A
Vicarage La., Heath End 96 1A
Vicarage La., Laleham 32 2B
Vicarage La., Leatherhead 69 4F
Vicarage La., Lower Bourne 96 5B
Vicarage La., Sendgrove 82 1C
Vicarage La., Shottermill 151 3E
Vicarage La., Wraysbury 13 2D
Vicarage Rd., Blackwater 60 1B
Vicarage Rd., Chobham 47 4D
Vicarage Rd., Crawley Down 149 3D
Vicarage Rd., East Sheen 19 1D
Vicarage Rd., Egham 13 4E
Vicarage Rd., Hampton Wick 36 1A
Vicarage Rd., Horley 128 2A
Vicarage Rd., Kingston 36 1B
Vicarage Rd., Lingfield 131 2E
Vicarage Rd., Staines 13 3F
Vicarage Rd., Sunbury 16 5A
Vicarage Rd., Sutton 38 5B
Vicarage Rd., Teddington 17 4F
Vicarage Rd., Twickenham 17 3E
Vicarage Rd., Waddon 40 5B
Vicarage Rd., Westfield 65 4D
Vicarage Way 7 3A
Vicars Oak Rd. 22 5C
Vickers Dr. North 49 3F
Vickers Dr. South 49 3F
Victor Rd., Fulwell 17 4E
Victor Rd., Penge 23 5F
Victoria Av., Hackbridge 39 5E
Victoria Av., Hurst Park 35 2D
Victoria Av., Long Ditton 36 3A
Victoria Av., Sanderstead 57 3F
Victoria Av., Whitton 16 1C
Victoria Av., York Town 43 5F
Victoria Cl., Horley 128 2B
Victoria Cl., Walton 33 5F
Victoria Cl., W. Molesey 35 2D
Victoria Cott., Kew 8 4B
Victoria Court 45 3D
Victoria Cres. 22 5C
Victoria Dri., Blackwater 60 1B
Victoria Dri., Southfields 20 2A
Victoria Gdns. 77 1E
Victoria Pl., Esher 52 1A
Victoria Pl., Ewell 54 4B
Victoria Rd., Addlestone 49 1F
Victoria Rd., Aldershot 78 5A

Victoria Rd., Cranleigh	**140** 1C	Virginia Water	**30** 3C
Victoria Rd., Crawley	**146** 4C	Viscount Gdns.	**49** 4F
Victoria Rd., Earlswood	**109** 1E	Viscount Rd.	**14** 2C
Victoria Rd., Farnham	**96** 4A	Vivien, Cl.	**53** 2E
Victoria Rd., Feltham	**16** 2A	Voewood Cl.	**37** 3E
Victoria Rd., Godalming	**119** 2D	Vogan Cl.	**108** 2C
Victoria Rd., Guildford	**101** 1D	Volta Way	**40** 4A
Victoria Rd., Horley	**128** 2B	Voss Court	**22** 5A
Victoria Rd., Kingston	**36** 1B	Vowels La.	**149** 5F
Victoria Rd., Knaphill	**64** 2A	Vulcan Cl., Sandhurst	**43** 4D
Victoria Rd., North		Vulcan Cl., Wallington	**57** 2D
Farnborough	**60** 5C	Vulcan Way, Sandhurst	**43** 4D
Victoria Rd., Oatlands Park	**33** 5F		
Victoria Rd., Owlsmoor	**43** 3E		
Victoria Rd., South Ascot	**28** 3C	**W**	
Victoria Rd., Staines	**13** 3F		
Victoria Rd., Surbiton	**36** 3B	Waddington Av.	**74** 3B
Victoria Rd., Sutton	**55** 1F	Waddington Way	**40** 1C
Victoria Rd., Teddington	**17** 5F	Waddon Cl.	**40** 5B
Victoria Rd., Tooting	**21** 5D	Waddon Court Rd.	**40** 5A
Victoria Rd., Twickenham	**17** 2D	Waddon Marsh Way	**40** 5A
Victoria Rd., Woking	**65** 2D	Waddon New Rd.	**40** 5B
Victoria Rd.,		Waddon Park Av.	**57** 1D
Woodmansterne	**73** 1F	Waddon Rd.	**40** 5B
Victoria St.	**12** 5C	Waddon Way	**57** 2E
Victoria Terr., Dorking	**160**	Wades La.	**17** 4F
Victoria Villas	**8** 5B	Wadham	**43** 3F
Victoria Way, East		Wadham Cl., Crawley	**147** 2F
Grinstead	**150** 3C	Wadham Cl., Shepperton	**33** 4E
Victoria Way, Walton on		Wadhurst Cl.	**41** 1E
Thames	**33** 5F	Wadhurst Rd.	**9** 1D
Victoria Way, Woking	**65** 2D	Wadlands Brook Rd.	**131** 5E
Victors Dri.	**16** 5C	Wagbullock Rise	**27** 3D
Victory Av.	**36** 3C	Waggon Cl.	**81** 5D
Victory Park Rd.	**49** 1E	Waggoners Hollow	**45** 3E
Victory Pl.	**23** 5D	Waggoners Way	**134** 5C
Victory Rd., Chertsey	**32** 4A	Waggoners Wells La.	**134** 5C
Victory Rd., Horsham	**158** 4B	Waggoners Wells Rd.	**134** 5C
Victory Rd., Merton	**20** 5C	Wagtail Cl.	**158** 2B
Victory Rd., Twickenham	**17** 2F	Wagtail Gdns.	**58** 3C
View Cl.	**77** 1E	Waite Davies Rd.	**24** 2C
View Terr.	**132** 3A	Wakefield Cl.	**49** 4F
Viewfield Rd.	**20** 1B	Wakefield Gdns.	**22** 5C
Vigilant	**23** 4D	Wakefield Rd.	**18** 1B
Viking	**26** 3B	Wakehams Green Rd.	**147** 2F
Village Gdns.	**54** 3B	Wakehurst Dri.	**147** 5D
Village Green Av.	**77** 2F	Wakehurst Mews	**158** 5A
Village Green Way	**77** 2F	Wakehurst Path	**48** 5B
Village Rd.	**31** 2E	Wakehurst Rd.	**21** 1D
Village Row	**55** 2E	Wakely Cl.	**77** 2E
Village St.	**125** 3F	Walburton Rd.	**56** 5C
Village Way, Ashford	**15** 4D	Walbury	**27** 2E
Village Way, Beckenham	**42** 1A	Waldeck Grn.	**22** 3B
Village Way, Camberwell	**22** 1C	Waldeck Rd.	**8** 2C
Village Way, Cranleigh	**140** 2C	Waldegrave Gdns.	**17** 3F
Village Way, Sanderstead	**58** 5A	Waldegrave Pk.	**17** 4F
Villers Av., Whitton	**16** 2C	Waldegrave Rd., Penge	**23** 5D
Villiers Rd., Elmers End	**41** 1F	Waldegrave Rd.,	
Villiers Av., Surbiton	**36** 3B	Twickenham	**17** 3F
Villiers Cl.	**36** 2B	Waldemar Av.	**8** 1A
Villiers Grove	**55** 3D	Waldemar Rd.	**20** 4B
Villiers Rd., Kingston	**36** 2B	Walden Cottages	**79** 4E
Vincam Cl.	**17** 2D	Waldens Park Rd.	**65** 2C
Vincent Av., Belmont	**55** 4F	Waldens Rd.	**65** 2C
Vincent Av., Tolworth	**37** 5D	Waldenshaw Rd.	**23** 2E
Vincent Cl., Chertsey	**32** 4A	Waldo Cl.	**21** 1F
Vincent Cl., Chipstead	**73** 3E	Waldorf Cl.	**57** 2E
Vincent Cl., Feltham	**69** 5D	Waldorf Heights	**60** 1B
Vincent Cl., Sandown Park	**35** 5D	Waldram Cres.	**23** 2E
Vincent Dri., Dorking	**105** 2F	Waldram Park Rd.	**23** 2F
Vincent Dri., Upper Halliford	**33** 2F	Waldron Gdns.	**42** 2B
Vincent Grn.	**73** 3E	Waldron Hill	**27** 1E
Vincent La.	**105** 1F	Waldron Hyrst	**57** 1E
Vincent Rd., Chertsey	**32** 4A	Waldron St.	**20** 3C
Vincent Rd., Dorking	**105** 1F	Waldrons, The, Croydon	**57** 1E
Vincent Rd., Kingston	**36** 2C	Waldrons, The, Oxted	**93** 4F
Vincent Rd., Stoke		Waldy Rise	**140** 1C
D'Abernon	**68** 1C	Wales Av.	**56** 1A
Vincent Rd.,		Walesbeech	**147** 4E
Woodmansterne	**73** 1F	Waley's Lane	**143** 2E
Vincent Rise	**27** 2E	Walford Rd.	**106** 3A
Vincents Cl.	**73** 3E	Walk, The, Tandridge	**93** 5D
Vine Cl., Stanwellmoor	**14** 1A	Walker Cl.	**16** 5C
Vine Cl., Surbiton	**36** 3B	Walker Rd.	**147** 4F
Vine Cl., Sutton	**38** 5C	Walkers Ridge	**44** 5B
Vine Cotts Rd.	**140** 1B	Walkerscroft Mead	**22** 2C
Vine Ho. Cl.	**61** 5F	Walkfield Dri.	**71** 2F
Vine La.	**114** 1C	Walking Bottom	**122** 1B
Vine Rd., Barnes	**9** 5E	Wallace Cl., Guildford	**80** 4C
Vine Rd., East Molesey	**35** 2D	Wallace Cl., Upper Halliford	**33** 2F
Viner Cl.	**34** 3B	Wallace Cres.	**56** 1A
Vineyard Cl.	**24** 2A	Wallace Fields	**54** 4B
Vineyard Hill Rd.	**20** 4B	Wallace Walk	**49** 1E
Vineyard Rd.	**16** 3A	Wallage La.	**148** 4B
Vineyard Row	**36** 1A	Waller La.	**75** 5D
Vineyard, The	**18** 1B	Wallingford Cl.	**27** 2E
Viola Av., Feltham	**16** 1A	Wallington	**56** 1B
Viola Av., Stanwell	**14** 2C	Wallington Rd.	**44** 3C
Violet Cl.	**39** 4E	Wallis Wood Green Rd.	**142** 2B
Violet Gdns.	**57** 1E	Wallner Way	**25** 2E
Violet La.	**57** 1E	Wallorton Gdns.	**9** 5D
Virginia Av.	**30** 3C	Walmer Cl., Crowthorne	**43** 1D
Virginia Beeches	**30** 2C	Walmer Cl., Frimley	**61** 3F
Virginia Cl.	**70** 2B	Walnut Cl., Carshalton	**56** 1A
Virginia Dri.	**30** 3C	Walnut Cl., Epsom	**71** 1E
Virginia Gdns.	**78** 1A	Walnut Dri.	**72** 5A
Virginia Rd.	**40** 1B	Walnut Grn.	**55** 5D

Walnut La.	**146** 2C	Warmington Rd.	**22** 1C
Walnut Tree Cl., Banstead	**55** 4D	Warminster Gdns.	**41** 1D
Walnut Tree Cl., Barnes	**9** 4E	Warminster Rd.	**41** 1D
Walnut Tree Cl., Guildford	**81** 5F	Warminster Way	**39** 1F
Walnut Tree La.	**49** 4F	Warner Av.	**38** 5A
Walnut Tree Rd.,		Warner Rd.	**24** 5C
Shepperton	**33** 2E	Warnham Court Rd.	**56** 2A
Walpole Av., Chipstead	**73** 2D	Warnham Rd., Crawley	**147** 5E
Walpole Av., Richmond	**8** 4B	Warnham Rd., Horsham	**158** 3A
Walpole Cres.	**17** 4F	Warple Way	**9** 1D
Walpole Gdns., Chiswick	**9** 2D	Warramill Rd.	**119** 1E
Walpole Gdns.,		Warren Av., Belmont	**55** 3E
Twickenham	**17** 3E	Warren Av., Bromley Hill	**24** 5C
Walpole Rd., Croydon	**40** 5C	Warren Av., North Sheen	**8** 5C
Walpole Rd., Old Windsor	**12** 2B	Warren Av., Selsdon	**38** 2C
Walpole Rd., Surbiton	**36** 4B	Warren Cl., Esher	**52** 1A
Walpole Rd., Teddington	**17** 4E	Warren Cl., Felbridge	**149** 1F
Walpole Rd., Twickenham	**17** 3E	Warren Cl., Sandhurst	**43** 4D
Walsh Cres.	**59** 4F	Warren Cl., Tulse Hill	**22** 2B
Walsham Rd.	**16** 2A	Warren Cutting	**19** 5D
Walsingham Gdns.	**54** 1B	Warren Dri., Crawley	**146** 3B
Walsingham Rd., Mitcham	**39** 3E	Warren Dri., Kingswood	**72** 4B
Walsingham Rd., New		Warren Drive North	**36** 4C
Addington	**59** 3E	Warren Drive South	**37** 4D
Walter St.	**36** 1B	Warren Hill	**71** 1D
Walters Mead	**70** 2B	Warren House Rd.	**25** 1E
Walters Way	**23** 1F	Warren La., Holland	**94** 5A
Waltham Av.	**81** 4E	Warren La., Oxshott	**52** 4A
Waltham Rd., Carshalton	**39** 4D	Warren La., Pyrford	**66** 2A
Waltham Rd., Caterham	**75** 4E	Warren Lodge	**72** 5A
Walton Av., New Malden	**37** 2E	Warren Mead	**72** 1A
Walton Av., North Cheam	**38** 5B	Warren Park, Thursley	**117** 5E
Walton Bridge Rd.	**33** 4F	Warren Park Rd.	**56** 2A
Walton Court	**65** 1E	Warren Pk., Kingston	**19** 5D
Walton Dri.	**28** 1B	Warren Pk., Warlington	**75** 2F
Walton Gdns.	**15** 4F	Warren Rd., Addiscombe	**41** 4D
Walton Green	**59** 3E	Warren Rd., Ashford	**15** 5F
Walton Heath	**147** 3F	Warren Rd., Banstead	**55** 5D
Walton La.	**33** 4E	Warren Rd., Colliers Wood	**21** 5D
Walton on the Hill	**88** 1C	Warren Rd., Coombe	**19** 5D
Walton Park La.	**34** 5B	Warren Rd., Farncombe	**100** 5A
Walton Pk.	**34** 5B	Warren Rd., Guildford	**101** 1D
Walton Rd., Leatherhead	**71** 4D	Warren Rd., Purley	**57** 4E
Walton Rd., Maybury	**65** 1D	Warren Rd., Reigate	**89** 5F
Walton Rd., Walton	**34** 3B	Warren Rd., Whitton	**17** 1E
Walton St.	**71** 5F	Warren Rd., Woodham	**49** 3D
Walton Terr.	**65** 1E	Warren Rise, Frimley	**61** 2E
Walton-on-Thames	**34** 5A	Warren Rise, Kingston	**37** 1D
Wanborough	**99** 2D	Warren Row	**28** 1A
Wanborough Dri.	**19** 2F	Warren, The, Ashtead	**70** 3B
Wanborough Hill	**99** 2D	Warren, The, Banstead	
Wanborough La.	**141** 1D	Newton	**72** 5A
Wandel Rd., Balham	**21** 3D	Warren, The, Carshalton	**56** 3A
Wandle Bank	**20** 5C	Warren, The, East Horsley	**84** 3C
Wandle Cl.	**78** 5C	Warren, The, Oxshott	**52** 4A
Wandle Court	**40** 5C	Warren, The, Worcester	
Wandle Court Gdns.	**40** 5A	Park	**54** 1A
Wandle Pl., Croydon	**40** 5C	Warren Way	**50** 1B
Wandle Rd., Crawley	**147** 4F	Warren Wood Cl.	**42** 5C
Wandle Rd., Hackbridge	**39** 5E	Warreners La.	**50** 3B
Wandle Rd., Morden	**38** 2C	Warrenne Rd.	**107** 1D
Wandle Rd., South		Warrington Rd.	**40** 5B
Wimbledon	**20** 5C	Warrington Spur	**12** 2B
Wandle Rd., Sutton	**40** 5A	Warwick	**27** 4E
Wandle St.	**40** 5C	Warwick Av., Staines	**14** 5B
Wandle Side	**39** 5E	Warwick Av., Thorpe Lea	**31** 1E
Wandle Way	**39** 3D	Warwick Cl., Ash	**97** 1D
Wandsworth Common		Warwick Cl., Camberley	**61** 1F
North Side	**20** 1C	Warwick Cl., Hampton Hill	**17** 5D
Wandsworth Common		Warwick Cl., S. Holmwood	**106** 5A
West Side	**20** 1C	Warwick Deeping	**48** 1B
Wandsworth High St.	**20** 1C	Warwick Dri.	**9** 5F
Wandsworth Plain	**20** 1B	Warwick Gdns., Lwr.	
Wansdyke Cl.	**61** 3E	Ashtead	**70** 2A
Wansford Grn.	**64** 2B	Warwick Gdns., Thames	
Wanstraw Gro.	**27** 4E	Ditton	**35** 3E
Wantage Cl.	**27** 2E	Warwick La.	**64** 3B
Wantage Rd.	**24** 1C	Warwick Rd., Anerley	**41** 2E
Waplings, The	**71** 5F	Warwick Rd., Ashford	**14** 4C
Wapshot Rd.	**13** 5F	Warwick Rd., Ash Vale	**78** 2C
Warbank Cl.	**59** 3F	Warwick Rd., Holmswood	
Warbank Cres.	**59** 3F	Corner	**125** 1D
Warbank La.	**19** 5E	Warwick Rd., Kingston	**37** 2D
Warbeck Rd.	**9** 1F	Warwick Rd., Lammas Park	**8** 1A
Warblers Green	**51** 5F	Warwick Rd., Redhill	**90** 5B
Warboys Rd.	**18** 5C	Warwick Rd., Sutton	**55** 1F
Warburton Rd.	**17** 2D	Warwick Rd., Thames	
Warbury La.	**63** 1F	Ditton	**35** 3F
Warcoppice Rd.	**91** 2F	Warwick Rd., Thornton	
Ward Cl.	**25** 1E	Heath	**40** 2A
Ward La.	**75** 1E	Warwick Rd., Twickenham	**17** 2E
Ward St.	**100** 1C	Warwick Rd., Woodcote	**56** 5C
Ward Stone Park	**27** 4E	Warwick Wold Rd.	**91** 3D
Wardle Cl.	**45** 2E	Warwicks Bench	**101** 2D
Wareham Rd.	**27** 2F	Warwick's Bench La.	**101** 2D
Warenne Rd.	**69** 5D	Warwicks Bench Rd.	**101** 2D
Warfield	**35** 1D	Wasdale Cl.	**43** 3E
Warfield Pk.	**27** 1F	Washford La.	**133** 5D
Warfield Rd., Bracknell	**27** 1D	Washington Cl.	**89** 4E
Warfield Rd., E. Bedfont	**15** 2A	Washington Rd., Barnes	**9** 3E
Wargrove Dri.	**43** 4E	Washington Rd., Kingston	**36** 1C
Warham Rd.	**57** 1E	Washington Rd.,	
Waring St.	**22** 4B	Worcester Park	**37** 5F
Warlingham	**75** 2F	Washpond La.	**76** 2B
Warlingham Rd.	**40** 2B	Wasp Green La.	**110** 4B
Warltersville Way	**128** 3C	Wassand Cl.	**147** 4E
		Wastdale Rd.	**23** 2F

Watchetts Dri. 61 2D
Watchetts Lake Cl. 61 1D
Watchetts Rd. 61 1D
Watchmoor Rd. 60 1C
Watcombe Cotts. 8 3C
Watcombe Rd. 41 3E
Water Field 71 3F
Water Field Green 71 3F
Water La., Abinger 104 5A
Water La., Albury 102 2B
Water La., Chobham 46 3C
Water La., Enton Green 118 5C
Water La., Farnham 96 3C
Water La., Great Bookham 85 1E
Water La., Hawley 60 3C
Water La., Haxted 113 5E
Water La., Kingston 36 1B
Water La., Oxshott 51 5F
Water La., Richmond 18 1A
Water La., S. Godstone 111 2F
Water La., Titsey 94 1A
Water La., Twickenham 17 2F
Water Mead 64 1A
Water Mill Way 16 3C
Water Rd. 55 1F
Water Side, Horley 128 2B
Water Tower Hill 57 1F
Water View 128 2C
Waterbank Rd. 24 4B
Watercress Way 64 2B
Waterden Cl. 101 1D
Waterden Rd. 101 1D
Waterer Gdns. 72 2A
Waterer Rise 56 2C
Waterers Rise 63 2F
Waterfall Cl. 30 2B
Waterfield Dri. 75 3E
Waterfield Gdns. 146 5A
Waterfields 70 3A
Waterham Rd. 27 3D
Waterhouse La., Burgh Hth. 72 4A
Waterhouse La., Godstone 92 4A
Waterhouse Mead 43 4E
Waterlea 147 5E
Waterloo Cl. 17 5D
Waterloo Cl., Wokingham 25 2F
Waterloo Cres. 25 2E
Waterloo Pl. 8 3C
Waterloo Rd., Aldershot 78 5A
Waterloo Rd., Carshalton 56 1A
Waterloo Rd., Crowthorne 43 2D
Waterloo Rd., Easthampstead 26 3A
Waterloo Rd., Epsom 54 4A
Waterloo Rd., Wokingham 25 3E
Waterlow Rd., 108 1C
Watermans Cl. 18 5B
Watermead 15 2F
Watermead, Tadworth 71 4F
Watermead Cott. 39 3E
Watermead La. 39 3E
Watermead Rd. 24 4B
Watermill Cl. 18 3A
Waterperry La. 47 3D
Waters Dri. 14 4A
Waters Rd., Downham 24 3C
Waters Rd., Kingston 36 1C
Watersedge 54 1A
Waterside 64 2B
Waterside Cl., Crawley 146 5A
Waterside Cl., Godalming 119 1E
Waterside Court 82 4A
Waterside Dri. 34 3A
Waterside La. 118 2C
Waterside Mews 81 4F
Waterside Rd., Guildford 81 4F
Waterside Way 20 4C
Watersmeet Cl. 82 3B
Watersplash Cl. 36 2B
Watersplash La. 29 1D
Watersplash Rd. 33 3D
Waterway Rd. 69 4F
Watery La. 31 4F
Watery La., Headley 133 2E
Watery La., Merton 38 1B
Wates Way 39 3E
Watford Cl. 82 5A
Wathen Rd. 106 1A
Watlings Cl. 41 3F
Watlington Gro. 23 4F
Watney Rd. 8 4C
Watney's Rd. 39 3F
Watson Av. 38 5A
Watson Cl. 21 5D
Watson Rd. 105 2D
Wattendon Rd. 74 1B
Watts La., Tadworth 72 4A
Watt's La., Teddington 17 4F
Watts Mead 72 4A
Watts Rd., Thames Ditton 35 4F
Watts Rd., West Heath 60 4C
Wavendene Av. 13 5E
Wavendon Av. 9 2D
Waverleigh Rd. 140 2C
Waverley 26 3B
Waverley Av., Coulsdon 74 1C
Waverley Av., Rose Hill 38 5C
Waverley Av., Surbiton 37 3D
Waverley Av., Whitton 16 2C
Waverley Cl. 61 1F
Waverley Court 158 5A
Waverley Dri., Ash Vale 78 3C
Waverley Dri., Camberley 44 5B
Waverley Dri., Chertsey 31 5F
Waverley Dri., Virginia Water 30 2B
Waverley Gdns. 78 3C
Waverley La. 96 4B
Waverley Rd., Ash Vale 78 3C
Waverley Rd., Bagshot 45 2E
Waverley Rd., Farnborough Park 61 5D
Waverley Rd., Oxshott 52 5A
Waverley Rd., S. Norwood 41 2E
Waverley Rd., Stoneleigh 54 2C
Waverley Rd., Weybridge 50 1A
Waverley Way 56 2A
Waverton Rd 20 2C
Wavertree Rd. 22 2A
Way, The 90 5A
Wayland Cl. 27 2E
Wayman Rd. 60 3B
Wayneflete Tower Av. 34 5C
Waynflete Av. 40 5B
Waynflete La. 95 4F
Wayside, Crawley 146 5A
Wayside, E. Sheen 19 1D
Wayside Court 64 1A
Weald Cl. 101 4D
Weald Dri. 147 5E
Weald Way, Caterham 92 2A
Weald Way, Woodhatch 108 2C
Wealdstone Rd. 38 5B
Weare St. 124 5C
Weasdale Cl. 64 1A
Weatherall Cl. 49 1E
Weatherhill Cl. 129 2D
Weatherhill Rd. 129 2D
Weaver Cl. 146 4A
Webb Cl. 45 3D
Webb Ct. 25 1F
Webbs Rd. 21 1D
Webster Cl. 52 5A
Websters Cl. 64 3B
Wedgewood 77 4E
Weighton Rd. 41 1E
Weihurst Gdns. 56 1A
Weir Av. 60 5C
Weir Pl. 31 1F
Weir Rd., Balham 21 2F
Weir Rd., Chertsey 32 4B
Weir Rd., Summerstown 20 4C
Weir Rd., Walton 34 3A
Weirbrook 147 5E
Welbeck 26 3B
Welbeck Cl., Ewell 54 2B
Welbeck Cl., Farnborough 60 5C
Welbeck Rd. 39 5D
Welcomes Rd. 74 1C
Weldon Dri. 34 2C
Weldon Way 90 3C
Welford Pl. 20 4A
Welham Rd. 21 4E
Well Cl., Camberley 61 1D
Well Cl., Horsell 64 2C
Well Cl., Streatham 22 4A
Well Farm Rd. 75 3D
Well House Rd., Eden Park 42 2A
Well La., East Sheen 19 1D
Well La., Haslemere 152 3A
Well La., Horsell 64 2C
Well Path 64 2C
Well Way 53 5F
Weller Cl. 147 4F
Weller Dri. 61 1D
Wellesford Cl. 72 2B
Wellesley Av., Hammersmith 9 1F
Wellesley Av., Richings Park 7 1B
Wellesley Cl., Ash Vale 78 2C
Wellesley Cl., Bagshot 45 2D
Wellesley Cres. 17 3E
Wellesley Rd., Ash Vale 78 2C
Wellesley Rd., Brentford 8 2C
Wellesley Rd., Croydon 40 4C
Wellesley Rd., Rushmore 116 5A
Wellesley Rd., Sutton 55 2F
Wellesley Rd., Twick. 17 3E
Welley Rd. 13 1D
Wellfield Rd. 22 4A
Wellhouse Rd., St. Helier 39 4D
Wellhouse Rd., Strood Green 107 2D
Wellington Av., Virginia Water 30 3B
Wellington Av., Whitton 16 1C
Wellington Av., Worcester Park 37 5F
Wellington Cl. 43 4D
Wellington Cott. 84 3C
Wellington Cres. 37 2D
Wellington Dri. 27 2E
Wellington Gdns. 17 4E
Wellington La. 96 1B
Wellington Rd., Ashford 14 4C
Wellington Rd., Caterham 74 4C
Wellington Rd., Crowthorne 43 2D
Wellington Rd., Croydon 40 4B
Wellington Rd., East Grinstead 150 2C
Wellington Rd., Feltham 15 1F
Wellington Rd., Fulwell 17 4E
Wellington Rd., Horsham 158 5B
Wellington Rd., Lammas Park 8 1A
Wellington Rd., Sandhurst 43 4D
Wellington Rd., Wimbledon Park 20 3B
Wellington Rd., Wokingham 25 2D
Wellington Road South 16 1C
Wellington Ter. 43 4D
Wellington Way, Horley 128 2B
Wellington Way, Weybridge 50 3A
Wellmeadow Rd. 24 2C
Wellow Wk. 39 4D
Wells Cl., Fetcham 69 5D
Wells Cl., Horsham 158 5A
Wells Cl., Redhill 90 3B
Wells La. 28 2C
Wells Park Rd. 23 3D
Wells Rd., Epsom 53 5F
Wells Rd., Merrow 82 4C
Wellwynds Rd. 140 2C
Weltje Rd. 9 2F
Welwyn Av. 15 1F
Wembley Rd. 34 1C
Wembury Park 130 3C
Wend, The 56 5C
Wendela 65 3D
Wendell Rd. 9 1E
Wendley Dri. 49 3D
Wendling Rd. 39 5D
Wendover Dri., Camberley 62 1A
Wendover Dri., Malden 37 3E
Wendover Pl. 13 4F
Wendover Rd. 13 4F
Wendy Cres. 81 4E
Wensley Dale 146 5C
Wensleydale Dri. 45 5D
Wensleydale Rd. 17 5D
Wentland Rd. 24 3C
Wentworth Av. 28 1A
Wentworth Cl., Ashford 15 4D
Wentworth Cl., Farnham 96 2C
Wentworth Cl., Long Ditton 36 5A
Wentworth Cl., Morden 38 4B
Wentworth Cl., Ripley 66 4B
Wentworth Cres. 78 3C
Wentworth Dri., Crawley 147 3F
Wentworth Dri., Virginia Water 30 3B
Wentworth Rd. 40 4B
Wentworth Way, Ascot 28 1A
Wentworth Way, Hamsey Green 75 1E
Wentworth Way, Sand'd. 58 5B
Werndee Rd. 41 2D
Wescott Cl., New Addington 59 3E
Wescott Cl., Purley 57 4F
Wescott Rd. 25 2B
Wesley Cl., Horley 128 2B
Wesley Cl., Reigate 108 1B
Wesley Dri. 13 5E
Wesse 72 4A
Wessex Av. 38 2B
Wessex Cl. 36 1C
Wessex Pl. 96 4A
Wessex Rd. 7 5C
West Av., Heath End 86 2B
West Av., Heath End 96 2B
West Av., Salfords 109 3E
West Av., Three Bridges 147 3E
West Av., Waddon 57 1D
West Av., Whiteley Village 50 3C
West Bank Rd. 17 5D
West Barnes La. 37 2F
West Bedfont 15 2D
West Byfleet 49 5D
West Cl., Ashford 14 4C
West Cl., Hampton 16 5C
West Cl., Heath End 96 1B
West Clandon 83 3D
West Dene Way 33 5F
West Down 86 2A
West Dri., Carshalton Beeches 56 3A
West Dri., East Ewell 55 3D
West Dri., Great Burgh 72 2A
West Dri., Streatham 21 4F
West Dri., Wentworth 30 4A
West End 46 4B
West End Gdns. 51 1F
West End Gro. 95 4F
West End La., Holloways Heath 153 2D
West End La., Millbridge 115 3D
West End La., Spreakley 114 3C
West End La., West End 51 1F
West End Rd. 45 4F
West Ewell 54 2A
West Farm Av. 70 2A
West Farm Cl. 70 3A
West Farm Dri. 70 3A
West Garden 27 1D
West Gdns., Ewell 54 3B
West Gdns., Mitcham 21 5D
West Glade 60 5B
West Green Dri. 146 4C
West Gro. 51 1D
West Hall Rd. 8 4C
West Heath 60 4B
West Heath Rd. 60 4C
West Hill, Ashtead 70 3B
West Hill, Dormans Pk. 131 5F
West Hill, East Grinstead 150 3C
West Hill, Elstead 117 2D
West Hill, Epsom 53 5F
West Hill, Oxted 93 3E
West Hill, Sanderstead 57 3F
West Hill, Southfields 20 2A
West Hill Av. 54 4A
West Hill Bank 93 3F
West Hill Cl., Brookwood 63 4F
West Hill Cl., Elstead 117 2D
West Hill Rd., Putney 20 1B
West Hill Rd., Woking 64 3C
West Hoathly Rd. 150 3C
West Horsley 84 3B
West House Cl. 20 2A
West Humble 87 4D
West La., East Grinstead 150 3C
West Lane, Abinger 104 3B
West Lees Cl., 106 3A
West Mead, Ewell 54 2B
West Mead, Farnborough 61 5D
West Mead, Woking 64 2B
West Mead Dri. 109 4E
West Meads 100 1B
West Moat Cl. 24 5B
West Molesey 34 2C
West Oak 42 1B
West Palace Gdns. 33 5D
West Parade 158 4D
West Park Av. 8 4C
West.Park Rd., Copthorne 149 1D
West Park Rd., Domewood 130 5A
West Park Rd., Epsom 53 4E
West Park Rd., Kew 8 4C
West Pl. 19 4F
West Rd., Brixton Hill 22 1A
West Rd., Brooklands 50 3A
West Rd., Camberley 44 5B
West Rd., Clapham 21 1F
West Rd., East Bedfont 15 1E
West Rd., Easthampstead 26 4A
West Rd., Guildford 101 1D
West Rd., Hawley 60 3C
West Rd., Kingston 37 1D
West Rd., Malden Rushett 53 4D
West Rd., Mead Vale 108 1C
West Rd., Mortlake 9 4D
West Rd., Reigate 108 1C
West Ring 97 1E
West St., Carshalton 56 1A
West St., Croydon 57 1F
West St., Dorking 105 1F
West St., Dormans Ld. 132 3A
West St., East Grinstead 150 3C
West St., Epsom 54 5A
West St., Ewell 54 3B
West St., Farnham 96 4A
West St., Haslemere 152 3A
West St., Horsham 158 5B
West St., Reigate 89 5D
West St., Sutton 55 1F
West St., West Green 146 4C
West St., Woking 160
West Side Common 20 5A
West Street La. 56 1A
West Temple Sheen 18 1C
West View 15 2E
West View Av. 75 2D
West View Rd. 75 3E
West Wates Cl. 27 1E
West Way, Crawley 147 3E
West Way, Lower Halliford 33 3E
West Way, Shirley 41 5F
West Way Gdns. 41 5F
Westacres 51 2F
Westbank Rd. 105 2F
Westbourne Av. 38 5A
Westbourne Dri. 23 3F
Westbourne Rd., Feltham 15 3F
Westbourne Rd., Penge 23 5F
Westbourne Rd., Staines 14 5B
Westbourne Rd., Woodside 41 3D
Westbourne Rd., York Town 43 4E
Westbrook Av. 16 5C
Westbrook Gdns. 27 1D
Westbrook La. 117 2D
Westbrook Rd., Godalming 118 1C

225
Westbrook Rd
Wilbury Av

Westbrook Rd., Thornton Heath **40** 1C
Westburg Cl. **75** 2D
Westbury Cl., Crowthorne **43** 1D
Westbury Cl., Shepperton **33** 3E
Westbury Rd., Anerley **41** 1F
Westbury Rd., Elmers End **41** 2F
Westbury Rd., Feltham **16** 2B
Westbury Rd., New Malden **37** 2D
Westbury Rd., Selhurst **40** 3C
Westcar La. **51** 2D
Westcombe Av., Croydon **40** 4A
Westcombe Cl. **27** 4E
Westcoombe Av., Cottenham Park **37** 1E
Westcote Rd. **21** 4F
Westcott **105** 2E
Westcott Rd. **105** 2E
Westcott St. **105** 2D
Westcott Way **54** 3C
Westcroft Gdns. **38** 2B
Westcroft Rd. **56** 1B
Westcroft Sq. **9** 2E
Westdean Cl. **20** 1C
Westdene Meadows **140** 1A
Westdown Rd. **24** 2A
Westerdale Dri. **61** 1F
Westerfield Rd. **34** 4C
Westerfold Cl. **65** 2E
Westerham Cl., Addlestone **49** 2E
Westerham Cl., Belmont **55** 3E
Westerham Rd., Limpsfield **94** 3A
Westerham Rd., South Street **77** 3F
Westerley Cres. **24** 4A
Western Av., Laleham **32** 2A
Western Av., Thorpe **31** 2E
Western Dri. **33** 3E
Western Parade **108** 2C
Western Perimeter Rd. **7** 5C
Western Rd., Bracknell **26** 1C
Western Rd., Cheam **55** 1E
Western Rd., Mitcham **39** 1D
Westfield, Ashtead **70** 2B
Westfield, Hoe **103** 5F
Westfield, Reigate **89** 4F
Westfield, Woking **65** 4D
Westfield Av., Sanderstead **57** 5F
Westfield Av., Woking **65** 4D
Westfield Cl. **55** 1E
Westfield Common **65** 5D
Westfield Dri. **69** 4D
Westfield Grn. **65** 3D
Westfield La. **114** 1B
Westfield Parade **49** 3F
Westfield Rd., Beckenham **42** 1A
Westfield Rd., Charlwood **127** 5E
Westfield Rd., Cheam **55** 1E
Westfield Rd., Croydon **40** 5B
Westfield Rd., Frimley **61** 2D
Westfield Rd., Hampton Wick **36** 3A
Westfield Rd., Mitcham **39** 1D
Westfield Rd., Slyfield Grn. **82** 3A
Westfield Rd., Walton-on-Thames **34** 4C
Westfield Rd., Westfield **65** 4D
Westfield Rd., West Green **146** 4C
Westfield Way **65** 4D
Westfields Av. **9** 5E
Westgate Rd., Beckenham **42** 1B
Westgate Rd., Ravensbourne **24** 5B
Westgate Rd., South Norwood **41** 2E
Westhall Park Rd. **75** 3E
Westhall Rd. **75** 2D
Westhumble St. **87** 4D
Westland Cl. **14** 1C
Westland Dri. **42** 5C
Westland Way **57** 2D
Westlands **158** 4C
Westlands Cl. **71** 1D
Westlands Way **93** 2E
Westleas **128** 2A
Westleigh Av., East Putney **20** 1A
Westleigh Av., Roehampton **19** 1F
Westleigh Av., Woodmansterne **73** 1E
Westmacott Dri. **15** 2F
Westmead **19** 1F
Westmead Dri. **109** 4E
Westmead Rd. **56** 1A
Westminster Av. **40** 1B
Westminster Rd., Crawley **147** 4F
Westminster Rd., Croydon **38** 5C
Westmont Rd. **35** 5E
Westmore Rd. **77** 4E
Westmoreland Dri. **55** 2F
Westmoreland Rd., Barnes **9** 4E
Westmoreland Rd., Sandhurst **42** 3C
Westmoreland Way **40** 3A
Westmorland Dri. **61** 1F
Westmorland Gdns. **54** 3A
Weston Av., Addlestone **49** 1E
Weston Av., Thames Ditton **35** 4E
Weston Av., W. Molesey **34** 2C
Weston Cl., Coulsdon **74** 3A
Weston Cl., Esher **35** 4E
Weston Cl., Godalming **119** 1D
Weston Fields **102** 3B
Weston Gdns. **66** 1A
Weston Green Rd. **35** 4E
Weston Grn. **45** 3F
Weston Gro. **42** 1C
Weston Lea **84** 1B
Weston Park **36** 1B
Weston Park Rd. **35** 4E
Weston Park Way **35** 4E
Weston Rd., Acton **9** 1D
Weston Rd., Bromley Hill **24** 5C
Weston Rd., Esher **35** 4E
Weston Rd., Ewell **54** 4B
Weston Rd., Guildford **81** 5E
Weston Rd., Woodbridge Hill **81** 5E
Weston Way **65** 1F
Weston Yd. **102** 3B
Westons Cl. **158** 2B
Westover Cl. **55** 3F
Westover Rd. **20** 2C
Westow Hill **23** 5D
Westow St. **23** 5E
Westview Gdns. **150** 3C
Westview Rd. **134** 5A
Westville Rd., Hammersmith **9** 1F
Westville Rd., Thames Ditton **35** 4F
Westward Ho! **82** 4A
Westway, Carshalton Beeches **56** 3A
Westway, Caterham **74** 4C
Westway, Copthorne **148** 1B
Westway, Parklangley **42** 3C
Westway, Raynes Park **37** 2F
Westway, Stoughton **81** 4E
Westway Cl. **37** 2F
Westway Gdns. **90** 4B
Westways **54** 1B
Westwell Rd. **22** 5A
Westwood Av., Norwood **40** 1C
Westwood Av., Woodham **49** 4D
Westwood Cl. **35** 5E
Westwood Hill **23** 4D
Westwood La., Christmaspie **98** 1C
Westwood La., Wyke **79** 4E
Westwood Park **23** 2E
Westwood Rd., Barnes **9** 5E
Westwood Rd., Coulsdon **73** 2F
Westwood Rd., Sydenham **23** 4E
Westwood Rd., Updown Hill **46** 1A
Westwood Rd., Windlemere **29** 5D
Wetherby Gdns. **78** 1A
Wexfenne Gdns. **66** 1B
Wexford Rd. **21** 2D
Wey Bank **66** 1C
Wey Bank Cl. **96** 3B
Wey Cl., Ash **78** 5C
Wey Cl., Camberley **44** 5A
Wey Cl., Godalming **119** 1E
Wey Cl., W. Byfleet **49** 5E
Wey Court, Ewell **54** 1A
Wey Court, Godalming **119** 1E
Wey Court, New Haw **49** 3F
Wey Hill **151** 3F
Wey Manor Rd. **49** 3F
Wey Rd., Catteshall **119** 1E
Wey Rd., Weybridge **33** 5D
Weybarton **50** 5A
Weybourne Pl. **57** 3F
Weybourne Rd., Aldershot **96** 1C
Weybourne Rd., Farnham **96** 2B
Weybourne St. **20** 3C
Weybridge **50** 1A
Weybridge Pk. **50** 1A
Weybridge Rd., Thornton Heath **40** 2B
Weybridge Rd., Weybridge **49** 1F
Weycombe Rd. **152** 2A
Weycourt, Godalming **119** 1E
Weydon Hill Cl. **96** 4A
Weydon Hill Rd. **96** 5A
Weydon La. **95** 5F
Weydon Mill La. **96** 4A
Weydown Cl., Guildford **81** 3E
Weydown Cl., Southfield **20** 2A
Weydown Rd. **151** 2F
Weyland's Cl. **34** 4C
Weylands Park **50** 2C
Weylea Av. **82** 4A
Weymead **65** 5F
Weymead Cl. **32** 4B
Weymede **50** 4A
Weymouth Av. **8** 1A
Weymouth Court **55** 2E
Weyside Cl. **50** 4A
Weyside Gdns. **81** 4F
Weyside Rd., Godalming **119** 1D
Weyside Rd., Guildford **81** 5F
Weysprings **151** 3F
Weywoods La. **96** 1B
Whaley Rd. **25** 1E
Wharf La., Pyrford **66** 2B
Wharf La., Send **65** 5F
Wharf La., Twickenham **17** 2F
Wharf Rd., Ash Wharf **78** 4C
Wharf Rd., Frimley Green **61** 4F
Wharf Rd., Guildford **81** 5F
Wharf Rd., Wraysbury **12** 2C
Wharf St. **119** 2D
Wharf Way **61** 4F
Wharfdale Gdns. **40** 2A
Wharfenden Way **61** 4F
Wharncliffe Gdns. **40** 1C
Wharncliffe Rd. **40** 1C
Whateley Rd., Camberwell **23** 1D
Whateley Rd., Guildford **81** 3E
Whateley Rd., Penge **23** 5F
Whatley Av. **38** 2A
Whatman Rd. **23** 2F
Whatmore Cl. **14** 1A
Wheat Knoll **74** 1B
Wheatash La. **32** 5B
Wheatfield Way, Horley **128** 2C
Wheatfield Way, Kingston **36** 1B
Wheathill Rd. **41** 2E
Wheatley **26** 3B
Wheatsheaf Cl., Horsell **65** 1D
Wheatsheaf Cl., Horsham **158** 3C
Wheatsheaf Cl., Ottershaw **48** 2C
Wheatsheaf La. **14** 5A
Wheatstone Cl., Mitcham **39** 1D
Wheatstone Cl., Tinsley Green **147** 1E
Wheeler Av. **93** 3E
Wheeler La. **118** 5A
Wheeler Rd. **147** 4F
Wheeler's La., Brockham **106** 1C
Wheeler's La., Epsom **53** 5F
Wheelers La., Smallfield **129** 3E
Wheelers Way **149** 1F
Wheelwrights La. **134** 5C
Whellcock Rd. **9** 1D
Wherwell Rd. **100** 1C
Whetsone Rd. **60** 5A
Whimmel Cl. **57** 4F
Whinfell Cl. **21** 4F
Whins Cl. **61** 1D
Whinshill Court **29** 4E
Whipley Cl. **82** 2F
Whisper Grn. **43** 5E
Whistler Cl. **147** 5D
Whistler Gro. **43** 5E
Whistley Cl. **27** 2E
Whitby Gdns. **38** 5C
Whitby Rd. **38** 5C
Whitchurch Cl. **97** 2D
Whitchurch Rd. **97** 2D
White Acres Rd. **61** 5E
White Beam Gdns. **60** 5A
White Beam Way **71** 4F
White Beech La. **138** 4B
White Cl. **15** 1F
White Cottage Cl. **96** 2B
White Down La. **104** 2B
White Gate Way **71** 3F
White Gates, Warlingham **75** 3E
White Gates, Woking **65** 3D
White Hart La., Barnes **9** 5F
White Hart La., Woodstreet Village **80** 5B
White Hart Meadows **66** 4B
White Heron Ms. **17** 5F
White Hill, Chipstead **73** 5D
White Hill, Windlesham **45** 1F
White Hill Cl. **44** 4A
White Hill La. **91** 3F
White Horse Dri. **54** 5A
White House Dri. **82** 5B
White House La. **81** 3F
White House Wk. **96** 1B
White Knights La. **50** 2B
White Knobs Way **92** 1A
White La., Albury **102** 2A
White La., Guildford **101** 1E
White La., Titsey **77** 5D
White La., Tongham **98** 1A
White Lion Wk., Guildford **159**
White Lodge **22** 5B
White Lodge Cl. **55** 2F
White Lodge Gdns. **109** 4E
White Oak Dri. **42** 1B
White Oaks **55** 5F
White Rd., Dorking **87** 5F
White Rd., Sandhurst **43** 5F
White Rose La., Farnham **96** 5A
White Rose La., Woking **65** 2D
White Way **86** 1A
White Way Court. **14** 5B
Whitebeam Dri. **108** 2C
Whitebridge Cl. **15** 1F
Whitecroft **128** 2C
Whitecroft Cl. **42** 2B
Whitecroft Way **42** 2B
Whitefield Av. **74** 1B
Whitefield Cl. **20** 1A
Whitefoot La. **24** 4B
Whitefoot Ter. **24** 3C
Whitehall Cres. **53** 1E
Whitehall Farm Rd. **31** 2D
Whitehall Gdns. **8** 3C
Whitehall La., Egham **13** 5D
Whitehall La., Ockham **67** 5E
Whitehall La., South Park **108** 2B
Whitehall La., Wraysbury **13** 1E
Whitehall Park Rd. **8** 3C
Whitehall Rd. **40** 3B
Whitehart Court **158** 4B
Whitehead Cl. **20** 2C
Whitehorse La. **40** 2C
Whitehorse Rd. **40** 4C
Whitelands Dri. **28** 1A
Whiteley Rd. **22** 4C
Whiteley Village **50** 3C
Whitemore Rd. **81** 3F
Whitepost Hill **90** 5A
Whitepost La. **114** 2C
White's Hill **154** 3A
Whites La. **63** 5E
White's Rd. **78** 1B
Whitethorn Av. **73** 1E
Whitethorn Gdns. **41** 5E
Whitewood **111** 5E
Whitewood Cotts. **77** 3E
Whitfield Cl. **152** 2A
Whitfield Rd. **152** 2A
Whitford Gdns. **39** 2D
Whitgift Av. **57** 1E
Whitland Rd. **39** 4D
Whitley Cl. **14** 1C
Whitlock Dri. **20** 2A
Whitmead Cl. **57** 2F
Whitmead La. **116** 2B
Whitmoor La., Jacobs Well **81** 1F
Whitmoor La., Sunningdale **29** 3E
Whitmoor Rd. **45** 3E
Whitmoor Vale Rd. **134** 3C
Whitmore Cl. **43** 4E
Whitmore Grn. **96** 2B
Whitmore La. **81** 1F
Whitmore Rd. **42** 2A
Whitmore Vale **134** 4C
Whitmore Vale Rd. **134** 3B
Whitmores Cl. **71** 1D
Whitnell Way **20** 1A
Whittaker Rd. **38** 5B
Whittel Gdns. **23** 3E
Whittington Rd. **147** 5D
Whittle Cres. **60** 3C
Whittle Way **147** 1E
Whitton Dene **17** 1D
Whitton Manor Rd. **17** 1E
Whitton Rd., Bracknell **27** 2E
Whitton Rd., Hounslow **17** 1D
Whitton Rd., Twickenham **17** 1E
Whitton Waye **17** 1D
Whitworth Rd., Crawley **147** 1D
Whitworth Rd., S. Norwood **41** 2D
Whopshott Av. **64** 1C
Whopshott Cl. **64** 1C
Whopshott Dri. **64** 1C
Whynstones Rd. **28** 3B
Whyte Av. **97** 1D
Whytebeam View **75** 2D
Whytecliffe Rd. **57** 4E
Whyteleafe **75** 2D
Whyteleafe Hill **75** 3D
Whyteleafe Rd. **75** 3D
Wick Cl. **150** 2B
Wick La. **12** 5B
Wick Rd., Egham Wick **12** 5B
Wick Rd., Hampton Wick **18** 5A
Wickers Oaks **23** 4D
Wicket Hill **114** 1C
Wicket, The **59** 1D
Wickham Av., Shirley **41** 5F
Wickham Av., Stoneleigh **54** 1C
Wickham Chase **42** 4B
Wickham Cl., Bagshot **45** 1E
Wickham Cl., Horley **128** 2A
Wickham Cl., Malden **37** 3E
Wickham Court Rd. **42** 5B
Wickham Cres. **42** 5B
Wickham La. **13** 5E
Wickham Rd., Beckenham **42** 1B
Wickham Rd., Camberley **44** 4B
Wickham Rd., Shirley **41** 5E
Wickham Vale **26** 3B
Wickham Way **42** 2B
Wide Way **39** 2F
Widgeon Way, Horsham **158** 3B
Widgeon Way, Roundshaw **57** 2D
Wiggle La. **90** 4B
Wigley Rd. **16** 2B
Wigmore La. **125** 3D
Wigmore Rd. **39** 5D
Wilberforce Way **27** 3D
Wilbury Av. **55** 3E

Wilbury Rd.	64	2C
Wilcot Cl.	63	1E
Wilcot Gdns.	63	1E
Wilcox Gdns.	33	2D
Wilcox Rd., Fulwell	17	4E
Wilcox Rd., Sutton	55	1F
Wild Wood Court	74	1C
Wildacres	49	4E
Wildcroft Dri., Dorking	106	3A
Wildcroft Dri., Eastheath	25	4D
Wildcroft Wood	118	5A
Wilderness Rd., Frimley	61	2E
Wilderness Rd., Onslow Village	100	1B
Wilderness Rd., Oxted	93	3F
Wilders Cl., Frimley	61	1E
Wilders Cl., Woking	64	2C
Wilderwick Rd.	132	4A
Wildfell Rd.	24	2A
Wildfield Cl.	80	5C
Wildridings Rd.	26	2C
Wildwood Cl., Catford	24	2C
Wildwood Cl., Cranleigh	141	2D
Wildwood Cl., Horsley	84	1C
Wildwood Cl., W. Byfleet	49	5D
Wildwood La.	140	4A
Wilford Rd.	40	3C
Wilfred St.	64	2C
Wilhelmina Av.	73	3F
Wilkins Cl.	39	1D
Wilkinson Way	9	1D
Willcocks Cl.	36	5B
Willett Rd.	40	3B
Willey Broom La.	91	1E
Willey La.	91	1F
William Booth Rd.	41	1D
William Ellis Cl.	12	1B
William Gdns.	19	1F
William Rd., Caterham	74	4C
William Rd., Guildford	81	5F
William Rd., Sutton	55	1F
William Rd., Wimbledon	20	5A
William Russell Court	64	2A
William St.	39	5D
Williams Cl.	49	1E
Williams La., Morden	38	3C
Williams La., Mortlake	9	5D
Williams Pl.	122	5C
Williams Ter.	57	2E
Williams Wk.	81	3E
Williamson Cl.	152	1B
Willingham Way	36	2C
Willington Cl.	44	5A
Willis Av.	56	2A
Willis Cl.	53	5F
Willis Rd.	40	4C
Willmore End	38	1C
Willoughby Av.	57	1D
Willoughby Rd., Bracknell	26	2C
Willoughby Rd., Kingston	36	1B
Willoughby Rd., Twickenham	18	1A
Willow Av.	38	1C
Willow Bank	18	3A
Willow Brean	128	1A
Willow Cl., Beare Green	125	2D
Willow Cl., Brentford	8	3A
Willow Cl., Byfleet	49	4E
Willow Cl., Carshalton	56	2B
Willow Cl., Colnbrook	7	3A
Willow Cl., Deadwater	133	5D
Willow Cl., E. Grinstead	150	1C
Willow Cl., Mytchett	61	5E
Willow Cl., Northgate	147	3D
Willow Cl., Woodham	49	4D
Willow Corner	127	4E
Willow Cotts.	8	3C
Willow Court	34	5A
Willow Cres.	60	3C
Willow Dri., Bracknell	27	1D
Willow Dri., Sendmarsh	66	5A
Willow Dri., Wanborough	79	5F
Willow End	36	4B
Willow Grn., N. Holmwood	106	3A
Willow Grn., West End	46	5B
Willow Hayne Dri.	34	4A
Willow Hayne Gdns.	54	1C
Willow La., Blackwater	60	1B
Willow La., Guildford	82	5B
Willow La., Mitcham	39	3D
Willow Mead, Wheeler St.	118	5B
Willow Mead, Woking	64	2B
Willow Mere	52	1A
Willow Pk.	78	5B
Willow Rd., Ealing	8	1B
Willow Rd., Kingston	37	2D
Willow Rd., Northbourne	100	5A
Willow Rd., Poyle	7	4B
Willow Rd., Woodhatch	108	2C
Willow Ridge	149	5D
Willow Vale	69	5D
Willow Way, Aldershot	97	1E
Willow Way, Ewell	54	2A
Willow Way, Fetcham	69	5D
Willow Way, Forest Hill	23	3E
Willow Way, Godstone	92	4B
Willow Way, Hale	96	2B
Willow Way, Slyfield Green	81	3F
Willow Way, Sunbury	34	2A
Willow Way, Twickenham	17	3D
Willow Way, Woking	65	4D
Willow Wk., Chertsey	32	4A
Willow Wk., Earlswood	109	1E
Willow Wk., Englefield Green	12	4C
Willow Wk., Sutton	38	5B
Willow Wood Cres.	40	3C
Willowbrook Rd.	14	3C
Willowdene Cl.	17	2D
Willowherb Cl.	25	1F
Willowmead Cl.	64	2B
Willows Av.	38	3C
Willows End	43	4D
Willows Path	53	5F
Willows, The, Byfleet	49	5F
Willows, The, Claygate	52	2B
Willows, The, Horsham	158	3B
Willows, The, Lightwater	46	3A
Willows, The, Weybridge	33	5D
Willows, The,	137	5E
Wills Cres.	17	1D
Willson Rd.	12	4B
Wilmar Gdns.	42	4A
Wilmer Cl.	18	4C
Wilmer Cres.	18	4C
Wilmerhatch La.	70	2C
Wilmington Av.	9	3D
Wilmot Rd., Carshalton	56	1A
Wilmot Rd., Purley	57	4E
Wilmot Way, Banstead	55	5E
Wilmot Way, Camberley	61	1F
Wilmots Cl.	89	5F
Wilmot's La.	129	1F
Wilna Rd.	20	2C
Wilson Av., Mitcham	21	5D
Wilson Dri.	48	1B
Wilson Rd., Aldershot	78	5A
Wilson Rd., Chessington	53	2E
Wilson Rd., Farnborough	60	5C
Wilson Way	64	1C
Wilsons	72	4A
Wilsons Rd.	134	4A
Wilton Av.	9	2E
Wilton Court	61	5E
Wilton Cres.	38	1B
Wilton Gdns., Walton	34	4B
Wilton Gdns., West Molesey	34	2C
Wilton Gro., Malden	37	3E
Wilton Gro., Merton	38	1B
Wilton Pl.	49	3F
Wilton Rd., Camberley	61	1D
Wilton Rd., Earlswood	109	1E
Wilton Rd., Mitcham	21	5D
Wiltshire Av.	43	1D
Wiltshire Dri.	25	1E
Wiltshire Gdns.	17	2D
Wiltshire Rd., Thorn. H'th.	40	2B
Wiltshire Rd., Wokingham	25	1E
Wilverley Cres.	37	3E
Wilwood Rd.	26	1B
Wimbledon	20	5A
Wimbledon Cl.	44	3B
Wimbledon Hill Rd.	20	4A
Wimbledon Park Rd.	20	3A
Wimbledon Park Side	20	3A
Wimbledon Rd., Camberley	44	3B
Wimbledon Rd., Summerstown	20	4C
Wimblehurst Rd.	158	4B
Wimborne Cl., Epsom	54	5B
Wimborne Cl., Hither Grn.	24	1C
Wimborne Av.	109	3E
Wimbourne Cl.	38	4A
Wimbourne Way	41	2F
Wincanton Rd.	20	2B
Winchcombe Rd.	39	4D
Winchelsea Cl.	20	1A
Winchelsey Rise	58	2A
Winchendon Rd.	17	4E
Winchester Cl., Esher	34	5C
Winchester Cl., Poyle	7	4B
Winchester Pk.	42	2C
Winchester Rd., Ash Wharf	78	4C
Winchester Rd., Hanworth	16	3C
Winchester Rd., Rushmoor	116	4A
Winchester Rd., Shortlands	42	2C
Winchester Rd., Twickenham	17	1F
Winchester Rd., Walton	34	4A
Winchester St., Acton	9	1D
Winchester St., South Farnborough	78	2A
Winchester Way	43	5D
Winchfield Rd.	23	4F
Winchilsea Cres.	35	1D
Winchstone Cl.	33	2D
Windborough Rd.	56	2B
Windermere Av.	38	2B
Windermere Cl., Farnborough	60	5B
Windermere Cl., Feltham	15	3F
Windermere Cl., Thorpe Lea	13	5E
Windermere Rd., Coombe	19	4D
Windermere Rd., Coulsdon	74	1A
Windermere Rd., Lammas Park	8	1A
Windermere Rd., Lightwater	45	3F
Windermere Rd., Norbury	39	1F
Windermere Rd., West Wickham	42	5C
Windermere Way, Reigate	90	5A
Windermere Way, Upper Hale	96	2A
Windermere Wk.	45	5D
Winders Hill	92	2B
Windfield	70	4A
Windfield Cl., Sydenham	23	4E
Windgates	82	4C
Windham Av.	59	3E
Windham Rd.	8	5B
Windings, The	58	4A
Windingwood Dri.	61	1F
Windle Cl.	46	2A
Windlebroof Green	26	1C
Windlesham	46	1A
Windlesham Court Dri.	29	5D
Windlesham Ct. Dri.	45	1F
Windlesham Gro.	20	2A
Windlesham Rd., Bracknell	26	1C
Windlesham Rd., Burrowhill	46	2B
Windlesham Rd., West End	46	4B
Windley Cl.	23	3E
Windmere Cl.	14	3C
Windmill Av.	54	4B
Windmill Cl., Caterham	74	4C
Windmill Cl., Epsom	54	4B
Windmill Cl., Horley	128	2B
Windmill Cl., Horsham	158	4C
Windmill Cl., Long Ditton	36	4A
Windmill Cl., Redhill	90	4A
Windmill Cl., Upper Halliford	33	1F
Windmill Court	147	3F
Windmill Dri., Clapham	21	1E
Windmill Dri., Headley Down	134	4A
Windmill Dri., Leatherhead	70	5A
Windmill Dri., Redhill	90	4A
Windmill End	54	4B
Windmill Field	46	2A
Windmill La., East Grinstead	150	1B
Windmill La., Epsom	54	4B
Windmill La., Long Ditton	36	3A
Windmill Rd., Aldershot	78	5A
Windmill Rd., Bracknell	26	1C
Windmill Rd., Brentford	8	2A
Windmill Rd., Chiswick	9	2D
Windmill Rd., Croydon	40	4C
Windmill Rd., Mitcham	39	3F
Windmill Rd., Sunbury	15	5F
Windmill Rd., Upper Halliford	33	1F
Windmill Rd., Wandsworth	20	1C
Windmill Rd., Wimbledon	19	3F
Windmill Way	90	4A
Windrush Cl., Bramley	120	1A
Windrush Heights	43	4D
Windrush La.	23	3F
Winds Ridge	82	1C
Windsor Av., E. Molesey	35	2D
Windsor Av., Malden	37	3D
Windsor Av., N. Cheam	38	5A
Windsor Av., South Wimbledon	38	1C
Windsor Cl.	100	1A
Windsor Court	16	5A
Windsor Court La.	47	3D
Windsor Cres.	96	2A
Windsor Dri.	14	4C
Windsor Gdns., Ash	78	5C
Windsor Gdns., Croydon	40	5A
Windsor Gro.	22	4B
Windsor Rd., Ascot	28	1B
Windsor Rd., Ascot Heath	10	5C
Windsor Rd., Chobham	47	2D
Windsor Rd., Fulwell	17	4E
Windsor Rd., Kew	8	4B
Windsor Rd., Kingston	18	5B
Windsor Rd., Lindford	133	4D
Windsor Rd., South Farnborough	78	1A
Windsor Rd., Staines	13	3D
Windsor Rd., Sunbury	16	5A
Windsor Rd., Thornton Heath	40	1B
Windsor Rd., Worcester Park	37	5F
Windsor Rd., Wraysbury	13	1D
Windsor Ride	27	4E
Windsor St.	32	3A
Windsor Walk, Lindford	133	4D
Windsor Way, Aldershot	78	5A
Windsor Way, Frimley	61	3F
Windsor Way, Woking	65	1F
Windsor Wk., Weybridge	50	1B
Windy Ridge	146	4B
Windy Ridge Cl.	20	4A
Windy Wood	118	3C
Wineacres Way	74	2A
Winern Glebe	49	5F
Winfield Grn.	125	3F
Winfrith Rd.	20	2C
Wingate Cres.	40	3A
Wingate Rd.	9	1F
Wingfield Cl.	49	3E
Wingfield Gdns.	62	1A
Wingfield Rd.	18	5C
Wingford Rd.	22	1A
Wingrove Rd.	24	3C
Wings Rd.	96	2A
Winifred Rd., Hanworth	16	4C
Winifred Rd., Merton	38	1B
Winifred Rd., Woodmansterne	73	1E
Winkfield	10	3A
Winkfield La.	10	2A
Winkfield Rd., Ascot	28	1C
Winkfield Rd., Windsor	11	1D
Winkfield St.	10	3A
Winkworth Pl.	55	5E
Winkworth Rd.	55	5E
Winlaton Rd.	24	4B
Winnington Way	64	2C
Winscombe	26	3B
Winsford Rd.	24	3A
Winsham Gro.	21	1E
Winslade Rd.	22	1A
Winslade Way	24	2A
Winslow Way, Hanworth	16	3B
Winslow Way, Walton-on-Thames	34	5B
Winstanley Cl.	51	5D
Winston Cl.	61	4E
Winston Dri.	68	2C
Winston Way	65	3E
Winston Wk.	115	1D
Winter Box W.	18	1B
Winter Rd.	22	1A
Winter Stoke Rd.	24	2A
Winterbourne Grn.	50	2B
Winterbourne Rd., Catford	24	2A
Winterbourne Rd., Thornton Heath	40	2B
Winterbrook Rd.	22	1C
Winterdown Gdns.	51	2F
Winterdown Rd.	51	2F
Winterfold	147	5E
Winterfold Cl.	20	3A
Winterfold Heath Rd.	122	3A
Winterhill Way	82	3B
Winters Rd.	36	3A
Wintersells Rd.	49	3F
Winterton Court	158	5B
Winton Rd.	96	3B
Winton Way	22	4B
Wire Mill	130	4C
Wisbech Rd.	40	3C
Wisborough Rd.	58	3A
Wiseton Rd.	21	2D
Wishanger La.	134	2A
Wishbone Way	64	1A
Wishmoor Cl.	44	4B
Wishmoor Rd.	44	4B
Wisley	66	1C
Wisley La.	66	1C
Wisley Rd.	21	1E
Witham Rd.	41	2C
Witherby Court	58	1A
Witherdale	128	2A
Witherslack Cl.	134	5A
Withey Meadow	128	3A
Witheygate Av.	14	5B
Withies La.	99	4F
Withies, The, Leatherhead	70	4A
Withies, The, Woking	64	2A
Withycombe Rd.	20	2A
Withypitts	149	5D
Withypitts East	149	5D
Witley	137	1E
Witley Cres.	59	2E
Wittenham Rd.	27	1E
Wittersham Rd.	24	4C
Wittmead Rd.	61	5F
Wiverton Rd.	23	5E
Wix Hill	84	4A
Wix La.	84	4A
Woburn Av., Farnborough	61	5E
Woburn Av., Purley	57	4E
Woburn Hill	32	5B
Woburn Rd., Crawley	146	5B
Woburn Rd., Croydon	40	4C
Woburn Rd., St. Helier	39	4D
Wodeland Av.	100	1B
Woking	65	2D
Woking Cl.	9	5E
Woking Rd.	81	3F
Wokingham	25	2E
Wokingham New Rd.	43	1D
Wokingham Rd.	26	1C
Wold Cl.	146	5B
Wold, The	76	4A
Woldingham	76	5A
Woldingham Rd., Caterham	75	3E
Wolfe Rd.	78	5A
Wolfington Rd.	22	4B

Wolfram Cl. 24 1C
Wolf's Hill 94 4A
Wolf's Row 94 3A
Wolf's Wood 94 4A
Wolseley Av. 20 3B
Wolseley Gdns. 8 3C
Wolseley Rd., Chiswick 9 2D
Wolseley Rd., Godalming 119 1D
Wolseley Rd., Hackbridge 39 4E
Wolsey Av. 35 3F
Wolsey Cl., Kingston 36 1C
Wolsey Cl., Stoneleigh 54 1B
Wolsey Cl., Wimbledon 19 5F
Wolsey Cres., Morden Park 38 4A
Wolsey Cres., New Addington 59 3E
Wolsey Dri., Kingston 18 4B
Wolsey Dri., Walton-on-Thames 34 4B
Wolsey Grove 52 1A
Wolsey Rd., Ashford 14 4C
Wolsey Rd., Esher 52 1A
Wolsey Rd., Hampton 17 5D
Wolsey Rd., Hampton Court 35 2E
Wolsey Rd., Sunbury 15 5F
Wolsey Rd., Whitton 17 1D
Wolsey Way 53 1F
Wolvens La. 105 4D
Wolverton Av. 36 1C
Wolverton Gdns. 128 3B
Wolves Hill 144 1A
Wonersh 101 5E
Wonersh Common Rd. 101 4E
Wonersh Way 55 3D
Wonford Cl. 88 1C
Wonham La. 107 1E
Wonham Way 103 4F
Wontford Rd. 74 1B
Wontner Rd. 21 3E
Wood Cl., Beckenham 24 5A
Wood Cl., Salfords 109 5E
Wood End, Ascot 28 3C
Wood End, Esher 35 5D
Wood End, Farnborough 61 5D
Wood End, Mickleham 87 1D
Wood End Cl., Coldharbour 66 1A
Wood End Cl., Woking 64 3B
Wood End Rd., Cobham 68 1B
Wood End Rd., Deepcut 62 3A
Wood La., Banstead 72 2B
Wood La., Caterham 74 5C
Wood La., Cove 60 5C
Wood La., Knaphill 64 2A
Wood La., Seale 97 3F
Wood La., Weybridge 50 3B
Wood Lodge La. 42 5B
Wood Rd., Biggin Hill 77 2E
Wood Rd., Farncombe 100 5A
Wood Rd., Frimley 61 2D
Wood Rd., Hindhead 135 4D
Wood Rd., Shepperton 33 3D
Wood Rd., Streatham Vale 21 5F
Wood Rd., Upper Hale 96 2A
Wood Riding 66 1A
Wood Rise 81 4D
Wood St., Ash Vale 78 3C
Wood St., Beddington Corner 39 4E
Wood St., Chiswick 9 2E
Wood St., East Grinstead 150 2C
Wood St., Kingston 36 1B
Wood St., Merstham 90 3C
Wood Vale 23 2E
Woodbank Rd. 24 3C
Woodbastwick Rd. 23 4F
Woodberry Cl., Chiddingfold 137 4E
Woodberry Cl., Sunbury 16 5A
Woodbine Cl., Sandhurst 43 4D
Woodbine Cl., Twickenham 17 3E
Woodbine Gro. 23 5E
Woodbine La. 37 5F
Woodbines Av. 36 2B
Woodborough Rd. 9 5F
Woodbourne 96 1B
Woodbourne Av. 22 3A
Woodbourne Dri. 52 2B
Woodbourne Gdns. 56 2B
Woodbridge Av. 69 2F
Woodbridge Court 158 3C
Woodbridge Gro. 69 2F
Woodbridge Hill 81 5E
Woodbridge Hill Gdns. 81 5E
Woodbridge Meadows 81 5F
Woodbridge Rd., Frogmore 43 5D
Woodbridge Rd., Guildford 81 5F
Woodbury Av. 52 2C
Woodbury Cl., Addiscombe 41 5D
Woodbury Cl., Westerham Hill 77 3F
Woodbury Dri. 55 3F
Woodbury Rd. 77 2F
Woodbury St. 21 4D
Woodby Dri. 29 4E
Woodcock Dri. 46 2C
Woodcock Hill 130 4C
Woodcock La. 46 2C
Woodcombe Cres. 23 2E
Woodcot Gdns. 60 5B
Woodcote, Cranleigh 140 1B
Woodcote, Epsom 71 2D
Woodcote, Guildford 100 2B
Woodcote, Horley 128 2C
Woodcote Av., Beddington 56 3B
Woodcote Av., Thornton Heath 40 2B
Woodcote Cl., Epsom 54 5A
Woodcote Cl., Kingston 18 4B
Woodcote Dri. 56 3C
Woodcote End 71 1D
Woodcote Green 56 3C
Woodcote Green Rd. 71 1D
Woodcote Grove Rd. 73 1F
Woodcote Hurst 71 1D
Woodcote La. 56 4C
Woodcote Park Av. 56 4C
Woodcote Park Rd. 71 1D
Woodcote Rd., Epsom 54 5A
Woodcote Rd., Wallington 56 2B
Woodcote Side 70 1C
Woodcote Valley Rd. 57 4D
Woodcrest Rd. 57 5D
Woodcrest Walk 90 4A
Woodcroft Rd., Crawley 146 5A
Woodcroft Rd., Thornton Heath 40 3B
Woodcut Rd. 114 1C
Woodend, Rose Hill 38 5C
Woodend, Upper Norwood 22 5B
Woodend, The 56 3B
Wooderson Cl. 40 2C
Woodfield 70 2B
Woodfield Av., Carshalton Beeches 56 2B
Woodfield Av., Tooting Bec 21 3F
Woodfield Cl., Coulsdon 73 3F
Woodfield Cl., Crawley 147 3D
Woodfield Cl., Lower Ashtead 70 2A
Woodfield Cl., Redhill 90 4A
Woodfield Cl., Upper Norwood 22 5C
Woodfield Gdns. 37 3E
Woodfield Hill 73 3E
Woodfield La. 70 2B
Woodfield Rd., Ashtead 70 2B
Woodfield Rd., Coulsdon 73 3F
Woodfield Rd., Crawley 147 3E
Woodfield Rd., Hinchley Wood 35 5F
Woodfield Rd., Rudgwick 157 2F
Woodfield Way 90 4A
Woodfields, The 58 4A
Woodford Gdn. 27 2E
Woodgate Av. 53 1D
Woodgates Cl. 158 4C
Woodgavil 72 1A
Woodger Cl. 82 4C
Woodhall Av. 23 3D
Woodhall Dri. 23 3D
Woodhall La. 29 5D
Woodham 49 4D
Woodham La. 48 5B
Woodham Park Rd. 49 3D
Woodham Park Way 49 4D
Woodham Rd., Catford 24 3B
Woodham Rd., Woking 48 5A
Woodham Rise 65 1D
Woodham Waye 48 5B
Woodhatch 108 2C
Woodhatch Rd. 108 2C
Woodhatch Spinney 74 1A
Woodhaw 13 4E
Woodhayes Rd. 19 5F
Woodhill, Sendgrove 82 1C
Woodhill La., Shamley Green 121 2D
Woodhill La., Spreakley 114 4C
Woodhouse La. 104 5A
Woodhurst La. 93 3F
Woodhurst Pk. 93 3F
Woodhyrst Gdns. 74 1B
Woodland Av. 140 1C
Woodland Cl., Crawley Down 149 3E
Woodland Cl., E. Horsley 84 2C
Woodland Cl., Ewell 54 2B
Woodland Cl., Weybridge 50 1B
Woodland Court 93 2F
Woodland Dri., Crawley Down 149 3E
Woodland Dri., E. Horsley 84 2C
Woodland Gdns. 58 4B
Woodland Gro., Farnborough 78 1B
Woodland Gro., Weybridge 50 1B
Woodland Hill 23 5D
Woodland Rd., Thornton Heath 40 2B
Woodland Rd., Upper Sydenham 23 4D
Woodland Rise 93 3F
Woodland View 100 4A
Woodland Way, Caterham 91 2F
Woodland Way, Kingswood 72 4A
Woodland Way, Monks Orchard 41 4F
Woodland Way, Morden 38 2B
Woodland Way, Purley 57 5E
Woodland Way, Tolworth 36 5C
Woodland Way, Tooting 21 5E
Woodland Way, West Wickham 42 5B
Woodland Way, Weybridge 50 1B
Woodlands, Ashtead 70 2B
Woodlands, Cannon Hill 38 2A
Woodlands, Normandy 79 4E
Woodlands, Pound Hill 147 3F
Woodlands Av., Earlswood 109 1E
Woodlands Av., Heath End 96 1B
Woodlands Av., Kingston 37 1D
Woodlands Av., West Byfleet 49 5D
Woodlands Av., Worcester Park 37 5E
Woodlands Cl., Claygate 52 2C
Woodlands Cl., Cranleigh 141 2D
Woodlands Cl., Hawley 60 2B
Woodlands Cl., Ottershaw 48 3B
Woodlands Cl., South Ascot 28 3B
Woodlands Ct. 43 3F
Woodlands Dri., Middle Bourne 115 1D
Woodlands Dri., Molesey 34 1B
Woodlands Dri., Ockley 124 5C
Woodlands Dri., South Godstone 111 2F
Woodlands Gro. 73 2E
Woodlands La., Shottermill 151 2E
Woodlands La., Stoke D'Abernon 69 2D
Woodlands La., Updown Hill 46 2A
Woodlands Pk., Addlestone 49 1D
Woodlands Pk., Merrow 82 5B
Woodlands Pk., West Humble 87 4F
Woodlands Rd., Ash Wharf 78 4C
Woodlands Rd., Barnes 9 5E
Woodlands Rd., Camberley 43 5F
Woodlands Rd., Earlswood 109 1D
Woodlands Rd., Effingham 85 2F
Woodlands Rd., Farnborough 60 4B
Woodlands Rd., Hambledon 138 2A
Woodlands Rd., Leatherhead 69 2E
Woodlands Rd., Slyfield Green 81 3F
Woodlands Rd., Surbiton 36 4B
Woodlands Rd., The Wells 70 1C
Woodlands Rd., Virginia Water 30 2C
Woodlands Rd., West Byfleet 49 5D
Woodlands Ride 28 3B
Woodlands Rise 93 3F
Woodlands Road East 30 2C
Woodlands Road West 30 2C
Woodlands St. 24 2C
Woodlands, The, Beddington 56 3B
Woodlands, The, Catford 24 2B
Woodlands, The, Esher 35 5D
Woodlands, The, Smallfield 129 2E
Woodlands, The, Upper Norwood 22 5C
Woodlands Walk 60 2B
Woodlands Way 70 1C
Woodlawn Cres. 17 3D
Woodlawn Dri. 16 3B
Woodlawn Gro. 65 1D
Woodlea Dri. 42 3C
Woodleigh Gdns. 22 3A
Woodman Court 99 5F
Woodman Cres. 49 5D
Woodman Rd. 73 1F
Woodmancote Gdns. 49 5D
Woodmancott Cl. 27 3F
Woodmansterne 73 1D
Woodmansterne La., Banstead 55 5F
Woodmansterne La., Carshalton 56 4B
Woodmansterne Rd., Carshalton Beeches 56 4A
Woodmansterne Rd., Streatham Vale 21 5F
Woodmansterne Rd., Woodmansterne 73 1F
Woodmansterne St. 73 1D
Woodmere 27 2E
Woodmere Av. 41 4F
Woodmere Cl. 41 4F
Woodmere Gdns. 41 4F
Woodmere Way 42 3B
Woodnook Rd. 21 4E
Woodpecker Cl. 57 4F
Woodpecker La. 126 3A
Woodpecker Mount 58 3C
Woodpecker Way 64 5C
Woodplace Cl. 73 2F
Woodplace La. 73 3F
Woodplace Ter. 73 3F
Woodquest Av. 22 1B
Woodridge Cl. 27 2D
Woodrow Dri. 25 2F
Woodroyd Av. 128 3A
Woodroyd Cl. 128 3B
Woodruff Av. 82 4B
Woodshaw Cl. 30 3B
Woodside 10 4C
Woodside, Blackwater 60 1B
Woodside, Fetcham 69 4D
Woodside, Horsley 84 1B
Woodside, Lwr Kingswood 89 2E
Woodside, Wimbledon 20 5B
Woodside Av., Esher 35 4E
Woodside Av., Walton 51 1D
Woodside Av., Woodside 41 3E
Woodside Cl., Caterham 75 5D
Woodside Cl., Chiddingfold 137 5F
Woodside Cl., Knaphill 64 2A
Woodside Cl., Tolworth 37 4D
Woodside Court Rd. 41 4D
Woodside Cres. 129 2E
Woodside Green 41 4D
Woodside La., Cheam 37 5F
Woodside La., Woodside 10 4C
Woodside Pk. 41 3E
Woodside Rd., Addiscombe 41 3E
Woodside Rd., Beare Green 125 2D
Woodside Rd., Chiddingfold 137 5E
Woodside Rd., Heath End 96 1B
Woodside Rd., Kingston 18 5B
Woodside Rd., New Malden 37 1D
Woodside Rd., Oxshott 52 5A
Woodside Rd., Purley 57 5D
Woodside Rd., Sutton 38 5C
Woodside Rd., Three Bridges 147 3E
Woodside Rd., Woodbridge Hill 81 5E
Woodside Way, Earlswood 109 1E
Woodside Way, Salfords 109 3E
Woodside Way, Wentworth 30 2B
Woodsome Lodge 50 2B
Woodspring Rd. 20 3A
Woodstock, East Grinstead 150 2B
Woodstock, W. Clandon 83 2E
Woodstock Av., St. Helier 38 4B
Woodstock Av., Twickenham 17 1F
Woodstock Cl., Cranleigh 140 2C
Woodstock Cl., Horsham 158 3B
Woodstock Cl., Woking 65 2D
Woodstock Gro. 100 5A
Woodstock La. 36 5A
Woodstock Rd., Bedford Park 9 2E
Woodstock Rd., Carshalton 56 1B
Woodstock Rd., Croydon 40 5C
Woodstock Rd., Woodmansterne 73 1E
Woodstock Rise 38 4B
Woodstock Way 39 1F
Woodstone Av. 54 1C
Woodstreet Rd. 80 4C
Woodstreet Vill. 80 4B
Woodsway 52 5B
Woodthorpe Rd. 14 4C
Woodvale Av. 41 2D
Woodvale Est. 23 2E
Woodview 53 4D
Woodview Cl. 58 5B
Woodville Cl. 17 4F
Woodville Pl. 74 4C
Woodville Rd., Ham 18 3A
Woodville Rd., Leatherhead 69 3F
Woodville Rd., Morden 38 2B
Woodville Rd., Thornton Heath 40 2C
Woodwarde Rd. 23 1D
Woodway, Camberley 44 5A
Woodway, Guildford 82 5B
Woodyard La. 22 2C
Woodyers Cl. 101 5E
Wool Rd. 19 5F
Woolborough Cl. 147 3D
Woolborough La. 147 3E
Woolborough Rd. 147 3D
Woolford La. 116 3C
Woolhampton Way 27 2E

Woolhams 92 1A
Woollards 78 4C
Woolmead 96 3A
Woolmer Hill Rd. 151 2D
Woolsack Way 119 2D
Woolstone Rd. 23 3F
Wootton Cl. 71 1E
Worbeck Rd. 41 1E
Worcester Cl.,
　Farnborough 61 3D
Worcester Cl., Mitcham 39 1E
Worcester Cl., Shirley 42 5A
Worcester Court 34 4B
Worcester Dri. 9 1E
Worcester Gdns. 37 5E
Worcester Park 37 5E
Worcester Park Rd. 37 5D
Worcester Rd., Cheam 55 2E
Worcester Rd., Guildford 81 4D
Worcester Rd., Reigate 89 5E
Worcester Rd., Wimbledon 20 4B
Wordsworth 26 3B
Wordsworth Cl. 147 3F
Wordsworth Dri. 55 1D
Wordsworth Mead 90 4B
Wordsworth Pl. 158 2C
Wordsworth Rd.,
　Beddington 56 2C
Wordsworth Rd., Hampton 16 4C
Wordsworth Rd., Penge 23 5F
Wordsworth Rd.,
　Weybridge 49 1F
Wordsworthy Av. 74 1C
Worldsend Hill 27 3E
Worlidge St. 9 2F
Wormley La. 137 2E
Worple Av., Isleworth 17 1F
Worple Av., Staines 14 5B
Worple Av., Wimbledon 20 5A
Worple Ms. 20 5B
Worple Rd., Epsom 71 1D
Worple Rd., Leatherhead 70 5A
Worple Rd., Raynes Park 38 1A
Worple Rd., Staines 14 5B
Worple Rd., Wimbledon 20 5A
Worple St. 9 5D
Worple Way 18 1B
Worplesdon 81 2D
Worplesdon Rd. 80 1C
Worplestone Rd. 81 3E
Worslade Rd. 20 4C
Worsley Bridge Rd. 24 5A
Worsley Rd. 61 3E
Worsted Green 90 3C
Worth Park Av. 147 3F
Worth Rd. 147 3F
Worthfield Cl. 54 2A
Worthing Rd. 158 5A
Worthington Rd. 36 4B
Wortley Rd. 40 4A
Wotton Way 54 3C
Wrabness Way 32 1B
Wrangthorn Wk. 57 1E
Wray Common Rd. 89 5F
Wray La. 89 3F
Wray Park Rd. 89 4F
Wray Rd. 55 3E
Wrayfield Av. 89 5F
Wrayfield Rd. 55 1D
Wraylands Dri. 90 4A
Wraysbury 13 1D
Wraysbury Rd., Hythe End 13 3E
Wraysbury Rd., Staines 13 4F
Wrecclesham 95 5F
Wrecclesham Hill 114 2B
Wrecclesham Rd. 95 5F
Wren Cl., Horsham 158 2B
Wren Cl., Selsdon 58 3C
Wren Court 78 4C
Wren Cres. 49 1F
Wren Way 60 3C
Wren's Av. 15 4E
Wrens Hill 69 1E
Wrenthorpe Rd. 24 4C
Wrights Rd., S. Norwood 40 2C
Wrights Rd., Wallington 56 1B
Wrotham Hill 139 5D
Wroughton Rd. 21 1E
Wroxham 26 3C
Wrythe Green Rd. 39 5D
Wrythe La. 38 4C
Wyatt Park Rd. 22 3A
Wyatt Rd. 14 4A
Wyatts Cl. 119 1E
Wych Elm Rise 101 2D
Wych Hill 64 3C
Wych Hill Estate 64 3C
Wych Hill La. 64 3C
Wych Hill Pk. 64 3C
Wych Hill Rise 64 3C
Wych Hill Waye 64 3C
Wyche Gro. 57 3F
Wychelm Rd. 46 4A
Wychurch Cl. 23 5E
Wychwood Av., Bracknell 27 2F
Wychwood Av., Thornton
　Heath 40 2B

Wychwood Cl. 16 5A
Wychwood Cl., Ash 78 5B
Wychwood Pl. 44 4C
Wychwood Way 22 5C
Wycliffe Gdns. 90 3C
Wycliffe Rd. 20 5C
Wycombe Pl. 20 1C
Wydehurst Rd. 41 4E
Wydell Cl. 38 3A
Wye Cl. 15 4E
Wyeth's Ms. 54 5B
Wyeth's Rd. 54 5B
Wyke Av. 79 4D
Wyke La. 79 5D
Wyke Rd. 38 1A
Wykeham Rd., Farnham 96 3A
Wykeham Rd., Merrow 82 5C
Wykehurst La. 122 5B
Wylam, Bracknell 26 3C
Wylev St. 23 2F
Wymering Court 61 5D
Wyndham Av. 51 5D
Wyndham Cl. 55 2E
Wyndham Cres., Cranleigh 140 1A
Wyndham Cres., Whitton 16 1C
Wyndham Rd., Kingston 18 5C
Wyndham Rd., Woking 64 2B
Wyndham St. 78 5A
Wynell Rd. 23 3F
Wynfields Cl. 61 5E
Wynnstow Pk. 93 4F
Wynsham Way 45 1F
Wynton Gdns. 41 3D
Wynton Gro. 34 5A
Wyphurst Rd. 140 1C
Wyresdale 27 3E
Wysemead 128 2C
Wyvern Rd. 57 3E

Y

Yaffle Rd. 50 3B
Yale Cl. 43 3E
Yard Mead 13 3E
Yardbridge Cl. 55 3F
Yardley 26 3C
Yardley Cl. 89 4F
Yarm Cl. 70 5A
Yarm Ct. Rd. 70 5A
Yarm Way 70 5A
Yarmouth Cl. 147 5E
Yarnold Cl. 25 1F
Yarrowfield 64 5C
Yatesbury Cl. 95 5F
Yattendon Rd. 128 2B
Yaverlands Dri. 45 3D
Yeats Cl. 108 2C
Yellowcress Dri. 63 1E
Yendells Cl. 88 5B
Yenston Cl. 38 3B
Yeoman Way, Salfords 109 3E
Yeomans Cl., Tongham 97 1E
Yeomans Cl., West Heath 60 4C
Yeomans Mews 17 1E
Yeomans Pl. 133 4F
Yeomans Way, Camberley 44 5B
Yeoveney Cl. 13 3F
Yeovil Cl. 78 1B
Yeovil Rd., Owlsmoor 43 3E
Yeovil Rd., South
　Farnborough 78 1B
Yetminster Rd. 78 1A
Yew La. 150 1B
Yew Tree Bottom Rd. 71 2F
Yew Tree Cl., Charlwood 127 4E
Yew Tree Cl., Chipstead 73 3E
Yew Tree Cl., Farnborough 60 5A
Yew Tree Cl., Horley 128 2B
Yew Tree Dri., Caterham 92 1A
Yew Tree Dri., Slyfield
　Green 81 3F
Yew Tree Gdns. 71 1D
Yew Tree La. 89 4F
Yew Tree Rd., Charlwood 127 4E
Yew Tree Rd., Dorking 86 5C
Yew Tree Rd., Milford 118 5A
Yew Tree Way, Addington 59 3D
Yew Tree Way, Hounslow
　Heath 16 1C
Yew Tree Wk., Effingham 85 2E
Yew Tree Wk., Frimley 61 2E
Yew Tree Wk., Purley 57 3E
Yew Trees, Shepperton 33 2D
Yew Trees, Thorpe 31 2E
Yewbank Cl. 74 1C
Yewdells Cl. 88 5B
Yewens 137 4F
Yewlands Cl. 72 1C
Yews, The, 15 4D
Yewtree Way 58 3C
Yockley Cl. 62 1A
Yolland Cl. 96 1A
York Av. 19 1D
York Cl., Byfleet 49 4F
York Cl., Horsham 158 4C
York Cl., Morden 38 2C

York Gate 74 4C
York Gdns. 34 5B
York Hill 22 3B
York Rd., Ash Wharf 78 4C
York Rd., Biggin Hill West 77 3D
York Rd., Brentford 8 2A
York Rd., Byfleet 49 4F
York Rd., Camberley 44 5A
York Rd., Cheam 55 2E
York Rd., Croydon 40 4B
York Rd., Guildford 100 1C
York Rd., Kingston 18 5C
York Rd., Selsdon 58 3C
York Rd., South Ealing 8 1A
York Rd., South
　Farnborough 78 1A
York Rd., Twickenham 17 4E
York Rd., Weybridge 50 1B
York Rd., Woking 64 3C
York St., Beddington
　Corner 39 4E
York St., Twickenham 17 2F
York Way, Chessington 53 2E
York Way, Hanworth 16 3C
York Way, Sandhurst 43 4D
Yorke Gdns. 89 5E
Yorke Rd. 89 5E
Yorkshire Rd. 40 2A
Yorktown Rd. 43 4D
Youlden Cl. 44 5C
Youldon Dri. 44 5C
Young St. 86 1B
Youngs Dri. 78 5C
Youngstroat La. 48 4A
Yukon Rd. 21 2E

Z

Zennor Rd. 21 2F
Zermatt Rd. 40 2B
Zigzag Rd. 74 1C
Zigzag, The 87 3D
Zinnia Dri. 63 1E
Zion Place 40 2C
Zion Rd. 40 2C

INDEX OF TOWNS AND VILLAGES

Abbotswood	82	4A	Chipstead	73	3E	Forest Green	123	4F
Abinger	104	5B	Chiswick	9	3D	Frensham	115	4E
Abinger Hammer	103	3F	Chobham	47	4D	Friday Street	104	5C
Addington	59	2D	Christmaspie	98	1C	Frimley	61	3E
Addlestone	49	1F	Churt	134	2B			
Addlestonemoor	32	5B	Clapham	21	1F	Gatton	90	2A
Albury	102	3B	Claygate	52	2B	Glanty	13	4E
Aldershot	78	5A	Cobham	51	5D	Godalming	119	1D
Alfold	156	2A	Coldharbour	124	2B	Godstone	92	4B
Alfold Crossways	140	5A	Colnbrook	7	3A	Gomshall	103	3E
Ascot	28	2C	Compton	99	3F	Grayshott	135	5D
Ash	78	5C	Copthorne	148	1B	Grayswood	152	1B
Ashford	15	4D	Coulsdon	74	3A	Great Bookham	85	1F
Ashtead	70	3B	Cranleigh	140	1C	Guildford	101	1D
Ash Vale	78	3C	Crawley	147	4D			
			Crowhurst	112	3C	Hackbridge	39	4E
Bagshot	45	2E	Crowthorne	43	2D	Hale	96	2B
Banstead	72	1C	Croydon	40	5B	Hambledon	137	2F
Barnes	9	4F				Hammersmith	9	2F
Beare Green	125	2D	Deepcut	62	4A	Hamsey Green	75	1E
Beckenham	42	1A	Dorking	105	1F	Harrow Common	76	1A
Bellfields	81	4F	Dormans Land	132	3A	Hascombe	138	1C
Belmont	55	2E	Dormans Park	131	5F	Haslemere	152	3A
Betchworth	107	1D	Doversgreen	108	3C	Hawley	60	2C
Biggin Hill	77	1E	Downside	68	2B	Haxted	113	5E
Bisley	63	1E	Dulwich	23	2D	Headley, Hants.	133	4E
Bletchingley	91	5F	Dunsfold	138	4D	Headley, Surrey	88	1A
Blindley Heath	111	5F				Headley Down	134	5A
Botleys	31	5E	Earlswood	109	1E	Heath End	96	1B
Boundstone	114	2C	Eashing	118	1B	Henfold	125	2E
Bracknell	27	2D	East Bedfont	15	2E	Hersham	51	1E
Bramley	120	1A	East Clandon	83	3E	Hinchley Wood	35	5F
Brentford	8	2B	East Ewell	55	3D	Hindhead	135	4D
Brockham	106	1C	East Grinstead	150	2B	Hoe	103	5F
Brook	136	2C	Easthampstead	26	3C	Holmbury St. Mary	123	1E
Brookwood	63	3E	East Horsley	84	3C	Hooley	73	4E
Buckland	88	4C	East Molesey	35	3D	Hookwood	127	3F
Bucks Green	157	2E	Eastwick	86	1A	Horley	128	3B
Burgh Heath	72	3A	Eastworth	32	4A	Horsell	64	1B
Burpham	82	3B	Effingham	85	2E	Horsham	158	4B
Burrowhill	47	2D	Egham	13	4E	Hurst Green	94	4A
Burstow	129	4E	Elstead	117	2D	Hydestile	119	5D
Byfleet	49	4F	Englefield Green	12	4B	Hythe	13	5F
			Epsom	54	5A	Hythe End	13	3E
Camberley	44	5A	Esher	52	1A			
Camberwell	22	1C	Ewell	54	3B	Ifold	155	4F
Capel	125	5D	Ewhurst	122	5C	Isleworth	17	1E
Carshalton	56	1A						
Caterham	75	4D	Fairlands	80	3C	Jacob's Well	82	3A
Catford	24	2B	Farleigh	58	5C			
Charlton	33	1E	Farnborough	61	5D	Kenley	74	1C
Charlwood	127	4D	Farncombe	100	5B	Kew	8	3C
Cheam	55	1E	Farnham	96	4A	Kingston-upon-		
Chelsham	76	2A	Felbridge	150	1A	Thames	36	2C
Chertsey	32	4A	Felcourt	131	4E	Kingswood	72	5A
Chessington	53	1F	Feltham	16	3A	Knaphill	63	2F
Chiddingfold	137	5F	Fetcham	69	5D	Knowle Green	14	4A
Chilworth	101	3F	Fickleshole	59	5F			

Place	Page	Grid
Laleham	**32**	2B
Langley Vale	**71**	3D
Leatherhead	**70**	4A
Leigh	**107**	4F
Lewisham	**23**	2F
Lightwater	**45**	3F
Limpsfield	**94**	3A
Lingfield	**131**	2F
Little Bookham	**85**	1F
Littleton	**33**	2D
Long Ditton	**36**	4A
Longford	**7**	4C
Lower Halliford	**33**	3F
Lower Kingswood	**89**	2E
Loxwood	**156**	4A
Lyne	**31**	4E
Martyr's Green	**67**	3F
Maybury	**65**	2E
Merrow	**82**	5C
Merstham	**90**	2C
Merton	**38**	1B
Mickleham	**87**	2D
Middle Bourne	**115**	1D
Milford	**118**	3A
Mitcham	**39**	1D
Morden	**38**	2B
Munstead Heath	**119**	3E
Mytchett	**61**	5E
New Addington	**59**	3E
New Chapel	**130**	3C
Newdigate	**125**	4F
New Haw	**49**	2E
New Malden	**37**	2E
Nork	**72**	1A
Normandy	**79**	4F
North Cheam	**38**	5A
Norwood Hill	**127**	2D
Nutfield	**91**	5D
Oakwoodhill	**142**	3C
Oatlands Park	**33**	5F
Ockford Ridge	**118**	2C
Ockham	**67**	4D
Ockley	**124**	5B
Old Windsor	**12**	1B
Old Woking	**65**	4E
Onslow Village	**100**	1A
Ottershaw	**48**	2B
Outwood	**110**	5C
Oxshott	**52**	5A
Oxted	**93**	3F
Parkgate	**126**	2A
Peaslake	**122**	1B
Pebble Coombe	**88**	3B
Penge	**23**	5E
Pirbright	**63**	5D
Pixham	**87**	5D
Plaistow	**155**	4D
Portmore Park	**33**	5E
Poyle	**7**	4A
Purley	**57**	4E
Puttenham	**98**	3C
Pyrford	**66**	2A
Quakers Plat	**132**	4A
Redhill	**90**	5B
Reigate	**89**	5F
Richings Park	**7**	1B
Richmond-upon-Thames	**18**	1A
Ripley	**66**	4B
Roehampton	**19**	2F
Roundshaw	**57**	2D
Rowledge	**114**	2C
Rowly	**121**	4E
Row Town	**49**	2D
Rudgwick	**157**	2F
Runnymede	**13**	3D
Salfords	**109**	4E
Sanderstead	**58**	4A
Sandhurst	**43**	4D
Seale	**97**	3F
Selsdon	**58**	3B
Send	**65**	5F
Sendmarsh	**66**	5A
Shackleford	**99**	5D
Shalford	**101**	3D
Shamley Green	**121**	2D
Shepperton	**33**	3E
Shepperton Green	**33**	2D
Shere	**103**	2D
Shipleybridge	**129**	5D
Shottermill	**151**	3E
Slines Green	**76**	2A
Smallfield	**129**	3E
South Godstone	**111**	3F
South Holmwood	**106**	5A
South Nutfield	**110**	1A
Staines	**14**	4A
Stanwell	**14**	1C
Stanwellmoor	**14**	1A
Stoke D'Abernon	**68**	2C
Stoneleigh	**54**	1B
Stoughton	**81**	4E
Streatham	**22**	3A
Sunbury on Thames	**33**	1F
Sunningdale	**29**	3F
Sunninghill	**29**	3D
Surbiton	**36**	3C
Sutton	**55**	1F
Sutton Green	**82**	1A
Tadworth	**71**	4F
Tandridge	**93**	5D
Tatsfield	**77**	3E
Thames Ditton	**35**	3F
The Chart	**94**	4C
Thorns Flush	**121**	5E
Thorpe	**31**	2E
Thorpe Lea	**13**	5F
Thursley	**136**	1A
Tilford	**116**	2A
Tillingbourne	**105**	4D
Tolworth	**36**	5C
Tongham	**97**	2E
Twickenham	**17**	3E
Twynersh	**31**	3F
Tyler's Green	**92**	3B
Upper Halliford	**33**	2F
Virginia Water	**30**	3C
Wallington	**56**	1B
Walton-on-Thames	**34**	5A
Walton on the Hill	**88**	1C
Wanborough	**99**	2D
Warlingham	**75**	2F
Warnham	**158**	2A
West Bedfont	**15**	2D
West Byfleet	**49**	5D
West Clandon	**83**	3D
Westcott	**105**	2E
West End	**46**	4B
West Ewell	**54**	2A
Westfield	**65**	4D
West Heath	**60**	4B
West Horsley	**84**	3B
West Humble	**87**	4D
West Molesey	**34**	2C
Weybridge	**50**	1A
Whiteley Village	**50**	3C
Whyteleafe	**75**	2D
Wimbledon	**20**	5A
Windlesham	**46**	1A
Winkfield	**10**	3A
Wisley	**66**	1C
Witley	**137**	1E
Woking	**65**	2D
Wokingham	**25**	2E
Woldingham	**76**	5A
Wonersh	**101**	5E
Woodcote	**71**	2D
Woodham	**49**	4D
Woodhatch	**108**	2C
Woodmansterne	**73**	1D
Woodstreet Village	**80**	4B
Woodside	**10**	4C
Worcester Park	**37**	5E
Wormley	**137**	2E
Worplesdon	**81**	2D
Wraysbury	**13**	1D
Wrecclesham	**95**	5F